Y0-EKP-528

Achtung! Moskito!

Achtung! Moskito!

RAF and USAAF Mosquito Fighters, Fighter Bombers, and Bombers Over the Third Reich

1941 - 1945

Martin W. Bowman

Schiffer Military History
Atglen, PA

Book Design by Stephanie Daugherty.

Library of Congress Control Number: 2009938721

Printed in China
ISBN: 978-0-7643-3347-7
We are interested in hearing from authors with book ideas on related topics.

Published by Schiffer Publishing Ltd.
4880 Lower Valley Road
Atglen, PA 19310
Phone: (610) 593-1777
FAX: (610) 593-2002
E-mail: Info@schifferbooks.com.
Visit our web site at: www.schifferbooks.com
Please write for a free catalog.
This book may be purchased from the publisher.
Please include $5.00 postage.
Try your bookstore first.

In Europe, Schiffer books are distributed by:
Bushwood Books
6 Marksbury Avenue
Kew Gardens
Surrey TW9 4JF, England
Phone: 44 (0) 20 8392-8585
FAX: 44 (0) 20 8392-9876
E-mail: Info@bushwoodbooks.co.uk.
Visit our website at: www.bushwoodbooks.co.uk

Grace

Her name was Grace; she was one of the best,
But that was the night I gave her the test.
I looked at her with joy and delight
For she was mine and mine for the night.
She looked so pretty, so sweet and slim,
And the night was dark, the light was dim.
I was so excited my heart missed a beat
For I knew that night I was in for a treat!
I had seen her stripped, I had seen her bare,
I felt her round and felt her everywhere,
But that was the night I liked the best,
And if you wait I'll tell you the rest.
I got inside her, she screamed with joy.
For this was her first night out with a boy.
I got up high and quick as I could,
I handled her well for she was good.
I turned her over upon her side,
Then on her back - that was all tried:
I pushed it forward; I pulled it back,
Then I let it go, until I thought she would crack.
She was one great thrill the best in the land,
The twin-engined MOSQUITO of Bomber Command.

Sergeant Harry Tagg,
1655 Mosquito Training Unit,
RAF Marham, April 1943
(via Daphne Light, ex-Marham WAAF).

ACKNOWLEDGMENTS

I am enormously grateful to the following people for making it possible to include as much diverse information and anecdotes on Mosquito operations. Michael Allen DFC**; Sidney Allinson; Don E. Aris; Jim Avis; Philip Back DFC; Captain "Buddy" Badley; David Backhouse; Norman Bacon; H. Barker; Len Bartram; Tim Bates; Derek "Taffy' Bellis DFC*; Air Vice Marshal H. Bird-Wilson CBE DSO AFC; Philip J. Birtles; Brian Whitlock Blundell; Barry Blunt BA Hons, Archivist to the Mosquito Aircrew Association; Dr Theo Boiten; Frank Bocock; Eileen Boorman; Warren Borges; Les Bostock; Terrence Boughton; Ed Boulter DFC; Bill Bridgeman; Tommy Broom DFC**; Squadron Leader Ed Bulpett RAF Retd; Jean Bunting; Jeff Carless; John Carnegie; Mike Carreck DFC; Derek Carter; George Cash; Peter Celis; Mrs. S. A. Chadderton; Johnny Claxton; Dorothy Chaloner; City of Norwich Aviation Museum; Gil Cohen; Bob Collis; Squadron Leader Joe Cooper AFC FC; Hank Cooper DSO DFC; Patrick Corness; Luc Cox; Des Curtis; Tom Cushing; Hans-Peter Dabrowski; Squadron Leader Mike Daniels; Cynrik de Decker; *Eastern Daily Press*; *Eastern Evening News*; Grenville Eaton; Roy Ellis-Brown DFC; Reg Everson; Leslie Fletcher; Stephen M. Fochuk; Mrs P. Jane Fox, *Legion* Magazine; J. D. S. Garratt DFC*; Rev Nigel Gilson; Air Vice Marshal L. W. G. "Bill" Gill DSO; GMS Enterprises; Val Grimble; Ken Godfrey; Ted Gomersall; Richard T. Goucher; Terry Groves; Cato Guhnfeldt; Peter B. Gunn, author of *RAF Great Massingham*; Alan Hague, Leo Hall; Lewis Heath; Gerhard Heilig; Vic Hester; Raymond Hicks; Wing Commander Gerry Honey OBE MRAeS MRIMgt Leslie "Dutch" Holland; George Honeyman; G. Horsfield; Richard Howard; Squadron Leader Stephen J. Howard; M. Howland; Dennis Hudson; Harry Jeffries; Wing Commander Howard C. Kelsey DSO DFC* Bernard M. Job; *Legion Magazine*; *Lancashire Evening News*; E. W. Lawson; Wing Commander R. W. Leggett; Frank Leyland, Andrew Long; Sister Laurence May; G. F. Mahony; Captain Bill McCash AFM; Basil McRae; Nigel McTeer; Noelle Meredith, PRM, The Royal Aeronautical Society; Neville Miller; W. H. Miller DFC; Denis Moore; Eric Mombeek; Wing Commander A. P. Morgan; F. G. Morris; Mosquito Aircrew Association; Jean Nater; Wing Commander George Newby; Wiley Noble; Merle Olmsted; J. A. Padilla; Charles Parker DFM; Wing Commander George Parry DSO DFC; Simon Parry, Air Research Publications; Derek Patfield; Squadron Leader Charles Patterson DSO DFC; André E. Pecquet; Allan Pudsey; Ralph Ramm; John Rayner; Barbara Rayson; John Rayson Harry Reed DFC; G.Av.A; W. F. Rhodes; The late Peter Richard; Alf Rogers; Group Captain J. K. "Sport" Rogers OBE FBIM; Squadron Leader Derek Rothery; Walter Rowley; Squadron Leader Philip Russell DFC; B. W. Salmon; Alan Sanderson; Squadron Leader E. J. Saunderson; James F. 'Bill' Setchell Jr.; George Sesler; Jim Shortland; Graham Simons; Wing Commander Joe Singleton DFC; Jerry Scutts; Richard T. Sizemore; Group Captain E. M. Smith DFC * DFM; Colonel R. Smith; Derek Smith; Mrs Ann Solberg Clark; Martin Staunton; Dr Robin Steel; Konrad "Bob" Stembrowicz; Gerald Stevens DFC; C. Tarkowski; Geoff Thomas; Squadron Leader A. M. Tomalin RAF; Henk Van Baaren; John Vasco; Paddy Walker; Colin "Ginger" Walsh; Peter Waxham; Alan B. Webb; Harry Welham DFC; Graham "Chalky" White; Brian Williams; Phylis and the late J. Ralph Wood; Squadron Leader R. G. "Tim" Woodman DSO DFC; W. C. Woodruff CBE FRAeS; and the *Worcester Evening News*.

Contents

CHAPTER 1

LOW LEVELLERS AND THE SHALLOW RAIDERS

Lie in the dark and listen,
It's clear tonight so they're flying high,
Hundreds of them, thousands perhaps,
Riding the icy, moonlit sky,
Men, machinery, bombs and maps,
Altimeters and guns and charts,
Coffee, sandwiches, fleece-lined boots,
Bones and muscles, minds and hearts.
English saplings with English roots
Deep in the earth they've left below,
Lie in the dark and let them go;
Lie in the dark and listen.
Lie in the dark and listen.

Noël Coward

Dark clouds covered eastern England on 15 November 1941 when Blenheim aircrews of 105 Squadron braved the raw wind to gather near the hangars at the 2 (Fighter Bomber) Group grass airfield at Swanton Morley, Norfolk, to see a grey and green shape approach the aerodrome from the northwest. First it flew over at about 500 feet, at a speed of 300 mph. Then it approached the Watch Office and hangar from the west and went into a vertical bank at a height of 2-3000 feet before turning a circle so tight and at such a speed that vapor trails streamed from its wingtips. This was followed by a normal circuit and landing. The rumors it seemed were true. For some time now the Squadron observers had attended conversion training on a new W/T and the gunners had started navigation courses, all amid speculation that they would be receiving a revolutionary type of aircraft built largely of wood to replace their outdated Blenheim IVs. Compared to the Blenheim IVs 105 Squadron was used to, this performance was quite breathtaking. The tall frame of Company Chief Test Pilot Geoffrey de Havilland Jr. emerged from the tiny cockpit of the "Wooden Wonder." He climbed down the ladder to be received like a conquering hero by Group Captain Battle OBE DFC, the station commander, and Wing Commander Peter H. A. Simmons DFC. Simmons' air and ground crews were equally ecstatic. During September and October 105 Squadron had flown anti-shipping operations from Malta. Losses were high. Returning to Swanton Morley, the surviving crews were due for a rest and in bad need of a morale boost. The arrival of the Mosquito provided it.

Sergeant Mike Carreck DFC was an observer in one of the newest Blenheim crews fresh from 17 OTU Upwood, 2 Group's finishing school. Pilot Officer Ronald Olney, first violinist in the London Philharmonic, and crew were one of the half dozen or so posted to 105 Squadron at Swanton Morley. Mike Carreck recalls:[1]

> "Waiting there for us were a very few survivors from 105's bloodbath in Malta where fourteen days was the lifetime of a Blenheim squadron. We rightly regarded these battle-scarred veterans with the deepest respect but they made us welcome. Life at Swanton Morley - a hell-spot only fifteen miles from Norwich but which might well have been in deepest Siberia - began sedately enough. Now and then we did a Blenheim cross-country as I handed my pilot course, compass and ETAs. Sometimes we ventured as far away as Lincoln. We flew to the range and dropped teeny-weeny bombs and once, special treat and with much trepidation, a 250 pounder. Dullish days but nights were duller still, as for recreation, romance and merriment one had to rely on nearby East Dereham where mothers locked away their daughters after tea and every door slammed tight shut on the dot of 1800 hours. Nothing to do but go shivering to our beds in our freezing Nissen huts. Excitement was somewhat lacking, except for a nonsense of a rumor going the rounds that we were to be re-equipped with a fabulous new aircraft. It was the fastest in the world, a day bomber that could out-fly any fighter and leave it wondering where we'd gone, that could fly five miles high into the stratosphere and had an incredible range of 1200 miles. We shrugged our shoulders. We'd believe it when we saw it, which we very soon did.

"On 15 November it came suddenly out of nowhere inches above the hangars with a crackling thunderclap of twin Merlins. As we watched, bewitched, it was flung about the sky in a beyond belief display for a bomber that could out perform any fighter. Well-bred whisper of a touch down, a door opened and down the ladder came suede shoes, yellow socks and the rest of Geoffrey de Havilland. We pushed and shoved around this impossible dream of an aircraft. No other word for it, it was beautiful. An arrogant beauty, job to do, get out of my way, slim sleek fuselage, high cocked 'to-hell-with-you' tail, awesome power on the leash in those huge engines, eager on its undercarriage like a sprinter on the starting blocks, couldn't wait to leap up and away.

"'Called a Mosquito,' they told us. Mosquito W4064 - it was to be shot down six months later on the squadron's first operation[2]. During those six months only seven more Mosquitoes joined W4064 so flights were few and far between; indeed we new boys had to wait weeks for our first. For us, back to Blenheims and Arctic nights, not counting a Station exercise when it was pretended that German paratroopers had landed and a batch of us were sent to guard the Sergeants Mess. We stretched out on the carpet, blissfully warm at last until somebody came in to wake us with the astounding news that the Japanese had bombed Pearl Harbor. We turned over to sleep our best night ever, the war was won...' Three to a crew in a Blenheim, only two in a Mosquito so sadly some of our navs and WoPs were surplus to requirements. Sadder still they were posted to Blenheim squadrons flying in the Sea of Carnage, attacks on North Sea convoys whose escorting flak-ships didn't bother to aim, just fired splash into the sea, a curtain of exploding steel through which the doomed Blenheim crews flew with unmatchable courage."

Among the gathered throng of seasoned pilots and their navigators at Swanton Morley on 15 November to admire the Mosquito's "beautiful shape" was Flight Lieutenant D. A. G. Parry, who, like his CO, was a veteran of two tours on Blenheims. He was always known as "George" because, like the autopilot of the same name, he always came home! Parry had recently completed two tours and was "resting" at 13 OTU at Bicester when he just happened to pick up the telephone and receive a call from Pete Simmons, who had been his "A" Flight commander in 110 Squadron at Wattisham. Simmons had rung to enquire when he was getting some more pilots, adding, "By the way George, I'm getting some fast aircraft. Do you want to come?" Parry quickly turned down a posting to a squadron equipped with Bisleys going to North Africa and joined Simmons at Swanton Morley. The CO's promise of "fast aircraft" had come true, although W4064 left almost as fast as it arrived. After lunch, Geoffrey de Havilland Jr. climbed back into the sleek Mosquito B.IV and was joined by Simmons, who took the right-hand seat for a joyride with a difference. de Havilland Jr. treated his passenger and the crews watching to an exhilarating display of aerobatics. When they landed, Simmons was reported to be "...looking a bit green around the gills, but it did not stop him talking about it in the Officers' Mess during lunch!"[3] The sleek new bomber had to return next day to Hatfield, where the first of a paltry ten B.IV bombers was coming off the production lines for adjustments. Not until July 1941 had it been decided to build Mosquitoes as bombers, and even then only converted photo-reconnaissance airframes.[4]

Meanwhile, 105 Squadron, now stationed at Horsham St. Faith, near Norwich, after Swanton Morley proved unsuitable for operations, had received only eight Mosquitoes by mid-May 1942, but 2 Group was anxious to despatch its new wonder aircraft on the first op as soon as possible. On 27 May it issued orders for 105 Squadron to prepare four Mosquitoes with bombs and cameras to harass and obtain photographic evidence in the wake of the "Thousand Bomber" raid on Cologne, scheduled for the night of 30/31 May. Squadron Leader Alan R. "Jesse" Oakeshott DFC, followed later by Pilot Officer William D. Kennard and Pilot Officer Eric R. Johnson, took off from Horsham before the "heavies" had returned. Pilot Officer Edgar A. Costello-Bowen and Warrant Officer Tommy Broom and Flight Lieutenant Jack E. Houlston and Flight Sergeant James L. Armitage followed them shortly before lunchtime the following day.[5] Oakeshott flew at 24,000 feet over the battered and blasted city and added his four 500lb bombs to the devastation; but with smoke reaching to 14,000 feet, his F24 camera was rendered useless. Kennard and Johnson failed to return, their aircraft being hit by anti-aircraft fire. Costello-Bowen and Houlston dropped their bombs from high-level into the smouldering and smoking ruins to prolong the night of misery for the inhabitants and bomb disposal teams and headed back to Norfolk. In the late afternoon Squadron Leader Peter J. Channer, who as a Blenheim pilot on 18 Squadron had received the DFC for the attack on the Knapsack power station at Cologne, took off from Horsham and flew in thick cloud to within 60 miles of the city. Then he dived down at almost 380 mph to low-level to take photographs of the damage. Channer quickly realized that this highly successful approach would be particularly effective for future Mosquito bombing operations.

On the evening of 1 June, two Mosquitoes returned to Cologne to bomb and reconnoitre the city. One of the aircraft failed to return. Then, just before dawn on 2 June, 18 hours after a "Thousand Bomber" raid on Essen, George Parry and his navigator, Flying Officer Victor Robson, flew a lone 2 hour 5 minute round-trip to Cologne. They carried four 500-pounders to stoke up the fires and a camera to observe the damage. However, thick smoke made the latter task impossible. (Robson had come to 105 Squadron from Coastal Command and, according to his pilot, "At night [he] was like a homing pigeon. No matter how bad the weather, he always pinpointed exactly.") The Mosquitoes were of course much faster than the "heavies" were and, as Parry recalls, "We were back having breakfast in the Officers' Mess while the 'heavies' were still overhead, heading for home." His curiosity was taken by a Whitley, which had aborted the raid with mechanical problems and was now taking off from Horsham with its bomb load still aboard:

> "I looked out the window and thought, it's not going to make it. It didn't. He went off nose-down towards the Firs pub on the road at the far corner of the airfield, and piled into a garage forecourt the other side. Luckily, it didn't explode. I rang the police and they cordoned off the area. Fortunately, the bombs did not go off."

In June the Mosquitoes of 105 Squadron continued their lone reconnaissance missions over Germany. On 8 June, 139 Squadron was formed at Horsham St. Faith under the command of Wing Commander Peter Shand DFC, using crews and a few Mk.IVs from 105 Squadron. One of the pilots transferred to 139 was Jack Houlston AFC, who was promoted to Squadron Leader. Houlston flew 139 Squadron's first operation on 25/26 June, a low-level raid on the airfield at Stade, near Wilhelmshaven, and returned after dark just as bombers for the third in the series of "Thousand Bomber" raids were taking off for Bremen. Two of 105 Squadron's Mosquitoes flew reconnaissance over the city after the raid and four more went to reconnoitre other German cities to assess damage and bring back photographs.

On 2 July the first joint attack by 105 and 139 Squadron Mosquitoes took place when four aircraft from 105 Squadron carried out a low-level attack on the submarine yards at Flensburg and two Mosquitoes in 139 Squadron also bombed from high level. Group Captain J. C. MacDonald DFC AFC, the Station Commander, and Wing Commander "Jesse" Oakeshott DFC failed to return. MacDonald and his observer, Flight Lieutenant A. E. Skelton, became PoWs. Oakeshott and his observer, Flying Officer Vernon "Titch" F. E. Treherne DFM were killed. Houlston came off the target pursued by three Fw 190s. Two more fighters chased Flight Lieutenant George Pryce Hughes MiD RCAF, who despite his name was an Argentinian, after he had been hit by flak over the target. Both pilots made their exits hugging the wave tops, and applying plus 12½lb of boost they easily outpaced their pursuers. On 11 July the Mosquitoes bombed Flensburg again as a diversion for the heavies hitting Danzig. Pilot Officer Laston made it home with part of his fin blown away by flak, but Flight Lieutenant George Hughes and his navigator, Flying Officer Thomas A. Gabe, were killed when their Mosquito crashed, possibly as a result of flying too low. Sergeant Peter W. R. Rowland, in DK296 borrowed from George Parry, flew so low that he hit a roof and returned to Horsham with pieces of chimney pot lodged in the nose. After he had landed Parry barked at Rowland, "I'm not lending you my aircraft again!"

High-level raids in clear skies were now the order of the day, and during July the first 29 "Siren Raids" were flown. These involved high-level dogleg routes across Germany at night and were designed to disrupt the war workers and their families and ensure that they lost at least two hours' sleep before their shifts the following day. Later that month came something different. George Parry was called into station commander Group Captain "Digger" (later Air Chief Marshal Sir Wallace) Kyle's office. "He asked if I would be willing to 'have a go' at flying the first Mosquito diplomatic run to Stockholm, to deliver ciphers and mail for the British Embassy." Parry said he would. DK301 was duly painted overall pale grey and its national insignia and codes removed, while he and Robson caught the train to London to be briefed by Air Ministry and Foreign Office officials. Parry continues:

> "At the Air Ministry they explained to us what was happening, and then we went to the Foreign Office for their briefing. They said there would be a van coming to pick us up and take us to Liverpool Street. When the van arrived it was filled with about 40 diplomatic sacks with labels clearly marked 'British Embassy, Stockholm.' What security! I got the driver to roll them together to hide the labels, and 'Robbie' got in the back and I sat up front. At Liverpool Street Station I went and saw the stationmaster and persuaded him to give us a first-class compartment all to ourselves and to make sure we were locked in. Then I rang Horsham and asked for a car to meet us at Thorpe Station, to take the bags and us to the base. As far as I was aware there were codes and ciphers in the bags.
>
> "At Horsham the bags were locked in the HQ building overnight. Next morning, 4 August, 'Robbie' and I, wearing our Sidcot flying suits over civilian clothes, boarded our grey Mosquito now loaded with about a 1000lb of baggage roped together in the bomb bay and rear fuselage, and prepared to fly to Leuchars for the over-water flight to Sweden. Everyone had been told that we were doing a special test and would be away for 48 hours. One of the ground crew looked at our footwear and told me much later that he had wondered why we were wearing black civilian shoes.
>
> "At Leuchars we rang the Foreign Office for the 'OK' to take off, but they could not apparently raise the Embassy in Stockholm. I had to get there before dark as we had no radio, IFF, or anything else; they had all been taken out to save weight and make room for the bags. After ringing again and getting no definite answer I finally decided I must take a chance and take off. We set off across the North Sea for Stockholm and arrived over Bromma Airport where I cut in front of a Luftwaffe Ju 52! We landed, and so did the Ju 52. A whole load of Germans came out of the transport and were extremely excited about our Mosquito. We were armed with incendiary devices to set it on fire if necessary, but the Swedes marshaled the Germans into the terminal and locked them in a room. Then the British Embassy staff, tipped-off by the Swedes that we had arrived, drove up and loaded up their cars with the diplomatic bags. A 24-hour guard by men in 'civvies' and armed with concealed revolvers was placed around the aircraft overnight.
>
> "We were taken to a large hotel in the middle of Stockholm, which overlooked a large lake. We had no money and were not allowed to buy anything but were taken out to dinner at a plush restaurant, where German Embassy staff and spies were pointed out to us by our hosts. We met a squadron leader who had been shot down in 1940 while flying Blenheims in 2 Group and had escaped after being taken prisoner by falling, unnoticed, out of the column he was in while being marched away to captivity and rolling into a ditch. He got as far as Stettin and got aboard a Swedish collier to Stockholm, where he gave himself up. He was an internee but was being looked after by the British Embassy. He wanted to get home. It was a bit tight and he would have to take turns on the oxygen mask, but I told him he could come home with us in the nose of our Mosquito. Next morning I started up one engine and all he had to do was nip in smartly, but the Swedes were not having it and they nabbed him! (He got back a year later.) On the way home we flew at 500-600 feet over the North Sea because of a weather front, and approaching Scotland two Hurricanes came out to intercept us. I had no IFF, so I opened up and left them behind and quickly landed at Leuchars."
> (Nine months later BOAC received Mosquito airliners and flew the route regularly.)

On 25 August Flight Lieutenant D. A. G. "George" Parry and Flight Lieutenant Victor G. "Robbie" Robson, and Flight Lieutenant Joseph Roy George Ralston DFM and Flying Officer Sydney Clayton DFM were detailed to raid two electric power stations. Ralston and Clayton had both been posted to the squadron in May 1942 after flying Blenheim IVs in 107 Squadron.

Ralston, a Mancunian from Moss Side, had enlisted in the RAF in 1930 as a technical tradesman. By 1938 he had progressed to become a sergeant pilot in 108 Squadron flying Hawker Hinds and Blenheims. Flight Lieutenant Edgar A. Costello-Bowen and Warrant Officer Tommy J. Broom were given a switching station at Brauweiler, near Cologne, but they hit a pylon and crashed at Paaltjesdreef Wood, at Westmalle, in the Belgian hamlet of Blauwhoeve, en route. Incredibly, both men survived and with the help of the Underground movement they evaded capture and were sent along the escape route to Spain. In October they returned to England aboard the battleship HMS *Malaya*.[6]

In September 1942 Marham was transferred to 2 Group, Bomber Command, and on the 13th 105 and 139 Squadrons received orders to vacate Horsham St. Faith by 28 September, as the Americans were due to arrive to base medium bombers there. The Mosquito Conversion Unit also moved to Marham with the two first-line squadrons. 105 Squadron were equipped with Mosquito Mk.IV bombers and 139 were then converting to this type from Blenheim V (Bisleys), while the Mosquito CU flew a mixture of Blenheims and Mosquitoes. (On 18 October the CU was renamed the Mosquito Training Unit.) On 19 September 105 Squadron attempted the first daylight Mosquito raid on Berlin. Amid the changeover, on 19 September six crews in 105 Squadron attempted the first daylight Mosquito raid on Berlin. Two pilots—Sergeant Norman Booth[7] and Flight Sergeant K. L. Monaghan—were both forced to return early. Flight Lieutenant Roy Ralston and Flying Officer Sydney Clayton bombed Hamburg after finding Berlin covered by cloud. George Parry and "Robbie" Robson were intercepted on two occasions by Fw 190s but managed to evade them. Parry jettisoned his bombs near Hamburg and turned for home, heading back across the north coast of Germany and into Holland. At 1000 feet, just off the Dutch coast, two 109s attacked, but although one of them scored hits, Parry dived down to sea level and soon outran them. Squadron Leader Norman Henry Edward Messervy DFC, an Australian from Point Cook, and his navigator, Pilot Officer Frank Holland, in *M-Mother* were shot down by a Fw 190 piloted by *Schwarmführer Oberfeldwebel* Anton-Rudolf "Toni" Piffer of 2nd Staffel/JG1.[8] The Mosquito crashed thirty kilometers NNW of Osnabrück with the loss of both crew. Messervy was a second tour man, having flown on 68 operations on Blenheims and PR Spitfires in 3 PRU in 1941. Only Warrant Officer Charles R. K. Bools MiD and Sergeant George Jackson succeeded in bombing the "Big City."

A few days later the expert low-level raiders in 105 Squadron were told to prepare for a long overwater operation, which would be flown at heights of just 50-100 feet. George Parry, now a squadron leader, would lead, with "Robbie" Robson as his navigator. The three other crews were Pilot Officer Pete W. T. Rowland and Pilot Officer Richard "Dick" Reilly, Parry's No 2; Flying Officer Alec Bristow and Pilot Officer Bernard Marshall; and Flight Sergeant Gordon K. Carter and Sergeant William S. Young. Their target was the *Gestapo* HQ in Oslo. The Norwegian Government-in-Exile in London had been made aware by reports from the Norwegian Underground that morale in their *Nazi*-subjugated homeland was at a low ebb. They also learned that a rally of *Hirdsmen* (Norwegian Fascists) and Quislings would take place in the Norwegian capital between 25-27 September, and it therefore seemed an ideal opportunity for the Mosquitoes to help restore national pride. As well as disrupting the parade, they were to bomb the *Gestapo* HQ between the Town Hall and the Royal Palace, which stands on a hill.

On 25 September the four Mosquitoes, their bomb bays empty, taxied out at Marham and took off for Leuchars, in Scotland, where the operation came under the control of Wing Commander Hughie Edwards VC DFC. The raid involved a round trip of 1100 miles with an airtime of four hours 45 minutes, the longest Mosquito mission thus far, with the crews using dead reckoning along the entire route. The Mosquitoes were refueled and bombed-up with four 11-second delayed-action 500lb bombs and they set off at low-level, 50 feet all the way, to Norway. They went through the Skaggerak, made landfall at the southern end of Oslo Fjord, and flew up the eastern side. As they flew up to a police radio station perched on a hill Parry hit the flexible 45 foot-high radio antenna, although it did no damage to his Mosquito. Crews had been briefed that there would be 10/10ths cloud at 2000 feet over Oslo, but it was a lovely day with blue sky. They had also been told that there were no fighters to worry about, but the Germans had brought a squadron of Fw 190s south from Stavanger for a flypast during the parade. They had landed at Fornebu and had only been on the ground a short time when the Mosquitoes swooped out of brilliant autumn sunshine over the center of Oslo at 3 PM. A lookout at the southern end of Oslo Fjord reported the bombers and two Focke Wulfs got into the action, although fortunately, the rest did not get off in time. The pilot of the leading fighter was 22-year-old *Unteroffizier* Rudolf "Rudi" Fenten, who had temporarily left his unit to train on and pick up the new Fw 190 at Sola/Stavanger. Flying the other Fw 190 was 24-year-old *Feldwebel* Erich Klein of 3./JG5 based at Herdla, near Bergen. Both pilots were very experienced. Fenten had been in the *Luftwaffe* since 1940, while Klein had joined it in 1937. Fenten at first thought that the twin-engined aircraft flying ahead of him in two pairs were part of the flypast. Then he realized they were too low and he chased after Carter's Mosquito; Fenten set his port engine on fire and he followed until the Mosquito exploded in front of him and crashed into Lake Engervannet, near Sandvika.

Parry, meanwhile, was concentrating on "buzzing" the parade and taking a line southwest over the center of Oslo for the bomb run. Pinpointing the *Gestapo* headquarters was simple enough. Parry was flying at 280-300 mph when he dropped his bombs. Erich Klein, meanwhile, went after Pete Rowland and Dick Reilly. The two aircraft chased around the fir trees north of Oslo for many minutes until Klein struck a tree with his wing and he was forced to return to Fornebu.[9] Some of the Mosquitoes' bombs did not explode, but everyone thought that it was a remarkably successful raid, especially since it was the first long-distance raid the Mosquitoes had carried out. All three crews were debriefed, and they flew back to Norfolk the next morning to rejoin the squadron at Marham. The postmortem and camera pictures taken on the raid revealed that at least four bombs had entered the roof of the *Gestapo* HQ; one had remained inside and failed to detonate, and the other three had crashed through the opposite wall before exploding.

October ushered in new tactics, as two distinct types of low-level attack eventually came to be developed by 105 and 139 Squadrons. These were the low level proper and the "Shallow Dive," which they frequently used together on the same target, starting at Liège on 2 October. Six to eight low-level raiders went in at the lowest level carrying bombs that exploded eleven seconds after impact, and they would be followed by the second formation of "Shallow Divers," who climbed up to about 2000 feet just before the target was reached. When over the target they peeled off and dived straight down on the target and released their bombs fitted with instantaneous fuses at about 1500 feet. Only a very restricted number of Mosquitoes could cross the target at low level before the leaders' bombs exploded, but a "Shallow Dive" formation enabled a target to be hit by a far larger number of Mosquitoes. October was a mix of low-level shallow-dive raids at dusk on targets in Belgium and Holland and high-level attacks on German cities. It was also a month when several crews were lost to the "Butcher Birds" of JG1 and JG 26. On 9 October Wing Commander Edwards and "Tubby" Cairns, as well as another Mosquito crewed by Warrant Officer Charles R. K. Bools MiD and Sergeant George Jackson set out to bomb Duisburg. *Feldwebel* Fritz Timm of 12./JG1 shot down Bools and Jackson over Belgium.[10]

At dusk on Sunday, 11 October, three pairs of Mosquitoes were despatched to bomb Hanover, but two of the Mosquitoes were intercepted by Fw 190As of II./JG26 while en route over Holland. *Unteroffizier* Günter Kirchner of the 5th *Staffel* took off from Katwijk and intercepted Pilot Officer Jim Lang and Flying Officer Robin P. "Tommy" Thomas two kilometers from Utrecht and shot them down. *Unteroffizier* Kolschek of the 4th *Staffel* was credited with shooting down Squadron Leader James G. L. "Jimmy" Knowles DFC and Flight Sergeant Charles Gartside. Lang and Thomas survived to be taken prisoner, but no trace was ever found of Knowles and Gartside.

Night Intruders were flown against targets on the continent. On 30 October Sergeant Reginald Levy and Sergeant Les Hogan and Flying Officer William "Bill" Blessing RAAF and Sergeant J. Lawson in 105 Squadron attacked the *Luftwaffe* night-fighter aerodrome at Leeuwarden, in Holland. They attacked successfully, but Levy was hit by flak from the ground defenses coming across the boundary of the airfield. The port engine was set on fire and the instrument panel and windscreen disappeared with the nose of the aircraft. Levy and his observer, Les Hogan, who was wounded in the arm, got back to Marham, but the Mosquito was completely demolished on landing. After three weeks in Ely hospital both men were back at Marham and operating again.

In November 139 Squadron ceased all operational work while the squadron was being fully equipped with Mosquitoes, and the whole month and the first few days of December was spent in bombing practice and formation flying. On 7 November Squadron Leader Roy Ralston DFM led six Mosquitoes at wave top height across the Bay of Biscay, the Gironde estuary, to attack two large German blockade-running motor vessels loaded with rubber. The operation had been mounted at short notice and preparation had been minimal, but the ships' crews were taken completely by surprise as the 500lb bombs fell full on them and things only got hectic afterwards, but no one stayed around for long. The Mosquito flown by Flight Lieutenant Alec Bristow and Pilot Officer Bernard Marshall was shot down by flak and they survived to be taken prisoner. Ralston was to become one of the most accomplished and skillful low-level bomber pilots of the war. A raid on 9 December demonstrates his quick thinking and rapid response to a given situation. He spotted a German troop train about to enter a tunnel on the Paris to Soissons railway line and immediately decided on a plan of action. Unlike the more conventional thinking of the "average" pilot he did not attack the train itself, but decided to create more havoc with an unconventional attack. He dropped down to tree top height behind the train and dropped a bomb into the mouth of the tunnel. He then quickly orbited the tunnel and bombed it at the other end before it emerged, thus effectively entombing the train, its crew, and cargo in the tunnel.[11]

Meanwhile, plans were well advanced for mounting 2 Group's biggest operation of the war; an attack on the Philips works in Eindhoven, Holland, from low-level. Although some industrial processes had been dispersed to other sites, Eindhoven was still the main center, especially for research into electronic counter-measures and radar. Preparations for Operation *Oyster*, the most ambitious daylight raid conceived by 2 Group, had been given the green light on 9 November. Originally plans called for the Strijp Group main works to be bombed by twenty-four Venturas, twelve Mitchells, and twelve Mosquitoes, while twelve Venturas and thirty-six Bostons would at the same time attack the Emmasingel Lamp and valve works half a mile to the east. The slower Venturas would lead the way at low level with HE and 30lb incendiaries before surprise was lost. On 17 November a full-scale practice was held on a route similar to the one to be used, with the St. Neots power station as the "target." Many basic lessons were learned, while other problems associated with a mixed force, such as the differences in bombing techniques and cruising speeds, were exposed. Rain was falling in East Anglia on the morning of Sunday, 6 December 1942, when 93 light bombers prepared to take off to attack the Philips works. At Marham Wing Commander Hughie Edwards VC DFC carried out the briefings. Eight Mosquitoes of 105 Squadron and two of 139 Squadron led by Edwards rendezvoused with the other bombers at a point over the North Sea. Then they trailed the Bostons and Venturas to the target despite the Mosquitoes' cruising speed of 270-mph, about 100-mph faster. The Mosquitoes were to make a shallow diving attack on the Strijp works, while the other bombers bombed from low level. Unfortunately the timings went wrong, and instead of being 60 miles behind the Mosquitoes caught up with the other bombers. As the Mosquitoes flew in over the Scheldt at 50 feet they began to "wobble," flying along at 160 mph and trying to maintain the speed of the leading bombers. They flew through a flock of ducks and one went through George Parry's windscreen, split his leather flying helmet and cut his head. He did not feel a thing, but his head went ice-cold. Robbie Robson was cut by flying glass, and thinking his pilot was "out" he grabbed the stick. Parry recovered and headed inland. Fw 190 fighters came up and Parry and Flight Lieutenant Bill Blessing, his No.2, broke away to decoy them away from the Venturas coming in over the coast behind. Parry went underneath a Fw 190 whose pilot did not see him and he and Blessing deliberately drew the 190s on themselves, then let them go chasing as they opened the throttles to full speed. The Mosquito IV was not quite as fast as the 190 at 20,000 feet, but at deck level it was about 5 mph faster. Parry was later able to rejoin the formation. Blessing, who turned into the fighter attacks and circled for ten minutes at 50 feet, decided to abandon the flight and made for home chased by the Fw 190, which only abandoned the pursuit about eight miles east of Vlissingen. Pilot Officers Jimmy Bruce DFM and Mike Carreck had an equally close encounter with another Fw 190 until the enemy fighter ran out of ammunition and they also headed back to Marham after first jettisoning their bombs.

The Mosquito flown by Pilot Officer John Earl O'Grady, who was on his first trip, was hit by flak and streamed smoke as they left the target area. O'Grady and his navigator, Sergeant George Lewis, died when their aircraft hit the sea. Nine Venturas and four Bostons also failed to return. The Philips works was devastated, essential supplies destroyed, and the rail network disrupted.[12]

After Eindhoven the Mosquitoes' targets were small in number raids on railway lines and yards in France, Belgium, and Germany. On 20 December 11 Mosquitoes of 105 and 139 Squadrons led by Squadron Leader Reggie Reynolds with Ted Sismore attacked railway targets in the Oldenburg-Bremen area in northwest Germany. One Mosquito came down so low that the crew read the name *Fritz* on a river-tug. The bombers swept over men working on a new barracks and one pilot reported later that "They were near the end of the work and we finished it off for them." Near Delmenhorst Reynolds planed off to attack a gasholder and his four 500lb GP bombs set the gasometer on fire. The Mosquito took a 40mm cannon shell in the port engine, which made the aircraft lurch drunkenly, but Reynolds managed to get the Mosquito on an even keel again. However, the anti-freeze mixture was pouring from the radiator and the cockpit filled with cordite fumes. His No.2, Warrant Officer Arthur Raymond Noesda, moved in closer to Reynolds. Together the pilot from Western Australia and his CO re-crossed the German coast over Wilhelmshaven Bay. Coastal batteries opened up on them and the guns of a warship joined in. Fountains of water rose on each side of the aircraft, which were down on the deck, but Reynolds got his crippled Mosquito back to Marham, where he landed wheels up. Squadron Leader Jack Houlston DFC AFC and his observer, Warrant Officer James Lloyd Armitage DFC, failed to return. They were buried in the Reichswald Forest war cemetery. Luck finally ran out for Noseda, who had flown Blenheims on suicidal anti-shipping strikes from Malta and his observer, Sergeant John Watson Urquhart, on 3 January when they were hit and killed by antiaircraft fire in the attack on engine sheds at Rouen.

In January 1943 attacks were maintained on rail targets on the continent. With no armament the Mosquitoes of course relied on speed and hedgehopping tactics. Sergeant Reginald Levy recalls that:

> "at that time the Focke Wulf 190 was appearing and they could get in one attack on us if they saw us first. The main casualties came from flying into the ground or sea, bird strikes and even from our own bombs. These were fitted with an 11-seconds delay but sometimes this didn't work or else you were unlucky enough to get the blast from someone else's bomb. I watched with apprehension, a bomb, from the machine in front of me, bounce high over my wing whilst attacking the marshalling yards at Terquier, France on 3 January. Just before that, on New Year's Eve 1942, I had been on another marshalling yard attack to Mouceau-sur-Chambres in Belgium. It was dusk and we ran into a snow storm and I flew between two huge slag heaps, only seeing them as they flashed past high above each wing. We then hit a bird, which smashed through the windscreen, covering my observer, Les Hogan and myself with feathers and blood. It was bitterly cold all the way back and although we bathed, scrubbed again the bird smell hung around and we were not the most popular partners at the New Year's dance."[13]

In January a fortnight's work went into low-level formation training for a raid on the Burmeister and Wain U-boat diesel engine works in Copenhagen, in occupied Denmark. Wing Commander Hughie Edwards VC DSO DFC and Flying Officer "Tubby" Cairns DFC would lead nine Mosquitoes of 105 and 139 Squadrons in a round trip of more than 1200 miles to the target. Edwards was to recall that on the 26th the weather "gave every promise of being satisfactory. After much speculation about the target the crews assembled in the briefing room at 0930 hours to see the tracking strings stretching right across the North Sea and Denmark to Copenhagen." Edwards thought that everyone "felt that here at last was a man-sized war-winning job." Unfortunately, the briefing was almost over when the trip had to be cancelled because of a sudden change in conditions over the target. They were promised that the weather conditions were almost certain to be perfect on the 27th, which they were, and in the early afternoon Edwards led nine Mosquitoes to Denmark. The Mosquitoes' war paint of dull silvery grey and green blended well with the cold, grey-green wave-tops and Danish countryside as they flew at low level in close formation to avoid attacks from enemy fighters. If it had been summer visibility would have been impaired by dust and squashed insects splattering their windscreens, but Edwards' only concern was that they were too far south and fuel consumption was a vital consideration. When the coast was eventually sighted the lighthouse on Braavardo Point showed up clearly. Edwards said that "this made it evident that we were 20 miles north of track. Then no sooner were we across the coast then we went straight over the top of Bröndurn aerodrome. This was a bad start, for we had hoped to get well across Denmark before the alarm went up." Near the coast light flak from ships opened up on the formation. Flight Lieutenant John "Flash" Gordon and Flying Officer Ralph Gamble Hayes thought their aircraft had been hit when the trailing edge of the starboard wing became enveloped in puffs of blue smoke. Thinking he had been hit by flak Gordon carried out evasive action, but he had caught the port wing in telegraph wires and damaged the aileron. This, together with the fact that the rest of the formation had gained a considerable lead, caused Gordon to decide to abandon, and he jettisoned his bombs at 16:09 hours and headed home. Edwards continues:

> "Cairns did a fine piece of work by steering a little north of east until we were across the neck of Denmark. This must have led the Germans to suppose that we were going for a target in the Baltic coast of Germany. We passed just south of the great bridge over Star Strom, then turned slowly north and ran up past Cliff Lighthouse. It was rather a thrill to look away to starboard and see Sweden. By the time we were halfway across Köge Bay we could see the outline of Copenhagen on the horizon. We flew up the east coast of Amagen and could clearly see ships in the canal separating it from the mainland. Then the Wing Commander opened his bomb doors and we packed in tight for the bombing run. The buildings of Burmeister & Wain came up just as we had seen them in the photographs and as we swept low over the roofs the bombs could be seen showering down - skidding, bouncing and crashing into the factory. Then, as we turned away across the spires of the city, the flak came streaming up from the ships in the harbor to the north. Only one aircraft was slightly damaged [Edwards' Mosquito received two holes in the starboard nacelle] but five minutes later a Mosquito went smack into a set of high-tension cables and blew up. [Sergeant James G. Dawson and Sergeant Ronald H. Cox were killed]. This was the worst of misfortune but the rest of us got safely away without further incident."

Sergeant pilot H. C. "Gary" Herbert RAAF in 105 Squadron and his navigator, Sergeant C. "Jakey" Jacques, flew number two to Wing Commander Edwards. Herbert wrote:[14]

> "Quite a long trip. When we eventually found the target it was getting dark but we hit it good and proper. We attacked between two big chimneys and hit the

machine shops and power station. Our bombs were delayed half-hour, three hours, six hours and 36 hours to disorganise the place for a while. Other kites had eleven second delay bombs as well as long delay. We got quite a lot of light flak as we left the target but kept on the housetops and nobody was hit. When we got well away it was pretty dark and one of the kites was hit and crashed in flames. Petrol was getting short so we throttled back to 230 mph and as we passed the last island on the west of Denmark we went straight over a machine gun post at 200 feet. It threw up a lot of flak but I jinked and dodged it OK. We came back quietly and landed in the dark at 8pm. One kite ran out of juice and crashed about twenty miles away killing [Sergeant Richard Clare and Flying Officer Edward Doyle of 139 Squadron, who hit a balloon cable and tree at East Dereham after the starboard engine failed]. Got a scare, on the way back we were struck by lightning twice and each time a ball of fire appeared on the wing and gradually died out. I looked at the wing but there wasn't a mark on it. Seems queer to me but the weather man said it had happened before so I couldn't have had the DTs. [Edwards landed with only fifteen gallons of fuel in his tanks; enough for about another six and a half miles]. Invited the Officers over to the mess in the evening to have a few drinks and fight the battle again. Nice evening. At the time for the bombs to go off we drank a toast to them. On Friday 30th some news came in from Sweden of our raid on Copenhagen. Apparently it was a huge success and the Diesel works were flattened. A sugar factory and another six-storey building burned to the ground. They thought our delay bombs were duds but they all went off OK on time."

On 30 January there was some trepidation among Mosquito crews at Marham who were due to raid Berlin to disrupt speeches in the city's main broadcasting station on what was the tenth anniversary of Hitler's seizure of power. Three crews in 105 Squadron led by Squadron Leader "Reggie" W. Reynolds DFC and Pilot Officer E. B. "Ted" Sismore would bomb Berlin that morning when *Reichsmarschall* Hermann Göring was due to speak. In the afternoon, three Mosquitoes of 139 Squadron would arrive over Berlin at the time Dr. Joseph Göebbels, Hitler's propaganda minister, was due to address the German nation at the Sports Palast. Reynolds had flown a tour on Hampdens and a tour on Manchesters. Sismore had flown on Blenheims on 110 Squadron and, while at the Blenheim OTU at Bicester and the Whitley OTU at Honeybourne, had flown on two of the 1000-bomber raids in 1942. Most of the pilots and navigators could not face breakfast. An exception was Flying Officer A. T. "Tony" Wickham of 105 Squadron, who was taking part in the morning raid with his navigator, Pilot Officer W. E. D. Makin. Wickham heartily drank three tins of orange juice and polished off half a dozen fried eggs. A month earlier, as a young pilot officer going on his first trip, a high level dawn raid on cities in the Ruhr (when casualties were particularly heavy), his reaction during a gloomy five o'clock breakfast had been quite different. Wickham suddenly burst out and said, "I suppose this is a death or glory effort?" Hughie Edwards lent forward, looked at him and said, "There is no glory in it and that's what makes it so worthwhile." Flight Lieutenant John "Flash" Gordon DFC and Flying Officer Ralph G. Hayes DFC, who three days earlier had returned with a damaged port wing, completed the trio of aircraft due in Berlin for "elevenses." The three Mosquitoes arrived over Berlin at exactly 11.00 hours and the explosion of their bombs severely disrupted the *Reichsmarschall's* speech. Listeners heard a few muffled words followed by confusion of many voices, then another shout or bang, after which the microphone was apparently switched off and martial music played. It was then announced that Göring's speech would be delayed for a few moments. But after three-quarters of an hour martial music was still being played!

That afternoon the three Mosquitoes of 139 Squadron arrived over Berlin at the time Göebbels was due to speak. They were flown by Squadron Leader Donald F. W. Darling DFC and Flying Officer William Wright, Flight Sergeant Peter John Dixon McGeehan and Flying Officer Reginald Charles Morris, and Sergeants Massey and R. C. "Lofty" Fletcher. The Mosquitoes dropped their bombs right on cue. However, the earlier raid alerted the defenses and flak brought down the Mosquito flown by Darling and Wright. Both were buried in Berlin's 1939-45 war cemetery. That night "Tony" Wickham treated British listeners to the BBC's 9 o'clock news to an account of the action. "Lord Haw Haw," trying to sound convincing in a German broadcast to any who cared to listen, announced that, "Thanks to the U-boat campaign Britain is so starved of materials that she has been compelled to build her bombers of wood." Reynolds was awarded the DSO, while all the other officers received the DFC and the sergeants, DFMs.

On the afternoon of 14 February, in what became known as the "Great Tours Derby," six Mosquitoes of 139 Squadron and a subsidiary formation of four Mosquitoes led by Squadron Leader Robert Beck "Bob" Bagguley DFC set out to attack the engine sheds in the French city. "Unfortunately, the weather marred the complete success of the show," reported Flying Officer William E. G. "Bill" Humphrey. "For though the leader and four aircraft of his formation succeeded in bombing their primary – the engine repair shops - from fifty feet, the rest of the formation was split up by cloud right down to the deck. Three of the remainder turned back but Flying Officer Pereira carried on by himself and carried out a Shallow Dive attack on the engine round house to the east of the town. He scored direct hits with at least two of his six bombs, one of which hit the turntable in the middle.[15] Flying Officer G. S. W. Rennie RCAF having lost the formation looked around for an alternative target and finally bombed a train with devastating results, hitting the engine with all four bombs in salvo. Everyone returned safely from this operation." The following evening, twelve Mosquitoes of 105 Squadron attacked the goods depot from low-level, and on the 18th twelve Mosquitoes made a shallow dive attack. Two aborted and one aircraft failed to return.[16]

On 14 February Hughie Edwards, who had been promoted Group Captain four days earlier, left 105 Squadron to take up a post at HQ Bomber Command prior to taking command of RAF Binbrook on the 18th.[17] Edwards' successor was Wing Commander Geoffrey P. Longfield, who on 26 February led an attack by twenty Mosquitoes of 105 and 139 Squadrons on the Rennes Naval Arsenal. Ten aircraft were to go in at low level led by Longfield and ten Mosquitoes of 139 Squadron were to follow just behind, climb to 2000 feet, and dive bomb behind the first wave. Longfield's navigator, Flight Lieutenant Roderick Milne, lost his bearings on the final run up to the target, which took the Mosquitoes to an airfield six miles south of the target. The airfield defenses sent up a hail of light flak as the Mosquitoes turned towards the target. On low level attacks the Mosquitoes had always flown in echelon starboard, and any left hand turns created no problems, as all members of the formation could keep the aircraft at his left in sight. However, Longfield, who had turned too far to the left, suddenly turned right again. In a sharp turn to the right as each pilot lifted his left wing to turn right his wing obscured the aircraft to his left because he could not drop down as in higher altitudes. Canadian Flying Officers Spencer Kimmel and Harry Kirkland, who were formating on Longfield, sliced into their leader's tail, and Longfield went up into a loop and dived straight into the ground west of Rennes St. Jacques. Kimmel lost height and disappeared below the trees at 300 mph. Longfield, Milne, Kimmel, and Kirkland all died. (On the way home a 139 Squadron Mosquito flown by Lieutenant T.D.C. Moe and his observer, 2nd Lieutenant O. Smedsaas, both RNAF, crashed and the two Dutchmen were killed.)

By the time the others reached the target Warrant Officer "Gary" Herbert, who before the operation had agreed to change positions with Kimmel, could see the dive-bombers already starting their dive. The Australian pilot knew his formation would be blown up by the 11-second delayed action 500lb bombs carried by some of the Mosquitoes if they went in. He therefore turned violently to the west and climbed to about 700 feet and dived below the other formation and got his bombs on the target. Others in his formation bombed alternative targets. Pilot Officer G. W. "Mac" McCormick, a young officer on only his fourth operation, did not see the dive-bombers until it was too late and he went in at low level. (139 Squadron were dropping 500lb MC - medium capacity - bombs with instantaneous fuses.) Herbert said, "God knows how he got through because photographs showed him right in the middle of the bursts. He came back with his radiators full of flock from bombed bedding stores. He used up a lot of luck today." Next day "Mac" McCormick and visiting Wing Commander John W. Deacon were killed on a training flight when the wing fairing broke up during a dive from 30,000 feet and they crashed a mile to the southeast of Marham at Brick Kiln Plantation.

On Sunday, 28 February, six of 105 Squadron's Mosquitoes led by Wing Commander Roy Ralston went to the John Cockerill Steel works at Liège. Four more led by Pilot Officer Onslow Thompson DFM RNZAF and Pilot Officer Wallace J. Horne DFC went to the Stork Diesel Engine Works at Hengelo, in what was the eighth raid on the Dutch town by Mosquitoes. At Liège the Mosquitoes bombed at about 200 feet and results were "good," but at Hengelo very little damage was done to the factories.

On 3 March Wing Commander Peter Shand DFC and Flight Sergeant Christopher D. Handley DFM led ten Mosquitoes of 139 Squadron to the molybdenum mines at Knaben, in South Norway. Molybdenum is a metallic element used in the production of high-speed steels. At the target Shand would lead the six Mosquitoes of the Shallow Dive section while Squadron Leader Bob Bagguley would lead the four Low Level attack aircraft. The formation set course over Marham at 1210 hours in good formation for Flamborough Head. Shand wrote:

> "We were ninety minutes over the sea at low level, during which time the 10/10 cloud gave way to a clear sky and brilliant sunshine. Track was maintained accurately by constant drift reading and a landfall was made within a mile of the appointed place. Visibility was exceptional and the snow capped mountains over which we had to climb presented a striking sight."

Flying Officer William S. D. "Jock" Sutherland, a Scot from Dollar whose navigator was Flying Officer George Dean, flew No.2 to Wing Commander Shand. They were very impressed by the scenery over Norway. Sutherland recalled:

> "Visibility was about twenty miles and there was no cloud. The snow-covered mountains with lakes dotted about made a very pleasant change after the long sea trip. We reached the target after climbing up and started our attack straight away."

The six Shallow Divers led by Shand commenced their climb and the remaining four Mosquitoes kept as low as possible on Sirdale Lake and overtaking them. They were seen to pass underneath the Shallow Divers just before reaching the northern end of the lake and then turn east, climbing steeply over the surrounding hills in line astern and stepped down. The Shallow Dive formation then turned east on to course. Bagguley's formation climbed up the rather steep crevice and the much-studied pinpoint of Risones was picked up. "From then onwards," said Bagguley, "it was a piece of cake. The target appeared just as per illustrations and was cleanly silhouetted against the snow of the surrounding mountains. We made a perfect run on and dropped our bombs from roof-top height." Flight Sergeant Peter McGeehan DFM and Flying Officer Reginald Morris DFC, flying at the rear of the Low Level formation, were not in a suitable position for an attack so they peeled off and took another run at it. McGeehan remarked:

> "During this time we saw the Low Level bombs going off, the Shallow Divers making their attack and Massey attacking the gun positions. It looked good and the stuff was still going off as we ran over, successfully this time."

As the Shallow Divers approached the target they saw brown and white smoke rising from the Low Level formation's bombs and only the roof of the target building was still visible. They commenced their attack immediately. Sutherland continues:

> "I followed the Winco in rather low and the debris from his bombs flew up at least 300 feet above us. After bombing we headed straight for home and could see smoke from the target rising to a very considerable height. Crossing the Norwegian coast going out we saw a Mossie being attacked by two 190s. We didn't wait to see the result. [18] We made a landfall at Hunstanton and landed at base at 1630. Altogether a very enjoyable and satisfactory trip."

Bomb bursts accompanied by orange flashes and a red glow were seen on and around the target, which resulted in the plant being enveloped in clouds of white and brown smoke and debris being blown to a height of 1000 feet. AOC Air Vice Marshal J. H. d'Albiac sent his congratulations for a "well planned and splendidly executed attack...Mosquito stings judiciously placed are very painful."

On 4 March Squadron Leader Reggie Reynolds DSO DFC led a successful attack by six Mosquitoes at low level from 50-200 feet on engine sheds and repair workshops at Le Mans. On 4 and 8 March 139 Squadron made two extremely successful attacks on Aulnoye. The first of these was directed against the railway engine sheds and a bomb manufacturing factory and was led by Squadron Leader Bob Bagguley DFC. Three Mosquitoes were employed on the Low Level attack on the railway target and three on the Shallow Dive. Bagguley's navigator, Flight Lieutenant Charles Hayden DFC, recalled:

> "A most pleasant trip. We made good landfall thanks to J. C. and my pilot and met no opposition the whole way to the target. The bombs made a wizard sight as they went up, making a sheer column of flame about 200 feet high. No opposition was encountered on the way out except some machine-gun tracer, which was seen going up at another Mossie. We landed in semi-daylight."

Sergeant Robert Pace and Pilot Officer George Cook, who were part of the Shallow Dive formation on the bomb factory, were flying their first raid. Cook recalled:

> "A most enjoyable first op. good to see bombs from two aircraft in front hitting the roof of the target and 300 foot columns of smoke after leaving target. Our photographs show direct hits from our own bombs."

On the second raid on Aulnoye on 8 March against the railway repair shops the six Mosquitoes of the Shallow Dive attack was led by Wing Commander Shand and the four in the Low Level section by Squadron Leader Bob Bagguley. One of the Shallow Divers was the Mosquito flown by Flying Officer Jock Sutherland and Flying Officer George Dean. Sutherland recalled:

> "We took off in good order, setting course for the enemy coast from North Foreland. Crossing the French coast slight A/A fire came up at the rear part of the formation. At le Cateau we turned on to a Northeast heading for the target climbing up to 4000 feet. The Low Level formation continued at 50 feet. As we were about to attack our target we saw a huge sheet of flame and black smoke where the Low Level boys' bombs were going off. Our target was bombed at 1855. There was no flak from the target area, which was covered with a slight industrial haze. We did not see our own bombs burst for once but got good photographs and saw a very thick cloud of smoke as we left the target. We came out at Termonds. Coming out of the coast there was a great deal of flak aimed in our direction from the shore on one side and ships on the other. I think we caught them with their trousers down, for they were too late. We landed away from base owing to bad weather and returned the following morning."

Another of the Shallow Divers was the Mosquito flown by Flight Sergeant Peter McGeehan DFM and Flying Officer Reginald Morris DFC. They were so engrossed in looking at the large sheet of flame and quantities of black and brown smoke coming from the engine sheds which had been bombed with excellent results by the Low Level formation that they overshot. They had to peel off to starboard and come in last before dropping their bombs on the target. Looking back after they had reached ground level again they could see a column of smoke 1000 feet high.

That same day three Mosquitoes of 105 Squadron bombed rail targets at Tergnier, 12 miles south of St. Quentin, in France, from low-level, and Flight Lieutenant Gordon led another pair of Mosquitoes in an attack on the railway shops at Lingen, in Germany. The Mosquito flown by Sergeant W. W. Austin and Pilot Officer P. E. Thomas was hit by flak and crashed on the return trip at Den Ham, in Holland. Both men survived and they were taken prisoner.

On 9 March the Renault Aero Engine Works at Le Mans was the target for fifteen of Marham's Mosquitoes. The whole formation was led by Squadron Leader Roy Ralston DSO DFM and his navigator, Flight Lieutenant Syd Clayton DFC DFM, at the head of five Mosquitoes from 105 Squadron who carried out the Low Level attack. A Shallow Dive section was led by Squadron Leader Bob Bagguley DFC at the head of ten aircraft of 139 Squadron. One of the "Shallow Diver" teams was Flying Officer Sutherland and Flying Officer Dean. Sutherland wrote:

> "Rather a ropey take-off. Squadron Leader Bagguley had trouble with his port engine and turned back. I took over the lead but Bob caught us up on the circuit and regained the lead. From then on it was a normal trip. Visibility was bad, but we spotted the target wreathed in smoke from 105's Low Level attack. We were greeted by plenty of accurate flak over the target, but managed to avoid same as we were diving fast. Coming out over the coast, we found an enemy convoy of twenty ships dead ahead. Big moment. We altered course to port, and the escort ship challenged us by lamp. We gave her a long series of garbled 'dits' and 'dahs' on our recognition lights and nipped smartly off. Base was reached without further incident."

"Bob" Bagguley and Flight Lieutenant Charles Hayden DFC were seen to bomb the target and, when last observed, "appeared to be sailing home in fine style," but they failed to return. No trace of the crew was ever found.

On 12 March twelve Mosquitoes of 105 and 139 Squadrons led by Squadron Leader Reggie Reynolds and Pilot Officer Ted Sismore were briefed to attack the John Cockerill steel and armament works in the center of Liège. The briefing officer stated that two crack fighter units had recently been moved to Woensdrecht, south of Rotterdam, and that they had recently been re-equipped with Fw 190s.[19] Allowing for several doglegs flight time to target was between 2 and 2½ hours. Attacks of this nature were normally planned for dusk or just before dark so that the Mosquitoes could return to England individually under the cover of half-light or darkness. Bombing had to be carried out very accurately indeed to keep losses to a minimum, and this task was given to the shallow dive section led by Squadron Leader John V. Berggren of 139 Squadron with his observer Flying Officer Peter Wright DFC. At 15.40 hours all twelve Mosquitoes took off. They headed south before flying across the Channel to France and up and over the cliffs to the west of Cap Gris Nez, then on across the heavily defended Pas de Calais at nought feet. Finally, the Mosquitoes seldom flying at more than 100 feet and keeping echelon formation on the leader, picked up the River Meuse, which led straight in to the target. At around five miles from the target 105 Squadron split from the rest of the formation and went straight in at low level to each drop their four 500lb 11-second delayed action bombs. These burst in the target area as Berggren and his six Mosquitoes hurriedly climbed to 3000 feet and then dived onto the target to release their four 500lb bombs with instantaneous fuses. Turning away to the north the crews could see a huge mushroom of smoke building up over the main target area. Leaving the target the formation broke into individual aircraft and raced for the Scheldt Estuary at 280 mph in gathering dusk. The Mosquitoes had to climb to 200 feet to avoid HT cables, which criss-crossed Belgium and France. The Mosquito flown by Sergeant Robert Pace and Pilot Officer George Cook was hit by flak and caught fire before it crashed on the runway of Woensdrecht airfield and was smashed to smithereens on impact, leaving a stream of burning debris in its wake.[20]

On 16 March sixteen Mosquitoes of 105 and 139 Squadrons led by Squadron Leader John Berggren DFC made low level and shallow dive attacks on roundhouses and engine sheds at Paderborn. Flight Lieutenant Bill Blessing DFC of 105 Squadron led the Low Level section. Berggren's navigator, Flying Officer Peter Wright DFC, recalled:

"Paderborn is quite a few miles east of the Ruhr, and it looked an alarmingly long way into Germany when we studied the route on the large-scale map in the briefing room. There were to be sixteen aircraft, which by our standards is a big formation. The target consisted of engine sheds, and they were to be attacked in two waves, first by six aircraft at low level and then by ten from about 1300 feet in a Shallow Dive. Apart from the bombing run, we were to fly at low level all the way. We, in our aircraft, were to lead the formation to a point about twenty-five miles short of the target, and then to climb to 3000 feet with nine others behind us, while the last six raced in ahead to bomb first from low level. The rest of us were to dive down to thirteen hundred feet before bombing. It was hoped that our bombs would begin falling just as the last of the low-level aircraft had got clear of the target. It would be too bad for him if we bombed a bit early. You can't see Mosquitoes when you are directly above them; their camouflage is too good. So, good timing would be needed if we were going to make a concentrated attack, and yet give that last man a chance.

"All went well till we were over the Zuider Zee, when we were intercepted by a formation of low-flying ducks. They attacked strongly, but inflicted only one casualty. Their leader crashed through the perspex of Sergeant Cummings' aircraft, and landed as a heap of blood and feathers on his observer's stomach. Two others hit his starboard engine nacelle. It was very draughty in that aeroplane (and messy, too), so it turned back for home. The rest of us managed to take the effective evasive action. We are better at avoiding birds than we used to be.

"We carried on very smoothly over the flat lands of Holland and North-West Germany. Occasionally we would lift a wing to avoid a church steeple. Visibility was just right - enough to map read by and no more. Between Minster and Osnabrück the country became hilly and the formation inevitably got more ragged. But everything was still very quiet. We crossed a big autobahn and began to climb, while the last six Mosquitoes stayed down. It's an uncomfortable feeling to be up at 3000 feet after a spell of low flying. You feel naked and motionless and a sitting target for the gunners. But it gets better when you dive on to the target and the earth comes close again and you recapture the feeling of speed.

"There was a lot of industrial haze drifting over from the Ruhr, and the target was difficult to see. Perhaps it was the haze that made the flak gunners so slow off the mark. They allowed half of us to bomb before they opened up. When they did open up, they were pretty good, and the boys at the back had a nasty few minutes. Flight Sergeant McGeehan was hit and did not return.[21] Sergeant Massey came back on one engine and did very well to make a crash landing at an aerodrome close to base.[22] We, personally, were lucky and were out of the target area in time. When we looked back the target was going up into the air, and above it the Mosquitoes were bucking like broncos to avoid the streams of orange balls thrown up at them from all angles by the Bofors guns.

"On the way home over Germany the mist got thicker and thicker and we all felt safer and safer. We saw two Junkers 52s and wished we had some guns. Nothing else happened, and we sneaked quietly out over the Dutch island, which we thought would give us the least trouble. I doubt if they could have seen us, anyway."

On 17 March Acting Wing Commander John "Jack" de Lacey Wooldridge DFC* DFM RAFVR took command of 105 Squadron. Wooldridge was born in Yokohama, Japan, on 18 July 1919 and was educated at St. Paul's School, London. As a composer he studied with Sibelius. Wooldridge had joined the RAF in 1938 and he flew two tours (73 operations) on heavy bombers prior to taking command of 105 Squadron, including 32 ops on Manchesters. For the last three months he had been attached to the tri-service PWD working on the FIDO fog dispersal system.[23]

On the 20th six Mosquitoes of 105 Squadron carried out low-level attacks on the engine sheds and repair shops at Louvain, in Belgium. Six Mosquitoes of 139 Squadron led by Flight Lieutenant Mike Wayman DFC and Flying Officer G. S. "Pops" Clear carried out a Low Level dusk attack on the railway workshops at Malines. This raid was unsuccessful, as Flying Officer Jock Sutherland recalled:

"Everything was OK until we reached the enemy coast. [Over Blankenburg] Mike Wayman was hit in the starboard engine. He tried to carry on, but after a couple of miles he peeled off and feathered his airscrew. We took over the lead. Near the target, the visibility closed in to 500 yards and we were unable to locate our exact position in the industrial haze and general filth. We eventually bombed a goods train. We boobed coming out and went slap across Antwerp aerodrome, where we got plenty of accurate flak. There we ran into trouble good and proper in the Flushing estuary, where everything opened up, including a convoy and escort. Fortunately we were not hit and landed OK at base at 2030 hours."

Wayman made it back to England, and he crashed at Martlesham Heath on overshoot; Wayman and "Pops" Clear were killed. Flying Officer Cussens and Sergeant Munro had also experienced "intense" flak crossing the coast at Blankenburg, which knocked out their hydraulics. They saw the target momentarily but were unable to open the bomb doors. Coming out they had more flak at Antwerp and an "incredible amount" at Beveland Island which shot away their rudder controls and port landing edge, causing the aircraft to stall at 180 mph when eventually landed at Marham. Flying Officer Brown summed up the operation thus:

'Never has the carefree attitude of some aircrews toward operating been more apparent! We stooged almost over Ostend to make a good landfall, pouncing on the target at thirty seconds' notice. A false alarm of 'snappers' after the target - which we missed - resulted in Mosquitoes pulling the plug in every direction and screaming about like a gaggle of alarmed hens; not to mention some cheery optimist who flew for fifty miles or so over enemy territory with his navigation lights on. The visibility was wicked; we went over Antwerp; we went over the mouth of the Scheldt; and back over this country, we went round from aerodrome to aerodrome with our wireless u/s, before base, which had spent a busy evening changing the flarepath about, condescended to receive us. What a life!"[24]

On 23 March ten Mosquitoes of 139 Squadron led by Wing Commander Peter Shand DFC and five of 139 Squadron led by Flight Lieutenant Bill Blessing DFC attacked the Compagnie Génèrale de Construction des Locomotives Batigniolles-Chatillon at St. Joseph, two miles northeast of Nantes, at low level. The raid had to be timed to perfection as the French factory workers finished work. Flying Officer J. E. Hay, a South African from Pretoria who was navigator to Pilot Officer T. M. Mitchell in the Shallow Dive section led by Wing Commander Shand, recalls:

"The Battle Order was issued early on the morning of the 23rd March and my pilot and I were on the list, which was a long one. All this, and the very long trainload of bombs being pulled along the tarmac, seemed to indicate a big 'do'. We entered the briefing room with more than the usual feeling of excitement that a formation made up of both Squadrons was to attack the St. Joseph Locomotive Works at Nantes - quite a deep penetration into enemy-occupied territory. We were airborne at 1350 and set course across the aerodrome about ten minutes later. The weather was good over base, but it had started to deteriorate before we reached the south coast. People at the seaside that afternoon must have been startled as the large formation went out over the Channel at nought feet. The weather improved for us over the Channel and on schedule the French coast was sighted - a low belt of sand dunes followed by wooded downs. We shot over these in tight formation and for once experienced no flak - we were over the first hurdle. From this point onwards the weather was perfect with excellent visibility and some cloud about 2000 feet above us.

"Our route across France lay over a series of hills and valleys. We skimmed over the hilltops, and flew down through the valleys and across the small towns. On one hilltop we saw three Huns make a dash for their machine-gun; we dived straight at them, and they threw themselves flat as we roared over the gunpit. There was nothing very dangerous in this, for we could see the tarpaulin cover still on the gun! Then, after almost thirty minutes of breathless chase across France, we swept into the broad plains of the River Loire to find the sun breaking fitfully through the clouds. At about a quarter to four the town of Nantes appeared ahead and we began to climb up to our bombing height, while Squadron Leader Blessing led 105 Squadron on ahead at low level. As we climbed away from the earth, we seemed at first to hover stationary in mid-air. Then we saw the first black puffs of anti-aircraft fire. As we peeled off for our dive, I saw 105 streaking across the target below us and then the vivid flashes of their bombs exploding. Within a few seconds we were diving fast after them and our bombs were following theirs. Then we went across the town and away to the south. Looking back, I could see the old works covered by an immense pall of smoke and I also caught a glimpse of six enemy fighters circling about twenty miles away to the west in the direction of St. Nazaire. They suddenly formed up and flew off north, apparently not having seen us. As we were racing south with a very pretty turn of speed, they were soon lost to sight.

"The job completed, we flew out over the Bay of Biscay in brilliant sunshine, heading for home. In every direction there seemed to be Mosquitoes just skimming the wave-tops. It was a grand sight! Shortly afterwards we all lost touch in a heavy bank of fog, and when we at last emerged from this the Cornish coast lay below us."

This raid was an outstanding success; not one bomb missing the target, and no building in the target area failing to be hit. Squadron Leader Berggren added, "the target...looked a good enough mess even before the second formation dropped their bombs."

Next day, 24 March, three Mosquitoes of 105 Squadron were sent on a *Rover* operation to shallow dive-bomb trains and railway lines within specified areas in Germany. On 27 March 139 Squadron dispatched six aircraft on another low-level raid on the Stork Diesel Works at Hengelo. The bombing results at debriefing were described as being uncertain, though photographs showed many near misses. On this occasion serious damage was done to the primary target, although nearby houses were hit once again. Henk F. van Baaren attended a funeral for the first time in his young life when a 17-year-old boy from his school and a member of the same gymnastic club that he attended was killed.[25]

On 28 March seven Mosquitoes led by Flight Lieutenant "Flash" Gordon were dispatched to attack the railway marshalling yards at Liège, but rainstorms reduced the evening visibility to half a mile, and instead he led the aircraft in an attack on a factory north of Valbengit Bridge at Liège. They were spotted by *Unteroffizier* Wilhelm Mayer of 6th *Staffel* JG26 heading towards Dunkirk at low level, and *Oberfeldwebel* Adolf "Addi" Glunz and three other Fw 190s of 4./JG26 were sent off from Vitry immediately. They intercepted the Mosquitoes after they had bombed. Glunz was credited with shooting down in the space of a minute the Mosquito flown by Flying Officer George Bruce DFM and Flying Officer Dick Reilly about 18 miles east of Etaples and Sergeant George Leighton and Sergeant Thomas Chadwick south of Lille. All four airmen were later buried in Lille Southern Cemetery. (Glunz finished the war with 71 confirmed victories.)

On 30 March ten Mosquitoes of 139 Squadron led by Wing Commander Peter Shand DFC set off to bomb the Philips Works at Eindhoven, which was about ready to begin full production again. One 139 Squadron Mosquito that was hit by flak on crossing the enemy coast lost its hydraulics and was unable to open its bomb bay doors to bomb and so abandoned the strike, leaving four aircraft to attack from low level and five in a shallow dive. The attackers switched back over Holland, dodging flocks of seagulls over the Zuider Zee and tearing over Eindhoven once more at zero feet. Pilot Officer T. M. Mitchell, who brought up the rear of the formation with his navigator, Flying Officer J. E. Hay, recalls:

> "We encountered very intense light flak at the coast. This was accurate and followed all the aircraft for about eight miles inland. We saw no further flak until the target was reached. The run-up was beautiful, the building being silhouetted against the sky. On reaching it we found it necessary to climb 50 feet in order to get over that blasted chimney, about which we had been warned. I saw the Wing Commander's bombs, which were timed to go off a short time after impact, fall into the buildings as we skimmed over the rooftops. Then I let our own bombs go right into the middle of the factory. As I circled after the attack I saw the whole building become enveloped in smoke with huge red flashes as the bombs exploded. On the way out the weather was very bumpy but we reached base without further incident. My navigator saw V-signs flashing from Dutch homes in the falling light."

Flying Officer Paney and Sergeant Stimson noticed a Dutchman hoeing in a garden. He glanced up once and then went on hoeing!

On 1 April six Mosquitoes of 105 Squadron led by Wing Commander Roy Ralston DSO DFM and Flight Lieutenant Syd Clayton DFC DFM, whose 100th op this was, set out with four of 139 Squadron led by Squadron Leader John Berggren. Their targets were a power station and railway yards at Trier and engine sheds at Ehrang respectively, which were bombed from 50-400 feet. Bombs from the first formation were seen to fall in the middle of the railway workshops, throwing up large quantities of debris followed by showers of green sparks. Bomb bursts were also observed on the power station followed by a sheet of flame which rose to a height of 100 feet. The attack by the second formation on Ehrang resulted in a huge explosion and a red flash from a coal container. One bomb was seen to bounce off railway tracks into a house, which was blown to pieces. On leaving the target area smoke was seen rising to about 1500 feet. No aircraft were lost, although Flying Officer Talbot's and Sergeant Sleeman's Mosquito of 139 Squadron, which was hit by blast from bomb bursts and also by flak, returned on one engine with gyro artificial horizon and turn-and-bank indicator out of action. They crossed the enemy coast one mile south of Boulogne harbor and flak "of various assortments" followed them up to five miles out. Talbot, who landed safely at Manston, concluded, "Ain't life grand!" In the messes that night crews celebrated Syd Clayton's award of an immediate DSO and wished him luck on his pilot's course. He had been waiting for three weeks to complete his century.

On 3 April Wing Commander Wooldridge led his first 105 Squadron operation and eight Mosquitoes carried out *Rover* attacks on railway targets in Belgium and France. All three of 105 Squadron's Mosquitoes returned safely from attacks on locomotive repair shed shops at Malines and engine sheds at Namur, but a Mosquito of 139 Squadron was lost. Flying Officer W. O. Peacock and his observer, Sergeant R. C. Saunders, were shot down by *Oberfeldwebel* Wilhelm Mackenstedt of 6./JG26 three kilometers south of Beauvais for the German pilot's sixth and final victory.[26]

On 11 April four Mosquitoes of 105 Squadron led by Squadron Leader Bill Blessing DFC and his navigator, Flight Sergeant A. J. W. "Jock" Heggie, ventured to Hengelo to bomb the Stork Works. This was the tenth and final low level attack by 2 Group Mosquito IVs on the long-suffering town. Light was failing and visibility was about three miles with 10/10ths cloud at 3000 feet when the formation was intercepted at 50 feet by two formations of three Fw 190s before reaching the target. One section of Fw 190s fired a burst of two seconds and then they broke off to starboard to attack two of the Mosquitoes. Flying Officer Norman Hull RCAF and Sergeant Philip Brown, No.3 in the formation, were intercepted by four Fw 190s who came in from starboard and opened fire for about fifteen seconds at a range of 350 yards. The Mosquitoes carried out evasive action by turning into the attack, weaving and gaining and losing height between 150-200 feet and increasing speed. After making one attack the enemy aircraft broke off and wheeled round to attack *Z-Zebra* flown by Flying Officer David Polgase RNZAF and his observer, Flight Sergeant Leslie Lampen, which had been hit by flak at the coast. *Z-Zebra* had one airscrew feathered, and with his speed greatly reduced Polgase and Lampen fell behind the rest of the formation. *Unteroffizier* Gerhard Wiegand of 2./JG1 shot them down. The Mosquito crashed in a wood near Bentheim, Germany, and both crew were killed. Flying Officer F. M. "Bud" Fisher, an American pilot from Pennsylvania, and Flight Sergeant Les Hogan were unable to bomb the primary target and attacked a train in the area instead. Blessing pressed home his attack from 50 feet and he dropped his bomb load directly onto the Stork Works, causing severe damage to the plant. The Resistance seems to have signalled London that the Stork and Dikkers factories should no longer be considered targets, as production of war machinery had stopped.[27]

On 19/20 April there were no Main Force operations, and six Mosquitoes of 2 Group failed to locate rail workshops at Namur in bad visibility and returned without loss. On the night of 20/21 April nine Mosquitoes of 105 Squadron and two from 139 Squadron led by Wing Commander Peter Shand DSO DFC carried out a bombing attack on Berlin. This was a diversion for 339 heavy bombers attacking Stettin and 86 Stirlings bombing the Heinkel factory near Rostock. The Mosquito "night nuisance" operations were also designed to "celebrate" Hitler's birthday. Over Berlin it was cloudless with bright moonlight, and the Mosquitoes dropped their bombs from 15,00-23,000 feet. Flak was moderate and quite accurate, but the biggest danger proved to be night-fighters. One of these was *Oberleutnant* Lothar Linke, *Staffelkapitän* 12./NJG1, who the night before had claimed to be the second *Nachtjagd* pilot to destroy a Mosquito whilst flying a standard Bf 110G.[28] Linke, again led by his night fighter controller *Eisbär* ("Polar Bear"), overtook Shand's Mosquito at high altitude and at high speed in a power dive, and shot the Mosquito down over the northern part of the Ijsselmeer at 0210 hours. Shand and his navigator, Pilot Officer Christopher Handley DFM, were killed.[29]

On 26 April two Mosquitoes of 105 Squadron led by Flight Lieutenant John "Flash" Gordon DFC and his navigator, Flying Officer R. Hayes DFC, were ordered to bomb the railway workshops at Jülich, near Cologne. This had always been looked upon as a particularly difficult target to find, as it had no easily distinguishable landmarks near it to assist the observer. Any errors in navigation would bring the aircraft dangerously near to Cologne to the east or Aachen to the west. Gordon wrote:

"Very shortly after briefing we were airborne, and after circling base a couple of times both aircraft set course for the Dutch coast. All the way over the North Sea I did nothing but sweat -' I hope we're not too high. Can any enemy ships see us? Down a bit. Altimeter reads just under nought feet. Hope to Heaven our landfall is OK. Worry! Worry! Worry!'

"At last the enemy coast loomed up, the spires of Gravenhage to the left, the Hook of Holland to the right. We were very low. Closer now. A latticed naval beacon went past to the left; we turned four degrees to port and straightened up for our run in. I saw the hummocks on the beach; the white foam breaking on the sands; soldiers running like the Devil for their guns - ' Look out for flak ' -we're over! Weaving madly, we shot over the sand-dunes and set a new course, flying as low as we dared over the glass roofs of the bulb nurseries and turning and twisting among the tall thin chimneys of the greenhouses. Soon we left the coastal towns behind us and, altering course southwards, roared across the level plains around the River Maas and past the tall smoking chimney of Eindhoven. Soon we could see rich black fields of ploughed earth, teams of chestnut Belgian horses and sleepy red-roofed hamlets. A quick glance behind showed us that Coyle, our No. 2, was just behind our tail.

"Another alteration of twenty degrees to port and we crossed the frontier into Germany, with plenty of dark cloud ahead and green plantations of young Douglas firs below. Then, in the gloom ahead we picked up the gleam of the Roer River, pin-pointed ourselves quickly, and made a slight alteration to bring us directly onto the target. A river and a railway crossing appeared immediately ahead - good show, we were dead on track. The little town of Jülich soon showed up, and in climbing to clear the buildings we saw the big railway sheds lying in a valley running southwards from the town. As I opened the bomb doors we dived straight for the target and waited until the serrated roofs were just in front of the nose. I got a quick impression of tall chimneys on either side, a small engine snorting and grunting on the sidings, stacks of white wood laid on long waggons and a group of workmen scattering in every direction - 'Look out, you blasted Huns! Here they come! Bombs gone!' My navigator slewed round in his seat and, looking back, shouted 'Yes! I can see where they've gone in. Up they go! Number 2's hit it as well!'

"No flak. I turned to starboard onto the next course and throttled back a little. Why all the hurry? Then we ran into a sharp rainstorm. I passed the target to starboard again, as I turned back and grey smoke was drifting slowly away. It began to get really dark on the way home, the dusk obscuring the power cables that raced underneath from time to time. A few lighted windows showed through the trees - it was too dark for a fighter interception now. I relaxed slightly. Everything seemed too easy, and there was plenty of cover in this semi-darkness.

"'Take care,' came a warning from Hayes. 'We're off track. Keep low - lower still.' Then, before we knew what had happened, we were over the middle of Eindhoven Aerodrome. Everywhere there seemed to be little spurts of fire from machine-guns and great gobs of flame from the Bofors. They all missed. As we sped on into the darkness the Huns lobbed a few long shots after us which fell around us, and then suddenly - we were hit. From the port wing, outboard of the engine, a little trail of vapor streamed back and slowly grew less and less until it died away. I checked over the instruments but could find nothing wrong and carried on, going fast. 'Is that the coast? Open up and go like Hell – or is it the coast? No. Just a bank of mist. False alarm - but it can't be far away now!

"Then far in front we saw a flock of white seagulls and knew that the sea was ahead. As we weaved our way across the dunes a feeble spurt of tracer swung lazily up from the left and followed us until we were out of range. It was lighter out to sea. Very pleasant it was to see the sunset in front of us to the west. Throttling back a few miles outside the coast, I climbed a few hundred feet and took things easy. We passed over one of our convoys off Norfolk, were challenged by a destroyer and replied to everyone's satisfaction.

"Far ahead we saw our own coastline and before long our own beacon gave us a friendly wink and our flarepath came into view.

"The Germans had dropped a shell into one of our petrol tanks, but by some stroke of luck it had not exploded."

Late in the evening of 27 May the final large-scale daylight raid by the Mosquito IVs of 2 Group took place when fourteen Mosquitoes were given two targets deep in Southern Germany. The briefing was very long and complicated. It meant flying at low level for well over three hours over enemy territory, of which a good two and a quarter would be in broad daylight. Six aircraft of 139 Squadron led by Wing Commander "Reggie" W. Reynolds DSO DFC and Flight Lieutenant Ted Sismore DFC set out to attack the Schott glassworks at Jena. A few miles further on eight Mosquitoes of 105 Squadron led by Squadron Leader Bill Blessing DFC and Flying Officer G. K. Muirhead were to bomb the Zeiss Optical factory, which at that time was almost entirely engaged in making periscopes for submarines. One of the 105 Squadron pilots taking part was Flight Lieutenant Charles Patterson, with the Film Unit cameraman Flight Sergeant Leigh Howard as his navigator. Patterson recalls:

"We saw the red ribbon running longer than we'd ever considered, right down into SE Germany near Leipzig and the target, the Zeiss optical lens works at Jena. It gave a great sense of anticipation and excitement that such a tremendously long trip was going to be undertaken but not undue alarm because it was so deep into Germany, an area that had never seen daylight flying aircraft before. We rather assumed that by going deep down not only could we achieve a great deal of surprise but there night be much light AA fire round this factory and what there was the gunners would be inexperienced.

"At 7 o'clock all around the perimeter the engines started up and everybody taxied out. Forming up on these trips with a full muster of Mosquitoes was quite a lengthy business, the leader circling slowly round and round the airfield for everybody to get airborne and catch up. 'The two formations swept across the hangars and the airfield at low level, an impressive sight and quite an exhilarating experience for the crews themselves. We settled down for the long flight right across to Jena in clear daylight as it was certainly a good 2½ hours before dusk. The Dutch coast was crossed with no difficulty but at the Zuider Zee we suddenly found ourselves flying slap into a vast fleet of little brown-sailed fishing vessels. In front of me the whole formation broke up and weaved in and around them, before we settled down again. On behind the Ruhr and down near Kassel we went, then on into the Thuringian Mountains where the Möhne and Eder dams are. Even then we were only two thirds of the way. You felt you were in a separate world, which has no end and will go on forever. On and on over the trees and the fields and the rising ground we went, mile after mile. Then suddenly, my navigator drew my attention to something. I looked across the starboard wingtip and I had a clear view of Münster cathedral quite a few miles away, the interesting thing being that I was looking up at the towers, not down on them!

"We carried on past Kassel then suddenly we came across all the floods of the Möhne dam raid which had taken place only ten days before. For twenty minutes there was nothing but floods. It was fascinating and confirmed in our minds what an enormous success the raid must have been. We flew between the Möhne and Eder dams and suddenly came over a mountain ridge and there was a dam [Helminghausen] beneath us. On the far side the front formation was just topping the far ridge when flak opened up. It didn't look very serious. An enormous ball of flame rolled down the mountainside, obviously an aircraft but it wasn't long after that I learnt that it was two Mosquitoes, which had collided. Whether one was hit by flak or whether it caused one of the pilots to take his eye off what he was doing and fly into the Mosquito next to him, nobody will ever know. But two had gone.[30]

"We flew on over this mountainous country, over ridges and down long valleys with houses on both sides. On my starboard wingtip we saw a man open his front door and look out to see these Mosquitoes flashing past. We saw the door slam in a flash of whipping past. Suddenly, the weather began to deteriorate and this had not been forecast. I think everybody was assuming that we'd soon fly out of it but it got worse and we were over mountains. We now began to fly right into clouds. Flying in formation in cloud and knowing you're right in the center of Germany gives you a rather lonely feeling. Blessing put on his navigation lights to try and enable us to keep formation. Everybody put on navigation lights. I was very nervous flying on instruments in cloud and although I did my best to keep the next aircraft in view, I lost him."[31]

H. C. "Gary" Herbert in the 105 Squadron formation adds:[32]

"A bit further on another 139 kite [*B-Beer* flown by Reynolds and Flying Officer Ted Sismore] feathered his port airscrew [after it took a hit and part of the aircrew entered then cockpit injuring Reynolds in the left hand and knee] and turned back. He got home OK. Just before we turned to make the last run up the valley to the target the clouds came right down to the deck and the formation had to break up. When the clouds broke I found the formation OK but three other kites were gone.[33] So six kites out of the formation went on to attack.

"Visibility was extremely bad and as we approached the target at nought feet we suddenly saw balloons over it. Then the fiercest cross fire of light flak I have ever seen opened up. I was last in the formation by this time. Free to go in how I liked I broke away and climbed up the mountain at the side of the town hoping to fox the gunners and dodge the balloons, which I expected would be spread across the valley. I didn't do either. As we went up the mountain they poured light flak down at us and we dived down the other side. The only thing to do was to weave straight in dodging the flak and praying not to hit a cable. We did that and as we screamed down the flak poured past us and splattered all over the town. They put a light flak barrage over the target hoping we would rim into it but somehow we dodged it and put our bombs fairly in the glass grinding section - a sixteen storey building. We were hit in several places on the way out.

"The heavy cross fire they put up over the glass grinding building (my target) was not directed at us but obviously to deter us from going through it. They don't know how close they were to succeeding! I was absolutely terrified and did not think anybody could get through that and survive and was sorely tempted to turn away and bomb an alternative target. The only thing that made me go through was the thought that I couldn't face men like Hughie Edwards, Roy Ralston, Reg Reynolds and say, 'I lost my guts and turned away.' I now know that heroes are really cowards whose conscience would not let them hold their heads high in the presence of real brave men. Subsequent reports confirmed that I was not the only one who was tempted to turn away.[34] However, we managed to get away OK and only ran into one lot of flak on the homeward journey. We dodged it OK. When we got back we found that our hydraulics were out of action and had to put our wheels and flaps dawn by hand. The throttles wouldn't close and I had to cut the switches to get in. Made it OK. Two other kites crashed when they got back and both crews were killed.[35] Another kite was missing, making five crews lost - our heaviest loss. It was certainly my stickiest operation and everybody else reckoned it was the stickiest too. There were so many aircraft pranged on the flarepath when we got back that we were ordered to go to an alternative aerodrome - Swanton Morley I think. We came back by car, which took many hours in the blackout. By that time all the Bigwigs from Headquarters who were there to decide whether we should continue as a low level squadron or be switched to PFF work had left."

The Men Who Built the Mosquito – and what strength! (BAe)

On 15 November 1941 de Havilland Chief Test pilot Geoffrey de Havilland Jr. facing the camera) demonstrated W4064 at the 2 (Light Bomber) Group airfield at Swanton Morley to Wing Commander Peter H. A. Simmons DFC CO, 105 Squadron, and his air and ground crews. That month the first B.Mk. IVs came off the Hatfield production lines and on 17 November, W4066 became the first Mosquito B.Mk.IV bomber to enter RAF service when it was received by 105 Squadron. Their first operation took place on 31 May 1942. B.Mk.IVs initially were so scarce that 105 and its sister squadron, 139, often shared the available aircraft for operations from Norfolk. (RAF Marham)

W4050 the prototype Mosquito, which first flew on 25 November 1940 and which in June 1942 was fitted with two-stage Merlin 61s. Standing on the left is John de Havilland. (HS via Ian Thirsk)

FB.VIs on the production lines at the Standard Motor Co works in Coventry. (via ARP)

NF.II DD630, part of an early batch built at Hatfield. As late as 1943-44 many surviving NF.IIs were refurbished, re-engined, had AI.Mk.IV and V radar sets installed and were given to 100 Group. A few aircraft were converted for photo-reconnaissance duties. (DH)

Mosquitoes being assembled at Downsview, Toronto. de Havilland Canada turned out a total of 1076 Mosquitoes. (via GMS)

Long range fuel tanks installed in the bomb bay of late-version PR Mosquitoes permitted 9-hour sorties over Europe. (via GMS)

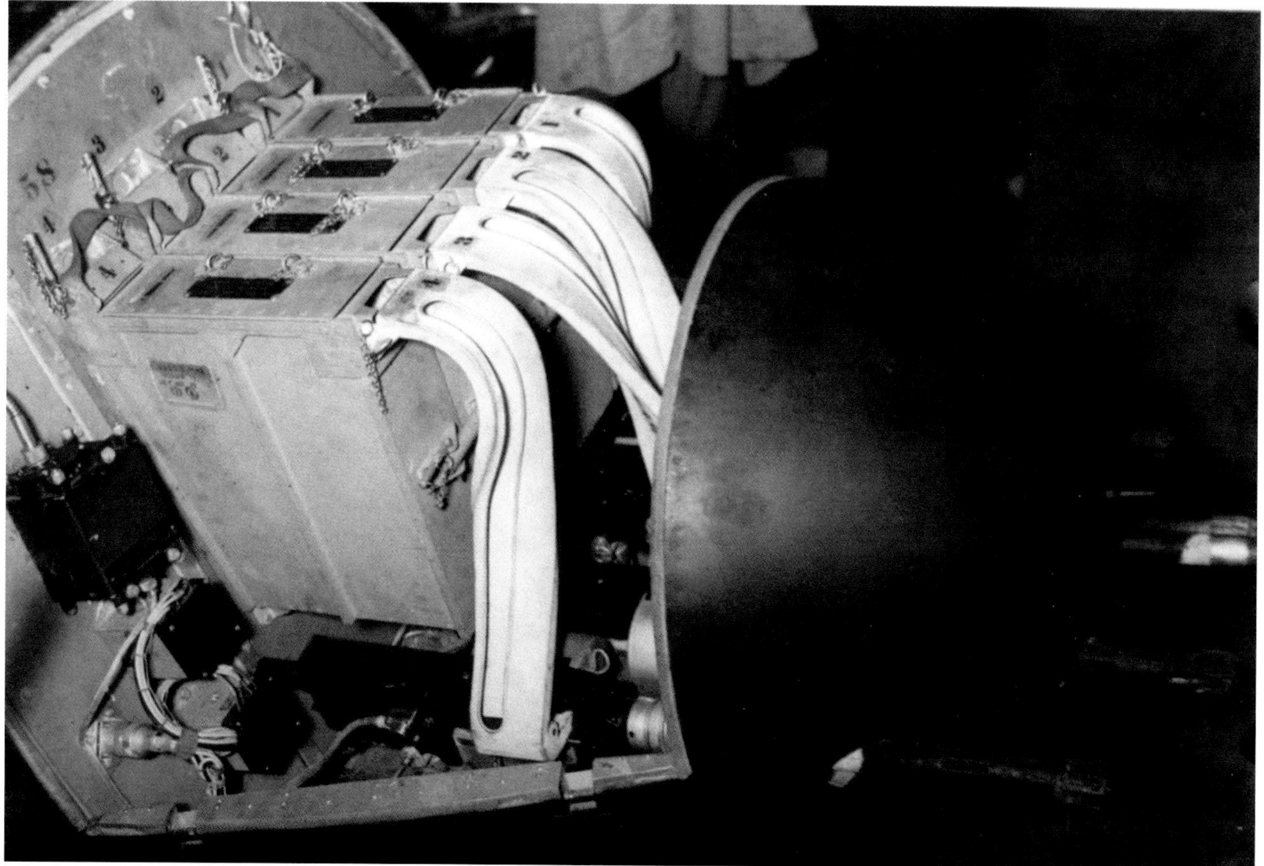

Browning Mk.II.303 inch machine gun installation showing the ammunition boxes (left) and the ammunition chutes. (via GMS)

A turbine in the central power station at Hengelo lies amid the wreckage following Squadron Leader George Parry's low-level dusk attack on 6 October 1942 in Mosquito B.IV DK317 GB-K. (via Henk van Baaren)

Damage to the Twenthe Central electricity station on 6 October 1942. (via Henk van Baaren)

B.IV DK337 GB-N of 105 Squadron at Horsham St. Faith on 22 September 1942 when it returned hit by light flak. DK337 took part in the daylight raid on Berlin on 30 January 1943 when Flight Sergeant Peter John Dixon McGeehan and Flying Officer Reginald Charles Morris flew it. DK337 later became Officer F. M. 'Bud' Fisher DFC, an American pilot from Pennsylvania's Mosquito and was named *Uncle Sam.* It failed to return from an operation to Duisburg on 31 August 1943. (DH)

Right: On 1 April 1943 six Mosquitoes of 105 Squadron led by Wing Commander Roy Ralston DSO DFM and Flight Lieutenant Syd Clayton DFC DFM set out with four of 139 Squadron led by Squadron Leader John Berggren. Their targets were a power station and railway yards at Trier and engine sheds at Ehrang respectively, which were bombed from 50-400 feet. Bombs from the first formation were seen to fall in the middle of the railway workshops, throwing up large quantities of debris followed by showers of green sparks. Bomb bursts were also observed on the power station followed by a sheet of flame, which rose to a height of 100 feet. The attack by the second formation on Ehrang resulted in a huge explosion and a red flash from a coal container. One bomb was seen to bounce off railway tracks into a house, which was blown to pieces. On leaving the target area smoke was seen rising to about 1500 feet. Locomotive wheels can be seen in the foreground.

British Prime Minister Winston Churchill flanked by Geoffrey de Havilland to his right and company chairman, Mr Alan S. Butler to his left, tours the Hatfield factory on 18 April 1943. (BAe)

An enemy flak gun emplacement opens up on a Mosquito during the low-level attack by four B.Mk.IVs of 105 Squadron on the Stork Diesel Works at Hengelo, Holland on 28 February 1943. The flying debris in the foreground is from a bomb burst through the roof of the Manemeyer electrical and mechanical equipment factory. The train is traveling along the Derventer to Zwolle railway line. (via Philip Birtles)

Still from the camera film aboard DK296/*G-George*, flown by Squadron Leader George Parry DSO DFC* with Flying Officer Victor 'Robbie' Robson DFC* who led the attack by four Mosquitoes of 105 Squadron on the *Gestapo* HQ at Victoria Terrasse (far left) in Oslo on Friday 25 September 1942. The large white building (top left) is the University. Middle right is the central cupola on which the pilots saw the *Nazi* flag flying. The photo shows a direct hit by George Parry and his bombs about to burst on the Victoria Terrasse (the bombs had 11-second fuses). Of the 12 bombs dropped, five did not explode and three went through the HQ building and exploded outside. (BAe Hatfield via Philip Birtles)

105 and 139 Squadron aircrew at RAF Marham after returning from Berlin on 31 January 1943. Seated, L-R: Flying Officer Flying Officer Ralph Gamble Hayes, Squadron Leader Reggie W. Reynolds and Pilot Officer E. D. Makin. Standing, left to right: Flying Officer Reginald Charles Morris, Flight Sergeant Peter John Dixon McGeehan; Sergeant Massey, Flight Lieutenant John Gordon; Flying Officer J. T. Wickham; Sergeant R. C. 'Lofty' Fletcher; Pilot Officer E. B. 'Ted' Sismore. Morris and McGeehan were KIA on 16 March 1943 and are buried at Den Burg, Texel. Either Morris or McGeehan carried this photo at the time of their death and it was found by German troops searching the wreckage of their Mosquito (DZ497). (via Theo Boiten)

Flight Lieutenant Victor 'Robbie' Robson DFC* and Squadron Leader D. A. G. 'George' Parry DSO DFC* of 105 Squadron in front of their B.IV *G-George* soon after the Oslo raid. (George Parry)

Returning from an attack on railroad maintenance facilities at Paderborn in the early evening of 16 March 1943 B.IV DZ497 XD-Q of 139 Squadron came under fire from *Kriegsmarine Flak battery 11./M.Fla.Abt.808* at Den Hoorn, Texel and at 1929 hours crashed 1200 meters south of this village. 21-year old Pilot Officer Peter J. D. McGeehan DFM RNZAF and his 33-year old navigator Flying Officer Reginald C. Morris DFC both died and were later buried in Den Burg cemetery. A member of the German island garrison is seen here with the wreckage. (Andreas Wachtel)

On 28 July 1942 Unteroffizier Karl Bugaj (seen here on his return being congratulated by other members of his Staffel) scored the first victory for 11th Staffel, JGI (and the second victory for IV. Gruppe) when he shot down Mosquito DK295/P of 105 Squadron from Marham over Mönchengladbach. The aircraft, which was on a sortie to Essen, crashed at Tilburg and the crew, Flying Officer Frank Watson Weekes RAAF and Pilot Officer Frank Arthur Hurley were killed and were laid to rest in the Reichwald Forest war cemetery. Bugaj who in March 1943 received the *Eisern Kreuz I* (Iron Cross First Class) was killed at Achmer flying Fw 190A-4 'Black 8' on a non-combat flight on 12 April 1943. (Eric Mombeek)

Right: On 6 September Feldwebel Erwin Roden of 12/JGI shot down B.IV DK322/P of 105 Squadron crewed by Sergeant K. C. Pickett (PoW) and his observer, Sergeant Herbert Edmund Evans (KIA), which crashed at 1830 hours near Tourines-La Grosse, Belgium. Thirteen days later, on 19 September, *Schwarmfurhrer* Oberfeldwebel Anton-Rudolf 'Toni' Piffer (far left with Oberfeldwebel Worth (12th Staffel Adjutant) Leutnant Eberhard Burath and Leutnant Hans Munz) of 2nd *Staffel*/JGI shot down DK326/M of 105 Squadron crewed by Squadron Leader Norman Henry Edward Messervy DFC RAAF and Pilot Officer Frank Holland (both KIA) of 105 Squadron. Leutnant Piffer was KIA by USAAF P-47 Thunderbolts on 17 June 1944 who shot down his Fw 190A-8 'White 3' near Argentan. Piffer was posthumously awarded the *Ritterkreuz* on 20 October 1944 for his 26 victories in the west. (via Eric Mombeek)

On 11 October 1942 DZ341/A of 105 Squadron flown by Pilot Officer Jim Lang (PoW) and Flying Officer Robin F. Thomas (PoW) and DK317/K flown by Squadron Leader James Gerald Leslie Knowles and Pilot Officer Charles Douglas Alan Gartside of 139 Squadron failed to return from a raid on Hanover. They were shot down over the sea by Unteroffizier Günther Kirchner (pictured) and Unteroffizier Kolschek of 5th and 4th *Staffel* II./JGI respectively. Lang and Thomas were captured and made PoW. Knowles and Gartside were KIA. A third Mosquito IV, DZ340, crashed at Marham on return. (via Eric Mombeek)

Roof top attacks on enemy targets were not only daring, they were timed to perfection. Here factory workers can be seen leaving off at the St. Joseph locomotive Works in Nantes on 23 March 1943 when three B.Mk.IVs of 105 Squadron, led by Wing Commander Peter Shand DFC and eight of 139 Squadron, led by Squadron Leader Bill Blessing DSO DFC RAAF bombed the factory. Shand led two more outstandingly successful attacks, to the Molybdenum mines at Knaben, Norway, on 3 March and a second raid on Eindhoven, 30 March. He and his navigator, Pilot Officer Christopher D. Handley DFM were KIA on the night bombing attack on Berlin, 20/21 April 1943 when they were shot down by Oberleutnant Lothar Linke of IV./NJG1, to crash in the Ijsselmeer on the way home. Squadron Leader Bill Blessing DSO DFC RAAF was KIA on 7 July 1944 on a PFF marking sortie over Caen. His navigator, Pilot Officer Douglas T. Burke managed to evacuate the aircraft before the Mosquito broke up. He awoke on a stretcher behind Allied lines.(via Philip Birtles)

Feldwebel Fritz Timm of 12/JG1 receives the *Eisern Kreuz II* (Iron Cross, Second Class) from his *Gruppenkommandeur*, Hauptmann Fritz Losigkeit after shooting down DK339 of 105 Squadron, crewed by Wing Commander Charles R. K. Bools and Sergeant George W. Jackson (both KIA) on 9 October 1942. Oberfeldwebel Timm was killed in his Bf 109G-6 *'Yellow 3'* (440939) on 28 May 1944 during combat with P-51 Mustangs of the USAAF at Elsdorf/Kôln. (via Eric Mombeek)

B.IV Series ii DK296/G of 105 Squadron, flown by Flight Lieutenant (later Squadron Leader) D. A. G. 'George' Parry DFC and Flying Officer (later Flight Lieutenant) Victor 'Robbie' Robson, highly-polished for extra speed, made its operational debut on 1/2 June 1942 in the wake of the 'Thousand Bomber' raid on Cologne. On 11 July *'G-George'* was badly damaged when Sergeant Peter W. R. Rowland flew so low on the raid on Flensburg that he hit a roof and returned with pieces of chimney pot lodged in the aircraft's nose. On 25 September Parry and Robson in DK296 led an attack by four Mosquitoes on the *Gestapo* HO in Oslo. *'G-George'* was flown by Squadron Leader Bill Blessing DSO DFC RAAF who crashlanded it at Marham and broke its back. The aircraft was duly repaired and on 24 August 1943 it was placed in store with 10 MU at Hullavington. The following month it was issued to 305 Ferry Training Unit at Errol, in Scotland, where it was given Red Air Force markings and used to train Soviet crews who were converting onto Albermarles. On 20 April 1944 DK296 was ferried to the Soviet Union by a Russian crew, being officially accepted on 31 August 1944 and subsequently serving with the Red Air Force. Its ultimate fate is unknown. (via Graham M. Simons)

B.IVs DZ353/E and DZ367/J of 105 Squadron in formation. DZ367 failed to return from Berlin on 30 January 1943 with the loss of Squadron Leader Donald F. W. Darling DFC and Flying Officer W. Wright. DZ353 later served in 139 Squadron and on 24 November 1943 joined 627 Squadron, 8 Group (PFF) as AZ-T. On 8 January 1944 it crashed on take-off at Vickers Armstrong, Weybridge when both undercarriage legs collapsed but Wing Commander G. H. B. Hutchinson and Flying Officer Freddie French were not seriously injured. Repaired and re-coded AZ-B, it failed to return from a raid on the marshalling yards at Rennes on 8 June 1944 with the loss of Flight Lieutenant Bill Steere DFM and Flight Lieutenant K. W. "Windy" Gale DFC RAAF. (RAF Marham)

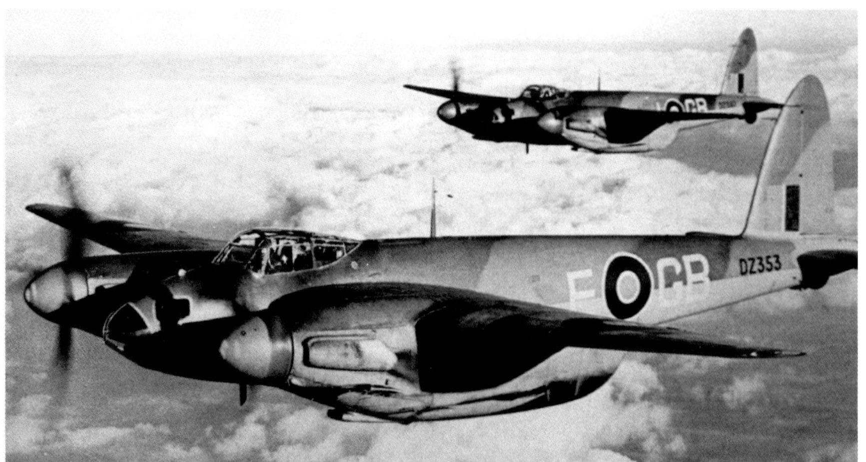

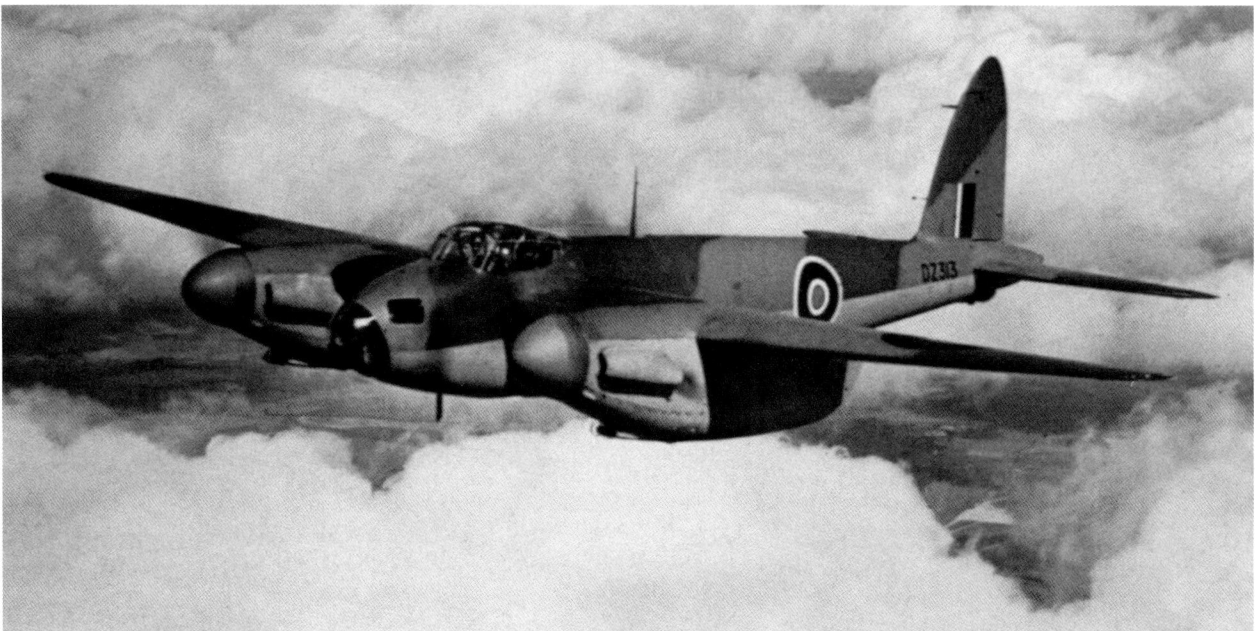

B.IV DZ313 of 105 Squadron and Flight Sergeant L.W. Deeth and Warrant Officer F. E. M. Hicks failed to return from the raid on Hanover on 20 October 1942. (via Shuttleworth Coll)

B.IVs DZ353/E and DZ367/J of 105 Squadron in formation. DZ353 flew its first operation in 105 Squadron on 23 October 1942 and later served with 139 and 627 Squadrons in 8 Group (PFF) before failing to return from a raid on the marshalling yards at Rennes on 8 June 1944. Flight Lieutenant Bill Steere DFM and Flying Officer 'Windy' Gale DFC RAAF were killed. DZ367/J flew its first operation in 105 Squadron on 16 November 1942 and was one of the Squadron's eight Mosquitoes that took part in the Eindhoven raid on 6 December 1942 when it was flown by Flight Lieutenant Bill Blessing and Sergeant J. Lawson. DZ367 failed to return from Berlin on 30 January 1943 when it was crewed by Squadron Leader Donald F. W. Darling DFC and Flying Officer W. Wright (both KIA). (via Shuttleworth Coll)

Flying Officer A. B. 'Smokey Joe' Stovel RCAF of 139 Squadron gets a light from his navigator Sergeant W. A. Nutter before setting off in B.IV DZ593/K on 27 May 1943 to bomb the Schott Glass Works at Jena with five other Mosquitoes. A few miles further on eight Mosquitoes of 105 Squadron bombed the Zeiss Optical factory. Stovel made it back and landed at 23.40 hrs. (via Peter Pereira)

Right: B.Mk.IV Series ii DZ367/J of 139 Squadron being bombed up in preparation for a raid. (Note that the shrouded exhausts have scorched the cowlings). DZ367 failed to return together with Squadron Leader Donald F.W. Darling DFC and Flying Officer William Wright on 30 January 1943, when 105 and 139 Squadrons were the first to bomb Berlin, during an attempt to disrupt speeches by Goering and *Nazi* propaganda minister, Dr. Joseph Göebbels at Nazi rallies in the capital..(via Shuttleworth Collection)

B.IV Series ii's of 105 Squadron at Marham on 11 December 1942. DZ360/A flew its first operation in 105 Squadron on 13 November 1942 and failed to return from a raid on the engine sheds at Termonde, East of Ghent on 22 December 1942 when it was hit by flak while crossing the French coast near Dunkirk. Flight Sergeant Joseph Edward Cloutier RCAF and Sergeant Albert Cecil Foxley were KIA when the Mosquito crashed at Axel just N of the Belgian border in the Netherlands. DZ353/F flew its first operation in 105 Squadron on 23 October 1942 and later served with 139 Squadron, becoming AZ-B of 627 Squadron but failed to return from Rennes on 8 June 1944 when Flight Lieutenant H. Steere DFM and Flying Officer K.W. 'Windy' Gale DFC RAAF were killed in action. DZ367/J flew its first operation in 105 Squadron on 16 November 1942. It was flown on the Eindhoven raid by Flying Officer W. C. S. 'Bill' Blessing and failed to return from Berlin on 30 January 1943 when Squadron Leader Donald F. W. Darling DFC and Flying Officer W. Wright were KIA. DK336/P, which flew its first operation in 105 Squadron on 16 September 1942 lost its starboard engine returning from a raid on Copenhagen on 27 January 1943, struck a balloon cable and a tree and crashed at Yaxham, Norfolk, killing Sergeant Richard Clare and Flying Officer Edward Doyle. DZ378/K, which flew its first operation in 105 Squadron on 14 December 1942 was damaged by flak and by bird strikes on the raid on a gasworks near Delmenhorst, Germany on 20 December 1942 and was relegated to Technical Training Command. DZ379/H, which flew its first operation in 105 Squadron on 8 December 1942 later joined 139 Squadron at Wyton and on 17 August 1943, the diversion for the Peenemünde raid, failed to return from Berlin when it was shot down by a night-fighter and crashed at Berge, Germany. Pilot Officer Cook, the American pilot from Wichita Falls, Texas and his navigator Sergeant D. A. H. Dixon were killed. (via Phillip J. Birtles)

B.IV DZ470 XD-N of 139 Squadron on the compass swing at Marham. (via Peter Pereira)

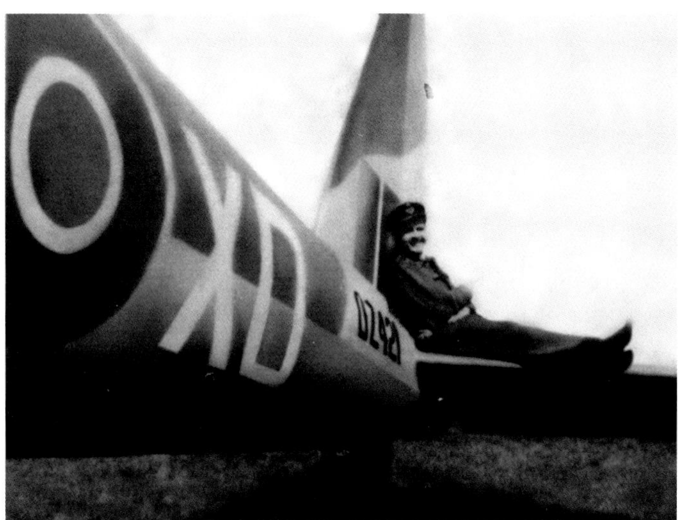

Flight Lieutenant C.Vernon Pereira, on the tail of his B.IV DZ421. (via Peter Pereira)

Wing Commander Hughie Edwards VC DFC (left) and his navigator, Flight Lieutenant C. H. H. "Bladder" Cairns, walk out to their B.IV at RAF Marham for a raid in 1942. (via Philip Birtles)

Wing Commander Hughie Idwal Edwards VC DFC, an Australian of Welsh ancestry was 26 years old when he took command of 105 Squadron in August 1942. He was only the second Australian to receive the VC (the first had been awarded to Lieutenant F. H. McNamara of the RFC in WW1) for his leadership on 4 July 1941 when he led 9 Blenheims on the operation to Bremen. On 10 February 1943 Edwards was promoted Group Captain and he became station commander of Binbrook. By 1944 he had taken up an appointment in ACSEA, and held the rank of Senior Air Staff Office until the end of 1945. Edwards was awarded the CBE in 1947 and in 1958 he was promoted to Air Commodore before retiring from the RAF in 1963. He returned to Australia, was knighted, and in 1974 became Governor of West Australia. (RAAF)

The 2 Group attack on the Philips Stryp Group main works at Eindhoven, Holland, in progress on 6 December 1942. 84 bombers, including eleven B.IVs of 105 and 139 Squadrons, took part in "Operation Oyster", as the operation was code-named. Ten Mosquitoes, eight Mk.IVs of 105 Squadron and two of 139 Squadron, led by Wing Commander Hughie Edwards VC DFC made a shallow diving attack on the Stryp works, while the other bombers bombed from low level. Squadron Leader Jack E. Houlston DFC AFC of 139 Squadron carried out bomb damage assessment. (via GMS)

In the operations room at Marham after the Jena raid are Flight Sergeant Leigh Howard (left) cameraman in DZ414 *O-Orange*, piloted by Flight Lieutenant Charles Patterson (middle), with Wing Commander Reggie W. Reynolds DSO* DFC, CO, 139 Squadron, enjoying a mug of rum from the jar. Reynolds' left arm is bandaged as a result of wounds sustained when the port engine propeller blade of DZ601 *B-Beer* took a direct flak hit. His wounds initially were dressed in flight by his navigator, Ted Sismore. (Charles Patterson)

Wing Commander Reggie W. Reynolds DSO DFC (at right) assumes command of 139 Squadron (note the unit's 'Jamaica Squadron' crest above the doorway at RAF Marham) in May 1943 from acting CO Squadron Leader Vernon R. G. Harcourt DFC RCAF (KIA 21 May 1943). (RAF Marham)

B.IV DZ464 *C for Charlie* of 139 Squadron, the only one of four to escape unharmed after a chase by two Fw 190s following an attack on Malines on 11 April 1943. This aircraft later failed to return on 21 May 1943 during an operation to the locomotive sheds at Orleans, its 17th trip. Squadron Leader Vernon R. G. Harcourt DFC RCAF and Warrant Officer J. Friendly DFM, a South African were KIA. (RAF Marham)

B.Mk.IV Series ii DK338 *O-Orange* flew its first operation in 105 Squadron on 16 September 1942 when six crews made dusk attacks on the chemical works at Wiesbaden at heights of 2500 to 4000 feet. On 1 May 1943 DK338 *O-Orange* took off for an operation to Eindhoven when an engine failed just after take off and the aircraft crashed about a mile west of Marham killing Flying Officer Onslow Waldo Thompson DFM RNZAF and his observer Flying Officer Wallace James Horne DFC. The aircraft had completed 23 successful sorties including one on 20 November 1942 by Squadron Leader Patterson and Flight Sergeant Jimmy Hill of the RAF Film Unit who took low-level reconnaissance photos of the Ooster Schelde estuary from Noord Beveland as far as Woensdrecht airfield to assist in planning for the Eindhoven operation. (RAF)

BI.V DZ367/J of 105 Squadron banking for the camera. (via Jerry Scutts)

Flying Officer William S. D. 'Jock' Sutherland, a Scot from Dollar, whose navigator was Flying Officer George Dean. Returning from Jena on 27 May 1943 they flew into high voltage overhead electric cables when attempting to land at RAF Coltishall and they crashed at Wroxham railway station. Both were killed. (RAF)

B.Mk.IV Series ii DZ467 GB-P of 105 Squadron failed to return from the attack on the Zeiss Optical Factory at Jena on 27 May 1943, the final large-scale daylight raid by 105 and 139 Mosquito Squadrons in 2 Group. It was DZ467's 19th sortie and Pilot Officer Ronald Massie and Sergeant George P. Lister were lost. Three out of the eight Mosquitoes of 105 Squadron despatched bombed the target, 45 miles from Leipzig, while three out of the six 139 Squadron Mosquitoes despatched, bombed the Schott Glass Works. (RAF Marham)

Aircrews in 105 and 139 Squadrons early in 1943 beside a B.Mk.IV at RAF Marham. Far left is Flight Lieutenant C.Vernon Pereira, a Trinidadian, of 139 Squadron, who flew 80 ops on Mosquitoes on 139 and 105 Squadrons and was awarded the DFC and Bar, talking to Flight Lieutenant John 'Flash' Gordon (head on one side, unfastening his Mae West). Behind Gordon is Syd Clayton. 139 Squadron flew their first operation on 2 July 1942 when two B.Mk.IVs carried out a high-level bombing raid on Flensburg. (RAF Marham)

Squadron Leader Charles Patterson. (Charles Patterson)

B.IVs of 105 Squadron at RAF Marham.

Squadron Leader Peter J. Channer DFC prepared for high flying in 105 Squadron. Channer's DFC had been awarded for his part in the raid on the power station at Knapsack near Cologne when he was a Blenheim pilot on 18 Squadron.

B.IV being bombed up at RAF Marham.

A B.IV of 105 Squadron over Marham in 1943. (RAF Marham)

Wing Commander Reggie W. Reynolds DSO* DFC CO, 139 Squadron, rests his bandaged hand on the damaged port engine propeller blade (both sustained as a result of a direct hit on the airscrew) and poses for the camera with Flight Lieutenant Ted Sismore DSO DFC in front of DZ601 *B-Beer* following the attack on the Schott Glass Works at Jena. This operation was the last big 2 Group raid carried out in daylight by 105 and 139 Squadrons. (via Philip Birtles)

Squadron Leader Roy Ralston DSO DFM and Flight Lieutenant Syd Clayton DFC DFM of 105 Squadron on 9 December 1942 following a very successful bombing raid which saw them lead two other B.Mk.IVs in a 'skip bombing' raid on the mouth of a French railway tunnel. The attack was designed to cause damage to both the tunnel and the track on the other side, thus making it difficult for the Germans to effect repairs. (via Philip Birtles)

B.Mk.IV Series ii DZ379/H flew its first operation in 105 Squadron on 8 December 1942 before being transferred to 139 Squadron at Wyton and on 17 August 1943, the diversion for the Peenemünde raid, failed to return from Berlin when it was shot down by a night-fighter and crashed at Berge, Germany. Pilot Officer Cook, the American pilot from Wichita Falls, Texas and his navigator Sergeant D. A. H. Dixon were killed. (Temple Press)

B.IV DZ353 GB-E of 105 Squadron in flight. (RAF Marham)

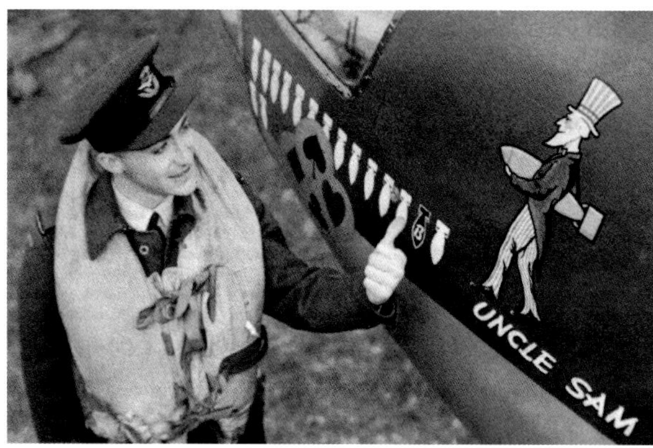

Flying Officer F. M. 'Bud' Fisher DFC, an American pilot from Pennsylvania, in front of his Mosquito DK337 GB-N Uncle Sam. On 22/23 September 1943 Fisher and his navigator, Flight Sergeant Les Hogan DFM were one of twelve *Oboe* Mosquitoes that visited Emden as a diversion for the Main Force attacking Hanover. They crashed while flying Mk.IX LR506/E one mile north west of RAF West Raynham and both men were killed. (RAF Marham)

Flight Lieutenant C.Vernon Pereira and Flying Officer Gilbert of 139 Squadron.

Air and ground crews at RAF Marham in 1943. (via Peter Pereira)

Flying Officer Ralph Gamble Hayes DFM (left), navigator and (right) his pilot, Flight Lieutenant John 'Flash' Gordon DFC of 105 Squadron who were killed on the night of 5/6 November 1943 over Norfolk. They tried to land at Hardwick, an American B-24 Liberator base used by the 93rd Bomb Group, when at 21:10 hours, they crashed into a field at Road Green Farm, Hempnall, about 10 miles south of Norwich. (RAF Marham)

Left: Flying Officer W.A. Christensen (left), navigator from New South Wales and (right) his pilot, Flying Officer Don C. Dixon, an Australian from Brisbane. (RAF Marham)

Below: Group Captain Wallace 'Digger' Kyle DFC (middle arms folded) with Squadron Leader Reggie Reynolds on his left and other crews who took part in the raid by seven Mosquitoes of 105 Squadron on the railway workshops at Thionville on the Moselle River abut 12 miles south of the Luxembourg border on 2 May 1943. Far left is Flying Officer F. M. 'Bud' Fisher. Ted Sismore who flew as Reynolds' navigator recalled that the raid was 'perfect' – 'no flak and no fighters – quite remarkable'. However some flak was encountered at the Channel coast and Pilot Officer B.W. Coyle, an Australian from Sydney and his observer, Sergeant P. H. Harvey had to land DZ521/V at North Weald after they came home on one engine.(RAF Marham)

Group Captain Wallace 'Digger' Kyle DFC, 2nd from left, with some of his fellow Australians at Marham. Far left is Pilot Officer B.W. Coyle. To Kyle's left are Flying Officer R. B. Smith, Flying Officer W.A. Christensen from New South Wales, Flying Officer Don C. Dixon from Brisbane and Warrant Officer H. C. 'Gary' Herbert. (RAF Marham)

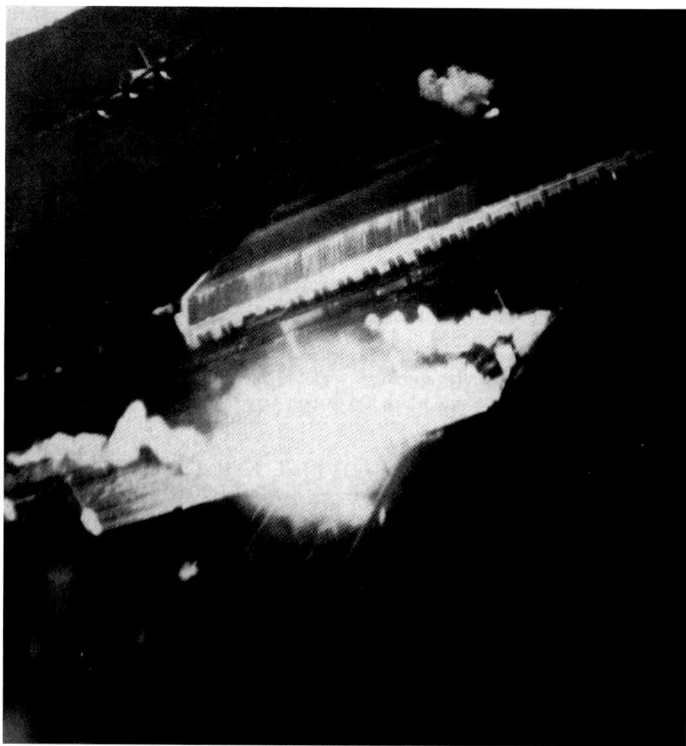

The dusk low-level attack on the engine sheds at Namur, Belgium on 3 April 1943 when Wing Commander John de L. Wooldridge DFC* DFM led his first 105 Squadron operation and eight Mosquitoes carried out *Rover* attacks on railway targets in Belgium and France. The flash of exploding bombs from Squadron Leader Reggie W. Reynolds' DZ458 GB-J illuminates the target. Top left can be seen Pilot Officer Ronald Massie and Sergeant George P. Lister's DZ519 GB-U over the sheds with its bomb doors open and bombs falling. All three of 105 Squadron's Mosquitoes returned safely from attacks on locomotive repair sheds shops at Malines and engine sheds at Namur but a Mosquito of 139 Squadron was lost.

Left: Wing Commander John de L. Wooldridge DFC* DFM CO, 105 Squadron, 17 March 1943-1944, in the emergency roof exit opening of his Mosquito IV. (Note the two-piece front windscreen, which was soon replaced by a bullet-proof fighter style flat windscreen, and the direct vision panel (forward of the blister) which opened inwards on each side). Wooldridge joined the RAF in 1938 and flew two tours on heavy bombers prior to taking command of 105 Squadron, including 32 ops on Manchesters in 61, 207 and 106 Squadrons. (via Philip Birtles)

B.IVs of 105 Squadron taxi out at Marham. Left is DZ367 GB-J.

Wing Commander John de L. Wooldridge DFC* DFM CO, 105 Squadron, 17 March 1943-1944 standing in front of his Mosquito Knave of Diamonds. Wooldridge survived the war only to die as a result of a car accident in 1958. (RAF Marham)

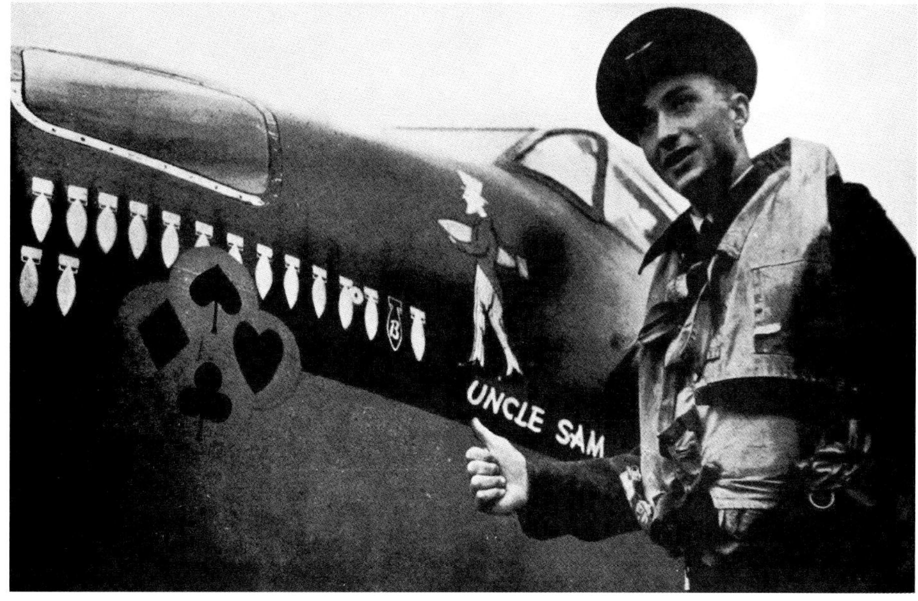

Flying Officer F. M. 'Bud' Fisher DFC, an American pilot from Pennsylvania, in front of DK337 GB-N Uncle Sam. On 22/23 September 1943 Fisher and his navigator, Flight Sergeant Les Hogan DFM were one of twelve *Oboe* Mosquitoes that visited Emden as a diversion for the Main Force attacking Hanover. They crashed while flying B.IX LR506/E one mile north west of RAF West Raynham and both men were killed.. (RAF Marham)

B.IV Popeye veteran of 105 Squadron at RAF Marham.

Left: A fitter works on the starboard Merlin of B.IV Series ii DK300 which had been delivered to Stradishall, Suffolk on 21 July 1942 to have *Oboe* radar equipment installed. The following month 109 Squadron moved to Wyton where DK300 and eight other B.IVs were used for *Oboe* trials. DK300 broke up in flight over Pidley in Huntingdonshire (now Cambridgeshire) on 22 July 1944 while serving with 1655 MTU. (via GMS) **Right:** The navigator of a B.IV Mosquito demonstrates how the Mk.IV bombsight was used, just as in heavy bombers. (Shuttleworth Coll).

Four 500lb tail-fuzed bombs with 11-second time delaying being fitted into the bomb bay of a 105 Squadron B.IV. (via Gary Herbert)

Squadron Leader Bill Blessing with his famous Mosquito B.IV THE KNAVE OF SPADES.

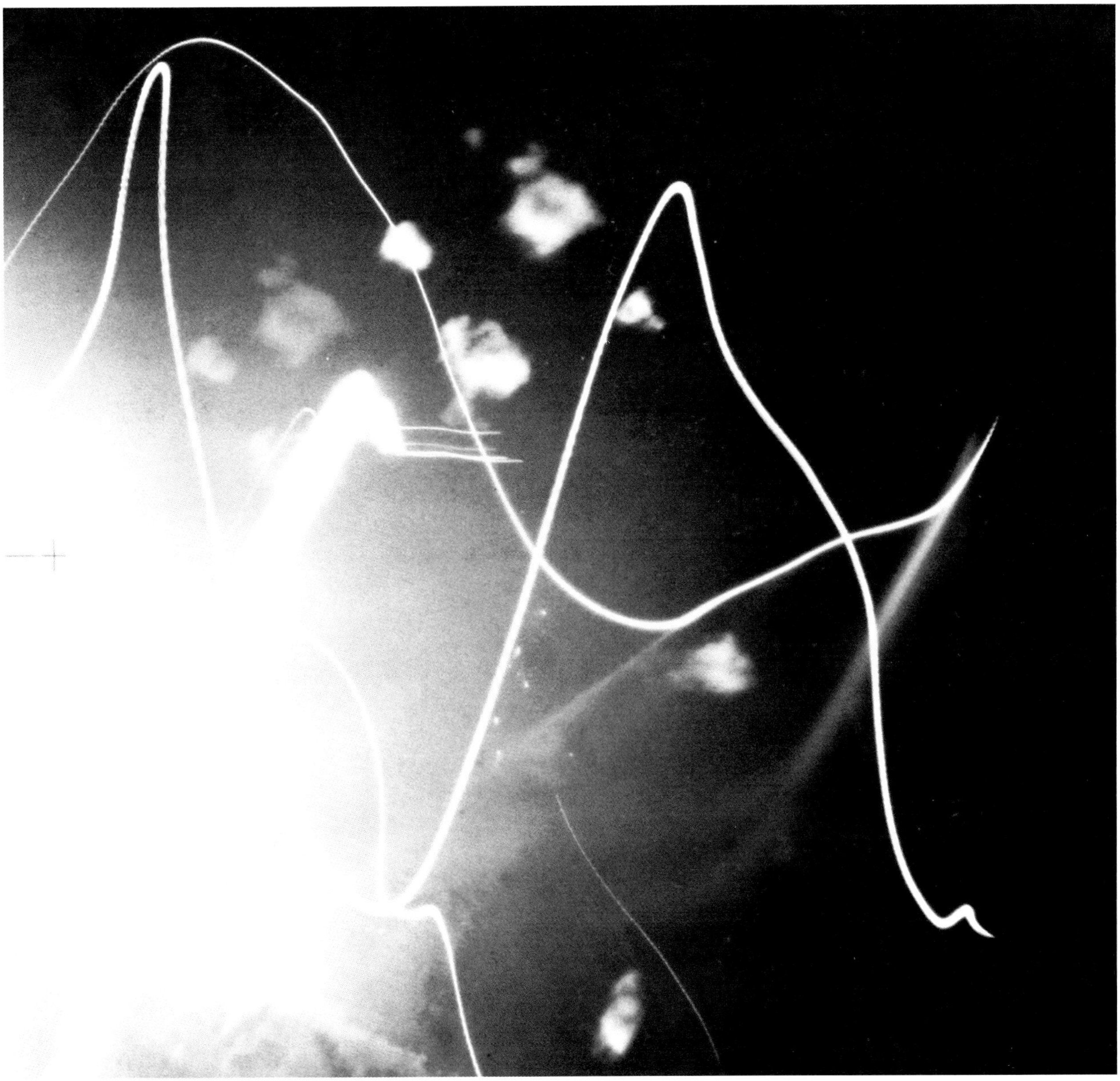

TIs over the Boulogne gun positions photographed from 15,000 feet on the night of 8/9 September 1943 when 257 Wellingtons, Stirlings, Mosquitoes and Halifaxes took part. OTU aircraft also took part and five B-17 Fortresses also flew the first American night-bombing sorties of the war with Bomber Command. No aircraft were lost. The target was a German long-range gun battery and the marking was mainly provided by *Oboe* Mosquitoes, some of whom were experimenting with a new technique but the raid was not successful. The marking and the bombing were not accurate and the battery does not appear to have been damaged.

Left: FB.VI crews study a map of the continent before setting off on another daylight operation (via Mick Jennings)

CHAPTER 2

DEFENSIVE AND OFFENSIVE NIGHT FIGHTING

Mossies they don't worry me,
Mossies they don't worry me,
If you get jumped by a One-nine-O,
I'll show you how to get free.
Keep calm and sedate,
Don't let your British blood boil.
Don't hesitate,
Just go right through the gate,
And drown the poor bastard in oil!

In the spring of 1942, following an attack by 234 RAF bombers on the old Hanseatic city of Lübeck, Hitler ordered a series of *Terrorangriff* (terror attacks) on England, mainly against cities of historic or aesthetic importance but little strategic value. In Britain they became known as the *Baedeker* raids, after the German guidebooks of the same name. Despite its historical significance, the cathedral city of Norwich made a tempting target for *Luftwaffe* raiders ever since the first *Baedeker* raid on the Norfolk capital on the night of 27/28 April 1942. Nine Beaufighters, ten Spitfires, and three AI.V radar-equipped Mosquito NF.IIs of 157 Squadron based at Castle Camps met the 28 *Luftwaffe* raiders. Meanwhile, 20 Ju 88s of *Kampfgeschwader* (KG) 30 laid mines off the coast. The enemy was picked up on radio at 2015 hours. Although radar contacts were made, the defending fighters failed to shoot down any of the raiders. From 2340-0045 hours the bombers rained down 41 tonnes of high explosive and four tonnes of incendiaries onto the city of over 126,000 inhabitants, causing the deaths of 162 people, injuring 600 more, and damaging thousands of buildings. Reports spoke of some of the bombers machine gunning the streets. The raid was the first sortie by I/KG2 since converting to the Do 217E. The *Holzhammer* unit, plus IV/KG30 and II/KG40, all based in Holland, would venture to England many times over the next 12 months. "Ack-Ack" batteries were drafted into and around Norwich and the fighter defenses gradually improved. The Mosquitoes suffered particularly from problems with cannon flash and exhaust manifold and cowling burning.

"A" Flight in 151 Squadron at Wittering had received its first NF.II on 6 April ("B" Flight had to wait until later to replace its Defiants). 151 were commanded by Wing Commander I. S. "Black' Smith DFC, a New Zealander, and the station commander at this time was Group Captain (later Air Vice Marshal, Sir,) Basil Embry.[36] On the night of 1 May Wing Commander Smith narrowly avoided a collision with a Dornier 217E-4. On 19 May a 157 Squadron Mosquito lost an engine and crashed at Castle Camps, killing both crew. 151 Squadron's first success came on the night of 29/30 May when Grimsby was attacked. Flight Lieutenant Pennington intercepted a damaged Do 217E-4 very early morning. Attacking with cannon from 400 yards hits were scored on the Dornier, which promptly took evasive action. Closing for a second attack from 80 yards the enemy returned fire. The Mosquito was hit in the starboard wing and tail and the port engine. Pennington's fire hit the port wing and engine of the enemy aircraft, which dived away on fire into the haze above the sea and contact was lost. The Mosquito flew 140 miles home on a single engine. Meanwhile, Pilot Officer John Alwyne Wain and Flight Sergeant Thomas Steel Greenshields Grieve intercepted an incoming Do 217 E4 of KG2 well out over the North Sea. Wain closed on the bomber and saw that it was carrying two large external bombs. He opened fire and the bomber immediately burst into flames and started to fall towards the sea. The crew claimed one "possible" enemy aircraft destroyed. Both attacks took place over the North Sea while the bombers were en route to raid Great Yarmouth. On 30 May, another Dornier of KG2 was almost certainly destroyed south of Dover by Squadron Leader G. Ashfield in a 157 Squadron Mosquito from Castle Camps.

On 24/25 June Wing Commander "Black" Smith DFC and his navigator, Flight Lieutenant Kernon-Sheppard, in W4097 intercepted three enemy aircraft off Great Yarmouth within 30 minutes. At 2330 a He 111 was intercepted at 8000 feet. The New Zealander closed to 300 yards before opening fire, but the Heinkel dived away trailing fuel from its port tanks as a second approach was made. Ten minutes later he was vectored on to a Do 217-E4 of II/KG40. This time Smith approached unseen to 100 yards before opening fire. Following a short burst of cannon fire the Dornier dived abruptly into the sea and exploded. At 2348 radar contact was made on a Do 217E-4 of I/KG2, and on closing a long burst was fired from 200 yards. The shells hit both the Dornier's wing tanks and the aircraft was engulfed in flames. Smith closed right in on the Dornier and fired a short burst into the stricken aircraft, which promptly went down into the sea.[37] Meanwhile, Flight Lieutenant Darling and Pilot Officer Wright engaged a Do 217 and a Ju 88, but both aircraft escaped without serious damage. The next night Pilot Officer John Wain and Flight Sergeant Tom Grieve claimed a He 111H-6 over the North Sea.[38] On 26/27 June, when He 111 pathfinders—Ju 88s of KüF1Gr 506 and Do 217s of I, II, and III/KG2—raided Norwich, Flight Lieutenant Moody and Pilot Officer Marsh claimed a Do 217 E4 of 3./KG2 flown by *Feldwebel* Hans Schrödel about 60-80 miles from the East Coast. It appeared to go down into the sea.

By 1942 RAF bombers had begun to suffer increasing losses due to *Luftwaffe* night fighter interceptions, and it was decided that RAF *intruder* aircraft roving over enemy airfields in France and the Low Countries could alleviate some of the attacks on the bomber streams. Blenheim Squadrons had pioneered offensive nightfighting in June 1940, in much the same vein as 151 Squadron, operating Sopwith Camels, had done in World War One. In November 1939 600 Squadron had become one of the first squadrons to use AI (Airborne Interception) radar (604 followed suit in July 1940). When the *Luftwaffe* began operating at night from France in 1940 the opportunity of attacking German aircraft on French airfields arose, but the only suitable aircraft available were Hurricanes and Blenheims, and later Havocs and Bostons. The first major support of bombers by night fighter squadrons was on the night of 30/31 May 1942 during the 1000-bomber raid on Cologne, when Blenheims and Havocs and Boston IIIs of 23 and 418 (City of Edmonton) Squadron RCAF intruded over Holland.[39] No radar-equipped aircraft were used as its operation over enemy territory was still banned. Mosquitoes were ideal for *Intruder* operations, and the FB.VI (in 1943) made possible *Intruder* sorties to as far afield as Austria and Czechoslovakia, but in 1942, squadrons re-equipping from other types had to soldier on with converted NF.IIs with increased fuel capacity and bereft of their Mk.IV radar. There were few NF.IIs that could be spared and any Mosquitoes that were available were welcome, whatever their pedigree. The same state of affairs concerning conversion to the NF.II persisted at Colerne where, in May 1942, 264 (Madras Presidency) Squadron began their conversion. On 30/31 May Squadron Leader C. A. Cook and Pilot Officer R. E. MacPherson scored the squadron's first Mosquito victory when they shot down a Ju 88A-4 of *KüFlGr 106* at North Malvern Wells. In December 1942 what few NF.IIs were available carried out *Night Rangers* to airfields in France from Trebelzue, Cornwall. *Rangers* were low level operations on moonlight nights, mainly against railway rolling stock and road transport, although one could shoot down enemy aircraft if they were encountered.[40]

On the night of 28/29 June an *Intruder* Mosquito of 264 Squadron from Colerne piloted by Flying Officer Hodgkinson forced down *Unteroffizier* Rudolf Blankenburg over Creil as he made for home in a KG2 Do 217E-2 after a raid on Weston-super-Mare. 264 Squadron had operated Defiant night fighters since early 1942, and on 3 May had received its first Mosquito. The squadron flew its first operational sorties on the type on 13 June. A second Mosquito "kill" occurred on the night of 30/31 July when a Ju 88A-4 was destroyed. During July-August III/KG2's much reduced bomber force continued to send single aircraft on daylight low-level or cloud cover "pirate" sorties against selected targets in Britain. They also made several small-scale night raids, during which they began to encounter, in increasing numbers, the Mosquito night fighter. Although 157 Squadron at Castle Camps had been the first to become operational on the NF.II, the enemy continued to elude them. To their chagrin, 151 Squadron Mosquitoes destroyed four more machines.[41] It brought 151 Squadron's claims by the end of the month to ten enemy aircraft destroyed.

In July 1942 23 Squadron, which had received a T.III for training on 7 June, began conversion to the NF.II at Ford, but these aircraft were at a premium because of the need to equip home defense squadrons. Eventually 25 of the modified NF.IIs would be issued to 23 Squadron, but for a time the only one available for intruding was *S-Sugar*. Appropriately, the Squadron's first NF.II *Intruder* sortie was flown in this aircraft on 5/6 July by the CO, the inimitable Wing Commander Bertie Rex O'Bryen Hoare DSO DFC,* and Pilot Officer Cornes.[42] "Sammy," who sported a large handlebar moustache "six inches, wingtip to wingtip," was one of the leading *Intruder* pilots of his generation, having flown first Blenheims, then Havocs on intruder sorties over the Low Countries. Despite losing an eye before the war when a duck shattered the windscreen of his aircraft, Sammy Hoare became one of the foremost *Intruder* pilots in the RAF. A legend in his own time, he had done heaven knows how many *Intruder* sorties both day and night from as early as 1941, during which he had destroyed and damaged eight more and left a trail of wrecked German aircraft on airfields in Germany and occupied territories. Most if not all of this was achieved with only one eye and without radar. He succinctly described *Intruder* operations thus:

> "I should like to tell you not to measure the value of this night fighter work over German aerodromes by the number of enemy aircraft destroyed. This is considerable, but our mere presence over the enemy's bases has caused the loss of German bombers without a shot being fired at them. Night-fighter pilots chosen for intruder work were generally of a different type to the ordinary fighter pilot. They must like night fighting to begin with, which is not everybody's meat. They must also have the technique for blind flying, and when it comes to fighting, must use their own initiative and judgment, since they are cut off from all communications with their base and are left as freelances entirely to their own resources. Personally I love it. Once up, setting a course in the dark for enemy-occupied country, one gets a tremendous feeling of detachment from the world. And when the enemy's air base is reached there is no thrill - even in big game shooting - quite the same. On goes the flare path, a bomber comes low - making a circuit of the landing field - lights on and throttle shut. A mile or two away, in our stalking Havoc, we feel our hearts dance. The throttle is banged open, the stick thrust forward, and the Havoc is tearing down in an irresistible rush. One short burst from the guns is usually sufficient. The bomber's glide turns to a dive - the last dive it is likely to make. Whether you get the Hun or miss him, he frequently piles up on the ground through making his landing in fright."[43]

Flight Lieutenant Ronald "Tim" Woodman, who flew Beaufighters and Mosquitoes on *Intruder* operations, adds:[44]

> "Individually in the moonlight we crossed the Channel into France. The French Resistance informed us that the midnight passenger train out of Paris to Rouen was

normally packed with German troops returning from leave. Shooting up the engines resulted in the first passenger coaches also being hit. The Resistance then informed us that, because of this, the rear coaches were reserved for officers. So we shot up the engine (steam would sprout out like hose-pipes and the engines would be put out of action and the lines blocked for some time), then came round again and shot up the rear coaches. The cine film had large trees silhouetted against the moonlight."

On 22/23 August 157 Squadron scored its first actual confirmed "kill" when the CO, 29-year-old Wing Commander Gordon Slade, and Pilot Officer Philip V. Truscott destroyed a Do 217E-4 6./KG2 flown by 29-year-old ex-Lufthansa pilot *Oberleutnant* Hans Walter Wolff, Deputy *Staffelkapitan*, 20 miles from Castle Camps. August opened with bad weather, low cloud, and poor visibility. 151 Squadron was detailed to intercept high flying German night raiders that were flying in over England on cloudy nights. Raiders coming in over the North Sea continued to be intercepted. In September 151 Squadron added two more Dornier Do 217E-4s to its "kill" total. The first of these, on loan to 3./KG2 and piloted by *Feldwebel* Alfred Witting, was shot down by Ian McRitchie on 8/9 September when the *Luftwaffe* attacked Bedford. During a raid on King's Lynn on 17 September Flight Lieutenant Henry E. Bodien DFC blasted a 7./KG2 Dornier piloted by *Feldwebel* Franz Elias. It crashed at Fring and all four crew were taken prisoner.[45] On 30 September 157 scored its first day combat victory when Squadron Leader Rupert F. H. Clerke, an Old Etonian and former PRU Mosquito pilot, downed a Ju 88A-4 off the Dutch coast.[46] It had been a particularly bad month for KG2, which on 19 August 1942, during the Dieppe operation, lost 16 Do 217s and had seven damaged. By October 157 Squadron had added three more enemy victories.

During 1942, some RAF night-fighter squadrons had re-equipped with the de Havilland Mosquito, "a lethal brute with no vices." In October of the same year Air Chief Marshal Arthur "Bomber" Harris, AOC RAF Bomber Command, advocated that Mosquito fighters should be used in the bomber stream for raids on Germany. Air Chief Marshal Sir W. Sholto Douglas, AOC Fighter Command, loathe to lose his Mosquito fighters, argued that the few available Mosquitoes were needed for home defense should the *Luftwaffe* renew its attacks on Britain.

Also in October 1942, 410 "Cougar" Squadron RCAF, which had been equipped with Beaufighters since February, moved from Scorton to Acklington to re-equip with NF.IIs. The Canadians had flown their Beaufighter IIs operationally for the first time on the night of 4 June. In two and a half months at Ayr and Drem in Scotland only eleven scrambles were made and only one enemy aircraft was located. When the Cougars moved to Scorton, in Yorkshire, on 1 September minus a number of crews who were killed in accidents, morale was low, but the Canadians finally secured a kill when a Ju 88 was attacked and crashed into the sea. Activity, however, remained low, but the re-equipment to Mosquitoes boosted spirits, although conversion was slow and the process was only finally completed in December. During December 1942-Janaury 1943 the Cougars flew 93 sorties against the "Jerry Weathermen" and "milk train" patrols which proved to be fruitless. On 13 January Flight Sergeant B. M. Haight and Sergeant T. Kipling were vectored onto a raider and they made a visual contact at 600 yards. Kipling identified it as a Do 217E from its silhouette against the clouds. One brief burst at 100 yards range produced a brilliant white flash on one engine. A second burst of 75 rounds from the Hispanos had no visible effect, but the Dornier disappeared into the clouds in a steep spiral dive and contact was lost. The Royal Observer Corps, however, saw the aircraft dive into the sea with a brilliant white flash and explosion five miles off Hartlepool.

On 15/16 January 1943 151 Squadron scored the first Mosquito "kill" of the New Year, when Sergeants E. A. Knight and W. I. L. Roberts shot down a Do 217E-4[47] during a raid on Lincoln. The Canadian Mosquito pilot aimed his first burst from quarter astern and hit the enemy's port engine. The pilot, Leutnant Gunther Wolf, dived and carried out evasive action. *Unteroffizier* Kurt Smelitschkj, the dorsal gunner, returned fire. Knight blasted the Dornier again and there was no more firing. His third burst caused pieces of the German bomber to fly off and it crashed at Boothby Graffoe, near Lincoln, killing everyone on board. On 17/18 January a NF.II of 85 Squadron flown by the Canadian CO, Wing Commander Gordon Raphael DFC,*[48] and his navigator, Warrant Officer W. N. Addison DFM, destroyed a Ju 88A-14 which fell over southeast England. 85 Squadron was a famous fighter squadron and its badge, the mysterious hexagon, the origin of which no one could trace, had distinguished itself in the First World War. It had borne the brunt of much of the early fighting in France and later it had won honors in the Battle of Britain. Converted to a night-fighter squadron, it was now stationed in the same North Weald sector from which the RAF had guarded the eastern approaches to London in the autumn of 1939. On 22 January a 410 Squadron RCAF Mosquito claimed a "probable" Do 217E and then there was a lull in the Mosquito "kills."

At the end of January 1943 Wing Commander John "Cats Eyes" Cunningham DSO* DFC*[49] assumed command of 85 Squadron at Hunsdon vice Wing Commander Raphael—"a vigorous young Canadian" who "strongly disapproved of drinking [which] had been weighing heavily upon the more light-hearted members of the squadron."[50] Cunningham had shot down 16 enemy aircraft while flying Beaufighters. This was due to a combination of flying skill and good shooting, as well as airborne radar operated by his navigator, 39-year old Flight Lieutenant C. F. "Jimmy" Rawnsley DFC DFM.*[51] Cunningham's miraculous night vision, the propagandists explained, was due to the fact that night-fighter pilots ate lots of carrots because they were good for night vision. This had its origins in the half-truth that a deficiency of certain vitamins could cause night blindness. Not unnaturally, the public, who knew nothing about airborne radar, went along with it, but the Germans were not fooled for a moment and Cunningham was saddled with the nickname "Cat's Eyes," which he detested. In the late 1930s Rawnsley, a Londoner, had been 18-year old Pilot Officer Cunningham's air-gunner in the two-seater Demon biplane fighters that 604 Squadron, Auxiliary Air Force, flew. It was the beginning of what was to develop into a close association as a team that lasted throughout the years of the war. Known to all as the "The Little Man," Rawnsley was appointed Navigation Leader at Hunsdon. Rawnsley's wife Micki had recently joined the ATS.

Cunningham and Rawnsley's first concern after their introduction to the Officers Mess in an old country house named "Bonningtons" was to get to know all those in the squadron. Of these, the first was the Adjutant, Flight Lieutenant T. J. Molony, known as Tim, "a massive and dignified man, urbane and very conscious of the niceties of decorum. In civilian life he was a director of Ladbrooke's, the turf accountants; and he had been with the squadron since the early days in France. He also laid claim to being the last man to bowl underarm in first-class cricket, playing for Surrey. Because of this distinction, Tim described himself, using a happy phrase, as 'the last of the lobsters....' The Engineering Officer, Flight Lieutenant J. Hoile, "was a good natured, hard working old sweat of a Regular who knew his job thoroughly and in every detail from spinner to tail wheel." The squadron Intelligence Officer was Flying Officer E. A. Robertson, "a wizened, dry old Scot." Robbie was in the fishery business and lived in Hull. The Senior Flying Control Officer was Squadron Leader M. H. Bradshaw-Jones, "a tallish, gaunt, piratical figure of a man" who would often pack a revolver and wear thigh-length boots. In the mess one night "Brad" quietly rode a solo motorcycle around the billiard table with four passengers on board. Before the war Brad—married and with two children—had been a keen amateur yachtsman. He had also raced in cars and on motorcycles. His business had been in manufacturing and wholesaling of fine silverware and in antiques. When war broke out he tried to join the RAF. Five times he was turned down on medical grounds, but he passed on the sixth try and went into Air-Sea Rescue, working with the high-speed launches. During the Battle of Britain he went through a dive-bombing attack one day while ashore at Gosport and he was badly injured, his spine being stretched. But he still went on with his work with the launches until he was shot up in one after the bombing of a convoy. The Bembridge lifeboat rescued him from that.[52] One of Rawnsley's first duties was to assess the value of the navigators in relation to the positions they held in each aircrew:[53]

> "Some had developed a patter that I could only describe as most extraordinary. It seemed to consist of a non-stop and bewildering stream of words somewhat like the chanting of a Dutch auctioneer trying to finish off the sale before closing time. It was not until I heard the retiring Navigator Leader in action that I discovered where it had all come from. He was a lively, vivacious man named C. P. Reed, a Flight Lieutenant. He was sharp featured and quick witted and a remarkably fast thinker. The words streamed out of him in a torrent and I wondered how any pilot could ever take it all in. But the amazing thing was that it worked and worked well. And what sort of argument could prevail against the unanswerable fact of success? All the same, I began with the newer navigators to use a more orthodox style, if only to simplify the interchangeability of crews. I had a pretty shrewd idea that Phil Reed owed his success more to his quick thinking than to his style.
>
> "There were among the aircrews some well-matched teams. Many of them merged their own pronounced individualities in achieving this. Flight Lieutenant W. H. 'Bill' Maguire - who had been in the millinery business before the war - was a jovial, prosperous looking man, an ex-instructor and a fine pilot. He had as his navigator a Welsh schoolmaster, Flying Officer W. D. Jones, a short, stocky man who was a great lover of music. Getting ready for a patrol always appeared to be an event with great relish in it for Bill Maguire, almost as if he were preparing for a feast, his eyes sparkling with anticipation, his bushy moustache bristling skyward. In his comfortable voice he would boom out 'Now ... where's that Jonesy man?'
>
> "In the quiet voice of Flying Officer George Irving, who came from Carlisle, there was just a hint of a border burr. His head of flaming hair naturally brought down upon him the nickname 'Red.' And there was always a suggestion of a smile in his twinkling, pale blue eyes, a smile always ready to break out in a flash of dazzling white teeth. He was navigator for Flight Lieutenant Geoffrey Howitt, a solid and imperturbable individual.[54]
>
> "Squadron Leader Wilfrith P. Green, A Flight Commander,[55] had as his navigator a typical NCO of the best type, Flight Sergeant A. R. Grimstone DFM. Known to everybody as 'Grimmy,' he was, although unburdened by any unnecessary ambition, keen, quick-witted and reliable. Peter Green was a slightly built, deceptively mild-mannered man, plagued with a nervous stammer, which, as I had noticed happened with other aircrew, was barely noticeable moment he left the ground. There was certainly no trace of nervousness about his flying. Another of the navigators, Sergeant Graham Gilling-Lax, had only been with the squadron for a very short time when we arrived. He was a NCO of a very different type and entirely different to the popular conception of what a Sergeant was supposed to be. Graying hair topped a long, scholarly face and he stooped slightly in a rather dignified manner. His voice was quiet and carefully and evenly modulated. I was not altogether surprised when I checked through the records to find that he had been a housemaster at Stowe. I seemed to have on my books an astonishing number of schoolmasters.
>
> "One of the more senior navigators - although young enough in years - was Flying Officer Frank Seymour Skelton.[56] I saw little of him as he was just finishing his first tour of flying and was about to go on a rest; but what I did see of him made a lasting impression. He had been through the complete navigator's course and at first he had been rather annoyed at having to specialize for night fighters, as that was by no means the job of his choice. Known to everybody as Bill, he was tall and handsome with veiled eyes well set in a leonine head. A rather drawling, undergraduate voice tended to complete an impression that Bill was taking the whole business far too languidly ever to be much good at it. I should have known better and subsequent events were to prove how wrong first impressions can sometimes be. In Bill Skelton, I felt, there could be more or less summed up the general standard of operating in the squadron: the basically fine material had been softened by prolonged and enforced inactivity. Most of them had got into the habit of doing only perfunctory night flying tests and their practice in the air was casual, even slapdash. It was the old and very sad story, all the result of a little too much of the playboy in their attitude towards things. I formed the impression that they were good, but not as good as they thought they were and by no means as good as they could be; and I became anxious to show up their shortcomings and my own, before the Luftwaffe did it for us."[57]

Early in February Cunningham and Rawnsley flew their first night flight in a Mosquito and eased themselves into their training regime. They decided that Rawnsley should control the interception during the early stages using their old and well-tried methods. Then, when they got close enough for any evasive action their quarry might take, Cunningham would take over. They carried out their first operational night interception in a Mosquito on 3 March when they flew *I-Ink*. Rawnsley picked up a contact in the London area and Cunningham closed to about 500 feet, but they were in dense cloud and they finally had to give up. They soon picked up another contact, however, and they followed it as it weaved its way outward bound between the swinging beams of searchlights. Cunningham looked up and saw a Dornier 217 twisting and turning ahead of them. They closed in for the attack, the twin fins of the Dornier standing out clearly. Rawnsley, whose faith in the AI had been quickly restored, had a perfect view of the enemy bomber. He realized that the clear, wide panel of bullet-resisting glass of the windshield was all that was between them and the target, and "any hot tomatoes they might want to throw back at them." But the Dornier crew did not see the Mosquito and Cunningham attacked. However, when he pressed the gun button nothing happened. He tried again, but still there was no response from the guns. And then somebody in the Dornier must have given the alarm. The long, slim bomber rolled right over to its left and plunged vertically downwards. Cunningham rammed *I-Ink's* nose over and Rawnsley was lifted from his seat as the Mosquito fell away, but he forced his face into the visor of the AI.Mk.V set and just held on. The Dornier went plummeting down for several hundred feet but they were still in contact. Then it leveled out and started to climb steeply, but the Mosquito was right behind it and a few minutes later Cunningham again had it in his gun sight. The Dornier was tantalizingly close, but again as he pressed the gun button nothing happened! A moment later the Dornier peeled off and away again, straight on down in a long, high-speed dive that kept the Mosquito well behind, and finally he was lost in the ground echoes and Rawnsley could see nothing more of him on the AI. At Hunsdon a quick examination revealed that a severed lead had put the Mosquito's gun-firing circuit out of action. 85 Squadron had put up eighteen sorties and Cunningham and Rawnsley were the only crew to see a raider.

At Hunsdon in March Squadron Leader Edward Crew DFC* joined 85 Squadron to take command of "B" Flight.[58] He had as his navigator Flying Officer Freddie French, who had never quite recovered from a Beaufighter crash at Middle Wallop in the winter of 1941-42, but he was determined to go on with his job. He was flying with a pilot who had only recently joined 604 Squadron and they had hit a hill near the aerodrome one night. The Beaufighter broke up and the pilot was killed, but Freddie was trapped in a part of the fuselage that had broken off. Badly injured, he lay there for some time before the rescue party arrived and hacked him out. Fortunately, the part of the aircraft that he was trapped in did not catch fire.

On 18/19 March *Fliegerkorps IX* set out to attack Norwich. Between 2255-2330 hours, 20 crews aimed 18 tonnes of high explosive and 19.2 tonnes of incendiaries on the part of the city that ran north and northwest of the large buildings in the city center. In all 3.3 tonnes actually fell on the streets, houses, and factories. Thirteen junior crews, who were on the raid to gain combat experience, attacked harbor installations at Great Yarmouth. Mosquito and Beaufighter night fighters had already taken off to intercept the bombers heading for Norwich. Flying Officer G. Deakin and Pilot Officer de Costa of 157 Squadron took off from Bradwell Bay at 2200 hours in their NF.II and they were vectored out to sea by GCI at Trimley Heath. Squadron Leader Kidd, the controller, directed the Mosquito crew towards an enemy aircraft approaching Orfordness. They got an AI contact with a Ju 88 at 9000 feet range. (Deakin eventually obtained a visual sighting at 2500 feet and recognized his prey.) The Ju 88 was climbing, so he opened up the throttles and climbed steeply behind him before opening fire with a long burst of four cannon and two Browning machine guns at 600 feet dead astern. The Mosquito pilot continued firing while the Ju 88 "corkscrewed" in vain. Deakin carried on firing into the doomed bomber until all his ammunition was exhausted. The enemy raider flew straight and level, then disappeared, falling into the sea about four miles off Southwold.

A Coltishall-based 68 Squadron Beaufighter flown by Flying Officer P. F. Allen DFC and Flying Officer G. E. Bennett destroyed a Do 217E, a 6./KG2 machine flown by *Hauptmann* Hans Hansen. In the meantime, a NF.II of 410 "Cougar" Squadron RCAF flown by Flying Officer D. Williams and his navigator, Pilot Officer P. Dalton, had taken off from Coleby Grange at 2245 hours and were directed towards "trade" in the King's Lynn area. Flight Lieutenant Tuttle at Orby Control directed the two Canadians towards a "bogey" three miles distant flying at 240 mph. Williams increased speed to 260 mph and Dalton picked up the contact at two miles range. Suddenly another contact appeared at 1000 yards, below and slightly to port. Williams put the nose down and at 8000 feet made out the unmistakable form of a Do 217 flying along at 2000 feet dead ahead. It was from I/KG2 and was being flown by *Unteroffizier* Horst Toifel. The fear and shock aboard the Dornier at that instant can only be imagined. Toifel must have seen his pursuer because he immediately carried out a half-roll and tried to dive before his gunner, *Unteroffizier* Heinrich Peter, the radio operator, Ludwig Petzold, or the observer, *Obergefreiter* Georg Riedel, could even think about opening fire. Toifel was so preoccupied with trying to lose the Mosquito that he had no time to sight and fire his defensive armament. Williams followed the Dornier down and held his fire as he did so. At 1800 feet the Mosquito pilot pulled out and shortly afterwards a huge ball of crimson fire could be seen directly below, near Terrington St. Clements. Williams could only think that the Dornier did not recover from its dive and therefore crashed.

On 28/29 March 1943 forty-seven bombers of *IX Fliegerkorps* bombed Norwich again. An NF.II of 157 Squadron flown by Flying Officer J. R. Beckett RAAF and Flight Sergeant Phillips took off from Bradwell Bay at 1940 hours and patrolled some 30 miles off Orfordness before they were vectored by HCI Trimley Heath on to an enemy aircraft approaching Lowestoft. Beckett had got contacts before on two of his previous twelve patrols, but so far had made no kills. After two momentary contacts on a fighter crossing rapidly from starboard to port, another contact was obtained dead ahead on an aircraft flying west at 12,000 feet. It was changing course and height as it approached the coast. With some difficulty the NF.II closed in to 1000 feet, where a visual sighting was obtained. Evasive tactics became more violent which made the target difficult to identify, but from its exhaust system, which glowed orange-red, it appeared to be a Dornier 217.[59] Beckett wrote:

> "The searchlights and ack-ack made identification difficult as we were also hit a few nines. After we closed op to our firing position to identify the plane positively as an enemy one, their rear gunner fired at us, but missed, firing too high. I returned the fire at once with two bursts of cannon fire at 300-400 feet range lasting about two seconds each. After that I saw hits and sparks on the rear of the aircraft and as a result the enemy fire stopped and the plane dived into the clouds a few hundred feet below us. Visual contact was lost but AI contact was held by Phillips from 10,000 feet down to 5000 feet with the Dornier turning hard to port. During that time we were constantly turning in left circles. Contact was lost when the enemy plane turned hard to port and left out screen."[60]

During February NF.IIs of 410 "Cougar" Squadron RCAF, the third Canadian night-fighter squadron to be formed, had moved south from Acklington to Coleby Grange for *Night and Day Rangers*. The moon period of March came and went while the *Night Rangers* cursed the weather, which made it impossible for them to operate. Nine *Day Ranger* sorties were dispatched on the 26th, 27th, and 30th, but eight were aborted at the Dutch coast because of unsuitable weather. The dangers appertaining to these operations were borne out on 6 April, when Flight Lieutenant C. D. McCloskey—one of 410 Squadron's original members—and Pilot Officer J. G. Sullivan were shot down and taken prisoner. Four days later Flying Officer J. E. Leach and Flying Officer R. M. Bull were killed in action over Friesland. *Ranger* operations began again when the moon period arrived in mid-April, and on the night of the 15th the CO, Wing Commander Frank W. Hillock, headed for the Ruhr. The weather was poor and, as the Mosquito skipped along at 300 feet over Holland, Hillock suddenly saw the eight radio masts of Apeldoorn station rushing towards him.

There was no time to climb and no room to fly between them, so he threw the Mosquito on its side and ripped through the antennae, tearing away several wires. On return to Coleby Grange it was found that one wing tip had been sliced off, and the other wing had been cut through to the main spar before the wire had broken; about 300 feet of well-made ¼-in copper cable was trailing behind the Mosquito! Despite this shaking experience, Hillock had coolly flown to his target before coming home.[61] Over the next four nights crews located a convoy off the Dutch coast suitable for a naval attack, strafed barges in Holland and a factory in Rees, and strafed rail yards at Cleve. On 20 April Flight Sergeant W. J. Reddie and Sergeant Evans went missing. There then followed a week of poor weather, which made it unsuitable for *Rangers*. Operations resumed again on the 30th, and during the moon period in May 410 "Cougar" Squadron RCAF extended its sphere of operations to include France and Belgium. Taking off at 1415 hours on the afternoon of 27 April, Pilot Officer M. A. Cybulski and his navigator, Pilot Officer H. H. Ladbrook, struck across the North Sea to Vlieland. They turned SE past Stavoren to Mepple, where they altered course eastwards and hedgehopping across northern Holland they reached Meppen, just across the German border. Here they flew down to the Ems canal to Papenburg, and then turned westward for home, where they landed at 1727 hours after covering more than 600 miles. Flying down the canal and railway lines between Meppen and Papenburg the Mosquito attacked five targets. First Cybulski damaged a tug and two barges, from which debris flew into the air, and then he riddled a locomotive and raked a line of six freight cars. Two military buses were shot up and, to end the strafe, pieces were shot off another locomotive, which was left wreathed in clouds of steam. Newspapers heralded the record flight, but the pilot's name had to be suppressed lest it bring reprisals upon his relatives in Poland; Cybulski's home was in Renfrew, Ontario, but his grandparents were Polish.

On 14/15 April 1943, during a raid on Chelmsford, Squadron Leader Wilfrith Green and Flight Sergeant A. R. "Grimmy" Grimstone DFM of 85 Squadron destroyed a Do 217E-4 of 4./KG40. Off Clacton Flight Lieutenant Geoff Howitt and Flying Officer George "Red" Irving destroyed a Do 217E-4 of 6./KG2 flown by *Unteroffizier* Franz Tannenberger. This was Howitt's third victory of the war, having destroyed two He 111s while flying Havocs in 1941. Flight Lieutenant James Ghilles Benson DFC and his navigator, Lewis Brandon DSO DFC, of 157 Squadron, intercepted a Dornier 217E-4 flown by *Unteroffizier* Walter Schmurr southwest of Colchester.[62] "Ben" Benson gave the 6./KG2 machine a three-second burst at 200 yards with his four cannon from astern and above but saw no results. He then fired a seven-second burst and saw strikes, first on the port engine and mainplane, which immediately burst into flames. These spread down the port side of the fuselage until the whole aircraft, including the tail, was ablaze. There was no return fire.[63] On 16/17 April Fw 190A-4/U8s of *Schnelles Kampfgeschwader* (SKG) 10, based in France, took part in attacks on London. The fast fighter-bombers, each carrying a 250-kg or 500-kg bomb on its centerline, had first been employed in March against Eastbourne, Hastings, and Ashford. To be better sited to meet the threat 85 Squadron had, in May, moved from Hunsdon to West Malling, and 157 moved from Bradwell to take their place. The mainstay of the *Luftwaffe's* raids on England at this time remained the Ju 88 and Do 217. On 24/25 April Flying Officer John Peter Morley Lintott and Sergeant Graham Gilling-Lax of 85 Squadron shot down a Ju 88A-14 of 8./KG6 and it disintegrated in the air, with the wreckage falling in Bromley, Kent. In April 604 Squadron at Scorton converted to the NF.XIII, and 256 Squadron began equipping with the NF.XII and 29 Squadron, who did likewise, followed them in May. In February-March 456 Squadron RAAF, which was largely equipped with Beaufighter Vifs, began to include some NF.II *Ranger* operations in addition to their day fighting role, first from Middle Wallop and then from Colerne. From late May they were successfully employed on *Intruder* sorties over France, attacking railway rolling stock and intruding on French airfields. In May 1943, 60 OTU at High Ercall was expanded and made responsible for all *Intruder* training.[64]

On the night of 4/5 May 1943 the bulbous glass-nosed Dornier Do 217K-Is of 6./KG2 taxied out at Eindhoven. On board one of them, *Oberfeldwebel* Heinrich Meyer and his three crew prepared to take off and join the circuit. Their bomb bay normally held either four 500-kg high explosive bombs or ABB500 incendiaries, and they were destined for Norwich. For the 4/5 May raid, III/KG2 at Eindhoven had only recently returned from a sojourn to Carcassonne when the French Fleet was on the point of defecting to the Allies. KG2 and II/KG40 would be joined on the Norwich raid by Ju 88As of I and III/KG6 based in Belgium. Six Mosquito night intruders were abroad that night and over Holland shortly after KG2 took off. Near Hilversum Meyer's Dornier was written off when it crashed. It was the start of a bad night for the famed *Holzhammer* unit. The remaining 42 Dorniers of KG2 and III/KG40 and 36 Ju 88s of KG6, including one aircraft that was to monitor the operation from Cromer, evaded their hunters and flew on low over the North Sea towards the Norfolk coast. Four of the Ju 88s had, at the same time, flown south to create a diversionary attack on the south coast of England. Over the North Sea the oncoming German bombers noticed about 40 RAF bombers at the same height, these being among 596 RAF bombers that had attacked Dortmund. The Do 217s and Ju 88s approached eastern England, hoping that the CHL stations would interpret their blips on the radar screens as "friendly" bombers. For a crucial period of time it seemed to have worked, because the German bombers carried on unmolested and then turned on a heading for Norwich, with their navigation lights on to further fool the defenders. Oberst Dietrich Peltz, "Attack Leader England," intended to deliver upon Norwich its heaviest raid of the war. That it did not happen was due to a fault in the target illumination and guidance system. The showers of flares were released well enough; in fact, John Searby, who was in one of the RAF bombers returning from Dortmund, diverted to look at the marker flares and was so impressed he "wished we had some to equal them." However, the parachute flares were dropped in the northwest of Norfolk, and the majority of the phosphorous and mixed incendiaries fell harmlessly in fields or did little damage.

Then the defenses were alerted. Aboard Do 217K-l U5+AA[65] *Leutnant* Ernst Andres sat in his contoured pilot's seat in close confinement with his crew: *Unteroffizier* August Drechsler, radio operator; *Obergefreiter* Wilhelm Schlagbaum, observer; and *Flieger* Werner Becker, gunner, who sat facing rearwards behind them in his dorsal turret. All four crew were keen to impress 31-year-old Major Walter Bradel, *Kommodore* of KG2, who was flying as an observer on the operation. Bradel, who had succeeded *Oberst* von Koppelow three months earlier, was probably flying on the raid to help restore shattered morale after heavy losses in his *gruppe*.[66]

Flying Officer Brian "Scruffy" Williams and his navigator, Pilot Officer Dougie Moore, in 605 Squadron, were complete opposites, but equally dedicated to their task. Moore was on his first tour, but the 21-year-old pilot had flown over 30 ops on Bostons in 418 (City of Edmonton) Squadron RCAF. Williams was an exceptional pilot. At 51 OTU, the CO, none other than Guy Gibson, had marked his Course Assessment "Above Average," but had added "May get overconfident."[67] Williams and Moore had taken off from Castle Camps about an hour and a half after the raid on Norwich and were stooging around Eindhoven when they chanced upon the returning Dorniers. The first aircraft could be seen circling the airfield with its red and green navigation lights on. Brian Williams recalls:

"It was bloody dark. There was no moon. I saw a Do 217.I fired but saw no strikes. Lost it! I'd probably frightened him to death! [The crew of Leutnant Alfons Schlander of 2/KG2 is also listed as being shot down near Eindhoven that night.] Then I saw a second one in the same circuit. It was a Do 217 and it also had its green and red navigation lights showing. I went in and made a beam attack. I fired my cannon and saw numerous strikes, but I didn't see it hit the deck so I later claimed a 'damaged'. I saw two more crossing in front of us but I didn't go after them because we had no chance of catching them, so I finished the patrol and flew home to base. While I was on home leave I received a 'phone call from the CO, Wing Commander C. D. Tomalin. He had rung to tell me that the Do 217 I had claimed as 'damaged' had crashed. Apparently, it had caused a furore in the German newspapers, which said that the Dornier was the one carrying Major Bradel. He was killed in the crash [at Landsmere, near Amsterdam] Leutnant Andres was seriously injured."[68]

Six more German aircraft were shot down by Mosquito *Intruders* before May was out.[69] On the 13th, 85 Squadron moved from Hunsdon to West Malling aerodrome, near the main London-Maidstone road, deep in the heart of the orchards and hop fields of Kent, which was occupied by Typhoons of 3 Squadron. The move coincided with some terrific action, for during May 85 Squadron claimed eight aircraft. On the night of 16/17 May the Fw 190A-4/U8 fighter-bombers of I/SKG10 came streaking in over the Straits of Dover. Much to the chagrin of 85 squadron, the Typhoons only were scrambled to meet them. The Mosquito crews waited almost an hour before they too were pitched into the fight after it was realized that the Typhoons, which did not have AI, were floundering. Squadron Leader Peter Green and Flight Sergeant A. R. "Grimmy" Grimstone DFM got off first and picked up a Fw 190 contact at three miles. The I/SKG10 machine had dropped his centerline bomb and was on his way back to France. He never made it. Green shot him down into the sea off Dover. Geoff Howitt and "Red" Irving shot down the second Fw 190 off Hastings. Flight Lieutenant Bernard Thwaites, a quiet, pale young fighter pilot with a look of confidence in his eyes, and Pilot Officer Will Clemo DFM*, his older, former schoolmaster navigator, chased an Fw 190 all the way to the French coast before being recalled to West Malling. He and Clemo kept a close eye on the horizon as they headed back to base. Clemo was a thoughtful man who took his pleasure in solitary nature study rambles. On the ground he sported an enormous pipe with a deeply curved stem and when he spoke, which was rarely, the words emerged reluctantly between puffs and in a gruff undertone. But there was a lively twinkle in his eyes that told of an alert brain working behind that dour façade, possibly savoring some secret joke.[70] In mid-Channel Clemo picked up a freelance contact crossing in front. Thwaites shot it down from 50 yards astern, collecting some of the debris in the air intake of one of his engines, but that did not prevent him from scoring three hits on another Fw 190, knocking a large piece off it to claim it as a "probable."

Flying Officer I. D. Shaw and Pilot Officer A. C. Lowton braved their own searchlights and brought down a fifth Fw 190 near Gravesend, returning to Hunsdon with their windscreen coated in soot and their rudder badly damaged.

Back at West Malling, to the accompaniment of *Yip I Addy 85*, Tim Molony ceremoniously presented the jackpot prize of bottles of whisky, champagne, and gin and £5 in cash to Peter Green and "Grimmy" Grimstone for being the first Mosquito crew to down a Fw 190 over Britain.[71] Squadron Leader Bradshaw-Jones gave a silver Mosquito. Congratulatory signals were received from the sector commander, Group Captain "Sailor" Malan DSO* DFC*[72] and Air Vice Marshal H. W. L. "Dingbat" Saunders at Group. There was soon more to celebrate. On the night of 19/20 May Flying Officer John Lintott and Sergeant Graham Gilling-Lax stalked a Fw 190A of 2./SKG10. Peering into his scope, he guided Lintott onto the tail of the Fw 190 and his pilot shot it down. Their victory was celebrated at West Malling, where a dance was in progress, and the remains of the Fw 190A were auctioned off for £105 in aid of the "Wings for Victory" appeal! On 21/22 May a Fw 190A was shot down into the sea 25 miles northwest of Hardelot by Squadron Leader Edward Crew DFC* and Flying Officer Freddie French. To complete a memorable month, on 29/30 May Lintott and Gilling-Lax shot down the first Ju 88S-1 to fall over England. It crashed at Isfield, Sussex.[73]

On 13/14 June Wing Commander John Cunningham and Flight Lieutenant C. F. "Jimmy" Rawnsley of 85 Squadron pursued a Fw 190A-5 of 3./SKG10 over his own airfield and shot it down. Rawnsley wrote:

"It was a Fw 190 all right. The single exhaust flickered below the fuselage; the short, straight wings still had the drop tanks hanging from the tips; the big, smooth bomb was still clutched fiercely to its belly... John very briefly touched the trigger, and the guns gave one short bark. The enemy aircraft reared straight up on its nose, flicking over and plunging vertically downwards. It all happened with an incredible speed. Standing up and pressing my face to the window, I watched the blue exhaust flame dwindle as the aircraft hurtled earthwards."[74]

The Fw 190, flown by Leutnant Ullrich, crashed at Nettlefold Farm, Borough Green, near Wrotham, but incredibly the pilot had been catapulted through the canopy in the death dive of the aircraft and was taken prisoner. Cunningham's seventeenth victory was his first on the Mosquito.

On 21/22 June Flight Lieutenant Bill Maguire and Flying Officer W. D. Jones of 85 Squadron bagged a Fw 190 of 2./SKG10 in the river Medway. On 9 July Geoff Howitt and "Red" Irving and Flight Lieutenant John Lintott and Pilot Officer Graham Gilling-Lax, the two standby crews at Hunsdon, were scrambled to meet a wave of sneak raiders coming in under cover of the bad weather. The cloud seemed to be almost down to the ground, blotting out Wrotham Hill nearby, but both crews took off and twenty minutes later crews at Hunsdon heard the sound of aircraft approaching, but now the notes of the engines varied, as if the pilots were jockeying for position. The Medway AA guns opened up, followed by a burst of machine-gun fire and the unmistakable throaty roar of cannon. Crews in the Officers Mess at "Bonningtons" rushed outside and strained their eyes, but they could see nothing in the driving rain that was now beating down around them. The note of the engines changed again and the drone rose to a howl, rising in pitch to a scream, and then it cut off abruptly with an ominous thump. There was silence as crews waited for news, and finally it came through on the telephone; a Dornier 217 had crashed near Detling. Lintott had obtained his fourth victory when he and Gilling-Lax shot down a Do 217K-1 piloted by *Oberleutnant* Hermann Zink of 6./KG2, which had just bombed East Grinstead high street and the Whitehall Cinema, killing 108 people and injuring 235 more. Zink and his crew were all dead. The GCI controller who had put Lintott onto the raider saw two blips on his CRT merge and stay together for seven minutes; then they had faded. Geoff Howitt and Irving had crept in under the weather and had landed safely at Bradwell Bay, across the other side of the Thames Estuary in Essex.

Shortly afterwards word came that Lintott and Gilling-Lax had been found two miles from where the Dornier fell. They were both dead in the wreckage of their Mosquito. Both men had just been awarded DFCs, and Gilling-Lax had recently been given his commission. They were a bitter loss to the squadron.

Two months earlier Flight Lieutenant Edward Nigel Bunting, a 27-year-old pilot and experienced night fighter from St John's, Worcester, had been one of the officers in 85 Squadron who operationally tested the high-altitude Mosquito NF.XV at Hunsdon. Bunting attained a record altitude of 44,600 feet on 30 March 1943, but the project was abandoned after the demise of German high-altitude raiding. On 13/14 July 1943, when KG2 headed for Cambridge, Bunting and Freddie French took off from the Somerfield wire mesh runway at West Malling at 2300 hours in their NF.XII and patrolled the Straits of Dover in search of enemy activity. Flying Officer Parr, at Sandwich GCI station, gave Bunting a vector towards a "customer" some 35 miles away. The Mosquito soon narrowed the gap to three miles and Bunting and French could see their prey well below them. French picked up another contact and Bunting pulled away, concerned that the red light he saw might be a decoy. French guided Bunting onto the higher, unlighted contact, which was at 25,000 feet. Climbing at full power Bunting gave chase for 15 minutes, opening and closing his radiator flaps to prevent overheating. When they were still at 7000 feet range they could see the enemy's two bright exhausts. Eventually, a visual was obtained against the bright glow of the northern sky at a range of 1800 feet. The Mosquito crew could make out the two engines trailing bright yellow exhaust flames with the narrow fuselage and twin barbettes bulging on either side. Rightly, they believed it to be a Me 410 *Hornisse* (Hornet). *Feldwebel* Franz Zwißler and *Oberfeldwebel* Leo Raida of 16./KG2 were flying it. Bunting closed to within 200 yards astern and worked his gun sight on to the target, but the Mosquito got caught in the Germans' slipstream and he could not aim his guns. Bunting dived below to recover and began easing up into position again before firing two short bursts. With flames streaming from the fuselage the Me 410 rolled over on its back and dived vertically into the sea five miles off Felixstowe. It was the first Me 410 to be shot down over Britain.[75]

For 410 "Cougar" Squadron RCAF June 1943 was a rather quiet and uneventful period as far as scrambles and *Rangers* were concerned. Coastal Command anti-submarine operations in the Bay of Biscay were being hampered by enemy counter air activity and 410 Squadron was requested to supply fighter support. (Another 410 *Intruder* detachment was temporarily established at Hunsdon.) Four crews were detached to Predannack for *Instep* patrols in company with Polish crews from 307 Polish Squadron, who began flying *Night Rangers*, and 456 Squadron RAAF. The Cougar crews remained at Predannack for a month and flew 20 patrols lasting between 4-5 hours' duration. On the afternoon of the 13th Pilot Officer R. B. Harris and Sergeant E. H. Skeel were accompanied by three other Mosquitoes on patrol when, SW of Brest, the formation intercepted four Ju 88s. Fw 190s then arrived on the scene and three aircraft, including the 410 Squadron crew, were shot down. The next morning, Pilot Officers J. Watt and E. H. Collis, with three Polish crews, sighted five *U-boats* in the bay. When the Mosquitoes were sighted they drew into a tight defensive circle. Two of the Mosquitoes attacked the *U-boats*, which sent up a considerable amount of flak. Strikes were made on the conning towers of the *U-boats*, and one Mosquito was damaged by flak. All the aircraft returned safely to Predannack. On the 19th, on another patrol with 307 Squadron, Flying Officers E. A. Murray and P. R. Littlewood of 410 Squadron encountered a Bv 138 flying boat as they zigzagged at low level over the Bay of Biscay. The Mosquitoes made two line astern attacks on the By 138, which attempted to climb into cloud cover. On the first attack one engine was hit and began to smoke; the aircraft, being unable to gain height, nosed down towards the sea. On the second attack the starboard engine was hit and caught fire. The aircraft then crashed into the sea. Three crew emerged and they scrambled into a dinghy. The last action occurred on 21 June when Pilot Officer C. F. Green and Sergeant E. G. White were members of a patrol that attacked two small armed merchant vessels or trawlers, both of which were damaged.

July 1943 was a month of high activity, thanks in considerable measure to enemy activity. On the 12/13th four Mosquitoes of 410 "Cougar" Squadron RCAF were scrambled from Coleby Grange to intercept an enemy raid on Hull and Grimsby. Squadron Leader A. G. Lawrence DFC and Flight Sergeant H. J. Wilmer intercepted a Do 217 over the mouth of the Humber, but after taking violent evasive action it got away after the crew had fired only one short burst at it. Flares, ack-ack, and searchlight activity made it impossible to continue the chase. The crew was then vectored onto another Do 217 and, following an AI contact and visual identification, the enemy aircraft was given a short burst of cannon fire. This had no effect and a second burst was given. This caused a huge flash in the Dornier's starboard engine, followed by clouds of smoke. In a diving turn with the engine glowing brightly the bomber went down, hitting the sea with a great splash. The enemy gunners had returned fire, but the streaks of red and white tracer passed under the Mossie's starboard wing. On the following night six crews were scrambled but no contacts were made.[76]

Early in July 410 Squadron received six FB.VI fighter-bombers for use on *Intruders* and *Ranger* operations. Flight Lieutenant Murray took charge of a special section formed to carry out these activities, the first sortie being made on the 15th. On a *Night Ranger* to France from Ford on the 18th, Pilot Officer L. A. Wood and Flying Officer D. J. Slaughter failed to return. Poor weather prevented any further ops until the night of the 25th, when 2 crews went on *Flower* sorties (Bomber Command support) to Deelen airfield, in Holland. The first crew, Norman and Hunt, saw visual *Lorenz* lit three times during their patrol and noticed bombs fall on or near the aerodrome, starting fires. An hour later they were relieved by Murray and Littlewood. Approaching Deelen, after orbiting a dummy aerodrome for a few moments the crew saw an aircraft come in and land. Thirty minutes later a second Hun appeared, flicking its navigation lights on and off. The crew came in behind a Do 217 and fired a 3-sec burst at the aircraft. Searchlights coned the Mosquito while the flak guns opened up. The port engine of the Dornier caught fire, and lit up by 5 searchlights it veered to the left, crashed, and exploded in flames on the airfield boundary. As the crew continued to circle the airfield a third aircraft made a hurried landing and, on reaching the end of the runway, the navigation lights were turned on. Murray came down in a sharp diving turn and fired a long burst at the aircraft, damaging it. The navigation lights were quickly doused and the enemy ground defenses immediately came into action again. Patrols were made on three nights between 28-30 July to Schleswig/Jegel, Gilze-Rijen, and Venlo airfields, all without success. The Cougars suffered a severe blow on the 30th when Flight Lieutenant E. A. Murray and Flying Officer P. R. Littlewood were killed at Honiley, Warks, when flying an Oxford on a navigation flight. Murray, a native of Stelleraton, Nova Scotia, was deputy flight commander of "B" Flight, whilst Littlewood came from Saanichton, Vancouver Island, BC.

Another of the Mosquito crews rapidly making a name for themselves on offensive night fighting patrols at this time was that of Flight Lieutenant James "Ben" Benson DFC and Flight Lieutenant Lewis "Brandy" Brandon DSO DFC of 157 Squadron. On the night of 3/4 July 1943, flying a NF.II, they shot down a Do 217 over St Trond. On 13/14 July Flying Officer Rae Richard Smart of 605 Squadron, flying a NF.II, destroyed a Do 217M-1 near Eindhoven. In July 456 Squadron RAAF and 605 Squadrons re-equipped with the FB.VI for Intruding, and 418 (City of Edmonton) Squadron RCAF flew the last of its Boston sorties and concentrated on *Flower* operations using the FB.VI. On 15/16 July Flight Lieutenant Bernard Thwaites and Pilot Officer Clemo DFM* of 85 Squadron shot down a Me 410 of V/KG2 flown by *Hauptmann* Friederich-Wilhelm Methner and *Unteroffizier* Hubert Grube, which was heading for London, into the sea off Dunkirk. Flying Officer Knowles of 605 Squadron shot down a Do 217M-1 flown by *Leutnant* Manfred Lieddert of 3./KG2 on 25/26 July when the target was again Hull. South African Wing Commander Geoffrey Park, CO of 256 Squadron, rounded off the month by shooting down *Oberleutnant* Helmut Biermann and *Unteroffizier* Willi Kroger in their Me 410A-1 on 29/30 July when the target was Brighton. They fell into the sea 20 miles south of Beachy Head.

One of the heaviest losses to befall KG2 in 1943 was on the night of 15/16 August, when it lost seven aircraft—six claimed by Mosquitoes—in a raid on Portsmouth.[77] On 22/23 August Geoff Howitt of 85 Squadron, now Squadron Leader DFC, and Pilot Officer J. C. O. Medworth took off from West Malling at 2330 hours in their NF.XII and went on patrol. Off Harwich they zeroed in on *Feldwebel* Walter Hartmann and *Obergefreiter* Michael Meurer's Me 410A-1 of 15./KG2. Howitt got a visual on the Messerschmitt's bright yellow exhaust emissions and closed in for the kill. It was difficult to get a sight of the silhouette, and at first Howitt thought his prey was a '210. Almost at once a stray searchlight beam illuminated the aircraft and he could quite easily see that it was a '410. With the German crosses easily visible, Howitt gave the Messerschmitt a short burst and it immediately burst into flames with a brilliant flash. Showers of burning pieces flew past the Mosquito in all directions. The Me 410A-1 fell away, its entire starboard wing on fire, and crashed at Chemondiston. Meurer baled out and came down at Stratton Hall, while Hartman's body was later found in a field, his parachute unopened.[78]

On the night of 24/25 August a NF.XII flown by 85 Squadron's Norwegian pairing—Captain Johan Räd and radio operator Captain Leif Lövestad—took off to look for "trade." Räd and Lövestad searched the night sky for a "kill." Lövestad worked the AI.VIII set and picked up a contact, a Messerschmitt 410. Räd fired four bursts into the enemy fighter, which exploded in a ball of fire. Blazing pieces broke off. Two explosions followed and a parachutist was spotted baling out. The victory was officially shared with Wing Commander R. E. X. Mack DFC of 29 Squadron, which claimed two more victories that night—their first Mosquito victories since converting from Beaufighters.[79] Tall and slim, Räd was a lively individual who had been an electrical engineering student and a pilot in the Norwegian Air Force Reserve when the Germans had invaded his country. He and fellow engineering student Per Bugge went into the Underground movement in Trondheim before setting sail six months later with eleven others for Britain. After nine days meandering around the North Sea and Atlantic Ocean they had finally landed in Scotland. Lövestad, a man with massive hands and broad shoulders, and a cheerful smile lighting a rugged, homely face, had started his career well before the war in the Norwegian Army, and had later changed over to the Air Force. He went through the air fighting in Norway, fighting as an observer in the Norwegian Air Force against the *Luftwaffe* until they had no aircraft left. Then he had gone underground, mapping and sketching the airfields the Germans were building and taking documents out to the coast for friends to smuggle across to England. In August 1941 Lövestad and 29 others set out for Britain across the North Sea in a small, dilapidated old fishing boat, following for reasons of safety the longest route from the Lofoten Islands to the Shetlands. The journey took them nine days. They missed the Shetlands and went sailing out into the Atlantic, but finally they decided to turn back and they landed near Scapa Flow, on the northwest corner of Scotland. For two days they rested in the shelter of a small bay and then they sailed on to Thurso, where they made their official landing. They even managed to sell the dilapidated boat to a Scottish fisherman even though it was rotten all through![80]

For a time Lövestad and Räd were the only two Norwegian airmen in Britain who had some training as pilots, and they were allowed to complete their instruction in England, rather than having to follow the usual course of going to Canada. Though he stood no more than shoulder high to Räd, Leif Lövestad had tremendous strength and had been known to change with ease a car wheel without using a jack. Sometimes in the evenings he said 'Now Johan…you must be tired. Why don't you sit down?," and he would lift his pilot at arm's length as gently as a baby and deposit him on the counter of the bar. Using the same strength Lövestad had battered his way through the side of their crashed Beaufighter at Middle Wallop and lifted the unconscious Johan clear of the wreckage as the flames sprang up around them. Soon they were joined at West Malling by three fellow countrymen: Claus Björn, Bugge's argumentative radio operator, who had reached England via Sweden, Russia, Japan, and the USA; and Lieutenants P. Thoren and Tarald Weisteen. Björn was trained as an observer in Canada. Per Bugge was a flaxen-haired giant whose rare words emerged reluctantly in a series of scarcely audible grunts. He appeared to be unshakable and was always pleasant and most courteous. He soon made a name for himself as an exceptionally capable pilot. Weisteen was small, dark, and slight of build. But his mind, like his features, was keen and taut. He had joined the Royal Norwegian Air Force before the war and was a regular officer. He had gone through the War Academy and was an established fighter pilot when hostilities broke out in Norway. It was said of him that he had had quite a time flying against the *Luftwaffe* in Gloster Gladiators until the resistance was overwhelmed, and then he managed to escape to England.[81]

In August 1943, when it was realized that the *Luftwaffe* were operating radar equipped night fighters against the "heavies" of Bomber Command, some AI equipped Beaufighters and Mosquito night fighters were released over enemy territory on *Mahmoud* operations as bait for enemy night fighters in their known assembly areas. With centimetric AI being used in Mosquitoes it was necessary to fit *Monica* tail warning devices, as the later Mks of AI did not scan to the rear. Mosquitoes pretending to be bombers were not successful, as the enemy soon recognized their speed difference. Nevertheless, on 15/16 August Flight Sergeant Brearley of 256 Squadron, flying a NF.XII, destroyed two Do 217M-1s over France. Six FB.VIs and six NF.II with AI fighters were available to 410 Squadron for *Flowers* operations in August in addition to the Squadron's usual defensive commitments. Twenty-five sorties, four by day, were made mainly during the last half of the month. The first part of the month had poor weather and much of this time was occupied with training. On a *Night Ranger* to France from Ford on 18 August Pilot Officer L. A. Wood and Flying Officer D.

J. Slaughter failed to return. Poor weather prevented any further operations until the night of 25 July, when two Cougar crews flew *Flower* sorties to Deelen airfield in Holland. Flight Lieutenant Murray and Flying Officer Littlewood orbited a dummy airfield for a few moments and saw an aircraft come in to land. Thirty seconds later another aircraft appeared, flicking its navigation lights on and off. The FB.VI crew came in behind a Do 217 and fired a three-second burst at the aircraft. Searchlights coned the Mosquito while the flak guns opened up. The Dornier's port engine caught fire and, lit up by five searchlights, it veered to the left, crashed and exploded in flames on the airfield boundary. As the FB.VI crew continued to circle the airfield a third aircraft made a hurried landing, and on reaching the end of the runway the navigation lights were turned on. Murray came down in a sharp diving turn and fired a long burst at the aircraft, damaging it. The navigation lights were quickly doused and the enemy ground defenses came into action again.[82]

On the night of 15/16 August two *Rangers* were made from Castle Camps to St. Dizier airfield. Lawrence and Wilmer dropped two 250lb bombs on the runway and, on the return flight, attacked a train near Paris. Pilot Officer Rayne Dennis Schultz, who was twenty years old and came from Bashow, Alberta, and Flying Officer V. A. Williams in FB.VI HP849 did not reach St. Dizier. Instead, they attacked three locomotives between Clermont and Poix and they bombed a bridge. On their way home, some 20 miles off Beachy Head, they spotted another aircraft, and on closing found it to be a Do 217M-1. The Do 217 under gunner opened accurate fire on the FB.VI and the enemy pilot tried to shake off the Mosquito. A long pursuit followed. Schultz's second burst hit the cockpit, where fires broke out and debris fell away. Three, or perhaps four of the crew were seen to bale out; then the Dornier turned for France in a shallow controlled dive. Schultz fired again; the starboard wing and engine broke away and, completely enveloped in flames, the bomber hit the sea, where it continued to burn brightly. After taking some cine films of the scene and reporting the position of the crew, Schultz headed for home to report their first victory. *Ranger* sorties were flown on the 16th, 17th, 18th, 23rd, 27th, and 29th (daylight); Flying Officers G. B. MacLean and H. Plant were lost on the 18th over Germany. There were also a number of scrambles, the most significant being on the 31st when five crews were dispatched—only one contact was made. Flying Officer F. W. Foster and Pilot Officer J. H. Grantham were hit by enemy canon and machine gun fire shortly after becoming airborne. Foster took immediate evasive action by climbing to 10,000 feet and the contact was lost.

On 17/18 August Flight Lieutenant David Henry Blomely of 605 Squadron in a FB.VI destroyed a Bf 109 east of Schleswig, and on 22/23 August a 29 Squadron NF.XII crew in HK164 destroyed a Me 410A-1 north of Knocke. Blomely was credited with another victory on 21 September when he destroyed two Ju 88s west of the Skaggerak.

For 410 "Cougar" Squadron RCAF, at least, the first three weeks of September were somewhat quieter than August. *Ranger* sorties were cancelled, but *Flower* ops continued. 15 sorties were made between the 3rd and 16th; attacks were made on St. Michel and Laon airfields and against railways targets. Pilot Officer J. E. Fisher and Sergeant D. Ridgeway failed to return from Melum on the 16th. This was the last night of FB.VI ops, which were transferred. *Ranger* and *Flower* ops ceased, and in their place *Mahmoud*, or offensive patrols over specific points in search of enemy aircraft, were made. Two specially equipped Mk IIs were used for these activities. During the period 17-23 September only a number of fruitless scrambles were undertaken, and on the 24th 410 "Cougar" Squadron RCAF started *Mahmoud* operations, but these were not successful until the night of 27/28 September. Flight Lieutenant M. A. Cybulski and Flying Officer H. H. Ladbrook, flying NF.II D7757, made a *Mahmoud* patrol of the Zeider Zee and Meppen area from Coleby Grange. The 90 minute patrol was unsuccessful, but on the way home an AI contact was made on a Do 217 which was then located flying east. The enemy pilot went into a steep climb with the Mosquito closing rapidly. A 3-second burst was fired and the enemy aircraft immediately exploded with a terrific flash and descended enveloped in flames. Burning petrol and oil flew back onto the NF.II, scorching the fuselage from nose to tail, the port wing inboard of the engine, the bottom of the starboard wing, and the port tailplane and the rudder, from which the fabric was torn away. Pieces of the Dornier struck the port oil cooler, resulting in the loss of oil and making it necessary to shut down the engine. Cybulski was completely blinded and Ladbrook had to take control of the aircraft for about five minutes until the pilot regained normal vision. Course was set for base, and the seriously damaged aircraft completed a hazardous 250-mile single engine return. The crew received immediate DFC awards. A further eight more *Mahmouds* were completed, all without incident, and between the 1st and 19th 26 scrambles were made. Coleby Grange was made unserviceable one night by enemy bombing activity. 410 "Cougar" Squadron RCAF moved from its base to West Malling, having completed a total of 286 sorties, of which 125 had been scrambles, 78 *Rangers*, 49 *Intruders* and *Flowers*, 20 *Insteps*, and twelve *Mahmouds*. Nine crews had been lost on operations and two in flying accidents. 410 Squadron moved again to Hunsdon in October 1943, then Castle Camps, where regular patrols were flown in defense of southern England.

Meanwhile, over England on 6 and 8 September 85 Squadron destroyed a total of five Fw 190A-5s. On 15/16 September Flying Officer Jarris of 29 Squadron shot down *Oberfeldwebel* Horst Müller and *Unteroffizier* Wolfgang Dose's Me 410A-1 of 15./KG2 off Beachy Head during a raid on Cambridge. A 9./KG2 Do 217M-1 flown by *Oberfeldwebel* Erich Mosler was also shot down by Flight Lieutenant Watts of 488 Squadron RNZAF into the sea southeast of Ramsgate. Flying Officer Edward Hedgecoe and Pilot Officer J. R. Witham of 85 Squadron destroyed a Ju 88A-14 of *6./KG6*. The Mosquito was crippled by return fire and the crew baled out, their aircraft crashing at Tenterden, Kent. Flight Lieutenant Edward Bunting destroyed a Ju 88A-14 of II/KG6.

By September 605 Squadron were flying *Intruder* sorties over Denmark and Germany. That same month Sammy Hoare assumed command of the Squadron, and he returned to combat operations on 27/28 September, whereupon he promptly despatched a Do 217 at Dedelsdorf for his seventh confirmed air to air victory. (On 10/11 January 1944 Sammy Hoare scored the County of Warwick Squadron's 100th victory when he and Flying Officer Robert C. Muir in an FB.VI shot down a Ju 188 4m east of Chievres. Sammy claimed a probable and damaged three aircraft in 1944 and shot down his 9th and final aircraft in March that year.) *Intruder* victories were now hard to find, and in fact none were recorded until Flight Lieutenant Blomely DFC destroyed a Bf 110 25 miles west of Aalborg on 9 November. Wing Commander Roderick A. Chisholm DFC and Flight Lieutenant F. C. Clarke of the FIU[83] destroyed a Bf 110 at Mannheim on 18/19 November. In November 1943 a 307 Squadron detachment at Sumburgh, Scotland, carried out *Rhubarbs* over Norway, destroying two He 177s and a Ju 88. When they returned south they continued intruding and later flew Bomber Support operations until March 1945.

In October the Norwegians of 85 Squadron had figured in two more victories. On 2/3 October Pilot Officer Tarald Weisteen and Freddie French destroyed two Do 217Ks during a raid on the Humber Estuary. On 7/8 October, when the *Luftwaffe* raided London and Norwich, Leif Lövestad was flying with Flight Lieutenant Bill Maguire, whose usual radio operator, Flying Officer W. D. Jones, was away on a Navigator Leaders Course. Maguire, who sported a bushy moustache, was an ex-instructor and a fine pilot who before the war had been a milliner. GCI control warned Maguire and Lövestad that two hostile aircraft were flying in line astern and a mile apart when they caught sight of an enemy aircraft in the moonlight showing reddish-yellow wingtip lights and a white tail light below its starboard quarter. At 2000 feet distance *Feldwebel* Georg Slodczyk of 16./KG2 put his Me 410A into a tight turn. In the back seat, *Unteroffizier* Fritz Westrich must have known there was a Mosquito on their tail. For several minutes Slodczyk and Maguire weaved and manoeuvred violently. Maguire turned tighter each time and was able to identify their prey. He gave the '410 a short burst using deflection and flashes appeared all along the German aircraft's fuselage and wing. Slodczyk desperately pushed his nose down and dived at full speed for the cover of cloud below. Maguire dived after him and pumped another burst into the '410 from 300 yards, just as Slodczyk disappeared into the cloud. (Westrich's body was picked up off Dungeness on 13 October and buried at sea.) Below, Squadron Leader Bernard Thwaites DFC and Will Clemo DFM,* who shot down an Me 410A flown by *Feldwebel* Wilhelm Sohn and *Unteroffizier* Günther Keiser of 14./KG2 (which crashed at Ghent), saw Slodczyk and Westrich descend in flames into the sea and were able to confirm Maguire's "kill."

On 8/9 October 85 Squadron claimed its first Ju 88S-1 when ten intruders flew in from Holland. Flying Officer S.V. Holloway and Warrant Officer Stanton shot their Ju 88S-1 of 8./KG6 down off Foulness. Flight Lieutenant Edward Bunting shot down a Ju 88S-1 of 7./KG6 into the sea ten miles south of Dover at 2020 hours for his third victory. *Feldwebel* W. Kaltwasser, *Obergefreiter* J. Jakobsen, and *Unteroffizier* J. Bartmuss were all killed. Summer and late 1943 had proved successful for the night fighter crews of 85 Squadron, but they knew that they could rely on the *Luftwaffe* to step up their efforts as the autumn nights began to lengthen. The Germans had already begun mixing Ju 88s in with the Fw 190 fighter-bombers, and word was that they could expect to meet the Ju 188, a faster and more powerful version of the Ju 88 with pointed extensions to the wings to give a better rate of climb. On 15/16 October thirteen enemy aircraft started towards England. Only eight of them crossed the coast, and of these three were destroyed. Maguire and Flying Officer W. D. Jones, now returned from his Navigator Leaders Course, shot down two Ju 188E-1s of 1./KG6 within the space of twelve minutes. One went into the sea off Clacton and the other crashed at Hemley, Suffolk, to become the first Ju 188 down on land in the UK.[84] Flying Officer Hugh Brian Thomas and Warrant Officer C. B. Hamilton got the third Ju 188E-1, which crashed at Birchington, for their first victory. On the last night of the month they had added to their score, downing a Ju 88G-1 of III/KG6 south of Shoreham.

On 15 October 1943 Wing Commander Cathcart M. Wight-Boycott DSO took command of 25 Squadron at Church Fenton, equipped with the NF.II.[85] Wight-Boycott recalls:

> "25 Squadron had been given the role of *Intruder* operations over Western Europe using bombs, for which crews, trained for night defense of the UK using AI.Mk. IV had no previous training or experience. Morale was not high. They had had a number of casualties. A' Flight Commander, Squadron Leader Brind RNZAF, had been intercepted returning from a low-level sortie and ditched. He and his navigator were taken prisoner. Just before I arrived a flight commander and his crew attempting a single-engined landing in had weather had been killed. A few days later another flight commander, Squadron Leader Matthews and crew, failed to return from a sortie over the Low Countries. A month later, the most experienced squadron pilot, Flight Lieutenant Baillie and Flying Officer Simpson, on their last flight before going on rest, also failed to return from a night sortie. It was not surprising that morale among aircrews was not high, especially as intelligence could not give any clue as to how these experienced crews had got into trouble.
>
> "The *Mahmoud*[86] Mosquitoes were only with us for a month before 25 Squadron moved to Acklington to re-equip with NF.XVIIs, which were fitted with AI.Mk X. During that time I flew two *Mahmoud* sorties. On the first one we were briefed to fly over the Low Countries and wait for a German night-fighter to get on our tail and then turn 360 degrees to get ourselves in position to get behind the German night-fighter. This manoeuvre was quite unsuccessful. Although I tried it three times in all, the German night-fighter remained on my tail and I had to take some pretty drastic evasion tactics to avoid being shot down myself. Our intelligence were quite unaware of the very efficient German ground control in the Low Countries.
>
> "My next sortie was to fly a pin-point near Bonn at 20,000 feet where I was told I would find a narrow vertical beam, around which there would be a German night-fighter orbiting waiting to he ordered by ground control into a heavy bomber stream. Nobody explained how a defensive night-fighter crew could possibly find the vertical beaus navigating by dead reckoning, no means of checking wind speed and direction, and unable to see the ground. Moreover, the crew had only experience of positioning by ground control - the navigator was Navigator Radar on hoard just to work a radar set. If this wasn't enough, no information was in the briefing on our own bomber routes and heights, and we arrived in the midst of our own bomber stream and were lucky not to he shot down by unfriendly 'friendly' rear gunners. In our efforts to avoid the stream, we became more and more lost and could never have got closer to our target than 50 miles. We decided optimistically to assume we were reasonably close to our target and set course for home (Coltishall) and with relief, recognized that we had reached the North Sea and would soon sight the Norfolk coast. We seemed to fly for hours and couldn't understand why we didn't reach the coast unless there was a 90mph head wind. We eventually had to break R/T silence and get a steer' from Coltishall which shoved that we were so far south we were flying west down the English Channel, any moment about to start a trans-Atlantic crossing! We had had no fix for over three hours. I was very relieved that shortly afterwards we left our *Mahmoud* operations behind."

Chapter 3

"Musical Mosquitoes"

Hinging on a bombers moon, wheeling on a cloud
Oboe's fingers nudging us on course
Living for the fight, living with the fright
Flying to the pulsing goads of Morse
But its dog-leg, half-turn, weaving through the fray
Every gunner wants to bring us down
Off to mark a target with a firework display
The Pathfinders are out to paint a town
Pick of the ranks
Mossies and Lancs
Kin of the wandering goose
Sing as we go
Look out below
Bennett's Brigade's on the loose

Bennett's Brigade, ***G. R. Reeves***

In April 1942 109 Squadron was established at Stradishall, Suffolk, to bring *Oboe* into full operational service as a navigation aid for Bomber Command before moving to Wyton in August, where at the end of the year it received the first *Oboe* equipped Mosquito B.IVs.[87] *Oboe* was first used on 20/21 December 1942 when the CO, Squadron Leader H. E. "Hal" Bufton DFC AFC and his navigator, Flight Lieutenant E. Lister "Ding" Ifould, as well as two other crews were sent to bomb a power station at Lutterade, in Holland, on the border with Germany. Bufton and Ifould, who had navigated one of the leading Lancasters on the famous Augsburg daylight raid of 17 April 1942, dropped the first Oboe-aimed bombs. Two other crews bombed on *Oboe*, but the equipment in the remaining three Mosquitoes did not function properly and their crews bombed targets of opportunity. All six Mosquitoes returned safely. Daylight PR photographs taken after the raid showed so many old bomb craters from an earlier raid on 5/6 October, when the pathfinder mistook Lutterade for Aachen, 17 miles away, that it was impossible to identify the *Oboe* results reliably. In fact, nine bombs fell together in open ground two kilometers from the power station. On 31 December 1942/1 January 1943, on a raid on Düsseldorf, sky-marking using *Oboe* was tried for the first time when two Mosquitoes of 109 Squadron provided the sky-markers for eight Lancasters.[88] The PFF markers' job was to "illuminate" and "mark" targets with colored TIs (target indicators) for the Main Force and other 8 Group Mosquitoes. The Path Finder Force had been formed from 3 Group using volunteer crews on 15 August 1942 under the direction of Group Captain D. C. T. "Don" Bennett and was headquartered at Wyton.[89] The tough talking Australian ex-Imperial Airways and Atlantic Ferry pilot wanted Mosquitoes for PFF and target-marking duties.

Starting on the night of 3/4 January *Oboe* Mosquitoes operated on two successive nights in attacks by the Lancasters of 5 Group on Essen and on 8/9 January against Duisburg. *Oboe* led operations against Essen were resumed on the night of 7/8th and then again on the nights of 9/10th, 11/12th, and 12/13th, when four PFF Mosquitoes and 55 Lancasters of 1 and 5 Groups attacked the city. The *Oboe* equipment of the first Mosquito to arrive failed and the other three Mosquitoes were all late. Because of this many of the Lancasters bombed on dead reckoning. On the 13/14th 66 Lancasters and three Mosquitoes visited Essen. Two *Oboe* Mosquitoes had to return without marking, and the sky markers of the third Mossie failed to ignite above the cloud, but the city was bathed in light. German aircraft even dropped decoy flares to try to distract the Lancaster crews. On 13 January the Path Finder Force became 8 (PFF) Group, and "Don" Bennett was promoted Air Commodore (later Air Vice Marshal) to command it.

On 16/17 January Berlin was bombed for the first time in fourteen months by 190 Lancasters and eleven Halifaxes. Air Marshal Sir Arthur Harris, C-in-C, Bomber Command sent them on their way with the words "Tonight you are going to the Big City. You will have the opportunity to light a fire in the belly of the enemy that will burn his black heart out." This raid marked the first use of purpose-designed Target Indicators (TIs) instead of modified incendiaries, which had previously been used.[90] Only one Lancaster was lost, but the raid was a disappointment. Thick cloud en route and haze over the target caused problems and the bombing was scattered. The Berlin flak had proved light and ineffective, and it was assumed that the greater altitude of the attacking force had surprised the German gunners. Harris repeated the raid on Berlin, sending 170 Lancasters and 17 Halifaxes back to the Big City the following night, when the weather was better.

On the night of 2/3 February 161 bombers, including 116 Lancasters and 35 Halifaxes, went to Cologene in another experiment using a four-engined bombing force with various forms of Pathfinder techniques. The night was cloudy and markers were dropped by both the *Oboe* Mosquitoes and ther H_2S heavy marker aircraft. Results were dsiappointing once again, with no clear concentration of markers being achieved and with subsqequent bombing well scattered. The *Oboe* Mosquitoes flew a series of minor operations against enemy targets throughout February, sending twos and threes to targets as far afield as Lorient, on the French Atlantic coast, to eastern Belgium and Essen, Düsseldorf, and Rheinhausen in Germany, as well as to night fighter airfields in Holland. On the night of 5/6 March it was the turn of Essen when 442 aircraft, 157 of them Lancasters and *Oboe*-equipped Mosquitoes, began what has gone into history as the starting point of the Battle of the Ruhr. The cascade that night included no less than 150 4000 pounders and two-thirds of the bombs carried were incendiaries. For most of the way out the route was cloudy, but fifteen miles from the target the weather cleared, although pilots reported valley mists were still seeping in from the river. The eight *Oboe* Mosquitoes marked the center of the city perfectly with Red TIs and the Pathfinder "backers up" arrived in good order and dropped their Green TIs blind on the target. Only if there were no reds visible were the Main Force to bomb the "Greens." These were followed by the first "Cookies," which wailed down and then erupted with violence and flame, and the raid was well under way. The valley mists and industrial haze did not affect the outcome of the raid, which was bombed in three waves with the Lancasters bombing last, the entire weight of the raid being concentrated into a volcanic forty-five minutes. Fifty-six aircraft turned back early because of technical problems and other causes. Fourteen aircraft were shot down and 38 other bombers returned with damage. Damage was modest, but a week afterwards the Air Ministry announced that 450 acres of Essen were a devastated area. Of the Krupps plant alone, 53 separate large workshops were affected by the bombing. Thirteen of the main buildings in the works were completely demolished or seriously damaged. Over 470 people were killed on the ground and over 3000 houses were destroyed, while over 2100 were seriously damaged. The havoc was caused by nearly a thousand tons of high explosive dropped by crews without them needing to see the target. "Essen," said the special Air Ministry announcement on 12 March "is now the second most blitzed town in Germany. Only in Cologne is there a greater area of devastation."

On 12/13 March 1943 Essen was again the target for 457 aircraft, one of the highest numbers for some time. The force included 152 Lancasters and ten Mosquitoes acting as Pathfinder markers using the *Oboe* technique of marking the target with special flares, directly controlled by radio beams from England. The role of the other aircraft taking part was that of fire raisers. They were to follow immediately after the first pathfinders had dropped their marker flares and drop incendiaries and 1000lb bombs to "stir things up" and light the fires for the following Lancasters to plaster them with their 4000lb Block Busters. It was estimated that the Krupps works received 30 per cent more damage on this night than the earlier raid that month. Sir Archibald Sinclair, the Secretary of State for Air, sent Harris an appreciative message. "Your cunningly planned and brilliantly executed attack on Krupps has destroyed no small part of Germany's biggest war factory. Congratulations to you and all under your command on this achievement in the teeth of Germany's strongest defenses."

On 26/27 March the raid on Duisburg by 455 aircraft was one of the few failures of this series of attacks on Ruhr targets. The night was cloudy, and for once accurate *Oboe* sky marking was lacking, because five *Oboe* Mosquitoes were forced to return early with equipment problems. A sixth was lost when Flight Lieutenant L. J. Ackland RCAF and Warrant Officer F. S. Strouts DFC RCAF were forced to ditch in the North Sea and both men were drowned. This aircraft was the first *Oboe* Mosquito lost on operations. Beginning on 27/28 March Berlin was attacked for two nights in succession. The first raid by 396 aircraft was a failure. The Pathfinders marked two areas but they were short of their aiming points by five miles. Consequently, none of the bombs came within five miles of the target area in the center of the city. Nine aircraft were lost. Another *Oboe* raid on Bochum on 29/30 March by 149 Wellingtons and eight *Oboe* Mosquitoes failed also. The night was moonless and cloudy. The Mosquitoes were unable to stick to their timetable and there were long gaps in the sky marking. Essen, the home of Krupps, was bombed by 317 aircraft with marking by ten *Oboe* Mosquitoes on 3/4 April. The weather forecast had predicted unfavourable conditions, and so the Mosquito force had planned for both sky-marking and ground-marking the target. As it turned out there was no cloud over Essen and the Main Force crews were confused to find that two types of marking were employed. Even so, bombing was accurate and over 600 buildings were destroyed and more than 500 seriously damaged. Fourteen Halifaxes and nine Lancasters failed to return. Thick cloud on the night of 8/9 April when the target was Duisburg ruined Pathfinder marking by ten Mosquitoes and the resultant bombing was scattered. On the night of 26/27 April, when the target was Duisburg again, 561 aircraft, including ten *Oboe* Mosquitoes and 215 Lancasters, 135 Wellingtons, and 119 Halifaxes were despatched. Seventeen aircraft were lost—ten of them to night fighters over the Netherlands—but all the Mosquitoes returned. The Pathfinders claimed to have marked the target accurately. More than thirty tons of bombs a minute for a space of three-quarters of an hour rained down on the important inland port, the largest in Europe, which handled about seventy-five per cent of all the cargoes passing along the Rhine. However, the bombing was not accurate, mainly because the Main Force may have bombed too early or dummy fires short of the target may have duped them.

On the last night of April, over 300 bombers headed for Essen, again to drop more bombs on its already devastated environs. Cloud had been expected over the target so a pathfinder technique based entirely on *Oboe* Mosquito sky-markers was planned. This was not expected to give such good results as ground marking, but the plan worked well, and 238 bomber crews reported that they had bombed the city to take the figure of bombs dropped on the long suffering city to 10,000 tons. At the time this was the heaviest weight of bombs dropped on any town in the world. Twelve aircraft failed to return. Half the losses were inflicted by night-fighters. The world's press took notice of the performance of Bomber Command and the *New York Times* commented in its leader:

> "Germany is apparently reaching the point where she cannot cope, materially or physically, with the effects of bombing. Her enemies did not wait to pummel her cities until the population was strained by years or war and the armies were scraping the bottom of the barrel for men and material. They waited because they were unable to hit sooner. But if Allied strategy had been dictated not by necessity but by a plan to reserve its full striking power until German force was spent, the results would be very much like what there are now."

The attack on Duisburg-Ruhrort on 12/13 May by over 570 aircraft saw more than fifteen hundred tons of high explosives and incendiaries being dropped. This was more than was dropped on Cologne in the thousand-bomber raid a year earlier. Whereas the Cologne raid had taken ninety-eight minutes, concentration at Duisburg-Ruhrort was so controlled that delivery was made in half that time, and the ten *Oboe* Mosquitoes did their work well. Zero hour was fixed for 2 o'clock. The first flares and bombs went down dead on time. The last aircraft was winging home forty-five minutes later. The night following over 440 bombers and ten *Oboe* Mosquitoes raided Bochum. The raid began well enough, but after 15 minutes what were thought to be German decoy markers drew much of the bombing away from the target.

Raids on Ruhr targets continued with Dortmund, the fourth heavy Bomber Command raid of May, on the night of the 23rd/24th. Of 829 aircraft (including thirteen *Oboe* Mosquitoes) despatched, 38 bombers failed to return. The Pathfinders marked the target accurately in clear conditions and the bombing which followewd went according to plan. More than two thousand tons of bombs, the biggest bomb load ever dropped anywhere in a single night, fell on the luckless city, and the great weight fell in less than an hour between one and two in the morning. The next morning came more accolades and another promise from the Commander-in-Chief, addressed to all crews in Bomber Command. "In 1939 Goering promised that not a single enemy bomb would reach the Ruhr. Congratulations on having delivered the first 100,000 tons on Germany to refute him. The next 100,000, if he waits for them, will be even bigger and better bombs, delivered more accurately and in much shorter time." On the night of the 25/26th, when a dozen Mosquitoes marked for the 759 bombers despatched to bomb Düsseldorf, 27 bombers were lost—21 of which were due to night-fighters. The raid was a failure due to the difficulty of marking in bad weather. Another raid on Essen on 27/28 May saw twelve Mosquitoes mark for over 500 bombers, but the weather was cloudy and sky-marking had to be used. The main bombing was scattered with many aircraft undershooting.

By contrast, the raid on Wuppertal on 29/30 May, when eleven *Oboe* Mosquitoes took part, was the outstanding success of the Battle of the Ruhr. Both Pathfinder marking and Main Force bombing was very accurate, and a large fire area developed in the narrow streets of the old center of the extended, oblong shaped town, which had a population of almost 360,000. Wuppertal had been formed in 1920 by the union of the adjacent towns of Elberfeld and Barmen, in the Upper Wupper Valley. The Barmen half of the town was the target for the 719 aircraft despatched on that Saturday night, which was moonless, and 292 of them were Lancasters. Sixty-two aircraft turned back early, but the remainder, aided by blind-marking systems, devastated about 1000 acres of Barmen's built up area. Nearly 4000 dwellings were destroyed and 71 industrial and 1800 domestic buildings were seriously damaged. Thirty-three bombers, seven of them Lancasters, were lost.[91]

On 11/12 June 783 aircraft, including thirteen Mosquitoes, attacked Düsseldorf. The Pathfinder marking plan went extremely well until an *Oboe* Mosquito inadvertently released its load of TIs 14 miles northeast of the city, which caused part of the Main Force to drop their bombs on open country. Even so, in the city itself damage was extensive and 130 acres were claimed destroyed. When over 700 bombers attacked Krefeld on the night of 21/22 June the raid took place in good visibility and the Pathfinders carried out an almost perfect marking operation. Ground-markers dropped by the dozen *Oboe* Mosquitoes were well backed up by the Pathfinder heavies and 619 aircraft were reckoned to have bombed these markers, dropping more than 2300 tons of bombs. More than three-quarters of the bombers achieved bombing photographs within three miles of the center of the city. A large fire ensued, took hold, and burned out of control for several hours; 47 per cent of the built up area was laid waste. About 72,000 people lost their homes; the largest figure so far in the war. The night following, 557 aircraft, including a dozen *Oboe* Mosquitoes, went to Mülheim, where the Pathfinders had to mark the target through a thin layer of stratus cloud. The marking proved very accurate, and large fires raged throughout the city, destroying over 1100 houses and damaging over 12,600 dwellings. The post-war British Bombing Survey Unit estimated that this single raid destroyed 64 per cent of the town of Mülheim.[92]

On 25/26 June 473 aircraft, including twelve *Oboe* Mosquitoes, were despatched to Gelsenkirchen for the first raid on this city since 1941. Cloud obscured the target, and the dozen *Oboe* Mosquitoes, for once, failed to produce regular and accurate marking since equipment in five of the aircraft was unserviceable. The raid was not a success and bombs fell on many other Ruhr towns. Three nights later only seven of the twelve *Oboe* Mosquitoes reached the target (Cologne), and only six of these were able to drop their markers. The weather forecast had predicted that the city would probably be cloud covered, although there might be a break, so the Pathfinders had to prepare for both ground marking and the less reliable sky marking. The target turned out to be cloud-covered, so sky marking system was used. This was seven minutes late in starting and proceeded only intermittently; despite all of this, the Main Force of nearly 600 bombers devastated Cologne in the most destructive raid on the city in the entire war. Thousands of buildings were destroyed, over 4300 people were killed, and about 10,000 inhabitants were injured, while 230,000 people were forced to leave their damaged dwellings. A follow up raid took place on 3/4 July when 653 bombers aimed their bombs at industrial targets on the east bank of the Rhine. Pathfinder ground marking by the Mosquito *Oboe* aircraft and the backers-up was accurate and much devastation was caused.

Meanwhile, on 4 June 1943 105 and 139 Squadrons at RAF Marham were taken off daylight operations prior to joining 8 (PFF) Group. On 4 July 139 Squadron left for Wyton to swap places with 109 Squadron and begin a new career in 8 Group as high-level "nuisance" raiders flying B.IX Mosquitoes. They would also be required to go in with the early markers and carry out diversionary attacks, acting as bait for the enemy fighters to keep them at bay during the main *Oboe* raids. *Gee-H* (from 1944, H_2S)-equipped B.IXs of 139 Squadron and *Oboe II*-equipped B.IXs of 105 Squadron spearheaded the Main Force bombing raids. 139 Squadron went in with the target-marking Mosquitoes of 105 Squadron, sowing bundles of "Window," which produced a "clutter" of blips on German radar screens to give the impression of a large bomber force. They made diversionary attacks called *Spoofs* on other targets to attract enemy night fighters anything up to 50 miles away from the Main Force during the attack. 109 Squadron, which was commanded by Wing Commander "Hal" E. Bufton DFC AFC, transferred their 18 Mosquito IVs and six IXs to Marham to join those of 105 Squadron, and the station now became home to the PFF *Oboe*-equipped Mosquito marking force.

Six Mosquitoes of 109 Squadron flew the squadron's first operation from Marham on the night of 8/9 July 1943 when the Main Force attacked Cologne for the third time in a week. Flight Lieutenant Stevens and Squadron Leader J. F. C. Gallacher DFC acted as primary marker. The *Oboe* sky marking was accurate, and over 280 Lancasters of 1 and 5 Groups devastated the northwestern and southwestern sections of the city. Over 500 people were killed and 48,000 more were bombed out, bringing the total number of displaced inhabitants that week to 350,000. The following night (9/10 July) 105 Squadron flew their first *Oboe* operation when Squadron Leader Bill Blessing and his observer, Flying Officer G. K. Muirhead, and Flying Officer William E. G. "Bill" Humphrey and his observer, Flight Sergeant E. Moore, went to Gelsenkirchen. Both crews had spent a month of training at Wyton. Ten other "Musical Mosquitoes" were flown on the Gelsenkirchen operation by 109 Squadron crews. The raid by over 400 Lancasters and Halifaxes was not successful. The *Oboe* equipment failed to operate in five of the Mosquitoes, and a sixth Mosquito dropped sky-markers in error 10 miles to the north of the target. A few nights later, on 13/14 July 105 Squadron operated Mosquito IXs for the first time when two *Oboe* Mosquitoes carried out a diversion for the main attack on Aachen by dropping Green TIs and a 500 pounder apiece over Cologne. Eleven other *Oboe* Mosquitoes went to Cologne ahead of the Main Force. Eight of the "Musical Mosquitoes" marked with Red TIs and three others dropped their mixed bomb loads of three 500 pounders and one 250lb bomb. Mosquito IXs could carry six 500lb bombs, including one under each wing, although for long range operations these were frequently used to carry additional wing tanks. At Aachen a strong tail wind brought the first waves of the Main Force into the target area before Zero Hour, so that when the first Pathfinder markers were released an unusually large number of heavies bombed in the first minutes of the raid. Visibility was good and large parts of the city appeared to burst into flames at once.

The best *Oboe* crews could place a bomb within a few yards of the aiming point from 28,000 feet. However, since they had to fly straight and level for several minutes in the final run to the target they were vulnerable to flak and fighters. Moreover, they could only approach a given target from two directions—in the case of Ruhr targets, almost due north or south—the Germans quickly realized this and set up searchlight cones over the aiming point, which they plastered with heavy flak. Another little trick was to position Ju 88s near the searchlight cones at a higher level than the Mosquitoes. Thus, when coned, a Mosquito might first be blasted with heavy flak and then the barrage could suddenly cease. If the pilot wasn't in a position to react instantly, the next happening would be a highly unpleasant squirt of cannon fire from the night-fighter. Meanwhile, the training of *Oboe* marker crews continued at Marham, where 1655 Mosquito Training Unit was tasked with instructing the specialist Pathfinder Force. All pilots had to complete a laid down syllabus of 30 hours flying: ten in the Dual Flight and 20 in the Bomber Flight, the latter complete with navigator. No pilot was allowed to touch the controls of a Mosquito until he had 1000 hours as first pilot under his belt and had been selected to fly Mosquitoes.

Flight Sergeant Edwin R. Perry, who had been posted to 1655 MTU in April and who teamed up with Flight Sergeant V. J. C. "Ginger" Myles, his observer, recalls:

> "Another 17 joined us to make up ten crews who were to be taught to fly the Mark IV Mosquito. When we joined 1655 initially it was to continue low level flying over the East Anglian countryside, initially using the Oxford. We were then formed into crews, (Ginger and I stayed together for the rest of our 8 Group experiences) and commenced a program of low level cross country exercises in the Mosquito flying at around 250 knots. Low level practice bombing also featured on the Whittlesey range near Peterborough. After the change in emphasis in training we concentrated on night flying which, with so many airfields in the country each with its own red two letter identification beacon within a few miles, was in many cases easier for the navigator to monitor his position than with day - navigation. There were also white aerial lighthouses of fixed position enabling accurate bearings to be made of these with a hand bearing astro compass. The aircraft was also being equipped with *Gee*, a piece of radar equipment which measured the distances from a master and two slave stations to give a very accurate position, but then limited in range up to 4° east longitude. *Gee* took up less room than the 1154/5 and was easier for the observer to use but had the disadvantage that the positions on the *Gee* grid map had to be transferred to the Mercators projection used for navigation. It was also known that VHF voice radio could be heard for long distances, up to 200 or more miles, and there was therefore no loss in establishing position on approach home when high altitude flying without MFDF or HFDF Morse code facilities.
>
> "After three weeks 1655 was detached to Finmere where we were the only unit. However we later flew back to Marham to complete the course, my pilot for that flight being Flying Officer Ivor Broom DFC (later Air Marshal Sir Ivor) who had made quite a name for himself in Malta. Normally his observer was an amiable Warrant Officer named Tommy Broom and it was claimed when they went on operations they went on a 'sweep'. Tommy really enjoyed his beer and raw onions, which was the normal supper in the Marham Sergeants Mess. He 'strained' the beer through a magnificent moustache but after one splendid drinking session. Tom went to bed and on awaking found some rogue (never identified) had removed one side while Tommy blissfully slumbered on. A side effect was that nobody recognised him when he turned up at the 'Flights' next morning! 1655 was a happy unit. When at Marham our free time was spent in Kings Lynn, where the Duke of York was a favored hostelry or we might go up the coast to Hunstanton or Sandringham. And so, at the end of 22.5 months service and 315.5 hours flying (50.45 at night), I was considered to be suitably trained for operational duties as an observer in Bomber Command Mosquitoes of PFF's Light Night Striking Force. Victor Miles and I were posted to 139 (Jamaica) Squadron on 17 July 1943 and we stayed there until 16 December 1943 at the very comfortable pre-war Sir Edwin Lutyens-designed station, Wyton."

Mosquito training and operational flying at Marham was interspersed with several accidents. On the afternoon of 15 July four Mosquitoes flew on ASR duty over the North Sea, searching in vain for a missing aircraft for three hours. On 18 July a Norwegian crew of Captain Stene and Lieutenant Lochen were killed when their Mosquito crashed near Cranfield during a cross-country navigation exercise. On 24 July another Mosquito was written off in a night landing accident. Next day Pilot Officer C. Prentice RNZAF and observer Pilot Officer J. L. Warner were injured when their Mosquito crashed on approach to Marham. The following day a 105 Squadron Mosquito suffered an undercarriage retraction on the ground at Foulsham. On the 26th, during a night flying test Flying Officer Bill Humphrey and Flight Sergeant E. Moore of 105 Squadron experienced an engine failure on take-off and the Mosquito crashed at Fincham.

Operation *Gomorrah*, the first of four raids on Hamburg, a city of nearly two million people, began on the night of 24/25 July. Since the city was far beyond the range of *Oboe*, over seventy of the attacking aircraft were equipped with H_2S[93] to help the Pathfinders mark and keep the city marked. Essen, which was the target for over 700 aircraft on the night of 25/26 July, was not beyond the range of *Oboe*, and seven *Oboe* Mosquitoes of 109 Squadron and four of 105 Squadron successfully marked the target for the Main Force. Twenty-six aircraft were lost, but the raid was a success, with much damage to Essen's industrial areas in the eastern half of the city. In the next raid on Hamburg, early in the morning of 27 July 550-600 bomb loads of high explosive and incendiary bombs were dropped by 787 aircraft, including 353 Lancasters, on the densely populated residential area east of the Elbe. Within a few minutes huge fires were burning all over the target area, and a firestorm of an intensity that no one would ever before have thought possible arose. Over four nights 3000 bombers dropped 10,000 tons of HE and incendiary bombs to totally devastate half of Hamburg and kill an estimated 42,000 of its inhabitants. After the fourth raid on 2/3 August by 740 aircraft, 900,000 inhabitants had lost their homes and had fled the city. By 6 August the battle ended, and 75 per cent of the city had been laid waste.

On the night of 30/31 July three of 105 Squadron's Mosquito IXs and six of 109 Squadron, each carrying four red TIs, departed Marham to mark Remscheid, on the southern edge of the Ruhr, which was the target for over 270 aircraft. Flying Officer Kenneth Wolstenholme with Squadron Leader J. F. C. Gallacher DFC flew one of the 105 Squadron Mosquitoes.[94] The *Oboe* ground-marking and the bombing by the comparatively small Main Force were exceptionally accurate, and 83 per cent of the town was destroyed. This brought the Battle of the Ruhr to an end after 18,506 sorties, in which 58,000 tons of bombs had been dropped for a loss of 872 aircraft. By the end of the month Marham Mosquito crews had flown 32 Mk IX sorties.

August 1943 proved a relatively quiet month for the Marham Mosquitoes, which operated a mix of target marking and bombing operations on just four nights while Bomber Command concentrated its main efforts on Italian targets at Milan, Genoa, and Turin. On 22/23 August, when the I.G. Farben factory at Leverkusen was the target for the Main Force, Marham despatched thirteen Mosquitoes. One of the six 105 Squadron Mosquitoes had a "technical failure" and was unable to bomb, so Flying Officer Ken Wolstenholme took over and marked. Each Mosquito dropped two Long Burn Red TIs and two red TIs, but *Oboe* was not operating as well as it should, and the Main Force bombing was directed against at least twelve other towns in and near the Ruhr instead. The I.G. Farben factory received only minor damage from the few bombs that did hit Leverkusen. At Brauweiler, the other "Musical Mosquitoes" of 105 Squadron also had problems marking with *Oboe*, and two Mosquitoes returned early with engine trouble. The four other Mosquitoes unleashed their 2000lb bomb loads visually.

On the following night, 23/24 August, when over 720 aircraft visited Berlin, Marham again provided the *Oboe* markers so necessary for the Main Force to do their work. Three of 105 Squadron's Mosquitoes and five of 109 Squadron were to mark the bombers' route by dropping Red LB TIs between the Dutch towns of Westerbork and Zweeloo, and Green TIs just over the German border at Georgsdorf, 270 miles west of Berlin, to keep the heavies. Despite reservations in some quarters, who feared it might alert enemy night-fighters, the object was to keep the bombers away from known flak areas and to achieve a heavy concentration of bombs at the target. Ken Wolstenholme and his observer, Squadron Leader Gallacher, were forced to abort after take off when a flock of birds smashed into their Mosquito, but the other Mosquitoes carried out their marking duties. The Main Force attack was partially successful, but 57 bombers were shot down by a combination of night-fighters and flak. A few nights later, on the 29/30th, four *Oboe* Mosquitoes visited Cologne, and Lieutenant "Bud" Fisher DFC USAAF and Flight Lieutenant Robert W. "Bob" Bray DFC in "*J-Jig*" and three other 105 Squadron Mosquitoes marked Duisburg. On 30/31 August 600 aircraft of the Main Force attacked Mönchengladbach and the neighbouring town of Rheydt. Marking by twelve *Oboe* Mosquitoes—four of 105 Squadron led by the new CO, Wing Commander Henry John "Butch" Cundall AFC[95] with Squadron Leader A.C. Douglas DFC and eight of 109 Squadron—was described as "excellent," and in particular Cundall and Douglas had only a 40 yard error.

On the night of 31 August/1 September over 620 bombers visited the "Big City" again. Three Mosquitoes of 105 Squadron and six of 109 Squadron route marked for the heavies by dropping red TIs near Damvillers, in northeast France, and Green TIs near Luxembourg. Bombing was carried out using H_2S equipment and TIs, but the latter were dropped to the south of Berlin, while the main bombing was up to 30 miles away and was unsuccessful. The enemy used "fighter flares" to decoy the bombers away from the target, and about two thirds of the 47 aircraft lost were shot down over Berlin by night-fighters. In a separate operation thirty OTU Wellingtons and six *Oboe* Mosquitoes and five Halifaxes of the Pathfinders bombed an ammunition dump in the Forêt de Hesdin, in northern France. All of Marham's Mosquitoes returned safely from the night's operations. During early September the *Oboe* Mosquitoes marked more "special targets." On the night of 2/3 September 30 OTU Wellingtons and six *Oboe* Mosquitoes and five Lancasters of the Pathfinders were despatched to ammunition dumps in the Forêt de Mormal, near Englefontaine in France, about 40km southeast of Valenciennes. Flying Officer Don C. Dixon, an Australian from Brisbane, and Flight Lieutenant Tommy W. Horton DFC of 105 Squadron carrying two red LB TIs and two red TIs, as well as four 109 Squadron Mosquitoes marked successfully. Crews dropped their TIs from 26,000 feet for the heavies' bombs fell squarely on the dumps. The following evening six *Oboe* Mosquitoes carried out a similar operation in the Forêt de Raismes, 10km northwest of Valenciennes, for 30 OTU Wellingtons and six Halifaxes. Flight Lieutenant Tommy W. Horton DFC and Lieutenant "Bud" Fisher of 105 Squadron and the four Mosquitoes of 109 Squadron again marked with two red LB TIs and two red TIs. On 8/9 September, when 257 bombers, including five American B-17 Flying Fortresses, attacked the German long-range gun batteries near Boulogne, the *Oboe* Mosquitoes marked the target with green LB TIs and red TIs. The marking and bombing was poor, and the gun batteries were largely untouched. Knowing that the Mk.I version of *Oboe* would soon be jammed, trials were begun with *Oboe* Mk.II (codenamed "Penwiper") on 11 September by Wing Commander H.J. "Butch" Cundall AFC with Flight Lieutenant C. F. Westerman in attacks on Aachen. (Aachen was the target for *Oboe* II trials again on 3 and 7 October.)

On 22/23 September twelve *Oboe* Mosquitoes visited Emden as a diversion for the Main Force attacking Hanover. Most of the Mosquitoes bombed on DR after the *Oboe* system failed. On 23/24 September the *Oboe* Mosquitoes were despatched to Aachen as the Main Force went to Mannheim. Two of 105 Squadron's Mosquitoes route-marked at a point near the Belgian-German border near Simmerath for six more Mosquitoes that successfully bombed the town. On 29/30 September four *Oboe* crews dropped 500lb and 250lb bombs on Gelsenkirchen, and nine *Oboe* Mosquitoes set out to mark Bochum with red TIs for 352 heavies. Many bombs fell accurately in the old part of the town. The Mosquito flown by Lieutenant "Bud" Fisher DFC and Flight Sergeant Leslie Hogan DFM crashed one mile northwest of RAF West Raynham, killing both crewmembers. Bad weather returning from Gelsenkirchen forced Squadron Leader Peter Channer DFC and Warrant Officer Kenneth Gordon to land at RAF Coltishall.

In October the *Oboe* Mosquitoes flew operationally on twelve nights during the month, 109 Squadron flying 101 sorties and 105 Squadron, 76. On 1/2 October a steelworks at Witten, northwest of Hagen, was ground marked with red TIs by 12 *Oboe* Mosquitoes for training purposes. Eight of the Mosquitoes bombed at Witten, and two whose *Oboe* system failed dropped their bombs on the fires at Hagen created earlier by 240 Lancasters and eight Mosquitoes of 1, 5, and 8 Groups. On 3/4 October twelve *Oboe* Mosquitoes attacked the Goldenbergwerke power station and Knapsack power station near Cologne, and four others carried out Mk.II *Oboe* trials to Aachen. Knapsack was attacked again on 4/5 and 20/21 October, and again on the 22nd, when twelve Mosquitoes of 105 and 109 Squadrons set out in the early evening. Flight Lieutenant Gordon Sweeney DFC and Flight

Lieutenant William George Wood of 105 Squadron failed to return. On 24/25 October raids were made on Rheinhausen and Büderich, and on 31 October Oberhausen was bombed.

On the night of 3/4 November twelve *Oboe* Mosquitoes ground-marked Düsseldorf for 589 heavies, and thirteen other *Oboe* Mosquitoes each carrying three 500lb MC and a 250lb GP bomb set out to attack the Krupps factory at Rheinhausen. Twelve Mosquitoes bombed successfully, while the unlucky 13th aircraft returned with two 500-pounders hung up in the bomb bay. On nights when the Main Force was not operating the *Oboe* Mosquitoes were despatched to keep the enemy defenses alert. On 4/5 November 24 Mosquitoes attacked a chemical works at Leverkusen and four Mosquitoes visited Aachen again, all returning without loss. On 5/6 November 26 Mosquitoes carried out small-scale raids on Bochum, Dortmund, Düsseldorf, Hamburg, and Hanover. Flight Lieutenant John "Flash" Gordon DFC and Flying Officer Ralph Gamble Hayes DFM in a 105 Squadron Mosquito were returning over Norfolk. They tried to land at Hardwick, an American Liberator base, when at 21.10 hours they crashed into a field at Road Green Farm, Hempnall, about ten miles south of Norwich. Both men were killed.

With no major raids planned for the Main Force the *Oboe* Mosquitoes spent most of November dropping their bombloads of six 500lb MC bombs on Dortmund, Bochum, Essen, Duisburg, Krefeld, and Düsseldorf, and using DR when *Oboe* failed. The operation to Essen on the night of 7/8 November was typical of the non-Main Force nights; apart from 35 aircraft minelaying off the French coast and a handful of OTU sorties, the only Bomber Command aircraft that were airborne were six *Oboe* Mosquitoes from Marham. The *Oboe* equipment failed because one of the ground stations was not in operation and the Mosquitoes were sent a recall signal. Two of the *Oboe* aircraft received the signal and returned, but the other four continued to the target and dropped their 24 500lb MC bombs from 32,000-35,000 feet on a DR run from the last *Gee* fix. Two of these Mosquitoes returned home on one engine and one of them put down at RAF Coltishall.

On the night of 9/10 November 18 *Oboe* Mosquitoes attacked blast furnaces at Bochum and a steelworks at Duisburg. The Mosquito flown by Pilot Officer R. E. Leigh and Pilot Officer J. Henderson of 109 Squadron was hit by flak at the target and they crash landed at Wyton on return. As the Mosquito touched down the tail assembly broke away from the fuselage but both men escaped uninjured. On 11/12 November Cannes was the target of the Main Force while 29 Mosquitoes raided Berlin, Hanover, and the Ruhr. Marham despatched twelve *Oboe* Mosquitoes to Düsseldorf. One of the four Mosquitoes of 105 Squadron each carrying four 500lb MC bombs was flown by Pilot Officer Angus Caesar-Gordon DFM and his second tour navigator, Flying Officer R. A. "Dick" Strachan, who were on their first Mosquito operation. Strachan recalled:[96]

> "The flak started about four or five minutes before the target and immediately it was apparent that it was intense and extremely accurate. *Oboe* entailed the pilot flying dead straight and level for ten minutes on the attack run. Suddenly a tremendous flash lit up the sky about 50 yards ahead of our nose and exactly at our altitude. Within a tenth of a second we were through the cloud of dirty yellowish-brown smoke and into the blackness beyond. I shall never forget the spontaneous reaction of both my pilot and myself. We turned our heads slowly and looked long and deep into one another's eyes - no word was spoken - no words were needed. Despite continued heavy flak, we completed our attack run and dropped our bomb-load on the release signal, within a quarter of a mile of the aiming point and, with luck, some damage to a German factory. Turning for home and mighty glad to be out of the flak, I glanced out of the window at the starboard engine and immediately noticed a shower of sparks coming from the starboard engine cowling. A quick glance at the oil temperature gauge showed that it was going off the clock. Only one thing for it and the pilot pressed the extinguisher button and then feathered the engine. The sparking ceased but we now had 300 miles to go and only one engine to do it on. I remember thinking this wasn't much of a do for our first operation. But at least we had a good deal of altitude and still had a fair amount of speed, even with just one engine. The danger was interception by a German night fighter and I spent a lot of time craning my neck around to check the skies about our tail. The other thing I remember was a terrible consciousness of our own weight, sitting as I was on the starboard side. However this feeling wore off and the remainder of the flight home to base was uneventful. Then came the strain of a night landing on one engine…again that awful awareness of how heavy I was… but after one anti-clockwise circuit, a superb approach and magnificent landing. I recall the great feeling of relief as the wheels touched the runway. I also remember the urgent desire to get my hands round a jug of beer to relieve the dryness in my throat and to celebrate a safe return from what was to prove my worst experience on Mosquitoes. Needless to say, the beer was not long in forthcoming."

On 12/13 November seven Mosquitoes attacked Düsseldorf, Essen, and Krefeld, and the night following, eight *Oboe* Mosquitoes attacked the blast furnaces at Bochum again. Both raids were flown without loss. On the night of 15/16 November ten *Oboe* Mosquitoes attacked the Rheinmetall Borsig AG ironworks at Düsseldorf and two others bombed Bonn. The Mosquito, flown by Flight Lieutenant J. R. Hampson and Pilot Officer H. W. E. Hammond DFC RCAF, was shot down. Both men survived, and they were later sent to *Stalag Luft III*. A flak shell exploded a few feet under Flight Lieutenant Humphrey's Mosquito and turned the aircraft upside down, and Humphrey was hit in the foot and leg. The Mosquito went into a spin, but the crew managed to make it home and Humphrey landed at Hardwick, whereupon one of his engines stopped.

On 17/18 November 83 heavies attacked Ludwigshafen. Twenty-one Mosquitoes visited Berlin and Bonn and the August Thyssen AG foundry in Duisburg, as well as the semi-finished products of the Bochumer Verein in Bochum. None of the Mosquitoes was lost. On the night of 18/19 November the Main Battle of Berlin began with a raid on the Big City by 440 Lancasters while another bomber force visited Mannheim and Ludwigshafen. Ten Mosquitoes went to Essen, and six each went to Aachen and Frankfurt. While returning from Aachen Flight Lieutenant R. B. Castle and Pilot Officer J. Griffiths, in a 105 Squadron Mosquito, overshot the landing area at Marham and crashed at 23.31 hours. They were not seriously injured, but the Mosquito was a write-off. On the next raid, on the IG Farbenindustrie AG chemical works at Leverkusen on 19/20 November, failure of equipment prevented most of the *Oboe* marking being carried out and the bad weather prevented other PFF aircraft from marking the target properly. As a result bombing was widely scattered and 27 towns, mostly well to the north, were bombed. On 22/23 November, when the Main Force raided Berlin, twelve *Oboe* Mosquitoes set out for Leverkusen again. Berlin was again the target for the Main Force attack on 23/24 November when six *Oboe* Mosquitoes braved the flak and searchlight defenses protecting the Goldenbergwerke power station at Knapsack, near Cologne, again. Pilot Officer Eric Wade BEM[97] and his observer, Pilot Officer Alfred Gerald Fleet, died when their Mosquito crashed at 19.50 hours five miles northwest of Swaffham at Contract Farm, Narborough. Throughout the rest of November the *Oboe* squadrons bombed familiar targets, such as the Krupps foundry at Essen, the Rheinmetall Borsig AG ironworks at Düsseldorf, and the steel producers Vereinigte Stahlwerke AG at Bochum.

On 3 December Marshal of the Royal Air Force, Lord Trenchard, made a lunchtime visit to Marham, and he congratulated the squadron on the excellent work they had done leading the Main Force in the Battle of the Ruhr. He also praised their current role of precision attacks on special targets. The *Oboe* Mosquitoes were operational on fifteen nights during December with return visits to targets such as Hamborn, Leverkusen, Krefeld, Düsseldorf Liege, Aachen, and Bochum. Usually the operations were flown without loss, but there were early losses. On the night of 2/3 December Flying Officer L. F. Bickley and Flying Officer J. H. Jackson of 109 Squadron failed to return from a raid by six *Oboe* Mosquitoes on Bochum. Both men evaded. Then, on the night of the 12/13th Pilot Officer Benjamin Frank Reynolds and Pilot Officer John Douglas Phillips of 105 Squadron were killed when they crashed at Herwijnen, in Holland, on the north bank of the Waal River. They had probably been hit by flak towards the end of the attack on the Krupps works at Essen. On the night of the 16/17th, when Berlin was the main target for the heavies, 35 Stirlings and Lancasters and 12 *Oboe* Mosquitoes were despatched to bomb two V1 flying bomb sites near Abbeville, in Northern France, at Tilley-le-Haut and in a wood at Flixecourt.[98] Neither raid was successful. The attack on Tilley-le-Haut by 26 Stirlings failed because the six *Oboe* Mosquito markers of 105 and 109 Squadrons could not get their green and yellow TIs closer than 450 yards from the tiny target. At Flixecourt the nine Lancasters of 617 Dam Busters Squadron dropped their 12,000lb *Tallboy* bombs accurately on the Green TIs and LB TIs placed by Squadron Leader Bill Blessing and Wing Commander F. A. Green DFC. But the markers were 350 yards from the V1 site and none of the Lancasters' bombs were more than 100 yards from the markers.[99] Five more raids on V-bomb construction sites were flown during the rest of the month, two each on the 22nd/23rd and 30th/31st and one on the night of 29/30 December, and only one site was bombed accurately.

Crew discipline and navigational accuracy were put to the test on the night of 23/24 December when 12 *Oboe* Mosquitoes were sent to raid Aachen and then to carry on to a second site to route-mark Berlin for 379 heavies heading for the Big City. Sixteen Lancasters were lost, and the losses would have been higher had it not been for the cloud covering the Berlin area, which grounded many German night-fighters and the diversion raid at Leipzig by seven Mosquitoes. There were no bombing raids on Christmas Eve, and only a few Mosquitoes were airborne on 28/29 December when operations resumed again after a period of bad weather. A raid by over 700 aircraft on Berlin on the night of 29/30 December had small numbers of Mosquitoes being sent to a number of targets in Germany and France without loss. This was followed on 30/31 December by the last raid of the year when 21 *Oboe* Mosquitoes were despatched to targets in Cologne, Duisburg, and the Vereinigte Stahlwerke AG steelworks at Bochum again. A further attempt was also made to mark a Vl flying bomb site at Cherbourg that had been missed on an earlier raid. Unfortunately, the markers were placed 200 yards from the target. All the bombs dropped by the ten Lancasters of 617 Squadron, though well grouped, and four 500 pounders dropped through 3/10th low cloud by Flying Officer Bill Humphrey and his observer Pilot Officer L. C. Poll of 105 Squadron missed the site completely.

In January 1944 the *Oboe* Mosquitoes were operational on 19 nights, with 105 and 109 Squadrons flying sorties on eleven nights during the period up to the 14/15th. It was much the same routine as in 1943, with area marking and attacks on industrial targets, such as the Ruhrstahl AG steel works at Witten, J.A. Henckels Zwillingwerke AG at Solingen, the Krupp AG works at Essen, the Verstahlwerke at Duisburg, and the Deutsche Edalstahlwerke AG at Krefeld. The Krupp Stahl AG works at Rheinhausen, the Rheinmetall Borsig AG ironworks at Düsseldorf, and the Mannesmannröhrenwerke AG iron and steel tube plant at Untererthal were also bombed, as were the Gutehoffnungshütte AG foundry at Obershausen and the Chemische Werke industrial chemicals plant at Hüls. No less than 21 V1 rocket sites were also visited by the *Oboe* Mosquitoes during January. Losses at night remained at a thankfully relatively low rate. Returning from a raid on Duisburg by five Mosquitoes on the night of 7/8 January a 109 Squadron Mosquito flown by Flying Officer C. R. G. Grant RAAF and Flying Officer K. F. Hynes hit a tree returning to Marham and crash landed at Narborough. Grant scrambled to safety, but a crane was needed to move the wreckage to allow Hynes to be freed. On the night of the 13/14th Flying Officer P. Y. Stead DFC and Warrant Officer A. H. Flett DFM of 109 Squadron failed to return from the night's operations when they were shot down at 26,000 feet by *Oberleutnant* Dietrich Schmidt of III./NJG1 flying a Bf 110. Flett was killed, but Stead survived and he was taken prisoner.[100] Squadron Leader J. Comer and his observer, Pilot Officer P. Jenkins DFM of 105 Squadron, were just setting out for Düsseldorf on the night of 20/21 January when at 20.43 hours their Mosquito became uncontrollable and they baled out over Norfolk. The aircraft crashed three miles east of Kings Lynn at Waveland Farm, Grimston. Returning home from their target on the night of 23 January Flight Lieutenant Kenneth Wolstenholme and Pilot Officer V.P. Piper crash landed at RAF Manston after their Mosquito lost elevator control.

By way of a change, on the night of 25/26 January 14 Mosquitoes of 105 Squadron were despatched to bomb the *Nazi* HQ at Aachen while 109 Squadron attacked four V1 sites in Northern France. Eleven of the *Oboe* Mosquitoes of 105 Squadron identified the target at Aachen, and amid light and accurate flak forty 500lb bombs were released through cloud. A number of hits were scored. Two days later the *Oboe* Mosquitoes returned to Aachen and dropped "spoof" green TI route markers just north of the town without loss, although Flight Lieutenant J. W. Jordan landed at RAF Manston with an overheating starboard engine. On the night of 28/29 January, while 677 aircraft headed for Berlin 23 *Oboe* Mosquitoes took off from Marham to bomb German night-fighter airfields in Holland. Six Mosquitoes of 109 Squadron were sent to attack Leeuwarden and four more to raid Deelen, while 105 Squadron despatched five to Gilze-Rijen. Six more went to Venlo and two visited Deelen.

On the night of 30/31 January 22 *Oboe* Mosquitoes attacked the G&I Jager GmbH ball bearing factory at Elberfeld when over 530 aircraft visited Berlin again. Warrant Officer I. B. McPherson's Mosquito received several flak hits in the port engine and Flight Lieutenant A. W. Raybould had the nose of his Mosquito shattered, but all aircraft returned safely. In February the ball bearing factory at Elberfeld was attacked on no less than eight more nights. Just before the third attack by eight *Oboe* Mosquitoes on 4/5 February, Flight Lieutenant John Fosbroke Slatter and his observer, Pilot Officer Peter Oscar Hedges, of 105 Squadron were killed on their NFT (Night Flying Test). During the late afternoon they were involved in a collision with a Boeing B-17G 42-97480 of the 337th Bomb Squadron, 96th Bombardment Group from Snetterton, Norfolk. The Mosquito came down at Colne Field Farm, near St. Ives, Huntingdonshire. Slatter and Hedges were killed, while the Fortress landed safely with minor damage.[101]

On 9/10 February, Flying Officer R. G. Leigh RNZAF and Flight Lieutenant M. R. Breed RNZAF of 109 Squadron were shot down over Holland. In the early hours of the 26th Flying Officer Taylor and Pilot Officer Mander of 1655 MTU crashed at Fincham, killing both crew. Much of February was spent bombing airfields at Gilze Rijen, Deelen, Volkel, St. Trond, Twente, Venlo, and Leeuwarden, all without loss, and V-l sites in northern France. On the night of 23/24 February, when 17 *Oboe* Mosquitoes raided Düsseldorf, the Mosquito flown by Pilot Officer L. Holiday DFM was hit in the fuselage and his observer, Flying Officer C. L. French, was wounded in the thigh. They continued to Düsseldorf nonetheless and bombed the target.

During the first five days of March, two of 109 Squadron's *Oboe* Mosquitoes acted as "formation leaders" for bomber units of the 2nd Tactical Air Force (2nd TAF) attacking flying bomb sites in Northern France. The formation bombed as soon as it saw the bombs of the *Oboe* Mosquitoes being released. Altogether eight of these daylight operations were flown, the first being to Conches on 1 March. That same night an operation to Stuttgart by over 550 aircraft of the Main Force was supported by eighteen *Oboe* Mosquitoes, which bombed German night-fighter airfields at Deelen, Volkel, Florennes, St. Trond, and Venlo. The operations were flown without cloud cover over Holland and only broken cloud to the west. It was on this night that 109 Squadron despatched its first Mosquito XVI sortie, to Deelen. Deliveries of the pressurised Mosquito B.XVI, an adaptation of the Mk.IX and powered by the more powerful two-stage 1680hp Merlin 77/73 engines, had begun on 19 December when two of the aircraft were received by 109 Squadron. The XVI also had bulged bomb boors to permit a 4000lb "Cookie" bomb to be carried.[102] All the airfields except Florennes, where *Oboe* failed, were bombed, and all the Mosquitoes returned safely, but a heavy snowstorm over Norfolk made landings very difficult.

Flying Officer Grenville Eaton, a 105 Squadron pilot, flew his first Mosquito operation on 1/2 March in "*A-Apple*," an *Oboe*-equipped B.IV. His observer was Warrant Officer J. E. "Jack" Fox, who had flown a first tour on bombers. Eaton recalls:

> "Venlo, the target, was a German fighter aerodrome on the Dutch border near Aachen. (The first few trips were usually to 'less difficult' targets but they were certainly no less important in countering the threat of fighters). With a full load of bombs, four 500 pounders, and of petrol, it took, perhaps, one hour following carefully planned and timed legs' all over East Anglia until setting course from Orfordness to the Dutch coast. Then, at the operational height of 28,000 feet, we flew towards the waiting point [where the track to the target extended backwards for a further 5 minutes] and there, at the precise appointed time [to hear the call-in signal in Morse], we switched on *Oboe*."

The navigator worked out the flight plan and calculated the time to set course in order to reach the target at the correct time. On marking sorties it was important that TIs were dropped at the correct time in order not to compromise the Main Force. Having worked out the time to set course, navigators actually did this with 6 minutes in hand to allow for any errors to the forecast wind, etc. Having settled into the flight and arrived at the ETA for the waiting point, crews usually had to make some sort of correction. If the full 6 minutes had to be lost the pilot did a 360 degree orbit, and most pilots became expert in achieving this in the 6 minutes. Lesser times to be lost were accomplished by making a dog leg. Grenville Eaton now had to find the beam and keep on it for perhaps 10-15 minutes to the target.

> "Thanks to *Gee*, Jack Fox's navigation was spot on and we had a good run to target. His signals gave him our distance to target and finally, the bomb release signal, like the BBC time signal, five pips then the sixth, a dash, to press to release the bombs. We had a clear run. Holding steady for some seconds after bomb release to photograph the bomb explosions, we turned smartly onto the planned course home, keeping our eyes skinned for fighters, flak and searchlights, around 360° above and below. A gentle, slow dive at top speed and we arrived at the Dutch coast around 20,000 feet and the English coast at 12,000 feet. We landed at 0330 hours. So, Jack's 31st and my first 'op' took 3 hours 25 minutes. A simmering feeling of incipient fear throughout had been kept in check by being fully occupied. Now, home, we felt a tremendous feeling of relief and achievement, especially when we were told at debriefing that we had achieved a 'Nil' target error on this, out first *Oboe* trip. Finally, a heavenly operational aircrew breakfast of bacon, eggs, toast, rum and coffee. Smashing!"

Weather conditions improved and the next night, 2/3 March, 105 Squadron flew its first Mosquito XVI sortie when six *Oboe* Mosquitoes formed part of the raid by 117 Halifaxes of 4 and 6 Groups on the aircraft assembly factory of SNCA du Nord, at Meulan-Les Mureaux. The factory, about 15 miles northwest of Paris, originally turned out Potez aircraft for the French Air Force and was now producing about 15 Messerschmitt Me 108s each month, as well as components for Bf 109s and Dornier Do 24s. Wing Commander H.J. "Butch" Cundall AFC and his navigator, Squadron Leader I.E. Tamango, flew the XVI (ML938), and they led four other Mosquito IXs of 105 and two of 109 Squadron. As usual the *Oboe* markers were to go in first and ground-mark the target with Red and Green LB TIs for the Halifaxes. Unfortunately *Oboe* failed, and Cundall relinquished primary marker duties to Flight Lieutenant E.M. Hunter with Flight Lieutenant Crabb and Flight Lieutenant Jacobs and Flight Lieutenant Tipton of 109 Squadron, who each dropped four Red LB TIs. Two 105 Squadron Mosquitoes flown by Squadron Leader L. F. Austin DFC with Squadron Leader C. F. Westerman DFC and Flying Officer Don C. Dixon and his navigator, Flying Officer W. A. Christensen, a fellow Australian from New South Wales, failed to drop their four Green LB TIs. The reserve aircraft flown by Flight Lieutenant Ken Wolstenholme with his observer, Flight Lieutenant V. E. R. Piper, dropped four Red LB TIs. The raid was successful, and the Halifaxes caused considerable damage to the main assembly shops, the factory testing hangars, and the seaplane base, while other parts of the plant were "extremely severely damaged."

On 5/6 March four *Oboe* Mosquitoes set out to mark Duisburg for three Mosquitoes carrying 4000lb "Cookies." Squadron Leader Peter J. Channer DFC was forced to abort before the target when his *Oboe* equipment blew up, though he managed to return safely to Marham. The other Mosquitoes encountered slight but accurate flak on the run-in to the target. Flight Lieutenant C. P. Gibbons' Mosquito of 109 Squadron was hit at 30,000 feet, but he was able to carry on. Flight Lieutenant G. W. Harding of 105 Squadron reported a cloud of smoke and a red flare hanging over the target. Meanwhile, plans unveiled on 4 March in preparation for the *Overlord* invasion planned for that summer had put in motion precision bombing attacks on railway networks and marshalling yards, ammunition dumps, and airfields in France. Seven rail targets at Trappes, Aulnoye, Le Mans, Amiens, Courtrai, Laon, and Vaires-sur-Marne were selected for all out attacks, which began on the night of 6/7 March when Trappes was marked by *Oboe* Mosquitoes to enable 261 Halifaxes of 4 and 6 Groups to bomb. Photo reconnaissance later revealed that the engine shed had been destroyed and six wrecked locomotives were seen lying in the almost demolished building. The water tower was completely destroyed; throughout the yards there was a heavy concentration of craters affecting tracks and all the internal lines were blocked. There was also considerable destruction and derailment of tenders and rolling stock. Seventeen direct hits on the main Paris-Chartres lines had put all but one line out of action. Attacks on Le Mans and also the road and rail junction at Aachen followed on 7/8 March. The Aachen operation was the second for Flying Officer Grenville Eaton and Warrant Officer Jack Fox, as Eaton recalls:

> "The target was Aachen, an important road and rail junction just inside Germany. I was feeling more confident. Crossing Holland at 28,000 feet, with a clear sky, we could see the distant Zuider Zee. We switched on *Oboe*, found we were early, so guided by the navigator, I wasted a precise number of minutes and seconds until finding and settling into the beam towards the target, about 15 minutes' flying time away. We noticed we were leaving long white contrails behind us - frozen water vapor crystals in the exhaust of each engine. Suddenly streams of cannon-shells and tracers enveloped us from the rear, hitting us in numerous places, but luckily missing Jack and me and the engines. I immediately dived to port, then up to starboard several times, then resumed height and regained the beam. The only protection was a sheet of steel behind my seat. Most instruments seemed to work, so we continued. Half a minute later, a second and noisier attack from the rear, so again I took evasive action, more violent and longer, and again regained height and beam. Now there was considerable damage to dashboard, hydraulics and fuselage. Shells had missed us, truly by inches. However, engines and *Oboe* still worked, so being so near we had to continue to target, deliver the load, and turn for home, changing course and height frequently, and assessing the damage as far as we could. Certainly, hydraulics, flaps, brakes, ASI and various other instruments were smashed - but we were okay.
>
> "At Marham, landing in pitch darkness was a problem, hut for safety I landed on the grass, by feel I suppose, at about 150 knots with no brakes. We hurtled across the aerodrome, just missing two huge armament dumps, straight on through hedges and violently into a ditch. Jack was out of the emergency exit like a flash. I could not move, could not undo the safety belt. Jack leapt back, released me and we scampered away to a safe distance in case of exploding petrol tanks, and emergency services were quickly there. Debriefing was interesting, as not only was our run 'seen' on the CRT, but our bombing error was precisely calculated and we wondered whether all operations were to be like this one! Incidentally, we never saw the attacking fighter. Our aircraft was a write off."[103]

On 11 March HRH the Duke of Gloucester, and accompanied by Air Vice Marshal D.C.T. Bennett CB CBE DSO, AOC 8 Group visited the station, and HRH inspected the aircrew who were presented to him by Wing Commander H.J. "Butch" Cundall DFC AFC. On 10/11 March three Mosquitoes of 105 Squadron attacked Duisburg again. Flight Lieutenant Ken Wolstenholme's Mosquito suffered flak damage to the starboard undercarriage door and starboard flap, but he returned safely to Marham.

Much of March 1944 was spent bombing French marshalling yards and Trappes, Le Mans, and Amiens. Diversionary attacks on Dutch airfields at St. Trond, Venlo, and Deelen were flown in support of Main Force operations to Stuttgart on the night of 15/16 March. Many of the heavies' bombs fell in open country southwest of the city due to poor marking. Amiens' marshalling yards were the main target for the *Oboe* Mosquitoes that night. Two aircraft were detailed to mark with four Red LB TIs and two 500lb MC bombs, but Flight Lieutenant Almond returned early with generator problems. Technical failures prevented both Flight Lieutenant Ken Wolstenholme and Flying Officer Holland from attacking, but Flight Lieutenant Bill Humphrey was able to make two runs, dropping two TIs each time with excellent results. There was some cloud and very thick haze over the target, and as only four sets of TIs went down at very irregular intervals it is doubtful whether much success was achieved. Some 132 Halifaxes and Stirlings were despatched and 105 heavies claimed to have dropped 605 tons of bombs. Little concentration of bombing was reported by the Mosquito crews, which in view of the poor marking was not surprising, but some of the Main Force were bombing to the northeast of the target before zero hour. Numerous searchlights were in operation and many fighter flares were seen. A subsequent Bomb Command report claimed that several parts of the northeast and southern areas of the yards were badly damaged while railway workshops, storage buildings, tracks, sidings, rolling stock, a road bridge, roundhouse, engine sheds, and lines under construction were all hit severely. Two Halifaxes and a Stirling failed to return, and in Amiens 18 French civilians were killed.

Further support operations were flown for raids on 18/19 March when Frankfurt was raided and St. Trond, Volkel, and Venlo were again attacked. On the 22/23rd it was the turn of Leeuwarden, Venlo, Deelen, and Juliandorp, and Marham despatched ten *Oboe* Mosquitoes. Nine of the aircraft carried six 500lb MC bombs, while Squadron Leader F. R. Bird and Flight Lieutenant Norman Clayes DFC carried three 500lb MC bombs and one White TI.[104] There was 10/10ths cloud at Leeuwarden, but four aircraft successfully attacked the airfield with good results. Bombs were seen to burst, and the TIs were seen to cascade as markers for Fighter Command Intruders. Three Mosquitoes attacked Venlo with excellent results through small amounts of cloud, but Flight Lieutenant J. H. Ford and his observer, Flight Lieutenant L. W. Millett, had a wing bomb hang up. They returned safely to Marham. Squadron Leader Wills and Flight Lieutenant Castle attacked Deelen through 5/10ths cloud with excellent results. But the Mosquito flown by Flight Lieutenant Charles Frank Boxall and Flight Lieutenant T. W. "Robby" Robinson DFC also suffered a wing mounted bomb hung up when the grease from the bomb release froze and the 500lb MC bomb refused to drop. Boxall was forced to return with it to Marham, where at 22.50 hours, on landing back, the bomb freed itself and exploded. The wing disintegrated, and Boxall died in the flaming aircraft. Robinson was injured, but he survived and was taken to the RAF Hospital at Ely, suffering from shock and severe burns to his left foot and minor burns on the right foot. He also had a fractured left clavicle and facial abrasions.

The *Oboe* Mosquitoes were now carrying "Cookie" bombs on a regular basis, and the bomb was known to be notoriously unstable. Also, the bomb bay doors were prone to creep, and if not fully open before the release point the bomb would take the doors with it. Not surprisingly, crews preferred Graveley's hard runway to Marham's grass airfield for "Cookie" carrying operations. A decision had been taken to close Marham and begin the construction of three concrete runways and bring the airfield up to the standard for heavy bombers. It was a massive undertaking that would involve 18 months work and a cost of £1,740,000. On 7 March 1655 MTU departed for Warboys, and two weeks later 105 Squadron began the move to Bourn, in Cambridgeshire, while in early April 109 Squadron began moving to Little Staughton.

Chapter 4

Find Mark and Strike

Cunning games of cat and mouse, nights of mortal chess
Blind man's buff with bullets for a lark
We drop window strips, foil the radar blips
They build decoy towns for us to mark
But its high cloud, ground mist, vision minus nil
Mute defenses hoping we'll go by
We've not the need to guess now we've mastered H2S
And our Wanganui candles ring the sky
Yellow and green
Calling the stream
Fling it out onto the glow
You don't have to care
When you're up in the air
For those in the cauldron below

Single star-shells blossoming, flak-flowers in the pyre
Twinning trails of burning buzzing bees
Cones of funnelled fire from the ground suspire
And 'keep the blighter steady' if you please
But its left trim, right trim, hold it, hold it, Now
Down the green and yellow markers go
Back and join the queue, still a job to do
Still a bombing run before we blow
Flying elite
Cock o' the fleet
Out for a tryst with the pack
Timing is tight
Must get it right
Or Gawd 'elp us when we get back

G. R. Reeves

Bennett's Mosquitoes were to prove so successful that, ultimately, eleven Mosquito-equipped squadrons operated in 8 (PFF) Group.[105] In addition, 1409 (Met) Flight was established at Oakington on 1 April 1943 using Mosquitoes and crews from 521 Squadron, Coastal Command at Bircham Newton. After having converted to the Mosquito at 1655 MTU at Marham, Flight Lieutenant Jack Richard "Benny" Goodman[106] and his navigator, Flying Officer A. J. L. "Bill" Hickox (after "Wild Bill Hickok" of American West fame) were posted in October 1943 to 139 Squadron at Wyton. Benny Goodman had completed a tour of 37 operations and 1300 hours on Wellingtons. "The average time for a trip to the Ruhr was 2½ hours, while a run to Berlin took about 4½ hours. To carry out such sorties in a Wellington had taken something like 5½ hours and 8 hours respectively. For this reason alone, Mosquitoes were greatly to he preferred to Wellingtons - it is better to be shot at for a short time than for a long time!" Bill Hickox had also completed a first tour on Wimpys, although he had been shot down and had to walk back through the desert. Their first operational sortie in a Mosquito took place on 3 November 1943, the target being Cologne. Benny Goodman recalls:

"Marking was to be done by 105 and 109 Squadrons, using *Oboe*. Our bomb load was four 500lb HE bombs and the attack was to be an all-Mosquito affair. Out first operational take-off in DK313 was only marginally longer than out take offs from Marham in Mosquitoes without bombs. The acceleration was rapid and in next to no time we were at the unstick speed of around 100 knots and climbing smoothly away. We climbed rapidly to 28,000 feet, leveled out and settled down to an economical cruising speed of around 250 knots (true airspeed). As we neared Cologne the first of the *Oboe*-aimed target indicators began to cascade down ahead of us. Bill took his place at the bombing panel and began the time honoured verbal directions: Left, left, Steady...' and ultimately, Bombs gone.' We then turned for home, more bacon and eggs, and bed. The post-flight interrogation was much the same as on any operational squadron in Bomber Command, with one important exception. 139's full title was 139 (Jamaica) Squadron and we were all offered a tot of rum on return from every operational sortie - the rum being provided by the good people of Jamaica. When I was on 139 we had with us a Jamaican named Ulric Cross, a flight lieutenant navigator, highly efficient and well liked. Later he became Lord Chief Justice of Jamaica.

"The best *Oboe* crews could place a bomb within a few yards of the aiming point from 28,000 feet. However, since they had to fly straight and level for several minutes in the final run to the target they were vulnerable to flak and fighters. Moreover, they could only approach a given target from two directions - in the ease of Ruhr targets, almost due north or south - the Germans quickly realized this and set up searchlight cones over the aiming point which they plastered with heavy flak. Another little trick was to position Ju 88s near the searchlight cones, at a higher level than the Mosquitoes. Thus, when coned, a Mosquito might first he blasted with heavy flak and then the barrage could suddenly cease. If the pilot wasn't in a position to react instantly, the next happening would he a highly unpleasant squirt of cannon fire from the night-fighter. The average time for a trip to the Ruhr was 2½ hours, while a run to Berlin took about 4½ hours. To carry out such sorties in a Wellington had taken something like 5½ hours and 8 hours respectively. For this reason alone, Mosquitoes were greatly to he preferred to Wellingtons - it is better to be shot at for a short time than for a long time!"

At Wyton, on 24 November 1943 "C" Flight in 139 Squadron and its B.IVs were used as the nucleus to form 627 Squadron at Oakington, near Cambridge. Benny Goodman and Bill Hickox were among the crews posted to the new squadron, as Bill Hickox recalls;

"We went down to the flights after breakfast as usual. We were called in by the Flight Commander and told to go back and pack our bags, as we were to take an aircraft [DZ615] to Oakington, where we were posted to a new squadron being formed, 627. We duly arrived at Oakington, where we were told that we would be operating that same night. So without having time to unpack our bags, or go through the normal arrival procedures, we went to briefing, where we learned that we would be operating to Berlin along with two other crews. This was only my second trip to the Big City, but everything went well."

Benny Goodman adds:

"It was a rule in Bomber Command that every new squadron became operational as soon as possible after it was formed and when we arrived, Bill and I found out that we were on the Battle Order for that night. The resident squadron at Oakington was No 7, a Lancaster squadron of the PFF force and on the day of 627's arrival, the station was a hive of industry. A Bomber Command maximum effort was in preparation and Lancasters were being made ready for ops that night. To the Oakington effort would now be added six Mosquitoes of 627 Squadron. As the day wore on it became apparent from reports from the Station met office that operations that night had become questionable; a warm front was spreading in from the southwest more quickly that had been expected. At tea time the Lancasters were stood down, but 627 remained on standby and after tea we were briefed for an-all Mosquito attack on Berlin in company with 139 Squadron.

"Early that evening Bill and I boarded DZ615 and set off for the 'Big City', a trip which turned out to he completely uneventful except that on returning to the airfield we were flying in thick cloud and pouring rain. We broke cloud at 500 feet, still in heavy rain, and approached and landed very carefully. On reporting to the Operations Room for debriefing, we were astounded to be told that DZ615 had been the only RAF aircraft over Germany that night. Ops had been cancelled by Bomber Command at a very late stage but two of us were already airborne and were left to get on with it. The other pilot had trouble with his aircraft and turned back, which left me on my own."

Bill Hickox has no doubts as to what gave 627 its "Esprit de corps":

"It seems to me that 627 had it from the very start. Mind you, we had everything in our favour. We were flying the finest aeroplane in the world (Ah, De Havilland) and lived in comfort in the pre-war messes of a permanent station near the beautiful city of Cambridge. Cambridge provided good entertainment for nights off, 'The Bun Shop', 'The Baron of Beef' and even 'Dorothy's Tea Rooms' being particularly memorable. Our CO, Roy Elliott, was the finest squadron commander I ever knew in a long RAF career. His Navigation Leader, William M. 'Bill' de Boos DFC, was a splendid Aussie character and even the Adjutant was a good type, as were all the other air and ground crews. We were a small, close knit community, proud of being members of PFF and of being part of the Light Night Striking Force operating practically every night, even when the Main Force were stood down. We didn't even mind being known as the 'Model Aeroplane Club.' On the rare occasions on which we were stood down, it was great to pile into the Hillman flight vans and blunder through the blackout until we came to the bank of a river, where we could pull ourselves across on a chain ferry to a delightful pub called the 'Pike and Eel'. How was it that it was always the Aussies who fell in on the return crossing?"

Benny Goodman continues:

"The winter of 1943-44 was famous - or infamous, depending on your point of view, because it saw the Bomber Command offensive against Berlin. Our C-in-c: said that if we could lay waste the Big City the Germans would he brought to their knees. Sixteen major attacks were mounted but Berlin was not destroyed. The truth is that the target area was too vast and the weather, which could often be worse than enemy action, was appalling. Bill Hickox and I took part in seven of these attacks against the German capital and also busied ourselves with spoof raids against other targets, for example Kiel and Leipzig. We knew only too well that we were engaged in a battle of attrition, as was the U.S. 8th Air Force, and the outcome could he defeat for the bombers.

"During the Battle of Berlin we lost Squadron Leader 'Dinger' Bell, our Flight Commander. However, he and his navigator managed to bale out and became PoWs.[107] At this time, Bill and I began to wonder if the sands were also running out for us when, on the way home from the Big City, the oil pressure on the starboard engine suddenly began to drop and the oil and coolant temperatures increased. Eventually the readings reached their permitted limits and I throttled back the engine and feathered the propeller. Now we were in the cart with a vengeance, for we had to lose height and were eventually flying along at a height and speed comparable to that of our heavy brothers, but with no means of defending ourselves if attacked. Moreover, since the only generator on the Mosquito was on the starboard engine we had to turn off our internal lights, the *Gee* box and our VHF set. So we drove on through the darkness with our fingers and toes slightly crossed and feeling very tense. Wouldn't you?

"Eventually our ETA at the Dutch coast came and Bill switched on the *Gee*. We were in luck; it worked, and Bill quickly plotted a fix. So far, so good. Next we turned the *Gee* box off and I called up the VHF guardian angels on Channel 'C' - the distress frequency. At once there came that voice of reassurance, asking me to transmit for a little longer. She then gave us a course to steer, and shortly afterwards said, 'Friends are with you.' Bill and I took a good look round and spied a Beaufighter, which stayed with us until we reached the English coast. We motored on eventually and got down fairly expertly which drew' from the imperturbable Mr Hickox the comment, 'Good Show'. Praise indeed.

"Shortly after this effort came another indication that Lady Luck was on our side. We were briefed for yet another trip to Berlin, but during the afternoon the raid was cancelled and a short-range attack on a Ruhr target was substituted. This was to he an all-Mosquito affair, led by 105 and 109 Squadrons. Our CO, Wing Commander Roy Elliott, decided that this was an opportunity for new' crews to have a go and Bill Hickox and I were stood down in favour of two 'makey-learns'. We had air-tested the aircraft that morning and were satisfied that it was in all respects serviceable. Yet as the Mosquito lifted off at night and entered the area of blackness just beyond the upwind end of the flare path both engines failed and there came the dreadful sound of a crash as the aircraft hit the ground. Both crewmembers were killed. Would this have happened if Bill and I had been on board? We shall never know."

By early 1944 suitably modified B.IV Mosquitoes were capable, just, of carrying a 4000lb "Blockbuster," although it was a tight squeeze in the bomb bay. To accommodate this large piece of ordnance the bomb bay had been strengthened and the bomb doors were redesigned. B.IVs did not prove entirely suitable, as Benny Goodman testifies:

"Our CO announced that we were to fly the 'Cookie-carrier' as much as possible and the most experienced crews were detailed to take her on normal operations. The night arrived when Bill Hickox and I were ordered to try our hand with this new' machine on a target in the Ruhr The aircraft looked like a pregnant lady, because its belly was markedly rotund. Take off was not difficult, hut quite definitely she was not a scalded cat. At 500 feet, as her tail came up I pushed the throttles quickly forward to the gate (plus 9lbs boost, 3000 rpm) and then clenched my left hand over the gate catch releases and eased the throttles to the fully open position plus 12lbs boost, 3000rpm). In '*G-George'* this would have resulted in a glorious acceleration and a hop, skip and jump into the air. Not so with our pregnant lady; she waddled along and took most of the runway before she deigned to unstick. Moreover, the climb was a sedate affair and sue took much longer to reach 25,000 feet than with our usual steed; and when we arrived there she took a long time to settle to a steady cruise. However, we eventually sorted ourselves out and headed resolutely for the Ruhr.

"In the target area I felt distinctly nervous. There we were, with the bomb doors open and Bill droning away with his 'Left, left...right...steady' and I just knew that every gunner in the Rohr could see the enormous bomb we were carrying and was determined to explode it and blow' us to smithereens. I looked at the bomb jettison handle in front of me - no delicate lever this; it was a solid bar of metal which, if moved, would manually release the massive catch holding the 'Cookie' and down the bomb would go. It the bomb doors had not been opened, that was hard luck - the 'Cookie' would still drop away and take the bomb doors 'with it! However, no such inglorious thing happened. Bill suddenly announced, 'Bomb gone' and as he did so the Mossie suddenly shot up like a lift. There was no delicate porpoising, as with four 500 pounders, the altimeter moved instantly through 500 feet of altitude. I had never seen anything like this before. More importantly, as soon as I had closed the bomb doors our fat little lady became almost a normal Mosquito and accelerated to a fast cruising speed."

The B.XVI, with its bulged bomb bay and more powerful two-stage 1680hp Merlin 72/76s or two 1710-hp Merlin 73/77s, giving a top speed of 419mph at 28,500 feet, first flew operationally on 1/2 January 1944 when 38 Mosquitoes attacked Hamburg, Witten, Duisburg, Bristillerie, and Cologne. On the night of 1/2 February 139 used H_2S for the first time, marking the target for a raid by twelve Mosquitoes on Berlin. At this time 139 Squadron, which had pioneered the use of Canadian-built Mosquitoes, was operating a mix of B.IVs, IXs, XVIs, and XXs. Mosquitoes dropped "Blockbusters" for the first time on Düsseldorf on the night of 23/24 February.

In Germany meanwhile, a new night-fighter, the He 219A-0 *Uhu* ("Owl"), might have turned the tide for the German night-fighter force had it been introduced in quantity.[108] On the night of 12/13 December 1943, when the Krupp Works at Essen was the target and I./NJG1 claimed four aircraft destroyed, one of them was a 105 Squadron Mosquito flown by Flying Officer Benjamin Frank Reynolds and Flying Officer John Douglas Phillips.[109] They were shot down and killed by Hauptmann Manfred Meurer flying a *Uhu*.[110]

At Coningsby, since the beginning of 1944 617 Dam Busters Squadron, now commanded by Wing Commander Geoffrey Leonard Cheshire DSO** DFC, had successfully employed the tactic of marking and destroying small industrial targets at night using flares dropped by a Lancaster in a shallow dive at low level. Cheshire, who was on his fourth tour, was born in 1917 at Chester and was educated at Stowe and Merton College, Oxford, where he was a member of the University Air Squadron between 1937 and the outbreak of war. At twenty-five he was the youngest group captain in the RAF, and he had dropped back to wing commander so that he could resume bomber operations.[111] Five years earlier he had an Honours degree in Law at Oxford, and at twenty-four, on leave in New York, he had met and married 41 year old Constance Binney, who had been America's top movie star. In England Cheshire liked a suite at the Ritz on leave and to bask in the Mayfair cocktail bar.[112] On the night of 8/9 February Cheshire had led a dozen of his Lancasters to bomb the Gnome & Rhône aero-engine factory at Limoges, 200 miles southwest of Paris. The factory was undefended except for two machine guns, and Cheshire made three low-level runs in bright moonlight to warn the 300 French girls working the night shift to escape. On the fourth run he dropped a load of 30lb incendiaries from between 50 and 100 feet. Each of the other eleven Lancasters then dropped a 12,000lb bomb with great accuracy. Ten of the bombs hit the factory and an eleventh fell in the river alongside. Obviously the Lanc had limitations in this role, so at 5 Group the

Air Officer Commanding, Air Vice Marshal The Honorable Sir Ralph A. Cochrane KBE CB AFC, urged on by Cheshire, allocated 617 a Mosquito.[113] The AOC was quick to appreciate that if a single aircraft could mark a target accurately for a squadron then it should be possible for a squadron of properly trained crews to mark targets with similar accuracy for the whole Group. The Lancaster was vulnerable to light flak at low level, and a more manoeuvrable aircraft was required for the operations Cochrane had in mind. Cheshire was aware of the limitations of the Lancaster and he had already decided that the Mosquito was the best aircraft for low level marking. He briefed the AOC on his ideas and Cochrane allocated 617 Squadron a Mosquito.

The Dam Busters' first Mosquito sortie was on 5/6 April when the seemingly fearless Cheshire and his chunky little navigator, Flying Officer Pat Kelly, marked an aircraft factory at Toulouse on his third pass with two red spot flares from a height of 800-1000 feet. Cheshire used this aircraft (ML976/N) on 10/11 April to mark a Signals depot at St. Cyr during a dive from 5000 to 1000 feet. This led to the meeting at Bomber Command HQ that resulted in 5 Group—the Independent Air Force, as it was known in Bomber Command—receiving its own PFF force, with 8 Group no longer enjoying its hitherto unchallenged monopoly over Pathfinder tactics. Nos. 83 and 97 Lancaster Squadrons moved from their respective Pathfinder bases at Wyton and Bourn to Coningsby to rejoin 5 Group as backers-up, and 617 Squadron (which received four FB.VIs/XVIs for marking purposes) and 627 Mosquito Squadrons were redeployed from Coningsby and Oakington respectively to Woodhall Spa. The two PFF Lancaster squadrons did not like the idea of marking being undertaken by the Mosquitoes. They saw themselves being reduced to "flare carrying" forces. Mosquito Crews were stunned into silence by the news that the new task would be "dangerous' and "possibly not altogether effective," and were struck by a feeling of "grim foreboding" that settled on the squadron "like a patch of low stratus." It soon became apparent that they were very much the poor relations at Woodhall. While the famous "Dambusters" "lorded it" in Petwood House, 627 were relegated to a batch of Nissen huts on the far side of the airfield. Their only amenity, apart from their own messes, was "a tiny one-roomed ale house down the road, run by a little old lady - the beloved 'Bluebell Inn.' The Mosquito crews even had to go to Coningsby for briefing and debriefing. Ground crews were dismayed to find that the mobile canteen now seemed to go round 617 Squadron's dispersal first, which was the rule rather than the exception, and that few NAAFI wads were left when their turn came." [114]

In the Station Cinema at Coningsby, Cochrane and Cheshire addressed the assembled Lancaster crews of 83 and 97 PFF Squadrons and Mosquito men of 627 Squadron as to their new role. Cochrane opened the meeting by saying that 617 Squadron had made a number of successful attacks on important pinpoint targets, and it was now intended to repeat these on a wider scale. The Lancaster Pathfinder squadrons were to identify the target areas on H_2S and were to lay a carpet of flares over a given target, under which 627 Squadron would locate and mark the precise aiming point. 5 Group Lancaster bombers would then destroy the target. Cheshire, a tall, thin, and imposing figure, took the stand in front of the assembled crews, who all knew of his legendary reputation in the RAF, and he explained carefully how the low-level marking business was done. What the Lancasters had to do was lay a concentrated carpet of hooded flares, the light from which would be directed downwards onto the target, making it as bright as day. The small force of Mosquitoes would orbit, find the aiming point, and then mark it in a shallow dive with 500lb spot-fires. Marker Leader would assess the position of the spot-fires in relation to the aiming point and would pass this information to a "Master of Ceremonies" in one of the Pathfinder Lancasters. The MC would then take over and direct the Main Force Lancasters in their attack on the target.

A number of the raids that were now taking place were in preparation for the invasion of France by the Allied forces. The invasion required destruction of the French railway system leading to the landing area. The best method of doing this was by employing heavy bombers, but grave doubts existed at the highest level as to the accuracy with which this could be done. Winston Churchill was adamant that French lives must not he lost needlessly, and eventually it was agreed that 5 Group should undertake a mass attack on a marshalling yard in the Paris area to prove the case one way or the other. Juvisy was selected as the target. The marshalling yard was attacked on the night of 18/19 April by 202 Lancasters led by Leonard Cheshire after the target was marked at each end with red spot-fires by four Mosquitoes of 627 Squadron.[115] The attack on Juvisy was a bombing classic. The railway yards were marked at each end with red spot-fires and the heavy bombers laid their cargoes between the target indicators. The bombing was concentrated, the yards were put out of action, few French lives were lost, and all but one Lancaster returned safely to base. The railway yards were so badly damaged that they were not brought back into service until 1947. On the 20th the target, just north of Paris, was the marshalling yards at La Chapelle. At the briefing the Lancaster crews were instructed not to bomb unless there was a certainty of hitting the target. It was policy not to hit the areas surrounding the marshalling yards, as these generally contained buildings occupied by French citizens. There was considerable opposition from enemy anti-aircraft guns as the Lancasters dropped their bombs from low level.[116] The real test of the new tactics had still to be made—against targets in Germany. 5 Group was therefore unleashed against three of these targets in quick succession: Brunswick on 22/23 April; [117] Munich two nights later;[118] and Schweinfurt on 26/27 April.[119] So far as Brunswick and Munich were concerned, considerable damage was done. In the case of Munich, 90 per cent of the bombs fell in the right place, doing more damage in one night than had been achieved by Bomber Command and the 8th Air Force in the preceding four years.

> "The flexibility and superiority of the new system was clearly revealed," recalls Benny Goodman "and, speaking for myself, I found the business of marking a German target no worse than marking anywhere else. The point was that enemy AA defenses in Germany were almost exclusively of the heavy variety, for use against relatively high-flying aircraft. There was not much light flak; this was concentrated in France and the Low Countries. Consequently, when the Mosquitoes of 627 Squadron circled Brunswick on 22 April, there was not much opposition from the ground. The aiming point was a large park and we plonked our four spot-flares into it with the greatest of ease."[120]

After these attacks the Group turned exclusively to support of the bombing campaign against interdiction targets for Operation *Overlord*. Benny Goodman continues:

> "1 May was another 'first' for Bill and me. The target was an engineering works outside Tours - the Usine Lictard works. We air-tested our faithful Wooden Wonder in the morning and then settled down to study

maps of the Tours area and photographs of the target itself. The factory had been bombed a few days earlier by 8th Air Force B-17s, but the photographs showed that nearly all the bombs had fallen in the surrounding fields. To drop bombs a few hundred yards from the aiming point might be good enough on a large area, but on a pin-point target like a factory the bombs had to be 'on the button'.

"We took off in the late evening and headed for France, climbing rapidly to 25,000 feet. The PFF Lancasters of 83 and 97 Squadrons had taken off about an hour before ms and were to drop a yellow target indicator 10 miles from Tours, from which the four low-level marker aircraft would set course accurately for the target area. Having dropped the yellow indicator for us, the Lancasters would head directly to the target, identify it on H_2S and discharge hundreds of illuminating flares above it. As Bill and I approached the final turning point, losing height steadily, the yellow TI suddenly cascaded down ahead of us. So far, so good. We flew over the TI and headed for the target. Approaching Tours a great carpet of light suddenly spread out in front of us; we lost more height and soon we were under the earner at 1500 feet and it was as bright as day. If a fighter appeared now, we would he dead ducks, and if there was light flak in the area we would certainly have a very tough time. Nothing happened. We circled around, and suddenly I saw the factory close by. I immediately pressed the transmit button on my VHF and called 'Pen-nib Three Seven, Tally Ho'. This was the laid-down method of informing the other marker pilots that the target had been found; they now withdrew from the illuminated area to give me room to manoeuvre and make my dive onto the factory.

"I circled around the works, losing speed and positioning the Mosquito for the dive, then opened the bomb doors and pressed the control column gently forward. Our speed increased and the target leapt up towards us, filling the windscreen. At about 500 feet I pressed the bomb release button and there was a slight jerk as the four spot-fires left their slips. I continued in the dive for another couple of seconds, selected bomb doors closed and turned sharply to the left in order to cheek our results. There was a red glow among the factory buildings and in fact the spots had fallen through the glass roof of a machine shop. This was splendid from my point of view - I had marked the target accurately - but as the spot fires were inside the machine shop they could not be seen clearly by the Main Force crews, now trundling towards Tours. Marker Leader (Roy Elliott) flew over the works and called in the next marker pilot to lay his red indicators in the yard alongside the machine shop. This was done. Marker Leader then called the Controller and told him that the target had been marked successfully. The Controller broadcast to the Main Force on W/T and VHF to bomb the clump of red spots, and this was done. The marking had taken less than five minutes, from my 'Tally Ho' to Roy Elliott's confirmation to the Controller that the target was ready for Main Force action. The low-level marking technique had been vindicated once more and the target was flattened."

During May-June Bomber Command was, apart from three major raids against German cities towards the end of May, fully committed to destroying the *Wehrmacht's* infrastructure in France, and bomber losses were relatively light. One exception, however, was on 3/4 May when 346 Lancaster crews, two *Oboe* equipped Mosquitoes, and four Pathfinder Mosquitoes of 617 Squadron (one flown by Wing Commander Leonard Cheshire, the "Marker Leader") were briefed for that night's operation. 617 Squadron were the experts in marking confined and difficult targets that could not be accurately located by purely radar aids.[121] There was the usual anticipation of the string drawing out the route to the target. It was a short string. Everyone gave a sigh of relief, as French targets were supposed to be easy. Then the Intelligence Officer introduced the reality; Mailly-le-Camp, a pre-war French Army tank depot near Epernay, east of Paris, about 50 miles south of Rheims. Many had never heard of it before. Crews were told that it was a *Panzer* depot and training center reported to house up to 10,000 *Wehrmacht* troops.[122] British Intelligence had received word that the Panzer Division was due to move out the next day so it had to be attacked that night. The penny dropped. It was just another raid, but this one really mattered. Crews were briefed to "'get the target' because there were French people all around it."

Flight Lieutenant J. R. "Benny" Goodman DFC [123] and his navigator, Flight Lieutenant A. J. L. "Bill" Hickox DFC of 627 Squadron flew on the Mailly Le Camp operation. Goodman recalls:

> "Cheshire was to lead the low-level marker aircraft and eight Mosquitoes of 627 Squadron were to be at a slightly higher level and were to dive bomb the light flak positions which were known to be around this depot. The raid was timed to begin at 0001 hours, when all good troops should be in bed. The Mosquito force arrived over Mailly, five minutes before zero hour as briefed. Although the target was marked accurately and Cheshire passed the order to bomb, confusion occurred. The first wave did not receive instructions and began to orbit the target. This was fatal and the German night-fighters moved in and began to shout down the Lancasters. Eventually the situation was sorted out and bombs began to crash down unto the depot. From our worm's eye view, Bill and I could see bomber after bomber coming down in flames towards us. We had a scary time as we dived on the light flak batteries, dropped out bombs singly on them, avoided light flak and burning Lancasters and contrived to keep ourselves out of harm's way. When out fourth bomb had gone I called Marker Leader and was told to go home. Bill gave me a course to steer for the French coast and I should have climbed to 25,000 feet but because of the mayhem in the target area I stayed at low level. All went well for a few minutes and then a searchlight shone directly on us, followed immediately by two or three more. Light flak batteries opened up and the pretty blue, red, green and white tracery associated with light AA fire came shooting up the beams and exploded all around us.
>
> "We were at 500 feet and I did not dare to lose height, not could I climb because this would have been a 'gift' to the German gunners. With Bill's exhortation 'watch your instruments' ringing in my ears I ruined steeply to port through 30 degrees, leveled out for a few seconds, then tolled into a steep turn to starboard

and repeated the performance. Although we were in searchlights and flak for quite a long rime, we were not being held by any one light or being shot at by any one gun for very long and we zig-zagged our way steadily towards the coast. It was a tense rime for us and we did not speak; we could hear the explosions around us from light AA shells but incredibly, were not hit. Deliverance came eventually as we breasted a low hill and ahead of us lay the sea. Now we were treated to a rare sight. The final group of searchlights was shining through the trees on top of the hill we had just passed and the beams were actually above us and lighting us on our way. We roared along a river estuary, below the level of the lighthouse at Le Treport and then were away over the 'drink' and climbing to safety, home and bed."

What had gone wrong?

It was a beautiful spring night, soft and starlit. Crews could see the shadows of aircraft above them. The Mosquito force arrived over Mailly five minutes before zero hour as briefed.[124] The target was marked accurately and Cheshire passed the order to the "Main Force Controller," Wing Commander L. C. Deane of 83 Squadron, to send in the Main Force, who were orbiting at a holding pattern to the north, and bomb. Deane instructed the wireless operator to give the "Start Bombing" order but the message was distorted. In some cases the VHF radio frequency was drowned out by an American Armed Forces Network broadcast. Crews heard only too well the tune "*Deep In The Heart of Texas*" followed by „hand clapping and noise like a party going on." Other garbled talk was in the background but drowned by Glenn Miller and his music. Some crews thought that the Germans were trying to jam their communications. Only a few Lancaster crews picked up the garbled message and went in and bombed. So too did a handful of other aircraft flown by experienced captains who realized that delaying dropping their bombs and circling the yellow datum point that had been laid near the village of Germinon could be disastrous. Deane knew that the delay in starting bombing by the Main Force was serious and he tried to send the message by Morse, but it failed to transmit. (It was found later that his radio was 30 kilocycles off frequency). Cheshire also tried to get through, but he was unable to do so either. He then tried to abort the raid but this failed. The first wave did not receive instructions and began to orbit the target and the German night-fighters moved in and began to shoot down the Lancasters.

The Deputy Controller, Squadron Leader E. N. M. Sparks of 83 Squadron, had been instructed to take over only if the Master Bomber was shot down or he was given instructions to do so. He was aware that Deane had not been shot down and that his messages somehow were not getting through, so Sparks took over and gave the order to bomb. The order was five minutes late, but that was an eternity to the waiting crews. "When the order to bomb was finally given the rush was like the starting gate at the Derby," recalled one pilot. In twenty minutes 1500 tons of bombs were dropped, but by this time nine Lancasters were crashing in flames. Many of the German soldiers on the ground sheltered in the woods when the first bombs dropped and then returned to the camp, thinking that the raid was over. They were not ready for the ferocity of the second wave and many were killed in the open. Some dived into the trenches, but many were buried alive as the sides of the trenches fell in on them or walls collapsed over them. Then the water tower was hit and the flood of water poured into the trenches, drowning some of the men who were trapped there.

It had been while crossing the English Channel that Flight Lieutenant Tom Bennett, navigator of the 617 Squadron Mosquito flown by Flight Lieutenant Gerry Fawke, realized how bright the moonlight was. An advantage of being in the second wave was that they could see the "party" starting well ahead of them, and the final run in could be made by visually steering towards the action. To Bennett the raid had seemed at first to be "progressing favourably," and everything had appeared to be "as normal as one would expect on a raid of this size." However, he was shocked when he saw that the Yellow route markers placed north of the camp at Germinon to mark the datum point were visible from "a long way off." If they could see them from that distance "so could the Germans." They were shocked again when bombs began falling as they tried to mark for the second wave. No one appreciated the chaotic conditions that were developing above.[125] For the first and only time they heard another voice across the ether. "Well get a move on, mate," said a calm but firm Australian voice. "It's getting a bit hot up here." This was the first indication they had that everything was not going according to plan. Satisfied with a job well done, the Mosquito crew readily obeyed their order to "cut and run," and Bennett set course for the return route. They had seen no aircraft shot down until they were on the first leg away from the target. Then they saw the first "ghastly" sight of a Lancaster hitting the ground and exploding in flames:

> "The fireball illuminated the pall of oily smoke that was always part of such a macabre scene. To our mounting horror and concern, that was not the only casualty. Again and yet again, the tragedy was repeated. I tried to convince myself that it was German night fighters that were being shot down but the funeral pyres were too large for that. When a fifth bomber was cremated beneath us Gerry said, 'Not a healthy area for a twin engined aircraft, Ben, let's find another way home.' It was pandemonium in the air, Lancasters were jinxing in the sky trying to escape from the Messerschmitts and Junkers. Our gunners were aiming at the enemy but they could only hold the fighters in their sights for a few seconds before they had flown on. We didn't waste time. We were as likely to be shot down by one of our planes. The Mosquito could have been mistaken for a German night fighter. I gave Gerry a rough course for the nearest safe part of the coast and then busied myself in the niceties of tidying up to ensure that we crossed the coast at a reasonably safe spot. I could not exorcise from my mind the glimpse of hell we had seen or the thought of the crews that had been flying the planes that had crashed…Our worst fears were confirmed later that day – 42 Lancasters missing; fourteen from 5 Group and 28 from 1 Group. My first reaction was that 5 Group had stirred the hornet's nest and 1 Group had taken the stings."[126]

On 11/12 May 429 bombers of the Main Force made attacks on Bourg-Leopold, Hasselt, and Louvain in Belgium. The target for 190 Lancasters and eight Mosquitoes of 5 Group was a former Belgian *Gendarmerie* barracks at Leopoldsburg (Flemish)/Bourg-Leopold (French), which was being used to accommodate 10,000 *SS* Panzer troops who awaited the Allied invasion forces. The weather was bad with low cloud and poor visibility, and a serious error was made with the broadcast winds. As a result, the aircraft were late over the target area and consequently flare-dropping was scattered and provided no adequate illumination. An *Oboe* Mosquito flown by Flight Lieutenants Burt and Curtis of 109 Squadron dropped a yellow marker. The Mosquito marking force of 627 Squadron arrived late over the target with the result that the *Oboe* proximity marker was seen by only one of the marking aircraft and the proximity marker, unfortunately, seemed to burn out very quickly. Flare dropping was scattered and did not provide adequate illumination of the target. Haze and up to 3/10ths cloud conditions hampered the marking of the target. The "Marking Leader" then asked the "Master Bomber" if he could drop "Red Spot Fires" as a guide for the flare force. The Master Bomber agreed and "RSFs" went down at 0024 hours in the estimated vicinity of the target. Unfortunately, the "Main Force" started to bomb this red spot fire immediately as it went down and half of the main force bombed this. The result of this was the five Mosquitoes of 627 Squadron returned to Woodhall Spa with their bombs and were unable to mark the target. Immediately the "Master Bomber" ordered "*Stop Bombing*," as he realized it was impossible to identify the target, but VHF was very poor, particularly on Channel "B," and the Germans had jammed Channel "A." Only half the main force received the "Cease Bombing" instruction, and 94 Lancasters bombed the target. At 0034 hours a wireless message "Return to base" was sent out to all crews.

5 Group was now used exclusively in support of the bombing campaign against interdiction targets for Operation *Overlord*, as Flight Lieutenant L. J. R "Benny" Goodman recalls:

> "1 June 1944 was the same as any other day at Woodhall Spa. Bill and I walked to the Flights after breakfast, found that we were on the Battle Order and went to the dispersal and tested *'G-George'*. We then strolled to the Operations Room and were told that the target was to he the marshalling yard at Saumur. The day proceeded normally, with detailed briefing about the target and a close examination of maps and photographs. At the end of the afternoon attended the AOC's broadcast link-up with the COs of all squadrons participating, then made ready to go. The operation was a copybook 5 Group attack, with no alarms and excursions. After landing, we switched off everything and climbed out as we had done so often before. *G-George* stood black and silent; the ground crew moved forward to ask if all was well; it was a lovely summer night. After debriefing we ate the usual bacon and eggs and went to bed. Maybe tomorrow there would be a stand-down for us. We did not know it, but in fact our tour was over. We had flown together against Fortress Europe thirty-eight times. Soon we would he instructors again and soon our work in 5 Group would he recognised by the award of a bar to the DFC to each of us. Paradoxically, however, Bill and I would never fly together again."[127]

A few days later an 8 Group weather report by Pilot Officer Joe Patient and Pilot Officer Norry Gilroy, a 1409 Met Flight crew, delayed the Normandy invasion by one day, and D-Day finally went ahead on 6 June. Four Mosquito crews in 627 Squadron at Woodhall Spa could pat themselves on the back for helping to remove one of the American objectives on D-Day, as "Benny" Goodman recalls:

> "The Americans were nervous about the long-range heavy gun battery at St Martin de Varreville behind what was to be *Utah* beach. This presented a threat to Allied shipping approaching Normandy and also to the troops landing on *Utah* beach. It was decided that 5 Group would attack this precision target, so on the night of 28/29 May, a force of 64 Lancasters, led by a flare force from 83 and 97 Lancaster Pathfinder Squadrons and four Mosquitoes of 627 Squadron, flew to St Martin de Varreville. The flare force identified the gun battery on their H_2S sets and laid a carpet of flares over the target. At Zero Hour minus five minutes, the Mosquitoes roared in at 2000 feet and identified the gun battery visually. The first pilot to see the target called, "Tally Ho" on his VHF radio to warn his companions to keep out of the way and then proceeded to dive at the gun, releasing a red TI at the appropriate point in the dive. His companions followed suit, making individual dives on the battery and creating a box of red TIs around it.[128] The Master Bomber now called in the Main Force, with each aircraft carrying several 1000lb armor-piercing bombs and the target was obliterated. On 6 June the 101st Airborne Division landed behind *Utah* beach as planned, but amid a certain amount of confusion. However, by 0600 hours Major General Maxwell Taylor had mustered one sixth of his force and with this he captured the exists from *Utah* Beach. An element of the 502nd Regiment had orders to overrun the battery and to crush the garrison if necessary but Captain Frank Lilleyman, the first US soldier to land in Normandy on D-Day, reconnoitered the battery and discovered that it had been bombed and abandoned as a result of the 5 Group attack on 28/29 May. A document captured soon afterwards revealed that the Officer Commanding, *Heer Kust Artillerie Regiment 1261*, reported the bombing attack had begun at 0015 hours, parachute flares having been dropped first in great numbers. He said that the battery had been hit 'with uncanny accuracy', approximately 100 bombs of the heaviest calibre having been dropped in addition to several hundred smaller ones. Very large bombs had made several direct hits on the gun casement and it had burst open and collapsed. As a result of the destruction caused by the attack he had cleared the remainder of the battery out of the position into three farms in the Mesier area."

On the night of 19/20 September the twin towns of Mönchengladbach and Rheydt were the targets for 227 Lancasters and ten Mosquitoes of 1 and 5 Groups. The designated Master Bomber was unavailable, and Wing Commander Guy Gibson VC DSO* DFC*, the famous Dambusters leader, and navigator Squadron Leader James B. Warwick DFC took off from Woodhall Spa in a 627 Squadron Mosquito[129] to act as Controller for the raid on Rheydt. It would appear that Gibson did not exactly endear himself to some of 627 Squadron's members, but then 617 Squadron always engendered fierce rivalries. Frank W. Boyle DFC* RFCF, a 627 Squadron navigator, encountered Gibson a few times at Woodhall. He reported that "he seemed a lost soul, particularly on the last occasion when he dropped in at the Mess; he was upset by the award of Cheshire's VC (and I would understand that after his own VC for the Dambusters raid), but he reckoned too forcibly and bluntly that, on the basis of Cheshire's citation, he would get a bar to his VC." Fellow 627 Squadron navigator Wallace "John-O" Gaunt DFC recalled:

"Guy Gibson was a brave man and did a good job leading the Dambusters, but he came back from the USA too full of his own importance. He walked into our mess one night and everybody was talking, playing liar-dice, drinking, etc, so he called out, 'Don't you know who I am?' He got very annoyed, as he had expected everyone to stand up and cheer him. In the end he was debagged and put outside. He persuaded our CO to let him fly a Mosquito – against his better judgment. A week or so later Peter Mallender and I were told that he wanted the aircraft we were due to operate that night. He did not return."[130]

The end came on Sunday, 25 April, with a raid by 482 aircraft on coastal batteries on the Friesian Island of Wangerooge and, in a fitting climax to bomber operations, on Hitler's mountain retreat at Berchtesgarden, in the southeast corner of Germany. The Obersalzberg, a beautiful mountainous region close to the Austrian border, was one that had long appealed to Hitler. Following the Munich Putsch and his imprisonment Hitler had stayed in the Obersalzberg, writing part of *Mien Kampf* there. Royalties from the book's sale had enabled the German dictator to buy a house called the "Berghof." After coming to power the building had been rebuilt on a lavish scale; the best known addition was the dramatically named "Eagle's Nest," a tea-house that had been built on Kehlshein mountain apparently as an isolated conference building. Hitler's home, referred to as the "Chalet" by the RAF, was the target for 359 Lancaster heavy bombers and fourteen *Oboe* Mosquito and 24 Lancaster marker aircraft. Included in the mighty force were thirty-three Lancasters of 9 Squadron and 617 of the "Dam Busters,' each carrying a potentially devastating 12,000lb *Tallboy* bomb in their long, rakish bomb bay. For once, the BBC was permitted to announce the raid while it was in progress. At least 126 Mustangs of 11 Group RAF and 98 P-51s from two American fighter groups provided escort relays along the route, a round trip of 1400 miles.[131]

One of the *Oboe* Mosquito markers was crewed by Flight Lieutenant Derek James DFC and Flight Lieutenant John C. Sampson of 105 Squadron. Sampson recalls:

"We took off at 0725 and the flight was 4 hours 15 minutes. We carried four red TIs to mark for the heavies. We flew at 36,000 feet because of the Alps and, since *Oboe* signals went line of sight and did not follow the curvature of the earth, the further the target, the higher one needed to be. (Following the Normandy invasion, *Oboe* ground stations were located on the continent thus increasing the effective range of the system). I heard the first two dots of the release signal and then nothing more. We were unable to drop and brought the markers back to base. On investigation, it was established that a mountain peak between the ground station and the aircraft had blocked out the signal. No *Oboe* Mosquito was successful this day."

Those who bombed the "Chalet" mostly missed, but the Berghof sustained much blast damage as a result of the bombs and the *Tallboys*. Only 53 bombers attacked their primary target, but at the SS barracks one building and several others were damaged. Six of the 3,500 who had sheltered in the air raid tunnels were killed. Soon after the raid the U.S. 3rd Infantry Division won the race to occupy Berchtesgarden and share in the spoils of victory.

Bomber Command's last bombing operations were flown that night when 119 Lancasters and Mosquitoes directed by the master bomber, Wing Commander Maurice A. Smith DFC, attacked oil storage depots at Tonsberg, in Southern Norway, and U-boat fuel storage tanks at Vallo, in Oslo Fjord. Operation orders for attacks on Heligoland on the 26th and 27th were each cancelled in turn.

With the Germans at the brink of defeat, thousands of people in the western and northwestern provinces of the Netherlands, which were still in German hands, were without food. Parts of the country had been under German blockade, and 20,000 men, women, and children had died of starvation during a very short period; the survivors were in a desperate plight. Dutch railwaymen had gone on strike in protest against German demands and, as a result, there was no distribution of food. Townsfolk went foraging in the country, and thousands camped in fields in search of food. Five slung panniers, each capable of carrying 70 sacks containing flour, yeast, powdered egg, dried milk, peas, beans, tins of meat and bacon, tea, sugar, pepper, and special vitamin chocolate were fitted into the Lancaster bomb bays. Orders were issued for each squadron to drop the panniers in their allotted area, which they would find "marked" by PFF Mosquitoes after liaison with the Dutch authorities and the underground movement.[132] Only the bedridden appeared to be confined to their homes as the Lancasters flew over to drop their loads and there was a sea of hands waving handkerchiefs and flags to greet the RAF bombers, while even some German gunners standing by their anti-aircraft guns waved solemnly in acquiescence.

The authorities tried to keep the drop zones clear, but there were a few incidents. A Lancaster of 186 Squadron, which were briefed to drop five large panniers each on Waalhaven aerodrome, near Rotterdam, dropped three packages, by which time crowds had swarmed across the field and they could not risk dropping the others. Another Lancaster could not get all its packages away because the bomb doors had been damaged by small arms fire. Back over Stradishall, the pilot found that he could not lower the undercarriage. While "jinking" his aircraft to jolt the wheels down a package fell, strewing tea, sugar, and tins over the countryside to the north of Stradishall, which caused something of a race between villagers and the RAF recovery party. Finally the pilot flew to Woodbridge and landed safely on the long runway. Next day one of this squadron's Lancasters was hit by two bags from an aircraft above, fortunately without causing damage. The drops continued for several days. Crews reported that on a number of houses messages had been whitewashed "Thanks RAF" and "Good Luck Tommy." Many crews gave their own sweet rations and their aircrew issue, wrapped up and tied by string to handkerchiefs or pieces of linen to make a parachute. They flung them from the open windows of their Lancasters with notes saying *Ver Het Kinde* – "For The Children." The sweets became a free for all! Stones marked out "TABAC," and a whip round of the cigarette ration was organized; it was dropped at the location the next day. A target indicator in the Rotterdam area fell by a house and set it on fire. One pannier dropped in a lake, but later crews reported rowing boats going out to salvage the contents. During the operation one Lancaster, after dropping 284 sacks, got into trouble over the North Sea on the return journey. A short in a microphone heater caused a fire in the rear turret and exploded rounds of ammunition. The pilot was able to land at Oulton without injury to any of the crew. During Operation *Manna* from 29 April to 7 May a total of 6684 tons of food were dropped in 3156 sorties by Lancasters and 145 flown in Mosquitoes.

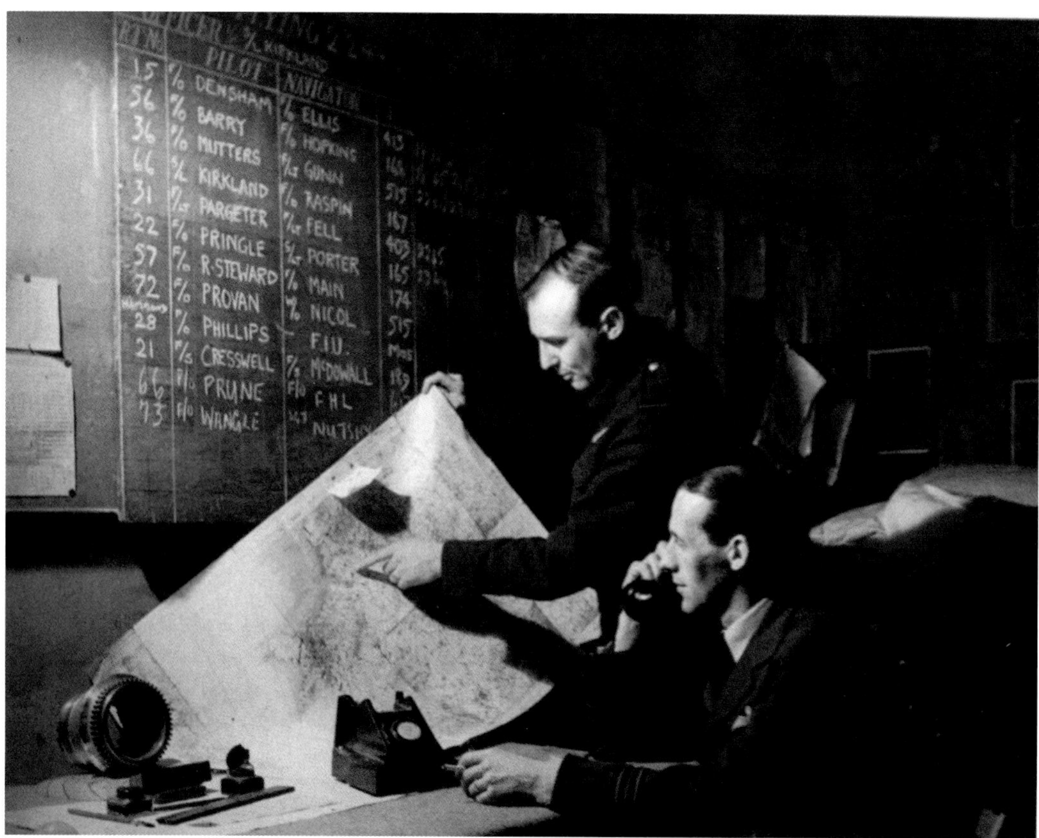

Squadron Leader Clive Kirkland 'A' Flight commander, 29 Squadron, is receiving the first warning of a possible approaching raider force. The two bottom lines on the blackboard were frivolous additions and have oblique references. Pilot Officer Prune seemed to serve on every RAF squadron. He dropped all the clangers and was responsible for all the mishaps. He never grew up and never got promoted. The polished souvenir in the bottom left hand corner was said to be a trophy belonging to Squadron Leader Clive Kirkland and which he had collected from a Fw 190 he had shot down. (Ken Lowes)

Servicing of a Mosquito the morning after operational flying. (Ken Lowes)

Flying Officers John Barry and Guy Hopkins of 29 Squadron leaving their crew room to take their Mosquito on the obligatory NFT (Night Flying Test). (Ken Lowes)

Flying Officer John Barry (left) uses his gloved hands to explain to the other crews in 29 Squadron how he shot down two enemy aircraft on 24/25 February 1944. On this, 'The Big Night' the squadron claimed nine enemy aircraft shot down plus one shared, two destroyed and two probables. Left to right beside Barry are navigator Flying Officer R. G. 'Bob' Stainton, his pilot Ernest Mutters, Flying Officer Guy Hopkins (Barry's navigator, who was a freelance journalist in Fleet Street in peacetime) and navigator Flight Sergeant McDowall. (Ken Lowes)

29 Squadron crews on readiness before twilight until dawn. The only card game that was universally played was Poker and there were few abstainers. L-R Guy Hopkins, Flight Sergeant Athol Cresswell, Sergeant Eric Haines Royal Artillery, Flight Lieutenant Reggie Pargeter, Flying Officer Bill Ellis, Flight Sergeant McDowall, Flying Officers Ron Densham (KIA over Arromanches on 6 June 1944) and John Barry, who is wearing special goggles with dark red lenses for darkness adaptation. When an aircrew was called out on a scramble, dashing out from artificial indoor lightning into the darkness outside was hazardous. The pictures on the walls are mostly pages from the American magazine *Esquire*. (Ken Lowes)

Flying Officer John Barry lends a hand during servicing of his Mosquito NF.XIX the morning after operational flying. (Ken Lowes)

Right: Flying Officer Guy Hopkins (left), Flying Officer John Barry (middle) and Squadron Leader Clive Kirkland standing in for the Intelligence Officer, who of course was elsewhere de-briefing other crews. Kirkland's hair parting was hurriedly altered and the Photoflood light so adjusted so that his features were in shade. (Ken Lowes)

Middle: Captain Ken J. W. Lowes the Army Liaison Officer, with crews of 29 Squadron. In the summer of 1943 Lieutenant Lowes was a troop commander in a searchlight regiment of the Royal Artillery. After attending an Aircraft Recognition Course he was interviewed by Wing Commander R. E. X. Mack DFC, CO of 29 Squadron at Ford near the Sussex coast in the regiment's operational area and invited to join his squadron as Liaison Officer. Lowes leapt at the chance; Mack's hope being that each side should have a fuller and more detailed understanding of the other's operational methods and equipment. Lowes was given unlimited access to the GCI station for the area at Durrington, Worthing. Here he could take a seat beside the controller on duty and his WAAF information assistance, the three of them around the radar tube or PPI (Plan Position Indicator). In shape this bore some resemblance to a single tympanum in an orchestra but the 20-inch horizontal upper surface was simply marked with the bare outlines of the coastline of Southeast England and that of Northern France. A long sweep hand resembling that of the second's hand of a wall clock left a blip representing an aircraft somewhere in the sky. This lasted a second or two and then faded. When added to other information giving height and range, the sum enabled the controller to interpret the track of each aircraft. This is in turn enabled him to get his Mosquitoes onto the track of what were considered to be enemy aircraft. On the night of 22/23 February 1944 Wing Commander Mack took with him the Squadron's Senior Navigator/Radar operator, Flight Lieutenant Bert Townsin (in NF.XIX HK371) and that night Lowes went to Durrington to observe events. He recalls. 'They were soon put on to the leading raider, the one most likely to drop 'Window' and therefore the reason for the Wingco's special interest. It was leading in a generally northwards direction and the Mosquito soon got in behind it and began to close the gap. The pattern of the pursuit was quite normal, until unbelievably, Mack's 'blip' split in two. The two halves began to lose height; eventually disappearing into what we knew was the sea. The obvious interpretation of these events was that the Mosquito had been shot in two, probably by rear-facing cannon fire. The tragedy I had just witnessed taking place on a flat sheet of glass bit deep into my consciousness and the echoes remained vivid forever. The rear fuselage and tail unit were recovered from the Channel. A report said that a Heinkel 177 had been shot down by anti-aircraft fire as it neared London and that the course and time corresponded with those of Mack's raider.' (Ken Lowes)

Left: Flight Lieutenant Ted Cox and Warrant Officer Kershaw of 29 Squadron who were credited with the destruction of a He 177 30-35 miles south of the Ford-Beachy Head area on the night of 24/25 February 1944. (Ted Cox via Theo Boiten) **Right:** 29 Squadron crews at RAF Ford on 24/25 February 1944 - 'The Big Night' - the squadron's most successful searchlight operation night with claims for nine shot down plus one shared, two destroyed and two probables. Back Row Flight Lieutenant R. L. Fell; Flying Officer John E. Barry; Flying Officer Guy Hopkins; Flying Officer Dicky Raspin; Warrant Officer Nichol. Front Row: Warrant Officer Kershaw; Flight Lieutenant Ted Cox; Flying Officer W. W. Provan; Squadron Leader Clive Kirkland; Flight Lieutenant Reginald Clive Pargeter. Pargeter and Fell were credited with a Ju 88A-4 of 8./KG6, which they shot down at Withyham, Sussex and a Ju 188, which fell at Thame and a Ju 88 damaged. Squadron Leader Clive Kirkland and Flying Officer Dicky Raspin's Do 217M fell at Dorking, Surrey. Flying Officer W. W. Provan and Warrant Officer Nichol's Ju 188E crashed at Framfield, Sussex. Flying Officer Barry and Flying Officer Hopkins' Do 217M crashed at Willesborough, Kent and they were also credited with a Me 410 probable. Ted Cox and Warrant Officer Kershaw were credited with the destruction of a He 177 30-35 miles south of Ford-Beachy Head area. (Ted Cox via Theo Boiten)

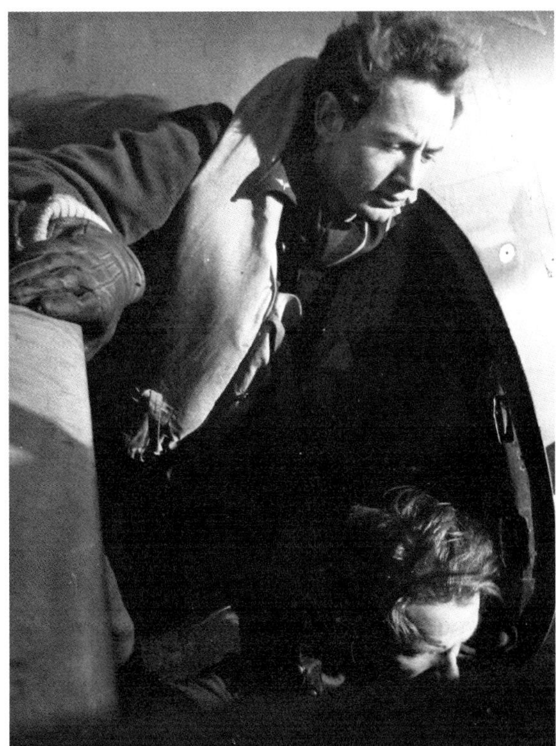

Flying Officer John Barry (top) and Flying Officer Guy Hopkins (below) showing how tricky it was getting into and out of the very small aircrew door into the close confines of the Mosquito cockpit. To bale out the pilot could only follow his navigator. On 7/8 June Flight Lieutenant Barry and Hopkins destroyed two Ju 188s to take the pilot's score to four. Barry and Hopkins died in a flying accident during a NFT while based at Hunsdon a few weeks after the invasion. (Ken Lowes)

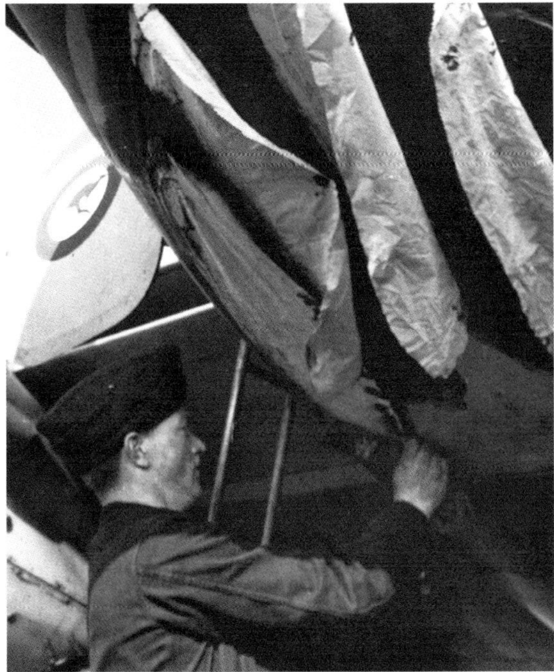

NF.XVII flown by the CO of 456 Squadron RAAF, Wing Commander Keith M. Hampshire DSO* DFC who finished the war with seven confirmed victories and one probable, all scored flying Mosquito NF.XVII aircraft. When the four cannons were fired the first shells burst through the streamlining material, which is being applied, and easily replaced the following morning. (Ken Lowes)

Naturally, anyone who knew or knows what a Mosquito was could tell you that it was affectionately known as the 'Wooden Wonder' but few apart from those who built them and a few RAF people, could have seen this. The picture, taken at Ford, shows where Wing Commander Keith MacDermott Hampshire's chunk of engine landed.

Flying Officers John Barry and Guy Hopkins of 29 Squadron ready for the off. (Ken Lowes)

Having flown his stint for the night, the pilot is nevertheless still on standby so he goes into the bunker to have a rest or any little nap that he can manage. After dawn he could go to his own bed in the Officers mess, a former girl's boarding school about a mile away and the aircraft noise was much less than in the bunker on the airfield. (Ken Lowes)

On the night of 24/25 February 1944 Squadron Leader Clive Kirkland and Flying Officer Dicky Raspin of 29 Squadron in NF.XIII HK413 shot down a Do 217M over the Dorking Hills, Surrey. Raspin got the chance to go souvenir hunting as the crash site was only thirty miles north of their airfield at Ford. Having taken this picture, Captain Ken Lowes, an Army liaison officer attached to the squadron, went towards the wreckage with a view to taking one or two close-ups. As he got nearer he realized that the aircraft was 'ticking' like an alarm clock! He gave tongue and bolted for safety. Kirkland and Raspin beat him to the car, which was behind Raspin and just off the picture on the left. They heard no more as they hurried away. (Ken Lowes)

Sergeant Eric Haines Royal Artillery and Captain Ken Lowes of the Essex Regiment, Royal Artillery beside a 29 Squadron Mosquito at Ford in 1943/44. Note the camera gun port on the right of the fuselage near the open door. (Frank Pringle)

Wing Commander John Cunningham DSO* DFC points out the 85 Squadron badge with its motto *Noctu Diuque Venamur* assisted by the Intelligence officer, Flying Officer E. A. Robertson at Hunsdon on 5 May 1943. (via Mick Jennings)

No.85 Squadron's Squadron Leader Wilfrith Peter Green, 'A' Flight CO, Wing Commander John Cunningham DSO* DFC CO, and Squadron Leader Edward Dixon Crew DFC*, 'B' Flight CO, at Hunsdon on 5 May 1943. Wing Commander Green DSO DFC finished the war with fourteen enemy aircraft and thirteen V1s destroyed - all while flying Mosquitoes. Wing Commander Crew DSO DFC* was credited with the destruction of twelve and one enemy aircraft shared destroyed, five damaged and twenty-one V1s destroyed. Group Captain Cunningham DSO* DFC was credited with twenty enemy aircraft destroyed, three probables and seven damaged. (via Mick Jennings)

DD737 an AI-equipped NF.II, was one of the first Mosquitoes issued to 85 Squadron when it converted to the de Havilland nightfighter from the Havoc at Hunsdon in August 1942. DD737 was delivered to 30 MU (Maintenance Unit) on 29 August 1942 and then to 85 Squadron on 21 September. It was passed to 264 Squadron on 13 March 1943 and then returned to de Havillands on 6 May. After languishing in various MUs it joined the Bomber Support Development Unit (BSDU) on 14 October 1944, before passing to 54 Operational Training Unit (OTU(at Acklington, with whom it was lost on 6 December 1944 when it failed to return from a cross-country exercise.(DH)

NF.XXX and air crews of 68 Squadron at RAF Church Fenton in 1945.Wing Commander L.W. G. Gill DSO arrived as CO ex-125 Squadron on 4 February 1945. This squadron Motto,*"Vzdy Pripaven"* (*"Always Ready"*) was not a Czech squadron as such but it had many Czech personnel who made a noteworthy contribution to its WWII history. From July 1941 till most of these remained were posted to the Czech depot on 2 May 1945.Awards to Czech personnel included a DFC to Flying Officer Mansfeld on 26 June 1942, a DFC to Warrant Officer Bobek and Squadron Leader Vesely in September 1942. (L.W. G. Gill DSO)

NF.II DD609 of 151 Squadron in all-black nightfighter finish and fitted with AI radar. On 18 February 1943 151 Squadron which had re-equipped with the NF.II at Wittering in April 1942, began *Night Intruder* operations over France flying Mosquitoes fitted with the *Monica* tail warning device. On 30 September 1942 Wing Commander Rupert F. H. Clerke, an Old Etonian and former PRU Mosquito pilot, flying DD607 destroyed a Ju 88. DD609 survived flying operationally with 151 Squadron and was allocated to 54 OTU in mid-1943. It was finally SOC in June 1945. (via GMS)

Wing Commander 'Bob' Braham DSO DFC** CO 141 Squadron who, on the night of 17/18 August 1943 flying a Beaufighter VIf and with Flying Officer W. J. 'Sticks' Gregory DFC (seen here, left) as his radar operator, shot down two Bf 110Gs of IV./NJG1 flown by Oberfeldwebel Georg Kraft and Feldwebel Heinz Vinke to take his score to 18 victories. Braham finished the war with 29 victories. Posted with Braham to 141 Squadron from 29 Squadron was Flying Officer William J. 'Sticks' Gregory DFC DFM his navigator and radio/ radar operator, who had partnered Braham in seven kills. Gregory earned his nickname as a result of having been a drummer in Debroy Somer's band. Flight Lieutenant Jacko Jacobs partnered Braham in four of his victories. Gregory partnered Braham in four of his 8 victories in 141 Squadron 14 June-29 September 1943 and Flight Lieutenant Jacko Jacobs partnered him in the other four. (IWM via Jerry Scutts)

25 Squadron pilots and navigators. Joe Singleton is standing tallest on the right hand engine mounting. Wing Commander Cathcart Michael Wight-Boycott DSO has his arms folded immediately beneath the nose of the Mosquito. He destroyed four enemy aircraft flying Beaufighters before taking command of 25 Squadron in September 1943. His first Mosquito victory was on 28/29 May 1944 when he and Flight Lieutenant D.W. Reid destroyed a Me 410. Wight-Boycott finished the war with a total of seven kills, two damaged and two V1s shot down (Wing Commander Joe Singleton Coll)

Flight Lieutenant Joe Singleton DFC and Flying Officer W. G. 'Geoff' Haslam of 25 Squadron. (Joe Singleton)

Wing Commander 'Bob' Braham DSO DFC* who finished the war with 29 victories. In December 1942, Wing Commander John Randall Daniel 'Bob' Braham DSO DFC* not yet 23, assumed command of 141 Squadron, then flying Beaufighters. An outspoken individualist, unsurpassed in his sheer aggressive fighting spirit and relentless determination, Bob Braham was already a living legend, having shot down twelve enemy aircraft, eleven of them at night. The son of a WWI RFC pilot, Braham shot down his first aircraft during the Battle of Britain and at 23 had become the youngest wing commander in the RAF. 'The Night Destroyer', as he was dubbed in the press, had an overdeveloped sense of modesty and could see no reason for the press having an interest in him. It is perhaps because he shunned publicity wherever possible, that he is not as well known as some other aces of WW2. In April 1943 Air Marshal Sir Trafford F. Leigh-Mallory AOC Fighter Command had been impressed with the aggressive spirit Braham had instilled in his squadron in so short a time and had informed him that 141 Squadron had been selected as the first *Serrate* squadron for Bomber Support operations over enemy territory. (IWM)

85 Squadron at Hunsdon in 1943. Flight Lieutenant Edward Nigel Bunting who had been one of the officers who operationally tested the high-altitude Mosquito NF.XV at the station and who reached a record altitude of 44,600 ft on 30 March 1943, is standing 4th from left. On 13/14 July 1943 Bunting, with his navigator Freddie French, shot down Me 410A-1 U5+KG, of 16./KG2 into the sea off Felixstowe. It was the first Me 410 to be shot down over Britain. (via Andrew Long)

This was taken in the mess at RAF Coltishall around midnight on 19 March 1944 following Flight Lieutenant Joe Singleton DFC and Flying Officer W. G. 'Geoff' Haslam of 25 Squadron's crash half a mile from the RAF station at the end of their successful operation when they destroyed three Ju 88s in quick succession. From left: Flying Officer Franklin; Flying Officer Grey; Singleton; u/k; Harwood and Haslam. (Joe Singleton)

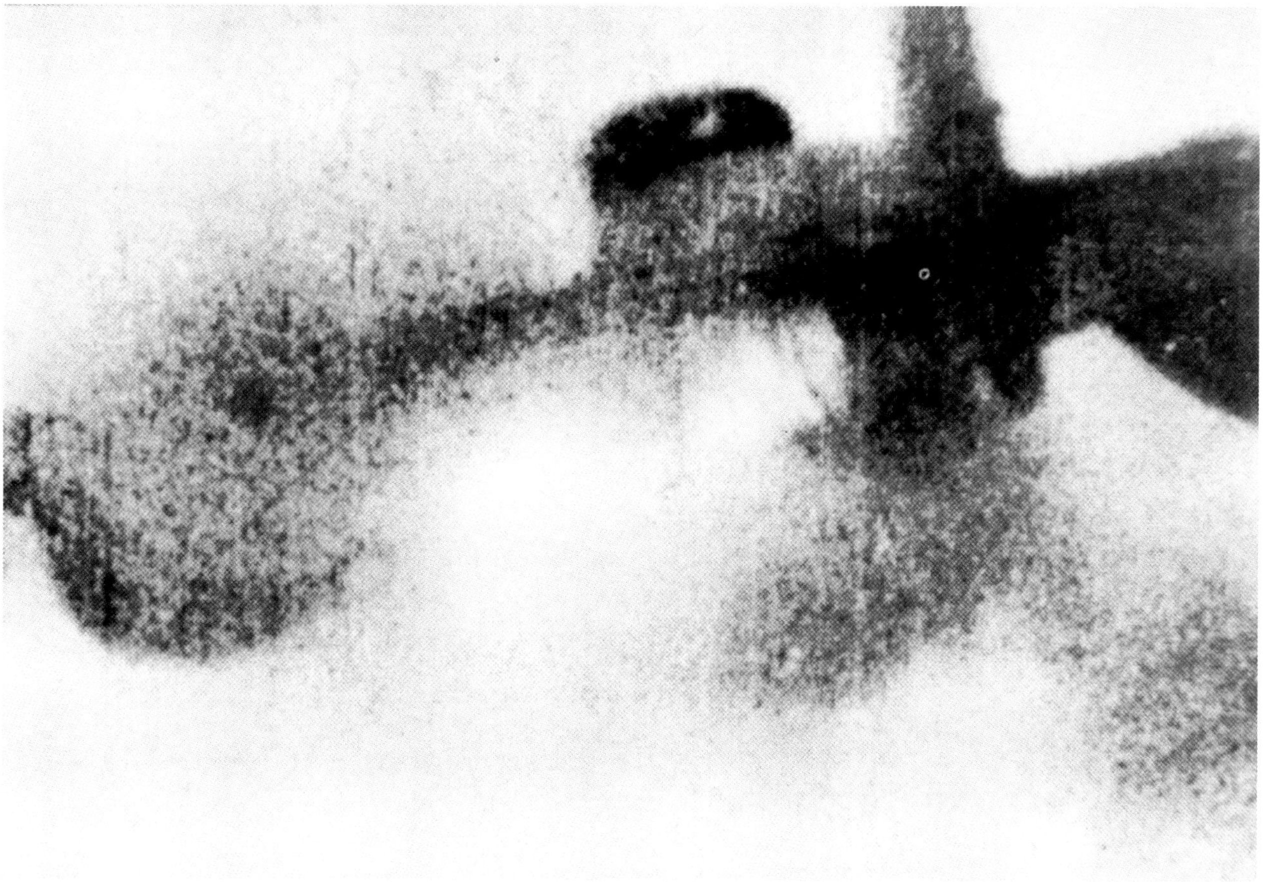

One of Joe Singleton and Haslam's Ju 88 victims caught on gun camera. (Joe Singleton)

On 16/17 June 1944 Flight Lieutenant M. M. Davison DFC (right) and Flying Officer A. C. Willmott DFC (left) of 264 (Madras Presidency) Squadron had to fly through the explosion of their Ju 188, which blacked the entire NF.XIII and burnt off the rudder fabric. They landed their Mosquito safely on a strip just behind the beachhead.

On 24/25 March 1944 Flying Officers Edward R. Hedgecoe and Norman L. Bamford of 85 Squadron were forced to fly through the fireball created by the sudden explosion of a II./KG54 Ju 88 that they had been attacking just seconds before. Upon returning to West Malling the true extent of the damage to their NFXII was revealed. (via Philip Birtles)

NF.II DZ757 RA-Q of 419 Squadron RCAF at Coleby Grange showing the effects of flying through the burning debris of a Dornier Do 217 destroyed by Flight Lieutenant M. A. Cybulski and Flying Officer H. H. Ladbrook on the night of 27/28 September 1943. They flew home on the starboard engine only. Five months earlier on the afternoon of 27 April Cybulski and Ladbrook intruded over Holland and Germany covering more than 600 miles. Flying down the canal and railway lines between Meppen and Papenburg, they attacked five targets. First Cybulski damaged a tug and two barges, from which debris flew into the air, and then he riddled a locomotive and raked a line of six freight cars. Two military buses were shot up and, to end the strafe, pieces were shot off another locomotive, which was left wreathed in clouds of steam. Newspapers heralded the record flight but the pilot's name had to be suppressed lest it bring reprisals upon his relatives in Poland. Cybulski's home was in Renfrew, Ontario, but his grandparents were Polish. The crew received immediate DFC awards for their efforts on 27/28 September when Cybulski was completely blinded and Ladbrook had to take control of the aircraft for about five minutes until the pilot regained normal vision. Course was set for base and the seriously damaged aircraft completed a hazardous 250-mile single engine return.

Squadron Leader Edward Bunting DFC and Flight Lieutenant C. P. Reed DFC of 488 Squadron RNZAF examine the remains of Ju 188E-1 3E+BK of 2/KG6 flown by Leutnant G. Lahl, which came down at Butler's Farm at Shopland, Essex. In the photo from left: Squadron Leader Bunting DFC is on the edge of the hole pointing, Flight Lieutenant Reed navigator; Flight Lieutenant J. A. S. Hall (who shot down a Ju 88 at Earls Colne), Air Marshal Sir Roderick Hill AOC ADGB, Wing Commander R. C. Haine, CO 488 Squadron and Flight Sergeant J. L. Wood. (ARP)

On 21/22 March 1944 Flying Officer S. B. Huppert and Pilot Officer J. S. Christie of 410 Squadron RCAF in NF.XIII HK456 shot down a Ju 88A-4 of 4./KG30 at Latchington, Essex. On 3 July 1944 Huppert, in NF.XIII MM570 destroyed a Ju 188 and a Me 410 before being shot down by defensive fire from the *Hornisse*. Huppert was killed but Christie baled out safely. (ARP)

The shattered remains of Me 410A-1 9K+KH of 1./KG51 which was shot down by Wing Commander E. D. Crew DFC* and Warrant Officer W. R. Croysdill of 96 Squadron on 18/19 April 1944. It crashed n the grounds of St. Nicholas Church in Brighton. The pilot, Hauptmann R. Pahl was found dead in the wreckage while the body of his *bordfunker*, Feldwebel W. Schuberth was washed up at Friston the following day. (H. Tappin via Theo Boiten)

ditto

Heinkel He 177A-5 *Greif* (*Griffon*) of II/KG40 at Bordeaux-Merignac. On 19 December 1943 1st *Staffel* of I/KG40, which had converted to the He 177 from the Fw 200 *Kondor* at Fassberg joined 3rd Staffel of I/KG100 at Châteaudun, also equipped with the He 177, for *Steinbock* operations against England. (ARP)

On the night of 24/25 February 1944 this Ju 88A-4 of 8./KG was destroyed by Flight Lieutenant R. C. Pargeter and Flight Lieutenant R. L. Fell of 29 Squadron at Withyham; one of six kills claimed by the squadron that night. (ARP)

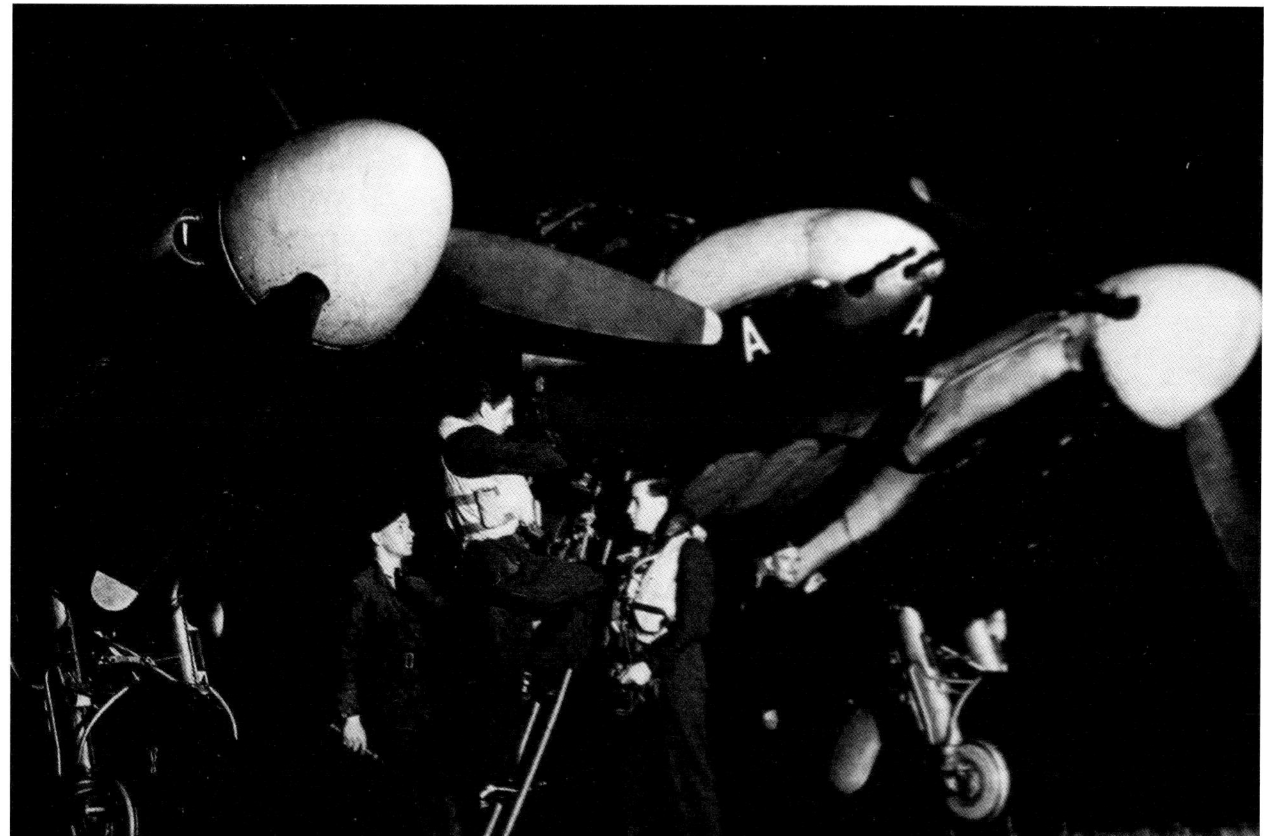

Sequence showing a night fighter crew getting ready for sortie in their NF.II. (via Jerry Scutts)

By 1943 several NF.II, XII, XIII, XIX, XVII and FB.VI squadrons were providing fighter support for Bomber Command main force operations and the intercept radar was continually improved. DZ659/G is a modified NF.II fitted with AI.Mk.X (US SCR 720/729 *Eleanora*) radar in the universal nose. AI.Mk.X radar, developed by the Radiation Laboratory, Massachusetts Institute of Technology and built by the Western Electric Co., had a range of 8-10 miles. (DH)

In August 1942 Ju 86Ps started flying over Britain at heights of up to 41,000 feet and dropped their bombs at will, immune from the Spitfires that attempted to intercept them. The answer was the Mosquito. MP469 was constructed as the prototype pressure cabin bomber and within a week the de Havilland experimental shop at Hatfield had converted the bomber by fitting a fighter nose and substantially lightening the airframe. On 15 September MP469 reached a height of 43,500 feet and was the answer to the Ju 86R. The following day it was flown to Northolt by Flying Officer Sparrow to join the High Altitude Flight of Fighter Command, but the call to intercept a raider did not come. In November the aircraft was fitted with AI.Mk.VIII radar in the nose and the four machine guns were installed in a blister under the fuselage. After radar trials at Defford, MP469 joined the FIU (Fighter Interception Unit) on 4 February 1943 but less than three weeks later it was with 85 Squadron at Hunsdon for operational trials, the squadron then being under the command of Wing Commander John Cunningham. The high-altitude fighter became known as the Mk.XV and four more joined MP469 at Hunsdon, although MP469 reached the highest altitude of 44,600 feet. In August it flew north to RAF Turnhouse to await the possibilities of raiders over Scotland. This remarkable aircraft ended its days as instructional airframe with the School of Aeronautical Engineering at Henlow. (DH)

Left: Wing Commander Keith MacDermott Hampshire DSO DFC RAAF (right) CO of 456 Squadron RAAF and his navigator, Flying Officer (later Flight Lieutenant) Tom Condon DFC inspect the wreckage of Ju 88A-4 of 6./KG6, which they shot down at Walberton, Sussex on the night of 24/25 March when ten enemy aircraft were claimed destroyed by Mosquito night fighters. The 29-year old Hampshire, born in Port Macquarrie, New South Wales and a resident of Peppermint Grove, Western Australia, and Condon had shot down two Ju 88s on 27/28 February 1944 off the southwest coast. On 27/28 March they destroyed Ju 88s 3E+FT of 9./KG 6 and B3+BL of 3./KG54 near Beer and Brewer Isle respectively. On 23/24 April they shot down another Ju 88 into the sea near Swanage and on 28/29 April they probably damaged a Do 217 86 miles off Durrington. On 22/23 May they destroyed a Ju 88S off the Isle of Wight and on 12/13 June they claimed another Ju 88 over the English Channel. Hampshire was a regular officer in the RAAF at the outbreak of war in the Far East and he was commanding 12 Squadron on Ansons and Wirraways when the Japanese attack began. He commanded an RAAF Boston squadron undertaking bombing and strafing sorties over New Guinea in 1942 to July 1943 for which he was awarded a DSO in May. He was then posted to the UK where in December 1943 he took command of 456 Squadron RAAF. A bar to his DSO followed in February 1945. (RAAF)

Right: In February 1944 125 (Newfoundland) Squadron at Valley in Wales began replacing its Beaufighters with the Mosquito NF.XVII. On 11 February Squadron Leader L. W. G. 'Bill' Gill and his navigator Flying Officer D. C. 'Des' Hutchins were in the circuit at Valley when a Blackburn Botha pilot trailing a drogue cable sliced six feet off the starboard wing of their Mosquito. Gill put down safely and three days later the repaired Mosquito was flying again. In April-May 1944 125 (Newfoundland) Squadron claimed ten victories over England. On 4/5 July 1944 Bill Gill flying the Mosquito and Des Hutchins working the AI.Mk.X took off from Hurn at 2220 hours and patrolled off Le Havre under FDT 216 control. They investigated a bogey four miles ahead crossing starboard to port and Hutchins obtained a contact to port, range 4_ miles slightly below their height at 6000 feet. Gill closed to 5000 feet range and obtained a visual on a target, which was turning gently to port. From 150 yards Hutchins with the aid of night glasses identified target as a Do 217 with what appeared to be bombs outboard of the engines. Gill fired two short bursts from 150 yards dead astern, both of which produced strikes on the fuselage. The enemy aircraft bust into flames and as he broke away Gill saw an explosion. He followed the bomber down and gave it a further short burst from 500 yards. It disappeared into cloud at 3000 feet in a very steep spiral dive and shortly afterwards there was a glow on the cloud as the enemy plane hit the sea. (AVM Bill Gill)

Junkers Ju 290 burning on the surface of the sea on 19 February 1944 after a successful *Instep* patrol by 157 Squadron Mosquitoes flown by Flight Lieutenant R. J. Coombs and Flying Officer G. H. Scobie and Flight Lieutenants R. D. 'Dolly' Doleman and Leslie Scholefield. (via Richard Doleman)

Wing Commander C. D. Tomalin DFC AFC (later Air Commodore Tomalin CBE DFC AFC FBIM) CO 605 Squadron May-September 1943 who was a well-known driving champion in pre-war days, about to take off on a *Night Intruder* operation in NF.II UP-L. His navigator on some of his operations in 1943 was 33-year old Robert 'Bob' Campbell Muir DFC who had trained for low level night intruding on Bostons in November 1942 at Twinwoods airfield near Bedford. Muir recalled: 'On 14 June 1943 in NF.II UP-L with Squadron Leader Tomalin we had been patrolling the Teuge and Deelen areas, searching for enemy barges. Finding two, we sprayed them with cannon fire scoring many hits and minor explosions. On turning for home amidst the flak there was an explosion near our tail and an aircraft, plainly German, on fire having been hit we believe by flak meant for us. He must have been tracking us. We refrained from claiming! On 30 August Squadron Leader Tomalin and I were in FB.VI UP-L. Bomber Command stated that reports from their crews claimed that enemy fighters could be clearly seen in the glare of burning cities, so would a Mosquito be missioned to test this out and of course attack the enemy aircraft? We staggered up to 26,000 feet, the utmost height achievable in this aircraft (service ceiling for a fully armed Mosquito). We were dangerously unstable, the air was full of smoke and we could not spot any enemy night-fighters. We experienced slipstreams from our bombers and were obviously a danger to them and ourselves. We decided therefore to return to base. We dropped down about 5000 feet and I set a 'guestimated' course for home and watched intently for any sign of *Gee* (radio beams transmitted as a navigation aid) - the range of which, was greater at high levels so we were told! After about a quarter of an hour I discerned the tiniest of blips and maneuvered the aircraft in all directions to prove it and joyously discovered one, which increased the size of the signal and eventually the second fixing blip appeared'. We were over Belgium! We had been caught in one of those fierce high level winds! My course for Base was unbelievable to Wing Commander Tomalin but to his great credit he accepted and we returned safely to base. In October 1943 Squadron Leader Tomalin and I had completed 35 operations. He received an immediate DFC and I was looking forward to a rest. [However] Wing Commander B. R. O'Bryen Hoare DSO DFC & Bar arrived to take over command from Squadron Leader Tomalin. He asked me to crew with him if he could get special dispensation from Air Ministry, which he did. I did not have the guts to say "NO!" (via Philip Birtles)

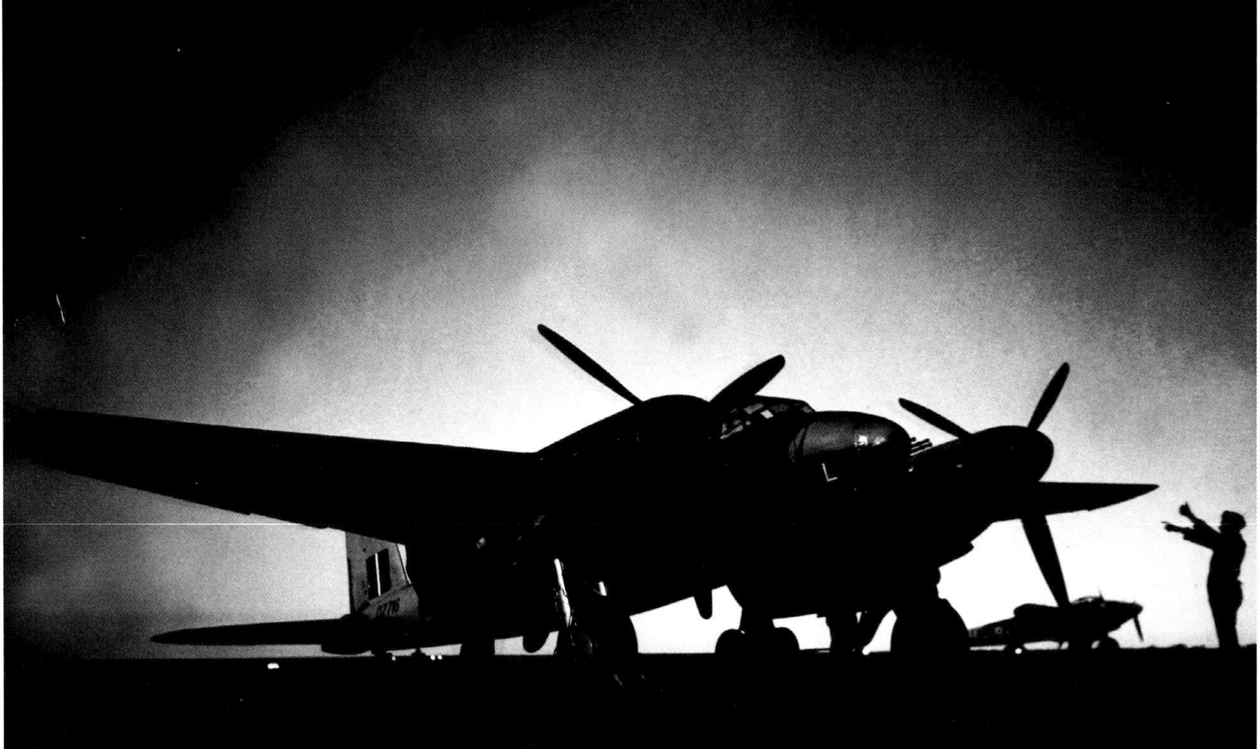

NF.II DZ716/UP-L of 605 Squadron prepares to start engines prior to another night operation over enemy territory. (via Philip Birtles)

NF.II DD739 RX-X of 456 Squadron RAAF in June 1943 during a flight from Middle Wallop. Below the cockpit is a small roundel with an Australian marsupial in red in the middle. DD739 passed to 157 Squadron and on the night of 3/4 July 1943 Flight Lieutenants James G. Benson DFC and Lewis Brandon DFC were flying this aircraft when they shot down a Do 217 at St Trond. (Dutch Holland via Basil McRae)

Another view of DZ659/G, a modified NF.II fitted with AI.Mk.X (US SCR 720/729 *Eleanora*) radar in the universal nose. DZ659/H was powered by two Merlin 21s. (DH)

Leavesden-built NF.36 prototype RL248. The NF.36 was a Night-fighter development of the NF.XXX, with improved AI radar and four 20mm cannon. (DH)

NF.XXX RK953 fitted with AI.Mk.X centimetric radar in a blunt thimble nose radome. This nightfighter development of the NF.XIX first appeared in March 1944 and attained service entry with 219 Squadron three months later. RK953 was one of 26 NF.XXXs delivered between April and June 1945 from the Leavesden works, the Mosquito subsequently seeing frontline service with 151 Squadron until the unit disbanded on 10 October 1946. After a long period in storage, the veteran nightfighter was passed to the RAF's Signals School on 21 August 1950. (DH)

Wing Commander Gordon Slade (right), CO 157 Squadron, with his adjutant (left) and engineering officer (center) at Castle Camps in 1942. Slade had joined the RAF in 1933 and four years later began a career as a test pilot at the A&AEE (Aircraft & Armaments Experimental Establishment) at Martlesham Heath. In September 1941 he was promoted to wing commander and attached to 604 Squadron at Middle Wallop, where he learned the art of nightfighting under the expert tutelage of John Cunningham before taking command of 157 Squadron in December 1941. On 22/23 August 1942 Slade and his radar operator, Pilot Officer Philip Truscott destroyed Do 217E-4 U5+LP of 6./KG2 flown by Deputy *Staffelkapitan* Oberleutnant Hans Walter Wolff over Worlingworth. By October 1944 Slade had taken command of 169 Squadron and in April 1945 he was promoted to group captain. After the war he resumed his career as a RAF test pilot, before joining the Fairey Group in 1965. He died in October 1981. (Brian Whitlock Blundell Collection)

NF.II DD723 briefly joined 85 Squadron in September 1942 at Hunsdon before suffering some damage. Soon after it was fitted with experimental Lancaster type power units with underslung 'chin' radiators and AI nose mounted radar and tested by Rolls-Royce at Hucknall during the latter part of 1943. Marshalls at Cambridge returned it to the RAF after overhaul in 1944. (BAe via GMS)

B.VI HP850 of 157 Squadron, which was transferred to 100 Group for bomber support operations in August 1944, by which time the squadron had re-equipped with the NF.XIX. (via Philip Birtles)

NF.XIII HK428 was delivered to 29 Squadron at Ford in January 1944 and Flight Sergeant Johnson shot down a Ju 88 on 17/18 June 1944. In October HK428 was badly damaged and after repair by de Havillands it was sent to the Central gunnery School at Catfoss. It was eventually SOC on 16 September 1946. The thimble nose houses the AI.Mk.VIII radar developed by the Telecommunications Research Establishment (TRE) and built by Ekco and GEC, entering service in 1942. AI.Mk.VIII had a wavelength of 10cm and a frequency in the region of 3 GHz and had a maximum range of 6½ miles. (DH)

85 Squadron at Hunsdon in 1943. Flight Lieutenant C. P. Reed DFC is 5th from left seated and Squadron Leader Edward Bunting DFC is 6th from left. (via Andrew Long)

Battle of Britain veteran Michael Hugh Constable-Maxwell (pilot) and his navigator Sergeant (later Flight Lieutenant DFC) John Quinton. They had teamed up in October 1941 when they joined 604 Squadron on Mosquito night fighters. Constable-Maxwell had gained the first of his three confirmed Mosquito victories on 30 March 1943 on 264 Squadron when he destroyed a He 111. His second victory in a Mosquito followed on 15/16 May 1944 when he destroyed a Ju 188 off the Isle of Wight. On 2/3 July 1944 Constable-Maxwell and John Quinton destroyed a Ju 88 and followed this on 8/9 July with the destruction of another Ju 88 over France. Constable-Maxwell returned to the UK in December 1947 and in April 1948 took leave of absence to go to Ampleforth Monastery as a novice, where he remained for the next four years. He returned to the RAF in November 1952, retiring from the service in June 1964. On 13 August 1951 while on a navigation course at 228 OCU at RAF Leeming in North Yorkshire, John Quinton was on board a Wellington detailed for an airborne interception exercise with a Martinet. During the exercise the Martinet and Wellington collided over the hamlet of Hauxwell near Richmond. The force of the impact caused the Wellington to break up and go out of control. Quinton picked up the only parachute within reach and clipped it on to ATC Cadet Derek Coates' harness. Pointing to the ripcord Quinton indicated that the cadet should jump. A large hole then appeared in the side of the Wellington flinging the cadet clear. Coates was the only survivor from the six men aboard the Wellington and he survived to tell the story of Quinton's unselfish act of bravery. Both men in the Martinet also died. For his heroism John Quinton was awarded the George Cross. Each year the Quinton Cup is awarded to the most efficient ATC Squadron in the Northwest region. Derek Coates emigrated to Perth, Australia. John Quinton lies buried in Leeming village cemetery along with three other members of the Wellington crew. (via Ron MacKay)

Crews of 456 Squadron RAAF at Colerne on 23 September 1943. L-R: Flying Officer M. N. Austin; Warrant Officer A. S. McEvoy; Flying Officer Richard S. Williams; Flight Lieutenant Gordon 'Peter' Panitz DFC; Pilot Officer G. Gatenby; Flight Sergeant A. J. Keating (kneeling); Pilot Officer J. M. Fraser; Flying Officer J.W. Newell; Pilot Officer A. M. Abbey and Flying Officer S. D. P. Smith. On the night of 14/15 May 1944 Flying Officer A. S. McEvoy and Flying Officer M. N. Austin destroyed a Ju 188A2. As CO of 464 Squadron RAAF Wing Commander Panitz was KIA on 31 August 1944 attacking targets in France. (RAAF)

85 Squadron line up. Back row, left to right: Flying Officer Robert O. Symon; Flying Officer Cleaver; Flight Lieutenant T. J. 'Tim' Molony, Adjutant, Flying Officer Bill Skelton DSO DFC*; Flight Lieutenant Branse Burbridge DSO DFC*, Squadron Leader F. S. 'Gon' Gonsalves DFC; Squadron Leader W. K. Davison DFC; Wing Commander John Cunningham DSO* DFC*; Captain Tarald Weisteen RNWAF; u/k; u/k; Flying Officer Ginger Farrell; Flying Officer Hugh Brian Thomas. Front row left to right: Flying Officer Custance; u/k; u/k; Squadron Leader C. F. 'Jimmy' Rawnsley. DFC DFM*; u/k.

Left: Pilot's instrument panel and stick in the cockpit of a B.35 RS709 the former G-MOSI, which was flown to the Wright-Patterson AFB from the UK in October 1984 and subsequently painted to represent NS519/P, a 653rd Bomb Squadron 25th Bomb Group PR.XVI for permanent display at the Air Force Museum. The instrument panels are coated in either plain matt black paint or a baked-on 'crackle' black to reduce reflections. (GMS) **Right:** Cockpit of NF.XIII HK524 of 29 Squadron in 1944 with the navigator's AI.Mk.VII radar on right. On the night of 7/8 August 1944 Flying Officer W.W. Provan and his radar operator, Warrant Officer Nichol destroyed a Bf 110 at Melun, west of Orly flying this Mosquito. (Frank Pringle)

Far Left: Wing Commander Paul V. Davoud DSO DFC and Flying Officer Keith Reynolds of 418 (City of Edmonton) Squadron RCAF. Davoud commanded the squadron from June 1943 to January 1944. (MAA)

Near Left: Headstone marker for Lieutenant Joseph Francis Black USN and Lieutenant Thomas Newkirk Aiken USN who as killed flying with 68 Squadron on 14 November 1944. (via Ian McLachlan)

L-r: Lieutenant Joseph Francis Black USN who as killed flying with 68 Squadron on 14 November 1944. (via Ian McLachlan)

Lieutenant Thomas Newkirk Aiken USN who as killed flying with 68 Squadron on 14 November 1944. (via Ian McLachlan)

Flying Officer Brian Williams of 605 Squadron, pilot of a very successful Intruder sortie over Holland on the night of 4/5 May 1943. (Brian Williams)

NF.II nightfighter Mosquito in all-black finish. (via Derek Smith) **Below,Left:** Flying Officer Michael John Gloster DFC* who with radar operator Pilot Officer James F. Oswald DFC*, claimed three He IIIs in one hour over the North African desert flying a Beaufighter VIf with 255 Squadron in December 1942 and seven more kills, two in North Africa and five over Western Europe in 1944 on Mosquito NF.XVII/XXXs with 219 Squadron. **Below:** Flying Officer (later Squadron Leader) Douglas Haig Greaves DFC* who claimed five victories in North Africa and the Mediterranean with radar operator Warrant Officer F. Milton Robbins DFC* while with 255 Squadron in 1942-43 and four more off the English coast flying Mosquito NF.XVII/XXXs in 25 Squadron in 1944.

Officers and aircrew of 418 'City of Edmonton' Squadron RCAF, Fighter Command at Hunsdon, Hertfordshire in October 1944. Center with Sid Seid's dog 'Mostitch' is Squadron Leader Russ Bannock DFC. The FB.VI Mosquito is FB.VI TH-J *J-Johnny* with 23 confirmed kills on the forward fuselage and the unofficial 'City of Edmonton' crest on the crew door. Below the door is Squadron Leader Ted Johnson DFC who destroyed the squadron's 100th air to air victory, a Ju 88 over Hailfingen with Flight Lieutenant Noel Gibbons DFC. (via Jerry Scutts)

Aircrew of 604 'County of Middlesex' Squadron in 1944 with Squadron Leader Dennis Chetwynd Furse DFC and Flight Lieutenant J. L. 'Johnny' Downs DFC to his right and flying NF.XIII fighters with the Universal radar nose.

Flight Lieutenant Johnny Downs DFC (left) with Squadron Leader Dennis Furse DFC who joined 604 'County of Middlesex' Squadron at Scorton in the winter of 1943 at Hurn airfield in May 1944. The crew were engaged in *Intruder* flights at night over Germany, which was 604 Squadron's major role at the time. The squadron was the first night fighter squadron into Germany after D-Day. Furse commanded the advance party (about six aircraft and crews) into France to Cherbourg/Maupertus about mid July 1944 (US Sector). On 6 August 1944 the whole squadron were assembled at Picauville, still in the US Sector. In September 1944 the squadron withdrew to Predannack, Cornwall to rest and re-equip returning to France, Lille/Vendeville from January to April 1945. Squadron Leader Furse and Downs stayed with the squadron throughout this period with Furse as 'A' Flight Commander. During his time with 406 ('Lynx') Squadron RCAF and 604 Squadrons Squadron Leader Furse claimed four victories.

Wearing large leather gauntlets, Wing Commander Vashon James 'Pop' Wheeler (he was born in 1898) DFC* MC* Order of St. Stanislaus (Russia) was CO 157 Squadron from 29 December 1942 to August 1943. He is seen here at Bradwell Bay with his navigator Flight Lieutenant Borridge. 'Pop' Wheeler had seen active service during World War I as a second lieutenant in the Rifle Brigade between 1916-18, and in 1919 was part of the ill-fated British Expedition to Russia in support of Czarist forces opposing the communist revolution. Learning to fly during the 1920s and duly becoming an airline pilot, Wheeler's multi-engine experience came in extremely handy when he was initially posted onto transport aircraft with the outbreak of war in Europe in September 1939. After completing a tour on Ansons, he flew a further 71 combat sorties on Hurricanes, Havocs and Beaufighters with 85 Squadron. He claimed two enemy aircraft destroyed in early 1941 whilst with this unit. Wheeler completed a further 29 defensive patrols with 157 Squadron, before flying the unit's first *Intruder* operation on 23 March 1943. On 26 February 1944 Wheeler took command of Lancaster-equipped 207 Squadron, 'Pop' flying on every operation the unit undertook until he was killed in action on the night of 22/23 March 1944 on a sortie to Frankfurt. It was his 158th operational flight. (Brian Whitlock Blundell Collection

Flying Officers Desmond T. Tull DFC and Peter J. Cowgill DFC of the Fighter Interception Unit are here flying NF.XVII HK360 accompanied by captured Me 410 TF209 (10259), which was used for comparison trials and is being flown by Squadron Leader J. Howard Williams and Flying Officer F. J. MacRae. HK360 came off the Leavesden production lines as a NF.II but it was flown to Marshalls at Cambridge for the fitting of SCR 720 radar and became an NF.XVII. SCR 720 (British designation AI.Mk.X) was developed by the Radiation Laboratory), Massachusetts Institute of Technology and built by the Western Electric Company. This radar entered RAF service in 1943. AI.Mk.X had a wavelength of 10cm with a range of 8 to 10 miles. HK360 was one of the first NF.XVIIs to enter service with 456 Squadron at Fairwood Common in January 1944. On 17 April the aircraft joined the FIU at Ford, which used Mosquitoes and other aircraft for test purposes and operational trials. During May-July 1944 Tull and Cowgill shot down four enemy aircraft and got one probable over Germany when they operated with 219 Squadron and they then destroyed four more enemy aircraft flying the Mosquito XIX and Beaufighter VI with the FIU, September-October 1944. On 18/19 December Tull and Cowgill, now with 85 Squadron, failed to return. Tull accidentally rammed Bf 110 G9+CC of Stab IV/NJG1 flown by Hauptmann Adolph Breves who was coming into land at Düsseldorf airfield. A large part of one of the wings of the 110 was torn off but Breves managed to land the aircraft without further damage. Tull and Cowgill were both killed. HK360 was SOC as obsolete on 31 January 1946.

NF.XXX MM813 of 219 (Mysore) Squadron undergoing routine servicing at Wittering in 1945. On 18/19 April 1944 Warrant Officer R. F. D. Bourke of 488 Squadron was flying this aircraft (then a XVIII) when he shot down a Ju 88 at sea. On 18/19 November 1944 Flight Lieutenant John Cyril Edwin Atkins DFC and Flying Officer D. R. Mayo of 219 Squadron were flying this aircraft when they destroyed a Ju 87. The aircraft next to MM813 is MM806.

Chapter 5

LNSF

Press on regardless - never mind the weather
Press on regardless - it's a piece of cake
Press on regardless - we'll all press on together
'Cos you're bound to see the Dummer or the Steinhuder Lake

(Tune "Poor Joey")

"Nuisance" raiding had begun in April 1943, and was so successful that by the summer a Light Night Striking Force (LNSF) of Mosquitoes was established. Mosquitoes went in up to an hour before the main attack, descended slowly, and released their *Spoof* cargoes of two 500lb bombs, two target indicators (TIs) or "sky markers" (parachute flares to mark a spot in the sky if it was cloudy), and bundles of "Window." German fighter controllers sent up their night fighters, so that when the "heavies" did arrive, the *Nachtjagdgeschwaders* were on the ground having to refuel. 139 Squadron first tried *Spoof* raiding on the night of 18 November 1943 when flares and bombs were dropped on Frankfurt. Various plain colors with starbursts of the same or a different color prevented the enemy from copying them.[133] On 26 November three Mosquitoes of 139 Squadron, flying ahead of the Main Force, scattered Window on the approaches to Berlin and returned to drop bombs.

692 Squadron was formed at Graveley on 1 January 1944. In the 12 months January-December 1944 five more Mosquito squadrons joined 8 Group.[134] Bennett wanted only experienced pilots with 1000 hours total time for his squadrons. Group Captain T. G. "Hamish" Mahaddie DSO DFC AFC, SASO at Group HQ in Huntingdon, was tasked with recruiting volunteer aircrew from the Main Force bomber groups. Sometimes pilots literally came knocking at his door. In June 1944 Philip Back and "Bing" Bingham, fed up flying Blenheims at Spittlegate and itching to fly Mosquito night-fighters, hitchhiked down the Great North Road to his office at 8 (PFF) Group HQ in Huntingdon. Back was educated at Harrow School and had joined the RAF in 1942 on a six-month university course, reading engineering at Corpus Christi College, Cambridge. He and Bingham found Castle Hill House, entered, and knocked on a door marked "Group Captain H. Mahaddie, SASO." Philip Back recalls:

> "There sat an imposing fellow with many 'gongs'. We saluted. He looked up over his glasses and said, 'What do you want?'
>
> "I said, 'We want a job Sir.'
>
> "'You'd better sit down. How many night flying hours?' he asked.
>
> "'Thirty!' I said.
>
> "Thirty? You mean 300, don't you?'
>
> "I simply said, 'Yes Sir!'
>
> "He asked us what was going on. When we had finished he said he would see what he could do. Two weeks later we were posted to 1655 Mosquito Training Unit at Warboys!"

Pilots and navigators were normally put in a large room and told to pair off. Philip Back had met and crewed up with 23-year-old Pilot Officer Derek Tom Newell Smith DFC (who had flown a first tour on Lancasters on 61 Squadron) after both men did a dinghy drill session in the Leys Swimming School at Cambridge. Back recalls: "on the bus back to base he said, 'We're crewed up?' I looked at his 'gong' and said, 'You bet we are.' We became an entity in the air and would fly all our ops together."

Derek Smith did not learn until much, much later that Philip Back had only 30 hours night flying experience, but the navigator never had the slightest cause to doubt his pilot's ability. "He was a natural who handled the 'Mossie' with a skill well beyond his experience and always did the right thing in our more 'hairy' moments."[135] Derek Smith, adds:

"There was something special about the bomber Mosquito pilot/observer relationship. On my Lancaster tour I flew in a very close-knit crew, which was all-sergeant until near the end, but I never formed any lasting relationship as close as I was to have with Phil. In the bomber 'Mossie' we sat side-by-side, almost shoulder-to-shoulder, sometimes for five or more hours, with a lot of decidedly unfriendly citizens down below for most of the time. They were no friendlier to the 'heavies' and although we relied as much on each other, we had so much more space and a little bit of the aircraft, which was ours. In the 'Mossie' every move, which was made was seen by the other, so maybe it served to weld us closer together as a unit."

Mosquito bombers flew a series of operations to German cities in March. On some nights, including 18/19 and 22/23 March, when Frankfurt was raided by the heavies, and Berlin on 24/25 March they acted as diversions for the Main Force effort with raids on German night-fighter airfields. The night of the 30/31st fell during the moon stand-down period for the Main Force, but the raid on Nürnburg, destination of 795 RAF heavy bombers and 38 Mosquitoes, went ahead as planned. The Met forecast indicated that there would be protective high cloud on the outward route when the moon would be up. A Met Flight Mosquito carried out a reconnaissance and reported that the protective cloud was unlikely to be present, and that there could be cloud over the target, which would prevent accurate ground marked bombing, but the raid went ahead. Jim Marshallsay DFC, an experienced PFF pilot in 627 Squadron at Oakington, was aloft in a Mosquito this night as a "Window Opener" for the heavies with navigator Sergeant Nigel "Nick" Ranshaw by his side as usual. Nestling in the bomb bay were four 500lb bombs. By the time the two airmen had joined 627 Squadron in November 1943 they had flown 14 LNSF trips in 139 Squadron, beginning with the big Hamburg raid of July 1943. Marshallsay recalls:

"Sometimes just a handful of Mossies would set out for the big German cities, usually in the 'moon period' when it was much too bright for the 'heavies'. If, on these trips the weather was cloudy, it was possible to take off, climb into cloud, travel to Germany, bomb the target on ETA and return to base, having seen nothing but the runway lights at base on take-off and landing. If however the night as clear, moonlight and stars, then you could get a hot reception from predicted flak and from the massive searchlight cones, especially at 'Whitebait', the code-name for Berlin. If you saw one of the attacking Mossies coned over the target, you took your chance, slipped in, bombed and slipped out again while the poor unfortunate in the cone was dazzled and blasted. When you got back for interrogation, if you had been the one in the cone, you got no sympathy from the other crews, just a lot of banter like, 'Brave lads, taking the flak from us.'

"The 30 March operation had started quite normally. We were airborne at 2300 hours. 'Window Opening' meant that we had to be over the target before the first of the Marker aircraft and scatter 'Window' to confuse the radar defenses. The Lancs of 7 Squadron had taken off from Oakington about half an hour before us. The track to the target was past Brussels, then almost East between Koblenz and Bonn, on the so-called 'long leg', then south to Nuremberg. As we turned onto this 'long leg' we realized that something was going badly wrong. The moon was much too bright for the heavies. The expected cloud cover was not there.[136] The main force was leaving persistent condensation trails, so there was a great white road in the air, leading into Germany. Combats soon broke out below us. As this was our 38th trip we knew what was happening to the heavies. First a long burst of tracer from the night fighter, then a ripple of flame from the wings of the Lanc or Halifax. A short interval — then a massive explosion and fire on the ground. Nick logged the first few crashes, but after we had seen 16 go down in 6 minutes, he stopped, preferring to use his time and eyes searching for fighters. We later learned that over 50 heavies had gone down on the 'long leg.'[137]

"Nuremberg, when we reached it, was covered in cloud.[138] We threw out our 'Window', dropped our bombs and circled to watch the attack develop, but little could be seen except for a few Wanganui flares. Nick said 'we're going straight home' and that is what we did. We turned the aircraft's nose towards Oakington and left at a great pace, landing at base at 03.17 hours, a trip of 4 hours 17 minutes. After interrogation we had our 'operational egg,' and as we left the mess to go to our beds, the first of the 7 Squadron Lancs were circling to land. The cloud base had lowered and there were flurries of snow in the air. Whereas we had taken the direct route to base from Nuremberg, the heavies were routed North of Paris, to Dieppe, Selsey Bill and home. The difference in flying times shows how fortunate it was to be operating in Mosquitoes."[139]

In April 1944, at 1655 MU at Warboys, Frank Diamond, a navigator who had flown a tour in Stirlings in 15 Squadron at Mildenhall, crewed up with Flight Sergeant Ron Hemming, and they were posted to 571 Squadron at Oakington. Frank Diamond recalls:

"As my pilot was not commissioned we did not share the same Mess. This was unfortunate but it did not interfere with our operational efficiency. We were destined to fly with the Pathfinders and operated alongside a Lancaster squadron with the role of providing some cover for the heavy bombers by creating diversionary trails and raids. Having in mind our wooden airframes, our friends on the Lancs dubbed us 'the model aeroplane club'. Our casualty rate was much lower than theirs was. This was acknowledged later in our tour when it was suggested that we could extend it from 30 to 50, and this we agreed to do. However, predicted flak and radar controlled searchlights were a threat up to 30,000 feet. We took MM156 to Berlin and on our approach a master searchlight caught us. Escape was made impossible as others immediately backed it up and we were held for 12 minutes into and away from the target area. At first we were fearful of being taken by a fighter circling above us. Just after releasing our 4000lb bomb and turning away there was a flak burst close to the tail. It had missed us. As we had now jettisoned our wing fuel tanks and no longer had the bomb, we could increase speed and dash for home. Speaking of the experience the following day I said that as a true veteran of flak in a Stirling over the Ruhr, that it was a bit close but really nothing that bad. However, I agreed to go to the hangar and take a look at the damage. The holes in the tail unit were being repaired. The jagged holes in the skin were being trimmed with a fine-toothed saw and inserts cut to fit and be glued in to place before taping with fabric and painting. I thought no more of it. We never flew that aircraft again but this was of little significance to my mind. The ground staff officer had taken a much closer look and found serious damage to the main structure in addition to the skin and he had ruled it unfit for further use. I now know that the Reaper was denied our scalps by a very narrow margin indeed. If that shell burst had occurred at a mere fraction of a second earlier it would have been a direct hit. And, at age 22 I would not have lived to enjoy a further 60 years or more.'

The German night-fighter force, meanwhile, was far from defeated. On the night of 10/11 June 1944 two Mosquitoes failed to return from a raid by 32 of the aircraft on Berlin. One of the German night-fighter crews on patrol this night was *Oberleutnant* Josef Nabrich and his *Bordfunker*, *Unteroffizier* Fritz Habicht of 3./NJG1, who were flying a cleaned up He 219 *Uhu* with the armor plating and four of the cannons removed especially for hunting Mosquitoes. Nabrich was looking to add to his claims for four bombers destroyed during May, including two in one night (on 24 May). This crew began their patrol high above the Zuider Zee until ground controllers reported the approach of a formation of Mosquitoes at a slightly lower altitude. Habicht looked at his *SN-2* radar display and directed Nabrich to reverse course towards a Mosquito flying east at high speed. Over Osnabrück the He 219 crew obtained visual contact and Nabrich closed to within firing range. He opened up with a short burst from the He 219's wing cannon. The starboard engine of the Mosquito[140] immediately burst into flames and started down in a spiral, out of control. Before Nabrich could attack again the Mosquito's bomb load exploded, and the blast caused the *Uhu* to stall. Nabrich finally managed to recover just above the cloud layer. Only pieces of the Mosquito were found, but the crew had baled out immediately after the first attack, convinced that a new anti-aircraft weapon and not a night-fighter had shot them down. Both men survived and were made PoW.

This same night a B.XVI[141] of 571 Squadron flown by Flight Lieutenant Joe Downey DFM was shot down returning from Berlin by *Hauptmann* Ernst-Wilhelm Modrow of I./NJG1 flying a He 219 *Uhu* "Owl" for his 19th victory. Downey's navigator, Pilot Officer Ronald Arthur Wellington, recalls:

"The attack on our aircraft consisted of a short burst of cannon fire, no more than five rounds. The starboard engine was hit and burst into flames. The aircraft immediately went into an uncontrolled dive and on receiving the order 'Bale Out' I made my exit from the normal escape hatch. At the time Joe was preparing to follow me. Very shortly after pulling the ripcord I saw the aircraft explode beneath me. It is therefore, very unlikely that Joe was alive when the remains of the aircraft crashed onto the dunes near Bergen, a small seaside town three miles northwest of Alkmaar."[142]

Airborne again on the night of 11/12 June, *Oberleutnant* Josef Nabrich and his *Bordfunker*, *Unteroffizier* Fritz Habicht of 3./NJG1, in their He 219 *Uhu* sought more victories as the LNSF sent 33 Mosquitoes to Berlin again as the heavies bombed rail targets in northern France. West of Salzwedel Habicht was able to pick up a Mosquito, so near that he could see it clearly without radar. Nabrich had difficulty getting into a firing position because the Mosquito pilot, Flight Lieutenant O. A. Armstrong RDFM MiD RNZAF of 139 Squadron, was carrying out wild evasive action. Finally, he gave the B.IV two bursts of 20mm cannon and DZ609 went down vertically and exploded seconds later, killing Armstrong and his navigator, Flying Officer G. L. Woolven. Now it was time for Nabrich to have concern. He had made his pursuit at full power, and seconds after the Mosquito went down the port DB603 engine of his He 219 seized. He feathered the propeller and was able to make a single-engine landing at Perleberg. *Generalleutnant* Josef "Beppo" Schmid sent Nabrich and Habicht a congratulatory telegram and a gift of several bottles.[143]

On 28/29 June 230 bombers hit the railway yards at Blainville and Metz for the loss of 18 Halifaxes and two Lancasters (or 8.7 per cent of the force),[144] while 33 Mosquitoes of the LNSF went to Saarbrücken and another ten were despatched to drop 4000lb "Cookies" from 32,000 feet on the Scholven/Buer oil plant in the Ruhr. All the Mosquitoes returned without loss, but Flight Lieutenant David "Russ" Russell and his navigator, Flying Officer "Barks" Barker of 109 Squadron, who had completed a tour in Stirlings and who were on their third Mosquito trip,[145] had a close shave after dropping their "Cookie," as Russell recalls:

"Heading for home at 30,000 feet it was clear and with bright moonlight. At almost one o'clock near Venlo on the German/Dutch border we were feeling relaxed and were trimmed for a gradual fast descent with an hour or so return to base. Suddenly and without warning lines of orange colored 'blobs' flashed past underneath, then gracefully and lazily fell away in the distance - quite fascinating. Shocked, we felt the dull thud of shells striking the Mossie. A fighter must have closed to within a hundred yards or so and attacked from below and dead astern. We must have been the perfect target, silhouetted against the light. Shells crashed between us, cold fluid from the compass got into my boots and poor Barker kicked his legs in the air. I opened up to full power and went into a tearing, climbing turn to starboard toward the attack but with the Mossie shuddering it became more of a sluggish stall turn. Looking around for some cover I could see a few wisps of cloud below us but they were so sparse that the moon shone through in a watery way. After a few more violent turns and looking around hopelessly for any sign of our attacker, who must have overshot, I leveled out hoping that we had shaken him off but the thud and clatter of shell strikes began again. This time our attacker seemed closer. He really 'caned' us. I responded like a scalded cat, turning toward him with full power and varying my height at the same time. After what seemed an age I leveled out cautiously, weaved and looked around, wondering if our tormentor was standing off to have another go. I was frustrated at not being able to make out any sign of him. We were still at about 23,000 feet and speed was now of the essence so I stuck the nose down and scarpered at about 400 or so. Either he had run out of ammunition or thought we had 'had it' and left us to our fate.

"I reduced speed and we assessed our damage. The radio and compass and the gyro were out of action and the port engine felt a little rough. There was the possibly that our fuel tanks were damaged but all the gauges seemed normal and all aircraft controls appeared OK. The intercom was still functioning. No physical damage to either of us but our real annoyance was, 'Why us?' I tried in vain to feather the port propeller so I decided to use the power for as long as possible. A windmilling or dead propeller may well have been the worst choice, particularly in view of the distance to cover. We set course for Woodbridge and hoped that the weather had improved. A feeling of calm after the storm now set in and with it reaction to the exertion of sheer survival against an unseen enemy. Poor Barks; he had just had to sit there hoping and I'd like to think, trusting in me! The adrenaline uplift and feeling of elation and achievement in beating the odds loosened our tongues on the return home.

"Crossing the Dutch coast at about 20,000 feet we received a farewell gesture of light flak, the tracer rising slowly and then increasing in speed as it neared us before falling away. I reduced power slightly to ease the loading on the port engine and we had a good look around. Weather conditions and visibility were good with 3-4/10ths broken cloud to the South but complete cloud cover was forecast at base. I decided therefore to head for Manston airfield in Kent, which like Woodbridge had three very long runways and grass undershoot and overshoot areas for emergencies such as ours. With some relief we made a straight-in approach in a gentle descent but at 16,000 feet flames started in the port engine cowling. Again feathering proved useless so I cut the fuel and the ignition off, reduced the revs and activated the fire extinguisher, all to no avail. Ditching was a possibility and so the roof panel was jettisoned but without radio and my own firm reluctance, I assured Barks that ditching was the last thing I intended. I was confident we would make the airfield and we could always bale out over land but the fire appeared to be gaining and spreading back over the wing and the inner wing tanks and control was beginning to fall off with a tendency to increase the rate of descent. Not trusting the hydraulics and with no flaps I advised Barker that we would land wheels-up to give us a better chance of getting out through the roof and away more quickly. At about 2000 feet I told him to fire off the colors of the day. Despite a marked increase in roughness on the closed down port engine I felt confident of hitting the threshold. At around 1000 feet and having crossed the coast we could see rooftops below from the glare of our burning aircraft. Final approach was made at about 500 feet with elevator control virtually non-existent and maximum trim. It was with an almost casual feeling of anti-climax that we glided, or fell the remaining few feet at about 160/170.

"We must have touched down on the grass undershoot area. Skidding and bumping along, our speed carried us to the threshold of the tarmac runway where the Mossie stopped suddenly, broke up and jack-knifed with the tail end of the fuselage folding forward, the tail-plane ending up against the trailing edge of the mainplane. Although my straps were secure they were not locked and I pitched forward, pranging my forehead on the screen frame. We appeared to be engulfed in fire and Barks left through the roof hatch. Dazed and my left foot jammed by the rudder, I thought about my new escape boots and was determined not to leave without them. Eventually I freed my foot and I clambered through the roof onto the starboard wing. It was hot and surrounded by glaring fire. I turned and escaped through a gap between the nose and the starboard engine. Jumping off the wing into darkness as the fire and ambulance crews ran toward me, all I could see behind was the huge bonfire of the poor old Mossie."14[6]

On D-Day Pilot Officer Ralph Wood RCAF was on a train heading for 1655 MTU Warboys. As a Flight Sergeant navigator Wood had flown 24 ops in Whitley and Halifax bombers July 1941-25 June 1942 and survived a terrible crash on a training exercise on 28 June which wrote off the Halifax in which he was flying. After a fortnight's sick leave he returned to ops, flew three more, and was credited with a full tour. Commissioned, he married his fiancée Phyl in Canada and returned to England to complete a second tour:

"I asked to be posted to a Mosquito bomber squadron and my strategy paid off. At Warboys I ran into Andy Lockhart, an old school chum from Moncton. We had gone to school together, worked together at Eatons on Saturdays and eventually joined the RCAF about the same time. Andy was selected as pilot material, trained as such, and kept in Canada as an instructor until now. While in Canada he earned the AFC for exceptional work while fulfilling his duties there. We were delighted at this chance meeting. Andy, about to do his first tour, would like to have me as his navigator because of my practical experience. I, in turn, would love to have him as my experienced pilot. Having earned the AFC sort of placed him high in my rating system. The only snag was that Andy had a RAF navigator, brought over from training in Canada. Now, fate stepped in and this navigator was told that he would have to stay on for more training, which he hadn't received in Canada. This consisted of a course in the use of the *Gee* Box, a navigational aid, and a bomb-aimer's course. Inwardly, Andy and I were delighted at this turn of events and so began the saga of the *Moncton Express* with the team of Lockhart and Wood.

"A month at 1655 MTU and we headed for our new squadron, 692, at Gravely, near Cambridge. We shared this station with 35 Pathfinder Squadron, which was flying Lancasters. A friendly rivalry existed between these two squadrons, especially when we were both frequenting the same local pub or the officer's mess. While our Mosquitoes roamed the German skies in all kinds of weather, the heavies (Lancasters and Hallybags) were more particular about when they went aloft. We took special delight in provoking the gentlemen who flew the heavies by singing our song, '*We Fly Alone*' in the pubs we both frequented. Our rewritten lyric of the jukebox favorite, '*I'll Walk Alone*'.

"Our Mosquito was an unarmed night-bomber. We had no guns, only our speed and manoeuverability to protect us. From Spruce to Bomber! The pilot and navigator sat side by side in this 'Wooden Wonder,' or 'Termite's Delight' as it was sometimes called. The pilots had a steel plate under their seats to protect them. Navigators had an extra sheet of plywood. We all had a nagging fear that our jewels might be shot off. The moral seemed to be that pilots make better fathers. I wore a Mae West (an inflatable life jacket) and a harness to which I would attach my parachute, which was kept on the floor near my feet. I sat on the dinghy, the little lifeboat all done up in a neat, square package. The rubber sucked out your piles if fear didn't. The hooks on my harness were snapped onto the dinghy damps. If I jumped, the dinghy came with me. With the parachute on my chest and the dinghy on my ass, I wonder if I could ever have squeezed through that small escape hatch. There we were, as snug as two peas in a pod. This was no place for claustrophobia. My lapboard, charts, maps and Dalton computer completed the picture. With a 4000-pounder aboard and the Mosquito tanked up for a 1200-mile sortie, the worst moment for the crew was take-off. Fused or unfused, a bomb of this size might go off on heavy impact.

"We were now part of the 'Light Night Striking Force,' and as such, flew quickly through any adverse weather to complete our task. As many as seventy Mosquitoes would each unload their 'Cookie', 4000lb of a high explosive! And this could happen every night of the week - in all kinds of soupy weather that kept the Halifaxes and Lancasters grounded. One of the dodges the 'Mossies' used to baffle the *Nazi* defense system was this; a few aircraft flew a feint at a certain target and fooled the German radar into thinking it was a raid in strength, while the main bomber force hit another city hundreds of miles away. 'Our first Mosquito op was on 6 July. Andy and I took off for Gelsenkirchen expecting anything and everything. It was an interesting trip (my 28th op of the war) and Andy's first over enemy territory. I think he thoroughly enjoyed it. On return to base we learned that we had picked up a bird on the way and it remained there firmly lodged inside the wing as it made a hole a foot wide on impact. We also brought back a piece of flak. Andy informed the intelligence officer at our debriefing that he had steered into some searchlights to see what effect they would have. When I regained my breath I pointed out very strongly that once caught in searchlights it was difficult to escape at high altitudes, and fighters would also have an idea as to the positioning of the Mosquito - meaning us. We went to bed, tired but happy, as the first trip - usually the worst mentally - was a success.

"The 'Light Night Striking Force' of Mosquitoes raided Berlin 170 times, 36 of these on consecutive nights. The Mossie could carry as big a bomb load to Berlin as the U.S. Flying Fortress, which needed an 11-man crew. The Mosquito flew so often to Berlin that its raids were known as the Berlin Express, and the different routes there and back, as platform one, two and three. On 7 July we went right to the Snake's home. We were quite keyed up too but were not letting on to each other. A typical trip to Berlin would be a feint attack on a couple of cities on the way to our target and throwing out 'Window' to foul up the radar. Once over Berlin we were usually caught in a huge cone of searchlights, so blinding Andy couldn't read the instruments. 'Are we upside-down or not?' he'd ask. I'd look down at the bombs exploding below and assure him that we were right side up. As the anti-aircraft crap seemed to surround us, Andy would throw our *Moncton Express* around the skies trying desperately to get out of the searchlights. On three occasions we lost an engine about now and had to limp home, as one set of searchlights passed us on to another set, and so on, until they ran out of lights. When over the target, we'd bomb and get out as fast as we could. This was when I'd sit in my seat, the blood draining out of my face and my stomach in tight knots. Jesus, this could be it, I thought. And after tight moments like this I'd say, 'Andy, pass the beads'.

"The trip was successful, but packed with excitement. As we did our bombing run into the center of Berlin our starboard engine seemed to catch fire. Andy feathered it immediately in case of fire spreading. We finished our run, dropped our cookie, and were immediately coned by a great number of searchlights. After five minutes we got out without damage. On the return journey we were coned and shot at again in the Hamburg district. Finally we reached the English coast and landed at the nearest airdrome with about 20 gallons of petrol left. We returned to base the following day after our engine was repaired. We have now been over the hottest target in Germany and feel quite good about it. One of our crews failed to return."

The operational use of the Mosquito bomber had forced the *Nachtjagd* to reconsider the *Wilde Sau*[147] method to hunt the high-performance aircraft at high altitude with Fw 190A-5s and A-6s and Bf 109Gs with *Neptun* AI radar and a long range fuel tank. *Oberleutnant* Fritz Krause, a *Staffelkapitan* in the experimental I./NJGr10 at Berlin-Werneuchen commanded by *Hauptmann* Friedrich Karl Müller,[148] whose main task this was, took off at 0040 hours on 8 July in "*Weisse Elf*" ("White 11"), a FuG 217 J2 (*Neptun*) equipped Fw 190A-5, and destroyed a Mosquito near Brandenburg as his only victory in this unit, as he recalls:

> "I was flying over Berlin at a height of 8500 meters when I saw a twin-engined plane flying west caught in the searchlights. I closed in until I was 700 meters above, gave full throttle and dived. I went in too low and opened fire from approximately 200 meters from below and behind and kept firing as I closed. My first shots hit the right motor and an explosion followed. There was a burst of sparks and then a thick white trail of vapor. As I had overshot I had to stop the attack momentarily and found myself on the right, alongside the enemy aircraft, whose cockade and external fuel tanks I saw clearly and so was able to identify it without a doubt as a Mosquito. I fired ESN to draw the attention of the flak and the searchlight to my presence. The enemy 'corkscrewed' in an attempt to evade. Because of the thick 'white flag' of vapor I was able to follow him, although he had already left the searchlight zone in a northwesterly direction. Following the trail, I managed to attack twice more. At the third attack I noticed a further explosion on the right wing and an even stronger rain of sparks. At 2000 meters he disappeared, turning at a flat gliding-angle under me. I did not see the impact on the ground as this was hidden from my angle of view. [149] On my return flight, passing Lake 'Koppeln I could estimate the crash-point as 60-70km NW of Berlin. When I returned to base a report had

already reached them about the crash of a burning enemy aircraft west of Kürytz. My own plane was covered in oil from the damaged Mosquito."[150]

On 10 July Andy Lockhart and Pilot Officer Ralph Wood RCAF were on the "Milk Run" again – Berlin or bust. Wood recalls:

"Of course, we had to get coned and shot at again over the target. As if that wasn't enough, the boys of Heligoland had a crack at us, too. The trip was exciting and a good one, but we lost a very fine crew. The pilot was our CO, a New Zealander. They think he got it near Cologne.[151] Andy and I saw a lot of action in that direction as we passed it. Andy liked the choice of names I used for the Hun when he let us have a barrage of flak. We were still keen and a bit more Berlin minded. We were coned for 9 minutes there this time. On return we just made the English coast and landed with 5 gallons of petrol left. We were getting along fine together and our teamwork was improving. One unusual return from enemy territory, and most satisfying, included a dive beginning at the French coast from 32,000 feet to 10,000 feet reached at Southwold on the English coast. This 88-mile journey was completed in eleven minutes, which was fast, even for a Mosquito. With our Cookie gone, our two 50-gallon drop tanks discarded, and our fuel load pretty well depleted, it wasn't too hard to accomplish this feat. Andy and I were at 25,000 feet completing our air test in preparation for the night's operation, when I happened to look up from my lap table. There was Andy, out cold and slumped over the controls. We were dropping like a lead weight - straight for the ground. My blood drained into my shoes as I managed to place my oxygen mask over his face in time for him to revive and pull the plane out of the dive. Thirty years after the war Andy reminded me of this long-forgotten incident. He told me that afterwards all I said was, 'Do you always take a turn that steeply?'

"Hanover on 14 July was ideal for our job. The target was fairly 'warm', as were places on the way home. However, it was our turn to have a quiet night and flak, searchlights, or fighters did not bother us. In fact, we quite enjoyed ourselves. We all came back to the base without casualties. (The first operation I ever did was to this target in a Whitley in July 1941). Berlin on 15 July on the 'Milk Run' again was my favorite dislike. On the way there, via the Ruhr, we managed to anger the … and they threw up everything they had at us. After what seemed ages, we shook them off and proceeded to the target, where we were fortunate in steering dear of trouble. Coming home, we had a few more taking pot shots at us, but returned to base okay. The fog at base caused us to land at our training station a few miles from base. Looking at our kite the next day we saw several flak holes; one below in front of us; one below and behind us on the bomb-bay doors; and one entered the engine covering underneath. 'A miss is a good as a mile' so here's the next trip.

"On 17 July it was Berlin again - making four out of six trips to the 'Big City'. This was more than I expected. It was a satisfaction to know that they respected our raids. That might be due to the fact that we carried a Cookie with us. If it didn't give them a headache, it would at least keep them awake! One lad on the way in was coned in about 100 searchlights and was getting enough shrapnel in his direction to sink the *Queen Mary*. The poor guy stooged over Hamburg by mistake. (I'd have to watch that; it might have been us!). At the target the boys were coned here and there but no flak was shot up the beams, which indicated that enemy fighters were present. At interrogation next morning we learned that those fighters chased a few of the boys persistently. Joe's halo (that's mine) must have been working overtime! It was a good trip for us, though. We were on again that night and we hoped it would be a short trip this time. 'No luck. It was Berlin again. The trip proved quite nerve-racking, as we were both on edge all the time due to not being able to get enough sleep and working rather hard lately. We were first over the target and got coned as we waited for the markers to fall. As we let our cookie drop, the markers dropped beside our bomb burst. Andy threw the kite around in every direction to get out of the searchlights. At one time he nearly stalled her and thought we were upside-down. I told him I could still see the searchlights by looking down, so we must be right side up. On the way out we were nearly coned again over Magdeburg. Andy was a little too quick for them this time and we returned home without further trouble, definitely all in and slightly fed up. Our leave on the 21st would certainly be welcome. So far we had been to Berlin five times out of seven trips."

By mid-July 1944 Pilot Officer George Cash, a 571 Squadron navigator, had been on ops for nearly a year, and "maybe [had] become somewhat 'flak happy' and blasé about things":

"During training and flying time, I had formed quite firm friendships with various fellows. Friends had gone on different postings from mine and we'd parted. Crews on ops had gone missing or had been killed. One was saddened for a short time but life went on and they went out of mind; that was the way of things. Like many others, I suppose, I thought that nothing would ever happen to me and that I would just go on until the end of the war, or until such time that I felt like packing up.

"On the evening of 18/19 July when my pilot, Squadron Leader Terry "Doddy" Dodwell and I went into briefing, I had no undue feelings of trepidation. Certainly not like the 'butterflies' that I had when I first flew on ops. Experience and knowledge of what to expect helped to ally ones fears, although, however experienced a man was I don't think that any airman could truthfully say that he did not feel some apprehension before setting out on a mission. At briefing I saw that 'A' Flight were going to the Ruhr and 'B' Flight to Berlin, and so I began to get out the charts for the Ruhr. However I noticed our names were not on the 'A' flight list and when I told 'Doddy' he said he had swapped with another crew and we were going to Berlin instead. A momentary cold shiver went down my spine! It was said that you did not volunteer for anything, unless you were mad, or going 'hunting'. If in the line of duty, you were detailed for a hazardous mission that was one thing, but you did not 'stick your neck out' and ask for trouble. For the first time in 50 odd trips, I had a premonition of doom.

"At dispersal Doddy was checking the instruments and running up the engines when there was a magneto drop on the port engine and so we had to clamber out and send for the flight van to take us around the drome to the reserve aircraft, *V for Victor* MM136. We settled and after hurried checks took off after the others. As we crossed the enemy coast, we began to siphon the fuel from the drop tanks and we settled at our operational height, 28,000 feet.

"Near Arnhem, a sudden stream of tracer shot past us announcing the presence of a night fighter. Doddy took vigorous evasive action never easy with a bomb load and for a few hectic minutes that seemed like an age, we ran the gauntlet of what we thought were two Ju 88s. We felt a few thuds in the fuselage but there did not appear to be any serious damage. At this point Doddy realized that he was losing precious fuel into the slipstream. He had not stopped the siphoning pumps and the tanks were overflowing. I switched them off and neither of us knew how much fuel had been lost. Somehow I wasn't particularly worried. I knew deep down that we wouldn't be needing it anyway.

"At the turning point in our route which was to take us on a dog-leg to Stendal, the starting point for the bombing run we decided to fly straight there to make up for all the lost time. I worked out a course to steer and then began to window 'like mad'. Unfortunately the route took us over the flak at Wittingen, which immediately opened up on us. Suddenly we found ourselves in a box of heavy predicted flak with shells bursting all around. Shrapnel rattled down on to the cockpit of the aircraft and we could smell the cordite. Doddy put the aircraft into a steep dive; a chunk of flak smashed through the fuselage and hit the *Gee* set putting it out of action. The evasive action finally took us clear of the flak and on an ETA for Stendal we climbed back to 32,000 feet. On course for the 'Big City' about 15 mins flying time away we could see the TIs going down as the raid began. Over on one side, we could see aircraft coned in searchlights and receiving a warm welcome from the defenses. We had hardly settled on our approach when we too, found ourselves coned. We were blinded by the brilliance of the beams. More evasive action was taken but the searchlights hung on. Doddy began to climb rapidly and just as I was beginning to wonder if we would ever get clear, the beams moved away. Strangely there had been no flak, but such was our relief, that we relaxed our vigilance - we ought to have known better!

"The TIs were now dead ahead, and nose down, gathering speed we were going in. I wrote in my log '0200hours target sighted. Preparing to bomb. "I undid my seat belt, and knelt down to go into the nose of the aircraft. Suddenly there was a thump, thump and a tremendous crump. As I straightened up again I could see that the port engine and wing was a mass of flames. I sat back on my seat and pulled up the flap to the escape hatch and it was then that I realized that I was alone in the aircraft. Doddy had gone out of the top escape hatch. Flames were licking around the side of the cockpit and the aircraft began to go down in a spin. I was pressed into my seat by the 'g' forces and I did what many in similar circumstances must have done - I prayed, 'God help me.'

"The spiralling stopped for some unknown reason; my mind was cool and clear despite the heat in the cockpit. Reaching behind my seat I pulled my parachute towards me, knocking my elbow on the damaged Gee set in the process. The parachute dropped into the escape hatch but fortunately it stuck halfway and I was able to retrieve it and clip it on. At this point I suddenly recalled an escape by a navigator described in the '*Tee-Em*' magazine, and so, instead of going through the navigator's escape hatch I climbed out of the cockpit and rolled on to the starboard wing before being swept away by the slipstream. After three seconds I pulled the release handle on the chute but it did not open so I reached up and pulled the flaps open. There was a clop, a slight jerk and I was floating down with a beautiful white canopy above me. Looking down, I saw the aircraft crash into a field in a blaze. The cookie had not exploded and I thought for a moment what would happen if I drifted down near to the aircraft and it blew up, but I drifted away from the scene. All of a sudden I found myself hanging from a tree in the darkness. I pressed the release button on the harness and fell about 10 feet into some bushes, which broke my fall. All I had were a few minor scratches and I was firmly on 'terra firma.'"[152]

On the night of 20/21 July the LNSF sent 26 Mosquitoes to raid Hamburg. One of the crews was Ralph Wood and Andy Lockhart of 692 Squadron, but as Ralph Wood said:

> "Fate was against our going us. Near Bremen we lost an engine, dropped our cookie and high-tailed it for home as fast as one engine would take us. We arrived back at base okay and found that our glycol had leaked out of the engine. We crossed the drome before landing and shot out the distress signal, which gave us priority in landing. Andy made a wizard one-engine landing (his first in a Mosquito at night). We were now ready to go on a much-needed leave as soon as we awoke."

Ralph Wood and Andy Lockhart's first op upon returning from leave was to Wanna Eickel on 5 August, but only after ops on six successive nights had been scrubbed at the last moment:

> "Wanna Eickel was in the center of the Essen district, a hot spot in Germany. Our halos were working overtime and apart from being coned, we were okay. Some of the boys caught a lot of flak. When we landed at base Andy made his approach with his wheels up. Just before we were due to touch down he opened up the throttle and went around the circuit again. (It gave me six new grey hairs). We went to Cologne three nights later. Everything went like clockwork. The bombing was very concentrated but Andy and I managed to steer clear of most of the opposition. It meant one-fifth of our tour was now finished. It was too good to last. On 10 August we went to Berlin. However, we had a good trip and weren't tampered with. We ran short of juice on the way home so we landed near the coast, refueled and came home later. Nothing much to tell about this trip, but that is always a good sign. As usual, there were plenty of fireworks over there. The night of 12 August was a lovely change as we had a long sea crossing and not too much time over enemy territory. The target was Kiel. It was rather warm too, as they threw up barrages of rockets, which burst too near for comfort. As they were rather demoralizing Andy kept

his eyes on the instruments and I kept mine on the target indicators. We ploughed through the barrage, bombed and headed for home. We had an oil leak in one engine and a flak hole in one wing. It was a good trip and the bombing was accurate.

"Our 13th trip on the 13th of the month was a honey. Everything worked perfectly. The target was Hanover. Our luck had been too good since our leave. It would soon be our turn to attract the searchlights, flak, rockets or fighters. We were in no hurry for it, though. We named our kite the *Moncton Express*. I hoped it was lucky. Two nights later, Berlin was the lucky city. We paid it a short visit with our usual calling cards of 4000lbs. It was a good trip, but we had a bit too much excitement attached to it. In short, our luck wasn't of the high standard it had been since our leave. We were coned for a hell of a long time between Hamburg and Lübeck. No flak came up so I strained my eyes looking for the inevitable fighters while Andy concentrated on getting us out of a cone of from 50 to 100 searchlights. As the night was black, the lights had a fine time with us. It sure made you feel naked! We were next coned over Berlin and again when we were nearing the enemy coast on the way home. I saw a fighter, but he evidently didn't see us. When we landed at base all our petrol gauges registered zero. And so ended another trip to the 'Big City'.

"On 16 August it was Berlin again. It was a good trip in spite of a lot of things going wrong. One of our compasses went unserviceable before we were airborne; then, over the North Sea we lost a carburetor stud on the port engine. Over Berlin we dropped our wing tanks along with the cookie as the ground crew had it wired up wrong. We were coned over the 'Big City' but got out of it in four minutes with only one hunk of flak in our wing. We had an uneventful trip home and were quite tired. A feed - our rum ration -and bed, all looked pretty good to us. Our next op, on 17 August, our third night running, we have a change of targets - Mannheim - a new one to us. It was a perfect trip in all respects. We weren't tampered with a bit, but the target was fairly 'warm'. Andy and I found that little things irritated us. We were due for a night off, I guess. *J for Johnnie* (*Moncton Express*) was as good as her name but another crew had it on our night off and succeeded in getting enough fighter cannon shells into it to warrant it unserviceable for some time to come. We had to borrow a kite to go to Cologne on 23 August. It was a bang-on trip with no complaints from our side. We lost one crew who crashed with their Cookie after take-off and very little remained. We missed our old kite but we hoped we could get a new one to replace it. On the 25th we were free. One of our flight commanders became a casualty when he returned short of petrol and crashed into a house. On 26 August we went to Berlin, which turned out to be rather pleasant in spite of our being coned over the target. Everyone got home okay. We were hit by flak and we lost an engine before reaching home. Andy made another single-engine landing.

"What a night our trip to Mannheim on 27 August was! One of our kites swung on take-off, caught fire and blew up. The cookie went off, but was not detonated, so it didn't cause too much damage. We saw all this as we were setting course over the airdrome. The crew got out when she caught fire and ran like merry old hell. The target was quite hot. On the way in we saw a fighter and later an aircraft shot down. Over the target one of our boys bought it. The searchlights and flak followed him all the way down. Slightly demoralizing. Andy and I had a smashing trip, though. The Hun was sending more fighters up after us as we were proving to be more than just nuisance raiders. According to a press report the Luftwaffe now rated Mosquitoes on night attacks so high that when and if a Jerry shoots down a Mosquito he was allowed to count it as two [sic]. Sometimes I wished we had some guns, too. We landed at another base because of the wreckage at our own base. A good night, but not good for the morale. Our op on 29 August to Hamburg was a good trip too but there was a little too much excitement to suit me. Apart from the odd piece of flak we picked up, we were untouched; but having a brush with a Jerry fighter was something different. As we left the target area a fighter got on our tail. We did tight turns and corkscrewed from 27,000 feet down to 8000 feet. He was still right with us on his instruments. After 15 minutes he gave up and we proceeded merrily homeward, a bit wiser from our experience. Lady Luck was certainly right beside us that night. We had flak holes in one petrol tank, wing, and the body near the tail. The trip to Düsseldorf on 31 August was a good one also. The moon was the brightest of the year. It was like flying in daylight and we could see the ground fairly well. Our ground speed was 450 mph as we had a good tail wind. After a few days of rotten weather we managed to get a trip to Hanover, on 5 September. There was not much to say about it except that it was a good trip and one more to add to our total."

Philip Back and Derek Smith were posted to 692 Squadron at Graveley on 5 September, and they flew their first op that same night with a 4000lb bomb in the bomb bay. Back recalls: "The bloody plane shot up about 200 feet when we dropped it over Hanover - no one warned me!"

On 8 September Ralph Wood flew his 50th op of the war when he and Any Lockhart were among those Mosquitoes that went to Nuremberg. Sardonically he wrote;

"Things are looking brighter. Tonight we had a long trip to Nuremberg. We had storms all along the route, but it was a good trip. We flew across liberated France, Holland and Belgium and saw some activity along the German frontier. We had a brand new kite tonight. It is *A-for Apple* and we're going to try and keep it. She took us to 29,000 feet with a cookie. We'll have to call her the *Moncton Express II* if we get her. Flight Lieutenant Wadsworth, a friend of mine, but a closer friend of Andy's, took off and one engine failed when he was only 500 feet up, so he landed with his wheels up risking the great chance of being blown from here to there. One has to be over 4000 feet up to drop a cookie or he'll get the blast, etc. The next day he was appointed Flight Commander, as there was a vacancy there."

On the night following (9 September) it was another new target for the Canadian navigator:

"This time it was Brunswick. The name almost made me feel homesick. It was a good effort and huge fires were seen as we left the target. Our new kite lived up to its previous performance. It was now ours and we named it *Moncton Express II*. We were nearly half-finished now. On 11 September it was the old 'Milk Run' again – Berlin. We had to land away from base, as an earwig plugged the starboard jettison tank. We had more trouble at the place we landed and didn't get home until 6 pm the next day. At 6:30 pm we were having our flying supper for another trip to the 'Big City'. We were coned near Hamburg on the way in and again over the target. Another one of our crews failed to return tonight. Our trip to Berlin on the 12th was quite respectable and we got back to base without any trouble. We were coned over the 'Big City', but managed to get out of it with a little effort. We were now over the hump and on our downward journey with 24 ops left to do."

The raid did not go nearly as well for Flight Lieutenant Norman Griffiths and Flying Officer Bill Ball of 571 Squadron in B.XVI MM127 *K-King*. Bill Ball wrote:

"There were wavering clusters of them all around the city, in the city and on the approaches to the city. A complete forest of blazing lights. Some were almost stationary, holding one or more of the early arrivals. Others were waving about like tall trees in a high wind, seeking the Squadron's Mosquitoes. Bombs were going down all the time as we approached. Great flashes and fires on the ground showed where the blockbusters were bursting. Flares and target indicators added to the illuminations. The whole sky on the bombing run and over the target was filled with vivid, vicious flashes and ugly grey and white puffs of smoke. The flak was crabbing nearer, bursting all around, a deadly barrage just above the cockpit, outside the port window and all along the starboard fuselage... it was so near I could feel *K for King* shuddering with the impact. So close I could see every detail of the cotton-wool puffs slowly unfolding!" (*K-King* limped back towards the English Coast on a rapidly depleting fuel supply and reached the coast at Bacton, Norfolk, after its crew had abandoned it over the sea. *K-King* came down in a beet field near the village of Bacton, having missed houses in the village by a fair margin.)

Warrant Officer Tommy Tomlinson and Flying Officer Dick Richards in B.XVI PF394 were also given "the full treatment," as Richards recalls:

"We dropped, but while still held in the glare the guns stopped. Twice fighters attacked us and the second attack smashed all our hydraulic systems. Eventually we got away and Tommy (I was lucky enough to do most of my trips with the tearaway Warrant Officer Tommy Tomlinson), remembering Magdeburg wanted to do another low level night X-country across Germany. (On 25 August to Berlin we had an engine shot out near Magdeburg. We returned the compliment with our 4000b cookie and turned for home. The aircraft would not hold height and we were contemplating jumping but with the throttle through the gate we staggered home at lowering altitude with Tommy loving every minute of it). I persuaded him that, with two engines operational it was silly to lose the advantage of height. He reluctantly agreed and eventually he made his usual immaculate landing at Woodbridge, but this time with no undercarriage or flaps and at a speed close to 200 mph."

Berlin at this time was the "favorite" destination for the Mosquitoes. "A" and "B" Flights at 8 (PFF) Group stations were routed to the "Big City" over towns and cities whose air raid sirens would announce their arrival overhead, although they were not the targets for the Mosquitoes' bombs. Depriving the Germans of much needed sleep and comfort was a very effective "nuisance" weapon, while a 4000-pounder nestling in the bomb bay was a more tangible "calling card." The "night postmen" had two rounds: after take-off from Wyton crews immediately climbed to height, departed Cromer, and flew the dogleg route Heligoland-Bremen-Hamburg. The second route saw departure over Woodbridge and went to the Ruhr-Hanover-Munich. Two Mosquito bombers which failed to return from the attack on Berlin on 13/14 September were claimed shot down SE of the capital by *Oberfeldwebel* Egbert Jaacks of I./NJG10 and at Braunschweig by *Leutnant* Karl Mitterdorfer of 10./JG300.[153] Two nights later, on 15/16 September, 490 aircraft bombed Kiel for the loss of four Halifaxes and two Lancasters. Three Mosquitoes and a Stirling of 199 Squadron in 100 Group were lost on Bomber Support and a Mosquito XX of 608 Squadron failed to return from a raid on Berlin.[154] *Leutnant* Kurt Welter claimed two of the Mosquitoes—one south of Berlin and the other north of Aachmer—and *Feldwebel* Reichenbach of 10./JG300 one other northwest of Wittenburg.[155]

On 15 September Andy Lockhart and Ralph Wood went to Berlin for the third time running, which Wood considered was "too much":

"Our journey there and back was fine and we missed all the hot spots. The target proved quite hot and we were coned for a while. It was a horrible naked feeling, especially as there was no flak in the cone, which got us. Hence, a damn good set-up for a cat's-eye fighter. It was okay, though, and we hoped for a smaller target the next time. On 16 September the 'old home province' (Brunswick) was our 'target for tonight'. It wasn't a very spectacular raid because of cloud. However, it was one trip nearer home, sweet home. This trip was a piece of cake and we had very little trouble. Berlin again on 18 September was anything but a nice trip. It was our 13th trip to the 'Big City'. We had the 'twitch' while waiting for take-off. Over Berlin we were coned and got caught in a huge barrage of flak. It was very unpleasant and ineffective. The following afternoon we were due to start a nine-day leave and we could certainly do it justice. Though we decided we might wait and go Wednesday morning, as we would like to have got 30 trips in before our leave, we went."

When Andy Lockhart and Ralph Wood returned from leave they went to Karlsruhe on 29 September and started their "last lap." Another crew took the *Moncton Express II* and failed to return. Ralph Wood recalls:

"We now had a new '*A-for-Apple*'. *Moncton Express III* seemed okay! Karlsruhe was a good trip. We could see that the target markers were well and truly placed. Our op to Hamburg on 30 September was another good trip, but we didn't deserve it as one of our crews left his radio on 'transmit' and talked about everything, telling when, why and how we were going to bomb Hamburg. They were waiting for us all right! Andy and I were in at the beginning and got Hell pasted at us. However, it was one trip nearer home and that's what we wanted. We lost one crew. *Moncton Express III* behaved quite well."

Chas Lockyer had flown a tour in Hampdens in 106 Squadron at Coningsby in 1941 before beginning his second tour of operations as pilot of a Mosquito B.XX in 608 Squadron at Downham Market. His navigator, "Jock" Sherry, another second tour man, was a big cheerful Glaswegian with a laugh that could stop a bus at 20 paces. He had completed a tour in Lancasters in 1943. Lockyer recalls:

"Naturally enough, with 635 Lancaster Squadron and 608 Mosquito Squadron sharing the same airfield at Downham Market there was a lot of good-humoured rivalry and banter between the respective aircrews. Our cause wasn't helped by some idiot naming the Mosquito squadrons of 8 Group 'The Light Night Striking Force', which left us wide open to sarcastic suggestions that the qualification for service on a Mosquito squadron was presumably an inability to see in the dark! It was later changed to 'The Fast Night Striking Force'; equally clumsy but less ambiguous. The Mossies were given a wide variety of tasks including such niceties as dropping route markers and target indicators over a false target while the main force pressed on elsewhere. With the introduction of the 'pregnant' Mosquito version [B.XVI, which the squadron began receiving in March 1945] adapted to carry a 'Cookie' (4000lb bomb, or 'blockbuster'), we became a reasonably lethal bombing force in our own right, particularly as we could operate in weather conditions that grounded the heavies."

The inhabitants of Berlin would be the first to acknowledge that 100 Mosquitoes each carrying a "Cookie" weren't the most welcome visitors night after night. When bad weather grounded the main force, small groups of Mosquitoes could be sent to a wide variety of targets in the *Reich*. Their objective was to get a large part of Germany out of bed and into the shelter so there were very few nights when the sirens were silent.

Lockyer's and Sherry's first operational trip in a Mosquito was to Berlin on 15/16 September, and they flew their second on 17/18 September, as Lockyer recalls:

"Our second trip, to Bremen, promised to be a bit of an anti-climax. The Intelligence Officer assured us that owing to the demand for manpower to stem the Allied and Russian advance women and old men were now manning the anti-aircraft guns. We'd just completed our bombing and camera run when all hell broke out around us as we were introduced to one of the problems of ops in Mossies. We were often used on diversionary raids involving extensive use of 'Window' to fool the enemy and tempt the fighters away from the main force of heavies. 'Window' could be used in a variety of permutations to confuse the enemy and give the controllers problems where to send up their fighters. One popular ploy was for the Mosquitoes to overfly the main force of heavies and heave out masses of these strips as the heavies either continued or diverted to its target while the Mossies carried on to an alternative target. Sometimes the Germans got it right and sometimes they didn't. But the net result as far as we were concerned was that only a limited number of us would finally bomb our particular target and Jerry was able to dispense with his usual box barrage and concentrate on one aircraft at a time. What was happening left us in on doubt that we'd drawn the short straw. Climb and dive, twist and turn as we might, the flak was deadly accurate and it was only a matter of time before the flying shrapnel found a vulnerable spot. That spot turned out to be the cooling jacket around the starboard engine and a violent juddering accompanied by belching smoke signified the imminent loss of interest of the engine in any further proceedings. Jock feathered the propeller while I throttled back and trimmed the aircraft for single engine flight and his finger hovered anxiously over the fire extinguisher button as we watched the trailing smoke but there was no fire. The smoke ceased and we breathed again.

"We were now faced with a further problem. As returning Mossies would be tracked by German radar they would soon know our course for home. We would be spotted as a straggler at our reduced speed and fighters would be sent up to intercept. Some more accurate flak near Groningen convinced us it would be unwise to continue on this course and a hasty cockpit consultation resulted in our turning due North to get out to sea as quickly as possible. This wasn't going to get us any nearer home but it would help to throw off the tracking radar and also deter the German night fighters, who were always reluctant to venture too far out to the sea. The bright red *Boozer* light receiver tuned to the transmissions of the different types of German radar in the cockpit soon turned to dull red and finally went out and we thankfully turned westward for home. On learning that we only had one engine, Downham control promptly diverted us to Coltishall on the well-worn principle, 'We're all right, Jack but if you're going to make a clobbers of your landing we'd rather you cluttered up someone else's flarepath rather than ours'. Welcome home!

"After two operations like this Jock and I were somewhat thoughtful about our chance of doing another 53 to complete the tour but the good old Law of Averages prevailed and the next half a dozen ops were comparatively uneventful."

On 2 October it was Brunswick again, and for Ralph Wood it proved to be a little "warmer" than usual:

"The full moon made you feel conspicuous. The fighters loved it. I hope we didn't have to go to the 'Big City' in this moonlight. It wouldn't have been the first time though. It was a good raid and all returned. The next night we went to Kassel. It was a poor trip all round. It brought us to two-thirds of our tour finished, so that was help, anyway. We saw a jet-propelled enemy fighter. Our op to the Kiel Canal on 5 October was the 'Daddy' of them all! After practicing for days, we took off to mine the Kiel Canal. We dropped our vegetable from a height of 100 feet It was wizard flying at rooftop level over the villages and farmhouses. The canal was well defended by light anti-aircraft guns and balloons. One searchlight got us and one gun opened fire at us head-on when we were about 200 feet off the deck. It was rather alarming but missed us. About a dozen were on the job and all got back, although one pilot flew back with a dead navigator beside him for company (gulp). We really enjoyed ourselves, but we certainly had the 'twitch' before reaching the target.

"9 October was a bit of a change with Wilhelmshaven our target. It was a nice easy trip and not much time over enemy territory. Our Wing Commander was going to try to put us on the battle order two nights running, then one off, until we finished, so we could get home for Christmas. (Maybe!) We still had 15 left to do. Our next one was on the 10th and the target was Cologne. Apart from the target itself we met with no opposition. Most of our trip was over Allied-held territory; that was nice. I could feel a string of Berlin trips coming up soon. We'd been too lucky lately. But the next, on 12 October, was a dirty weather trip to Hamburg. The target area was clear, though and we got heavily coned and hell shot at us. I was glad to see that last of this place. It was a good trip, though. Another one of our crews failed to return, making it seven crews lost since we arrived on 6 July. It was Cologne again on 13 October. We had 13 trips to do and it was Friday the 13th! But we fooled them and took off at 4:30 on the morning of the 14th and went to Cologne. Shocking hours, but then it was another trip and an uneventful one at that.[156] On the 15th we went to Hamburg and received the usual 'warm' welcome they handed out to us there. This was now ten trips since our last leave and no Berlin trips yet. Our luck couldn't last much longer.

"Our trip on 16 October was another short dash over the allied front to raid Cologne again. It was a nice little trip, but we came close to some flak over the target. It was a very dark night and one of our crews flew into the deck as he prepared to land at base. The kite was completely wrecked but Fate brought the crew through with only minor injuries. A few trees broke their speed, enabling them to survive. We were now in the 'fast forties'. Two nights later it was Hanover and a damn good prang. We weren't touched the whole way there and back. Next day Andy and I received the immediate award of the DFC, which was for our part in the raid on Kiel on 5 October. The weather had been against us of late but we managed to get to Hamburg on the 22nd. We took off at five in the afternoon and got back at 8:30. Coming home through a violent storm we were flying up and down like a bird in a chimney. The storm pitched us all over the place. At one time there were big circles of electricity around the tips of the propellers as we made our way through the clouds. It was an eerie sight. As we left this electrical field there was a very loud explosion. I was certain we had blown up and started looking frantically for my parachute. On our return to base we found it completely socked in with fog. Our station was equipped with FIDO, a device for burning fuel oil on either side of the runway The heat from this burning fuel would raise the fog enough for us to land in safety. We sure as hell appreciated this invention, as we had nowhere else to go. We all got down in one piece. It was a new experience for both of us. The target was unusually 'warm' but the gunners were rather clueless.

"My 70th op, on 23 October, was to Berlin or bust. We had a very pleasant trip there and back, watching others get into trouble instead of ourselves. The target itself, however, proved very, very warm. It was such that we were really shaken for a few minutes. Personally, I was just waiting for a hit in a vital spot, which I expected at any moment - then to see if I could bale out. In short, the gunners below were in top form. We were over the 'Big City' at 7.30 pm. Andy and I now had seven more to do and then it would all be over."

Others this same night were just starting their tour. On 23/24 October "A" and "B" Flights in 128 Squadron at Wyton were assigned different cities: "A" Flight were given a *Spoof* raid on Wiesbaden, while "B" Flight were allotted Berlin.[157] One of the new crews in 128 Squadron who made the trip was Flying Officer Herbert "Ed" Boulter[158] and Sergeant Jim Churcher, who boarded B.XXV *D-Dog* (128 Squadron was equipped with B.XVIs and B.XXVs). All 8 (PFF) Group airmen had to undergo decompression tests, but although the XVI was pressurized crews never used it on operations. Boulter notes. "You couldn't drop 'Window', and we were afraid to use pressurization in case we were holed. We could still fly at 30,000 feet and above on oxygen."

Another new crew, Flight Lieutenant James Duncan AFC and his navigator, Sergeant Charles Parker, went out to their Mosquito for their flight to the "Big City." Parker, a Londoner, had experienced "The Blitz" as a 17-year-old and was determined that "these people had to pay for this," and had joined the RAF. At Warboys he had crewed up with Flight Lieutenant Patrick James Duncan AFC, whom he had flown with on navigational training flights in Oxford. "Dunc" had simply asked, "Are you willing to risk your life with me, sergeant?" Parker took one look at his AFC ribbon and had said, "Yes!" Parker was apprehensive:

> "The 'Mossie' was considered a 'lady' and as such needed careful handling. Normally, a pilot would do a 'second dickie' flight, but you couldn't do this in a 'Mossie' so Berlin was our first op together. We took off at 1714 hours. It was dark until we reached the searchlight batteries.[159] Berlin had radar searchlights. We'd be stooging along when suddenly the icy-blue searchlight in the distance would swing over to us and immediately all the others would latch on until we were coned by white light. It was like daylight in the cockpit. Two minutes caught in the beams seemed like two days. I'd duck down. Pat would lose 10,000 feet in diving. Then the flak would get closer. If you couldn't hear it, then it wasn't intended for us - it had someone else's name on it. If you could smell it, well…it was bloody close.
>
> "At ETA I said, 'We should be there by now Pat.' He banked and looked down. We were at 25,000 feet and there, only 15 miles in the distance, was the start of the raid so I was quite pleased we were that close. We didn't have a Master Bomber that night. Another PFF's TIs went down, bursting at different heights. (We seldom got an overshoot on the TIs; normally they slipped back: human nature.) We'd been told to drop our four 500lb MCs[160] on the green markers. I flicked the bomb selection switch and immediately got down into the glass nose. It was difficult. You could quite easily get snagged on the oxygen knob and the Window chute sticking up on the door underneath my feet. Window came in a brown wrapper with a loop

around it. The idea was to hold the loop while shoving Window out. Usually, there were upwards of fifty bundles piled up in the nose and all had to be thrown out in two minutes before using the bombsight.

"Half crouching, I'd throw out the 'Window', then switch on the Mk 14 automatic bombsight. On my knees now, I peered into the illuminated cross, shaped like a sword, the point to the front. The bomb release cable in my right hand was like a bell push. I gripped it and directed Pat on the intercom: 'Right, right, left, steady, steady...Bombs Gone!' With four bombs you didn't have the gigantic leap you had with a 'Blockbuster'. You didn't wheel away. We still had to fly straight and level for the camera in the rear to take its two photos. Activated by the bomb release it took the first frame, and with the shutter open a time switch shot the second half-a-minute later as the bombs exploded. The flight lasted 4 hours, 20 minutes. When we got back to Wyton we landed and sat in the cockpit a moment, shook hands and said something like, 'Well, that's the first of many - we hope!'

"On a later op, when we were 'windowing' for the 'heavies', seven minutes were allowed because we carried 250 bundles. I felt OK but I heard Pat ask, 'You all right Charles? Your oxygen's off!' I'd knocked the knob to 'Off' with the edge of my 'Mae West' as I clambered into the nose. He turned it back on and I came up gulping for air. OK again, I started back down to the nose. Pat said, 'You going back down there?'

"'What do you think we're here for?' I said."

During October 11 Mosquitoes of the LNSF were lost on operations. New squadrons joined the force, with 142 Squadron reforming at Gransden Lodge on 25 October and flying their first operation when their only two Mosquito B.XXVs were despatched to Cologne. At Gravely, meanwhile, Andy Lockhart and Ralph Wood were on the last lap. Ralph Wood recalls;

"My 71st op was on 24 October. Three nights running and this was supposed to be the 'Big City', but it was changed at the eleventh hour, and we went to Hanover instead.[161] Not a very spectacular raid but it was one more nearer Home Sweet Home. On the way back we saw several jet-propelled enemy fighters. We did the odd bit of weaving and avoided any trouble, which may have been waiting for us. We couldn't get back to base as the weather had damped in there. We arrived back the next day at 3 pm. Op No.72 three days later, on 27 October, was Berlin again, but the reception committee was not on its toes that night. As a matter of fact, the whole trip was rather uneventful. Flak at the target was moderately heavy. We were briefed for the 'Big City' again on 28 October but it was cancelled at the last minute and instead we went to Cologne where about 700 heavies had been that afternoon. When we got there at 2030 hours it was burning merrily. The river showed up well and you could distinguish the streets by looking at the rows of burning buildings. We saw a rocket (V2) take off and climb to 50,000 or 60,000 feet before losing height in the direction of London.

"It looked like we were going to finish the hard way. On 30 October it was Berlin again and my heart was really in my mouth as we lost our starboard engine and came home nearly all the way on one engine. I had visions of finishing my tour in Stalag Luft III but Andy did good job as usual and we made a one-engine landing at base. It was his third such landing. I wrote, 'Here's to an easier trip tomorrow night. (Three more)'. We got a break. It was a short trip to Cologne. We went in two hours before the heavies. I got the 'twitch' five minutes before reaching the target because I saw a jet fighter take off beside us and climb up above us. A lovely silhouette we must have been with the cloud below and the moon and fighter above. Still, we had a good trip and he didn't pick on us. The weather on return was pretty putrid but Andy got us back to Mother Earth in one solid piece. We saw another rocket at the same place and about the same time. Our nerves are a little on edge and it didn't take much to irritate us. We were getting very anxious to finish. Another crew failed to return. The pilot was a good friend of ours. Nine crews had gone missing in the four months we'd been at Gravely. Now I had got the 'twitch'! Our target on 2 November was Osnabrück, a place I always wanted to visit because they usually had a crack at us on the way home from Berlin if we came out that way. The raid wasn't brilliant but we got there and back. We saw two jet fighters on our way home. The twitch was doing fine. We not had one more to go.

"It was Berlin on 3 November, our 17th there and I hoped the last; the one that I'd wanted to write about for quite a while. We took off at midnight. I'd never felt so keenly about a trip in all my life. I certainly lived every moment of it. There were numerous fighter flares and fighter contrails all the way there and back. We saw one jet fighter. The moon was rather bright too. The raid was wizard though. Andy and I exchanged congratulations and shook hands on it before we got out of the kite. Gosh, we were a couple of happy kids. *Moncton Express III* came through with flying colors. I could have written pages about our feelings, our 'twitch' and our relief when we got back again but so ended my second and last tour. Our *Moncton Express* had carried us out safely and back again for our fifty trips together, to all those places on the map of Europe. For this I was grateful, and I admired Andy's skill as a pilot.

"Suddenly it broke through my slightly spinning head that I had now completed 77 ops and for me my war was finally over. It looked like I'd made it after all, though why, I couldn't understand. All I knew for certain was that I was very glad to be alive. I'd come very close several times to discovering all about death. Perhaps in the years ahead I might be lucky enough to find out something about life."[162]

Despite the intensity of raids, "Don" Bennett's LNSF Mosquito squadrons had the lowest losses in Bomber Command (one per 2000 sorties). Early in November 1944 Sergeant John Clark, a Scottish navigator, was at 1655 OTU at Wyton awaiting a posting to an operational Mosquito squadron in 8 (PFF) Group. Clark recalls;

"RAF Warboys was just like so many other airfields in wartime - some Nissen huts and hangars strung together by concrete paths. There were so many aircraft flying that day it seemed as if the whole of East Anglia was one large airfield. I was told to report to an assembly hut, or

Briefing Room, the next day. There were about 20 of us, of whom half were pilots, half navigators. For some it was their second tour of operations. For a few it was their third tour. DSOs and DFCs seemed to be commonplace among them. Not a few had what was known as an 'operational twitch'. Their eyes and heads involuntarily flicked from time to time. I stood well back in deference to all this array of talent. I was, and felt, a very 'sprog' sergeant.

"A group captain, with so many gongs displayed on his chest that he must have been flying one wing low any time he took to the air, jumped up on a table and addressed us in no uncertain manner. We were, he said, a specially picked lot and would augment the LNSF, which was already causing the 'Hun' night fighters a few headaches. He warned us, however, that their flak was more accurate than it had ever been. The Germans knew they were losing the war but they were going down fighting, especially since they had been presented with unconditional surrender terms. He made the analogy of a wounded animal being more vicious when hurt. As an afterthought he tossed in the information that we would be carrying no guns whatsoever. We would have to rely on our speed to keep clear of trouble. A gasp of incredulity greeted this revelation. After a few more remarks of this nature he announced that he wanted us all crewed up within three or four days. It reminded me of those announcements in the quality newspapers: 'The engagement has been announced, and a wedding will take place.' It was going to be a whirlwind courtship.

"I was still standing at the back of the Briefing Room when a squadron leader, complete with 'operational twitch', came up to me. He had a scar, which he must have collected on one of his previous operations, across his forehead, and a DSO and DFC and bar across his chest. He looked me up and down. 'You've been saying nothing all this time, but I think you've been taking it all in. I like that. Think about it.

"I did. A cat, so legend states, has nine lives. I wondered how many he had and how many he had used up so far. Just then a little warrant officer, the only non-commissioned pilot in the room, came over to me. His shoulder flashes identified him as a New Zealander. His accent was as sharp as his profile. 'I hear you're a Scot. Will you be my navigator?'

"For some reason which I could never explain, I answered, 'Yes.' We shook hands on the deal and introduced ourselves.

"'I'm Bill Henley,' he said. 'I've been instructing for the last 18 months. This will be my first tour on ups.

"'Same here, only I haven't been instructing. You could say I've been like a spare one at a wedding - just hanging around. Let's have a beer and talk things over.'

"We popped up to the bar in the Sergeants' Mess and gave each other a potted history of our service careers so far. He came from Auckland and had a brother who had been killed in the fighting in Crete in the Middle East campaign. Good God, I thought. Is no family going to be untouched by this war? I had just heard that my sister, who had become a driver in the ATS, had nearly been drowned driving a DUKW from the Ayrshire coast to the Isle of Arran.

"I pulled a bit of a face. 'Too bad about your brother. Let's try to get you back to New Zealand in one piece when this war is over. Who knows, we may get our commissions, and a gong to go with them.' What a load of bull, I thought. Still, it was better to look on the bright side. 'By the way, I've got to report for *Gee* training this afternoon. I've never used the thing before.'

"He smiled. 'And I've got to familiarize myself with the Mosquito. I've never flown one before.'

"A week or so later I joined Bill at Wyton, a permanent station with brick buildings and tarmac roads which seemed to ooze luxury compared with the muck and mess of Warboys. I walked round the aircraft we had been allocated to make our first familiarization flight together.

"'She's got beautiful lines, hasn't she?' I observed. 'Except for this extended belly, which makes her look pregnant.'

"'Yes,' Bill replied. 'Pregnant with celestial fire. It's extended so that it can carry the 4000lb bomb. The bomb looks like an extra large can of beans and the casing is just about as thick as a bean can. The rest of it is all explosives. We'll have to handle it rather carefully - no belly landings - and if we drop below 4000 feet, we're liable to get our tail blown off.'

"'Are we? So now you tell me!'

"I clambered up the steps after him, into the cabin of the aircraft. 'They don't give a navigator much room to navigate.' I looked at the foldaway navigation table complete with anglepoise shaded orange light on my right, as I sat on the rather uncomfortable seat with part of the bomb bay under it. 'I've got to get us to Germany - and back - using this,' I said, pointing to the table. 'I see I'm considered more expendable than you.' At the back of his seat, armor-plating rose above his head. In my part it stopped at my waist; the rest of the space above the armor-plating was crammed with Bendix radio and LORAN. The *Gee* box was positioned behind the pilot's seat and was easily accessible.

"The ground crew, who had been standing patiently, waiting for us to get settled, folded the telescopic ladder, stowed it away and slammed the main door shut. I in turn fitted the floor under my feet, slipping my parachute and navigation bag behind my legs. This routine was going to take some getting used to. With the aid of the ground starting 'ack' the two engines coughed into life. The ground staff waved us off the dispersal pan and in no time, it seemed, we were lined up, looking down the runway. Bill pushed open the throttles and the two Merlin engines took us by the seat of our pants and pulled us down the runway.

"Then it happened. The aircraft swung to the right. Fortunately, our wheels were off the ground and by a quick piece of avoiding action, we missed a hangar and pointed our nose skywards.

"'Sorry about that.' It was Bill's voice over the intercom. 'It's never done that before, and I'll make sure it doesn't do it again.'

"I tried to be jocular. 'That's what the man said when his horse dropped dead. Anyway, why worry? We missed the hangar by about 500 yards.' What a lu-lu of a take-off! I wondered what kind of driver I had chosen - or had he chosen me? As the months rolled on,

Bill was as good as his word. Our aircraft never again swung on take-off.

"One morning, the whole of the OT Course was summoned to present itself in the Briefing Room. The group captain with all the medals on his chest strode in and, without preamble, congratulated us on having completed the course. It was too bad that we had lost one crew during that time. It was unusual at an OTU. There had been no case of 'OTU-itis'. Our postings were on the notice board outside the Crew Room. We were being spread among the other Mosquito squadrons in 8 Group. He left as abruptly as he had arrived. 'What on earth is 'OTU-itis?" I asked a seasoned-looking navigator.

"'Well, to put it crudely, some of these intrepid bird-men like to wear a brevet.' He pointed to his wings. 'And pick up a few free beers in their 'local'. However, when the chips are down, they suddenly discover that they have an incurable disease which their great uncles, or some other relative in the family, had picked up fighting in the Afghan wars or somewhere else in the British Empire. They call off flying before they have to face the flak and the fighters. The powers that be treat them pretty roughly. They're stripped of their rank and brevet, then their documents are stamped 'LMF' - Lack of Moral Fibre. They usually become shit-house cleaners-out.'

"We found that along with another crew we had been posted to 571 Squadron at Oakington, halfway between Cambridge and Huntingdon, where we would share the airfield with 7 Squadron Lancs. On 5 November we presented ourselves to the squadron adjutant of 571, Flight Lieutenant R. Stanton. Evidently our credentials had gone before us. We had been allocated to 'A' Flight; the other crew to 'B' Flight. We were introduced to the 'A' Flight commander, Squadron Leader Norman A. J. Mackie DSO DFC*[163] and his Australian navigator, Flight Lieutenant Angus MacDonald RAAF DFC DFM. 'Ah yes, you're the new boys. We'll put you on ops tomorrow night.' He looked at his navigator. 'How say you, Blue?'

"'Yes, the usual treatment. Blood them early. They can take the old lady *L-London* for their first trip.'

"He sounded quite laconic about it, as if he were allocating us an ice-cream cart for a day's 'jolly' at some fairground. "Didn't he realize we had waited years for this minute?

"Next morning we were taken out to a dispersal pan where *L-London* stood. She was painted all-over black and the flight commander's navigator hadn't exaggerated when he said she had completed over 100 trips, if the bomb insignia stencilled on the side of the aircraft were to be believed.

"There's no practice bombing; it's been scrubbed,' said the 'Chiefy' who was waiting for us. He and Bill discussed a few technical points before Bill signed the Form 700, accepting the aircraft. [Before an op a crew would complete a NFT, or Night Flying Test in the aircraft they would fly that night]. After an impeccable take-off we headed for the Norfolk coast. I undid my waistband harness and, with a bit of difficulty, crawled underneath the dashboard on my side, to check the course-setting bombsight, which jutted out over the Perspex nose. There was also a bomb 'tit' hooked innocuously on the side of the fuselage, and the fuse-setting switches, which activated the three fuses on the 'Cookie'. I glanced through the two Perspex panels set in either side of the nose. The propellers were churning the air at what seemed only a few inches from my earholes. If one of those props detached itself and flew off, I would be like a piece of corned beef - all ground up. Rubbish! I thought. They'll fly forwards, not sideways. Anyway, they won't fly off.

"'Everything OK?' asked 'Chiefy' when we got our feet on the ground again. We gave him the thumbs-up sign. 'We'll see you later,' we added.

"It's your first trip, isn't it? Good luck. She'll get you back.' He nodded at the aircraft.

"Bill looked at me. 'No messing - Briefing is at half-past three with take-off about half-past five. In between those times we get supper - bacon and eggs, I'm told.'

"Hmmm. It's almost worth going for that alone.'

"At the appointed time we assembled in the Briefing Room. We immediately felt isolated from the outside world. Special policemen stood at all the entrances with revolvers hanging from their waists. On a raised platform at one end of the room, some sitting and some standing, were the commanding officer, the flight commander, the intelligence officer and the Met officer. On the wall behind them, illuminated by strong lights, were maps of the UK, France and Germany. Superimposed on them were tapes indicating our route out and back.

"'OK chaps, settle down.' It was the intelligence officer. 'Your target, as you can see, is Gelsenkirchen.'

"'Where the hell's that?' I muttered. A Canadian sitting next to me leaned over and whispered, 'It's in the Ruhr - the 'Happy Valley' in other words, just north of Essen. It'll be a doddle.'

"Reassured on that point I concentrated on what the intelligence officer was saying.

"We're taking you west of London, then over France to Germany. You'll attack the target from the southwest to take advantage of the winds on your leg into the target. The raid is of a diversionary nature. The 'heavies' are bombing here.' His pointer jabbed at a different spot.[164] 'Because it is a diversionary attack you will Window most of the way into the target – navigators please note.

"'Jeeze,' said the Canuck out loud. 'Why don't you stick a brush up our ass, then we can sweep the floor when we crawl through to the bomb-sight to drop our 'Cookie."

"The remark received a ripple of laughter, which the intelligence officer ignored. 'The target will be marked by *Oboe* markers, so I'll be looking for some good photographs on return.' He waffled on for some time about searchlights, flak, etc., and was followed by the Met man who assured us that the airfield would be wide-open on our return and that the winds were in fact blowing from the southwest. Wing Commander R. J. Gosnell DSO DFC, the CO, affirmed that the 'Graveyard' airfields of Woodbridge and Manston would be wide-open for any aircraft that couldn't make it back to base. 'However, I'll be waiting for each of you here. Good luck!' he wound up.[165]

"As it turned out we sat waiting for an hour-plus, looking at each other and the wall opposite, each minute seeming like an hour. Now I knew in some degree what the soldiers of the First World War must have felt like when they knew they were going 'over the top' when the whistle blew. Bill produced a shiny black pair of sheepskin flying boots. 'I got them in New Zealand and decided I wouldn't wear them till I did my first op.' They looked pretty swep-up compared with my battered old escape-type boots, so-called because there was a single-bladed knife in a small pocket in the leg of one of them. The idea was that, should I have to bale out and resort to walking back, I could cut the leggings off and make them resemble civilian shoes.

"After what seemed like aeons of time the WAAF orderly came round the rooms to tell us that the flight trucks were waiting for us. We climbed aboard, stopping at the Crew Room to pick up our parachutes, 'Mae Wests' and escape packs; then, crew by crew; we were dumped at our respective aircraft. I made a cursory check of the fuses on the bomb while Bill did the rest of the checks; then I followed him, navigation bag slung over my shoulder, into the cockpit. It seemed to get smaller each time I got into it, especially with the bundles of 'Window' stacked all over the place. How we would get off the ground with 100-gallon drop tanks fixed underneath each wing and a 4000lb load of explosives underneath us I refused to contemplate, consoling myself with the thought that it had been done many times before. Bill, with the aid of the ground crew, started the engines and I switched on my navigation light, spreading my charts over the navigation table. The other aircraft were 'crocodiling' their way to the end of the runway. It was comforting to see we were not alone. Their navigation lights were shining and they were being given a green flare from a caravan at the threshold of the runway. Our turn came. Bill gave the engines everything they had and trundled off.

"'Come on, you son-of-a-bitch, get airborne,' I heard myself muttering into my face mask as old *L-London* bounced once, then twice, then bounced no more. We were off the deck. I noted the time in my Log. We passed over a railway line, which ran at right angles to the runway. There was a train puffing sedately along the track. We must have missed it by 10 or 20 feet. I don't know if we frightened it but it certainly frightened us.

"We turned on-course, climbing steadily, listening subconsciously to the beat of the props and the throb of the engines. The blue flames of the engines spurted from the exhaust stubs in an asymmetrical pattern. While they were alarming to look at, it was very reassuring to see them. I checked our course on the climb. We were bang on track. I turned the light down on my navigation table and looked outside again. 'Here comes Eastbourne and Newhaven, and there's Brighton on our right. We'll be crossing the coast in a few minutes. I'll switch off the navigation lights.'

"We leveled off at 25,000 feet. Although we were over France, heading for Germany via Belgium, I still had the feeling we were over enemy territory in spite of the fact that we were passing over places occupied by our own troops. A layer of stratus cloud covered Northern France and Flanders. Probably it was best that way; so much killing and death had taken place there over the years. The cloud cleared as we approached the Ruhr Valley. We seemed to be alone, with no other aircraft around, but when we turned in on our long run-up to the target the flak and searchlights opened up on us. I gave Bill his course to fly after we had dropped the bomb, then folded away my table.

"Now to get rid of this 'Window'. I adjusted the wooden chute. Breaking open two bundles of Window, I placed them in the chute and pressed it down through the floor and through the trapdoor of the outer fuselage. Unfortunately, in my haste and the confined space, I found I had pushed the 'V'-shaped chute out into the outside air, with the 'V' scooping up the air instead of sucking it out. A 300+ mph gust of air blasted the whole cockpit with silvery metal strips of paper. I quickly remedied the situation, chucking down the remaining bundles, which slipped out of sight into the night air.

"'What on earth's going on?' asked Bill. He looked like a mock-up of Santa Claus sitting in a heap of glistening metal.

"'I'll clear it up after we've got rid of the bomb,' I said. It would have been quite funny if we hadn't been flying in one of the most heavily defended parts of Germany. I disconnected my intercom, dived under the sea of tinsel, and replugged it into a socket in the nose of the aircraft.

"'How do you read me?' I asked.

"'Five by five. How me?'

"'Ditto. We seem to be on track. The red TIs have gone down on time. Remember to fly straight and level for half a minute after the bomb's gone - photographs, remember. I'm fusing the damned thing now.' I pushed the fuse switches. "'Bomb doors open - confirm?'

"Bill parroted the phrase back to me. I watched the TIs as they came closer. I was told later that there was flak and searchlights all over the place, but I didn't notice any. My eyes were riveted on the TIs as they started to slide down the wires of the bombsight.

"'Left, steady!' Bill nudged the aircraft to the left so that the TIs came back to the center of the bombsight.

"'Steady, steady, we're nearly there.' As the TIs reached the crosswire I pressed the bomb tit.

"Bomb gone! Bomb doors closed.' It was like reading from a prepared script. The first part of the script was totally unnecessary as the aircraft reared up like a startled horse as the 'Cookie' fell away into the night sky.

"Hold that course,' I said as I waited for the camera lights to wink. There were flashes on the ground below. Which one was ours? Only the 'boffins' at base could say.

"OK, the camera's worked. Head for base.' My mouth and throat were dry and devoid of all saliva. Whether it was the tension of it all or the oxygen blowing into my mask, I didn't know, but I made a mental note to carry some chewing gum on our next trip. How totally impersonal it all seemed. I didn't really think of the German civilians who would be on the receiving end of the load of explosives I had released on them. For the first time I noticed the flak sparking around. None, as far as I could see, had hit us. My sympathies, if I had any, were for Bill who had to sit like an automaton, viewing the whole scene and having to follow my instructions. There was no automatic pilot fitted to the aircraft. He had to fly it manually.

"I scrambled back to my seat and looked ruefully at the sea of tinsel covering the cockpit. I gathered most of it up and stuck it down the chute as we flew over Holland. I reckoned I was going to have some explaining to do to the ground crew when we reached base. I turned to the *Gee* box. The two matchsticks, or, to be more correct, the two blips, were flickering brightly on their time bases and getting stronger the nearer we got to England. I took a fix and gave Bill an alteration of course. We were going to come in over the Cromer beacon.

"I turned on the navigation lights and switched from the main tanks to the outer drop tanks. Bill always liked to keep 25-30 gallons in each outer tank, which he used for landing. I stuck my forehead against the *Gee* box visor again and started to home in on the two coordinates I had memorized. I was very tired, although we had been airborne for less than four hours.

"Visibility was very good, and every airfield in East Anglia seemed to be flashing its green Morse code beacons giving its identity. We joined our circuit and came in over the runway threshold onto a very nice three-pointer landing. I noted the time in my log.

"At the dispersal pan the ground crew undid the catch of the outer fuselage and set the telescopic ladder in position. 'Watch out!' I yelled, as I lifted the trapdoor in the floor. They got a deluge of tinsel on their heads. It blew away in the early November breeze, which drifted across the airfield. I hurriedly explained the reason for the loose Window, which seemed to have covered everything. They took it in their stride and assured me I had not been the first navigator to make that mistake. Bill was telling the ground crew that as far as he knew we hadn't been hit by flak. I interrupted him. 'A very gentle christening, don't you think?'

"'Tell that to my grandmother - you weren't sitting where I was.

"There was a moral there somewhere, I felt. Just then the crew truck drew up. We piled aboard and headed for the debriefing. A mug of coffee heavily laced with rum - a double shot for me as Bill didn't drink it - beckoned. At the debriefing the other crew, who had joined the squadron at the same time as we had, were having some difficulty deciding where they had dropped their bomb. The navigator had a rather glazed look in his eyes. His Log Sheet and charts looked as if they had been stuffed in his pockets at some point on the trip. He stated, categorically, that no TIs had gone down and that he had dropped his load 'by guess and by God' at his ETA over the target. On a replot of his navigation it was decided - and later confirmed by his photographs - that he had done some 'TNT ploughing' on the North German Plain. How he had managed it no one could understand.

"I felt quite an 'operational type' after the trip. It had been pretty easy going as far as I was concerned, and I felt quite chuffed when the flight commander took us to one side and congratulated us on the photographs we had brought back."

On 6/7 November RAF Bomber Command sent out two major forces of bombers. Some 235 Lancasters of 5 Group, together with seven Mosquitoes again attempted to cut the Mittelland Canal at Gravenhorst, but crews were confronted with a cold front of exceptional violence and ice quickly froze on windscreens. Only 31 Lancasters bombed before the Master Bomber abandoned the raid due to low cloud. Ten Lancasters FTR from the Mittelland debacle. Meanwhile, 128 Lancasters of 3 Group carried out a night *Gee-H* raid on Koblenz. Eighteen Mosquitoes raided Hanover and eight more went to Herford, while 48 Mosquitoes of the LNSF carried out a *Spoof* raid on Gelsenkirchen to draw German night-fighters away from the two Main Force raids. The Gelsenkirchen raid began as planned five minutes ahead of the two other attacks, at 1925 hours. The city was still burning as a result of an afternoon raid that day by 738 RAF bombers. From their altitude of 25,000 feet the Mosquitoes added their red and green TIs and high explosives to the fires. A few searchlights and only very light flak greeted the crews over the devastated city. The twelve B.XXs in 608 (North Riding) Squadron began returning over Norfolk shortly before 2100 hours to Downham Market. They had to contend with cloud and icing conditions as they descended over the flat landscape. The Canadian-built Mosquito flown by Pilot Officer James McLean, a 26-year-old Scot from West Lothian, and his observer, 21-year-old Sergeant Mervyn Tansley, from Fulham, in London, began to ice up badly. McLean lost control during his descent through cloud and the Mosquito struck overhead electric power cables before crashing into Bawdeswell village church. Both whirling propellers sheered off the engine nacelles and fell into neighbouring gardens, where a tree was cut down as if hit by a chain-saw. The remains of McLean and Tansley were not recovered from the wreckage until nine days later.

The "Big City" remained top of the target list in November 1944. Flying Officer Leslie Fletcher, a B.XVI pilot in 571 Squadron at Oakington, recalls:

> "Berlin was a formidable target but in truth I didn't think it posed as many problems as the Ruhr targets. I think that I was coned on the outskirts of the city on about every trip that I made. I was held right across the city but as long as you varied your course and height and kept going the situation did not present too much of a problem. The flak fire was always intense and unpleasant. The most memorable feature of the Berlin operations was the long drag across the North German plain. On most occasions the return route was fixed between Münster and Hanau which were two well defended areas. We used to complain about this because we often strayed into one or the other of their flak belts. Even so the complaints fell on stony ground and the same routes continued to be used."

On 11/12 November Flying Officer Leslie Fletcher and his navigator, Flight Sergeant McCorkindale, in B.XVI PF381 encountered a fighter at 2310 hours just after they had cleared their target at Berlin. Fletcher recalls:

> "It was the only encounter we had with a night fighter whilst we were on operations. There had been some talk about a number of German night fighters being stripped down to reduce their weight to enable them to chase the Mossie. They were being orbited at 20,000 feet over Berlin to deal with an ever-increasing number of Mosquito attacks. On this particular evening I was being held in the normal searchlight cone and we had just completed the bombing run when to my surprise I saw a stream of tracer passing over my head. My immediate reaction was to dive and turn into the fire to force him to

break off. I couldn't see the fighter as I was blinded by the glare of the searchlights. A black shape flashed over the cockpit, uncomfortably close, and disappeared. The distance between the aircraft must have been very close as the turbulence the Mossie all over the place. I opened up the throttles and dived away. There was no further sign of pursuit."

Elsewhere 139 Squadron was not so lucky; they lost one Mossie to a night-fighter and had two more damaged by flak. The rest of the Squadron made uneventful returns to base.

After their first op, on 6/7 November Johnnie Clark and Bill Henley had to wait four nights before they again went through the ritual of a bombing trip. This time they went to Hanover "with a nice civilized take-off time at six o'clock." Then followed two more trips in succession to Hanover, as Johnnie Clark recalls:

"On our third trip, on 23/24 November, we flew into a cone of searchlights quite early; Bill, who could raise or lower his seat, decided to do the latter until we had passed through them. There was no flak; an indication that fighters were on the prowl. I looked back into the night sky. We weren't making any contrails and I told him so. A few minutes later we were shrouded in darkness again, except for the dim amber light which shone on my navigation table. Bill raised his seat so he could better spot any attack, which might come from a night fighter. In doing so his oxygen tube was pulled out of his mask and fell to the floor. At first, neither of us noticed it; then the aircraft started to wallow all over the sky and went into a steep dive. I looked up and saw that Bill's head had sunk onto his chest. He was rapidly passing out. Then I spotted the oxygen tube lying on the floor. I grabbed the control column with one hand and steadied the aircraft. With the other I ripped off his mask and my own and quickly fastened mine to his face. At the same time I switched the oxygen to emergency and stuck the tube, which was lying at his feet, into my mouth. There was nothing in the rulebook about this, I thought. What a carve-up! We readjusted our masks and attained some degree of normality. We had overshot our turning point and were out of the main stream of bombers. I gave him a course to fly direct to the target.

"The aircraft was climbing again to our bombing altitude when the first burst of tracer bullets flicked past our wings. A fighter was on to us. 'He's a bloody poor shot, whoever he is,' I mumbled. 'Perhaps it's because we are climbing that he didn't give us the knockout punch.' Bill, as so often happened, didn't say anything. I stuck my nose into my charts and tried to ignore it. After all, that was Bill's department. He seemed to be tossing the Mosquito all over the sky. However, I couldn't ignore the second attack; the tracer bullets seemed to be going in one side of the wings and out the other. The engines were maintaining their steady beat, as did the propellers. I glanced at all the luminous dials on the dashboard and they were remaining steady. Then I noticed our green navigation light shining from our [starboard] wing tip. I looked past Bill's head and saw the red one shining on his side. He was busy with the evasive action.

"'Hell's bells, Bill. We've got our nav lights on! No wonder the bastard is picking on us. He must think we're crazy. We must have knocked them on in that mix-up with our oxygen masks.'

"I quickly switched them off and returned the oxygen supply to normal, while Bill pulled the engine throttles back through the 'gate', where he had thrust them at the first attack. After all, it was like driving a car at full speed with the choke out: it didn't do the engines any good at all.

"'Do we press on or abort the trip altogether?' I asked.

"'The engines seem to be OK and we aren't losing any petrol. Any sign of that fighter?' asked Bill.

"'Not that I can see. Let's carry on.

"We dropped our 'egg' and came back via the Cromer beacon, as usual. On the dispersal pan I moved to the grass verge, spat out the chewing gum, which I had rolled around in my mouth since take-off, and at the same time stripped and wiped the curd, which had formed on my lips. I lit a cigarette. Hell, it tasted good. Bill came over to me. He had been discussing the damage with a rigger. We had collected quite a few bullet holes in the wings, but nothing vital had been hit. 'We were lucky,' I remarked.

"'Yeah, we'll need a lot more luck before this tour is over. Thanks a lot for noticing the oxygen tube. I was pretty 'gaga' by that time.'

"I made light of it. 'If you go - we both go; whereas if I catch a packet you can always get back to England using that little information card I give you before each trip, and which you slip into the top of those shiny black flying boots of yours.'

"I had just finished lunch the next day when Bill came over to me. 'We are on the Battle Order for tonight, Johnnie. Briefing is at three o'clock.' At the appointed hour Bill and I presented ourselves for briefing.

"'Ye Gods,' muttered Bill. 'Do you see where we are due to go tonight? Berlin.' The route tapes were pinned to the map.

"'So, it's the "Big City" tonight,' drawled the Canadian at my elbow. 'With *Spoof* attacks on Hanover and Magdeburg, I wonder where the 'heavies' are going tonight? Is this your first to the 'Big City'?' I nodded. It was funny how everyone took the same place at briefing. Still, it was more comfortable that way.

"The intelligence officer soon filled us in on where the 'heavies' were bombing that night. They were coming in on a northern route and were going to saturate Potsdam. We were going to bomb the center of Berlin, with a view to drawing off some of the flak and searchlights from the Main Forces. The Germans may have had a 'busted flush', to use the Canadian's poker language, but they were still a force to be reckoned with; a fact which the paratroopers' disastrous landing at Arnhem was but one example. Their fighters, flak and searchlights were others. That we were winning no one doubted, but it was going to take a big heave yet. The Germans were fighting for their lives with their own lives.

"We were given our time on the target, which would be marked by the H_2S Mosquitoes of 139 Squadron. H_2S was airborne radar. *Oboe* aircraft couldn't mark as far as Berlin. Their activities were confined to the Ruhr and its environs, although their range was extending as the armies on the ground advanced. The *Oboe* marker was very accurate and very 'hush-hush'.

"You'll find the flak and searchlights really concentrated around the 'Big City,'' remarked the intelligence officer. Cold comfort for us, I thought, as the briefing progressed. When it ended I turned to the Canadian. You been there before?'

"He nodded. 'Two or three times, and as yet not a scratch to show on us.' He pointed to his pilot. 'We're hoping our luck lasts.'

'We got airborne just after five o'clock, thanks to the short days at the end of November. Running up to Hanover, the *Gee* blips grew fainter and eventually guttered out like two spent candles. After collecting our share of flak over that city we pointed our nose towards Magdeburg. There was no need to navigate to it as the Americans had been there during the day. The place was still burning. We turned towards the northeast and headed for the 'Big City'. The TIs went down on time and I noticed another bunch on my left. Potsdam was being marked for the Main Force of 'heavies'. They were operating much lower than we, the Mosquitoes were. Then the searchlights came into play. First the bluish ones, operating singly and radar-controlled, wandered haphazardly, or so it seemed. Suddenly, one of them darted sideways and caught a Lanc in its beam. The Lanc dived and wriggled left and right, but hadn't a hope as 20 or 30 other searchlights immediately lit the sky around it. It was caught in a wigwam of light. Then the sparks of flak began to burst around the aircraft. Some of the flak shells must have hit the starboard wing, for within a minute flames were rolling over the wing and the Lanc started to spin round and down ever so slowly, I thought. I heard myself yelling into the microphone which was clamped to my face, 'Bale out, you stupid bastards. You haven't a hope. Don't you know you're on fire?'

"As if they had heard me, the silk parachutes began to appear in the searchlight beams. I started to count them - one, two, three - then no more. Four hadn't made it. As if to underline the whole affair which was unfolding, the aircraft seemed to disintegrate as it went down. The three parachutes hung like stationary mushrooms in the cone of light. Just then there was a flash and what looked like an explosion. Two aircraft must have collided in mid-air. There would be no parachutes coming out of that, I reckoned.

"As we were running up to the target a bunch of searchlights caught us. It had been sheer good luck on their part that they did so, since all the pale blue ones were latching onto the Main Force on our right. I was completely blinded by the light and couldn't see the TIs, far less bomb on them. 'I've overshot the TIs - we'll have to go round again,' I said into my mike, adding automatically, 'Bomb doors closed.'

"'Oh, bloody hell,' replied the somewhat strained voice of Bill. 'Which way do you want me to turn the damned thing?' It was the first and only time I had ever heard him swear. After a moment's thought I replied, 'Make it a wide right turn. All the others will be making a left turn after dropping their loads. We don't want to run into any of them.' Bumping into another aircraft's slipstream was no fun either, as I had found out over Hanover when night fighters had attacked us. Our right turn seemed to fox the searchlights. Presumably, they had anticipated we would be making a left turn, heading for home. Anyway, we lost them, and were shrouded in darkness again.

"I resolved to concentrate on the markers and ignore what was going on around me. This I found rather hard to do; it was difficult to tell which were bombs bursting and which were aircraft either on fire or blowing up. It seemed to me that Dante had underestimated his description of Hell. I went through the patter on our second run-in, dropped the TIs, waited for the photographs, then headed for the Cromer beacon and home. 'Sorry about the run-in to the target. I couldn't see a thing; the searchlight blinded me,' I said rather lamely.

"'Not to worry Johnnie, we're still in one piece. It was a good idea of yours to make a right turn - it caught the Jerries on the wrong foot.'

"I didn't explain to him that I had been thinking more of the aircraft following us than of the German defenses.

"We landed safely. Bill, following the laid-down instructions, opened the bomb doors at dispersal before cutting the engines. I was doing my usual - having a pee and spitting out the wad of chewing gum which had kept my mouth moist during the trip - when an armorer of the ground staff approached me. 'I say sergeant, come and see this. It looks a bit queer to me.

"'Nothing wrong I hope?' We ducked into the empty bomb bay together.

"'Do you know where you collected that?' He pointed to the whole side of a flak shell embedded in one of the main spars.

"'Over the 'Big City' I suppose,' I answered. Bill had joined us and was looking curiously at the splinter. 'I never felt a thing hit us during the whole trip. It must have gone through the bomb doors or the fuselage. Isn't there a hole somewhere?'

"'That's what's making me wonder. There's not a mark on the outer skin of the aircraft at all,' replied the armorer.

"I looked at Bill and found him gazing at me. 'Are you thinking what I'm thinking?'

"I shrugged. 'I don't know, but I reckon we could only have collected it after I'd dropped the bomb and before you'd closed the bomb doors - a matter of seconds.'

"'That's what I thought,' said Bill. 'Thank God the bomb had gone.' We turned to the armorer, who was looking as if he had seen a couple of ghosts. 'Yes, a matter of seconds - the difference between the quick and the dead.'

"At the debriefing my Canadian oppo said, 'I hear you went round the target twice tonight?'

"'That's right. I liked the look of the place,' I answered, dryly."

Chapter 6

The Fast Night Strikers

We fly alone, when all the heavies
are grounded and dining
692 will be climbing.
We still press on.

It's every night but though they
never can give us a French route
To the honour of 8 Group
We still press on

It's always the Reich, no matter how far
One bomb is slung beneath
The crew they are twitching
It's not fear of ditching
It's twelve degrees East –
One engine at least!

We fly alone, although tonight
you can see it's a stand-down
But tomorrow the big town
We still press on.
We Fly Alone

On 25/26 November 128 Squadron at Wyton formed part of a force of 68 Mosquitoes that attacked Nuremberg. One of the aircraft that took part was *D-Dog*, flown by Ed Boulter and Jim Churcher. In the bomb bay was a 4000lb bomb, which they released from 25,000 feet. Boulter recalls:[166]

> "Suddenly, an unseen German night fighter put several shells into the Mosquito. The starboard engine began to run rough. We lost coolant and the engine began to register high temperature and low oil pressure. I feathered the prop. It was all quite 'light-hearted' at this point because the Mosquito could perform marvellously on one engine. However, 20 min passed and the port engine began to behave in the same way! Things were getting a bit hectic! I swapped engines all the way back, feathering one to cool down the engine and then switching to the other when it got hot. Near the coast of France we were talking to Manston Emergency, and they tried to persuade us to fly 'the 10 miles remaining'. (We actually had 25-30 miles to go). It was 4am; 7000 feet over Dunkirk and both engines were trailing 40 foot-long flames. A 'Mossie' does not glide too well! I throttled back and we baled out. We came home on an MTB on the 27th."[167]

On the night of 27/28 November, when 67 Mosquitoes raided Berlin, Pat Duncan and Charles Parker also had trouble with a Cookie when they went out to their Mosquito for their thirteenth operation. They watched their ground crew winch the 4000 pounder into the bomb bay. It was almost in position when CRASH! The back half fell down. Parker recalls:

> "I did the 100-yard sprint. Pat was more philosophical and stayed put. I stopped. I felt a bit stupid! The Squadron Leader 'B' Flight arrived. He told us to take the spare aircraft into the hangar, but we said it hadn't been bombed up. (A 4000-pounder had to be dropped on the night. We were not allowed to land with one because it would strain the fuselage.) The Squadron Leader ordered it bombed up and told me to go to the Briefing Room and work out a direct course to Berlin. I drew up a new course. Cromer direct to Berlin, calculating an extra five knots' airspeed on top of our average cruising speed. Even if we left in the next 10 minutes we would arrive 20 minutes after everyone else had left! Pat was halfway up the ladder when I got back to the reserve aircraft. I said, 'Pat, hold it. This is just madness.' In his perfect King's English he said, 'Come on Charles - we're going.' 'I am no hero. Flying alone over Berlin was not my idea of fun. Perhaps the thirteenth was at the back of my mind. I argued. We didn't go that night."

On 30 November the LNSF mounted the second major daylight raid of the month when five Mosquitoes from 128 Squadron were part of a force of 20 Mosquitoes from their unit and 571, 608, and 692 Squadrons despatched to the *Gessellschaft Teerverwertung* in Meiderich, a suburb of Duisburg. "Sky markers" defeated the solid cloud cover, and smoke seen rising to 10,000 feet was testimony to their bombing accuracy.

Returning from Berlin on 6 December, Flight Lieutenant Pat Duncan and Sergeant Charles Parker encountered severe problems with wind changes and gusty conditions. Low on fuel, they sent out a Mayday call, adding cryptically "*Gravy is low! Gravy is low!*" Charles Parker studied his maps and made his calculations, but the wind played havoc with their Mosquito. He could have sworn it was Grimsby when he saw fishwives on the quay below as they passed over the coast, but it was actually a French port! They finally put down at Friston, on the south coast, with less than 20 gallons of fuel remaining in the 12 tanks.

On the night of 9/10 December *Feldwebel* Reichenbach of 4./NJG11 claimed a Mosquito near Berlin, but the 60 Mosquitoes that attacked the "Big City" returned without loss. Two nights later, when 89 Mosquitoes went to various city targets, one of the aircraft that failed to return from the raid on Hamburg was claimed by *Oberleutnant* Kurt Welter of II./NJG11.[168] *Unteroffizier* Scherl of 8./NJG1 claimed a Mosquito east of Hagen on the night of 12/13 December when 540 aircraft attacked Essen, but though six Lancasters were lost, all 28 Mosquitoes that attacked Essen and 49 others that raided Osnabrück returned safely.[169] Another daylight raid was despatched on 11 December when two waves drawn from 128 Squadron raided Hamborn. When the 13th day of December broke it was under a very heavy frost, and towards mid-morning thick fog enveloped stations in Norfolk and operations were scrubbed very early. That night 52 Lancasters and seven Mosquitoes of 5 Group flew to Norway to attack the German cruiser *Köln*, but by the time they reached Oslo Fjord the ship had sailed, so instead other ships were bombed. On 15/16 December 327 Lancasters and Mosquitoes of 1, 6, and 8 Groups raided Ludwigshafen for one Lancaster lost.

"Being on a squadron" recalled Johnnie Clark, "was to be quite remote from the rest of the world. Time passed quickly, except for that gap between briefing and take-off, which seemed an eternity. Bill, thanks to his magpie instincts, had a gramophone and a large pile of records. At first he and I sat on our beds listening to the records. Then one or more crews engaged in flying on the same trip would slip into our room and listen to Bing Crosby, Vera Lynn, the Ink Spots *et al.* Singing the sentimental songs in vogue at that particular time took our minds off the trip that lay ahead. Usually, one of the tunes swung around in our heads subconsciously while we were airborne. To get the wrong tune didn't help when you were waiting to be pounced on over Germany. Once Bill remarked, 'I've never heard a nightingale since I came over to the 'Old Country.' Ann Shelton had just warbled out about the one that sang in Berkeley Square. 'There's still time,' I answered. Someone else joined the conversation. 'Can anyone tell me why we are doing formation flying on our night flying tests? It frightens me fartless all this tucking up to one another. At least at night I can't see you lot. This formation lark puts you too close to me.

"We found out pretty soon. Seemingly, the CO hadn't gone batchy as we had thought. We had done a trip to Hagen and another to Berlin, and were waiting to take off again to the 'Big City' when we were summoned to the Briefing Room on the morning of 11 December. We were told that we were going to take part in a bombing raid on a distillation and coking plant at Duisburg.[170] It was going to be marked by *Oboe* aircraft. The idea was that we were going to form in pairs behind the markers, then when they opened their bomb doors we would open ours, and when we saw their bomb drop, we'd press the bomb tit and release ours. That meant that upward of two-dozen 4000lb bombs would hit the coking plant together. In order that those following would see when the marker bomb was released, the formation would step down 50 or 100 feet behind the aircraft in front. It also kept the following aircraft out of the slipstream of those ahead. It worked like a charm, except that the likes of us, who were in the middle of the formation, found ourselves flying through a cascade of 4000lb bombs. Those, allied to the numerous flak bursts, combined to make us long for the cloak of darkness. No wonder the daylight boys reported heavy flak. To our knowledge, the idea was never repeated. What the effect of it was we never found out - Berlin was a 'piece of duff' by comparison.[171]

"I decided one thing after the trip and discussed it with Bill. 'Do you think you could wind the aircraft up 1000 feet above our flight-planned level on our next op?' Bill looked at me and I explained my reasoning.

"'That sounds like good common sense,' said Bill. 'I think I can. It'll keep us out of the others' paths.'

"'Good. I'll speak to the photographic section about our change of altitude, then they can adjust the camera for the extra 1000 feet.' Apparently, I hadn't been the first to think of the idea. The corporal winked and smiled. 'You've decided to join the other clever buggers up top. I don't blame you.'

"The next night [12/13 December, when 49 Mosquitoes were despatched] we flew to Osnabrück, bringing our tally of ops into double figures. We completed the trip and we went on the beer with the boys the next night. The day following the flight commander wanted us in his office. We laid on all the bullshit we had ever been taught - marching in, saluting, and banging our feet in the approved manner.

"'What in God's name are you playing at? Sit down,' came the laconic request from the flight commander. His Aussie navigator had his ample bulk parked on the seat in the corner of the office. 'By the look of them they must think they're going to be put on a fizzer,' he said. 'Park your asses on these chairs.' A burnt matchstick protruded from the corner of his mouth. We sat on the edge of our chairs, not quite knowing what was coming.

"'You've been posted,' said the flight commander.

"'We looked rather crestfallen. 'Cheer up. I've been asked to supply two crews for 162 Squadron which is starting up at Bourn.'[172] He doodled with a pencil on the blotting pad in front of him. 'It's being reconstituted as a Pathfinder Mosquito squadron. I was warned that they didn't want any rubbish, so it's quite a compliment to you both.'

"'Yeah,' added his navigator. 'They don't want kangaroos that can't jump. You're good 'press on' types with lots of ops left in you.

"'It's a bit of a shoestring airfield compared with here,' broke in the flight commander, 'but you'll get used to it. By the way, I've recommended you both for commissions.'

"They wanted their pound of flesh, however and a week before Christmas 1944 [on 17 December, when

44 Mosquitoes took part in a 'spoof' raid] we were detailed for a trip to Hanau. We took off, in heavy fog, dropped our 'Cookie' on the target and returned with some degree of apprehension gnawing at us. We needn't have worried for a wind had picked up, blown the fog away, and substituted snow and sleet instead. We landed safely. We left the next day, 18 December. The Canadian navigator and his pilot were the other crew who were posted. After a lot of asking and swearing we found the adjutant's office. He was in a complete muddle. I noticed he was wearing wings above his breast pocket, which I found reassuring. I reckoned if he could have jumped into an aircraft and got the hell out of the place, he would have been a happy man.

"'What a shambles the whole thing is,' he said. 'It's a silly question I know,' remarked Bill, 'but there are aircraft here for us to fly, I suppose?'

"The adjutant looked up from his jumble of papers. 'Yes, that is one thing that is not in a muddle. There are a lot of brand new Mk.XXV 'Mossies' in the hangars or on dispersals waiting for you. We've got to get operational in a couple of days. That's an order from God himself.' He jerked his thumb in the vague direction of Huntingdon. We presumed he was referring to our intrepid AOC.

"'By the way, there's a meeting of all you members of the squadron in the Briefing Room at six o'clock tonight, so don't get ideas of going out on the piss to Cambridge or the Caxton Gibbet. See you then.'

"We nodded, left him to untangle his knickers, climbed aboard the 30-cwt truck and directed the driver. The billets were warm, even if they were a bit rudimentary. NCOs and officers mucked in together, at least as far as living accommodation was concerned, and we were all on 'Bill and Ben' terms within the hour.

"The CO [Wing Commander C. J. D. Bolton DFC] looked as if he had just left the Upper Sixth. His display of 'gongs' disproved that. Our flight commander, on the other hand, wouldn't have looked out of place in a comfortable chair by the fireside, wearing a pair of slippers. He must have seen 30-35 summers - aged by our standards. The rest of the bunch seemed to be a cross-section of the Commonwealth and the Colonies. Besides members from every county in Great Britain, there were Australians, Canadians, New Zealanders, a South African; 'Ossie', a Scots tea planter from Ceylon, and a sugar planter from Jamaica. There was even a Czech. How he arrived in the squadron only he knew. We were going to meld into a new squadron. All of us had flown on ops before. It was satisfying to know that Bill and I were no longer 'sprogs' but had several trips under our belts.

"We were operational in two days, but without night flying tests on our aircraft. The foggy weather precluded that. We were called to briefing on the afternoon of 21 December. We had to do a *Spoof* raid on the important marshalling yards at Cologne/Nippes. The 'heavies' were going to bomb it again an hour or two later, the idea being to help cut the jugular vein feeding the Ardennes offensive.[173] Apparently, it was far more ferocious than had been anticipated at first, and had caught the Allies on the wrong foot. When the intelligence officer said we would drop 'Window' on our way into the target, Bill smiled at me and asked if I was going to make a Father Christmas of him again.

"Just after six o'clock we groped our way onto the runway and got airborne safely. The fog had been swirling across the field in banks; sometimes it was clear, sometimes it cloaked everybody and everything. It had been an on-off trip from the start. The Met men could give no assurance about the fog, either on take-off or return. The 'heavy' boys were going to follow us after an interval, so that each time our trip was delayed, the Main Forces had to fall back in time.

"The weather over the target was pretty bloody. Snow showers drifted across the Cologne area and it seemed as if the defenses hadn't much heart for putting up a barrage. It must have been cold and bleak on their gun-sights that night. I threw the Window out on the run-up to the target, making sure the chute was positioned correctly, and dropped four 500lb bombs on the Tis, which had been put down by the *Oboe* markers; then headed for base. Before we crossed the r coast at Cromer we heard over the R/T that all was not well. All the fields were out owing to fog, although some aircraft had got into Wyton, which was still producing some holes in the fog. But many were running around East Anglia like scalded cats. I used this expression to Bill. He glanced in my direction. 'Have you ever landed at an airfield using FIDO?'

"'No, have you?' Woodbridge and Manston had it. Flicking through the sheets of flimsies I was reading, I said, 'There's one at Foulsham.' FIDO consisted of two raised pipes running either side of the runway and well back from it. There was a crossbar at either end and the theory was that oil was injected into the pipes, which had holes in them, at various intervals. The oil was then set on fire and the resultant heat lifted the temperature and with it the fog that blanketed the runway. It was a dangerous and expensive way of getting aircraft down in foggy weather. I glanced at the petrol gauges. We still had plenty of juice left. If the worst should happen and we couldn't get into Foulsham, we could always head south. 'Let's have a stab at Foulsham.'

"We crossed the coast, and I didn't have to give Bill a course to steer as we could see the red glow of the burning oil that showed we were on track for Foulsham. From the chatter on the R/T it was evident we were not the only ones with the idea. We joined the queue circling the airfield, being tossed around by the turbulence of the upcurrents from FIDO. At least, we hoped it was the upcurrents and not the slipstream from some other aircraft, which had forgotten to switch its navigation lights on. At last our turn came, and Bill pointed the aircraft's nose at what seemed to be a raging inferno. He kept the gyrocompass lined up on the main runway. It was no easy task as the nearer we got to the flames the more the turbulence tossed us around. When we had almost given up hope of getting down we burst through the fog and saw the runway ahead of us. Bill had more nerve than I would ever have had. I would have overshot and abandoned the landing. He pulled back on the steering column and we thumped onto the tarmac. The flames from FIDO were licking up on both sides of us but, although dazed by the experience, we obeyed the R/T injunction from the control tower to clear the runway as quickly as possible as there were other aircraft following on behind us. With the aid of a 'Follow Me' van and the torches wielded by ground crew, we got to an overcrowded dispersal pan and cut the engines. We found that our aircraft and the ground crew were covered in thick oily flecks of soot.

"It sticks like shit to a blanket,' said one of the distraught ground crew, whose face looked as if he had been made up for a Black and White Minstrel Show. Bill phoned base to say we were safely down, and we slept where we could find a place on the Mess floor. Next morning, in gin-clear conditions, we flew over to Bourn. As we rumbled down the runway at Foulsham we caught a glimpse of a Fortress lying across the FIDO installation. He hadn't quite made it."

From time to time many enterprising COs devised schemes (some "cracked-brained") for improving bombing accuracy and results, or for meeting emergency calls. One such scheme that December was the "Formation Daylight." The idea was for an *Oboe* equipped aircraft to act as "Lead Ship" (to borrow the American term) for a small force of Light Night Striker Mosquitoes, each carrying 4000 pounders to attack small, vital targets in daylight, thus achieving, it was hoped, great precision. Two 582 Squadron Lancaster B.VIs, specially adapted for the leadership role, were at first allocated. The Lancaster VI was good for 28,000 feet, but its cruising speed was incompatible with the Mosquito IX or XVI. It was to carry an extra *Oboe* pilot and navigator of 109 (Mosquito) Squadron to fly the specialized bombing run. This arrangement was not popular with the *Oboe* Mossie crews.

One of these was Flight Lieutenant Bob Jordan and Ronnie Plunkett of 105 Squadron at Bourn, who were asked to operate the *Oboe* on the operation on 23 December, an attack on the Cologne/Gremburg railway marshalling yards to disrupt enemy reinforcements for the Battle of the Bulge. Twenty-seven Lancasters and three Mosquitoes would make the raid. (Another fifty-two Mosquitoes would visit the rail yards at Limburg and forty more were going to Siegburg.) Jordan and Plunkett were to lead the second formation of ten, while Squadron Leader Robert A. M. Palmer DFC* of 109 Squadron and his crew would lead the first formation in an *Oboe*-equipped Lancaster borrowed from 582 Squadron. Palmer, who was 24 years old and had been promoted to squadron leader at age 23, had completed 110 sorties at this time, having been on bombing operations since January 1941. At Graveley, Jordan and Plunkett were detailed to fly on Lancaster PB272 *X for X-Ray* of 35 Squadron, flown by Flying Officer E. J. Rigby and his usual crew. Jordan and Plunkett were to take over the aircraft 60 miles out from the target to operate the *Oboe*. *X for X-Ray* was airborne at 1038 with eleven 1000lb MC on the racks. Their outward run was normal, except that two Lancs touched wings and went down. When the two Mosquito men took over, their aircraft came under predicted heavy flak and caught fire, which the crew was able to extinguish. Since they were not "on the beam" they did not get a release signal and had to jettison the bomb load from 17,000 feet.

"We had a clear view of Squadron Leader Palmer leading the first formation just ahead," recalls Plunkett, "and his aircraft came under intense AA fire. Smoke billowed from the Lanc and I wondered why he did not bale out there and then because there seemed to be no hope for them. A German fighter then attacked them but they carried on and completed their bombing run. The Lanc then went over on the port side and went down. I cannot think what, other than sheer determination, kept him on the bombing run. He carried out his duty in textbook fashion. After this we went down to 6000 feet and Rigby did a good job getting us all back to Manston."[174]

The "Formation Daylight" attacks on Siegburg and Limburg, meanwhile, were, after a change of heart, finally led by *Oboe* Mosquitoes, not Lancasters, as Flight Lieutenant John Garratt, a navigator in 109 Squadron at Little Staughton, recalls:

"After some bright spark suggested using an *Oboe* Mosquito as 'Lead Ship' - the obvious choice in the first place, my pilot, Flight Lieutenant C. M. Rostron DFC and I were detailed as 'Lead Ship' crew! The target was a small installation at Siegburg in western Germany. Our bomb load was four 500lb MC (surprisingly!) and our kite, XVI MM123. We were to take twelve Night Light Strikers carrying 4000 pounders. Most of East Anglia was fog-bound and the heavies were stood down, but we could land on FIDO at Gravely if we had to. We were to rendezvous with the strikers off Orfordness and proceed in a loose gaggle to the 'Turning-on-Point' for the bombing run where the strikers would close in to a tight formation of Vics astern of the lead ship, with bomb bay doors to open two minutes before release point. (The bomb doors on the Mosquito were notoriously prone to creep and if not fully open when the 'Cookie' went, they went with it!) The striker's navigators were to release on visual cue from the lead ship, which I thought was the weak link in the scheme.

"We took off at 1455. Just enough time to reach the target in daylight. To my surprise we met the strikers on time and in position as planned and flew across Holland into Germany to the 'Turning-on-Point' where the *Oboe* ground stations called us in and we began to transmit, creating the beam. The run down the beam went OK. There was little opposition and the striker pilots' station keeping I thought, remarkable, particularly since we had had no formation practice. Our timing was bang-on and the release signal came loud and clear Immediately after bomb release we broke formation in an orderly manner (bearing in mind it was now getting dark, even at 30-odd thousand feet), and flew back to base singly. All kites returned safely. At debriefing we were told our error off AP was small and the timing spot on. Despite enquiries, I never learned whether the operation was considered a success. The intelligence hods never told us much, safe in their ivory towers. However, we never flew another 'Formation Daylight.'"

A successful daylight raid *was* carried out on 31 December against the Oslo *Gestapo* Headquarters in Victoria Terrasse (last bombed by 105 Squadron Mosquitoes on 25 September 1942) by the low level Mosquito diver specialists of 627 Squadron, as Flying Officer Robert G. "Bob" Boyden DFC* RCAF recalls:

"I was a Canadian bomber pilot attached to the RAF's 627 Squadron. We were flying the fabulous Mosquito bomber and after nearly a year of constant practice, I was a confident pilot. The Mosquito had become a part of me. Wing Commander Cheshire had developed our unique dive-bombing technique and we had done quite a number of dive marking trips for the heavy bombers - Lancasters, Halifaxes and Stirlings. We used visual means of marking, instead of the technical equipment used by 8 Group. This took a great deal of practice and our accuracy had become so dependable that we grew from a "toy airplane" to a lethal weapon. A quick, accurate placing of our target indicators and bombs would keep the damage centerd on the main target and that is why we were chosen for the Oslo raid.

"We followed the same routine procedure, getting ready for the big one. Our target practices over the Wash increased a little and the aircraft we were slated to fly were checked out. My aircraft was DZ611 and I had flown her on a number of previous trips. We didn't get all excited about this target beforehand, as the crews knew nothing of what the upper ranks were planning. Our first information about the trip to Oslo was that we were to fly to Peterhead in the Northern part of Scotland, which would be our advance base. Peterhead was an American base for B-17s and would cut off at least two hours flight time and give us a good start. The trip would be a long one - four to four and a half hours - and that can be very tiring if weather conditions require continuous instrument flying or if there are a few unfriendly happenings along the way. Briefing told us that Oslo was the target - not target for tonight - as this would be a daylight raid, which we did not do very often. In fact, I believe I flew only three trips in daylight. It's quite different, as you feel you stand out like a sore thumb. At this time of our action against the enemy we flew to our destination at 28,000 feet and around the target would descend to 3000 feet to look over the area for a pre-determined aiming point. We would then dive to 1000 feet or 500 feet levels. After we had done our marking, we would climb back to 28,000 feet and return to base. This time the target had flak positions and the German Navy was in the Oslo Fiord. Wing Commander Curry was our new CO and would lead the group, which was made up of two flights of six Mosquitoes each. Flight Lieutenant Peter Mallender would lead the second wave. Flying Officer Willis was my new replacement navigator and we hadn't done very many trips together. He had been Squadron Leader's Churcher's navigator and needed some more trips to wind up his tour of operations. Warrant Officer Fenwick had retired after another 30 flights in his second tour of operations and had left the Squadron.

"I left Woodhall Spa with a full load of gasoline and two 1000lb bombs. The two hour flight to Peterhead was uneventful but the air was rough along the coastline as we came in to land and to my embarrassment I came in pretty heavily. Why is it that it seems everyone is watching at a time like that and no one ever seems to notice when you "grease it in"? The Mosquito wasn't a nose wheel job so it had to be landed in a three point position.

"We were up bright and early the following morning as our target arrival time was 11.00 hours. Much to my surprise Wing Commander Curry wanted us to take off in a V formation, three at a time. I was No.3 on his starboard side, behind and to the right of his wingtip. I can only guess that he wanted to do this because the Americans were masters of formation flying and our Wing Commander had embellished our skills over a glass of black and tan the previous evening. I had flown formation in our early training days but hadn't done any for a long time. During the night two to three inches of snow had fallen leaving a nice light cover on the ground. When our leader opened up his throttles for take-off the resulting blizzard astonished even a good Canadian prairie boy like me. It was complete black-out and strictly instrument flying and as soon as we were airborne I pulled sharply to starboard. We waited for the other nine to take-off - at least we had cleared the runway for them - and form up into the echelon position. I have yet to hear or read any comments about this spectacular take-off. We climbed 12,000 feet on a heading of 045° NE and started our trip to Oslo.

"The North Sea is a long trip and we had been told that the water was so cold we would last only two minutes in it. I don't remember worrying too much about it - it was such a beautiful day. We relaxed and enjoyed the scene just below us - snow covered mountains and bright sunshine. Flying Officer Willis and I did not talk much, if at all. Each of us absorbed in our own thoughts, thinking of what could happen and Willis no doubt wondering what this bastard was going to do next.

"We cleared the Norwegian coast, with the Oslo Fjord to our right. The target was ahead of us but not in sight, lost in the haze. Suddenly bursts of flak came up, seemingly one for each aircraft and right on altitude. This was the first time that I had seen, heard and smelled flak all at the same time and we flew through the cloud. Wing Commander Curry called out for us to descend on target, probably with his usual 'Tally Ho'. He started to dive with us following his movements. No.2 disappeared from my view and left a gap between the leader and myself. He told No. 2 to close in and after a couple of instructions like that I realized I was the one he called No.2. I had already pushed up my throttles at the start of the dive to close the gap. I broke radio silence to tell him I was No.3 and closing fast. Everything happened so quickly: we had, of course, fooled the flak defenses by our diving attack and at last - the target. Bomb doors open, wait for right moment, push the button, and hold at 1000 feet. I felt two concussions that closely followed one another. There was no smoke, no dust. I then pushed lower over the city and I remember seeing an open-air skating rink with people skating around, unaware of the chaos and explosions behind them.[175]

"Suddenly No.4 was descending down on top of us. Once again I had to break silence and suddenly what seemed to be a mountain loomed up right in front of us and as we changed our straight and level to a steep climb, flak came off the mountain, then we were up and over. Curry ordered us to break up, every man for himself. I was doing a left-hand turn to head back when I saw a valley to our right. I slid down into the valley and kept at a low level. We passed over the coast and I began the climb back to our operational altitude of 28,000 feet. There wasn't a cloud in the sky and no enemy aircraft were in the vicinity. I didn't know until years later that the second wave did not drop their bombs. All they saw was smoke and dust at the target site and would not risk killing Norwegians."[176]

Flight Lieutenant Peter Mallender in *D-Dog* was briefed to lead the second wave of six aircraft, which were ordered not to bomb unless they could see the target.[177] Mallender recalls:

"I was instructed to follow our intrepid leader after an interval of five minutes. I did and the German naval gunners quickly learned how fast a Mosquito could travel in a dive. All the aircraft in my flight were hit."

Mallender's Australian navigator, Flight Lieutenant Wallace "John-O" Gaunt DFC, who had completed 33 operations on Wellingtons in 466 Squadron, recalls:

"We had been briefed to expect flak from the hillside of the fiord. In fact the Prinz Eugen with its flotilla of destroyers was just to starboard of our low level mid-day attack and they were most unfriendly. We suffered massive damage and I got a cannon shell through by right leg - exposing but not breaking the bone. I later found a small arms bullet in the left-hand breast pocket of my battle dress. It had traveled through the tube of gentian violet and a field dressing."

Mallender continues:

"It missed the back of my head and went out through the Perspex top. Another hit removed the whole of the curved part of the port leading edge outboard of the engine leaving the very flat and un-streamlined bare main spar to face the force of wind of a Mosquito in a dive. I did manage to regain control from the violent yaw to port by slapping the starboard Merlin right back. I called to my No.2 to take over and I flew through the smoke and dust still obscuring the target. I cleared flying low over the Royal Palace and poor old 'D-Dog' received another load of shot from a machine gun sited on the roof, just beside a huge Red Cross. 'D-Dog' still wanted to make circles to port and I thought that perhaps I would have a little more control if I were to jettison the drop tanks. I tried that; the starboard tank dropped away but apparently the wiring to the port drop tank had been severed and that one stayed there. The yaw was exacerbated by this and my right leg was very cramped but pushing as hard as I could we sidled our way home to Scotland after I had jettisoned our bomb load after crossing the Norwegian coast near Stavanger. ("John-O" Gaunt adds, "Peter was doubtful whether the aircraft would make it back to UK so flew north for several minutes debating whether to turn right and head for Sweden, but the engines kept going and we gained height slowly, so went west over the mountains.")

"I stuck John in the backside with the little tube of morphia that we carried. Even so he managed to remain conscious and helped me to get home until I told him that I could see the Scottish coast. I had managed to crawl up to 5000 feet whilst crossing the sea and thought that it was about time I found out if I was going to be able to land the old lady. I dropped fifteen degrees of flap and throttled back the port engine a bit but before I had time to ease back to reduce speed much she shook violently and I noted that we were still flying at one forty knots. All the other aircraft had got safely home so I had the runway to myself. Rather unwisely, I now admit, I put the undercarriage down and the pre-stall shaking began immediately. I put down about fifteen degrees of flap (previous experiments had taught me that this seemed logical), I jettisoned the top hatch and powered her over the boundary at something near one forty knots. She stayed down all right but was burning up runway much too fast. I touched the brakes and that did it. She spun round and around like a Dervish, collapsed the under-carriage and finally came to rest in what I thought was a heap of ply, balsa wood and aluminium. I was really quite pleased to see George Curry's grinning visage looking down through the open hatch. He helped me out and together we lifted from his seat a very comatose, if rather battered, navigator."

"John-O" Gaunt, who was put into an ambulance and taken to a Naval Hospital just north of Aberdeen, concludes. "They sewed me up in the last hours of 1944. Got a bar to the DFC for that escapade - notified by telegram whilst in hospital."[178]

Back to night operations again, and on the night of 31 December 1944 77 Mosquitoes were despatched to Berlin and twelve to Ludwigshafen. One of them was *Z-Zebra*[179] of 128 Squadron, which was flown by Flight Lieutenant Leicester G. Smith RNZAF, who with his navigator, Warrant Officer Bill Lane, completed 52 operations on the Mosquito B.XVI from October 1944 to April 1945. Twenty of these were to Berlin. Smith recalls:

"The big 'Cookie carrier' B.XVI was a wonderful aircraft to fly and although it had a pressurised cabin it was not used on operations in case of internal damage from flak. Take off time was 1615 hours. The flight plan kept our aircraft to 10,000 feet to 6° East and an indicated airspeed of 215 knots at that height. It was a glorious evening for flying, as so many evenings were and mainly over 7/10ths cloud. The reason given was to miss the cumulo-nimbus cloud tops. We climbed to operational height and leveled out at 26,000 feet. Flak was heavy between Lübeck and Hamburg (commonly called the Gap). Shrapnel was whistling around everywhere but our sympathy went out to one Mosquito crew who was coned by at least 20 searchlights. Flak was bursting all around him, at least 2000 feet above and below. I was about two miles north of this aircraft and he flew straight through it all. It was an unforgettable sight. Otherwise we had a comfortable run to the Big City. Over Berlin all was quiet as the target indicators, reds and green, went down. A warning was issued that fighters were in the area but none were seen. Bill reported contrails 2-3000 feet above. We put our 'Cookie' down on schedule, took the photo and had a relatively quiet flight back to England. We were coned by many searchlights over the Woodbridge area (must have been an army exercise), landing at Wyton from an operation of five hours airborne."

One of the 692 Squadron crews who were laid on, unexpectedly, for the operation to the "Big City" was Pilot Officer Ron H. M "Percy" Vere and his navigator, Flight Lieutenant (later Squadron Leader) J. F. P. Archbold, who recalls:

"The crew conference was at midday and navigation briefing at 13.15 so there was just time for a meal before getting ready. Our aircraft was *K-King* (MM224), Burbidge and Ramage's kite. Rumor had it that everyone who flew *K-King* except those two had something happen to them. We hoped that we were the exception! After the meal I went down to the billet to put on my old blue sweater, check scarf and flying boots and then bike to the crew room for briefing. Phil Earnshaw was doing the nav, briefing and a hell of a route it was too! Tonight's op was a maximum effort with twelve kites on the Battle Order. There was something else in the air too. Wadsworth, Burbidge, Crow, Nairn and two others hung about as if waiting for a briefing after we came out. Ron had been out to the kite to ground run it and put in the kit. I didn't have the time.

"The route out was via Cromer, over the North Sea, with a turn towards Heligoland, then north of Lübeck before turning SE to Berlin. The return route was south of Magdeburg, through the gap between Osnabrück and Münster before turning west for the English Coast. This was a route I did not like. We were going in north of Hamburg and the gunners there were pretty hot. They got bags of practice anyway so I hoped it was 10/10[ths] there. We plotted tracks, working out courses and times and recording them in the log, sorting out maps and charts. Then, after about three quarters of an hour we checked our work against the Master Log for any errors (on either side) and then sat back and waited for the main briefing to begin.

"In came the Met man. He started drawing in his cloudscapes on his briefing board. It didn't look too good to me: 8/10[ths] Stratocu over the sea, clearing over the Third Reich. It looked as if we could be shot at! The drivers airframe [pilots] drifted in and sat down with their navs and the CO followed them. We got on with the main briefing. It was 14.15. First, Flying Control (Squadron Leader 'Lemnos' Hemming, a pioneer in photographic reconnaissance in 1940 with Sidney Cotton. We knew him as 'Popeye' because he wore an eyepatch. He told us the runway would be the long one; no obstructions. There were no other comments. Then Met gave his story. 'Target will be clear; no cloud from the time you cross the coast in 'till you come out again. Base would be clear for the return. Forecast winds are up in the seventies and eighties.' My guess was that they may well be a little stronger than he told us. Now Intelligence: 'Usual place chaps; you've all been there before, so I can't tell you anything you don't already know. Target height, 17,000 feet.'

"The CO, Wing Commander 'Joe' Northrop DSO DFC AFC in his slow methodical way told us the tactics and the type of the TIs to be dropped. We were to bomb the highest concentration of Red TIs, or failing that, the highest concentration of Greens, or on good DR. Finally the CO detailed take-off times for each aircraft. Ours was 16.08 and the full number of aircraft would set course at 1617.

"Well, it all seemed pretty straightforward so far. I caught Percy's eye and grinned. He was a bit cheesed off because his wife had come down for the New Year's Eve party and we were only put on this trip at the last minute. I could see us belting back tonight! Well, that was the end of the briefing. It was now about 14.45 and we all trooped out to the crew room where old Chiefy Tite had organized tea and sandwiches for us. Having munched these we went to the locker room and collected Mae Wests and navigation bag, signed for the escape kit pack and straggled out to the crew buses waiting to take us out to our aircraft. Our dispersals were at the East end of the airfield, south of the main runway. The bus duly deposited us at *K-King*. First thing to do was to stow the 'Window' bundles in the nose while the skipper went to sign the F700; then cram the nav bag in on top. After this I had to check that the DR compass master unit was serviceable, that the oxygen cocks were turned on and the camera magazine was fitted; all this is in the rear hatch. Next I had to see that the navigation lights were working and that the safety pins had been taken out of the Cookie - an awkward job, this. You had to use a torch and peer through a small circular hole at the lug. All done; time for a last smoke.

"Percy was round the back having his operational pee, which he never missed. The usual curious hush had settled on the aerodrome just before the kites started up. There just wasn't a sound. A train whistled in the distance and then the silence descended again. I looked at my watch: 20 minutes to take off, time to get in. I took a last drag at my cigarette. Ron was getting himself strapped in. It took him some time to do this. And I put on my parachute harness after slipping a piece of gum into my mouth and got in myself. "Have a good trip, Sir" said the rigger, as he stowed the ladder and shut the door. Good lads, our ground crews. Bill Brodie the duty CO came round to each kite in turn to see if everything was OK. We gave him a thumbs up and he went to the next kite. We were eighth off, so it was about time we started up. The first kite had already done so Ron ran up the engines and I checked the Gee and Loran to see if they were working. All were OK and I switched them off until we were airborne. The first kite taxied out in the dusk of this December afternoon. After a while we waddled forward, checked the brakes and moved slowly out on to the perimeter track and on in the queue to the take off point. A last check: petrol on outers, pitot head heater on, nav lights and oxygen on, radiator shutters open. We got a flashing green Aldis from the ACP's caravan and taxied on to the runway. We could see the tail light of the kite in front climbing away. Ron taxied forward a little to straighten the tail wheel and then said, 'OK, boy, here we go.' And we were off.

"The next few moments were pretty tense. We had the maximum load of fuel and bomb aboard. You hoped she won't swing or burst a tyre because you had a rather unpleasant companion about 6" underneath where we were sitting. Then the tail came up and we watched the airspeed creep up to 120 knots; full boost and 3000 revs. The red light at the end of the runway came rushing up and the kite heaved herself off the deck. (You could almost hear her grunt). Then the skipper gave the word to raise the undercarriage. We listened anxiously to the engines. A misfire now would be decidedly unpleasant -but they didn't miss (we had a damn good groundcrew) and we climbed away to the delay pattern. We passed over Little Staughton, 10 miles from base at 1500 feet before turning back towards base, still climbing, to set course with the others.

"We crossed the coast at Cromer and headed for Heligoland. At 1712 we began climbing to 20,000 feet. we were gaining a lot of time. The kite wouldn't go less than 190 knots at 10,000 feet. That was 15 knots too fast and we now had nine minutes in hand and had to lose some time. We decided to orbit to lose four minutes. We got back on course and ten minutes later started to climb again to 27,000 feet. During this time we transferred fuel from 100 gallon drop tanks to the outer tanks. This was done automatically and a red light came on when the drop tanks were empty and you switched off the transfer switch. Slap bang over Heligoland six rocket shells rose up on the starboard beam about two miles away and we altered course slightly to the north and pressed on. At 1805 the Yellow route marker went down dead ahead and fairly close. Good, that meant that we were pretty well leading the stream behind the markers. Gee was no longer available now and I worked feverishly to average a wind velocity to apply to courses ahead. We crossed the German coast 25 miles NW of Brunsbüttel. All cockpit lights were out now; both of us keeping our eyes skinned for flak and searchlights. It was very dark now and the low cloud had completely dispersed. The kite was going like a bomb - wizard. Aha, there were the first searchlights, ahead and to starboard and there was flak too, 88mm stuff and rockets. You could see the rockets coming up as little red points of light moving very slowly at first. Then they suddenly sped up to your level and burst with an angry red flame. Not near us though. The searchlights were coning over to starboard. They were too far off to see if they'd got someone but it looked like it.

"At 1814 we crossed the Kiel Canal and we were right in the searchlight belt. A master searchlight picked us up and three or four others swung over on to us immediately. The bright red lamp of the '*Boozer*' came on, indicating that we were being tracked by radar-controlled flak. Ron stuck his head well down in the cockpit and did a corkscrew while I kept watch aft. Wow! Just as well we did that a burst of rockets came up just where we were a few seconds before. No sign of any fighters - touch wood. Hello, someone else was coned to starboard. It looked like a Mossie too. I'll bet they were twitching like we were a moment ago. We've lost the searchlights now, or they lost us. We seemed to be getting past the worst of it and the time was 18.20. Ahead and a little to port went the green route markers. We seemed to have lost a bit of ground doing avoiding action. We still had to get past Lübeck. At 1825 the marker leader broadcast a 'Zephyr' message: 'Wind 345°/90 knots.'

"Lübeck was comparatively quiet, thank the Lord. Just past there, on course, someone yelled, 'Snappers' (enemy fighters spotted). Another colossal corkscrew and bags of rubbernecking, but we saw nothing. We resumed course and tried to get some LORAN to check position but there were no signals visible, only grass. We expected the red route marker any minute now. When it came I'd switch on the bombsight, which must be done at least 15 minutes from the target so that it could warm up.) The reds went. It was 1840 and we'd just crossed over 10/10^{ths} cloud below, which looked like going all the way to the 'Big Town'. So much for the Met briefing but a bit of luck for us. I switched on the bombsight and got the 'Window' ready to push out through the wooden 'Window' chute down through the small hatch in the floor.

"Our ground speed on this leg was about 338 knots (about 390 mph). We began windowing with 8 minutes to go. The chute was on the floor between your feet and you had to bend almost double to drop the bundles. You could hear a crackle on the R/T as they opened up in the slipstream. Back breaking job, this and it made you sweat like blazes. Five minutes to go. We should see the first TI in a minute. Out went the last 'Window' bundle. I stretched up and had a look out. We were still over 10/10^{ths} cloud. Good. The first TI was slightly over to port. I dived into the bombing position. 'Dive' is a misnomer. With all the kit I had on it was more like a wrestling match! I switched on the sighting head and put the final wind velocity on the computer box and waited for the TIs to come into view. All the nose except for the optically flat, heated bombing window was frosted up so I couldn't see very far ahead. A couple of minutes to go now.

"'More red and green TIs going down', said Ron.

"'Bomb doors open. Bomb doors open' I repeated and I heard the rumbling roar as they opened and the wind whistled in the bomb bay.

"'I'm running up on a bunch of three', said Ron. 'Can you see them yet?'

"I craned my neck close to the window and looked ahead sideways. 'Yep, I can just see them.' I said. 'OK now, left-left, left-left, steady. We're running up nicely. Keep weaving a bit, we've a minute or so to go yet'. I got the TIs up on the centerline of the graticule and thumbed the release switch. I would press this when the markers reached the cross line. A couple of big white flashes under the cloud up ahead showed that the first two cookies had gone down. I noticed them almost subconsciously.

"'A little bit of flak to starboard,' said Ron.

"'OK, keep going', I said. 'Right, r i g h t a little - steady now, steady...BOMB GONE!' and I pressed the tit. There was a thud underneath as the lug sprang back and released the bomb. The camera whirred and the red light on the selector box came on. We had to keep straight and level for 45 seconds to get a photo of our bomb burst in relation to the TIs so as to be able to plot the accuracy later. I scrambled back into my seat and looked down the window chute. The wait seemed endless.

"'Bomb doors closed', said Ron. The camera green light came on. 'Hold it', I said. There was a great flash under the cloud. 'There she goes; OK, lets get the hell out of here' and we turned southwest to get out of the target area. I turned off the bombsight and bomb selector switches, and looked aft. Some flak was coming up now and some searchlights were on under the cloud. It must have been pretty thin, but they were quite ineffective. More bomb flashes appeared as the TIs drifted slowly down into the cloud tops. It looked like quite a concentrated effort. Just after turning we saw a kite (possibly a cats-eye fighter, a 190, or a 109) shoot over us in the opposite direction leaving a contrail. He didn't appear to have seen us but we kept a sharp look out just in case there were any more. Things being quieter now I entered the time, height and heading of when we bombed.

"Ron said, 'Check the petrol, will you?'

"I did so and found that we had about 330 gallons left; a little less than we expected, but OK. At 1919 I tried to get some LORAN but the signals were very weak and I discarded them. I would try again later. Just then the expected green route markers appeared ahead, so we were OK and pretty well on track. At 1924 we altered course and we crossed the Dutch coast at 2022, altering course slightly to the north for Woodbridge and still keeping our height above 23,000 feet. We switched on the IFF and 'identify' on Channel D, making a VHF broadcast: 'Lounger *K King* identifying, out'. (This was for the Fighter Command plot so that we are not mistaken for an enemy aircraft.) I got a string of fixes across the North Sea. The crossing always seemed to me to be one of the longest parts of the trip. The Scu cloud that had reappeared over Holland near the coast was about 4-5/10ths but it dispersed completely before we got to Woodbridge, leaving a clear night. I worked out the ETA coast as 2049 and Ron increased speed a little. At 2038 he said he could see lights ahead and when I looked out for a minute or two later I could see the semi-circle of sodium lights which marked the Woodbridge circuit dead ahead. We coasted in at 2046 and began to lose height slowly, switching on the navigation lights as we did so. We were really moving now, with a ground speed of 260 knots. ETA base was 2100. I began to relax a little.

"Ron changed frequency from Channel D to Channel A (base frequency) to listen out for other aircraft. All the way in from the coast were airfield after airfield, each with its Drem system of lights illuminated and one or two searchlights (called Sandra lights) over the top, forming a sort of canopy. Someone once said that airfields in East Anglia were as thick as fleas on a dog's back. He was right. We began to look for the base lights and I set up homing co-ordinates on the *Gee*. At 2056 we sighted two Sandra lights in an inverted V with a flashing white light in between them (this was the Station identification letters GR in front of Flying Control; all Station idents were lit but ours was the only one in this area to have them flashing). As soon as we saw this, Ron prepared to call up Flying Control and I started packing up my kit. As we did this, two other kites called up almost simultaneously - Chandler and Ginger Wood in *J-Johnny* and another kite. We came tearing up behind them. As we arrived over the airfield, Chandler called, '*J Johnny,* funnels' and landed. The other kite called 'downwind'. We now called up: 'Control from Lounger *K King* over'. Control replied, 'Lounger K King, prepare to land, runway 270, QFE 1029, over'. We replied, '*K King* preparing to land, out', which meant that we acknowledged permission to land and were listening out. Someone else called up just behind us.

"I switched on the downward identification light and opened the radiator shutters. We reduced height to 1500 feet and turned downwind. Ron lowered the undercart, put down some flap and called, '*K King* downwind, out'. This was not acknowledged by Control. Instead they called the next aircraft and told it to prepare to land.

"Now we were turning across wind and one quarter flap was lowered. Two green lights showed that the undercart was down. The circuit lights were visible over the port wing tip and the funnel lead-in lights appeared, with the Station ident letters GR illuminated on the outer circle at their head. We turned into the funnels at 900 feet and called '*K King,* funnels, over'. Control replied, '*K-King,* land, out'. Had the runway not been clear we would have been told to overshoot and come in again.

"The runway lights appeared now, narrowing into the distance. Two flashing lights either side of the threshold were the glide path indicators, or GPIs, which showed the correct glide path. Now Ron hunched himself over the stick, put down full flap and concentrated on his landing. We went sliding in at 125 knots. The runway lights came up quickly at the end. We gave the usual heave as Ron checked her and closed the throttles, touching down on the main wheels at about 95 knots and trundling down the runway to the accompaniment of the usual crackles and pops from the exhausts of those wonderful Merlins. We turned left at the end of the runway, pulled up the flaps and called, '*K King* clear' and then taxied back to dispersal with the engines purring away as if they'd only just started up. At dispersal we were waved in by the groundcrew and we stopped and opened the bomb doors. (You got reproachful looks from the groundcrew if you forgot this, for they then had to pump them down by hand; a tedious exercise). Ron pulled the cutouts and the engines rumbled to a stop. We switched everything off and climbed out stiffly with a mutual grin of congratulation at completing another trip safely. This was our 27th. We collected our kit and stalked over to the waiting crew bus laden with parachutes and harness, nav bag, camera magazine and the rest and were driven back to the crew room for interrogation.

"Back at the crew room we dumped our kit and went in to be interrogated. First, the CO had a word about the trip in general, then Intelligence. They wanted to know in detail about the bombing: how concentrated was it; was there much opposition; what were the relative positions of the TIs you bombed - draw a sketch of them as you saw them please - and a host of other details? While this was going on coffee and rum was brought in and the second cigarette lit. Boy, did the first one taste good! Following this the navigators had to hand in their maps, charts and logs and pass on details of radar coverage, *Gee* jamming, hand over signals flimsies and camera magazine, while the pilots signed the Form 700 and told the engineers about any snags. At last all was done and it was h'way to the Mess for bacon and eggs and the New Year's Eve party."180

Quite late on New Year's Eve, 18 crews in 692, 571, and 128 Squadrons were called to a briefing for details of a raid starting at first light on New Year's Day. At Oakington five crews in 571 Squadron were briefed, as Flying Officer Douglas Tucker DFC, one of the pilots, recalls:

"Until we called to the briefing room, everything had been very hush-hush. No one seemed to know anything definite or even if there was to be a raid at all. Because of the secrecy preceding the flight I did not take Sergeant Bert Cook, my own navigator (who had already completed 24 trips with me). Instead I took Flight Sergeant Fred David. We all soon knew what was in front of us. The German Army was hard pressed bringing equipment and men to the fighting front, mainly by rail. It was reasoned that if this rail traffic could be delayed even for a day or two, the confusion this could cause would be quite substantial. There was little point in bombing railway tracks because even if the rails were hit it was a relatively short time before the craters were filled in and new track laid. It was decided that if it were possible to bomb 24 strategic tunnels at precisely the same time, it would be bound to cause considerable confusion and inconvenience at the very least. How to achieve this was the next problem. Even using the latest bomb sights, it would have been impossible to bomb from normal height and get the result, which was so essential. To fly across enemy territory in daylight would have been hazardous, especially when the desired effect would not be achieved. The decision was made to use Mosquito bombers, which were very fast and could out-pace most fighters.

"Most of our aircraft were equipped with drop tanks; these were two torpedo shaped tanks, one on each wing; which gave us greatly increased range. Although the tanks could be jettisoned at the press of a button, we were told not to drop them unless an extra-speed emergency that required a few extra knots (our speed indicators were calibrated in 'Nautical Miles Per House' - knots). Our particular model of Mosquito carried no armor plating or armament. This saving of weight gave us an increase of speed, so we relied on this to keep us out of trouble, combined with our usual operational height in excess of 25,000 feet, which was twice as high as most of the heavy bombers flew to drop their bombs. What type of bomb would be needed? We normally carried the one 4000lb HE bomb, shaped like an oversize dustbin. Because of the relatively thin casing, they exploded on impact. On this operation, we were to drop our bomb as low as it was possible for us to fly in, aiming for 50 to 100 feet above ground level. A 4000lb bomb with orthodox casing was selected and fitted with a 30-second delay fuse. This would avert any possibility of us being blown apart by the blast. For some weeks, we had been practicing low level bombing with small practice bombs. We were told that it was just a general exercise. In the event, this practice was of little use as the targets [in the Eifel and Ardennes area] were on a completely flat piece of ground and train tunnels are usually on the edge of hills, or hilly areas. To make a direct hit would require flying towards the mouth of the tunnel, dropping the bomb and hopefully pulling up at the last second to clear the hill.[181]

"We had been flying low for some time before reaching the area of the tunnel, map reading frantically as the ground sped underneath us. We looked for landmarks such as railway lines, rivers, canals and villages etc. Suddenly, just ahead of us was the tunnel and just as quickly we had passed it. We were covering the ground at approximately one mile every nine seconds. Two German soldiers had stopped their motorcycle and sidecar on a bend of a hill. One was astride the motorcycle and the other stood by his sidecar. It would have been difficult to have missed them, as they were less than 100 feet away from me when I passed over them. They must have heard the roar of low flying aircraft and stopped just as I flew past. I throttled back, lowered the flaps slightly and turned to the left to complete a circle in the hope of locating the end of the tunnel again. After 360 degrees we located the tunnel mouth. Now we would have to complete another circuit to make preparations for dropping the bomb. On the down leg I opened the bomb bay doors. This did nothing to improve the flying characteristics of the aircraft. At our normal bombing height of five miles this made little difference, except that it was more difficult to hold a steady course, but at ground level it was a different sensation altogether.

"We came round for our third run towards the tunnel entrance. As we circled close to the hill we were suddenly confronted with a wood on a rise in the ground. Instinctively, I pushed both throttle controls forward hard and pulled the control column back equally hard. The aircraft continued towards the ground and the trees for what seemed a lifetime, until it wallowed not flew over the obstruction. Apart from shattering raw nerves, it also meant that we would have to do another circuit. So far we had met no opposition from either the air or the ground, but every second we spent in the locality increased the risk of attack. It would have been quite difficult for anyone to hit us, as we were in and out of trees and often below the top of the hill but there was always the chance that someone was just around the corner with a machine gun. It wasn't until the fifth time that we were at the correct height, position, speed etc and at last I was able to press the bomb release button. I pulled the aircraft up just clear of the surrounding land, closed the bomb bay doors and then decided to do one more circuit to have a look at the result of our efforts. As we headed back towards the tunnel entrance the bomb exploded with a cloud of smoke earth and bricks.

"We had hit the target.[182]

"Now our task was completed we realized that we had been in the area far too long. In actual time, the whole episode was only a matter of minutes, but whilst it was happening it seemed like an eternity. I decided to start back by flying at maximum speed in the general direction we had come-in, keeping fairly close to the ground. On our normal night time raids we were given courses and heights and speed to fly at, both to and from the target and we were not allowed to deviate unless there was some exceptional reason. On this trip we were given a free hand on our return journey to decide what height and courses we should take depending on prevailing conditions based on weather, enemy opposition etc. as long as we approached the English Coast within a certain corridor. Our route home took us back along the railway line from the tunnel we had bombed. Within a few minutes, we sighted a train steaming in the direction of the tunnel. They certainly would have a delay. We could take no action against the train, or anything else for that matter .We had dropped our one and only bomb and we carried no armaments except for our revolvers. I continued at low level. I didn't want to risk climbing and thus reducing our speed considerably. I waited until we reached what appeared to be a quiet patch of country and started a shallow climb, maintaining as high a forward speed as possible. Luck was still with us. We did not see any opposition, although it was quite likely that a ground barrage had opened up on us after we had gone past, but we saw nothing and suffered no damage, we considered in this case 'ignorance was bliss.'

"Soon the North Sea was visible. So far we had been flying in the general direction of the East Coast. Now we could relax a little, we set course to cross the area allocated to us. As we approached England we discovered that a thick blanket of fog covered the land. There was no shortage of fuel but if we flew on to our base near Cambridge and then had to divert to another airfield there was a possibility of running low. A landing at Manston, an emergency airfield on the coast of Kent was the safest solution. The station was equipped with FIDO. (Fog Installation Dispersal 01) and if our reasoning were correct, it would be switched on in these conditions. It was. FIDO consisted of metal tubes similar to scaffolding drilled with many holes. This tubing was fixed to each side of the runway and petrol was pumped through the pipes at a rate of 1000 gallons per minute and ignited. The whole system burned with a roar like a gigantic blowlamp. I had not seen FIDO in operation before and it proved to be a most amazing sight. It was just like looking down a giant map, which was covered by a sheet of cotton wool except for a square that had been cut out with scissors. The airfield was completely fog-free, with the sun shining on the runways. We landed without any problems and taxied to the far end of the runway, clear of the pipes. It was essential that the aircraft was not allowed to veer on landing. The heat was so intense that it could be felt through the cockpit windows with the plane in the middle of the runway.

"On landing we contacted our squadron by phone to let them know we were back safely, then a visit to the mess for a hearty breakfast, the second that day. A further call to the squadron confirmed that all fog had cleared and with the aircraft re-fuelled, we took off and headed for Oakington. After de-briefing I met Bert Cook, who was most upset to have missed the trip. He informed me that he would be flying that evening with another pilot. We were a small squadron with no surplus crews. He said that after the night's trip he and I would be back together again. Neither of us particularly liked flying but we had built up a certain affinity and closeness that can only be produced by working under conditions such as we had during our 24 operational flights.

"We were never to fly together again. Bert Cook and his temporary pilot were both killed that night coming back from the raid."

One bomb, dropped by B.XVI ML963 *K-King*, crewed by Flight Lieutenant Norman J. Griffiths and Flying Officer W. R. "Bill" Ball, totally destroyed a tunnel at Bitburg. Bill Ball wrote:

> "At 100 feet the ground simply raced beneath us like lightning. From the big railway junction, dead on ETA the tunnel came up in a flash and we could just not position ourselves in time. We undershot the target and went around again and thus time ran up, dead in line, astonished that the ack-ack batteries had not yet been alerted, we rapidly reached the target, dropped the 4000lb bomb and soared almost vertically to get away from the blast and when had gained height, we looked back and saw a great column of brown-black smoke and sizeable debris rumbling upwards. A mixture of bricks and shattered masonry rising falling and scattering wide. Norman and I agreed that it would be some time before trains ran again on that line."

After returning from Edinburgh on Christmas leave, Johnnie Clark had met up with his pilot Bill Henley and had flown the "long slog" to Berlin. The Scottish navigator had hitch-hiked to Peterborough and then stood in the corridor of a crowded, dirty train all the way to Edinburgh, where he had the usual wartime Scots New Year. His sisters and his father guessed he was flying on operations but had not mentioned it to his mother. At the end of his leave he caught the Colchester night train from Waverley Station, which was looking even dirtier than on those occasions earlier in the war. He knew he'd be flying that night and would need his wits about him. He got a cup of tea from the engine driver of the train which connected with the Colchester one and he arrived back at base about midday. Bill Henley, who had spent his leave with some distant relatives of his in Kent, told him that he had done the night flying test without him and that they were due in the Briefing Room at three o'clock. They were airborne just before 18:00 hours. Clark had tried to ignore the searchlights and box barrage flak over Big B, concentrating on his charts illuminated by the small navigation light which stretched over them. They had dropped their bombs, got their photographs, and had headed for home. Clark turned the oxygen up and found that it perked him up quite a bit. While they were emptying their bladders at the edge of the dispersal pan after landing, Henley had told him that it was their thirteenth trip. "Oh was it? Superstitious are you?" Clark had asked. "No," said Bill Henley, "I just thought you'd like to know." Clark spent New Year's Eve drinking beer in the Caxton Gibbet with the rest of the squadron who were not on ops. Bill Henley, who, ever diligent, told him that they were on the Battle Order next day and they had to report to briefing at six o'clock that night. News that their 14th op [on 1/2 January] would be Hanover met with the usual comments. "Christ, not that bloody place again. It's been burning for days," said the Canadian out of the corner of his mouth. Clark continues:

> "At 20:45 hours we got airborne and climbed to our cruising altitude via the Cromer beacon. There were quite a few snow clouds around but the steady

beat of the engines and the propellers was reassuring. I switched the taps from the 100-gallon drop tanks to the main fuel supply. The changeover went smoothly and after crossing Holland we saw Hanover burning long before we got there. We knew it was no Spoof fire, as the Germans needed every bit of fuel they could get their hands on for domestic use and for armaments. I moved the wad of chewing gum to the other side of my mouth as I pointed out the blaze to Bill. 'There's the target. Seems as if we're only going to stoke up the blaze and turn over the rubble. I'll get up to the nose and prime the bombs. You OK?'

"'Yes. Just awaiting your directions. They may have lost their night fighters but their flak looks pretty hot.'

'I glanced around. The sparks from the 'ack-ack' peppered the sky. What was it some cynic had said: 'The flak was so thick I cut my feet walking on it.' Hell knows what the Yanks thought looking at all the black powder puffs of smoke that those sparks left in the sky. Still, that was their pigeon. We did not attract any searchlights and in the anonymity of darkness we dropped our bombs on the target, then headed for base.

"I don't know how long it was after we left the burning city that it happened. It may have been two minutes; it may have been 10. The aircraft gave a lurch and the engines began to splutter. I quickly raised my eyes from the navigation table and looked at Bill, who was scanning the dials on the dashboard in front of him. 'What the hell's the trouble?'

"Quick, switch on to the drop tanks again.'

"'I switched the levers over and the engines coughed a bit then resumed their steady beat. 'No fuel starvation there,' I muttered. The fuel in the 'drops' we worked out at between 55 and 60 gallons. Not enough to get us back to England. 'Just in case, make the heading 250°. We don't want to ditch in the North Sea in this weather. That heading should take us towards Holland and Belgium.'

"I tried the port engine's main tank again, but the engine spluttered and died almost at once. Bill had put the aircraft into a nose-down attitude to keep up the speed and prevent it from stalling while we switched tanks.

"Let's have it on the 'drop' again,' said Bill.

"When the port had picked up we tried the starboard one, with the same result. Bill sucked in his breath. 'I'll keep it on the starboard engine until it dies on us, then go on the port one. I'll keep the speed up by losing height.'

"We were down to about 18,000 feet from our original 26,000 feet. Although outwardly calm, we knew that when the petrol in each of the drop tanks had gone we had to go as well. It was galling to us to know that although we were sitting on plenty of 'juice', we couldn't get to it. The flak had seen to that; it must have cut the pipes from the main tanks, as the gauge showed that we still had plenty of fuel in them. We settled on the starboard engine only until it packed up, our reasoning being that we wouldn't be chopped to pieces by a whirling propeller when we baled out, as the escape hatch was situated on the starboard side under my feet. We sat and waited for it to die on us. Each minute took us nearer the Allied lines and away from Germany. Their citizens, so we had been told, were not averse to hanging any aircrew from the nearest tree or lamppost, if aircrew dropped among them.

"The port engine was purring away by now. We would have to get out soon. Neither of us showed any panic even though we felt it. It was the waiting that was the worst aspect of the whole thing. If we could have jumped and got it over with we would gladly have done so, but every minute we stayed in the air meant we got nearer to safety and freedom. We were caught between instant action and playing the waiting game. We knew we were going to 'hit the silk', as the Yanks said, eventually.

"I started to get ready to jump, clipping on my chest parachute. I realized I hadn't had it checked since I drew it from the Parachute Section at Wyton several months previously. I hoped it would open when I pulled the D-ring. Then I smashed my elbow through the *Gee* box radar tube, realizing after I had done it how stupid a thing it was to do. After all, if the aircraft were going to crash, the Gee box would be mangled up with the rest of it.

"Bill made one transmission on the R/T, giving our call sign and saying we would be baling out in the next few minutes. Bloody hell, was this really happening to us? I turned and bent down to lift the floorboard under my feet so that I could get to the outer door. It had a pedal attachment to it. One press of the foot on the pedal and the whole door was supposed to jettison. Nothing happened. I pressed again. Then realized the door was jammed. In leaning forward to reach the handle to release one side of it, I caught my parachute D-ring in the edge of my folded-up navigation table. The result took me by surprise. A small spring or something forced out the pilot 'chute and the main canopy spilled out in front of me. I gathered up the folds of the 'chute in one arm, edged round the hole where the floor had been and faced the tail of the aircraft. I didn't want to break my back when I dropped out. Then I told Bill about the outer door having jammed. 'I'll have to unhook it and let it swing in the wind. What height are we now?'

"Bill grunted. '10,000 feet, and all the needles are knocking on the stop.'

"'I'd better go now and leave you some time to get out.' I pushed the lever holding one side of the door. It swung open. I looked at the dark void under my feet. I noticed flames flickering from the starboard engine. 'Hell - we're on fire! I'm on my way now. Good luck. See you back at base.' Sheer bravado on my part, as I didn't think either of us would make it.

"'Hey!' Bill shouted. 'You've got your oxygen tube and intercom flex caught between yourself and your parachute!'

"I raised my thumb in acknowledgement, unhooked one side of my 'chute with one hand and tore off my helmet and oxygen tube. My other hand was clutching my spilled 'chute. I stuck my legs into the black void under me and slipped off the edge of the floor into the night.

"After landing, I gathered my parachute and dusted the snow off my battledress. I was in Holland. Almost at once, two British soldiers approached me and ordered me to put up my hands. Apparently, I'd landed in a minefield and they didn't believe I could have come from this direction! I suppose the frozen ground kept the mines inert!

"Eventually, I was flown to Alconbury and thence returned to the squadron at Bourn. I removed the symbolic axe from my pillow, put there by the other crews. After all, I hadn't got the 'chop' yet. My back was acting up a bit and my testicles felt as if they had been thumped by a truncheon. I was told Bill was in hospital in Belgium with frostbite in both feet. His flying boots came off when his 'chute opened and he had to walk quite a way through the snow in his stockinged feet before he met up with the 2nd Army. Consequently, he lost the skin off both his feet. I remembered the pride and joy Bill had for his shiny black boots he had brought all the way from New Zealand. The adjutant had offered to fix me to fly with another pilot till Bill came back, but I said, 'Like hell you will.' The thought appalled me. 'I'll wait for Bill to get out of the 'boneyard.'"

"Bill arrived a week or so after me. He seemed more perturbed about losing his flying boots than by the frostbite. We compared notes. He gave me the impression that he was highly delighted that I had insisted on waiting for him to return. I brushed his remarks aside by mangling part of the marriage ceremony by saying, 'Till death us do part.'"

By 5 January 1945 Flying Officers Philip Back and Derek Smith in 692 Squadron at Graveley had flown over 30 ops together. The start of January was hectic for them. Derek Smith wrote to his sister. "We've done three trips in the last three nights to Berlin, Hanover and Nürnberg. It's a nice way of spending New Year's Eve, going to Berlin. Still, there was a party in the Mess when we got back so we had a slap-up meal and a good time." Phil Back and Derek Smith had set off for Berlin in *T-Tommy*. Back wrote:

> "We had feathered one engine over Holland due to lack of power and lost some height. At about 27,000 feet the other engine stopped. We discussed baling out but it looked such a bloody long way down and we were over the sea, we decided to try and get down. We could see the lights of Woodbridge. We crossed the coast at about 18,000 feet and requested permission to land.
>
> "'What is your trouble *T-Tommy*?'
>
> "'We have lost both engines - long pause - 'Land, *T-Tommy*.'
>
> "We got into the circuit about 12,000 feet on the upwind cross-leg - lost all the rest of our height to cross the boundary high and very fast, wheels down and a bit of flap. God knows what our speed was. I know it was over the limits for the aircraft. The next morning I got a bollocking from the engineering officer, for they had found nothing wrong. We were collected on 6 January in the Oxford and the next day I flew back to Woodbridge and flew *T-Tommy* home to Graveley. A day or two later I got another bollocking from Wing Commander Joe Northrop. I was expecting a Green endorsement in my Log Book and was somewhat miffed at completing a dead-stick landing, in a 'Mossie', at night, losing about 15,000 feet in one enormous circuit and getting the wheels down - and getting my balls chewed up for doing so!"

Derek Smith adds. "It was a remarkable bit of flying and really deserved a medal. I can only think our otherwise amiable Wing CO guessed we had been a little too high!"

During January-May 1945 LNSF Mosquitoes made almost 4000 sorties over the dwindling *Reich* for the loss of 57 "Mossies" shot down or written off. The LNSF bombed Berlin on 61 consecutive nights. When, on 14/15 January 83 Mosquitoes raided Berlin and Ed Boulter of 128 Squadron piloted B.XVI MM204 to the Big City, a new navigator, Sergeant Chris Hart from Derby, was in the right-hand seat. Boulter recalls:

> "Weather predictions were so bad the Main Force heavies didn't go on ops that night. It was decided that six Mosquitoes from each of the six squadrons would go to Berlin so it could be reported that 'Last night our aircraft bombed Berlin.' The wind velocity predicted was 120 knots from the west. This was wrong. It was considerably more. So we all arrived at Berlin sooner than expected and I overshot the city. At this time I was surprised to see two searchlights pointing up. They then descended pointing westward to Berlin. This happened twice. Then the penny dropped. I can only assume that the searchlights belonged to the Russians. They pointed up, down, twice, to Berlin. We had to go back now that the PFF markers were down. Right speed, right heading, height, 4000lb bomb.
>
> "Over Woodbridge the cloud base was 1100 feet. I must have heard it on the radio. The weather had changed to heavy drizzle and fog. I did three approaches on the SBA and didn't on any approach see a light. By this time battling the headwind left us very short of fuel. I think I heard on the Wyton circuit two Mosquitoes crash, both out of fuel. It was fair bedlam on the radio. I thought things were getting a bit serious. I was just commencing a climb away from Wyton when the voice of my flight commander came on the radio, "Bertie, this is Ivor Broom. This is not a request, this is an order. You are to climb to a safe height and bale out. He repeated this to any other aircraft airborne. (I found out later that the lights had been lit on the short runway - the wrong runway. Ivor and Tommy had landed and Ivor went into the tower and chucked out the Wing Commander CO).
>
> "I'd run every tank dry except the inner tanks. I throttled back near Thurligh and prepared to bale out. Chris Hart went out. I remembered that you should never bale out of a Mosquito without getting hold of the D-ring first. My solution was to hang onto some bit of the navigator's seat, my right hand on the D-ring, with legs bent, and jam my back to the door. To leave the aircraft I just had to straighten my legs and the slipstream pulled me out. It took the skin off my shins. I landed and walked down to a farmhouse and knocked on the door. A first floor window opened. I explained that I'd baled out of a Mosquito returning from Berlin. I asked if I could use the telephone. In a clear voice he said, 'There's a phone box down the road 100 yards on the right!' And the window slammed shut!
>
> "I had no money. As I walked along the road I was approached from the rear by a US staff car leading a track and searchlight followed by an ambulance. The Americans put me out of my misery and took me to Thurleigh and the warm. They didn't find my navigator

until the next day. He had wrapped himself in his chute and locals found him next morning, still asleep! "[183]

On 25 January 1945 163 Squadron reformed at Wyton in B.XXVs under the command of Wing Commander Broom.[184] Flight Lieutenant Pat Duncan, who was promoted Squadron Leader and given "B" Flight and Ed Boulter, plus their navigators, were among those posted to the new unit. Ed Boulter recalls:

"Ivor was Ivor. You couldn't have a better CO. Ivor told us all individually, I was chuffed and very pleased to be asked because I was going with Ivor, and Tommy Broom, who was promoted to squadron leader. Ivor took the nucleus from 128 Squadron but he couldn't take all the best guys. He had to take some of the dross as well! He had to have new crews from 1655 or other squadrons. After it happened it was quite incredible. We never separated completely. We still felt part of 128 - they almost melled from a social point of view into one. There was no rivalry whatsoever. All the high jinks were on 128. I can't remember even changing rooms."

Wing Commander Broom had instructions from Air Vice Marshal Bennett for 163 Squadron to become operational immediately, and 163 Squadron flew its first operation on the night of 28/29 January when four B.XXVs dropped "Window" at Mainz (a spoof raid for the attacks by 602 aircraft on Stuttgart). On the night of 29/30 January, when 59 Mosquitoes were despatched to Berlin and 50 reached and bombed the city without loss, Philip Back and Derek Smith in 692 Squadron flew their fortieth op, with their second operation to Berlin in 48 hours, in *K-King*. Derek Smith recalls:

"We returned to be greeted by the news that FIDO at Graveley was u/s and we were diverted to Bradwell Bay. Bradwell closed in and Coltishall advised that we should 'Get down where you can', which we did at Hethel, a USAF base [home to the 389th Bomb Group and B-24 Liberators] near Norwich. We were treated with the usual American hospitality but memory of the operational meal remains in both our minds - it was roast pork with gooseberry jam! Next morning our *T-Tommy* came up with a very bad mag drop so we were taken by jeep to Philip's home at Brundall for lunch and the weather closed in so we stayed the night. Next morning Philip's father took us by car to Norwich where we were picked up by American transport for a run-up of the now serviceable *T-Tommy* but we were at Hethel for another night due to continuing bad weather. On 1 February we woke to a sunny morning and after a good breakfast at Hethel, we were back at Graveley by 0940 to find ourselves on the Battle Order for Berlin that night. Because of the problems at Hethel, *T-Tommy* had to be checked so we were in *K-King,* Burbridge and Ramage's aircraft which had an indifferent reputation put about by them, I suspect, to keep it out of other hands!

"The trip was fairly routine until we lost an engine near Hanover and again the weather was u/s with low cloud and snowstorms over East Anglia and the 8 Group area, so once more it was a matter of getting down where we could. The Mossie flew very well on one engine but it could be tricky to land especially at night and in the poor weather conditions, so we proceeded with care losing height gradually knowing we were over East Anglia. Eventually we saw a rocket come up through the low cloud and, losing more height, spotted a runway [Rougham near Bury St. Edmunds and home to the 94th Bomb Group) very well illuminated by wartime standards. Phil was quickly into the approach only to find a Fortress being landed, hence all the illumination. However, short of fuel, on one engine and in a snowstorm it was no place for the faint hearted. So Phil went in over the Fortress with rather too much height and speed. We hit the runway past halfway but with hardly a bump, shot off the end over a wide grassed area and ditch, to be brought to a halt at the perimeter by a row a tree stumps. One of which impacted with the starboard wing and slewed us around by 90°. Apart from two small cuts on my forehead neither is us were hurt. So we were very smartly out and taking off at speed in case of fire, only to be halted by the sound of voices behind us. We returned to find the aircraft was across a road with an Armstrong Siddeley car between the port engine and drop tank. We found four very lucky occupants, badly shocked but not too badly hurt although one did need hospital treatment for a head wound requiring forty stitches. Then, almost immediately, we found ourselves surrounded by GIs brandishing rifles as they though us to be a Messerschmitt 410 intruder. On this occasion we did not receive the usual American hospitality probably due to our -unannounced arrival and were left to make our own way back to Cambridge by train to await being picked up by car. Of course we were lugging our flying "gear and received some odd glances from other passengers. However, we made our way to the University Air Squadron and were lavished with their hospitality. Of course, we were not very popular with Burbridge and Ramage but everyone was pleased to see us in one piece, especially the 'Wing Co' who put us in the Battle Order for the next two nights! However, they were Wiesbaden and Dortmund, rather easier than the six to Berlin up to that ending up at Rougham. This latter Philip described as being due to the bad judgment of a single engine approach. Many Mossie aircrew did not survive to tell the tale of single engine landings. So in my view, as the only witness, to land from a steep approach at night in a snowstorm and to be able to walk away' was a small miracle aided by airmanship of the highest order."[185]

In February the LNSF flew 1662 sorties. The 1/2 February attack on Berlin was the largest Mosquito bombing attack on the Reich capital since the formation of the LNSF. Some 122 aircraft were dispatched in two waves to bomb Berlin. No aircraft were lost. Flight Lieutenant Norman Griffiths and Flying Officer Bill Ball of 571 Squadron flew B.XVI MM169. Bill Ball recalls:

"Now Group, having decided that sleep was not very important - what with there being a war on and all that unpleasantness, sent us off at 0210 - a time when not even milkmen are awake! Nevertheless, according to my Log sheet, we took off on time, and set off for Orfordness, a distance of 57 miles. Thus, with all that 4000lbs of heavy 'luggage' on board, plus Norman's 12 stone seven, the journey would take 18 minutes. My goodness! It sometimes takes longer than that to get served in the 'Officers Mess'.

'The second leg was to a point known as 'A', near The Hague, which was on a track of 091 for 89 miles, and it should take eighteen minutes. In fact it took us nineteen. Now at 20,000 feet, and with a 60 mph wind from the west, Norman was as silent as the Sphinx, minding his own business, concentrating on all around him, while I was wrestling with *Gee*, LORAN and lots of paper and pencil work. We then set course for 'B', a point just south of Magdeburg. The leg from 'A' to 'B' was quite a long one, namely 298 miles and estimated to take exactly 58 minutes. Our *Gee* set was on its best behavior, and we reached our turning point on time, and made for point 'C'. This was a mere 23 miles, to the southwest of Brandenburg and took only five minutes. The time, by my gold watch and chain was now 0351. *Gee* and LORAN were still active. Unfortunately, my anglepoise lamp suddenly ceased to function. However, Norman came to the rescue, he handed me a torch. He, very kindly hit me on the head with it, because I couldn't see in the sudden darkness. You will appreciate that this was not an ideal situation. To be fair, here was a hard-pressed 'clerk', struggling with a torch in one hand, pencils in the other, twisting around in the confined space to twiddle with the *Gee* set knobs and the LORAN.

"Now the serious business commenced. At 0351 we altered course for the target, only 40 miles away. As we approached, we were met by millions of roving searchlights. I could have read a newspaper, had I thought to bring one. In a moment or two I'd be going 'up front' to get ready for bombing. (Incidentally, I contend that there is nowhere lonelier - not even on a desert island - than where the (euphemistic) 'observer' had to be at a time like this). I left my comfortable seat and went forward into the nose of the Mossie to lay prone on my stomach by the bombsight. There was only a sheet of Perspex between eternity and me. I could see the whole galaxy of 'stars' exploding above and beneath me, as well as a few more straight ahead, where we had yet to go. Now there was a clatter of metal pieces falling on to the root of our cabin, as if someone was knocking, trying to come in and out of the murderous action. The searchlights were still roving around, as if they'd lost something. Meanwhile, I was concentrating on the bombsight. Then, at the crucial moment, with couple of 'left, left, steadies, and another 'steady' - or it might have been a 'right,' I pressed the teat that unleashed the 4000lb of luggage we'd brought half way across the world - well, say 600 miles of it.

"My relief was paramount as I felt MM169 *C for Charlie* leap into the air when relieved of its deadly burden. Now the Yellow TIs were going down and disappearing into some scattered cloud. We bombed at 0359. The flak was rather troublesome, but sporadic; some over there, some over here, some to starboard, but too high. We had time to notice that one Mosquito was caught in a cone of searchlights. We hoped and prayed that it got away. Glimpses of the ground through the scattered cloud showed areas of fire smoke and ruin. But Norman was on his way. He banked quickly, then dived and leveled out on a course of 323, making for the next turning point. More TIs were still going down amid the smoke. We were two minutes away, but still the flak was spattering the sky."

On the night of 2/3 February, while two other forces bombed Wiesbaden and Wanne-Eickel, 250 Lancasters and 11 Mosquitoes of 5 Group attempted to bomb Karlsruhe. Cloud cover over the target caused the raid to be a complete failure, and the Mosquito marker aircraft that dived over the city failed to establish the position of the target. To make matters worse, 14 Lancasters were lost on the raid. German cities were continually bombed early in the month, and all were marked by Mosquitoes of 8 and 5 Groups. On 5/6 February 63 Mosquitoes attacked Berlin. By way of a change, on 7/8 February 177 Lancasters and 11 Mosquitoes of 5 Group attacked a section of the Dortmund-Ems canal near Ladbergen with delayed action bombs, but all missed their target. Meanwhile 38 Mosquitoes attacked Magdeburg, 16 bombed Mainz, and 41 others attacked five different targets. On 8/9 February Mosquitoes of 5 and 8 Groups marked Pölitz oil refineries for 472 Lancasters, 12 of which were lost. The first wave's objective was marked by the 5 Group method and the Pathfinder Mosquitoes of 8 Group marked the second. The weather was clear and the bombing was extremely accurate, and severe damage was caused. On 10/11 February 82 Mosquitoes bombed Hanover and another eleven raided Essen. The night following (12/13 February) 72 Mosquitoes attacked Stuttgart and 15 others hit Misburg and Würzburg.

At Woodhall Spa on 13 February Flight Lieutenant William Worthington Topper RAFVR and his navigator, Flying Officer Victor W. "Garth" Davies, went to the ops room to be told, "It's Dresden tonight and Topper will lead." A fair-haired giant of a man, Davies had teamed up with Topper in June 1944; Topper could see why he was called "Garth." He was straight out of the "Jane" cartoon strip in the *Daily Mirror*. Davies was a second tour navigator who in December 1943, while flying on 466 Squadron, had been shot down over Belgium in a Halifax, picked up by the Resistance, and who then walked back over the Pyrenees into Spain and back home via Gibraltar. He had never been far afield in his youth, but walked for miles, and this and his mother's strict upbringing, which included Senna Pod tea every Friday, stood him in good stead in the five days and nights walk through the Pyrenees in continuous rain. While Garth was the country lad, Topper was the "posh city gent" who owned an open top Bentley that his dog "Rostov" rode in standing erect in all his glory, as the two aircrew motored over the Pennines. Topper and Garth Davies had their differences, settled many times over pints of beer, and they became, like many Mosquito crews in wartime, almost inseparable. In addition to Topper and Davies, seven other crews in the marking team carried a further nine Red TIs, as well as two Yellow and eight *Wanganuis*. Inaccurate markers were to be scrubbed with yellows.[186] Bill Topper recalls:

> "We went into briefing where we heard that the defenses were not known (the city had received attention once before, early in the war - but by common consent it had been considered a 'safe' one, full of art treasures and architecturally superb). There would probably be light flak from trains in the marshalling yards as the Germans were sending supplies up to the front, about 70 miles East. The Russians had asked for the target because of this. There were a lot of refugees moving West. If we got into difficulty, that is where we should head, West, in no circumstances force-land to the East. The problem was

going to be a weather front with 10/10 cloud over the target - unless it cleared as we got there."

For most of the participating aircrew the Dresden raid would just be another bombing attack.[187] Dresden would be bombed in two RAF assaults three hours apart, the first by 244 Lancasters of 5 Group and the second by 529 Lancasters of 1, 3, 6, and 8 Groups. 5 Group was to attack at 2215 hours, using its own pathfinder technique to mark the target. This was a combination of two Lancaster Squadrons (83 and 97) to illuminate the target with Primary Blind Markers and parachute flares to light up the target, and 627 Mosquito Squadron to visually mark the aiming point with TIs from low level. The aiming-point was to be a sports stadium in the center of the city situated near the lines of railway and river, which would serve as a pointer to the Stadium for the Marker Force, especially since it was anticipated that visibility might not be too good. There were six such stadiums in the area, so particular care had to be exercised. At 2213 hours 244 Lancasters, controlled throughout by the Master Bomber, would begin their attack. A second raid was timed for 0130 hours on the 14th by another 529 aircraft of Bomber Command.[188] Calculations were that a delay of three hours would allow the fires to get a grip on the sector (provided the first attack was successful) and fire brigades from other cities would concentrate fighting the fires. In this second attack target marking was to be carried out by 8 Pathfinder Group. Bill Topper continues:

"We were operating at the limit of our fuel, which didn't allow a very good dog-leg to disguise the target.[189] We went towards Chemnitz and at the last minute altered course a few degrees and went down fairly rapidly from 30,000 feet to 5000 feet at which point I called the Controller, who was Maurice Smith of 54 Base, to say I was clear of cloud cover. Garth said we would be there in one minute, packed all his navigational gear away, put the bag on his knees, his usual habit, with the Target map on top. This had concentric circles 100 yards apart surrounding the marking point, which was the center of the middle stadium of a line of three across the city. In the event the bad weather front cleared as we got there and 5 Group Lancasters had no trouble in seeing the TIs. And then, as if by magic, the green flares were coming down from the two Lancaster Pathfinder Squadrons of 5 Group, which were flying at about 12,000 feet. Down below was the city, as though in bright moonlight, with the river winding through it and there were the three sports stadiums. By now we were down to 3000 feet and Garth had selected the switches on the bomb panel. I called out 'Tally Ho!' and down we went, Garth calling out each 100 feet as the altimeter unwound itself. At 700 feet I pressed the button and away went a 1000lb Red. Immediately there came a brilliant flash under the aircraft - the first photograph had been taken. We continued down to about 400 feet where we leveled out, counting the flashes. Six. Up with the nose. Full power to regain height quickly. But there was no need. There was no flak. The city was undefended. (The opposition started the next day, at home, at Westminster.[190]) The Controller and one of the markers assessed the TI as 100 yards East and backing up was called for. One by one they called up, went in, cleared and climbed away while the red splash in the stadium widened and intensified."

Marker 8 was Flying Officer Ronald Wingate Olsen and Flying Officer Frank Leslie "Chipps" Chipperfleld, who had both been awarded the DFC flying on 619 Squadron, and were last to mark in *Y-Yankee*.[191] They were in their bombing dive when the Master Bomber called, "Markers to clear the target area," followed by "Main Force come in and bomb," Olsen recalls:

"Having released my markers and pulling out of my dive, two things caused consternation - first there, right in front of me were the spires and turrets of Dresden Cathedral, secondly, some of the Lancasters were a bit quick to drop their 'Cookies', much to my discomfort. The aircraft was rocked and buffeted just like a row boat in a heavy sea. It was on this occasion that I learned why the safety height to fly when 4000lb bombs were exploding was a minimum of 4000 feet. This was the only occasion when I pushed the throttles through the gate to get extra power from the engines to get out of the area as quickly as possible.

"The return journey was uneventful after we had been given 'Markers go home' by the Marker Leader. On landing Chipps and I were tired. De-briefing, followed by a meal and back to the billet to get some much needed sleep. Later we realized that this operation was the longest time we had been airborne in a Mosquito - five hours forty minutes, close to the maximum fuel endurance."

Topper concludes:

"Controller asked for the area to be cleared - a few moments later the bombs started to erupt in patches over the still silent - to us - city. I asked permission to send the marking team home, got it, and passed it over. One by one the markers acknowledged. Garth and I continued to fly round the city at about 1500 feet. It had attractive bridges across the river and many black and white buildings. The bombing intensified and we climbed higher and away. There was a brilliant blue flash -probably a power station - and I commented on this to the Controller. A little later he said I could go - I acknowledged. Garth gave me the course to steer. As we climbed up the glow on the ground spread as we went into thin cloud, then disappeared as the cloud thickened. At 30,000 feet there were stars overhead and three hours of flying to be done. We were airborne for six hours. 5 Group's raid was at 2100 hours and four groups of Bomber Command arrived at midnight to add to the flames already growing. The Americans followed up at 0800 hours the next day to add to the destruction, which PRU photographs, taken later that day, showed to be very extensive. As an operation it was markedly successful. Nothing went wrong - the marking went smoothly, the bombing was accurate and there were very few casualties in the bomber force. The Mosquitoes were aided by the newly installed Loran sets, which enabled reliance on radar to be greatly extended as they went further east and out of *Gee* range. Navigation was excellent - spot on by all navigators - and the backing-up by all markers first rate. Little did we all think as we climbed down from our aircraft that the following days were going to see an outcry, which was to continue for months and years."[192]

So great were the conflagrations caused by the firestorms created and the great heat generated in the first attack that crews in the second attack reported the glow was visible 200 miles from the target. In a firestorm similar to that created in Hamburg on 27/28 July 1943, an estimated 50,000 Germans died in Dresden.

Bill Henley and Johnnie Clark did not get off the ground until the middle of February, although they did a couple of air tests combined with practice bombing, just to break them in. When they finally presented themselves at briefing, they found that the usual place had been left for them. Some faces were missing and they would never see them again:

"Hiya flight sergeant," Clark said to the Canadian. "It's an honour to have you sitting next to me, Sir."

"'Spherical objects to you,' came the reply.

"'My, you've improved your language, too!'

"'Like hell I have. Look at where we're going tonight [14/15 February] - Dessau. That's southwest of Berlin - it's like an elephant's foreskin: a bloody long haul.'

"'We kept the idle banter going while the various bigwigs had their say. As we climbed from the runway, Bill switched on his microphone. 'Nervous?' he asked.

"'No more than usual,' I replied. 'It's a pity we didn't land a short trip, though, to break the ice. How are you?'

"'I'll have to get used to these boots I've been issued with - otherwise I'm OK.'

"'We chattered on much more than usual until it came to changing the fuel intake from the outer drop tanks to the main supply. We were both listening to the throb of the engines and the beat of the propellers. Everything went according to the textbook. By the time we had crossed the Dutch coast we were behaving like an experienced crew and not like a couple of scared rabbits.

"We dropped our bombs on time and headed for base. We had encountered flak over the target and were skirting Hanover and the flak barrage that rose so accurately from there, when our starboard engine started vibrating, sending shudders through the aircraft. 'Curse that damned place Hanover,' I thought.

"'I think it's the prop that's copped it,' said Bill. 'The engine revs seem to be all right. I'm going to feather it.' He pressed the button. The engine went dead and the prop rigid. The aircraft stopped vibrating, and Bill started slowly to lose some height and to keep the forward speed up.

"'Shall we head for home or what?' he asked.

"'I don't think we should head for base as the Met men said there was a cold front line squall stretching across the North Sea. We would have to go through it. That would be no fun with both engines, but on one - well, it's anyone's guess.' "I had hoped we would fly over the top of it.

"'Where to, then?' His voice was as sharp as a pin.

"'Manston in Kent. That way we'll fringe the south end of it, I hope.'

"St. Elmo's Fire was flickering its blue veins across our Perspex windscreens when we dipped into the cloud. We were tossed around like a bottle on a surf-pounded beach. Lightning hit the cabin repeatedly, followed by thunder almost immediately. How the aircraft stuck together only God and the manufacturers knew. We bounced out of the storm as quickly as we had gone in. We landed on our one engine. The starboard prop had a jagged hole in one of its blades and was twisted like a badly broken leg. The fact that it and the lightning storm hadn't broken up the aircraft was a tribute to the people who had built it as much as to Bill, who had kept the thing in the air until we reached this graveyard called Manston. We could find no other damage.

"I turned to Bill. 'I'm going to report sick. My ears are all bunged up and I have a bad cold. At least, that's my story. It will get us off flying for a week or so.'

"'You do that Johnnie. I'll back you up if necessary.' We were both rattled and twitching a bit, and we knew it. There was nothing wrong with my ears. Strange, I reflected; had anyone suggested three or four months before that I would be contemplating doing such a thing, they would have received a rather dusty answer in reply. However, once I had stepped into the Clearance Center I felt ashamed. Aircrew were lying on stretchers. They had burns, flak wounds, arms bandaged and legs in splints. I felt a complete fraud. I said to Bill, 'Come on, let's go to the Mess.'

"Back at Bourn, a 'Wing Ding' had been laid on in the Mess. What started off as a civilized party developed into a real 'thrash'. 'Ossie', the Scots tea planter from Ceylon climbed onto the bar counter.

"'Right!' he bellowed. 'I think we all need a bit of practice at landing on FIDO. I'll be the controller.' Newspapers and magazines were confiscated from the lounge, rolled up and placed in almost parallel lines on the highly polished Mess bar floor. Tins of Ronseal were sprayed on the papers. 'Let's make it realistic,' said someone. 'Get the feather cushions from the lounge and we'll have 10/10ths feather visibility.'

"The idea was to slide down the polished line between the burning papers and have the air full of feathers at the same time. 'Ossie' bellowed out the time-honoured phrase, 'Come in Number One, your time is up!' Whereupon the CO whipped down the burning line of newspapers on his bottom and crashed into the stove at the other end. The atmosphere of the burning papers plus the clouds of feathers made the bar almost untenable.

"It could have been worse. They could have burned the place down. At one party a bunch of aircrew from another squadron had found a pile of bricks, sand and cement. Contractors were building an extension to the Mess. The chaps used the lot and bricked up the CO's car, which was parked outside. The contractors had been reported ass saying that they hoped they were better flyers than they were bricklayers.

"At briefing the following afternoon on 19 February my Canadian oppo flopped into the seat beside me. 'Jeeze! Look where we're going tonight - way down south,' he said. I followed the tapes on the Master Plan. It looked a little place southwest of Berlin called Erfurt. Why it was going to receive the heat-treatment from us was explained by the intelligence officer. It was a center for light engineering, and in order that we hit it fair and square we were going to go in at 7000 feet; abnormally low for us. No flak or opposition was expected. We duly bombed Erfurt and left it blazing. I saw what I took to be a church steeple tumble into the flames and secretly hoped that the few faithful left in that town were tucked up in their shelters and didn't suffer the indignity of dying in the House of God.

"On the way back, over Holland, we spotted what we thought was a jet aircraft boring its way through the atmosphere. It was heading straight for us. It rose level with us and continued on upward, arching northwest on its sightless way towards England. It was a V2. I quickly spotted the place from which it had been launched. I was not the only navigator to do so, and I understood the place was located the next day and bombed out of existence.

"We were full of coffee and rum when 'Ossie' and his navigator arrived at the debriefing, having bombed the town by themselves, as they had been about an hour behind us. They, like us, reported no opposition. 'By God,' 'Ossie' said in his blunt way, 'I can't see that town contributing much to the Nazi war effort now. It was burning beautifully when we attacked.' He gave a graphic description of the carnage we had created. The powers that be hadn't thought so, however, and we did two more trips to Erfurt with similar results. Each load we dumped on the place contained one long-delay bomb, which must have disturbed the residents for many hours after the raid. We puzzled over our trips there, as it stretched our flying endurance quite a bit. It wasn't until after the war that I saw films of the gas ovens in the concentration camps, with the trade plates on them stating that they had been built in Erfurt."

On 20 February, when 1283 bomber sorties were flown 66 Mosquitoes went to Berlin. On of these, Mosquito B.XVI MM202 *V-Victor*, was flown by Flight Lieutenant Leicester G. Smith RNZAF and his RAF navigator Warrant Officer Bill Lane, who were flying their 31st operation in 128 Squadron. Smith recalls:

"Our flight time was 4 hours 15 minutes. Many and varied are the experiences Bill and I shared over enemy territory, but that evening we certainly had our fair share. We were over the Big City at 2010 hours. We had quite a fire raging in the cockpit prior to the release of our 'Cookie' and on our bombing run. I didn't realise its importance as, at the time, my attention was on the controls, but seeing the flames a foot in length urgent action was required. At the time we were at 27,000 feet, ahead of schedule by 3 minutes, so climbed the aircraft for the bombing run. Within a few seconds the cockpit was filled with black smoke following from the flames, which Bill thought at first was from the outside. My first action was to dive the aircraft, thinking incendiary bullets from an enemy fighter had hit us. The flames were out before Bill could use the fire extinguisher and with target indicators ahead, we dropped the 'cookie'. The resulting dive found the aircraft at 22,000 feet, so I turned onto 296 degrees and on the way out an enemy fighter jumped us, as indicated by the white flashing *Boozer* light in the cockpit. I took evasive action but as nothing happened I climbed back to operational height. All told a very busy 5 minutes. However, I am a little ahead with my story. It had been a wonderful night flying the German skies with, at times, cirrus cloud for protection, but on the whole quite clear. Flying in near Hanover the plotting became serious, as the contrails were plainly visible to the enemy. At 2000 hours I switched over to the main fuel tanks, with *V Victor* cruising at a steady 180 knots, while Bill computed his final course to Berlin. In the distance and at operational height, we could plainly see the lights of the advancing Russian Army approximately 50 miles away and east from Berlin. To the north the Germans had lit their Dummy City, so that before our ETA it was quite a pretty sight. However, with our own red and yellow target indicators clearly visible, on these we bombed Berlin.

"It was during our bombing run that the fire started and so did the problems. In fact, who would feel secure at the thought of haling out over Big City with all the 'cookies' bursting. But my chief concern was getting *V Victor* back to good flying condition. We had lost 5000 feet in the dive. At a steady 200 knots and back at 26,000 feet turned onto a course of 285 degrees. Near Hanover the guns were opening up on the incoming wave of Mosquitoes, one of which nearly hit us. Seeing the black outline rushing towards our aircraft at an incredible speed, I just had time to ease the control column back and fly over the top of the other aircraft. Left to ourselves, the enemy plotting ceased and then was able to enjoy the glory of the German skies.

"With no navigational equipment serviceable, Bill pinpointed himself over the Dutch coast, the water shone in brilliance, giving perfect relief to the coastline. Over the North Sea we received a Vector from 'Largetype' to steer 305 degrees, only 20 difference from Bill's original course. Returning to clear sky over England, landing at Wyton 2153 hours, after circling base for 15 minutes.

"Because *Gee* and LORAN navigational aids went unserviceable at the same instant, it was assumed that was probably the cause of the fire. On return the aircraft was checked and no sign found of a fire from the motors. We were both very relieved and again our faithful friend, *V Victor*, brought us safely home.'

During February 1945 Ball and Griffiths completed thirteen Mosquito operations, eight of which were to the "Big City." Bill Ball recalls:

"The highlight of this busy month must be two visits to Berlin in less than 24 hours. In fact, it took only 20 hours. On Wednesday the 21st Norman and I went down to see if our names were on the Battle Order. We had not operated on the night before, so it was quite on the cards that our names would appear. Yes, there they were, so that meant an hour's Air Test. We were booked for, and presented with, that old war-horse, '*C' for Charlie*. It was a fine sunny day, so, about lunchtime, we took him for a run and I think he enjoyed it. At least, everything belonging to him seemed to be in good working order according to Norman who knows about such complicated things. No good asking me. I couldn't pass an opinion; I couldn't drive a Mosquito!

"Anyhow, after that exercise in the fresh air with *Charlie*, we pottered around, waiting for briefing. We felt sure the target for tonight would be the 'Big City'. We had not visited it since the 14th. In the event we were not 'disappointed'. At Briefing it was announced that Berlin, was indeed the target. Take-off time would be 2155 hours.

"After all the preliminaries - the 'hearty supper', the careful preparation of maps, charts and log sheets, the truck arrived to take us all to collect parachutes, parachute harness, Mae West, etc., then out to dispersal, dropping us off, two by two, at the appropriate flying machine. The next 45 minutes gave the pilots time to check their aircraft from stem to stern, kick the tyres to see if they were blown up. They would also check that the pitot-head cover had been removed. Had a short conversation with the invaluable and dedicated ground crews. All this Norman did, then he climbed the small ladder at the entrance to the aircraft and settled himself comfortably at the controls. Now, it was my turn; laden with parachute, Mae West and bulging navigation-bag. I closed the lid of the hatch and shut out the rest of the world. Well, it felt as claustrophobic as that.

'We were waiting now for take-off time and out at dispersal, there was a series of ear-splitting roars, as the pilots ran up their engines prior to take off. As Norman did so, I could feel the two powerful Rolls-Royce Merlins fighting against the brakes, juddering outrageously, eager to get away - until the pilot eased off.

'As the hands of our watches approached take-off time, we made for the beginning of the runway to wait for the green Aldis from control. It came and we raced off down the runway, gathering speed all the time. It was now 2155. We circled base, climbing. At 2205 we left for Southwold on the coast a distance of 60 miles on a track of 087. The route out was towards Bremen, some 245 miles on a track of 080, which took 60 minutes to complete. Thirty miles from Bremen a change in course indicated by a Green Route Marker was made. The route went near Oldenburg, then east of Stendal. The final approach to the city from the northwest was 48 miles long on a track of 153.

'As the second wave arrived over the city the defenses became very active and a large number of fighters were also deployed around the Berlin beacon. The searchlights were active sweeping the skies and working into numerous cones and fighter flares illuminated the whole city. In the clear conditions crews could see all the usual spoofs on the bombing run and as they bombed many of the Y TI bomb bursts were visible, scattered around the markers. As crews left the target they could see that many small fires had started to burn at various points around the aiming point. In MM169 Norman and Bill saw the Y TIs going down at 0013 hours. The supercharger blowers on the aircraft would not engage and they approached at 23,000 feet. The flak was too high, being aimed at the Mosquitoes flying above them at 28,000 feet. On this occasion this was a relief to the crew and they completed the bombing run at 0016 hours. Once away from Berlin crews turned towards home on a route which went near Magdeburg and as they approached, masses of searchlights lit up the sky away to starboard. Some stray flak aimed possibly at someone who had strayed off course went up. The route then went via Halberstadt, Hanau, Amsterdam, The Hague and finally Woodbridge. Crews crossed the coast at about 0151 hours and arrived back at base around 0200 hours.

"Having returned from Berlin shortly after 2am on this Thursday morning, I suppose it must have been at least 3 am by the time we all got to bed. All those, that is, who were on operations, together with those indispensable bodies engaged on night-flying duties. Our 'supporting cast', I would call them, in the nightly melodrama. It was with some surprise, therefore, to discover that Norman Griffiths and I were on again. But, as I tell myself, we are after all, merely 'pawns' in the game, and we can be moved around like chess pieces - Berlin one night, Hamburg the next night, and Bremen the next. Still, it was without any surprise at all to learn at Briefing that the target was, once again, Berlin! (We must be making quite a nuisance of ourselves over there waking up all the citizens and sending them scuttling to their deep shelters, night after night.)

"However, after briefing, it was the usual drill - a quick meal, collect parachute and other important gear. Then we're delivered by truck to our waiting Mosquitoes. Tonight *C for Charlie* was resting after his labors a few hours ago. We were given his understudy, MM185 *E for Edward*. Norman made the usual inspection outside the aircraft, but it was seldom that anything needed attention. Once on board, he carried out the cockpit-drill. Then, as take-off time approached, ran up the engines in turn and our wooden cabin throbbed and shuddered violently as the two 1680hp Rolls Royce Merlins screamed to a high pitch while its slender wooden body shuddered in response along its entire length. When Norman was satisfied with their performance, he signalled 'chocks away' to the ground crew. Then, with our 'Cookie' having been loaded earlier, we trundled slowly to the runway in use.

"Norman aligned his aircraft in the center of the runway. I could see the grim outline of his serious face, concentrating hard. Then, as the green Aldis flashed its signal, the two Merlins roared again - the yellow and blue flame belching angrily, as our Mosquito, disregarding its heavy load of 8.5 tons, its speed built up and the ASI leapt into action at eighty. As the ASI showed '100' we lifted off into the hands of fate. With the undercart retracted, we were on our way to that beleaguered capital, 600 miles to the East.

"We were airborne at 1809 and circled base, climbing all the time, then set course for Southwold, a familiar 'port of call'. We reached Southwold a little late and then altered course. There was a lot of bumpiness, no doubt caused by someone's slipstream. On this jaunt we saw Red Route markers going down but these should have been Green! At 2001 we saw Yellow Route Markers going down. At 2012 there was some flak ahead, but we took no notice. We were not there yet! We were still a couple of minutes away. We altered course for Berlin and we could see odd bits of flak bursting - some to the left of us, some to the right, but none of it in the center, but all too high. I watched with much interest, as the cotton-wool puffs seemed to unfold and float slowly away, leaving its bright 'star' glowing harmlessly just above us. But the smell of cordite drifted on for a while and we could sometimes smell it.

"I was now in the nose of the aircraft, waiting for the target to reach us down the drift wires. We had come down from some thin cirrus above and I had a bird's-eye view. I could see some other 'Pilgrims' making 'progress' over the target, but the searchlights had now lost them. Everywhere seemed brightly lit, until the beams swung away to pester some other crews. I can see a number of Cookie bursts below. As we were on the bombing run I felt much as a turkey must feel as Christmas approaches. Still, the 'oven door' was not yet ready for us and we escaped without even a scorch mark. As I pressed the bomb release I had shouted, 'Bomb gone!' Suddenly, I felt critical of myself. I had thought that was a ruddy silly thing to say! Norman knew damn well it had gone, from the moment *Edward* jumped a couple of yards into the air! Anyhow, we were just turning away from the target when I caught a glimpse of a seemingly tiny river wending its way. It looked silvery in all the reflected light. I broke the silence. "'Norman, that's the River Spree on which Berlin stands.'

"In spite of still being in that dangerous area, he quipped: 'Is that so? Well, I think it's stupidly named, because it's not the place where our crews would want to go for a 'merry frolic', or even a 'drunken carousel'. No not for me, it's a little dangerous around here'. [Despite a lot of fighter activity 571 crews had no contact with the enemy. The bombing on this occasion was considered to have been fairly accurate]. The homeward route was via Stendal. Soon after leaving the target, we were in for a 'rude' awakening. Suddenly there was an almighty 'rat-a-tat. This knocking or banging was to the rear of *Edward* and the aircraft shuddered and shook, violently. Never mind, the main thing was that we were still flying. Then, immediately Norman shouted, 'Good God! What was that?' Well he already knew what it was. He knew damn well that it wasn't the postman, especially at that time of night!

'The Dutch Coast was reached at 2157 and the last lap commenced. This joyous fact prompted Norman to break into conversation: 'How are we doing?' End of said conversation. I replied, 'Okay! Won't be long now!'

"We reached base at 2211 and landed at 2215. As soon as Norman had landed he taxied off the runway and made for dispersal, anxious to see what damage had been done to *Edward's* rear. The two or three groundcrew were waiting to hear if all was well with their charge, torches at the ready. Norman spoke to them and led the way to the rear end. We were not surprised to see the sizable hole in the starboard tail plane, caused by the flak when we heard the almighty bang. Attracted by the several flashing torches, two or three other crews came to see what the 'panic' was. One 'joker' grinned, and said: 'I say Norman that's going to 'mugger-up' your No Claims Bonus!' So ended the memorable 'Two ops on Berlin in 20 hours by 571 Squadron.'"

In all, 77 Mosquitoes went to Berlin on 21/22 February. No aircraft were lost. On the following night, 73 Mosquitoes went to the 'Big City' without loss, although one of four Mosquitoes was lost on a raid on Erfurt. In March 163 Squadron alone visited Berlin 24 times. On 6 March 48 Mosquitoes led by *Oboe*-equipped Mosquitoes of 109 Squadron to provide marking bombed Wesel, which was believed to contain many German troops and vehicles. One of the most dramatic marking operations of the war occurred on 14 March when a Mosquito of 5 Group and eight *Oboe* Mosquitoes of 105 and 109 Squadrons set out to mark for 5 Group Lancasters in attacks on the Bielefeld and Arnsberg viaducts. Four Mosquitoes attempting to mark the Arnsberg viaduct for 9 Squadron failed in the attempt with no damage to the viaduct. Three of the *Oboe* Mosquitoes were unable to mark the Bielefeld viaduct for 617 Squadron, but B.XVI MM191, flown by Flying Officer G. W. Edwards of 105 Squadron, succeeded in getting his markers on target and more than 100 yards of the Bielefeld viaduct collapsed under the explosions.[193] The largest operation ever on Berlin occurred on the night of 21/22 March when 138 Mosquitoes attacked in two waves. Only one aircraft was lost.

On 27/28 March three Mosquitoes of the Light Night Striking Force were missing from a raid on Berlin,[194] and a 627 Squadron Mosquito was lost during a 5 Group minelaying operation in the River Elbe. One of the Berlin losses was a Mosquito of 692 Squadron which was lost without trace and the other two were involved in a collision. Flight Lieutenant Leicester G. Smith RNZAF and his RAF navigator, Warrant Officer Bill Lane of 128 Squadron, in Mosquito B.XVI MM202 *V-Victor*, who were on their 44th op, were on the outward leg to Berlin over Holland at 25,200 feet under a full moon when at about 20.00 hours they were involved in a collision with Mosquito RV326 of 571 Squadron. Smith recalls:

> "We were waiting for the arrival of the Yellow Route Markers, which was but a couple of minutes away when the collison occurred. There was a sudden jolt, the sensation of which was like being bounced off a trampoline. The aircraft started to go into a spin to the right with the nose well down and for a time out of control."

RV326 spun in, crashing in a cornfield near the village of Zevenhuizen, or Seven Houses, near Groningen. Flying Officer Gordon "Huddy" Hudson AFC RNZAF and his Canadian navigator Flying Officer Maurice G. Gant, who were on their 11th consecutive sortie to Berlin, were killed. They were later buried in a single coffin in the local cemetery of Leek.195 Smith's starboard propeller had been torn away before it could be feathered and it cut a huge hole in the fuselage near the nose and splintered the cockpit windscreen. A small explosion followed and a fire broke out, but Smith quickly extinguished it with the graviner and, after falling to 16,000 feet, Smith was able to jettison his "Cookie" and regain control. He nursed V-Victor back across the North Sea and put down safely at Woodbridge.

Throughout the attack on Berlin the searchlights were active across the city and a jet fighter was spotted in the area of the 128 Squadron bombing run. Flight Lieutenant Jim Dearlove and Sergeant Norman Jackson's Mosquito was coned on the bomb run and it was attacked by a Me 262 of 10./NJG11 just after they had dropped their "Cookie." He fired two short bursts of cannon fire that missed the Mosquito, and Dearlove was able to take evasive action and escape. Two other Mosquitoes which failed to return were claimed shot down by Me 262 jet fighters. *Oberfeldwebel* Karl-Heinz Becker flew one of 10./NJG11's three Me 262A-1as this night and claimed his sixth victory. At 2138 hours and flying at 27,600 feet Becker clearly saw the RAF aircraft and opened fire at 150 meters whilst pulling up the nose of his aircraft. He hit the Mosquito squarely. Pulling away to the left Becker observed large burning parts of the Mosquito falling and scattering the ground near Nauen.[196]

Returning from leave, Bill Henley and Johnnie Clark congratulated each other on winning their "gongs" [DFCs]. Clark recalls:

"Bill's commission had come through a week or two beforehand, so we were feeling pretty much on top of the world. We were preparing to get our heads down knowing we would be flying the next night, probably to Berlin. We'd done 15 trips to the 'Big City' so far. The Air Council seemed bent on sending Mosquitoes to Berlin every night and we were told, when we turned up for briefing the next day, that our target was the usual. We were to go over the target on our tod. Ten past three in the morning was our time.

"That night was a night to remember. As we flew over north Germany, heading for what had been Hamburg and before we turned and pointed our nose at Berlin, we could see the whole of Heligoland, Denmark and south Norway, with the moon reflecting off the North Sea which looked like polished steel against the dark ground. The searchlights caught us, followed by the flak. We ran the gauntlet. I dropped our bombs and we emerged unscathed.

"On landing back at base we had our routine pee. The pee tube in the aircraft froze up if we used it. We were then driven to an Intelligence hut where a group descended on us. They were tired and jaded, unlike us. We had been flying on oxygen for 4½ hours, then jacked-up with coffee heavily laced with rum. That and the knowledge that another op was behind us, made us feel like spring lambs, which was more than could be said of the Intelligence mob. We dictated our report and headed for the billet. We crept into our beds and went out like lights.

"Life went on as if the war was going to last forever. Things were changing a bit, however. At each briefing to the 'Big City' (where else?), we were issued with a plastic label which we hung around our necks. It was imprinted with a Union Jack and stated in Russian that we were Englishmen. We were told that if we were shot down and didn't finish up a mangled heap, we were to raise our hands above our heads. What would happen if we landed among a bunch of fanatical Germans was never mentioned. As most of the Russians, so the story went, couldn't read, it was a case of heads you win, tails I lose - and a lump of lead was waiting for us wherever we landed. When I strung one of these labels, complete with white tape, around my neck, I felt like an evacuee from the 1940 era.

"The Allies had crossed the Rhine and had fanned out over Germany. The 'Huns' were still fighting, albeit in their own Fatherland. We did get a break and bombed Nurnberg one night. Strange to think it was in that city that the Nazis' evil dream had all started which turned the world upside down. Then we bombed Berlin again. It was our last trip there, and we discarded our plastic labels with the Union Jack and switched our efforts to Munich, with just one break in Kiel. Why Kiel, no one knew; not even the intelligence officer. We were sent back to Munich as a farewell punch. Perhaps we were helping the Yanks. We didn't know.

"Bill and I compared notes. We had completed 40 trips; 18 of them had been to Berlin during the non-stop bombing of that city by Mosquitoes. We were told that Mosquitoes had visited the 'Big City' nearly 40 nights on the trot. We had grown older, if not wiser, during that time. Any other target offered to us had become quite a novelty.

"One night, after a late trip to Munich at the end of April, we were walking back to our billets with bed very much in our thoughts. 'Listen,' I said, and held my finger to my lips. 'You said you had never heard a nightingale when we played that record of the one that sang in Berkeley Square. Well, you're hearing one now.' Through the stillness of the morning one was singing as if there were no tomorrow. 'Now you can tell your folks back home that you have heard one.' We stopped and listened. All thought of sleep had left us."[197]

On the night of 3/4 April 95 Mosquitoes went to Berlin, eight to Plauen, and five to Magdeburg. A Mosquito of 139 Squadron flown by Canadian Squadron Leader Roy Dow DFC and Flight Lieutenant J. S. Endersby was shot down on the raid on Magdeburg by a Me 262 of 10/NJG 11 for the only loss of the night. Roy Dow was on his 90th op.[198] The last attack on the "Big City" by Mosquitoes took place on the night of 20/21 April when 76 Mosquitoes made six separate attacks on the German capital. Flying Officers A. C. Austin and P. Moorhead, flying Mosquito XVI ML929, claimed the last bombs dropped on the Big City when they released four 500 pounders at 2.14 AM British Time. All the aircraft returned safely. Two Mosquitoes were lost on 21/22 April when 107 Mosquitoes bombed Kiel. Another attack was flown against Kiel on 23/24 April by 60 Mosquitoes who returned without loss.

On 25/26 April twelve Mosquitoes dropped leaflets over PoW camps in Germany telling Allied prisoners the war was almost over. It was feared that the enemy might stage a last stand in Norway when ships laden with troops began assembling at Kiel. Therefore, on the night of 2/3 May three final raids by 142 Mosquitoes from eight squadrons in 8 Group (and 37 Mosquitoes of 100 Group) were organized. In the first raid, a record 126 aircraft from 100 Group led by sixteen *Oboe* Mosquitoes attacked airfields in the Kiel area with Napalm and incendiaries. In the second and third attacks, one hour apart, 126 Mosquitoes of 8 Group bombed through thick cloud using H_2X (the U.S. development of H_2S) and *Oboe*. That same night Ed Boulter (who had flown 19 operations to Berlin), Duncan, and Parker all flew their fiftieth operations when they took part in the raids. It was the last Bomber Command raid of the war.

In the period January-May 1945 LNSF Mosquitoes had flown almost 4000 sorties. Altogether, 8 Group's Mosquito squadrons flew 28,215 sorties, yet they had the lowest losses in Bomber Command; just 108 (about one per 2800 sorties), while 88 more were written off on their return because of battle damage. This is an incredible achievement, even more remarkable when one considers that well over two-thirds of operations were flown on nights when the heavies were not operating.

Ely Cathedral, a reassuring wartime landmark for homecoming bomber crews, was the setting for a special RAF service on 15 August 1992 marking the foundation of the Pathfinder Force 50 years earlier. Mrs Lys Bennett, widow of the late Air Vice Marshal "Don" Bennett, was in the congregation with about 800 former air and ground crews. The Reverend Michael Wadsworth, who lost his father in Pathfinder operations over southern Germany in 1944, gave the sermon. He said that of 93 seven-man Lancaster crews posted to the unit between June 1943 and March-April 1944 only 17 survived. "Nevertheless, there was a strange alchemy about bomber operations," he said, "They were a special breed."

Above: Juvisy marshalling yards, Paris, before and after the attack by Bomber Command on 18/19 April 1944. A number of the raids that were now taking place were in preparation for the invasion of France by the Allied forces. The invasion required destruction of the French railway system leading to the landing area. The best method of doing this was by employing heavy bombers, but grave doubts existed at the highest level as to the accuracy with which this could he done. Winston Churchill was adamant that French lives must not he lost needlessly and eventually it was agreed that 5 Group should undertake a mass attack on a marshalling yard in the Paris area to prove the case one way or the other. Juvisy was selected as the target. The marshalling yard was attacked on the night of 18/19 April by 202 Lancasters led by Leonard Cheshire after the yards were accurately and effectively marked at each end with red spot flares by four Mosquitoes of 627 Squqdron, 5 Group and by three *Oboe* Mosquitoes of 8 Group. The bombing was concentrated, the yards were put out of action, few French lives were lost and all but one Lancaster returned safely to base. The railway yards were so badly damaged that they were not brought back into service until 1947. (Group Captain J. R. 'Benny' Goodman)

Right: Group Captain Leonard Cheshire VC DSO** DFC CO 617 'Dam Busters' Squadron who on 5/6 April 1944 successfully marked an aircraft factory at Toulouse from 800-1000 feet with two red spot flares on his third run. Cheshire used the same Mosquito on 10/11 April when he marked the St. Cyr German signals' depot during a dive from 5000 to 1000 feet. These successes led to 617 Squadron receiving four FB.VI and B.XVIs, which were first used for marking the Paris-Juvisy marshalling yards, 18/19 April with three *Oboe* Mosquitoes of 8 Group. Munich was hit heavily on the night of 24/25 April when Cheshire in Mosquito NS993, dived from 12,000 feet to 3000 feet and then flew repeatedly over the city at little more than 700 feet, coming under fire for 12 minutes as he left the target area. Cheshire's contribution to the success of the Munich operation was mentioned in his Victoria Cross citation, 8 September 1944.

Oberleutnant Fritz Krause, *Staffelkapitan* I./NJGr.10, (later *Kommandeur* III./NJGII) stands beside his Fw190A-5 of the *Wilde Sau Staffel*, one of the *Nachtjagd* units used mainly to hunt Mosquitoes at night at high altitude. The Fw is fitted with *FuG 217 Neptun J* radar and a long-range belly tank. Over Berlin on the night of 20/21 April 1944 Krause shot down a 239 Squadron Mosquito crewed by Squadron Leader E.W. Kinchin and Flight Lieutenant D. Sellars. Surviving the war with a score of 28 night victories, Krause was awarded the *Ritterkreuz* (Knight's Cross) on 7 February 1945. (via Hans Peter Debrowski)

Below: Fw 190A-5 *'Weisse Elf'*(*'White 11'*) Werk Nr. 550143 fitted with FuG 217 J2 (*Neptun*) AI radar, flown by Oberleutnant Fritz Krause (later *Kommandeur* III./NJGII) of I./NJGr.10 at Werneuchen in 1944. Originally, *Neptun* was designed as a tail, warning radar for twin-engined aircraft and the J2 version was used as an AI radar in single-seater fighters. At 0040 hrs on 8 July 1944 Krause took off in *'White 11'* from the research station at Werneuchen, NE of Berlin and near Brandenburg he intercepted Mosquito B.XVI MM147 of 692 Squadron , which after his three attacks went down and crashed W of Granzow, 9km NNW of Kyritz at 0155 hrs. The pilot, Flight Lieutenant P.K. Burley DFC was KIA. Flight Lieutenant E.V. Saunders DFC, navigator, survived and he was taken prisoner. It was Krause's only *Abschuss* in I./NJGr.10. Three days later at 0120 hrs on 11 July Krause was shot down over Berlin by his own flak and he had to bale out of his Fw 190. (Fritz Krause)

Wing Commander Guy Gibson VC DSO* DFC* born in Simla, India in 1918, joined the RAF in 1936 after leaving St. Edward's School, Oxford. At the outbreak of war he held the rank of Flying Officer and in August 1940 he completed his first tour as a Hampden bomber pilot on 83 Squadron. He was promoted to Flight Lieutenant and won his first DFC (he was awarded a bar the following year). He was posted to instruct at an OTU before transferring to Fighter Command and a posting to 29 Squadron equipped with Beaufighters. In 99 operational sorties he claimed four enemy aircraft destroyed and was promoted to Squadron Leader with a bar to his DFC on completion of his second tour in December 1941. In March 1942 he returned to Bomber Command, was promoted Wing Commander and posted to take command of 106 Squadron. He was awarded the DSO with a bar in 1943. On 16/17 May 1943 he led 617 Squadron's 19 Lancasters in the famous operation against the Ruhr dams. Gibson awarded the Victoria Cross for his leadership on the raid. Later sent to America as an air attaché but he begged the Air Ministry to allow him to return to operations. On the night of 19/20 September 1944 the designated Master Bomber was unavailable and Gibson and 23-year old navigator Squadron Leader James Brown Warwick DFC, an Irishman and veteran of two tours, took off from Woodhall Spa in B.XX KB267/E., a 627 Squadron Mosquito, to act as Controller for the raid on Rheydt. While returning over Walcheren both engines of Gibson's Mosquito cut (according to Anton de Bruyn, a night watchman at the local sugar factory in Steenbergen, who witnessed the incident) and the aircraft crashed near the sea wall killing both crew. Gibson and his navigator are buried at Bergen-op-Zoom. The most likely theory for the incident is that the fuel transfer cocks were not operated in the correct sequence and the engines ran out of fuel. (IWM)

B.Mk.XVI MM224 P3-*K-King* of 692 Squadron, which was crewed by Pilot Officer R. H. M. "Percy" Vere and Pilot Officer J. F. P. Archbold to Berlin on 31 December 1944, their 27th operation. On New Year's Day 1945 Flight Lieutenant Burbidge and Flight Sergeant Ian Ramage used MM224 as 17 Mosquitoes, each carrying a 4000lb delayed-action bomb, made precision attacks on railway tunnels which were being used to support the German Army in the Battle of the Bulge. Returning from Berlin on 1/2 February 1945, MM224 was written off in a crash at Bury St. Edmunds (Rougham) airfield, when, with no hydraulics, Flying Officer Philip Back and Flying Officer Derek Smith overshot the runway and collided with a car. (via Cliff Hall)

Above, Left: PRU photo of St. Cyr airfield and Signals depot which was bombed on 10/11 April 1944 by 17 Lancasters and one Mosquito of 617 Squadron and again on 25 July 1944 by 94 Lancasters and six Mosquitoes of 5 Group. (via Derek Patfield) **Above, Right:** Tours marshalling yards which were bombed on 19/20 May 1944 when Bomber Command resumed operations with raids by 900 aircraft on five separate rail targets in France, two French coastal gun positions at Le Clipon and Merville and a radar station at Mont Couple. At Le Mans 112 Lancasters and four Mosquitoes attacked rail yards and caused serious damage. The railway yards at Orléans were bombed accurately by 118 Lancasters and four Mosquitoes without loss but a similar force found that their target at Amiens was cloud-covered and the Master Bomber ordered the attack to stop after 37 Lancasters had got their bombs away. The most difficult sorties of the entire night were flown by 113 Lancasters and four Mosquitoes of 5 Group who attempted to bomb the railway installations in the center of Tours where a previous raid by 5 Group had destroyed the St. Pierre-des-Corps yards on the outskirts of the town. Both the marking and the bombing force were ordered to carry out their tasks with particular care and to be prepared to wait until the Master Bomber was satisfied that the surrounding housing areas were not hit. Much damage was caused to the railways but some bombs did fall to the west of the target. (via Derek Patfield)

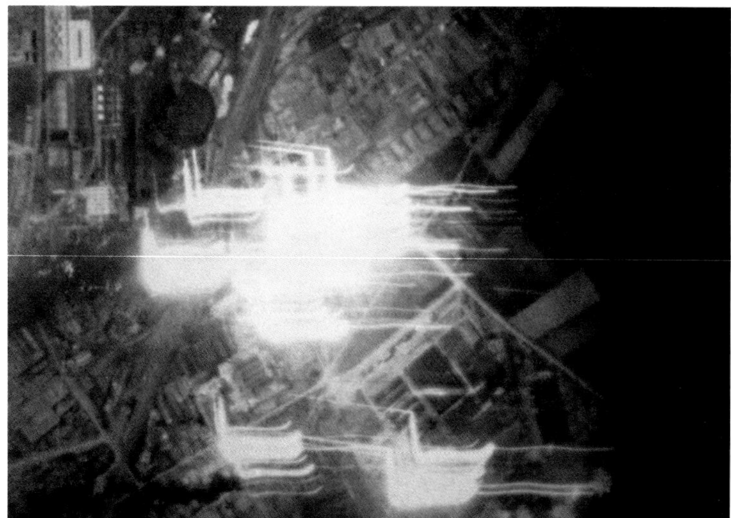

Left: The Lyons engine factory taken from 10,700 feet during the marking by 8 Group Mosquitoes on 25/26 March 1944. In 8 Group, marking for the LNSF and the Main Force was carried out by 109 and 105 Squadrons using *Oboe* and 139 Squadron, using H_2S. In 5 Group the target areas were identified on H_2S and a carpet of hooded flares laid making it as bright as day. This enabled a small number of 627 Squadron low-level visual marker Mosquitoes - four or possibly six - to orbit, locate and mark the precise aiming point in a shallow dive with 500lb spot-fires. The target would then be destroyed by 5 Group Lancaster bombers. (Jim Shortland)

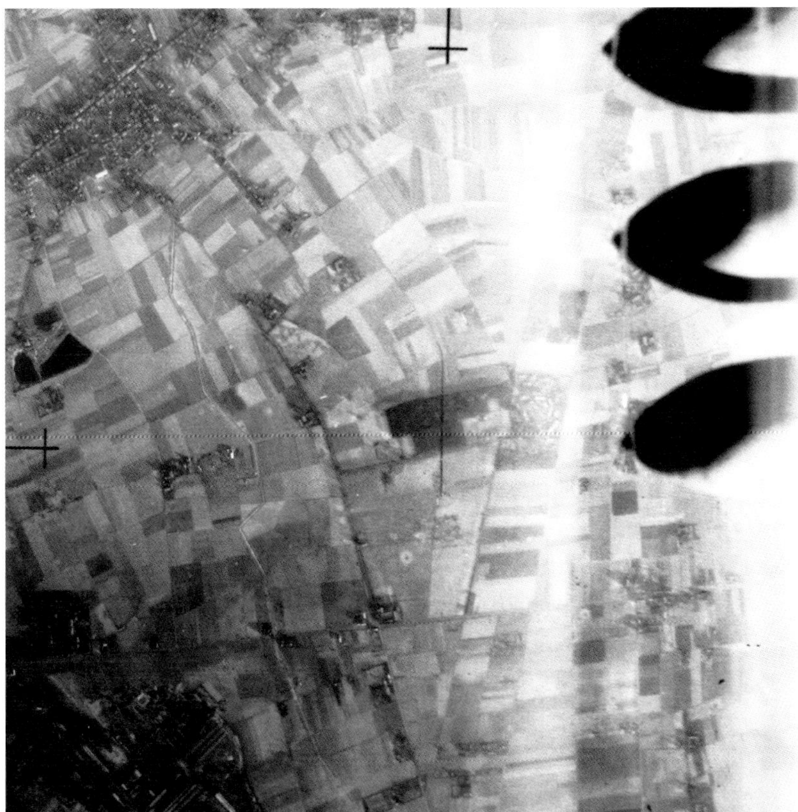

Flying Officer Philip Back (left) and Flying Officer Derek Smith DFC of 692 Squadron in front of *T-Tommy* at Graveley. (Derek Smith DFC* Coll)

On 27 December 1944 200 Lancasters and 11 Mosquitoes of 1, 3, 5 and 8 Groups attacked the railway yards at Rheydt. One Lancaster was lost and one Mosquito crashed behind the Allied lines in Holland. This photo taken from a Lancaster at 19,000 feet shows the bombs going down. (via Derek Patfield)

1655 MTU at RAF Marham in July 1943. L-R: U/K; U/K; Flight Lieutenant Tommy J. Broom DFC Chief Ground Instructor; Flying Officer Sydney Charles Bertram Abbott DFC RAAF, an Oxford Flight pilot; 1943 Squadron Leader Edgar Alfred Costello-Bowen AFC, Chief Flying Instructor at 1655 MTU; Wing Commander Roy Ralston DSO DFM CO; Flight Lieutenant 'Robbie' Robson, Navigation Officer; Pilot Officer K. L. Monaghan, Dual Instructor; Flight Lieutenant Ivor Broom DFC AFC, Dual Instructor; Flight Lieutenant Hoare, Radar and *Gee*; Flying Officer Grant an Oxford pilot. Costello-Bowen, who had evaded capture following his crash with Tommy Broom in August 1942, Flying Officer Abbott and Corporal Frank Richard Magson were killed on 9 August when Abbott was piloting a 487 Squadron Ventura flown in by Group Captain Percy Pickard DSO** DFC who had landed at Marham to get a few hours in on a Mosquito. The Ventura stalled on final approach and crashed at Larch Wood, 1½ miles Northeast of Beechamwell, Norfolk. all three men were laid to rest in the local cemetery in Marham village four days later on 13 August. (via Tommy Broom)

Bombing up a Mosquito with a 'Cookie' for a night raid on Berlin.

Far Left: Flight Lieutenant Ivor G. Broom and Flight Lieutenant (later Squadron Leader DFC**) Tommy Broom. Tommy and Ivor (no relation) flew 58 operations (21 to Berlin) with 571, 128 and 163 Squadrons in 8 Group Pathfinder Force. Ivor later became Air Marshal Sir Ivor Broom KCB CBE DSO DFC** AFC. (via Ed Boulter)

Near Left: Pilot Officer Bill Henley. (via Anne Solberg-Clark)

Mosquitoes of 128 Squadron at dispersal at Wyton.

B.Mk.XVI ML963 *K-King* on a test flight from Hatfield on 30 September 1944. Major repair work on the aircraft had recently been carried out following severe flak damage sustained on the operation to Scholven, 6 July 1944, when it was flown by Warrant Officer Russell Longworth and Pilot Officer Ken Davidson. (ML963 had also been damaged on 12 May, on a raid on Brunsbuttellkoog, repaired on 25 May and returned to the Squadron on 26 June). ML963 returned to the squadron on 18 October 1944. ML963 was assigned to 109 Squadron on 9 March 1944, transferring to 692 Squadron on 24 March, before becoming 8K-K in 571 Squadron on 12 April and which flew this Squadron's first sortie on 12/13 April 1944, to Osnabrück. On 1 January 1945 it was flown by Flight Lieutenant N. J. Griffiths and Flying Officer W. R. Ball on the precision raids against the railway tunnels in the Eiffel region during the Battle of the Bulge. Their 4000lb delayed-action bomb totally destroyed a tunnel at Bitburg. On 20-24 March 1945, now coded '*F-Freddie*', ML963 flew six consecutive ops to Berlin. On 10/11 April 1945, having flown 87 ops, ML963 failed to return from Berlin following an engine fire. The 'Cookie' was jettisoned and Flying Officer Richard Oliver and Flight Sergeant Max Young, who baled out near the Elbe, returned safely. (Charles E. Brown)

Johnnie Clark (via Anne Solberg Clark)

Pat Rooney caricature of Johnnie 'Equiper' Clark. (via Anne Solberg Clark)

Flight Lieutenant Ed Boulter and his navigator, Sergeant Chris Hart DFM of 163 Squadron in front of Canadian built B.Mk. XXV KB403 *'B-Bertie'* at Wyton. 163 Squadron Re-formed on 25 January 1945 mostly from 128 Squadron aircraft and personnel, under the command of Wing Commander Ivor Broom DFC, flying their first LNSF operation on the night of 28/29 January when four B.XXVs dropped 'Window' at Mainz ahead of the PFF force. *'B-Bertie'* was flown by Boulter and Hart on 17 LNSF operations. (Ed Boulter Coll)

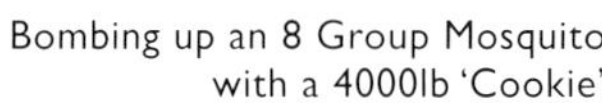

Bombing up an 8 Group Mosquito with a 4000lb 'Cookie'

St-Leu-d'Esserent flying-bomb site, which was bombed accurately and without loss on 4 July by 17 Lancasters, one Mosquito and one Mustang. The site, north of Paris, housed a flying bomb store in a large cave on the site. The aim of the attack was to collapse the roof of the caves, which had been estimated to be about 25 feet thick. A subsidiary aim of the raid was to devastate the road and rail communications running between the caves and the river. Aircraft of 5 Group with some Pathfinders, attacked St-Leu-d'Esserent immediately after the 617 Squadron attack. 208 Lancasters and 13 Mosquitoes, mainly from 5 Group but with some Pathfinder aircraft attacked the site again on 7/8 July. The bombing was accurately directed on to the mouth of the tunnels and on to the approach roads, thus blocking access to the flying bombs that were stored there. On 5 August 1944 St-Leu-d'Esserent was one of several flying bomb sites bombed by 742 aircraft including 16 Mosquitoes. (via Derek Patfield)

Squadron Leader Norman A. J. Mackie DSO DFC* and his Australian navigator Flight Lieutenant Angus MacDonald RAAF DFC DFM at Oakington late in 1944. (John Clark)

A 'Cookie' arrives for loading into a 128 Squadron Mosquito at Wyton.

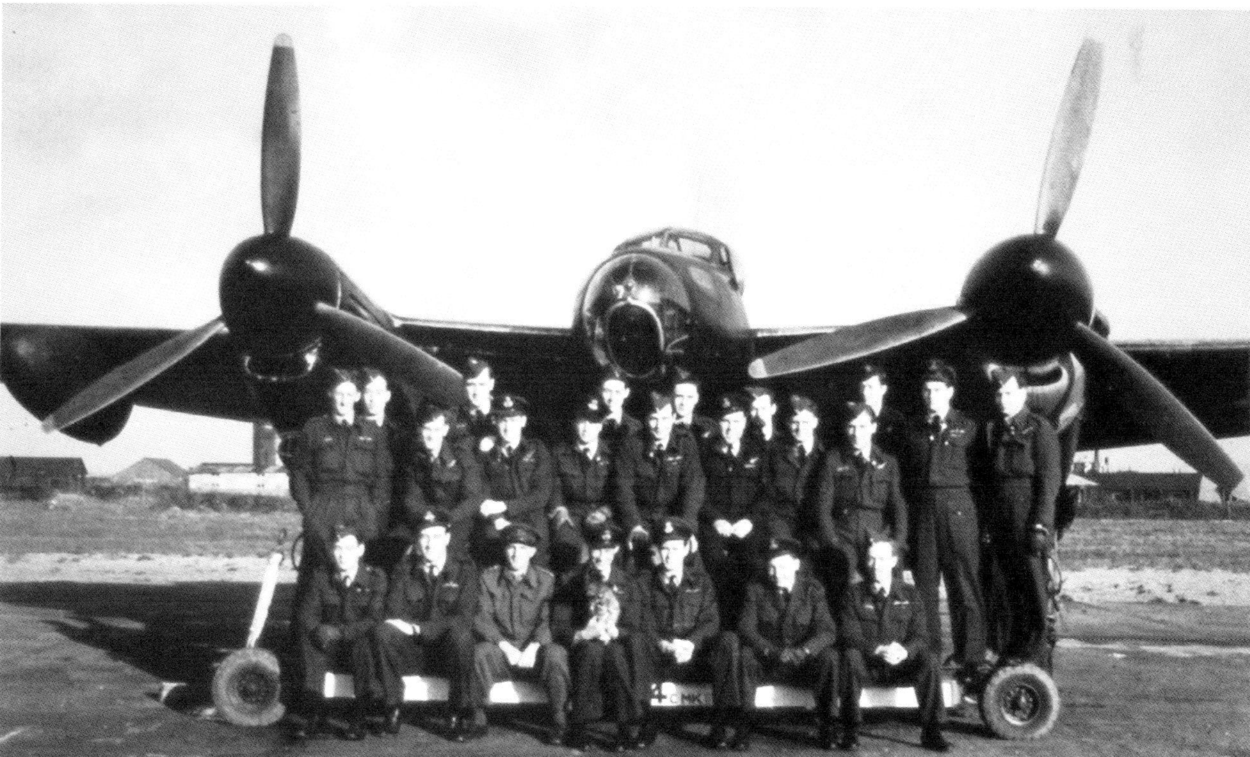

Oakington 1944 showing aircrews of A' Flight 571 Squadron with 'A' Flight commander, Squadron Leader Norman A. J. Mackie DSO DFC* (center, hands on knees), in front of *L-London,* a Mosquito given to all new crews. When Pilot Officer Henley and Clark flew *L-London* on their first operation, it had already done 120 ops and 'knew its way there and back'. (John Clark)

B.Mk.XVI RV297 M5-F of 128 Squadron taxies out at Wyton on B the night of 21/22 March 1945 when 142 Mosquitoes of 8 Group (PFF) made two raids on Berlin. Only one 8 Group Mosquito was lost. The LNSF of Mosquitoes raided Berlin 170 times, 36 of these on consecutive nights.

Moving a 'Cookie' into position.

Oakington 1944 showing ground crews of 'A' Flight 571 Squadron with 'A' Flight commander in front of L-London. (John Clark)

Flying Officer McEwan DFC and Flying Officer Harbottle DFC* watch as B.XVI MM199 M5-Q *'Q-Queenie'* is loaded with a 4000lb 'Cookie' bomb. Note also the 50-gallon wing tanks. On 28/29 August 1944 McEwan returned from a raid on Essen with his 4000lb bomb still aboard. (via Jerry Scutts)

Flying Officer Derek Smith DFC of 692 Squadron. (Derek Smith)

Canadian built B.XX KB326 ACTON ONTARIO CANADA was the first of two such aircraft to arrive at Hatfield on 12 August 1943. The B.XX was basically a Canadian-built B.IV. (via Jerry Scutts)

Flight Lieutenant Frank Griggs DFC RAAF and Flight Lieutenant A.P. 'Pat' O'Hara DFM of 109 Squadron in front of their distinctively painted B.IV Mosquito at RAF Marham, Norfolk in 1943. This crew flew *Oboe* operations until January 1944 when Griggs was repatriated to Australia, O'Hara finishing his second tour (he and Griggs had flown on Stirlings) flying with various pilots, including Wing Commander Peter Kleboe, Commanding 'A' Flight. On 25 October 1944 they marked Essen with red TIs. As O'Hara leaned forward and pressed the lever to open the bomb bay doors a piece of flak came through the windscreen and tore the left epaulette off his battle-dress. Kleboe's face was peppered with fragments of perspex and he was practically blinded. Despite this the Mosquito got back to Little Staughton, and it was landed safely. Kleboe was KIA on the Shellhaus raid, 21 March 1945. (Pat O'Hara DFC* DFM)

AVM Donald C. T. Bennett, C-in-C, 8 Group (PFF) an Australian ex-Imperial Airways and Atlantic Ferry pilot, and his staff officers at a briefing session. Formed originally from 3 Group, using volunteer crews, 8 Group started as a specialist PFF force on 15 August 1942 and on 13 January 1943 it became 8 Group (PFF). By March 1945 8 Group numbered 19 squadrons, ten of them equipped with Mosquitoes. (via Tom Cushing)

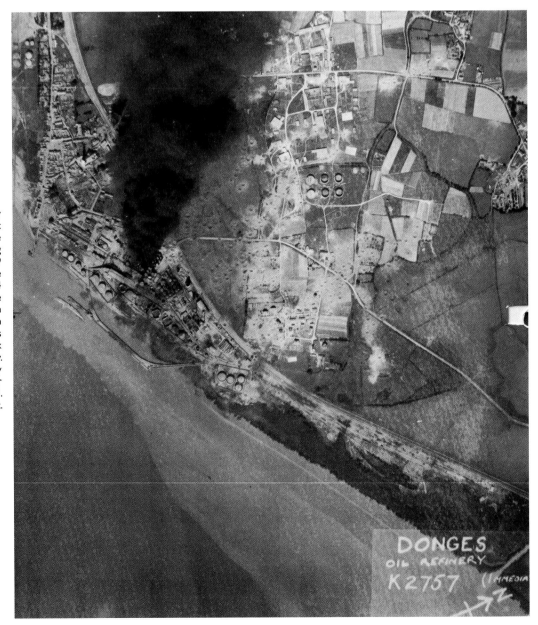

Donges oil refinery and storage depot near the mouth of the River Loire burning after the raid by 119 aircraft including five Mosquitoes on 23/24 July 1944. This was the start of a new campaign against oil targets in the occupied countries and the bombing took place in good visibility. The target was severely damaged and a tanker was hit and capsized. No aircraft were lost. (via Derek Patfield)

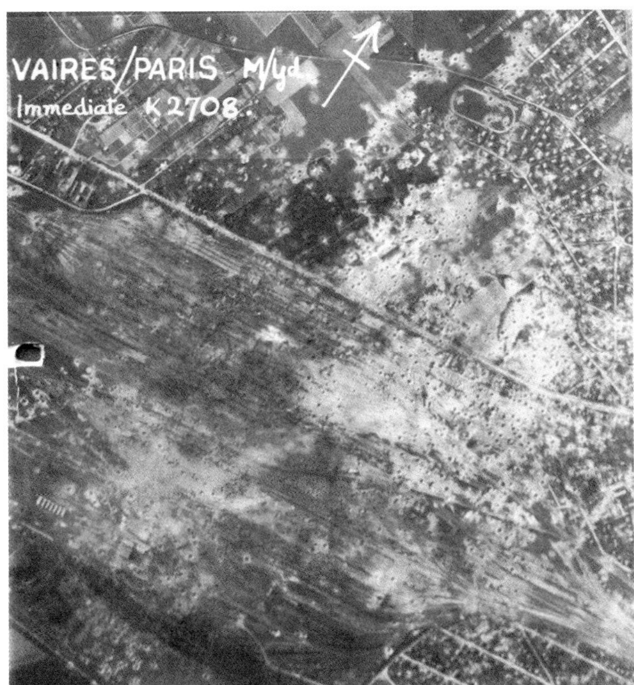

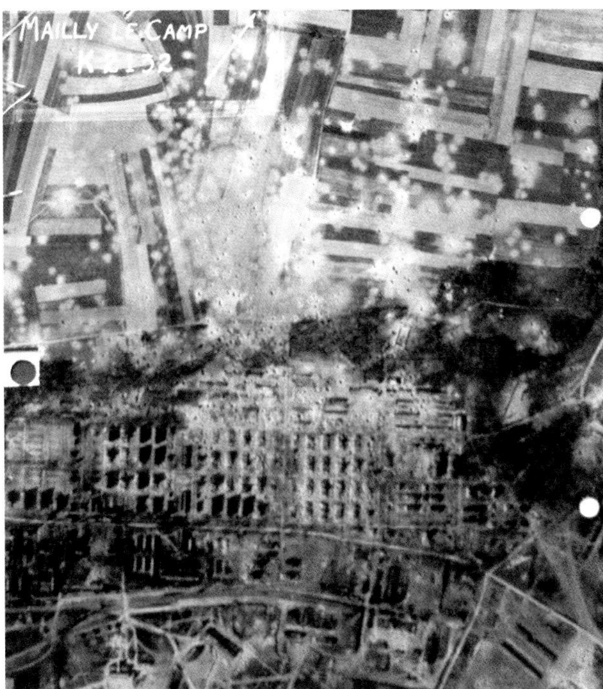

Left: On 29/30 March 1944 70 Halifaxes and eight Mosquitoes of 4, 6 and 8 Groups attacked the rail yard at Vaires on the outskirts of Paris in bright moonlight. The bombing was very accurate and two ammunition trains, which were there, exploded. It was reported that 1270 German troops were killed. One Halifax was lost. The yards were bombed again on 27/28 June by over 200 Lancasters and nine Mosquitoes of 1, 5 and 8 Groups and were particularly accurate. On 12 July 1944 153 Lancasters and six Mosquitoes carried out a daylight operation on the rail yards at Vaires but the target area was covered by cloud. The Master Bomber sent the code word 'Buttermilk' to abandon the attack after two of the Mosquitoes had marked and twelve of the Lancasters had bombed. The final raid on Vaires was on 18 July 1944 when 110 aircraft including five Mosquitoes of 4, 6 and 8 groups bombed the yards. Two Halifaxes were lost. (via Derek Patfield) **Right:** Mailly-le-Camp after the raid on the night of 3/4 May 1944 by 346 Lancasters, 14 Mosquitoes and two PFF Mosquitoes. Despite good marking the Main Force delayed its attack and paid dearly, losing 42 Lancasters, or 11.6 per cent of the force, probably all to *Nachtjäger*. 1500 tons of bombs were dropped with great accuracy and hundreds of buildings and vehicles, including 37 tanks, were destroyed. (via Derek Patfield)

Orléans marshalling yards, which were bombed on five occasions in 1943-44. The first was by four Mosquitoes on 21 May 1943. Then on 19/20 May 1944 it was bombed by 118 Lancasters and four Mosquitoes of 1 and 8 Groups and again on 22/23 May by 128 aircraft including eight Mosquitoes. Most of the bombs fell on the passenger station and the railway repair workshops. The yards were bombed again on 10/11 June and finally, on 4/5 July by over 280 Lancasters and five Mosquitoes of 1, 6 and 8 Groups. (via Derek Patfield)

Bf 110G-4s of 8./NJG1 or '*Zirkus* (Circus) *Schmidt*' during a daylight training flight over France in the summer of 1944 and taken from the Bf 110 flown by 8th *Staffelkapitän* Oberleutnant Dietrich Schmidt. Clearly visible are the large *SN-2* antennae and long-range drop tanks for *Tame Boar* missions on these night-fighter aircraft. G9+RS, nearest to the camera, was the mount of Oberfeldwebel Ruge and the furthest away is flown by Leutnant Rolf Ebhardt. (Dr. Schmidt-Barbo)

Canadians Flight Lieutenant Andy Lockhart and his navigator, Flight Lieutenant Ralph Wood in 692 Squadron flew 50 operations in Mosquitoes, including 18 of them to Berlin. (Phyllis Wood)

Caricature of Ralph Wood (Ralph Wood)

A 4000lb Cookie being hoisted aboard a Mosquito.

On 24/25 March 1945 two Mosquitoes were claimed destroyed by Me 262 jet fighters of 10./NJG11 (Me 262A-1 single-seater jet of *Kommando Welter* with nose mounted FuG 218 *Neptun* radar and four 30mm Mk.108 cannon pictured). Oberleutnant Kurt Welter claimed one and another was credited to Feldwebel Karl-Heinz Becker. (Hans-Peter Dabrowski)

Bf 110G-4 of II./NJG6 at Grossachsenheim airfield one moonlit night in September 1944. (dr. Gunther Lomberg)

Dornier Do 217N-2 3C+IP of 6./NJG4 on 2 May 1944. By early 1944 the heavily armed but relatively slow Do 217 was largely phased out of operation in *Nachtjagd* and relegated to the training role. (Anneliese Autenrieth)

Ju 88G-1 night fighter.

Ju 88 nightfighter.

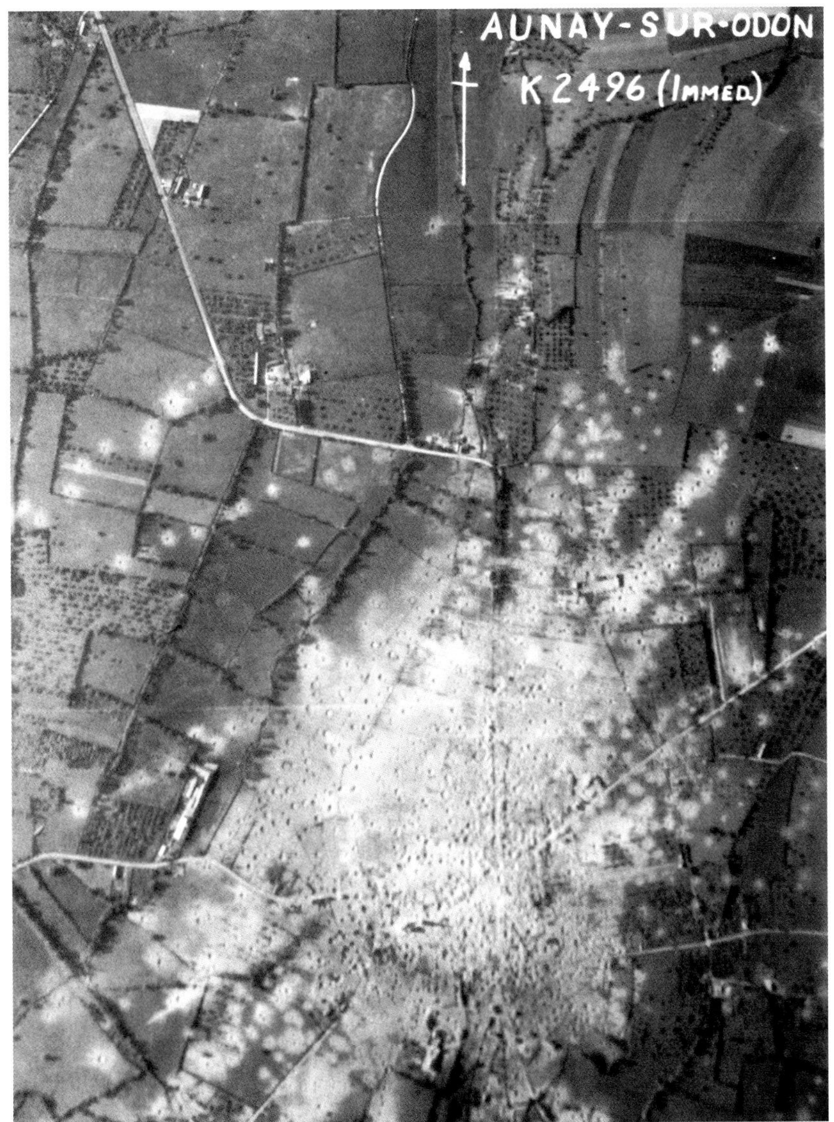

German troop and vehicle positions at Aunay-Sur-Odon (pictured) and Évrecy near Caen were bombed on 14/15 June 1944 by 337 aircraft including 14 Mosquitoes. These raids were made prepared and executed in great haste, in response to an army report giving details of the presence of major German units. The weather was clear and both targets were successfully bombed. The bombing at Aunay, where 5 and 8 Groups shared the marking was particularly accurate. No aircraft were lost. (via Derek Patfield)

After running out of fuel this Bf 110G of III./NJG6 made an emergency landing at Tapoleu airfield in the summer of 1944. Note the aerial array associated with the FuG 220 *Liechtenstein* SN-2d AI radar, its antenna dipoles mounted at a 45-degree angle. SN-2d incorporated a tail warning capacity. (Georg Punka)

Bf 110G-4 fitted with FuG 220B *Liechtenstein* SN-2b and FuG 212 *Liechtenstein* C-1 *Weitwinkel* (Wide-Angle) central array in the nose. SN-2 was not affected by Window and the *Serrate* homer fitted to the Mosquitoes of 100 group. (Hans-Peter Dabrowski)

The Heinkel He 219 *Uhu* (*'Owl'*) might have turned the tide for *Nachtjagd* had it been introduced in quantity. Fast (670 km/h at 23,000 feet), maneuverable and heavily armed with four or six forward firing cannon and a twin 30mm Mk.108 *Schrage Müsik* installation, the *Uhu* was *Nachtjagd's* only aircraft capable of meeting the Mosquito on equal terms. But by the time the first He 219A-6 Mosquito hunters (with all engine and ammunition tank armor and oblique armament removed) was delivered, use of the *Uhu* against the Wooden Wonder had officially been banned. On 23 April 1944 a daylight raid by the American 15th Air Force halted production of the He 219A-0 at Vienna-Schwechat and in May 1944 the 219 was officially abandoned in favor of the Ju 88G series.

Bf 110G-4d/R3 fitted with FuG 220 *Liechtenstein* SN-2d. (Hans-Peter Dabrowski)

On the Messerschmitt Bf 110G-4d/R3 the FuG 220 *Liechtenstein* SN-2d AI radar's low drag antenna dipoles were mounted at a 45° angle to avoid the trajectory of the two nose mounted 30 mm Mk.108 and twin 20 mm MG 151/20 cannon in the ventral tray. (via Hans-Peter Dabrowski)

Junkers Ju 88G nightfighter in flight.

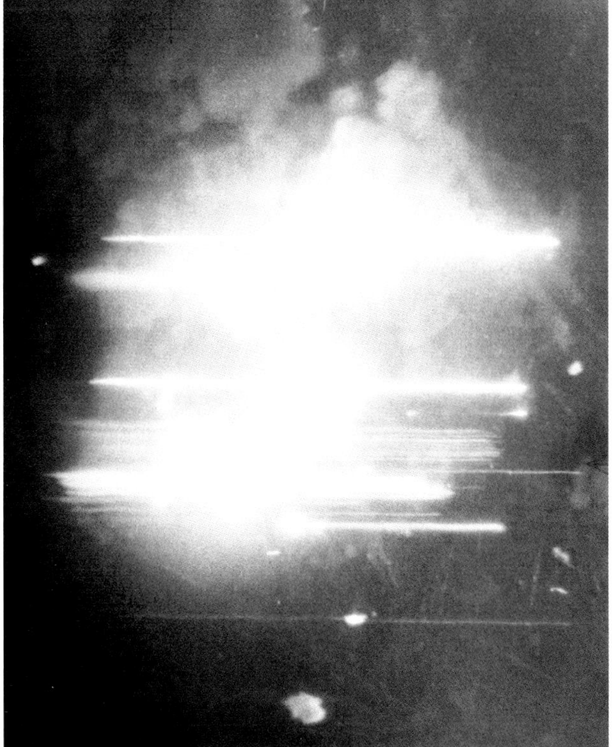

A 4000lb Cookie going down over a German target. (via Derek Patfield)

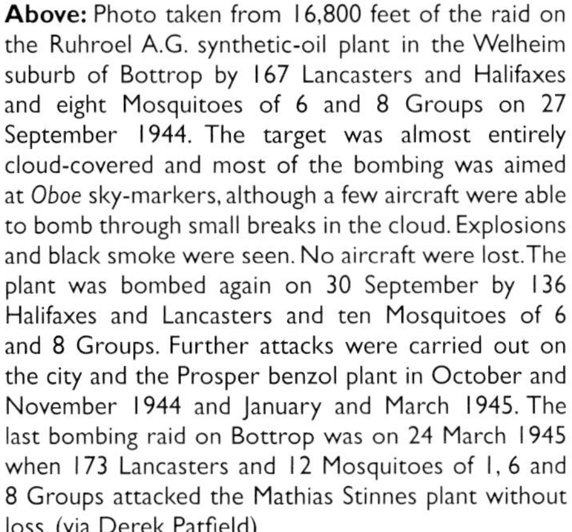

Above: Photo taken from 16,800 feet of the raid on the Ruhroel A.G. synthetic-oil plant in the Welheim suburb of Bottrop by 167 Lancasters and Halifaxes and eight Mosquitoes of 6 and 8 Groups on 27 September 1944. The target was almost entirely cloud-covered and most of the bombing was aimed at *Oboe* sky-markers, although a few aircraft were able to bomb through small breaks in the cloud. Explosions and black smoke were seen. No aircraft were lost. The plant was bombed again on 30 September by 136 Halifaxes and Lancasters and ten Mosquitoes of 6 and 8 Groups. Further attacks were carried out on the city and the Prosper benzol plant in October and November 1944 and January and March 1945. The last bombing raid on Bottrop was on 24 March 1945 when 173 Lancasters and 12 Mosquitoes of 1, 6 and 8 Groups attacked the Mathias Stinnes plant without loss. (via Derek Patfield)

Heinkel He 219 *Uhu* (Owl) nightfighter. (Hans-Peter Dabrowski)

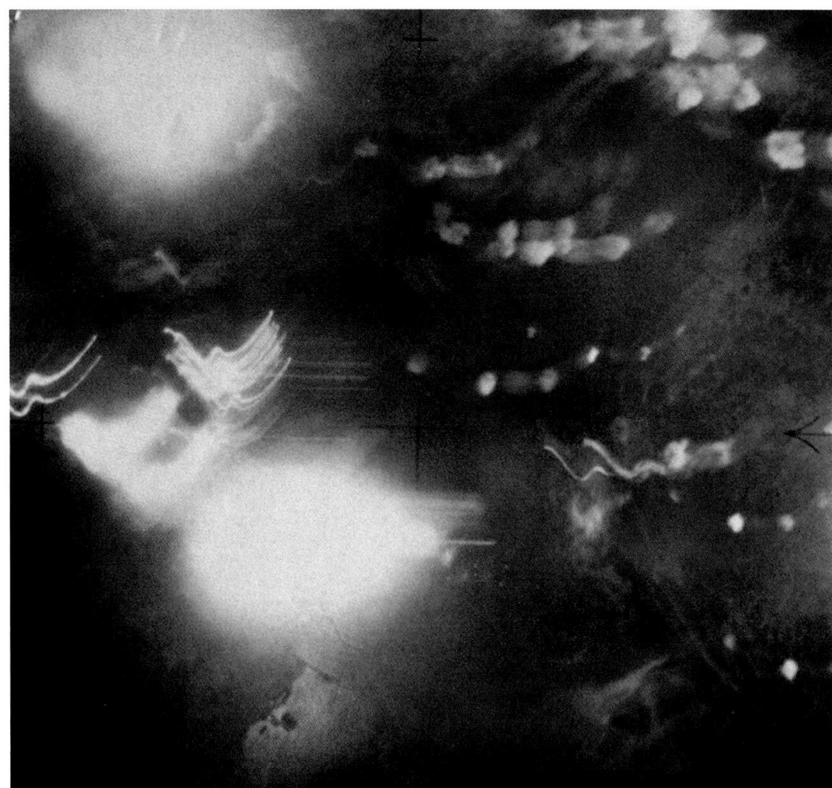

Night raid on Kiel on 23/24 July 1944 by 519 Lancasters, 100 Halifaxes and ten Mosquitoes in the first major raid on a German city for two months and the first by the RAF on Kiel since April 1943. The elaborate deception and RCM operations combined with the surprise return to a German target completely confused the German fighter force and only four aircraft, all of them Lancasters, were lost, a loss rate of 0.6 per cent. The bombing force appeared suddenly from behind a *Mandrel* jamming screen and the local radio warning system only reported it as being a force of minelaying aircraft. Some 612 aircraft then bombed in a raid lasting only 25 minutes. All parts of Kiel were hit but the bombing was particularly heavy in the port areas and all of the important U-boat yards and naval facilities were hit. 315 people were killed and 439 injured. The presence of about 500 delayed-action bombs or unexploded (UXBs) duds caused severe problems for the rescue and repair services. There was no water for three days, trains and buses did not run for eight days and there was no gas for cooking for three weeks. (via Derek Patfield)

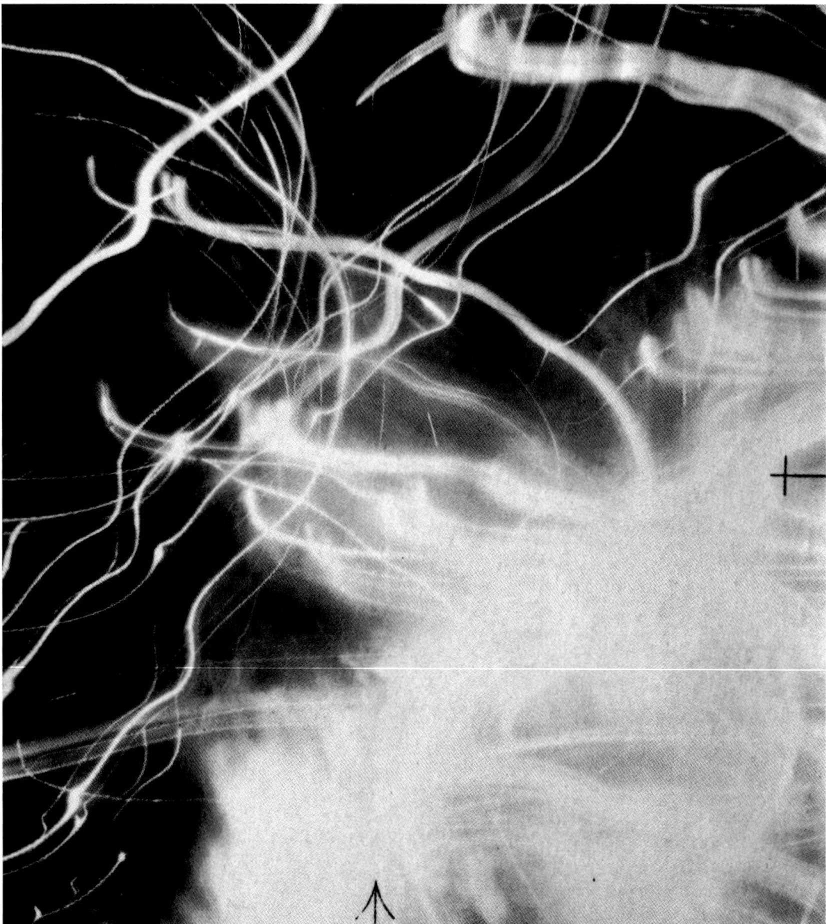

Night raid on Plauen by 307 Lancasters and eight Mosquitoes of 1 and 8 Groups on 10/11 April 1945 in progress. The bombing fell around the railway yards in the northern half of the town. The railways were hit and 365 acres, 51 per cent, of the town's built-up area were also destroyed. (via Derek Patfield)

The second in a series of terrifying area-bombing raids on German cities, which had thus far escaped the bombing, went ahead on 23/24 February 1945 when over 360 Lancasters and 13 Mosquitoes carried out the first and only area-bombing raid on Pforzheim, a city of 80,000 people, from only 8,000 feet. Some 1825 tons of bombs were dropped in just over twenty minutes. More than 17,000 people were killed and 83% of the town's built up area was destroyed in 'a hurricane of fire and explosions'. Ten Lancasters failed to return. (via Derek Patfield)

Cologne cathedral blackened by Allied bombing. (via Derek Patfield)

A 4000lb bomb being released by B.XVI MM200/X of 128 Squadron. During the final months of the war, Mosquitoes of the Light Night Striking Force were the scourge of the battered German cities, especially the *Reich* capital. Berlin, suffered severely at the hands of 4000lb Cookie-carrying LNSF Mosquitoes. These 'nuisance' raids culminated in a devastating series of 36 consecutive night visits against Berlin, beginning on 20/21 February 1945. Of 1896 sorties flown, only 11 Mossies failed to return from the 'Big City'. MM200 overshot landing on one engine at RAF Valley, Wales on 27 August 1945. (Graham M. Simons) **Below:** 4000lb Cookie going down over the target. (via Derek Patfield)

Left: Photo of the raid on Düren on 16 November 1944 taken from 12,000 feet and showing a Lancaster crossing the smoke clouds caused by the bombing. (via Derek Patfield)

Right: On 16 November 1944 RAF Bomber Command was asked to bomb three towns near the German lines which were about to be attacked by the American First and Ninth Armies in the area between Aachen and the Rhine. Some 1188 Bomber Command aircraft attacked Düren, Jülich and Heinsburg in order to cut communications behind the German lines. Düren was attacked by 485 Lancasters and 13 Mosquitoes of 1, 5 and 8 Groups, Jülich by 413 Halifaxes, 78 Lancasters and 17 Mosquitoes of 4, 6 and 8 Groups and Heinsburg by 182 Lancasters of 3 Group. Three Lancasters were lost on the Düren raid and one Lancaster failed to return from the raid on Heinsburg. Some 1239 American heavy bombers also made raids the same area, without suffering any losses. The combined bomber forces dropped more than 9,400 tons of bombs. The RAF raids were all carried out in easy bombing conditions and the three towns were virtually destroyed. Düren, whose civilian population was still present, suffered 3127 fatal casualties - 2403 local civilians, 398 civilians from temporarily staying in Düren and 326 unidentified, of whom at least 217 were soldiers. Heinsburg, described in the British press with other targets as 'a heavily defended town', contained only 110 civilians and a local military unit of one officer and a few soldiers; 52 of the civilians were killed. The American advance was not a success. Wet ground prevented the use of tanks and the American artillery units were short of ammunition because of supply difficulties. The infantry advance was slow and costly. (via Derek Patfield)

4,000lb 'Cookie' bombs in train for loading aboard B.XXVIs of 692 Squadron at Graveley, formed there on 1 January 1944 with B.IVs and flying its first LNSF operation on 1/2 February, three B.IVs going to Berlin. By early 1944 suitably modified B.IVs were capable, just, of carrying a 4000lb Blockbuster, although it was a tight squeeze in the bomb bay, which was strengthened and the bomb doors re-designed. 692 had the distinction of being the first Mosquito squadron to drop a 4000lb bomb over Germany when DZ647, a modified B.IV, released one during a raid on Düsseldorf on 23/24 February 1944. B.XVIs were used from June 1944 until October 1945. (via Tom Cushing)

The devastated city of Cologne. (via Derek Patfield)

Cologne cathedral among the ruins. (via Derek Patfield)

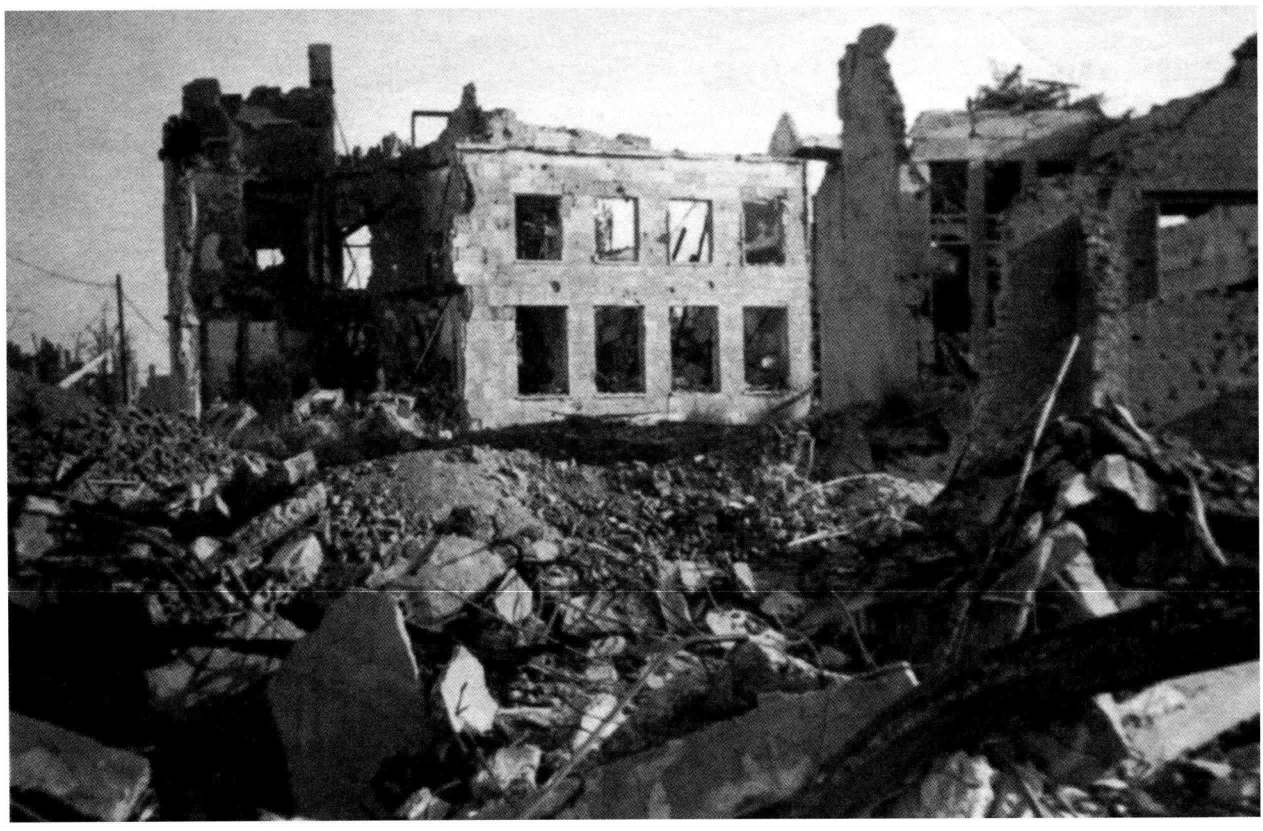

Street scene in Düren in 1946. (via Derek Patfield)

Flight Lieutenant Alfred J. Cork DFM of 109 Squadron in January 1945, a month after being shot down, on 27 December 1944 during an *Oboe* marking operation to Rheydt during the Battle of the Bulge when 200 Lancasters and eleven Mosquitoes attacked the marshalling yards. Cork and his pilot, Flight Lieutenant Hodgson took off from Little Staughton at about 1300 hours in ML961 *T-Tommy*. After take off it soon became apparent that the cabin heating was not working properly if at all. Soon after crossing the coast the windows became completely frosted over and visibility was virtually nil but they pressed on. They completed the release run and Cork believes that he had already received the release signal and he released the first TI when a burst of machine gun (or cannon) fire hit them. He could still see nothing through the iced up perspex. 'Hodge' signalled to him that they were out of control and pointed to the escape hatch. At that moment, a second burst of gunfire hit them and the aircraft went into a dive. Cork got out. Sadly, Hodge didn't. Cork's parachute opened and one of his highly prized pre-war fleece-lined all-leather flying boots fell off. He was angry – those boots were a mark of seniority! (Latecomers had to make do with canvas legged boots!) Cork was picked up and transported back to England. (A. J. Cork DFM)

Canadian built BXX KB268 of 627 Squadron, 8 Group during a visit to a USAAF base in East Anglia during the war. Behind is the 392nd Bomb Group's garishly painted assembly ship. (Author's Coll)

8 Group Mosquitoes taxi out for another raid on Berlin.

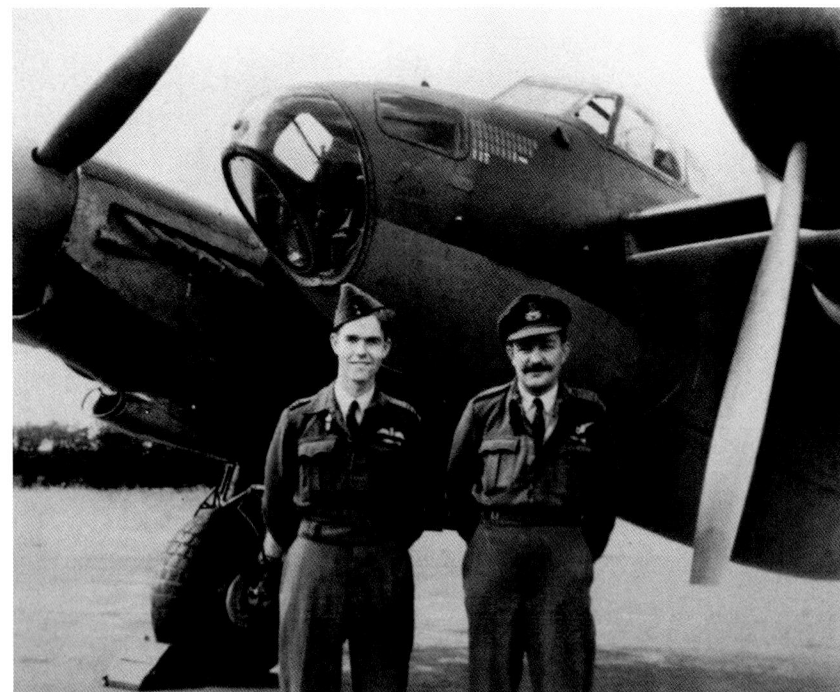

Flight Lieutenant Ivor G. Broom and Flight Lieutenant (later Squadron Leader DFC**) Tommy Broom (note the crossed broomsticks on the nose!). Tommy and Ivor (no relation) flew 58 operations (21 to Berlin) with 571, 128 and 163 Squadrons in 8 Group Pathfinder Force. Ivor later became Air Marshal Sir Ivor Broom KCB CBE DSO DFC** AFC. (via Rolls-Royce)

An 8 Group Mosquito ready for a night raid on Berlin.

Mosquitoes of 128 Squadron taxi out for Berlin.

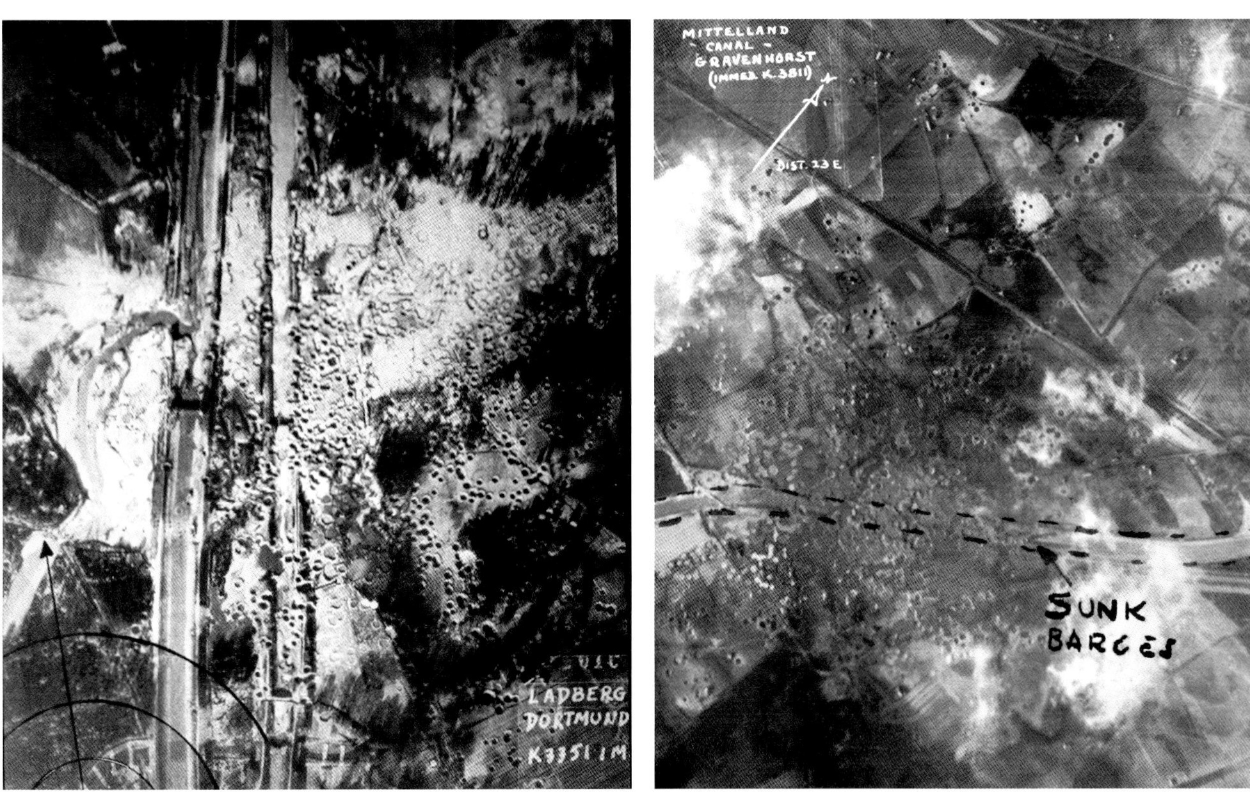

Top Left: Aftermath of the raid on the Dortmund-Ems canal at Ladbergen on 4/5 November 1944. Three Lancasters from the 174 despatched by 5 Group failed to return from the raid on the canal. On 6/7 November when 235 Lancasters and seven Mosquitoes of 5 Group again attempted to cut the Mittelland Canal at Gravenhorst, crews were confronted with a cold front of exceptional violence and ice quickly froze on windscreens. The marking force had difficulty in finding the target due to low cloud and the bombers were told to bomb at low level. Only 31 Lancasters bombed before the Master Bomber abandoned the raid due to low cloud. Forty-eight Mosquitoes dispatched to Gelsenkirchen on a 'spoof' raid to draw German night fighters away from the Mittelland attack and a 3 Group raid on Koblenz, had better luck. Gelsenkirchen was still burning as a result of that afternoon's raid by 738 RAF heavies. Ten Lancasters FTR from the Mittelland debacle. **Above:** Flooding from the breach in the Dortmund-Ems Canal. The Mittlelland Canal was attacked again on 21/22 November and this time the canal banks were successfully breached near Gravenhorst. Fifty-nine barges were left stranded on one short section alone and the water draimned off over a thirty mile stretch. Near Ladbergen the Lancasters, some of them flying as low as 4,000 feet, also breached the Dortmund-Ems Canal in the only branch of the aqueduct which had been repaired since the last raid and the water once again drained out of the waterway. (via Derek Patfield) **Top Left** The results of the attack on the Mittelland Canal at Gravenhorst. (via Derek Patfield)

Flight Lieutenant D. W. Allan DFC, navigator and Flight Lieutenant T. P. Lawrenson, pilot, in front of B.IX LR503 GB-F of 105 Squadron on the occasion of its 203rd operation. LR503 eventually set a Bomber Command record of 213 sorties but was lost on 10 May 1945 along with the crew Flight Lieutenant Maurice Briggs and John Baker, when it crashed at Calgary during a goodwill tour of Canada. (via Norman Booth)

Flight Lieutenant Leicester G. Smith RNZAF, a B.XVI pilot in 128 Squadron at Wyton, who with his RAF navigator Warrant Officer Bill Lane completed 52 operations October 1944-April 1945. Twenty of these ops were to Berlin. (Leicester G. Smith)

Christmas 1944 and a 4000 pounder inscribed *Happy Xmas Adolf* is wheeled into position to be hoisted aboard B.XVI MM199 M5-Q *'Q-Queenie'*, a 'Cookie carrier' of 128 Squadron at RAF Wyton, flown by Flying Officer B. D. McEwan DFC and Flying Officer Harbottle. MM199 FTR from the raid on Hanover on 4/5 February 1945 when at 1948 hours, it was hit by flak from the 8th Flak Brigade and exploded, pieces falling down over a wide area NW of Ronnenberg, 9km SW of Hanover. Flight Lieutenant J. K. Wood RAAF, pilot and Flying Officer R. Poole, navigator were killed. (via Jerry Scutts)

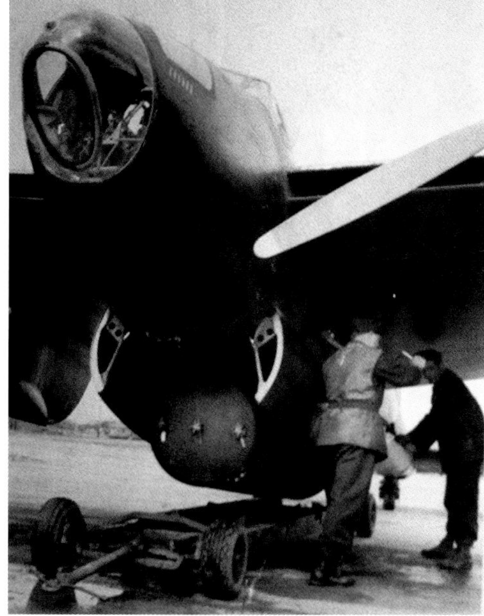

Loading up a Mosquito with a 'Cookie' ready for the Big City. (Phyllis Wood)

Group Captain Menaul DFC, Station Commander at RAF Graveley in front of a 692 Squadron Mosquito.(DH)

B.XVI ML963 *K-King*, which flew 571 Squadron's first sortie on 12/13 April 1944 to Osnabrück. (Charles E. Brown)

SAUMUR
TUNNEL.
RECONSTRUCTION REPORT
No. K.S.1476.

On 8/9 June 1944 483 aircraft attacked rail targets at Alençon, Fougères, Mayenne, Pontabault and Rennes to prevent German reinforcements from the south reaching the Normandy battle area. Three Lancasters and a Mosquito failed to return. That same night the first 12,000lb *Tallboy* bombs developed by Dr. Barnes Wallis were used when 25 Lancasters of 617 Squadron dropped these fearsome weapons on the a railway tunnel near Saumur to prevent a panzer unit moving up to the Normandy front by train. The target area was illuminated with flares by four Lancasters of 83 Squadron and marked at low level by three Mosquitoes. The *Tallboys* were dropped with great accuracy and the tunnel was destroyed in a 'miniature earthquake'. (via Derek Patfield)

1409 (Met) Flight was established at Oakington on 1 April 1943 using Mosquitoes and crews from 521 Squadron, Coastal Command at Bircham Newton. Bill Woodruff is first in the front row. Second from left is Bob Taylor. Fourth from left is Squadron Leader the Hon. Philip I. 'Blister' Cunliffe-Lister DSO the CO and former CO of 521 Squadron, Coastal Command that was used to form the flight. To his left is Squadron Leader Denys A. Braithwaite DFC*. The new Flight soon settled down to its routine work of gathering meteorological information of all sorts and from then on an aircraft of the Flight was invariably out ahead of any major force of Bomber Command, obtaining absolutely up-to-the-minute information of the weather over and approaching the target. Squadron Leader Braithwaite was posted out on 2 May to 139 Squadron and he was replaced by Squadron Leader the Hon. Philip I. 'Blister' Cunliffe-Lister DSO. The Squadron soon had eight operational aircraft and by the end of May three MR.IX Mosquitoes had arrived and were modified for meteorological use. The unit being equipped with seven MR.IX aircraft by August. Squadron Leader Cunliffe-Lister DSO and Pilot Officer A. P. Kernnan in LR502 failed to return from a "*Pampa*" to Osnabrück on 28 July. Fortunately they both managed to bale out and were taken prisoner. Flight Lieutenant Val S. Moore RNZAF took over command on 28 November (Bill Woodruff)

Squadron Leader Tommy Broom who is smoking a cigar, and friends at a social 'bash' at Wyton. Tommy flew 58 operations (21 to Berlin) with 571, 128 and 163 Squadrons in 8 Group Pathfinder Force and was awarded no less than three DFCs. (Tommy Broom)

1409 (Met) Flight PR.IX ML897/D complete with 161 operational bomb symbols. (via Jerry Scutts)

ML963 BK-K *K-King* in flight. (Charles E. Brown)

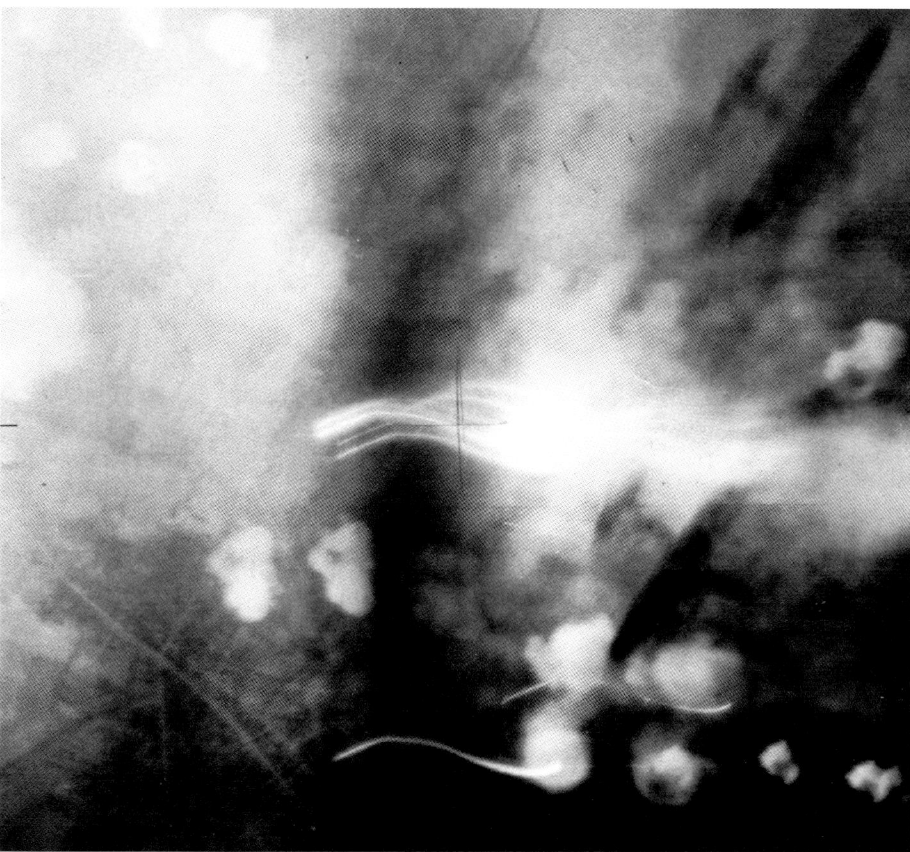

Target photo taken on 10/11 April 1944 from 11,000 feet of the raid by 148 Lancasters and 15 Mosquitoes of 3, 6, and 8 Groups on the rail yards at Laon, France. One Lancaster was lost and the marking was not completely accurate with only a corner of the rail yards being hit. Note the silhouettes of two Lancasters crossing the target below. (via Spud Taylor)

Below: At Wyton in 1944 Wing Commander Eric E. 'Rod' Rodley waves off 128 Squadron B.XVIs fitted with 50-gallon underwing drop tanks setting off for the thirtieth successive night to Berlin. As a 28-year old Flying Officer on 97 Squadron, Rodley had flown Manchesters and then Lancasters on operations, including the suicidal daylight low-level raid on the MAN factory at Augsburg. Mosquitoes flew so often to the 'Big City' that its raids were known as the Berlin Express and the different routes there and back, as Platform One, Two and Three. 128 Squadron reformed as a Pathfinder unit in 8 (PFF) Group on 15 September 1944 equipped with B.XXs before standardizing on the B.XVI. (via Jerry Scutts)

On 4/5 June 1944 six Mosquitoes attacked Argentan in northern France and it was one of the communications targets bombed on the night of 5/6 June on the eve of D-Day. At Argentan, Châteaudun and Lisieux, much damage was done to railways as this target photo shows. (via Derek Patfield).

Post strike photo of the Rheine marshalling yards, which were bombed on 15/16 September 1944 by eight Mosquitoes and again on 16/17 September when during *Market-Garden* four airfields in Germany and Holland were bombed by 200 Lancasters and 23 Mosquitoes of 1 and 8 Groups. On 6/7 November 11 Mosquitoes attacked Rheine again and finally, on 21 March 1945 178 aircraft including 12 Mosquitoes, of 4, 6 and 8 Groups, carried out an accurate attack on the railway yards and the surrounding town area. One Lancaster was lost. (via Derek Patfield).

The men who flew the Mosquito.

1409 (Met) Flight at Oakington in front of a MR.IX. Fourth from left is Squadron Leader the Hon. Philip I. 'Blister' Cunliffe-Lister DSO the CO. To his left is Squadron Leader Denys A. Braithwaite DFC*. (Bill Woodruff)

Climbing into the Mosquito via the small crew door in full flying kit was always very tricky. Baling out was equally difficult.

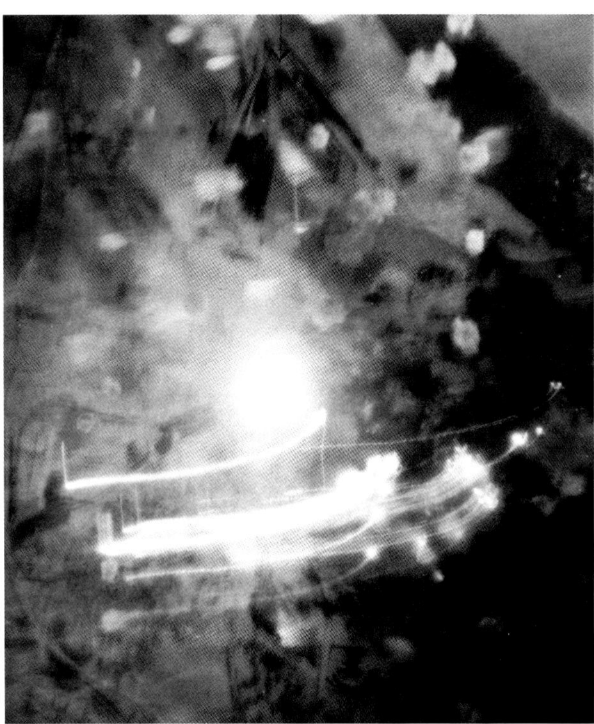

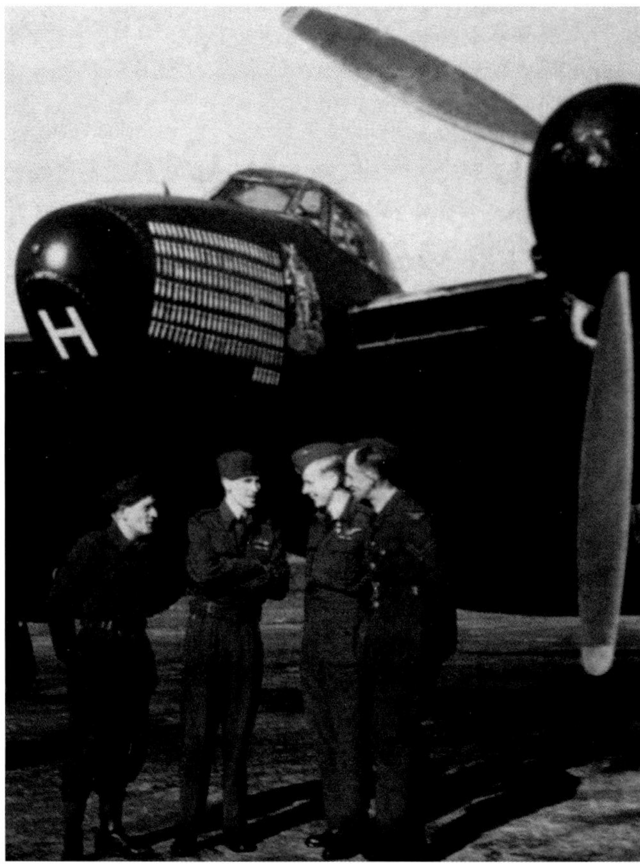

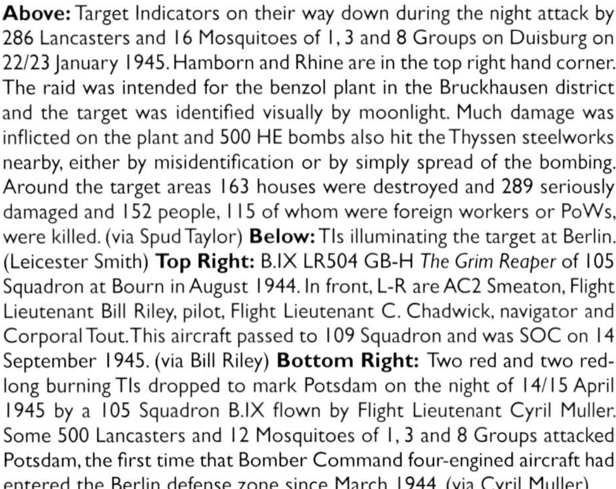

Above: Target Indicators on their way down during the night attack by 286 Lancasters and 16 Mosquitoes of 1, 3 and 8 Groups on Duisburg on 22/23 January 1945. Hamborn and Rhine are in the top right hand corner. The raid was intended for the benzol plant in the Bruckhausen district and the target was identified visually by moonlight. Much damage was inflicted on the plant and 500 HE bombs also hit the Thyssen steelworks nearby, either by misidentification or by simply spread of the bombing. Around the target areas 163 houses were destroyed and 289 seriously damaged and 152 people, 115 of whom were foreign workers or PoWs, were killed. (via Spud Taylor) **Below:** TIs illuminating the target at Berlin. (Leicester Smith) **Top Right:** B.IX LR504 GB-H *The Grim Reaper* of 105 Squadron at Bourn in August 1944. In front, L-R are AC2 Smeaton, Flight Lieutenant Bill Riley, pilot, Flight Lieutenant C. Chadwick, navigator and Corporal Tout. This aircraft passed to 109 Squadron and was SOC on 14 September 1945. (via Bill Riley) **Bottom Right:** Two red and two red-long burning TIs dropped to mark Potsdam on the night of 14/15 April 1945 by a 105 Squadron B.IX flown by Flight Lieutenant Cyril Muller. Some 500 Lancasters and 12 Mosquitoes of 1, 3 and 8 Groups attacked Potsdam, the first time that Bomber Command four-engined aircraft had entered the Berlin defense zone since March 1944. (via Cyril Muller)

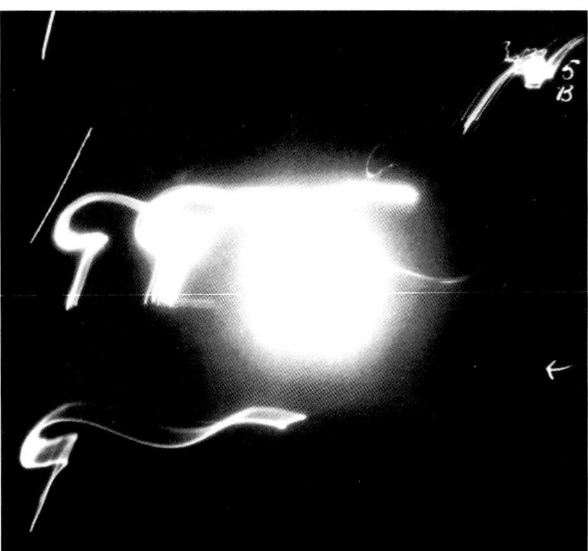

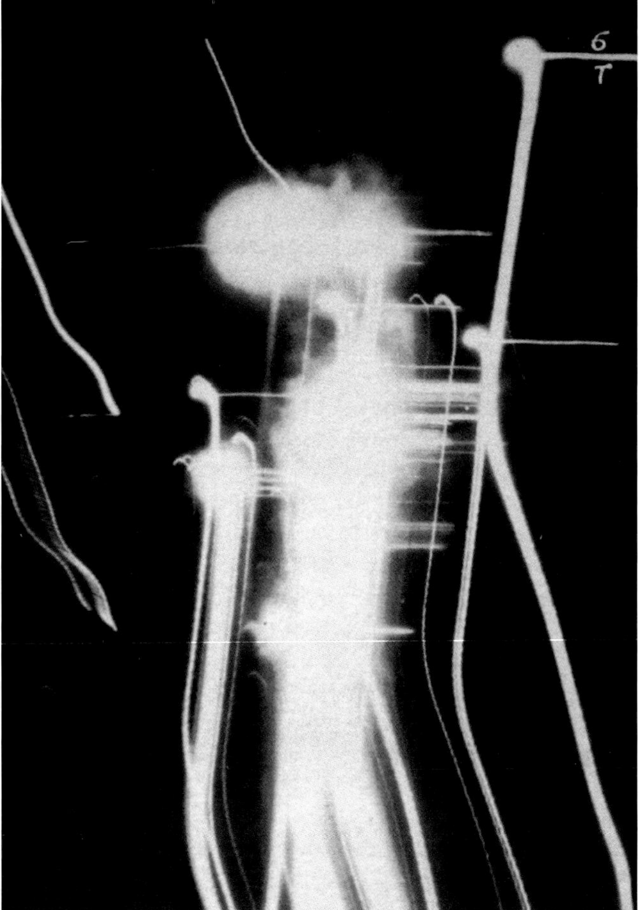

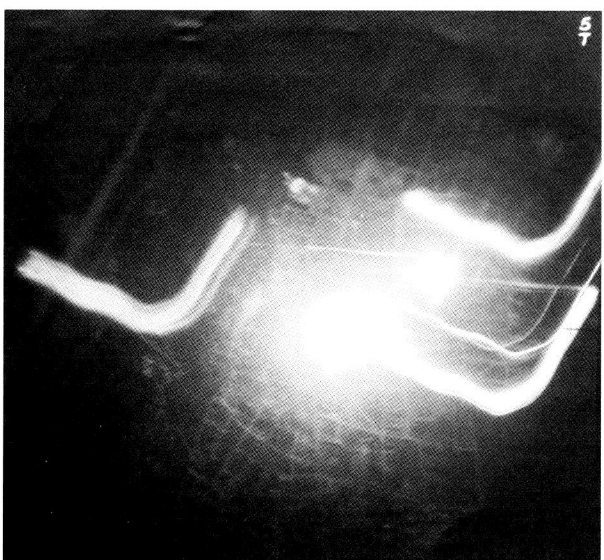

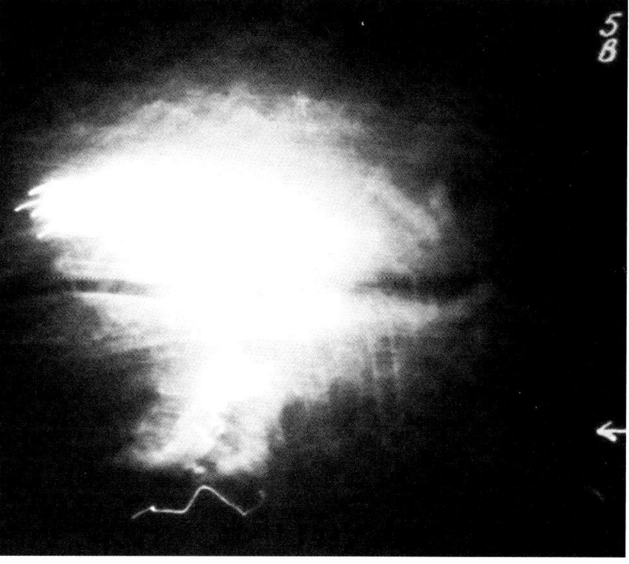

Left: Munich pictured from 20,000 feet on the night of 16/17 April 1945 when Pilot Officer Bill Henley and John Clark were one of 23 Mosquito crews in 8 Group who flew to the city. That same night 19 Halifaxes and four Pathfinder Mosquitoes went to Gablingen airfield and 64 Mosquitoes attacked Berlin. (John Clark) **Right:** Berlin shudders under the impact of bombs and flares on the night of 14/15 April 1945. This photo was taken from Pilot Officer Bill Henley and John Clark's Mosquito at 23,000 feet while the raid by 62 Mosquitoes was in progress. (John Clark)

Post strike photo of Hanau which was bombed on 6/7 January 1945 by 482 aircraft of 1, 4, 6 and 8 Groups, the last named supplying 14 Mosquitoes for the raid. Six heavies were lost .the attack was aimed at that part of Hanau in which an important junction in the German railway system was situated. Many bombs did fall in this area but a large proportion fell in the center of the city and to the north into an area of countryside and villages. Approximately 49 per cent of Hanau was destroyed. A raid by 24 Mosquitoes was made on Hanau on the night of 16/17 March 1945 without loss and on 18/19 March the last raid on the city was made by 277 Lancasters and eight Mosquitoes of 1 and 8 Groups. This was another accurate area raid with 50 industrial buildings and 2240 houses destroyed. The *Altstadt* was completely devastated and approximately 2000 people were killed of whom 1150 were regular residents of Hanau. (via Derek Patfield).

Top Left: Post strike photo of Frankfurt-on-Main which was bombed repeatedly during the war, including eleven times in 1944 and on five occasions in 1945 by the heavies and by 8 Group Mosquitoes. on the night of 12/13 September 1944 378 Lancasters and nine Mosquitoes attacked Frankfurt in the last major RAF Bomber Command raid on the city during the war. Frankfurt was bombed for the last time by RAF Bomber Command on 7/8 March 1945 when ten Mosquitoes attacked the city. (via Derek Patfield). **Top Right:** The destruction of Dresden photographed a short time after the city was devastated by 796 Lancasters and nine Mosquitoes on the night of 13/14 February 1945 when 8 Group provided standard Pathfinder marking, and by 311 bombers of the 8th Air Force the following day. (via Derek Patfield) **Bottom:** The bombing of the small island of Heligoland on 18 April 1945 when a daylight attack was made on the *U-boat* base, the airfield and the town by 969 aircraft - 617 Lancasters, 332 Halifaxes and 20 Mosquitoes. A total of 11,776 bombs were dropped on Heligoland between 1224 and 1325 hours. Bombing was accurate and the target areas were turned almost into crater-pitted moonscapes. Ninety-five per cent of all the houses on Heligoland were destroyed leaving 2000 civilians homeless. Fifty German soldiers were killed and 150 injured. Three Halifaxes were lost. Between August 1944 and April 1945 one third of all Bomber Command sorties were flown in daylight, which underscored both the overwhelming allied air superiority and almost complete impotence of the Luftwaffe by this time. (via Derek Patfield)

128 Squadron air crews and WAAFs celebrate VE-Day 8 May 1945 at RAF Wyton. Ed Boulter is second from left, front row. In the second picture the squadron are joined by visiting Russian general staff, AVM 'Don' Bennett (with glass raised above the head of one his two children) Group Captain Dixie Dean DSO DFC, the station commander (in the foreground looking to his right). A Pathfinder demonstration was given but only after the Soviet embassy allowed one Russian general to fly in a Lancaster, provided that 'Don' Bennett piloted it. The other general and some of the six colonels flew in another Lancaster. (via Ed Boulter)

Chapter 7

The "Baby Blitz"

Touch me gently, wake me softly
Let me start to sing,
Free to use my strength and power
Throbbing on the wing.

Let me roar my throaty war-song
As we start to rise,
Challenging the unseen dangers
Lurking in the skies.

Keep me happy as we settle
Steadily to fly
Purring like a drowsy kitten
Loudly in the sky.

Let me never fail my masters
In the searchlight's glare;
Let me keep them safely airborne
In my loyal care.

Let me help them do their duty
On their awesome flight,
Let me bring them through the hazards
of the savage night.

Winging through the cloudy darkness
I will sing my song,
Reaching lip to dawn's pale sunlight
Though the night was long.

Let me sing of men returning
Safely homeward bound,
Then my thrusting heart shall sing
In glorious joyful sound.

Song Of The Merlin,
Audrey Grealy.

On the night of 21/22 January 1944, 92 German bombers headed for London in the first of a series of revenge raids on Britain codenamed Operation *Steinbock* and directed by *Generaleralmajor* Peltz, *Angriffsführer* (Attack Leader) England. Peltz had assembled a small fleet of all types of bombers and fighter-bombers for dive-bombing over England as retaliation for RAF heavy bomber raids on German towns and cities. Each raid carried out by the *Kampfgeschwaders* normally bore emotive code-names like *Munich* and *Hamburg* to remind the *Luftwaffe* crews that they were embarked on revenge raids for the round-the-clock bombing of centers of German population. As the *Luftwaffe* became short of aircraft, new types, like the Heinkel He 177 *Greif* (*Griffon*), were now employed on bombing raids against English cities. Pathfinders led the German bombers, including 15 He 177A-3s of I/KG100 to London, and *Düppel* (German "Window") was scattered by the attacking force in an effort to confuse the radar defenses. The first He 177 to be shot down over the British Isles, a He 177A-5 of I/KG40, fell to the guns of a Mosquito NF.XII flown by Flying Officer H. K. Kemp and Flight Sergeant J. R. Maidment of 151 Squadron from Colerne.[199] Altogether, the first *Steinbock* raid cost the *Luftwaffe* 21 aircraft.

German units were rested until the night of 28/29 January, when 16 Me 410s and ten Fw 190 fighter-bombers raided East Anglia, Kent, and Sussex again. One Me 410 was destroyed by a Mosquito, but one of the defending fighters was lost in action. The following night the *Luftwaffe* force also included He 177s of 3./KG100 and I/KG40. Some 130 of the 285 enemy aircraft tracks penetrated inland, 30 reaching London. Bombs were dropped in a wide swathe across Hampshire, the Thames Estuary, and Suffolk. A Mosquito of 410 "Cougar" Squadron RCAF flown by Lieutenant R. P. Cross RNVR and Sub-Lieutenant L. A. Wilde RNVR, and equipped with AI.VIII radar, was just gaining height after taking off from Castle Camps at 2030 hours when they received a vector from Flight Lieutenant Parr at GCI Control at Trimley Heath. A "bogey" had been picked up on radar, and Parr told Cross to climb to 15,000 feet. Wilde picked up the "bandit" (a Ju 88) at 2039 hours, three miles distant (the AI.VIII radar set had a range of 6½ miles straight ahead) flying west. Cross closed in behind the unsuspecting raider. A five-minute chase ensued and finished with Cross lifting his nose up and blasting the Junkers with two short bursts of 20mm cannon fire. Cross and Wilde did not see any hits on the Ju 88 when firing. A Ju 88A of 3./KG54, which crashed at Barham, Suffolk, about this time, fell to a 68 Squadron Beaufighter.

On the night of 3/4 February 240 enemy aircraft operated in two phases over London and southeastern England. 95 went inland, 17 reached London, and 14 were lost. Six squadrons of Mosquitoes met them. 410 "Cougar" Squadron RCAF got six NF.XIIIs off from Castle Camps. Canadians Flying Officer E. S. Fox and Flying Officer C. D. Sibbett took off at 0400 hours and were vectored by Sergeant Burton at GCI Trimley, who gave them a "bandit" crossing starboard to port. Sibbett worked his AI.VIII radar set until he obtained a contact 3½ miles distant at 18,000 feet. Fox turned to port and closed to 2000 feet. The German intruder was dropping *Düppel* and

Sibbett lost contact temporarily, as his screen became cluttered with pulses. He radioed Control, but before they could respond contact was regained and Fox set off in pursuit.

The Mosquito pilot closed to 200 feet and the German, a Do 217, immediately began violent evasive action to shake off his pursuer. Fox gave the Dornier a one-second-burst, but the shells missed as he peeled off to starboard. Fox turned right, then left, and regained contact again. He stalked the enemy bomber for 10mm and maintained visual contact despite continued violent evasive action on the part of the German pilot. The Canadian closed to 200 feet and gave him a two-second burst. A large piece flew off the enemy aircraft and it exploded. Fox orbited and watched the flaming wreckage hurtle down into the sea. It impacted and exploded with such force that the tops of the clouds were illuminated over a wide area. (The only Do 217M-1 lost this night came from 8./KG2, but crews of 85, 410 "Cougar" Squadron RCAF, and 488 Squadron RNZAF each claimed one!)

Fellow Canadians Flying Officer W. G. Dinsdale and his observer, Flight Sergeant J. E. Dunn, also of 410 Squadron RCAF, picked up a radar contact and closed to 2000 feet slightly below the "bandit," which was flying at 15,000 feet at about 220 mph near Stapleford Tawney. Dinsdale drew to the left to prevent overshooting his prey. It was a Ju 88 flying straight and level, seemingly oblivious to the Mosquito's presence. However, just as Dinsdale turned into an attacking position the Ju 88 peeled off violently to port and headed directly for them! It flew dangerously close underneath, and its fin or tailplane clipped the Mosquito's starboard propeller as it passed. Dinsdale temporarily lost control, regained it again, and dived the aircraft to the left. Despite Dunn getting several more contacts, the enemy aircraft disappeared before the Canadians could attack again. They could only claim a "damaged."

A NF.XIII flown by Flying Officer Hugh Brian Thomas and Warrant Officer C. B. Hamilton of 85 Squadron at Biggin Hill was climbing to 20,000 feet when they received a vector from the Sandwich controller to intercept two contacts. One turned out to be a friendly fighter and the hunt was called off. Then another contact was obtained and the hunt was on again. This time it was a German bomber. At 1500 feet the "bandit" was made out to be a Do 217. Thomas closed from 300 to 100 yards before opening fire. In three very short bursts, each lasting just 2½ seconds, 120 20mm rounds were pumped into the hapless Dornier. Thomas observed strikes, and with the third burst the Dornier exploded and the starboard engine erupted in flames. Thomas broke off, his windscreen covered in oil, and watched the German aircraft fall away, well alight. It hit the sea 20 miles east of the Naze and lit up the clouds with an orange glow. Thomas and Hamilton returned to Biggin and were told to orbit the station, as "hostiles" had been reported overhead, but flying debris from the Dornier had penetrated the Mosquito's port engine and five miles west of the base Thomas feathered the propeller and landed. Thomas ended his tour in the summer of 1944 having scored four victories and earning the DFC. He returned to the squadron in April 1945 as a Flight Lieutenant and claimed his fifth victory west of Lutzkendorf flying a NF.XXX.

The fourth "kill" of the night went to Dutchman Flight Sergeant Christian J. Vlotman and his navigator, Sergeant John L. Wood, of 488 Squadron RNZAF at Bradwell Bay. On his AI.VIII, Wood picked up a Do 217 gently weaving at 17,000 feet, 2½ miles distant. Vlotman was directed by ground control until he was able to make contact at about 1000 yards. The Dutchman closed to 300 yards dead astern and let fly with his four 20mm cannon. His port inner stopped, fouled by loose rounds, but the shells had done their work. The Dornier peeled off to port, its left side and engine aflame. Vlotman followed the stricken fighter-bomber down and gave it two more short bursts to make the "kill" certain. It spun violently down, shedding pieces of debris. The enemy cockpit was well alight, and no crew were seen to bale out as it went down over the North Sea, 40 miles off Foulness Point, Essex.

The fourth major *Steinbock* attack took place on the night of 13/14 February, and Mosquito crews were again triumphant. One of the victors was Flight Lieutenant Rayne Schultz DFC of 410 "Cougar" Squadron RCAF, who took his score to five. On the night of 10/11 December 1943 he and Flying Officer V.A. Williams had scored a hat trick of victories. They downed three Do 217s of KG2, for which they had received DFCs. Schultz's victory on 13/14 February was a Ju 188, which was shot down about 20 miles off East Anglia. Fellow Canadian Squadron Leader James Dean Somerville of 410 "Cougar" Squadron RCAF, who was 25 years old and came from Esshaw, Alberta, destroyed a Ju 88S-1 of Major Helmut Schmidt's I/KG66 pathfinder unit, and it fell at 2110 hours at Havering-Atte-Bower, Essex. Flight Lieutenant Edward Bunting DFC and Phil Reed, now of 488 Squadron RNZAF and a 96 Squadron pilot, scored a victory apiece to take the total to eight enemy aircraft that failed to return. Five Ju 88s from KG6 went into the sea and a Ju 188 crashed in France on return. Altogether, the raiders attacked targets in Britain on eight nights in February, including a devastating raid on London on the 18th whose success owed much to the Ju 88 pathfinders of KG6 and KG66. Fortunately for British civilians, the intended wholesale use of V1 flying bombs had not materialized and *Luftwaffe* morale was further sapped by the poor performance of the He 177.

On the night of 20/21 February, 95 German raiders crossed the English coast between Hythe and Harwich, heading for London.[200] Mosquitoes of 25 Squadron, which had arrived at RAF Coltishall, near Norwich, on 5 February, were alerted. At 2110 hours Pilot Officer J. R. Brockbank and his navigator-radio operator, Pilot Officer D. McCausland, took off in their NF.XVII codenamed *Grampus 16*. Flight Lieutenant Joe Singleton and his observer, Flying Officer W. G. "Geoff" Haslam, also took off at about the same time. Both aircraft were equipped with AI.X radar, and a NF.XVII had yet to shoot down an enemy aircraft at night. As soon as they cleared the circuit both aircraft were handed over to GCI at Neatishead, from where the controllers gave them their instructions. *Grampus 16* was told to climb to 17,000 feet, while Singleton (*Grampus 20*) was ordered to climb to *Angels 18* (18,000 feet). At 2143 hours he was passed on to the Chain Home Low (Radar) Station at Happisburgh, who gave him new vectors after they had picked up a "bogey" going eastwards at *Angels 10*.

Meanwhile, at 2137 hours Brockbank and McCausland obtained a contact at seven miles range on an aircraft crossing from left to right. Brockbank throttled to 2,650 revs at +4 boost and gained gradually on the target. His prey was a Ju 188E-1 flown by *Leutnant* Ewald Bohe of 5/KG2. Bohe weaved gently at first and then made more violent manoeuvres in an effort to shake off the Mosquito. Brockbank closed in several times to 1000 feet, but he could not get a visual on the target and was forced to break off each time. McCausland lost contact, but Neatishead restored it after a further vector. At this point a single searchlight pierced the gaps in the cloud and illuminated the fighter. Bohe "corkscrewed" violently and tried to outdistance his pursuer, but Brockbank stuck doggedly to his task, chasing the German for 25 minutes and gradually closing the gap. At 600 feet he could make out the enemy's exhaust glows. The Ju 188E crossed gently from port to starboard, and as it was crossing back Brockbank fired two short bursts. Tenaciously, he closed to 75 feet and poured more rounds into the hapless German. It caught fire, flew straight and level for a few seconds and, blazing furiously, commenced a deep death dive through the clouds to crash at Park Farm, Wickham St. Paul, Essex. Both the artificial horizon and direction indicator aboard the Mosquito were put out of action after the cannon were fired, so *Grampus 16* headed back to Coltishall, where the time of the "kill" (2203 hours) was logged; the first "kill" attributed to a NF.XVII.

Singleton, meanwhile, had pursued his enemy aircraft at 9000 feet over the sea to 50 miles east of Lowestoft. Haslam used night binoculars to make a positive identification of the enemy aircraft. (It was a Do 217K-1 of 7./KG2.) At 2236 hours Singleton despatched *Oberleutnant* Wolfgang Brendel and his crew into the sea with a two-second burst from dead astern. Brendel, *Feldwebel* Bruno Preker, *Oberfeldwebel* Bruno Schneider, and *Unteroffizier* Heinz Grudßus were all posted as "Missing." Then Singleton and Haslam picked up the chase again and pursued *Unteroffizier* Walter Schmidt's KG2 Do 217M-1 to within 20 miles of the Dutch coast before they had to return to Coltishall, low on petrol. All in all, a successful night for the Battle of Britain station.

The following night, 22/23 February, He 177s of I/KG100 based at Rheine and 3./KG 100 from Châteaudun were included in the all-out assault on England. Mosquito nightfighter teams like Flight Lieutenant Bill Baillie and his navigator-radio operator, Flying Officer Simpson, were always on the lookout for "bogies" in their part of the sky. They had taken off from Coltishall at 2125 hours and had not been on patrol long when Flying Officer Humphries, one of the controllers at the radar station at Happisburgh, told them that there was the possibility of "trade" southwest, traveling west about 20 miles away. They were vectored to within three miles of the contact when the radar station said they could not give much more help. At three minutes after midnight Simpson picked up two blips on his AI.X cathode ray screen at two miles range, 10-15° above at 17,000 feet. Baillie set off in hot pursuit, and within minutes had narrowed the range to just 2000 feet. He could see the exhausts and resins of the rear aircraft. At this point the rear blip veered away to the left and the other went slightly to the right as the enemy aircraft carried out mild evasive action. Had they picked up the Mosquito's presence? Baillie and Simpson peered ahead through the narrow windscreen of their fighter. Immediately they looked away, dazzled momentarily by groping searchlight beams, which bathed the Mosquito in bright light before they were eventually extinguished.

Their night vision restored, Baillie and Simpson strained in the direction of where their quarry should be. Baillie narrowed the gap, closing to 400 yards from the blip. And there it was! At 14,000 feet they made out a rough outline against the night sky; a large black silhouette of fuselage and engines ploughing along, intent on death and destruction. It motored on as if it owned the sky. Even the exhausts emitted no flames. They were at one with the black expanse and dark grey cloud shapes. Baillie stared intently. "It's a Dornier Do 217," he reported, and closed to just 200 feet astern. In fact it was a He 177A-3 of 3./KG100 flown by *Oberfeldwebel* Wolfgang Ruppe. At just 23 minutes after midnight Baillie opened fire, sending the He 177 down in flames to fall in the vicinity of Wolsey House Farm, Yoxford. It lay scattered over an area about a quarter of a mile across. The only survivor was the rear gunner, Emil Imm, who floated down in his turret and lived to tell the tale. He was found next morning by workmen who revived him with coffee from their flasks.

Oberfeldwebel Ruppe's He 177 was one of 150 *Luftwaffe* bombers which crossed East Anglia on the night of 22/23 February 1944. By and large they got through. Only two Me 410s were lost. One fell to Squadron Leader G. L. Caldwell and Flying Officer Rawling of 96 Squadron at Framfield, Sussex; the other to AA fire at Radnage, Buckinghamshire. Squadron Leader C. A. S. Anderson and his observer, Flight Sergeant G. P. I. Bodard, of 410 "Cougar" Squadron RCAF were on interception patrol at 20,000 feet in their NF.XIII from Castle Camps. They were vectored north by Trimley GCI, who told them to climb to 23,000 feet to investigate a "bogey" near Earls Colne. Trimley told the two Canadians to descend to 18,000 feet, and it was at this point that Anderson and Bodard made contact. A German raider was flying along two miles in the distance, well below the height of the approaching Mosquito. The Trimley controller had done his job well.

Anderson closed, but before he could line up his guns he had overshot the bomber. He orbited and Bodard picked up the "bogey" on his screen again, range ½-mile, and still below. The same thing happened again! Anderson orbited a second time and Bodard made contact, range ¾ mile. Anderson closed slowly this time to 500 feet and obtained a visual. The twin-engined enemy machine began carrying out a wild evasive action, and visual contact was lost several times until Bodard managed to hold the contact and Anderson could close to 50 feet. It was a Ju 88A-4 of 9./KG6, one which had taken off from Melsbroek to bomb London.

Astern and below, Anderson lined up to fire. Just as he was about to launch a fusillade of 20mm cannon and HEI rounds the Ju 88 pilot peeled off violently to the left and spoiled his aim. However, Anderson managed to get in a short burst from 150 feet and he was pleased to see some of the rounds find their mark on the fuselage and starboard engine, which caught fire. The Junkers leveled out and Anderson attacked again, this time from 75 yards. The stricken bomber was hit further and the German crew, impotent it seemed, must have known they were doomed. The pilot refused to give up the struggle, however, and turned to the right as Anderson pumped more shells into the target. Small explosions danced on the Junkers' fuselage and, finally, it burst into flames. It spun away into the night and broke up before plunging into the North Sea.

Bodard returned to Trimley GCI control. Flight Lieutenant Carr calmly informed the Mosquito crew to go to 17,000 feet; he had picked up another "bogey" over Essex. Range, three miles. Anderson closed in while climbing, but the enemy aircraft was too high and he undershot. Bodard lost contact and asked Trimley for help. Can gave them a vector of 270°, and Anderson closed on the enemy to 500 feet. A visual was obtained, but this "kill" was not going to be any easier than the previous one, and the enemy pilot immediately carried out evasive action. Contact was maintained, however, and Anderson closed to 150 feet, keeping underneath and to one side, just to be on the safe side. The two Canadians made the bomber out to be a Ju 188E-1. Immediately, the German bomber dived to the left. Anderson gave a short burst from 50 yards and the rounds struck home on the side of the Junkers' fuselage and wings. The wounded animal took further violent evasive action and lost height, but the Mosquito crew would not be shaken from their stride. Anderson pumped more bursts into the Junkers and a fusillade, which struck the cockpit area, seemed to signal the end of the German bomber. It dived steeply, leveled out momentarily, and finally spun in, out of control. Anderson followed it down and pulled out at 6000 feet when he recognized that the Junkers was finished.

With characteristic understatement, Britons by now called the Operation *Steinbock* raids the "Baby Blitz." Mosquito nightfighter crews encountered all manner of German bomber and fighter types, including Do 217s, Me 410s, and even the occasional Fw 190 and He 177. On 23/24 February three enemy aircraft were lost and a Do 217 fell to AA fire. The following night Mosquito crews claimed three "probables" and eight enemy aircraft shot down.[201] *Steinbock* raids continued over East Anglia and London throughout the remainder of February and into March. The "Baby Blitz" showed no sign of easing up, and 70 aircraft attempted to bomb London on 1 March. Only 10 managed to evade the defenses and reach the capital, however.

On the night of 14/15 March, 140 German raiders crossed the coast of eastern England in four waves. Two-thirds of the force crossed between Cromer, in Norfolk, and Shoeburyness, Essex, while a smaller wave crossed over Sussex. Some of the bomber force used skill and daring to infiltrate British airspace under cover of returning Mosquitoes, and *Düppel* was dropped to complete their disguised approach. Most of the invading bombers crossed the coast between Great Yarmouth and Southwold at heights ranging from 14,000-24,000 feet before turning south for London and its environs. The incursions were met in some strength by a determined force of Mosquitoes. Seven of 410 "Cougar" Squadron RCAF at Castle Camps were scrambled to intercept. 1st Lieutenant Archie A. Harrington and Sergeant D.G. Tongue destroyed a Ju 88A-4 of 2./KG54,[202] which fell at Hildenborough, Kent. Harrington, who was 29 years old and came from Jamesville, Ohio, was a USAAF officer attached to the RCAF to gain night fighting experience. (Over Germany on the night of 25/26 November they intercepted and shot down three Ju 88G night-fighters to take their score to seven.) Squadron Leader Peter Wilfrith Green DFC got a Ju 88 for his fourth victory of the war and his first since joining the Canadian squadron from 85 Squadron in the spring.[203] A Ju 188E-l flown by Leutnant Horst Becker of 4./KG6 fell to the guns of Flight Lieutenant Edward Bunting of 488 Squadron RNZAF. It broke up in the air and crashed in flames at White House Farm, Great Leighs, near Chelmsford.[204]

Meanwhile, Joe Singleton and his observer, Flying Officer Geoff Haslam, of 25 Squadron had taken off from Coltishall at 2105 hours for a *Bullseye* exercise (when training aircraft from the bomber OTUs were engaged by the sector searchlights and subjected to dummy attacks by night-fighters). Singleton had just returned to the squadron after instructing, being promoted to Flight Lieutenant and receiving the DFC. Sector Control passed them on to Neatishead GCI. At 18,000 feet Singleton asked his controller if there was any "*trade*?" There were "*possibilities*" came the reply, and a few minutes later, on a vector of 140°, Singleton and Haslam obtained a head-on contact at 4½ miles. Singleton went in pursuit guided by Haslam, who was able to make contact and hold it. The enemy plane was at about 16,000 feet, flying along at approximately 240 mph. The two men observed that it was taking the normal "corkscrew" evasive action. Singleton closed to 1000 feet. Haslam raised his night binoculars to his eyes. "It's a Ju 88!" he said.

At this the Mosquito went in closer until Singleton was within 75 yards of his quarry. A three-second-burst of 20mm cannon—less than 120 rounds—produced a big explosion. Fire erupted on the left-hand side of the Junkers' fuselage and Haslam and Singleton could quite clearly see the black crosses on the underside of the port wing as the stricken bomber toppled over and fell, burning fiercely. The leading edge of the Mosquito's starboard mainplane took some of the flying debris from the doomed '88 as it disappeared into 8/10ths cloud at 5000 feet. Almost immediately the clouds were illuminated by the blaze from the Junkers, which crashed into the North Sea five miles east of Southwold. (The Ju 88 was from KG30, which lost a second aircraft this night.)

On 19/20 March, Singleton and Haslam were among the aircrews at readiness in 25 Squadron at Coltishall who were alerted to intercept a force of about 90 bombers over the North Sea, heading for Hull. Singleton and Haslam had taken off from Coltishall at 2055 hours in NF.XVII HK255. Neatishead radar told them to "hurry and climb to 16,000 feet," as a contact had been made. At about 8000 feet the CHL station at Happisburgh gave them a vector towards 12 "bandits" crossing up ahead of them. At 16,000 feet Haslam established contact on his American-made AI.X radar at 8½ miles range (the AI.X set had a range of 8-10 miles in an arc at most altitudes). Singleton wrote later:

> "We turned to port and followed, closed the range and obtained visual 10° above at 1600 feet. We identified it as a Junkers and closed to about 100 yards. I gave him a 2½-second burst from dead astern. It exploded. As we were still closing we had to pull up steeply to avoid collision; debris from the enemy aircraft spattered our aircraft. We orbited and watched the enemy aircraft go down in a steep dive to port in flames. When it had dropped to about 5000 feet it broke up completely, and several burning pieces hit the sea, and cast a glow over a wide area."

Their first victory of the night had gone down at 2120 hours, 56 miles NNE Cromer. After fixing the position with Neatishead, Singleton and Haslam were given a vector by Happisburgh. Haslam got a contact at 4 ½ miles range, crossing slowly from right to left. Singleton closed in behind and slightly below the intruder and obtained a visual at about 1500 feet. The unsuspecting machine (Ju 88) was not making any evasive manoeuvres. At 2127 hours, Singleton took careful aim from 100 yards dead astern and fired a 2½-second burst. The center of the Ju 88's fuselage exploded and the aircraft went down almost vertically before it fell into The Wash, where it continued to burn fiercely on the surface for a few seconds. Singleton orbited the scene and obtained a fix of the position from Neatishead, 65 miles NNE Cromer.

Almost immediately, Haslam obtained a third contact at four miles range. He watched it crossing hard right to left on the scope of his AI.X and directed Singleton accordingly. The pilot made a hard turn left and followed the blip at 230 IAS and at a height of 16,000 feet. This Ju 88 put up a fight. It carried out a series of quite violent evasive manoeuvres and changed height several times as the Mosquito closed to 1500 feet. At 21:33 hours Singleton fired a 2½-second burst at 125 yards dead astern. The German's starboard engine emitted a myriad of sparks, which danced along the nacelle until it erupted in flames. The Ju 88 pilot fought frantically, but uselessly, with the controls as his aircraft dived like a shot pheasant. Singleton delivered the *coup de grâce* with a 3-second burst at 500-600 yard range and the aircraft disintegrated into a blazing inferno. Burning debris flew off in all directions as it plummeted into the sea, 63 miles NNE Cromer at 21:33 hours. The water engulfed the flaming bomber and eventually snuffed out its flames and the lives of the crew, if they were not already dead.

Singleton leveled out, but both engines were running very roughly. The needle on the port radiator dial quivered on 1400, while the starboard indicated 1 20g. Singleton immediately throttled back, opened his radiator flaps, and succeeded in cooling the engines slightly. Happisburgh was informed by radio that the "Mossie" had engine trouble, and they responded quickly by giving the ailing night-fighter a vector and telling the crew to go over to GCI at Neatishead. They crossed the coast at 5000 feet. By now the port engine was very hot and was emitting a succession of sparks, so Singleton feathered the prop. He flew on towards Coltishall with both engines throttled as far back as was practical without losing too much height. The radiator temperatures were by now reading 130-140°, and he told Haslam to get ready to bale out.

Singleton called Coltishall and asked for the aerodrome lighting to be switched on so he could see the base from the coast and make a direct approach. Both engines were still running, but very roughly, and the aircraft was gradually losing height. Singleton had decided to land with wheels and flaps up. At about 1000 feet the starboard engine seized and burst into flames. Haslam operated the starboard engine fire extinguisher while Singleton switched on the port landing light. He tried to get more power from the port engine, but this also seized. At 140 mph Singleton leveled out and suddenly felt the aircraft hit the ground. Haslam opened the top hatch and jumped out; Singleton followed a few seconds behind him. They ran about 25 yards from the wrecked Mosquito, which had come down at Sco Ruston, half a mile from Coltishall, and sat down.

Singleton saw that the engines were burning at the cylinder heads and went back and climbed into the cockpit to switch off petrol and other switches and look for the fire extinguisher. He could not find it, so he clambered down and threw clodfulls of earth onto the engines and had extinguished the flames in the starboard Merlin by the time the fire tender and ambulance arrived. Singleton and Haslam were treated for slight head injuries. On examination, it was found that both glycol tanks, which had been holed by flying debris from the Ju 88, caused the engine trouble. Singleton and Haslam's three Ju 88 victories (probably all from II/KG30), which they destroyed in the space of an incredible 13 minutes, and the loss of six other aircraft could have done little for the morale of the *Luftwaffe* raiders. They aborted the raid and no bombs fell on Hull![205] Next day, C-in-C Fighter Command, Air Marshal Sir Roderick Hill visited Coltishall. Singleton was awarded an immediate DSO, a DFC for Haslam followed, and both men were posted to HQ Fighter Command in April for special duties, which were to take a Mosquito XXX to the USA. The events of the night of 19/20 March took Singleton's score to seven aircraft destroyed; plus he had three damaged, and on 23 June, just before the trip to the USA, he destroyed a V1. The purpose of the trip to America was threefold. They were to obtain agreement for many modifications to the SCR 720 radar, required by the RAF to be undertaken during production in the States, rather than in the UK after delivery.[206] They were also to test and assist in the development of new radars and to demonstrate the Mosquito, as well as to liaise with the night-fighter training establishment of the USAAF, U.S. Navy, and U.S. Marine Corps.

On 21/22 March 25 Squadron Mosquitoes were on patrol again as raiders attempted another strike on London. Some 95 aircraft crossed the Suffolk coastline and headed towards an area southeast of Cambridge, where they were to make their turn south and head for the capital. Part of the force acted as a diversion, approaching between Great Yarmouth and Felixstowe. Two Ju 88s flying at 23,000 feet were intercepted by Flight Lieutenant R. L. Davies and his navigator, Flying Officer B. Bent, aloft in their NF.XVII from Coltishall. Davies shot down the first '88 into the sea 35 miles southeast of Lowestoft. Two of the crew parachuted out before the aircraft disintegrated and disappeared into cloud at about 7000 feet. The second Ju 88 gave its presence away by firing a Chandelier flare and was promptly despatched into the sea 25 miles southeast of Southwold.[207] Meanwhile, Fw 190s and Me 410s had taken off from bases in France and were also en route to London. 410 "Cougar" Squadron RCAF and 488 RNZAF Squadrons orbited over their patrol sectors until directed by their GCI stations on intercept paths. A 410 Squadron RCAF Mosquito flown by Flying Officer S. B. Huppert and Pilot Officer J. S. Christie shot down a Ju 88A-4 of 4./KG30 at Latchingdon, Essex, and a 456 (RAAF) Squadron Mosquito destroyed a Ju 88 off the south coast; but there was also plenty of "trade" over Essex for the marauding Mosquitoes of 488 Squadron RNZAF at Bradwell Bay.

Flight Sergeant Christian J. Vlotman and his navigator-radio operator Sergeant John Wood were scrambled at 2335 hours under Trimley Control. Flight Lieutenant Parr vectored them towards the incoming raiders over the sea near Herne Bay. At about 500 feet range they spotted a Ju 188, which was the leading aircraft of the attack, dropping *Düppel* in profusion. Vlotman opened fire from dead astern and despatched the Junkers into the sea. He was next directed to another contact heading in a westerly direction. The controller vectored him to within six miles of the aircraft, a Ju 88 of II/KG54 which was flying at 16,500 feet. Vlotman approached slowly, got to within 500 yards and, although he could not positively identify it, could quite clearly see that the enemy machine was dropping vast quantities of *Düppel*. Vlotman opened fire with his four cannon from 200 yards. The Ju 88 shuddered under the impact of the rounds and fell into the sea near Herne Bay. Fragments of metal and Plexiglas peppered the dome and radiator of the Mosquito and holed the starboard glycol tank. Coolant spilled away into the night, and when the glycol temperature rose to 150° Vlotman knew it was time to feather the starboard engine. He landed back at Bradwell on one engine, none the worse for wear.

Squadron Leader Edward Bunting DFC in 488 Squadron RNZAF and his navigator, Flight Lieutenant C. P. Reed DFC, had also been scrambled from Bradwell. Bunting obtained a contact at 1¾ miles, slightly above, and immediately went below. He throttled right back and closed rapidly to 2000 feet on a 9./KG30 Ju 88A-4 from Varêlbusch flown by *Oberfeldwebel* Nikolaus Mayer dropping *Düppel*. Searchlights flicked on and a shaft of bright white light latched onto the enemy aircraft and held it. Other beams coned Bunting's Mosquito. As Reed radioed for a "douse" Mayer wriggled and wrestled like a caged predator in his attempt to escape the groping fingers of light, before finally eluding the Mosquito crew's attentions. The Mosquito dived onto the fleeing Junkers, who steadied into a mild, drunken weaving, and fired a burst of machine gun fire into the bomber from 200 yards astern. It caught fire in the left wing root and engine and flames appeared. Encouraged, Bunting again took aim and gave the Ju 88A-4 another burst from 300 yards. Bunting's camera gun recorded the image of the plane turning over on its back and commencing its flaming death dive over Suffolk. What it could not capture was the resulting crash, a split-second later at Blacklands Hall, Cavendish, in Suffolk, where the bomber's fuel tanks exploded and its engines buried themselves deep into the soil. *Feldwebel* K. Maser and *Feldwebel* Karl-Heinz Elmhorst had baled out and were taken prisoner. Mayer and *Oberfeldwebel* W. Szyska died in the crash.[208]

Meanwhile, Bunting and Reed orbited the scene of their "kill" and were then *Gauntletted* southeast. Reed reported "Window," and they eventually made contact at 3¾ miles range. Bunting closed fairly fast to 4000 feet when searchlights suddenly illuminated him again. They obtained a "douse," but the enemy aircraft, a Ju 188E-1 of 2./KG6 flown by *Leutnant* G. Lahl, had begun very violent evasive action. They nearly overshot beneath him, although the Mosquito was only doing 130-mph IAS. Lahl peeled off to port; Bunting turned hard left. Reed regained contact on his AI.VIII at about 4000 feet and followed him on his scope. They pursued Lahl through a hard, climbing turn to the right, and Bunting took a quick shot at 300 yards, but he could not get enough deflection and his shots missed. The two adversaries gyrated in tight turns and another steep climb before Bunting got into the favoured astern position. Peering through his gun-sight with its diffuser, he repeatedly pumped short bursts into the '188 from 250 yards. It dived, hit the ground, and exploded near Butler's Farm at Shopland, Essex, shortly after 01:10 hours.[209]

Another Ju 188E-1 flown by *Unteroffizier* Martin Hanf of 5./KG2 was lost on the night of 24/25 March when it was intercepted over the North Sea by a NF.XVII flown by Flight Lieutenant V. P Luinthune DFC and Flying Officer A. B. Cumbers DFC of 25 Squadron at Coltishall. Strikes, followed by the vivid orange glow of an explosion, signalled the end of the Junkers. Hanf and his four crewmen died in a watery grave 45 miles southeast of Lowestoft. A total of 10 enemy aircraft were claimed destroyed by Mosquitoes that night. Mounting losses—Mosquitoes shot down nine enemy raiders attacking mainly London and Bristol during 23-28 March 1944—meant that KG2 had to operate a diversity of types despite the fact that *Oberst* Dietrich Peltz, "Attack Leader England," had wanted KG2 re-equipped with Ju 88s. He disliked the Do 217, which he considered unsuitable for night raids over Britain and more suited for use as a day bomber over the Eastern Front.

On 13/14 April 96 Squadron shot down a German raider, and on the night of 18/19 April, when the last "Baby Blitz" raid was made on London, a further eight fell to the Mosquitoes.[210] From 20-30 April, Mosquitoes claimed 16 enemy raiders as *Steinbock* raids were made on Hull, Bristol, Portsmouth, and Plymouth using He 177s, Ju 188s, and Do 217s. Mosquitoes shot down nine raiders on 14/15 May when over 100 *Luftwaffe* raiders attacked Bristol. A Ju 188 and three Ju 88s were destroyed on 22 May when Portsmouth was again the target.

On 28/29 May Wing Commander Cathcart M. Wight-Boycott DSO, CO 25 Squadron at Coltishall, and Flight Lieutenant. D. W. Reid were directed by Neatishead GCI towards a "bogey" over the North Sea. It was a Me 410 *Hornisse* of KG51 flown by *Feldwebel* Dietrich and *Unteroffizier* Schaknies, which was returning from an intruder mission in the Cambridge area. At 0239 hours Dietrich had attacked a Stirling I of 1657 OCU on approach to Shepherd's Grove. The pilot, Flying Officer W. A. C. Yates, and all the crew were killed when it crashed on a dispersal, hitting and badly damaging another Stirling to such an extent that it too had to be written off. Dietrich and Schaknies sped off towards the coast and headed home. They did not make it. Wight-Boycott (who, on 23/24 June would add a Ju 188 destroyed to his score) approached the Me 410 almost at sea level and fired a half-second burst into it from 700 feet. Dietrich and Schaknies fell into the sea 50 miles off Cromer. The wreckage could be seen burning on the water from 20 miles away.

It was the final day of the "Baby Blitz."

Chapter 8

Star and Bar

You may cuss the Tiger Moth, while you're blowing off the froth
From your tankard of good honest English beer, man,
But they put me through my paces in the great wide open spaces
When they trained me on the AT and the Stearman.
Yes, I trained out in the States, out in Arizona, mates,
In a place that was as hot as Satan's kitchen,
And it did no good to fret when you fairly dropped with sweat;
'Cause they only tell you, "Brother, quit your bitching!"

David Livingstone-Spence

America wanted Mosquitoes, but Robert A. Lovett, Assistant Secretary of War for Air, suspected that Britain wanted to keep them all because "it was the one airplane that could get into Berlin and back without getting shot down." Major General Henry "Hap" Arnold and other USAAF officials saw the Mosquito for the first time on 20 April 1941 at Boscombe Down. The prototype, painted bright yellow, and which had first flown at Hatfield a year before, gave a dazzling performance in front of the Americans, whose country was not yet in the war. General Arnold's aide, Major Elwood Quesada, no doubt excited by the Mosquito's rolling climbs on one engine, recalled: "I was impressed by its performance [and] the appearance of the aeroplane…all aviators are affected by the appearance…an aeroplane that looks fast usually is fast, and the Mosquito was…It was highly regarded, highly respected!"

On 4 December 1941, three days before America declared war on Japan, a request was sent to Britain for one airframe, this to be evaluated at Wright Field. In the summer of 1942, Colonel Elliott Roosevelt brought two squadrons of F-4 Lightnings and a squadron of B-17F "mapping Fortresses" to Britain. The President's son was preparing his group for the invasion of North Africa and was to work with the RAF until ready. Given a Mosquito B.IV for combat evaluation, Roosevelt discovered that the aircraft outperformed his F-4s and had five times the range. The first of the Canadian-built Mosquitoes had already given demonstrations at Wright Field. It was so good that General Arnold ordered that no U.S. aircraft were to be raced against the Mosquito, to avoid embarrassing American pilots! Arnold asked that Mosquitoes be obtained to equip all American photo-reconnaissance squadrons in Europe—almost 200 aircraft for 1943 alone! In 1943 30 Mosquitoes were diverted from British production after the Canadian allocation of 120 for the Americans had been reduced to just 60 B.XXs because of RAF demands. These, plus 11 Canadian-built F-8 models, were delivered to the 802nd (later 25th) Bomb Group at Watton. However, these were not as popular with the pilots and navigators as the British-built Mosquitoes, and they were soon reassigned to a bomb group in Italy.

The 802nd, with the 7th Photographic Group, became part of the 325th Photographic Wing, commanded, since August 1944, by Colonel Elliott Roosevelt. Many personnel who were transferred into the 802nd Bomb Group had to be retrained. Mechanics who had never seen a Mosquito night bomber attended a two-week course at the Rolls-Royce engine school in Derby. Others attended the airframe school at the de Havilland factory in Hatfield. Most of the aircrew, many of whom were P-38 Lightning pilots from the 50th Fighter Squadron in Iceland, and who were used to the P-38's contra-rotating propellers, had never experienced the take-off and landing characteristics of the Mosquito bomber, especially its high landing speed and tendency to swing on take-off. They had also to remember to open the radiator shutters just prior to take-off to prevent the engines overheating.

The 652nd Bomb Squadron was equipped with the B-17 and B-24, while the 653rd Bomb Squadron used Mosquito TIII and PR.XVI aircraft on meteorological flights known as *Bluestockings*, gathering weather information from over the continent. PR.XVIs used a two-stage, two-speed supercharger that would cut in automatically at altitude. The superchargers were independent on each engine, and a small difference in adjustment caused one to change gears hundreds of feet before the other. The resulting "bang" and surge of power to one engine could wrest control from the unwary pilot and give the impression that the aircraft had been hit by flak. Several Airspeed Oxfords and three dual-control Mosquito T.IIIs were assigned for training. The 654th, or the "Special Squadron," flew day and night *Joker* photo missions and scouting sorties just ahead of the main bombing force, transmitting up-to-the-minute weather reports back to the task force commander to prevent him leading his bombers into heavy weather fronts.

Pete Dustman, an American pilot from the western Rocky Mountains in Idaho, who while serving as an instructor at RAF Leconfield early in the war had met and married Lorna, his English wife, wanted night-fighters when he finished training. His roommate wanted training command. "You guessed it," says Dustman, "I was posted to Upavon to become an instructor on Oxfords and my roommate went to night fighters." After various assignments 2nd Lieutenant Dustman wound up ferrying B-17s, B-24s, Dakotas, the P-47, and one Boulton Paul Defiant that the U.S. borrowed to tow targets and then didn't use. On one trip he heard about the formation of a Mosquito base at RAF Watton, so he made a stop on his next delivery to talk to the commander. Since he had flown English aircraft Dustman was immediately accepted, and he joined the 25th Bombardment Group and was assigned to the 654th Bomb Squadron, as he recalls:

"As I joined the squadron they were working to modify the Mossie to fit chaff dispensers, night photo equipment with 24" cameras for high altitude (24,000 feet), and to install radar on the Mickey ships. In the interim we had one B-25 and three B-26s to take night photos at 12,000 feet, short range, slow and low. I flew five in the B-25 and three in the B-26 over France to cover railways at night and the building of the new V1 sites. I flew my first mission in a day photo Mosquito along the French coast. I imagine it was a just a feint to keep the Germans guessing, which is about all it did as the groundcrew forgot to turn on the cameras before we left. As others on their first mission, I flew my first trip with my heart going at top speed, but I saw nothing except a few clouds along the route. Other missions of the 654 were a bit more exciting. Two missions that I flew verified the old saying that 'flying is 90% luck and 10% skill', although that might be overstating the skill part. On my 28th on 21 February 1945 I started out on a routine night photo mission with a target at Memel, west of Hamm in the Ruhr Valley with Lieutenant Len Erickson as navigator. The scheduling team had fouled it up as I was approaching Essen at the same time as the RAF was having a major strike in the same area. It was interesting to watch, as we were getting ready to start our run-in at 22,000 feet. Naturally everything was lit up with flares going down and flak coming up. As I started my photo run and dropped my first of a string of 30 flares, flying straight and level to keep the camera in focus, I heard a loud English voice say, 'Mossie rock your wings'. We assumed that a British night fighter was on our tail but couldn't make contact. I didn't want to miss the pictures, so I kept going hoping to complete the mission. Then again I heard the same voice saying 'Blue Leader, this is Blue 4, 'This Mossie won't rock his wings' and the faint reply, 'Shoot the bastard down then'! My wings were rocked vertical and sideways with flash bombs going in every direction, with no pictures taken that night. I did have words at debriefing on return that night about their scheduling.

"On a night flight over Germany to take photos, a new navigator was with me. His training had been primarily on radar, with very little on navigation. On this flight we had a strong wind shift (now known as jet stream shift) which was unexpected. The navigator thought it was just the *Gee* navigation system that had messed up and didn't consider the wind shear accurate, although the Gee was good for the target run. On retur he did not allow for the wind shift and we drifted so far south that we missed not only our base in East Anglia but England! Since our radios had also packed up, we let down hoping to find land and get our position in the moonlight, but the top of one cloud was just like all others. I kept trying the radio and finally received a steer of due north, landing at Bournemouth with 10 minutes of fuel left. Since the navigator had also forgotten the camera switches, the mission was a complete loss.

"I flew a compiled total of 54 missions in the Marauder, Mitchell and Mosquito aircraft and completed the tour without a hole in an aircraft or having to land with an engine shut down. Of the 23 aircrew forming 654 Squadron I was the third and last to finish a tour of duty and the last of the original crews."

The *D-Day* invasion was determined by intelligence gathered on *Dillies* (night photography missions of coastal defenses). A local storm front, forming suddenly east of Iceland on 5 June, and monitored by the *Bluestockings*, postponed the invasion for one day until 6 June. On *Joker* missions the Mosquitoes dropped 1000,000-candlepower-type M-46 flash bombs to illuminate and obtain evidence of enemy troop movements and bridge construction conducted under the cover of darkness.

The Mosquito was also used on *Skywave* long-range navigation missions using *LORAN* (the RAF did not begin using the *LORAN* system to any extent until after the end of the war); daylight missions codenamed *PRU*, using still and motion-picture photography; and H_2X *Mickey* flights. Mosquitoes brought back bomb-approach strips, or target run-ups, which were used to brief the key radar navigator-bombardier of the bomber mission and to sight the bomb target through the overcast during the actual bombing. Three *Mickey* sorties flown at night failed to return, and later, four P-38 Lightnings were assigned to escort the H_2X missions going in at high altitudes.

American Mosquitoes accompanied Project *Aphrodite* and *Anvil* pilotless drone operations using war-weary B-17s and PB4Y-1 Liberators respectively. Each aircraft was packed with 18,000lbs of Torpex, a nitroglycerine compound, and was flown to a point over the English coast or North Sea where the pilot and co-pilot baled out, leaving the drone to fly on and be directed onto its target (normally a V1 or V2 site) by remote control via a Ventura "mother ship." Strike analysis depended upon the films brought back by the accompanying Mosquitoes to determine the success or failure of the mission.

Each *Aphrodite* and *Anvil* mission was preceded by a *Bluestocking* weather reconnaissance flight over the target by a 653rd Bomb Squadron Mosquito. After the drone was airborne, a Mosquito in the 654th Bomb Squadron joined the mission carrying an 8th Combat Camera Unit (CCU) crewman. The mission was to fly close to the drone and to photograph its flight and its effects. These photographs were used to analyze all angles of the flight and to improve methods and equipment used on such missions. Some of the 8th CCU cameramen came from the Hal Roach Studios in Hollywood, where they trained alongside movie stars making training films, such as Ronald Reagan (the Administrative Officer), Alan Ladd, Van Heflin, John Carroll, and others.

On 4 August 1944, of four *Aphrodite* B-17s, or "Babies" despatched to *No-ball* sites in the Pas de Calais, one crashed in England, killing its pilot; the second refused to dive over the target and was destroyed by flak; the third overshot and the fourth undershot. On 6 August two *Aphrodite* drones crashed and exploded. The missions were photographed by Staff Sergeant August "Augie" Kurjack and Lieutenant David J. McCarthy in 25th Bomb Group Mosquitoes. Kurjack ran about 50 feet of movie film of the crash in England. McCarthy's Mosquito, flown by Lieutenant Robert A. Tunnel, picked up some flak and flew home on one engine.

The U.S. Navy's first Project *Anvil* mission went ahead on 12 August. Some 21,170lbs of Torpex was distributed throughout the PB4Y-1 Liberator, together with six demolition charges each containing 113lb of TNT. The pilot for the *Anvil* mission was Lieutenant Joseph P. Kennedy Jr, at 29, the eldest son of Joseph Kennedy, the former U.S. Ambassador to Britain, and who had flown a tour of missions from Dunkeswell with VB-110. "Bud" Willy was co-pilot. Their target was a secret weapon site at Mimoycques, which concealed a three-barrelled 150mm artillery piece designed to fire 600 tons of explosives a day on London.

A Mosquito flown by Tunnel, with McCarthy in the right-hand seat, followed behind the formation of two Ventura "mother ships," Kennedy's Liberator, a navigational B-17, a P-51 Mustang, and a P-38 Lightning. The mission proceeded satisfactorily to Blythburgh when, at 1500 feet two explosions ripped the Liberator asunder. McCarthy reported:

> "We had just decided to close in on the 'Baby'. I was flying in the nose of the plane so that I could get some good shots of the 'Baby' in flight ahead of us. The 'Baby' just exploded in mid-air. As we heard it I was knocked halfway back to the cockpit. A few pieces of the 'Baby' came through the Plexiglas nose and I got hit in the head and caught a lot of fragments in my right arm."

McCarthy crawled back to the cockpit and lowered the wheels. Tunnel concludes:

> 'I didn't get a scratch but I was damn near scared to death. The Mosquito went up a few hundred feet and I didn't get any response from my controls. I was setting to reach for my parachute but decided to check the controls again. This time they responded and I decided to try and make a landing. One engine was out and the other was smoking. We were near a field so I headed straight for it. We made a good landing and then the second motor cut out. I had just enough speed left to get the Mosquito off the runway, but I couldn't taxi onto a hardstand. I'm sure glad that the pictures of our previous mission were good because I don't think we're going to get that close to the 'Baby' again.'

A dozen drone missions were flown before the British advance overran the Pas de Calais area. Several attempts were made to convert Mosquitoes into "mother ships," but they were not used operationally.

On 13 August Dean H. Sanner and Kurjack filmed the flight paths of *Disney* glide bombs released from under the wings of B-17s at *U-boat* pens at Le Havre, France, and photographed any damage to the submarine pens. The 18-feet-long, 2000lb bombs powered by a rocket motor in the tail had been invented by Captain Edward Terrell RN, and were designed to pierce 20 feet of concrete before exploding. The first was not going to hit anything, so Sanner broke off the pursuit and climbed back to follow the second glide bomb. At the Initial Point the second bomb was released and he zigzagged back and forth considerably to hold the faster Mosquito behind the slower glide bomb. As Sanner flew over the bomb it exploded. The blast blew him out of the aircraft. His cameraman was killed. Sanner suffered a broken leg and injuries to his right arm and was captured within the hour. He finished the war in *Stalag Luft I*.

In September 1944 the Allies attempted to capture bridges on the Rhine in Holland at Veghel, Grave, Nijmegen, and Arnhem, using Britain's 1st and America's 82nd and 101st Airborne Divisions. Operation *Market-Garden* was planned to cut off the German Army in the Belgian sector and save the bridges and the port of Antwerp for the American army units and British XXX Corps advancing north from the Dutch border. Claude C. Moore, a Mosquito navigator, recalls:

> "On the night of 16 September three 'Mossie' crews were called in and told that we would go out early next day at staggered intervals. No details. One plane was to take off at 2am, one at 4am, and one at 6am. Next morning, just before take-off, we were given the details - the Nijmegen-Arnhem area. Find the base of the clouds in the area. How thick and how low? Go down to the deck if necessary. Radio back that information.
>
> "We were the last flight, at 6am. Jimmy Spear was the pilot. The sky was already light when we left. It was only a matter of minutes from Watton to Holland. We skimmed across at 2000-3000 feet. Soon we were at the target area, which, I learned later, was where the parachute drops were made and the glider-borne assault troops were landed. There were large clouds, intermittently broken, so we descended. At around 500 feet we were finding the base of the clouds. Apparently High Command was not waiting for our information; there were planes everywhere. I had never seen so many fighters up close. Below us, above us, around us, on every side they were climbing, diving, milling like a swarm of angry bees. They were really beating the place up.
>
> "We reported thick, low, occasionally broken, white clouds and smaller, grey puffs of clouds, and gave the cloud base as approximately 400-500 feet. The smaller, grey puffs of clouds were spaced all around. Only, I finally realized, they weren't small clouds. They were shell bursts. We were being shot at!
>
> "I was startled to see a plane coming off the deck, climbing straight at us and closing - a snub-nosed, radial-engined plane. From the markings and the silhouette I took it to be from Hermann Goering's own elite group - cowling painted in a distinctive yellow-and-black checkerboard pattern. 'Focke-Wulf 190' flashed through my mind. *'Damn,'* I thought. 'This is it!' I'm sure that, mentally, I was frozen in space. But the next thing I knew, the snub-nose had zoomed past us. I did a double take. It was a P-47 Thunderbolt.
>
> "We stayed in the area a little longer, made a few more weather reports, then headed back to Watton. At the base we were debriefed. We went over to the Combat Mess for breakfast and settled into the day's routine."

On 18 September the Germans counter-attacked and forestalled an American attempt to capture the bridge at Nijmegen. Just over 100 B-24 Liberators dropped supplies and ammunition to the American Airborne forces at Grosbeek, in the Nijmegen-Eindhoven area. Five Mosquito weather scouts were despatched to Holland. 1st Lieutenant Robert Tunnel and his navigator-cameraman, Staff Sergeant John G. Cunney, failed to return. Both men are now interred in the American War Cemetery at Neuville en Condroz, Belgium.

Bad weather during Operation *Market-Garden* made regular air reconnaissance over the Arnhem bridge impossible, so on 22 September three 25th Bomb Group Mosquitoes were despatched. Lieutenant "Paddy" Walker's navigator, Roy C. Conyers, recalls:

> "We were to dip as low as possible to try to establish by visual observation who controlled the bridge, the Germans or the British. I thought that this regularity was crazy and mentioned it to Edwin R. Cerrutti, 654th navigator. His only comment was that the German Command wouldn't believe that we were that stupid."

As "Paddy" Walker flew over the north end of the bridge just below the fog, at under 500 feet, he and Roy Conyers could see Germans running for their anti-aircraft guns. Walker remembers:

> "Ground fire began almost immediately. This continued as we flew over and past the other end, on towards the coast. Tracer fire could be seen coming up around us and the plane was hit. I saw the left wing drop tank disintegrate, and jettisoned both. The right engine was shut down and the propeller feathered. The fire went out, but the engine was inoperative. I was flying as low and as fast as possible to get out of range. As we crossed the coast additional fire was received, spurts of water coming up near the plane from the barrage; however, we were not hit. After we got out of range, I climbed up into the weather to gain enough altitude to make an emergency Mayday radio call, to get a 'steer' to the nearest base where the weather was suitable to land. We steered to Bournemouth. My Mayday call was answered by the sweetest girl's British accent – 'Tommy' Settle, a beautiful blonde WAAF at Tangmere. During the days that it took to repair the plane she and I became better acquainted."

On 25 September another *Bluestocking* mission was launched as evacuation of the surviving paratroops from Arnhem began. 1st Lieutenant Clayborne O. Vinyard and his navigator, 1st Lieutenant John J. O'Mara, took off at 0126 hours in fog so thick they could only see 300 yards in front. They flew too deep into Germany, reaching the Frankfurt area before turning back. They descended to 18,000 feet, but a night-fighter got on their tail and shot them down. Both men baled out and later joined Dean Sanner at *Stalag Luft I*.

Some 352 *Chaff* (Window) dispensing sorties, codenamed *Gray-Pea*,[211] were carried out by Mosquitoes of the 653rd and 654th Bomb Squadrons using an electric dispensing mechanism in their bomb bays. Captain Roy Ellis-Brown DFC was returning from a "*chaffing*" mission for 8th Air Force bombers to St. Vith and Abois when he spotted a flight of P-51 Mustang escorts below him. "One of these jocks called me and said, 'Don't worry old boy, we will protect you on the way home.' I replied, 'Thanks, I'll slow down so you can give me cover!'" Feathering one engine and pulling full power on the other, the Mosquito pilot dived and performed a slow roll past the Mustang formation, pulling up in front. "I then called the leader and said, 'Sorry old chap. Will have to cut in the port engine as the 'Mossie' rolls a bit on one fan. Also have a hot date tonight!'" Ellis-Brown restarted the engine, and as he opened the throttles his observer reported that the Mustangs' engines were smoking as they tried to catch up. "As I landed, the P-51s overflew the base at low-level, in a beautiful beat-up. I think we made our point."

Another extrovert was Flying Officer Vance "Chip" Chipman, a former racetrack driver from Chicago who had joined the Royal Canadian Air Force when war started in Europe. To some he was "a strange chap in USAAF uniform with both RAF and USAAF wings. His chest was splattered with combat decorations and he sported a long handlebar moustache. In a crisp British accent he introduced himself, mentioning that he would be assisting in Mosquito pilot training." On 1 November, during an H_2X photography mission to Schweinfurt, enemy fighters shot down Chipman's Mosquito. He became a prisoner of the Germans, although he once tried to escape by stealing a Bf 109. He was recaptured before he could start the engine.

On 6 November 1944 Otto Kaellner's Mosquito crashed in England following a *Mickey* night radar-mapping mission using the H_2S radar system to Cologne. *Mickey* flights were temporarily suspended and, beginning on 19 February 1945, the 654th Bomb Squadron switched to light weather missions. On 24 March a daylight mission was tried. A Mosquito piloted by Lieutenant C. B. Stubblefield and his navigator-radar operator, 1st Lieutenant James B. Richmond, flew ahead of the 8th Air Force bombers, escorted by eight P-51 Mustangs from Wattisham. They would be led to the German fighters as they started their climb to attack the bombers. Unfortunately, a 9th Air Force P-47 shot down the Mosquito. Stubblefield was killed and Richmond was made a PoW.

Next day 1st Lieutenant Bernard J. Boucher and his navigator, Louis Pessirilo, were killed during a *Bluestocking* mission over Germany. Five other Mosquitoes on weather reconnaissance returned safely. On 3 April six *Gray-Pea* Mosquitoes were detailed for *Chaff*-screening for the 8th Air Force, five more scouted for the B-17s, and seven flew weather reconnaissance over the continent and seas around Britain. Lieutenant Colonel Alvin E. Podojski, pilot and group deputy commander, and Captain Lionel A. Proulx, navigator, were leading a flight of four Mosquitoes on a *Gray-Pea* mission over Kiel when they were attacked by German fighters. Their Mosquito received damage and they limped to Sweden.

Some 74 Mosquito *Red-Tail* sorties (named after their red tails, so colored to distinguish them from enemy aircraft) were flown from bases in East Anglia, each carrying the Command Pilot of 8th Air Force bombing missions. On 4 April 1945 1st Lieutenant T. B. Smith and Colonel Troy Crawford, CO 446th Bomb Group, were shot down by B-24 Liberator gunners who mistook their Mosquito for an Me 262 as the formation headed for the jet airfield at Wesendorf. Crawford was captured, but was freed later by some Germans who realized that Germany had lost the war. He returned to the USA.

John W. "Jack" Green, a pilot in the 653rd squadron, recalls:

> "My navigator Johnny Mink and I were diverted on one occasion to Exeter in the southwestern region of England. Two other weather mission aircraft were also diverted there. The three weather missions in one night had to be staggered to obtain insight into the movement of foul weather in the area. Our descent began at approximately 20,000 feet into the cloud layer that covered all of England. Our vectors or headings for us to fly were established by three receiving stations and

were set to circle us down and into the somewhat narrow valley in which the airfield was located. To circle us down required a triangulation plotting from the three, registering our direction from each. Directional lines of the three must cross to determine our point of location.

'Ceiling was at 500 feet, well below the level of the tops of the surrounding mountains. As the descent progressed the radius of the circle we were in became shorter and shorter. Finally vectors were coming one after another acknowledgement was transmitted. As, for example, when receiving a bearing or heading of 270 degrees our acknowledgement would be as: 'Roger, two-seven-zero'. Then immediately we heard: 'Turn now to two-one-five degrees'. Each bearing one right after another. We received then acknowledged as we circled all the way from 20,000 feet to 500 feet, the ceiling level.

"Then came touchdown. After we parked, a staff car drove us to the front of operations command and there we were greeted by a Wing Commander with, 'Wot? A Yank flying a Mosquito?' After pleasantries and curiosities were satisfied and after being introduced to his stag we were escorted to the main vector unit where we could meet the officer in charge, the one who had made the quick triangulations. With a degree of pride, I believe, and interest in us, he explained how all had been done on the board in front of him. It was quite remarkable that he could receive directional lines from two other stations and plot our next bearing so rapidly. He had been very busy!

"In January 1945 flying with Lieutenant Ralph E. Fisher, I returned from a mission with one engine out, dead tired, at four in the morning. There was no airfield open in all of the UK, a not uncommon occurrence for the 653rd. We were directed to head for Manston on the southeast tip of England on the surmise that the weather there might break and open for us. As we approached the coast the ceiling lifted to 200 feet with visibility a quarter of a mile. But then, as we descended, we were informed that Manston had closed in again. It was suggested that we fly west on the chance that there would be an opening-- somewhere. We were 200 feet off the deck of the sea, south of the cliffs of Dover, in black conditions, nothing visible and still on one engine. Imagine again relying in the dark, on altimeter settings at 200 feet, hoping that you are indeed, clearing the deck. And the coastline and cliffs of Dover off the starboard wing! And, what about the feeling of my navigator? This was Fisher's first flight with me.

"We flew for about fifteen minutes when 'Blue Frock', code name for Manston, called us back. They reported visibility had improved to a quarter of a mile again so back we went. My approach was 'hot'. I planned it that way. With only one engine it would be necessary for Lieutenant Fisher to hand pump the landing gear down and commit to some flaps for the round out before arriving at approach speed. It worked.

"After all that, and being dead tired, we learned that there was a small US contingent stationed at Manston to handle those Yanks landing in emergencies. We were directed to a Nissen hut where a USAAF supply sergeant furnished OD blankets. And then told us to find a cot somewhere? The treatment received from the USAAF supply sergeant and his telling us to look for a cot somewhere, after his supplying us with the thinnest of OD blankets, could only be something of a shock to us. We had not been treated so before. But we ate the standard scrambled eggs that were furnished before turning in. We had been spoiled by the far different treatment we had always received when diverted. Usually, and hopefully, it was always an English airfield, where the Mossie could be handled and serviced by those familiar with it. Perhaps our reception at English aerodromes would be considered unusual by our standards. This was wartime. But that in itself underscores how considerate and hospitable the English everywhere were and especially when encountering the Yank flier. Even civilians in the countryside extended themselves within the limits of their capabilities, on might think. Frequently, the extension seemed to go way beyond that.

"But it was nearly morning and a moment of glory came at eight o' clock. Not being able to sleep, I needed my diversion kit, which had been left in the aircraft. I went off to 'ops' for help. Where had we parked the Mosquito? The duty officer, a WAAF, asked for the number of our aircraft, then left the room. She came back shortly with wide, wide eyes. 'You're a 'Paint Jar!'' 'Yes-?' 'I've always wanted to meet a 'Paint Jar'. On a number of occasions 'Blue Frock' people had been startled late at night or in early morning when, with no radio-activity, weather being so bad that no one was flying, yet a 'Paint Jar' would be heard calling for a vector. 'Paint Jar' was a mystery. Just who were they, those 'Paint Jars', the only ones aloft in such miserable weather? And on their secret missions? 'Paint Jar' was the call sign of the 653rd Squadron. My call sign was 'Paint Jar 57'. And of course my chest puffed up a bit! But I was too tired to follow up."[212]

By early 1945 several anti-*Nazi* agents were ready to be parachuted into Germany from American aircraft, but there were problems. In France agents had successfully used the long-established, but weighty *S-Phone* device; but making air-to-ground contact with the agents once they had landed in Germany was more difficult. A large and heavy suitcase was highly suspicious and safe houses were few and far between. And anyway, the *S-Phone* had an effective range only up to 10,000 feet—well within reach of the German flak batteries. Stephen H. Simpson, a Texan scientist with the honorary rank of Lieutenant Commander, and Dewitt R. Goddard came up with a transmitter-receiver system so small that the agent in the field could easily carry it, yet it could transmit a radio beam so narrow that it was practically immune to detection by the German "*Gonio*" (Radio-goniometry) vans. The new system was named *Joan-Eleanor*, after Major Joan Marshall, a WAC and Goddard's wife. Goddard and Simpson's invention was modified and installed in a Mosquito after all unnecessary equipment was removed. An oxygen system was installed in the bomb bay and adapted to accommodate the *Joan-Eleanor* device and an operative. Eventually, five Mosquitoes were made available for *Joan-Eleanor* and agent-dropping missions, the latter being known as *Redstockings* in the hope that the German *Abwehr* would think they were connected with *Bluestocking* weather missions. Lieutenant Marvin R. Edwards, a navigator who served on B-24 and Mosquito flights, recalls:

> "The *Joan-Eleanor* radio equipment was battery operated. The transmission and receiving package carried in the Mosquito weighed about 40lbs. It could pick up a voice on the ground in the 60-mile radius of the cone at 40,000 feet. Beyond that, the *Joan-Eleanor* radio transmission and receiver equipment would not work. The transmitter and receiver were called *Eleanor.* The OSS agent on the ground carried the *Joan* section, which beamed UHF transmissions. It only weighed about two pounds and it measured only 6.5 inches x 2.25 inches x 1.5 inches. While the transmitter used by the agent on the ground spread to about a 60-mile circle at 40,000 feet. The cone narrowed to just a couple of feet at ground level. Therefore the chance of the conversation being picked up by German direction finders was almost nil. The special operator in the Mosquito recorded the conversation that took place on a wire spool, which was rushed to OSS HQ for analysis. It was then immediately given to the Allied High Command, who used the information tin planning future operations and strategy against Germany."

On 22 October the first test flight was made with Steve Simpson and his equipment in the rear fuselage. On 10 November 1944 the first agent, codenamed *Bobbie*, was dropped during the night at Ulrum, on the German border with Holland. *Bobbie* was Anton Schrader, a 27-year-old Dutch engineer and the son of a Netherlands governor-general in the Dutch East Indies. An agent was given a line of 100-150 miles, anywhere along which he could use his radio. He was never to use it in the same place twice. He should broadcast from a 50-yard clearing in a forest because trees and shrubbery would quickly absorb the spreading frequency waves. The BBC would broadcast an innocuous sentence—"Mary needs to talk to you Thursday the 10th."—at a pre-arranged time. This meant a mission would fly the line on that date after midnight and call continuously. When the agent responded he was acknowledged and the aircraft continued for 20 miles. The point was then orbited at a radius of 20 miles as the Mosquito flew in a 40-mile circle above 30,000 feet. By using direction finders in the Mosquito, the contact man located the point from which the agent was transmitting. By using synchronized instruments the contact man in the plane could direct the pilot.

Simpson's first two attempts to contact *Bobbie* failed. Both missions were flown in Mosquito NS676, the second of two Mosquitoes supplied by the RAF, crewed by Captain Victor S. Doroski, pilot, and Lieutenant Bill Miskho, navigator. On the first try the Mosquito's elevator controls jammed and control of the aircraft was wrenched from Doroski's hands. On the second effort *Bobbie* could not be contacted. On 22 November Simpson made a third attempt to make contact with *Bobbie*. Mosquito NS707 was used as NS676 had been badly damaged on landing after the abortive second trip. As they crossed the Dutch coast Doroski lost height, and the *Redstocking* Mosquito started circling at 30,000 feet at a pre-set time and at an established rendezvous point to enable Simpson, crouched in the bomb bay, to record the conversation on the wire recorder There was no response from *Bobbie*. Simpson ordered Doroski down to 20,000 feet in an effort to pick up the agent's signal, but still there was no response. Below the Mosquito there unfolded a barrage of fireworks. The aircraft shuddered with each burst. Simpson shouted on the intercom, "We're in a storm, Captain. You'd better get us out of here!"

"Commander, that's no storm. We're being shot at!"

Doroski climbed back up to 30,000 feet and cruised around the area again. At midnight Simpson finally made contact with *Bobbie*. Through heavy static the agent informed Simpson that he was "quite all right." He said that a *Panzer* regiment was headed towards Arnhem and pinpointed a railway bridge over the Ems Canal at Leeuwarden. If Allied bombers destroyed the bridge, he said, they would paralyze traffic from this key junction into Germany. *Bobbie* finished abruptly "I am standing here near German posts. It is very dangerous." Simpson said goodbye and told Doroski to head for home. (Doroski was subsequently lost on a night-photography *Joker* mission on 8 February 1945.)

On 12 December the seventh mission in contact with *Bobbie* was flown. Simpson's pilot was "Paddy" Walker, and Captain Bill Miskho flew as navigator. *Bobbie* told Simpson that the IX SS Panzer Division was in a rest camp in the area but had been ordered to move in 48 hours. He added ominously that, "it is almost impossible as all railroads, cars, trucks and buses have been taken over and are moving troops and supplies. Something big is about to happen." The message was clear and in English. After receiving and recording the full communication from *Bobbie* the Mosquito headed for Watton. On arrival, the recording wire was transported to London and reported to Secret Intelligence, but the significance was not realized. On 16 December Field Marshal Karl von Rundstedt's *Panzer* divisions attacked the Allied front line in an area of the Ardennes where American units were in rest and rehabilitation. The German offensive achieved complete surprise and caused widespread confusion and a salient, or "bulge," was opened. The Ardennes Offensive had proved that the German Army was yet capable and agents were needed in Germany. *Bobbie* was later apprehended by the *Abwehr* who used him to transmit deceptive intelligence, but by a pre-arranged code OSS knew that he had been "turned" and contact missions continued to be flown regularly by the 25th Bomb Group. However, the stripped-down Mosquito flew above 45,000 feet to avoid German night-fighters and interceptors. Two months later *Bobbie* returned to England equipped with a German radio, having persuaded the *Abwehr* that he would make a good double agent!

Lieutenant Marvin R. Edwards adds:

> "These Mosquito missions involved a crew of three, the pilot, the navigator and a special operator who spoke to the agent on the ground. A compartment was designed to hold this operator in the belly of the aircraft. Once I was shown how the Mosquito navigation equipment operated I had few problems. The navigator on the B-24 had to not wear an oxygen mask but a heated suit and heavy gloves as well. The outside temperature at 20,000 feet in December was well below zero Fahrenheit. The navigator's desk on the B-24 was located over the nose wheel and there was no air seal! Thus the temperature where the navigator stood was the same as outside the plane. Some of the navigational work required removing the gloves and thereby risking frostbite. Thus the Mossie heating system was a refreshing change. Mosquitoes used were Mk VIII and the IX. They had Merlin 72 engines. Heat in the pilot-navigator cockpit area stayed at room temperature. These models were not pressurised so oxygen masks had to be used. We later learned that the Mossie as not designed to carry a passenger in the modified compartment. Happily, except for the great discomfort of the special operator, the plane handled well on most occasions. We all noted that the engines in American aircraft seemed to roar, while

the Merlins seemed to purr. We were also impressed with the automatic supercharger that was activated at about 20,000 feet, as we climbed to an altitude of 28-40,000 feet. The thrust was so strong that it seemed as though we were taking off again. Once we reached 40,000 feet we felt secure. The German flak could not reach us. The only German planes that presented any threat were jet fighters the Germans developed near the war's end. Their numbers were very limited. Since our plywood plane was at such a high altitude, we felt that the German radar would have difficulty in spotting us. This was important. To maintain both our speed and altitude, our Mossie was stripped of what was considered all excess weight. We had no armament of any kind. Even our IFF (Identification Friend or Foe) was removed. Eliminating the IFF did present a problem on occasion when we returned to England.'

On 21 January 1945 a team codenamed "*Troy*" was dropped into Stuttgart. They were followed on 28 February by a second team codenamed "*Anzio*," who were also dropped into Stuttgart. On the night of 1/2 March 1945 a lone A-26 Invader dropped two agents codenamed "*Hammer*" near Berlin (the Mosquito could carry only one agent). The mission required two weeks of preparation, which included collecting all information from British sources regarding territory covered in flight. The crewmembers were familiarized with enemy gun batteries, enemy flying fields, and enemy radar installations, enemy fighter control points, and enemy navigational aids. Drop-points near large watercourses, which could be seen in the dark of the moon, were selected. Specialized navigational equipment was installed. The selected course was plotted on a special LORAN and *Gee* trainer attached to a link trainer. Days were spent by the two navigators and the pilot in training for a fully co-ordinated exercise. The mission was flown on a moonlit night at fence-top level all the way. The flight took a zigzag course, following rivers and other features discernible at night. It skirted mountains and defensive areas. It was piloted by Robert Walker. One navigator, John W. Walch, sat in the nose reading maps and observing the terrain. Another navigator, William G. Miskho, operated specialized equipment. The weather was good of course. A weather observation flight to Berlin in a Mosquito had proceeded the mission and reported conditions as clear and favourable. The mission was successful. On 12 March a *Redstocking* Mosquito flying 30,000 feet over Berlin successfully established contact with one of the agents by using *Joan-Eleanor*. The total exercise resulted in one of the most valuable intelligence commitments of the war.

On 13 March operations moved to Harrington, where 492nd Bomb Group *Carpetbagger* Liberators commanded by Colonel Hudson Upham were used on covert missions. B-24 and B-17 night leaflet crews arrived from Cheddington at the same time and chaos ensued. Mosquito maintenance suffered drastically and, eventually, RAF ground personnel were brought in to maintain the aircraft. OSS regained control over all Mosquito operations and 25th Bomb Group pilots and navigators flew the aircraft until enough 492nd Bomb Group personnel were available. A 492nd Bomb Group pilot and navigator carried Commander Simpson on their first communications mission on 31 March 1945.

One of Lieutenant Marvin R. Edwards' most meaningful rendezvous Mosquito flights was in mid-April 1945:

"Our assignment was to fly in orbit at a point in the Munich area. There had been reports that the German military were planning a last ditch stand in the mountains near Munich known as the 'Redoubt'. That concept was first talked about after the failure of the last massive German counter attack in December 1944 in the Battle of the Bulge. Certain members of the German High Command had believed that underground fortifications and factories connected by tunnels could be constructed in the Alps. They believed that such a complex would be impregnable, even from air attacks. Many of those defending the facility would be German SS Storm Troops. Shortly after the war's end, in May 1945, I went to OSS HQ in Grosvenor Square in London. I was informed that the OSS agent contacted in Bavaria had reported that there would be no organized resistance by the Germans in that area. The plan never got off the ground. The Germans offered no resistance to the American army assigned to that sector of operations."

On 12 April 1945 President Roosevelt passed away in Warm Springs, Georgia. His son was relieved of his command and a recommendation for a Presidential Citation for the 25th Bomb Group was discarded. Requests for awards for the 325th Photographic Wing, signed by Elliott Roosevelt, were returned, stamped "*Denied*." After 3 May 1945 *Redstocking* missions became an all-492nd Bomb Group operation. Animosity between Upham's Bomb Group and OSS reached a peak, and negotiations at the highest level were held in London to resolve the matter. The outcome was that the 492nd Bomb Group extended its B-24 operations to include central Germany and beyond. And, as Lyon had proved unsuitable for *Carpetbagger* operations, new bases were established at Bron Field, Dijon in France, and at Namur, Belgium. OSS was anxious to despatch their growing number of anti-*Nazi* agents to Germany. *Carpetbaggers* flew 11 *Redstocking* missions (and 12 communications missions from England, only two of which were successful). Between 19 March and 28/29 April 1945, 31 successful *Joan-Eleanor* missions and 47 unsuccessful *Redstocking* sorties were flown.

***

1st Lieutenant André E. Pecquet was posted to the 856th Bomb Squadron as a *Joan-Eleanor* operator on 21 March 1945 after decompression testing in London. He recalls:

"My departure from London was delayed because Cmdr Simpson lacked personnel, and the few people working under him were too busy to be able to train anyone. Also, the *Joan-Eleanor* project was transferred around the 19th from Watton to Harrington, thus creating additional work. Cmdr Simpson did not receive adequate co-operation from Harrington. Due to the lack of experienced ground crews, the maintenance of the Mosquitoes was also poor."

Jean M. Nater was also posted to the 856th Squadron as a *Joan-Eleanor* operator, where he met André Pecquet and Calhoun Ancrum:

"Pecquet told me some harrowing details of his work with the Maquis in the Vecors. He had flown also and trained with Mosquitoes. He had been with US armor, so he wore his hat on the left side of his head.[213] We often spoke French together. He really didn't like flying in Mosquitoes. It upset him, but he did it.

"Calhoun Ancrum was a quiet, serious young man. He spoke several languages, Russian included. He had flown a couple of successful *Joan-Eleanor* missions but he never talked about these, nor about himself. Stephen Simpson showed me the *Joan-Eleanor* equipment, how it was used, some of the technical details (in very general terms); and he told me of his own experiences as a *Joan-Eleanor* operator over Germany. He noted that the equipment worked well but that it could be improved. He was particularly dissatisfied with the wire recorder. 'The spools can work loose, then you have wire all over the place,' he said. And he was unhappy with the cramped space for the *Joan-Eleanor* operator behind the collapsible fuel tank in the bomb bay. George Fogharty, another quiet man, undertook further training.

"I met the 'Mossie'. It was an impressive machine. Small, slim and sleek. Our models, mostly older photo-recce veterans, had been stripped of all arms and armor and the bomb bays had been stripped of bomb racks. Navigational equipment was left intact and there was tail-warning radar to tell the pilot if there was anything on his tail. To fit in the *Joan-Eleanor* operator, his radio receiver and wire recorder, our squadron riggers had adapted a small hatch on the starboard side of the fuselage just aft of the wing. They had fitted a makeshift seat close to the bottom of the fuselage; this was hinged and held together with parachute elastic cords so that you could pull it down to sit on. Great in theory, but when you shifted your backside, the seat tended to collapse. Imagine yourself all togged up in an electric flying suit covered with a pile-lined flying suit, wearing felt flying boots, a chest-pack 'chute and an emergency oxygen flask strapped to your leg; hunched over in a crouch in front of a radio with dials and an antenna, which had to be rotated and a wire recorder, which was apt to shed a spool! It was not very comfortable. The thing that bothered me most was the long-range bomb bay fuel tank. It was just forward of me and my gear, looking much like the rear end of an elephant backed up against a low fence. Because the *Joan-Eleanor* operational flight usually lasted between five to six hours, the ground crew would top up the tank to its full capacity.

"As we climbed fast up over the Channel, the fuel would expand and be sucked into my compartment, where it would bubble in the bottom of the glass camera port just under my feet. Being on oxygen, you couldn't smell the stuff. The mere sight of it forced you to make an important decision: tell the pilot and have him abort the mission; or tell him, adding that you'll stay for the ride. As we gained altitude and reached our operational altitude of about 35,000 feet the temperature inside the fuselage was about -20 degrees and the danger of an internal explosion was greatly diminished."

Jean Nater flew on two "live" high-altitude training flights: one in an A-26C Invader, and a second on 19 April in a Mosquito. He managed to contact and record messages from an "agent" somewhere on the ground. Meanwhile, on 23/24 April André Pecquet flew his first mission, to *Farmer-Chauffeur*—a 6 hour 50 minute flight in a Mosquito flown by Lieutenant Knapp with his navigator, Lieutenant Jackson. Pecquet recalls: "The first two hours were unpleasant as liquid gas, due to some leakage, was floating all over my compartment. I made contact with both *Farmer* and *Chauffeur*."

Nater's first operational flight was scheduled for the night of 24/25 April. Nater says:

"Although the war in Europe was visibly coming to an end, it was still almost dogma among Allied commanders that the German Army, particularly the *Waffen* SS, would mass in southern Bavaria and the Austrian Alps for a Wagnerian final battle. If we could get agents into the Alpine Redoubt, we would be well placed to defeat Germany's final stand. Our target this time was south of the Munich area. After a light supper (belly gas is to be avoided at high altitude in unpressurized aircraft) we were kitted up and taken out to PR.XVI NS707 waiting on the runway. The pilot was 1st Lieutenant James G. Kunz, whom I knew, and the navigator Flight Officer Bob Green, recently assigned to the squadron and on his first mission.

"I was helped to squeeze into my compartment. The hatch was closed and I locked it from the inside and quickly tested the *Joan-Eleanor* equipment. I had been issued for the first time with silk gloves to wear under my heavy, heated flying gloves, and these made it much easier to manipulate the *Joan-Eleanor* gear As usual, the 'Mossie' got off fast. We flew south over the Channel and over France began steadily climbing to our operational altitude. Cold, noisy, but steady. I turned on my tiny lamp (no gas bubbling in the camera port, thank God) and tested the equipment again. The intercom was on and I could hear the pilot checking our position. Kunz said, 'We're at altitude, but still some way to go.' Time went by. Suddenly, I heard a French-accented voice asking us to identify ourselves or 'We will open fire.' Kunz cut in. 'That's French AAA - I won't answer them. They'll open fire, but the bursts will be way, way below us.' Then he announced, 'We can see the bursts below us.'

"It was dark and I was cold. Kunz suddenly announced, 'Tail radar has gone on! I'll do a quick 360°.' A '360'? I soon learned what it meant. We turned sharply and I was pushed down into my bench. It collapsed. Still we went around. We leveled out just as quickly. Kunz said, 'Jesus! Something's flown past us! It had a tail light! Maybe it was one of the new Messerschmitts we've heard about!' Was it true, or was Kunz just keeping me awake?

"At about 22.00 hours Kunz said, 'Time's right; we're on target. Do your stuff Jean. I'll fly a large figure-of-eight.' So it began. I turned on the Joan-Eleanor There was static in my headphones. The set was working. I began turning the antenna. It was functioning. I began calling the agent's code-name, repeating it twice and then identifying myself with a name I had been given. I repeated this procedure several times in German. If the agent was at the rendezvous, at this time, remembered the code name, his transmitter was working, and there was no German military within 50 yards, he must hear me and respond. Silence. Nothing. I tried again and again. Green checked our position. We were where we were supposed to be. Kunz changed the flight pattern. Around and around and back and forth we went for 15-20 minutes. Nothing. Kunz suggested we return to base.

I made one more call. No answer. I agreed with Kunz. I was sweating and cold.

"My altimeter stayed at 35,000 feet for a long time before moving down. Kunz told me we were deep into France so he'd come down lower I must have fallen asleep. The bouncing and whipping of the aircraft woke me. The altimeter had us at 5000 feet. I asked Kunz where we were and he replied, in a tone of great relief, that we would be crossing the Channel soon, then he'd go down lower. I watched the altimeter come down and then level out at 1000 feet. Despite the bouncing and shaking, I felt much better. The altimeter started down again, to 500 feet. In my mind's eye I saw the water below and the cliffs of Dover before us. The altimeter went below 100 feet and then lifted. 'We're over the coast,' said Green. We climbed to 3000 feet. Smoother, much smoother.

"About 10 minutes after crossing the coast, one of the engines began to miss and the aircraft shuddered. Kunz ordered Green to switch on the reserve fuel. I assume he complied, but the engine did not pick up. Instead it started to shake itself loose. Kunz began calling for an emergency landing. Two stations answered him and gave him a 'fix' so the navigator could work out a course. Kunz told them that we were at 'Angels Three'. Then he saw the port engine begin to burn. He ordered us to bale out. 'Green's out! Jean, Jean, when are you going?' I told him, 'I'm going!'

"In theory, the *Joan-Eleanor* operator was to 'kick out the hatch' and go out head first, but going out into the roaring darkness head first was something I could not do. I went out feet first and got stuck in the hatch with my legs banging outside on the fuselage. My 'chute had stuck on the hatch frame. I tried to disengage it with my hands. As I did so I smelt smoke. I was terrified that my searching fingers would spill the 'chute inside the aircraft. '*Relax,*' I thought. Then I was outside on my back, the aircraft going away from me with the port engine burning. I pulled the ripcord. A long, strong tug on my shoulders and body and a God-given quiet. My 'chute had opened!'

"Jean Nater landed near an ammunition depot not far from Farnham and was taken to RAE Farnborough. Kunz was all right, but Green was missing. Kunz told Green before he baled out that he had not done up the legstraps of his parachute harness. Green pulled the harness up between his legs but probably went out without buckling the legstraps. After a brief physical examination, Kunz and Nater joined the search for Green in the open, partially wooded countryside. They found his open 'chute high in a tree. His body was found the next day. At Harrington, Kunz told Nater that the port engine had been retrieved by RAF engineers and taken apart. A steel projectile had pierced the jacket of the supercharger and lodged there, effectively sealing the jacket. Over England the projectile had worked loose, causing the carburetor to explode. Kunz reasoned that the 'projectile' could only have come from the aircraft that had been on our tail while we flew over Germany."

* * *

On 27/28 April 1945 André Pecquet flew his second *Farmer-Chauffeur* mission with Lieutenant Knapp and Lieutenant Jackson:

> "Gas again leaked all over the rear compartment but stopped after an hour The weather was very bad during the 7 hour 40 minute flight and we flew at 32,000-35,000 feet. No contact with either team was made in spite of a thorough search over a wide area."

On 30 April Jean Nater flew his last Mosquito operational mission. He recalls:

> "We staged at either Dijon or Lyon, and had a light but excellent dinner in some OSS-requisitioned French country manor house. This time our target was in the Breganz area. The flight from the OSS French base to the target area and then to Harrington took 5 hours 25 minutes. Over the target at 35,000 feet we flew figures-of-eight and I called someone on the ground. I called and called. There was no answer. Time was running short so we turned for home. Not long after this, there was smoke in my compartment. I immediately informed the pilot. He confirmed that he and the navigator could also smell smoke. I then noticed that some liquid - probably gas - was bubbling in my camera port. I told the pilot. He asked, 'Do you want to bale out?' What a question at 35,000 feet! It would mean turning on the emergency oxygen flask strapped to my leg, getting out of that damned hatch, and then free-falling for a count of 10! I asked the pilot where we were. 'Over the Alps,' he replied! Visions of mountain peaks, snow and ice. 'No, not this time,' I told the pilot. I would stay...In time the smoke disappeared and the camera port cleared. The only instrument I had was the altimeter. When I could see it going down to 3000 feet staying there for a while, while we turned, the engines changing their tune, feeling the flaps come down - then I knew we were home!"

On 1 May 1st Lieutenant André Pecquet flew another mission in search of *Chauffeur* with Lieutenant Kunz and navigator Lieutenant Edwards, but the interphone, VHF, and radio equipment "blew out" and they were compelled to return after 40 minutes. Pecquet recalls:

> "We tried another plane, but because of several mechanical defects we were unable to take-off. The plane was repaired, but while taxiing we discovered that one engine was out of order. By then it was too late for a fourth attempt. This was my last mission. The surrender of Germany took place a few days later."

The 25th Bomb Group expected to be sent to the Pacific, but soon orders arrived to return their Mosquitoes to the RAF. Lieutenant Warren Borges wrote: "We came home…after flying our beloved Mosquitoes into a field ('Boondocks'…the grass was two feet high!) in Scotland - what a sad day!"

Quietly, without ceremony or flag waving, the Americans' involvement with the Mosquito was over.

PR.XVI of the 25th Bomb Group in D-Day invasion stripes over the Norfolk countryside. (Ken Godfrey via George Sesler)

Part of the *Joan-Eleanor* equipment. (Author)

PR.XVI NS590/B in D-Day invasion stripes over Norfolk. (Ken Godfrey via George Sesler)

PR.XVI 'M' in flight. (Ken Godfrey via George Sesler)

PR.XVI NS590/B with D-Day invasion stripes. (Ken Godfrey via George Sesler)

Bad weather during the *Market-Garden* operation made regular air reconnaissance impossible so 654th Squadron PR.XVIs were instructed to fly over the Arnhem bridge 'every hour on the hour.' On 22 September Lieutenant Robert P. Pat 'Paddy' Walker (pictured left with Sergeant Scott a War Correspondent with *Stars & Stripes* and Roy Conyers on 20 June 1944) and Lieutenant Roy C. Conyers flew over the northern end at under 500 feet to try to discover who had control of the bridge. Their Mosquito was hit by return fire but Walker managed to make it back to England and he landed safely at RAF Tangmere. On the 20 June D-Day +14 mission Scott rode home in the nose of the Mosquito after the crew, low on fuel, put down at an airstrip near the Normandy beach head. NS559/M was refueled by hand using Jerry cans earmarked for General Patton's tanks. Paddy Walker flew 57 missions, his last PR.XVI on OSS duty. Early on *D-Day* NS559 was flown on a photography mission by Lieutenant Colonel George Doherty and Major John 'Knobby' Walch, who was KIA with two other crew aboard an A-26 Invader mission for OSS on 19 March 1945. (Pat Walker via Ken Godfrey)

Near Right: Lieutenant Walter D. Gernand (right), 654th Bomb Squadron, and his cameraman, Sergeant Ebbet C. Lynch, 8th CCU **[far right]** were the first casualties in the 25th Bomb Group. They were killed returning from a mission over the D-Day beaches, 6 June 1944, when PR.XVI RS555 hit a railway embankment near High Wycombe. (via George Sesler)

25th Bomb Group personnel with French Armed Forces officers during an awards ceremony. L-R: Lieutenant Colonel John B. Larkin, Lieutenant Colonel John R. Hoover, General Martial Volin, Lieutenant Colonel Alvin E. Podwojski and Lieutenant General James E. Doolitle. From late in November 1944 some 25th Bomb Group aircraft and personnel were on detached service at Station A-83, the former Luftwaffe base near Valenciennes in northern France. (via George Sesler)

Cornelius A. Engle (left) and Len A. Erickson, a navigator in the 654th Bomb Squadron. (Erickson)

Crews and *Joan-Eleanor* operators of Harrington, 1945. L-R: Flight Officer Bob Green, navigator (who was recently assigned to the squadron and was on his first mission on 24/25 April 1945 when he was killed after baling out of PR.XVI NS707); Lieutenant Calhoun Ancrum (*Joan-Eleanor* operator); Lieutenant Kingdom Knapp (MIA Korea in an A-26); unknown pilot; 1st Lieutenant André E. Pecquet, (*Joan-Eleanor* operator). (André Pecquet)

Captain Richard Wright, 653rd Bomb Squadron and 25th Bomb Group Assistant Navigation Officer in the last months of the war (left) and Cornelius A. Engle in the 653rd Bomb Squadron.

Above: 25th Bomb Group PR.XVIs in flight. (Ken Godfrey via George Sesler)

Left: 25th Bomb Group PR.XVI at dispersal at Watton. (Ken Godfrey via George Sesler)

Below: J. E. 'Gene' Goodbread, pilot and Warren R. Barber, navigator in the 653rd Bomb Squadron were returning from a night mission on 25 July 1944 and crash landed at North Pickenham, a B-24 base in Norfolk. The landing gear caved in on the third bounce and the Mosquito slid off the runway onto the grass.

Night Joker photo of Nippes and Essen, Germany on 4/5 October 1944 using M46 photo flash bombs of 700,000 candlepower, 12 of which could be carried in the bomb bay of a PR.XVI. The system was perfected in 1943 by the RAF using two PR.IXs to test the American flash bombs, which were three times brighter than the British equivalents, once the cameras and the flash bombs had been harmonized. On 25 October the Mosquito flown by 1st Lieutenant George M. Brooks and 2nd Lieutenant Richard C. Taylor failed to return from a Night Photography (*Joker*) mission to Duisburg. Brooks was killed but Taylor survived and he returned. (Wright Booth via George Sesler)

Captain Lionel A. Proulx, navigator and Lieutenant Earl L. Muchway, pilot walk to their waiting Mosquito at Watton. The crew were leading a flight of four Mosquitoes on a *Gray-Pea* mission over Kiel on 3 April 1945 when they were attacked by German fighters, forcing them to land in Sweden. (via Ken Godfrey)

On 13 August 1944, 1st Lieutenant Dean H. Sanner and 8th CCU cameraman Staff Sergeant Augie Kurjack filmed a GB-4 *Batty* 2600lb glide-bombing mission to Le Havre. (The GB-4 had a TV camera installed under the nose and could be guided onto a target from 15 miles distant after being launched from the external wing racks of a B-17). Sanner, in MM370, followed the launched bombs down and was knocked out of the sky by the explosion of the second *Batty* as he overflew at low level. The blast threw Sanner out but Kurjack was killed. The first photo shows Sanner closing in on B-17G 42-40043 and the second is of Sanner on the steps of MM370 in happier times. (USAF)

A 492nd Bomb Group PR.XVI taxies out at Harrington in May 1945. After 3 May 1945 653rd Bomb Squadron *Redstocking* missions became an all-492nd Bomb Group operation. (André Pecquet)

Ex-RAF PR.XVI NS619, still in its overall PRU blue scheme, at its dispersal at Watton. 25th Bomb Group PR.XVIs were used on all manner of weather-reconnaissance, spying and PR missions by the 653rd and 654th Bomb Squadrons. (via Ron Mackay)

H2X PR.XVI NS538/F taxies by at Watton. NS538 exploded in the air near Newmarket during a local test hop on 8 September 1944 killing Flight Officer Russell C. Whitner and Master Sergeant Raymond C. Armstrong in the 654th Bomb Squadron. (via Steve Adams)

Left: American airmen flew Mosquitoes from RAF Watton in Norfolk and from Italy. Major (later Lieutenant Colonel and Group CO 4 November 1943-18 January 1944) James F. Setchell (left) and Captain J. C. Alexander of the 3rd Photo Group, 12th Air Force, are pictured in front of their Canadian-built F8-DH 43-34926 (KB315) *The "Spook"*, one of six converted from the B.VII. In March 1943 680 Squadron and the 3rd Photo Group formed the North African PR Wing under the unified command of Lieutenant Colonel Elliot Roosevelt. (J. F. Setchell Jr) **Right:** *The "Spook"* was named in honor of James F. Setchell's son James 'Bill' F. Jr, both of whom are seen here! (J. F. Setchell Jr)

PR.XVI MM386 was delivered to the USAAF at Burtonwood on 4 May 1944 and was assigned to the 653rd Bomb Squadron at Watton, where it was coded 'U'. Combat missions were usually signified on the nose, as here, by a cloud with a red lightning flash. Sometimes, a mosquito caricature with a telescope, a modified representation of the official 653rd Bomb Squadron badge, was used. (Jack Green via George Sesler)

1st Lieutenant Claude C. Moore, a navigator in the 654th Bomb Squadron. On 9 April 1945 1st Lieutenant John A. Pruis and Claude Moore took off on a *Gray-Pea* mission with three other Mosquitoes to escort a long, maximum-effort mission by B-17s of the 1st Air Division to Oberpfaffenhofen in southeastern Germany. This was Pruis' third Mosquito mission with the 25th Bomb Group. Three days earlier they had escaped from their crashing Mosquito at Watton. Moore had completed a tour in B-24 bombers. On the 9 April mission they were attacked by P-51s and Pruis slumped over the wheel. Moore tried to help Pruis but he was unable to move him. The Mosquito began a right hand spin with the right engine in flames. Moore experienced a difficult time reaching for his chute behind the pilot. It took the strength of both arms to grasp the pack and pull it toward him. He then attempted to connect it to his harness but, due to the centrifugal forces, he managed to connect only one side. He had more trouble than he thought he should and later, in the hospital, he learned the reason for his awkwardness. He had shrapnel wounds in his left arm from aircraft cannon shells. Moore eventually got out and then he noticed the bleeding from his left upper arm and forearm. As he descended fighter planes circled him. They were P-51s with the roundel markings of the Free French Air Force. These Mustangs circled only minutes then left the vicinity. Moore had not seen the aircraft that had fired at their Mosquito but he knew that the shells entered the fuselage diagonally from the left rear side. He knew that Pruis and the starboard engine had received the brunt of their effects. Moore's parachute caught in the top of a tall tree, leaving him hanging by the risers 50 to 75ft above the ground. He passed out soon after hitting the trees and when consciousness returned Moore unfastened the harness of his chute but with difficulty. His hands were burned raw; his arm was bleeding and his face felt like it was on fire. His back, left ankle, knee and foot were injured. Luckily soldiers of the 103rd Infantry Division rescued him. Moore remained the better part of two years in hospitals. For several months after his arrival at the hospital in Reims the doctors concentrated on his broken back, a ruptured cartilage in his knee, an injured ankle and the shrapnel wounds in his arm. He was then transferred to two burn centers in England where his hand, face and scalp received skin grafts and other attention. Later, he was transferred to the States where he received attention at two more hospitals. When married years after the mission he was still wearing a body cast. Pruis is buried in Lorraine American Cemetery, France. **Bottom Right:** L-R: 1st Lieutenant Claude C. Moore, 654th Bomb Squadron; Flight Officer James D. Spears, 654th Bomb Squadron; Warren R. Barber, 653rd Bomb Squadron; Robert C. Taylor, 653rd Bomb Squadron. Spears and his navigator Lieutenant Carroll Bryan were KIA on 23 December 1944 when their Mosquito crashed at Debden on a local training flight. (Warren Barber Coll)

PR.XVI NS591/S of the 25th Bomb Group landing at Watton on 22 February 1945. (via Philip Birtles)

On 12 August 1944 PR.XVI NS569/N flown by Lieutenant Robert A. Tunnel, 654th Bomb Squadron (left) with photographer Lieutenant David J. McCarthy (right) was sent upwards a few hundred feet when the PB4Y-1 *Anvil* mission drone flown by Lieutenant Joseph P. Kennedy Jr and "Bud" Willy, exploded, putting out the Mosquito's port engine and peppering the aircraft with flying debris. McCarthy managed to lower the wheels and Tunnel landed at Halesworth just before the starboard engine cut. (via George Sesler)

PR.XVI NS569/N of the 654th Bomb Squadron, 25th Bomb Group at Watton with a 652nd (H) Bomb Squadron B-17 behind. (Flight)

PR.XVI NS591/S of the 25th Bomb Group landing at Watton on 22 February 1945. (via Philip Birtles)

Air and ground crews in the 654th Bomb Squadron pose for the camera with 60lb Type M-46 photo flash bombs of 700,000-candle power. The PR.XVI could carry six of these in the forward half of the bomb bay and six in the rear half. (via Ken Godfrey)

Bob Peterson, pilot and Raymond Smith, navigator in the 653rd Bomb Squadron. (Warren R. Barber)

1st Lieutenant Harry J. Anglum Jnr, Roy C. Conyers and Robert P. Walker leaving a A-26 after a flight.

Right: 1st Lieutenant Malcolm J. 'Mac' MacLeod, who had flown in the RAF and Claude C. Moore. McLeod and 2nd Lieutenant Edward G. Fitzgerald, Meteorologist-Navigator **[Left:]** 653rd Bomb Squadron, were both killed on 22 November 1944 on a *Bluestocking* weather meteorological flight when they crashed at Saham Toney in severe weather. Both men are buried in Madingley Military Cemetery at Cambridge. The 653rd *Bluestocking* Squadron suffered a run of fatal crashes. On 1 November 1st Lieutenant Robert C. Grimes and 1st Lieutenant Clarence W. Jodar were returning from a *Bluestocking* mission in a furiously stormy night when a wingtip clipped a tree and they crashed inverted. Both men were killed and Jodar is buried at Cambridge. Then on 22 November MacLeod and Fitzgerald and 1st Lieutenant Russell E. Harry and 2nd Lieutenant Milford B. Hopkins were killed returning from another *Bluestocking* mission in much the same circumstances. Harry's aircraft crashed at Thompson near Watton. Just a few weeks earlier Hopkins and Clarence Jodar had celebrated with friends the arrival of their first born sons. (Warren Barber Coll)

Near Right: Lieutenant Elbert F. Harris, navigator and Lieutenant Ronald M. Nichols, pilot **[Far Right]**, the weather scout crew on the second *Frantic* shuttle mission, August 1944, who were shot down by a P-51D Mustang of the 357th Fighter Group while returning over France on 8 August. Harris baled out and with the help of the French Resistance, returned on 6 September. Nicholls was killed in the encounter. (via George Sesler)

PR.XVI NS748 lost its tail and rear fuselage in this crash at Watton in April 1945. (via Ken Godfrey)

Lieutenant Raymond G. Spoerl (right) with an u/k airman at Watton.

On 18 September 1944 1st Lieutenant Robert A. Tunnel (pictured) in the 654th Bomb Squadron, with 19-year-old Staff Sergeant John 'Buddie' G. Cunney, 8th CCU cameraman **[below]** failed to return from a PR mission to the Nijmegen-Eindhoven area where a supply drop was to be made by Liberators to the US Airborne. Tunnel was blinded by a searchlight, lost control and crashed on Plantlunne airfield. Both he and Cunney were killed and they are interred in the American war cemetery at Neuville en Condroz, Belgium. (via George Sesler)

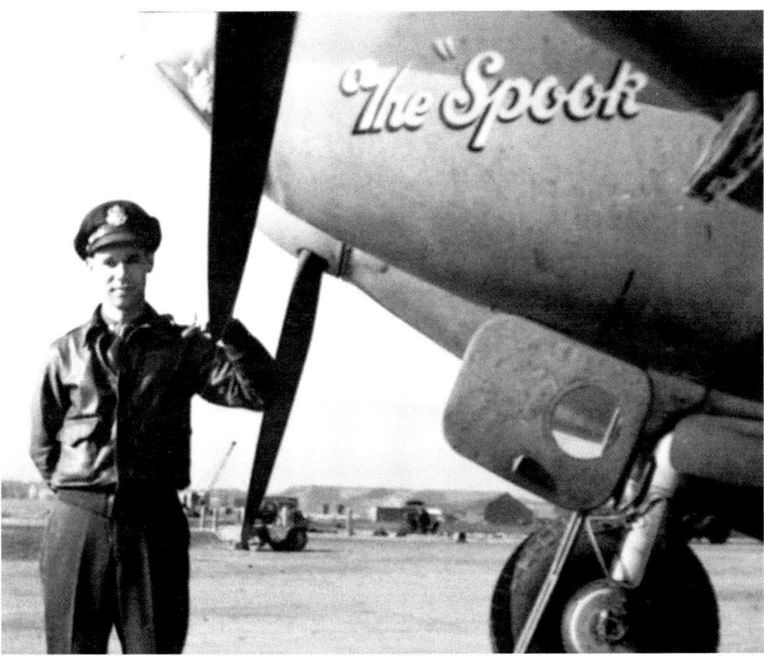

James F. Setchell with *The "Spook"* at Prestwick, Scotland in October 1943. (J. F. Setchell Jr)

Lieutenant Dean Sanner at Watton on 8 April 1944.

PR.XVI NS519/P in the 653rd Bomb Squadron was used by Lieutenant Earl L. Muchway and Lieutenant Lionel Proulux, one of two Mosquito crews that accompanied the B-17s on the disastrous *Frantic Joe* shuttle mission to Russia, Italy and England, 21 June-5 July 1944. After take off from San Severo, Italy on 5 July NS519 was forced to abort at 25,000 feet when the port propeller ran away. A RAF unit repaired the aircraft and the crew returned to Watton a few days later. (via George Sesler)

654th Squadron Photo Lab personnel show off their aerial cameras, which they operated, from onboard Mosquitoes at Watton. Camera equipment used consisted of the Fairchild K series in the 6, 12 and 24-inch models. Also used was the British F camera with its 36-inch lens. For BDA, the Fairchild K20 and K21 hand-held cameras were carried. The radar or *Mickey* camera, which provided a photo log of radar imaging, used by the 654th Squadron, was a development of the Camera Repair Dept at Watton. (via Ken Godfrey)

A crashed 25th Bomb Group *Red Tail* Mosquito at Watton. In November 1944 the 25th Bomb Group lost five Mosquitoes and seven crew killed while two more survived and were taken prisoner. A B-24 Liberator in the Group's 652nd Bomb Squadron also failed to return from a SHARON weather flight from Lagens in the Azores and the crew were interned in Portugal for a time. (via George Sesler)

654th Bomb Squadron officers in front of a PR.XVI Mosquito with the Watton control tower behind. (via Sesler)

PR.XVI still in its RAF PR blue scheme, which crashed at Watton on 20 February 1945. (Ken Godfrey via George Sesler)

PR.XVI NS553, still in its RAF PR blue scheme, suffered a starboard undercarriage failure after putting down in emergency at the 96th Bomb Group B-17 Flying Fortress base at Snetterton Heath in Norfolk. (via Dick Jeeves)

Lyndon F. Lakeman in the 654th Bomb Squadron beside a Mosquito at Watton. (Ken Godfrey via George Sesler)

PR.XVI *Greex* attached to the 492nd Bomb Group, at Harrington, Northamptonshire in May 1945 for a clandestine *Red Stocking* mission over Germany. (André Pecquet)

A 25th Bomb Group Mosquito crash near Long Melford on 6 March 1945. (via Bob Collis)

H_2X PR.XVI NS538/F with Photo Lab personnel, Carl J. Wanka and John W. Ripley. *Mickey* ships were fitted with modified B-17 H_2X sets for preparing photographic records of radar bombing approaches to high-priority targets deep inside Germany. The H_2X radar scanner was placed in a bulbous nose, the amplifiers and related equipment in the nose and bomb bay, and the radarscope in the rear fuselage. There was a tendency for the *Mickey* set to arc or even explode, when first turned on. The radar drew a heavier current than the Mosquito's electrical system. (via George Sesler)

Reynolds and William H. Rice repairing cameras in the 654th Bomb Squadron facility at Watton. (via George Sesler)

Lieutenant Colonel Leon W. Gray, CO. 25th Bomb Group with General James Doolittle, 8th Air Force at Watton in 1944. (via George Sesler)

Above: Len A. Erickson, a navigator in the 654th Bomb Squadron and Albert D. Rasmussen and two other officers playing cards at Watton. (Erickson) **Below:** In the grandstand on 17 October 1944 watching the US Navy Blue Devils against the Watton football team. The Navy came from behind in the last minute to win 13 to 7. (via George Sesler)

Major Albert S. Straff, Ground Executive; Colonel Elliott Roosevelt, Wing CO and Lieutenant Colonel Leon W. Gray, CO. 25th Bomb Group at Watton. (via George Sesler)

Lieutenant Colonel Leon W. Gray, CO. 25th Bomb Group (23 September 1944-14 April 1945) (left); Major Albert S. Straff, Ground Executive; Lieutenant General James E Doolittle, Major Alvin E. Podwojski, CO, 652nd Bomb Squadron, later Lieutenant Colonel, deputy Group CO and Colonel Elliott Roosevelt, Wing CO, at Watton. (via George Sesler)

Mosquito crash at Watton on 7 December 1944. (via George Sesler)

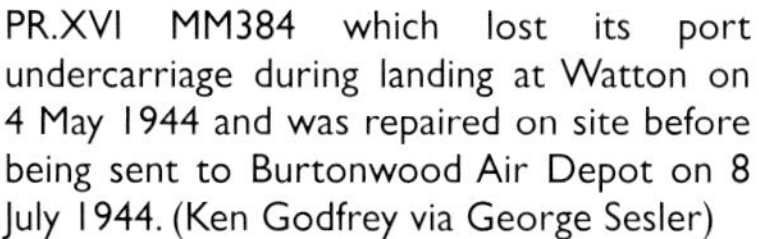

PR.XVI MM384 which lost its port undercarriage during landing at Watton on 4 May 1944 and was repaired on site before being sent to Burtonwood Air Depot on 8 July 1944. (Ken Godfrey via George Sesler)

Remains of a Mosquito at Watton being cannibalised for spare parts. In the background is B-17G 44-8507 in the 652nd Bomb Squadron, which was assigned to the 8th Air Force in October 1944. Unlike this Mosquito it survived the war and was flown back to the USA where it was broken up at Walnut Ridge in December 1945. (via George Sesler)

Above: Lieutenant Len A. Erickson in the 654th Bomb Squadron who flew the incident-filled *Chaff*-dispensing missions on 20 March 1945 with his pilot, Lieutenant Norman R. Magee. They were forced to feather their starboard engine propeller and drop out of the flight but they returned to Watton alone. (Erickson)

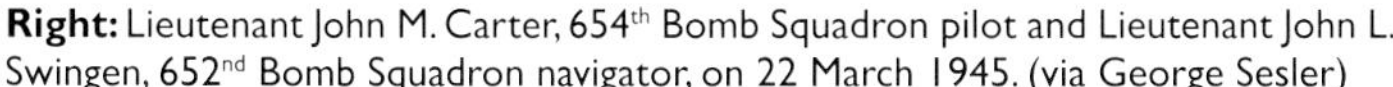

Right: Lieutenant John M. Carter, 654th Bomb Squadron pilot and Lieutenant John L. Swingen, 652nd Bomb Squadron navigator, on 22 March 1945. (via George Sesler)

654th Bomb Squadron, 25th Bomb Group at Watton. (via George Sesler)

PR.XVI MM388/U in the 653rd Bomb Squadron, 25th Bomb Group. (Jack Green via George Sesler)

2nd Lieutenant Vance J. Chipman (at the back with his pet monkey) a pilot in the 654th Squadron who flew *Chip's Chariot* was a former racetrack driver from Chicago who had joined the RCAF when war started in Europe. To some Chipman was '...a strange chap in USAAF uniform with both RAF and USAAF wings. His chest was splattered with combat decorations and he sported a long handlebar moustache. In a crisp British accent he introduced himself, mentioning that he would be assisting in Mosquito pilot training.' On 1 November 2nd Lieutenant Vance J. 'Chip' Chipman and 1st Lieutenant William G. Cannon took off on a *Mickey* mission to take H_2X photos for a bombing run to Schweinfurt. They never returned from their mission. Fifty miles from Schweinfurt the run was completed and on leaving the Mosquito received a direct AA hit. The right engine caught fire and Cannon was hit by shrapnel in his right leg and on the back of his head. Chipman gave the order to bale out but received no reply from Cannon, who had the usual difficulties in exiting the Mosquito but his descent was smooth. The impact with the ground in the black of night was unexpected and rough and broke his injured leg in three places. He had landed near an anti-aircraft battery whose crewmen found him within minutes. They placed him on a mattress and carried him to their battery office. They called a doctor, who arrived after two hours, set Cannon's leg and bandaged it. Next day Cannon was shipped to a PoW hospital at a prison camp. Chipman meanwhile, exited the bottom hatch, opened his parachute and from his descending parachute watched his aircraft explode. After landing he took stock. He had lost one tooth, split his lip, cut his tongue and torn a ligament in his left leg. He had retained his escape supplies during his jump, however and Chipman made his way toward France during the night and sought available hiding places during the day. From some farmer's storage hill he filled his trouser leg pockets with raw beets and potatoes. From a small shop he stole a bicycle. With the use of the bicycle he was covering distance until an aged tyre blew out. Thereafter he walked pushing the bicycle. One night Chipman passed two German soldiers who became suspicious and shone their torch on him. Seeing the blood and torn military clothing they took him to a Luftwaffe aerodrome and locked him in a cell. Later he was given the freedom of a hallway. A day or two later at breakfast he found a door unlocked. Walking out the door he made his way to one of several Bf 109s parked in a blast bay. He planned to start the aircraft and head for England and everything seemed to be working smoothly but he found that a lone person inside the aircraft could not start a Bf 109. Chipman was still trying when he was discovered and hustled back into the guardhouse. A guard, using a one-inch rubber tubing, beat Chipman over the head until he was unconscious. When he recovered he was taken to the *Dulag Luft* in Frankfurt where he was interrogated. Chipman answered all questions with the usual name, rank and serial number but perhaps in a frivolous manner. Thus, in an effort to make him talk, his captors gave him a doped cigarette. It made him very dizzy and very sick but he did not lose his control. Rather, he answered their questions with imaginative and ridiculous accounts of activities as if it were the effect of the drug. This included a revelation about a flying submarine. From Frankfurt, Chipman was taken to *Stalag Luft III* at Sagan. (via Ken Godfrey)

PR.XVI NS590/B of the 654th Bomb Squadron showing the newly applied stars and bars although the overall PRU blue paint scheme has failed to totally cover the old RAF roundels. This aircraft crashed at Watton on 5 May 1945. (Ken Godfrey via George Sesler). **Middle Left:** PR.XVI RF992/R in the 654th Bomb Squadron flown by Roger W. Gilbert and his navigator was Lieutenant Raymond G. Spoerl, which returned from a *Chaff* mission on 20 March 1945 with battle damage to the wings, fuselage and paneling caused by attacking Me 262 jets. Spoerl reported that the jet was firing at them and Gilbert broke as hard as he could to the left. they had turned about 45° when they began taking 30mm hits in the cockpit, the instrument panel, the observation canopy and in the left wing. The battle damage on the left wing helped them turn even tighter to the left, taking them out of the line of fire. The 30mm shells had worked the wing over, however. they were going down out of control in a tight spiral. The jet flashed by us on their right. Spoerl, who had been monitoring the Me 262's activities from the observation bubble and without his safety belt, was thrown to the floor by gravity forces. This occurred as the cannon fire punched the hole in the observation bubble. As Gilbert looked down at Spoerl on the floor he thought that he had been shot. Gilbert was concerned that he could not get out of the tight spiral because of the damage to the left wing, but with a high power setting on the left engine the Mosquito straightened up. By keeping a much higher power setting on the left engine than the right, the Mosquito flew fairly well and, with the lifting of gravity forces, Raymond Spoerl lifted himself up and proved to be OK. Taking inventory of the damage, they found that the entire left wing tip was lost. The flap and aileron extended perhaps two feet beyond the shredded main structure of the wing. The ailerons that had been jammed temporarily in the left turn position now worked only part way and the radio was inoperative. They had dropped 8000 feet below the flight, could not communicate and were no longer part of the team. They were on their own as they turned toward Watton. Gilbert did not experience further control problems unless his speed slowed to 170 mph. Then the aircraft would fall off to the left. Without the radio they could not communicate with the Watton control tower. To alert their personnel to their problems Gilbert raced across the field and by the control tower with the damaged wing on a level with and near its windows. Fortunately the control tower personnel saw it. Gilbert circled the field and set the wheels down at the edge of the runway at just above 170 mph. They stopped comfortably and taxied to their dispersal area. (Gilbert)

PR.XVI 'J' in the 25th Bomb Group starts its engine at a dispersal at the 466th Bomb Group B-24 Liberator base at Attlebridge, Norfolk, prior to a *Red Tail* mission with the 8th Air Force in 1945. Some 74 Mosquito sorties code-named *Red-Tail* (after the red tails painted to distinguish them from enemy aircraft) were flown from bases in East Anglia carrying the Command Pilot on 8th Air Force bombing missions. (via Mike Bailey)

PR.XVI NS569/N in the 654th Bomb Squadron, 25th Bomb Group at Watton. (USAF)

Chapter 9

"Divers" and "Doodlebugs," Widows and Orphans

A 'Sprog' was what they at first called me
Meaning that on an Op I had never flown
'Flak' was the term used for anti-aircraft fire
Aircrew spoke a are lingo of their own

'Flak Valley', I learned was the Ruhr Valley
Where many bombers had been mortally hit
With 'Ack-Ack' guns it was heavily defended
The flak was so thick you could taxi on it

'No Ball' targets were the V-1 launch sites
From where was launched a pilotless plane
Doodle Bug' or 'Flying Bomb' we called them
A new weapon that brought death and pain

Aircrew Lingo,
Sergeant George 'Ole' Olson RCAF

It had been intended that V1 flying bombs would rain down on Britain as part of the *Steinbock* offensive but, fortunately for the civilian population of this island, problems delayed the anticipated "rocket blitz" until 13 June 1944. On this day ten V1s were catapult-launched at the capital from sites in northeastern France. The *Vergeltungswaffe 1* (Revenge Weapon No 1), or Fieseler Fi 103 *Kirschkern* (Cherry Stone), was a small pilotless aircraft with a 1870lb high explosive warhead that detonated on impact.

Flight Lieutenant Vic Hester, a Mosquito pilot with 138 Wing at Lasham, recalls:

"Word came down from Group HQ that the Prime Minister wanted a close-up cine film of a buzz bomb to show on Cinema newsreels, in an endeavour to reassure the public that this new German weapon did not baffle us. The fastest aircraft that could carry a trained cameraman equipped with a 35mm cine camera was the Mosquito. DZ383 a modified B.IV Series II, which had an all-perspex nose, was occupied by a cine cameraman from Pinewood studios. The modified nose allowed the cameraman to squat and hoot his films at any angle. We also fixed up a 400 feet-reel camera, fixed to shoot straight ahead. We rigged up a simple gun sight for the pilot so that he could operate this particular camera. Our task was to take 35mm cine footage of selected raids by any squadron in 2 Group. This unusual Mosquito could carry either 4x500lb bombs in the fuselage or extra fuel tanks extending the range by some 300 miles. In fact these extra fuel tanks, when new, carried 80 gallons of Courage's Best Bitter to our colleagues stationed on B 5 landing strip near Bayeaux, France, in August 1944. I've continued to be amazed how short a time it took for the British Army and Air Force to consume over 600 pints of beer! 'We were not on the strength of any of the three squadrons that made up 138 Wing, so we could not use any known squadron letters on our aircraft, so a question mark was painted in place of a letter. The first attempt by a Polish airman went wrong, as he got the question mark the wrong way round on one side!

"Between 18 June and 3 July 1944 I piloted Flying Officer Oakley on sixteen flights in DZ383 and DZ414, flying mostly out of Biggin Hill, trying to get some good close-ups of these flying bombs. (We used two different Mosquitoes because our high speed dives were stripping off some of the fabric wing covering and the first aircraft had to go to Lasham for the airframe fitters to get to work with new fabric and the dope brush). Buzz Bombs, or rather their launching pads were not new to us. We had been bombing them since the previous year. The main building of these launching pads was about the size of a small haystack plus the take-off ramp. There were perhaps over one hundred of these sites known in the RAF and US 8th and 9th Air Force as *No Ball* Sites. Over 90% were destroyed by allied airforces. Remembering the damage done in the south of England by the remaining 10% one cannot help thinking of the effect upon our war effort had the whole 100% been available to the Germans. 20% of these rocket sites were destroyed by Mosquito attacks. The German Ack-Ack defenses of these rocket sites increased as the construction advanced until they became very heavily defended when they approached operational ability.

"The buzz bomb was a liquid fuelled rocket and by the time they were crossing into southern England they would be flying at about 2 or 3000 feet and at a speed of about 350-mph. They were small and black and did not stand out as well as an aircraft. If you wanted to spot them easily you needed to be slightly lower than they were, so to catch them against the skyline; however if you followed such a procedure you had insufficient speed to catch them. How most flights ended up was that Spitfires would dive from about 5000 feet and if they spotted a target they would pull out of the dive when in line with the target, alert the Tempests, that were faster. They started from 7000 feet and using the line of the Spitfire would dive to the attack. Our photographic Mosquito started diving from 10,000 feet and if we spotted a target would pull out of the dive at the last moment in an endeavour to maintain enough speed to keep up with the target for a short while. The 'G' forces experienced whilst pulling out of the dive made it almost impossible for the Cameraman to hold and sight the heavy 35mm camera of the period. We took many pictures of the ground, with the occasional frame or two of a buzz bomb.

"After about five days Oakley thought he might have got something worth processing, so after landing at Biggin Hill amongst all the balloons that were also trying to catch the buzz bombs, we rushed up to Shepherds Bush Film Studios to get our films processed. Whilst waiting, Oakley took me off to a local pub that he used regularly before the war. The landlord welcomed Oakley with considerable gusto and asked what he was doing in Shepherds Bush. Oakley told him that we had been trying to get a close up of a buzz bomb for some days. The landlord looked at his watch and then said that if we would accompany him to the roof of his five storey building, in about ten minutes, there would be one passing over. We did in fact accept the offer and sure enough got the best shot so far achieved. We did in the end, get a good air-to-air shot of a buzz bomb being shot down."

Incredible as it now seems, RAF Mosquito interceptor crews were not appraised of the coming V1 threat. Flight Lieutenant R. W. "Dickie" Leggett, who with Flying Officer Egbert J. "Midi" Midlane was stationed at Hurn, near Bournemouth, explains:

"It is absolutely absurd to think that here we were in a front-line squadron [418] and we hadn't been briefed about 'buzz bombs'. On the night of 18/19 June we had just done a normal routine patrol, had landed and were refuelling, when we were intercepted and told to hurry up and get off again to intercept some 'pilotless aircraft'! We were very disbelieving and said some pretty rude things to the IO. We were put on patrol by a GCI station at about 1500-2000 feet. It was still dark. After about 45 minutes of absolute boredom (we were already pretty fed up after the previous two to three-hour patrol where nothing had happened) everything happened at once! The GCI station got a contact. At the same time this device with this great big flame came within 300 feet, going across at 90° to us. We were worried and awake. I turned the aircraft around as best I could and my navigator immediately got a contact on his radar. We were cruising at around 220 mph. I immediately put on full throttle, but of course this thing' was doing 400 mph+ and left us looking rather stupid! We took a great interest for another hour or so, but no more came along so we went back and reported what we'd seen. We were furious at not being briefed."

The first V1 destroyed by a Mosquito was launched on 14/15 June 1944 and fell to Flight Lieutenant Rayne Schultz DFC, who was on a freelance sortie over the sea when he was passed by a "queer aircraft" flying in the opposite direction. Schultz, who had scored his sixth victory on 10/11 April when he downed a Ju 188, turned and gave chase, going through the "gate" as he did so, and shot it down. He flew straight into the debris and returned to Manston with little skin left on his Mosquito. Ben Johnson, a Fitter IIE, recalls:

"Both engines later had to be changed. Within a matter of about two weeks, every aircraft was u/s as engines were swapped for American Packard-built engines, which took about 15 hours per 'kite'. We were sent some WAAFs to help out, but with the restrictions on what they were allowed to do, it only made for harder work to keep to our targets. Just prior to this all Rolls-Royce engines had to have the Sun wheels in the reduction gears changed."[214]

On 25 June 1944 85 and 157 Squadrons in 100 Group were switched to anti-*Diver* patrols. (By the start of 1945 85 Squadron were still using AI.VIII radar sets, but at least their Mosquitoes were made more powerful with the injection of nitrous oxide (better known as "laughing gas") with petrol to give the added power needed to catch the V1s.) They operated against the "Doodlebugs" until 20 August, when both squadrons resumed bomber support duties from Swannington.

Flight Lieutenant R. W. Leggett recalls:

"The *anti-Diver* patrols were a free-for-all. You had to dive down on these things at an enormous rate of knots - absolutely flat-out - and do the best you could. There was no real control about it. (Our XVII didn't have the power of the Mosquitoes with injection.) Because it was a free-for-all, when we got close, to avoid collision with other night fighter chaps going in, we were briefed to switch on our navigation lights. Colliding with another aircraft was embarrassing. However, all the Fw 190s had to do was hover around, knowing some fool would have his nav' lights on. It was a fairly obvious cat and mouse' game. Chaps didn't come back from these V1 things; a couple of friends in particular. It is my opinion they rather stupidly put on their nav' lights, lined up, and got one up the backside from a Fw 190. Easy! This was all part of the anti-*Diver* game. I could see the other aircraft coming in with their lights on. Very useful for me to see them, but I wasn't going to put my nav' lights on and I didn't bother to tell them!"

By the end of June 1944 605 Squadron had shot down 36 "Doodlebugs," and in July the squadron destroyed a further 29. One of its pilots was Flight Lieutenant Brian "Scruffy" Williams. On 6/7 July 1944 Williams and Warrant Officer S. F. Hardy took off at 0145 hours to carry out a *Diver* patrol. In all, they saw eight V1s. At 0205 hours Williams attacked and destroyed the first of three, eight miles south of Dungeness at 6000 feet. His second "Doodlebug" exploded after a burst from 500 yards astern, five miles north northwest of Le Touquet, and the third exploded 15 miles east of Dungeness. On 18 August Brian Williams sighted a group of eight "Doodlebugs" crossing the French coast between Le Touquet and Boulogne at 2000 feet. He attacked and shot down two. He exploded the first with a short burst from dead astern, about four miles off Dungeness, and he destroyed the second with two short bursts from astern and slightly above about 10 miles northwest of Le Touquet.

For four weeks starting on 28 June 1944 125 Squadron and six Northrop P-61 Black Widows of the Scorton-based 422nd and 425th Night Fighter Squadrons, 9th Air Force, carried out comparative night-fighter trials from Hurn. (A further detachment also operated from Ford starting on 15 July against V1s.) The two P-61 squadrons, the only ones to operate in Europe during WWII, had arrived in England during March-June 1944, being based originally at Charmy Down. Flight Lieutenant Richard W. "Dickie" Leggett recalls the arrival of the gloss-black aircraft and their crews, who were commanded by Colonel Winston W. Kratz of the 481st Night Fighter Operational Training Group:

> "They were super aircraft and the Americans were great chaps, but we pulled their legs unmercifully because they'd had no luck in shooting down any enemy aircraft. They were unlucky. Personally, I believe it was because they did not have the opportunity, background or feeling for this war. It was not something that could be learned in the classroom. They were not teams like we were in the Mosquito, where a pilot and navigator were an entity."

On 5 July a NF.XVII flown by Squadron Leader Eric Barwell DFC of 125 Squadron[215] flew a combat evaluation demonstration at Hurn against Lieutenant Donald J. Doyle. The P-61 proved faster at 5,000 feet, 10,000 feet, 15,000 feet, and 20,000 feet, out-turning the Mosquito at every altitude by a big margin. The P-61 also far surpassed the Mosquito in rate of climb. The Americans concluded, "We could go faster and slower, up or down. Faster than the pride of the British - a most enjoyable afternoon."

Flight Lieutenant "Dickie" Leggett, who also flew a mock combat exercise in daylight with the P-61, confirms its speed advantage:

> "We started at 1000 feet and had a formal dogfight, getting GCI to set us up about 20 miles apart. We intercepted each other using our AIs. Then we climbed at 5000 feet intervals to gaps until we reached 30,000 feet. My navigator made notes. Although I outmaneuvered the Black Widow, it was slightly embarrassing at our 5000 feet gaps to find it always seemed to be waiting for me. His engines were more powerful. This gave him an extra advantage in the rate of climb, but, surprisingly, not in maneuverability."

On 15 July the 422nd NFS flew the first P-61 operation from England, and on the very next night scored the first "kill" when it downed a V1. On 5 August the 425th NFS shot down a V1, and two days later the 422nd got its first manned aircraft. (The 425th had to wait until Christmas Eve 1944 before it got its first manned aircraft 'kill.") R. W. Leggett concludes:

> "We had so many night fighters messing about we often spent the night chasing our chums, especially if the IFF was not turned on. As there were normally about 100 Mosquitoes and 20 Germans, the 'bogey' nearly always turned out to be a Mosquito. Black Widow crews were keen to fire. They were so trigger-happy that it became embarrassing. Much later, I heard one 'kill' on my R/T one night. He fired, then I heard him claiming a '410. 'I've hit it! It's on fire! It's going down in flames!' Then I heard the RAF pilot's voice say, 'He missed by at least six feet! I'm not hit. I'm not going down in flames!' It was a Mosquito!"

By September the Allied advance had overrun launching sites in the Pas de Calais. (Thankfully for the troops hitting the beaches all along the Normandy coastline on *D-Day*, 6 June, they had no need to fear bombing by the V1s.) However, the Allied advance had not wrong-footed the *Luftwaffe*, who mounted a new terror blitz from the skies by air-launching "Doodlebugs" from aircraft over the North Sea. In 1943 experiments at the German research establishment at Peenemünde, on the Baltic coast, where V2 rockets were being built and tested, resulted in several He 111s being modified to H-22 standard to carry a V1 under its wing.[216] By August 410 V1s had been air-launched against London, Southampton, and Gloucester. All of them were fired from Heinkel He 111s of III/KG3 based at Venlo and Gilze Rijen in Holland. Normally, the Heinkels took off at night, flew low over the North Sea to evade radar, and climbed to 1475 feet before firing their missiles from approximately 50 miles offshore.

In September 1944 the Allied advance forced III/KG3 to abandon its bases in Holland and move to airfields in Germany. Only the radar-equipped Mosquito and Tempest V night-fighter were able to counter the new threat. On 25 September Mosquitoes downed their first He 111H22s over the North Sea, the "kills" being credited to "Mossies" of 409 and 25 Squadrons. On the night of 28/29 September 25 Squadron at Coltishall had further success. A NF.XVII flown by Wing Commander L. J. C. Mitchell and navigator Flight Lieutenant D. L. Cox operating the fitted AI.X took off at 0055 hours to intercept some anticipated "trade" over the North Sea. At 3500 feet, 40 miles east of Great Yarmouth, they saw a V1 being launched from a Heinkel. Mitchell carried out a diving turn on the enemy machine. At the same time *Greyfriars* Control informed them that the Heinkel was also turning to port. Mitchell lost height to 600 feet in a turn and Cox made contact at 2½ miles range. Mitchell closed at 200 feet above the sea and obtained a visual at 1300 feet. Cox raised his night glasses and confirmed the "bogey" as a He 111H22 Mitchell and gave it a short burst from 400 feet dead astern. It exploded, flinging debris into the night sky and into the path of the onrushing Mosquito. Mitchell yanked the stick hard right and then turned back to see the German aircraft crash in flames into the sea, where it burned for two to three minutes before sinking beneath the dark waters.

Mitchell and Cox returned to their patrol line and saw another V1 being launched. Losing height, Mitchell sped off after the "Doodlebug," informing *Greyfriars* Control of his bearing. They vectored him towards the source of the launch. Cox eventually obtained contact on a converging course. He waited patiently until the range closed to about one mile and then carried out a hard turn to port, so as to close in behind the enemy machine. The Mosquito lost height to 150 feet and pounded over the waves at 220 mph as the Heinkel sailed along at a leisurely 180-190 mph, seemingly oblivious to its imminent demise. At 1500 feet range the Mosquito crew got their visual confirmation that it was a He 111. Mitchell let loose with a short burst from 600 feet. Pieces flew off the He 111's right wing and Mitchell added to its misery with another short burst, this time from 400 feet. The port engine burst into flames and the Heinkel crashed in flames into the sea. Mitchell searched for survivors until 0615 hours, but his action had been total.

On 5 October a 25 Squadron Mosquito brought down another Heinkel He 111H-22 over the North Sea. 125 (Newfoundland) Squadron bagged another of the V1 launchers on 25 October, and on the night of 30/31 October were out again seeking Heinkels over the North Sea. Squadron Leader L. W. G. "Bill" Gill and his navigator, Flight Lieutenant D. A. Haigh, took off from Coltishall at 0725 hours in a NF.XVII and were vectored by Hopton Control at full speed towards some "trade" reported to the east. Contact was obtained at 2½ miles range and Haigh instructed Gill to turn hard right. At 7000 feet range they obtained a contact again. Gill got a fleeting glimpse of the Heinkel as it passed above them on the opposite vector. He closed rapidly to 4000 feet and started to get fleeting sightings of the bomber as it passed through broken cloud. By now the Heinkel had released its flying bombs and was turning left and starting to descend slightly. Gill closed range rapidly to 1000 feet and opened fire with a long burst. Haigh and Gill saw the shells hit home around the right engine and fuselage, and pieces of debris scattered in all directions as the Heinkel dropped like a winged bird. Gill gave it another burst and saw hits strike the tail. Gill was now overshooting so he broke away.

To his chagrin, the Heinkel went down to sea level, straightened out, and climbed slowly, frantically seeking cover in the cloud. It was a futile gesture; cloud was no hiding place for a searching AI.X radar and its trained operator. Haigh busily operated his AI set until he regained contact with the fleeing Heinkel at 4000 feet range. Gill closed in, determined to finish off the Heinkel once and for all. In desperation *Feldwebel* Theodore Warwas, the pilot of the 4./KG53 machine, carried out violent evasive action and climbed slightly with one of his Jumo 211 engines smoking. Gill mercilessly pumped another long burst into its sides from 1000 feet range. This time the German aircraft floundered, caught fire, and went straight down into the sea.

Eleven minutes later Gill and Haigh carried out an attack on another He 111H-22. Although Gill obtained strikes before his ammunition ran out, he and his navigator were unable to confirm if it had crashed into the sea because of the 600 feet cloud base and prevailing scattered heavy rainstorms in the area. Gill and Haigh were credited with a "damaged" to go with their earlier He 111 "kill."[217]

Despite the losses during October, I/KG53 (III/KG3 redesignated) was joined by II/KG53 and III/KG53 for further air launching of V1s. On the night of 5/6 November a 68 Squadron NF.XIX fitted with AI.X and piloted by Flight Sergeant L. W. Neal took off from Coltishall to intercept incoming "trade" over the North Sea. Flight Sergeant E. Eastwood, his navigator, obtained a contact at 1½ miles range, flying at an altitude of 1000 feet. Cloud was 10/10ths at 2300 feet, but Neal and Eastwood had no difficulty finding the V1 launcher, which was traveling at 150-mph. Neal dropped to 1000 feet and, closing to 2500 feet range but flying at 160 mph indicated, overshot and returned to patrol. They picked up contact again at two miles and closed to 1000 feet, then 500 feet. At 1500 feet altitude they watched the He 111 release its flying bombs. For 20-30 seconds the Heinkel followed in the path of the V1s before gradually losing height and turning hard to starboard. The two sergeants followed on AI and obtained a visual at about 200-yard range, 900 feet altitude. Neal gave the enemy bomber a two-second burst and the aircraft dived steeply to starboard and crashed into the North Sea. A red glow was visible for 15 miles.

On the night of 10/11 November 125 Squadron at Coltishall despatched a Mosquito at 18:25 hours to intercept a contact over the North Sea. Flight Lieutenant G. F. Simcock and his navigator, Flying Officer N. Eric Heijne, took off in their NF.XVII, call sign *Goodwill 27*, and headed out across the inhospitable waters, vectored first by Neatishead GCI then Hopton CHEL. Simcock wrote later:

> "I saw what proved to be flying bombs being released and asked Hopton if any information available. Control had no information so turned in direction of flying bombs. We obtained a contact on target crossing from starboard to port, going east, but Hopton turned us away from this and then back towards it again. As we were turning back, I saw, slightly behind us, a Heinkel 111 by the light of its flying bomb. Turned towards it and obtained contact at three miles range, our height being 1000 feet and target's about 1500. Target did a wide turn to port and slowly lost height to 200 feet, approx. ASI 200. Followed on AI through heavy shower and closed in, getting visual at 800 feet. Target was then down to 150 feet, ASI 150. I originally intended to shadow e/a on AI hoping that he would gain height on approaching coast, but as there was more dirty weather ahead, decided to open fire at once rather than risk losing contact. Opened fire with a long burst at 600 feet, closing to 400 feet approx. Target then at 100 feet height. Many strikes were seen on port engine and port wing root and port side of fuselage. There was a large whitish-yellow flash from the port engine and a large piece flew back from it. My observer reported seeing another flash from the port side of the fuselage, but I did not see this. E/a immediately slowed down and went into a steep port bank. I had to break away - ASI then 140 - to avoid collision. Broke to starboard and then turned back to port again and attempted to regain contact. We searched area thoroughly at about 75 feet, scanning up, but no contact obtained. The sea was very rough with 'white horses' and it was extremely dark, so consider it unlikely, as it was not on fire, that I would be able to see it hit the sea. I claim one Heinkel 111 probably destroyed."

Although Simcock was only able to claim the Heinkel 111 as "probably" destroyed their victim, a Heinkel 111 of *Gruppe Stab* I/KG53,[218] was shot down. What is more, the all out raids this night by KG53 cost them three Heinkels.

At 0130 hours a second Heinkel[219] was shot down by Flight Lieutenant Douglas Greaves DFC and Flying Officer F. Milton Robbins DFC of 25 Squadron under Bawdsey CCI. They obtained a sighting of the enemy aircraft at 200 feet and Greaves opened fire with a long burst from dead astern. The Mosquito crew saw strikes, which were followed by a sheet of flame about the starboard engine and wing root. Wreckage was left burning on the sea in the Thames Estuary area when the Mosquito resumed its patrol. It was the pairing's ninth victory of the war, and they had also scored a probable and one damaged.[220]

Twenty-five minutes later a second 4 *Staffel* machine[221] was shot down by Flight Sergeant A. R. Brooking and Pilot Officer R. B. Finn of 68 Squadron. They saw four V1s released, and Finn obtained an AI contact flying at 700 feet with a speed of 180 mph. This led to a visual sighting at 1200 feet. Flying through patchy cloud, Brooking closed to 600 feet and opened fire. The crew saw hits, pieces flew off the starboard wing root and fuselage, and a glow of burning was visible inside the fuselage. Brooking broke off the combat to avoid flying wreckage and a few seconds later he and Finn saw the Heinkel burning on the sea.

On the night of 14/15 November KG53 launched thirty-seven missiles during three attacks from off the coast of Lowestoft, Bawdsey, and to the south of these two places. Weather conditions were poor with low cloud over the North Sea, rain, sleet, and snow. In all, eleven V1s got through the defenses and eight reached London. Off Southwold the AA defenses shot down a Mosquito of 25 Squadron flown by Wing Commander W. J. Mitchell and Flight Lieutenant D. L. Cox while they were returning short of fuel, and the aircraft crashed in a field east of Thetford Norfolk after the crew had baled out. Mitchell sprained his ankle. A second Mosquito, a NF.XVII call-sign "Ferro 17" crewed by two U.S. naval airmen (Lieutenant Joseph F. Black and Lieutenant Thomas N. Aiken) and attached to 68 Squadron, took off from Coltishall. A very short time later Ground Controllers at Neatishead warned them of an approaching enemy aircraft. Black turned the Mosquito onto the interception course as relayed by the ground controller, and shortly afterwards Aiken made contact on his AI set with the Heinkel, which they saw release a V1 before they could close with it. Black and Aiken ignored the enemy bomber and chased the *Diver* into the AA gun strip, where they too were shot down. The *Diver* fell harmlessly southwest of Berkhampstead in Hertfordshire. The Mosquito crashed in a field at Home Farm, Somerleyton, 18 miles from Lowestoft, and both Americans were killed. Joe Black was due to marry his English fiancée, Nancy Annan, a WREN who had worked at Bletchley Park on the top secret *Ultra* Project. Both airmen were posthumously awarded the U.S. Air Medal and the Purple Heart.[222]

On the night of 17/18 November 456 Squadron RAAF at Ford, in Sussex, flew anti-*Diver* patrols for the first time, sending five Mosquitoes on sorties to just off the Dutch coast. Two nights later a 456 Squadron RAAF NF.XVII flown by Flying Officer D. W. Arnold and his navigator, Flying Officer J. B. Stickley, chased and finally caught up with an He 111 75 miles east of Lowestoft. Their quarry was a Heinkel 111H-16 of 5th *Staffel*, KG53 flown by *Feldwebel* Rudolf Ripper. Arnold fired his cannon from 400 yards. Ripper's ventral gunner returned fire, hitting the Mosquito in the right propeller. Debris embedded itself in the leading edge of the right wing. As the Heinkel turned away Arnold fired another burst and the starboard engine caught fire. He fired a third burst. Climbing suddenly to 1200 feet, the still burning He 111 started to break up before falling over to the right in a stall turn into the Zuider Zee. The waves almost immediately snuffed out the shower of sparks and doused the flames. On the night of 22/23 November Warrant Officer J. L. Mulholland and Flying Officer J. D. James of 456 Squadron RAAF chased a Heinkel, which they saw launch a V1 from under its port wing. The Mosquito crew did not break off the chase until they were twenty miles into Holland, when bad weather finally forced them to abort and return to Ford. The night following Mulholland and James failed to return from their patrol after chasing their quarry down to 50 feet off the sea.

Another 456 Squadron RAAF crew, Flying Officer F. S. Stevens and his observer, W. A. H. Kellett, chased their quarry in the early dawn of 25 November. They took off from Ford at 0625 hours, and the two Australians saw four bright flashes on the horizon about 1000 feet below them. Stevens dived to 1500 feet, and Kellett obtained two contacts at about two miles range. They chose the nearest blip, which appeared to be taking evasive action and was flying east, back to Holland. Stevens dived the Mosquito until he was just 500 feet above the sea and then set off in pursuit. This He 111 settled onto a course for home at 500 feet, changing height every now and again and weaving continuously. Kellett's C-scope had malfunctioned, so very slowly Stevens closed the gap between them and the retreating Heinkel until they could see the enemy machine just 800 feet in the distance. All at once the Heinkel turned violently to starboard. Stevens carried out a half-orbit and contact was immediately regained. There was no cloud but it was very dark, and the two Australians had difficulty making out the fleeing bomber. There was no mistaking its return fire though. Twice the Heinkel's gunners opened up from 800 feet, but Stevens bravely closed in still further to 600 feet, and they were able to identify it positively as a He 111. It was flying at 900 feet. Stevens opened fire with a two-second burst from his cannon and the enemy's left engine immediately burst into flames. He closed to 150 feet, a second two-second burst going right through the fuselage, which erupted in flames, illuminating the peculiar dull light grey tail fin with its evil black swastika outlined in white. Stevens broke to starboard. The flaming torch fell, shedding a dozen or so bright green incandescent balls in its fiery wake before it hit the water about 10 miles west of Texel. German ASR picked up all the crew.

The *Luftwaffe's* air launched *Diver* offensive tailed off considerably in December, and for the first two weeks of the month interceptions were nonexistent. After a four-night pause KG 53 launched 45 V1s thirty miles off the Norfolk coast on the night of 17/18 December. It was cold, with little wind and heavy cloud cover, and visibility over the North Sea was poor. In the early morning a Mosquito (call sign *Goodwill 4*) flown by Pilot Officer K. D. "Denny" Goodyear and Pilot Officer J. Burrows of 125 Squadron from Coltishall were patrolling under control from Hopton, a Chain Home Low Station on the Suffolk coast near Great Yarmouth. At 0610 hours *Goodwill 4* was vectored towards three He 111H-22s at a range of 2½ to three miles. After about eight minutes one of the Heinkels broke away to starboard and Goodyear followed. In an attempt to evade the pursuing Mosquito the Heinkel pilot began to climb and then dive, all to no avail. With daylight now on their side, the Mosquito crew visually identified the Heinkel from 1000 feet. Closing fast,

Goodyear opened fire from below and astern. He and his navigator witnessed the resulting flash from the Heinkel's starboard engine. The enemy machine dived from an altitude of 700 feet to 300 feet in a matter of seconds and then climbed up steeply to between 5000 and 6000 feet with the Mosquito close on its tail. At a range of 200 yards Goodyear could see the white glow of an intense fire burning in the engine he had hit. He opened fired again, but within seconds his Mosquito went into a violent uncontrollable spiral as the aircraft flew through the slipstream of the Heinkel, and he only managed to regain control just 200 feet above the icy waters of the North Sea. So violent was the encounter that the "G" force had broken loose a large part of the radar equipment in the nose of his Mosquito. This in turn had rendered the electrical system to his guns useless, putting them all out of commission. It would have been futile for Goodyear and Burrows to continue the pursuit, so they returned to Coltishall and claimed one Heinkel "probably destroyed."

At 0550 hours on 23/24 December Dick Leggett and "Midi" Midlane, back in Norfolk after their stint at Hurn, took off from Coltishall in their NF.XVII, call sign *Goodwill 37*. They knew they would soon find some "trade" over the North Sea. Leggett explains:

> "The British 'Y' Service would get information that V1-carrying Heinkels would be taking off, and we'd be told that at such and such a time they would be in place. No other op was as tidy as this. We looked at our watches and thought, 'My goodness, they'll be here in another few minutes'; and sure enough, right on the button, it would all happen. It was a question of whether you'd be the lucky one because there were lots of us. I looked at my clock and knew that at around 0230 hours there would be several Heinkels in the usual place. The enemy obviously did not know we were going to meet him. Being in a position to stab him in the back in the dark was a nice way to fight a war. One was mentally tuned to this. We felt sorry for our bomber chaps. We in the night fighter force didn't have to drop bombs on women and children. We had to kill Germans who were trying to do things to our women and children with nasty weapons. It was a very clear and clean way to fight. Sure enough, almost on the dot we saw the flash of a V1 being launched. At the same time ground control said they had contact. Tally-ho!
>
> "There might be 12, 13, 14 of these Heinkels, all doing it at once. It was a timed op. Then they'd turn to port. I don't know why but they always did this. Then they would go down very rapidly and head for home. Our job was to lose height quickly, go below 100 feet. and pick up the Heinkel. The Mk.X was a good AI, but there were a lot of sea returns and it depended on the expertise of the navigator. I had a very good one. Sure enough, the Heinkel turned left and at two to three miles we got a contact. It wasn't a good night. There was rain and 'stuff' about. The Germans only came when the weather was bad.' Leggett took off after the Heinkel, using his highly accurate radio altimeter to maintain position and height behind the fleeing German. 'We started to close. It was still dark and there was a lot of cloud. You knew perfectly well that on our straight and level course behind him we would get a tremendous wash from his engines. I felt it. Then for some reason, he started to turn away slightly, as if he had an indication that we were behind him. It foxed us a bit. Eventually, it settled down again. I closed in on him. It was in cloud. Guns and sights were harmonized at about 200 yards but we could not get a visual, although we could feel his slipstream. We dropped away and my navigator picked up contact again. Some people might have lowered their undercarriage at this point, but I didn't like to. I had as much flap as I dared and managed perfectly well. We waited and we waited. Off Den Helder I was getting concerned. We'd followed him for fully 55 minutes. We waited as patiently as one can in this situation and eventually, as the dawn was coming up; I closed in at 300-yardd range. [The exhaust emissions at 300 feet altitude belonged to a Heinkel 111H-22 of 7./KG53 *Legion Kondor* flown by *Unteroffizier* Robert Rosch.] I fired my cannon in his slipstream and had to put on a lot of throttle to prevent a stall. I got a number of strikes on it and that was it. The Heinkel went in very quickly. When we broke away the cloud base was only at 200 feet. It was a beautiful morning." The Heinkel made it back to Holland but crashed on landing at Leck, killing four of the crew.

Of 50 Fi 103s that were air-launched from Heinkel He 111s against Manchester on Christmas Eve 31 crossed the coast, but only one actually exploded in the city. A 68 Squadron NF.XVII, call sign *Ferro 26* and crewed by Flight Sergeant A. Bullus and his navigator, Flying Officer L. W. Edwards, in charge of the AI.X scope, pursued one of the Heinkels under Orby radar control. The Heinkel, which was flown by *Unteroffizier* Herbert Neuber of 7/KG53, was successfully intercepted over the North Sea and a visual sighting was obtained. Bullus fired the first of three two-second bursts of 20mm cannon fire from 200 feet and his shells struck the starboard wing root, fuselage, and port engine. The Heinkel burst into flames, did an uncontrolled climbing turn to port, and peeled off into the sea, where it as seen to be on fire for at least five minutes.

The air-launch Heinkels carried out their last major raid on England on the night of 3/4 January 1945 when 45 *Divers* were launched. RAF night-fighter crews made no claims, but three Heinkels failed to return. Two nights later a Heinkel of 7th *Staffel* KG53 failed to return. A Heinkel of 9th *Staffel* flown by *Hauptmann* Siegfried Jessen—the *Staffel* commander— and his crew was shot down and all killed near Josum airfield by a Mosquito XXX *Intruder* flown by Wing Commander Russ Bannock DFC* RCAF and Flying Officer Bob Bruce DFC of 406 ("Lynx") Squadron RCAF. It was his eighth victory of the war and his second since taking command of the Squadron. On 6 January Warrant Officer A. R. Brooking and Pilot Officer R. D. Finn in a Mosquito of 68 Squadron, who failed to return, claimed the last He 111H-22 to fall to RAF guns. On the night of 12/13 January two Mosquito crews of 68 Squadron made contact with a Heinkel of KG53 but were unable to press home the advantage. The final air-launched flying bomb attack on England took place the following night, 13/14 January, when 25 *Divers* were launched, but only seven got through.

On 3 January Dick Leggett and "Midi" Midlane were sent to the Fighter Interception Development Squadron at Ford to take part in Operation *Vapour*. Leggett recalls:

"We were pleased to learn that that the 'boffins' were planning a possible answer to the menacing Heinkels and their underslung V1 missiles. Immediately on arrival we met other night fighter friends and were quickly ushered into a briefing room to meet the head 'boffin', Mr. E. J. Smith. He then introduced us to the captain and crew of a Coastal Command Wellington, which we had noticed on landing, but had no idea of its significance. The Wellington had been equipped as an airborne GCI station, with Mr Smith as radar controller. The Wellington would fly at 50 feet above the surface of the sea and locate 'bogeys', while we Mosquito hounds, flying at 500 feet above the 'Wimpy' at intervals of a mile, would be directed against the V1-carrying Heinkels.

"After several *Vapour* practice patrols, on 14 January six of us flew to Manston for the first op patrol off the Dutch coast. Our navigators used a 'mother beacon' and the Alto position behind the Wellington at one-mile intervals. The whole 'shooting match' flew a 50-mile patrol north to south, parallel to the Dutch coast. Intelligence had told us that something was going to happen. Mr Smith put us onto an unidentified aircraft, flying west at about 270° at 100 feet. It was an absolute set-up. Within a few minutes 'Midi' obtained a firm contact on his AI.X and took over from Mr Smith. I was ready, excited and thought; 'This will be easy meat.' Speed was synchronized with the target at 120 mph on a course towards Norfolk at a height of 250 feet. With my gun button to 'Fire', we struggled through the severe downwash of slipstream from the target and quickly achieved a visual sighting while closing to about 100 yards. To our utter disappointment, the aircraft was a Warwick! In strong language I announced my frustration to Mr Smith who replied, 'Shoot it down as it must be hostile.' A fierce argument followed as he explained the target was not responding to IFF, so get on with it! We stupidly nudged closer and closer in an attempt to convince ourselves it was an enemy aircraft. We virtually flew in formation with it, reaffirmed there was no V1 missile underslung and that it was a Warwick. I wanted to tell the pilot how lucky he was that I hadn't fired! We were in the wrong position and we missed the Heinkels going out and we missed them coming back! It was the last night they came."

Altogether, about 1200 V1s were air-launched against Britain, although of these only 638 approached the coast. KG53 ceased operations having lost 77 Heinkels, 16 of them claimed by Mosquitoes.

During the remaining months of the war 25, 68, 96, 125, 151, 307, 406 ("Lynx") Squadron RCAF, and 456 Squadrons, Fighter Command, and 141, 239, 515, 169, 157, 85, and 23 Squadrons in 100 Group flew Bomber Support, "*Lure*," and *Intruder* operations to pre-selected airfields on the other side of the "bomb line." Flying Officer Basil McRae, a 25 Squadron NF.XXX pilot, explains:

"On Bomber Support operations, the objective was to protect our bombers from attack by enemy fighters from airfields adjacent to the target area. By timing our arrival some 10 minutes prior to the colored TIs being dropped by the pathfinders and the subsequent arrival of the main bomber force, we would orbit allocated airfields. During the bombing we would continue to orbit the designated airfields, my navigator, Flying Officer Frank Sweet, keeping a watchful eye on the AI.Mk.X radar tube for any activity from below. The time spent over the target area, often without incident, could become rather tedious and I would look for targets of opportunity on the way home. Roads and autobahns showed up well in moonlight and vehicles could he seen quite distinctly from 500 feet.

"Operation *Lure* was designed to intercept enemy fighters should they he following our bombers returning from the target. For this purpose we would join the rear of the stream and by throttling back and lowering a few degrees of flap, we could simulate the bomber's speed. Equipped with rear facing *Monica*, it was my navigator's function to watch for any unidentified aircraft approaching. In the event, it was open throttles, raise flaps, smart 180 degree turn, make contact with our Mk X radar and intercept, or perhaps I should say, investigate'. Sometimes, they turned out to he a crippled Lanc or a Halifax.

"Our final operations were night intruding to strafe pre-selected airfields. Due to the rapid advance of the Allied armies designated airfields for attack had to be 'cleared' just prior to briefing. On 22 April 1945 Frank Sweet and I were disappointed to learn that the airfield allocated had not been 'cleared'. The airfields that had were being visited at hourly intervals, so I sought and got permission to attack Neuburg airfield half an hour later, when, hopefully, the element of surprise would he on our side. We lost Gee en route to the target and as I recall we located the Danube and proceeded to navigate visually below the cloud base of around 1500 feet. We located what appeared robe a marshalling yard with many white wagons bearing the Red Cross. It was rumored that much ammunition was transported this way and having circled the area a couple of times, I was tempted to have a go'! Frank was not in agreement, saying that they might have been legit'. Ar this juncture a break in the cloud allowed bright moonlight which revealed our target airfield, which we had been over flying whilst circling. Many parked aircraft were plainly visible. The instant I pressed the firing button, intense fire was returned from all sides; tracer shells seemed to be everywhere. I managed to silence one gun position, but not before being hit, which caused an almighty shudder throughout the aircraft. It was then time to disengage and head rapidly for cloud cover and a worrying return to base, where, fortunately, the damage to the Mosquito was not very serious, the butts of the cannons having taken most of the impact. This proved to be our last operation of the war.

"Despite the dangers Mosquito intruders faced, nightfighting was the safest part of the war. You were the aggressor."

Chapter 10

The Serrate Squadrons Strike

Bomber Command laid on a raid
To be carried out with 100 Group's aid,
But Bomber Command considered the weather was poor
So Group took a hand at alerting the Ruhr.
They put up a suitably placed Mandrel Screen
Through which, so they hoped, not a thing would be seen.
They sang to the Hun a Serrate serenade
Round the beacons they danced a Perfectos parade.
They intruded up high, they intruded down low
(Just to be beastly they'd put on this show)
The 'Window' force 'Windowed' 100 per cent
And came through the Screen with offensive intent.
The Hun plotted hundreds of heavies around,
But hadn't a hope of control from the ground.
He put up some fighters and led them astray
In a huge mass of blips that faded away.
Our immediate analysis shows in the main
That the poor bloody Hun had been fooled once again.

Wing Commander L. W. Wells

German revenge weapons aimed at southern England had proved such a menace that in June 1944 some *Intruder* Mosquitoes from 100 (Special Duties, Bomber support from May 1944) Group in Norfolk had been detached to West Malling for *anti-Diver* patrols. 100 Group had been formed on 23 November 1943 under the command of Air Commodore (later Air Vice Marshal) E. B. Addison after it became obvious to all that the RAF needed a specialized bomber support force.[223] From stations in Norfolk 100 Group despatched Wellington, Halifax, Fortress, and Liberator aircraft on radio countermeasures (RCM) while its Mosquito squadrons flew day and night intruder operations, which were extended to include loose escort duties for the Main Force. The first unit to move to 100 Group, from 3 Group at Gransden Lodge, was 192 Squadron, which took up residence at Foulsham on 7 December.[224] West Raynham would be the new home for 141 Squadron, which would become the first operational squadron in 100 Group, and the squadron would move to Raynham on 3 December. There, 141 Squadron really got down to conversion from Beaufighter VIs to Mosquitoes. On 6 December, the advance party of 239 Squadron, which had been training at Ayr and Drem for *Serrate* (a device designed to home in on German night-fighter radar transmissions)[225] Bomber Support operations, joined them at West Raynham.[226] In the first week of December 169 Squadron, the third unit equipped with *Serrate*, moved from Ayr to Little Snoring.[227] On 12 December 1473 Flight arrived at Foulsham from Little Snoring, and in April 1944 the Special Duty Radar Development Unit equipped with Mosquitoes arrived to become the Bomber Support Development Unit on 1 May.

141, 239, and 169 Squadrons were destined for an *Intruder* role in 100 Group. *Intruder* aircraft had already proved their worth on bomber support operations. In June 1943 141 Squadron Beaufighter VIfs fitted with AI.IV *Serrate* and *Gee* had been the first unit to be used in this role. In September 141 Squadron converted to the Mosquito NF.II. On 25 November 192 Squadron, equipped with Mosquito B.IV, Halifax, and Wellington X aircraft for the electronic intelligence (Elint) role (monitoring German radio and radar), moved to Foulsham from Feltwell. At West Raynham 141 Squadron, equipped with the Beaufighter VI, arrived on 4 December. On the 10th 239 Squadron's Mosquitoes joined them. Three days later Foulsham and Little Snoring were transferred from 3 Group to 100 (SD) Group. 192 Squadron, together with 169 and 515 Squadrons, were absorbed by the new force. On 3 March 515 Squadron became operational on the Mosquito in 100 Group.[228]

The first 100 Group operation was flown on the night of 16/17 December 1943, when two Beaufighters and two Mosquitoes of 141 Squadron were despatched in support of the "heavies" raiding Berlin. All three *Serrate* squadrons operated for the first time on 20/21 January when 769 aircraft attacked Berlin. At Little Snoring that night Wing Commander Edward John "Jumbo" Gracie DFC, Commanding Officer of 169 Squadron, and his navigator, Flight Lieutenant Wilton W. Todd, climbed aboard the only squadron Mosquito Mk II fit for duty. 239 Squadron also could only muster one Mosquito; Flight Lieutenants Jackson S. Booth DFC and Tommy Carpenter flew the sortie. "What did you get?" they were asked on their return to West Raynham. "Back!" they said. A number of contacts with bogeys were made but no enemy aircraft fell to the guns of the Mosquitoes. Thirty-five bombers, however, were shot down by the German defenses, which operated the *Zahme Sau* tactics to excellent effect.[229] Window seemed to have been rendered counter-productive by the German night-fighter force. On the night of 21/22 January 648 RAF bombers attacked Magdeburg. Twenty year old Flight Sergeant Desmond Byrne Snape RAAF and Flying Officer I. H. Fowler RCAF of 141 Squadron, one of five Mosquito II crews airborne this night (the fifth was from 239 Squadron), tussled with a Ju 88 during their patrol in the Brandenburg area. German night-fighters shot down fifty-seven bombers in the raids on Magdeburg, Berlin, and on flying bomb sites in France. These were the heaviest losses in any night of the war so far. Major Prince zu Sayn Wittgenstein, *Kommodore* of NJG4 and a night-fighter ace with 83 or 84 victories, shot down four or five of the bombers flying a Ju 88G this night and was then shot down and killed by the rear gunner of a Lancaster. *Hauptmann* Meurer, Commanding Officer of I/NJG1, was also killed when his He 219 *Uhu* (Owl) was accidentally rammed by a Bf 110.

On 28/29 January seven Mosquitoes were dispatched from West Raynham,[230] and Flying Officer Harry White DFC and Flying Officer Mike Allen DFC scored their fifth victory of the war.[231] By 1943 they had become known in Bomber Command as "The Old Firm," since they had already been a team for more than two years. Experienced as they were in combat, however, both were barely 20 years of age. Allen picked up AI contacts on an enemy aircraft, which turned out to be a single-engined machine, probably a Bf 109. White dispatched it with a five-second burst of 20mm cannon fire from astern and below. The enemy aircraft burst into flames and exploded, diving through haze. The other success of the night went to Flying Officers N. Munro and A. R. Hurley of 239 Squadron, who destroyed a Bf 110 near Berlin. Theirs was the first Squadron victory using *Serrate*.

On 30/31 January 169 Squadron scored its first victory in 100 Group when Berlin was attacked by a force of 534 aircraft. Two Mosquitoes were put up by 169 Squadron, including *P-Pluto* flown by the "B" Flight Commander, Squadron Leader Joseph Aloysius Hayes "Joe" Cooper and his navigator, Flight Lieutenant Ralph D. Connolly, an Income Tax Inspector from Dulwich, London. Joe Cooper recalls:

> "I had to orbit fifty miles from Berlin on one of the German beacons. We tootled along and just got into position when I picked up a blip in front of me. He was orbiting slowly Turning down the gunsight I could see the shape. There was no moon and it was very, very dark. I got into position, slightly below, and astern, went up to him and gave him the treatment; cannon - a lot of cannon. We were at about 25,000 feet. He was a complete flamer. Actually I gave him a bit more. 'That's for Coventry' I said. But I got in too close. I was mesmerized by it all. Rafe said, 'Look out Joe, you're going to hit the bastard.' I pulled the 'pole' back hard and the result was I stalled and went into a spin. We were not allowed to spin or acrobat the Mosquito because of our long-range belly tanks, which moved the center of gravity of the aircraft. I put on the usual drill: full opposite rudder, stick forward. I'd done this before but never in a Mossie. Went straight into a spin the other way! I went into the spin about five times, heading for the ground all the while. During the spins I could see this 110 out of the corner of my eye; most extraordinary!
>
> "One's thoughts were, what a bloody shame. This is going to be the first Hun the Squadron's got and I won't be there to tell the boys. I wonder who's going to hit the ground first, him or me? What a bloody shame the boys aren't going to know. I told Rafe, 'Bale out. We've had it!' He had an observer-type parachute under his seat. In the spin he couldn't bend down to pick it up! He took his helmet off and put it on again. I said, 'Get out!' Rafe replied, 'If you can get us out of this spin, I could!' I thought, 'I'll try something else.' I centralized the pole and the rudder and eased it out of the dive. At 7000 feet I straightened up. I had not been frightened but boy was I frightened now. Our radar blew up in the spin. I said to Ralph 'You can kneel and look backwards and keep an eye out for the Huns!' We had light flak all the way back to the coast. Approaching Snoring I called up the tower 'Is Squadron Leader Ted Thorne in the tower?' I asked. 'Yes,' they said. I said, 'Tell him he owes me ten bob.' (I had bet Ted ten shillings I would get a Hun before him!) Ted took the camp Tannoy - it was one in the morning - and announced, 'For your information everybody Squadron Leader Cooper is coming into land and he's got the first Hun!' When I landed there were 300 airmen and WAAFs around *P-Pluto!* Most extraordinary! I gave them a little talk and off we went."[232]

The next major raid by RAF Bomber Command took place on 27/28 January when a force of 515 bombers attacked Berlin. Again, losses were high. Thirty-three Lancasters were shot down. No. 141 Squadron dispatched seven *Serrate* Mosquitoes, and 239 and 169 Squadrons sent off three and two Mosquitoes respectively. However, none of the Mosquitoes recorded any successes, mainly because five crews experienced engine failures and had to abort, while two other aircraft suffered AI failures. On 28/29 January seven Mosquitoes were dispatched from West Raynham. One returned early with equipment failures, and 22-year-old Flight Lieutenant Basil "Johnny" Brachi and his navigator, 37-year old Flying Officer Angus P. MacLeod of 239 Squadron, failed to return. During a patrol to Berlin their Mosquito lost its starboard engine over enemy territory and then the port engine started cutting out and finally quit over the North Sea. Crews in 239 and 141 Squadrons conducted an extensive sea search, but the two crewmen were never found. (MacLeod's body was later washed ashore in Holland where he is buried.) Joining the search between 1710 and 2120 hours were Harry White and Mike Allen, who had only just returned from their successful sortie at 0600 hours. Both men had joined 141 Squadron at the same time as Brachi and MacLeod. White and Allen had picked up AI contacts on an enemy aircraft which turned out to be a single-engined machine, probably, a Bf 109. White had dispatched it with a five-second burst of 20mm cannon fire from astern and below. The enemy aircraft burst into flames and exploded, diving through haze. The other success of the night went to Flying Officers Munro and Hurley of 239 Squadron; the first Squadron victory using *Serrate*.

On 30/31 January five Mosquitoes of 141 Squadron were on patrol and one of the crews destroyed a Bf 110. Two aircraft returned early with engine trouble, while Flight Lieutenant John C. N. Forshaw and Pilot Officer Frank Folley discovered to their dismay that the cannons would not fire when Forshaw had a Bf 110 in his sights at a range of 900 feet. Howard Kelsey and Smitty Smith chased six or seven *Serrate* contacts at heights varying from 22,000 to 6000 feet but failed to get close to their prey to open fire. After thirty minutes over the target their AI began to develop a "squint" so they turned for home.

There were no major raids undertaken by Bomber Command during the first two weeks of February 1944, but the *Serrate* squadrons were tasked to support a raid by small forces of Mosquitoes on Berlin, Aachen, and Krefeld on 1/2 February. Four enemy aircraft were shot down in February. Three of them were accredited to crews in 169 and 239 Squadrons, but the first kill that month came on 15/16 February when 891 bombers resumed the attack on Berlin in the biggest raid on the capital so far. Harry White DFC and Mike Allen DFC returned to West Raynham from a patrol to the Big City with a claim for a *Beleuchter* (illuminator) He 177, which was dropping flares in an attempt to reveal targets to the *Wilde Sau* night-fighters. The He 177 spiralled down on fire followed to 12,000 feet by the Mosquito before the Heinkel disappeared in cloud. It was the sixth enemy aircraft destroyed by the White-Allen partnership.[233]

On 20/21 February, when the bomber force went to Stuttgart, Flying Officers E. A. "Tex" Knight and D. P. "Paddy" Doyle of 239 Squadron shot down a Bf 110. On 28 February night-fighter ace and A&AEE test pilot Wing Commander R. Gordon Slade arrived to take command of 169 Squadron. With him came his navigator, Philip Truscott.[234] On 23/24 February a 141 Squadron crew was shot down while supporting the Bomber Command raid on Schweinfurt. On 25/26 February Flying Officers N. Munro and A. R. Hurley, who had scored the first *Serrate* 239 Squadron victory on 28/29 January, crashed in Norfolk on returning from operations. Munro was killed in the crash and Hurley died a few hours later. February had proved a bad month for the three *Serrate* squadrons, and to compound it, seventeen Mosquitoes had returned early with engine failures.

In March 1944 the *Serrate* Mosquito squadrons destroyed six aircraft.[235] Four of the victories went to 141 Squadron crews. On 18/19 March Flying Officer Harry White DFC and Flying Officer Mike Allen DFC destroyed two Ju 88s during a patrol in the Frankfurt area, which was the target for 846 bombers. Flying Officer John Forshaw and Pilot Officer Frank Folley also bagged a Ju 88.[236] On 19 March Harry White and Mike Allen went to 100 Group HQ at Bylaugh Hall to receive congratulations for their double victory from Group Captain Roderick Chisholm, the Senior Air Staff Officer. Chisholm said that they would be sent to 51 OTU at Cranfield on 23 March to give a talk on the Squadron's operations in an attempt to try and gain volunteers for new *Serrate* crews, particularly from among the flying instructors on the completion of their rests.

On 22/23 March, when Bomber Command again dispatched 816 aircraft to Frankfurt, Squadron Leader F. W. Kinchin and Flight Lieutenant D. Sellars of 239 Squadron destroyed a Bf 110.[237] The following night Flight Lieutenant Butler and Flight Sergeant Robertson of 239 Squadron were lost on a support operation for Mosquitoes bombing Dortmund. The night of 24/25 March was one of mixed fortunes. Bomber Command dispatched 811 bombers to the Big City in a finale to the Battle of Berlin; seventy-two bombers failed to return. (The Berlin offensive cost 625 bombers shot down, 2,690 crews killed, and 987 crews made prisoners of war.) To these cold, harsh statistics can be added the loss of the *Serrate* crews who supported them. Flight Lieutenant Armstrong and Flying Officer Mold of 239 Squadron were posted missing, later to be declared PoWs. Flight Lieutenant Howard C. Kelsey DFC* and Flying Officer Edward M. Smith DFC DFM were credited with the destruction of a Fw 190 over Berlin. On 25/26 March the marshalling yards at Aulnoye, in Northern France, were the target for 192 bombers. A 141 Squadron crew—Flying Officer Francois Emile D. Vandenplassche, a Belgian, and his navigator, twenty year old Flying Officer George Mamoutoff, the son of Russians living in London—lost their port engine when it caught fire during a patrol to Aulnoye. Mamoutoff baled out at 1400 feet and the Belgian followed.[238]

On the afternoon of 30 March Mosquito crews in 100 Group were briefed for the part they would play in the raid that night on Nürnburg. Flight Lieutenant "Tim" Woodman of 169 Squadron recalls:

> "Briefing showed the bombers' track going south across France, then turning east to a point north of Nürnburg where the bombers turned again on to their target. They were to leave the target in a southwesterly direction, then out west and north and back to England. We immediately protested that as the bombers entered Germany between Mannheim and Frankfurt they would be passing between two German marker beacons which would be heavily stacked by German night-fighters waiting to pounce. And having established the track of the bombers other night-fighters would be vectored in from the north and up from the Munich area. Only a month earlier I bad shot down a 110 which was orbiting, along with other night-fighters, the south one of these two beacons. We knew from a captured map sent to us by the Resistance the positions of twenty-two of these German night-fighter marker beacons. Our request that the track of the bombers be changed was passed to the SASO, Air Commodore Rory Chisholm DSO DFC at 100 Group, who passed it on to Bomber Command. But they refused to change.
>
> "At the next briefing our escort counter-measures patrol lines were on the map, planned by Group. I saw that my route and patrol was at 20,000 feet from the North Sea down over the Netherlands, then west of the Ruhr and to cross ahead of the bomber stream as it entered Germany, to take up a patrol on its south side at ten miles range. I was to engage any German night-fighters approaching from that direction. We were informed that the main bomber formation would have climbed to 15,000-20,000 feet and that it would he some five miles wide. To me it was utterly incomprehensible: I was being treated like a destroyer escorting a convoy At ten miles range I would only have some two minutes to try and intercept on a dark night before a German night-fighter entered the bomber stream where contact would be lost. I begged Group to let me get ahead of the bombers (fly in low down undetected) and go straight to one of those marker beacons, with another crew flying to the other one, and shoot at least one down and scare off the rest. Again the Group SASO tried with Bomber Command and again our request was turned down. We foresaw a night of heavy casualties, possibly as great as some recent ones, which had reached seventy plus bombers, shot down. The Station Commander Group Captain Rupert Leigh (he had done a couple of *Serrate* operations himself), enjoined us all to press on even if we had radar failure which in the past had been an acceptable excuse for abandoning an operation and returning to base. Even one Mosquito's presence might save a bomber or two.
>
> "I took off and climbed out over the North Sea. It was a dark night; the moon would rise after the raid was over. At 18,000 feet flames and sparks burst out from the inner side of the starboard engine and back across the

wing. This was a disaster. I throttled back the engine, cut my speed almost to stalling, but did not stop the engine. The fire died down and I now had to make a possible fatal decision. The engine instruments were OK. Go on or go back? The golden rule was, never open again an engine, which has been on fire. But I did. I had lost height to 13,000 feet, carefully opened up the throttle and the engine roared away smoothly No sign of fire so I decided to press on. Over the Netherlands my observer, Pat Kemmis DFC, spotted on radar another aircraft coming up behind me. I guessed, rightly, that it was Flying Officer Harry Reed from my squadron who had caught up with me. He was indeed trying to intercept me thinking I was much further ahead. I put the nose down and at full throttle lost him but ran into flak over Aachen, which I had to avoid. Back at 20,000 feet again and expecting shortly to cross ahead of the bomber stream Pat started picking up radar contacts coming from the right. It was the bombers. We had lost time getting there and they were being carried along on a wind which was much stronger than forecast. There was nothing for it but to cross through the stream. This required skilful monitoring of the CR screens by Pat as he could see a dozen or more blips at the same time, whilst I saw the dark shapes of the Lancs and Halifaxes crossing below, ahead and above me. And instead of the bomber stream being five miles wide it was more like fifty. Some had already been shot down and before I reached the far side of the stream they were being shot down on my left.

"On the south side of the stream Pat immediately picked up *Serrate* contacts but before I could intercept these Hun night-fighters they had entered the bomber stream. I went back in among the bombers and told Pat to get me a *Serrate* contact dead ahead. But for the final interception it was necessary to switch over to AI.Mk. IV radar and each time Pat did so he had a dozen or more blips on his screens - bombers plus among them the German night-fighter. Masses of Window were also being tossed not of the bombers, which also jammed our radar. We tried three times but each time came up below a bomber, the rear gunner spotting us the third time, his tracer coming uncomfortably close whilst his pilot did a corkscrew. It was hopeless; we were doing more harm than good. Ahead bombers were being shot down one after another, some going all the way down in flames, some blowing up in the air, the rest blowing up as they hit the ground. I counted forty-four shot down on this leg to Nürnburg. What was happening behind I could only guess.

"I flew on to Nürnburg and saw that the bombing had been widespread, a number of fires in the city, with a separate area where bombs and incendiaries had obviously landed in the countryside. I prowled around until the last of the bombers had gone but got no more *Serrate* contacts. Then I saw the odd bomber still being shot down to the southwest as they were making their way home. I flew down that way towards Stuttgart, then ahead and low down I saw a bomber on fire. I went down to his height, 8000 feet and it was a Halifax with its rear turret on fire. I kept formation with him but far enough away for the crew not to see me until the fire died down and went out. Silently wishing the crew the best of luck (they did in fact make it back) I turned and went back to Nürnburg. I was inwardly raging at the incompetence of the top brass at Bomber Command.

"Back at 20,000 feet again I prowled over the city again hoping the odd German might still be around. Pat picked up a contact on radar I intercepted it but it was another Mosquito. I called them up and told them I was on their tail but got no reply Later I discovered there were two other Mosquitoes over Nürnburg at that time: Flying Officer Mellows from my own Squadron and a Mosquito from 192 Squadron, also from 100 Group.[239]

"It was time to start the long haul back with the moon already up and the clouds closing in, Near Frankfurt my starboard engine caught fire again and this time I had to shut it down and feather the prop. We could maintain a height of 7500 feet, just above the clouds, with Pat keeping a lookout to the rear for anyone on our tail. But all the Huns had landed, sated with kills. Back at base they discovered that the engine exhaust gasket had been blown doing a lot of damage from the intense heat inside the cowling. But for the delay of the earlier fire I am sure I would have ignored orders, got ahead of the bombers and tackled those German night-fighters on one of those beacons. For the next couple of raids on Germany I was invited to Group by Air Commodore Rory Chisholm DSO DFC to help plan *Serrate* operations, and on my future operations I was permitted to freelance."[240]

In April 1944 the Bomber Support Development Unit (BSDU) was formed at Foulsham for trials and development work on radar and various apparatus carried by aircraft of 100 Group. The BSDU operated a mixture of aircraft, including the Beaufighter, Stirling, Halifax, and Mosquito. On 11/12 April Squadron Leader Nevil Everard Reeves DFC* and Warrant Officer A. A. O'Leary DFC* DFM of 239 Squadron destroyed a Do 217. It was Reeves' and O'Leary's tenth victory of the war, the previous nine having been shot down in the Mediterranean with 89 Squadron. On 18/19 April Harry White (promoted Flight Lieutenant on 14 April) and Mike Allen of 141 Squadron gave chase during a *Serrate* patrol to Swinemunde and the western Baltic, but their intended victim escaped. Their ninth kill would have to wait just a little longer. Altogether eighteen Mosquitoes operated from West Raynham this night, including ten from 141 Squadron, its best effort so far. On 20/21 April, when the Main Force went to Cologne, Harry White and Mike Allen were one of eight 141 Squadron Mosquitoes dispatched to patrol over France. (Five B-17s of 214 Squadron, including one captained by the Commanding Officer, Wing Commander McGlinn, flew their first jamming operation this night. 214 Squadron's role was to jam enemy R/T communication between the *Freya* radar and the German night-fighters. Among other counter measures, they also jammed the *FuG 216 Neptun* tail warning system.) Harry White wrote:

> "We took off and set course over base at 6000 feet at 2252 hours and continued uneventfully on course until 2350 hours when our first *Serrate* contact was obtained to starboard and below, crossing starboard to port. We gave chase going down hill and obtained an AI contact at 12,000 feet range, which was found to he jinking considerably. Height was decreased to 12.000 feet and range closed to 1500 feet when *Senate* and AI contacts faded. We turned starboard and back to port hoping to regain contact - no joy. Enemy aircraft switched off *Serrate* as we broke away. Throughout this attempted interception our elevation was

behaving most erratically and it is believed that the enemy aircraft was directly below us at 1500 feet when contact faded, the usual reason for fading blips.

"The gyro having spun during the interception, I had little idea of where this interception had taken me, so set course towards the estimated position of Paris which I hoped shortly to see illuminated and fix my position. At 0020 hours various contacts were obtained on the bomber stream leaving the Paris area. Window was much in evidence. At 0025 hours an AI contact at 15,000 feet to port and below was obtained a few miles west of stream and chased. We decreased height and followed contact through gentle port and starboard orbits reducing height to 12,000 feet and eventually closing range to 600 feet where I obtained a visual on four blue-white exhausts, later positively identified at 300 feet as a Ju 88. For five minutes I followed enemy aircraft patiently through gentle port and starboard orbits at 200 indicated air speed, eventually opening fire, still turning, at 500 feet with a one-second burst allowing 5° deflection; no results. Enemy aircraft, completely clueless, continued to orbit. Apparently clueless also, I tried again with a one-second burst. Again no results. A third burst was fired as enemy aircraft peeled off to starboard and disappeared from view I have no idea why I continually missed enemy aircraft and can only attribute it to the dot dimmed out from the gunsight and gremlin interference.

"At 0100 hours, being in the proximity of the bomber stream, second attack on Paris, we obtained another *Serrate* contact starboard and below which we followed for three minutes. This *Serrate* momentarily faded and enemy aircraft was presumed to be orbiting, at least turning. This was confirmed within a few seconds by a head-on AI contact at 15,000 feet range well below. We turned behind and closed rapidly to 600 feet, and there obtained a visual on four quite bright blue exhausts, identified from 300 feet as a Do 217 now flying at 10,000 feet. Enemy aircraft was now turning very gently to port and was followed for five minutes not wishing to repeat above. At 450 feet only exhausts could be seen, though these, unlike the Ju 88, quite clearly. Not wishing to approach closer I opened fire at this range with a two-second burst and was gratified to see enemy aircraft exploded with a blinding flash and disintegrate. Several pieces were flung back at us and I instinctively ducked as they splattered over the windscreen and fuselage. Apart from two broken Perspex panels, which were causing more noise than worry, we appeared to be OK but visions of damaged radiators caused some concern for the first minutes. We had no trouble in that respect and returned uneventfully to base."[241]

The Mosquitoes had done their work well. Only eight bombers were lost on the attacks on the French railway yards. The other confirmed victory this night went to Flight Lieutenant Gordon D. Cremer and Flying Officer R. W. "Dick" O'Farrell of 169 Squadron, who flew a *Serrate* patrol in support of the bombers targeting Köln. Their report was as follows:

"Airborne at 0110 hours and except for intense enemy activity over this country first patrol point was reached uneventfully, both searchlight and flak activity were non-existent. After patrolling a beacon for ten minutes without incident we headed towards cologne along a line from the NW which we did for five minutes afterwards turning starboard to a westerly course. Shortly after making this turn at approximately 0234 hours obtained an AI contact at maximum range…we closed to 9000 feet astern of (enemy) aircraft. He took evasive action consisting of climbing and diving turns to port and starboard. However with good AI interception and full throttle the range was reduced rapidly and seven minutes after original contact a visual was obtained ahead and above. Despite navigator's early warning to throttle back I was approaching much too fast. I saw the aircraft silhouetted slightly above against cirrus cloud and instantly recognized it as a Me 110 by its tail fins. To avoid overshooting I pulled up to port losing visual momentarily and then turned starboard and regained visual. As the (enemy) aircraft was diving away to starboard I closed astern and gave a short burst at about 100 to fifty yards range from slightly above. Strikes were seen instantaneously inboard of the port engine followed by a large flash of flame which clearly illuminated the cockpit, fuselage and tailplane. We then overshot, but in passing both my observer and I were easily able to recognize the enemy aircraft as a Me 110 in the glare of the flames. I turned first to port and then to starboard and my next visual of the aircraft was its vertical descent in flames. It disappeared through the clouds whose tips were at 10,000 feet and a few seconds later there was the reflection of an explosion, followed by a red glow on the clouds. No return fire experienced. When last seen the cockpit was enveloped in flames as the enemy aircraft dived vertically into cloud and this fact, coupled with the explosions and red glow seen immediately after this through cloud is taken as the basis for the claim of one Me 110 DESTROYED." [Cremer fired just forty rounds of 20mm ammunition to shoot down the enemy aircraft.]

On 22/23 April, Flight Lieutenant Tim Woodman and Flying Officer Patrick Kemmis of 169 Squadron were aloft again as the bombers went to Düsseldorf. Tim Woodman recalls:

"The Y-Service had informed us that when the bombers were approaching targets in northern Germany and the Ruhr, night-fighter squadrons in the Munich area were being directed to the suspected target area. On this night, therefore, I flew from the Ruhr towards Munich as the bombers approached the Ruhr We picked up a *Serrate* contact coming towards us and when it was within AI range turned port and came up underneath him. He had not spotted us on his radar. It was a 110 with a small white light on his tail. And there were four other aircraft flying in formation with him, two to port and two to starboard. I switched on the gunsight but it did not light up. I changed the bulb and it still did not work, so I banged the sight with my gloved fist and the socket and bulb fell out on its lead, blinding me with its brilliant white light as it lit up. I switched off and fired a short burst at the 110 tail light but with no strikes.

"We were fast approaching the Ruhr searchlight zone so I fired a longer burst, stirring the stick as I did so to spread the shells. There were a number of strikes and the 110 seemed to have blown up. Black sooty oil covered my windscreen and when we got back we found the nose and starboard wing damaged. Pat, on radar, said he could see large pieces going down to the ground. But the Ruhr searchlights were after me and I did not want them to recognize me as a Mosquito. The Y-Service came to my aid. I reached back and pressed the trigger of a fixed Verey pistol. Red and green Very lights spread across the night sky. The searchlight crews counted them and doused their searchlights. I had fired off the German 'colors of the day', the Y-Service supplying us with this information. It was the only time I did so. Immediately after the war I was sent to Germany and Denmark to test fly their aircraft and to cheek up on their radar and other electronic devices. This particular Me 110 I was told was probably a *Nachtjägd* night-fighter escorting Me 109 *Wilde Sau* fighters to the bombers' target area. Seeing their escort aircraft shot down they would all have dived down to ground level, not knowing what was behind them. Maybe this is what my observer saw on radar."[242]

On 23/24 April, during a *Serrate* patrol to the Baltic, Flight Lieutenant Graham J. Rice and Pilot Officer Ron Mallett of 141 Squadron shot down a Fw 190 employing *Zahme Sau* tactics against RAF bombers carrying out mine laying in the Baltic. It was Rice's second victory in the Squadron. A few nights later, on 26/27 April, when Bomber Command attacked Essen, Flying Officers William Ranson Breithaupt RCAF and J. A. Kennedy of 239 Squadron crew shot down a Bf 110 in the Essen area. It was the first of their five victories. Breithaupt had joined the RCAF in August 1941 and was finally off the mark after having no victories flying with 488 Squadron RNZAF and 409 "Nighthawk" Squadron RCAF. One of 141 Squadron's ace night-fighting crews was lost when Squadron Leader John Forshaw, "A" Flight Commanding Officer, and his navigator, Pilot Officer Frank Folley, failed to return.[243] On the night of 27/28 April, a Mosquito B.IV of 192 Squadron had just touched down at Foulsham when a returning Halifax landed on top of it. Fortunately, none of the crews suffered injury. On 19/20 April German intruders bombed the station and put it out of action.

On 8/9 May the largest operation of the night was an attack by 123 aircraft on rail yards at Haine-St-Pierre, which cost six Halifaxes and three Lancasters.[244] One of the bombers that failed to return was a 405 "Vancouver" Squadron RCAF Lancaster flown by Flight Lieutenant Chase.[245] From their Mosquito Flight Lieutenant Tim Woodman and Pat Kemmis of 169 Squadron, supporting the operation, could clearly see the bombers, as many as ten at a time, but no sign of German night-fighters. He and Kemmis "sniffed around" for 109s and 190s over the target area but they saw none. Woodman then saw three Halifaxes "weaving like dingbats" up at 6000 feet. Below the leading bomber he and Kemmis could see a twin-engined aircraft climbing up to attack. It was a Bf 110 of I./NJG4 flown by *Leutnant* Wolfgang Martstaller and his radar-operator/air gunner, who had taken off from Florennes at 0300 hours. They had just shot Chase's Lancaster down[246] and were after another victim. Martstaller, however, was unable to pick off another of the bombers because he was attacked immediately by Woodman and Kemmis. The Mosquito pilot fired a two-second-burst and Martstaller dived into the darkness, Kemmis following him on *Serrate*. Martstaller soared up in a steep climb and Woodman fired from 800 yards. This time he opted out and took the Mosquito on a chase across the French countryside at treetop height. Though they could not see him as he flew away from the moon they easily followed him on *Serrate*. Martstaller went into a steep dive to almost zero feet ("at night!"), but still he could not escape the Mosquito's attention. The German made the mistake of flying towards the moon and Woodman saw the moonlight glint off his wings. He fired and got some strikes on his fuselage and wings as he flew across a wide-open space, which looked like an aerodrome. Martstaller went into a steep turn and, firing 50 yards ahead of him to allow for deflection, Woodman hit him again. White smoke poured from the 110's port engine, and closing to 150 yards Woodman gave him another two second burst and hit him again. Martstaller was fortunate to spot a field in which to belly-land. He and his *Bordfunker* were slightly injured from shrapnel. Next day they discovered that a large explosion they had seen two miles away was "their" *Viermot* "with seven crewmembers burned to death." Martstaller ended his letter, "*We were so happy!*"[247]

At 0010 on 10/11 May Flying Officer Vivian Bridges DFC and Flight Sergeant Donald G. "Spider" Webb DFM of 239 Squadron attacked another Bf 110 of I./NJG4 near Courtrai, setting one engine on fire.[248] It crashed at Ellezelles, Belgium. *Oberleutnant* Heinrich Schulenberg, pilot, and *Oberfeldwebel* Hermann Meyer, *bordfunker*, baled out near Flobeq. Meyer recalled: "We were shot down with one engine on fire. We could save ourselves by baling out, and came down near Flobeg. I was wounded on the skull and was badly concussed. I spent three weeks in hospital at Brussels and then had four weeks leave at home."

On 11/12 May 429 bombers of the Main Force made attacks on Bourg-Leopold, Hasselt, and Louvain in Belgium. Harry White and Mike Allen reached double figures by bringing down a Ju 88 a few miles north of Amiens, while Belgian pilot 44-year old Flight Lieutenant Lucien J. G. Le Boutte and his navigator/radio operator, Flying Officer H. Parrott, destroyed a Ju 88 thirty miles southwest of Brussels.[249] Their victim was a 6./NJG2 machine flown by Wilhelm Simonsohn, who had taken off from Köln-Wahn, a satellite field to the main base at Köln-Butzweilerhof. Simonsohn recalls:

"We started around 2200 in Raum Brussels and flew at a height of 6500 meters (20,000 feet) towards the Channel coast. At times, we saw flak shells exploding. However, compared to the large attacks on the German cities and the huge fires there, this was a quiet area. We were about 1½ hours in the air and now patrolled at a height of around 6000 meters (18,000 feet). There were some clouds above us when suddenly a chain of tracer bullets struck our port engine, coming in from the left side. I immediately did a steep dive, hoping that the enemy would break off his attack. The flames from the engine blinded our eyes, which were used to the darkness. I yelled through my microphone at my throat, "Bale Out!" Franz [Unteroffizier Franz Holzer, flight engineer] kneeled at the escape hatch, pulled the red handle and flew out of the plane together with the hatch. Günther [Unteroffizier Günther Gottwick, wireless operator-air gunner] who was sitting with his back towards me, dived towards the hatch and also disappeared. Meanwhile, I loosened my straps, but our aircraft was in a high-speed dive by now. I tried to pull the stick towards me in an effort to reduce the speed. I think that during this maneuver the left wing broke off, probably as a result from the attack. The aircraft, or what was left of it, was out of control.

"I broke through the cockpit canopy and catapulted myself into the night air. I waited for about five seconds before I pulled the ripcord, then I pulled (I did that so hard that I had the ripcord in my hand!) and there followed a huge jolt. I will never forget that feeling, while I was hanging under that chute and listening to the air flowing through the silk. Far away from me, I saw burning pieces of my aircraft falling towards the earth. Below me in the light of a white signal flare, I saw another parachute. I pulled my own signal pistol to respond, but it fell out of my hand, which had become stiff in the descent. The landing was without any problem. I landed in the yard of a farm near Mechlen, north east of Brussels. My chute fell down - there was no wind - and I heard the raid sirens wailing. Next morning I met up with my crew. We were together again, slightly shocked, but happy and we were then transported to Brussels."[250]

Although they carried out all the normal tasks of *Intruders*, 23 and 515 Squadrons also performed any odd task dreamed up by 100 Group HQ, the Station Commander, Squadron Commanders, or even, on occasion, the crews themselves. All were likely to form a part of the curriculum. The *Intruder* crews of 23 and 515 Squadrons were excellent pupils. On 12/13 May 515 Squadron carried out anti-flak patrols on the Kiel Canal in support of twenty-two mine laying Mosquito aircraft of 8 Group by drawing fire from the gun emplacements to themselves and away from the mine-layers. The support given by the squadron has been classified as one of the most important mine-laying operations of the war. Ten Mosquito crews in 515 patrolled the heavily defended canal area. By drawing the fire away from the mine-layers or strafing the gun positions from very close range they silenced the opposition and enabled the mining of one of Germany's most important waterways to be achieved with the loss of just one 8 Group Mosquito.

Viv Bridges DFC and "Spider" Webb DFM added another victory on 12/13 May when 239 Squadron dispatched *Serrate* patrols to Belgium in support of the bombers raiding Hasselt and Louvain again.[251] Also, Flying Officers Bill Breithaupt and J. A. Kennedy DFM shot down a Bf 110 in the Hasselt-Louvain area. On 15/16 May Pilot Officers Wilfred Handel "Andy" Miller and F. C. "Freddie" Bone of 169 Squadron destroyed two Ju 88s and a Bf 110 near Kiel when Mosquitoes of 8 Group mined the Canal. This brought the Welsh pilot and the 38-year-old Birkenhead policeman's score to five enemy aircraft destroyed while in 100 Group[252] and eight all told. Warrant Officer Les Turner and Flight Sergeant Frank Francis, who had just joined 169 Squadron, had been scheduled for their *Freshman* trip that same night, but as Turner recalls:

"It was thought that the penetration was too deep for an inexperienced crew. The crew that replaced us (Miller and Bone) had a field day that night - two Ju 88s and a Bf 110 - an unbroken Squadron record). For the whole of 1943 I had instructed on Blenheims at Grantham. At the end of 1943 I returned to 51 OTU (having gained my first experience of radar-controlled night interception flying on Blenheims and Havocs there in the summer of 1942), this time on Beauforts and Beaufighters (which brought me to April 1944 and to 169 Squadron and Mosquitoes. I found it to be a Rolls-Royce of an aeroplane, easy to fly, forgiving on mistakes and, at that time, a joy because of its high power-to-weight ratio. I had never enjoyed flying more although, until then, I thought the best was a Beaufighter. Seated centrally between those two great radial engines gave a sense of power, which was to be experienced to be believed! At OTU I had crewed up with a radar-navigator Frank Francis and it was with him that I did my first tour of thirty-five trips on Bomber Support Duties. Although perhaps we had little in common on the ground, he was an excellent Radar Screen 'Reader' and our successes were in no small part due to his expertise. 169 Squadron was equipped with rather aging Mosquito II with forward and rearward-looking radar (AI.Mk.IV) and armed with four 20mm Hispano-Suiza cannon. Serviceability was a continuing problem until at the end of June 1944 we got Mosquito VIs. As well as radar we also had *Serrate*. This was a homing device, which was supposed to lock on to German night-fighter radar transmissions. It could not give range or altitude, merely direction, and while it worked after a fashion in practice (we did a two-week course on Beaufighters before going to the squadron) one instance where we got *Serrate* indication, proved abortive.

"After about a fortnight's practice both day and night we set out on our *Freshman* op on 19 May. The '*Freshman*' was to Dieppe and Amiens and was totally uneventful over enemy over enemy territory but I frightened the life out of myself as we were climbing over southern England to our patrol. There were a number of 'cu-nimbs' - storm clouds - around us and as we reached 12,000 feet there was an enormous flash of lightning away to starboard. At that moment, the Auto-gear change of the supercharger operated with its usual 'thump'. Such was the state of my nerves, I was sure that we had been struck by lightning until rational reason returned a few seconds later!"

Two more Bf 110s were shot down on 22/23 May.[253] Two nights later, Bill Breithaupt and J. A. Kennedy DFM added a Ju 88 to their score and damaged a Bf 109 fifteen miles ESE of Bonn and Northwest of Aachen respectively. Meanwhile, in the Aachen area Hughes and Perks and Flight Lieutenant Dennis John Raby DFC and Flight Sergeant S. J. "Jimmy" Flint DFM destroyed two more Bf 110G-4s.[254] On 27/28 May 239 Squadron sent up eight Mosquitoes on Bomber Support.[255] Meanwhile, Flight Lieutenants Harry White DFC,* now OC Station Flight, and Mike Allen DFC* were one of seven Mosquito crews in 141 Squadron that supported the Main Force raids on Aachen and Bourg-Leopold. At 0235 hours, a little to the west of Aachen, Allen obtained two AI contacts at 14,000 feet and 12,000 feet, crossing right to left. At a range of 8000 feet the two blips merged into one and Allen remarked to White: "A bomber's about to be shot down in front of us at any minute." "Still crossing," White wrote;

"We turned to port in behind this contact and at 1200 feet, obtained a visual on two white exhausts. We had not increased speed as range was closing quite rapidly. But as we assumed the line astern position, the exhausts faded from sight and range was increased to 8000 feet before, at full throttle, we were once more able to decrease the range slowly to 1200 feet again, obtaining a visual on two white exhausts. We closed to 600 feet where I was able to identify this target as a Me 109. I closed further to 300 feet and opened fire with a two-second burst from 15° below. It exploded with a colossal flash, which completely blinded me for about a minute and a half. I asked Mike to read my instruments for me but his attention was at that moment elsewhere. The flash had attracted his attention from his box and he looked out in time to see a second Me 109 slip slowly by under the starboard wing. With his head now well in the box, Mike commenced reading off the range as this 109 emerged from minimum range behind. But even the best navigator cannot carry out an interception with the help of a blind pilot and the range had increased to 6000 feet astern before I could even see my instruments. We turned hard port but contact went out of range at 14,000 feet."[256]

A 515 Squadron Mosquito flown by Flying Officers David Kay Foster and twenty-year old Robert Stanley Ling, which took off from Little Snoring at 0155 hours and was detailed to patrol Leeuwarden, failed to return. They were shot down by airfield defense flak and crashed into a hangar on the airfield. Both are buried in Leeuwarden Northern General Cemetery. Flying Officer R. K. Bailey and his navigator, Flying Officer J. F. M. White, also failed to return, as Bailey recounts:

"Intelligence had declared Leeuwarden to be the main reaction base of the German night fighter force for operations that night. We were detailed to arrive at Leeuwarden when the German fighters would be reacting to the radar indication of the approach of the main force of bombers (we crossed the North Sea at sea level to avoid detection). The plan of operations worked for no sooner had we reached the Leeuwarden area than the navigator called '*Serrate contact*'. We followed this target in a climbing orbit to 11,000 feet where in conditions of high haze and resultant poor visibility I sighted a Me 110 directly ahead and at very close range. Two bursts from the four 20mm cannon resulted in an explosion and showers of debris into which we flew. The navigator called out another *Serrate* contact, which I had to ignore being engaged in feathering the propeller of the starboard engine, which had overheated and stopped. Assessing the situation the navigator said he would give a course for our base in Norfolk. I asked him instead for a course to Calais and thence to Manston, Kent, to avoid a North Sea crossing in a damaged aircraft, the extent of which was unknown. Ten minutes later the port engine failed and I ordered bale out. Within seconds the navigator was gone and I made to follow diving headfirst across the cockpit to the escape hatch. I had trimmed the rudder for asymmetric flying when the starboard engine failed but I omitted to neutralize trim when the port engine failed. The result was a steep spiral dive. Meanwhile I was trapped having caught the top section of the hatch. I was head and shoulders out in the slipstream with my legs and torso in the aircraft. I was almost reconciled to this situation when a stupid thought crossed my mind that when the aircraft struck the ground I would be sheared in two! This possibility brought about a frenzied new effort. Suddenly I was free from the whistling slipstream and falling in space. I pulled the ripcord and the parachute opened; I said a prayer of thanks. Some seconds later I made contact heavily with the ground."[257]

In all, 239 Squadron destroyed ten aircraft during May and now led the three *Serrate* Mosquito squadrons with nineteen victories; 141 Squadron had thirteen and 169 Squadron at Little Snoring had twelve. Replacements arrived at West Raynham during May-June. Two of them, Warrant Officer A. L. Potter and his navigator, Flight Sergeant R. E. Gray, had only just joined 141 Squadron when they were killed on a training flight on 24 May when their Mosquito crashed at North Farm, Clenchwarton, near King's Lynn. In April-May 1944 three new Mosquito night-fighting squadrons had joined 100 Group. NF.XIIs and XVIIs of 85 Squadron and NF.XIXs of 157 Squadron flew in to the recently completed base at Swannington, while 23 Squadron arrived from the Mediterranean to operate from Little Snoring. The previous incumbents, 169 Squadron and 1692 Flight, moved to Great Massingham. Wing Commander John Cunningham had commanded 85 Squadron, and 157 had been the first to be equipped with the Mosquito. Now, 85 and 157 Mosquitoes were equipped with the first AI.X radar sets.

On 30/31 May 239 Squadron at West Raynham dispatched ten Mosquitoes on *Serrate* sorties. Bridges and Webb, and Flight Lieutenants Denis Welfare and David B. "Taffy" Bellis shot down a Bf 110 apiece. Bellis recalls:

"It was in January 1944 that I first heard of 100 Group. I was stationed at TRU Defford, nr Worcester at the time and was on "rest" after completing a tour of ops at Malta with Denis Welfare. Defford was basically a research station at which new airborne electronic equipment was being tested and life was pleasant, but rather boring. I flew about ten hours a month and there was plenty of time for bridge and sampling the beer and food at the local pubs, especially the 'White Lion' at Upton-on-Severn. By the end of 1943 I longed for an operational squadron again, for the camaraderie that went with it and for the addictive excitement of flying over enemy territory. Thus it was with relief that I was told in January that my posting had arrived. The signal from the Air Ministry read something like, "You are posted to 100 Group and you will report to O/C 239 Squadron at West Raynham as soon as possible". I had never heard of 100 Group before; nor had other aircrew at Defford. We all thought there was a mistake; there could not be 100 groups in the RAF! "Jumbo" Harkness, one of the flight commanders at Defford, said that 239 was a Special Duties Squadron and I had visions of flying VIPs or even dropping agents over occupied Europe.

"Denis Welfare had received the same posting and we arrived at West Raynham, where we soon found what 100 Group was about. By the autumn of 1943, a large part of the Luftwaffe had been concentrated over Western Europe and its night fighters had developed tactics and electronic equipment that were causing serious losses to RAF bombers on their night operations over Germany. Consequently, 100 Group was formed as a matter of urgency to counteract the Luftwaffe night fighters by jamming their ground control, organizing spoof raids and by attacking the night fighters at their bases and in the air.

"When we arrived at West Raynham, 239 Squadron, which was previously on low level reconnaissance, was being reformed and re-equipped with Mosquito IVs for offensive night fighting. Like other crews joining 239 at the time, Denis and I has no experience of offensive night fighting. Our first squadron in 1942 was 141 at Tangmere and Acklington, flying Beaufighters on defensive night flying duties. This was followed by a tour with 272 Squadron in Malta, also flying Beaufighters, but this time on daylight operations against German and Italian supply lines between Italy and North Africa.

Consequently, Denis and I spent the first few weeks at West Raynham on familiarization courses on Mosquitoes and the specialized electronic equipment that they were fitted with, i.e. AI (Airborne Interceptor), *Serrate*, and *Gee* navigational aid.

"We had some experience of the AI.Mk.IV since our days on 141 Squadron. This airborne radar enabled us to pick up an "echo" from another aircraft and to home accurately on to it. The range of this radar was equal to our altitude - the echoes from the ground below "drowned" out everything else further away. Thus, successful defensive night fighting depended on ground control guiding us to within, say, 10,000 feet of an intruder. There was, of course, no such ground control to assist a Mosquito night fighter over Germany and the chances of a crew picking up a German fighter on AI was negligible. This is where *Serrate* came in. A radio receiver in the Mossie picked up *Liechtenstein* radar transmissions from a German night fighter and enabled the Mossie to home in on it - usually a Me 110 or a Ju 88 - until it came into AI range. The *Serrate* receiver had two screens - one giving the vertical and the other giving the horizontal direction of the source of the radar transmission. The Mosquito would home onto the transmitting aircraft until it came within AI range, when the *Serrate* was switched off. *Gee* was also new to me. It made navigation easy; in fact, the old-fashioned skills that I used over the sea and deserts of North Africa on my previous operational tour were now sadly obsolete.

"Ground and air exercises followed thick and fast during February and we were operational by the middle of March. Operations were of two categories. The first was to patrol known German night fighter beacons. These were locations where German night fighters were held in readiness until their Ground Control decided where the main bomber stream was going. Here we used AI alone and success obviously depended on our navigation being correct, on the Luftwaffe using a particular beacon on a given night and on our luck - the sky is a big place and 10,000 feet range for our AI was not much. The second category of operation was to patrol in the vicinity of the bomber stream, using both AI and *Serrate*. Success was a matter of luck - a German fighter using his own radar at the right time and place. Our first op was on 19 March, when we patrolled Holland and France with no contacts. Similarly no luck with further patrols during the following weeks. Success came at last on the night of 31 May when we picked up a *Serrate* transmission north of Paris. Our first priority was to make certain that the transmission did not come from a fighter homing on us from behind! We then maneuvered our Mossie to get behind the transmitting aircraft. To our dismay, it switched off its radar before we were in AI range. However, we kept on the same course and picked up an AI contact a minute or so later and converted this to a visual and the shooting down of a Me 110."

Welfare and Bellis and 239 Squadron enjoyed more success on 5/6 June, the eve of *D-Day*, when twenty-one *Serrate* Mosquitoes were dispatched to northern France.[258] One of the dozen Mosquitoes dispatched by 141 Squadron (two returning early) was crewed by Wing Commander Winnie Winn, the new Commanding Officer, and R. A. W. Scott. Ten 515 Squadron Mosquitoes on *Ranger* patrols patrolled and bombed enemy airfields in France and strafed road, rail, and canal traffic. Two of 515 Squadron's FB.VIs were shot down. Squadron Leader Shaw and his navigator crashed near Dusen, and Squadron Leader Butterfield and his navigator were lost off Dieppe. The *Luftwaffe* put up just fifty-nine fighters to intercept the invasion forces, but only one claim was submitted by a *Nachtjager* pilot. *Hauptmann* Strüning of 2./NJG1 flying a He 219 Owl claimed it. *Hauptmann* Eberspächer, a fighter-bomber pilot flying a Fw 190G-3 of III./KG51, claimed three more victories over Normandy.

That same night the Mk.X radar-equipped NF.XVIIs of 85 Squadron and 157 Squadron's NF.XIXs at Swannington officially began operations when sixteen sorties were flown.[259] Twelve Mosquitoes in 85 Squadron operated over the Normandy beachhead, while four in 157 Squadron patrolled night-fighter airfields at Deelen, Soesterberg, Eindhoven, and Gilze Rijen in Holland. "On 5 June" recalls Flying Officer Robert O. "Bob" Symon of 85 Squadron:

> "Wing Commander Michael Miller and myself were transferred to Colerne, arriving at one pm. There was quite an uproar when nobody was allowed to leave the airfield, no 'phone calls to wives to say they would not be home for dinner. We flew patrols seventy-five miles inland over the beachhead. We had four Mossies making a line covering the territory on the British and Canadian landings. Michael and I were the first on patrol, Pavilly-Bernay. This was the beginning of an invasion and there was nothing in our part of the sky. One searchlight groped around for less than a minute and then went out. The real sight was on our way back to Colerne after our relief had taken over. On the return to base looking north over the water we could see for miles the tugs and gliders making their way over the Channel: a fabulous sight."

On 8/9 June West Raynham was the scene of mixed emotions. Flying Officer A. C. Gallacher DFC and Warrant Officer G. McLean DFC in 141 Squadron told of the destruction of an unidentified enemy aircraft over Northern France after they had chased it into a flak barrage at Rennes, where it was brought down by a single burst. A popular Free French crew, Flight Lieutenant D'Hautecourt and his navigator, Pilot Officer C. E. Kocher, returned from their seventh operation, patrolling over their homeland, on one engine and died shortly after swinging off the runway and crashing into two fighter aircraft. Both Frenchmen had only been with the Squadron since February.

That same night Warrant Officer Les Turner and Flight Sergeant Frank Francis flew their fourth trip, which Tuner said:

> "...made up for the lack of incident on their previous two outings. While somewhat south of Cherbourg - this was again a Beachhead area operation - I noticed that the glycol coolant temperature was rising 'off the clock'. I assumed the worst - a pump failure, possible seizure and maybe fire - and feathered the engine. We set a rough course for UK - 'steer North and you are bound to hit something' - and when we were with radio range of Tangmere got them to give us a course. We then settled down to what turned out to be one hour fifty minutes of single-engined flying at the recommended 170 mph (IAS) at 12,000 feet. We had picked what turned out to be one of the worst nights of the year, from the point of view of weather. In fact one of the crews of a neighbouring squadron baled out when they were unable to get in and

were nearly out of fuel. Tangmere kept hold of us all the way. We transmitted for radio fixes every few minutes sand eventually I was instructed to commence a controlled descent of say 300 feet a minute until instructed further. I had a marked reluctance to lose height with only one engine and in cloud, and when we reached, I believe, 1400 feet, I asked urgently if further descent was safe. I was assured that it was and we broke cloud at 600 feet over Dante's Inferno - actually the paraffin flares of FIDO at Hartford Bridge. We were given permission to land immediately and executed a very tight circuit to hold the (literally) flarepath in view. We had to lower the undercarriage by pump and this took so long that we didn't have tome to get the flaps down! We touched down reasonably well but at 150 mph. Another pilot in the tower said later that it looked like a take-off! When, after about two-thirds of the runway had gone past, the tail-wheel touched down. I locked the brakes but the runway ended and we careered on what seemed like ploughed land for another 100 yards or so when we hit a drainage ditch, slewed to port a bit and stopped. The tremendous silence after the noise of the landing was broken only by the 'chufferty-chuff' of the one Merlin, which was still ticking over. The crash crew arrived almost at once and we clambered down, relieved, somewhat breathless but unhurt. The Mossie suffered a damaged undercarriage and in view of its years was I believe, subsequently written off."

Also on 8/9 June, Wing Commander Neil Bromley OBE and Flight Lieutenant P. V Truscott of 169 Squadron, which had recently moved from Little Snoring to Great Massingham, shot down a Dornier in the Paris area.[260] Flight Lieutenant Clements and Pilot Officer Pierce of 141 Squadron safely abandoned their Mosquito in the Wisbech area after losing their port engine over Reading while returning from a sortie to northern France. A 239 Squadron crew overshot the West Raynham runway with the starboard throttle jammed and crashed in a field, but both crew scrambled out unhurt. Next day Flight Sergeant Humpreys and his navigator set off from Massingham on a cross-country flight. Near Gayton Mill, Humpreys lost control and the 169 Squadron Mosquito crashed. Humpreys was killed, but his navigator managed to bale out successfully.

On the afternoon of 11 June, during another training flight, a Mosquito crewed by Flight Lieutenant P. A. Riddoch and his navigator, 33-year old Flying Officer C. S. Ronayne, a new crew who had just joined 141 Squadron, disintegrated in mid-air two miles south of Chippenham village between Mildenhall and Newmarket. Riddoch was blown out of the aircraft and his parachute opened in the action. He suffered a dislocated right shoulder, fractured jaw, and lacerations to his face and eyelids, but recovered in the White Lodge EMS Hospital at Newmarket. Ronayne was found dead from multiple injuries. (A subsequent enquiry found that the cause of the accident was structural failure.) That night Irishman Wing Commander Charles M. Miller DFC,** Commanding Officer of 85 Squadron, and Flying Officer Robert Symon in a NF.XIX fitted with AI.X shot down a Bf 110 over Melun airfield. Miller wrote in his report:

"We took off from Swannington at 2215 hours on an Intruder Patrol to Bretigny and Melun. While orbiting the town of Melun at 3000 feet we passed over the airfield and were momentarily lit up by searchlights. Shortly afterwards, another aircraft was engaged and it fired a recognition signal - a number of white stars. We turned towards this and a contact was obtained 30° starboard, same level and two miles range."

Symon continues:

"I saw the blip on my tube and I had us in position in two and a half minutes behind. We made a very simple interception. Michael insisted that I keep my eyes on the tube even when he had a visual, well that is quite proper, but when I protested that we had closed inside minimum range and there was nothing to look at he relented and said I could look out. So I looked out and saw a completely empty sky. He pointed upwards with one finger and there it was - a Bf 110: I felt that I could have stood up and autographed its under-side."

Miller continues:

"We gave chase, the enemy aircraft firing further recognition signals and from 600 feet got a visual of the enemy aircraft silhouette. Closing in to about fifty feet and immediately below, we recognised a Me 110; small fins and rudders, long nose, square wing tips, and drop-tanks. No exhausts were visible from below but a stream of small sparks was seen. We dropped back to about 150 yards, height now about 2000 feet and pulled up behind, but the silhouette having become rather indistinct, I fired in anticipation of its position. No strikes were seen at first, but by raising the firing point strikes became visible and the aim was steadied. A fire started in the port engine, which spread over the fuselage. Large pieces of flaming wreckage flew back, and enemy aircraft dived vertically downwards, exploding on impact with the ground, about ten miles NE of Melun airfield at 0035 hours. No return fire was experienced."

Miller fired ninety-two 20mm SAPI and ninety 20mm HEI rounds to down the Bf 110, although his port outer gun stopped after two rounds because of a loose bullet or round striking the body of the gun by the chamber entrance. Symon concludes, "When we got back to Swannington we found that we had opened the scoring, which I thought was a right and proper thing for the CO of 85 to do! (I regret that 108 days from this event my pilot was compelled to retire due to illness.)"

Denis Welfare and Taffy Bellis of 239 Squadron were also on patrol, between Paris and Luxembourg, on radar watch for night-fighters. Bellis recalls:

"We picked up a German airborne radar transmission about ten miles away on our *Serrate* apparatus and homed on to it. We made a contact 10,000 feet away with our own AI and in a few minutes converted it to a visual, showing clearly the twin fins and faint exhausts of a Me 110. We attacked from about fifty yards and the Me immediately blew up. Our Mossie flew into debris and was enveloped in burning petrol. Fortunately, the fire did not get hold, but our Mossie was clearly damaged. We jettisoned the escape hatch ready to bale out quickly and called UK on the Mayday channel. The emergency control at Coltishall was most helpful with radio bearings, etc. However, Denis was able to control the aircraft and our *Gee* navigation equipment seemed to be working OK. Thus we decided to dispense with Coltishall's help and return to base, where eggs and bacon never tasted so good! I shall never forget Denis' skill, the ability of the Mossie to take punishment, the spectacular film from the camera gun of the engagement and last but not least, the discomfort of flying 300 miles home in a plane without an escape hatch."

Meanwhile, the first airfield intrusion results with AI Mk X were very promising, and it was found that at a height of 1500-2000 feet AI contacts at ranges of three miles or so could be obtained and held. During June, from 176 sorties dispatched, of which 131 were completed, thirty-eight AI contacts were reported leading to the destruction of ten enemy aircraft and the damaging of three others. All these combats, save one of those leading to damage claims, resulted from sixty-two sorties flown between the nights of 11/12 June and 16/17 June. On 12/13 June Flight Lieutenant James G. Benson DFC and Flight Lieutenant Lewis "Brandy" Brandon DFC of 157 Squadron shot down a Ju 188 at Compiègne during a low-level patrol of three airfields near Rheims (Laon-Athies, Laon-Couvron, and Juvincourt). Finally, Brandon could see the blip on his AI.Mk.X coming in to 800 feet. Then came the words he was waiting for:

"'Okay, have a look now. It's a Jerry all right. Looks like a Junkers 188.' I looked up, my night vision needing a few seconds to adjust itself. I saw a dark shape, which gradually resolved itself into a Junkers 188. We were almost directly underneath it, just about 400 feet below. Ben eased back the throttles gently; lifted Eager Beaver's nose slightly and at 150 yards' range fired a three-second burst at the Junkers. There were strikes on the starboard wing roots and the starboard engine caught fire. A further two-second burst blew pieces off the port wing tip. A short third burst produced strikes on the burning starboard engine. Then the whole of the port wing outboard of the engine broke off and passed under us. A second later the Junkers hurtled straight down in flames and exploded on the ground. I had been entering up my log and then took a *Gee* fix, which showed us to be over the Forest of Compiègne. It had taken just under four minutes from obtaining contact on this second aircraft to seeing it hit the ground. From the light of the burning starboard engine we had seen a swastika on the tail and dark green camouflage on the upper surface of the wing.

"The time for the finish of our patrol had been up some minutes so we set course for base, which was reached without further incident. We landed just after thee am and everyone was highly delighted that the score at Swannington had been opened for 157 Squadron. For our part, it was certainly satisfying to have had an early success with Mk 10 on this new job. As for our ground crew, they had painted a swastika on Eager Beaver almost before we were out of the cockpit.[261]

"It is not perhaps very well known how successful the Mosquitoes who provided the Bomber Support as fighters in 100 Group were during the latter part of World War II. There were three stages in their harrying of the Luftwaffe night fighters. Some squadrons sent low-level fighters to patrol the known German night-fighter airfields. Others provided high level patrols near their assembly points, about 40 miles from our bomber stream, in order to shoot them down before they reached it, and a third wave of low level Mossies would arrive at their airfields as they were returning. At RAF Swannington in Norfolk we shared the station with 85 Squadron. In the comparatively short time we carried out high level patrols, our score was 37 German night fighters destroyed, six probables and 13 damaged. We lost only seven, one of which was shot down by one of our own aircraft. The crew got back luckily and of course had several rounds of drinks from the offenders. 85 Squadron were even more successful and one of their Mossies bagged four German night fighters in one sortie. Very soon after the Bomber Support began operating, the Luftwaffe pilots started to use the phrase *Moskitopanik*! and *Ritterkreuz Height*! The later referred to the fact that after carrying out their attacks against our bombers, they would immediately drop down almost to ground level, i.e. *Ritterkreuz* height in order to avoid the dreaded Mosquitoes. I believe they lost a few more planes with their low flying back to collect their *Ritterkreuz*."[262]

On 13/14 June, their fifth trip, Warrant Officer Les Turner and Flight Sergeant Frank Francis of 169 Squadron in a FB.VI took off from Great Massingham at 2320 hours still looking for their first victory. They set course at 5000 feet over base at 2331. Turner reported:

"In good visibility obtained visual of English coast and subsequently of enemy coast, which we crossed at 0005 at 15,000 feet. Tuned on to Southerly course and during this log we observed no sign of activity. We then turned west and lost height down to 5000 feet in the hope of finding some joy. The lights of Paris were observed three miles port of track so we climbed to 9000 feet and orbited lights on the off chance of arousing some re-action. This was however unavailing so we climbed on a Westerly course to 12,000 feet where an AI contact was obtained 8000 feet in front showing 20° starboard at 0112 hours. We turned towards aircraft, which was traveling in a Northerly direction at approximately 250-mph. A contact was showing considerably below, we lost height down to 8000 feet from which point aircraft began to weave violently tuning alternately port and starboard through 1800 at speed approximately 350 mph and losing height to 5000 feet at 12lbs boost and 2800 rpm. We closed to 2000 feet after approximately six minutes. Then enemy aircraft flew into a patch of cloud and as range closed rapidly, I throttled back obtaining visual at 1300 feet of enemy aircraft above and to port, positively identifying plan view as a Ju 88. We overshot slightly so I let enemy aircraft come ahead and followed portly visually and portly I through wispy cloud. When this was cleared I closed to 300-400 yards and opened fire on port engine, which immediately burst into flames. Enemy aircraft turned port and in avoiding enemy aircraft, which was now burning fiercely, I turned port and on to my back, thus upsetting gyro instruments. I regained control on natural horizon and saw enemy aircraft hit the ground and explode at 0122 hours. We then set course towards northerly sky and when instruments had settled down, set course of 350° for coast, which we crossed three miles

West of Dunkirk at 0200 hours. No *Serrate* indications were observed throughout the trip."

Satisfied with their night's work but reaching the shores of England, they were warned that there were German intruders about. With a pessimism, which is probably part of his character, Turner was convinced that they would not make it back to report the combat! They did though. Turner had fired sixty rounds of cannon with no stoppages to down the Ju 88.

On 14/15 June Flight Lieutenant J. Tweedale and Flying Officer L. I. Cunningham of 157 Squadron shot down a Ju 88 trying to land at Juvincourt. Flight Lieutenant H. B. Thomas and Pilot Officer C. B. Hamilton of 85 Squadron also brought down a Ju 88 near Juvincourt. The third victory of the night went to Flying Officer Branse A. Burbridge DFC and Flight Lieutenant Frank Seymour "Bill" Skelton DFC of 85 Squadron, who destroyed a Ju 188 for their sixth victory of the war. Burbridge and Skelton bagged another Ju 88 on 23/24 June. The 23-year old Bransome Arthur Burbridge and 'Bill" Skelton were deeply religious. Burbridge had been a conscientious objector on religious grounds for the first six months of the war before joining up. They had served individually on Havocs in 85 Squadron in October 1941 and January 1942 respectively. They only crewed up on their second tour on the Squadron in July 1943. Their first victory was a Me 410 *Hornisse* (Hornet) on 22/23 February 1944. A first-class team in every sense of the word, the two men were totally dedicated to their task. Many more victories were to follow, but these were put in abeyance when both Mk.X Squadrons packed their bags on 25-27 June and left Swannington to return to West Malling for anti-*Diver* patrols since the V1 offensive was now threatening London and southern Britain. Mk.X radar was accurate enough to track flying bombs, but the Mosquitoes had to be modified to cope with the rigors of anti-*Diver* patrols. They received strengthened noses to match the Doodlebugs' extra turn of speed and stub exhausts were fitted in place of the exhaust shrouds. Engine boost pressure was adjusted to plus 24lbs and the Merlin 25s were also modified to permit the use of 150-octane petrol so that the aircraft could reach around 360 mph at sea level. Just over 130 successful *Intruder* patrols out of 176 dispatched had been carried out by the two squadrons before they were transferred (they would not return to Swannington until 29 August).

Another inspired 85 Squadron pairing was Squadron Leader F. S. "Gon" Gonsalves and Flight Lieutenant Basil G. Duckett, an architect by profession, married with one child, a son. Basil Duckett had been trained as a navigator and had finished that off with a course in AI at Prestwick. He was a quiet, gentle man who could always be relied upon for pleasant, interesting companionship. Always unobtrusively in the background, generally listening rather than talking, he became affectionately known to all of the crews as "the Distinguished Stranger."[263] On 15/16 June Gonsalves and Duckett were on patrol over Belgium. Gonsalves reported:

> "I arrived some nine minutes late on my patrol line owing to some difficulty in finding my last pinpoint just north of St. Trond. Eventually decided to do an east to west patrol between two white beacons as St. Trond airfield was not lighted. At 0140 hours Flight Lieutenant Duckett reported he had a contact over to port and 10° above (two miles range) and almost immediately afterwards the Visual Lorenz and flarepath were put on at St. Trond just a mile or so to port. I followed the contact in a wide orbit of the airfield and closed to 800 feet, 15° below where I could see a silhouette but could not identify. I closed to 200 feet and right below and recognized a Me 110 with long-range tanks. Then dropped back to 600 feet and fired a one-second burst which produced a strike on the back of the fuselage – closed in to 400 feet and gave a further burst which blew up the starboard engine. I broke to starboard to avoid the debris flying back and watched the enemy aircraft going down in a starboard turn until finally it hit the ground and blew up in the dispersal area east of the airfield. My height was 3500 feet. Time 0147 hours.
>
> "I then resumed patrol and at 0154 hours Flight Lieutenant Duckett again reported contact. This time head-on at one mile range, 15° above. Closed in to recognize another me 110 also with long-range tanks. Height 4000 feet. Fired short burst with no results; closed in too fast and found myself flying in formation with him 100 yards away on my port side. Turned back port and gave a good long burst and pulled my nose right through his line of flight. Concentration of strikes seen on upper part of wing outboard of the port engine but no fire. As I was aiming at the top of the fuselage, this struck me as quite odd so I pulled up my nose to have another look at the enemy aircraft but unfortunately he must have been going down because visual was lost and contact could not be regained. No fires were seen on the ground after this combat. One Me 110 destroyed. One Me 110 damaged."[264]

The following night, 16/17 June, a Ju 88 of I./NJG2 that crashed in the Pas de Cancale was possibly shot down by Flying Officers Andy Miller DFC and Freddie Bone of 169 Squadron.[265] On 17/18 June, at 0230 hours Flying Officer Philip Stanley Kendall DFC and Flight Lieutenant C. R. Hill DFC of 85 Squadron reached their patrol area, the airfield at Soesterberg, at 0100 hours. Their combat report says:

> 'The airfield was not lit, so we proceeded to Deelen, where similar conditions prevailed. At 0126 hours Soesterberg lights were seen to be lit and an aircraft with navigation lights was seen landing. While flying towards the airfield, a red Verey light was seen, shot from the ground, and almost immediately another aircraft was seen to put on navigation lights and start to fly round again. W gave chase, putting down wheels and flaps to reduce speed and, with an IAS of 140, intercepted the aircraft at 700 feet, just as it was turning onto the flarepath to attempt to land again. Two bursts were given, one second and two seconds, with half-ring deflection, range 150 yards closing to 100 yards, strikes being seen on the wing and in the fuselage. The aircraft caught fire and climbed to 1500 feet, still burning navigation lights, and then dived vertically and exploded on the ground 200 yards short of the end of the runway at 0130 hours. We broke away, retracted the undercarriage and flaps and climbed to 3000 feet and took cine shots from approximately three miles range of the aircraft burning on the ground. Patrol was continued near Soesterberg till 0150 hours when course was set for base. Landed 0243 hours."[266]

Also this night Flight Lieutenant Geoffrey E. Poulton and Flying Officer Arthur John Neville of 239 Squadron came across some Ju 88s orbiting a beacon and fired at two of them. Neville recalls:

"We claimed one destroyed after it plunged earthwards thoroughly on fire, and the second likewise plunged down with one engine on fire which fairly soon went out. This we claimed as damaged and both were credited to us."[267]

Several enemy aircraft were claimed destroyed by 515 Squadron during June, including two He 111s, a Ju 34, a Bf 110G, and a Ju 88. The Bf 110G-4[268] was destroyed at 1519 hours on 21 June by Squadron Leader Paul Wattling Rabone DFC and Flying Officer Frederick C. H. Johns DFC during a *Day Ranger* to northern Holland and the Friesians. The Bf 110, flown by 21-year-old *Unteroffizier* Herbert Beyer of 8./NJG1, had just taken off from Eelde airfield. Rabone and Johns came in from astern and promptly attacked with a 3½-second burst of cannon. No strikes were observed so Rabone fired again. This time the two-second burst hit the starboard engine and pieces flew off before it crashed on the northern side of Eelde airfield. Later, Rabone wrote graphically:

"Before the Hun got his breath back a delightful third burst of cannon was presented at fifty yards range at a height or about 100 feet. This created havoc - the Me 110's starboard wing and starboard engine burst into flames, the port engine belched forth black smoke, and the enemy aircraft dived into the ground enveloped in a mass of flames, smoke and destruction. Mosquito landed at Little Snoring at 1630 hours after a most enjoyable afternoon's sport."[269]

On 24 June Wing Commander J. R. D. "Bob" Braham DSO DFC* and his navigator, Flight Lieutenant D. Walsh DFC, flew in to West Raynham to begin their *Day Ranger* on 25 June to Denmark (one of several such "arrangements" Braham had made since leaving 141 Squadron).[270] Braham, who had 29 victories, completed an attack on a German staff car on a road on Fyn Island when two Fw 190s attacked him. In one of them was *Leutnant* Robert Spreckels. The Mosquito's port wing and engine were set on fire. Braham tried to crash land on the shore of a fjord when he was attacked again, but he managed to set it down and fortunately the aircraft did not explode. Walsh and Braham made a run for it and got behind sand dunes. Troops from a nearby radar station advanced towards them and opened fire with automatic weapons. Unhurt, Braham and Walsh were marched away into captivity. At 1000 hours next day an ASR search was initiated and 141 Squadron crews took part, including Paddy Engelbach and Ron Mallett, but their search was in vain. That night Flight Lieutenant Denis Welfare DFC* and Flying Officer Taffy Bellis DFC* shot down a Ju 88 near Paris.[271]

On 27/28 June the Mosquito *Serrate* squadrons helped support 1049 bombers making attacks on V-l sites and other targets in northern France. At West Raynham eleven Mosquitoes of 141 Squadron and eight Mosquitoes of 239 Squadron took off between 2200 and 2305 hours and set out across the sea towards France to provide bomber support. At 2235 hours Wing Commander Charles V. Winn and his navigator/radio operator, Flight Lieutenant R. A. W. Scott, led 141 Squadron off, followed at ten and five minute intervals by the remaining ten Mosquitoes. Flying Officer W. P. Rimer and Warrant Officer H. J. Alexander had to return soon after take off when their AI set failed. Pilot Officers Coles and J. A. Carter patrolled Beacon *Mücke* hoping to pick up signals from German night-fighters (otherwise known as "bashing the beacons"), but also had to abort after both *Serrate* and AI went unserviceable. Problems with engine vibration and instruments and R/T failure made a return to base equally expedient. Francois Vandenplassche and Pilot Officer M. K. Webster were one crew who patrolled and chased but returned empty handed. It was Vandenplassche's first operation since his return to the squadron after his evasion from occupied France when he baled out on 25/26 March 1943. Meanwhile, Squadron Leader Graham J. Rice and Flying Officer Jimmie G. Rogerson had had better luck. Rogerson recalls:

"It was now approaching half way house, with unlucky number thirteen of the thirty operations making up the full tour behind us. Action was just around the corner. On 27 June we were given another of the one-hour beacon patrols, taking in two of them in Northern France code-named *Emil* and *Goldhammer*. We took off just after the last of midsummer's long daylight had faded and a bright full moon was rising into a cloudless sky, made our way across the North Sea to Flushing, and began our stipulated patrol soon after midnight. The skies were crystal clear, brilliant from the harsh illumination of an un-obscured moon, but otherwise apparently empty. After some twenty minutes of stooging calmly up and down, quite unexpectedly a sudden burst of four red stars, exactly like one of Standard Fireworks better rockets, exploded in the air away to our right, followed almost immediately by four more of the same, now slightly closer. Not our own chosen color combination for the night. My driver promptly turned towards this pretty display of pyrotechnics to investigate, myself with eyes glued to the radar screens searching for non-existent *Serrate* indications. Half a minute later, I had it. A good clean blip, racing out of the ground response and down the time base so rapidly that we were obviously meeting whatever it was head on.

"Waiting until the range had closed to 4000 feet, I gave instructions to haul round to starboard through 180°, so that if all went according to plan we would finish up directly behind our customer and in a position to chase and intercept. Which is exactly what happened. The Mosquito completed its turn to show me my contact directly ahead at a distance of two miles but well below our own altitude of 15,000 feet. On this occasion I was really going to have to apply myself. The target ahead was weaving steadily about to right and left, added to which it was a question of reducing our height whilst trying to follow spasmodic twists and turns and close the distance respectfully between us. After ten minutes, during which time we found that we had descended 4000 feet, Graham obtained a visual thanks to the clean brilliance of the white moon on an aircraft flying at least 1500 feet ahead of us.

"At that precise moment, our target took a gentle turn to port and finally steadied to fly directly into the full blinding glare. There was no doubt whatsoever about its identity. The marked dihedral of the longer than average wingspan and the engines close-set to the fuselage shouted Ju 88. But any hopes of closing to a position where my driver could see properly to open fire would have to be deferred. It was back to the radar screens and follow the blip for very nearly quarter of an hour, and that I can tell you was an irritatingly long time. Finally, it turned once more, this time out of the glare altogether, and we were able to close without more ado right in to firing range. Seizing the opportunity whilst we had it, we opened fire at once in two short bursts. Large pieces flew off-and passed uncomfortably close above our heads just as they had with the 110 up at Hamburg and this time-both engines burst into flames simultaneously. The sequence of events, which followed, is yet another that is burnished into my memory like a roll of ciné-film. So well alight was the Ju 88 that the black crosses on its wings were clearly visible as it went down beneath us in a steep dive to port, where it disappeared into the only bank of cloud anywhere in sight, almost as though it were seeking refuge.

"Just as we thought we would not see it again and so be unable to vouch positively for its destruction, it suddenly reappeared out of the cloud in a zooming vertical climb, ablaze from end to end. It described a perfect loop directly above and then came down straight at us, as though by some will of its own it was bent upon revenge by taking us with it in a mid-air collision. Its fiery downward path surged desperately close behind our port wing, and for one awful moment I was absolutely convinced that it would hit us! The whole astonishing performance seemed to last for ever as we sat there watching its progress in open mouthed amazement. Yet in the event I suppose it cannot have taken more than a couple of minutes before it all ended with a huge explosion as it hit the deck in the Cambrai area of Northern France." It was their third victory.

Warrant Officers Harry "Butch" Welham and E. "Gus" Hollis used their well-established rapport to track and hunt an AI contact five miles north of Eindhoven. Their Mosquito, DZ240, was the same aircraft they had used to shoot down their first enemy aircraft on 14/15 June when a Me 410 had fallen to the Mk II's guns. Clearly painted in large white letters on the pilot's side of the Mosquito's nose was the double entendre "*SHYTOT*." Welham reduced height to 14,000 feet and closed in on the contact. He recalls:

"The target, a Ju 88, appeared dead ahead, slightly above but we looked as if we were going to overshoot. Gus came on the intercom and in his lilting Welsh accent said, 'Throttle back, pull the nose up, Butch.' His nose was in his set, keeping track of the fir-tree-shaped blip on the *Serrate* scope. 'Left, left, right, right,' he ordered. 'Thirty degrees above. Dead ahead, 2000 feet.' I steered to the ideal spot, 400 yards behind (the four 20mm Hispanos were synchronized for 400 yards). I lined him up through the circular gunsight, my right thumb ready to press the firing button on top of the stick and aimed between the cockpit and engine. Gus said clearly, 'Go on, shoot!' I said, 'OK,' and let fly a two-second burst. As the cannons fired beneath our feet the seats vibrated and dust flew up from the floor all around the cockpit. A fire started in the engine and the wing and the kite went down in a spiral burning all the while, exploding on the ground about six miles south of Tilburg.

"We continued to patrol and at about 0143 hours about ten miles west of Gent, we chased another AI contact at maximum range. It developed into a series of tight orbits and contact turned out to be 2000 feet behind. We did a exceedingly tight turn and it brought 141 Squadron's total victories to seventeen."[272]

Evans recalls:

"I was returning from accompanying the bomber force to Stuttgart. Near the Channel on the French side we picked up an IFF contact which turned out to be a Fw 190. I shot it down from behind but unfortunately it exploded covering my aircraft with burning petrol. This burnt off a great deal of the doped control surfaces, which were not wood, and made the aircraft difficult to control. I made a very fast landing at Manston after numerous trials at height to determine at what speed I lost control."

Flight Lieutenant Donald Ridgewell "Podge" Howard and Flying Officer Frank A. W. "Sticky" Clay destroyed a Ju 88 near Brussels. Howard reported to Flight Lieutenant C. H. F. Reynolds, the Intelligence officer:

"Mosquito took off West Raynham 2311 hours on a *Serrate* patrol in support of the bombers on Vitry le Francois, crossing in at St. Valery and contacting the bombers at 0106 hours. After intercepting and obtaining a visual on a Lancaster at 0120 hours well away from the bomber stream and at 14,500 feet (6000 feet above the other bombers), Mosquito went on to Vitry le Francois. After patrolling there for eight minutes while the bombing was in progress, it was decided to set course for the French coast as the port engine was running very badly. At 0210 hours when north of Laon at 16,000 feet, 0215 hours, an AI contact at 6000 feet ahead and to the East was picked up but it faded almost at once. When about five miles North of Cambrai, still at 16,000 feet, 0215 hours, an AI contact was observed nearly head-on, 12,000 feet range, crossing gently port to starboard below an estimated course of 130°. Mosquito, which was on 320°, allowed contact to pass below and then turned round starboard, gradually losing height to 8000 feet and then climbed to 12,000 feet. During this climb Mosquito found it was impossible to gain on contact which was doing 260 ASI but fortunately it turned port on to 050°, reduced height and eventually settled down straight and level at 9500 feet. This enabled Mosquito to close in to 1500 feet where a fleeting visual was obtained on the silhouette of an aircraft 20° above. At 1000 feet range a clear visual was obtained on what the pilot believed to be a Ju 88 but in order to be quite certain, Mosquito was brought in to within fifty feet and any doubt of the target's identity was removed. Dropping back to seventy-five yards dead astern and slightly below, a one-second-burst of cannon caused strikes on the fuselage and E/A's port engine blew up. As E/A dropped away to port, Mosquito put its nose right down and with another one sec burst set E/A's starboard engine on fire. E/A then turned slowly to starboard, well on fire, and dived vertically into the ground where it exploded. No lights had been visible on E/A and no return fire was experienced. Claimed as a Ju 88 destroyed (Cat. A (1). E/A was shot down from 9,500 to 9000 feet at 0230 hours a few miles NE of Brussels.

"The AI became u/s after the cannon had been fired and three minutes later the starboard coolant temperature was seen to be 160°, flames started spurting along the starboard engine and fumes gilled the cockpit. Pilot feathered the starboard propeller and turned on to 290° climbing into cloud at 10,000 feet re-crossing the enemy coast at Knocke at 0255 hours. The port vacuum pump was u/s and gyro instruments would not perform. The starboard engine having been put out of action, all electric services had to be switched off to conserve the supply of electricity. Later the navigator tried to get a *Gee* fix, but could not get a normal picture and a fix was unobtainable. R/T was switched on and a 'Mayday' call to Kingsley was given on Channel 'D' with IFF on Stud 3. But after two transmissions and when Kingsley had given a vector to Manston, R/T became completely u/s. Mosquito was holding hard at 10,500 feet so an approximate course of 260° was maintained until Sandrs lights were seen and the Manston pundit was identified. Mosquito fired the colors of the day several times and then made a perfect landing at Manston at 0330 hours. A number of pieces of '88' and a handful of 'Window' (broad) have been recovered from Mosquito's starboard engine."

Two crews failed to return to West Raynham: Flight Lieutenant Herbert R. Hampshire and Warrant Officer Alan W. Melrose, who were on their last operation; and Paddy Engelbach and Ronald Mallett DFC, all of 141 Squadron. Engelbach and Mallett patrolled north Holland for an hour, and the navigator could tell they were being picked up by a German night-fighter. The pilot turned south then Mallett suddenly ordered, "Hard on to the reciprocal." Engelbach wrote:

"As I threw the aircraft over I asked if there was anything behind. The answer was a series of judders as my tail was shot off and I went into a spin. I pulled the aircraft out but was immediately hit again. At about 2500 feet the aircraft disintegrated and I was thrown out through the canopy. I opened my parachute after a long search for it, and my fall was broken at about twenty feet and I landed unhurt. Mallett was killed. The Germans said that the aircraft that shot me down was a Heinkel 219."[273]

On 27/28 June 100 Group Mosquitoes claimed six enemy aircraft shot down. Pilot Officer Clinton Warren Chown DFC RCAF and Sergeant D. G. N. Veitch of 515 Squadron set off from Little Snoring to patrol Gilze-Volkel-Venlo-Eindhoven. After three quarters of an hour, during which they bombed Venlo airfield and created a substantial fire emitting flashes for the odd fifteen minutes, they returned to Eindhoven for a second look. There was no cloud and visibility was "good." At 0213 hours they were over the airfield, which had its north-south flarepath well lit. On their approach, four red cartridges were fired from the air and the runway lights changed pattern. Four airfield identification bars were lit at the southern end, and then almost immediately three of the bars were switched off and a single red cartridge was fired from the ground followed by a white light flashing. Just then, a green light flashing dashes appeared in the air to the west of the airfield. Chown and Veitch, their Mosquito at 1500 feet, gave chase and spotted the outline of an aircraft with a green bow light and red downward identification light under the tail. They closed to 200 yards and recognized it as a Ju 88 (300651 B3+LT of 9./KG54 flown by *Unteroffizier* Gotthard Seehaber, which was returning after a mine laying operation in the invasion area). Chown delivered a stern attack with a two-second burst of cannon fire, which recorded one strike on the fuselage. Chown closed to 150 yards and delivered a second stern attack with a burst of about three seconds. The Ju 88 immediately exploded and scattered debris through the sky as it disintegrated before crashing into a house, killing three children. Chown and Veitch orbited the scene and took photos of the burning enemy night-fighter before breaking away and returning home.[274]

In June almost all the contacts obtained over enemy territory had been by the Mosquitoes' AI radar with its limited range. This was due to the success of beacon patrols. It became clear in June that the enemy was making more and more use of his assembly beacons in France. The area of these beacons proved to be the most profitable type of patrolling for the *Serrate* Squadrons. Many of the Mosquitoes' successes at the beacons were obtained before the enemy fighters had attempted to intercept the bombers.

On 28/29 June Pilot Officer Harry "Shorty" Reed and Flying Officer Stuart Watts of 169 Squadron picked up an AI contact two minutes after their arrival at Beacon *Mücke*. Reed turned hard to starboard in an attempt to get behind the enemy aircraft. After losing the contact twice through fading and interference, it was eventually picked up again at a range of 15,000-feet dead ahead and just below, after two hard orbits and some weaving. Harry Reed closed to about 5000 feet after some difficulty due to unreliable elevation signals. The Mosquito's height was now 12,000 feet. A visual was obtained at 3000 feet, and the enemy aircraft continued weaving. Harry Reed called "bogey bogey wiggle wings," but there was no reply. It had to be an enemy aircraft. Then it fired off four star red cartridges. Range was reduced to about 150 feet when the enemy aircraft was recognised as a Bf 110 with external wing tanks. Harry Reed fired two two-second bursts and the Bf 110 exploded. The Mosquito's AI and *Serrate* failed immediately after the guns were fired. The Bf 110 was seen to go down in flames until it entered cloud at 4000 feet. A bright flash followed on the ground. With their radar now u/s Harry Reed and Stuart Watts turned for home.

June seemed to offer much for the *Serrate* squadrons. For instance, 239 Squadron reported 89.7 per cent of sorties completed (compared to only 62.5 per cent in January) and registered eleven victories. But 141 and 169 had shared only eight evenly between them. July would be the same for the *Serrate* Mosquitoes. Both 141 and 169 notched six victories, while 239 Squadron racked up seven without any operational losses.

On 30 June/1 July Flight Lieutenant Dennis Raby DFC and Flight Sergeant S. J. Flint DFM of 239 Squadron destroyed Ju 88 711114 of 5./NJG2 over France. They stalked the Junkers and were fired at by the enemy air gunner, but his tracer passed harmlessly over the top of the Mosquito. Raby fired a two-second burst from 450 feet and saw strikes all along the port fuselage and wing, and the port engine burst into flames. He pumped another two-second burst into the doomed Junkers, which exploded, scattering debris into the path of the charging Mosquito. As it fell vertically to earth Raby continued to pepper the machine, finally breaking away just before another explosion tore the wings off the night-fighter. It crashed southeast of Dieppe in a massive explosion.[275]

P-61 Black Widow night fighters with D-Day invasion stripes on the wings. (USAF)

In November 1943 Air Commodore (later AVM) E. B. Addison established 100 Group HQ at Radlett, Hertfordshire and in December moved his HQ to Norfolk, first to RAF West Raynham and in January 1944, to Bylaugh Hall, where the headquarters remained until the end of the war. Previously Addison had commanded 80 Wing RAF, which, as a wing commander, he had established at Garston in June 1940. (Addison)

Flight Lieutenant R.W. 'Dickie' Leggett (left) and his navigator Flying Officer Egbert J. Midi' Midlane of 125 Squadron. ('Dickie' Leggett) **[Below]** Heinkel 111H-22 releasing a V1.

Bylaugh Hall, 2 Group and later 100 Group HQ.

Flight Lieutenant C. G. A. Drew (left) and Flight Lieutenant A. B. A. Smith being debriefed by Flight Lieutenant C. H. F. 'Buster' Reynolds the Intelligence Officer, at West Raynham following a *Night Intruder* sortie. (Tom Cushing Collection)

This graphic photograph shows the damage suffered by NF.XXX NT252 as a result of Flight Lieutenant Paul Mellows and Flight Lieutenant S. L. 'Dickie' Drew's combat with a Bf 110 near Stuttgart on the night of 1/2 February 1945. Mellows had opened fire at 300 feet range from slightly below with a two-second burst from which, a small explosion sent debris flying back. A second burst resulted in a very large explosion and for a few moments the Mosquito was enveloped in flame, the heat of which was felt in the cockpit. Mosquitoes were famed for their strength - NT252 operated after the war with 609 Squadron until 1948! (Paul Mellows)

192 Squadron 'C' Flight air and ground crew at Foulsham in December 1944. The role of 'C' Flight varied. Sometimes it flew with the Main bomber stream to and over the target and the navigator/special operator had a triple role – navigation within *Gee* range (thereafter by dead reckoning), jamming over the target, identifying, if possible and photographing any radar signals on the CRT radar oscilloscope and recording on wire any radar and R/T that could be picked up. 192 Squadron had German speaking 'bods' operating in the Halifaxes whose aim was to confuse utterly the German ground/air and air/ground R/T. the 192 Squadron Mosquitoes would, on these occasions, orbit the target while the raid was on with the jammer switched on. The fuzes had a bad habit of blowing at crucial moments and it was a 'hell of a job' changing them in the cramped cockpit of the Mosquito because the fuzes were directly behind the navigator's head. The jammers used were *Piperack* and towards the end of the war jamming over the target was a routine task. Then again, sometimes the Mosquito crew flew alone, patrolling the V2 launching sites, trying, unsuccessfully, to lock on to the frequency of their controlling wavelength. Sometimes too the Mosquitoes went on spoof raids, agha9in recording enemy reactions. (Ted Gomersall)

192 Squadron 'C' Flight air and ground crew at Foulsham in December 1944. L-R: Bishop; Taylor; Hicks; Allen; Stead; George; Ted Gomersall and Phillips. (Ted Gomersall)

Left: Flying Officer Viv Bridges DFC and Flight Sergeant Don 'Spider' Webb DFM of 239 Squadron who on 10/11 May 1944 destroyed Bf 110 Werk Nr.740179 3C+F1 of I./NJG4 piloted by Oberleutnant Heinrich Schulenburg near Ellezelles, Belgium. Two nights later they shot down Ju 88C-6 Werk Nr. 750922 of 5./NJG3 flown by Unteroffizier Josef Polzer at Hoogcruts near Maastricht. On 31 May/1 June Bridges and Webb scored their third kill (a Bf 110) followed on 7/8 July by another Bf 110 near Charleroi for their fourth and last victory of the war. (Don Webb Collection)

Pat Rooney caricature of Tommy Smith. (Tommy Smith)

Flying Officers 'Ali' Barber (left) and Peter W. R. Rowland (right) of 192 Squadron in front of their Mosquito IV. On his first tour in the expert low-level raiders of 105 Squadron Rowland had flown the first op on Berlin and the low-level raid on the *Gestapo* HQ in Oslo, Norway.

Wing Commander Howard C. Kelsey DFC* drawn post war by *Wren*. The award of the DSO was gazetted after the war. On 23/24 December 1943 in Beaufighter VIF V8744 of 141 Squadron at RAF Wittering Flight Lieutenant Howard Kelsey and Pilot Officer E. M. Smith scored the first 100 Group victory when they shot down a Ju 88 of 4./NJG1 based at St. Trond. It crashed near Bergisch-Gladbach, near Cologne. Oberleutnant Finster, pilot and *Staffelkapitan* was KIA. Feldwebel. S. E. Beugel (WIA) baled out. (Tom Cushing Collection)

'D' Flight, 192 Squadron at RAF Foulsham in May 1945 in front of XVI DT-M flown by Flying Officer Reay and Pilot Officer Eric Clarkson. L-R; Front: G. Dolby; Pilot Officer Eric Clarkson; Flying Officer Reay; Flight Lieutenant 'Hank' Cooper DSO DFC; Flying Officer Don Kelt; E.A. Jones or Dan Tucker; T. L. Dray; A. Parker; u/k; Flight Lieutenant Allan E. Roach DFC RAAF; C. Pushon

Flight Lieutenant Allan E. Roach DFC RAAF and Flight Lieutenant 'Hank' Cooper DSO DFC navigator-radar operator at RAF Foulsham in 1944-45. (Hank Cooper Coll)

Ted Gomersall, navigator-special operator and his pilot, Charlie 'Bud' George of 192 Squadron at RAF Foulsham. This photograph was taken for the French Resistance in 1944 to guard against infiltration by Germans if they were to be shot down. (Ted Gomersall)

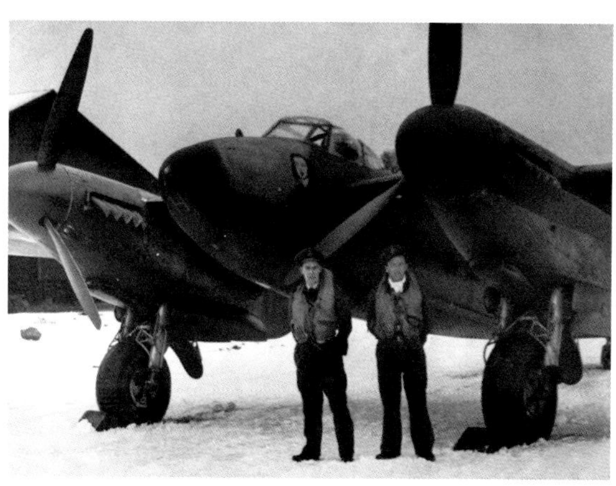

Flight Lieutenant 'Hank' Cooper DSO DFC navigator-radar operator and Flying Officer Don Kelt RNZAF of 192 Squadron in front of B.IV 'H' at Foulsham, Norfolk during the winter 1944-45. This dedicated ELINT (electronic intelligence) squadron within 100 Group also operated Halifaxes and, for radar and radio investigation, NF.II DZ292. All their aircraft were fitted with various receivers for the detection of German nightfighter AI frequencies over the continent, which they recorded on *Bagful* and *Blonde* recording equipment. ('Hank' Cooper Collection)

Group Captain Sammy Hoare (seated, 2nd row, middle) and other personnel at Little Snoring. Robert 'Bob' Campbell Muir DFC is third from right in the same row. In September 1943 Sammy Hoare assumed command of 605 'County of Warwick' Squadron's and he returned to combat operations on 27/28 September whereupon he promptly dispatched a Do 217 at Dedelsdorf; his seventh confirmed air-to-air victory. On 1 January 1944 Bob Muir flew as "Sammy" Hoare's navigator in FB.VI UP-L. 'Intelligence informed us that there was enemy flying training near Kastrup, (Copenhagen, Denmark) but there was strong frontal, 10/10 low cloud conditions and a pretty fierce northeasterly wind. Sammy decided to "have a go", so off we went. Flying blind, I fixed on *Gee* continuously until out of its range - refining our course accordingly, and was able to calculate the wind speed and direction to apply to the remaining sea miles on DR. After 2 hours 30 minutes "blind" flying we cleared the front and there was Kastrup about 2 miles to port! A relieved pilot said, "Well done, Bob", but there were no flying activities so we returned to Base. On 10/11 January 1944 we flew an op in FB.VI UP-R. We had received intelligence that there were German aircraft flying training at Chievres. I plotted several legs so that we would arrive from the South and hopefully would be mistaken for one of their own German aircraft. It was a beautifully clear full moonlight night and as we approached the airfield at Chievres we spotted a Ju 188. Coming up from about 1500 feet Sammy leveled off behind it and fired two bursts of cannon, the aircraft crashed to the ground. This was County of Warwick' Squadron's 100th 'Hun'! On 24 March 1944 in FB.VI UP-R again we flew an *Intruder* to Stendal and Burg. One Me 109 destroyed at Burg, whilst taxiing after landing. Port engine failed at Salzwedel, so 450 miles to Woodbridge on one motor. To keep the aircraft trimmed I had to position myself half way out of my seat in a back-straining position with both feet on the rudder-bar. I remained in this position for three hours! Using my comprehensive flight plan I dog-legged the "sitting duck" of an aircraft back to Woodbridge. [Sammy claimed a probable and damaged three aircraft in 1944 and shot down his 9th and final aircraft in March that year]. On 25 February Sammy Hoare [**Near Right**] and I flew a *Night Ranger*. One motor failed at Lake Cheim. Restarted after 20 minutes but only half capacity. 1 x 100-gallon tank refused to jettison and we were failing to make height. Luckily it fell off when the mountain peaks were VERY NEAR! It was a clear moonlit night so I had to map read through the Alpine valleys to our French base! If I say so myself, IT WAS NO MEAN FEAT! We flew another *Night Ranger* on 23 March to Celle and Wesendorf carrying 80 4lb incendiaries, which were dropped on dispersal areas at Wesendorf. Fires started. I flew my 59th and last operation on 3 April 1945 with Squadron Leader Griffiths DFC. It was a fire blitz on Lübeck/Blankensee. Master Bomber, auspices of 100 Group. Timing to the minute was vital because of other Mosquitoes following. We marked hangars and drome buildings at precise timing with 80 x 4lb incendiaries from 700 feet. Good fires started.' (Robert 'Bob' Campbell Muir DFC)

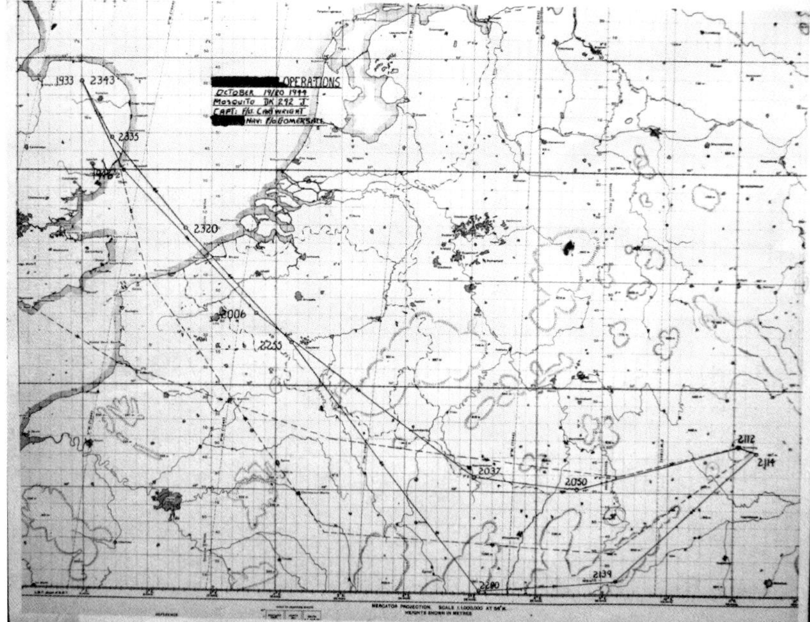

Map showing the route taken on 19/20 October 1944 by Flying Officer Cartwright and Flying Officer Gomersall in DK292/J when 19 Mosquitoes went to Hanover, 18 to Mannheim, eight to Düsseldorf, five to Pforzheim and four to Wiesbaden. One Mosquito failed to return from the raid on Pforzheim. DK292/J failed to return on 26/27 November 1944. (Gomersall)

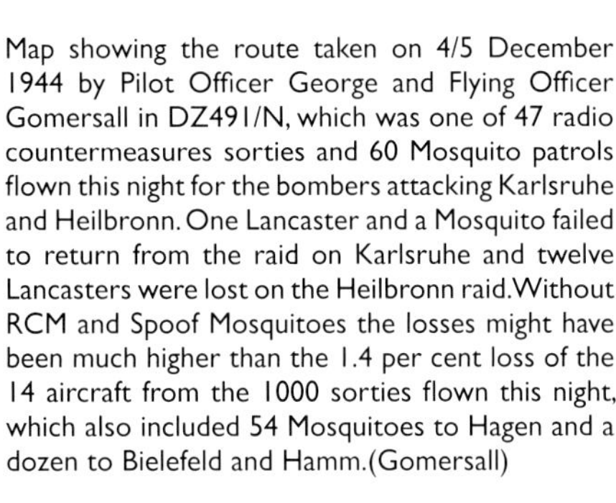

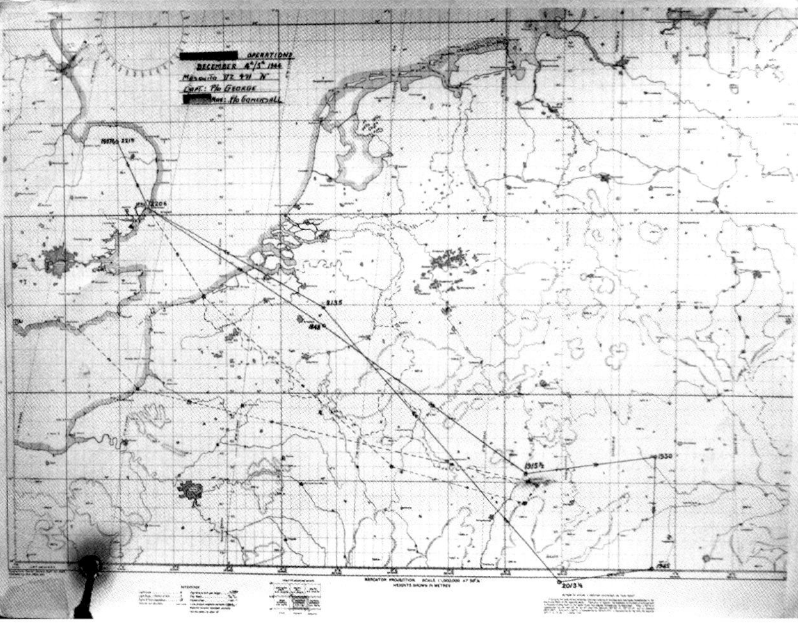

Map showing the route taken on 4/5 December 1944 by Pilot Officer George and Flying Officer Gomersall in DZ491/N, which was one of 47 radio countermeasures sorties and 60 Mosquito patrols flown this night for the bombers attacking Karlsruhe and Heilbronn. One Lancaster and a Mosquito failed to return from the raid on Karlsruhe and twelve Lancasters were lost on the Heilbronn raid. Without RCM and Spoof Mosquitoes the losses might have been much higher than the 1.4 per cent loss of the 14 aircraft from the 1000 sorties flown this night, which also included 54 Mosquitoes to Hagen and a dozen to Bielefeld and Hamm. (Gomersall)

W4052 the fighter prototype in all-black night fighter scheme in flight. This aircraft differed from the bomber prototype in having two uprated Merlin 21s of 1460hp and a flat bulletproof windscreen. Constructed at Salisbury Hall it was flown out of a field adjacent to the assembly hangar on 15 May 1941 by Geoffrey de Havilland Jnr. W4052 completed handling trials at Boscombe Down by the end of July 1941 and from 1942 onwards was used to test various modifications, such as 40mm cannon, underwing bomb racks and drop tanks, barrage balloon cable cutters in the wing leading edges, Hamilton Standard airscrews and braking propellers, drooping aileron systems for steeper approaches and a larger rudder tab. W4052 joined the FIU at Ford and was eventually scrapped on 28 January 1946. (BAe)

On 27/28 May 1944 A 515 Squadron Mosquito flown by Flying Officers David Kay Foster (**Left**) and 20-year-old Robert Stanley Ling, which took off from Little Snoring at 0155 hours and was detailed to patrol Leeuwarden, failed to return. They were shot down by airfield defense flak and crashed into a hangar on the airfield. Both are buried in Leeuwarden Northern General Cemetery. (via Theo Boiten)

Wing Commander 'Sticky' Murphy DSO DFC earlier in the war, in Malta. (via Tom Cushing)

239 Squadron aircrew and groundcrews at West Raynham. Top row, left to right: Sergeant West; Warrant Officer Dave Brochie; Warrant Officer Chalky White; u/k Belgian; Pilot Officer Paul Falconer; Flight Lieutenant R. C. 'Killer' Kendall DFC; Pilot Officer Jamie Jameson; u/k; Flying Officer Frazer; u/k; Warrant Officer Chick Ellinor; Sergeant Peel; u/k. 2nd row left to right: u/k; Flying Officer 'Spider' Webb; Cliff Rind RCAF; Flight Lieutenant Woolton; Flight Lieutenant Smith; u/k; Da Costa; u/k; Flight Lieutenant Freddy Wimbush; Rowley; Flying Officer Pete Poirette; u/k; Terry Glasheen RAAF. 3rd row, left to right: u/k; radar officer RAAF, Flight Lieutenant Al Deere; Flight Lieutenant Hawley Adjutant, Wing Commander Walter F. Gibb DSO DFC CO; Squadron Leader Dennis Hughes DFC; Flight Lieutenant Dennis Perks DFC; u/k; u/k. Front row, left to right: u/k; Flight Sergeant Dai Rees; Flight Sergeant Ferguson; Flight Sergeant Andrews; Flight Sergeant L. 'Spic' Spicer; Flight Sergeant Arthur Briggs; Flight Sergeant Brogan; Warrant Officer Tony Tanner; Warrant Officer 'Dagwood' Wooding. Wing Commander Gibb and Flying Officer Kendall destroyed two Ju 88s on 5/6 March 1945. Squadron Leader Hughes and Flight Lieutenant Perks shot down a Ju 188 at Nürnburg on 16/17 March. (Graham Chalky White)

Personnel at Swannington enjoying the snow during a brief respite from the war in the winter of 1943/44.

Wing Commander J. A. Mackie (left) CO 157 Squadron from August 1943 to March 1944, with his navigator-radar operator, Flight Lieutenant Leslie Scholefield DFC. (Brian Whitlock Blundell Coll)

Badly damaged NF.XXX NT252 as a result of Flight Lieutenant Paul Mellows and Flight Lieutenant S. L. 'Dickie' Drew's combat with a Bf 110 near Stuttgart on the night of 1/2 February 1945. Mellows had opened fire at 300 feet range from slightly below with a two-second burst from which, a small explosion sent debris flying back. A second burst resulted in a very large explosion and for a few moments the Mosquito was enveloped in flame, the heat of which was felt in the cockpit. Mosquitoes were famed for their strength - NT252 operated after the war with 609 Squadron until 1948! (Paul Mellows)

239 Squadron at West Raynham in late spring 1944. The Squadron CO, Paul Evans, is fifth from left, front row. (Tap Tappin Coll)

Left: Squadron Leader Herbert 'Tap' Tappin DFC and Flying Officer I. H. Thomas of 157 Squadron at Predannack in 1943. On 8/9 February 1944 they destroyed a Blohm und Voss Bv 222 Viking six-engined flying-boat of 1.(F)/129 during a *Night Ranger* to Biscarosse Lake in France. (Brian Whitlock Blundell Coll)

Right: Wing Commander J. A. Mackie (left) CO 157 Squadron from August 1943 to March 1944, with his navigator-radar operator, Flight Lieutenant Leslie Scholefield DFC. (Brian Whitlock Blundell Coll)

Wing Commander 'Sticky' Murphy DSO DFC (left, center) and Group Captain Bertie Rex O'Bryen 'Sammy' Hoare DSO DFC* (right center) during a function at Little Snoring with local farmer, Mr. Whitehead (right) where Murphy commanded 23 Squadron and Hoare was Station Commander. (Tom Cushing Coll)

Sticky Murphy pulls down the dice in the bar at Little Snoring. The bar was designed by Flight Lieutenant Wilton W. Todd who also designed the memorial to the fifty murdered RAF airmen at Sagan in Upper Silesia, Poland. Todd was shot down flying as Wing Commander 'Jumbo' Gracie's navigator on 15/16 February 1944 in the Hanover area. Gracie was killed. A scrubbing brush counterbalanced the large dice. When the 23 or 515 Squadrons were 'on ops' the dice was lowered. As in 'Dicing with death' a lowered scrubbing brush meant that all ops were cancelled – 'scrubbed'. This was usually the sign of a good 'booze-up'. On the night of 24/25 March 1944 76 prisoners escaped from the North Compound of *Stalag Luft III* before *'Harry'* (the name of the tunnel) was discovered. (*'Tom'* had been discovered in the summer of 1943 and was blown up by the Germans. *'Dick'* was used subsequently to store tools and equipment for *Harry*.) 50 of the escapers who were captured, including Squadron Leader Roger Bushell SAAF, who as 'Big X' organised the successful escape and Brettell, who was caught together with Flight Lieutenants R. Marcinus, H. A. Pickard and G. W. Walenn near Danzig, were taken to remote spots and shot in the back of the head by the *Gestapo*. Only Bram van der Stok, Royal Netherlands Navy; Flight Lieutenant Jens Einar Mueller, Royal Norwegian Air Force and Flight Lieutenant Peter Rockland RAF made 'home runs'. (Jean Bunting/Tom Cushing Collections)

Squadron Leader Philip Russell DFC who assumed command of 23 Squadron at Little Snoring on the death in action of Sticky Murphy. (Philip Russell via Tom Cushing)

Pilot Officer Leslie George 'Dutch' Holland of 515 Squadron at Little Snoring, 1944 in front of his FBVI, *D-Dog*, which is equipped with AI.Mk.XV ASH (Air-Surface-H) radar. ASH was a wing mounted radar but could not be fitted to the Mosquito wing so it was installed in a 'thimble' radome in the nose. FBVI PZ459 assigned to 'A' Flight, 515 Squadron at Little Snoring, where it was coded 3P-D *'D-Dog'* and flown almost exclusively by Holland and Flight Sergeant Robert 'Bob' Young. Note the AI Mk XV ASH (Air-Surface H) nose radome. ASH was designed as a wing-mounted radar but it was found to be unsuitable for the Mosquito's slender wing, so it was installed in a "thimble' radome in the nose instead. Following service with 515 Squadron, 141 Squadron briefly used PZ459 before it was placed in storage and was eventually sold as scrap in July 1947. (Leslie Holland)

Pat Rooney caricature of Pilot Officer Leslie George 'Dutch' Holland of 515 Squadron. (via Holland)

NF.II DZ238, which carried the name *Babs* in white on the nose, of 23 Squadron in July 1942. Intruder operations became a deadly Mosquito specialty when small numbers of NF.IIs with the radar equipment removed, known as NF.II Specials, operated over Europe and in the Mediterranean. (via Kelvin Sloper)

FB.VI RS566 of 515 Squadron at dispersal at Little Snoring in late 1944. Issued to the unit almost straight from the Hatfield factory, this aircraft later served briefly with 141 Squadron until it transitioned to NF.XXXs in April 1945. Following a brief spell in storage, RS566 was one of around 57 FB.VIs sold to the *Armée de Pair* in August 1947. (Tom Cushing Collection).

Flight Sergeant Frank H. Baker, navigator-radar operator, and his pilot Flying Officer (2nd Lieutenant) R. D. S. 'Hank' Gregor, USAAF of 141 Squadron. On 14/15 March 1945 'Hank the Yank and Frank' were on a lone ASH patrol in the Frankfurt-Mannheim area in support of the bombers attacking Zweibrücken near Saarbrücken, when they shot down a UEA coming into land at Lachen airfield. The enemy aircraft exploded under their nose just as they began pulling out after closing rapidly to 100 feet. The explosion illuminated the area, and almost at once they drew light flak and were coned by a searchlight, which Gregor dodged by turning into it and diving. This victory was 141 Squadron's final air-to-air kill of the war (Molly Baker Collection)

Squadron Leader R. G. 'Tim' Woodman DFC. On 30 March 1944 he and his observer, Flying Officer Pat Kemmis DFC had a very eventful night in their Mosquito night fighter while the fatal raid on Nürnburg by bomber Command was in progress. A devastating loss of 95 bombers was recorded; Woodman saw 44 of them go down. Flying with 169 and 85 Squadrons Woodman destroyed six aircraft in 1944 including, on 8/9 May at Braine-le-Comte, a Bf 110 of I./NJG4 flown by Leutnant Wolfgang Martstaller. Before their combat with Woodman he and his *bordfunker* had taken off from Florennes and at 0300 hours shot down Lancaster III ND587 of 405 'Vancouver' Squadron RCAF. The Bf 110 belly-landed in a field. Martstaller was KIA in a crash at St. Trond aerodrome on 18 August 1944. In 1945 Woodman took his final score to eight enemy aircraft destroyed and one damaged while flying NF.XXXs in 85 Squadron and BSDU. (Tim Woodman)

Left: Squadron Leaders Giles 'Ben' Benson DSO DFC* and Lewis Brandon DSO DFC* who shared in eight victories flying in 157 Squadron 1943-45. Benson, whose first victory with Brandon as his radar operator was in a 141 Squadron Beaufighter If on 15/16 February 1940 scored his 9th victory on Christmas Eve 1944 when he destroyed a Bf 110. Benson finished the war with ten victories, four damaged and six V1s destroyed. (via Theo Boiten)

Mike Seamer Allen DFC** of 141 Squadron who shared in 12 victories with Harry White DFC**. (Mike Allen DFC**)

Leutnant Wolfgang Martstaller, pilot, I./NJG4. (Cynrik de Decker via Roland Charlier)

B.IV DZ535 of 192 Squadron flown by Flight Lieutenant Roach RAAF DFC and Flying Officer Hank Cooper DSO DFC, which on 23 September 1944 crash landed in a field on one engine at Briston, Norfolk and went through a hedge. ('Hank' Cooper Collection)

Wing Commander Bertie Rex O 'Bryen 'Sammy' Hoare DSO DFC* one of the leading *Intruder* pilots of his generation. In April 1944 Wing Commander Hoare assumed the post of Station Commander at Little Snoring. Despite losing an eye before the war when a duck shattered the windscreen of his aircraft, Sammy Hoare became one of the foremost *Intruder* pilots in the RAF He had commanded 23 Squadron during March-September 1942 and on 6 July had flown the Squadron's first Mosquito *Intruder* sortie. In September 1943 he had assumed command of 605 Squadron, destroying a Do 217 on his first operation, and in January 1944 had notched the Squadron's 100th victory when he downed a Ju 188. At Snoring, 23 and 515 Squadron crews took bets on which one of Sammy's eyes, one blue, one brown, was real. Sammy's main feature was his moustache, which was six inches, 'wing tip to wing tip'.

Wing Commander K. H. P. Beauchamp DSO DFC, CO, 157 Squadron, with his navigator Flight Lieutenant Leslie Scholefield DFC at Swannington, Norfolk in late 1944. On 12/13 December 1944 they damaged a Bf 110 SE of the Ruhr during a chase, which took them over Aschaffenburg airfield during a patrol in support of Bomber Command attacks on Essen. Scholefield initially got a contact at six miles range, which Beauchamp chased, before dropping back to 600 feet astern and firing two short bursts. Strikes were seen on the starboard wing, followed by a large shower of sparks but visual contact was then lost. As was so often the case, the firing of the guns had also upset the AI radar resulting in the target being lost. Beauchamp and Scholefield had better luck just over a week later, however, when they destroyed a Ju 88 West of Koblenz on 21/22 December. (Mrs. Edna Scholefield)

Air crew of a 23 Squadron FB.VI *Intruder* at Little Snoring. (Tom Cushing Coll)

Bomber Support Development Unit, which was formed at West Raynham on 10 April 1944 to develop, test and produce a wide variety of radar and radio equipment for 100 Group. BSDU moved to Foulsham and finally, in December 1944, to Swanton Morley where this photo was taken. Front row 8th and 9th from left: Flying Officer Frank.W. Sticky Clay, navigator; Flight Lieutenant Donald R.'Podge' Howard, pilot. They destroyed a Fw 190 while with 239 Squadron on 14/15 October 1944. Squadron Leader N.A. Reeves and Flying Officer Phillips of BSDU destroyed a Bf 110 west of Giessen on 6/7 December 1944. Squadron Leader B. Gledhill (front row 11th from left) Wing Commander Rupert F. H. Clerke DFC the CO (front row, 12th from left). Clerke flew the first operational sortie, on 4 July 1944, when he and Flight Lieutenant Wheldon investigated V1s. (RAF Swanton Morley)

NF.IIs and XIXs of 157 Squadron at Swannington, Norfolk in May 1944. Far left is Leavesden-built NF.II HJ911. The NF.IIs used by 100 Group units in December 1943 had previously seen much use with Fighter Command and serious reliability problems were experienced both with their Merlin 21s and AI radar. As the first in a batch of 34 NF.IIs delivered to the RAF between September and November 1942, HJ911 had served with 157 Squadron for almost two years by the time this shot was taken, and it went on to serve with 141 and 307 Squadrons and 1692 Flight before being struck off charge on 19 February 1945. Its sole nocturnal success came on 27/28 June 1944 when 141 Squadron's Squadron Leader G. J. 'Jimmie' Rice and Flying Officer J. G. 'Graham' Rogerson destroyed a Ju 88 over Cambrai. (BAe)

Harry White and Mike Allen of the BSDU had a narrow escape on 2/3 January 1944 after taking off from Swanton Morley in NF.XXX MM797 in support of a raid by the Main Force on the Ruhr. Glycol started pouring out of the port engine shortly after taking off and White had to skillfully put the aircraft down in a field. The trapped airmen were rescued by three locals. (Mike Allen)

FB.VI PZ181/E of 23 Squadron at Little Snoring. On 8 October 1944 Flight Lieutenant F. T. L'Amie and Flying Officer J. W. Smith of 515 Squadron were flying PZ181/E when they destroyed a Bf 109 at Eggebeck, Denmark. (Tom Cushing Coll)

As one of 100 Group's most successful pilots, Harry White had joined the RAF as a 17-year old in 1940, having lied about his age. On 4 August 1941 he crewed up with 18-year-old Mike Seamer Allen at 54 OTU at Church Fenton. The following month the two of them were posted to 29 Squadron at West Malling, where they started defensive night patrols in Beaufighters. White was eventually commissioned as a pilot officer on 26 March 1942 and after scoring three kills and two damaged in July/August 1943 both he and Allen were awarded DFCs and Bars followed in April and October 1944. White and Allen's first Mosquito victory came on 27/28 January 1944 when they destroyed a Bf 109 near Berlin. On 15/16 February they claimed a He 177 *Beleuchter* (Illuminator), which was being used in conjunction with single-engined fighters conducting *Wilde* and *Zahme Sau*, tactics against RAF bombers. The pair continued to score until their lengthy tour with 141 Squadron came to an end in July 1944, by which time their tally had risen to 12 destroyed and three damaged. Their final claim was for a Ju 88 damaged whilst flying an NF.XXX with the BSDU in January 1945. (Mike Allen DFC**)

Above: Squadron Leader Robert Daniel 'Dolly' Doleman of 157 Squadron who on 19/20 October 1944 with his radar operator Flight Lieutenant D. C. 'Bunny' Bunch DFC (right) in a NF.XIX shot down a Ju 88 and claimed a Ju 88 'damaged' on their High Level Support Patrol to Nürnburg. Doleman finished the war with ten and two shared victories. (Doleman)

Flight Lieutenant Kenneth D. Vaughan and Flight Sergeant Robert Denison MacKinnon of 85 Squadron and ground crew at Swannington. (Vaughan Coll)

Mosquito NF.XXX of 85 Squadron in 100 Group taxi-ing at RAF Swannington, Norfolk. 85 Squadron and 157 Squadrons had recommenced *Intruder* operations in 100 Group from Swannington in August 1944 after their brief sojourn south to West Malling in July for a month on anti-*Diver* patrols against V1s. 85 Squadron began receiving NF/XXXs in September 1944 and 157 Squadron, in February 1945. These squadron's last bomber support operation was flown on the night of 2/3 May 1945. 157 Squadron disbanded at Swannington on 16 August 1945 but 85 Squadron continued operating Mosquitoes in front line service until November 1951. (IWM)

157 Squadron gathered on the steps of the Officers' Mess (Haveringland Hall) at Swannington. Front row left to right: Flight Lieutenant J. R. V. Smythe; Stevens; Chisholm; Wing Commander H. D. U. Dennison (CO, March-June 1944); 'Towser'; Flight Lieutenant J. O. Mathews DFC; Squadron Leader Giles 'Ben' Benson; Squadron Leader Dolly Doleman. Others identified are Wylde (back row, 3rd from right); to his right is Flight Lieutenant Lewis Brandon; Smythe's navigator, Flying Officer Waters, (2nd from far right). (Richard Doleman via Theo Boiten)

NF.XIX of 157 (Special Duties) Squadron at its dispersal near St. Peter's church, Haveringland on whose land part of RAF Swannington airfield was sited. Note the white band around the base of the church tower for identification purposes.

NF.XXXs of 157 Squadron from Swannington over the Norfolk countryside. NF.XXXs began to equip 157 Squadron in February 1945. (Richard Doleman)

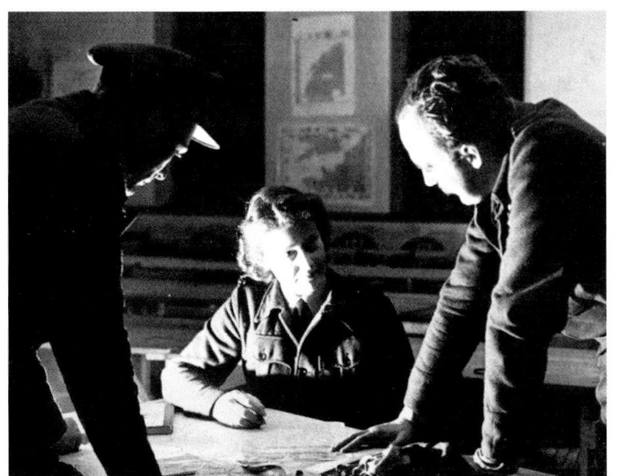

Belgian Flying Officer Henri F. M. E. Cabolet and Flight Lieutenant R.V. D. Smith of 239 Squadron are interrogated at West Raynham by Section Officer Jean Barclay following the completion of a sortie. (Tom Cushing Collection)

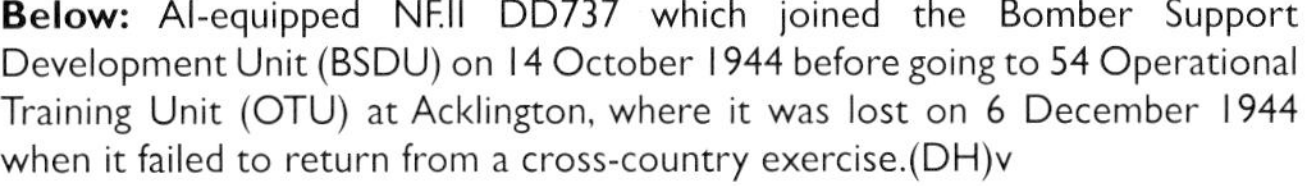

Below: AI-equipped NF.II DD737 which joined the Bomber Support Development Unit (BSDU) on 14 October 1944 before going to 54 Operational Training Unit (OTU) at Acklington, where it was lost on 6 December 1944 when it failed to return from a cross-country exercise.(DH)v

NF.IIs first equipped 157 Squadron on 13 December 1941. DD750, which served with 157, 25, 239 and 264 Squadrons, is fitted with AI.Mk.IV "arrowhead" and wing mounted azimuth aerials. All four machine guns were deleted to make room for *Serrate* apparatus. The all-black scheme could slow the aircraft by up to 23 mph. The first NF.IIs that 100 Group received in December 1943 had seen long service and the Merlin 21s were well used. Finally, in February 1944, all re-conditioned engines were called in and while stocks lasted, only Merlin 22s were installed. (via Philip Birtles)

Leavesden-built NF.II HJ911, which Squadron Leader Graham J. Rice and Flying Officer Jimmie G. Rogerson of 141 Squadron flew when they destroyed a Ju 88 at Cambrai on the night of 27/28 June 1944 and a Bf 110G-4 which crashed 5km west of Chievres, Belgium, thought to be Wrk Nr 730006 D5+ of 2./NJG3. The pilot and Gefreiter Richard Reiff, who was wounded, both baled out safely. Obergefreiter Edmund Hejduck was killed.

Squadron Leader Graham J. Rice (left) and Flying Officer Jimmie G. Rogerson (right). (Richard Doleman)

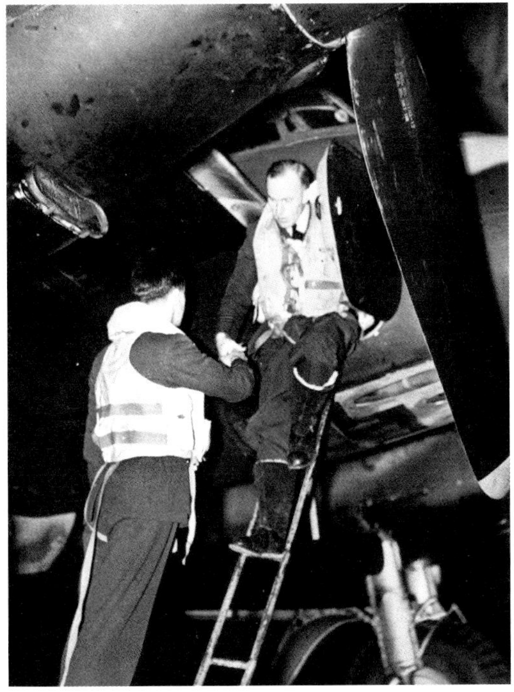

Flight Lieutenant (later Squadron Leader DFC and 'A' Flight Commander) Geoffrey E. Poulton and Flying Officer (later Flight Lieutenant DFC) Arthur J. Neville of 239 Squadron, who destroyed a Ju 88 and damaged another near Eindhoven on 17/18 June 1944.

Squadron Leader 'Dolly' Doleman and his dog 'Towser' with Jimmy Mathews' dog 'Shadow'. (via Richard Doleman)

'A' Flight 157 Squadron at Predannack in December 1943. Flight Commander Squadron Leader James G Benson can be seen smiling in the center of the shot, while Brian Blundell is in the top row holding 'Dolly' Doleman's dog 'Towser'. On Blundell's right are Flight Lieutenants Brooks (Doleman's navigator). Hull (Blundell's navigator) and Huckin, who and his navigator Edwards, ditched in the Bay of Biscay during their tour with this unit following combat. They quickly evacuated their sinking aircraft and got into their dinghy, before transferring to a lifeboat dropped by an air-sea rescue Warwick. The pair then sailed to the Cornish port of Newlyn. Huckin and Edwards were subsequently decorated for their daring escape. (Brian Whitlock Blundell Collection)

NF.XIX TA446/Q of 157 Squadron, RAF Swannington, which made an emergency belly-landing at the 44th Bomb Group, 8th Air Force base at Shipdham, Norfolk on 17 January 1945 following an in-flight engine failure following Flight Lieutenant A. Mackinnon and Flying Officer G. Waddell's encounter with a Ju 188 which they shot down at Fritzler. (Jacob Elias)

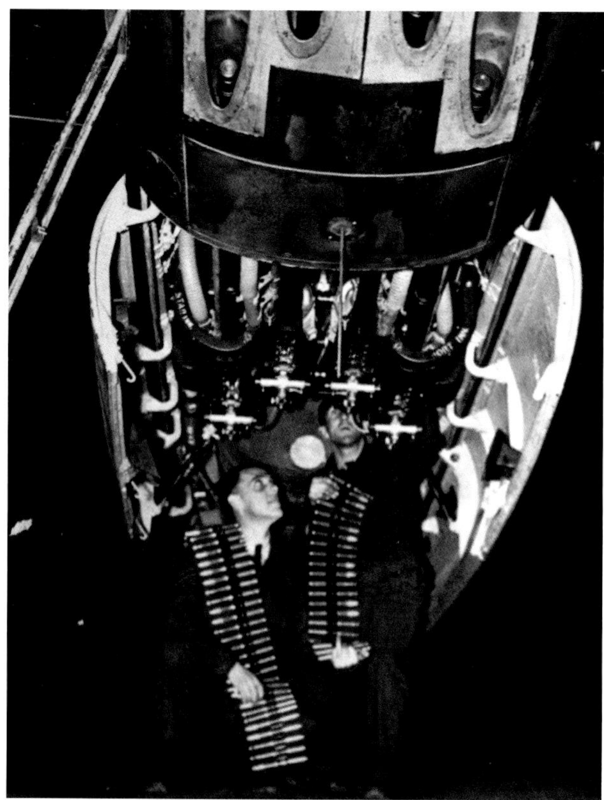

Armorers with 20mm belts around their necks at the request of the cameraman attend to a FB.VI fighter-bomber armed with four 20mm cannon and four .303 inch machine guns. The FB.VI could also carry two 250lb bombs in the bomb bay plus two more under the wings. (Tom Cushing Coll)

'A' Flight 157 Squadron at a misty Swannington in the winter of 1944/45. Flight Commander Squadron Leader Giles 'Ben' Benson DSO DFC* is seated in the middle in front row with Brian Blundell, Hannawin and Sib Davidson to his left. Bill Tofts is seated immediately behind Davidson. (Brian Whitlock Blundell Coll)

Near Left: 'Dolly' Doleman (2nd from left) when a member of 1452 Flight (Havoc Turbinlite) at West Malling, Kent. Roberts, third from right, went onto Typhoons and post war became a captain for BEA. Fourth from left is Thomas who later crewed with Tap Tappin. (via Theo Boiten)

Below: Squadron Leaders Giles 'Ben' Benson DSO DFC* (holding propeller) and Lewis Brandon DSO DFC* to his left with Flight Lieutenant Barry Hull, Brian Blundell and his navigator Gilbert 'Gib' Davidson at Predannack in 1943. (Brian Whitlock Blundell Coll)

Bottom: BSDU at Swanton Morley 1944-45. In the latter, they were still expected to continue flying on operations because the new equipment could only be adequately tested on the job. The BSDU operated a mixture of aircraft, including the Beaufighter, Stirling, Halifax and Mosquito. A modified *Serrate* Mk.IV homer was tested and flown operationally by the BSDU. There was also increased German jamming and interference of the old AI.Mk.IV sets and although frequencies were changed from 193 MHz to 188 MHz, it was not a success and introduced complications in interrogating IFF and beacons. At the BSDU at Swanton Morley pilots such as Tim Woodman, Squadron Leader Gledhill, Flight Lieutenants Neville and Carpenter, specialist radar observers, checked out ASH, *Perfectos*, *Piperack*, centimetric homer and other electronic devices.

239 Squadron personnel outside their crew room at West Raynham. They are, from left to right, at the rear, Squadron CO, Wing Commander W. F. Gibb DSO DFC (who on 5/6 March 1945 with Flying Officer B. C. Kendall DFC destroyed two Ju 88s at Nürnburg to add to their Bf 110 and Fw 190 claims during February), unknown, Dicky Da Costa, Warrant Officer Tanner (obscured, and wearing dark glasses). Flight Sergeant Briggs, Flight Lieutenant Wimbush and Warrant Officer 'Chalky' White. Front row, left to right, unknown, Squadron Leader Holderness (who, with Flight Lieutenant W. Rowley, destroyed a Bf 110 on the night of 7/8 February), Peter Poirette and an unknown Australian (Graham 'Chalky' White)

Captured Ju 88G-1 4R+UR of III./NJG2 now part of 1426 Enemy Aircraft Flight at Duxford during a visit to Little Snoring. (Paul Mellows)

157 Squadron Mosquito in the snow at Swannington. (Whitlock Blundell Coll)

85 Squadron crest.

Snowball fight at Swannington in the winter of 1944-45.

192 Squadron crest.

85 and 157 Mosquito crews at Swannington. (Dolly Doleman)

85 and 157 Mosquito crews at Swannington. (Dolly Doleman)

Left: 'B' Flight, 169 Squadron at Little Snoring, Norfolk sit for the camera in front of a 515 Squadron Mosquito. Back row L-R: Pilot Officer Harry 'Shorty' Reed; Logan; D. C. Dunne; Bob Tidy RCAF, Flight Lieutenant S. L. Dickie Drew. Middle row, L-R: P. A. J. 'Pete' Dils; Warrant Officer Hays; Flying Officer Pat Kemmis; Len 'Tiny' Giles; Flying Officer Stuart Watts; Robinson; Flight Lieutenant R. W. 'Dick' O'Farrell. Front row L-R: Flight Lieutenant Ralph Connolly; Flight Lieutenant R. G. 'Tim' Woodman; Squadron Leader J. A. H. 'Joe' Cooper, 'B' Flight CO; Flying Officer Gordon F. Cremer; Flight Lieutenant A. Paul Mellows. 'B' Flight had a very successful period January-August 1944. On 30/31 January Cooper and Connelly shot down Oberleutnant Karl Löffelmann of *Stab* III./NJG3. During February-May Woodman and Kemmis destroyed four Bf 110s and in August, a Fw 190. On 20/21 April Cremer and Flying Officer B. C. Farrell shot down a Bf 110 and in June-July Harry 'Shorty' Reed and Flying Officer Stuart Watts destroyed a Bf 110 and a Ju 88. Mellows and Drew had to wait until 31 December 1944/1 January 1945 before they got their first victory, a He 219A-2 in the Köln area, their second kill - a Bf 110 - following on 1/2 February 1945. (Joe Cooper)

Right: Oberleutnant Karl Löffelmann served in 9./NJG3 and *Stab* III./NJG3, being credited with one night *Abschuss* before he was killed flying Bf 110G-4 Werk Nr. 740081 D5+LB on 30/31 January 1944 when he was attacked by Mosquito NFII HJ711 VI-P flown by Squadron Leader Joseph A. H. 'Joe' Cooper and Flight Lieutenant Ralph Connelly of 169 Squadron at Leuenberg near Werneuchen, 20 km E of Berlin. Feldwebel Karl Bareiss, *Bordfunker* and Oberfeldwebel Oscar Bickert, *Bordschütze*, both WIA, baled out. It was 169 Squadron's first victory in 100 Group. (Steve Hall via John Foreman).

Flight Sergeant R. B. 'Doc' Dockeray DFM and Pilot Officer Terry A. Groves DFC of 515 Squadron destroyed a Bf 110 in the air and damaged several Bf 109s on the ground, during a legendary *Day Ranger* with Flight Lieutenant F. T. L'Amie and Flying Officer J. W. Smith on 29 October 1944 that resulted in nine aircraft shot down and five damaged. (Tom Cushing Collection)

Messerschmitt Bf 110G-4d/R3 night fighters of 7./NJG3 with FuG 220 *Liechtenstein SN-2d* AI radar, its antenna dipoles mounted at a 45° angle. *SN-2d* incorporated a tail warning capacity. This type of radar equipment, which required a larger (*grosse Hirschgeweih*/'Big Antlers') antenna array than the 212C-1 *Liechtenstein Weitwinkel* (Wide-angle) was fitted to the Bf 110G-4 from September 1943 onward. (Theo Boiten Coll)

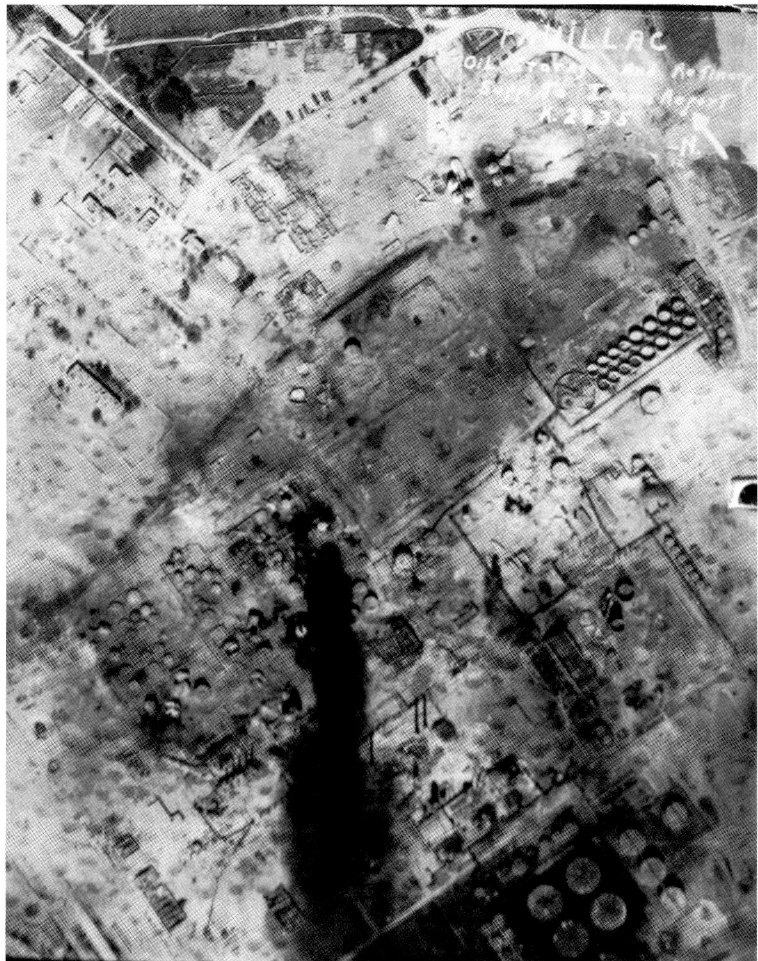

On 4 August 1944 288 Lancasters of 1, 3 and 8 Groups attacked Bec-d'Ambes and Pauillac (pictured) in clear conditions and without loss. 27 *Serrate* Mosquitoes were used as escorts to the bombers attacking these two targets, the first use of 100 Group Mosquito fighters in this way. They did not encounter any German fighters. (via Derek Patfield)

Messerschmitt Bf 110G-4 night fighter in flight.

Line up of 515 Squadron Mosquitoes at Winkleigh, Devon prior to an escort mission for Lancasters attacking Bordeaux on the night of 11/12 August 1944. The second Mosquito from the left is one flown Squadron Leader Mick Martin DSO DFC RAAF. (Tom Cushing Collection)

On 30 September Squadron Leader Henry Morley and Flight Sergeant Reg Fidler of 515 Squadron were returning from a *Day Ranger* to the Munich-Linz-Vienna area in FB.VI PZ440 when their aircraft was hit by a Swiss 20mm flak battery whilst flying between Konstanz and Zurich at a height of just 200 feet. With its port engine knocked out, the Mosquito was intercepted by four Swiss Morane MS.406 fighters and escorted to Dubendorf airfield, over which PZ440's starboard engine also quit, forcing Morley to crash-land near Volketswil. Both men suffered only minor injuries. (via Tom Cushing)

On 23/24 December 1943 when 390 bombers raided Berlin, Flight Lieutenant Howard Kelsey DFC and Pilot Officer Edward M. Smith of 141 Squadron, pictured here in front of their Beaufighter VIF V8744 at RAF Wittering, scored the first 100 Group victory. They shot down a Bf 110 G-4 of 4./NJG1 based at St. Trond and it crashed at Unteresbach, near Cologne. Oberleutnant Lenz Finster, pilot and *Staffelkapitän* was KIA. Feldwebel Siegfried E. Beugel, *Bordfunker* (WIA) baled out. (Tom Cushing Collection)

Aircrew at Little Snoring. Left to right: Frank Bocock; Pilot Officer A. Harvey (both 515 Squadron); Flight Lieutenant Bill Gregory (23 Squadron); Squadron Leader Tweedale. (Frank Bocock)

Squadron Leader Russell and family members on the occasion of his DFC award ceremony at Buckingham Palace. (Russell Coll)

Result of the collision at RAF Foulsham on 27 April 1944 when Halifax III MZ564 of 192 Squadron landed on top of Mosquito BIV DZ377 from the same squadron. (via Alan Hague)

Flight Lieutenant T L'Amie with his original navigator, Pilot Officer S. H. 'Frank' Lindsay in front of PZ344/E which, L'Amie and Flying Officer J. W. Smith were flying on 29 October 1944 when they destroyed a Fw 190 and a Ju W34 in the air and a Bf 109 in the process of taking off and three 109s on the ground. (Tom Cushing Coll)

Warrant Officer Harry 'Butch' Welham of 141 Squadron, who destroyed a Me 410 on 14/15 June 1944 and a Ju 88 on 27/28 June. His radar operator was Warrant Officer E. J. 'Gus' Hollis. (Harry Welham)

Mosquito men at Little Snoring. (Tom Cushing Coll)

NS993 P3-T flown by Flight Lieutenant Arthur S. Callard and Flight Sergeant E. Dixon Townsley, which was lost on the *Day Ranger* on 30 September 1944 when it was force landed in Switzerland. Both crew were interned. This very same Mosquito had been used on the Munich raid of 24/25 April 1944 by Leonard Cheshire, who dived from 12,000 feet to 3000 feet and then flew repeatedly over the city at little more than 700 feet, coming under fire for 12 minutes as he left the target area. Cheshire's contribution to the success of the Munich operation was mentioned in his Victoria Cross citation, 8 September 1944. NS993 was pressed into service by the *Kriegstechnishe Abteilung* (KTA) and was modified as a test bed for the Swiss SM-1 turbofan version of the Armstrong Siddeley Mamba, which was intended to power the Swiss-deigned N-20 jet fighter. After use NS993, together with PR.IV DK310, which force-landed in Switzerland on 24 August 1942, was stored in a hangar for a number of years before it was scrapped. (Tom Cushing Coll)

Prelude to a *Night Intruder* at Little Snoring. In front of PZ338 left to right: Wing Commander Freddie Lambert; Squadron Leader Ginger Farrell; Flying Officer R. J. 'Whiskers' Lake AFC (Lambert's navigator) and Pilot Officer Terry Groves. On 15 June Lieutenant Peter Twiss Royal Navy and Flying Officer R. J. Lake AFC of the FIU destroyed a Ju 88 at Laon airfield and on 7 August they destroyed a Ju 88 at Melun-Bretigny. On 6/7 September Wing Commander Freddie Lambert and Flying Officer R. J. 'Whiskers' Lake AFC returned with a claim for a Bf 109 believed destroyed in the Grove-Copenhagen area. 'There were not many who flew continuously on operations, paying little or no attention to the matter of going on a rest. One of those who did was Ginger Farrell, who made a name for himself as an outstanding personality of 85 Squadron. Rather than protesting or being carried off anywhere, Ginger kept quiet about it all, and just went steadily on his way. I think that perhaps his record in the war was one of the most stalwart; and although he appeared at the time to be under no undue strain, after it was all over he was called upon to make a formidable settlement. Ginger had joined the RAF at the age of 18 soon after the war started and after completing his training as a pilot he was posted to 8; Squadron. He flew with the squadron at Hunsdon from September 1941 until April 1942 and he was then posted to a Defiant squadron, also flying from Hunsdon. He spent the next eight months flying mostly on night co-operation with the searchlights. In December 1942 he returned to 85 Squadron, and he continued with it until September 1944, when he went to one of the Mosquito *Intruder* squadrons as a Flight Commander. Ginger was on the sick list for a short time in May 1945, and after that he was sent to a headquarters staff job on a convalescent rest. But that lasted only a month. He then went back to 85 and eventually, at the age of 23 became CO of the squadron. And he had also by that time become married. Immediately after leaving the RAF - of the six years he was in the Service practically the entire time had been on intensive and operational night flying - Ginger went straight to work studying to become a doctor. He passed all his examinations and started up in practice. And then came the settling of the account with an almost complete breakdown in his health. It will always be to his credit that this misfortune did not impair in any way Ginger's never-failing cheerfulness.' (Tom Cushing Coll)

Squadron Leader Ginger Farrell and Pilot Officer Terry Groves pretend to wave off Wing Commander Lambert and Flying Officer 'Whiskers' Lake AFC for the cameraman but the wheels are still chocked! (Tom Cushing Coll)

Squadron Leader Harold 'Mick' Martin DSO* DFC* (right) of 'Dambusters' fame with Wing Commander Freddie Lambert, CO, 515 Squadron at Little Snoring, Norfolk in spring 1944. Martin was supposed to be 'resting' after a Lancaster tour in Bomber Command, but instead he flew many Mosquito Intruders and destroyed an unidentified enemy aircraft on 26 April 1944 and a Me 410 over Knocke in Belgium on 25/26 July. Flying Officer J. W. Smith was his navigator on both occasions. Harold Brownlow Morgan Martin, born at Edgecliff, New South Wales on 27 February 1918 had been pronounced unfit to fly because of asthma but he worked his passage to England, where he joined the RAF in 1940. Martin was commissioned in 1941. He then served with 455 Squadron RAAF, was transferred to 50 Squadron, with whom he flew a further 23 operations and was then taken off operational flying and awarded the DFC. He was probably the RAF's greatest exponent of low-level bombing. Flight Lieutenant 'Mick' Martin DFC RAAF flew *P-Popsie* on the Möhne dam raid, for which he was awarded the DSO. Exactly four months after the famous Ruhr dams raid, on the night of 15/16 September 1943 when 617 Squadron, were tasked to carry out a raid on the banks of the Dortmund-Ems Canal at Ladbergen. Martin spent an hour and a half plunging at 150 feet in the fog around the canal trying to find a good enough sight on the few spots where the high earth bank was vulnerable. Finally, on the thirteenth run Flight Lieutenant R. C. 'Bob' Hay DFC*, his South Australian bomb aimer and the Squadron Bombing Leader since 617 Squadron's formation, got a glimpse of water in the swirling fog and they at last dropped the bomb. A little later they hurtled back across the canal and saw the water boiling where the bomb had exploded, a few feet from the bank, just a few feet too far, because the bank was still there. Mick Martin was awarded a bar to his DFC. In January 1944 Martin was awarded a bar to his DSO. On 12/13 February 1944 in an attack by ten Lancasters of 617 Squadron with 12,000lb blockbusters on the Anthéor Viaduct, when running in to attack at under 200 feet through heavy fire, Martin's Lancaster was hit repeatedly. 'Bob' Hay was killed and the engineer wounded. The bomb release was destroyed and the controls badly damaged. Martin succeeded in flying the crippled Lanc back through severe electrical storms to Elmas Field at Cagliari in Sardinia, where he made an excellent landing in difficult circumstancesMartin was awarded a second bar to his DFC in November 1944 after he had completed two tours on heavy bombers and one as a Mosquito *Intruder* pilot. By the end of the war he was the only Australian airman to have won five British awards in the conflict. He was granted a permanent commission in 1945 and commanded 2nd TAF and RAF Germany from 1967 to 1970, retiring from the RAF in 1974 as Air Marshal Sir Harold Martin KCB DSO* DFC** AFC. He died on 3 November 1988. (Tom Cushing Collection)

Escape photo of Warrant Officer E. J. 'Gus' Hollis of 141 Squadron. (Harry Welham)

Below: 141 Squadron enemy aircraft scoreboard 3 July 1943 to 6 October 1944 at West Raynham. (Author)

DATE	CREW		DESTROYED	Probably Destroyed	Damaged
3·7·43	F/O White	F/O Allen			1 ME 110
13·7·43	F/S Frost	Sgt Towler			1 ME 110
15·7·43	F/O White	F/O Allen	1 ME 110		
9·8·43	W/C Braham	F/L Gregory	1 ME 110		
12·8·43	S/L Davis	F/O Wheldon	1 JU 88		
15·8·43	F/L Kelsey	Sgt Smith	1 JU 88	1 ME 110	1 JU 88
17·8·43	W/C Braham	F/L Jacobs	2 ME 110's		
17·8·43	F/O White	F/O Allen	1 JU 88		1 ME 110
6·9·43	F/O White	F/O Allen	1 JU 88		
27·9·43	W/C Braham	F/L Jacobs	1 DO 217		
29·9·43	W/C Braham	F/L Jacobs	1 ME 110		1 JU 88
16·12·43	S/L Lambert	F/O Dear			1 ME 110
24·12·43	F/L Kelsey	P/O Smith	1 JU 88		
28·1·44	F/O White	F/O Allen	1 ME 109		
30·1·44	F/L Rice	F/O Rogerson	1 ME 110		
15·2·44	F/L Forshaw	P/O Folley			1 JU 88
15·2·44	F/O White	F/O Allen	1 HE 177		
18·3·44	F/O White	F/O Allen	2 JU 88's		
18·3·44	F/L Forshaw	P/O Folley	1 JU 88		
24·3·44	F/L Kelsey	P/O Smith	1 FW 190		
26·3·44	F/O White	F/O Allen			1 JU 88
20·4·44	F/O White	F/O Allen	1 DO 217		
23·4·44	F/L Rice	P/O Mallett	1 FW 190		
11·5·44	F/L LeBoutte	P/O Mallett	1 JU 88		
11·5·44	F/L White	F/L Allen	1 JU 88		
27·5·44	F/L White	F/L Allen	1 ME 109		
8·6·44	F/O Gallacher	W/O McLean	1 U/I EA		
14·6·44	W/O Welham	W/O Hollis	1 ME 210		
27·6·44	W/O Welham	W/O Hollis	1 JU 88		
27·6·44	S/L Rice	F/O Rogerson	1 JU 88		
4·7·44	F/L Peterkin	F/O Murphy	1 ME 410		
7·7·44	S/L Rice	F/O Rogerson	1 ME 110		
18·7·44	F/O Gallacher	W/O McLean			1 ME 410
20·7·44	F/O Lagouge	F/O Vandenberghe			1 ME 110
23·7·44	P/O Gregory	P/O Stephens	1 JU 88		
28·7·44	W/C Winn	F/L Scott			1 JU 88
28·7·44	F/L White	F/L Allen	2 JU 88's		
28·7·44	P/O Gregory	P/O Stephens	1 JU 88		
10·8·44	F/L Thatcher	F/O Calvert			1 ME 110
16·8·44	W/O Lampkin	F/S Wallnutt	1 ME 110		
11·9·44	F/L P A Bates	P/O Cadman	1 ME 110		
6·10·44	F/L Gallacher	P/O McLean	1 JU 88		

23 Squadron at Little Snoring on 26 November 1944. George Stewart on top of his Mosquito. Left to right: Wing Commander Sticky Murphy; Flight Lieutenant Curd; Flying Officer Joynson; Flight Lieutenant Griffiths; Squadron Leader Philip Russell; Pilot Officer Cocky Cockayne; Flight Lieutenant Tomny Smith; Flying Officer Lewis Heath; Warrant Officer Rann; Flight Lieutenant Jock Reid; Flight Lieutenant Bill Gregory; Lieutenant Christie; Pilot Officer George Sutclffe; Flying Officer Atherton; Flight Sergeant Freddie Howes; Pilot Officer Paul Beaudet RCAF, Pilot Officer Neil; Flight Sergeant Chessel; Pilot Officer Berry; Flight Sergeant Alex Wilson; Flight Sergeant Don Francis; Flight Lieutenant Buddy Badley; Flight Sergeant Tommy Barr; Pilot Officer Kit Cotter; Flight Sergeant Thompson; Flight Sergeant Jock Devlin; Flight Sergeant Jimmy Weston; Flying Officer Spetch; Flight Lieutenant Tommy Ramsay; Flight Sergeant 'Benny' Goodman; Flight Sergeant Jimmy Gawthorne; Flight Sergeant Sid Smith. Joynson and Spetch went missing on 28 October. (Tom Cushing Collection)

NF.XXX of 239 Squadron flown by Warrant Officer Graham 'Chalky' White over Hamburg at the end of the war just after hostilities had ended. (Graham White)

Above: BSDU maintenance hangar cartoon.

Lancaster *P-Popsie* of 617 Squadron with the Mosquito flown in by Squadron Leader 'Mick' Martin DSO DFC RAAF during a visit to the Dambusters in Lincolnshire while he was attached to 100 Group in Norfolk. Martin flew *P-Popsie* on the Möhne dam raid, for which he was awarded the DSO. (RAAF)

On 4/5 November 1944 Squadron Leader Branse Burbridge DSO* DFC* and Flight Lieutenant Bill Skelton DSO* DFC* of 85 Squadron shot down three Ju 88s and this Bf 110 of 6./NJG1 north of Hangelar airfield. The Messerschmitt crashed into the Rhine at 0150 hours, killing pilot Oberleutnant Ernst Runze, although radar operator Obergefreiter Karl-Heinz Bendfeld (WIA) and the gunner baled out safely. Burbridge and Skelton finished the war as the top scoring nightfighter team in the RAF, with 21 aircraft destroyed, two probables, one damaged and three V1s also destroyed. (IWM) **Below:** Mosquitoes taxi out at snowbound Swannington in late 1944. **Opposite:** Route map for a Spoof flight by a RAF B-17 of 100 Group on the February 1945 raids on Pforzheim and Dresden. The notation for the Pforzheim raid on 23/24 February mentions that it was 'a very good prang but quite a few of our boys down. Probably fighters. Diverted to Carnaby base'. Ten Lancasters were lost and two more crashed in France. In all 54 RCM sorties and 25 Mosquito patrols were flown this night. The Dresden notation mentions the first wave on 1st RAF attack on 13/14 February when 65 RCM sorties and 59 Mosquito patrols were flown. (Ted Gomersall)

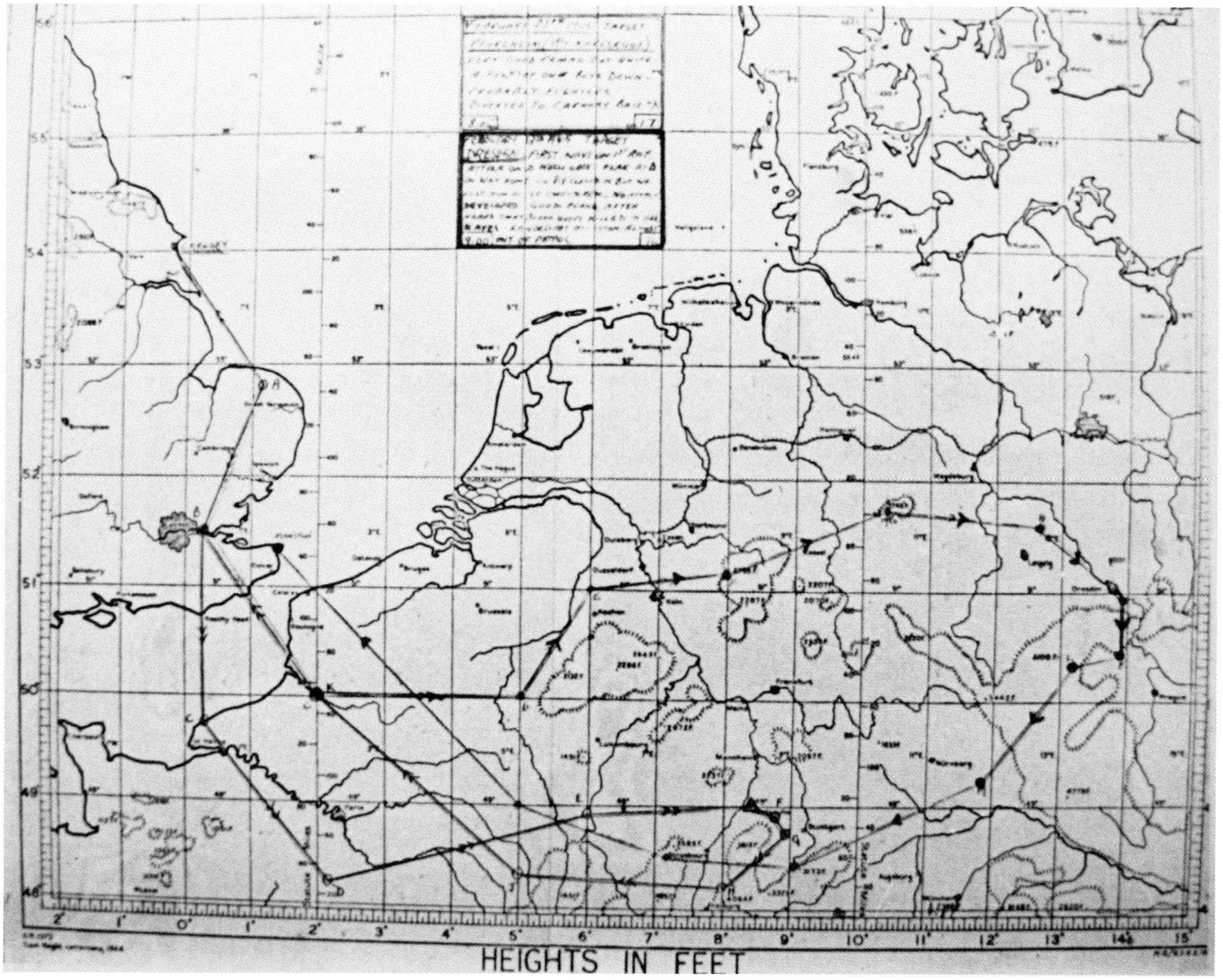

HEIGHTS IN FEET

B Flight, 169 Squadron at Little Snoring sit for the camera in front of a 515 Squadron Mosquito. Back row L-R: Harry Reed; Logan; D. C. Dunne; Bob Tidy RCAF, Dickie Drew. Middle row, left to right: P. A. J. 'Pete' Dils; Warrant Officer Hays; Flying Officer Pat Kemmis; Len 'Tiny' Giles; Flying Officer Stuart Watts; Robinson; Flight Lieutenant R. W. 'Dick' O'Farrell. Front row L-R: Flight Lieutenant Ralph Connolly; Flight Lieutenant R. G. 'Tim' Woodman; Squadron Leader Joe Cooper, B Flight Commander; Flying Officer Gordon F. Cremer; Flight Lieutenant A. Paul Mellows. (Joe Cooper)

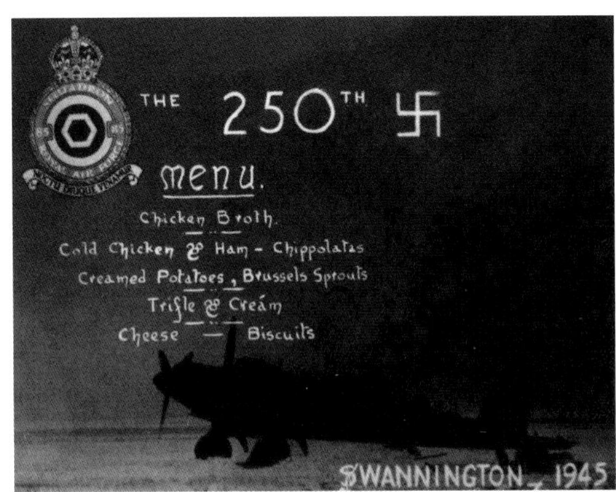

Swannington Menu card celebrating 85 Squadron's 250th aerial victory.

'Hun' scoreboard at Swannington showing aerial kills for 85 and 157 Squadrons in 1944. (Author)

Parade at Little Snoring led by Squadron Leader Russell DFC. (Russell Coll)

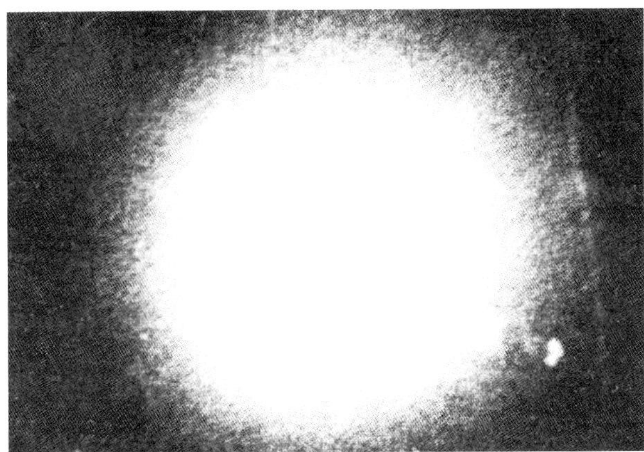

Camera gun frame showing the last moments of a Dornier Do 217 shot down 6 miles N of Prague-Ruzyne, Czechoslovakia on 24/25 April by Wing Commander Howard C. Kelsey DFC* CO 515 Squadron and Flight Lieutenant E. M. Smith DFC DFM in FB.VI RS575/C. Their victim was one of *Nachtjagd's* most distinguished aces, Major Rudolf Schoenert, *Kommodore* of NJG5, who had shot down four Russian bombers east of Berlin earlier that night, for his 62nd-65th victories. Schoenert and his crew all baled out safely. Kelsey and Smith therefore had the distinction of scoring 100 Group's first (in a Beaufighter) and last victories of the war. It took Kelsey's overall score to 8 destroyed, 1 probable, 2 damaged and 3 destroyed on the ground. (Tom Cushing Collection)

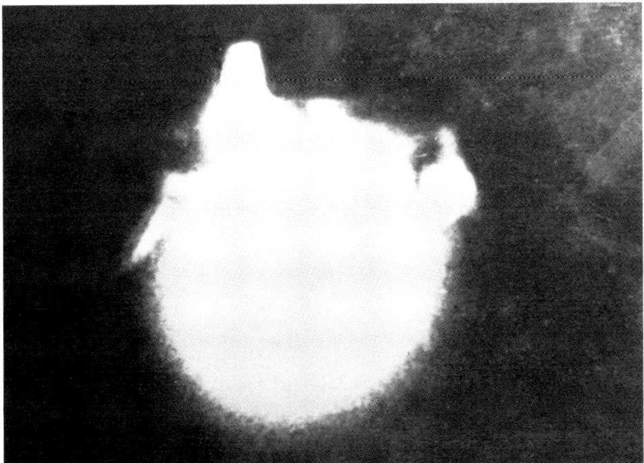

The instant a Bf 110 probably 730370 2Z+EL of 3./NJG6, flown by Oberleutnant Willy Rathmann, fell victim near Stuttgart to the guns of Flight Lieutenant Paul Mellows who was flying NF.XXX NT252 with Flight Lieutenant S. L. 'Dickie' Drew as his radar operator on the night of 1/2 February 1945. The Bf 110 crashed 25km south of Stuttgart. Oberleutnant Willy Rathmann, with no victories, Feldwebel Erich Berndt, *Bordfunker* and Obergefreiter Alfred Obry, *Bordschütze* were KIA. (Paul Mellows)

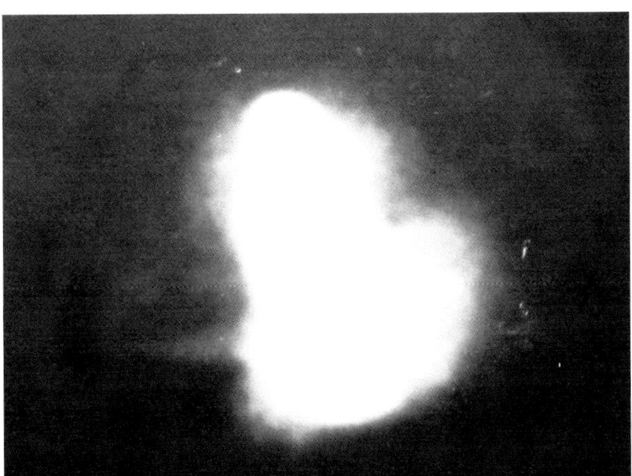

On 13/14 April 1945 Flight Lieutenant Kenneth D. Vaughan and Flight Sergeant Robert Denison MacKinnon of 85 Squadron in NF.XXX NT334/S destroyed a He 219 *Uhu* near Kiel. On the third occasion that Vaughan closed range to 1000 feet Vaughan thought that their twin-engined quarry had caught fire but MacKinnon got his head out of radar set and confirmed that it was the exhaust glow of his BMW 109-003 turbojet below the fuselage. Vaughan immediately pushed the Mosquito's throttles fully open before giving the *Owl* a half-second deflection shot on his jet at about 900-feet range. However, this burst produced no strikes, so he got dead astern in the turn and at 700 feet range fired another burst, which caused a large explosion and strikes on his starboard side. Vaughan gave him another burst 'for luck' and another explosion appeared on the port side. The *Owl* burned from wingtip to wing tip and went down in a spin to starboard. (K. D. Vaughan via Theo Boiten)

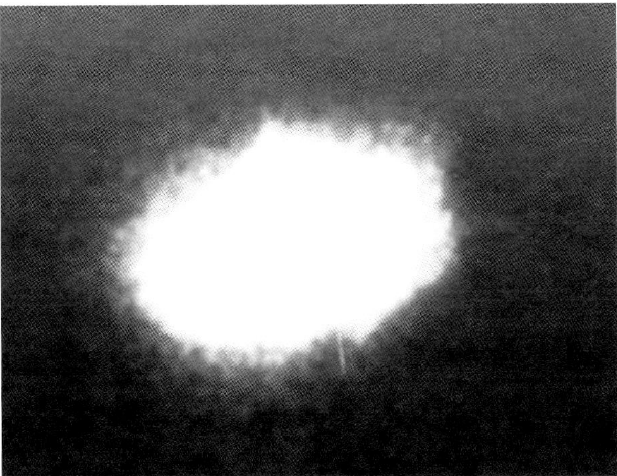

On 16/17 January 1945 Flight Lieutenant Kenneth D. Vaughan and Flight Sergeant Robert Denison MacKinnon of 85 Squadron in NF.XXX NT334/S destroyed a He 219 *Owl* of 2./NJG1 flown by Leutnant Otto Fries. Fries and his *Bordfunker* Feldwebel Alfred Staffa survived when they ejected from their doomed aircraft. On 19/20 May 1944 they were the second aircrew ever to eject under combat conditions after their He 219 suffered an in-flight engine fire. (The first to use ejection seats in combat were Unteroffizier Herter and Gefreiter Perbix of 2./NJG1, who ejected from their He 219 on 11 April 1944. They each received 1000 *Reichmark* from Professor Dr. Heinkel.) (K. D. Vaughan via Theo Boiten)

Chapter 11

Moskitopanik!

"It is not perhaps very well known how successful the Mosquitoes who provided the Bomber Support as fighters in 100 Group were during the latter part of World War II. There were three stages in their harrying of the Luftwaffe night fighters. Some squadrons sent low level fighters to patrol the known German night fighter airfields. Others provided high level patrols near their assembly points, about 40 miles from our bomber stream, in order to shoot them down before they reached it, and a third wave of low level Mossies would arrive at their airfields as they were returning. Very soon after the Bomber Support began operating, the Luftwaffe pilots started to use the phrase Mosquitopanik!"

Lewis Brandon

The mere presence in the circuits of "Mr Micawber-like" Mosquitoes "waiting for something to turn up" as they lurked one by one to cover the whole night period was enough to cause morale-sapping "Moskitopanik" throughout Germany in the summer of 1944. On 4/5 July Warrant Officer R. E. Preston and Sergeant F. Verity of 515 Squadron took off on a *Night Ranger* to Coulommiers airfield via Southwold and North Beveland. They reached the enemy night-fighter base at 0205 hours, but the base was inactive, so they stooged around for three-quarters of an hour before returning. This time their approach signalled the double flarepath to be lit. Obviously, the base anticipated that one of its fighters was returning. Preston reduced height to 1000 feet. Verity obtained a visual sighting of the enemy aircraft at 300-400 yards range. It was a Ju 88, and it was on a southerly course at about their height. Preston gave chase, but the Junkers started weaving before turning starboard and diving. Undeterred, Preston followed. As the Ju 88 pulled out of its dive at treetop height it appeared right in his sights, and Preston gave it a three-second burst of cannon at 200 yards. It set the Ju 88's starboard engine on fire and the aircraft instantly disintegrated, scattering burning debris into the air like an exploding firework. Preston circled the scene before bombing the airfield with two 500lb GP bombs, which exploded on the south side of the airfield. There was no opposition and only four inefficient searchlights vainly probed the cloudy sky. Not satisfied with their night's work, Preston and Verity attacked two small freighters moored side by side in the Zuid Beveland Canal at the Westerschelde lock gates with a three-second burst of cannon fire. Strikes were seen on the bow of one of the ships.

On 5/6 July 1944[276] Wing Commander Alan Michael "Sticky" Murphy DSO* DFC *Croix de Guerre with Palm*, the 23 Squadron CO, and three other Mosquito VIs flew the first Squadron *Intruder* operation from Little Snoring since embarkation leave, with sorties against enemy airfields. Flying *Intruder* operations from Sicily and Sardinia, in the Mediterranean, the audacious and admired Wing Commander's Mosquitoes, or "Murphy's Marauders" as they were known, had been more akin to his private Air Force.[277] Crews quickly loved him for his humanity, his daring leadership, and natural charm, bombing, strafing, and intruding from Bordeaux, on the Atlantic coast to Udine on the borders of Austria and Yugoslavia. At Little Snoring, the ebullient coryphaeus and his daring crews took the friendly Norfolk hamlet by storm and the locals to their hearts. Always one for a drink and a party, Sticky's discordant rendering of "*Rip My knickers Away*" heralded the real singing sessions. What he lacked in melody, which was to the tune of "*Yip Aye Addy Aye Ay...*," he made up for with his usual attack. "*We're a Shower of Bastards*," the traditional squadron song, usually followed. One of the navigators, Bucky Cunningham, was a professional cabaret musician and songwriter, and he added original material to the repertoire, such as "*My Gal Sal is the Queen of the Acrobats*" and "*She's got Two of Everything*." 23 Squadron would leave its mark in social as well as operational circles, and Sticky's exploits remain legendary in the memories of the local people of that time. Snoring's Station Commander was none other than the redoubtable Wing Commander B. R. "Sammy" O'Brien Hoare DSO DFC,* who had assumed the post in April.[278] By late 1944 Sammy Hoare was still flying occasional sorties and showed no signs of losing any enthusiasm. Briefings were sometimes a bit daunting when particularly "dicey" jobs were "on," but Sammy's attitude of courtly chivalry never waned. Stroking his immensely long moustache (you could see both ends at once from behind), he would conclude with, "Let us sally forth and do battle with the Hun," or, on one memorable occasion, a quote which should be engraved in stone: "Gentlemen, there will be flak; almost certainly quite heavy flak. If you cannot go over, you will go under. If you cannot go under, you will go through!" At Snoring, 23 and 515 Squadron crews took bets on which one of Sammy's eyes, one blue, one brown, was real.

The main role of 515 and 23 Squadrons was flying low-level day and night *Intruders*, mostly concentrating on active German night-fighter bases. Although 515 Squadron had been based at the remote Norfolk outpost since 15 December 1943, it had only been introduced to this role early in March 1944. Before then, 515 had operated from Northolt, Heston, and then Hunsdon, during which time it had conducted *Moonshine* operations using Defiant aircraft. *Moonshine* was the code-name given to an operation which was calculated to alert the enemy defenses by causing the approach of a large force of aircraft to be registered on their early warning radar equipment. The large force was, in fact, one Defiant carrying special radar devices. These tests were highly successful, and a Flight called the Defiant Flight was formed in June 1942 and attached to RAF Northolt, under the direction of 11 Group, Fighter Command. From September-December 1942, as 515 Squadron and equipped with Defiant Mk IIs, operations with *Moonshine* equipment were conducted which succeeded in confusing the enemy. On occasions, 300 plus enemy fighters were drawn up by the *Spoof* entirely in the wrong position to ward off bombing attacks by other British aircraft. In December 1942, the role of the Squadron was changed to manipulating a *Mandrel* screen by night, in support of the bomber offensive. *Mandrel* was an American jamming device and was used ahead of RAF night raids and U.S. 8th Air Force daylight raids. Eight pre-determined positions were patrolled nightly by 515 Squadron, which operated from forward bases at West Malling, Tangmere, and Coltishall. This work continued until July 1943, when it was decided to re-equip the Squadron with Beaufighters.

Five crews in 23 Squadron took part in an uneventful *Night Ranger* on 6/7 July. On 7 July Sticky Murphy and his trusty navigator, Jock Reid, flew *a Day Ranger* to France and attacked a convoy of nine vehicles, claiming one destroyed and a damaged railway engine near Ath. Eight other crews flew patrols that night over France, Holland, and Belgium, and carried bombs for the first time. Flight Lieutenant D. J. Griffiths destroyed an enemy train. Pilot Officer K. M. Cotter RNZAF bombed Eindhoven, but no results were observed due to flak from the airfield. Warrant Officer T. Griffiths bombed Le Culot and a large red glow was seen. Flying Officer D. Buddy Badley RNZAF bombed a railway junction near Barnefeld. No flashes were reported, but great volumes of smoke appeared. Only the weather stopped 23 Squadron flying on 9-11 July and adding to the impressive score of enemy vehicles it had run up in the Mediterranean.

On 7/8 July Squadron Leader Graham J. Rice and Flying Officer Jimmy G. Rogerson of 141 Squadron, meanwhile, had taken off from West Raynham at 2317 hours on a *Serrate* patrol in support of Bomber Command attacks on St. Lou D'Esserent and Vaires. Rice reported:

> "Enemy coast was crossed on track between Calais and Dunkirk at 0005 hours and patrol was uneventful until approximately twenty miles south of Abbeville at 0030 hours and 15,000 feet when an AI contact was soon dead ahead and slightly below. Aircraft turned hard port and contact passed overhead, when a visual was obtained on very brought exhausts. At 1000-feet range contact was soon to be a twin engined aircraft traveling at high speed on a NNE vector and looked similar to a Mosquito. Aircraft switched on *Canary* but contact made no response. Contact was followed at full throttle but after two or three minutes it went right away and disappeared in interference and could not be recognised. As contact took no evasive action at any time and made no response to canary, it is thought contact was probably a Me 410.
>
> "Mosquito turned back on track and five minutes later when vectoring 147° a head-on AI contact was obtained dead ahead and below. Contact was allowed to come in to 4000-feet range and Mosquito went into a hard turn through 180° and obtained contact dead ahead and still below at 8000-feet range. Contact was weaving gently and made two hard turns of 90° to starboard with aircraft following hard and losing height to come in from below. No response was made by contact when Mosquito switched on *Canary*, after about ten minutes' chase a visual was obtained at 2000-feet range at 10,000-feet height. Closing in quickly to 600 feet contact was seen to be an aircraft with twin fins and exhausts peculiar to a Me 110. At this moment enemy aircraft apparently became aware of the presence of Mosquito and took hard turn to starboard. Mosquito gave 1½ ring deflection and opened fire with a four-second-burst at 600 feet range. Strikes were seen all along the top of the mainplane leading to a large explosion in the fuselage which as quickly well on fire. The E/A was now definitely established to be a Me 110. E/A turned over on its back and passed underneath Mosquito and was followed down to 3000-feet range on AI then blip disappeared. Mosquito straightened up and orbited to look for E/A and immediately a terrific explosion was seen directly below. Scattered pieces of E/A were seen floating down in flames and one large remnant hit the ground with a further explosion. Combat took place at approximately eight miles NW of Amiens at 0050 hours at 10,000 feet. After combat AI was no longer wholly serviceable but improved after half an hour and aircraft made for the target area. Numerous green star cartridges were soon fired in the air on many occasions and aircraft attempted to investigate several times without success. Stoppages on port guns caused by foreign matter in breech. Claim one Me 110 destroyed Cat A (1)."[279]

During a *Day Ranger* on 10 July 515 had more success. At 1503 hours Flight Lieutenant R. A. Adams and Pilot Officer F. H. Ruffle and Flying Officers D. W O. Wood and Bruton took off and crossed Happisburgh before heading across the North Sea at zero feet for their patrol area in northern Holland and northwest Germany. Both Mosquitoes roared in over the Dutch coast and "beat up" a German Army encampment at Herslake, fifteen miles west of Quakenbrück, soon after crossing into Germany. Strikes were recorded on huts and the Mosquito crews reported general confusion among the "Bosche privates." After this exhilarating interlude both crews flew in the direction of Schwishenahner airfield. At 1637 hours and at zero feet a Ju 88 night-fighter, clearly on a NFT, was spotted three miles in the distance at 800-feet altitude making its approach to land. The Junkers, quite unconcerned, turned left and lowered its undercarriage. Wood and Bruton approached to within about 250 yards, and from below and astern pumped a two-second burst of cannon into the enemy machine. Its starboard engine immediately burst into flames and started down. The airfield defenses opened up on the Mosquitoes with some light flak. Adams and Ruffle went in and finished it off with a further burst of two-three seconds of cannon fire. The Junkers hit a tree near the airfield and exploded. Both crews landed safely back at Snoring at 1814 hours.

Another German prize fell into the RAF's lap when *Obergefreiter* John Maeckle landed his Ju 88G-1 night-fighter 4R+UR of III./NJG2 at RAF Woodbridge on 13 July. The crew had taken off from their base at Twenthe at 2305 and had become lost in thick cloud, which had a ceiling of about 14,000-feet. For forty-five minutes the *Bordfunker* tried to establish radio contact but without success. After four hours in the air and very low on fuel Maeckle told his crew they might have to bale out. However, the flight engineer informed him that he had not packed his parachute. Maeckle decided to get the Ju 88 down. He wrote:

> "Fuel gauges showing empty and descending at six feet per second, we broke through the clouds at 600 feet and miraculously discovered we were coming down right on top of an airfield. I did not waste any time landing the aircraft. When I saw the big white flashing light on the control tower and all the four-engined airplanes, I had no doubts where we were. After we touched down, the plane rolled to a complete stop in the middle of the runway with both engines dead. While bright spotlights aimed at our plane, we sat there for twenty minutes or longer before we were finally approached by an armored vehicle and thus had plenty of time to burn classified material and demolish valuable instruments. We were happy to be alive and well, especially the flight engineer."

Gerhard Heilig, a special operator with 214 Squadron from March to July 1944, heard a different story. He recalls:

> "The Ju 88 did not get lost but was misled by our own people. On one of my leaves I had lunch with my father at a Czech émigré's club in Bayswater. Amongst the group of his friends there was a WAAF sergeant and I made polite conversation with her. To my opening questions she replied that her work was so secret that she could not even tell inc where she was stationed. However, before nmany minutes had passed, I knew that her job was my own counterpart on the ground with 100 Group. When I started to gnu, she told me indignantly that it was nothing to laugh about, it was all terribly important but she was mollified when I told her that I was in the same racket. She then told mile the following story.
>
> "Receiver operators passed Luftwaffe radio traffic to a controller who then issued co-ordinated false instructions to transmitter operators designed to cause confusion to the enemy. One night there was nothing happening whatsoever. Then the controller was roused from his torpor by repeated calls for a homing, which evidently remained unanswered. Mainly in order to relieve the utter boredom of a routine watch he decided to give the lost sheep a course to steer - to Manston airfield in Kent. The German pilot had been faced with the prospect of having to abandon his aircraft and was going to buy everyone concerned a beer on his return to base. He came down safely - to find himself a prisoner and could hardly be expected to keep his promise to stand drinks all round. The aircraft was a Ju 88 stuffed with the latest German equipment, quite a catch for Intelligence. The capture of this aircraft was made public at the time, but not how it had all come about."

Scientists from TRE investigated the Ju 88's FuG 220 *Liechtenstein SN-2*, *FuG 227/1*, and *FuG 350 Z Naxos* radars, the last two types being previously unknown to the RAF. They confirmed *Serrate*'s ineffectiveness and discovered that the *Nachtjagd* was using the *FuG 227/1* equipment to home on to the *Monica* tail-mounted warning device, and the *FuG 350 Z Naxos* to home on to H_2S radar bombsight transmissions. RAF bombers were ordered immediately to restrict the use of H_2S while *Monica* sets were removed from the Lancasters and Halifaxes. Window was modified to jam the new *Liechtenstein* radar.

In July 515 flew over forty *Day* and *Night Rangers*. The third victory that month occurred on a *Day Ranger* on 14 July when Wood and Bruton again figured in a shared kill, this time with Flight Lieutenant A. F. Callard and Sergeant Townsley. Their victim was a Ju-W34 single-engined four-passenger transport, which was unfortunate enough to be in the wrong place at the wrong time as the pair of Mosquitoes approached, twelve miles east of Stralsund. Callard and Townsley went in first and gave it a one-second burst from about 150 yards. At this range the Mosquito was hit by flying pieces of debris but no lasting damage to the British machine was done. The Ju 34, on the other hand, never stood a chance. It went into an almost vertical climb and stall-turned before "fluttering" to the ground. There was no telling what high-ranking officers were on board, if any, but just in case, Wood and Bruton made absolutely certain by giving the smouldering embers a one-second burst until it exploded. None of the occupants would be keeping their appointment at a top-level meeting or climbing into their night-fighters later that evening, that was for sure.

No. 23 Squadron was getting its eye in too. On the morning of 14 July, Sticky Murphy with Squadron Leader H. F. Smith carried out a *Ranger* patrol and took the opportunity to shoot up some German troops on the beach at Stadil. Another famous pilot at Little Snoring at this time was Squadron Leader Harold B. M. "Mick" Martin DSO DFC, who had joined 515 Squadron in April and was supposed to be "resting" after flying Hampdens and Lancasters.[280] Group Captain Leonard Cheshire has written:

> "I learned everything I knew of the low flying game from Mick. He was the ideal wartime operational pilot. He had superb temperament, was quite fearless and innovative in his thinking. He was meticulous in his flying discipline and never did make a mistake."

On an operation over the Ruhr, Cheshire broke silence to enquire about the weather. From a Mosquito came Martin's voice. "What the hell are you doing?" Cheshire asked. "Sticking my neck out for you types," replied Martin, who was strafing a night-fighter airfield!

That night (14/15 July) Warrant Officer Turner and Flight Sergeant Francis of 169 Squadron took off in their FB.VI from Great Massingham at 2310 hours and set course at 2315 hours over base. They crossed the English and enemy coasts on ETA and arrived at their Orbit point and patrolled for eighty minutes with no activity except for two fleeting AI contacts at maximum range, which disappeared into ground returns before any pursuit action could be taken. Turner continues:

> "At 0113 hours whilst on vector towards prang at Auderbelck obtained AI contact at maximum range ahead, well to port and slightly below, at patrol height. Turned port immediately and dived and after a few minutes chase closed range to 3000 feet where target was held in dead ahead position. It was then ascertained that target was on port orbit and on closing to 2000 feet visual was obtained on white light at first believed to be a tail light. Closed visually and when necessary on AI and on nearly overshooting saw that light was exhaust flames. Since target speed was approximately 160 mph. throttled hand back and closed slowly in with my navigator calling out airspeeds. We closed to a position about twenty feet below enemy aircraft winch was recognized as a Me 109. I then dropped back to 150 feet end opened fire,

seeing strikes on starboard wing, and then fuselage caught fire. Enemy aircraft turned on its back and black crosses, blue camouflage and twin radiators could be seen as it passed underneath. A bright flash was seen as aircraft hit the ground. We took a *Gee* fix and plotted his position. The combat took place at 0128 hours at 13,000 feet, confirmed by Warrant Officer Schoolbread in Mosquito 169/G. Our patrol time being up we set course for Le Touquet at 0131 hours and returned to base uneventfully. '80 Rounds of cannon fired. - No stoppages. Camera exposed. One Me 109 destroyed Cat 1 (A). Slight damage to Mosquito from fragments of enemy aircraft."

On the night of 23/24 July[281] Pilot Officers Doug Gregory and D. H. Stephens of 141 Squadron returned from their patrol triumphant. The intelligence officer at West Raynham compiled their report during de-briefing:

"Mosquito took off from West Raynham 2310 hours and set course for patrol area crossing enemy coast at 2350 hours proceeded to *Chameleon* and then to *Willi*, arriving at 0025 hours. Shortly after leaving *Willi* on the way to *Biene* at 15,000 feet, AI contact obtained on aircraft crossing starboard to port way below at maximum range. We turned in behind it and lost height. E/A was doing mild evasive action and half orbits. Chase continued for ten minutes with A/C closing range giving fleeting visuals at 600 feet. Closed further to 300 feet and E/A was identified as a Ju 88. We were now at 9-10,000. On identification panic set in and we desperately tried to get the sights on. Meanwhile, greater panic took hold of the 88 'type' who promptly peeled off and visual and contact was lost, although we also peeled off. Taking a psychological view of the situation we orbited for ten minutes, hoping he would return; sure enough he did and came in head-on well below. We opened up everything and got on to his tail. He was going very fast still weaving and it took us ten minutes to close range and get another visual when we again identified contact as a Ju 88. Due to slightly faulty elevation he appeared much more above than was expected.

"Pilot said, '*He's miles above.*'

"Navigator said, '*Gee, have a go*', whereupon we stood on our tail and at a range of approximately sixty yards, let fly with a one-second burst, which exploded E/A's port engine. We continued upwards in a starboard climbing turn and watched the 88 spiral down in flames and, after going through cloud blew up on the ground with great gusto and much flame. He was still burning on the ground when we left ten minutes later. Patrol completed we returned to base through the usual channels. Claim One Ju 88 destroyed." Gregory fired forty-eight rounds to down the Ju 88, which crashed south west of Beauvais.

On 25/26 July Micky Martin and Flying Officer J. W Smith flew a *Night Ranger* to Stuttgart and Boblingen. They arrived over the area shortly after midnight and stooged around "for as long as possible," but the patrol was uneventful and he headed home. Just after crossing the Belgian coast at Knocke at 0350 hours in very hazy conditions an aircraft was seen about one mile to port flying very fast. Martin swung the Mosquito around to dead astern and below the illuminated aircraft at a height of about 3000 feet. He closed to fifty yards and identified it as a Me 410. Martin gave the *Hornisse* a burst of cannon fire from astern and slightly below at seventy yards. He was so close the tail light of the Me 410 literally blotted out the spot on his ring sight. Martin recorded:

"This inconvenience was adjusted with no trouble at all, and, with the ring-sight moved to the Hun's starboard engine, a short second burst of cannon *set* the engine well alight. This obviously shook the Hun, and he speedily dived to port, but an almost simultaneous short second burst of cannon, directed on the port wing, blew the wing off, and the enemy aircraft, burning well, went down in a screaming dive. The 410 was seen to crash on the sea, and continued burning."

Also on 25/26 July Flight Lieutenant D. J. Griffiths and Flight Sergeant S. F. Smith of 23 Squadron recorded the Squadron's first air-to-air victory since returning from the Mediterranean with an unidentified enemy aircraft at Laon Pouvron. The following night, 26/27 July, Sticky Murphy and Jock Reid, one of six Mosquito crews of 23 Squadron aloft from Snoring, damaged a Ju 88 during their patrol to Châteaudun/ Orléans airfield. Flying Officer K. Eastwood and Flight Lieutenant G. T. Rogers bombed Clastres airfield and shot up railway trucks and a factory building. On 4 August, 13 Mosquitoes of 23 Squadron led by Sticky Murphy and ten of 515 Squadron led by Station Commander Sammy Hoare flew to Winkleigh, in Devon, to escort Lancasters attacking Bordeaux in daylight. When the Mosquitoes arrived over the target smoke from bombs dropped by the Lancs was at 11,000 feet. They flew back over Vannes and Paimpol, covering the bombers, and landed at Winkleigh for the night. Next day at lunchtime all the Mosquito crews returned to Snoring in great spirits.

The previous day's operation was to be run again. Twelve crews in 23 Squadron, including Sammy Hoare flying with Flight Lieutenant W Gregory as his navigator, and seventeen in 515 Squadron flew out and met the Lancasters returning from Bordeaux. Unluckily, Hoare had to abort with a jammed elevator after two hours and landed at Colerne, where all crews returned safely by 2130 hours. Everyone returned to Snoring on 6 August at lunchtime and were rewarded with a "stand down."

On 28/29 July parity with 239 Squadron was almost restored when 141 destroyed three aircraft in one night. None other than Flight Lieutenants Harry E. White DFC* and Michael S. Allen DFC* emulated Booth's and Dear's feat, getting two Ju 88s in the Metz-Neufchâteau area. In the same area, Pilot Officers Doug Gregory and D. H. Stephens destroyed their second Ju 88 of the month, as Gregory recalled:

"We took off from West Raynham at 2315 hours, set course for enemy coast, crossing in at Overflakee at 16,000 feet at 2357 hours. Route uneventful until leaving *Ida* on way to *Christa*. At 0031 hours at 16,000 feet we got an AI contact slightly port and below crossing port to starboard. We turned in behind him and went down. A/C then led us on a vector of 210°M. we closed and after an eight-minute chase obtained visual. Closing still further we got into various positions and finally when about 200 feet directly below, identified A/C as a Ju 88. He was flying quite straight at 14,000 feet without a clue.

"We pulled up to his level and at approximately 100 yards and let fly with a 1½-second burst. Our shells apparently found their mark for his port engine immediately gave up the ghost and burst into flames and smoking pieces came back at us. We broke off to port and watched him burning satisfactorily and going down. He entered cloud at 8000 feet and after a few seconds he lit up the cloud as he exploded on the ground. Time was now 0045 hours and his grave may be found sixteen miles NW of Metz. We then set course for base via Overflakee, crossing out at 0140 hours. Here endeth the second lesson."[282]

When 239 Squadron was told, at the end of July, that it was to be called upon for greater efforts in order to offset a shortage of trained crews and a lack of serviceable aircraft in the two sister squadrons, the general opinion was that nothing better could happen. At the beginning of August, however, German-originated radar, which had begun to bother crews in June, became rapidly more troublesome, and the next four months the maximum detection range of 10,000 feet became a rarity. Even the most experienced and successful crews returned from sortie after sortie with reports of jamming so intense that, as one navigator remarked, it was flooding the tubes and spilling over the cockpit.

Twenty-six aircraft were claimed destroyed by 100 Group Mosquitoes in July 1944.[283] In August 23 Squadron continued daylight operations with a series of *Day Rangers* (operations to engage air and ground targets within a wide but specified area).

100 Group Mosquito victories were on the wane, largely due to successful German counter-measures to the *Serrate* homing device used in the Bomber Support units. In August, 331 *Serrate*/AI.Mk.IV sorties yielded just eight successful combats. Just one was claimed by 141 Squadron, while 239 Squadron, which completed 93 per cent of all sorties it dispatched, destroyed only three but lost two crews: one killed in landing, the other disappearing without trace on a non-operational night flight. Four were destroyed by 169 Squadron. Tim Woodman and Patrick Kemmis destroyed a Fw 190 near Abbeville on 9/10 August when the heavies attacked V-l sites in the Pas de Calais.

On 26/27 August Warrant Officer Les Turner and Flight Sergeant Frank Francis destroyed a Ju 88 near Bremen to add to the Bf 109 they had shot down on 14/15 July. Turner reported:

"Took off from Great Massingham at 2235 hours in Mosquito T, setting course immediately over base, crossing English and Enemy coasts on ETA. Nothing of note occurred until we reached a position at 2345 hours at 20,000 feet. Considerable searchlight activity was observed to port. It was apparent there were obviously aircraft of some sort concerned as we decided to investigate and forthwith 'mucked-in' with a Hun searchlight co-op exercise. Occasional fleeting, AI contacts were obtained all showing hard above. From this, the position of the cone and the firing of apparent colors of the day, it was assumed that there were some aircraft, possibly single-engined, at about 25,000 feet, which made chances of interception very slim with a Mosquito VI. Having ourselves been coned on two occasions, and discretion being obviously the better part of valor, we proceeded to leave that area and attempt to reach our scheduled patrol area.

"At 0030 nothing further having been seen, we turned on a reciprocal westerly course and after about twenty minutes flying, obtained at 20,000 feet, a forward AI contact at maximum range. Target appeared to be crossing port to starboard on estimated course of 030°. We chased for approximately five minutes reducing height to 14,000 feet where target was held in dead-ahead position at 1000-feet range. A visual was obtained and range reduced to 500 feet where aircraft was positively identified as a Ju 88. We allowed target to pull away to 1000 feet range when we opened fire, the port engine immediately bursting into flames. Target turned gently starboard into a diving turn, leaving a long spiral of grey smoke. We followed, firing intermittently, observing strikes all over the fuselage. A tremendous flash was seen as aircraft hit the ground. A westerly course was set for base, which was reached at 0225 hours without further incident."[284]

The two other 169 Squadron victories in August went to Flying Officers Andy Miller DFC and Freddie Bone DFC. Their Bf 109 over Dijon on 10/11 August was their tenth victory of the war. Their eleventh, scored the following night, was not confirmed until after the war, for Andy Miller and Freddie Bone failed to return from a patrol near Heligoland. Andy Miller recalls:

"Freddie picked up a contact crossing slightly 'at quite a lick'. We eventually caught up with it. Vertically above it I identified it as a He 219. I dropped back to about 150 yards and gave it four two-second bursts. We were hit by debris and lost coolant in both our engines. I glided in over the coast of Holland and Freddie baled out at 1200 feet and I followed, at 800-900 feet."

Freddie Bone was captured early next morning and later sent to *Stalag Luft III*. Andy Miller evaded. For four weeks he was sent along the Dutch Underground. Then the network was betrayed. He was among evaders captured at Antwerp and handed over to the *Gestapo*. At *Dulag Luft* the pilot of the He 219 he had shot down in August confronted him! He wasn't too pleased and his arm was in a sling. Andy Miller was sent to *Stalag Luft I*. Freddie Bone DFC* returned to the police force after the war and was promptly put back on the beat!

In September three Mosquitoes were lost. On 6/7 September Neil Bromley and Philip Truscott were killed by flak near Oldenburg during a night bomber support operation for Mosquitoes bombing Hamburg. (Wing Commander I. A. Heath assumed command of the Squadron on Bromley's death.) Flight Lieutenant A. S. Callard and Flight Sergeant F. D. Townsley flew an *Intruder* to Grove and Schleswig/Jägel, returning with claims of one Arado 196 floatplane destroyed and another damaged after sighting five moored in line just off shore at Aalborg. Shore batteries opened up with intense light flak, but Callard and Townsley made it safely back to Snoring with a holed starboard outer fuel tank. Meanwhile, Wing Commander Freddie Lambert and Flying Officer R. J. "Whiskers" Lake AFC returned with a claim for a Bf 109 believed destroyed in the Grove-Copenhagen area.

"Mick" Martin and Flying Officer Smith had a very adventurous op to München and Wien on 9/10 September. They made four circuits of Tulin airfield to make sure the coast was clear before strafing aircraft on the ground. One aircraft was left burning. A second strafing run was made and another "vivid" fire was seen among the parked aircraft. In the Salzburg area on the way home they attacked and destroyed a train which "blew up in a terrific explosion followed by vivid blue sparks." Martin and Smith flew on, pausing to rake installations at Cheim airfield with cannon fire before moving on to the southeast end of Lake Constance, where a seaplane base was also strafed. At Mulhouse, Mickey Martin strafed the marshalling yards and had a pop at railway stations, buildings, and lights. The former Dam Buster reported that "strikes were recorded in most cases."

239 Squadron lost Bill Breithaupt DFC and Flying Officer J. A. Kennedy DFM DFC on 12/13 September. Their grave was found on 15 January 1947, when it was determined from witnesses that they had been shot down by a Bf 110, but had in turn brought this down before their Mosquito crashed. It was their fifth victory. The German crew had baled out safely and they had confirmed the story. Flying Officer W. Osborne and Flight Sergeant Acheson were also lost. Despite 93 per

cent of all sorties being completed, 239 Squadron had nothing to show. In fact, the 240 sorties flown during the month by the *Serrate* squadrons bore little fruit. On the 7th Flight Lieutenants Paul Mellows and S. L. "Dickie" Drew of 169 Squadron damaged a Ju 88 fifteen miles south of Wilhelmshaven. The only successful combat during the month was on 11/12 September when Flight Lieutenant Peter Bates and Pilot Officer William Guy Cadman of 141 Squadron destroyed a Bf 110 south of Mannheim. Despite these successes there were obvious signs that the German defenses were countering the Mosquitoes' *Serrate* homer. On 26 September, Squadron Leader Tim Woodman, who had taken over "B" Flight in 169 Squadron from Joe Cooper, found that there were "plenty of Huns airborne" during a sortie near Frankfurt but found that his "radar [was] completely jammed."

Group obviously took notice of the changing fortunes, for that month the *Serrate* squadrons began much practice (more hours of practice flying were actually recorded than on operations in August) and low flying in anticipation of a new role that was to be found for them. In September, the three *Serrate* squadrons joined 85 and 157 Squadrons, which had returned to the fold at the end of August following their anti-*Diver* patrols at West Malling, on low-level strafing and *Intruder* attacks over enemy territory. No.85 Squadron, which had destroyed thirty-three V1s, and 157 Squadron's Mosquitoes retained the modifications they had received for anti-*Diver* operations except the stub exhausts, which were replaced again with shroud exhausts. Both AI.Mk.X Squadrons were also used on high-level patrols, and the results for both kinds of operation were very encouraging. From 167 Mk X high-level patrols, forty-seven suspicious AI contacts were reported leading to twelve successful combats. Ben Benson and Brandy Brandon, who had destroyed six V1s, opened the scoring for 157 Squadron since returning to Swannington by destroying two Ju 188s at Zeeland on 11/12 September. A Bf 110 was knocked down on 12/13 September by Squadron Leader Robert Daniel "Dolly" Doleman and Flight Lieutenant D. C. "Bunny" Bunch, and Flight Lieutenant Vincent and Flying Officer Monoy destroyed a Me 410 *Hornisse* on 29/30 September. In 85 Squadron Branse Burbridge and Bill Skelton destroyed a Ju 188 on 11/12 September, the first squadron victory since returning to Swannington.

85 Squadron destroyed another six enemy aircraft by the time the month was out. These included two Bf 110s, which fell to the guns of Flying Officers Alan J. "Ginger" Owen (whose brother Don was killed early in 1944 while flying as a navigator on the squadron) and S. Victor McAllister DFM on 17/18 September.[285] On 28/29 September Flight Lieutenant M. H. C. Phillips and Flight Lieutenant Derek Smith destroyed a Ju 188. Phillips, whose father was an Admiral, had joined the RAF straight from school and was known to everybody as Micky. His operator was, in view of his lack of height, somewhat suitably nicknamed "the Gremlin" by his lanky pilot. Phillips always had his long hair hanging down over one eye. It was as if he had a fixed aversion to having it cut. John Cunningham, his CO, would look steadfastly at him for a while without saying a word, then he would firmly press sixpence [5p] into the youthful pilot's hand and issue a quiet reminder to have his hair cut by merely saying, "The next time you are in town."[286]

Besides patrols in the target areas after bombing and around the assembly beacon, escorting the stream was tried with the Mk.X-equipped Mosquitoes of 85 and 157 Squadrons flying at ten to fifteen miles from the mean track. A number of contacts were also obtained on the rearward looking *Monica* equipment carried by the AI.Mk.X high-level *Intruders*. It was found that these contacts could generally be evaded fairly easily, but that it was often difficult to convert them to forward AI.Mk.X contacts—only about a quarter of the *Monica* contacts reported were converted. Thus, it appeared that the main value of *Monica* was the prevention of surprise attack from the rear rather than as an additional interception aid. The Mosquitoes of 85 and 157 Squadrons did not, in general, find much activity at the airfields to which they were sent. They did, however, achieve three successful combats from thirteen AI contacts.

A few weeks earlier, 141 Squadron had at last begun receiving Mosquito FB.VIs. 169 Squadron had had them since June, and 239 had received just one on 31 December 1943. The Mk VI was standard *Intruder* equipment in 100 Group and 2nd TAF. Meanwhile, a modified *Serrate* Mk.IV was being tested and flown operationally by the BSDU. There was also increased German jamming and interference of the old AI.Mk.IV sets, and although frequencies were changed from 193 MHz to 188 MHz, it was not a success and introduced complications in interrogating *IFF* and beacons.

On 2 September Wing Commander Winnie Winn had held an aircrew conference at West Raynham, giving a lecture on the operational aspect of low flying. Another was given two days later, although the first victory of the month on 141 Squadron was the result of an AI contact on a *Serrate* patrol on 11/12 September when Bomber Command visited Darmstadt. Flight Lieutenant Peter A. Bates and Pilot Officer William G. Cadman obtained a head-on AI contact ten miles northwest of Frankfurt at 2350 hours at 18,000 feet. Both aircraft went into a dogfight lasting some twenty minutes, with neither aircraft getting anywhere. *Canary* was tried without result, but eventually the contact made off to the northwest. A chase lasting five minutes ensued, but the contact eluded them. Bates and Cadman returned to the target area, and as the bombing had ended, decided to fly slowly westward in the hope of deceiving enemy fighters that it was a straggling bomber. Twenty miles west of Darmstadt a backward AI contact was picked up 12,000 feet behind crossing starboard to port. Bates turned and followed. For almost twenty minutes the Mosquito tailed the enemy machine through twists and turns towards Darmstadt. Eventually, Bates closed to 900-feet range and a visual was obtained on two exhausts. Bates and Cadman dropped back, but the visual was lost. Closing again, a pale bluish-white light was seen underneath the dim silhouette of an aircraft. At that moment, the enemy aircraft opened up from the upper gun position and tracers hit the Mosquito's starboard drop tank. Bates pulled up, visual was regained on the exhausts, and he gave the enemy aircraft a burst of two-three seconds of cannon fire from 600-feet range. The enemy's starboard engine exploded and Bates had to pull up to avoid a collision as it passed underneath. It was then that they could see in the light of the explosion that it was a Bf 110. Cadman watched the contact going down on his AI set before the Bf 110 hit the ground and exploded. Five other victories that month can be attributed to Mosquitoes of 85 Squadron. During the month, *Intruder* and escort operations for the four-engined bombers in 100 Group were the order of the day, or rather the night.

Bob Symon of 85 Squadron recalls:

> "The 12th of September 1944 was a frustrating night's work. I found two sitting duck targets, a Ju 88 and a Me 110. For the first one the gun-sight suddenly flared up and wrecked Michael's (Miller) night vision. We fired some rounds waving our nose around hopefully but saw no strikes. The second sitting duck was equally fortunate - gunsight dead. The 15th of September the trip to Kiel was short on targets for us but we found that we were an excellent target for them. I have never felt so embarrassingly naked as I did on top of that searchlight cone. Like taking over from Eros in Piccadilly Circus on boat-race night with all the car headlights trained on me. I was thankful that Michael had done two tours in Wellingtons and was quite at home taking evasive action. This was my first experience of this treatment:

at one moment one is being pushed through the bottom of the aircraft and the next one is picking up pencils, bits of paper, a bar of chocolate and whatever is floating around in the cockpit. To give the Germans their due I confess that they were pretty good with their heavy metal. When one can hear the shell explode over the engine noise it must be pretty close."

On 12/13 September Pilot Officer Chris Harrison and Flight Sergeant Mike Adams flew an *Intruder* patrol to Hanau/ Langendiebach and damaged an enemy night-fighter coming into land at the airfield. Searchlights and light flak became very active and patrol time was up, so the pair decided to set course for home and comfort!

On 13/14 September Flight Lieutenant Bill House and Flight Sergeant Robert Denison MacKinnon of 85 Squadron patrolled Germany looking for a ninth victim to add to the tally. 85 Squadron had been short of navigators when MacKinnon had been posted to the squadron straight from training, and he had never been to Night Flying Training School. In fact, he had never been in an aircraft that had occasion to fire any guns. MacKinnon recalls:

"I guided Bill onto a Me 110 near Koblenz and managed to get behind it without the crew being aware of us. Bill opened fire and I thought it was us who were being attacked. The noise, to me, was terrifying but to the enemy it must have been terrible. The whole plane just blew up in front of our eyes."

Their victim was a Bf 110G-4[287] of 5./NJG1 piloted by *Oberleutnant* Gottfried Hanneck, a very experienced pilot who served with various *Luftwaffe* units flying forty different aircraft types for five years before he joined 5./NJGl at Deelen in April 1944. On his fourth operational sortie, on the night of 11 May 1944 he shot down his first RAF night bomber and had gone on to claim another five "*4-Mots*" [four-engined bombers]. He recalls:

"After the successful invasion by the Allied Armies in the summer of 1944, the second *Gruppe* of *NJG1* was posted from Deelen to Düsseldorf airfield at the end of August 1944. The big problem of our night fighter controllers at this time was the loss of the radar stations in France and along the coast of the Canal. Thus, the preparations by the RAF for incursions over the *Reich* could not be established in time and effective countermeasures could not be prepared anymore. Instead, our leadership, suspecting a RAF raid, had to scramble a number of night fighter crews and keep them in the air in case a raid developed. Thus on 13 September 1944 me and Unteroffiziers Erich Sacher, radar/radio op and Willi Wurschitz, who on this mission served as air gunner but normally was a radar operator, were ordered to take off and fly to a radio beacon in the Frankfurt area and await further developments. We took off at 2234 in our Me 110. Once we had arrived at the radio beacon, we flew around in wide circles and listened to the messages from our controllers on the radio frequency relating the developments in the air. Then my radar operator reported a blip on his *SN-2* radar set - he could not quite determine it but gave me courses to steer to the target. The target flew in a Westerly direction at a distance of about 6000 meters. It could be a homebound enemy aircraft. I followed it and tried to reduce the distance by increasing my airspeed. The blip on the radar screen however did not become clearer, and since we had been chasing it for about twenty minutes and by now had probably arrived over the frontline, we had to turn around and return to the radio beacon.

"At this very instant we were fired upon and I saw many hits striking in the wings of my aircraft. The control column was shaking, a clear indication that the controls were heavily damaged, and I ordered my crew to 'prepare to bale out'. At this time, the intercom was still functioning and my crew was not injured. After I told my crew to prepare to bale out, we received another burst of gunfire and the 110 immediately caught fire in both wings and the pressure on my control column was completely gone. The aircraft was plunging down out of control! There was only one option left to save our lives: the parachute. I counted for four or five seconds to give my crew the opportunity to 'hit the silk', and then I opened the roof of my cockpit and jumped out through the ball of fire. Again, I counted for several seconds before I pulled the chord of my parachute, for fear of colliding with my crashing plane. The canopy unfolded and I floated down towards the dark earth. In order to be able to estimate my height, I fired off a Verey light towards the ground. It fell into a meadow, and I swung to and fro three or four more times before I hit the ground. I glanced at my watch and saw it was 2335 hours. I had come down East of Pruem in the Eifel. I had suffered second and third degree burns to my head and hands, and stayed in cover at the edge of a small wood for the remaining hours of darkness, as I did not want to walk into the arms of enemy soldiers. At the break of dawn I sneaked to the East and soon I ran into German soldiers. My crew had been killed in the crash. In this way, a RAF long- range night fighter 'revenged' my six night kills of four-engined bombers."[288]

On 16/17 September, Bomber Command's operations were in support of the Allied airborne landings at Arnhem and Nijmegen, in Holland. Six Mosquitoes of 239 Squadron supported attacks on German airfields in Holland and Germany during the night and 141 took part at dawn on the 17th. Winnie Winn and five other Mosquito crews carried out a low-level attack on Steenwijk, one of three airfields bombed during the night. Four Mosquitoes were damaged by flak. Winnie Winn damaged a twin-engined Junkers on the ground, and buildings and personnel were strafed. Trains were attacked on the way home.[289] Six more Mosquitoes from 239 Squadron kept up the momentum, with support raids on the airfields again the following night. At last light on 18 September, two Mosquitoes of 141 Squadron flew protective patrols for nine Fortresses of 214 and 223 Squadrons supplying a *Mandrel* screen off the Dutch coast and the action was repeated again at first light on the 19th. The Fortresses were covered by two 141 Squadron Mosquitoes again at last light on the 22nd. By the end of September, the score for the two *Serrate* squadrons at West Raynham stood at thirty-eight destroyed by 239 Squadron and twenty-five destroyed by 141 Squadron. Despite the problems with *Serrate*, these sorties still predominated; 141 Squadron, for instance, flying sixty-two *Serrate* sorties on eleven nights and fourteen *Intruder* sorties.

On 26/27 September Squadron Leader Henry Morley and Flight Sergeant Reg Fidler took off on an *Intruder* to Zellhausen airfield, where they destroyed a twin-engined aircraft (possibly a He 111) on its approach. Three days later they flew to the forward airfield at St Dizier with Arthur Callard and E. Dixon Townsley in *T-Tommy* for a *Day Ranger* to the München-Linz-Wien area. The two Mosquitoes took off at twelve noon and headed for Holzkirchen airfield, twenty miles south-southeast of München. Morley and Fidler attacked, firing a four-second burst, damaging and probably destroying on the ground two Siebel SI 204 radio, radar, and navigation trainers. Their drop tanks gone, Morley and Fidler parted company with Callard and Townsley. On the way back they strafed a number of Ju 86s parked on the perimeter of München/Neubiburg airfield. They were between Konstanz and Zurich when, at 200 feet Morley and Fidler's Mosquito was hit by 20mm flak from a Swiss battery. Morley feathered the port propeller. Four Swiss Morane 406 fighters appeared and formated on the damaged Mosquito, which was losing height. The firing of Very cartridges and their general behaviour indicated that they wanted the Mosquito to land at Dubendorf. However, when over the airfield the Mosquito's starboard engine also quit and Morley crash-landed near Volketswil. Both men suffered only minor injuries.

The crew of *T-Tommy*, meanwhile, had continued their *Day Ranger* with an attack on a seaplane base at Prien. Callard and Townsley attacked at 500 feet and destroyed two Do 24 floatplanes moored near the shore. Satisfied with their work, they carried on to the Salzburg area and investigated a small grass airfield at Friedberg, about twenty miles northeast of Salzburg. They spotted a Bf 109G parked near a hangar and attacked it. The Messerschmitt exploded and pieces hit the low flying Mosquito. They were returning to base when, passing Prien again, wreckage of their earlier handiwork was seen floating in the water. Callard and Townsley immediately went in to attack the remaining Do 24, which was sunk by a burst of cannon from 200 feet. At about 1435 hours, when south of München at zero feet, *T-Tommy's* starboard radiator began running hot. Southeast of Lake Constance, as the temperature rose and the needle went off the clock, Callard shut down the right engine and feathered the propeller. He found it difficult to gain height on the one good engine, which was worrying because of the hilly terrain.

Almost an hour later, when north of Zurich, four Swiss Bf 109 fighters slowly overtook and formated on *T-Tommy*. Two flew off the right wing and the other pair took the left wing. The Swiss made no attempt to attack, and the Mosquito crew pretended to ignore their presence, but the Swiss fighters closed in and indicated that they had to land. This was done safely on one engine at Dubendorf, near Zurich, at about 1600 hours. Morley and Fidler were removed to hospital in Zurich and then interned along with Callard and Townsley. All four men later escaped from their captivity and got back to England.

Bob Symon of 85 Squadron recalls:

"On 27 September 1944 we did an Intruder patrol to Ober-Ulm. Nothing seen. Very thundery. This was my last flight with Michael and his last too. He has done two tours in Wellingtons, and I think that this was his third tour with night fighters. He was sent to see the MO after we came back from this flight and was sent to hospital for examination. They found he had diabetes. When one considers the work he has done since the beginning of the war it is a wonder he lasted that long. Captain Svein Heglund of the Norwegian Air Force came to the Squadron at the beginning of October. He had no Nav/Rad waiting for him and I was asked to show him around until his Nav/Rad turned up. After a couple of flights we got on so well that I went to the CO and asked him to let me have him permanently. We flew our first op on 14 October, a bomber support run to Brunswick. We had one chase but it was one of ours. We did four more Ops in October, all of them different. The first was hunting for Heinkels, which launched flying bombs from over the North Sea. This involved flying at less than 500 feet on a bumpy windy night. We never found anything, but I was mightily impressed by the way Svein handled the Mossie. The next one was supporting our minelayers in the Kattegat. We had one chase but it was, again, one of our own. The next was a low level ranger patrol to Vechta/Diepholz, which we didn't reach as the radar set gave up and died. It was a bright night so we stayed low and kept our eyes open for a likely target on the ground. At one point we were shot at by light flak which seemed to cover the ground for miles around. Tracer was coming from all sides and I wondered how we were going to get out of this mess. My unflappable Norwegian put our nose down and all was peace. I said, 'Thank God we are clear of that horrible place.' - 'Not Yet' said Svein, 'but at this height if they shoot at us they will shoot each other.' At this point my breathing got back to normal and the adrenaline took over. Hedge hopping by moonlight! We had a pot shot at a train and missed, I think we had more luck with a car, we hoped it was full of Gestapo agents. As we turned away a pair of cooling towers faced us: no room to climb over, so go between. Svein had to bank a bit to get through. This brought us to a small town. I looked up at the church clock as we passed - it was just after ten pm. I did some research with the map and decided that we had passed over Meppen. I don't think I want to do that over again. The final op on the 31st was a bomber support run to Frankfurt."

On 26 September 23 Squadron flew a *Day Ranger* with two Mosquitoes against Grove aerodrome in Denmark. One of the Mosquitoes was flown by Bud Badley, the other by Canadian Flying Officers George Stewart and Paul Beaudet. Stewart recalls:

"I'll never forget trying to find Grove aerodrome. Just before our attack on the *Freya* radar installation. Before we knew it, we were right in the center of it at nought feet. The Germans were as surprised as we were. First thing I saw was an erk adjusting camouflage netting covering an aircraft in one of the dispersal bays. Then I saw an 88 on what appeared to be the horizon and climbed slightly to attack. As I started to fire, an erk from the 'kite' ran like hell, off to the left. We attacked the *Freya* and stirred up hornets' nest. We took a .303 in a feathering button, and Bud Badley had an engine shot op and diverted to Woodbridge on one fan and no rudder control. Both aircraft were damaged, one almost a write-off, so after that we stuck to straight intruding and night targets."

Meanwhile, on 20 August 85 and 157 Squadrons had resumed Bomber support duties from Swannington. Even so, 100 Group Mosquito victories were on the wane, largely due to successful German counter-measures to the *Serrate* homing device used in the Bomber Support units. During August 100 Group Mosquitoes claimed only eight aircraft destroyed. Between 6/7 and 12/13 September eight more German night-fighters fell to 100 Group Mosquitoes. Leslie "Dutch" Holland, an FB.VI pilot in 515 Squadron, describes Mosquito *Intruder* operations:

"The object was to cause as much disruption as possible to German night-fighter operations. On fairly deep penetrations requiring the fuselage fuel tank, no bombs were carried but the 20mm guns could be used whenever there were signs of enemy activity. It was also a part of the briefing for all *Intruders* to attack transport of all kinds. However, this was not entirely a one-sided activity. Many trains carried light flak batteries, which made it foolhardy to make the simpler lengthways attack. It is very much easier to aim the length of a train and much more difficult to get elevation and range in a crossing attack, even in daylight. In addition, night trains were more likely to be carrying some very explosive loads. All fuel for V2 rockets was taken to launch sites by rail. Activity of this type occurred on most sorties and only occasionally got a mention in our logbooks if really positive results were observed. While on patrol at an airfield, light flak was usually encountered and at some airfields various devices were kept in readiness for the protection of aircraft landing or taking off. These included flak screens on the final approach path, which probably accounted for several *Intruders* who went missing. We were repeatedly reminded at briefing to be wary of following an aircraft into the runway threshold and to refrain from continuing an attack below 200 feet. But at such times the eyes are not on the altimeter but at the gunsight and it is easy to misjudge height, especially on a dark night with ground details not too clear. Discretion gets elbowed aside.

"A five-hour flight without much activity on the patrol and two hours each way out and back tends to get a bit tedious strapped to the seat the whole time. But the need to stay alert and keep a look out does not cease until the wheels are firmly on the ground. The aircraft were eventually fitted with *Monica,* a rearward looking radar which was intended to indicate the presence of an aircraft behind, but it gave so many false alarms that it became a normal practice to try a couple of turns to see if the pursuer followed exactly. If it did, it was pretty safe to assume that it was a spurious 'ghost'. There will always be the one occasion when the cry wolf' is not to be ignored. There were also rumors of balloons on lengths of wire and I am bound to say that some of the 'ghosts' behaved very much as if they were just that.

"All navigation after crossing the coast was by contact flying, or if the ground was obscured, by dead reckoning. Contact flying means simply map reading and endeavoring to anticipate prominent ground features. It is an art, which improves with experience, but I had been fortunate in having been on a two-week course in 1942 at No. 2 School of Air Navigation at Cranage, which specialized, in low-level pilot navigation. It taught how to look ahead for the next line features; how to assess, reasonably correctly, the size of area features like woods and lakes and built-up areas and how to work out course corrections in one's head. That was in daylight. At low level at night it's a different story but that course provided an invaluable grounding.

"We flew several sorties to patrol night-fighter airfields such as Marx and Varel near Wilhelmshaven; Vechta and Quakenbrück, north of Osnabrück and near the Dummer Lake; Hanau; Lippstadt: Erfurt and Schwabisch Hall. The Dummer Lake was one of a pair in Northwest Germany, which were easily identified landmarks. In impromptu sessions round the piano in the mess "Press on Regardless - never mind the weather" a little ditty commemorating the fact was a regular favorite. Among other things, which we saw, in our comings and goings there were of course several sightings of flying bombs. Although the jet flame could be seen from a long way off in clear conditions it was extremely difficult to assess the actual distance. On more than one occasion we witnessed the launch of a V1 in the middle of the North Sea. But a bit of simple trig' will show that apart from failing to make our own target on time, it would be an impossibility to make an interception of an object traveling on its own vector at around 400 mph.

"One sortie brought us back on a course to pass northwestwards, well clear to the east of Antwerp. This was at the time when it was the principal supply port for the Allied armies. We picked up a V1 and set off after it but it was too low for us to range it in the ground returns on the ASH. However, it ought to be possible to tell if one was within about 400 yards, or so one would think. A handy patch of moonlight suddenly revealed that we were going along a heavily wooded valley at treetop height. This was not the spot to generate a cataclysmic explosion even if one could be sure of doing so and it was deemed prudent to delay the attack until circumstances were more propitious. Further progress in our stalk was made inadvisable by the rise of a wall of tracer ahead. We had crossed it clear into the Antwerp *Diver* defenses and our only option was a very steep turn out of it. All *Diver* defenses were ordered to shoot at everything but everything - flying below a certain height unless specifically ordered (for which on a later occasion I had reason to be thankful)."

By the end of September 100 Group Mosquitoes had claimed 14 aircraft destroyed.[291] In October another 17 were claimed.[292]

October saw a great decrease in the effectiveness of the enemy opposition to the night bomber. This was a combined result of the Allied advance into the continent and the technical and tactical countermeasures employed. The enemy warning and inland plotting systems were thrown into confusion. The low-level and high-level *Intruder* played no small part by causing the enemy to plot hostile aircraft over very wide areas, as well as forcing him to broadcast frequent warnings of the presence of hostile aircraft to his own fighters. In fact, 100 Group fighters made a very important contribution to Bomber Support. The fighters also took part in the Window feints, flying with them to add to the effect of deception and then fanning out to take advantage of enemy reaction.

In October the *Serrate* Squadrons led the rest of the field with six enemy aircraft destroyed to the AI.Mk.X Squadrons' five. 141 Squadron shot down three enemy aircraft (although these were accomplished using AI and not *Serrate*) and 239 Squadron also scored three, while 169 Squadron damaged three enemy aircraft that month. This Squadron was in the process of having nine of its *Serrate* homers replaced by *Perfectos*, a homer that gave a bearing on the enemy night-fighter's IFF set and had a range of forty miles. Stopgap arrangements were made to fit some of 141 Squadron's Mosquitoes with ASH (Air-Surface H). This was a centimetric radar originally developed in the USA as an ASV (air-to-surface-vessel) radar for U.S. Navy aircraft and the Fleet Air Arm. ASH was a wing mounted radar, but it could not be fitted to the Mosquito wing so it was installed in a "thimble" radome in the nose.

The first of the victories by 141 Squadron occurred on 6/7 October when Flight Lieutenant A. C. Gallacher DFC and Pilot Officer G. McLean DFC destroyed a Ju 88 during a *Serrate* patrol to Dortmund and Bremen.[293] The night following (7/8 October), Flight Lieutenant Jimmy Mathews and Warrant Officer Alan "Penny" Penrose of 157 Squadron picked up a contact at six miles range west of Neumünster while on a high level support sortie. Mathews narrowed the range, and as they got a visual at 1000 yards the target straightened out. It was recognized as a Me 410 with long-range tanks. Mathews opened fire with a short burst from 100 yards dead behind. Strikes were seen and a small explosion occurred in the starboard engine. Another burst and the starboard engine caught fire. It dived, burning to the ground, and exploded. Flight Lieutenants Paul Mellows and S. L. "Dickie" Drew of

169 Squadron on a Support patrol to Egmond returned with a claim for a Ju 88 damaged. Mellows wrote:

> "Mosquito arrived in Patrol area at 2005 hours, flying at 15,000 feet. Two beacons flashing 'QC' and 'CT' respectively were observed near two airfields fifteen miles to the North so Mosquito proceeded to the area to investigate. At 2022 hours an AI contact was obtained hard port at maximum range, our height being 14,000 feet. Mosquito closed to 7000 feet when target commenced hard urns to port through a number of orbits. Enemy aircraft then straightened out and climbed at low IAS and Mosquito closed to 100 feet to identify enemy aircraft as Ju 88 vertically above height 18,500 feet in climbing at 140 IAS to attack, Mosquito dropped back and opened fire at 500 feet. Time 2037 hours. Strikes being observed between the starboard engine and fuselage. Enemy aircraft immediately peeled off to port and visual was lost, but contact was held at 10,000 feet range and Mosquito closed again losing height to 14,000 feet and obtained another visual while in hard starboard turn, at 500 feet on enemy aircraft which was losing height and turning starboard. However visual could not be held and no further AI contact was obtained on enemy aircraft, which was inside minimum range. Mosquito continued to patrol the area, where three aerodromes were now lit, until 2120 hours at heights ranging between 7000 and 15,000 feet, numerous sisters were seen to be fired mostly well below but no further contacts were obtained. Course was then set for base. Rounds fired. 140. No Stoppages. Claim, one Ju 88 damaged Cat.III (B)."

On 19/20 0ctober, when 853 bombers raided Stuttgart and Nürnburg, 141 and 239 Squadrons dispatched a total of twenty-six Mosquitoes. Warrant Officer Falconer and Flight Sergeant Armor of 239 Squadron shot down an enemy aircraft, and two Ju 88s fell to the guns of 141 Squadron. A Ju 88 was claimed by Pilot Officer J. C. Barton and Flight Sergeant R. A. Kinnear as "damaged" which they attacked on three separate occasions, ten-fifteen miles north of Nürnburg. Squadron Leader Goodrich confirmed this as a victory upon their return to West Raynham. His inspection revealed the leading edge of the Mosquito's starboard spinner and starboard mainplane were extensively covered in oil from their victim, while several indentations in the aircraft were found to be caused by flying debris.

Flight Lieutenant G. D. "Charlie" Bates and Flying Officer D. W. Field destroyed the second Ju 88 approximately ten miles southeast of Karlsruhe after a ten-minute chase. Charlie Bates gave the Ju 88 a two-second burst of cannon fire from 300 feet dead astern. After what seemed like "hours," the enemy aircraft's starboard engine burst into flames and the Ju 88 pulled up in a hard starboard turn. Bates turned hard port and came in to deliver a second attack. However, the Junkers was by now well alight, and after firing red and white Verey lights went into a steep dive into cloud. Two seconds later two explosions of great force were seen below the second one lighting up the whole cloud. The Ju 88 split into three pieces, which were picked up on AI, scattering themselves into the night.[294] Four aircraft were destroyed by 85 Squadron and 157 Squadron scored one victory, a Bf 110, which fell to the guns of Flight Lieutenant Jimmy Matthews on 7/8 October. On 14/15 October and again on 19/20 October Branse Burbridge and Bill Skelton destroyed a Ju 88. On the latter Squadron Leader Dolly Doleman and "Bunny" Bunch DFC shot down a Ju 88 and claimed a Ju 88 "damaged." Doleman wrote in his report:

> "We were airborne Swannington at 1924 hours on High Level Support Patrol to Nürnburg. Patrol was uneventful from 2056 hours to 2102 hours when a contact was obtained head-on, same height, at four miles range at Beacon *Fritz*. Turned round on to a target at approximately the same height. Closing in with visuals at 2000 feet when we went through searchlight cone. Target pooped off some colors, about six stars, mixed green and white, illuminating us. Searchlights doused. Target on course of 310, which seemed very 'phoney', so closed to 400 feet and identified as a Ju 88. Dropped back to about 800 feet and in spite of having a screened sight, when I put spot on him he disappeared. Had a squirt and missed. Target continued straight and level. Repeated process with strikes all along fuselage from dead astern. Target just seemed to drop straight down and went into 10/10[ths] cloud at 8000 feet, contact disappearing from C scope on –15 with extreme speed. Fanned around, then did a reciprocal at about 11,000-12,000 feet. Contact obtained port, turning port at four miles. Closed at full boost and revs and identified another Ju.88 with night glasses at 14,000 feet, about 600-feet range. Had a squirt with no results, and target peeled off port down to 10,000 feet. Followed on AI and closed into 800 feet on target, climbing port. It leveled off again at 14,000-feet, so had another squirt. Target again peeled off to port to 10,000 feet, and again contact held. Climbed and closed to about 800 feet at 12,000 feet, squirted once more with mass of strikes on port wing root, and thereabouts. Target slowed down very quickly and in spite of throttling right back overshot to starboard, as he dived to port. Inaccurate traces came from dorsal position. Much profanity as we thought he had got away. But when he was below at about 7000 feet range on *Monica*, he caught fire and went down burning though not fully alight, in a 45-degree dive, the flames spreading quite nicely until he hit the deck, somewhere near a steady searchlight. No more joy, so set course for base at 2200 hours. Flight Lieutenant Bunch was 'wizard' on the infernal machine, never making a mistake. I should like to add that the night glasses are really invaluable, being an incurable optimist I had them slung rang my neck before starting the patrol - in any case that is about the only place vacant in the flying power house."[295]

The *Serrate* Mosquitoes carried out a number of Day and Night *Intruder* operations during the month. On 17 October, Tim Woodman flew a daylight *Intruder* sortie to northeast Germany. He recalls:

> "Squadron Leader Mike O'Brien DFC, a pilot from 23 Squadron, came as my observer and Pilot Officer Pierre Dils DFC (Belgian) as my No. 2. Fifty miles off the Danish coast Dils saw two men in a dinghy. They did not wave and looked like 'krauts'. I sent him back to call up and radio their position. The Germans were informed as they were too far out for our rescue services. We pressed on alone, crossing into the Baltic without any trouble. Flew past German airfield at Eggebeck, which looked deserted. Low-level flak with tracer had me doing ducks and drakes at fifty feet to avoid it. Crossed into the main coast at Barth. What I thought was a forest fire lookout platform in the conifers proved to be a sentry post at Barth *Stalag Luft I*. Barthropp was a prisoner there and a test pilot with me at Boscombe Down after the war. He said I had flown right over the camp at midday.) Some fifty miles inland I shot up a long train of tanker wagons (empty)

plus the loco. On the way out I shot up the Heinkel factory at Barth. No aircraft on the airfield or in the air. Was able to put some cannon shells into a converted M/Y, which had shot at me on the way in. Crossing Schleswig-Holstein there was a small passenger train entering a small station. I shot up the engine. Passengers got out and started to run across a field. I dived down on them as they stared terror-struck at me. 'Don't shoot,' Paddy O'Brien said. 'They're nice people up here.' I had no intention of doing so, only giving them something to tell their grandchildren about. We found machine-gun bullets in our starboard engine, probably from a sentry on one of those platforms at Barth, when we got back."

Warrant Officer Turner and Flight Sergeant Francis of 169 Squadron, meanwhile, had been piling up their ops, and on 22/23 October they flew their 32nd trip, a *Serrate* patrol to Denmark. It was to prove a rather frustrating patrol, as Les Turner confirmed in his combat report:

"We took off from Great Massingham at 1744 hours in Mosquito Y reaching Patrol area at 1915 hours, without event. At 1920 hours whilst on course West of Nissun Fiord height 15,000 feet, contact was obtained at maximum range showing hard starboard and below. Pursuit action was immediately taken and for the next five minutes we indulged in tight turns eventually reducing range to 2000 feet where a visual was obtained of an aircraft believed to be a Ju 88 standing on its port wing, also tight turning. The enemy aircraft must have seen Mosquito and peeled off whereat we lost some range. Contact was held and after a further three minutes of hectic dog-fighting range was once again closed to 2000 feet where aircraft was identified as a Ju 88 traveling at about 150 mph. We throttled back and put down full flap opening fire at about 400 yards observing large strike on port wing root. Enemy aircraft peeled off starboard and an ineffective burst was fired leaving Mosquito in an awkward position at about 145-mph - full flap and being curiously knocked about by slipstream from the Ju 88. We followed down on AI to about 4000-feet height where contact was lost in ground returns.

"We patrolled off the coast for another thirty minutes with no further joy. Course was set for home at 2005 hours and reached without further event at 2120 hours. Rounds fired:- 160 of cannon, including one one-second burst by accident during chase. Camera exposed. WEATHER:- Moonlight, Clear, some scattered low cloud. CLAIMED one Ju.88 damaged (Cat.B.)."

Though they could only claim a "damaged," Turner was convinced this aircraft crashed subsequently, as there was a fire on the ground some ten minutes after the attack. He adds:

"I am fairly certain that the R/T listening group known as the 'Y Service' monitored the German R/T and confirmed this combat. For security, there was no mention of this on the paper. I am also fairly certain that this aircraft crashed subsequently. There was fire on the ground some ten minutes after the attack. On a personal level, I was commissioned. Frank was promoted to warrant officer and we were awarded the DFC and DFM respectively. These awards were effective before my commission and Frank's promotion, hence the DFM rather than DFC."

On the 23rd Squadron Leader Tim Woodman flew another daylight *Intruder* to northeast Germany:

"Squadron Leader Mike O'Brien was again my observer another volunteer crew - a black West Indian Flying Officer pilot - as my No.2. I let them lead the way across the North Sea, doing the *Gee* navigation. They brought me right up the main street of Westerland, the *Nachtjägd* fighter base on Sylt, forty miles from where I had intended to cross in! I flew down the coast with white very lights being fired by shore stations. Surprise factor was essential and we had lost that. Suddenly all hell broke loose as a number of Oerlikon cannons fired at us from Eggebec, no longer deserted. Total blue skies too, no cloud cover. I decided to abandon. Told the West Indian to break to starboard, hit the deck and pour on the coal to the North Sea. Took me twenty minutes to catch him up. He looked like he intended to make it all the way to Barbados. Some hits on my Mosquito from machine gun bullets."

Squadron Leader O'Brien and his navigator, Flight Lieutenant P A. Disney, who had flown with Woodman on 6 October, were killed on their 23 Squadron *Intruder* op on 22 March 1945.

On 28/29 October Flight Lieutenant Donald R. "Podge" Howard and Flying Officer Frank A. W. "Sticky" Clay, who had shot down a Fw 190 over Holland a few days earlier on 14/15 October after a considerable dog fight, destroyed a very slow flying Heinkel 111 at Stendal-Handorf. The Heinkel exploded with such force that it was probably carrying a V-l flying bomb, which would account for its slow flying speed. On 29/30 October six crews in 239 Squadron made low-level *Intruder* patrols over northwest Germany and left a trail of destruction, including nine trains, a lorry, and a marshalling yard. Eight Mosquitoes of 141 Squadron also operated. Gallacher and McLean of 141 Squadron were gratified to see clouds of steam as "their" train stopped with seven wagons damaged. Six other 141 Squadron crews destroyed or damaged locos and trains this night. On 29/30 October fifty-five Mosquitoes operated on *Serrate* and *Intruder* patrols. On the night of 30/31 Ocotober, when 905 aircraft attacked Köln, fifty-seven Mosquitoes patrolled the night sky. Squadron Leader D. F. Hughes and Flight Lieutenant R. H. Perks of 239 Squadron returned with bullet holes through the tail unit and both wings, including one through the port wing tank. Flight Lieutenant F. Wimbush and Pilot Officer Fraser "tangled" for thirty-five minutes with a German fighter.

One of the most successful *Day Rangers* was flown on 29 October 1944 by Flight Lieutenant F. T. L'Amie and Flying Officer J. W. Smith and Pilot Officer Terry A. Groves DFC and Flight Sergeant R. B. "Doc" Dockeray DFM of 515 Squadron. Between them, they left a trail of destruction across Bavaria and on to Prague, destroying nine aircraft (three in the air and six on the ground) and damaging five more. Both crews took off at 1420 hours from St Dizier and crossed liberated territory south of Nancy at 8000 feet. Allied ack-ack fired at them as they sped overhead, but no lasting damage was sustained. At zero feet at Heehingen, thirty miles south-southwest of Stuttgart, a Fw 190 was spotted to port on a reciprocal course. L'Amie and Smith did a climbing turn and came behind the Fw 190. They attacked below and astern, with L'Amie giving the enemy machine a one-second burst of cannon fire from about 100 yards. The Fw 190 immediately burst into flames and disintegrated. At Ingolstadt, just minutes later, a Bf 110 was seen at about 500 feet. This time it was the turn of Terry Groves and "Doc" Dockeray. They got astern and fired three bursts of cannon fire from 100 yards. Pieces fell off and the Messerschmitt crashed to the ground and continued burning.

The two Mosquitoes continued on their patrol. At Straubing at 1632 hours a Ju 34 crossed from starboard to port at a height of about 1000 feet. The pilot spotted the Mosquitoes and took evasive action, but L'Amie and Smith got into position and made a starboard quarter attack from fifty yards range. L'Amie gave the Junkers a one-second burst of cannon and it exploded in flames. Then the starboard wing blew off and the rest of the transport aircraft disintegrated. L'Amie and Smith flew through the burning oil and petrol, which severely scorched the fuselage and rudder surfaces of the Mosquito. Flying debris from the Ju 34 punched a small hole in the tail plane, but the Mosquito remained airworthy and L'Amie and Smith were ready for more. Just over a quarter of an hour later they attacked a Bf 109 taking off from a grass airfield in the Beroun area. The Bf 109 stopped and swerved to port and, although a number of strikes were seen all around the enemy aircraft, they could not confirm its destruction.

About a dozen Bf l09s were seen parked on the grass airfield and both Mosquito crews went in to attack. Altogether four strafing runs were made on the enemy field, and they left nine burning fiercely with three damaged. A hangar was set alight by the fires and burst into flames. L'Amie and Smith claimed three Bf 109s destroyed and two damaged. Terry Groves and Dockeray also claimed three Bf 109s destroyed and two damaged. There was no opposition, save for a lone machine-gunner who put a hole in Groves' starboard engine cowling. Terry Groves and "Doc" Dockeray landed at Juvincourt at 1905 hours and L'Amie and Smith put down at Amiens/Glisy thirty minutes later, both crews well satisfied with their work.[296]

During November 1944 there was not one single *Serrate* contact during the month's operations by any of the three *Serrate* Mosquito Squadrons (141, 169, and 239). The situation had been getting worse since the summer of 1944. Although 141 Squadron had successfully destroyed three enemy aircraft in air-to-air combat on *Serrate* operations in October, these were all through AI contacts and not *Serrate*. It was a poor month for all three *Serrate* squadrons, with only five enemy aircraft being destroyed, three by 141 and two by 239 Squadron. The former had only one *Serrate* contact all month, and 169 and 239 had only four between them.[297]

Canadian airmen on *Intruder* work flew a first tour of 35 sorties, followed by a period usually as instructors at OTUs on in operational planning at group HQ, then a second tour of 25 trips would round out their operational obligation and they would be eligible for a posting home. George Stewart and his navigator, Paul Beaudet, were an experienced Mosquito crew with 23 Squadron, RAF, which shared Little Snoring with another RAF Intruder Squadron, 515. Stewart writes:

> "Paul and I did our first tour in 11 weeks and we were still raring to go, so we applied for and were granted an extension to our first tour of 15 trips. We thought that by being very quiet about it, we would be able to sneak in an extra ten sorties without anyone noticing and, therefore, we could say that we'd done our two tours and so we'd get back home sooner. This plan didn't work, and as soon as we finished the extra 15 we were off operations. But for now, let's get on with today's trip. This is 4 November 1944 and Charlie, our batman, has just come into our Nissen hut with a cup of tea for us. He says, 'Good morning gentlemen. It is now 7.30 and we are having a nice day." He wasn't so clever, but he was great to us guys. When any of us had joy, he was just as proud and happy as we were. Tea is quite a ritual by now and it certainly warms you on a cold morning in an equally cold Nissen hut, which always is cold and damp. There is no running water so we quickly wash in basins and put on our 'battledress' ready to cycle over to the officers' mess about a mile away. I just heard the sound of our flight commander's jeep starting so I made a mad dash outside to ask him (Flying Officer Griffiths) to please be sure that Paul and I will be put on the roster for tonight's flying. There was a general rule of thumb where we would operate for two nights in a now, then a night off, and a week's leave every six weeks. Paul and I decided that we would rather do three nights on, then one night off. We found that we were a bit edgy on the first night, not edgy, but alert on the second night and except for being a bit tired we were fine for the third night's work.
>
> "Six or eight of us cycled to the mess just in time to enjoy our ersatz scrambled eggs and sausages and loads of tea with toast and jam, all generously mixed with conversation about last night's flying. Any joy (damage to the enemy), anyone missing, etc, and so our day begins. The notice board in. the mess has briefing time posted for 14:00 hours so there are a few unrushed hours ahead to comfortably fit in all we have to do. The CO and flight commanders have left to go out to our flight offices, so gradually we all mount our trusty bikes and follow them out there, too.
>
> "The aircraft 'status report' is drawn up, showing which aircraft are available today, and which ones are for any reason not serviceable. Our flight commander has listed beside the aircraft registration the names of the 'on duty' crews, and Paul and I note that we are again assigned PZ448, which happens to be our own regular kite. We are happy! Our aircraft has been topped up with fuel, oil, glycol and with ammunition. Since we didn't fly the day before we prepare to do our traditional NFT (Night Flying Test), a short hop to give us the feel of the aircraft and which often reveals some little snag that can be fixed up before our 'Op'. The 'Mossie' is such a delightful aircraft to fly that we look forward to any excuse that would allow us to fly her - a pilot's dream, mine at least! These few minutes of happy romping around in a Mosquito are among the best memories I canny with me, flying just for the sake of flying. I remember one day, closing in on an American Flying Fortress for a bit of formation fun. Imagine my surprise when Paul told me to look out on my right - there, large as life, was another Fort. The two Fortresses and I beat up Fakenham in formation, echelon starboard with me in the center. It must have looked hilarious to see the three of us three nuts in such an unbalanced formation of three.
>
> "I was soon called 'The Mad Stewart' - the guy most likely to get the chop on a night flying test. As it was, I was near the top of everyone's short list. I used to dogfight and formate on aircraft in sight. One day Kit Cotter, a NZ pilot, and I mixed it with a couple of Mustangs and did very well. Another day a Havoc gave me a lovely trimming and another day we whipped the pants off some Thunderbolts. A favorite sport was low flying, which we did lots of, and playing around in and out of fluffy clouds. To shake up the ground crew, I used to dive very steeply at the aerodrome, then climb vertically - soon nobody would ride with me except for a few who had done so before. They were swell guys and always called us 'George and Paul.' On the NFT's we used to drop fellows off at various places when they were going on leave. One day, returning from one of these nuns, we beat up Lush's (Mrs. Colquhoun's) place in fine style, creating wing tip vortices on the pullouts, and low enough to recognize the people in her garden. She told us later she thought we were going to hit the trees and Fee (Mrs. Colquhoun's nanny) said she thought we were alight.

She had seen the wing tip vortices. Another time Paul and I visited a friend at Tholthorpe in Yorkshire and on leaving got permission to beat up the aerodrome. Harry Facey saw the beat-up and said he thought we'd had it a couple of times.

"We get the aircraft all set for the night's work, parachute in position all ready to snap on, and this done we make our way back across the field for lunch on briefing. With briefing called for 14:00 hours, all aircrew and people involved, like meteorology and intelligence bashers, as well as flight commanders and COs, - head for the squadron intelligence library and briefing room behind station headquarters. The on-duty aircrews wait in the intelligence library until the planning is completed and usually there is a lot of speculation going on about where tonight's raid will be directed, plus the expected amount of armchair quarter-backing.

"The orderly officer has just opened the door to the briefing room, and that is our signal to file in. It is a large room something like a classroom with a slightly elevated 'stage' at the front, behind which on the wall is a large map of Europe. The target board is just off to one side of this stage, and as expected, we find it is covered. Squadron Leader Charlie Price, our senior intelligence officer, has mow mounted the podium and a hush fills the room. 'Good afternoon, gentlemen. Today's briefing will now begin. Will you please close the door, orderly officer, and I will call the roll.' He calls the names of each crew operating tonight and we answer, 'Sir' when he says 'Flying Officer Stewart and Flying Officer Beaudet'.

"Charlie has retired to the back of the stage and with his pointer he tells us which target our heavy bombers are pranging tonight, how many are being used and the routes to and from the target. He mentions the tactical purpose of the raid, such as the demolition of certain industries, on the demoralizing saturation bombing of a large city. He tells us about other groups supporting the raid such as pathfinders, and then he explains how we are going to be deployed. Our aircraft will be used to patrol enemy night fighter aerodromes near the target and on the way to and from the raid. At last the target board is uncovered, and we all too quickly look for our names, then our target and finally our patrol times. Charlie reads each one out and makes certain that the crew concerned understands cleanly his job, his target, his patrol time and his armament, whether on not he is carrying two 500lb bombs.

"'Stewart and Beaudet, you are to patrol Andorf aerodrome from 20:15 hours until 21:15 hours and you will carry bombs. If you have time, take a look at Marx and Varel while you are in the area. Is that clear?'

"'Yes Sir!' We reply.

"The meteorology basher has his turn, telling us about tonight's winds and weather, and usually we have lots of both. He tells us what moonlight we can expect and gives us an idea of weather at base upon our return. Tonight is no exception and we are warned about very strong winds.

"Charlie Price has now asked Wing Commander 'Sticky' Murphy to say a few words: 'All night, chaps, you know what you are expected to do; get cracking, use your heads and don't stick your necks out. Be sure to keep a sharp lookout behind and watch out for that wind to change direction and strength!'

"Charlie says, 'Gentlemen, we will now synchronize our watches. Half a minute before 14:56. I'll begin counting at ten seconds to go - ten, nine, eight, seven, six, five, four, three, two, one - 14:56 - good luck chaps!'

"Mass briefing thus concluded, each Mosquito crew pains off to plan its own particular sortie, since each operates independent of any other.

"My navigator, Paul, has started to spread out his maps, trip log, Dalton navigational computer (a visual calculator) and Douglas protractor. My job is to draw flying nations, enemy colors of the period (ESN's) if they are known, so that we can fine them from our Very pistols if need be. These are nicknamed 'sisters'. I also draw escape kits in which we find small compasses, German aircraft cockpit checks (on nice paper), concentrated food portions, first aid materials, and pills to keep us awake should we need them, as well as water purifying tablets.

"I pull out the files on Andorf, Marx and Varel aerodromes and note their layouts and remember where their defenses are marked, as well as station buildings, ammo dumps etc. I note too, the heights of nearby obstructions. The main function and type of aircraft used there is night fighting Ju 88s. I also draw out our phony passport pictures and negatives. Paul has by now drawn in his tracks to our target and I note that we will cross the Dutch coast at 3500 feet. We are going to cross the Dutch coast at Noord Egmond at 1500-2000 feet, diving and weaving from 3500 feet. We are going to cruise at 240mph indicated airspeed, starting out at 6000 feet over base, steering 102° magnetic, our true airspeed works out to be 260mph and, with this wind, our ground speed will be 310mph. Therefore, 23 miles in 4½ minutes to the British coast where we will dive quickly to 500 feet over the English Channel and head for Noord Egmond, 134 miles (31 minutes) away, with a ground speed of 262mph.

"Weaving over the Dutch coast, Paul and I will cruise on to our target, varying height from about 2000 to 4000 feet, keeping a constant lookout behind for any Ju 88s on Fw 190s on our tail. Our next turning point is on the Leda River, southwest of Emden, then we turn north into the patrol area just above the Jade Canal (which leads into Wilhelmshaven). If Aldorf isn't lit on is hand to locate, we may have to continue on to the north coast, pinpoint our location and backtrack to our target. We add up the anticipated times including this latest possibility and find that we have 75 minutes, so subtracting that from our slated time on target of 20:15 we therefore must be off the ground at 19:00 hours. Our trip is now planned; all we have to do now is to fly it!

"Paul had put all his gear into his locker and we cycle over to the mess just in time for tea at 16:00 hours. We will miss dinner at the regular sitting because we are flying so early, so we gorge ourselves with tea, toast and cake - just delicious! Thus sated, we don our red goggles to adjust our 'visual purple' for night vision and relax for an hour, reading on chatting. The first emotion a crew feels at a time like this is the expectation that this sortie could mean 'joy' (hacking down an enemy aircraft), the second, death, on a cold jump into the night and a very uncertain future.

"Sitting in the mess until time to go, we feel slightly cold and alone and in our minds, our beds down at our hut seem to us to be so warm and enticing. It's kind of strange, this feeling before doing a trip. We know that a Mosquito will be patrolling Germany with us in change tonight, but somehow it doesn't seem quite real; certainly not one's present self, rather some other being which takes over our bodies on such occasions and makes us carry on automatically. We sort of detach our souls and minds and mentally tuck them in bed until our return when happily they re-unite. It is just as though we are being taken along by someone else and there is nothing we can do about it. To all outward appearances we aircrew here in the mess are very offhanded about the whole thing and the impression we might give is that we couldn't care less - not so! Actually we don't sit down and dread what's to be done, because it is really fascinating work and, as we do it, it is a lot of fun and is very exciting at times. Usually the twitchy feeling is felt now more than on the actual trip. Our job is a lonely one and the fact that we will likely be the only British aircraft within maybe 100 or so miles makes this feeling more intense. It is a most disconcerting sensation to consider that we might be shot down and just dissolve into the night on, sinking onto the Channel on North Sea without anyone seeing us go, leaving no trace behind. We are lucky tonight because we have such a short time to wait before going out to our aircraft.

"'Well Paul,' I say, 'it's 5:45. We'd better get down to the aircraft.' So, hopping on our bikes, we cycle to our locker room, stopping off at the intelligence section to place our valuables in our little bag and collect Paul's navigation equipment, nations, etc. We ride on, with Paul bitching about how awkward it is to carry this stuff, and ride a bicycle too! At our lockers by our flight office we crawl into our escape boots and don our Mae West's. I sign out and we pile into the 15-hundredweight van, which takes us around the perimeter track to our dispersal area and our aircraft. I walk over to Chiefy's office and sign the L 14 and then back to the aircraft.

"Out there in the cool darkness, it's like a world of our own because it all seems so unreal, so quiet, so private. Usually by this time a certain amount of anxiety has crept into our souls and down our respective spines and often has the effect of making us a bit high strung and cranky. I remember giving Paul proper hell just before our first trip because he wouldn't undo his tie (one of the rules when flying over water). It causes us to shiver slightly even though we don't feel cold. We don't talk much; usually silence prevails. Now we come to our much-practiced ritual before an operation; that of walking back to the tail of the aircraft to christen the tailwheel with urine for good luck! Fifteen minutes to go we climb aboard telling the ground crews to douse their flashlights because they'll spoil our night vision. I suppose they sensed our anxiety. When Paul started to get in, he'd complain about the one I'd 'cut' in the doorway of the kite. And gosh, did my dinghy ever stink! Small wonder after sitting on it for four on five hours at a time without moving from it. It never took Paul very long to get out after landing.

"We strap in; our ladder is removed, collapsed, and handed to Paul, who snaps it in its place on the door, after the door is closed and latched. The external starting batteries are plugged in, the engines are primed and we are ready to start. The odd few minutes before starting drag like hours, then, eight minutes before takeoff, I yell, "Contact starboard" and we start our engines. With both engines going and the radio heating up we feel much better and our anxiety fades away. The ground crew has unscrewed the undercarriage locks and removed the starting batteries and they wave us out to the perimeter track where we follow the blue lights around to the take-off position. After I do a quick run-up and cockpit check I flash our downward recognition light to signal that we are ready to go. A green light is flashed from the control tower and we line up and take off. All signals before an 'Op' are visual only, so that the enemy can't tell by radio chatter when we depart. It's pretty black outside now and we don't feel too comfortable until we have 1000 feet under us. The aircraft feels quite 'loggy' with full 50-gallon drop tanks plus the added weight of two 500lb bombs. It is 1900 hours and as we climb and turn to set course over the field I flash 'V' as we pass over.

"The time is 1906 and at 5000 feet over Happisburgh light at the British coast we alter course slightly for Noord Egmond, diving to 500 feet and switching off our navigation lights. It is fascinating to see the brightness of the phosphorescence in the water below us. On a black night like this, it really shows up!

"'Four minutes to go George,' says Paul. This is my signal to climb quickly to 3000-4000 feet, ready to dive and weave our way across the Dutch coast just ahead. We can hear the enemy scanning us for almost as soon as we climb; it sounds 'insect-like' in our earphones and it imparts a nervousness all of its own. Diving and gently weaving we are safely across and level off between 1500 and 2000 feet. The scanning has stopped now and we set course for our next turning point. Flying along like this over enemy territory, seeing the odd rotating beacon and distant searchlight is a truly physical sensation even present, and as we pass over the Zuider Zee we can see the riding lights of many small fishing craft. There is our landfall now coming up on the east coast of the Zuider Zee and we alter course for our previously mentioned turning point on the Leda Canal. We can now rely only upon waterways as landmarks, because everything else below us is pitch black.

"'Look back, Paul' I say, as I pull sharply up and Paul scans behind for enemy aircraft. (We did see a Ju 88 on one trip when we did this).

"'There is Zuidlaander, George, we are night on track,' says Paul. 'Let me know when you see the Dortmund Ems Canal.'

"We soon are there and shortly afterwards arrive at the turning point on the Leda River. I hum a few bars of 'This is a lovely way to spend an evening' and Paul makes a rude comment. 'OK George, steer 05 and look out for the Jade Canal.'

"'OK Paul, have a look behind.'

"Five minutes later, over the Jade Canal we can see ahead of us in the distance the landing pattern of lights (visual Lorenz) that the Germans use to guide their aircraft in for a landing. It is Andorf, nicely lit up to welcome us, night on the money at 20:15 hours. 'OK Paul, load up a sister just in case we need it.' I dive the Mossie to 500 feet so that we can look up and see any aircraft silhouetted in the gloom. Parallel searchlights challenging aircraft on downwind leg with one holding and the other dipping. 'There goes an ESN (Sister), Paul. Someone is on the downwind leg.'

"We race around the circuit and see some navigation lights on the final approach. So, turning my gun safety switch to firing position, we close in on him as he turns his landing lights on and get a quick shot as he silhouettes himself against his own light, a Ju 88. Strikes appear on him all around the nose area and by now he must be very low; then suddenly, the whole field is plunged into total blackness, as Paul and I speed up and around the airfield. Imagine our surprise, when looking up we see another aircraft on the downwind leg. I pull up sharply and overshoot his tail, execute a sharp wingover and close in to fire a quick burst of cannon at him, noticing strikes all over the starboard wing and cockpit area and pieces falling off. It is a He 111 and there are huge sparks trailing behind him as we pass. We see him no more.

"We hang around the area for a while and keep getting challenged by the searchlights, and one such time we fine off a 'sister' and the lights are doused. 'There goes their visual Lorenz on again Paul,' I say, and as our patrol time is coming to an end I turn away, and quietly climb to 6000 feet, ready to dive back in and bomb. Very often they will switch off all lights as we increase power to climb, because they know what's coming. OK, we're there now, and our bomb doors are open, our bombs are armed, and we roll into our dive, aiming at the runway - 5000 feet, 4000 feet, 3000 feet. We ease out of the dive at 3000 feet and release our bombs just as the searchlights reach up to grab us and we weave and skid gently out of their nays, looking to see our bomb strikes. We notice too, that there is an extra string of lights beside the main flare path and a lot of activity at the upwind threshold of the runway; must be where our Ju 88 went in. There are our bomb bursts right on the runway. All lights now are doused as we weave and dive away from the airfield and set course for home.

"'OK George, steer 2930M. We're going for a 'Gee' fix in the North Sea. ETA 22 minutes - 76 miles away against a headwind.' This I do, and now we can both relax a bit.

"At 2135 hours we reach our invisible destination and Paul says, 'OK George, alter course to 2630M.'

"I say, 'OK Paul, look behind.' We are headed for the British coast, 204 miles, 61 minutes away. Fatigue has caught up with me so I say, 'Paul, hang on to this for a bit while I nest my eyes, will you please?' So he reaches over and flies with his left hand as I lean my head back to rest. 'Cats-eye' intruding requires tremendous concentration, and is very tiring. I sometimes wonder anxiously as I lean back like this if I will be alert enough to land the aircraft safely, because I am so tired now and we will start to accumulate a film of salt on our windscreen which will further reduce my visibility.

"We are now 40 miles from the British coast, which is near enough to make our initial radio contact and, as Paul turns on our IFF, I say, 'Hello, Largetype, this is Cricket 34, identifying, and my cockerel is crowing' (IFF turned on). They reply, 'Roger Largetype out.'

"Ten minutes later, as we cross the coast - a most welcome sight - I transmit, 'Cricket 34 drying my feet and changing frequencies.' 'Roger, 34, goodnight.'

"'Goodnight Largetype, and thank you. Cricket 34 out.' Now is the time to call base, turn on my navigation lights and turn my IFF off. 'Hello Exking, Cricket 34 drying my feet, clear the circuit.'

"'Hello 34, you are clear to the circuit. Call overhead at 3,000 feet.'

"'Roger Exking, 34 out.' England is very black at the moment and it seems so unlikely that in all the dankness below an airfield can suddenly light up.

"'George,' Paul says, 'we are just coming over base now.'

"'Hello Exking, Cricket 34 over base at 3000 feet. May we have the flare path lit, please?'

"'Roger 34, Exking out.'

'I now descend quickly to 1500 feet on our downwind leg, drop the undercarriage, check my fuel, RPM, radiator flaps open, then turn smoothly to port, on final, keeping my airspeed at 150mph all the way around. 500 feet above ground, full fine pitch, I drop my flaps, trim off the control pressures, and adjust power to hold 140mph and a nice sink rate. The threshold of the runway is coming up quickly now, so I allow my speed to slacken to 130 as I cross, then throttling right back, we hold off as we sink gently to touch down with the tail wheel low. Not a three-pointer, but much smoother and always in control. Turning off at the end of the runway I call 'Cricket 34 clear. Goodnight, Cobby,' to which the controller replies, 'Roger 34. Goodnight old chap.'

"I taxi along the perimeter track to our dispersal area, where our ever-faithful ground crew has been standing by for our return. Our marshaller waving his illuminated wands guides us into position. Brakes on, engines at 1000rpm, radio off, rad flaps closed, pull out the idle cut-off knobs, and when both props are stopped, gas off, switches off, throttles closed, and all the lights off, Paul opens the door, hands down our ladder and prepares to disembark. The ground crew says, 'Chocks in place.' Then: 'Any joy?'

"'A bit.' I say, 'brakes off.' Paul is now climbing down the ladder and the gyros are still humming as I unstrap and remove my helmet. 'Ouch!' My bloody ears hunt from the damned earphones pressing against them. And my face is tender and perspiring where my oxygen mask has been touching it. What a relief to get it all off. My bottom is now feeling the effects of sitting on a most uncomfortable dinghy for so long, and as I climb down, my circulation starts up again, and I long to stretch. This I do as soon as I get out, taking a much savored deep breath and head back to re-christen our tailwheel before the 15-hundredweight arrives (often with a WAAF driver) to take us back to the flight office and our lockers. We are now feeling very slap happy with fatigue and happiness to be back and we laugh at anything and everything as we chat with our ground crew and then with the other crews on the way. Paul and I put our gear into our respective lockers and then we mount our bikes and cycle back to the intelligence section for debriefing. Paul, as usual complaining bitterly about his bulky navigation-bag being so awkward to carry on a bike.

"With a cup of hot tea and a cookie, we relax and wait to be de-briefed and all at once the world seems to be a better place. The intelligence officer motions Paul and me over to a seat and we tell him all about our trip as he makes notes. This soon concluded, we hand in our escape kits, retrieve our valuables and head for the officers' mess, where with the other crews we have a most welcome meal of eggs and bacon and toast and tea. There is lots of chatter as we linger over this treat and then delicious fatigue creeps over all of us and we gradually break up and bike back to our huts, so to bed, tired but relaxed and happy.

'The night after we damaged the 88 and III Smitty said he couldn't get near the place. Instead of just challenging searchlights, they had searchlights whose beams contained steady bursts of 20mm. We must have upset them pretty well."[298]

CHAPTER 12

"*RITTERKREUZ HEIGHT*" OF DIE!

Ritterkreutz Height referred to the fact that after carrying out their attacks against our bombers, German fighters would immediately drop down almost to ground level, i.e. Ritterkreutz height in order to avoid the dreaded Mosquitoes. I believe they lost a few more planes with their low flying back to collect their Ritterkreutz.'

Lewis Brandon

November 1944 saw the same pattern of operations, with bomber support and night and day *Intruder* and *Ranger* patrols. 85 Squadron continued its run of success with a superb individual effort during a night *Intruder* on 4/5 November when Bomber Command's main thrust was against Bochum, with smaller raids on the Dortmund-Ems Canal and Hanover. Three Bf 110s were claimed shot down, one each by Wing Commander K. H. P. Beauchamp and Flying Officer Mony of 157 Squadron, Flight Lieutenants N. W. Young and R. H. Siddons of 239 Squadron, and Squadron Leader Tim Woodman and Flying Officer Arthur F. Witt of 169 Squadron.[299] By far the greatest achievement this night though went to Squadron Leader Branse Burbridge DSO* DFC* and Flight Lieutenant Bill Skelton DSO* DFC*. They were airborne from Swannington at 1731 hours on a high-level *Intruder* patrol south of Köln. They crossed the enemy coast and headed into Germany. Burbridge wrote later:

> "We were returning to our patrol point from Limburg at 15,000 feet, on a north westerly course, when Bill reported contact at 1904 hours, range four miles, crossing starboard to port at about our level. We turned in behind it, flying west, looking vainly for Type F response while closing in. I obtained a visual at 1500-feet range. At 1000 feet, I believed it to be a Ju 88, and using night binoculars Bill identified it as a Ju 88G. I fired a short burst from 500 feet, producing strikes on the port engine. A dull flame appeared. A second short burst gave the same result, and a fire slowly developed in the engine as the enemy aircraft lost height. Soon it began to dive steeply, exploding on the ground at 1909 hours.
>
> "By the time we had climbed up again to our patrol point, the markers were beginning to appear in the target area, so we set course towards it. On returning to a reciprocal brief investigation of further flares southwest of us was fruitless, but at 1953 hours Bill reported contact at four miles range. We dived after it and found that it was taking regular evasive action by losing height at high speed, weaving up to 45° in either direction. After about five minutes we had lost height to 7000 feet, and I obtained a visual at about 1200-feet range. Again no Type F response or exhausts were seen. We closed in and identified the target with binoculars as a Ju 88. At 500-feet range, having finger trouble, I pressed the camera button by mistake, but the absence of thunder and the mocking buzz of the camera on the R/T put me right. A short burst (cannon) gave strikes and a flash from the port engine and fuselage, but owing to the dive I lost the visual against the darkness of the ground. Bill regained contact, and although the evasion of the enemy aircraft had increased and became irregular, we closed in again to visual range of about 1200 feet after a further five minutes, our height now being 3000 feet. Another short burst at 2002 hours at the same engine produced the same results, and once again the visual was lost below the horizon. We searched around, but were unable to pick him up again; our position was roughly five miles SE of what we took to be the dummy flarepath of Bonn. At 2005 hours, an aircraft

exploded on the ground some distance ahead of us. Two minutes later I saw what I believed to be another crash on the ground.

"We now proceeded to regain a bit of height, and when at 8000 feet, set course from the last named position to join the bomber homeward route near Duren, which point we reached at 2020 hours. It was our intention to fly on the reciprocal of the route, towards the target, and to intercept contacts coming head on: these would most likely be hostiles attempting late route interceptions, as the bombers should all have been clear. After two minutes flying on 50° my attention was attracted by a recognition cartridge (red and white) fired about twenty-five miles east of us. We hurried in its direction losing height on the way, and shortly the red perimeter lights of an airfield appeared. Then I saw the landing light of an aircraft touching down east to west at 2028 hours.

"A minute later we had a snap contact and fleeting visual of an aircraft above us, but were unable to pursue it. On commencing a right-hand circuit of the airfield, however, Bill obtained a contact (on the north side of the aerodrome) at two miles range and at our height, which was about 1000 feet above the ground. Following round the south side, we closed in to identify a Me 110. He must have throttled back rather smartly when east of the airfield for we suddenly found ourselves overtaking rapidly, horn blaring in our ears, and finished up immediately below him about eighty feet away. Very gradually we began to drop back and pulling up to dead astern at 400-feet range, I fired a very short burst. The whole fuselage was a mass of flames, and the Me 110 went down burning furiously, to crash in a river about five miles north of the airfield, which we presumed to be Bonn/Hangelar. The time was 2032 hours.

"We flew away to the north for a few minutes, and then turned to approach the airfield again. As we did so Bill produced yet another contact at two miles range, 80° starboard. When we got in behind him he appeared to be doing a close left-hand orbit of the airfield. Again we followed round the west and south sides, and as he seemed to be preparing to land, I selected ten degrees of flap. I obtained a visual at 1500-feet range; no a/c was visible, so I took the flap off again. We identified the target as a Ju 88 and a very short burst from dead astern, 400-feet range, caused the fuselage to burst into flames. The cockpit broke away, and we pulled up sharply to avoid debris. Crosses were clearly visible in the light of the fire, and the Ju 88 dived towards the airfield. He finally turned over to starboard and exploded in a ploughed field just north of the aerodrome at 2040 hours.

"We could see intruder warnings being fired from aerodromes in every direction by this time, and although we tried to investigate one further recognition signal some distance from us, we obtained no joy, and presumed that we had outstayed our welcome.'

Burbridge and Skelton landed back at Swannington at 2223 hours and submitted claims for one Bf 110, one Ju 88, and one Ju 88G destroyed, as well as one Ju 88 probably destroyed. Their Bf 110 victim was a II./NJG1 machine that crashed into the River Rhine near Hangelar airfield at 2150 hours. *Oberleutnant* Ernst Runze, pilot, was killed, and *Obergefreiter* Karl-Heinz Bendfeld, radar operator and the *bordschütz*, baled out safely.

The popular press dubbed Branse and Bill the 'Night Hawk Partners." Such was the need for morale-boosting headlines. James Lansdale Hodson, a newspaper reporter, visited Swannington and in his subsequent article attributed the reasons for Burbridge and Skelton's great success to:

> "...intelligence. They knew before they set out precisely where they will be at a certain time. They carry a picture in their head of the whole night's operation... the various bomber streams, times, targets. They try to read the enemy mind...they visualize at what time he will discover what is happening, how far he will be misled, what he will do, what airfields he will use, what times he will rise whether he will fly, what his tactics will be. They act accordingly. If one expectation fails, they know which next to try. After they had shot down three on the night they shot down four, Burbridge said, 'Time we were starting for home, Bill.' To which Skelton replied: 'Well if you like, but I've got another Hun for you.' They went round after him and destroyed him too. Then they had a further look round, 'But,' says Burbridge's combat report, 'We found no joy and presumed we had outstayed our welcome.'"[300]

Two nights later, on 6/7 November, the bombers attacked the Mittelland Canal at Gravenhorst. It was one of the worst night's weather Tim Woodman had ever flown in:

> "We left the target area and flew into a cold front of exceptional violence. We were thrown all over the place, ice quickly froze on the windscreen and static electricity began to spark about the cockpit. We would drop like a stone and I feared my wing tips would come off. Down at 800 feet the ice cleared but it was too dangerous so close to the sea so I went back up to 2000 feet. Flying Officer Witt had his straps loose in order to operate the *Gee* set but after he had hit the top of the cockpit for the third time I told him to lock his straps and I would fly due west until we reached better weather. I listened out on the radio. Other crews were obviously in dire trouble from the nature of their calls. Outside the propellers were whirling discs of violet fire, the aerials on the wings glowed violet like neon tubes. 'The inside of the windscreen was a lattice of static and, as I leant forward concentrating on the instruments the static struck across like pinpricks on my face. We dropped out of the sky in another violent air disturbance, the instruments went spinning and we waited to hit the sea. Arthur Witt then said, quite calmly. Another one like that...why not let the controls go. Then it will all be over. I am quite easy about dying. We made it after some more dicey episodes. But poor Arthur was killed a fortnight later flying with another pilot. Eleven aircraft were lost due to the weather, including two 100 Group Mosquitoes."[301]

On the night of 6/7 November 100 Group crews claimed two Ju 188s, a Bf 110, and a Ju 88 and Ju 188 as probables.[302] Squadron Leader "Dolly" Doleman and Flight Lieutenant "Bunny" Bunch DFC of 157 Squadron at Swannington received confirmation of a Bf 110 destroyed. Doleman reported:

"We were airborne at 1734 hours and before reaching our patrol point obtained a contact to starboard on 090 just by the Rhine. Chased and obtained a visual on exhausts like a Mosquito, but on closing in to identify definitely, aircraft did steep turn to port. Chased on AI on target, which was taking evasive action, and obtained a second contact head-on, which we chased and got a visual on a Me 110 going west. The position and time are somewhat uncertain after the first chase. Minimum range on weapon was poor, but opened fire on a visually estimated range of 500-600 feet with a short burst. Strikes and explosion occurred instantaneously and poor Hans went straight down in flames.

"Contacts were obtained on bags more, Mosquitoes and the odd bomber throwing out Window, and also on two aircraft (at different times) going North West at very high speed. Mosquito flat out but contacts drew steadily away. One visual obtained on two pairs of exhausts, one of these at 6000-feet range. Do not know what there were but most certainly they were not Mosquitoes on one engine.

'Returned from these chases towards Koblenz, and was followed h some crab in a friendly for about fifteen minutes, in spite of 'G' band, Type 'F' and calling on Command Guard. At 2040 hours set course for base as supplies of chewing gum were running low. Saw one beacon lit up. No contacts obtained and *Monica* was u/s by then anyway. Near Brussels was challenged by an American on Channel C and put navigational lights on as second American was advising our chum to '*shoot the basket down*' - only he didn't say '*basket*'. Landed base with nasty smell of burning in cockpit at 2155 hours. Claim one Me.110 destroyed.'

When the fitting of AI.Mk.X into 100 Group Mosquitoes began there were not sufficient equipments available for the whole force. Tim Woodman recalls:

"Although 85 and 157 Squadrons had been attached to 100 Group since May 1944 with ten centimeter AI we considered they were not shooting down the numbers of Hun night fighters they should have. Our Mk IV radar was completely jammed over Germany. Only half a dozen crews of 85 and 157 were getting scores; two or three doing quite well. I challenged the SASO, Air Commodore Rory Chisholm, to let two of 169 crews have the use of 85 Squadron's aircraft for five ops each, guaranteeing to shoot down a Hun apiece. We went over to Swannington, myself to fly with Flying Officer Simpkin, an 85 Squadron observer, plus Mellows and Drew from 169. What a delight to have ten centimeter radar which could range up to eight miles ahead and no jamming. Mellows proved my challenge by shooting down a Heinkel 219 on the second of his five ops. I failed but nearly got a Ju 88 on my fifth op on 2 January. Chased three Huns but had partial radar failure. Shot at Ju 88 as it entered cloud. Followed him down through, shooting blind on radar. Clear below cloud. A light on the ground and another pilot said he saw an aircraft crash. Made no claim, however, and climbed back up as unsure of the height of the ground."

This was Tim Woodman's fifty-first op, and his last with 169 (85). He was assessed as a "Bomber Support Pilot: Exceptional." He received a commendation from 100 Group's AOC for meritorious service and was appointed to be operational test pilot at the BSDU at Swanton Morley. At BSDU Woodman, Squadron Leader Gledhill, and Flight Lieutenants Neville and Carpenter, specialist radar observers, checked out ASH, *Perfectos*, *Piperack*, centimetric homer and other electronic devices, and flew eight more operations.

ASH was not so elaborate an AI as the Mk X, and was expected to be much better than Mk IV for bomber support operations. It was decided to equip 23, 515, and 141 Squadrons with it. On 8 November, Mr Willis of Western Electric and Mr. Glen Turner, the U.S. technical representative, visited West Raynham. The reason for their call was to inspect the ASH AI.Mk.XV installation, which had been fitted to an Anson (and an Oxford) for testing by 141 Squadron. Some weeks later, on 21 November, Flight Lieutenant R. A. W Scott DFC and Flying Officer William G. Cadman DFC flew in the Anson on ASH training and obtained excellent results, especially at minimum range. Two days later aircrew at West Raynham were shown a two-hour film on ASH. ASH required a very high degree of skill for successful operation. With a very highly skilled operator, 100 Group hoped that it might become a really valuable weapon in bomber support.[303]

"On 16 November 1944" recalls Bob Symon of 85 Squadron, "We were airborne 0010 hours a bomber support ops for the Dortmund raid. No reaction, no searchlights no gunfire. The met briefing before we left warned us that Swannington probably would be clamped down on return. When we were over the sea on the way back all our electrics went out, no radio, no blind flying panel. We were above cloud at around 10,000 feet. Svein reckoned that our only way out was to fly until we were sure of being over land, pointing our Mossie towards the sea and making a jump for it. I wonder who has tried this one? I recall one peculiar event coming back one night from a bomber escort trip to Dortmund. The weather forecast was for cloud over the east of England with a base of 500 feet and a ceiling of 10,000 feet odd. We were just short of the coast when all the electrics quit on us: no instruments, no radio. Without the blind flying panel there was not much future in flying down through the cloud. I suggested to my pilot that our Mark X AI (which has its own generator and was functioning) could give me a good enough clue as to whether we were nose up or nose down or which wing was up or down. A short check on my claim satisfied us that a controlled downward spiral was possible and we proceeded to do so until the ground return suggested that we were at about 3000 feet. At this point the tube told me that we were in a straight steep dive. I protested but was calmly informed that there was a hole with a light beyond and he was going for it. And so we landed at Coltishall."

On 25 November, two Mosquitoes of 141 Squadron carried out low-level night *Intruder* sorties to enemy airfields in Germany. One crew returned early after failing to find Sachsenheim airfield, but Flying Officer R. D. S. Gregor USAAF and his navigator/radar operator, Flight Sergeant F. S. Baker, attacked vehicles en route to Hailfingen and Eutingen. The latter was all lit up, but there was no sign of any aircraft, so they blew up some more vehicles before returning to Norfolk. Low-level and high-level *Intruders* continued to be flown during the month and, starting on 25 November, two 500lb MC bombs were carried by 141 Squadron Mosquitoes for the first time on attacks on German airfields. Alternatively, eight 40lb bombs could be carried. The small 40lb bombs caused little damage, but helped disrupt the German night-fighter airfields. Also high-level bombing sorties were flown using *Gee* navigation fixes to pinpoint targets, to help foster the impression that the 100 Group *Spoof* Window-dropping aircraft were, in fact, a bombing force, and so divert German night-fighters from the main attack by the heavies and by Mosquitoes of 8 Group.

On 30 November Wing Commander Howard Kelsey DFC* and Flight Lieutenant Edward M. Smith DFM of 169 Squadron destroyed a He 177 on the ground at Liegnitz. That night Squadron Leader F. S. Gonsalves and Flight Lieutenant Basil Duckett of 85 Squadron destroyed a Ju 88, and Flying Officers R. J. V. Smythe and Waters of 157 Squadron destroyed a Ju 188. 141 Squadron dispatched eight *Intruders*. Pilot Officers F. A. Lampkin and Bernard J. Wallnutt were shot down during their patrol to Diepholz airfield. Lampkin was last heard transmitting "Winball 20 pranging in Holland." Wallnutt was killed and Lampkin was made PoW. Eight *Day Intruder* sorties and thirty-five *Night Intruders/Rangers* and night bomber/*Intruder* sorties were flown during November by 141 Squadron. On 2/3 December two Mosquitoes in 141 Squadron carried out the last *Serrate* patrols of the war, having been the first to fly *Serrate* sorties on 14 June 1943 from Wittering. No. 239 would continue with *Serrate* patrols for a little longer during December 1944 and, starting on 7 January, some of their Mk.VIs were transferred to 141 Squadron as 239 received new NF.XXXs. Some patrols using Mk.IV *Serrate* were carried out by 169 Squadron at Great Massingham right up until the end of the war. Mosquitoes from 141 Squadron would start ASH operations in December, thus joining sister squadrons 23 and 515 at Little Snoring. Since late 1944, both squadrons had begun training with ASH for low-level raids on German airfields. For many months with and without ASH, these two squadrons had been long established in this deadly, incisive form of airborne warfare. Wing Commander "Sticky" Murphy, whose panache and aggressive leadership had created a fresh élan that boded ill for the *Reich's Nachtjagdgeschwader gruppen*, led 23 Squadron.

The large-scale use of the Mosquito late in 1944 forced the *Nachtjagd* to re-think their tactics, and this seriously reduced their efficiency. One *Geschwader*, with a strength of about 100 crews, lost, in three months, 24 crews killed, ten missing, and 15 wounded. It was around this time that the real "*Moskitopanik*" started, and from then on all the normal run of crashes through natural causes were attributed to the Mosquito. "*Moskitopanik*" reached a peak during December 1944 when 36 enemy night-fighters were shot down.[304] The Mosquito's increased reputation heightened the German night-fighter crews' despondency, and their demoralization was complete late in 1944 when they had to resort to throwing out *Düppel* (Window) as a routine to mislead and distract the Mosquito night-fighters. *Hauptmann* Heinz-Wolfgang Schnauffer, the top scoring German night-fighter pilot, with 121 victories, attributed his continued survival to the fact that he did not only weave but actually carried out what he described as "steep turns" from take off to landing. He even continued to weave when in AI contact with a bomber. His impression was that none of the top German night-fighter pilots dared to climb until the last moment and all remained very low, or at "*Ritterkreuz Height*," as if they flew higher they would never survive to receive the decoration. Schnauffer recalled that the only time that they felt at all free from RAF fighters was in the bomber stream, but he said because of the threat of Mosquito intruders "it was impossible to relax even then."

Hauptmann Hans Krause, with 28 destroyed, quoted an instance in the Ruhr when he was intercepted in the target area and was pursued for 45 minutes, having frequent visuals on a Mosquito as it came into range. He took violent evasive action in azimuth and height, and by going through cloud, but this failed to shake off the fighter. He finally succeeded in evading only by flying to a district in the Ardennes that he knew really well, flying, as he said, "Down a valley below the level of the hills." This confirmed in his mind the exceptional standard of the British AI radar. German night-fighter crews now flew at tree-top height to the beacons. This caused many accidents, and German night-fighters often flew into the ground. An alternative technique of returning to base, provided the pilot could come straight in and land, was to approach straight from 10,000 feet. When possible, Krause preferred to do this for, as he said, "It had the added advantage that if you were shot down by a Mosquito you had plenty of time to bale out."

Throughout 1944 the Fortresses of 214 Squadron and the Liberators of 223 Squadron had been "jostling" for every major bombing raid. By December all were of still greater assistance, being fully equipped with *Carpet* (anti-*Würzburg*) and *Piperack* (anti-*SN-2*), besides *Jostle* (anti-HE and anti-VHF). Mosquitoes began operating this month as jammers. Their role was a dual one. They flew to target areas on routes, that took them well clear of the Main Force, and on the way they made "Y" recordings of enemy R/T traffic. Arriving at the target area, they jammed the enemy AI with *Piperack* and they stayed there until well after the attack was over; thus covering the withdrawal of stragglers. It was intended to increase and prolong the AI jamming in the target areas to which the enemy fighters would ultimately gravitate. During December, the *Mandrel* screen and Window Forces also kept up the good work of confusion and diversion. The Ruhr was still the favorite target, and Window flooding continued to be used with success. Even though 141, 169, and 239 Squadrons would not shoot down any enemy aircraft during the month, their part in the overall scheme of things was of great importance. This started on 1/2 December when a *Spoof* Window attack on the Ruhr by forty-nine aircraft of 100 Group with no losses among the eighty-one heavies that attacked Karlsruhe, Duisburg, and Hallendorf was supported by *Intruder* and high-level patrols by the *Serrate* Squadrons. They would continue this type of operation throughout the month.

The following night, 2/3 December, was again judged successful, with only two aircraft missing from the 504 dispatched to Hagen and Giessen. The operation was supported by 110 aircraft of 100 Group, losing one aircraft (Murphy) and claiming two aircraft destroyed in the air. Low-level *Intruder* squadrons bombed enemy airfields and strafed rolling stock. On patrol at Fassberg airfield, Flying Officers F. X. A. Huls and Joe Kinet of 515 Squadron saw four twin-engined aircraft on the ground and attacked them. Two He 177s were set on fire and claimed as destroyed. A Ju 88 was destroyed by Flight Lieutenant W. Taylor and Flying Officer J. N. Edwards of 157 Squadron a little to the east of Stagen at 2136 hours.[305] Captain Tarald Weisteen in 85 Squadron obtained a contact at five miles going west across the target area. Range was closed to 4000-5000 feet, and at 2000 feet it was identified as a Bf 110. The Norwegian opened fire at 200 yards and portions of the aircraft broke off, and the starboard engine caught fire before the Bf 110 spun down. The explosion could be seen through the cloud half a minute later.[306] A 223 Squadron Liberator rear gunner obtained a visual on an aircraft carrying an orange light on the starboard quarter, which closed very fast at 2000 yards. He ordered the pilot to corkscrew starboard and nothing more was seen. It was presumed to be a German jet.

There were no 100 Group operations on 3/4 December. An outstanding piece of *spoofery* was on 4/5 December when 892 heavies set out for Karlsruhe, Heilbronn, Hagen, and Hamm, in the north and south of the Ruhr. The Window Force[307] went straight into "Happy Valley" supported by PFF marking and held not less than 90-100 fighters in the area until much too late for their deployment against the heavies. Losses to the Main Force were kept to fifteen aircraft, or 1.5 per cent of the force. On this night 100 Group Mosquitoes shot down five and probably destroyed another. The AI.Mk.IV Squadrons obtained numerous contacts in the Ruhr area, but AI was mainly unworkable due to heavy interference from "Window." Contacts in the south showed great superiority in speed and in all cases drew away from the aircraft. Low-level *Intruder* squadrons, meanwhile, bombed airfields, but results were unobserved due to adverse weather conditions. The AI.Mk.X Squadrons recorded victories. Flight Lieutenant W. Taylor and Flying Officer J. N. Edwards of 157 Squadron obtained a contact in the Frankfurt area at 4½ miles range. Taylor chased it for ten minutes, the enemy all the time taking violent evasive action. He closed to 1500 feet and identified it as a Bf 110. At 250 yards he gave it a two-second burst from dead astern. The Bf 110 burst into flames and dived, and exploded on the ground near Limburg. Flight Lieutenant Jimmy Mathews DFC and Warrant Officer Penny Penrose DFC, meanwhile, obtained a contact in the Ruhr area at five miles range and chased it for forty minutes before it was identified as a Ju 88. Mathews dispatched it near Dortmund.

The twenty-three year old Flight Lieutenants Richard "Dicky" Goucher and thirty-three year old C. H. "Tiny" Bullock of 85 Squadron completed their patrol and set course for Swannington. These men had crewed up in North Africa in 1943 and they would remain together until the end of the war, being posted to 151 Squadron at Hunsdon on 18 January 1945. Thoughts of home were abandoned when a *Monica* contact was obtained. Tiny Bullock successfully converted it to a forward contact at 8000-feet range. The enemy aircraft was going in the direction of Karlsruhe at 2000 feet. In the light of flames from Karlsruhe Dickie Goucher identified it as a Bf 110. He gave it two bursts without apparent result, but a third put out the port engine. The fourth caused the aircraft to explode, and it crashed in the vicinity of Germersheim, close to a red beacon. Almost immediately another contact was obtained at four miles range. After several orbits around the beacon visual was obtained on a Bf 110 at 2000 feet. Two short bursts caused the enemy aircraft to explode and crash in approximately the same place as the first one. Goucher and Bullock's Mosquito was struck by flying debris but returned to Swannington safely.

The German night-fighter force was run ragged by 85 Squadron. Captain Svein Heglund DFC and Flying Officer Robert O. Symon, who were airborne in their NF.XXX from Swannington at 1730 hours on a High Level Support Patrol in the Karlsruhe area, reached their patrol at 1855 hours. Contacts were obtained on bombers and later two targets, with violent evasion, were chased eastwards. At 2005 Schwabish Hall airfield was seen lit and several fleeting contacts appeared well below. Heglund went down to 2500 feet to investigate but all lighting was doused. The Norwegian regained at height, and at 2015 hours, northeast of Heilbronn, Symon obtained a contact. Captain Heglund continues:

> "We had just regained height at 10,000 feet, after investigating Schwabish Hall airfield and were flying on about 260° when, at 2015 hours, my N/R said he had contact and told me to turn 100° port. Our position then was about ten miles North East of Heilbronn. Contact was then obtained six miles ahead and well below. The aircraft was doing a mild corkscrew on an easterly course and we came in behind at 4000 feet (about 2500 feet. above the ground). The aircraft being chased was traveling very slowly - 190-200 IAS - and we overshot, recognising it as a Me.110 by its square wingtip and two fins and rudders, as we pulled away to starboard 400 feet away. Contact and visual were momentarily lost but contact regained and maintained to bring a further visual at 400 feet. We were still overtaking and I lost the visual in making further S turns to lose speed, and remained behind the enemy aircraft. Contact was maintained, the whole time and finally the visual was obtained at 400 feet, and held steady. I fired a one-second burst obtaining strikes immediately on the starboard engine and wing root. The enemy aircraft burst into flames, lighting up the crosses on wings and fuselage and showing up the Radar aerial display on the nose. Enemy aircraft sideslipped into the ground near Rothenburg where it exploded. Time 2025. At 2026 course was set for base via Frankfurt area where several airfields were seen active. Unfortunately petrol was low and we had to land at Brussels at 2200 hours. After refuelling, we took off 2320 and landed back at base at 0010 hours.'

Heglund, who expended just twenty-four rounds of SAPI and sixteen of HEI, put in a claim for a Bf 110 destroyed. Robert O. Symon DFC recalls that:

> "Captain Svein Heglund DFC* who joined 85 Squadron (and his fellow group of Norwegians) in October 1944, was a delightful and modest young man, who, I found later, was Norway's Ace. As a point of interest check the number of rounds it took my friend to bring down three 110s compared with the number of rounds fired to bring down No.1. I can only assume that this was the first for Swannington and he was going to be sure that it would never fly again."

Flying Officers "Ginger" Owen and Victor McAllister DFM, also of 85 Squadron, got an AI contact in the Ruhr area at four and a half miles range and chased it for twenty-six minutes before a visual on a Ju 88 was obtained before shooting it down. It was 85 Squadron's 100th enemy aircraft at night. Their victim was probably Ju 88G-1 714152 of 6./NJG4, which crashed near Krefeld. *Unteroffizier* Wilhelm Schlutter, pilot, was wounded, and *Unteroffizier* Friedrich Heerwagen, radar operator, and Gefreiter Friedrich Herbeck, air gunner, were killed.

Flight Lieutenant Edward R. Hedgecoe DFC finished an uneventful patrol except for chases and visuals on other Mosquitoes before setting course for home. However, a minute later a contact at four miles head on was obtained. The thirty-four year old former accountant officer had re-mustered to aircrew and joined 85 Squadron, where he crewed up with Flight Lieutenant Norman Bamford. On 24/25 March they had a narrow escape when their Mosquito, *O-Orange*, had been severely scorched, with the rudder fabric being burned away following their shooting down of a Ju 188 at 300-feet range off the south coast. Hedgecoe had nursed *O-Orange* back to base, where a piece of debris from the Ju 188 was removed from the port wing. He and Bamford both received the DFC after this encounter. This harrowing experience appears to have had an effect on Hedgecoe, who now employed a more judicious approach on the bogey behind which he turned and gave chase for eight minutes. Over Detmold airfield at a range of 1000 feet, at 6000 feet the unmistakable outline of a Ju 88 was made out. Its identity was confirmed at 300 feet. Dropping back to 150 yards, Hedgecoe gave it three short bursts and saw strikes all over the aircraft. Burning debris flew in all directions. Hedgecoe overshot and was unable to regain contact before a shortage of petrol forced him to set course for Brussels/ Melsbroek to refuel. He put in a claim for a Ju 88 probably destroyed.

On 5/6 December, 553 aircraft attacked Soest, Duisburg, Nürnburg, and Mannheim. Seventy-six aircraft of 100 Group supported the operation, which cost one heavy bomber. Reports indicated "there was probably no fighter reaction. Only a few contacts were obtained. This was probably due to adverse weather conditions over enemy airfields."

A very severe ground frost heralded a bright and clear morning on 6 December, and all anticipation was for a maximum effort. Low-level *Intruders* bombed and strafed enemy airfields, but the weather conditions were not good for this type of operation. That night, 1291 aircraft attacked Bergesburg, Osnabrück, Giessen, Berlin, Schwerte, and Hanau. Eighty-nine aircraft of 100 Group supported the operations and lost one aircraft. The heavies lost twenty-one of their number, or 1.7 per cent of the force. Squadron Leader Neil Reeves DSO DFC and Flying Officer M. Phillips, attached to the BSDU, were carrying out a *Perfectos* patrol when they obtained a contact west of Giessen at twelve miles range. They followed and eventually got a visual on a Bf 110. After a long chase they shot it down. It was the first victory for *Perfectos*.

Bad weather did not prevent 157 and 85 Squadrons from running up the score. Flight Lieutenant Jimmy Mathews DFC and Warrant Officer A. "Penny" Penrose DFC of 157 Squadron obtained a contact at range. They chased the contact for thirteen minutes through several orbits and changes of height. A visual was gained at 1000 feet range on a Bf 110 with long-range tanks. He closed to just fifty yards and gave it a one-second burst, scoring strikes all over the fuselage. The Bf 110 burst into flames and crashed at Limburg. A second contact at five miles led to a visual on a Ju 88 at 1500-feet range. Mathews gave it a short burst from close range and the enemy aircraft broke its back and crashed fifteen miles southwest of Giessen. Their Ju 88 victim was 712268 of I./NJG4, which crashed near Giessen, killing the air gunner, *Gefreiter* Alfred Graefer.

Squadron Leader Dolly Doleman and "Bunny" Bunch of 157 Squadron were airborne from Swannington at 1835 hours in their "plywood pantechnicon" and set course for patrol. Doleman continues:

> "Got hung up in the bomber stream West of the Rhine, and saw the flares being laid on Biesson. We saw bags of four or five-star reds being fired from the Frankfurt searchlight belt so bogged off to have a look. No joy so returned to Giessen, which was being inundated with incendiaries (wizard alliteration) and saw lashings of Lancs flying across the target. We stayed overhead to see if we could pick off someone trying to pick off a Lanc, but nothing happened so went NW to clear the bomber stream. We had just arrived, at 2030 hours when we picked up an almost head-on contact at 15,000 feet at six miles, same level. Target dived to 11,000 feet on bomber withdrawal route then did a figure of eight and stooged off eastwards. Closed in and identified as a Me 110 and shot it down at 2040 hours in Kitzingen area. Night glasses were used to advantage. We had a persistent *Monica* contact before and after the happy event and as he wouldn't close to less than 8000 feet we had to turn and try to catch him. He must have seen what we were trying to do, for he had no forward contact but saw the Hun colors fired in the direction he should have been, but out of range. Looked in at an aerodrome near Zelhausen and later at Bonn, but no bon, as they say, so returned to base, where we landed at 2320 hours - the landing as usual, being the most exciting thing of the evening for Bunny. Claim one Me 110 destroyed." [Doleman fired 52 SAPI and 48 HEI rounds to dispatch the enemy night-fighter.]

Flight Lieutenant Edward R. Hedgecoe DFC of the Fighter Interception Unit at Ford was attached to 85 Squadron at Swannington for a ten-day period. Hedgecoe took off in *O-Orange*, an 85 Squadron NF.XXX, with Flight Sergeant J. R. Whitham as his radar operator. They obtained several contacts at 15,000 feet. One was selected and chased westwards for ten minutes. A visual was obtained at 800 feet on a Bf 110 (an 8/NJG4 machine flown by *Hauptmann* Helmut Bergmann, a *Ritterkreuzträger* with thirty-six victories). Hedgecoe gave it a one-second burst between the exhaust flames. It crashed and exploded on the ground twenty-five miles west of Münster. Several more contacts were obtained in the target area; one at four miles coming towards the Mosquito was selected. After a five-minute chase a visual was obtained on another Bf 110. A one-second burst produced strikes and a flash on the port engine. Visual was lost. When it was regained, the Bf 110 was going very slowly with its port engine feathered. Hedgecoe closed in again, but overshot due to ice on the windscreen. He tried a second time, but the Mosquito stalled and the enemy aircraft was lost. He claimed it as a "damaged." Hedgecoe and Whitham's second "victim" may have been Bf 110G-4 740078 G9+HZ of 12./NJG1, which crashed ten kilometers NW of Handorf. This aircraft was flown by twenty-three year old *Hauptmann* Hans-Heinz Augenstein, *Staffelkapitan* 12./NJG1, who was found three days later in a ditch, his parachute unopened. *Feldwebel* Günther Steins, his *bordfunker*, was killed when he was hurled from the aircraft in the crash. Augenstein had forty-six night victories, including forty-five RAF night bombers, and had been awarded the *Ritterkreuz* on 9 June 1944. *Unteroffizier* Kurt Schmidt, *bordschütze*, who was WIA, baled out and survived. (A Ju 88 was also claimed as "damaged" by Fortress gunner Flying Officer Corke of 214 Squadron while on *a Jostle* patrol.)

For two nights following 100 Group flew no operations. Then on 9/10 December, when seventy-nine aircraft of 8 Group attacked Duisburg, Koblenz, and Berlin, 100 Group dispatched sixty-eight aircraft. One of their number, a Halifax of 171 Squadron piloted by Warrant Officer Powe RAAF, failed to return from Windowing Koblenz. All Mosquito patrols were "completely uneventful," probably due to adverse weather conditions over Germany. No operations were flown the following night for the same reason. The morning of 11 December was much milder and warmer in contrast to the previous day's sleet and rain, but that night's operations were also scrubbed. Late that evening the Met gave crews the "gen" that it was to be "a lovely day tomorrow," but then it broke dull and wet.

That night, 12/13 December, 592 bombers attacked Essen and Osnabrück. (Six aircraft, or one per cent of the force, failed to return.) Ninety-one aircraft were dispatched. 100 Group and 192 Squadron played its first operational role as an airborne jammer when the first Mosquito fitted with two channels of *Piperack* operated. (In time, all the squadron's Mosquitoes would be fitted with *Piperack*. The aircraft played a dual role. Signals investigation continued to and from the target, while *Piperack* itself was used over the target.) 100 Group shot down five more German night-fighters.

The AI.Mk.IV squadrons, meanwhile, obtained only two contacts, but no combats resulted and in the main, the low-level *Intruder* squadrons were once again defeated by the weather. Not so 85 and 157 Squadrons. In 85 Squadron Flight Lieutenant Edward R. Hedgecoe DFC and Flight Sergeant J. R. Whitham destroyed two Bf 110s and Squadron Leader Branse Burbridge DSO* DFC* and Bill Skelton DSO* DFC* added a Ju 88 and a Bf 110 to their rising score. Hedgecoe and Whitham in *O-Orange* obtained a contact at six miles range, head on and below them. Violent evasive action followed before Hedgecoe was able to close to 1000 feet and obtained a visual. He closed right in and positively identified it as a Bf 110. Hedgecoe dropped back to seventy-five yards and fired a short burst, which caused an explosion in the fuselage. The Bf 110 dived steeply, burning furiously, and disappeared into 10/10ths cloud at 7000-8000 feet, twenty miles south of Hagen. A second contact was obtained at four miles range, slightly above them and orbiting. It eventually settled down on a course towards Essen. Hedgecoe closed the range to 2000 feet and saw exhaust flames at 1000 feet. Obtaining a visual, he closed right in and recognized it as a Bf 110. A two-second burst from 100 yards caused the enemy aircraft to disintegrate and fall vertically in approximately the same area as the first one. (At the end of the month Hedgecoe and Norman Bamford were posted to 151 Squadron at Hunsdon, where the promoted Hedgecoe was a flight commander. On 1 January they both died in a crash-landing on their first flight with the squadron. Hedgecoe had shot down eight enemy aircraft and Bamford had taken part in the destruction of ten. The award of a Bar to Hedgecoe's DFC was Gazetted in March.)

Squadron Leader Branse Burbridge DSO* DFC** and Bill Skelton DSO* DFC** were on patrol when a contact was obtained at 7000 feet and 2½ miles. Burbridge followed it at a low air speed through port and starboard orbits. A visual at 1000 feet confirmed the contact as a Ju 88. Burbridge gave it a 1½-second burst from 500 feet and set one of the engines on fire.[308] Flying towards Essen, another contact was obtained at four miles and 12,000 feet. Burbridge and Skelton dashed towards the target area at high speed and climbing. Luckily a burst of flak illuminated a Bf 110, and Burbridge closed to 400 feet for final identification. He gave the Bf 110 a ½-second burst from 500 feet and the enemy aircraft exploded before spinning down in flames, the tail unit breaking off. It crashed about two miles west of Essen. Burbridge and Skelton finished their second tours early in 1945. Both were awarded Bars to their DSOs to go with the Bars they had already been awarded to their DFCs. Burbridge and Skelton finished the war as the top-scoring night-fighter crew in the RAF with a final total of twenty-one victories. Bob Braham and Wing Commander John Cunningham both destroyed nineteen enemy aircraft at night. Post-war, Branse Burbridge became a lay preacher, while Bill Skelton was ordained as a clergyman in the Church of England and became chaplain at Clare College, Cambridge.

Captain Eric Fossum and Flying Officer S. A. Hider, another Norwegian crew in the strength of 85 Squadron, obtained a contact crossing port to starboard. A hard turn brought the contact dead ahead at a range of 4,500 feet and he closed in. At 300 feet the silhouette was made out to be that of a Ju 88. Fossum dropped back to 600 feet and fired a short burst. Strikes on the tail unit were seen and debris flew off. A further burst produced more strikes on the fuselage and the Junkers spun to port. A few seconds later a faint glow was seen through the clouds.

Wing Commander K. H. P Beauchamp DSO DFC, Commanding Officer of 157 Squadron, and his navigator, Flight Lieutenant Leslie Scholefield, patrolled uneventfully until the Main Force bombing commenced. At 1925 hours the markers were seen on Essen and Osnabrück. At 2010 hours at 12,000 feet Scholefield got a contact at six miles range, 30° to starboard and going away to starboard. Beauchamp wrote:

> "I turned after it, and abased for twenty-five minutes, first on course 120 and then on 150, and descending during chase to 10,000 feet, just above cloud tops. At 2035 hours the target did a port orbit over a lit airfield, believed to be Aschaffenburg. I closed to 200 feet below and. on the quarter and identified it as a Me.110 with long-range tanks, and burning an orange light inboard of the starboard engine. Identification was checked by Flight Lieutenant Scholefield using night binoculars. I dropped back to 600 feet astern and fired two short bursts at 2037 hours, 10,000 feet. Saw strikes on the starboard wing and there were two large showers of sparks. Immediately after this, visual was lost and as the AI had been upset by firing the guns, contact was also lost. I patrolled in the area hoping to regain contact. We had had two forward *Monica* contacts during the chase and got another AI contact at 2040 hours, which was followed down to 5000 feet and lost in violent manoeuvres. I claim one Me 110 damaged."

The thirteenth day of December broke under a very heavy frost, and towards mid-morning fog "thick enough to shame any Manchester could boast about" enveloped stations in Norfolk, and operations were scrubbed very early. Therefore, 100 Group did not support Bomber Command operations in north Denmark and Norway that night, nor *Gardening* operations in the Kattegat on 14/15 December. On 15/16 December seventy-three aircraft were used to support main force operations against Ludwigshafen, Osnabrück, Hanover, and Duisburg. Seven Mosquitoes of 141 Squadron led a *Spoof* raid and dropped 500-pounders and 250lb yellow target indicators through solid cloud over the target. *Spoofing* was adjudged successful; only one heavy bomber was lost in the main attack on Ludwigshafen. Only two AI contacts leading to chases were made. The following night 100 Group stood down again.

On 17/18 December ninety-six aircraft in 100 Group, including a *Spoof* raid by four Mosquitoes of 141 Squadron on Mannheim, supported a massive operation by 1174 aircraft that bombed Ulm, München, Duisburg, Hanau, Münster, and Halendorf. Three Bf 110s were destroyed on the night of 17/18 December. Dickie Goucher and Tiny Bullock obtained a contact about forty miles from Ulm. Their prey was above them, and because of evasive action was at first thought to be a Mosquito. Goucher closed to 2000 feet and got a glimpse of a green resin light. At 1000 feet he obtained a visual and Dickie Goucher closed to 400 feet. It was a Bf 110. A short burst set fire to the port engine and the Bf 110 pulled up and dived, hitting the ground about eight miles from Ulm, where it continued to burn.

This night 157 Squadron also reaped rich rewards. About five miles west of Duisburg Warrant Officer D. A. Taylor and Flight Sergeant Radford obtained a contact at eight miles range and 13,000 feet. Taylor chased it for five minutes, closing to 1500 feet, and obtained a visual on a Bf 110. Closing to 300 feet, he pumped a two-second burst of cannon into the Bf 110's airframe and it exploded, covering the Mosquito with oil and debris. It crashed northwest of Neiss. Thirty miles north-northeast of Ũlm another Bf 110 was shot down by Flight Sergeant Leigh. One of the crew baled out before it crashed in flames. A Ju 88 was damaged by Squadron Leader James Ghilles Benson and Flight Lieutenant

Lewis Brandon during a dogfight lasting an exhausting forty minutes after obtaining the contact near a cone of searchlights. Lewis Brandon recalls:

"We had not chased a Hun for over a month and were hoping our luck would change. It was a long way to go, two solid hours each way for only a twenty-minute patrol. We wasted no time and made straight for our patrol point, crossing in over the Belgian-Dutch border and plodding on over land at 15,000 feet until we reached our destination. For twenty minutes we scoured the skies between Stuttgart and Ulm without anything appearing on our AI, although we saw lots of activity where the bombing was taking place. We tried flying at 10,000 feet and 18,000 feet, but there was just nothing doing for us. We had plenty of petrol left so we decided to go out of our way a bit and see what we might find in the Frankfurt-Koblenz area. This proved a happy decision. As we approached Frankfurt at about twelve thousand feet I got a contact on an aircraft flying south. It was well above us so we whipped around and climbed after it. Whatever it was, it was certainly flying fast and high. Try as we could, we just could not catch it. Eventually, when we were up to nearly twenty thousand feet, we lost him, still well above us and going like a bat out of hell. It seemed as if this was just not our night. Round we turned, heading for Frankfurt again, when we spotted a cone of searchlights shining up into the sky near Wiesbaden. We made for these, and a minute later I had another contact. Our combat report read as follows:

"Contact obtained near a cone of five steady searchlights. Our height 16,000 feet. We followed down to 6,000 feet and up again to 12,000 feet. Target weaving violently and making steep turns in either direction. Then followed down to 2500 feet still on AI and we found ourselves on the circuit of a fully lit airfield. Visual obtained on Junkers 88G, indicated air speed 320 mph, height 2500 feet. At this time certainly not more than fifty yards away and below the enemy aircraft. I raised the Mosquito's nose and was about to open fire (despite the fact that I thought we were too close,) when we were illuminated by a searchlight. At this moment the Junkers 88 fired a four-star cartridge - two reds, two whites. These completely blinded me. As I knew we were dead behind him, I opened fire but saw no strikes. Then I saw the enemy aircraft, illuminated by the falling cartridges below and peeling off to port. I jammed the nose down and had a quick shot which produced several strikes outboard the starboard engine. He continued steeply down to port and we followed him round to the other side of the airfield, going very fast.

"We were again illuminated, this time by two searchlights. The enemy aircraft fired another cartridge, which illuminated it, and it was seen above us and slightly behind. Our height was then only 800 feet. We could not get into firing position and contact was lost. Several white cartridges were fired from the airfield, which we continued to patrol for some time afterwards without obtaining contact again. Excellent work by Flight Lieutenant Brandon, who kept contact despite violent and continuous evasive action of every sort, especially when below 2500 feet. The dogfight on AI before the visual lasted for nearly forty minutes. Claim: one Junkers 88G damaged."

On 18/19 December 308 bombers attacked Gdynia, Münster, Nürnburg, and Danzig. Forty-eight aircraft of 100 Group supported the operation. Four heavies and a Mosquito flown by Flying Officers Desmond T. Tull DFC and Peter J. Cowgill DFC of 85 Squadron failed to return. Tull accidentally rammed Bf 110 G9+CC of *Stab* IV/NJG1 flown by *Hauptmann* Adolph Breves (with *Feldwebel* Telsnig, *bordfunker*, and *Unteroffizier* Ofers, *bordschütze*), who was coming into land at Düsseldorf airfield at 2230 hours. A large part of one of the wings of the 110 was torn off, but Breves (who finished the war with eighteen victories) managed to land the aircraft without further damage. The Bf110 was repaired and test flown on 31 December. Tull and Cowgill, who were both killed, are buried in Reichswald Forest Cemetery, near Kleef.

Low-level *Intruders* reported no combats, and the AI.Mk.IV squadrons did not operate. The one victory this night went to Flight Lieutenant William Taylor and Flying Officer Jeffery N. Edwards of 157 Squadron. At first their patrol was uneventful. Having set course for base, they ran into Window, but were able to pick up a contact at about six miles range. Their target was climbing steeply and orbiting. At 2000 feet and 800 above they obtained a visual. Taylor was nearly overshooting so he dropped back and weaved gently. Another visual was obtained 30° above him. After chasing for another five minutes the contact was identified as a He 219.[309] Taylor opened fire from 250 yards, but the Mosquito was caught in the enemy night-fighter's slipstream and his shooting was erratic. Strikes were observed, and minor explosions appeared in the fuselage before the Owl turned slowly to port and peeled off. Visual was lost, but the Heinkel was followed on AI until contact was lost at 12,000 feet. A few seconds later it exploded on the ground at Suedlohn. (*Unteroffizier* Scheürlein (pilot) baled out safely. *Unteroffizier* Günther Heinze (radar op.) was KIA.) Taylor and Edwards were killed on 22/23 December when they crashed while attempting to make an approach to land at Swannington after informing Flying Control over the R/T that they had no aileron control.

Bad weather interfered again before operations resumed on 21/22 December. Only 28 aircraft supported 475 heavies attacking Köln, Bonn, Politz, and Schneidemuhl. Three bombers failed to return. Low-level *Intruder* and AI.Mk IV Mosquitoes did not operate. The only contact of the night was obtained by Wing Commander K. H. P Beauchamp DSO DFC and Flight Lieutenant Leslie Scholefield DFC of 157 Squadron south of Bonn. Beauchamp reported:

"We had completed our patrol uneventfully at 1852 hours and were on the way home at 12,000 feet, just west of Koblenz when my navigator got a contact 60° to port at five miles range, going port. This was chased on an initial heading of 150°, turning port slowing on to 060°. We were losing height and eventually overtook him at 4000 feet having been flying at 300 mph for most of the time. A visual was obtained at 2500 feet and was identified as a Ju 88 in the light of a half-moon from 200 feet on his starboard quarter below. I dropped back to 200 feet dead astern and fired a short burst, causing strikes. Enemy aircraft immediately peeled off port and went down on to the top of some stratus cloud, which appeared to be just above ground level. I thought he had dived right through this as I had lost visual contact, but as there was no resultant explosion I followed down and regained a visual on him as he was weaving away violently just above cloud. I closed in on his port quarter and slightly above, opening fire at about 600 yards, as I was anxious to inflict further damage before he could make good his escape. Strikes were obtained from this burst and from two more, the last of which set his port engine on fire. I pulled up and did a port orbit over him watching the fire increase until the enemy aircraft flew into the ground in a shallow dive and exploded. In view of the length of time of the combat and his final behaviour of the enemy aircraft it seems likely that the crew had time to escape by parachute." [Beauchamp fired 176 rounds of SAPI and 172 rounds of HEI to down the Ju 88.]

More Ju 88 losses occurred on the following night (22/23 December) when forty-five aircraft were dispatched to cover 274 heavies attacking Koblenz and Bingen. High-level ASH patrols were carried out but no contacts resulted. The mercurial AI.Mk.X squadrons worked their magic once again with a wizard prang or two. Branse Burbridge, and Skelton and Dolly Doleman, and "Bunny" Bunch DFC of 85 Squadron destroyed a Bf 110 and a Ju 88 respectively. Doleman reported:

"Arrived at patrol at 1825 hours and at 1835 hours obtained contact. We were at 15,000 feet and chased it up to 20,000 feet, just north of Bingen. As staggering up the last few thousand feet a *Monica* contact whistled in, and position became so uncomfortable, we had to leave the original contact and try to catch the other type. As we turned to port the *Monica*, which had been frantically jammed, cleared (we think the first contact might have been a *Dinah* [sic] Mosquito) and we saw the type behind showing IFF. After several conversations on the R/T, starting with 'Please go away' and finishing '_______ *off, you silly* ______' we neared the bomber stream and dived into a cloud of Window where we lost him. This had wasted about twenty minutes of valuable time, and as bombing had finished we went along north of Frankfurt to have a look at Limburg. This proved a good bet, as we obtained a contact at ten miles range and well below. We were at 15,000 feet and time 1925 hours. We closed range and descended to 8000 feet and obtained visual at 3000 feet; the target by this time was doing a hardish port turn. Identified at 1500 feet from below in the turn as a Ju 88 then the silly clot slackened his turn and we were able to close in nicely to 500 feet and prang him with only ½-ring deflection. The fuselage and port engine burst into flames. We hung behind just to make sure, but he dived straight in five miles west of Limburg at 1935 hours. We wished him a Merry Christmas on the way down - literally cooking his goose for him.

"No more joy, so left patrol at 1949 hours. Saw a buzz bomb in Malmedy area on way back. Just getting nicely in position when some brown job opened up with one solitary gun, missed the buzz bomb and frightened us away. I hope it landed on their headquarters. Landed base 2107 hours." Claim one Ju 88 destroyed."[310]

Flying Officers A. J. "Ginger" Owen and J. S. V. McAllister also went on the rampage, scoring a hat trick of victories with two Ju 88s and a Bf 110. First they shot down a Bf 110 north of Saarbrücken. Then a *Monica* contact was obtained almost immediately afterwards. It was converted to AI at 14,000-feet range. At 1200 feet visual was obtained and confirmed as a Ju 88 on closing dead below it. Owen gave it a "medium" burst from 150 yards which set the port engine on fire before it crashed in the same area as the Bf 110. Twenty minutes later, a third contact was obtained four miles ahead. Closing to 2000 feet, a visual was obtained well above him. It was another Ju 88 and it was taking evasive action. A short deflection burst scored strikes on the port wing and pieces flew off. The Ju 88 dived vertically and contact was lost at 7000 feet. Four minutes later an explosion occurred on the ground.[311]

Flight Lieutenant Hannowin obtained a visual on a Ju 88, but contact was lost because of violent evasive action by the enemy aircraft. For 24 minutes Warrant Officer Taylor chased a contact. When a visual was obtained it was seen to be a Ju 88 throwing out *Düppel* (Window). The Mosquito overshot and contact was lost. A 199 Squadron Stirling crew obtained a visual on a Fw 190 dead astern at 450 yards. Both the rear and mid-upper gunners opened fire before the enemy fighter could attack.

On 23/24 December 61 aircraft of 100 Group supported operations by Bomber Command when 105 heavies attacked cities in Germany. Low-level *Intruders* had no combats, but took advantage of the moonlight to bomb and strafe a variety of aerodromes and any other targets. Again, the aerial victories went to the Swannington squadrons. A contact was obtained by Flight Lieutenant G. C. Chapman and Flight Lieutenant J. Stockley of 85 Squadron at eight miles range and 11,000 feet in the Mannheim area that turned out to be a Bf 110. After a prolonged dog fight Chapman finally shot it down just south of Mainz. Flight Lieutenant R. J. Smythe and Flying Officer Waters of 157 Squadron destroyed a Ju 88 about ten miles west of Koblenz.

On 24/25 December 100 Group supported Christmas Eve raids by 104 Lancasters of 3 Group on Hangelar airfield, near Bonn, and 97 Lancasters and five Mosquitoes of 1 and 8 Groups on the marshalling yards at Cologne/Nippes. At Cologne good *Oboe* marking resulted in an extremely accurate bombing raid. Losses were five Lancasters shot down during the raid and two more crashed in England. In support of these two raids, 42 RCM sorties were flown and 42 Mosquitoes of 100 Group patrolled the *Luftwaffe* night-fighter bases and radio beacons along the route taken by the heavies.[312] The Mosquito squadrons in 100 Group celebrated the festive season in style, claiming four Me 110s and one Ju 88 shot down. Low-level *Intruders* covered enemy airfields and carried out *Ranger* operations in the Breslau area. Locomotives, rolling stock, and motor transport were bombed and strafed by the Mk IV AI Mosquito squadrons operating as low-level *Intruders*. Meanwhile, Wing Commander Howard C. Kelsey DFC, the new 515 Squadron Commanding Officer, and Flying Officer Edward M. "Smitty" Smith took off from Little Snoring in the afternoon for a night *Intruder* operation. Edward Smith recalls:

"We had been interested in night-fighter training areas and felt the Breslau area might be fruitful. We landed at Laon/Juvincourt to refuel as this station was supposed to provide facilities for Bomber Command aircraft. On arrival we found some panic on there as the Battle of the Bulge had just started. However, we managed to make arrangements to refuel and have a quick meal before starting off at 1650 hours across S Germany, passing near Bayreuth all quite low level; 200-300 feet."

The Commanding Officer and his navigator reached Rosenhorn airfield at 1952 hours. It was not lit, but several aircraft were seen parked around the perimeter. Kelsey made several low runs over the airfield but, as there was some ground haze with poor visibility, he decided to continue his patrol and return to Rosenborn later. They had the same problems at Ohlau airfield so they returned to Rosenborn. Several Ju 52 transports were seen parked at the south end of the airfield while a single He 111 was parked on the north side near a radio station. Kelsey took the Heinkel first, broadside on, from 1300 feet down to 150 feet, breaking off at 200-feet range. Kelsey's cannon shells ripped into the Heinkel but it did not catch fire. Then the crew turned their attention to the Ju 52s and a lone Ju 88. Again Kelsey attacked from broadside on, breaking off the attack at 200 feet range at a height of 150 feet. Kelsey claimed one Ju 52 and the Ju 88 as "damaged." Smith adds, "On the way back we damaged two trains severely in the Prague area."

The AI.Mk.X Mosquitoes, meanwhile, enjoyed almost total air superiority over the *Nachtjägdgeschwader* this night. Squadron Leader James Benson DFC* and Flight Lieutenant Lewis Brandon DFC* of 157 Squadron in Mosquito XIX were airborne from Swannington at 1819 hours on High Level Support Patrol for Bomber Command attacks on Cologne and Hangelar. Lewis Brandon recalls:

> "We decided to have our Christmas dinner on Christmas Eve. As a maximum effort had been asked for from the station for the night's operations, we were very pleased that we all had an early time for takeoff. It was arranged that dinner would be held back until we returned, giving us something to look forward to. We left Swannington at 16.30 hours on our way to Limburg. We had put in quite a lot of flying time in that area during the past few weeks and considered ourselves rather as specialists around Frankfurt - a couple of Frankfurters almost.
>
> "We had been on patrol at 14,000 feet for about half an hour when we obtained a contact. We were just north of Limburg and the aircraft was well below us. Down we went pretty smartly to 8000 feet after a target that was flying level at that height but weaving quite violently. As we closed in, Ben had fleeting visuals two or three times. Each time, however, he could not hold on to them nor could he identify the aircraft. We continued to follow him on AI, and he turned through two complete orbits before settling down on a North Westerly course. Shortly afterwards we saw some target indicators go down ahead of us. We had closed in on the aircraft and Ben got a visual on a Messerschmitt 110 at a range of two thousand feet, silhouetted against the light of the target indicators. 'Okay. I can see him all right now', said Ben. 'Just look at that. No wonder we've taken such a while to close in.' As I looked up, I saw the Messerschmitt go across us from starboard to port. It went a fair way out to port, then went right up on one wing and came back in front of us, crossing the other way in this violent weave. Ben followed it through several of these weaves, fairly well throttled back and far more gently than the Messerschmitt. Then, from about 150 yards he gave it two short sharp bursts, firing at the exhaust flames. The second burst set the port engine and the whole of the port side of the fuselage alight. We dived under some large pieces of debris that came flying back and heard them swoosh above the cockpit. The Messerschmitt was well alight now and going over to our starboard. We saw it hit the ground and explode near a small town by the name of Dottesfeld [about ten miles west of Mainz], where we could see it burning brightly.
>
> "'About bloody time we shot one down again,' remarked Ben. 'Look at it burning. I wonder if the camera gun would pick that up?'
>
> "'Why not have a go?' I suggested. So we did. We had a good look around to see that there was no high ground and Ben did two runs right down to within a few hundred feet of the burning aircraft. All in vain though, nothing appeared on the film when it was developed. We landed back at Swannington at five minutes to nine. Dinner had been laid on for half past so after a pretty rapid debriefing we set off for the mess. We were fortified with the news that, in addition to our Messerschmitt, Jimmy Matthews and Penrose had destroyed a Junkers 88.[313] As can be imagined, this gave the squadron something to celebrate. Four enemy aircraft destroyed in one night was by no means a record, but this had been accomplished on Christmas Eve, just before a party."

Benson concludes: "About time too after two damaged recently."

Another success went to Captain Svein Heglund DFC and Flying Officer Robert Symon of 85 Squadron, who obtained an AI contact at 1850 hours. Heglund reports:

> "We were flying in a South Easterly course away from target area and towards a visual beacon in Wiesbaden area when we obtained a contact head on and below at 6 miles range. We turned port and dived, leveling out at 14,000 feet, coming in behind an aircraft doing a mild corkscrew, range 1½ miles. We chased rapidly to 3000 feet and aircraft climbed rapidly to 14,000 feet, weaving all the time. A visual was obtained at 2000 feet, on a faint outline and a dim white light inboard of the starboard engine. Following the white light through several turns range was closed to 150 feet, when aircraft was recognised as a Me.110 by twin fins and rudders, general outline and large drop tanks. We dropped back to 600 feet and fired a ½-second burst obtained strikes on starboard wing root. Aircraft exploded immediately and we dived hard to avoid flaming debris which showered back over us.
>
> "We once again turned on original South easterly course and almost immediately obtained another contact dead ahead at six miles, height being 15,000-feet, traveling on the same course as ourselves. We increased speed and went into a shallow dive slowing overhauling the aircraft, which was traveling at about 300 mph IAS. Shortly before arriving at the beacon and when we had closed range to 2500-feet, aircraft dived hard to starboard then climbed hard, contact being lost for some seconds. Contact was regained and aircraft dived hard again turning as it did so. Contact was finally lost. During the last part of the chase the port engine was getting very rough, cutting intermittently and vibrating. Claim: one Me.110 destroyed. Aircraft landed base 2041 hours." It was Heglund's 14th victory of the war, having scored twelve and 1/3 kills flying Spitfires with No.331 Squadron.

Squadron Leader Dolly Doleman and Flight Lieutenant Bunny Bunch of 157 Squadron were airborne from Swannington at 1626 hours at the start of a very auspicious high Level Support Patrol for Bomber Command attacks on Cologne and Hangelar. Doleman wrote:

"Just before reaching patrol had a Radar dogfight with something. We presumed this to be either friendly or single-engined. We found on landing this was R.S.D. Reached patrol area and saw an aircraft hit the deck dead below us near Siegen. Things seemed pretty dead, so went towards Cologne and just as we arrived, obtained a contact: range 6 miles well below. Overhauled fairly quickly and just managed to slow down into an ideal position, where we identified an Me 110 doing an orbit at 9000 feet. I think the crew must have been full of the festive spirit as we were directly up moon at 600 feet when we opened fire with very long burst. The pride of the Luftwaffe caught fire immediately but we gave them another burst just for fun, and he went down and pranged just west of Cologne at 1905. We immediately had another contact at 10 miles' range, well above. Chased this at full bore and luckily the tyke dived down and we closed in very rapidly, eventually slightly overshooting. About fifty yards to port, having a wizard view of another Me 110. We did a hard port orbit and picked him up at three miles - by this time we were at 8000 feet, going NW slap across the Ruhr - closed in and identified again and opened fire from about 500 feet with long burst. He caught fire and pieces of debris fell off including one quite large piece. He continued flying evenly so we gave him three more bursts, when he went down in the Duisburg area at 1921 hours. We headed west, as we could not fix on *Gee* and found ourselves near Krefeld as flew straight home. Cannot write any more as there is a party on in the mess. Claim two Me 110s destroyed. Aircraft landed at base 2024 hours."[314]

Meanwhile, Flying Officer Frank Bocock and Flight Sergeant Alf "Snogger" Rogers of 515 Squadron had found little joy in recent weeks. Alf Rogers recalls:

"A typical night intruder op. began by crossing the North Sea at less than 500 feet. In this way they were too low to be detected by German radar. The Dutch coast was crossed at a point five miles north of the town of Egmond. From there on navigation was by map reading which could be difficult on a dark night. Water features showed up quite well so these were used as pinpoints. After crossing the coast the next turning point was the distinctive mouth of the Ijsell River on the eastern side of the Zuider Zee. Then on to the Dortmund-Ems Canal, next Dummer Lake, then Steinhuder Lake. Depending on which aerodrome was being visited the Intruder would turn off at one of these points and head for the target.

"If the target was in southern Germany the route would be via Belgium. This involved another problem as the Allied armies moved in. They created several 'Artillery Zones' where the gunners were free to fire on any aircraft flying lower than 10.000 feet. Intruders never flew higher than 2000 feet so they had to avoid these Zones to avoid being shot down by what is now euphemistically called 'Friendly Fire'. Sometimes the target was Lista in Norway. This involved a 500-mile sea crossing where *Gee* was not available. Then it was a matter of trusting that the Met Officer had been accurate in forecasting the wind velocity and that the navigator had worked out his flight plan correctly. Occasionally *Intruders* carried bombs, HE or incendiary, in which case the primary target was the Luftwaffe base. Failing that any other legitimate' target that presented itself was attacked. So Low Level *Night Intruders* contributed to the safe return of many a bomber crew.

"One night in December we were assigned an *Intruder* target at Giessen in southern Germany. The previous few days had been very wintry and there was good deal of snow on the ground. The snow plough had been busy keeping the runways usable. As we walked out to dispersal the sky was heavy with more snow and as we climbed into our Mossie the snow began to fall heavily. We settled ourselves into the cockpit, started the engines and began to move off. After we had moved just a yard or two Frank said 'Can you see anything at your side?' I said 'No - but I have an uneasy feeling that we are not right.' Frank said - 'So have I -we'd better stop.' He put the brakes on and we strained our eyes in an effort to see something through the darkness and the falling snow. We spotted a ground crew coming round in front of us carrying two marshalling torches. He stood with his back towards us, put both torches together and shone them straight ahead. In the light of the torches we were just able to see directly in front of us a petrol bowser. The ground crew pointed us in the right direction and we began to creep around the perimeter track.

"We had not gone far when over the R/T a voice from Control said, 'Aircraft on runway - return to dispersal.' So it seemed that ops were scrubbed. We were about to turn round and return when another voice on the R/T said 'It's all right control, we can cope.' After that silence. We didn't quite know what to make of that so Frank called Control and asked 'Do we go or don't we?' Back came the reply 'You can go if you like.' - Go if you like! - On ops! We decided that having gone so far we might as well continue. So we taxied round and took off along the snow covered runway.

"We always flew over the sea at a maximum of 500 feet so it was no problem to stay below cloud at first. But eventually we had to climb in an effort to get above the weather. Being a low-level squadron our engines had a rated altitude of 2000 feet. On this occasion we climbed steadily up through the cloud but never quite out of the top. There was a spectacular display of St. Elmo's Fire and serious icing. Icing on the control surfaces prevented any manoeuvering and we had no alternative but to fly straight and level hoping to run into clear skies. When we did eventually run out of the cloud we had passed our target area. There was no possibility of carrying out a low-level *Intruder* so once we were free of the ice we just had to turn round and come back. In a way that was worse. On the outward flight we had pressed on in the hope of finding better weather. Now we knew exactly what lay ahead - all the way back to base. We had not encountered enemy action, but that was one occasion when we were glad to get back home."

Bocock and Rogers flew their nineteenth operation on 28/29 December, a flak patrol off Jeloy island, in Norway, in support of a raid on Oslo Fjord by sixty-seven Lancasters and one Mosquito of 5 Group. Strong winds blew Bocock and Rogers south to the northern tip of Denmark on the way home. On the 30th they flew all the way to Stavanger, where they dropped flares over Lista airfield only to discover there were no aircraft, "not even a light." Adding to their frustration was the fact that no RAF bombers were headed that way either. (Much later, Frank Bocock was told that agents were being dropped in Norway that night.) Long missions over water were flown at 150 feet above the surface of the sea using the radio altimeter. In complete contrast, their op on 7 January to Hailfingen in *J-Jig* was at very high level indeed! Bocock was forced to climb to 23,000 feet to get above cloud. The heating failed and the temperature registered -37°C outside, or 70° of frost. Rogers was so cold that he wrapped his hands around the bulb on the *Gee* box to try to warm them. They landed back to Snoring after four hours. Bocock and Rogers came through, but there were periods when the "chop rate" became very high. Frank Bocock adds, "You learned not to be so damned inquisitive some times."

On 31 December/1 January five aircraft were destroyed. Crews of the *Gruppenstab* and the VIIIth and IXth *Staffeln* of III./NJG2 at Marx/Varel were given the usual meteorological and signal briefing on 31 December, and the Commanding Officer told the crews that "in view of the suitable weather conditions, an RAF raid was to be mounted that night." At 1800 hours his eight Ju 88s were ordered to take off. The first to take off was 4R+CS and sat at the end of the runway awaiting the signal when a Mosquito *Intruder* dropped a bomb which exploded on the runway about thirty meters from the Junkers. No damage was apparently suffered by 4R+0S, and it took off after a short delay. The crew made for Hanover and soon they saw the first cascade flares. On arrival they saw the incendiary bombs and fires. A four-engined bomber was seen to be held in searchlights and heading southwest. The *Naxos* and *SN-2* of 4R+0S had been u/s for some time and the four-engined aircraft was lost. The Ju 88 first turned west-northwest in the hope of finding the bomber stream, but after fifteen minutes the starboard engine cut out. It was a coolant leak caused by the *Intruder's* bomb.

The *Intruder* was crewed by Lewis Heath and Jack Thompson of 23 Squadron, which had taken off from Little Snoring at 1700 hours on 1 January. The Ju 88 pilot turned due east to return to Marx/Varel, but soon afterwards the crew, believing themselves to be over German territory and anxious to find their exact whereabouts, fired a recognition signal followed by two "reds," which they repeated. They were then surprised by a night-fighter attack from aft. The pilot lost control and all the crew baled out. They all landed in Allied territory and were taken prisoner. The foregoing was extracted from one of the crew on interrogation. Subsequently Air Commodore Chisholm hoped that Flying Officer Heath would be credited with a destroyed enemy aircraft, as it was considered that 4R+S was hit by splinters from bombs dropped on the airfield by the Mosquito crew before take off.

The last of 39 *Luftwaffe* aircraft to fall to 100 Group in December were two Ju 88s and a He 219 *Uhu* on New Year's Eve. On this night Flight Lieutenants A. P. Mellows and S. L. "Dickie" Drew of 169 Squadron, attached to "B" Flight 85 Squadron at Swannington to try interceptions with AI.Mk.X, also had good fortune on their patrol that same night. Mellows recorded:

> "We took off at 1654 hours on a High Level Support Patrol west of the Ruhr. Patrol was reached at 1758 hours and at 1808 hours AI contact was obtained at six miles range and ceased turning slowly port and climbing from 15,000 feet to 18,000 feet. While this contact was still well above another came in at three miles range from the west nearly head on. This was found to be at our height so we turned starboard as it passed us and came in 4000 feet. behind. A visual was obtained at 2000 feet on four white exhausts and on closing to 400 feet twin tail fins were seen. Shortly after black crosses on the blue under surface of the wings were seen in the light of a searchlight. On the strength of this I fired a two-second burst from slightly below causing debris to fly off and a small fire in the fuselage. Another two-second burst caused an explosion by the light of which Flight Lieutenant Drew clearly saw the dihedral and slanting fins of a He.219, which I confirmed. A further short burst set him well alight and from 1000 feet to starboard we saw him climb for a few seconds before plunging to earth, where he exploded with a bright orange flash at 1824 hours in the Köln area. Throughout the combat the He 219 was flying straight and level and appeared to have no knowledge of our presence. Mosquito landed Manston 2005 hours and crew returned to base 1.1.45."[315]

Two of the New Year's eve victories were the first using ASH. The first went to Squadron Leader C. V. Bennett DFC and Flight Lieutenant R. A. Smith of 515 Squadron. In the Lovns Bredning area during an *Intruder* patrol to Grove, Bennett and Smith's Mosquito was fired at with tracer from *Oberleutnant* August Gyory's Ju 88 of 4./NJG2. Bennett returned fire at 400 yards with a two-second burst of cannon and strikes were seen on the port wing. A second burst cut the Ju 88 in two. Gyory spun in and dropped into Lim Fjord. 515 Squadron received a congratulatory signal from Air Vice Marshal Addison, "Heartiest congratulations on opening the batting for the Ashes." During the New Year's party that followed they were joined by Squadron Leader J. Tweedale and Flight Lieutenant V. Cunningham of 23 Squadron, who scored their Squadron's first victory using ASH, having destroyed a Ju 88 of NJG5 at Alhorn. (On 13 January Bennett and Smith were lost when they went down in the North Sea on the way home.) It brought the number of victories during the month to thirty-seven. It is no coincidence that 85 Squadron, which claimed eighteen victories, and 157 Squadron, which claimed thirteen, were the only squadrons in 100 Group that were equipped with the excellent Mk X AI radar. *Intruder* incursions over *Luftwaffe* bases were being made with haunting regularity, and there was much "joy" as the predators enjoyed rich pickings from among the returning flocks of unsuspecting, weary *Nachtjagdgeschwader* crews.

Sixteen aircraft were claimed shot down by 100 Group Mosquitoes in January 1945. On 1/2 January Mosquitoes on bomber support covered heavy operations over Germany. Eight crews in 85 Squadron participated in a maximum effort in the Kiel and Ruhr areas while the Main Force attacked the Mittelland Canal, as well as rail yards at Vohwinkel and Dortmund. Dickie Goucher and Tiny Bulloch chased a contact for eleven minutes before obtaining a visual; it was a Ju 188. Goucher gave the Junkers a couple of bursts and it fell in flames, crashing ten miles north of Münster. Almost immediately, Tiny Bulloch got a second blip on his Mk X scope apparently dropping *Düppel*. Goucher got closer and they could see that their enemy was a Ju 88G. Dickie Goucher gave it a long burst from dead astern as the Junkers turned to port. Flying flaming debris struck the Mosquito, causing it to vibrate badly and lose height. Goucher jettisoned his drop tanks and the port tank came over the top of the wing, damaging the tail plane and at the same time shearing off the pitot head. They landed safely at Brussels/Melsbroek and were flown home in a C-47 the next day. Their second victim was a Ju 88G-6,[316] which crashed at Dortmund.

Four Mosquitoes of 239 Squadron carried out low-level *Intruder* patrols. One of these, flown by Flying Officers Walker and J. R. Watkins, crashed on return at Narford Hall, just north of RAF Marham, and both were killed. One of the six Mosquitoes dispatched by 141 Squadron on a high-level ASH patrol was forced to land in France with oxygen trouble. Another, flown by Flight Lieutenant Ron Brearley and Flying Officer John Sheldon, took off at 1710 hours on a low-level *Intruder* patrol to the airfield at Luneburg. They crossed in at Egmond, Holland, at 1749 hours at 200 feet and flew to Luneburg, arriving at 1846. The airfield was lit on their approach, but the lights were doused as they arrived. Brearley orbited for ten minutes, and as there was no activity flew off to the south. At 1906 hours he approached the airfield again and again it was lit. The Mosquito orbited about one mile away and the crew saw the exhausts of an aircraft taking off but this was then lost. Four searchlights were exposed around the airfield, two pointing in their direction. Brearley and Sheldon continued to patrol the airfield until 1940 hours. When crossing Luneburg airfield at about 100 feet they saw two very small green lights moving along the flarepath. It was an aircraft which had just landed. They executed a tight turn and came in over the flarepath and over the aircraft. Brearley opened fire. Many strikes were seen all over the enemy aircraft but it did not burn. They turned again, giving a longer approach, and once more Brearley opened fire on the German aircraft. Again many strikes were seen resulting in pieces being scattered in all directions. This time the German night-fighter burst into flames and burned furiously. Searchlights were exposed all over the area and flak came up all around them. Brearley took evasive action and then stood off and watched the enemy plane burn before setting course for home at 1945 hours.

White and Allen continued flying ops in to 1945. On the night of 1/2 January they took off on a High Level *Intruder* in MM797, known as the "dreaded XXX" because of its recurring engine problems. They crossed the Dutch coast near Ymuiden at 15,000 feet at 1803 hours and patrolled uneventfully until 1830 hours. When a wide, straggling bomber stream was contacted at 1915 hours at 15,000 feet Mike Allen soon obtained two AI contacts: one to port, one to starboard, at seven miles range. They chased the first contact that was weaving violently, until White closed the range to 3000 feet. They obtained a fleeting visual, but the enemy aircraft took evasive action and extended the range to 3000 feet. The two adversaries jockeyed range constantly until, at 200 feet, White could identify his quarry as a Ju 88. Allen confirmed it using night glasses. White dropped back to 250 feet and opened fire. Several strikes were seen, followed by an explosion, and small pieces were seen to come away. The flash caused Harry White to lose visual contact, and as the Ju 88 broke away in a hard diving turn to starboard his navigator tried to follow it on AI but without success. White fired a second short burst at the estimated position of the aircraft but was unable to confirm results. It went down in the record books as a "damaged." If it had not been for stoppages in both port cannon they might have been more successful.

Next day, 2 January, they wanted to go again and try to find another Ju 88 to make up for the one they had lost. Flight Lieutenant Dennis Welfare and his navigator, "Sticky" Clay, also wanted to go, so he and Harry White tossed a coin to see who would fly the op. It was the first time White ever tossed a coin for an op and he won. There was no time for an NFT (Night Flying Test) before briefing so White and Allen decided to take it on the op without one. They had never done this before in three and a half years of night fighting. At 1715 hours White and Allen took off again in MM797 in support of a raid by the Main Force on the Ruhr. It was their 91st op. When glycol started pouring out of the port engine shortly after take off, White pressed the feathering button and jettisoned the long-range drop tanks. He was at 600 feet; too low to think about turning to get back into Swanton Morley and too low for either of them to bale out. When he found the propeller of the dead engine would not fully feather he knew he could not maintain height for very long. He realized his only chance was a belly land into a field, if he could spot one in the gathering darkness. The field would have to be almost in their line of flight because to turn would mean losing precious height and it would have to be soon. White wrote later to Rodney Allen, Michael's brother:

> "To my mind, no-one can learn much from what happened before we touched down. The Pilot's Notes will tell you what to do - it is not possible to make a mistake. But there is always something to learn from any accident. And the first thing is never take off at night without having done an NFT during the day. This was the first time we had tried and it stood fair to be the last.
>
> "The touchdown, which soon became inevitable in the half light, was very heavy, much heavier than it should have been with the possible excuse that a glide approach with such a load at 140 mph could be otherwise."

Mike Allen recorded in his logbook, "Harry put up a terrific show in crash-landing the kite in a field in the half light and very poor visibility." Mike Allen had jettisoned the perspex canopy cover over the top of the Mosquito's cockpit just before they touched down. All that should have been necessary was a rapid abandoning of MM797 and an Olympic dash for the nearest ditch in case the aircraft exploded in flames. Unfortunately both men were trapped. As they bounced across the field White's seat had shifted on its mountings. They both knew that they had not long before MM797 blew up. Fortunately Herbert Farrow, a farmer, James Andrews, one of his labourers, and Walter William Ward, known as "Old Walter," had seen the Mosquito crash. They hurried to the scene and at the risk of their own lives tried to pull the men free. At one point Allen remembered hearing one of the men say, "I think she's going to go up now!" He thought it was too. Virtually giving up the struggle, he sat back and started to contemplate what death would be like. He felt a warm sense of anticipation; in fact, he was looking forward to it. It was going to be good. He also made a mental note he would probably find out what had happened to his parents. [His parents had been killed on 28 October when a V2 rocket exploded in Ashford, Middlesex. His younger brother Rodney, who was in the house, escaped injury. (Sadly, he was killed post-war flying a Meteor from RAF Stradishall.)] Allen felt exhilarated by the prospect of dying in the next few seconds. Harry White, who had certainly not given up, rudely awakened him. He kept urging his navigator to greater efforts with equally forthright language. The Mosquito had now been on the ground for three minutes and time was running out. In a superhuman effort the two airmen and the three rescuers succeeded in pulling White and Allen out of the Mosquito. Then, in compliance with Harry White's shout to "Run before she goes up!," they all sought the safety of a ditch. During the whole time there were explosions of ammunition and the flames grew in intensity. A second or two after all five men had flattened themselves in the ditch the petrol ignited and the Mosquito exploded. Allen knew they owed their lives to the three men. On 8 May Farrow, Andrews, and Old Walter were awarded the BEM. It was bitter for Mike Allen to learn from Herbert that, after the war was over, he and Walter Ward and Jimmy Andrews received their BEMs in the post! However, Herbert did not seem to be too troubled by this. What he really seemed to value was his silver tankard![317]

On the night of 5/6 January Captain Svein Heglund DFC and Flying Officer Robert O. Symon of 85 Squadron in their NF.XXX flew an eventful High Level Support Patrol to North Osnabrück. Heglund and Symon were airborne from Swannington at 1955 hours. Patrol was reached at 2100 hours, and after fifty minutes a contact was obtained and chased for twenty minutes, finally being identified by exhausts and behaviour as a Mosquito. At 2225 hours in Patrol area a head-on contact was obtained and chased on 240°. Heglund reports:

> "After having patrolled beacon in Münster/ Osnabrück area without any contact we set course for Hanover and arrived just as the target indicators were sent out. We got contact, which we chased in a westerly direction for twenty minutes with everything pushed forward. We just got a visual of exhaust flames, which looked like a Mosquito and took it for one of the pathfinder force and turned back towards target.
>
> "At 2223 hours we got another head-on contact north of Osnabrück and turned in behind it. It was slightly above and we closed in to about 2000 feet, when my operator lost contact owing to scanner trouble. We made one orbit and picked up contact again at four miles' range. We closed in again and got visual of Me.110 recognising square wings and twin fins and rudders. As we were slightly overshooting I weaved underneath enemy aircraft keeping visual contact all the time. At 500 feet range I pulled up behind it and gave it is a short burst, which caused an explosion in fuselage. Lots of smoke and debris was flying off and enemy aircraft continued flying straight and level. I rather think the crew was killed right away. I fired another burst, which missed and noticed small explosions going on all the time. The third burst put enemy aircraft we'll on fire and it crashed on the ground with a large explosion at 2230 hours. We got two more contacts afterwards, which turned out to be Mosquitoes and then set course for base.
>
> Claim: one Me.110 destroyed. Mosquito landed base 2355 hours."[318]

Another top scoring team, Flight Lieutenants "Ben" Benson DSO DFC* and Lewis "Brandy" Brandon DSO DFC* notched their ninth combined victory on 5/6 January, shooting down He 219A-0 190188 G9+CK of 2./NJG1.[319]

On 12 January two FB.VIs of 169 Squadron gave high-level and ASR support for a raid by thirty-two Lancasters of 9 and 617 Squadrons and one Mosquito on *U-boat* pens and shipping in port at Bergen, Norway. Two Mosquitoes of 169 Squadron flew long-range escort for an ASR operation. Nearing the target, NS998 encountered five Fw 190s. Undaunted, he attacked two of them and damaged one. In NT176, Squadron Leader John Wright was chased by the Fw 190s. Two days later, the first five NF.XIX Mosquitoes arrived at Great Massingham from Swannington and joined A Flight for high-level patrols and intruding. A Flight had been flying *Serrate* patrols since November, while B Flight, which operated Mk VIs, used *Serrate* and *Perfectos*.[320]

On 14/15 January, the main Bomber Command thrust was aimed at a synthetic oil plant at Leuna, near Merseberg, railway yards at Grevenbroich, and an oil store at Dulmen. Ron Brearley, with John Sheldon of 141 Squadron, again proved successful. Brearley wrote later:

> "We contacted the bomber stream at the front line and overhauled them at a height of 20,000 feet. On reaching the target area we proceeded eastward through defended area between the banks of searchlights for seven-eight minutes, then struck north in the hope of intercepting enemy fighters from the Berlin area. An airfield was seen lit, subsequently identified as either Jüterborg or Pretsch, but which doused on our approach.
>
> "We patrolled, sweeping north and south for some time, noting three horizontal searchlights pointing south near Wittenberg. At 2130 hours, fifteen minutes after the Merseberg bombing had finished, an ASH contact was achieved at 13,000 feet, 2½ miles, which we followed down to 6000 feet before losing it in ground returns. Enemy aircraft was losing height rapidly and obviously heading for aforesaid airfield which was plainly visible and which now fired a green Very light. (The flarepath was unusually wide, about 300 yards with aircraft landing close to left hand line of lights. Hangars and buildings plainly seen in light of flares). Smelling blood and knowing that none of our *Intruders* was operating thus far afield, we rapidly knocked off the remaining height and orbited the airfield at 1500 feet. Navigation lights of an aircraft were seen on the approach, between the 'artificial horizon' and flarepath, at 2135 hours, so with a twitching thumb we turned hard port and came down in a diving quarter attack opening fire at 500-600 yards with half ring deflection. Strikes were seen in line with the enemy aircraft, but on the ground as he neared the runway. This was easily countered by raising the nose and continuing to squirt. Many strikes were seen on him and he hit the deck just off the flarepath, bursting into flames immediately. By the light of flares which had been put up, enemy aircraft was seen to be a twin engined job, but these things happen much too quickly for positive identification.
>
> "While doing a hard turn over the airfield after this encounter another set of navigation lights was seen at the other side of the circuit, so we kept on the hard turn and bared after him, determined to get as much joy as we could with our seriously diminishing petrol. Deflection and range estimate being somewhat difficult at night we allowed home *one* and a half rings for luck and fired at 500 yards as we closed in on him from the port side. After a two or three second burst some strikes were seen on him and flame streamed out behind him. Enemy aircraft dived away as we passed behind him and, as e watched, in a somewhat expectant manner, for him to prang. Instead he made a panic circuit and tried to land in spite of reds, which were being popped off from the ground. He failed to make it and opened up again, Just as our attention was distracted by some flak, which hurtled up at us, necessitating evasive action, with the result that we did not see him again. However, yet another 'bod' was *seen* almost instantly, with his navigation lights on, and once again we gave chase. After our first burst at him he was evidently stirred by strong emotions, for he commenced weaving violently, and we followed as best we could, squirting as opportunity offered in the pious hope that something would hit him. Much to our regret no strikes were observed and he eventually pulled his finger out and switched off his lights.

"As our petrol supply was really getting low we had to set course for home immediately, feeling somewhat peeved that we could no longer take advantage of such promising opportunities. Height was gained at 8000 feet and while still well in enemy territory another enemy aircraft was seen burning navigation lights crossing to port some distance away. We turned after him but he soon switched them off and we turned back on course, as a long ASH chase could not be contemplated even if we could have picked him up, in view of diminishing petrol. What a situation! Several lighted airfields were seen on the way back, and about 0600E port radiator temperature was seen to be high (110°) Immediately throttled it back to -4 boost and reduced revs in order to nurse it. Temperature remained constant until 0400E when it shot up right round the clock. Feathered the propeller and proceeded to base to find cloud down to 700 feet and bad visibility. In view of this we had *no* alternative but to belly-land on the grass. *Gee* of course expired with the port engine and we were 'homed' by Coltishall and base. 215 gallons of petrol in tanks after landing."

Brearley and Sheldon, who were uninjured, submitted claims for one twin-engined aircraft destroyed and one damaged.

In January, Flight Lieutenant Kenneth D. Vaughan and Flight Sergeant Robert Denison MacKinnon of 85 Squadron shot down two enemy aircraft, the first of these being a Ju 188 on the night of 14/15 January while on a High level Patrol supporting the raid on Merseburg. Vaughan wrote:

"Whilst on High level Patrol supporting attack on Merseburg at 2125 hours on last leg of patrol navigator reported contact 4½ miles eleven o'clock port side crossing starboard to port, above. Our height 15,000 feet. Chased target flying straight in Southwesterly direction gradually losing height. Closed in on target to identify. At range of 100 feet directly beneath, identified target as Ju 188 by pointed wings, under slung engines, no protruding leading edge between engines and fuselage and no exhausts. I increased range to 600 feet and fired a one-second burst dead astern, which produced a large explosion from starboard engine. I pulled away to starboard, but seeing no further results followed again on AI and closed in to 900 feet firing a two-second burst which produced no strikes. Closed in to 600 feet on target now rather rapidly losing height and decided to make certain this time. I fired a one-second burst, range 500 feet, producing strikes and explosion again in starboard engine with pieces flying off past Mosquito. Target then disappeared straight down to explode on ground right beneath us at 2143 hours lighting up countryside and cockpit of Mosquito with large orange glow. We orbited fire on ground. I claim one Ju 188 destroyed. Mosquito landed base 2315 hours."[321]

Their next victim, a He 219, was shot down on the night of 16/17 January during a High-Level Support patrol in the Frankfurt area. When Bomber Command attacked Magdeburg, oil plants near Leipzig and Brux, in Czechoslovakia, on 16/17 January and 100 Group again flew support, Flight Lieutenant Kenneth D. Vaughan and Flight Sergeant Robert Denison MacKinnon of 85 Squadron were airborne from Swannington at 1902 hours for their High Level Support in the Frankfurt area. Vaughan reported:

"We had completed uneventful patrol East of Frankfurt supporting raid on Zeitz and set course for base at 2140 hours. At 2145 hours, on vector 290° navigator reported contact 3½ miles range crossing starboard to port. We closed in on target, losing height to 10,000 feet, IAS. 260. At 4000 feet range two pairs of brilliant white exhausts could be seen. We closed to 150 feet below and astern and identified target as He 219 by twin fins and rudders, narrow wings with marked tapor on trailing edge outboard of engines, long nose and those brilliant exhausts. Confirmation was obtained as to target's identity from my navigator using night glasses. I dropped back to 600-feet range astern and fired a two-second burst between the pairs of exhausts but no strikes were seen. Closed in to 400 feet range and fired another two-second burst. Immediately a large explosion occurred in the port engine and we pulled up to starboard to avoid debris, which was coming back at us, and passed over enemy aircraft which went down to port with port engine on fire. We did a quick starboard orbit and saw burning fragments of aircraft falling and small fires starting on ground suggesting it had disintegrated in the air. Claim: one He 219 destroyed." Mosquito landed base 2345 hours."[322]

This same night five Mosquitoes of 239 Squadron made a *Spoof* bombing raid on Stuttgart, while eleven Mosquitoes of 141 Squadron patrolled to Zeitz and Magdeburg. Two of the three crews detailed to patrol the Magdeburg area were Flight Lieutenant D. H. Young and Flying Officer J. J. Sanderson and Flying Officer R. C. Brady and Flight Lieutenant M. K. Webster. Young wrote up his combat report in a laid back manner thus:

"We patrolled to the north and east of Magdeburg watching it burn somewhat and we continued patrolling the furnace until 2220 hours when we decided to follow up the bomber stream and set course in that direction. Just as we were leaving Magdeburg at 2225 hours, our height being 20,000 feet, a contact was obtained on the starboard side going further starboard. We followed it round the southern side and up the western side of the still furiously burning target, the searchlights very kindly pointing at the aircraft we were chasing. After about half a minute all the searchlights doused simultaneously, (no doubt the Boche told them to put those **** lights out). Shortly after this, having followed him round on to a NE heading (weaving slightly) and closed to about 2000 feet. I saw a bluish green light being situated inboard of the starboard engine nacelle. I pulled the nose up and pressed the button and precisely two rounds came out. We both nearly burst into tears. Then for some inexplicable reason, I tried the gun master switch and found that it had been flicked off so I put it back on again. By this time I had dropped back to 800 feet but the Bf 110 continued flying straight and level. I was now afraid I should lose it any second so I closed in again as fast as possible - much too fast - and found myself about to ram the brute so I got him in the sight and opened fire again at what must have been fifty feet. He immediately exploded in a blinding flash, so I pulled back the stick and bounced over the top. A little later I saw the explosion on the ground where he crashed, blew up and burned furiously. We orbited the crash and put its position down. The ASH was now unserviceable so we set course for base and landed at 0033 hours."

Brady and Webster, meanwhile, were also heading for Magdeburg. As Webster went over to ASH on the "downward tilt," the Dummer and Steinhuder lakes were picked up and valuably assisted navigation. They also used the H_2S side of ASH to reach their patrol point, which was the Brandenburg Lake. They obtained an ASH contact at a range of five miles, well above them and crossing from port to starboard. Brady recalls:

"We chased and after following the aircraft through some mild evasive tactics, obtained a visual, fifteen minutes after the initial contact, at 17,000 feet and 1000 feet range. It was a Halifax. We followed it for a few minutes and it appeared to be orbiting the target of Magdeburg. We carried on with our patrol. At 2245 hours whilst patrolling on a westerly vector south of Magdeburg at 14,000 feet, a contact was obtained at four-five miles well above and crossing gently to port from starboard. We gave chase and the aircraft appeared to be flying more or less straight and level. Range was closed to 2000 feet behind, height 17,000 feet. At this point the aircraft appeared to get backward warning of us and began to take violent evasive action, in a way of tight turns with loss of height. We managed to hang on to him but about 1½-miles range. This continued for some time until finally the other aircraft seemed to give up and flew straight and level. We positioned ourselves dead behind him and at 1-mile range and rapidly closed in and obtained a visual at 1000-feet range. My 'good man' had the night glasses and identified the aircraft as a Me 110. Upon closing in I noticed a dim yellow light showing from outside the starboard engine nacelle of the enemy aircraft. Range was further closed to about 200 yards and below, so that looking up I was able to confirm the aircraft as being a Me 110. I was still tending to overshoot and was a little to port. I gave the enemy aircraft a one-second-burst using 20° deflection from 200 feet and strikes were observed on the side of his fuselage. The enemy aircraft immediately fired off colors, which lit up the side of the aircraft. I turned away to port to allow the Bf 110 to get ahead of me, which he did, still flying straight and level - quite clueless. We came in behind him and slightly above and at 200 yards opened up with a five-second burst. Very many strikes were seen on the cockpit and thereabouts. Bits flew off and much black smoke belched out, then the port engine burst into flames. The 110 spiralled down burning furiously and hit the ground with a terrific explosion. It crashed approximately 25 miles SW of Magdeburg at 2310 hours. We were very short of fuel by this time and headed straight back for base, landing at 0115 hours."

On 16/17 January Flight Lieutenant Tommy Smith in 23 Squadron, who by now was within two operations of completing his second tour, and his navigator, Flying Officer "Cocky" Cockayne, were on ops. Tommy Smith recalls:

"It was a dirty night - thick as a bag up to 16,000 feet - and we went on an ASH patrol to Stendal fighter airfield near Berlin. I used a square search system for nearly an hour, but picked up nothing and when the time was up, we set course for home. At the point when we should have been over the area of the Steinhuder Lake, we came across an airfield where aircraft with nav lights on were taxiing. This was unheard of. I went in to have a bash. There was a chap sitting at the taxi point. He was my target: his nav lights and the hooded runway lights were *on*. I opened up and saw a good cluster of cannon strikes on the aircraft, and was about to break away when I saw exhaust flames of another aircraft half way up the runway. God, someone's taking off! I'll have him,' I thought. (I was trained to recognize an aircraft by the number, type and disposition of its exhaust flames and I reckoned it was a Ju 88.) So instead of breaking off; I closed in and opened up. My muzzle flashes lit up the Hun right under my chin! (I was so close I was practically looking at the back of the pilot's head.) It wasn't a Ju 88; it was a Me 109! (What I had taken for exhausts of two engines, were the flames from either side of one engine.) Because of the difference in line between my gunsight and the guns beneath my feet, I was shooting low, being *so* close, and ripped the bottom out of the Me 109. He crashed at the end of the runway.

"However, as I was pursuing this chap, I had passed between two flak towers at the downwind end of the runway. Light flak [from eight guns, the Germans said later] had the cannon flashes to aim at, and my Mosquito was hit coming in over the perimeter track at a height of about 200 feet in a dive. Flak set my right engine on fire and I automatically feathered the prop and pressed the extinguisher button. I zoomed up to 1000 feet. My mind was running on how to get organized to fly home on one engine, when, all of a sudden the other engine stopped! The first engine was blazing merrily and the prop was feathering and un-feathering. I said to Cocky, '*That's it! Bale Out!*' It's not easy to get out of a Mosquito. Cocky was having trouble jettisoning the hatch door. Time and height were running out. I switched on the landing lights. Treetops showed up below. We were too low. I shouted, '*Knock it off. Do your harness up.* Cocky didn't answer. A burst of flame lit up the open hatch. He had baled out. I found out later that his parachute didn't open fully, and he had broken his neck.

"The forest came up and I was skimming *over* the treetops, and preparing to stuff the nose in while I still had flying speed. I could feel the 'whiffle', which indicated the approach of the stall. Suddenly, there was a field covered in snow. I stuffed it in at about 200-mph. Next thing, I was hurtling along the ground heading for more trees. I thought it was a wood but it was only a line of trees; a windbreak! The trees ripped off the outer wing sections and something, possibly a stump, knocked a hole in the cockpit alongside me. I still had my hand on the throttle control and it was ripped away by the tree stump! Then I was out of the trees and into the snow again before the aircraft came to a stop. A feeling of relief came over me. All I could think was 'a forced landing in the dark! What fantastic luck to be alive!'

"All I had to do now was lift the roof emergency hatch, climb out, and run away. Except that in the crash, the whole of the seat had come adrift and shot me underneath the instrument panel, and the cockpit cabin was full of earth. The left rudder bar had taken my foot back under the seat and locked it. I had some grim moments trapped in the middle of a bonfire trying to extricate my foot. By the time I got out of the hole the port radiator and its contents were burning fiercely right outside the hole. I crawled out badly burned, and stuffed my face and hands into the snow. When I got up, I found I had a broken leg, caused by the rudder pedal. [He had also lost an eye]. By the light of the fire I could see a farmhouse and crawled over to it. Two soldiers hiding in the hedge, expecting the bombs to explode, carried me into the barn and about an hour later a Luftwaffe ambulance from Fassberg collected me. I was sadly aware that my wartime flying was over."[323]

On 21/22 January 239 Squadron attempted its first AI Mk.X patrol when three Mosquitoes from West Raynham supported an attack on Kassel by 76 Mosquitoes, but the NF.XXX returned early with radar problems. The two 141 Squadron Mosquitoes completed their patrols. The following night, fourteen Mosquitoes from 141 Squadron and three from 239 Squadron supported Bomber Command operations to Duisburg. One crew reported their first sighting of an enemy jet aircraft. German jets could certainly outpace the Mosquito, but their introduction had been too little too late, and while on occasions they caused havoc with the U.S. daylight bombing missions, they were less effective against the Mosquitoes at night.[324]

More of a problem was the bad weather, January being the worst month since 100 Group began operations in December 1943. There were sixteen days of snow. A big freeze from 19-31 January prevented many operations. However, 100 Group Mosquitoes destroyed seventeen enemy aircraft and damaged three in January. One of the latter was credited to Flight Lieutenants Paul Mellows and S. L. "Dickie" Drew of 169 Squadron, attached to "B" Flight 85 Squadron at Swannington on 28/29 January using AI.Mk.X. At 2050 hours they took off for a high-level support patrol to Stüttgart for some "beacon bashing." Mellows reported:

"Shortly after completing patrol on Beacon *Fritz* a single white flare was observed to the North West, presumably over Darmstadt. We proceeded in that direction and Biblis airfield was seen to be lit and had a. canopy of four searchlights 2 miles to the West. From 6000 feet three single-engined aircraft on the airfield were soon outlined against the snow. As there were no signs of airborne activity and time was short it was decided to make an attack. The airfield was approached from the Southwest and one single-engined aircraft, believed to be Fw.190, was attacked with two 3-second bursts from height of 1500 feet to 1000 feet. No results were observed, from first burst, but strikes were seen on and around fuselage from second burst. Defenses opened up when we were over the center of the airfield, but without results."

By the end of the month re-equipment with ASH was almost complete. All of 141 Squadron's AI.Mk.XV radar and the *Monica* Mk.IX backward AI ASH had been fitted, and the squadron had only experienced four early returns from eighty sorties; a great tribute to the radar mechanics and their abilities in difficult conditions. In February ten German aircraft were destroyed by Mosquitoes of 100 Group, plus a probable on 1/2 February. This night *Oberleutnant* Gottfried Hanneck of 5./NJG1, who had been shot down by House and MacKinnon on 13/14 September 1944, returned to Bf 110 operations at Düsseldorf airfield after seven practice flights in January with a new crew of *Feldwebel* Pean, radio/radar operator, and *Unteroffizier* Gloeckner, air gunner. Hanneck recalls:

"We arrived on 1 February to fly on operations again. By this time, the night fighter control organization was experiencing severe problems when trying to assess the plans of the enemy, as we had lost the complete advanced defense line (Holland, Belgium and France were already occupied by the enemy). Therefore, on this day a number of crews were ordered to fly to several night fighter beacons, and wait there at the height at which the bombers were expected to fly in. I received orders to take-off[325] at 1945 hours, proceed to a beacon in the Frankfurt area and wait for any reports of enemy aircraft movements. Thus, we were flying around in wide circles and figures of eight in the prescribed area and waited for the enemy reports. These however, did not reach us, but something else did - the enemy in the shape of a Mosquito (which we were expecting because who else would have come?), which completely by surprise gave us a short burst of fire. We were hit. The intercom was put out of action, and the landing light in the wing came on. I stood the aircraft on its nose to avoid a second attack and to find shelter in a layer of clouds beneath us. My crew, who couldn't contact me any more, must have assumed I was hit as I was slumped over the control column. They baled out - and landed safely.

"I was now alone in the machine. I safely reached the layer of clouds and was now confronted with the question: should I bale out or attempt a crash-landing? There was no question that I should continue with my flight without any radio contact and with the light on. I decided to crash-land. I could only switch off the light by stopping both engines and glide towards the ground in an aircraft which weighed several tons. But where should I land? Fortunately, I could distinguish between the dark forest and the snow-white fields and I steered towards such a field where I let the tail unit touch the ground first (to avoid nosing over) and then with retracted undercarriage, slid over he ground on the motor gondolas. I had come down 2 kms west of Kettershausen in the Westerwald. The time was 2110 hours. My face slightly hit the gun sights but I was able to scramble out of my seat and withdraw from the machine through the snow and shouted for help. A farmer "collected" me on his horse-drawn sleigh and took me to the nearest Army post. There I received first aid, and large quantities of Cognac as a remedy for the shock and pain. Then I was transported to the nearest hospital which was at Wissen on the Sieg."[326]

Also on 1/2 February meanwhile, Flight Lieutenants Paul Mellows and Dickie Drew of 169 Squadron, who were still operating with 85 Squadron at Swannington, had taken off at 1700 hours for a High Level Support Patrol at Stüttgart, the scene of their eventful night intruder operation a month earlier. Mellows reported:

"We arrived at our patrol point at 1845 hours, and after 10 minutes proceeded in a north-westerly direction. A Red star cartridge was soon to be fired some way off to the north so we proceeded to investigate, losing height to 10,000 feet. A head-on contact was obtained and after being once lost was converted to an intermittent visual on a blue light at 2000 feet range, height then being 11000 feet. We closed on AI to 1000 feet where navigator identified it as a Me.110 with the aid of night glasses. Target was climbing and weaving 30° each side of course. We closed to 200 feet to confirm and opened fire at 300 feet from slightly below with a. 2-second burst from which a small explosion sent debris flying back. A second burst resulted in a very large explosion and for a few moments the Mosquito was enveloped in flame, the heat of" which was felt in the cockpit. We broke to starboard and watched enemy aircraft flying straight but losing height with starboard engine well on fire, in the light of which a black cross and all details of the aircraft were plainly visible. A further explosion occurred whilst it was going down, and enemy aircraft eventually exploded on the ground at 1910 hours. As combat had affected rudder control, the patrol was terminated."[327]

On 2/3 February Wing Commander Kelsey DFC, Commanding Officer of 515 Squadron, and Flight Lieutenant Smith DFC patrolled Gütersloh to no avail before obtaining a visual on a Ju 88 near Vechta. From astern and below Kelsey dispatched the Junkers with a short burst of 100 rounds of cannon fire. The starboard engine burst into flames, the port wing outboard of the port engine fell off, and pieces of debris flew back and damaged the Mosquito's air intake and undercarriage doors. Kelsey managed to land safely at Little Snoring.

That same night Pilot Officer Les Turner flew his first op of his second tour. He says:

"I can recall nothing but a feeling of pleasure that we had reached the end of my first tour unscathed. After Christmas at home I was posted to the BSDU at Great Massingham, flying Ansons loaded with pupil navigators learning ASH radar. My original navigator, now Flight Lieutenant Jimmy Wheldon, was there as an instructor and, somewhere along the line, we agreed to rejoin 169 Squadron, then equipped with Mosquito XIXs with Mk.X radar, for a second tour. Jimmy had served in another 100 Group squadron as the wing commander's navigator and I was quite flattered that he wished to fly with me again! Needless to say, he was an excellent radar operator and I always felt safe in his hands.

"We trained throughout the second half of January 1945 and did our first op on 2 February. This was to the Ruhr and the logbook records one chase without results. Trip No.2 was another 'Beacon' patrol, where German night fighters were supposed to assemble, but we had no contacts. Jimmy then took some leave to complete his studies for and sit his LLB Finals. He was an intellectual throughout and after the war attained a high position in the Civil Service. To keep me occupied I was attached to Massingham's Gunnery Flight and it was there that I experienced my second incident of engine failure, only this time, rather unnervingly, as passenger. I must confess that I had less than 100% faith in the pilot's ability but, by leaving him to control the flying and with me dealing with undercarriage and flaps and keeping up a running commentary on our approach speed, we landed without incident. Jimmy and I were 'squeezed in' trip No.3 to Mannheim on 13 February and then it was back to the Gunnery Flight. I didn't distinguish myself particularly at practice air-to-air firing, although I once shot the drogue off, having 'led' too much with the sight!"

Meanwhile, on 7/8 February 239 Squadron crews were prominent when the Main Force targets were Cleve and Hussum. Flight Lieutenants Anthony J. Holderness and Walter Rowley DFC of 239 Squadron had taken off from West Raynham at 2025 hours and reached their patrol area at Zandvoort at 2117 hours. The pilot's report of the sortie and successful combat is as follows:

"We carried out the first part of our patrol quite uneventfully, before and while the targets, Cleve and Hussum were being bombed. Towards the end of the bombing we moved closer in to the targets and were doing a short 'square search' patrol when, at 2200 hours 13,000 feet, we got a contact at 2240 hours at about six miles range, and heading towards the targets. It was only slightly above but difficult to close, as it was taking what appeared to be precautionary evasive action, diving and climbing through a series of steep turns. Throughout this part of the chase our altimeter was reading anything from 11.000 to -15,000 feet. Several times I caught sight of the exhausts glow, but was unable against the starlit sky to hold them for-more than a few seconds at a time. After about ten minutes of this, when we had closed to 1000 feet we suddenly found ourselves overshooting very fast and some way above, and had to turn 60° to port, then back onto our original course to recover the blip. This time the contact was headed away from the target, flying on an easterly course and at a height of about 12,000 feet. The pilot must have thought either that there was no longer any need to evade, or that he had shaken us off because he was flying straight and level. We closed in fairly fast and from only about 200 feet below and behind identified as Me 110. I dropped back to about 250 yards and opened fire. Quite a lot of debris flew back past us and the port engine immediately caught fire. Then the nose came up and he went into steep climb, which I tried to follow, still firing. Although I throttled right back we were - rapidly overtaking him and had to pull away quickly to starboard. Just then he seemed to stall and flick over to port. I turned as slightly as our low airspeed would allow and saw him diving very steeply with the port engine now a mass of flame. My navigator could still see burning pieces coming off when he went into the cloud. Almost simultaneously there was a terrific white flash, which lit up the clouds. We followed through about 3000 feet of cloud to come out at 4000 feet on the altimeter, and there it was, burning immediately beneath us, and only about a mile from a white beacon flashing the letters 'L F.'"

The A Flight Commander in 141 Squadron, Squadron Leader Peter Anthony Bates DFC and his navigator, Flying Officer William Guy Cadman, who had destroyed a Bf 110 on 11/12 September, failed to return from an ASH patrol to Ladbergen on 7/8 February.[328] On a happier note, on 13 February Harry White and Mike Allen were posted back to 141 Squadron at West Raynham. They had flown twenty-one and twenty operations respectively while with BSDU, testing new radar equipment for 100 Group. In September both men had received a second Bar to their DFCs.[329]

On the night of 13/14 February 1945, when the bombers' targets were Dresden and Leipzig, Flight Lieutenant Donald R. "Podge" Howard DFC and Flying Officer "Sticky" Clay DFC of BSDU at Swanton Morley were airborne in their Mosquito XIX. Howard joined 239 Squadron on 2 May 1944 and completed thirty-two operational sorties by 9 November 1944, during which time he destroyed three enemy aircraft and damaged eight trains. During four other sorties he damaged eight trains in Holland and Germany. He was awarded the DFC on 9 November 1944.

"Sticky" Clay recalls that at BSDU:

> "...my time was enjoyable. The nature of our operations was such that we (more or less) planned our on trips after seeing the morning Bomber Command Broadcast, which gave details of the targets for the night. It was nice too, to try out various 'boxes' dreamed up by George Baillie (one of the boffins), and then use them operationally. I remember him sitting on a chair on the perimeter track with earphones on, listening to pulses emanating from a sort of Walls Ice Cream tricycle being ridden around the other side of the airfield by some poor 'erk'." [George Baillie was one of the small group of scientists that pioneered electronic warfare at the Royal Aircraft Establishment, Farnborough, in the late 1930s. Inspired by Group Captain "Addy" Addison, Baillie's team anticipated that the *Luftwaffe* would use radio beams to guide bombers to targets in Britain. As a result of their dedicated efforts in the run-up to the outbreak of war, the RAF was amply prepared for the "Battle of the Beams," and in 1940 radar started to be introduced in night-fighters. At the height of the Battle of Britain Baillie was posted to Radlett, Herts, where Addison had formed Bomber Command's 80 Wing to counter enemy beams. Equipment was scarce, but Baillie employed all the ingenuity for which the cash-starved Farnborough scientists were renowned to turn hospital radiotherapy sets into beam-benders. After America's entry into the war Baillie paid regular visits to the United States to pass on Britain's growing expertise in electronic warfare. His overall contribution to the development of Britain's radar capabilities played a significant part in the eventual success of 100 (Bomber Support) Group.]

Howard and Clay's patrol 13/14 February was to prove very rewarding, as Howard reported:

> "Aircraft BSDU/H was airborne Swanton Morley at 1906 hours to carry out a patrol of beacons *Kolibri*, *Ida*, *Elster*, *Nachtigall* and *Otto* with AI.Mk.X and *Serrate IV* with lowered frequency band of 80 megacycles. Beacon *Kolibri* was reached at 2011 hours (six minutes after start of *Mandrel Screen*) and proceeded to *Ida* where at 2015 signals were heard of *Serrate IV* (77.5 m/cs). The D/F on this low frequency was very suspect and we were not surprised when we found we could not D/F these signals. It was however an indication that Huns were around. We then set course in an easterly direction and the signals' strength increased. We obtained a Mark X contact about five miles 30° to port and down. We turned after it and lost height and eventually discovered it was in a climbing port orbit and the range closed fast. The A/C did not show Type F and by now the George box [George Baillie] was trilling furiously (still in dashes) and A/C apparently leveled out. A visual was obtained on an A/C at 1000 feet and at 600 feet in a rate 1-1½ turn to port the A/C was recognised as a Me 110. At a range of about 600 feet with a ¼ ring deflection a short burst was fired but no strikes seen. Increased deflection and fired another burst which caused strikes all over starboard engine, wing root and starboard side of cockpit. A fire started in starboard wing root and the Me 110 turned over to port burning well and dived straight down and entered cloud; shortly after there was a vivid white explosion on the ground at 2033 hours, our height being 12,000 feet. Claim - one Me 110 destroyed.
>
> "Two minutes after this type had bought it, another Mark X contact appeared crossing starboard to port and above range 12,000. Turned after it and range closed fast and after turning about rate one for about two complete circles and got visual on an A/C at 1000 feet with George box still pushing out its very loud Hun note. At 600 feet this A/C was identified as another Me 110 in a port turn. Opened fire at 600 feet and missed and the Hun promptly rolled into a starboard bank during which he presented no deflection and he received a one second burst which caused strikes on the cockpit fuselage and port wing root. The type then dived away to starboard and we gave him another burst, which set his port engine on fire and caused bits to fly off. He then dived vertically into cloud, burning very well. We had to pull up and out of our dive and we didn't see it hit the deck but as the cloud was only about 5000 feet and he was well on fire this is claimed as a Me 110 destroyed. Cat A (1).
>
> "At 2040 hours, 5000 feet. We obtained yet another Mark X contact almost at once. But although we chased him in an easterly direction for about twenty minutes at full bore we could not overtake him so we decided he was very fortunate and returned to our patrol area and came back to base via *Kolibri* and West Kappelle."[330]

On 14/15 February Bomber Command attacked Chemnitz and an oil refinery at Rositzm near Leipzig. Leslie Holland of 515 Squadron recalls:

> "Our designated patrol airfield was Hailfingen, in the area east of Stuttgart where nearly every town ends with 'ingen'. After we had mooched around the vicinity of the airfield for the best part of an hour Bob announced that he thought there was something on the *Monica*. A port turn caused an increase in range whereupon I immediately opened the taps and made the turn as steep as possible. The blip disappeared so we started a starboard turn to make a sweep. A head-on contact came up on the ASH at about two miles closing fast. As he appeared to be on a parallel course slightly right we went straight into a hard right turn. The bogey must have done exactly the same because he failed to appear on our screen after the turn. Reverse course again and have another go. Sure enough, another head-on. Port turn this time and lose him again. Suddenly, Bob yells into the intercom, 'He's coming in from....'

"WHOOSH, and a Heinkel 219 flashes by under our nose about twenty feet away - the radar operator clearly visible in the after part of the canopy No time to depress the nose and have a squirt, not even to get the ginger on the button. And he's in a 600 bank to his right going to my left, so he's probably got *Liechtenstein* radar with all-round performance superior to our miserable little ASH. So the only course is to try and outguess him and at the same time bear in mind that we have now been making inroads at full throttle into our get-home fuel. We make a sweep and try to make a bit of westing. But a break in the clouds reveals that the North Star is to port. I've been steering by the directional gyrocompass and it has spun in the tight turns. A quick look at the compass, which has just about settled down confirms the 'astro' observation and we are actually working our way deeper into enemy territory.

"Obviously, our adversary had been expecting us to do exactly as we had intended so we must have ended up going in opposite directions at a separating speed of something over 500 mph. We never saw each other again, which may be just as well considering the performance of his mount and the great superiority of his radar.

"Another anti-flak covering mine laying in Oslo fiord at Rygge was made. It was very near the scene of our previous sortie. The cloud cover was low and on this occasion *we* made our approach over the mountains of southern Norway There was a good moon but letting down into the fiord through a gap in the clouds was a trifle nail biting. Near the southeast coast we intercepted a Halifax while still below cloud and passed fairly close to him without being seen. The minelayers were supposed to be Lancs so I expect he was from 38 Group on some clandestine activity."

While 141 did not score during February they destroyed *two* enemy aircraft on the ground, damaged two more, and destroyed a train and damaged nine more. On 13 February two of 141 Squadron's favorite sons, Squadron Leader Harry White DFC** and Flight Lieutenant Mike Allen DFC,** had arrived back at West Raynham after their stint with the BSDU. On 21/22 February they flew their first operation since rejoining the squadron but drew a blank. On 23/24 February a 239 Squadron Mosquito flown by Flight Sergeant Twigg and his navigator, Flight Sergeant Turner, overshot as it was landing on the FIDO strip at Foulsham and hit a parked Halifax. Twigg was killed and Turner was injured. Worse, four Halifaxes of 462 Squadron RAAF failed to return to the airfield after a Windowing operation in the Ruhr. The following night, Warrant Officer E. W "Bunny" Adams and Flight Sergeant Frank A. Widdicombe of 515 Squadron damaged a Ju 88 in the circuit at Bonn. Adams throttled hard back and lowered his flaps to avoid overshooting and gave the Junkers a two-second burst before he was forced to pull away hard to starboard to avoid hitting the ground.

Dutch Holland's last trip in February was another unusual one, in that it was a close escort for a raid on Wilhelmshaven by Liberators of the 492nd Bomb Group, 8th U.S. Air Force. Leslie Holland recalls:

"It was a sort of trial run to see how they made out on a night sortie and involved about three dozen B-24s. We were to rendezvous with them at a DR position half way out at 20.000 feet and run chose escort rather hike riding herd. We picked them up easily on our little sets then shut them down after getting visual contact. There was no difficulty in running up one side of their stream, turning and coming back for another run. There was no room to speak of but enough starlight to see them clearly from about 100 yards on the beam. As we neared the target, we widened our sweep to about ½-one mile in order to intercept any interceptors. (Our radar was now switched on again or in the official code of the period, we were 'flashing our weapon.') Our separation from the stream incidentally kept us nicely clear of the large-calibre flak, which was now coming up by the bucketful. They turned for home without any spectacular disasters. We resumed our role of guard dogs back to our rendezvous, feeling we had done a fairly good job even if we hadn't run into any fighters, but, after our return, a message came through from the American group, 'Where the hell were you guys?' Ah well, I suppose night vision isn't learned in a day (or night). This addendum is of course slightly apocryphal and they were grateful for our support.

"On 2/3 March there was a full moon, which was a deterrent to a Main Force effort but on such occasions experienced intruder crews were allowed to go on a *Night Ranger*. Generally a distant target would be chosen at which worthwhile aircraft could be found on the ground or even with luck in the air. All such ventures had to be approved by Group HQ and they were usually given the OK if not either too footling or too foolhardy - like an attack on the *Tirpitz*. Several hours would be spent poring over intelligence reports and air photographs. Our little efforts were very tame in comparison. The target selected as our primary was a seaplane base on the Baltic coast at Tarnewitz near Wismar, calling at Gustrow, Ludwiglust and Schwerin. We found no seaplanes although it was brilliant moonlight, bright enough for us to dodge high tension cables and watch our shadow to be sure one didn't become two without our noticing. Bob was keeping a very sharp lookout behind while I did some very easy map reading. However, it was not entirely a fruitless trip because Hagenow provided so many trains in its yards that we used the last burst of our cannon ammo on the water tower which showed gratifying evidence that next day's traffic would be a trifle interrupted."

On 3/4 March 1945, when RAF Bomber Command sent two large forces of bombers to raid the synthetic oil plant at Kamen and an aqueduct on the Dortmund-Ems canal at Ladbergen, 100 Group dispatched 61 aircraft on RCM sorties to hamper the enemy radar, flak, and night-fighter defenses. This was the night that the *Nachtjagd* mounted *Unternehmen* [Operation] *Gisela*, although *Oberst Generalmajor* Dietrich Peltz committed only 142 Ju 88G night-fighters to the intruder operation. This was far too small a force to inflict a serious blow against the returning RAF bombers. The Ju 88s penetrated the airspace over some of the 100 Group stations and over Norfolk, and further afield they succeeded in shooting down 24 RAF aircraft.[331] Dutch Holland and his navigator, Bob Young, had just landed at Little Snoring from an air-interception training exercise, left their fully armed Mosquito on its dispersal hard stand, parked their gear in the 515 Squadron hut and were sauntering back up the lane towards the Messes. Dutch Holland recalls:

"There were several returning aircraft in the vicinity all making very familiar noises when we noticed that one was being followed by an aircraft with a distinctly unfamiliar note. I had just time to say to Bob, 'By God it's a Jerry!' when a stream of tracer streaked across and, as they *were* only at about 1500 feet, [we] could *see* the flicker of strikes. The stricken aircraft had its landing lights on ready for joining the circuit and was naturally not expecting any trouble. The lights went into a descending curve out of sight behind the trees. No flak. No fire."[332]

During early March 1945 *Luftwaffe* intruders made a brief but damaging reappearance over eastern England, and many Mosquito crews talked confidently of getting more victories. During the month 100 Group Mosquitoes shot down thirteen aircraft. At West Raynham, the nights went by with excitement at fever pitch because 239 Squadron was chasing its fiftieth victory.[333] March produced rich pickings for the Mosquito *Intruders*. On 6/7 March Flying Officer S. J. Bartlam and Flying Officer A. A. Harvey of 515 Squadron flew a *Freelance* low-level *Intruder* patrol of the Baltic coast in support of an attack by 336 aircraft of 5 Group on Sassnitz. At Griefswald, Bartlam and Harvey attacked north to south and many strikes were seen on a Ju 52, an unidentified aircraft, and a tractor. Bartlam pulled out of his dive at 400 feet and flew on to Barth, where a second aircraft was damaged. The lights at *Stalag Luft I* at Barth were doused during the main attack by the heavies and again when Bartlam and Harvey attacked the airfield. It must have been a tonic for the PoWs at the infamous *Stalag Luft*.

On 7/8 March a heavy bombing raid on Dessau destroyed the first two prototypes of the Ju 88G-7 high-performance night-fighter *Moskitojäger* (Mosquito destroyer). Flying Officer Lewis Heath and Flight Sergeant Thompson of 23 Squadron enjoyed a fruitful patrol. Lewis Heath wrote:

"Mosquito took off from Little Snoring at 2044 hours and arrived in patrol area at 2225 hours and ten minutes later both Burg and Stendal lit up A/F flarepath and perimeter lights. Two green Vereys and two flares were fired from each airfield as Mosquito approached. Mosquito continued patrol and each time the airfields were approached the green Vereys and white flares were fired. At 2325 hours an enemy aircraft was observed taking off from Stendal, burning navigation and downward recognition lights. Mosquito was then about ten miles south of Stendal at the time, 'going through the gate', reached airfield as enemy aircraft was just airborne. Mosquito gave two two-second bursts at enemy aircraft at 600 feet height, 1½ rings deflection, 250 yards range, but no strikes seen. Mosquito overshot and enemy aircraft turned port climbing rapidly, making left-hand circuit of airfield. Mosquito turned quickly inside enemy aircraft and came in astern. Enemy aircraft was still burning all lights which made recognition difficult (downward recognition light was very bright). Closing into 150 yards, same height, half ring deflection, Mosquito fired a two-second burst. Strikes seen on port wing, root and fuselage and identified as Fw 190. Immediate flash and enemy aircraft peeled off to port from 1200 feet, exploding on the ground six miles south of airfield three seconds later and 2330 hours. Mosquito immediately left patrol area with enemy aircraft still burning. Claim one Fw 190 destroyed (Cat.A.1). Mosquito landed at 0117 hours."[334]

On the following night, Flight Lieutenant Ian Dobie and Warrant Officer A. R. "Grimmy" Grimstone DFM of 85 Squadron destroyed a Ju 188 near Hamburg. On 14/15 March they were shot down by American flak near Koblenz. "Grimmy" Grimstone had gone to 96 Squadron with Peter Green, but in August, when his pilot had taken over command of 219 Squadron, "Grimmy" had gone on a rest before returning to 85 Squadron. Dobie was thrown clear and came down safely on his parachute and wandered into the American lines. Grimstone was found with his parachute open but burnt, still attached to his body within fifty yards of the wreckage.

On 12/13 March, when the heavies bombed Lutzkendorf, Flight Lieutenant J. W. Welford and Flying Officer R. H. Phillips of 410 "Cougar" Squadron RCAF in a NF.XXX claimed a Ju 88 "probable" in the Dunkirk area. On 14/15 March American pilot Flying Officer (2nd Lieutenant) R. D. S. "Hank" Gregor and his navigator/radar operator, Flight Sergeant Frank H. Baker, returned victorious from a lone 141 Squadron ASH patrol in the Frankfurt-Mannheim area in support of the bombers attacking Zweibrücken. Near Saarbrücken they picked up a contact coming into land at Lachen airfield and opened fire from 2000 feet. They rapidly closed range to 100 feet, and just as they started to pull out the enemy aircraft exploded under the nose of their Mosquito, illuminating the area. It was 141 Squadron's final air-to-air victory of the war. That same night Squadron Leader Dolly Doleman and Flight Lieutenant Bunny Bunch DFC of 157 Squadron were airborne from Swannington in their Mosquito XIX at 1847 hours. Doleman recorded:

"We found that the *Gee* was u/s but we dared not change aircraft as Bunny had just given a lecture saying that *Gee* was merely an aid to navigation. We D/R'd onwards and checked position with the prang at Zweibrücken and picked up the 5 Group bombers shortly after. We escorted them uneventfully, looking for the odd airfield, but none were lit. We were investigating a small Squadron Leader line pointing from somewhere near Nürnburg to the target (Lutzkendorf) when contact was obtained, six miles head - on 20° to port. We closed to 1500 feet. At 10-11, 000 from a violently moving target, orbiting and climbing and diving. Unfortunately all this was taking place in the darkest patch of sky over the whole of the continent. After sitting behind him in formation for about fifteen minutes we pulled up very close and identified as a Ju 88G by the square top of the fin and elevators set forward. Pulled up and target became an indistinct blur. Had a crack at that from short range even closer. Strikes were soon, but impossible to say whereabouts they were. We were within minimum Mk.X range and Flight Lieutenant Bunch obtained his next contact about 2000 feet, 90° starboard. We whipped around but he must have gone down on the deck, as no further contact was obtained. Bags of blasphemy. Went on to target but no further joy, so set course base and landed base 0055 hours, brassed off to hell."

The following night, 15/16 March, Captain Eric Fossum and Flying Officer S. A. Hider of 85 Squadron closed in below a contact at 200 feet in the Hanover area. Hider used his night glasses and identified the bogey as a Ju 88. Fossum dropped back to 600 feet astern and level and pumped a two-second burst into the enemy machine. Strikes could be seen between the fuselage and port engine. The Norwegian fired a second burst. This time the Junkers exploded and the port engine burst into flames. Hider, watching the dying moments through his glasses, saw one crewmember bale out of the doomed machine. Fossum, however, closed in for a third burst at 600-feet range. He did not want any of the crew to escape. Fossum blasted the machine again until a bright explosion appeared in the fuselage, but Hider, still peering through his night glasses, saw two more crew abandon the doomed Ju 88 before the coup de grace. On the same night, Flight Lieutenant Jimmy Mathews and Warrant Officer Alan Penrose of 157 Squadron bagged a Ju 88 twenty miles south of Würzburg.

On 16/17 March 231 Lancasters of I Group and forty-six Lancasters and sixteen Mosquitoes of 8 Group attacked Nürnburg and 225 Lancasters and eleven Mosquitoes of 5 Group bombed Würzburg. Thirty aircraft were lost mainly to German night-fighters that found the Bomber Stream on the way to the target. Squadron Leader D. L. Hughes and Flight Lieutenant R. H. Perks of 239 Squadron destroyed a Ju 88 flown by Major Werner Hoffmann (fifty-three victories) near Nürnburg. On 18/19 March Flight Lieutenant V. D. Win RNZAF and Flying Officer T. P. Ryan RNZAF of 85 Squadron destroyed a Bf 110. Wing Commander W. F. Gibb and Killer Kendall of 239 Squadron shot down a He 219 *Uhu* at Witten to take their score while with the squadron to five.[335] Warrant Officer Taylor and Flight Sergeant Radford of 157 Squadron destroyed a Ju 88. *Nachtjagdgeschwader* crews had little defense against the Mosquitoes. Even their *SN-2* AI band could now be jammed since several Fortresses of 214 Squadron had each been fitted with six installations of the latest development of *Piperack*. (An American development of the *Mandrel IV* device. Known as *Dina II* when used against the *FuG 220* AI radar, the device was known as *Piperack*.)

Advances by the Allied Armies made most of the month's operations comparatively deep penetrations, and it was not easy to confuse the German plotters once the Main Forces had passed the early stages of their routes over enemy territory. This was overcome in the latter part of the month by splitting the Window Force, and by operating the *Mandrel* aircraft in the double role of *Mandrel* and Window. By these means, and with the co-operation of the American 492nd Bomb Group, it was possible to make several feint attacks simultaneously on widely separated areas. The supporting fighters of 100 Group could do little about enemy fighters, which occasionally got into the stream and shot down a number of bombers. They were flying well away from the bomber stream owing to the difficulty of operating AI in the midst of the Window and bomber echoes. It became clear that AI Mk X could be used for close escort provided the Mosquitoes flew above the bombers, where the H_2S and Window interference was least. It was decided to try again a close escort of the stream, and it was hoped that with experience the crews would become better able to operate among Window and bomber echoes. The first close escort of the bomber stream was carried out in March.

Bomber Command's tactics of deception and radio countermeasures had reached a fine perfection. Just how fine can be assessed from one typical night operation on 20/21 March when no less than three feint attacks took place in support of the Main Force attack on the synthetic oil refinery at Bohlen, just south of Leipzig, by 235 Lancasters and Mosquitoes. The Window Force left the Main Stream soon after crossing the front line and made for Kassel, which was bombed. Further on, when closer to the true target, another Window Force broke off and bombed Halle. The third feint force was provided by the *Mandrel* screen which, after the passage of the heavies, re-formed into a Window Force and attacked Frankfurt with flares.

The Main Force's Zero Hour was set at 0340 hours on the 21st. Almost simultaneously, 166 Lancasters headed for the oilfield at Hemmingstedt, in Schleswig-Holstein, far to the north of the first target. This force's attack was to commence at 0430, and together with the other attack involved Bomber Command's main effort. In the meantime, the evening's diversions began with a large-scale nuisance raid on Berlin: 35 Mosquitoes of the Pathfinder force bombed the city beginning at 2114 hours. Just after 0100 hours the main Bohlen force crossed the English Channel on a southeasterly heading, while a few miles to the south a feinting formation, comprising 64 Lancasters and Halifaxes from training units, crossed the Channel on an almost parallel course. It was here that the complications for the German radar operators began. By 0205 an 80-mile long *Mandrel* screen comprising seven pairs of Halifaxes from 171 and 199 Squadrons was in position over northern France, throwing up a wall of radar jamming through which the German early-warning radar could not see. Shortly after crossing the coast of France, the Bohlen force split into two streams, hidden behind the *Mandrel* screen. 41 Lancasters broke away and headed off to the northeast, and these were to cause considerable difficulties for the Germans.

While the bomber formations were still approaching the German frontier, fourteen Mosquito fighter-bombers of 23 and 515 Squadrons were fanning out in ones and twos and making for the airfields the German night-fighter force was expected to use that night. Once there, they orbited overhead for hours on end, dropping clusters of incendiaries and firing at anything that moved.

At 0300 the training aircraft, which had by now almost reached the German frontier near Strasbourg, turned about and went home, their work done. At the same time, the two formations making their separate ways to the Bohlen refinery burst through the *Mandrel* jamming screen. Seven Liberators of 233 Squadron and four Halifaxes of 171 Squadron went five minutes—about 18 miles—ahead of the larger Bohlen force, laying out a dense cloud of Window which effectively hid the bombers following them. Once over the Rhine, the more southerly of the two streams of bombers turned northeast straight towards Kassel. So far, there was no way in which the German fighter controller could tell the real target for the night. In fact, at the time the bomber forces crossed the German frontier, the German fighter-controller of the Central Rhine defense area, Major Rüppel, seriously underestimated the strength of the two approaching formations: he thought each force involved about thirty aircraft, and both might well be Window feints. As the reports from the ground observation posts began to come in, however, it became clear that the southernmost of the two was much larger than he had estimated. No amount of jamming could conceal the roar of 800 aircraft engines.

Also successful this night were Flight Lieutenant G. C. Chapman and Flight Sergeant Jimmy Stockley of 85 Squadron, who took off from Swannington at 0145 hours in their NF.XXX on a high-level escort of the bombers to Bohlen. While en route to patrol a *Perfectos* contact was obtained at 0255 hours just after passing Hamm at twelve miles range and 12,000 feet. Chapman wrote later:

> "Range was closed to one mile but no AI contact was obtained, and the range started to increase again. So, deciding that the contact must be below we did a hard diving turn to port, down to 9000 feet and finally, D/F'd on to the target's course at seven miles range. We closed in to six miles range and an AI contact was obtained at six o'clock. The target was climbing and we closed in

rapidly and obtained a visual at 900 feet, height 13,000 feet. The target was still climbing straight ahead and was identified with the night glasses as a Me 110. It had a pale blue light between the starboard nacelle and fuselage. I closed in to 600 feet and pulled up to dead astern when the Hun started to turn to port. I gave it a ½-ring deflection and a three-second-burst, whereupon the enemy aircraft exploded in the port engine in a very satisfactory manner, with debris flying back. It exploded on the ground at 0305 hours twenty-five to thirty miles NW of Kassel. All this excitement was too much for the Perfectos, which went u/s unfortunately, so we set course for the rendezvous with the bomber stream."

Chapman and Stockley reached the bomber stream at 0322 hours. Their patrol was uneventful until the stream left the target at 0400 hours. Chapman continues:

"I noticed to port and fifteen miles south a ball of yellowish flame take off and climb very rapidly (Plauen airfield). I thought it was a flare or a V2 (a little out of position) until it started emitting a meteor tail several hundred feet long. We turned port towards it, and lost height to 7000 feet, that being the height of this phenomenon as far as I could judge, and continued watching. It traveled in a NW direction very fast and suddenly to our astonishment fired off some RPs [rocket projectiles], four single and one pair, in the general direction of the departing bomber stream. We were pretty amazed at all this and decided that it must be a Me 163. I continued turning port and got behind it. It was vectoring 275° by this time and doing about 260 IAS and using the AI to check range we closed in to 1000 feet and visually identified a twin-engined aircraft with rocket apparatus slung under *the* fuselage - a He 219. [The He 219 V14 *Uhu* carried a BMW 109-003 turbojet, used in the He 162 *Salamander* program, below *the* fuselage]. Considerable quantities of flames and sparks were flying back preventing me from identifying the tail unit, so I decided to open fire at that range. I gave it several longish bursts as two of *the* cannon had stoppages and was gratified to see an explosion take place somewhere in the fuselage and debris fly back. The enemy aircraft nosed straight down through the patchy cloud and exploded on the ground with a tremendous glare."[336]

On 24/25 March, Pilot Officer F. X. A. Huls and Flying Officer Joe Kinet of 515 Squadron flew a *Night Ranger* to the Stendal area. Their presence caused consternation. Or did it? The flarepath was lit and doused three times but was identified as Buch landing ground, classified as a dummy in the Intelligence Section's "List of Airfields, Vol 1 Germany" back at Snoring. Huls and Kinet dropped two flares and went in at 500 feet to spot three Fw 190s dispersed at the runway threshold. Both men were convinced the dummy landing ground was being used as an airfield, and Huls climbed to 1500 feet and picked out one of the Fw 190s, which he gave a long burst of cannon fire before pulling out at 500 feet. The Fw 190 began to burn fiercely and emit a column of smoke. Huls leveled out and the AA defenses opened up, but they were well clear before any hits could be registered. Not content with their night's work, on their way home they dropped forty 4lb incendiary bombs on the east-west flarepath at Hustedt airfield, north of Celle, which was lit up, and caused fires on the south side of the flarepath. Meanwhile, Flying Officer E. W. "Bunny" Adams and Flight Sergeant Frank A. Widdicombe, who had damaged a Ju 88 the previous month, really went to town on their *Night Ranger* to the Müchen area after a refuelling stop at Juvincourt. They made three low runs over Erding airfield, and on the third their shells overshot and struck a hangar, but a line of at least six aircraft were seen in the southwest corner. Adams and Widdicombe attacked from north to south and sprayed the entire line. The second aircraft exploded and disintegrated, and this was claimed "destroyed," with four claimed as "damaged."

On 30/31 March Leslie Holland and Bob Young were assigned to another anti-flak job:

"As it was not at such a great distance," recalls Dutch Holland, "there would be time to look for a bit more trouble elsewhere. Then minelaying was to be carried out in the Weser between Bremen and Bremerhaven, so we were expecting to run into some pretty hot opposition. As it turned out, it proved to be a somewhat tame affair with nothing like the reaction we had provoked up the Oslo Fiord. As a secondary operation we had elected to poke our nose in at Nordholz, a few miles further north near Cuxhaven. Our briefing maps had been pretty specific about aircraft parking stands in among the trees on the north side of the field. It was easy enough to find after having detoured out to sea round Bremerhaven and looked pretty bare of any game. But we had some flares and incendiaries on board. The flares were dropped first over the middle of the field and showed that nothing had been carelessly left out in the open. So, try the coverts next and see what we could draw from them. The incendiaries were duly laid in a string across the shrubbery on the north side and *OHO*, what have we here?

"In amongst the parking bays, several twin-engine aircraft without propellers and no reflections from their noses. More than likely Me 262s. This is where the handiness of the Mosquito comes in because a lot has got to be done before the fires go out. Steeply round for a low run with a short burst, which hits a trifle short but just time to correct and cover the pens with strikes. Round for another run and by this time the gun crews, probably a trifle out of breath, have got to their posts and are answering back. But this is too good to miss, so back for a couple more runs by which time there is a confused cloud of smoke and fire. We reckon we have done enough to claim one Me 262 destroyed and two damaged, and head for home once more. And on the way out we see an odd thing, a submarine flying a balloon. We don't know whose it is, so refrain from attacking and do not call attention to it until debriefing. My guess is that it was an Allied submarine with an aerial raised by the balloon for signals monitoring.

"Somewhere in Holland, flying at about 1000 feet we were startled to see a V2 rise off its pad about a mile in front of us. I slipped off the safety catch but it rose at an unbelievable rate into the clouds at about 2000 feet, lighting up the whole sky in a weird flickering brilliant violet glow. NW couldn't trace the pad but made a note of the map references so that someone could come and have a look in daylight; but some of the sites were mobile. I have also been near *to* being on the receiving end of those beasties and the sudden arrival has a shocking effect much worse than the ones you hear coming."

Mosquito PR.XVIs replaced the Mk.IVs in 192 Squadron; their aircraft had been fitted with *Dina* and *Piperack* jamming equipment earlier that year. With the front line beginning to advance further into Germany the Mosquitoes' targets became more and more distant. On 1/2 April 1945 four 515 Squadron Mosquitoes took part in a *Night Ranger* operation in the München and Augsburg-Ingolstadt areas from their forward base at Juvincourt. Howard Kelsey and Smitty Smith stooged around many airfields in the München area but found no fighters and failed to make any ASH contacts. Kelsey attacked a factory with incendiary bombs and caused terrific explosions and a large fire. Bunny Adams and Frank Widdicombe attacked seven Bf 109s on the ground at Erding with cannon fire and damaged one before attacking Lechfeld airfield, causing fires and explosions. Squadron Leader John Penny, Flying Officer Whitfield, and Lieutenant Emil J. Van Heerden SAAF and Flying Officer J. W Robson attacked Leipheim airfield. The South African and his navigator were killed when an AA battery manned by Hitler Youth shot down their Mosquito. Penny proceeded to Neuburg, where he found nothing. Returning to Leipheim, he bombed the dispersals with incendiary bombs and attacked and damaged a truck at Ertingen before turning for home. Operations were flown even further afield to the Czech border, as Leslie Holland recalls:

> "Several Main Force attacks were made on points where there were railway concentrations in order to disorganize the movement of troops from the eastern front. In support of one of these we were assigned to patrol the airfield at Plauen, which is pretty near the Czech border. As it happened, the winds took advantage of the 2½ hours to target to increase and get round to the south. I couldn't claim with confidence that we had located our assigned airfield because a large marshalling yard, which appeared beneath us that, we were at Pilsen. There was a great deal of activity and it seemed a good idea to illuminate the scene a little better. There were, we thought, a flare and incendiaries in the fuselage bay, but dropping these from 500 feet gave us a considerable surprise. The flare turned out to be a 250lb bomb with contact fuse but fortunately splinters and debris passed us by. The incendiaries proved more true to form. (In fact the load had been changed after the briefing.) At the least we certainly made a hole in the tracks and carried on the good work by damaging some of the locos and rolling stock with cannon fire.
>
> "Having more or less established our position (as we thought), it was then necessary to think about the rather long trek home. Shortly after this, an area of scattered conflagrations to starboard of our track led us to make a tentative identification of Leipzig, which had been the Main Force target. This meant that it was Chemnitz and not Pilsen, which we had treated, in such cavalier fashion and we were making both much more nothing than we wished and slow progress over the ground. After about another hour it was becoming apparent that our fuel state would need careful management. In view of the increased and adverse wind it seemed best to keep at a fairly low altitude and pull back the revs a bit. Much later, the north German islands began to drift past aggravatingly slowly. It now looked as though we might have a problem and some nice calculations began to occupy the fingers of both hands. It would be very much touch and go. Fifty miles out, the gauges were pretty near their marks. A Mayday from here should get us a clear run through the Norfolk anti-*Diver* belt. This would ensure a straight descending run into the first airfield that could receive us - Coltishall. The fuel pressure warning lights were on during the approach and the touch of the wheels on the asphalt was accompanied by the exaltation we had been delaying for the last five minutes. As we turned off the runway *the* engines stopped."

On 3/4 April eight Mosquitoes of 157 Squadron made a *Spoof* raid on Berlin in support of 8 Group Mosquitoes. Over the Big City, Flight Lieutenant J. H. Leland was coned by the searchlights and a Me 262, seeing its chance, made four attacks on the Mosquito. Two strikes were recorded on Leland's engines, but he escaped his pursuer after spinning his aircraft and heading flat out for friendly territory.

On 4/5 April 141 Squadron dispatched its first Mosquito XXX sortie when three joined twelve from 239 Squadron in a bomber support operation for the heavies attacking synthetic oil plants in southern Germany. Squadron Leader Tim Woodman and Flight Lieutenant Neville, who were serving at BSDU, destroyed a Bf 109 west of Magdeburg (Woodman's seventh confirmed victory of the war). This same night, Flight Lieutenant C. W "Topsy" Turner and twenty-year old Flight Sergeant George "Jock" Honeyman, from Edinburgh, both of A Flight in 85 Squadron, took off from Swannington at 2238 hours for a high-level escort of the Window Force. Escort was only a loose term because in the dark it was not possible to fly any kind of formation over long distances. Turner and Honeyman were new boys who had joined the squadron in November when they were somewhat dazzled by the arrays of "gongs" worn by aces such as Burbridge and Skelton (DSO* and DFC* each) and A. I. "Ginger" Owen and McAllister (DFC* DFM). These crews finished the war with twenty-one and fifteen victories respectively. They flew their *freshman* op on the night of 29 December 1944 and would fly seventeen ops together on the Mosquito. It was Turner's first tour as a pilot. He had been a gunner on Hampdens and had been shot down twice.

Topsy Turner piloted the Mosquito on a course of 090°. On crossing into enemy territory at the Dutch coast they began their climb to their tasked height of 20,000 feet. After nearly two hours they reached their patrol area northwest of Magdeburg. All the time Jock was scanning the AI and all the other interception aids. Their Mosquito was equipped with Mk X radar, which George Honeyman considered "probably the best AI of WW2":

> "It could be operated down to circuit height of 1000-1500 feet. In addition, there were two additional displays. *Perfectos*, a small-diameter cathode ray tube fitted in the AI visor, displayed enemy *IFF* transmissions. Only left or right indications were given but the transmitting aircraft could be detected at a much greater range than was possible using AI which relied on the echo from the fighter aircraft's own transmission. *Monica*, fitted at the bottom of the instrument panel, showed on its display aircraft coming from behind from a range of one-two miles. Every day the Y-Service provided the enemy colors of the day and we carried similar cartridges for the Very pistols, to try to confuse enemy Bofors fire, which was usually encountered on *Intruder* sorties at low level over enemy airfields. The only navigational aid was *Gee,* which could only be received as far as Holland because of enemy jamming. From there it was DR based on a detailed flight plan."

At approximately 2238 hours Jock Honeyman picked an AI contact and immediately began his commentary to Topsy, who had a visual range of only 800-1000 yards, depending on moonlight conditions:

"Contact 3¼ miles, 200. Starboard, crossing starboard to port... Turn port...Go down. Range now two miles, 100. Starboard - harder port. Target now 12 o'clock, 5° above, one mile. Level off, ease the turn. Now steady; 800 yards 12 o'clock, 15° above; 600 yards, 12 o'clock 150 above - throttle back; 12 o'clock, 20°, minimum range - hold that speed. Can't you see him?' Topsy called 'Visual."

He opened up the throttles and slowly closed in on a gently weaving target, adjusting his gunsight and switching on his camera-gun. At 100 yards there was no Type F response (an infrared telescope which could pick up a light source fitted under the tail of RAF bombers but invisible to the naked eye because the light was covered by a black shield, known as Type Z). Using night binoculars, the target was identified from underneath as a Ju 188. Topsy dropped back to 200 yards to open fire when a black object, possibly a single-engined fighter, whistled across their bows at about 100-feet. Both men ducked smartly. Turner continues:

"After multiple curses and bags of brow mopping, we saw our quarry still ahead and I opened fire from 200 yards astern with 5° deflection, obtaining strikes on the port engine. Two more short bursts made the Hun burn nicely. It spun and crashed, burning fiercely on the ground, west of Magdeburg."

At 0130 hours *C-Charlie* landed back at Swannington after four hours forty minutes in the air. This was their one and only kill of the war.

On 9/10 April Wing Commander Kelsey DFC,* the Commanding Officer 515 Squadron, and Flight Lieutenant Edward M. "Smitty" Smith DFC DFM flew an *Intruder* to Lübeck, a night-fighter base that was still active. Smith recalls:

"After a while we spotted a Ju 88 taking off in dark conditions and had difficulty keeping it in radar contact and slowing down sufficiently to keep behind it. The Ju 88 was climbing very hard (probably with flaps). However, it was shot at and we saw several strikes. (After the war I was with 85 Squadron at Tangmere and visited Lübeck and whilst there I was told there was somewhere about, the remnants of a Ju 88 from the appropriate time.) After that all was quiet and we headed off towards Hamburg. I spotted an aircraft coming in behind us. We feinted to the right then circled hard to port, coming in behind him in part moonlight. We had no trouble in shooting the Ju 188 down. We continued over Hamburg and dropped the *Intruder* load of two 500lb HE and 160 incendiaries."

This was Howard Kelsey's fourth victory in 100 Group and his seventh overall, plus four aircraft destroyed on the ground and one "probable." Air to air victories were now few and far between, but on the night of 13/14 April Flight Lieutenant Kenneth D. Vaughan and Flight Sergeant Robert Denison MacKinnon returned triumphant with a claim for the destruction of a He 219 V14 carrying a BMW 109-003 turbojet below the fuselage. Vaughan wrote:

"We planned to cross the enemy coast at Westerhever at 2320 hours mid then proceed to a point twenty miles SW of Kiel, which was the target for the main bomber force. We had originally intended to cover the bomber route out from the target area to the enemy coastline for a period of thirty-five minutes. We were then aiming to do a *freelance* patrol in the Luneburg area. After being on patrol for forty minutes we were still getting groups of bomber contacts. As there was apparent ground activity with searchlights and ground flashes on the bomber route, which were definitely not gun flashes but some sort of indicating aid to the Hun night-fighters, we decided to continue patrolling the same area. However, this area quietened down considerably and after many alterations of height etc, on patrol, at 2020 hours, height 18,000 feet, just when our time limit on patrol had expired, my navigator obtained a crossing starboard to port contact at five miles range 35° above. We chased our target in a port turn on to a southerly vector with the range rapidly reducing to 9000 feet and the target losing height at a rather low air speed, 220-230 IAS. The target kept up a continuous weave but settled down at about 10,000 feet. We closed range to 1000 feet but experienced difficulty in getting behind him owing to his weaving activities. I got a visual on a pale blue light. But the aircraft did a peel off to port and range went out to 5000 feet. We followed on AI, which incidentally was very ropey, in turns. Again we closed on the hard weaving target. I got fleeting visuals on bright exhausts at one stage, at about 2000-feet range, but still could not get comfortably settled astern. Three times we closed in to 1000-feet, the target peeling off on every occasion. The blue light was visible on most of these occasions from just astern but I was unable to follow visually owing to the target' s activities.

"We could identify target as a twin-engined aircraft on our very few opportunities. On one occasion, my navigator confirmed this with night glasses. On the third occasion that we closed range to 1000 feet, the target, to me anyway, appeared to catch fire underneath the fuselage. I got my navigator's head out of the box to confirm this and very quickly and brightly he yelled 'That's his jet', which jolted me out of my fire theory very quickly.' The Target again started one of his routine turns and I immediately pushed the throttles fully open +12 and already using 28,000 revs, and gave a ½-second deflection shot on his jet at about 900 feet range. However, this burst produced no strikes, so I got dead astern in the turn and at 700 feet range, fired another burst, which caused a large explosion and strikes on his starboard side. I gave him another burst for luck and another explosion appeared on the port side and the E/A burned from wing tip to wing tip, going down in a spin to starboard and hit the deck at 0031 hours. From it's general appearance and behaviour, particularly the two of a jet we consider this A/C was a He 219, and we claim it as destroyed. We then set course for base. No *Perfectos* throughout patrol. The Hun did not seem to have any - tail warning device, but was apparently carrying out the usual evasive action". CLAIM: one He 219 destroyed. A/c landed 'Swannington 0211 hours.'

There were definite signs that the end of the war could be in sight, but as Leslie Holland in 515 Squadron recalls:

"Wing Commander Kelsey and 100 Group between them seemed determined that we should not become bored during its last throes. On 15/16 April Schleissheim airfield at Munich was selected for special attention probably because it was a likely transit point for German staff movements now that Allied armies were closing in from east and west. Be that as it may, it was supposed to have been a co-ordinated attack but I do not recall it as having been a particularly well-planned operation. We had the usual feeling that it was Bob and I alone against the Third Reich. In the absence of any general target illumination we used our own incendiaries to light up the area round the airfield buildings. Incidentally, it's a hell of a long way to Munich and we just took it for granted that we would find the place. That we did so without any great difficulty is a credit to Bob. Features on the airfield were recognizable from the photos we had studied at briefing. The object of the exercise being to create mayhem, we used our 20mm guns on the airfield buildings, concentrating on the control tower, which cannot have been too pleasant for its occupants.

"After this little gesture, we climbed to about 2000 feet and flew round Munich trailing our coat, looking for anything that might turn up. Having left behind the light flak at low level which had been hardly enough to mention, it was noticeable that the heavy guns undoubtedly disposed round the city did not seem over-concerned with one or two relatively innocuous Mosquitoes droning around, even though we might have been pathfinders. They probably couldn't set their fuses for that level. We once flew at about 2000 feet right across the Ruhr (accidentally) without a shot being fired. Bob said it was because they couldn't believe that a hostile aircraft would do anything so stupid. There might have been balloons but the thought didn't occur to us at the time.

"While over the northern purlieus of Munich, Bob picked up a contact on our level, range about one mile and out to our right. Having turned sharply towards the supposed position of the bogey (it could have of course been one of our own aircraft), a light came into view, which was evidently on the aircraft we were tracking. It was not difficult to get into a position behind it but we came near to running into it as it was evidently doing very much less than our 240 mph. A wide S turn brought us back behind it and although our speed was very much reduced, we were still too near and closing too fast. As we passed beneath, the fixed landing gear of a Ju 52 could be seen distinctly but the white light made it almost impossible to pick out any other features against the moonless sky. It seemed to he doing about 120 mph in a slow turn round an airfield beacon, probably in a holding orbit until things had settled down at Schleissheim.

"It didn't take too long to decide that although it was a transport aircraft and might be unarmed (some did carry defensive armament) there was no doubt in our minds that the chance that it could be carrying top brass or war material meant that it must be attacked. The next approach brought us into firing position and a burst of 20mm was aimed at each of the wing engines. As we passed, it had already begun a descending turn and there appeared to be fire in the wing engines. We did not see it again and the trace disappeared from our radar.

"[No.] 515 had more casualties than any other squadron in 100 Group. I suppose there was a tendency to avoid dwelling on the fact if someone 'got the chop'. It just seems that it didn't happen very often and most of our particular mates came through OK."

There remained one more task in the wide-ranging activities of 515 Squadron before hostilities ceased when, on 14/15 April, 515 Squadron and 23 Squadron flew the first Mosquito Master Bomber sorties in 100 Group. They dropped green TIs and orchestrated attacks by eighteen Mosquitoes of 141 and 169 Squadrons which carried a new, even more sinister form of aerial bomb for the first time, going under the code-name *Firebash*. The aerial bomb in question was napalmgel (petrol thickened with a compound made from aluminium, naphthenic, and palmitie acids to which white phosphorous was added for ignition). Winnie Winn DFC, 141 Squadron Commanding Officer, had asked for and received Napalmgel from the American 8th Air Force. Winn obtained permission for his squadron to drop the gel in Mosquito 100-gallon drop tanks, providing he could obtain his own supplies. He made a call to the Eighth Air Force and 40-gallon and 50-gallon drums of napalmgel soon began arriving at West Raynham, courtesy of the Americans. At first armorers pumped it into drop tanks using hand pumps, but then the Americans obliged with petrol-driven mechanical pumps and the operation became much easier. LAC Johnny Claxton, who at that time was one of the longest-serving members of 141 Squadron's ground crews, recalls that a one pound all-way phosphorous fuze was fitted in each tank to ignite the napalmgel on impact. The fuze was called all-way because no matter how the tank fell the fuze would ignite the contents.

In the afternoon of 6 April, Wing Commander Winn carried out the first of three trials of types of napalmgel when he flew low and parallel with the main No. 1 runway and dropped 100-gallon drop tanks on the grass. These trials caused enormous interest, and the station and aircrew crowded in the control tower while the ground crews climbed on to the roofs of the hangars in order to get a better view of the explosions. It was decided that crews who would drop napalmgel required no additional training because they had carried out enough low-level attacks with bombs or cannon over many months; no special tactics were to be employed. Enthusiasm and keenness to get on the night's napalmgel program reached a fever pitch. When six aircraft were asked for a dozen were offered—and accepted! Petrol and range was reduced so that each Mosquito could carry two 100-gallon drop tanks of napalmgel but, even so, they would have to land at Juvincourt, Melsbroek, or Mannheim. No one was unhappy about this arrangement, as it offered the possibility of being stranded on the Continent for days![337]

On the night of 14/15 April eighteen FB.VIs and NF.XXXs were dispatched from West Raynham. Twelve were from 141 Squadron and six from 239 Squadron, some of which were detailed to provide support for the 512 bombers attacking Potsdam, just outside Berlin. This was the first time the Big City had been attacked by heavies since March 1944, although Mosquito bombers had continually attacked it. Seven Mosquitoes of 141 Squadron flew high-level AI.Mk.X patrols in support of the Potsdam raid, but also covered the remaining five 141 Mosquitoes that would carry out the first napalmgel *Firebash* raid on night-fighter airfields at Neuruppin, near Potsdam, and Jüterborg, near Berlin.[338]

Winnie Winn and R. A. W Scott in a Mk VI led the formation of five napalmgel aircraft to Brussels/Melsbroek. Here they refueled before setting course for the Berlin area, where they were to be supported by bomb and incendiary carrying Mosquitoes of

23 Squadron, which also supplied the "Noload" leader, the Master Bomber, for the Neuruppin raid. Master of Ceremonies Squadron Leader H. V Hopkins provided "excellent support," and Winn dropped his canisters from 800 feet. Two more Napalm-carrying Mosquitoes followed him, and all six napalm bombs exploded near the hangars and engulfed the airfield in flame and smoke. A row of six buildings burned merrily and lit up the night sky as all three Mosquitoes, unburdened now, returned to strafe the airfield with cannon fire. Red tracer every fifth shell zeroed in on buildings and bowsers, one of which exploded in a huge flash of flame near a hangar. One of the Mosquito crews strafed the hapless base three times from 2000 feet to 500 feet in all, helped in no small measure by TIs dropped just southeast of the airfield by the Master Bomber.

At Jüterborg, Flight Lieutenant M. W Huggins, the Master of Ceremonies, and Flying Officer C. G. Stow, a 515 Squadron "Sollock" aircraft (Master Bomber), were unable to help much, and no TIs were seen to drop, which scattered over about a ten-mile area. Ron Brearley and John Sheldon and Flight Lieutenant E. B. Drew and Flying Officer A. H. Williams thundered low over the German countryside and had to toss their napalm bombs on the estimated position of the airfield. One of Brearley's drop tanks hung up so he dropped the port tank containing fifty gallons of napalmgel from 300 feet and headed west. (Returning with a napalmgel tank still attached was, as one could imagine, "pretty dicey." On a later *Firebash* op one tank that would not release over the target fell off on the West Raynham runway on the aircraft's return. These hang-ups occurred due to deposits of napalm on the release unit, and at the joint between the tank and the mainplanes.) Drew, meanwhile, was forced to climb to 5000 feet and position on *Gee*, following the failure of the TIs and flares, before he dropped down to 1000 feet and roared over the base with the two 100-gallon drop tanks ready to rain death and destruction. The two firebombs exploded among rows of buildings in the northwest corner of the airfield and were still burning thirteen minutes later as he twice strafed buildings amid light and inaccurate flak. All five fire-bomber Mosquitoes landed back at Melsbroek for refuelling before returning to West Raynham, no doubt highly delighted with their night's work.

The second *Firebash* raid by 141 Squadron was flown on 17/18 April. Bomber Command was also abroad this night, with attacks by 5 Group on railway yards at Cham, Germany. Five 141 Squadron Mosquitoes, each armed with 100-gallon napalmgel drop tanks and led by Wing Commander Winnie Winn, were to head for Schleissheim airfield, just north of München, after a refueling stop at St. Dizier. However, after landing at St. Dizier, Winn was delayed with refueling problems when petrol had to be brought sixty miles by road. He decided that by the time they got off and found the target they would be unable to see the markers, and opted for an attack on München instead. However, a bad storm front scrubbed this option and he and Scott were forced to return to England.

The three remaining napalm-armed Mosquito crews battled through solid cloud and violent thunderstorms to Schleissheim, but Rimer and Farnfield were forced to abort after losing *Gee*. After vainly trying to climb above the thick cloud, Squadron Leader Thatcher was also forced to abandon the mission. Another crew, Flying Officer J. C. Barton and Sergeant L. Berlin, fought their way through the storm front and hurled their napalm bombs among airfield buildings; then, obtaining permission from the 23 Squadron Master Bomber, they strafed the airfield on a return low-level run. Roy Brearley and John Sheldon climbed to 10,000 feet to escape the worst of the weather and, diving down on pinpoints provided by "Noload," they added fuel to the flames with their two napalm bombs. They fell among two hangars and exploded. They called up the Master Bomber before returning and strafing hangars, buildings, and rolling stock, then exited the area to allow 23 Squadron to add their bombs and incendiaries to the conflagration. Meanwhile, Mosquitoes of 85 Squadron patrolled Schleissheim and Firstenfeldbrück airfields. Wing Commander W. K. Davison, 85 Squadron Commanding Officer since Wing Commander E. S. "Gon" Gonsalves DFC had been posted in January, destroyed a Ju 88 in the München area using *Perfectos*.

On 18/19 April 1945 24 Mosquitoes[339] flew to the forward base at Juvincourt, in France, for a *Firebash* raid on München/Neubiberg airfield. The raid was in full swing when 141 Squadron, led once more by Winn, arrived at München/Neubiberg with their napalm loads. Flight Lieutenant C. G. A. Drew and Pilot Officer A. H. Williams were ready to commence their-low level bomb run at 700 feet, but had to wait 25 minutes before they could take their turn. To add insult to injury one of their firebombs refused to release. Drew climbed to 7000 feet and tried to shake it loose, and finally got it safely away just north of Munchen. On the instructions of "Noload Leader," the Master Bomber, Warrant Officer Ronald G. Dawson and Flying Officer Charles P. D. Childs, an all New Zealand crew in *Winball 7*, went in for their fire-bombing run. The 24-year old pilot and his 32-year old navigator/radar operator had joined 141 Squadron on 22 January and this was their tenth op. It was the last they would complete. As they hurtled into the attack they heard in their headphones the Master Bomber's warning of accurate light flak but pressed bravely on. Just as they reached their drop point *Winball* 7 was hit by flak. The New Zealanders' Mosquito appeared to climb, and some ten seconds later crashed in flames near an autobahn northwest of the airfield. One of the tanks seemed to ricochet into the air and fall back into the burning pyre. They were the last casualties of 141 Squadron in WWII.

On 19/20 April, three squadrons of Mosquitoes flew a napalm raid against Flensburg airfield, on the Danish border. Six Mosquito FB.VIs of 515 Squadron marked the target with green TIs and flares, and dropped incendiaries and 500lb HE bombs. The Commanding Officer of 515 Squadron Howard Kelsey, and Smitty Smith, was Master Bomber. Three FB.VIs of 169 Squadron took off from Great Massingham and flew to West Raynham to load up with napalm tanks for their first napalm attack. The same aircraft also carried two 500lb bombs beneath their wings. No. 141 Squadron was unable to carry bombs on its NF.XXX Mosquitoes as well as napalm tanks because they did not have bomb racks nor the release mechanisms fitted in the bomb bay behind the cannons. For the same reason 169 Squadron were unable to use their NF.XIX Mosquitoes. The attack was very successful, with good work by the Master Bomber. Flensburg was plastered and strafed from end to end, and smoke and flame made observation of the final result difficult. Count Bernadotte, the head of the Swedish Red Cross, was at this time using the airfield to fly back and forth between Sweden and Germany for secret negotiations with Heinrich Himmler, who hoped to extract a separate surrender. The Count, and his chauffeur, narrowly escaped death during the attack.

Also on the night of 19/20 April Flight Lieutenant "Podge" Howard DFC and Flying Officer Frank "Sticky" Clay DFC of BSDU returned triumphant to Swanton Morley from a patrol to South Denmark and Island of Fyn airfields in a NF.XXX with a claim for a Ju 88.

Further napalmgel attacks were carried out on 22/23 April. Jägel was attacked by NF.XXXs of 141 Squadron. Three Mosquitoes of 169 Squadron and four Mosquitoes of

515 Squadron, led by Master Bomber Squadron Leader J. H. Penny and Flying Officer J. H. Whitfield, dropped green TIs and incendiaries. Flak greeted them, and a 141 Squadron Mosquito flown by Flight Lieutenant G. M. Barrowman and Warrant Officer H. S. Griffiths suffered severe damage in the starboard wing and inner fuel tank. They returned to England hugging the German and Dutch coasts, keeping the Friesians in sight to port, and landed safely at Woodbridge. Five Mosquitoes of 23 Squadron with napalm tanks, and five Mosquitoes of 23 Squadron with Squadron Leader H. V. Hopkins as Master Bomber bombed Westerland airfield on Sylt. Hopkins, aware that his TIs would not be seen because of the thick cloud over the target, instructed the Deputy Master Bomber to drop incendiaries. By 23 April the British Second Army had arrived opposite Hamburg, and on the next day its advanced units were on the west bank of the Elbe ready for the last thrust to Lübeck and Kiel. On 23 April, as part of the support operation for the ground troops, five Mosquitoes of 23 Squadron flew to Melsbroek with six napalm Mosquitoes of 141 Squadron led by Wing Commander Winnie Winn refueled and crossed to Lübeck. That night they plastered the airfield with HE, incendiaries, and firebombs under the direction of Master Bomber Squadron Leader D. I. Griffiths of 23 Squadron. The whole attack took just ten minutes; the airfield was left burning and devastated. All aircraft returned safely despite light, accurate flak put up by the defenders. That same night thirty Mosquitoes and seven Lancasters dropped leaflets over eight PoW camps. The war was drawing to a close, and the morale of the men behind the wire soared, while at home some worried that there would be no more opportunities to fly their Mosquitoes in anger.

On 24/25 April six Mosquitoes of 141 Squadron carried out a napalm attack on München/Neubiberg airfield again. The 515 Squadron Master Bomber, Squadron Leader J. H. Penny and Flying Officer J. H. Whitfield, again marked for them; other 515 Squadron aircraft flew support. During the patrol Flight Lieutenant J. Davis and Flying Officer B. R. Cronin claimed eight enemy aircraft damaged on the ground during their six strafing and bombing runs with two 500lb and eighty 5lb incendiaries over Kaufbeuren airfield. The aircraft were in the moon shadow of the hangar and positive identification was therefore impossible. A fire broke out in the hangar and could be seen through the open doors. Meanwhile, at Neubiberg, Squadron Leader Harry White DFC** and Flight Lieutenant Mike Allen DFC** also claimed the destruction of a single-engined enemy aircraft on the ground; it was also the last recorded victory for 141 Squadron in WWII. White and Allen dropped their napalm bombs with the safety pins still in, but they exploded on impact and caused "a good fire." White and Allen landed at their forward base at Juvincourt, an area they had patrolled in Beaufighters from August 1943. Wing Commander Howard C. Kelsey DFC* and Flight Lieutenant E. M. Smith DFC DFM of 515 Squadron destroyed a Dornier Do 217 at Libeznice, six miles north of Prague. They thus earned the distinction of getting the first (23/24 December 1943) and the last air to air victories in 100 Group.

On 25/26 April the *Firebash* Mosquitoes attacked München/Reim airfield while four Mosquitoes of 515 Squadron, with Lieutenant Wally Barton SAAF as Master Bomber, attacked Landsberg airfield. Mosquitoes of 169 Squadron also took part in the raid on Landsberg. Flying Officer J. K. "Sport" Rogers, navigator to Flight Lieutenant Phil Kelshall, recalls:

> "For this operation we flew to RAF Oulton where our drop tanks were filled napalm. We returned to Massingham where the aircraft, a FB.VI (224) was armed with two 500lb bombs and cannons loaded with ammo. In the afternoon we flew to Juvincourt where we refueled and waited for nightfall - the operation took place in moonlight, so navigation was easy. We flew at low level and made initial rendezvous with all the other aircraft at the north end of the Ammer Lake and checked in with Master Bomber.
>
> "At the agreed time made by the Master Bomber we made rendezvous over the airfield. We had all been assigned a call sign in numerical order. At the appropriate time, the Master Bomber called in the first aircraft to drop napalm tanks - calling '01 clear' as it dropped its tanks and then at ten second intervals the remainder of the aircraft followed to drop their napalm tanks. This routine was adopted to avoid collision over the target area, which in this raid were the hangars and adjacent aircraft parking areas, which had been previously illuminated with flares and target markers. Also in attendance were anti-flak aircraft to suppress the flak. Having dropped the napalm, we returned to orbit the airfield and when the last aircraft had completed its drop of napalm, the Master Bomber called for the 500lb bombs to be dropped in the same sequence as before. Having completed the bomb-drop and again returned to orbit, the Master Bomber called for cannon fire, again in the same sequence - the target area was a mass of flame by this time and the cannons were used to spray the area in the pass over the target. This completed the operation and we returned to Juvincourt -elapsed time three hours forty minutes - where we stayed the night and returned to Massingham the next day."

On 26 April another consignment of 100-gallon drop tanks arrived at West Raynham. Word spread quickly that a final *Firebash* fling was in the offing. On 2 May the British Second Army, having crossed the Elbe, now moved on to Lübeck, and units of the British 6th Airborne Division reached Wismar, on the Baltic, and made contact with the Russian Army. The war was all over bar the shouting, but Leslie Holland in 515 Squadron wrote:

> "May 2nd and still, as far as we were concerned, there was no let up in the determination to break the regime that had been our mortal enemy for so long. Crusaderish? It was a pretty general feeling among aircrews at that time now that the end was in sight. With only five days to go before VE Day 515 undertook just one more very hairy job."

Large convoys of ships were now assembling at Kiel, on the Baltic, and it was feared that they were to transport German troops to Norway to continue the fight from there. It was decided, therefore, that Mosquitoes of Bomber Command should attack Kiel on 2/3 May, and this would be the very last operation of the war for Bomber Command. Some 126 Mosquitoes from 8 Group would follow in the wake of sixteen Mosquitoes of 8 Group. Thirty-seven Mosquitoes of 23, 169, 141, and 515 Squadrons in 100 Group would make attacks on airfields at Flensburg, Hohn, Westerland/Sylt, and Schleswig/Jägel. Hohn and Flensburg airfields would be bombed with Napalm and incendiaries directed by a Master Bomber. Support for the night's operations would be provided by twenty-one *Mandrel*/Window sorties by 199 Squadron Halifaxes, while eleven Fortresses of 214 Squadron and nine B-17s/B-24s of 223 Squadron would fly Window/jamming sorties over the Kiel area. At Foulsham, ten Halifaxes of 462 Squadron would carry out a *Spoof* operation with Window and bombs against Flensburg, while some of the nineteen Halifaxes of 192 Squadron carried out a radio search in the area. Others were to drop "Window" and TIs, and some also carried eight 500lb bombs. Five Mosquitoes of 192 Squadron were also engaged in radio frequency work.

At North Creake, Air Vice Marshal Addy Addison was present during the take off of thirty-eight aircraft of the Southern Window Force of eighteen Halifaxes from 171 Squadron and ten from 199 Squadron, also heading for Kiel on *Mandrel/* Window operations. Addison expressed his satisfaction at the size of the final effort. All told, a record 106 aircraft of 100 Group took part. Eight NF.XXXs of 239 Squadron took off from West Raynham for high-level and low-level raids on airfields in Denmark and Germany, while six Mosquitoes of 141 Squadron were to make napalm attacks on Flensburg airfield, with fourteen napalm-armed Mosquitoes attacking Hohn airfield. Master of Ceremonies at Flensburg would be Flying Officer E. L. Heath of 23 Squadron, while Master Bomber at Hohn was Squadron Leader D. I. Griffiths. Four Mosquitoes of 23 Squadron would drop incendiaries on Flensburg prior to the arrival by 141 Squadron, and seven more from 23 Squadron would bomb Hohn with incendiaries before the arrival of 141 Squadron's Mosquitoes. Meanwhile, 169 Squadron's Mosquitoes, plus four from 515 Squadron with Flight Lieutenant McEwan as Master Bomber and Flying Officer Barnes would raid Jägel. Four other Mosquitoes of 515 Squadron, with Wing Commander Howard Kelsey as Master Bomber, would drop incendiaries on Westerland airfield on Sylt.

Dutch Holland, in 515 Squadron, has written:

> "Just what was brewing at the Westerland I have never been able to find out precisely. It couldn't have been that it was a particularly active night-fighter base because I don't remember any patrols being assigned there, but it was believed that suicide missions were being planned by the Luftwaffe, presumably against heads of state or centers of government. Whatever it was it must have been something out of the ordinary to make it necessary to try and burn up everything on it. At the briefing it was announced that a new type of bomb would be used, referred to as 'thermite'. It was a 50-gallon cylinder carried on the wing racks. A warning was given that it would ignite on contact and great care must be exercised not to cause premature ignition. In other words 'For God's sake don't have a prang with these on board!' Each aircraft was detailed to take up an assigned position round the island at a designated time; great emphasis on the time. At a given signal the attack would commence with a bomb run by the Commanding Officer, followed by the rest at very short intervals, criss-crossing the field from different directions at height intervals of 50 feet. Bob and I were to come in No.3 at 150 feet.
>
> "It was still full daylight when we left Little Snoring in a loose gaggle, each making for his own pinpoint and ETA and there was still enough light to make out the odd island as we approached Sylt. A marker was to be dropped on one of them to ensure complete synchronization at the target. All aircraft duly arrived at their stations and the minutes began to drag by. For some reason Kelsey wasn't ready to open the attack and we were acutely aware that immediately the airfield became encircled by orbiting aircraft the Jerries must have been fully alerted and dashed out to man every gun on the place. The covers were off and there was one up the spout of every weapon they possessed when the cue to start was finally given. I don't know what form the signal took, as I was too uptight to record an impression. The runs were to follow in very quick succession a matter of seconds only and after that each aircraft was to engage the defenses.
>
> "The first one in was greeted by a cone of tracer that looked like a tent of sparks flying upwards, meeting and then spreading like the poles of a teepee. Thinking to take advantage of their diverted attention I cut in at full belt to cross the airfield, heading for some large hangars clearly visible in the southeast side but by the time we were half way, the whole shower swung in our direction. Things happened pretty fast from then on. I pressed the release when I judged the aim about right and almost immediately as we turned sharply away the whole hangar erupted in an enormous ball of fire out of the roof, doors and windows. I couldn't help hoping even at that moment that there was nobody in it but all else was driven from our minds by a sharp BONK in the tail, at which the aircraft began to vibrate violently and the stick to try and shake itself out of my hand. (The cause of the vibration was that the starboard elevator had been shot through at the spar and the resulting overbalance was causing a flutter It was gradually coming and just lasted out the return to Snoring.)
>
> "Clearly this was no time to think about giving supporting fire, which turned out to be about as dangerous from risk of collision as from flak. So we excused ourselves and informed the assembled host that we had been hit and were pulling out. Still at about 100 feet we turned seawards and immediately found ourselves flying horizontally down the beams of a battery of searchlights. If they did shoot anything further in our direction we were heartily glad not to see any tracer probably on account of the brightness of the lights. There was a bank of mist offshore a mile or two and the shadows of our aircraft in several discs of light were plain to see on its surface. Anything in the way of violent evasive action was out of the question and the minute it took to reach cover seemed like an hour. Losing all visual references on entering the mist then rendered us dependent on instruments, which were all snaking about so much that only the artificial horizon could be seen at all clearly. However, taking stock and realizing that apart from whatever was causing the alarming vibration, all else seemed to be more or less in order. We found that by reducing speed down to about 150 mph it was possible to gain a little height and think about a course for home. Bob, I may say, appeared to remain unperturbed throughout apart from impolite observations about the parentage of some anti-aircraft personnel."

Kel Purdie, a navigator/radar operator in 515 Squadron, who like his pilot, Jack Flanagan, was a New Zealander, recalls:

"Jägel was more hair-raising than anything that had gone before and having regard to the state of the war, seemed to us to be rather pointless and fraught with danger which we did not want at that stage. From recent experience we knew that German ground defenses had been concentrated in the small area of northern Germany still held by the Germans, with all the airfields bristling with AA defenses. This was to be a mass attack by three squadrons. Jack and I circled in our holding position waiting for our call from the master bomber. At one stage there was a large oily explosion on the airfield, which looked like a plane going in and this did nothing to calm the jitters. In due course we received our call and Jack carried out his usual dive bombing routine, going in at plus 12 boost. As we approached the perimeter the flak ahead was intense and suddenly Jack pulled away and told the master bomber that he would make a second run. He remarked to me that with so much flak coming up ahead of us he did not like our chances, so on his next call he opened up through the gate to plus 18 from a slightly higher altitude and in we went. This time most of the flak was coming up behind us and we made it through without a scratch - and so we began the long haul home across the North Sea. I could not help but wonder if Jack's action in aborting the first run had kept us off the casualty list. In fact, one plane was lost, two came home on one engine and others were damaged."

Warrant Officer Les Turner, who made the trip with Flight Lieutenant Jimmy Wheldon as navigator, recalls:

"By now I had enough of destruction and, while I could see the surrounding buildings, I decided to drop the Napalm on the airfield. The war was obviously not going to last much longer. The opposition was quite intense and as I followed Flying Officer Keith Miller (later to become famous as an Australian Test cricketer) the light flak aimed at him was passing worryingly close to us. One of Keith's drop-tanks hung up and slewed him to starboard. But for this he reckoned that he would have got caught in the flak.[340] As it was we regrettably lost one of our crews - such a waste so near the end. During the napalmgel attack on Jägel, Flying Officer Robert Catterall DFC and Flight Sergeant Donald Joshua Beadle of 169 Squadron were killed when their Mosquito was shot down by flak. During a run on Westerland, a Mosquito in 515 Squadron flown by Flight Lieutenant Johnson and Flying Officer Thomason was hit but the pilot landed safely at Woodbridge on one engine."[341]

Leslie Holland of 515 Squadron recalls:

"There followed three weeks of flights to observe bomb damage in Germany and a few practice flights before 515 broke up and we took our aircraft up to Silloth and left them forlornly standing in a row. That flight doesn't appear in my logbook. While the House of Commons was being told on the afternoon of the 7th that cessation of hostilities was imminent, they may have heard a Mossie go over at 500 feet. If they or the milkman whose horse gave him a bit of trouble at Sudbury Hill wondered who was the lunatic up there, well, now they know."

Les Turner adds:

"On the day before VE Day we did a sight-seeing tour covering Aachen, Cologne, Dusseldorf, the Mohne Dam, Dortmund and Duisburg. The destruction was appalling and a sense of the terrible waste hung over a number of us over the Victory celebration days. We repeated the trip a week later - it was for the (?) benefit of ground crews who had, of course, seen nothing of this. We did some desultory flying throughout June and I last flew a Mosquito on 17 July 1945. One of my duties on 169 Squadron was to collect, on his return from PoW release, Pilot Officer (then Flying Officer) Miller, who had the successes in May 1944 and had subsequently been shot down. I flew the Oxford very carefully. The responsibility of getting him back safely seemed very great indeed. My total flying time on Mosquitoes was 350 hours, the majority at night."

"Dutch" Holland concludes:

"May 9th dawned bright and clear with only one drawback. I was orderly officer. I was awakened by a sergeant of RAF Police standing beside my bed staring straight ahead through the peak of his cap announcing that it was believed that an officer from Little Snoring had made off with the Union Jack, which had been flying at the King's Lynn Steam Laundry. If it were returned, no more would be said. If the sergeant would give me a few minutes I would join him in the search for said item. He dutifully departed and as I was hoisting myself out of the pit, noticed that my bed had for a quilt a very large Union Jack. It was quite a night."

During 25 June-7 July 1945 Exercise *Post-Mortem* was carried out to evaluate the effectiveness of RAF jamming and *Spoof* operations on the German early warning radar system. Simulated attacks were made by aircraft from four RAF groups, including 100 Group, the early warning radar being manned by American and British personnel on this occasion. *Post-Mortem* proved conclusively that the countermeasures had been a great success.

On 25 June Tim Woodman flew to Germany and Denmark with Flight Lieutenants Neville and Bridges:

"At Grove I was walking back across the airfield after inspecting some of their aircraft when I passed four Luftwaffe airwomen in white shorts and grey skirts. Typical frauleins. They stood smartly to attention but looked pretty boot-faced at having lost the war. 'OK sweethearts,' I said, Your time will come again.' How right I was.

"But what disasters they must have gone home to."

100 Group was disbanded on 17 December 1945. While it had developed electronic warfare to an almost state-of-the-art technology in just 18 months, its Mosquito force had accounted for many valuable German night-fighters and airfields.

Chapter 13

2nd TAF and The German Winter of Discontent

My mistress is the sky,
She calls forever "Fly".
Often she treated me shamefully –
Tried putting me to the core
Yet still I cry for more
And yearn for her embrace,
Her clear and open face
Above the cloud and rain
O let me fly again.

My Mistress,
Jasper Miles

From 1943 to 1945 Mosquito FB.VI, and later NF.XII and NF.XIII squadrons, in 2nd Tactical Air Force also intruded over the Reich, bombing and strafing German lines of communication and *Luftwaffe* airfields. In 2nd TAF the FB.VI is probably best remembered for daylight precision operations, particularly pinpoint raids on *Gestapo* buildings in occupied Europe. 2 Group had been transferred to 2nd TAF on 1 June 1943. Air Vice Marshal Basil Embry replaced Air Vice Marshal d'Albiac at HQ, Bylaugh Hall, with the task of preparing 2 Group for invasion support in the run-up to Operation *Overlord*: the invasion of France. Embry was an excellent choice for the newfound role. He successfully fought off an attempt to re-equip 2 Group with Vultee Vengeance dive-bombers and saw to it that his Lockheed Ventura-equipped squadrons were re-equipped with the Mosquito FB.VI, which was armed with four cannon for night *Intruder* operations.

Re-equipment began in August 1943 with 140 Wing at Sculthorpe, when 464 RAAF and 487 RNZAF Squadrons exchanged their obsolete Lockheed machines. 21 Squadron closely followed them; in September, all three squadrons moving to Hunsdon in December 1943. On 15 October 138 Wing at Lasham began operating FB.VIs when 613 (City of Manchester) Squadron joined 2 Group. In December 305 (Polish) Squadron converted from the Mitchell, and in February 1944 107 Squadron converted from the Douglas Boston. It was planned to transfer 138 Wing to airfields in France when the outbreak from the Normandy beachhead came. Early in 1944 85 (Base) Group was formed for the purpose of providing fighter cover over the continent leading up to and after *D-Day* by the transfer from Fighter Command to 2nd TAF of 29, 264, 409 "Nighthawk" RCAF, 410 "Cougar" Squadron RCAF, 488 RNZAF, and 604 Squadrons. In January 1944 the first to transfer to 85 Group was 264 Squadron, which went to 141 Wing. (The last, 219 Squadron, would transfer from Fighter Command to 147 Wing on 26 August.) As part of the newfound offensive, the main work for the FB.VIs of 138 and 140 Wings was *Day* and *Night Ranger* operations and *Intruder* sorties from England.

One of the Mosquito intruder pilots at this time was American 1st Lieutenant James Forrest "Lou" Luma[342] of 418 (City of Edmonton) Squadron RCAF, stationed at Ford, Sussex. Luma recalls:

"Ford was located on the beautiful south coast of England. Like many RAF aerodromes, it consisted of two paved runways at right angles to each other. Circling the perimeter of the aerodrome was a paved taxiway. The aircraft were parked in blast bays located outside this perimeter. Blast bays were 'U'-shaped revetments that protected the aircraft from all but a direct hit by a bomb. The blast bays were in clusters with a taxiway leading from each cluster to the perimeter taxiway. The taxiways and runways were lighted at night but only when aircraft were using them. Life at Ford was good. We had a comfortable officer's mess and were billeted in private homes that had been taken over by the government. We had our own rooms and were awakened and brought tea in the morning by a batman, who was a RAF enlisted man.

"418 Squadron consisted of 'A' Flight and 'B' Flight, which alternated duty. Fin [Colin Finlayson] and I were posted to 'A' Flight. The squadron's Mosquitoes had the paintings of Al Capp's *'Li'l Abner'* characters on them; each aircraft had a different character from Dogpatch. The aircraft that was assigned to Fin and me - *'D for Dog'* - had a painting of *Moonbeam McSwine* on it.

"Sometimes when we were on standby, we would conduct a night-flying test. Fin and I would fly the airplane for 30 minutes or so to determine its mechanical fitness. Sometimes we would also practice air-to-air gunnery, using a camera gun. At other times we would do an in-flight compass swing. After landing we would leave our parachutes and helmets in the seats in order to save time in case of a scramble. The 'erks' (ground crew) would correct any mechanical problems we might have experienced and would top off the fuel tanks. The erks were a hard-working, dedicated, loyal part of the team, and they did not receive the recognition they deserved. At least not from me. I was too young and egotistical to think that anyone other than myself was contributing to any success that I might achieve.

"After we had finished our night-flying test, we would have supper at the officers' mess before reporting in at the ops room for the night's duty. The ops room was a medium-size room with reasonably comfortable chairs to lounge in while we were on standby. It had planning tables for the navigators, and the walls were plastered with silhouettes of German aircraft for boning up on aircraft recognition. We killed time by reading, talking, and listening to the radio. Sometimes we would listen to the English-speaking 'Lord Haw Haw,' who broadcast Nazi propaganda from Germany. The music on his station was usually better than what the BBC offered.

"Usually we were given our targets as soon as we arrived at the ops room, and would plan our flight accordingly. At other times, we reported to the ready room and remained there on standby, waiting for a scramble. We were dressed and ready to go. Pilots had flying gloves made of thin chamois that fit tightly to the hands. The preferred style of flying boots had a dress shoe on the foot with fleece-lined uppers. In the event you baled out over occupied territory, you would cut off the uppers after you were on the ground by using a small knife carried in a pocket in the boots. This left you with black, low-cut dress shoes that could pass as part of your civilian attire when being helped by the Underground to get out of the country. Each crewmember carried a packet containing the currency of the country they would be flying over (usually French francs) and a map printed on cloth."

Luma carried out his most memorable flight on the night of 21/22 January when 648 bombers attacked Magdeburg. (Berlin was also bombed in a diversionary raid by Lancasters and Mosquitoes and flying bomb sites were also hit.) Luma's 17th operation was the one that entitled him and his navigator to have their first swastika painted on the side of their FB.VI, as he recalls;

"My navigator, Fin was sick so another navigator, Flight Lieutenant Al Eckert, was assigned to my plane. We took off from Ford at 2215 hours on a *Flower* to Hildesheim, Germany, near Hanover. By now ops were pretty much routine for me. On each of my early flights I fully expected that I would see an enemy aircraft but it didn't happen. Now I was pretty much resigned to the fact that I might put in a whole tour without ever seeing an enemy aircraft. It was possible; some of our crews did come up scoreless. When Al and I took off, there was no reason to believe that this wouldn't be just another uneventful op. The weather was sour with a lot of low cloud and haze, which made navigation difficult. We reached an airfield that was lighted with perimeter lights. After orbiting the airfield we found a pinpoint that fixed the airfield as Wunstorf. Shortly after that we saw two bright lights on the other side of the airfield. We came in to meet them very nearly head-on. They proved to be on an aircraft that had just taken off from the base. We were at 1500 feet and the enemy aircraft passed over us at 2000 feet. As he passed over us we identified him as a twin-engine aircraft with one white light just under the nose and one under the tail.

"We did a quick orbit to port, coming in behind him and chased him for 15 to 20 miles. As we closed, he was climbing through about 4000 feet. In my excitement at seeing my first enemy aircraft, I very possibly came close to losing the opportunity to chalk up my first kill. I had overestimated our closing speed and overshot him. As I threw down the landing gear to slow us down, the thought that my buck fever was going to cost me the chance of destroying my first enemy aircraft left me with a sick feeling in the pit of my stomach. With the gear down, the Mossie rapidly slowed but we were still not in a position to shoot at him. We were directly below him. By now the nervous excitement had disappeared. I did a quick turn to port, followed by one to starboard. This brought us under his tail - about 500 feet below and 250 to 100 yards behind. I was calm, and I knew we had him in the bag. We were in position. I pulled back on the stick, placed the center of the gunsight slightly forward of and midway between the points where the exhaust flames emerged from the engines. Then I fired all my cannon and machine guns. Strikes on the fuselage were followed by a big ball of fire, which enabled us to identify the aircraft as a Me-210. A large piece broke off to the left and he went down. Al Eckert saw him go in, explode and burn on the ground. After our return to base the erks found two pieces of plywood from the enemy aircraft embedded in the leading edge of the Mosquito's starboard wing.

"Not long after destroying the Me-210 there was an article in the Air Ministry Weekly Intelligence Summary about a Luftwaffe ace by the name of Major Prinz Heinrich zu Sayn-Wittgenstein, a highly decorated Luftwaffe night-fighter pilot who was killed in air combat on the night of 21/22 January 1944. The Intelligence Summary went on to say that he had shot down 83 aircraft. It also said he had shot down five RAF aircraft within a few hours of meeting his death. I found it interesting that I was the only RAF/RCAF pilot who had shot down an enemy over the Continent that night."[343]

In the 2nd TAF the FB.VI carried out precision attacks, often on individual buildings, by day and night. Probably the most famous of these was Operation *Jericho*, which went ahead on 18 February 1944 after snowstorms and thick cloud had led to several postponements. In January information had been received in London that over 100 loyal Frenchmen, among them Monsieur Vivant, a key Resistance leader in Abbeville, were being held in captivity in Amiens prison. Several attempts by the Resistance had been made to rescue them but had failed. Dominique Ponchardier, the leader of the local Resistance, requested an urgent air strike to break open the prison walls. There would be casualties, but better to die from RAF bombs than be shot by a German firing squad. A dozen prisoners were due to be executed on 19 February. The prison was built in the shape of a cross and surrounded by a wall 20 feet high and 3 feet thick. The plan was to breach this wall by using 11-second bombs dropped by five FB.VIs of 464 RAAF led by Wing Commander R. W. "Bob" Iredale and six 487 Squadron RNZAF led by Wing Commander Irving S. "Black" Smith. The concussion from the bomb explosions should open the cell doors to give most of the prisoners a chance to escape. Wing Commander "Black" Smith recalled: "After four years of war just doing everything possible to destroy life, here we were going to use our skill to save it. It was a grand feeling and everybody left the briefing room prepared to fly into the walls rather than fail to breach them." If the first two waves of Mosquitoes failed, six FB.VIs of 21 Squadron led by Wing Commander I. G. "Daddy" Dale had orders to flatten the prison complex.

Embry was forbidden to go on the raid because of his previous exploits in France, and Group Captain Percy C. Pickard DSO DFC, CO 140 Wing, was in overall command of the raid. He and his navigator, Flight Lieutenant J. A. "Peter" Broadley DSO DFC DFM, flew in *F-Freddie* (HX922), a 487 Squadron Mosquito, and flew with the 464 Squadron formation. (Pickard, a brave and revered leader, as a Flight Lieutenant he, Wellington, and *F-Freddie* had appeared in the British wartime film *Target for Tonight*.) Corporal Ralph Hunt, a wireless operator-mechanic at Hunsdon who carried out the Daily Inspection (DI) on the Mosquitoes, making sure his CO's GEC VHF set was in "bloody good order," remembers, "He was always smoking his pipe like a factory chimney, but in a hangar one day he'd ticked off an erk for smoking a cigarette!"

Flight Lieutenant Tony Wickham, in DZ414/O, a specially equipped Film Photographic Unit Mosquito IV with a cameraman, Pilot Officer Leigh Howard, would film the bombing operation. Typhoon IBs of 174 (Mauritius) Squadron and 245 (Northern Rhodesia) Squadron at Westhampnett were detailed to provide the Mosquitoes with escort cover.

The formation of 19 Mosquitoes took off from Hunsdon at 1055 hours with snow falling and headed for their rendezvous with the Typhoons over Littlehampton. Over the Channel the weather improved, but by then Flight Lieutenant E. E. Hogan and Flight Sergeant D. A. S. Crowfoot, and Flight Sergeant A. Steadman and Pilot Officer E. J. Reynolds, in 21 Squadron, were forced to return. Two Typhoons in 245 Squadron aborted with fuel problems and 174 Squadron failed to make the rendezvous at all. About 10 miles from the target Flight Lieutenant B. D. "Titch" Hanafin and Pilot Officer C. F. Redgrave of 487 Squadron RNZAF were forced to abort because of an engine fire. The remaining Mosquitoes descended to 100 feet, and they pressed on at no higher than tree top level, avoiding power lines and known flak batteries. The formation swept around to the south of Albert, and the crews picked up the long, straight tree-lined road to Amiens. Descending to 10 feet, their propellers swirled wispy snow clouds in their wake. The poplars on the road ended abruptly and a mile in the distance the prison stood out in fresh snow. The Mosquitoes split up and attacked in four waves from two directions at 1201 hours, precisely as the guards were eating their lunch.

The first bombs were dropped on the outer walls on the east and north sides of the prison by the four 487 Squadron FB.VIs led by Wing Commander "Black" Smith. The five FB.VIs of 464 Squadron and Pickard's Mosquito closely followed them. Their target was the main building, and the guards' quarters at the east and west ends of the prison. Eight Typhoons of 174 Squadron provided escort over the target while six Typhoons of 245 Squadron covered Wing Commander Daddy Dale's four remaining 21 Squadron Mosquitoes, which orbited ten miles to the north, ready if needed. The first bombs blew in almost all of the doors and the wall was breached. Wing Commander R. W. "Bob" Iredale said later, "I pinpointed the guards' quarters, let go my bombs so that they would skid right into the annex, with the sloping roof of the prison inches from the belly of my plane as I climbed over it." Flight Lieutenant Tony Wickham made three passes over the ruined jail, which was now disgorging smoke and flame and fleeing men, and Pilot Officer Leigh Howard filmed the flight of the prisoners.

Pickard was the last over the prison and, after dropping his bombs, he circled the area at 500 feet to assess the results. Satisfied that the Mosquitoes had done their work, the success signal *RED-RED-RED* was radioed to Daddy Dale so that they could return home. Almost immediately Fw 190s of II/JG26 attacked the Mosquitoes and took on the Typhoons. *Feldwebel* Wilhelm Mayer[344] singled out *F-Freddie* and sent it crashing in flames, and Pickard and Broadley were killed. Leutnant Waldemar "Waldi" Radener of 7./JG26 shot down a Typhoon flown by Flying Officer J. E. Renaud north of Amiens, and the pilot was taken prisoner. Squadron Leader Ian McRitchie and Flight Lieutenant R. W. "Sammy" Sampson's Mosquito in 464 Squadron RAAF was downed by flak. The Australian second flight leader was wounded in 26 places and he crash-landed at over 200 mph near Poix. McRitchie survived and was taken prisoner, but Sampson was dead. Hanafin, meanwhile, was limping home on one engine. He was again hit by flak, which paralyzed one side of his body. He was met and escorted home by "Black" Smith, and he made a perfect landing at a forward airfield in England. Foul weather over the Channel claimed another Typhoon flown by Flight Sergeant H. S. Brown.

Corporal Hunt remembers the "general air of sadness" back at Hunsdon: "Everyone was miserable. We went into mourning. It was a sad night, but at a meeting we were told that we must carry on. When you are 20 years old, like I was, it was 'tough luck'; but when someone didn't come back the attitude was always, 'it's him and not me.'" Group Captain Peter Wykeham-Barnes DSO DFC* became the new 140 Wing Commander.

In March 1944 Dominique Ponchardier sent the following message to London:

> "I thank you in the name of our comrades for the bombardment of the prison. We were not able to save all. Thanks to the admirable precision of the attack the first bomb blew in nearly all the doors and 150 prisoners escaped with the help of the civilian population. Of these, twelve were to have been shot on February 19. In addition, 37 prisoners were killed; some of them by German machine guns, and 50 Germans were also killed."

On 15 February George Murray and Harry Batt and Gordon Bell-Irving[345] and Bert Hott and Flight Lieutenant J. L. "Les" Bulmer, navigator, and his pilot, Flight Lieutenant Ed McQuarrie RCAF, had joined 21 Squadron at Hunsdon. This was a surprise to them for, having completed the *Night Intruder* course at 60 OTU High Ercall, they expected to join one of the three *Intruder* squadrons: 418 (City of Edmonton) Squadron RCAF, 605 (both in the UK), or 23 in Malta. Les Bulmer remembers the move:

"When we joined 21 Squadron's principal occupation was attacking V1 (*Noball*) sites at low level. We had no experience of low-level navigation so we spent all of February practising low-level cross-country and formation flying. On 18 February we watched all three squadrons of the wing take off in a snowstorm for what we later discovered was the Amiens prison raid. The only time I saw the 140 Wing CO, Group Captain Charles Pickard, was in the Mess the night before the raid. The whole squadron was sworn to secrecy when we heard he was missing in case he had got away but it was not long before we received news that he was dead."

Flight Lieutenants Les Bulmer and Ed McQuarrie RCAF flew their first 21 Squadron operation, a *Night Intruder*, to the airfield at Montdidier on 2 March:

"Although we were new boys, because we'd been trained as *Night Intruders* we had more night-flying experience on Mosquitoes than the old hands. We took off at 1955 and returned at 2155. It was uneventful. I was not sure what to expect as we crossed the French coast but I rather imagined it would be flak and searchlights all the way in and all the way out. Instead there was just total darkness, with the odd glimmer of a light and nobody seemed to be interested in us at all - or was a night-fighter creeping up on us? I kept constant lookout rearwards. The night was very dark and *Gee* was jammed once we crossed the coast, so navigation had to be by dead reckoning. We were somewhere in the area but could not locate the airfield and the Germans would not co-operate and put on the lights for us, so we returned home somewhat disappointed.

"2 Group Mosquitoes tried various techniques in attacking *Noball* sites. The normal method was to go low-level all the way but this had resulted in aircraft sustaining damage by 20mm flak when crossing the coast. On 4 March we were one of four aircraft to attack two sites. Our target was near Esclavelles and we took off at 0810. *Noball* targets were far too small to get four aircraft over them within eleven seconds, which was the delay we had on the 500lb bombs. The squadron CO, Wing Commander 'Daddy' Dale, led with 'A' Flight Commander Squadron Leader Joe Bodien as his No.2. As a 'sprog' crew we were to stick with Flight Lieutenant Mike Benn, who was one of the squadron's most experienced pilots.[346]

"We crossed the Channel at low level and climbed as we reached the coast to about 3000 feet to avoid the flak. There we split into pairs for our respective targets and got down on the deck. Not long afterwards I noticed a red glow on the edge of a wood on the starboard side. This became several red balls that traveled rapidly towards us. It was then that I realized what flak looked like from the wrong end. The stream of 20mm appeared to be heading along the wing and into the cockpit, so Mac and I instinctively ducked. Luckily it passed overhead and we went thankfully on our way.

"At briefing we had arranged to fly beyond the target, turn and attack on the way out. We arrived at the turning point but nothing happened. There was strict radio silence so we couldn't ask Mike and his navigator, Flying Officer W. A. Roe what they were doing. We just had to stick with them and hope that they knew where they were. Eventually they did start to turn and all hell broke loose. In fact, Roe had missed the turning point and when he did eventually start to turn he led us into a real hornet's nest. Everything happened so fast but we suddenly found ourselves in a valley with a railway in the bottom and rows of huts up the valley sides. I don't know what the area was but they obviously objected to our presence and the sky erupted in 20mm flak from all directions. Mike Benn started to climb out of harm's way and we followed behind but were surrounded by streams of tracer and we had an uncomfortable few seconds when flak intended for Mike was crossing in front of our nose, while that for us was crossing just behind the tail. Mac said, 'Sod this, I'm going down" and shoved the stick forward. As he did so there was a loud bang. I checked to see if we were on fire or losing fuel but everything was normal.

"By this time we had lost sight of Mike Benn and were somewhere southeast of the target. If we tried to make the target on our own we might arrive just as his bombs were due to explode, so we headed for a secondary target in a wood. We duly dropped our four 500-pounders on a hut in the wood and fled at high speed towards the coast. We flew low over a large château outside which German troops were milling around, then I told Ed to climb before we hit the coast. Unfortunately I left it too late and we were on top of the coast as we started to climb. Up came the flak, hosing around us and down went the nose as we sped out to sea, weaving like mad and followed by the now all too familiar tracer. Soon we were clear and heading for home, somewhat relieved to find ourselves still in one piece.

"When we got back to Hunsdon we found that a 20mm shell had come up underneath us from the port and entered the starboard nacelle. It blew a large hole in the inboard side of the nacelle and a smaller one in the outboard side. Shell splinters had knocked chunks out of the starboard flap and out of the fuselage side just about where I was sitting. I was thankful that a Mosquito had a thick skin; if it had been metal I would probably have had a sore bum. The shell struck in the only part of the nacelle where it couldn't do any damage - in the rear fairing. Any further forward and it would have smashed the undercarriage.

"For another *Noball*, on 7 March, to near Les Essarts, our leader was Flight Lieutenant Duncan A. 'Buck' Taylor, with Squadron Leader Philippe Livry-Level as his navigator.[347] We decided to stay high after crossing the coast, identify the target, dive on it, then climb back up to 3000-4000 feet until clear of the coast on the way back. There was a flak position on the right of our approach to the target, so we arranged that we would both fire our cannons as we dived, hoping that this would make them keep their heads down until we were clear. Everything went according to plan and we arrived over the target and went into a steep dive, both of us firing cannons on the way down. There was no problem from the flak position but as we pulled out of the dive and released the bombs a burst of 20mm shot up vertically in front of us. Buck was clear but we had no choice but to fly through it. As we climbed away I looked back to see the whole site erupt as 4000lb of high explosive went off. I must say that I've always had a grudging admiration for the guy who shot at us. To be blasted with eight cannons and yet have the nerve to jump up and let fly at us, presumably aware that he was about to get eight 500lb bombs around his ear holes took some courage.

"Ed said, 'Check around. I think we've been hit.'

"There was so much racket from the cannons as we dived that I hadn't heard any bang but I checked for fire and loss of fuel. The fuel gauges were reading normal, so we joined up with Buck for the return trip. We climbed to 4000 feet and stayed there until clear of the coast, then dropped down to sea level over the Channel. Soon after we were clear of the French coast Buck's aircraft fired off a Very cartridge and he was obviously in trouble. I checked the list of the colors of the day but the one he'd used wasn't on it. We were puzzled and expected him to ditch at any moment but nothing happened. I tackled Philippe at debriefing and he explained that he had to have a smoke - he used a long cigarette holder - and since the designers of the Mosquito had forgotten to include an ashtray in the specification, he was forced to improvise. An empty Verey cartridge case would fill his requirements, so he emptied one! Smoking in or near an aircraft was strictly forbidden but Philippe was a law unto himself.

"Ed had been right in thinking that we'd been hit - a 20mm shell had exploded in the port spinner. It appeared that bits of it had gone rearwards through the engine, because the bottom cowling had a number of carbuncles that weren't there when we started. And yet the engine and propeller pitch mechanism had functioned perfectly, which gave me a great deal of confidence in the Merlin. I was beginning to think that if these sort of trips were the norm then sooner of later a shell would find a vital spot and our chances of completing a tour of ops looked none too promising. In the event these were the only times that we sustained damage although they weren't the only times the enemy took a dislike to us and let fly.

"Our next two ops were also against V1 sites but employed a very different technique. Six aircraft, in two vies of three, joined up with two Pathfinder Mosquitoes fitted with *Oboe,* at the coast. We followed the lead *Oboe* aircraft up to 20,000 feet while the second *Oboe* aircraft tagged along behind in case of equipment failure in the lead aircraft. We had an escort of six Spits, which was some comfort. The idea was that we would maintain close formation on the *Oboe* aircraft. His four bombs were set to drop in a stick and the boffins had calculated that, by the time the third bomb appeared out of the bomb bay, we would have woken up and released our bombs also. So the leader's third bomb was supposed to be on target, with the first two undershooting and the last one overshooting. The only snag with this system was that *Oboe* required that we fly in tight formation, straight and level for ten minutes until bomb release. This was not exactly amusing, since the Germans were somewhat hostile and slung a lot of heavy flak at us as we approached the target east of Abbeville. It was a long ten minutes, sitting there at 20,000 feet, having to take everything that was thrown at us and not being able to take avoiding action. You just prayed that your name was not on any of the bits of metal that were being flung into the sky. The Spits, wisely, kept well clear of the formation at this time, as did the stand-in *Oboe* aircraft, which only closed in tight at the last minute.

"With bombs gone we turned for home. From that height Dungeness looked so close. The rest of the formation had adopted a 'last man home's a sissy' attitude and were hell bent for the English coast. With wartime camouflage it was difficult to see an aircraft from above; it merged very effectively with the ground below. So suddenly Ed and I found ourselves all alone in the sky and, reckoning that we'd outstayed our welcome, stuck the nose down and went, hell for leather for Dungeness and safety. We were traveling so fast that even with the throttles right back and the undercarriage warning horn blowing continuously the ASI was indicating well over 300 mph. And I was wondering at what speed the wings came off. Part way across the Channel we caught up with another Mosquito and tried to maintain some form of decorum by flying in formation with him. One of the Spit escort managed to catch us up in mid-Channel and stayed with us until we crossed the Kent coast when he did a victory roll and headed for his base, wherever that was. At de-briefing the flight leader, Squadron Leader Ritchie issued a rocket. He said we'd behaved like naughty schoolboys who'd been breaking windows and then run away. I don't think we cared that much, as long as wed broken the right windows. Sadly, we hadn't. The much-vaunted *Oboe* had caused us to drop our bombs several miles, I believe, from the target. So, as a penance for our sins, we had to go out next day and do it all over again and this time we did all come back together. For the rest of March and the first half of April our ops were all *Night Intruders* on airfields in Holland and France. We never spotted any aircraft but we did bomb and strafe the runways and dispersals. At Evreux the Germans were most co-operative and switched the lights on for us. We made what we thought was a bombing attack - that is, until we got back to base and I got out to find a dark object hanging under each wing, which shouldn't have been there. Ed had forgotten to select the bombs."

The last raid on Hengelo by twelve Mosquitoes of 140 Wing, 2nd TAF took place on 18 March 1944. Although the Stork Works was no longer on the target list there was still the important target of Hazemeyer. The low-level raid was led by Wing Commander R. W. "Bob" Iredale DFC and involved four aircraft from each of 487 Squadron RNZAF, 464 Squadron RAAF, and 21 Squadron RAF at Hunsdon. A Mosquito of 487 Squadron aborted its sortie five miles SW of Lowestoft after an engine failure, while another hit a tree when it took evasive action to avoid hitting another Mosquito. Three remaining aircrews bombed the target at 16.36 hours and very good results were claimed. The whole area was seen to have numerous fires. 464 Squadron bombed a minute ahead of 21 Squadron, and crews succeeded in hitting the central part of the main building and setting it on fire. Fifteen-year old Henk F. van Baaren was among those who took shelter in the cellar at the family shop in Hengelo. He recalled:[348]

> "Some bombs fell in the town center, one killing a German officer in the street. A couple of houses were damaged and two civilians were reported as having been killed. After the raid I saw two girls running away from the bombed center area of the town. There was blood all over their faces and dresses but later I heard that they had been in a grocer's shop when the blast of the exploding bombs had blown debris from tomato juice and jam containers over them! Later when my father and I were talking together on the pavement in front of his shop window, there was a loud bang followed by the sound of broken glass. At that moment an ammunition train near the railway

> station exploded and the force of the huge blast blew out our shop window scattering glass all over us. Buildings in a large area around the station, including much of the main shopping center, the main offices of the Stork Works and other factories nearby had all their windows shattered. Two German guards were killed and a number of soldiers were injured. The German AA gunners, having been in action on the roof couldn't leave their positions after the bombing as numerous fires surrounded them. The German fire brigade arrived to rescue them but when they connected the hoses to the fire hydrant they couldn't get any water. They were rather irate and angry and accused the local firemen who were called in from other factories nearby of sabotaging the supply! Peace was eventually restored between the two parties and the AA crews were rescued. The fire brigade report reads: 48 250kg HE TD 11 bombs dropped of which forty were on target; twelve bombs hit the factory interior at 1636 hours after which the factory clocks stopped! It took until 3 am to extinguish the last of the fires in the factory."

464 Squadron had also bombed the primary target, but the Mosquito flown by Squadron Leader W. R. G. "Dick" Sugden and Flying Officer A. H. "Bunny" Bridger was hit by flak in the starboard engine, which caught fire. The Australian crew crash-landed in Albergen, not far from the target area, and they were slightly injured. Luckily Dutch farmers living nearby helped them out of the aircraft, but they were disturbed to discover that there were still bombs on board. Some Germans who quickly arrived on the scene took Sugden and Bridger prisoner. They were taken to hospital for a check up and three weeks later Sugden was sent by train to Amsterdam, and from there with a group of American aircrew to Frankfurt. He ended up in *Stalag Luft I* Barth, where he was reunited later with "Bunny" and with his former commander, Squadron Leader Ian McRitchie DFC, who had been shot down on the Amiens prison raid in February, which Sugden and Bridger had also flown. The Russians liberated all three airmen on 1 May 1945.

More low-level pinpoint daylight raids, for which 140 and 138 Wings would become legendary, took place in 1944. In April Mosquitoes of 2nd TAF were once again called upon to fly a very important low level strike mission, this time to Holland, when 613 Squadron, commanded by Wing Commander R. N. "Bob" Bateson DFC, was directed to bomb the "Huize Kleykamp" in The Hague. Before the war the five-story, 95 feet high white building on Carnegie Square had been used for art exhibitions. Now occupied by the *Gestapo*, it housed the Dutch Central Population Registry and duplicates of all legally issued Dutch personal identity papers so that identity cards falsified by the Dutch Underground could be checked and recognized as false. Jaap van der Kamp and a few other Underground members had managed to infiltrate the Bureau staff in the building and sketches of the interior layout and its immediate surroundings were prepared. The "*Huize Kleykamp*" was strongly defended day and night, and the ID card duplicates were stored in heavy metal cupboards so a raid by the Underground was just not possible. In mid-December 1943 London received word from Holland requesting that the building be destroyed from the air. It would be the most difficult job that a bomber squadron had ever had to face.

Light anti-aircraft weapons defended the "Huize Kleykamp," and it was tightly wedged among other houses in the Schevengsche Weg, which made accuracy very difficult, and heavy civilian causalities could be expected. By March 1944 there was no alternative; the building had to be destroyed. Planning for the raid therefore had to be meticulous. The attack would have to be carried out when the building was occupied on a working day so that the files would be open and the card indexes spread out on desks, otherwise they could not be destroyed by fire. The Dutch underground was not overly concerned with the deaths of the Kleykamp personnel, as they were regarded as collaborators anyway. Finally, the time of the attack was scheduled for midday so that most civilians would be off the streets and having lunch. A scale model of the building, perfect in every detail right down to the thickness and the composition of the walls, was built. Meanwhile, scientists developed a new bomb, a mixture of incendiary and high explosive, which was designed to have the maximum effect on the masses of *Gestapo* files and records. Bateson picked his crews carefully and put them through weeks of intensive training. Embry insisted that the mission could not go ahead until visibility of at least ten kilometers was available. At last, on Tuesday, 11 April, all was ready.

In the early morning Bateson led six Mosquitoes off from Lasham and set course very low over the North Sea to Holland with Spitfires for escort. The Mosquitoes climbed and flew a feint from the head of Goeree via Lehornhoven to the Reeuwijk Lakes, near Gouda. No.2 in the second pair led by Squadron Leader Charles Newman and Flight Lieutenant F. G. Trevers was Flight Lieutenant Ron Smith in HP927:

> "I was completely occupied in flying the aircraft at very low level in formation and listening to Flying Officer John Hepworth, my navigator, on what landmark to expect next. The way in was deliberately made very roundabout in order to confuse the enemy of our objective and to achieve maximum surprise."

As they approached the Dutch coast Bateson and his navigator, Flying Officer B. J. Standish, noticed something strange. There were no recognizable landmarks; they found themselves flying over a vast expanse of water, dotted with islands where no islands should have been. Unknown to the aircrew, the Germans had opened the sluice gates on the River Scheldt, inundating a large area of the flat Dutch countryside. There was relief all round when, after flying on for a few more minutes, they finally got their bearings and leaned that they were on track for the objective. As they approached The Hague the Mosquitoes split up into pairs, following in line astern, sweeping across the rooftops, the narrow streets shuddering to the din of their engines. Bateson and Flight Lieutenant Peter Cobley, the first two FB.VIs, lined up to attack while the other four circled Lake Gouda, allowing the 30-second 500lb delayed action bombs carried by the first two aircraft to explode. The third and fourth aircraft carried incendiary, and the fifth and sixth aircraft two HEs and two incendiary. Rob Cohen, an ex-student at the Delft Technical University who had escaped to England by canoe, flew one of these Mosquitoes. Bateson's Mosquito streaked towards the target, bomb doors open, its port wing tip missing the tall spire on top of the Peace Palace diagonally opposite the "*Huize Kleykamp*" by inches. Cobley, following Bateson, saw the leader's bombs drop away. He had a hazy impression of a German sentry throwing away his rifle and running for his life, and then he saw Bateson's three bombs quite literally skip through the front door and the large windows of the first floor of the building. A. Korthals Alter wrote later:

> "Immediately after there were two large explosions. A streetcar about to turn into the Javastraat, stopped and the conductor, driver and passengers ran for cover. At the corner of Scheveningsweg and Laan Copes van Cattenburgh people lay flat on the ground. The only sound that followed

after the explosions was that of broken glass and a dull rumbling noise resembling a distant thunderstorm. During the first few moments, people were so bewildered that no one uttered a sound. Only when the second Mosquito came rushing in and heavy explosions were again heard did people realize what was happening. 'They are bombing' they called out. A frightful noise then announced the second attack."

Cobley dropped his bombs in turn, pulling up sharply over the roof of the building. Two minutes later, with dense clouds of smoke already pouring from the shattered building, the second pair of Newman and Smith made their own attack. One of the Mosquito crews could barely see the target. After a further interval the third pair, led by Flight Lieutenant Vic Hester and Flying Officer Ray Birkett, finished off the mission by dropping HE and incendiary bombs. By now little of the Kleycamp building remained, and Hester's bombs flew through the air and hit the Alexander barracks. Cohen, whose bomb drop failed, but who took photographs, was killed later that summer on a sortie over France. Flight Lieutenant Ron Smith's final recollection was of coming out over playing fields filled with footballers before crossing the coast north of the city to be escorted home by waiting Spitfires.

The *Gestapo* building had been completely destroyed and the majority of the identity papers destroyed. The card files lay buried under the burning wreckage or fluttered over the Schaveningsveg, carried by the heat of the fire. The state police who rushed to the scene forced passers-by to pick up the file cards from the street and even made them search the wreckage, threatening them with their cudgels. Most realized why the raid had occurred, and they slyly dropped file cards into the flames or destroyed the photos. Fire brigade personnel hosed people away from the devastated building instead of trying to save people in the Kleycamp. Among the dead lay Van der Kamp and some of his fellow Dutch Underground workers. Buildings that surrounded the Kleycamp had suffered only slight damage, but 61 civilians were killed, 24 seriously injured, and 43 slightly injured. All six Mosquitoes got back safely without a shot being fired at them. Five weeks later a report reached the RAF that the operation had been highly satisfactory. For his leadership of this operation Bateson was awarded the DSO and received the Dutch Flying Cross from Prince Bernhard of the Netherlands. An Air Ministry bulletin later described the raid as "probably the most brilliant feat of low-level precision bombing of the war."

One of the main proponents of *Day Ranger* operations over France and the Low Countries was 418 (City of Edmonton) Squadron RCAF, which had re-equipped with Mosquitoes in March 1943 and had flown *Flower Intruder* operations out of RAF Ford, Sussex, using AI.Mk.IV and Mk.VIII. 418 Squadron flew their first FB.VI operation on 7 May 1943. Since January 1944 the Canadians had reaped a rich harvest of victories on day and night *Rangers*, and the high point came in April-May when they shot down 30 aircraft in the air and destroyed a further 38 on the ground. By May the Canadians, based at Holmsley South, had claimed 100 victories, and would have the distinction of destroying more enemy aircraft both in the air and on the ground than any other Canadian squadron in both night and daylight operations.

Flying Officer Bernard Job, Flying Officer Jack Phillips' navigator in the squadron, recalls:

"Being one of the pioneers in Intruder operations, the squadron worked at perfecting techniques aimed as surprising and intercepting enemy aircraft over their own airfields at night and generally disrupting airfield activity. Given opportunity, ground targets were strafed. The absence of AI equipment in the aircraft plainly made the task of interception much more challenging, but, as results showed, hardly impossible, given the acute observation and perseverance demonstrated by crews. What made this type of offensive operation so different from many others was that, having been assigned designated patrol areas, often a group of airfields in France or Germany, crews were then free to plan their own routes to and from these areas. Intruder aircraft almost always flew at low altitude, firstly in order to avoid unwanted enemy radar detection but also to arrive on target at something like aerodrome circuit height. There were of course, variations on the theme of *Night Intruder* patrols. One of these was that of a *Ranger* where by a single Mosquito penetrated freelance deep into enemy territory, even as far as Poland and southern Bavaria. Later, *Day Rangers* took place, usually by pairs of aircraft surprising and destroying enemy aircraft both in the air and on the ground, far afield. The Baltic States became a favorite run, thereby exploiting the Mosquito's long endurance at low speed."

On 27 January 1944 Flight Lieutenant James Johnson RCAF and Pilot Officer John Caine and Pilot Officer Earl Boal in FB.VIs attacked Clermont-Ferrand airfield. Johnson shot down a Ju 88 and damaged a Ju 86 and shared in the downing of two Ju W34s with Caine, who also destroyed a Ju 88. By 8 May Caine had destroyed 12 aircraft on the ground or water, with five more damaged on the ground or water. (In April-May 1945 Caine, now with 406 "Lynx" Squadron RCAF and flying NF.XXXs, destroyed a Ju 88 on the ground and damaged four other aircraft on the ground.) In the meantime, 418 (City of Edmonton) Squadron RCAF had also been busy. On 21 March American Lieutenant James F. Luma and Flying Officer John Finlayson and Flight Lieutenant Donald MacFadyen and "Pinky" Wright flew a long-range *Ranger* over France. Luma and Finlayson attacked Luxeuil airfield, where they shot down a Ju W34 liaison aircraft and a Ju52/3m transport and damaged two Gotha Go 242 glider transports and two Bf 109s on the ground. MacFadyen and Wright shot down a Blohm und Voss Bv 141 that was coming into land.[349] Moving on to Hagenau airfield, MacFadyen proceeded to destroy nine Gotha Go 242 twin-boomed troop transports and a Do 217 on the ground. MacFadyen later operated in 406 ("Lynx") Squadron RCAF, where he flew the NF.XXX on *Night Intruders*, finishing the war with seven aircraft and five V1s destroyed, and five aircraft destroyed and 17 damaged on the ground. Luma finished his tour in April and was awarded both a British and U.S. DFC.

On 14 April Squadron Leader Robert Allan Kipp and Flight Lieutenant Peter Huletsky of 418 Squadron RCAF shot down two Ju 52/3mg6e minesweepers of the *Minensuchgruppe* fitted with degaussing rings. They also destroyed two Do 217s on the ground and they damaged a third. Kipp was born on 12 October 1919 in Kamloopa, British Columbia, joining the RCAF in June 1940 and being commissioned on completion of training. He served as an instructor until 1943 when he departed for the UK. Finally, in November he joined 418 Squadron. Bob Kipp's brother also served on 418 Squadron as a navigator.[350] Meanwhile, Flight Lieutenant Stanley Herbert Ross "Stan" Cotterill DFC and "Pop" McKenna destroyed four in a night sortie. Flight Lieutenant Charlie Scherf DFC RAAF in three months (27 January-16 May 1944) racked up 23 destroyed, thirteen of them in the air.[351] Scherf, a 27-year old pilot from Emmaville, New South Wales, had worked as a grazier on the family sheep ranch before joining the RAAF in September 1941. He was promoted Squadron

Leader at the start of May and received a bar to his DFC with a DSO following in June. A month later he left the UK via the United States for his native Australia, where he instructed at 5 OTU Williamstown, near Newcastle NSW, still on Mosquitoes.[352]

The main work for 138 and 140 Wings also was *Day* and *Night Ranger* operations and *Intruder* sorties from England. On 12 April Flight Lieutenant J. L. "Les" Bulmer and Flight Lieutenant Ed McQuarrie of 21 Squadron were intruding over the airfield at St. Dizier when a searchlight was turned on them:

> "We took exception to that," recalls Les Bulmer, "so we flew right down the beam, firing our cannons as we went. That soon put it out. Didn't do our night vision a lot of good, though - we were almost blinded for a while. On our return journey we ran into searchlights near Abbeville and there were so many that we were in and out of them for about ten minutes. There was no sign of flak so I kept a sharp eye out for night-fighters but didn't see any. I was beginning to wonder where I'd taken us, because a concentration of searchlights such as this was normally reserved for large cities and I was convinced that we were nowhere near a town, let alone a city.
>
> "All was revealed when we got back to de-briefing. While we'd been away the flak map had been changed and where before there had been no flak position, there was now a large green area with '800' marked against it. This meant that we had just flown through a large defended area with 800 light AA guns in it. It seems that the Germans, in a bid to stop the destruction of their individual V1 sites, had concentrated a number of them into one large area heavily defended against low-level attack. I think someone might have told us before we took off.
>
> "For the second half of April Ed and I were on a *Gee-H* course at Swanton Morley. This was to be our precision blind-bombing aid. Although I got good results in practice raids on Boston Stump and the central tower of Ely Cathedral, on operations it - and sometimes I - was something of a failure, so this piece of equipment was not much used. In fact I only carried out three *Gee-H* sorties. On the first the equipment packed up. On the second we dropped our bombs from 20,000 feet on the Seine crossing at Duclair - at least that was where they were supposed to go. I have a feeling that they were nowhere near. The third and last I put down in my log-book as *Gee-H* trouble but some unkind person came along afterwards, crossed out *'Gee-H'* and inserted 'finger' and drew a small picture of Percy Prune's award of the highly Derogatory Order of the Irremovable Digit."

FB.VIs of 2nd TAF continued their night fighting role and bombing of German targets in France and the Low Countries. On the night of 19/20 May, when RAF Bomber Command carried out raids by 900 aircraft on five separate rail targets in France, Wing Commander Norman John "Jack" Starr DFC and Pilot Officer J. Irvine of 605 Squadron in a FB.VI flew a successful *Intruder* sortie over France.[353] Starr and Irvine took off from Manston at 0100 hours for their patrol, and they headed for the vicinity of Florennes, where landing lights were obligingly switched on as a twin-engined aircraft prepared to land. Starr and Irvine, whose Mosquito was at 2000 feet, were assisted further when a searchlight on the NW side of the airfield was switched on and began sweeping the area before it was switched off, the operators presumably satisfied that there were no intruders following the landing aircraft. Starr dived to attack while his prey, oblivious to the Mosquito's presence, blinked its landing light on and off sufficiently for Starr to estimate his position on the runway. Just as he was about to open fire the German aircraft switched on its landing light again and appeared to be traveling at about 20 mph. Starr gave the aircraft a 1½-second burst of cannon only, and strikes were seen in front of the machine and then strikes all over the aircraft. (Starr and Irvine were unable to identify their victim.) By this time the Mosquito was very close to the ground in the dive and Starr had to pull out very sharply. As he pulled out Starr and Irvine saw the German machine catch fire and all the airfield lights were switched off. They orbitted the airfield and saw a motor vehicle with powerful headlights on dash up to the now blazing aircraft, and the fire crew took about 12 minutes to extinguish the flames.[354]

There were other tasks for 2nd TAF Mosquito fighter-bombers in the build up to *D-Day*, as R. W. Smith, a FB.VI pilot in 613 "City of Manchester" Squadron, recalls:

> "Sometime before D-Day, the squadron was asked to provide two aircraft to fly on a mission which, except for the aircrew concerned, was kept completely secret. One aircraft had a pilot and navigator, and the other a pilot and a visiting passenger in the shape of an Australian wing commander. Subsequently, after D-Day we learned that the passenger was General Browning in fact, and that the mission had been to fly over the airborne and parachute dropping grounds in Normandy. On the night of the D-Day landings and for many nights afterwards, the squadron's chief role was patrolling over and behind enemy lines, attacking troop movements and anything in the way of enemy activity on the ground. Our mode of entry and exit was via the sea corridor between Alderney and the Cherbourg Peninsula, entering France at Granville and then making our way to the 'Tennis Court', which was our patrol area. It did not always work out according to plan. On our first patrol, which was in the Caen-Vire area, we found ourselves in solid cloud between 2000 to 3000 feet a soon as we crossed the coast. We could not get below the cloud because in places the ground rises to almost 2000 feet. The *Gee* was being jammed so badly that the screen was covered with 'grass' and John [Flying Officer Jack Hepworth] was unable to verify our position. After stooging around our patrol area for the required time and seeing nothing, it was time to return home. We decided to fly so many minutes due west to bring us over the sea and then fly north for home. This we did, and after turning north we broke cloud into a lovely clear night immediately to be caught in a cone of searchlights when flying at a height of 4000 feet. At the same time all hell seemed to be let loose with tracer coming up from all sides. Instead of being over sea, we were approaching Cherbourg. We just put the nose down and went weaving and skidding in a dive, passing over the breakwater of Cherbourg at about 400 feet. We landed at Lasham unscathed.
>
> "During the period 5 June-11 July John and I completed 17 operational sorties - all at night. In June these sorties were all in the Normandy area attacking roads, bridges, marshalling yards and any lights or movements Seen. Sometimes we would rendezvous with Mitchells dropping flares for us to operate under in certain conditions. My chief recollections are of the fires, which seemed to be burning night after night at Caen and Vire.

Lasham airfield is several hundred feet above sea level and, unless the cloud base was on the deck, we usually tried to return to base rather than to divert to Hartford Bridge; if we were diverted, we got less sleep and still had to get back to Lasham next morning. So, with low cloud over England, we tried to fly back under it and in so doing sometimes encountered the Navy. The Navy was quick on the draw and didn't seem to recognise the colors of the day. We would quickly disappear into cloud and settle for Hartford Bridge? From 6 July onwards we went further afield to places south of Paris, Châteauroux, Orleans, Nantes, La Rochelle, Le Mans, Tours, Rouen, Evreux and Dreux, still on the hunt for bridges, railways, trains and transport."

On the night of 5/6 June on the eve of D-Day, all six of 2nd TAF's FB.VI squadrons in 138 and 140 Wings carried out defensive operations over the invasion coast. In 85 Group at this time were 264 and 410 Squadrons in 141 Wing at Hartford Bridge and 488 Squadron RNZAF and 604 Squadron in 147 Wing at Zeals. At West Malling were 29 and 409 Squadrons in 148 Group, while in 11 Group ADGB, in southern England, there were 605, 96, 125 (Newfoundland), 219, 456 Squadron RAAF, and 418 (City of Edmonton) Squadron RCAF Squadrons. Fewer than fifty enemy aircraft plots were made on 5/6 June.[355] Then things heated up.[356] 264 Squadron flew jamming patrols before they went looking for enemy fighters. There was also another role for the Mosquitoes, as Bernard Job of 418 Squadron recalls:

"The squadron was stationed at Holmsley South near Bournemouth and six aircrews were detailed to act as 'Flak bait' to cover the paratroop and glider drops in the Cherbourg Peninsular, by drawing searchlights and flak away from these more vulnerable aircraft. So successful was this that two of the six were hit, one so badly that it crash landed near base and burnt up. The crew ran!"[357]

"When D-Day arrived," recalls Les Bulmer, "21 Squadron was out whenever weather permitted patrolling behind the battlefront looking for anything that moved. The night of *D-Day*, the 6th, we were briefed to patrol the Caen-Lisieux-Boisney road to stop German reinforcements reaching the beachhead. We were told that there was a corridor across the Channel in which every aircraft must stay on outward and return flights. Our night-fighters were patrolling on either side of the corridor and were likely to regard any plane that was found outside the designated area as hostile. As we left the English coast a hail of flak went up from a ship in mid-Channel right where we were headed. Pretty shortly down went an aircraft in flames - it looked like one of our four-engined bombers. It seemed that one of our own ships (the Royal Navy got the blame) had parked itself right on the path that every aircraft going to and from the Continent that night would be following. And, in true naval fashion, it let fly at everything that went over. We decided to risk the night-fighters rather than fly through that lot and did a wide detour."

On the night of 6/7 June Flight Lieutenant Stanley H. R. "Stan" Cotterill DFC and "Pop" McKenna of 418 Squadron equaled the squadron record set by Robert Kipp during May when they took off from Holmsley South at 2218 hours to fly a *Flower* patrol to Orléans and Châteaudun. They arrived at a pinpoint on the Loire at 2344 hours and proceeded to skirt the town of Orléans. They then swung north to commence their east-to-west patrol of Orléans and Châteaudun airfields. On the first leg of their patrol they observed a large orange colored fire at Terminiers, and shortly afterwards saw an aircraft orbiting Châteaudun at 800 feet and burning navigation lights. They recognized it as a Ju 52, and Cotterill fired a two-second burst of cannon and machine gun fire at an angle of 30 degrees astern and to port from 200 yards. Strikes were seen on the port wing and engine. A further four-second burst from 75 yards almost dead astern caused a small explosion and they broke to starboard. Cotterill and McKenna watched it crash and burst into flames two miles west of the airfield and then went down to photograph the burning wreckage.

They set course for Orléans using the fire at Terminiers as a pinpoint when within five miles they noticed considerable activity at Orléans airfield. The V/L was on and the runway lighting but no beacon. One aircraft was landing and two more were circling preparatory to doing so. All were burning navigation lights. Cotterill attacked the second aircraft, a Ju 52, which was apparently going round again at 500 feet. He fired a three-second burst of cannon and machine gun from 150 yards, 20 degrees astern and to starboard. The enemy aircraft blew up instantly and crashed 40 yards north of the east to west runway three-quarters of the way along. On breaking away to port the Mosquito crew observed the last of four aircraft break away from the circuit, douse all lights, and head south. At once they took up the chase and overshot, as they were diving underneath trying to keep a visual. They noticed a series of "dits" being flashed from three downward recognition lights in white, and as they throttled back they managed to pull in behind, obtaining a clear silhouette of a Ju 188. The enemy aircraft took violent evasive action, but Cotterill and McKenna managed to maintain contact and, as he straightened out, fired a three-second burst from 30 yards astern and slightly below. Strikes were seen on the port engine and fuselage and fire started in the belly. The Mosquito's windscreen was covered in oily liquid and debris started hitting their starboard wing. They broke to starboard and followed the enemy aircraft as it glided gently down into a field, the fire illuminating the terrain for several hundred yards. On impact the whole aircraft burst into flames. As they were now south of the town, Cotterill and McKenna returned to the airfield, where they noticed that the V/L had been turned off but the runway was still lit. A large white floodlight had been installed on the left side and about 15 yards from the beginning of the runway. They then decided to bomb the runway in use and dropped two 500lb GP eleven seconds delay, from 500 feet. As they broke away to port, their bombs were seen to explode on the runway and a third of the way along. Immediately afterwards they noticed an aircraft with navigation lights on and a large landing light shining practically straight down from the nose, making an approach to land about 300 feet above and 1000 yards away from the runway. They swung round to port and closed to 100 yards, recognizing the enemy aircraft as a Ju 52. Cotterill opened fire at this range with a four-second burst from an angle of 20 degrees astern and to port, with strikes being seen on the port engine and fuselage. By this time the aircraft was only 100 yards from the perimeter track and 100 feet high. It crashed and blew up on the edge of the runway. As all their ammunition had been used up by that last burst they set course for home.

In night operations on 7/8 June 1944 Mosquito night-fighter crews in 29, 307, 406 ("Lynx") Squadron RCAF, and 418 and 456 Squadrons made claims for ten enemy aircraft destroyed, one probably destroyed, and three damaged. Five crews in 29 Squadron took the lion's share with claims for five destroyed, one probably destroyed, and two damaged. Flight Lieutenant George E. Allison and Flying Officer R. G. "Bob" Stainton, his 34-year old navigator, claimed a Ju 52 and a UEA destroyed. Flight Lieutenant John Barry and Guy Hopkins claimed two Ju 188s destroyed. Flying Officer

Frank Pringle and his navigator, Flying Officer Wain Eaton, flying a NF.XIII equipped with AI.Mk.VIII radar and armed with four 20mm cannon, took off from West Malling at 22.53 hours for an *Intruder* patrol on German airfields at Evreux, St. André, Dreux, and Chartres, just west of Paris. Pringle recalls:

> "Intruding back in 1941 and '42 had been successfully carried out by both German and RAF crews, but radar-equipped RAF fighters were not permitted to cross the enemy coastline until Overlord. In the buildup to the invasion, 29 Squadron had been working-up with low level night navigation at 240 mph in order to sharpen up rusty navigation skills, with the radar operators peering for hours into their PPIs (Plan and Position Indicators) guiding their pilots to make interceptions at all levels. Early 1941/42 Mk.IV airborne radar had height limitations due to obstructing ground returns, but this had now been replaced with the efficient and reliable Mk.VIII that could take on low level targets.
>
> "The squadron had new aircraft and had been equipped with tents and motor transport with which they had 'shaken down' at Drem and had practiced night landings on grass with the minimum of lighting aids in preparation for full mobility when sent to Europe. Although a dim view was taken of the tents, morale was good.
>
> "As we lined up on runway 23 Wain crouched beside me on his miserable hard seat, with his flight plan and computer handy and with only his knees as a worktop - inches away from the mask covering the PPI tube. It was all a very tight fit in Mae West and flying harness, while stuffed in his boot was a torch and in another pocket his emergency pouch containing a silk map of Europe, foreign currency, glucose tablets etc. - but no condoms. Sewn into his jacket and trousers were a couple of miniature compasses.
>
> "Crossing out at the south coast over Beachy Head, I descended to below 500 feet to cross the Channel. Fifteen minutes later, I increased power for a quick climb to 3,000 feet before stuffing the nose down for maximum speed to nip over the French coast at Fécamp, north of the Seine, at 300 feet. We were now on the first leg to Evreux, which came up at 23.43 hours, the beacon flashing 'ZP'. There was no sign of activity at either Evreux or St. André.
>
> "At 23.55 a Visual Lorenz was lit at Dreux. This was a long approach lighting aid, sometimes several kilometers in length, to make German pilots make a snappy approach and landing without having to wander around circuits. After a short while Wain obtained a contact at three-quarters of a mile, crossing fast at 90 degrees and descending through 1500 feet. We turned hard to port, lost radar contact, but obtained a visual on a landing light from an aircraft touching down. I gave it a quick burst of fire, saw some strikes and claimed it as damaged.
>
> "Bearing in mind that this was the first time I had fired my cannons at low level at night, I was scared of flying into the ground. On a previous occasion when I had fired cannon in daylight, at a practice target off the Clacton pier area, the perspex radar dome in the nose of the Mosquito had disintegrated and a hunk of debris had pierced my leading edge radiator. All the port engine coolant went overboard. I had sweaty hands that it might happen again.
>
> "We now climbed to 2000 feet and stood off to watch down-wind, hoping for more contacts in the direction of Chartres to the south. Meanwhile the VL at Dreux stayed lit.
>
> "At about 00.30, colors of the period were gently fired off from an aircraft nearby, but we failed to get a contact in spite of several orbits. Suddenly, south of Dreux, I saw an aircraft below - to my astonishment with a navigation light on! I made a quick beam attack down to low level with a five-second burst, again with numerous strikes. After breaking away there was a brilliant flash south of the airfield. We now observed a bright fire that had not been there before and in line with the runway. Bright objects were shooting off it in all directions. After emptying my remaining cannon rounds into this area, I made a couple of ciné camera runs over the site and claimed it destroyed, seeing inaccurate light flak coming up from a position south of the airfield.
>
> "We set course for base via the Seine and crossed out north of Lillebonne at 00.55, making landfall at Beachy Head and we touched down at West Malling at 01.46 hours, ready for bacon and eggs.
>
> "The weather over France had been good, with a slight ground haze and with cloud at 4000 feet. All our cannon had fired, using 352 rounds of SAPI (semi-armor piercing incendiary) and 344 of HEI (high explosive incendiary). At 44 rounds per second this would take just fifteen seconds."

Also on 7/8 June, 70 Mosquitoes of 107, 305, and 613 Squadrons operating to the west on rail targets at Argentan, Domfort, and Lisieux, sealing approaches to the bridgehead in Normandy. The opportunity for breakout and the eventual invasion of Germany was now within reach, and 2nd TAF would go all the way with the ground forces. On 11 June six Mosquitoes of 464 and 487 Squadrons led by Wing Commander Bob Iredale and Flight Lieutenant McCaul attacked petrol tankers in a railway marshalling yard at Châtellerault at the request of the Army. Wing Commander Mike Pollard of 107 Squadron and his six Mosquitoes arrived at 2244 hours to find fires burning in an area 300 x 200 yards with smoke rising to 4000 feet. That night attacks continued on railway targets and 50 aircraft from 88, 98, 107, 180, 226 and 320 Squadrons bombed the railway junction at Le Haye, west of Carentan. Two nights later 42 Mosquitoes of 107, 305, 464, and 613 Squadrons strafed and bombed troop movements between Tours and Angers-Vire, Dreux and Falaise, and Evreux and Lisieux. "The scene over France," continues Les Bulmer, "had changed completely. Whereas before *D-Day* there had been almost total darkness, now there were lights everywhere and most of the Normandy towns burned for several nights. Navigation was much easier; you just flew from one fire to the next."

On 14/15 June Mosquitoes wreaked havoc on the continent, and eight enemy aircraft were shot down over the continent by 2nd TAF Mosquito crews,[358] including one by Squadron Leader Russ Bannock RCAF and Flying Officer Bob Bruce, their first victory since joining 418 Squadron a few days earlier.[359] Bruce recalls:

> "We wasted no time and after practice trips on the first three days set off on our first *Intruder*, a two-hour patrol off Bourges-Avord airfield. Luck was with us and after some time we spotted the exhaust of a night-fighter as it passed overhead. We picked it up as it turned on final approach but had to break off to the south due to heavy anti-aircraft fire. Fortunately for us the pilot switched on his landing lights. We attacked in a shallow dive and fired a burst of cannon and machine guns. As it exploded and caught fire we

recognized it as a Me 110. We were subjected to a barrage of AA fire from the north side of the airfield and we turned sharply to the left to avoid this wall of fire but Russ was reefing so hard on the elevator we did a high-speed stall just as we almost turned 180 degrees... We exited to the west of the field still carrying two bombs under the wings and by the time we reached Holmsley South our fuel reserves were getting low. It was a memorable first trip."

On 18/19 June the only ADGB success was achieved by 32-year old Wing Commander John Topham DFC,* CO of 125 (Newfoundland) Squadron, and Flight Lieutenant H. W. "Wilber" Berridge DFC, who claimed two Ju 88s off the beachhead to take his score to thirteen.[360] Topham and Berridge, a 32-year old ex-printer and former air gunner, had crewed up on Beaufighters on 219 Squadron, and they had shared in nine victories during 1941-42. Lieutenant Archie Harrington of 410 "Cougar" Squadron RCAF claimed a Ju 88 destroyed, as did Flying Officer G. E. Edwards. Flying Officer Sid Seid and Pilot Officer Dave McIntosh of 418 Squadron were sent out on an Anti-*Diver* patrol that night, having had a careful briefing from Squadron Leader Russ Bannock and Flight Lieutenant Don MacFadyen, who had devised tactics for V1 interceptions. They were advised to climb to 10,000 feet, wait for an incoming flying bomb, and then dive flat-out, hoping that, at 400 mph, they could catch it.

Accordingly they climbed away from Holmsley South, heading for the Channel. Seid decided to remain at 2,000 feet, however, then followed an hour of "stooging around" waiting just inshore of Le Havre. Suddenly they caught sight of a red glow below and ahead, and Seid rammed the throttles forward, the Mosquito accelerating to 350 mph and the crew watching in frustration as the missile simply ran away from them.

Dave McIntosh then reminded his pilot of their Flight Commander's advice. Seid pulled up the nose and they ascended to 10,000 feet, with McIntosh getting a sore neck from craning around in the darkness. Suddenly Seid saw another, stood the Mosquito on its nose, and down they went, the speed building up fast. With the ASI needle hovering around 400 mph they found themselves hurtling past it before Seid could line up for a shot. Regretfully, they abandoned this attempt and climbed again to 10,000 feet. Dave McIntosh described what happened next:

"Another hour went by arid we were thinking of doing another stooge before heading home, when we spotted a third doodlebug. 'By God, this time,' Sid said.

"The speed went up as we went down. I looked at the clock. It read 350 mph. I looked out along my wing. It was flapping like a seagull working in a hurricane. My stomach gave another wrench. Christ, the wings will come off and we'll go straight in. I didn't take any comfort from what had happened to Tony Barker and Gord Frederick, his navigator. They hit the drink so hard the cannons pulled them through the floorboards of the cockpit and clear of the Mosquito. They got into their dinghies and a rescue plane picked them out of the Channel two miles off the Dieppe beaches. It takes all kinds.

"Down, down, down. We were gaining some because the fire coming out of the ass end of the V1 was getting bigger. The Mosquito was screaming in every joint. Sid had both big, hairy hands on the stick. When he began **to** pull hack I thought the wings would never stand it. But we began to level out and the clock said 400 mph. Sid pulled and pulled and she kept coming out of the dive. I tore my eyes away from the shaking wing and looked ahead. It was just like looking into a blast furnace.

"'We're too close,' I screamed. I shut my eyes as the cannons began banging away. I was thrown against my straps because the cannons going off cut the speed down suddenly.

"When the explosion came I thought I was going to be dead. The goddam thing went off right in our faces. I opened my eyes and caught a glimpse of things whirling around outside the window. Black things and blobs of smoke.

"'I can't see,' Sid said.

"'OK, boy,' I said. 'Just keep her like that. You can cut your speed, though.' He throttled back. After those hours of darkness, he had been blinded for a few seconds by the flash. Why we hadn't been smashed up by all that flying debris, I don't know. We had flown right through it."

They returned to base to discover that the entire aircraft was blistered black. Every inch of paint had been burnt. Next day, after the crew had gathered to inspect the blackened aircraft, Seid gave a hilarious account of the encounters, ending by saying, "I don't know how you are supposed to tell how far away you are. I thought we were about 300 yards away. Jesus, we weren't three yards away. I'm going to wear dark glasses at night after this."[361]

On the night of 22/23 June Flight Lieutenant Mike Benn DFC was killed. He took off on his 31st Mosquito operation with his navigator, Flying Officer W. A. Roe, on a *Night Ranger* from Thorney Island in FB.VI *G-George*. On becoming airborne he found that his ASI (airspeed indicator) was not working, and so he radioed Control that he had problems and was returning to base. Another Mosquito crew was able to formate with *G-George* and led them into the approach to ensure that they were at the right speed, but Benn's approach was such that he touched down too far down the runway. He overran the end of the runway and the Mosquito went over the low sea wall at the airfield boundary and bounced on the shingle strip. The undercarriage and wheels were torn off as they hit the barbed wire fence entanglement beyond the shingle and the tail dropped when it hit the mud flat. The fuselage snapped completely off near the tail fin and the aircraft's nose dropped and dug into the mud, bringing the aircraft to a halt about thirty yards from the sea wall. Bill Roe survived, but the sudden stop caused the armor plate behind the pilot's seat to hurl itself forward, and this broke Mike Benn's back. They were in shallow water, and Roe managed to keep Benn's head above water and carried him some way back to the airfield before the ambulance finally found them. Benn died the following day in St Richard's hospital, Chichester. The Squadron records stated, "Michael was a favorite of the Squadron and his death is a great shock to us all."[362]

On 24/25 June 1944 488 Squadron RNZAF crew Flight Lieutenant George Esmond "Jamie" Jameson DFC RNZAF and Flying Officer A. Norman Crookes, his navigator from Derbyshire, were on patrol from Zeals in NF.XIII[363] *R for Robert* over France covering the advance of the Army near Lisieux. Crookes picked up a stray contact 20 miles SW of Bayeaux and closing in quickly, Jameson shot down a Me 410.[364] Four nights later, on 28/29 June, Jameson and Crookes destroyed a Ju 88 ten miles NE of Caen as it was about to bomb British Forces landing at Arromanches. Crookes' DFC was announced for his share in three of Jameson's victories. In June 488 Squadron RNZAF was credited with nine victories over the Beachhead area. At the end of July the New Zealand squadron moved to Colerne near Bath, where Jameson was devastated to learn that his both his brothers had been killed. His elder brother was serving with the New Zealand Army in Tunisia and his younger brother died in a Beaufighter during training at East Fortune. Tragically a cable from New Zealand informed Jamie that his father had died on hearing the news of the death of two of his sons. Jameson's mother immediately appealed to the New Zealand Government to allow Jamie to return home and take over the family farm of nearly 2000 acres in Rotherham near Canterbury. The High Commissioner, Mr. (later Sir William) Jordan, visited 488 Squadron RNZAF and told Jamie that he had done more than his duty and that he should return to his mother. Jamie was persuaded to apply for a passage on the next ship repatriating time-expired New Zealanders and Australians via the USA and Panama. However, before Jameson departed he was determined to avenge the untimely deaths of his brothers.[365] On the night of 29/30 July the Kiwi and his faithful navigator Crookes took off in *R for Robert* to patrol the Coutance-St. Lô area. They returned having claimed three Junkers 88s and a Dornier Do 217 destroyed. Their second victim was confirmed destroyed by a navigator of 410 'Cougar' Squadron RCAF who saw the Ju 88 hit the ground 5-6 miles south of Caen, explode and burst into flames. Jameson fired 320 20mm shells to destroy all four aircraft in the space of just twenty minutes, a feat which took the New Zealander's score to nine e/a destroyed.

2nd TAF and ADGB destroyed at least 230 aircraft at night over the Channel, France, the Low Countries and Germany, June 1944-April 1945. In the run up to *D-Day*, 29 Squadron of the ADGB had been the first Mosquito unit equipped with the superior AI.Mk.VIII radar to be released for intruding over the Continent. Whilst still equipped with Beaufighter VIFs, the unit had had its first taste of offensive night operations in spring 1943 when it began *Night Rangers* over airfields in German-occupied France. After converting to the Mosquito in the summer 29 Squadron reverted to defensive operations in the ADGB, finally mounting its first *Intruder*s over France on the night of 14 May 1944. Flying Officer R. G. 'Bob' Stainton in 29 Squadron at Hunsdon has vivid memories of a narrow escape he and his pilot Flight Lieutenant George E. Allison had during a *Night Intruder* on the night of 5/6 July 1944 in NF.XIII MM553:

> "We night-prowlers liked the 'blanket of the dark' better than any romantic moonlight and this night we were to visit the Coulommiers district again - Bretigny, Melun, Orly. There was a full moon. It was like daylight, as it had been on the night of the Nuremburg raid. The moon shone on French villages, woods and roads a thousand feet below us; for we had decided that at this height a 'cat's eye' Fw 190 had less chance of spotting us, although light flak had more and we were still not low enough to escape German radar detection. No aerodromes seemed to be lit - ominous inactivity amid the luminous tones of a countryside so peaceful and still. The Seine was a bent silver ribbon but we saw one aerial beacon flashing. This was awkward, as was the fact that Bill Provan366 had already been a nuisance, shooting at trains and stirring up wasp nests. It was our choice of height, however, that directly led to trouble. We failed to pinpoint an important small lake and shortly after narrowly missed the Melun wireless masts. At least we now knew exactly where we were.
>
> "Suddenly, near Bretigny, we were lit by a searchlight and tracer shells passed behind the tail. 'What's the time, Bob?' It was 0242 and we were both wishing the clock would go faster, when there was a series of explosions under us. We felt the shock and shudder of their impact. Other tracers wove light-tracks behind and above and as suddenly stopped. The Mosquito was shuddering (us with it). It even seemed to me that the fuel cocks were hot. I got my parachute on as George, without speaking, though I could hear him snort, dived almost to the ground. For a second I wasn't sure that he had control and began feathering the port propeller. There was no further attack. We managed to make a little height, 1800 feet and in spite of a spasmodic shaking at the tail-end of the fuselage the aeroplane seemed to be holding her own. To lighten the load we dropped the wing-tanks and fired our cannon with empty bravado over that tranquil landscape. Headway was slow at 170 IAS (with the wind from port and against us, our ground-speed was about 145 mph) but it gave me time to double-check our course and track and ETA at the coast. We prayed for accuracy and that no part of the ship would fall off. I kept my parachute on, hoping that no predator would creep up behind us for we could not have taken evasive action. And how that black hole in the propeller-blade eyed us! We decided that if we met flak at the coast we would bale out. 'We'll paddle round to the beach-head in the dinghy.' Mild laughter. To our relief, neither event occurred.
>
> "The crossing seemed age-long and George asked every few minutes exactly how far we had to go. However we did not quarrel. At last we could see the flashing 'K' of the Friston beacon west of Birling Gap. 'May Day! May Day!' There was no reply. We reached Ford to my wry satisfaction exactly as calculated and from 1800 feet went straight in to land at 170 knots. High speed is vital when you have only one engine and too slow a turn becomes an immediate and fatal stall. The wheels were down but we used no flaps. Half way along the runway the wheels still had not touched nor had the speed dropped. We both lifted the undercarriage lever. She dug her nose in like the ,wheels' in a wheel-barrow race, hit something, threw her tail up and turned an exact somersault amid a splintering of wood and perspex. Something cold and sharp closed on my left hand, twisting it behind me. We were stuck fast, upside down. Metal creaked, petrol escaped with an overpowering stench. There followed the long drawn-out waiting for the gas to burst into flames as it touched hot metal. I remember only one thought: 'At least you had your cricket.'367 No? No fire? An age of waiting followed while I struggled in vain to free my left arm and the sweat dripped from my face.
>
> "Forty-five minutes later the blood-wagon and crash crew arrived and began trying to hack us free. It was some time before they realized that if the aeroplane was upside down they were trying to cut their way through the guns. Someone had an attack of good sense and broke open the escape-hatch. It was the doctor. He also stuck a needle into my elevated bottom. They freed my arm. We were both very wide awake when they pulled us clear and I remember lying on the stretcher in a delicious twilight of sensation, comfortable and still conscious enough to appreciate this unbelievable freedom. Only later did I discover that the crash crew had stolen my torch, commando knife and the box of escape equipment we always carried."368

Until suitable airstrips could be made ready, the Mosquito wings flew operations from Thorney Island and Lasham. Some spectacular pinpoint daylight operations against specific buildings were flown. On 14 July, Bastille Day, the Mosquitoes of 2nd TAF were called upon for an important task in France, as Gordon Bell-Irving explains:

"AVM Basil Embry came to Thorney Island to brief us for a daylight low-level attack on a special target at Bonneuil Matours, near Poitiers. He was a formidable presence. We were told that the raid was on a *Gestapo* barracks and was to punish those responsible for the murder of some British prisoners of war who had been dubbed to death with rifle butts in a nearby village square."[369]

The Mosquitoes' target was a collection of six buildings inside a rectangle just 170 x 100 feet, close to the village, which had to be avoided. Bell-Irving continues:

"There was no model of the target for us - there hadn't been time to prepare one. Basil's final words before sending us on our way were, 'If you get shot down and taken prisoner don't shoot your mouth off about retaliation. You can't out-piss a skunk!' This struck me as being colorful but anatomically incorrect. I expect he'd heard it from a Texan.

"The raid went quite smoothly. We took off in the late afternoon to hit the target at dusk, when the occupants of the barracks would be having dinner. There were 18 aircraft with crews from 21, 464 and 487 Squadrons led by Group Captain Peter Wykeham-Barnes DSO DFC* and Flying Officer Chaplin.[370] At about 2000 feet we skirted the Cherbourg Peninsula, and on passing a little too close to the Channel Island of Alderney our tidy formation was fired on by a heavy shore battery. Considering our altitude and range this came as a surprise. We scattered in a relatively disciplined way and reformed as soon as we were out of range. I think we made our landfall near St Malo and went down to about 50 feet from there until just short of the target, where we climbed to bombing height; our bombs were fused for a 25-second delay. Bert Holt, my navigator, and I were among the first to bomb, and as we dived on the target I noticed a 20mm gun-firing tracer rather wildly from the roof of the target building. Looking back after bombing there was a lot of smoke and no sign of tracer. We did not re-formate after bombing; it soon became dark and we returned to base independently. The rest of the trip was uneventful and all crews returned safely. Whoever was in the barracks, we were told that 150 had been killed in our raid.' The Mosquitoes in shallow dives had dropped nine tons of bombs on the barracks while they were eating dinner. Three trains were attacked on the return flights for good measure."

On 30 July the SAS learned that 2000-3000 Germans were massing for an anti-Maquis/SAS sweep, and the majority were billeted in the Caserne des Dunes barracks at Poitiers. This resulted in a raid by 24 FB.VIs of 487 and 21 Squadrons escorted by Mustangs on 1 August. Meanwhile, the SAS learned that the survivors of the 158th Regiment were now in the Château de Fou, an *SS* police HQ south of Châtellerault. This and Château Maulny, a saboteur school was attacked by 23 FB.VIs of 107 and 305 Squadrons on Sunday 2 August. It is estimated that 80 per cent of the regiment were killed, so that unit paid dearly for its actions. That same day, 613 Squadron attacked a château in Normandy, which was used as a rest home for German submariners. It appeared that Sunday was chosen because on Saturday nights the Germans had a dance, which went on rather late. The FB.VIs attacked early in the morning, with rather devastating results. AVM Embry under the alias "Wing Commander Smith" and the Station Commander, Group Captain Bower, took part.

On 25/26 July when 412 Lancasters and 138 Halifaxes returned to Stuttgart and other large forces bombed Wanne-Eickel and flying bomb sites in France two 2nd TAF[371] Mosquito *Intruder* crews were successful over the continent. On 26/27 July Squadron Leader R. S. Jephson and Flying Officer J. M. Roberts of 409 Squadron RCAF destroyed a Ju 88 over Caen but their NF.XIII was brought down by the flying debris and both men were killed in the crash. The only other Mosquito claim was a Ju 188 at Melun by Flying Officer Frank E. Pringle and Flying Officer Wain Eaton of 29 Squadron.

In July Squadron Leader David F. Dennis DSO DFC became the CO of 21 Squadron. He had rejoined the squadron when the build-up to D-Day was in progress and on 29 July he flew his first night operational sortie of his third tour. Having carried out an interdiction sortie in Southern Germany with his navigator Flying Officer Grantham his Mosquito was hit by flak, which put one engine out of action. The propeller refused to feather and only by maintaining full power on the other engine could he maintain flight, albeit in a slight descent. Arriving in darkness at the recently recaptured area around Caen in northern France he found an emergency landing strip and put the aircraft down without injury to himself or the navigator but the Mosquito was a write off. The next night he was back at Thorney Island carrying out night flying training and at that time it was not unusual to carry out two x two hour thirty minute operational sorties in one night.

Meanwhile, the first PR XVI production examples had been urgently despatched to 140 Squadron at Hartford Bridge where they supplemented PR.IXs on reconnaissance and mapping duties as part of the build up to D-Day. 140 Squadron provided photo coverage throughout the winter of 1944-45, moving to France in September to keep in touch with the action. [372] Flying Officer Arthur T. Kirk, a pilot in 140 Squadron, recalls:

"At the end of July 1944 Sergeant Mike Pedder, my navigator, and I set off on our first trip over France. Our target was a stretch of country between Grand Courronne and Hautor. The excitement got to Mike a bit, and he kept looking round behind. I said, 'Look Mike, I've been on night-fighters, and it's no good you looking round behind. If there's anything up our rear end, we'll know about it soon enough!' It did the trick and we settled into the task. On our second op we photographed the road between Thury-Harcourt and Caen, as our troops were bogged down and needed information about opposing forces. The third trip was to the Falaise area, which was soon to be a scene of bloody carnage as German armor was caught and savaged by rocket-firing Typhoons and other fighter-bombers. We returned to find our cameras had obtained only three photographs instead of the dozen expected from each camera. It appeared that this had occurred on all of our sorties so far as, somehow, we had got the camera programming sequence wrong. After a sort-out, we did a lot better.

"In August 67 of 140 Squadron's long-range mapping sorties were at night. We carried out three night operations, two of them along the River Orne, and another from Barentin to Pavilly, when we saw Rouen under the shellfire. Mike navigated using *Gee*, sometimes *Rebecca*, or even *Oboe*. We carried 12 flashes in the belly of the Mossie, and as they were released, they exploded at the set height, operating the camera shutters by photo-electric cells. On a good op we got 24 pictures of troops, trucks, trains and armored columns. Sometimes we'd be sent to photograph river crossings supposedly in use by the Wehrmacht anything the Army wanted to know about movement in the area, or was considered important to the overall strategy, we photographed. We plotted our track to enter France unnoticed if possible, with Fecamp, on the coast, being a favorite landfall. The 'natives' didn't seem to be too unfriendly there!

"Occasionally, we would be frustrated by jamming or on-board malfunctions and we had to rely on more basic techniques: dead reckoning or map reading if conditions allowed. We were not the only aircraft inhabiting the night sky. Sometimes we would see Bomber Command unloading their deadly cargoes, from the target indicators, splashes of vivid reds, greens or yellows saturating the aiming points, followed by exploding bombs, flak and searchlights probing until they' lit one or more of the bombers like a moth in a candle-glow. Once or twice we saw them pounced on all and sundry and, amid the flashing streams of tracer and bilious smoke, catching fire. We always looked for parachutes and hoped they all got out. On night reconnaissance we didn't lose a crew, or have one injured, while I was with the unit, although aircraft did suffer damage through flak. The Mosquito was an elusive bird, even more so at night!"[373]

In August '77 enemy aircraft were destroyed in the air by the seven night-fighter and fighter-bomber squadrons of 2nd TAF. On 1/2 August Canadians Squadron Leader James D. Somerville and Flying Officer G. D. Robinson of 410 'Cougar' Squadron RCAF in NF.XIII MM477/U equipped with AI.VIII shot down of a Ju 88 NE of Tessy at 0100 hours. Somerville reported:

"We took off from Colerne at 2310 hours and went to Pool 2. Handed over to Robust and given vector of 100 degrees then over to Circular and later to Radox GCI. We intercepted a Stirling on southerly vector and then told to vector 190 degrees, 140 degrees and finally 230 degrees from the Seine estuary. Control told us they had a Stirling. In the meantime having crossed inland we pulled over to starboard of the Stirling and was immediately given patrol vector of 280 degrees. After flying on this course for 2/3 minutes chandelier flares were seen N/W of us. Immediately Radox told us to vector 320 degrees as my "turkey was gobbling" and they could not help us much. Whilst still on 320 degrees contact was obtained 3 miles range 5 o'clock 40 degrees. Closed in to 2000 feet, when visual was obtained on an a/c weaving 30 degrees on either side of 320 degrees. A straight course was flown on visual when a/c cut across in front of Mosquito on one of the jinks, range dropped to 600 feet. A/C now identified as Ju.188. The enemy crew evidently saw us at approximately the same time and did a violent peel off to starboard, but luckily peeled off directly into the chandelier flares and visual was maintained during the dive. E/A pulled up into steep climbing port turn. We turned a little harder than E/A and the range dropped to approx. 900 feet where I opened fire allowing 1 ring deflection. After what appeared a short burst the port wing of the E/A disintegrated outward of engine nacelle. The E/A flicked over into a steep half spiral to starboard and dived vertically into the ground approx. 10 miles N/E Tessy, There a violent explosion followed. No return fire experienced. Landed back at Colerne 0500 hours."

The night following, 2/3 August 1944, Squadron Leader F. J. A. Chase and Flying Officer A. F. Watson of 264 Squadron got their 5th enemy aircraft since *D-Day* when they destroyed a Ju 188 (or 88) 10m west of Argentan. Somerville and Flying Officer Robinson of 410 'Cougar' Squadron RCAF in MM477/U scored their third victory when they shot down a Do 217 6 miles Northwest of Pontorson at 2255 hours. Somerville wrote:

"I was first given vector of 190 degrees after a group of bogies then vectored 170 degrees and finally on 150 degrees from 20 miles NE of Avranches. Contact obtained 3 miles range 50 degrees off and to starboard height 7000 feet ASI 220 mph. Target was doing a gentle weave. I closed to 1000 feet and identified as a do 217 by pulling off to starboard and getting a silhouette against a bright northern sky. I pulled back into line astern and opened fire at approximately 800 feet. It appeared that E/A must have seen me at the exact split second as I opened fire as it started a fairly hard starboard turn. On the first burst half of the E/A port tail plane and the port rudder flew off and evidently I must have holed his oil tank, because my windscreen and A/C became smothered in oil. I experienced great difficulty in maintaining a visual through the film of oil. E/A then started doing a steady starboard orbit and losing height rapidly, as if the pilot had been killed or was having difficulty in controlling his A/C. After the first burst the combat developed into a dog fight, as return fire was experienced from the dorsal and ventral guns of the E/A. No hits appeared to register although the fire appeared to be uncomfortably close. I reopened fire every time I got close enough to see the E/A through oil, which was gradually clearing due to the slipstream, at the same time E/A kept firing back at me. It appeared that the E/A dived vertically into the ground from 3000 feet at the precise moment when I had used all my ammunition. I orbited port and saw the E/A strike the ground and burn furiously. (Position approximately 6 miles NW Pontorson). No parachutes were seen to leave the E/A but my navigator on the last burst told me he saw the other half of the tail plane leave the E/A. Intermittent flak was experienced throughout and on returning to base found that my main plane had been hit by a 13mm shell inboard of the port engine nacelle."

Flight Lieutenant "Jamie" Jameson DFC's tenth victory on 488 Squadron RNZAF came on the night of 3/4 August when he shot down a Ju 88 which was about to dive-bomb British Army troops near St. Lô. He fired just 60 20mm cannon shells to down the Junkers. Next day came news of his sailing date for New Zealand. On 6 August Jameson and Norman Crookes took off on their last sortie together in *R-Robert*. The Controller informed them that "Bandits" were making for the front-line. Jameson gave a "*Tallyho*" (enemy sighted) over his R/T and he claimed a Ju 88 damaged 5 miles west of the Vire before notching his 11th victory, a Ju 88 15 miles east of Avranche. *"R" for Robert* landed back at Colerne to a rapturous welcome. Jameson returned to New Zealand and the award of a DSO followed. Crookes, who after the war became a teacher in Kent, received a bar to his DFC. Jamie's score made him the highest scoring New Zealand fighter pilot of the war.[374]

On the night of 5/6 August Flight Lieutenant John A. M. Haddon and his navigator-Flying Officer Ralph J. McIlvenny flying XIII MM514 took off on a night patrol. Haddon wrote;

"McIlvenny and I had taken off from A8 at 2200 hours on our first night sortie from the American beachhead, and ground control was using us to calibrate some new radar on the British beachhead. Our patrol line lay about 50 kilometers south of Caen at about 5000 feet. Unknown to us a Junkers 188 was on a westerly course, fairly well east of the British Sector. An 88/188 would follow him some twenty minutes later. Both could have been aiming at targets anywhere in the American Sector. Patton had just made his breakout of the beachhead towards Rennes in the extreme west but the Canadian and British forces were still being held fast somewhere south-of Bayeaux and Caen. Falaise was still in enemy hands. We could see ground artillery fire from that Sector. It was a brilliant moonlit night, a little before midnight. Control told us there was trade coming up flying much higher than we were and gave us several southerly courses to steer. Because we had been unusually low and had to climb as we tried to reach our target -we found ourselves having difficulty catching up with it, but it made things easier by gradually turning from west to NNW towards the general direction of our own airfield. We-were pretty sure we were after a fellow Mosquito and that our interception would be no classic encounter - just another tail chase. Controllers who put you in such a position weren't high on aircrew popularity lists.

"Mac had the bogey on radar for some minutes before I saw a tiny speck ahead in the sky at a distance of 3500 feet. At 2000 feet Mac voiced the opinion that it could be a Ju 88. He was using night glasses. Pilots seldom believed that navigators could tell a Lancaster from a Lysander but, as Mac was much above average, discretion became the better part of valor. We slid well to one side and below so that we weren't silhouetted against the moon as we had been, which also gave us a chance to see the aircraft from the best angle. As we closed it was clear that our target was a 188 and that he didn't know we were there, a very desirable situation. Keeping it that way, I got in to 800 feet and checked for the tenth time that the guns were set to fire, the props were in near fine pitch and the gunsight dim enough to see through. I then pulled up behind him and opened up. I first hit his port engine, then the fuselage, and we ducked when something left the aircraft. It was on fire on the way down, then its pyrotechnics blew up and finally it went in near somewhere called Domfront.

'Before we had time for the usual mutual admiration to begin we got a call from Ops to turn south east again because there was more trade at 25 miles and below us. I put the nose hard down and eventually Mac got a number of contacts. I ended up overshooting and needing more help from Ops and Mac. It was clear that this was no sitting duck. He knew we were there and what he had to do about it. After several visuals on an 88 that was all over the sky, doing steep turns, climbing and diving, I finally managed to hold him visually, and fly as in a day combat. Now night aerobatics are not to be recommended because you topple your major instruments and lose them when you-need them most. It is also very easy to lose speed and spin-in. However, Mac and I had developed a drill for such circumstances and he called height and airspeed to me every few seconds so that we would not fly into the ground. As I tried to turn inside the 88 to get my gun-sight on him I found him flying in a very tight turn, much too low for comfort. Suddenly he went on his back and dived, perhaps having stalled. Shortly afterwards there was a great flash from the -ground and both Ops and Mac lost contact. Later the French Underground confirmed time and place near Antrain where it had gone in."

On the night of 6/7 August Wing Commander J. D. Somerville DFC RCAF and Flying Officer G. D. Robinson DFC RCAF of 410 "Cougar" Squadron RCAF in NF.XIII MM566/R equipped with AI VIII shot down a Ju 88 at St. Hilaire to take their personal victory score to four. Somerville wrote:

"Took off from Colerne at 0050 hours/landed back at 0325 hours. I was put on patrol east-west (south of St. Malo). I was given a vector of 060 degrees. After being on this vector for a short time *Tailcoat* told us to vector 280 degrees, as he had something for us. I did several one-off vectors until finally on 240 degrees contact was obtained at 2 miles range, 30-35 degrees above, 12 o'clock. My observer told me to climb hard as E/A was considerably above us. Our height was 4000 feet. My starboard engine was missing badly but we managed to climb to about 5500 feet where a visual was obtained about 1000 feet above, dead ahead. Flak was starting to emanate ahead of E/A, which seemed to frighten him somewhat and he did a turn to port and started to let down slowly, which suited us as the starboard engine was giving considerable difficulty. When I saw him start to turn I cut across the inside of his turn and pulled in to about 900 feet, slightly below, where I recognized him as a Ju 88. Pulled in a little close and saw two large bombs carried externally inboard motors. Pulled up and opened fire at approximately 700 feet. a few strikes were seen on the starboard engine, which caught fire. E/A did a wide sweeping spiral to port from 3000 feet and struck the ground with an extremely violent explosion, scattering debris over a large area. Tailcoat fixed us at 180 degrees beacon FM 55 miles (St. Hilaire du H. area). No return fire or evasive action experienced. I claim 1 Ju 88 destroyed."

On 6 August 604 (County of Middlesex) Squadron at Zeals, which had joined 141 Wing, 2nd TAF, in April, transferring to 147 Wing 85 (Base) Group, on 3 May, became the first Mosquito fighter squadron to move to France, when it transferred to A.8 at Picauville on the Cherbourg Peninsula. On 11 August 264 Squadron joined 604 Squadron at Picauville. Flight Lieutenant John A. M. Haddon of 604 Squadron recollects:

"By the time 2nd TAF came into existence the Allies had had four years of night warfare experience to devise airfield systems that could function well at night as well as protect aircraft on the ground from attack. Largely they used wide dispersal, aircraft blast sheltering and minimal visibility from the air as defensive systems. As aircraft became heavier, grass surfaced fields fell out of use. By D Day engineers had perfected systems of construction that could carry entire airfields overseas, not too different in facilities from any modern field of that time. One invasion airfield, A.8 west of St. Mere Eglise in the American sector was built in about 48 hours, including runway, dispersals, taxi paths, control and refueling, using a base of sand covered with tar paper. Designed to last 30 days, it lasted 55 or so and was home to three American day fighter-bomber squadrons and two RAF night squadrons. The RAF was doing night cover from A8 because someone, quite wrongly, had convinced the planners that the US night fighters were inadequate. I heard that the A8 designer was a Canadian. Again by 2nd TAF time, aircraft carrying heavy radar and equipped with cannons firing 2400 rounds of 20mm ammunition a minute could be operated out of such fields in all-but-total darkness. As far as I know there was only one fatal crash in the 55 days of A8's existence.

"Like most wartime flying operations, the longer a night-fighter crew had survived, the longer it would continue to survive. Crews of 604 and 264, the first night squadrons on the beachhead, had no less than One full tour of duty each behind them. As I recollect it, 604 shot down some 50-60 hostiles for the loss of two or three crews from D-Day to VE Day. Life for aircrew wasn't all that bad in Normandy. There were so many experienced crews available, and food was so much easier to furnish in the UK than on the beachhead, that for one period we got ten days home leave every three weeks. As usual, staff seemed to get better quarters than fighting forces. At A8 the staff lived in the former German Army Commander's HQ, known as the 'Château', while aircrew were put into a centuries old, partly burned-out insect-ridden farmhouse known to us as the 'Shiteau'. We eventually rebelled and moved into tents.

"Although fast scrambles had been (additional ways of getting night-fighters airborne, the usual procedure was to have aircraft constantly on patrol at about Angels 10, positioned to intrude into hostile air space when required, with minimum loss of time. The speed difference between a Ju 88 and a Mosquito was sufficiently slight that the long stern chases of earlier years were out of the question. Security considerations had prevented the very latest airborne radar from-being operated from-bases so close to enemy lines, so the squadrons operating from Normandy had to use a radar that could only see in a cone (like an ice cream cone) looking forward, which limited their interception capabilities. I now forget the maximum range of that radar but probably it was two or three miles.

"A time-saving manuever, if a ground controller had been good enough to put you onto a bandit on a closing angle, was to wait for your RO to get radar contact and assess the targets course and speed as it came towards you. Then at the critical moment determined by the RO, turn hard across the face of the bandit and continue turning until hopefully it re-appeared in the radar cone in front of you. If you turned too soon, you got in front of him, not a good thing if he was also a night fighter; if you turned too late it meant a long stern chase. It was the RO's skill and the crew's total integration that determined success or failure. Most crews had spent years perfecting their techniques. On a good moonlight night a normal night fighter pilot could (visually) see an aircraft as a dot at about 4000 feet; on a black night 1500-2000 feet was pretty good. The RO's job was to get his pilot to that range, nicely positioned for the kill. Under the operating conditions of normal static warfare, ground control could reasonably assure a crew whether or not a target was hostile. Under invasion conditions such as Sicily or Norman4y, the chances of a target being hostile were perhaps ten or twenty-to-one against. I was told that when we were airborne at H-hour-6 of D Day and over a beachhead and sea area thirty miles long by twenty miles deep. There were up to 20 other TAF night fighters-as well as Dakotas towing gliders, the odd bomber and quite a few-Fighter Command aircraft trying to get into the act. My logbook shows much the same to be true for the next two weeks as we covered the fleet and invasion area. Sorting things out wasn't easy. Experienced night crews knew that it was vital to treat any interception as a technical exercise and make full identification, rather than go blustering in and shooting down some unfortunate Allied crew while the adrenaline was flowing. The only exception to this identification-first principle came from US anti-aircraft gun crews on the beachhead who generally fired at anything within range, especially before they got used to having night fighters based in their midst."

On the night of 6/7 August Mosquitoes of 2nd TAF claimed nine enemy aircraft over France. Among the missing was Hauptmann Helmut Bergmann, a *Ritterkreuzträger* and *St.Kpt* of 8./NJG4 with 37 kills, during a sortie in the Invasion Front area of Avranches-Mortain. No trace was ever found of his Bf 110G-4 or his crew.[375] On the night of 7/8 August, when 1019 heavy bombers blasted the Normandy battle area Mosquitoes of 2nd TAF claimed ten more victories,[376] almost one for each bomber lost. On 8/9 August 2nd TAF Mosquito crews scored another three victories,[377] as 170 Lancasters and ten Mosquitoes of 1, 3 and 8 Groups attacked oil depots and storage facilities at Aire-sur-Lys and the Fôret de Lucheux in France for one Lancaster lost.

On the night of 14/15 August Squadron Leader Somerville DFC and Flying Officer G. D. Robinson DFC of 410 Squadron RCAF in NF.XIII MM477/U equipped with AI VIII went in search of their fifth victory. Fifteen miles due West of Le Havre they picked up a contact as Somerville relates:

"I pulled in behind the E/A, range about 1½ miles and started to close. E/A at this time began to climb and do about a rate half turn to starboard. We maintained contact on the AI, closing the range till finally the E/A leveled off at approximately 10,500 feet after turning a complete 360 degrees. At this time I was very well shrouded. The range at this time was about 1800 feet, almost directly above. I started to pull up and on decreasing the angle off the exhausts disappeared, visual being lost. However the visual was regained at approximately 800 feet range 20 degrees off. I pulled into 600 feet and recognized E/A as a Ju 88. During this period my navigator was getting his Ross Night Glasses and from directly underneath the E/A he confirmed my recognition. At this range I noticed two heavy calibre bombs slung externally inboard of the engines. I dropped back to 450 feet, pulled up to dead astern and opened fire at this range. The fuselage of the E/A burst with a violent explosion and disintegrated into the air. No return fire was experienced. The majority of the debris fell off to port. I pulled up in a very steep climb and broke to starboard. I asked control for a fix and was given 15 miles due west of Le Havre. Time 2325 hours. I claim this E/A destroyed." Somerville was promoted to wing commander and given command of 409 Squadron RCAF.

On 18 August at Lasham 613 Squadron crews, like those in 305 (Polish) and 107 Squadrons, had been granted a 24-hour stand down by Group to celebrate 138 Wing's thousandth sortie since D-Day and no-one was expecting to fly again until the 19th. H. Mears, a navigator in 613 Squadron, recalls:

"A station party was organized in the Airmen's' Mess, together with the necessary bars. We had quite a heavy night, getting to bed about 2am. About 10.00am, we were rudely awakened from our slumbers by a Tannoy announcement ordering all of Black Section (us) to report to the crew room. After a quick wash, we staggered into the daylight for a quick cuppa in the mess, then over to the crew room. The 'doc' was doing a good trade dispensing what he called 'Hangover pills'. Many chaps were missing; sleeping out with wives or whatever. My own driver [pilot] was missing so I flew out with Squadron Leader Bell-Syer, known as the 'Count', whose observer was missing."

Fifteen FB.VI crews in 613 Squadron led by Squadron Leader Charles Newman were to carry out a daring low level attack on a school building at Egletons, 50 miles SE of Limoges, believed to be in use as an *SS* troops barracks. AVM Basil Embry and Group Captain Bower, as usual, went along. Mears continues:

"We had drop tanks fitted to the aircraft, so we knew that it was going to be a long ride. However, we eventually started off in formation, low level, across the Channel and on the deck down to the target. The use of wing tanks necessitated emptying the outer tanks, going onto the inners then going back to outers when they were emptied, making a final change to inners."

Fourteen of the Mosquitoes located and bombed the target, scoring at least 20 direct hits and the target was almost completely destroyed. One Mosquito, crewed by Flight Lieutenant House and Flying Officer Savill, was hit in the starboard engine over the target area and failed to return but the crew survived and returned to the squadron just five days later.

On 26 August 219 Squadron joined 147 Wing, 85 (Base) Group, 2nd TAF and on 3 September 264 Squadron made a move to Caen/Carpiquet with the first patrols flown over the Paris area and later over Brussels. The only real excitement was when Flight Lieutenant Moncur and Flying Officer Woodruffe did not return from a low flying exercise on the afternoon of the 19th. They did come back a week later having been shot down in the St Nazaire area. On the 14th 264 Squadron flew back to Predannack - ostensibly to re-equip, but anyway by then the war had got too far out of sight. Victories in September and October did not match those scored in June and July but the night-fighters nevertheless maintained a credible response. During September they destroyed 28 enemy aircraft of many types, and in October, a further 15 were destroyed. On 25/26 August 138 Wing took part in all-out attacks in the Rouen area on troop concentrations and vehicles that were attempting to retreat across the Seine. Attacks continued on the night of 30 August against railways in the Saarbourg and Strassburg areas. "August was a very busy month for 21 Squadron," wrote Les Bulmer:

"With the breakout from the beachhead things moved very swiftly and we harried the Germans in retreat. Sometimes it was sheer slaughter as we found roads jammed with enemy transport just waiting to be set on fire. Ed and I flew eighteen sorties that month, sometimes two in one night. On the 18th we took off at 0010 for our thirty-ninth op and were back at Thorney Island by 0145. We re-fuelled and re-armed and were off again at 0350, landing again at 0530. After de-briefing and a meal, we snatched a few hours sleep before attending briefing for the next night's raids. We were off at 2310 that night and back at 0110 on the 19th. Once again we refueled and re-armed and were off at 0415, returning at 0550. So in less than thirty hours we had carried out four operations. Coming back over the Channel on the last one I must have dozed off because I awoke with a start when the aircraft gave a violent lurch. Ed had also fallen asleep and woke just in time to stop us spiralling into the sea."

On 26 August, the day after Paris was liberated, Les Bulmer and Ed McQuarrie had a change from beating up transport, as Bulmer explains:

"The Army wanted the railway bridge at Rouen destroyed to impede the German retreat. It was too small a target for the heavies, so 21 Squadron was asked to have a go. It had to be a night attack because the enemy was bound to defend it with everything he had. Four aircraft, working in pairs, were allotted to the task. One of the pair would fly at around 3000 feet and drop flares for the other one, which would be waiting underneath. After dropping his bombs the two would change places. Since we were carrying flares in the bomb bay, we could only carry two bombs each under the wings. Flight Lieutenant Swaine and another crew took off first. We, together with our partner Flight Lieutenant Winder, left at 2235, thirty minutes or so later. On the way over to France Swaine called up on the R/T to say that it was pretty hot in the target area. He'd been hit and he recommended that we abort. Ed and Winder had a brief conversation and decided to give it a whirl - I was more than happy to call it a day but I wasn't consulted.

"We had been selected to do the first flare drop, so went in at about 3000 feet. The enemy took a dislike to us at Cap d'Antifer as we crossed the coast, then we settled down for a straight run in to Rouen. I had my head stuck in the *Gee* set following a *Gee* line that should take us over the bridge from the Northwest. Ed was concentrating on following my instructions to stay on the line and waiting for me to give him the order to drop the flares. Thus neither of us was aware of what was going on around us. This was just as well, because afterwards Winder said that he could see exactly where we were above him because of the flak that was following us in. Ignorance is a wonderful thing at times. Our three flares went down right on target but by the time we had turned to watch Winder attack, two flares had gone out - presumably shot out - and another had its parachute damaged and fell to the ground on the east bank of the river. However, this remaining flare gave enough light for us to see Winder's bombs burst on the Southwest end of the bridge. Ed stuck the nose down and we dived on the bridge before our one remaining flare expired. We let go the bombs just as the flare went out so I couldn't see the results and then we called up Winder to tell him that he needn't bother to drop his flares. I think he was as relieved as we were to get the hell out of it. I don't suppose we did much damage to the bridge - if any. But at least we tried.'

Though V1 patrols had occupied most of 418 Squadron's time in July and August they were interspersed with other types of activity, 418 reverting, in September to *Rangers* and abortive *Big Ben* patrols (trying to "jam" V2 rockets). 418 finished the war with the distinction of destroying more enemy aircraft both in the air and on the ground, than any other Canadian squadron, in both night and daylight operations as Bob Bruce, Russ Bannock's navigator, recalls:

"We did *Flowers* harassing enemy bases in support of the invasion or of bombers and *Day Rangers* hunting in pairs. These were carried out at low level, and ideally with cloud cover at 1000 feet or more, to facilitate evasion if attacked. Our first of these was on 27 June 1944 led by Flight Lieutenant Clarence Murl Jasper (Long Beach, California) and his navigator O. A. J. 'Archie' Martin DFC of Ottawa, Canada. 'Jas' was one of several American pilots who joined the RCAF and he was awarded the DFC in September. Crossing Denmark at treetop height, we found a Ju 88 crossing the Baltic, close to a fair sized vessel. Jasper destroyed the Junkers in the air, but was caught by the ship's fire. I vividly recall his blazing tailfin above the seemingly static ship. The damage was limited and he flew home successfully.[378] *Night Rangers* and *Flowers* gave similar opportunity, if we were lucky enough to detect enemy aircraft. For a higher success rate AI was needed, with which 406 ('Lynx') Squadron RCAF were equipped. But we were lucky sometimes, and Russ's shooting was deadly. Sometimes bad weather intervened. On 15 August en route for Avignon we met such thunder and up draught over the Massif Central that we had to pull out and return. We had gained 4000 feet over the mountains in a few seconds; we might equally have lost them. Russ compared the stresses he encountered there with the worst ever in his subsequent career as a test pilot. (On another trip to Breslau in October we flew 5.25 hours without a pinpoint and of course no result. Good D.R. depends upon accurate flying.)

"We did two other *Day Rangers*, one to Copenhagen with Sid Seid (another Californian) and Dave McIntosh with gratifying result, the other alone arriving at Parow, on the Baltic coast at sunrise. We found an OTU in full operation. After destroying two Me 108's in the circuit we were attacked by another older type Me 109. We broke off at treetop height but our port engine caught fire (due to debris holing the radiator). We feathered and returned on one engine landing back at Hunsdon after 7 hours 15 minutes. 418 had established a high success rate in *Day Rangers* during the first six months of 1944."[379]

138 Wing received incoming reports on 25/26 August of a concentration of troops and vehicles in the Rouen area and off attempts to retreat across the Seine. This now seemed to be a critical area and could well be a pivot to the successful advance of Allied troops into Belgium and Germany. An all-out attack in this zone was set for the night of the 26/27th. One of the crews that took part was Flight Lieutenant Eric "Tommy" Atkins DFC* KW* (*Krzyz Walecznych*, the Polish Cross of Valor) and his navigator, Flight Lieutenant Jurek Majer, in 305 Polish Squadron at Lasham. They were, at this time, veterans of 25 *Night Intruder* operations. The night before they had been searching the railways between Belgium and Germany for trains carrying V1s or V2s and had attacked one in the darkness but could not determine the extent of the damage. As they were searching the scene, a German aircraft suddenly attacked them. Luckily, their attacker missed and Atkins was able to do a tight turn and give a burst of gunfire in return before returning to Lasham "in a state of some excitement." Atkins recalls:

"Being small and light, the Mosquito could fall foul of bad weather conditions. On the other hand, in emergency conditions when caught in flak, searchlights or being attacked by enemy aircraft, it could be flung around the sky in almost impossible maneuvers that a pilot might think twice about in daylight. The Mosquito responded to the controls like a thoroughbred racehorse, with speed, precision and a sixth sense of judgment linked to that of the pilot. I have also known the Mosquito to turn in such a tight circle at night to get away from searchlights and flak beamed onto it, that it virtually 'disappears up its own orifice. A Mosquito could fly well on one engine, providing you had the speed and height to gain a level flight over a long distance. Many a Mosquito pilot flew from Germany on one engine but the landing could be tricky and you never knew whether the other engine would overheat and pack up! A Mosquito would also do a safe belly landing, providing you remembered to come in without any undercarriage and flaps - then it would probably turn over. I landed at night on a grass 'drome at Epinoy, France, with no undercarriage, no flaps and a bomb aboard! The only annoying thing was that the ambulance and M.C. took over half an hour to reach us. They were waiting to see whether the bomb went off! The aircraft had only minor damage and was soon returned to service again. Other Mosquitoes landed with half a wing missing. Despite its wooden construction the Mosquito had strength and endurance and was easier to repair. You simply spliced another wing on! The speed of the Mosquito also meant that the operational time was less (unless you were *Ranging*).

"We were told that on returning to Lasham and our tent that we would he needed again that night, 26/27 August for the all-out attack at Rouen. We tried to get some sleep during the day but we were pretty tense still after the NFT of our aircraft and as we entered the briefing tent in the late afternoon. The briefing was fairly simple - we had to tour the Rouen-Gisors-Dieppe area and bomb and strafe anything that moved, and in particular, the mass of vehicles trying to retreat across the Seine. A second operation that night was also expected of us! It was a good night for flying, not much cloud and with our 'cats eyes' we could pick out shapes on the ground. We flew quite low, at 800 feet in the darkness and picked out roads and railways. We had flares and cannon and we had been told that there might also he illumination from pathfinders, hut not to depend on it as the battle looked like being prolonged. My worry was that with so many Mosquitoes in the same area we had the further concern of avoiding each other! We soon picked out the convoy and some of the vehicles were already on fire. We bombed by the light of our flares and then turned around to gun the area again - the smoke rising up seemed to fill the cockpit and warned us that we were too low in the darkness. Our deed done, we turned for home. At that moment, a dark shape dived in front of us, missing us by inches. 'Another damned Mosquito!' said Jurek.

"When we got back to Lasham the ground crew was standing ready to reload tanks, guns etc, proud to be taking their part in the operation. We were quickly debriefed and then into our Mosquito and away again. This time we attacked a road junction clogged full of enemy transport, just outside Rouen. They were a 'sitting target', although the light flak coming up at us did hinder a straight bombing run and we had to come round again. We had scored some serious hits and once again our ammunition and bombs were expended and we started for Lasham and our cold, dank rents.

"On the ground Jurek looked at me and grinning, said, 'What about doing what you English call a 'hat trick'? I said it was OK by me if we could get turned around in time. The ground crew was magnificent and it was almost like a professional 'pit stop'. This time there were many aircraft in the area. We decided to bomb a goods train, which we found in the Rouen-Rheims-Givet area. We obtained a 'near miss' but damage had been done and on our way back we expended all our remaining ammunition on the conflagration around Rouen and the Seine. It was, indeed, the 'Rout of Rouen'. We congratulated the ground crew and ourselves and after debriefing, flung ourselves on our bunk beds in the tent and slept and slept! Our next operation was to be on the railways at night around Saarbourg and Strasbourg on 30 August, which indicated how successful our Army advance had become and our far from unsuccessful efforts to support them!"

2nd TAF received the highest possible commendation for these attacks, and this support continued. On 31 August a huge petrol dump at Nomency near Nancy was destroyed and twelve FB.VIs of 464 Squadron attacked a dozen petrol trains near Chagney from between 20 and 200 feet (and caused widespread destruction. Wing Commander G. Panitz, the CO, failed to return, but the Panzer divisions in the Battle of Normandy were deprived of millions of gallons of much needed fuel.

At 5 AM on 31 August 1944 Squadron Leader Stanislaw Grodzicki and his navigator Flight Lieutenant Adam Szajdzicki in 305 (Polish) Squadron had just landed back at Lasham after a 4-hour patrol over northeast France. They were one of six Mosquito crews put on the Battle Order for the day's operation:

"I had got up late from bed," remembers Adam, "and was in rather a hurry to get to the Mess for lunch. I collected my bicycle from behind the tent.

"'Adam,' I heard the voice of Squadron Leader Grodzicki, my pilot, say. 'Where are you going?'

"'To lunch,' I said.

"'Forget it. Take your things and come quickly for the briefing. We are flying with five Mosquitoes. Orlinski is leading.' Wing Commander B. Orlinski was our CO at the time.

"'Hard luck,' I said. 'There goes my lunch.'

"But the news excited me because it could be an interesting operation. I went back and collected my bag, which was lying under my bed where I had left it earlier in the morning. The ops tent was not very far away, and arriving there I found that some of our crews were already there, and others were arriving. Everybody was asking the same question: 'Where? What?'

"The map on the wall was marked with a red thread for our track. The route out was over Portland Bill, Guernsey, Arromanches, then south of Auxerre, north of Langre, ending just north of Epinol. A US flag was pinned in Auxerre indicating that there were American forces. The flight plan was already written on the board for us to copy. To the briefing came the Group Captain, our CO and two assistant officers. One of them I knew from previous briefings. The other, a 'new face", held a big roll of papers under his arm.

"Wing Commander Orlinski called the briefing to order and began: 'Gentlemen, our destination is Nomexy where there are reservoirs estimated to hold more than 3 million gallons of German petrol, which must be destroyed. We will fly six aircraft, and not five as stated in the order.'

"He named the sixth pilot, Flight Lieutenant Smith, who had only recently joined our squadron and was known among us as 'Matilda' because he used to sing or whistle the song, which had a Central American rhythm – '*Matilda, Matilda, took your money and went to Venezuela'*. He was the only Bahamian crewmember among us. He appeared, beaming with pleasure. It was his second or third operation. Orlinski said that we were flying in pairs stacked to the rear. But before the last check-point we would separate and increase the distance between the aircraft to four miles apart because we would be attacking our target from low level, one by one and our bombs were fitted with 11-second delay fuses. He added, 'I don't want any of you getting blown up by our own bombs. The navigation to the target will be done by my navigator and I will tell you about the start later.'

"Now the 'new face' stepped forward. 'Well, gentlemen, here is your target.' With those words he opened the papers. These were the photographs of our destination. He passed them around, saying, 'Please have a good look at them, and memorize them well to make sure that you will find your target.' After a while he continued. 'The photos were taken on the same track as you will be heading for the target. There is also a photo of the last checkpoint. That is the photo with four large buildings beside the loop in the river bend. Now from that check-point, which we will call zero point, you will have to take a course of 022 for 4 minutes, then - Bang!' - you will be over your target. I am afraid that the target will not be too visible from the zero point.' He was finished.

"The zero point was very good indeed and could not be mistaken. I tried to memorize the details that were not shown on the map. The three big petrol reservoirs stood on the eastern side of a railway line running north from Epinol to Nancy on an azimuth of about 35-170 degrees. Beyond was the river lined with high trees. I was impressed with the preparations that had been made for this raid. Drawing our track through the target I thought that it had been well chosen. On that approach we probably would not see the light between the tanks and it would present a more certain target for our bombs. The navigation officer gave us the exact run-in time from the zero point, and Orlinski assigned each crew a position in the formation. We were No 2.

"He continued, 'At 1500 hours proceed to your aircraft, start engines on my signal. We will start rolling right away to avoid overheating the engines, as it is very hot today. The start will be in pairs with the second pair accelerating when the first is at the end of the runway. After take-off, turn left. Remember to empty the drop tanks as soon as possible. In the bomb bay are two bombs with 11-second delay fuses.

Remember you will be dropping them from low level so don't get too close behind one another. Over the UK and the Channel we will fly at 2000 feet and later over France we will come down to 200 feet. At this time we have had no reports of German fighter activity along our route, but you never know - so watch it! Keep total radio silence. Only break it in an emergency. Any questions? Oh yes,' he added. 'There will be the usual man with the Aldis lamp at your dispersal point. Signal him when you are ready and obey his signals.' For the benefit of the CO and Matilda, the briefing had been conducted in English.

"'We are ready, sir,' said Orlinski, saluting the CO.

"The CO returned the salute and said to us, 'Good luck, boys. Let's go to our aircraft.'

"I checked the contents of my navigation bag, collected the flares of the day, and put one of them into the top of my left boot. I stuffed my pistol into the top of the right boot. Then, from the box I collected a chute and the harness with the dinghy attached to it and the bag. This made a very heavy load and it was not easy to carry it the 100 or so yards across the clearing, where our aircraft was standing. Just before leaving the briefing tent, I snatched up the photo of the target and pushed it inside my battledress blouse.

"At *Z-Zebra* the ground crew were waiting, and reported that the aircraft was OK. Stan, my pilot, went to check the aircraft logbook and I dropped my gear on the ground and went to check the suspension of the bombs. I gave them a friendly tap, and wished them a good journey and a good landing.

"Stan and Adam went through their take-off checks and finally, at 1535, taxied out to the runway. Adam looked back at the 'wonderful line of Mosquitoes' and one by one they took off.

"It was quieter in the cockpit now as the aircraft climbed in a wide left turn. There was only the noise of the wind outside, and the hiss of the fresh air in the ventilators. After one circuit No 1 waggled his wings and we set course for Winchester, leveling off at *Angels Two* [2000 feet]. Then we changed course south for Portland Bill, and Portsmouth, full of all sorts of shipping, slipped by on the port side. Craft of all sorts were heading to and from Normandy, some of them towing barrage balloons.

"We followed No.1 to Arromanches. I spotted three Dakotas heading northwest, probably flying home the wounded. I watched the sky for bandits and noted the course and height changes in my log. Dropping to 300 feet and increasing speed, we passed Auxerre on the port beam and the ground whistled by. We were keeping well clear of the built-up areas because the Germans could still be there, even though the briefing map showed that the Americans had captured the area. We also knew that our own ack-ack chaps were a bit 'trigger-happy'.

"I pushed the safety switch to arm the bombs, logged the time and shouted to Stan to tell him. The loop in the River Maine came in sight and Chaumont was visible on the port beam. Up to now everything was going fine and quietly - we were 2 minutes early. The ground sped by beneath us as I searched the sky for bandits - thank God none were visible. I pulled out the photograph of the target and tried to sort out the details in my mind. This was my last chance to do it. We just had to find the bloody target! I kept repeating this over and over again. I checked my watch again -in 3 minutes we should be at the zero point. Ahead appeared the four buildings, then the bend in the river, just as the photo showed.

"'We are coming to point zero, dead ahead. Can you see it?' I said to Stan.

"'OK,' he said, steering the aircraft slightly to the right and increasing the distance from No 1 to make sure that we were making 022 degrees over the zero point.

"'OK,' said Stan again. 'On course.'

"I opened the bomb doors as we flew over the zero point and noted the time. But we could not see the target ahead. Instead there was a hill. Orlinski changed course to about 060 degrees and headed towards Epinal on our starboard. Stan spotted him and shouted, "'Where is No 1 going? Are you sure we are on the right track?'

"'Check that you are on 022 degrees,' I replied. I gave a quick glance at the photo and saw that there were vineyards on the slope of the hill between the zero point and the target. I saw vineyards on the hill in front of us. I suddenly realized that French farmers, logically, had probably planted the vineyard on the south slopes of the hill facing the sun.

"'Another 2½ minutes to go,' I said. 'The target must be over the hill.'

"'Are you sure?' asked Stan.

"'That's the course they told us to steer. One and a half minutes to go. There is some flak on the far right.'

"I had a feeling that soon our Mosquito would start chopping up the vines, we were flying so low. We were going parallel to the slope of the hill.

"'Forty-five seconds to go,' I called.

"Stan pulled up the Mossie over the top of the hill. 'Oh Santa Madonna! What a sight!'

"Straight ahead and below were the reservoirs, standing at an angle to our course, just like the photo. Stan pushed the stick sharply forward and I shot out of my seat, my head hitting the canopy.

"'Bombs gone!" called Stan, putting the starboard wing down and pulling the aircraft up. I spotted the bombs. The right one was slightly ahead of the others and seemed to be going for a break between the tanks. Damn! The second one was heading directly into the middle tank. I held my breath. Is it going to be a direct hit? Oh no! God! It's gone over the tank. Damn! I realized that when we were over the hill and climbing that we had not enough time and distance to put the aircraft into a steeper dive; therefore the bombs had been released too high. One had exploded in the river, one in a field behind it. I was absolutely disgusted. All that way for nothing!

"'They missed the tanks,' I told Stan.

"'Look out for our Mosquitoes and their whereabouts,' requested Stan, pulling the aircraft up into a very tight left turn. The G-force was pushing me into my seat. I felt a pain in my bottom; the dinghy was not very comfortable as a seat cushion. I wanted to stand up to have a better look around. I was worried about our starboard side because aircraft could be coming from that quarter. Looking over the port wing I saw the river approaching, and through the canopy I saw the burning tanks. We passed over the river, then over the railway, and at that moment a Mosquito passed right under us. Bombs were bursting in the railway yard as we climbed, always in that sharp turn. We flew over the town's houses, then some trees and a hill, while another Mosquito was pulling away from the yard.

"The tanks were coming up at 10 o'clock. The G-forces became less tormenting. Stan put the Mossie into a dive and the turn became gentler but steeper. The tanks were at 12 o'clock when Stan opened fire with the cannons. Suddenly the aircraft started to shake and the airspeed dropped by 40 mph. Tracers hit the ground in front of the tanks on the far left, and slowly rose until they pierced the tanks. A red tongue of fire burst from the lower part of the tank, and as the aircraft slid further to the right the tracer hit the central tank. This also burst into flames, as did the third tank, which blew up sending a great cloud of black smoke into the air. We were heading straight for it.

"'Oh God! That smoke will cover us.'

"The Mosquito stopped shaking and the next instant we ran into the dark cloud. The cockpit became dark and smelly for a few seconds before we came out into the clean fresh air beyond. The smell persisted as we made a wide left circle, while happily admiring the fire and looking to see if there was anything else that we could destroy. At that moment a Mosquito passed over the yard.

"'Hey, Blue chaps,' came a voice on the radio, "there is smoke towards the north.'

"Before we had finished the circle I spotted another Mosquito passing along the yard. In turn we came in line with the rail line. Stan pushed the stick forward and started diving toward the freight cars standing on the rails, opening fire on them. I noted some flashes on the cars but this time we did not manage to start new fires. Stan was preparing himself for the third run when on the radio came Orlinski's voice.

"'Blue, Blue, return to formation over point zero.'

"Stan immediately set course south. Suddenly, on the radio came the song, 'Matilda, Matilda, took your petrol and went to Venezuela. Ha ha!'

"I counted six Mosquitoes making formation as we set course for home, along the same route as we had taken on the way in. The return flight went quietly and we landed at base at 1955.

"At the de-briefing Flight Lieutenant Leimiesozonek, Orlinski's navigator, explained that they had turned eastward after the zero point because he could not see the target ahead. He had turned towards what he thought was a camouflaged target. We found out that the second pair had followed No.1, thinking that we were wrong. The third pair did not follow us over the hill because they couldn't see the target, so they went around the hill to look for it; these were the Mosquitoes I spotted flying over the rail lines. For his efforts Stan was awarded the '*Virtuti Militarui*' decoration and I was awarded the '*Krzyz Walecznych*' (Cross of Valor)."

Life for Dave McIntosh was never dull flying with Sid Seid. McIntosh recalls that:

"Shortly after dawn on 15 October 1944, Sid and I were flying in a Mosquito fighter over our target, Stargard, a German airfield northeast of Berlin. We were a long way from home (Hunsdon, an airfield thirty miles north of London) and still had farther east and north to go to a second target, Kolberg, another German aerodrome, before we could head back to England. 'Heading back' were the sweetest two words, I knew during the war, apart from 'arrival Hunsdon' (or any other friendly base). We were in the process of attacking Luftwaffe planes on the ground-we had seen none in the air, thank heaven - and there was a whole array of them for our picking: Messerschmitt fighters, Junkers night-fighters, Stuka dive-bombers and Focke Wulf fighters. We had flown low (treetop) level, pulling up over power lines, and had so completely caught the Jerries by surprise that a hundred of them were drawn up for what we surmised was a Sunday morning (which was what it was) church parade. I say surmise because neither Sid nor I ever went to church (in his case, synagogue) except, perhaps, to give the squadron padre a lift. Occasionally when he was particularly down in the mouth because of heavy non-attendance at his services in gymnasium, hangar or open air. Fear of death in war might have driven some fliers to God, but it didn't drive them to church.

"Sid dived at one group of planes, aiming at the wing roots where the fuel were located, and blazed away with our 20mm cannon. He blew up a Messerschmitt with a one-second burst on our first run. We got turned around for another run at the field and Sid fired a two-second burst at three planes, one exploding. As he finished the salvo, he spotted two more planes, one a Stuka, on the south side of the field. He got in a quick burst and the Stuka exploded just as we started going over on our port side. We were only 20 feet off the deck and when Sid tried to correct our roll we stalled and the stick flew out of his hands.

"We should have been dead right there and then, spread in little pink and red pieces all over Stargard airfield. If the Germans could find anything at all to pick up, the two of us would have fitted easily into one shoe or cigar box. But the Mosquito in an unexplained flick righted itself and we were flying straight and level at a height often feet. The explanation for this baffling Mosquito self-maneuver didn't interest me; only the result did. Later, I wondered vaguely whether our plane's call sign, *Credo 29*, had anything to do with our survival: Belief, resulting in a perfect cribbage hand. When my nerves steadied (as much as they ever did-a controlled jangle) a few minutes later as we raced over the sunlit autumn leaves toward Kolberg, I said to myself: "Boy, the rest of your life is pure gravy. Every minute after flicking out of the lethal stall is an unearned bonus."

On 31 August Mosquito fighter-bombers destroyed a huge petrol dump at Nomency, near Nancy, and twelve FB.VIs of 464 Squadron attacked a dozen petrol trains near Chagney from between 20 and 200 feet and caused widespread destruction.

At Hunsdon in summer 1944, Pilot Officer Dudley Hemmings' pilot in 464 Squadron completed his tour with him and was rested. The young navigator met Squadron Leader Don Wellings DFC, "a tall, unassuming man," who had completed a tour on Blenheims at a night-vision course:[380]

"During the period June to October 1944 Don and I did 35 ops, thirty at night, five day low level trips. We commenced our first ops on the V1 flying bomb sites in Northern France. The targets were difficult to locate in the woods, the ramps not much longer than a cricket pitch. I must say was scared on my first trip when we saw the heavily defended French coast ahead 50 feet over the sea. Low-level tight formation in Vics or Boxes was a must for the squadrons. This was difficult for some pilots to do continually. Wellings was a fearless man and could fly a perfect course from his navigator. During night attacks in Normandy with me he would press hard to destroy the target going as low as possible for accuracy - hence I would yell out to him altimeter readings fearing he was getting too low for my liking!

"A typical night op. Take off Lasham 2300 hours. Sixteen minutes to Littlehampton on the coast, across the Channel at 50 feet. When the French coast was coming up we climbed to 3000 feet, crossed the coast in a weaving dive to escape any flak then down to about 1500-2000 feet and patrolled a given area in the battle zone. Eventually to find a moving train or transport column, climb a bit and drop a flare over the targets. It would burn on a parachute for about seven to ten minutes turning night into day. Bomb the train - engine if possible - the train would stop - rake the train with machine guns and cannon and set it on fire. Sometimes got flak and the cockpit filled with cordite smoke, which nearly made me sick as I called out altimeter readings to Wellings in our dives. I would identify the location with a *Gee* fix if possible and when all armaments expended set course for the French coast and back to base. Then a de-briefing - bacon and eggs - and on to our camp stretchers for sleep around 3 AM."

Early in September the focus of the war changed dramatically. One of the first to hear about a new highly secret operation was Vic Hester, who had completed a tour as a pilot with 613 Squadron in June 1944 after 31 operations, and whose navigator, Ray Birkett, had left to do training duties. Hester recalls:

"I remained with 138 Wing at Lasham flying DZ383 a modified B.IV Series II, which had an all-perspex nose, occupied by a cine cameraman from Pinewood studios. The modified nose allowed the cameraman to squat and shoot his films at any angle. We also fixed up a 400 feet-reel camera, fixed to shoot straight ahead. We rigged up a simple gun sight for the pilot so that he could operate this particular camera. Our task was to take 35mm cine footage of selected raids by any squadron in 2 Group. This unusual Mosquito could carry either 4x500lb bombs in the fuselage or extra fuel tanks extending the range by some 300 miles. In fact these extra fuel tanks, when new, carried 80 gallons of Courage's Best Bitter to our colleagues stationed on B 5 landing strip near Bayeaux, France, in August 1944. I've continued to be amazed how short a time it took for the British Army and Air Force to consume over 600 pints of beer! 'We were not on the strength of any of the three squadrons that made up 138 Wing, so we could not use any known squadron letters on our aircraft, so a question mark was painted in place of a letter. The first attempt, by a Polish airman went wrong, as he got the question mark the wrong way round on one side!

"On 4 September my cameraman Ted Moore and I were detailed to attend a briefing at RAF Netheravon, which was filled to over capacity with tugs, gliders and their crews.[381] We were briefed by most senior Army officers on operation *Market-Garden* and thereafter confined to camp.[382] After two days of bad weather we were allowed to return to our base on no more than normal wartime security, believing, at that time, the operation to be cancelled. Imagine our surprise when, roughly two weeks later, we were briefed locally for the same operation. The date was different; but the dropping zone was the same and the drop-time was similar. I still have doubts that our security was not jeopardized in those two weeks."

On 17 September operation *Market-Garden* took place. Thirty-two FB.VIs of 107 and 613 Squadrons in 138 Wing were detailed to attack a German barracks at Arnhem, while 21 Squadron at Thorney Island bombed three school buildings in the center of Nijmegen, which were being used by the German garrison. Both raids were to eliminate the opposition before the airborne forces went in later that day. Flying Officer Nigel L. Gilson, a navigator in 107 Squadron, had been spending a day's leave in Winchester and was all set for an enjoyable evening to round it off at a dance hall in Basingstoke. However, a friend gave him the news that he had to return to Lasham immediately as the squadron was confined to barracks overnight:

"We were met by the usual expectant rumors, but could still learn nothing definite except that we were to be up for briefing at 0530. Ours was a quiet Mess that night, only admin officers were drinking more than lemonade and all air crews were in bed by about 10 - most unusual for us!' Rising before midday was a bit of a strain, but 0530 on Sunday found us all milling around the briefing room with an exceptional complement of 'braid and scrambled egg' among us. The tense gaiety and laconic humor of briefing are something one remembers but can't adequately describe. I can recall only two things. The CO's description of the purpose of the Arnhem landing (for that was the cause of the trouble): 'If this one comes off the war will be over in 14 days'; and his description of the anticipated reception of the paratroops: 'They expect to slide down stocks of 40 millimeter.' A minor flap broke out while navigators struggled with maps, rulers, protractors and computers, working out tracks, courses, winds and other essentials to the successful combat of hostile gremlins, until at last there was a welcome break for a hasty bacon and egg breakfast. It was a hectic and hilarious meal, then we were back for a final route check and squadron briefing on formation and tactics."

Vic Hester continues:

"We were briefed for two tasks that day: First was to film the 613 Squadron raid, then after that, photograph the airborne drop at Arnhem. We took our usual four bombs in case we found an opportune target. Whilst in our aircraft sorting out our cameras etc just prior to 'engine start time' the Wing Intelligence Officer appeared and gave us an extra brief. 'Can you take off at once and attack an undefended telephone exchange in a disused barracks in the town of Arnhem?' He handed us a map of the town and the position of the barracks, adding that they had just found out that the German land-line communications would need to go via that exchange when the Para drop began. What could be simpler? We loved undefended targets and were used to hitting small buildings.

"We took off about five minutes ahead of 613 Squadron. I think they probably thought my watch was wrong. Upon arrival over Arnhem we found the target. Good Boy. Good Boy. We made live one bomb only. The target was a haystack size building just inside the main gate of the barracks. Why not treat this attack as a practice bombing exercise and make four runs? We slowly descended for the first, and when we were established in a shallow dive, Ted Moore in the nose said, "Jesus Christ, look at that!" Now Ted was a very cool, quiet South African who seldom got excited about anything, so I realized that something was afoot. Taking my eye of f the target, I saw that we were gently approaching twenty *Tiger* tanks - all manned and firing at us!

"We dropped our one bomb from an approach pattern we would not have used had we known the target was defended. As a result our aircraft was hit and I got three bullets in my left leg, which stopped my left foot from working. Ted kindly fastened a field dressing around the outside of my trousers and we continued the exercise. Fusing the other three bombs, we made a further attack on the telephone exchange, but did not wait to see if we had hit the target. We were now too late to film the attack by 613 Squadron, so with regret, we continued to the Para dropping zone, found, and filmed considerable German armor etc surrounding the dropping area, and decided to head for home. There was no way I could break radio silence and even if I had, no single aircraft transmission could have put a stop to such a large operation as *Market-Garden*. On arrival back at Lasham, our AOC, AVM Basil Embry, was on base. With no food for several hours, I hobbled into de-briefing. Noting my state, Basil Embry handed me a half-pint glass full of issue rum, and proceeded to take our report. Ted Moore went off the process the films, which were flown to Monty within hours."

Meanwhile, at Lasham the Mosquitoes of 138 Wing had taken off, but only after a few last minute hiccups, as Nigel Gilson recalls:

"Time for take-off was altered twice, but at last we went to our aircraft where tired ground crews, who'd been working half the night, were just finishing bombing and arming up. Flying Officer Phil Slayden, my pilot, and I sat on the grass waiting for the signal to get into our aircraft. In the peace of a brilliant Sunday morning war seemed very far away. Only Dougie, who'd come to the squadron the day before, remarked on the incongruity of it all; the strains of '*Abide With Me*' from a nearby hangar service sounded too ominous to his unaccustomed ear to pass unnoticed! The ground crew gave us the usual strict orders to do a good job with their aeroplane and wished us a brief but sincere "Good luck", and we taxied out. We took off into a clear sky already filling with squadrons of ungainly gliders and tugs, took up formation and set course. Soon the English draughtboard gave place to a sea of rippled blue, and finally that to the deeply cut green flats of Holland.

"Arnhem identified itself for us - the natives, or their uninvited guests were distinctly hostile - but we rejoiced in our speed and ploughed in. At first one could watch things quite objectively; one gun team was firing explosive shells, with tantalizing persistency, right on our track, and I wondered absent-mindedly by how much they would miss us. Then we dived to attack. I bent to switch on the camera, began to rise and then instinctively ducked again, only to be conscious of an explosion and a shower of perspex splinters. I jerked up, looking anxiously at Phil, and heaved a sigh of relief when I saw that he was OK and that we were climbing again. At least, I think we were climbing - neither of us was quite sure what happened in those 30 seconds. A glance showed that the gun team had been robbed of their prey by the dive, and the shell had burst above us, merely shattering our cockpit cover.

"Suddenly Phil called, 'Hey, the bomb doors are shut, we couldn't have dropped the bombs!'

'I jammed them open and he pressed the tit to drop the bombs; we looked behind for the flash, but there was none, and then we remembered that we'd opened the doors before the dive and must have closed them instinctively during the attack. But the look behind had shown us one thing - an aircraft with our markings suddenly catching fire in the starboard petrol tank. The flames spread rapidly to the port, covering the cockpit; the aircraft lost height and finally hit a house and overturned into the river. We shall not forget that quickly. Woody and Mac were in that mass of flame.

"It was only a matter of minutes before we were over the Zuider Zee again, flying below formations of gliders and tugs. We felt sorry for them - they hadn't our speed, they had to fly straight though the flak, and their occupants had to go down on 'chutes or without engines or guns - no future in that.

"The CO called up to check formation. As we called 'Here' to our own call sign we waited anxiously to hear who was missing. Two failed to reply - two out of 14. Woody and Mac, Ted and Griff had bought it - tough luck; we should miss them."

Dudley Hemmings and Don Wellings, who in August had moved to 613 Squadron, recalls:

"The attacks were scheduled to begin five minutes before midday Dutch time to soften the German defenses ahead of the invading paratroopers. As was usual with all Mosquito daylight raids, low level flying and careful routing into the targets to gain surprise was essential for success. Whilst by late 1944 the Luftwaffe had diminished in the air, enemy anti-aircraft guns were still heavy around German held positions. The task given the Section led by Squadron Leader Don Wellings DFC and I as his navigator, was to attack the barracks in the center of Arnhem."

The thirty-two FB.VI Mosquitoes of 107 and 613 Squadrons in 138 Wing were to attack in shallow high-speed dives at between 800 and 1500 feet two German barracks complexes in Arnhem, the Willemskazerne in the center of the town and the Saksen-Weimarkazerne in the northern outskirts. Fifteen Mosquitoes of 21 Squadron in 140 Wing were to bomb three school buildings in the center of Nijmegen, which were being used by the German garrison. One of the crews who took part was Canadian Flight Lieutenant Ed McQuarrie RCAF and his navigator Flight Lieutenant "Les" Bulmer, who were flying their last operation as a crew. Bulmer recalls;

"It was to be quite an exciting finish to our tour together. Both raids were to eliminate the opposition before the airborne forces of *Market-Garden* went in later that day. We were still based at Thorney Island, so we would have quite a way to go to reach the target. As a result we had to carry wing tanks, which meant that our bomb load was confined to two 500-pounders in the bomb bay. At briefing we had the usual 2 Group model of the town so that we could familiarize ourselves with the target and the run-in over the town. There would be fifteen aircraft in five sets of three in echelon starboard. Wing Commander David F. Dennis DSO DFC DFM led with 'Jock' Murray as his No 2. We led the third echelon with Flight Lieutenant Bert Willers as our No.2. To ensure that all fifteen aircraft would be clear of the target before the bombs exploded the leading aircraft (the first ten) had 25-second fuses, whereas the rear echelons had the normal eleven-second delay. To stay clear of trouble we planned to fly across the Channel and up to the front line at high level. Once over enemy territory we would drop down to the deck and head for a road that ran northwest from Cleve into Nijmegen. The road would give us an accurate run-up to the target, which consisted of three large buildings forming a semi-circle facing the direction from which we planned to attack, so it would be easy to identify."

On 17 September 1113 medium and heavy bombers escorted by 330 fighter aircraft carried out bombing attacks to eliminate the opposition before the airborne forces of *Market-Garden* went in later that day. The first airlift alone involved 360 British and 1174 American transport aircraft and 491 gliders, accompanied by 910 fighter escorts. During the course of the operation 20,190 parachutists, 13,781 glider-borne troops, 5230 tons of equipment and stores, 1927 vehicles and 568 pieces of artillery were landed behind the German lines. The bombing strikes included seventeen Mosquitoes of 107 Squadron and sixteen Mosquitoes of 613 Squadron at Lasham and sixteen Mosquitoes of 21 Squadron at Thorney Island. 107 Squadron finally began taking off at half-minute intervals at 1051 hours after a few last minute hiccups as Dudley Hemmings continues:

"We formed up in tight formation and set course for Southwold on the English coast for the 750 miles round trip. Across East Anglia we had a marvellous view of the sky filled with the great armada of some of the 2000 transports and gliders en route to their drop zones several miles west of Arnhem. Crossing the English coast at Southwold we soon left the brave Red Berets behind and skimmed over the North Sea at 50 feet and 250 mph - IFF off and bombs switched to 'Fire'. As lead navigator I was map reading each pinpoint every two minutes to keep on track knowing there were seven crews behind relying on our lead. Our routing into Arnhem was circuitous and required good timing, pinpoint map reading and the use of *Gee* over the 130 miles of sea to the Dutch coast. Midway over the North Sea we turned slightly to port at a DR position in order to cross the Dutch coast one-mile south of Egmont, a position presumed undefended. Landfall without incident was made as planned and we swept across the lowlands of Holland, lifting up over some high-tension lines east of Alkmaar. At a headland on the Zuider Zee near Hoorn we turned south east to cross 32 miles of the Zuider Zee, making for a checkpoint at Nijkerk where a railway ran 90 degrees to our track. We crossed the town of Nijkerk at house top level and looking behind us it was good to see the flight still in close formation.

"We were now eight minutes to our time on target. About ten miles west of Arnhem we turned on an easterly course and climbed rapidly to 3000 feet, the others breaking the box formation to line astern. I had an oblique photo of a model made from aerial photographs and knew that a white gravel road led straight to the barracks. We flew in a shallow dive down this road. I pointed out the target to Don Wellings and we dropped our bombs from 1000 feet. The Mossies behind us did likewise. We carried instantaneous bombs on this trip and could not bomb at low level for fear of blowing up either the following aircraft or ourselves. When really low level bombing was done, eleven-second delay bombs were carried. Pilot aimed bombing became quite accurate after much practice by pilots on the bombing ranges back in England. Up came some flak and with the bomb doors open Wellings opened up with the firepower in the nose as our bombs were released. The Section followed us in. Until now the crews had maintained radio silence but soon after flattening out past the target I heard one of our crews over the radio call out 'We've got it!'"

In 21 Squadron, meanwhile, Ed McQuarrie and "Les" Bulmer had taken off at 1045 for Nijmegen and the Mosquitoes formed up into tight formation. Bulmer continues:

"Somewhere short of the front line we shed our drop tanks - empty tanks could be lethal if hit by flak. Just after crossing the front line we came under heavy ack-ack fire near Weert. There was nothing we could do to avoid it, as this would have destroyed the formation. But this didn't stop No.2 in the second echelon from trying to weave. He was a bigger menace than the flak. As far as I know nobody was hit, although a message came over the R/T calling someone by name - which we didn't catch - telling them that they were on fire. I think it probably came from some other formation because there were no signs of fire in ours. But I reckon it caused a mild panic among all our crews. On the deck it was hard work for the pilots trying to keep one eye on the ground and the other on the rest of the formation. Somewhere along the way there was a cry of 'Wires, wires!' and we had to climb to get over an electricity pylon. I was amazed to see that Willers on our right seemed to fly underneath! In fact, I found out afterwards that he'd taken advantage of the droop in the cables to stay low.

"Our turning point on the Cleve-Nijmegen road came up, which we planned to follow into Nijmegen but we carried straight on, then circled starboard to come up on Cleve from the east. I had no idea what was going on. Every navigator in the formation, except the leader, must have been wondering what the hell was happening. I could hardly believe my eyes when the leading aircraft opened their bomb doors. Ed followed suit and I yelled at him that this wasn't the target and not to release our bombs. Poor Ed was totally confused and probably thought I had gone off my head since the leaders were obviously intent on bombing whatever was coming up. After what seemed ages but was probably only seconds the leader's bomb doors closed and I breathed a sigh of relief as we shot over Cleve. On the straight road, with houses on either side and a larger building, which could have been a church or chapel, people were standing watching us go over. I looked back to check that the rear echelons had noticed that bomb doors had been closed and saw to my dismay a large cloud of black smoke. Some of the rear six aircraft had let their bombs go. (According to later official reports three aircraft bombed a barrack square in Cleve and machine-gunned troops.)

"Southwest of Cleve is the Reichwald, a large forest and we proceeded to career around this. By now there was not much formation left, just a gaggle of aircraft milling around waiting for someone to make a decision. Suddenly I saw two aircraft haring off in the right direction - one of them, I later discovered, was Jock Murray. I told Ed to follow and we chased after them, with everyone else tagging along behind or beside us. We were now fifteen aircraft all flying individually towards Nijmegen. And we had no means of knowing whether any of the leading planes were the ones with the short fuses.

"We sped up the road to Nijmegen and I could see the bridge over on the right. Then we were over the town looking anxiously for the target. It seemed to be chaos, with Mosquitoes going in all directions, flak coming up and Mustangs milling around above us. I noticed one Mosquito climbing away to the north and wondered where the hell he was going. Then another Mosquito shot underneath us almost at right angles. I shall never know how he found room between the rooftops and us and I wondered why he was going in that particular direction. Then I realized that he'd seen the target and was heading straight for it. I yelled to Ed to pull round and pointed to the target, by now almost on our port wing tip. He put us into a tight turn but we couldn't make it in time. We shot over the town and I recall the railway station with crowds waiting on the platform and what appeared to be a green-colored train alongside. In a flash we were clear and out over farmland where we dumped our bombs and fled. On the way in and on the way out the farmers and their families were standing in their doorways waving like mad - probably cheering on 'the brave RAF' while we were thinking, 'what the hell are we doing here, let's get the hell out of it.' The element of surprise is essential on low-level attacks and there is no going round again unless you have suicidal tendencies so we found a convenient wood and jettisoned our load. In the confusion we forgot to put the arming switches to 'OFF' so I just hoped that no one would be passing that way within the next 25 seconds. (We weren't the only ones to blow holes in the countryside. At the subsequent inquest there were several photographs taken by rearward-facing cameras showing jettisoned bombs exploding. There were a few caustic comments from the flight commanders about this. Fortunately we didn't have a camera on board so we managed to conceal our misdemeanor.) We found another Mosquito, which seemed to be going in the same direction as us, so we joined him for the journey home. This was uneventful; we didn't even get shot at over Weert this time. Maybe the Germans didn't consider two aircraft to be worth wasting ammunition on. And besides, we were heading for home.

"We returned to Thorney Island (one crew was missing) where the full story of the confusion over the target route unfolded. Wing Commander Dennis had a bird hit his windscreen just before reaching the turning point. In retrospect it might have been wiser for him to pull out and hand over to Jock Murray immediately but he chose to carry on, not being able to see properly and hence the mess we finished up in. Only five aircraft claimed to have located and bombed the target. Most of the rest did as we did and dumped them in fields, apart from those who had already got rid of theirs over Cleve. I've always felt that it was a mistake to have fifteen planes in one formation. The usual formation on previous raids of this sort was groups of six in two vics of three. Because each of the following echelons had to be stepped down on the one in front to avoid slipstream problems, it meant that the leader had to keep a reasonable height above the deck, otherwise the rear echelons would be ploughing a furrow across the countryside. In the event, it was impossible to avoid hitting slipstreams and we were being thrown all over the place and at treetop height this is not the healthiest of situations. It was only later that we learned that the German troops were not in their barracks anyway, so all we succeeded in doing was probably to kill a few innocent Dutchmen and some German civilians. Such is war. In wartime I suppose you can't very well admit to the world that you made a cock-up."

Hemmings concludes.

"Safely back at Lasham after three hours in the air a debriefing, some discussion of the other Sections' experiences (two aircraft failed to return), a beer at 'The Swan' in Alton nearby clouding the knowledge that tomorrow was another day, another 'op'. As to whose bombs hit the barracks or went astray I do not know. It is best not to know as a number of Dutch civilians were killed during the raid. For navigator and pilot on such missions it was purely a test of one's navigational and flying skills, a hope .of survival under fire, a task completed as ordered and a mental isolation from the outcome on the ground. When my CO told me my operational tour was completed and to take Rest Leave Wellings said to me that the CO had told him the same. While he insisted I go Wellings stated that he would ask to stay on because he wanted to 'see out the war'. Sadly, when I was on leave he took a new navigator and went missing on 9 October 1944."

The Arnhem operation was the last one for Ed McQuarrie and for Les Bulmer, or at least he thought so at the time:

"Ed had done the requisite fifty trips and I'd managed 52 because Ed had an argument with a motor cycle early in our tour and finished up in hospital. While he was in there I did two trips with an Irishman, Flying Officer Smith. Ed and I went on two weeks leave and I expected that we would be sent on rest to an OTU but I was in for an unpleasant surprise when I returned to pick up my kit and move on. While I was away 2 Group had moved the goal posts. A tour was now 85 ops with a month's leave around the halfway mark, 200 operational hours or twelve months on the squadron, whichever came first. I was told to take another fortnight's leave and come back for another 35 trips. It was rather like being given the death sentence. Having survived 52 ops I couldn't believe that my luck would last for another 35. I never saw Ed McQuarrie again and it is only in recent years that I learned that the RCAF would not go along with the extended tour and Ed was shipped back to Canada."

On 18 September the Germans counter-attacked and forestalled an American attempt to capture the bridge at Nijmegen. *Market-Garden* has been described in an official report as "by far the biggest and most ambitious airborne operation ever carried out by any nation or nations."[383]

Altogether, nine Mosquito bomber squadrons now equipped 2nd TAF. In September 1944, following the outbreak from the Normandy beachhead, plans were in progress to move them to airfields in France. As part of the newfound offensive, Mosquito squadrons outside 2nd TAF also made daylight *Rangers* from France and intruder sorties over the Continent.

On 2 October 1944 Flying Officer Roy Emile Lelong of 605 Squadron took off from his forward base at St. Dizier and over the Baltic went looking to add to his score of three victories. It proved a very fruitful sortie for the 27-year old New Zealand carpenter from Auckland and his navigator Pilot Officer J. A. McLaren DFC who sighted enemy seaplanes in Jasmunder Bay. Lelong claimed five Dornier Do 24s destroyed and two damaged and a Blohm und Voss Bv 138 damaged in the air. Lelong returned to base on one engine where his camera gun film revealed that he had shot down the Bv 138 and that five Do 24s had been destroyed, one probably, and five damaged on the water.[384]

At this stage of the war the *Luftwaffe* had become increasingly wary in its use of its dwindling aircraft resources. Consequently, the Allied air forces had to employ imaginative tactics to find and destroy them. Since the Luftwaffe was doing less and less flying, Flight Lieutenant F. A. "Ted" Johnson DFC RCAF and his navigator, Flight Lieutenant N. J. "Jimmy" Gibbons, of 418 Squadron had speculated that it should be possible to catch them on the ground at night. After some experimentation they had established that on nights when there was a full moon there was sufficient light to carry out an air-to-ground strafing attack in a shallow dive from about 1500 feet above ground level. Any higher and it was difficult to see objects on the ground, while any lower would give insufficient time to aim the Mosquito's guns, fire a burst and pull out from the dive before striking the ground. Best visibility was obtained by positioning for the attack with the moon on the opposite side of the target. The Mosquito crew had studied intelligence reports of *Luftwaffe* flying activity and had noticed that in recent weeks there had been several indications of aircraft flying in the vicinity of Erding airfield deep within Germany on the far side of Munich at the limit of the Mosquito's range. They had calculated that if they pre-positioned their aircraft from their operational base at Hunsdon to Ford airfield in Sussex and refueled and launched from there with full tanks, they could make the round trip. So at the next full moon phase they re-checked all factors, obtained authorization for the operation, on the night of 2 October 1944, moved their Mosquito to Ford in the late afternoon, refueled, then took off at 2015 into a hazy autumn night. The moon had not yet risen but it would be up in an hour and the Met forecast had said that although there was a weather front over Germany it should be well east of their target by the time they arrived and the skies should be clear.

The Met man was wrong. After flying for three hours at 500 feet AGL in the hope of avoiding being picked up by German radar, Johnson and Gibbons arrived in the area to find the sky completely obscured by thick, low-hanging clouds. There would be no help from the moon. Determined not to return without trying to attack their target, they flew north of the enemy airfield to a predetermined sharp bend in the Isar River, which could be seen even on this moonless night and using an accurate course heading, airspeed and time made their first abortive pass. The Germans did not react as they overflew the airfield, so Johnson and Gibbons speculated that no radar alert had been given to the defenses and, indeed, they might still be uncertain if this was a hostile aircraft or one of their own with radio communications problems. As their Mosquito streaked close to 300 mph through the night sky a few miles east of Munich, searchlights flicked on to the southeast at Erding airfield and nervously probed the dark clouds above. Johnson said, "Jim, turn our navigation lights on and off a few times. The natives are getting restless." A few flashes of the nav lights and the German crews doused their searchlights and waited and wondered.

Again they reached their pinpoint over the river bend and carefully turned so that when they re-crossed in a southerly direction they would be on the desired course at exactly the selected height and airspeed. The Mosquito passed over the river - precision was essential to success under these adverse visibility conditions. Gibbons clicked his stopwatch and breathed into the microphone mounted in his oxygen mask. "Two minutes 28 seconds to go."

Ted Johnson grunted acknowledgement and re-checked that the safety guards were off on both the cannons and the machine guns. He tweaked the dimmer control lower on the reflector gunsight to reduce the dim glow of the circle of light with its central dot on the windscreen that was his aiming guide. He needed the gun sight as dim as possible to maximize his chances of seeing something on the ground in the target area. Dim outlines sped under the Mosquito as the two Merlin 25s growled their power across the night sky. Wispy cloud flicked by. Tension in the dimly lit cockpit mounted as the crew strained forward in their safety harnesses, striving to see objects on the ground. The airfield ahead remained totally blacked out. There was no sign of hostility. Johnson re-checked speed, course and altitude. Gibbons glanced at his stopwatch and said, "30 seconds," then began a countdown at 10-second intervals. As he called out "10 seconds," Johnson replied, "Airfield in sight!" and eased forward slightly on the control column, anticipating the need to initiate a quick dive as soon as a target was seen. His right thumb and forefinger tensed over the button and the trigger on the control column that would fire the cannons and machine guns. Suddenly the vague outline of a single-engine aircraft sitting on the airfield swept under the Mosquito's nose and the pilot made a spasmodic movement to start a dive but in the same second knew it was too late. 'Damn!' was all he said as the airfield continued to race away beneath and the indistinct outlines of hangars on the southern boundary were left behind. Still no reaction from the airfield defenses.

The Mosquito made a wide sweeping turn westwards and continued around on to a northerly heading. Gibbons spoke. "What kind of aircraft was that?"

Johnson replied, "I'm not sure. Could have been a Me 108, an advanced trainer. I couldn't see in time. Let's have one more go." A green Aldis-type hand-held signal light directed a series of dots and dashes toward them from the airfield control tower. The Mossie crew was unable to decipher the message since, whatever it was, it was in German. "Jimmy," said Johnson, "I think they believe we want to land. Give them a few more flashes on the nav lights, then leave them on steady." Then, as an afterthought, he added, "Make damn sure you switch them off the instant I fire the guns!"

Over the kink in the river they commenced their third run. Johnson eased the Mossie down 100 feet hoping to improve the ability to see objects on the ground, and concentrated on holding the air speed and heading. He turned the ultraviolet cockpit instrument lighting a notch dimmer and eased forward on the hard dinghy pack that was numbing his buttocks after 3 hours. The airfield ahead remained in total darkness. A trickle of sweat itched its way down the pilot's back. His open mike picked up the navigator's rapid breathing. "20 seconds to go," said Gibbons tensely. A moment later Johnson saw the blurred outline of a tree on the airfield perimeter and realized that he had seen it on their second pass. The parked aircraft had to be just ahead! Without waiting to actually see his target he pushed the Mossie's nose down into a shallow dive and at the same moment saw the shadowy outline of the German aircraft. Rapidly he brought the central 'bead' of his reflector gunsight on to it and squeezed both triggers.

The cockpit floor vibrated under their feet from the thunderous bellow of the four 20mm cannon, each spewing rounds at the rate of 600 a minute. Simultaneously the four-.303 machine guns chattered their deadly hail. Streams of glowing tracers lashed forward from the Mosquito's nose and immediately a pattern of strikes from the mixture of ball, incendiary and explosive shells were seen to envelope the German aircraft. The stench of cordite fumes filled the Mossie's cockpit.

On the ground the suspicious anti-aircraft crews were tracking the mysterious intruder in their sights, and instantly the Mosquito fired they loosed a barrage at it. Yellow, white and red fiery streams venomously arced through the darkness, clawing to destroy the attacker. As they pulled from the dive, the Mosquito crew heard a loud bang. Their aircraft shuddered. They had been hit! Johnson concentrated on controlling his aircraft and keeping as low as he dared without running into the hangars on the edge of the field. The German flak continued to hose up at them from all sides, but he knew that they could not fire too low lest they strike their own buildings. The volume of incendiary bullets slashing the sky actually provided enough light to see the oncoming hangars well enough to pass over them with minimum clearance. Rapidly they swept away from the hostile area and the ground fire ceased. It as only then that Johnson glanced out toward the left wing-tip and exclaimed, "My God, Jimmy, you forgot to turn the nav lights out!" The Mosquito was vibrating badly. The rudder pedals were tramping back and forth so furiously that the pilot could not hold them, and he finally withdrew his feet from the battering. Slowing the aircraft reduced the severity of the vibrations somewhat, but did not stop them. Anxiously the navigator peered toward the tail of the Mosquito, but was unable to see the extent of the damage. Johnson set course to pass south of the heavy defenses around Munich, then turned for England while watching the engine temperature gauges for any sign of overheating, and the fuel gauges for loss of fuel. At the reduced speed it would take over 3 hours to reach home base. Would the Mosquito hold together that long?

Knowing that they had thoroughly stirred up the enemy defenses, they kept as low as they dared and maintained a watchful eye over their tail for German night-fighters. It was a long flight home. The official maximum endurance of this version of the Mosquito was 6¼ hours. They landed back at Hunsdon after 6 hours 15 minutes! The fuel gauges all read nearly zero. Upon wearily clambering down from the cockpit, Johnson and Gibbons were able to see by the aid of their ground crew's flashlights the damage to their beloved Mosquito. The tailplane and elevators were sieved with shrapnel holes, there was a ragged 1 feet hole in the starboard tailplane, and the rudder was but a skeleton of ribs, but it had brought them home. As they trudged towards the operations room for de-briefing by the Intelligence officer, they heard one of the ground crew remark, "They sure build these Mosquitoes tough!" In all Johnson flew 43 operations as a pilot with 418 Squadron, but none were as eventful as this.

Late in October another daring low-level raid, this time on Aarhus University, the HQ for the Gestapo in the whole of Jutland, Denmark, was ordered. The University consisted of four or five buildings just next to an autobahn, which ran ten miles in a straight line up to the buildings. In College No.4 was also the HQ of the *S.D.*, the police service of the *Nazi* party. The precision attack was scheduled for 31 October by 25 FB.VIs of 21, 464 and 487 Squadrons, each carrying 11-second delayed action bombs. Included in the Mosquito formation, which was led by Group Captain Peter Wykeham-Barnes was AVM Basil Embry and his navigator, Peter Clapham. On 30 October the crews at Thorney Island had no idea what their target was, as Les Webb, Ern 'Dunks' Dunkley's navigator in 464 Squadron recalls:

"The Flight Commanders were called in by the CO, Wickham Barnes. 'Dunks', an Australian, was one of the Flight Commanders. They were told that we were going on a special raid and he wanted each flight commander to pick six crews, see that their planes were all right, tell them to carry an overnight bag and they'd get instructions to go off tomorrow. Nobody knew where." The crews were to fly to Swanton Morley, in Norfolk. "The advantage of doing it from Swanton Morley were two-fold. One was that it was nearer to the coast but the other one was the that it was a Mosquito training area so if anybody was looking they were used to seeing Mossies in that area."

Humphrey-Baker, in 487 Squadron, who was Wing Commander "Peter" Thomas', adds, "On 31 October we took off from Thorney Island at 7 am, landing at Swanton Morley to refuel and to link up with aircraft from 21 Squadron." Les Webb continues:

> "We all flew up singly and landed at Swanton Morley. After we landed we were told that we were now under guard. We couldn't go out, we couldn't make telephone calls and there would be an early dinner. The food at Swanton Morley was out of this world; it was absolutely superb. Immediately after dinner a little Dane who had been parachuted into Denmark, who then got all the information and then had come out by submarine, briefed us. His information enabled a large model to be constructed showing all the surrounding area and even the colors of the roofs. It was an incredible model."

Escort was provided by eight Mustang IIIs of 315 (Polish) Squadron, 12 Group, which flew to Swanton Morley from their base at Andrews Field in Essex, led by the CO, Squadron Leader Tadeusz Andersz. One of the Mustang pilots was Flight Lieutenant Konrad "Wiewiorka" (Squirrel) Stembrowicz, who recalls:

> "We landed at Swanton Morley early on the morning of 31 October. One or two of our Mustangs damaged their tailwheels on the grass field and were not ready in time for the escort. Eight of us refueled and took off again to rendezvous with the Mosquitoes over the North Sea. When we saw them they were at 100 feet above the waves. Our two Finger Fours formated 50 feet below to starboard and slightly south of them. We crossed Denmark and dropped our auxiliary 90-gal petrol tanks, which by necessity were only half-filled. Mine fell near a Danish cottage surrounded by a mass of brown, yellow and orange chrysanthemums. People ran out of the house and waved their arms and large white tablecloths as we all roared past. Approaching Aarhus the Mosquitoes lifted slightly. They were to attack down a street west to east. The leading section of four Mustangs went left and we followed."

Humphrey-Baker in 487 Squadron continues:

> "We were carrying wing tanks, which would be abandoned, over the North Sea. It was rather alarming to see these grey torpedo-like shapes whipping by in close proximity. As we approached the target already shrouded in smoke, I could see that the right hand building, which

we had to attack, had the center section completely destroyed while the two end sections were still standing. As we crossed the target I felt the aircraft being hit on the starboard side. Soon afterwards Peter Wykeham Barnes called Peter to feather the starboard prop, as the engine was on fire. Once we were on one engine we headed for "Sally", our code name for Sweden. I read later that we had been hit by debris from an exploding bomb, all of, which had delayed action fuses to allow each box of six aircraft to pass without risk. We crossed the Kattegat and reached the coast without further incident and upon finding a suitable field, Peter brought the aircraft down for a very efficient wheels-up landing. Once the shaking had ceased it was very quiet. Peter placed the firebomb in the navigator's bag and the plane was soon in flames and we took off up a hill towards some trees.

"With surprising speed a squad of grey clad soldiers arrived with an antiquated fire engine in tow. They waved guns at us and we thought it advisable to stop. We were rather amused at their efforts to quell the flames, as the weak jet from their machine would not reach the aircraft. They soon made it clear that their concern was to know if there was anybody else in the aircraft or if there were still bombs aboard. We were taken to a neighbouring farmer whose wife prepared an excellent meal at short notice. We were then taken to Gothenburg and placed in a large room at the top of a tall hotel. The room was equipped with a telephone directory and from this we were surprised to learn that there was in fact a British Consulate in the town and we resolved that we would try to reach it if the opportunity presented itself."

"Dunks" Dunkley in 464 Squadron continues:

"We made landfall at a lake where we made a rate one turn. The first six aircraft took off for the target followed at short intervals by the other three boxes of six. It was a very well planned run really, except that the wind was blowing right down the autobahn. The blokes who went in first had a good picture of the target, whereas those following had dust and smoke obscuring the target. By the time we got there the place was a mess. There was a hospital not very far along the road on the other side and a lot of people must have got a hell of a shock from the noise but not a single bomb landed in the hospital area."

"Dunks" Dunkley's navigator, Les Webb, continues:

"'Daisy' Sismore was leading. As we crossed the coast there was a small village a few miles inland and as we flew across, he flew straight over the village and went on. The other three formations did a circuit and then the next one peeled off. We were the last ones in. We orbited until it was our turn. In a field below were a couple of farm horses with a plough that seemed to be on their own. By the time we had done three circuits, everybody realized that we were RAF aircraft and they were waving and cheering in the streets. The interesting thing was that a farmer dressed in blue dungarees and blue hat who must have ducked down between the two horse stood up and held the horse's heads at the salute as we went past. I thought that was superb.

"We went in, in formation, echelon starboard. We turned and saw the building. The problem now was we had broken up into pairs, whether intentionally or not and we were flying Number 2 at that point because Bedford, Bill Langton's [the CO, Wing Commander A. W. Langton DFC] navigator had called that he had handed over to somebody else. Clayton had gone up to the number 1 and Dunk and I were flying Number 2. By the time we got to the target we were flying with Clayton, coming in together. We were slightly starboard. The smoke from the site, unluckily, was blowing towards us and as we entered the smoke it was pretty obvious that the left-hand building was more damaged than the right hand building. Clayton saw it before we did because he was slightly ahead of us. In all his glory he made a smart turn onto the target, which left 'Dunks' with absolutely nowhere to go. 'Dunks' did a brilliant bit of flying. He just went *oomph, oomph* and we went under Clayton, across and then swung round. We were at nought feet and two people on the main road to Aarhus dived into the gutter! We still had time to drop our bombs on the target, then off and away. We formed into formation again before we got to the coast and went out over the North Sea again. The Mustangs were still with us and later they went off and left us. We came straight home to Thorney. On the way home 'Dunks' lost track of the CO and called over the radio, 'Has anyone seen the old man?' He came back saying, 'We are not home yet, shut up!' The whole flight took four hours 45 minutes."

Inside one of the college buildings, 40 year old Pastor Sandbäk, arrested in September on suspicion of complicity in acts of sabotage, was about to have his final interrogation, the longest interrogation being 39 hours without any rest, after days of whipping and tightening of string around his handcuffs. "Suddenly, we heard the whine of the first exploding bomb while the planes thundered across the University. Werner, my interrogator's face, was as pale as death from fright. He and his assistants ran without thinking of me. I saw them run down a passage to the right, and instinctively I went down to the left. This saved my life. Shortly afterwards the whole building collapsed. Werner and his two assistants were killed. I heard two bangs and everything went blank. When I awoke again I was buried under bricks." Pastor Sandbäk was later spirited across to Sweden.

The operation was carried out at such a low altitude that Squadron Leader F. H. Denton of 487 Squadron hit the roof of the building, losing his tail wheel and the port half of the tail plane. Denton nursed the Mosquito across the North Sea and managed to land safely. Flight Lieutenant Stembrowicz concludes: "We saw explosions and very light ack-ack coming up in the Mosquitoes wake. All of us went to the right and put ourselves between the Mosquitoes and the German airfields. This time we were higher. We saw no fighters and the flight home was uneventful." The university and its incriminating records were destroyed. Among the 110-175 Germans killed in the raid was *Kriminalrat* Schwitzgiebel, head of the *Gestapo* in Jutland and *SS Oberstum Fuhrer* Lonechun, Head of the Security Services.

Later that evening, in Gothenburg, a young officer collected Wing Commander "Peter" Thomas and Humphrey-Baker. He informed them that he was a schoolmaster doing his period of compulsory service. Baker recalls:

"He was to escort us to Falun where we would be detained for an indefinite period. He was very pleasant and we all got on very well. He escorted us to the railway station and while he was busy getting our tickets, we took off at speed into the night. After the brilliant lights of the station the square outside looked very black. It was raining and the macadam glistened in the light of the high street lamps. We raced across the empty space, Peter was to my left and we had not gone far when he took a flying leap over a low parapet and disappeared a second later I heard a loud splash. I thought that this was in keeping with Peter's somewhat flamboyant style. Peter was blond and handsome and played the role of a RAF Wing Commander excellently. His wife was equally glamorous.

"Within a few seconds of our escape I was on my own. I ran on for a few yards to a bridge. I ran across and doubled back on the other side of the canal. I called out to the soggy Peter to see if he was OK or if he needed help. He told me to carry on, which I had every intention of doing, as I could dimly see people appearing on the other side of the canal. I ran on and followed the road round to the right. I continued until came to a junction and turned right and scion came upon a woman about to enter her home. I asked her in what I fondly thought was a mixture of German and Swedish where the British Consulate was. She replied in English, 'Why should I help you?' which was not surprising, as I must have been somewhat bedraggled and hatless. I mumbled that I was in a hurry and wet. She replied that it was only a few doors further on. So to my intense surprise and relief I had located it in what seemed to be a very short time. I really do not think I could have run more than 1km. The Consul's son opened the door and I was taken in. It was a remarkable stroke of luck to get there so quickly and at night. Soon afterwards with Schnapps in hand we saw a guard being posted at the gate. The Consul had no option but to return me and a few Schnapps. Later I arrived at the Police station in the company of the Consul and his son to find a somewhat disconsolate Peter Thomas sitting wrapped in a blanket.

"We had wrongly thought that if we could reach the Consulate we could be repatriated. This of course would only have happened if we had escaped from occupied Europe, but did not apply to anyone stupid enough to escape from the hospitable hands of the Swedes. We were handed back to our chagrined guard who could not understand why we should have wanted to run away from him. We were escorted back to the station by the Consul, placed on a train and locked into a very comfortable sleeping compartment. On arrival at Falun we had to go before a local doctor for an FFI inspection. I was somewhat alarmed at his vigorous approach and was relieved to depart still entire, although I was also amused at the wooden trumpet with which he tuned in to my heart. Everything possible seemed to be made of wood in Sweden. I recall watching the local businessmen stoking up the boilers mounted on the back of their Volvos to generate the producer gas, which powered their vehicles. In thick overcoats and wearing gloves they would shove wood into the little furnace and then slowly drive away. 'We were lodged in a pension at Korsnas run by Miss Sundberg, a very nice old lady. There were about 16 of us, mostly Australians I think, including the crew of a Lancaster that had been damaged on the final successful attack on the *Tirpitz*.[385]

"The numbers dwindled rapidly as the rate of repatriation had increased following an influx of German soldiers from Finland. There was also a large camp of about 600 Americans nearby. Peter Thomas who had to go to Malmo to move a Mosquito said that there were over one hundred serviceable American aircraft at the Lingschoping airfield where they would arrive in droves.

"Among the attributes of our pension was a still made by earlier residents and a stock of München Lowenbrau beer. It was my first introduction to this beer and I have enjoyed it ever since, when I can find it. We were given a lot of freedom and I very much enjoyed my time in Falun. Meeting some members of the Danish Resistance movement, which of course we had set out to help, heightened my enjoyment. They took me around and we had a great time until we had to return to Stockholm prior to flying home. Peter Thomas as a result of his senior rank stayed at the British Consulate while I was sent to a dirty and evil smelling hotel. I protested immediately, but was told we would be leaving that night. Fortunately my Danish friends had given me the address of the local Danish Resistance office in Stockholm, which I quickly visited. They were eager to help and took me to a nicer hotel where I spent several nights until flown out. I also met a charming young Danish girl Henny Sindunq, a resistance worker from Copenhagen. She took me around Stockholm and we had supper together every evening until like Cinderella I had to leave to head out to the airport in preparation to flying home. Fortunately the weather was bad and we were returned to our respective lodgings in the small hours of the morning. Henny would dutifully turn out the next day and we would dine-at a different restaurant of her choice. This went on-for four or five nights until we finally crept off in a very cold DC 3 finally landing at Wick in Scotland after an absence of 24 days."[386]

By November 1944 107, 305 (Polish) and 613 Squadrons of 138 Wing finally arrived in France, to be based at Epinoy near Cambrai, France. By this stage of the war the *Panzers* and other German troops were being given no respite in the daylight raids by Mitchells and Bostons and the nightly visits by Mosquitoes. Flight Lieutenant Eric Atkins DFC* KW* on 305 (Polish) Squadron, recalls:

> 'Prisoners captured complained, 'We are attacked all day and then the Mosquitoes harass and bomb us at night. We cannot '*em Schläfchen machen*' (take a nap) or '*eine Scheiesse machen*' (have a crap) - we are caught with our pants down!' Nowhere was this more apparent than when we attacked the *Panzer* billets on the night of 6/7 December 1944 in the village of Wassenberg, just south of Mönchengladbach, on the edge of the Ruhr itself. The attack on the billets would be my 78th operation, the 26th in my third tour. My navigator was Flight Lieutenant Jurek Majer, a Pole who spoke little English. There was talk that I would be stood down after this operation, and this made the raid even more significant. As all aircrew know, it can be a superstitious moment when you wonder whether you will 'get the chop' on the last one.
>
> "However, there was no time to worry about the consequences to me of the operation - there was much to do! The Met officer warned us that although the weather was set fair for the night, snow was on the way. (December's weather was the worst of an already bad three months. On some nights we operated when visibility at the base was

less than 800 yards.) Our route to the target took us near Brussels. It was a very dark night, but the radar kept us on the track. There seemed to be a lot of activity about. I was probably more finely tuned" than normal on this trip and thought I saw enemy aircraft on our beam, but Jurek just grunted and got on with his navigation. There was not normally a lot of conversation in our Mosquito - we both had our jobs to do and we reserved speech for when action was needed - no idle chatter!

"My thoughts drifted to three operations ago, 29 November, when we had attacked Hamm, in the east Ruhr area. The weather had been appalling, and the flak over the target was heavy. After bombing, something had gone wrong with our aircraft, the electrics and hydraulics were amiss, and I had to "belly-flop" at night at our new base at Epinoy near Cambrai, France, a grass aerodrome on a slight hill. Without flaps we floated almost off the top of the hill before I forced it down. I hoped nothing like that would happen to us tonight!

"Jurek said that we were approaching the German border and now we saw much more activity - searchlights and tracer fire. We were flying at about 3000 feet.

"'Look out for flares and a river,' said Jurek. We had HE and incendiary loads, flares, cannons and machine guns. We were not the only ones attacking this target, and it should have been well lit up. However, we were among the first in. I came down much lower, soon picked up the Roer River and then saw the target. There were no flares at the time, but there was a glow and Jurek confirmed that it was Wassenberg. We could see the fires starting as we did our first run. In the light of the flares we dropped we came round again and bombed and strafed the target. All hell seemed to be let loose below and heavy flak was coming up just south of us. There was some rain about and I remember thinking that it might put the fires out!

"We did another run strafing with cannon fire. 'That's enough,' said Jurek. 'Save some for the others!'

"A black shape zoomed up and passed our nose. 'What the hell's that?' I cried, then realized that it was probably another Mosquito going in to attack.

"We had overstayed our welcome. Flying straight and level in the darkness, heading for base, we checked our instruments, oil pressure and engine temperatures. I had flung the Mossie around rather a lot, and sometimes engines overheat, then you have to shut one down. However, everything seemed all right and Jurek grunted the course back to base. It had been a very successful operation. The Panzers had been caught with their 'pants down!'

"After we had landed and been de-briefed, the station commander told me that it had been my last operation. They were standing me down on my 78th -' enough was enough!' I was very disappointed, however, to lose Jurek - he had to carry on with another pilot to finish his second tour."

On 21 November, 136 Wing was created within 2nd TAF by the arrival, from Fighter Command, of 418 and 605 Squadrons, which transferred to Hartford Bridge. That month 14 enemy aircraft fell to the guns of the 2nd TAF Mosquito night predators. The signs in December 1944 were that the weather and other factors would limit Mosquito night-fighter activity over the *Reich.* [387] Only three Ju 88s and two Bf 110s were destroyed 4-18/19 December. On the last named, Flight Lieutenant Charles Emanuel 'Pop' Edinger RCAF and Flying Officer C. C. Vaessen of 410 'Cougar' Squadron RCAF in NF.XXX MV527 shot down a Ju 88 south of Bonninghardt. Wing Commander James D. Somerville DFC, now in command of 409 Squadron, scored his sixth confirmed victory, flying NF.XIII MM456 with Flying Officer G. D. Robinson DFC, when they despatched a Ju 88 in the Kaiserworth area. Somerville wrote:

> "While patrolling at Angels 10 under 15119 Control (Squadron Leader Allen) we were vectored south as the Hun was reported to be active in the American Sector. We were then advised of trade and after receiving initial vectors of 130 and 280, we were vectored 190. Controller advised us that he was keeping us on a slightly converging course to bring us in behind the target beyond the 'Hot Spot' at the same time, instructing to reduce to Angels 7. We started down but as the Control then advised that the target had started to climb, we leveled out at Angels 9. AI contact was obtained at a range of 5 miles and closing rapidly, I obtained a visual at 1600 feet. Closing to 800 feet below and directly beneath, both my navigator and I recognized the target as a Ju 88, flying at approximately 160 mph indicated, which necessitated my lowering my undercarriage to prevent overshooting. At this juncture, the E/A turned west and started to dive. I followed, and overtook the E/A with an indicated speed of 270 mph. I closed to 600 feet and pulled up, but did not fire as I momentarily lost visual owing to a dark cloud in the background. I closed to within 300 feet and opened fire. I observed strikes on the fuselage but no flames. I attempted to re-open fire but my guns had jammed so I continued to follow the aircraft down, which by this time was doing hard evasive – making hard peel offs to starboard and port, until it finally dove in from 1500 feet. My navigator and I both saw it hit the ground and explode with a brilliant flash but it did not appear to burn on the ground."

In December 464 RAAF and 487 RNZAF Squadrons sent advance detachments to Rosières-en-Santerre, France. In February 1945 the two squadrons, along with 21 Squadron, all of 140 Wing, left southern England and landed at Amiens-Rosières-en-Santerre. Their arrival coincided with the first anniversary of the Amiens raid by 140 Wing Mosquitoes in February 1944, when the "walls of Jericho" had come tumbling down.

The *Luftwaffe* was powerless to stop the inexorable advance westwards but there was one last attempt to try to halt the allies. Since 20 December 1944 many *Jagdgeschwader* had been transferred to airfields in the west for Operation *Bodenplatte,* when approximately 850 *Luftwaffe* fighters took off at 0745 hours on Sunday morning 1 January 1945 to attack 27 airfields in northern France, Belgium and southern Holland. The 4-hour operation succeeded in destroying about 100 Allied aircraft, but it cost the *Luftwaffe* 300 aircraft, most of which were shot down by Allied anti-aircraft guns deployed primarily against the V1s.

Sergeant John Walsh, a Liverpudlian and a navigator in 487 Squadron, and his pilot, Flying Officer John Patterson, flew their first operation, a three-hour round trip from Thorney Island to Arsbeck, on 21 January 1945. Walsh had trained at Greenwood, Nova Scotia and training losses had been high, many of the Canadian-built Mosquitoes ending up in the Bay of Fundis. However, the 21-year-old "Scouser" was "desperately keen' to fly the 'fast weapon'" Losses climaxed near the end of his training and he had been one of only four to volunteer for Mosquitoes. Leeds-born "Pat" Patterson had been an instructor in Canada, where he had met and married a delightful Canadian girl. Both men had teamed up at High Ercall. "Ginger" Walsh recalls:

"Northwest Germany was divided into three, one for each Mossie wing, then into three again, one for each squadron. 2nd TAF Spitfires and Mustangs, which attacked the German Army on the ground during the day, returned with details of troop concentrations and targets, which we then bombed by night. Our main target was anything that moved, especially trains and transport but you were bloody lucky to find a moving target at night! Trains were a high priority but they were blacked out and we were lucky to see them. On the Arsbeck op we flew at about 1000 feet through low cloud to the target. I navigated all the way using maps 'illuminated' by a tiny pin-prick of light from my torch filled with three layers of paper in the bottom to retain our night vision and prevent us from being seen from the air or the ground. (*Gee* could not be used too far into Germany before it got interfered with and 'railings' confused the two-three 'spikes'. I had to take the best signal, the best 'cut'.) Moonlight was a bastard. You could count the rivets. Over Germany on moonlit nights I felt that I had no clothes on. Our mates in the squadron had been to Arsbeck earlier and had started fires. We would bomb on the *Gee-set* co-ordinates. I selected the four bombs, fused them and 'Pat' pressed the 'tit' on his spectacle control column.

"On the way home 'Pat' saw a train for what was the only time. The first I knew was that the Mosquito was suddenly standing on one wing! We had been told that if we saw a train we were to go straight in - no messing! "Pat" circled (he was following his instincts) for the best position, then adopted a shallow dive and went in, all four .303 and four cannons blazing. By now I was 'climbing out of the roof'. The sky filled with 40mm flak. I soon learned that German ack-ack gunner's were mustard! In the cockpit cordite fumes and dust filled the air. 'Pat' broke off immediately and on my advice flew to the west! On reflection it had done us good. It was thought provoking.

"It was a terrible night. Ron Batch, a fellow navigator I'd been with at navigational school and had known for eighteen months, who had already flown two ops, failed to return. He and his pilot had 'got the chop'. Forty-eight hours later Ron's father, a Metropolitan Police Inspector, came to see me. He wanted to know what area of Germany Ron had been flying over and any other details; Ron was his only child. I could tell him nothing. It really carved me up.

"We got shot up ourselves one night. We got back and landed and the props had barely stopped when our two faithful ground crew opened the door (we never bothered with the ladder). They asked if we'd hit anything. They were always so thrilled, so keen, that we should be successful. They asked, 'Were we fired at?'"

"I said, 'Yes, I think it was the British Army!'

"'Were we hit?'

"I said, 'No.'

"Then they pointed to a hole beneath the wing! I looked and was thrilled. It was strangely exciting! However, next day they could see that the hole had been caused by oil dripping from the guns - our Mossie was a clapped-out machine and had flown many ops."

During January 2nd TAF Mosquitoes exacted a measure of revenge, starting with the shooting down of three Ju 88s on 1/2 January by Flight Lieutenant R. J. Foster DFC and Flight Lieutenant M. F. Newton DFC of 604 Squadron. By the end of the month 2nd TAF Mosquito night fighters had shot down 17 enemy aircraft, including, on 23/24 January, two Junkers, which were despatched by 409 (Nighthawk) Squadron NF.XIIIs. At this time Ju 88S-3s of 1./KG66 and *Lehrgeschwader 1* were carrying out bombing and mining operations against river traffic in the Scheldt estuary in an attempt to stem the flow of supplies to Antwerp. Pilot Officer M. G. Kent and Pilot Officer Simpson in NF.XIII MM466 shot down a Ju 88 of LG 1 over the mouth of the Scheldt.[388] While there is some doubt about which was Kent and Simpson's victim, there is no question, which Ju 188E-l was shot down three miles west of Dienst by the CO, Wing Commander James D. Somerville DFC and Pilot Officer A. C. Hardy.[389] The Ju 188E-l[390] flown by Obergefreiter Heinz Hauck was on a clandestine mission for KG200's *Kommando Olga*. Hauck took off from Rhein-Main and he successfully dropped two agents near Gilze Rijn in the liberated part of Holland before heavy AA bursts and searchlights gave away their position to the Nighthawk crew, who were returning from patrol at 8000 feet. Somerville and Hardy were directed by '*Rejoice*,' a GCI station, towards the bogey, now six miles distant at 4000 feet. Somerville reduced height and Hardy was further assisted by "*Bricktile*" and then "*Laundry*," GCI stations, until they came upon the Ju 188E-1, which was now flying at 3000 feet. Hardy had difficulty keeping their quarry out of the ground clutter on his AI.Mk.VIII scope at their height of 2500 feet until finally, he got a contact at two miles. Somerville closed to 1500 feet for a positive identification. Satisfied, he closed still further and opened fire with his cannons at 200 feet. His first burst set fire to Hauck's port engine and the 20mm shells caused a brilliant explosion, which forced the Mosquito pilot, momentarily blinded, to break away. Somerville came in again for a second burst as Hauck desperately dived and stall turned in a vain attempt to extinguish the flames. Somerville's second burst missed but his third ripped the Ju 188's port wingtip off and the enemy aircraft dived steeply into the ground. It was Somerville's seventh and final victory of the war.[391]

On 6 February 1945 21, 464 and 487 Squadrons of 140 Wing left southern England and moved to Amiens and Rosières-en-Santerre. Les Bulmer in 21 Squadron recalls:

"Personnel were scattered around the airfield in villages. The admin types naturally picked the best château for themselves. 21 Squadron aircrew were billeted in a château in Warvillers. It served as the Mess and sleeping quarters were in an orchard at the rear. These were wooden huts thoughtfully provided by the Germans. There was even a small dance hall suitably decorated with Luftwaffe murals. It wasn't the Ritz but at least it was better than the tents we'd had at Gravesend and Thorney Island and which we were led to believe we would have to use in France. Actually, we did cheat a little at Thorney Island. As winter developed, so came the gales and one night one of the senior officers lost his tent. Since there was a large empty Mess on the other side of the airfield it seemed only logical to fill it. So we did, still sleeping on our camp beds so that we could continue to qualify for the 'hard living' allowance."

The arrival of the Mosquito squadrons at Amiens and Rosières-en-Santerre coincided with the first anniversary of the Amiens raid by 140 Wing Mosquitoes on 18 February 1944, when the walls of *Jericho* had come tumbling down. Pickard's widow was flown out especially from England to visit her husband's grave and for the mass in Amiens Cathedral. "Ginger" Walsh was among the personnel who attended and afterwards he visited the wall, now patched, through which the French Resistance had escaped:

"The bulk of our squadron was billeted in Amiens. At first I slept at Meharicourt, near the bomb dump in what had been the Luftwaffe hospital site at the airfield. *Wehrmacht* and Luftwaffe personnel too badly wounded to be evacuated were still there. Later the local village butcher adopted a friend Bob Belcher and me and we were billeted at his elderly mother's small château. Near our base was a huge First World War cemetery filled with thousands of white crosses. We buried Flying Officer Joe Coe and his fellow New Zealander Squadron Leader pilot there after they crashed on take-off one day and their bombs and fuel load exploded. Joe had already lost his fingers and been badly burned in a Wellington crash earlier in the war. At their funeral a group of French schoolchildren sang 'God Save the King.'"

One of the crews in 305 Squadron at Epinoy at this time was pilot Flight Lieutenant Reg Everson, an ex-railway policeman and his navigator Flight Lieutenant Tony Rudd, a university graduate. They had crewed up at 2 Group GSU at Swanton Morley in September 1944. Everson recalls:

"At Epinoy our enthusiasm was somewhat dampened when we found the airfield covered with six feet of snow and we spent most of the daylight hours using shovels to help clear the runways. Eventually flying was possible, taking off along runways with snow piled high on either side. It did, however, concentrate the mind and made the pilots even more careful than ever to avoid a swing on take-off. Night patrols were carried out most nights, incurring a number of casualties, attacking enemy road and rail transport when possible and bombing rail junctions on *Gee* when bad weather prevented visual sightings. One night we returned from patrol to find 10/10ths cloud at 200 feet over the base. As our *Gee* set had gone 'on the blink' I declined the offer of a diversion to Brussels (I learned better later) and received permission to land at base. This proved somewhat 'hairy' but landing was completed without damage. No operations were carried out for the next few nights, diverted aircraft having to return to base and the weather remained such that even the birds were walking. Normal service was resumed until 13 February when the squadron had a break from operations to practice for a daylight formation operation - *Clarion*. As it was to be a twelve-aircraft formation some crews (including us) were not involved. However, on the day of the operation, 22 February, it was decided to increase it to maximum effort and all crews and serviceable aircraft were to be involved. Without the benefit of practice we had an unenviable position, 18th in an eighteen-plane formation."

Wilf Jessop, a navigator in 418 Squadron, recalls:

"After testing the aircraft for night flying and with fine weather, we expected to do our usual night patrol. However, operations were cancelled and bad weather given as the excuse but navigators were instructed to report at 0630 hours the next morning with long-range maps. We were cautioned about security. AVM Basil Embry, Officer Commanding 2 Group appeared next morning and explained our part in Operation *Clarion,* which was to attack road junctions, railways, transport and buildings in North Western Germany aiming in twenty-four hours to decimate German ground transport. Nine thousand Allied aircraft were to take part in the operation."[392]

Clarion was intended to be the coup de grace for the German transport system with 9000 Allied aircraft taking part in attacks on enemy railway stations, trains and engines, cross roads, bridges, ships and barges on canals and rivers, stores and other targets. It was to be the last time that the Mosquitoes operated in daylight in such numbers.

Les Bulmer of 21 Squadron adds;

'We fielded sixteen aircraft, eight from each flight. The squadron was allocated an area between Bremen and Hanover in which any form of transport was to be attacked. This area was sub-divided between 'A' and 'B' Flights and these two areas in turn were divided again so that groups of four aircraft each had their own particular patch to cover. As by now we were one of the more experienced crews on the squadron, we were to lead four aircraft to the farthest areas just to the north of Hanover. The whole squadron took off at 1130 and formed up in two sections of eight, 'A' Flight leading. We flew northeast to the Zuider Zee, then turned east. Over the Dummer Zee "A" Flight left us to fly northeast to their area. "B" Flight continued east and shortly afterwards four aircraft turned away northwards, leaving us and our brood of three to carry on eastwards to our patch, which covered the area bounded by Nienburg, Schwarmstedt, Hanover and Wunsdorf. Over Schwarmstedt we found two engines and a freight train in the station, so we dived on them with cannons and bombs followed by our No.2, Pilot Officer Bolton. The other two aircraft left us to find a train of their own to play with. We got cannon strikes on the engines and Bolton reported large clouds of steam as we pulled away. We continued around our area but saw nothing worth attacking, so set off westwards for home. Just south of the Dummer Zee we found another train at Lemforde and turned to attack it but they'd already seen us and sent up a hail of 20mm flak, so we decided to give it a miss. Soon afterwards, a single-engined aircraft appeared heading in the opposite direction and above us. He apparently didn't see us and we didn't stop to identify."

Reg Everson and Tony Rudd in 305 Squadron meanwhile also braved flak. Wing Commander S. Grodzicki DFC led 305 Squadron and Squadron Leader P. Hanburg led the British Flight. For half an hour the Mosquitoes of 305 Squadron wreaked havoc in the Bremen-Hamburg-Kiel region. The German ground defenses were strong. Ten aircraft suffered damage and one with a British crew was lost; the pilot was killed and the navigator taken prisoner.

Reg Everson recalls:

"We flew in close formation at 4000 feet until we crossed the enemy lines when we encountered some light flak bursting at that height. We took evasive action and rejoined the formation as soon as we were clear of danger. When we arrived at the area Stade, River Elbe, we broke into 'pairs'. I was No.2 to Warrant Officer Smith. Our main targets were barges and shipping, secondary targets being warehouses, trains and road transport. During our patrol we attacked railway trucks. The eighteen aircraft did considerable damage and eight of them were damaged by ground fire. We then set course for base, formating on Warrant Officer Smith at low level. Shortly after leaving the patrol area we passed over a machine gun post and Smith's aircraft was hit and caught fire; we saw it make a crash-landing. Not being sure of our exact position and as we had used up all our machine gun ammunition and cannon shells, I climbed to a safer height of 4000 feet, at which we could get an accurate *Gee* fix. We soon found out where we were! The guns of Bremerhaven opened up and the air was filled with black puffs of exploding shells. A sharp diving turn to port down to nought feet followed, for a re-assessment of the situation. Bremen was to our south, so a course was set for Zwoller on the River Yssel, which was the 'Bomb Line' for the day. Once we felt safer from immediate danger we made a tentative climb to 4000 feet to enable us to use *Gee to* keep away from further "hot spots". Shortly after reaching this height an American Mustang formated on our starboard wing. A cigar-chewing pilot waved a friendly greeting before peeling off to go about his own business. As we approached Zwoller I opened the throttles to maximum boost, put the nose down to get maximum speed and crossed the River Yssel as quickly as possible. The rest of the trip was uneventful."

P. D. Morris, pilot of a Mosquito FB.VI in 613 (City of Manchester) Squadron at Epinoy near Cambrai, France, on 22 February recalls:

"My navigator Ron Parfitt and I had flown together on every operation since arriving in France on 19 November 1944. Six days after arriving at Epinoy we did our first night operation - the first of forty. However, on 22 February we were briefed for our first *Day Ranger* sortie against the enemy. All the squadrons were to take part and the area given to Ron and me to patrol was the very north of Germany up in Schleswig Holstein near the Danish border. Our job was to patrol a large area and bomb, machine gun and cannon any enemy transport or personnel we spotted. After being able to cause a little havoc on various targets, the time came for us to make our way home. To do so, we were to go directly west until we reached the North Sea and to fly back to friendly territory before crossing to land back again. We were flying fairly low, roughly at about ten-fifteen feet, as it was safer. As we crossed over very low-lying fields that were separated by dykes, which were about the same height as that at which we were flying. I was looking well ahead when I suddenly saw a German soldier 300 yards ahead who was having the audacity to be firing from the top of the dyke directly at us. This I thought was not good enough so I armed first my four machine guns and then my four cannons. After that I took a very careful bead on this presumptuous fellow. When about one hundred yards from him I pulled both triggers but all that emerged from my guns was complete silence! However, I was determined at least to frighten him badly, so I passed over him a few feet over his head and saw him fall flat on his face. I feel after that he must have headed for the nearest Schnapps! When we got out over the sea I decided to try out the guns again, so having armed them, I pulled the two triggers and both guns fired perfectly. My aircraft was and until that moment not known as any particular friend of the Germans! This soldier, if still alive, must be among the luckiest imaginable!"

At 1117 hours Wilf Jessop and his pilot Wing Commander Jack Wickett led 418 Squadron's twenty aircraft in formation at a height of about 1000 feet from Hartford Bridge to Aldburgh and then over the North Sea to Holland at fifty feet above the waves:

'Whilst over the sea we sent three aircraft back home. One was hit by birds and damaged. Two collided due to ballooning drop tanks during the tricky and dangerous manoeuvre of skidding out of formation during the drop and skidding back in. We climbed just before reaching the Dutch coast then dropped down to fifty feet again to avoid German radar. When the formation reached the East Coast of the Zuider Zee Wickett ordered the seventeen aircraft remaining to split up and go for their individual targets. We cruised along at 240 mph, 50-100 feet above the ground. At about 1230 hours our aircraft was hit by light flak near the Dortmund-Ems canal southeast of Osnabrück before reaching our target. The aircraft was on fire and as the wheels and flaps were hanging our hydraulics had probably been damaged. My pilot broke radio silence to say we had been badly shot up and would try to land in a marshy area. I had given him a course of 270° magnetic for home but he could not keep the aircraft in the air and made, in the circumstances, a marvellous landing alongside the canal. The whole of my side of the cockpit caved in and, with our cannon shells and machine gun bullets exploding, I got our rather sharpish, not having a parachute hanging on my backside to hinder me. My pilot, sitting on and fastened to his parachute, was having difficulty getting out.

"I have a faint recollection of helping him, knowing we were sitting on top of two 500lb bombs ready to explode. Both out we ran like the clappers away from the aircraft - the direction did not matter! We got about sixty yards away when the bombs went off We were glad of the eleven second delay fuses on them. Armed Germans quickly picked us up and it was then that I found I had only one boot on. We were taken to a barge on the canal where my pilot was briefly questioned. Most of the Germans on the barge were quite young, about fifteen and manning an anti-aircraft gun. Towards late afternoon we were marched off in the direction of the remains of our aircraft and I had visions of us being disposed of near it. I mentioned this to my pilot but we decided to hang on a bit. We arrived at a factory, which was shut and our guards could not get in so they took us back to the barge. I think they thought they could hand us over to someone else. Some of them lost a bit of sleep that night guarding us. I found out much later that this operation turned out to be the costliest to date for 418 Squadron - four aircraft failed to return to base."

Les Bulmer returning to base noticed that all the way back to the Zuider Zee Pilot Officer Bolton was staying well back behind them:

"We couldn't figure out why he didn't stay close. (At the de-briefing he explained that we were being shot at at several points on the way out and he didn't really want to get involved. Fortunately for our peace of mind, Bert and I were totally unaware of this.) Just short of the Zuider Zee we spotted two trucks on the road north of Elspeet. We were almost over the top of them before we noticed them and did an imitation of a *Stuka*, with an almost vertical dive, to give them a blast of cannon. Several characters left them a bit sharpish. I only hope that they were Germans and not Dutch. From there we had an uneventful trip back to base, where we landed at 1450. 21 Squadron was one of the lucky ones that day. We lost only one aircraft, Fielding-Johnson and Harbord. 464 lost two and 487 took a hammering and lost five. I believe that this was principally because they chose to take the long route around the coast and got caught by flak and fighters as a result. 2 Group lost twenty-one Mosquitoes on *Clarion* with forty damaged. I think it taught the 'powers that be' a salutary lesson that the Mosquito was not, after all, invulnerable."

Hugh Henry Fielding Johnson had joined 21 Squadron in March 1944 and he flew his first operation on 26 March with his navigator Flying Officer L. C. Harbord. Fielding Johnson was known on the squadron as "Fee-Gee" (or "Fiji") and he sported a typical RAF moustache. "Fee-Gee" also wore a navigator's or an air-gunner's brevet above his right breast pocket, perhaps out of respect for his illustrious father, Squadron Leader W. S. Fielding Johnson who was also a pilot and a qualified air-gunner? At fifty-two Squadron Leader Fielding-Johnson was the oldest air-gunner on operations in the RAF serving as gunnery leader of a 2nd TAF Mitchell squadron taking part in an attack at Venlo in Holland. His aircraft was severely hit by flak over the target. The captain gave orders to jump. Johnson climbed down from his upper turret and, at 8000 feet, jumped. As he said later, "This was the thing I have always wanted to do. As soon as I had pulled the cord I found the sensation quite splendid."

"Thankfully" continues Bulmer, "we returned to night patrols and did our 23rd and last op together on 10 March. I had been on the squadron for thirteen months and had completed 75 ops. After acting as 'officers under instruction' at a court-martial in Lille, we returned to the squadron to find that we were posted to No.1 Ferry Unit at Pershore. Peter Kleboe had arrived to take over the squadron, Wing Commander V. R. Oates having failed to return from an op on 12 March. We left 21 Squadron on 18 March. As we climbed aboard the Anson to take us back to the UK the adjutant came out to see us off and whispered that the *Shellhaus* raid was on again and was due in the next few days. My feelings were mixed when I heard this. I'd missed out on all the much-vaunted 2 Group pinpoint raids except the attack on the barracks in Nijmegen at the beginning of *Market Garden* and that had ended in a complete fiasco. On the other hand, I would probably be pushing my luck to do just one more op. It was with sadness that I heard of Peter Kleboe's death three days later. I'd only known him for a few days but I liked him and reckoned he would be good for the squadron. With three COs lost in just over six weeks, 21 Squadron was going through a bad patch. But such is war."[393]

140 Wing now were required for another special pin point bombing operation, this time to Denmark. Special Operations Executive (SOE) in London had received intelligence that various Resistance and political prisoners held captive n the *Gestapo* HQ in the Shellhaus building in Copenhagen were to be shot on 21 March. The Free Danish Resistance movement had made repeated requests that the RAF should attack the building even though most of the prisoners were held in the attic to thwart any attempt to bomb the HQ.[394] Air Vice Marshal Basil Embry DSO** DFC* AFC CIC 2 Group, considered the implications. He decided to send the low level experts in 140 Wing, some of whom had flown on the Amiens prison raid and the attack on the *Gestapo* HQ in The Hague, to make a daring pinpoint attack on the Shellhaus.

On 20 March 18 FB.VIs of 140 Wing plus two FPU (Film Production Unit) specially modified Mosquito BIVs were detached from their base at Rosiéres en Senterre to RAF Fersfield in Norfolk. The move was made so that the route over the North Sea to Denmark would avoid flying over enemy-held territory with all the attendant risk of flak and radar detection. However, this stretched the Mosquitoes' range to the limit of endurance, a total flight time of over five hours. Group Captain R. N. 'Bob' Bateson DSO DFC AFC and Squadron Leader Ted Sismore DSO DFC, the leading tactical navigator, in R5570 would lead the operation. Air Vice Marshal Embry, alias "Wing Commander Smith," would fly in PZ222, a Mosquito loaned by 107 Squadron, in the first wave, with Squadron Leader Peter Clapham as his navigator. The crews were briefed intensely on 20 March and before take-off the next day, and kept in a confined and closely guarded area away from the other personnel on the base.

The twenty Mosquitoes would attack at minimum altitude, in three waves of 7, 6 and 6 aircraft respectively. Included in this total was one FPU Mosquito IV (DZ414/O) flown by Flight Lieutenant Ken Greenwood and Flying Officer E. Moore of 487 Squadron, which carried two 500lb HE and two 500lb M.76 incendiaries, and was to fly with and bomb with the first wave. The second FPU Mosquito IV (DZ383/*Q-Query*) flown by Flying Officer R. E. "Bob" Kirkpatrick of 21 Squadron and Sergeant R. Hearne of 4 FPU. Kirkpatrick, an American from Cleveland, Ohio, had joined 21 Squadron in August 1944 after completing training in Canada and flying Beaufighters in a Coastal Command OTU. His first attempt to start his military career on 8 December 1941 had been rebuffed at the US Marines recruiting office when he was told that he had a heart murmur. Bob crossed the border to Windsor, Ontario and upon questioning his physical condition, he was told, "If you can see lightning and hear thunder you can be a pilot!" He would probably see more than his share of both on *Carthage* because he and Hearne had the unenviable task of flying behind the third and last wave to film the results. In total the 20 Mosquitoes carried a lethal load of 44 500lb bombs. Because of the very low levels flown, to prevent damage to aircraft following the leading aircraft of each wave had 30-second delayed action bombs and the remainder, 11 second delayed action bombs. A proportion of the first and third waves carried M76 incendiaries.

At Fersfield the Mosquito crews were joined by 31 Mustang pilots from 64, 126 and 234 Squadrons (11 Group Fighter Command) who flew in from RAF Bentwaters. The fighters that were to escort the Mosquitoes and eliminate flak positions in the target area, were led by their Belgian Wing Commander (later Lieutenant General Avi e.r.) Mike Donnet CVO DFC CG. Born of Belgian parents in Richmond, England in 1917, Donnet had escaped to England on 5 August 1941 after Belgium had capitulated, in a two-seater Stampe biplane with a fellow officer. Twelve Mustangs of 126 Squadron would escort the first wave; six from 64 Squadron; two from 126 Squadron would escort the second wave and eight Mustangs of 64 Squadron, the third wave. Three Mustangs from 234 Squadron would sweep from ten miles north (Værløse air base) towards Copenhagen.

At 0855 on 12 March 21 the formation was airborne, forming up over Fersfield - five minutes later it crossed the English coastline northeast of Norwich, with a direct course for the first checkpoint some 375 miles away at Hvide Sand in Denmark. The weather was stormy, with surface winds gusting at 50 knots, making it difficult to control the aircraft. After crossing the North Sea at 50 feet to avoid radar detection, the windshields had become coated with salt spray, which reduced visibility - some pilots tried slowing down so that they could clear patches of their screens with gloves or cloths.

The checkpoint was dead-on with the force making landfall at Hvide Sand at 10.20. Three Mustangs were forced to turn back due to bird-strike damage. Over Jutland, the aircraft, still flying at minimum height, begun to attract attention of Danes and Germans alike. The *Jagdfliegerfuhrer* (German Fighter Control) received continuous reports as they flew across Denmark. The formation flew on by way of Give and along the northern side of Vejle Fjord to Juelsminde and then across the Great Belt. On the island of Zealand the checkpoint was Tissø, an almost circular lake chosen as an easy landmark. Here the formation spilt into the three wave formations ready to be escorted by the Mustangs. The first wave, lead by Group Captain Bateson, set course for Copenhagen at minimum altitude with an escort of eleven Mustangs, one having been forced to return due to bird strike damage. Flying on Bateson's port side was Air Vice Marshal Embry and Peter Clapham in PZ222/H. The remaining aircraft carried out "rate-one turns" (orbits) of the lake, once for the second wave, twice for third and three times for the remaining FPU Mossie. This gave a distance of approximately nine miles between each wave, an interval of approximately two minutes flying time.

On the outskirts of Copenhagen the first wave began to pick out the details of the target area. Despite the bumpy conditions Ted Sismore identified the target by the green and brown stripes and Bateson led his force over the rooftops. The aircraft began to move into attack formation, bomb doors were opened- bombs fused and speed was increased to 300 mph. The escorting Mustangs increased speed and began to seek out their targets - the flak positions, most being unmanned at the time. The first wave continued their run-in towards the final checkpoint when 800 yards from the target tragedy struck. The leading aircraft of the second flight (SZ977, the fourth Mosquito in the first wave, behind Bateson/Sismore, Carlisle/Ingram (PZ306) and Embry/Clapham (PZ222) collided with a 130 feet high floodlight pylon in the marshalling yards at Enghave and went into a vertical dive. The pilot, Wing Commander Peter Kleboe DSO DFC AFC aged 28, was the newly appointed CO of 21 Squadron. (On 2 February 'Daddy' Dale and Hackett, his navigator, went missing on a night patrol. On 6 February the squadron transferred to Rosières-en-Santerre and shortly afterwards Wing Commander V. R. Oates took over command. He failed to return from a sortie on 12 March and Peter Kleboe arrived to take over the squadron). His navigator was Canadian Flying Officer Reg Hall aged 30. Flight Lieutenant T. M. "Mac" Hetherington RCAF and Flight Lieutenant J. K. Bell, in HR162, were flying No.6 on the starboard side of, and slightly behind, Kleboe's aircraft. Hetherington observed:

> "We watched each other and attempted to follow the leader by 'biting hard into his tail' and at the same time, staying clear of his slipstream. We followed each other like shadows. We were altogether; 12 feet feet lower than the first three aircraft. We knew that we had to turn, but apparently Wing Commander Kleboe had not seen the pylon or had reacted too slowly. Suddenly, through the side window I observed Kleboe's aircraft climb at a very steep angle and fall off to port. Squadron Leader A. C. Henderson[395] and I instinctively threw our aircraft to starboard and continued on towards the target."

Flight Lieutenant Ken Greenwood, in DZ414/O, flying on the port side of Kleboe's aircraft, was just 25 feet away on Kleboe's port side. He adds:

> "Some 10-15 seconds before the accident, bomb doors had been opened, copying the leader. Kleboe's aircraft lost height, some 15 feet, and I suppose by peripheral vision I saw the pylon and realized that he was going to fly into it. As the aircraft struck the pylon, part of the port engine was damaged. The Mosquito rose almost vertically and then rapidly to port. I had to take violent evasive action to prevent a mid-air collision and swung to hard to port."

Kleboe's two bombs struck a building in Sdr Boulevard (one, a dud, failed to explode) and eight civilians were killed. The Mosquito was observed waggling its wings and trailing smoke before it crashed into a garage on *Frederiksberg Allé* adjacent to the *Jeanne d'Arc School*. The force of the explosion from the fuel created a huge pall of black smoke. Kleboe and Reg Hall were both killed. They were later buried in Bispebjerg Churchyard. The remaining aircraft of the first wave continued over the target area. Group Captain Bateson being the first to attack with his bombs going in between the second and third floors of the west wing at 11.15 - right on schedule.

Air Vice Marshal Embry and Squadron Leader Peter Clapham and Squadron Leader Tony Carlisle and Flight Lieutenant N. J. "Rex" Ingram got their bombs away. Carlisle followed with Embry directly behind and observed the Air Vice Marshal's bombs strike the building at street level. Henderson, and "Mac" Hetherington, each put their two bombs through the roof of the *Shellhaus*. Embry moved into Henderson's flight path, which forced him to go over Embry. Henderson's navigator, Bill Moore, said, "Look, the old man's going sightseeing!" After getting their bombs away, the first wave scattered and exited Copenhagen at roof top height in a northwesterly direction over the city and made for home. Until now, the Germans had not sounded the air-raid warning. The Danish Civil Air Defense had also followed the path of the aircraft, realizing the danger to the city it tried to persuade the Germans to sound the alarm. By the time the Germans took action, bombs were already smashing into the *Shellhaus*. Official records have revealed that the German officers responsible for this negligence were court-martialled.[396]

The second wave of six Mosquitoes of 464 Squadron RAAF led by Wing Commander Bob Iredale DSO DFC RAAF and Flying Officer B. J. Standish in SZ968 arrived over Copenhagen some two minutes behind the first. By this time the sky over Copenhagen was being criss-crossed by flak. The leading three crews were distracted by the smoke coming from Kleboe's wrecked aircraft as this was greater than that coming from the *Shellhaus*. Confusion reigned and the force was split into two. A split-second decision had to be made. Iredale broke off his attack and circled to come in again. At the same time the three remaining Mosquitoes of "*Blue Section*" led by Flight Lieutenant Archie Smith DFC and Flight Sergeant E. L. Green in PZ309, had realized the mistake and located the target slightly to the right of their track. Smith made two orbits of the target area before bombing. His bombs struck the outside of the east wing, destroying a pillbox situated on the corner. In the confusion it appears that one aircraft bombed the school by mistake, the remainder (together with the Mustang escort) began to circle the area to clarify their position.

In the first manoeuvre some Mosquitoes were too far left of the target and only those aircraft closest to *Shellhaus* were able to bomb. Both Iredale, who got his bombs away on the east end of the *Shellhaus*, and Smith, who also attacked a flak position at Hundested, managed to bomb *Shellhaus*.

During his orbit Flight Lieutenant W. Knowle Shrimpton DFC and Flying Officer Peter R. Lake RAAF in PZ353 in the No.2 position behind Iredale in the second wave, came into conflict with the incoming third wave. Shrimpton explains:

> "We came up to the lake where we would drop our wing tanks. I had to keep the Mosquito level and straight during this part of the operation, no skidding, so that the tanks would fall away cleanly without rolling into the tailplane. This was no easy task due to the extremely high turbulence. Peter was then concentrating more on map reading whilst I concentrated on accurate flying. I prayed that he had memorized the track. Then on the outskirts of the city I recognized the first landmark shown on the briefing model. Flying became precise; height 50 feet, engine revs, and boost. We wanted 320mph but settled for 305 to 310, which was about all we could get. I set the bomb fuses and opened the bomb bay doors. We were getting close. Flak was looping over the target from the right with not much room over Shellhaus. The next event was a shock. Peter yelled, 'Don't bomb, smoke to port!' He signalled to me that something was wrong. Were we on target? This all took place some 10-15 seconds from what we believed to be the target. Enough time to see that the building in question was not damaged but not enough to evaluate all the facts. Therefore, I aborted the attack, cleared the building and closed the bomb doors. Throttling back and keeping low, I commenced a left-hand orbit. After a moment we had left the flak area and I reduced the rate of turn. We then had the opportunity to access the situation and make a plan. The building, which we were confident was the target was not damaged, no fire or smoke. We decided that the preceding aircraft had probably bombed the wrong target. Was the fire a decoy?
>
> "We decided to get ourselves into position for another run up to the target. Then, realizing that we were alone without orientation of our position, we commenced another orbit. After about 325° we both became re-orientated, first by Peter's recognition of the run up track and as a result of that, my identification of the target. Here we determined that Shellhaus had been hit. We could see dust and smoke. I continued to turn on the run-up and as we came in we both agreed that the job had been done. We observed heavy damage to the base of the building and lots of dust and smoke. More bombs might have unnecessarily endangered the Danes in the building so we aborted the attack. Later, on the long flight home, there was a distinct sense of failure or at least disappointment that we still had our bombs."

Two of the Mosquitoes from "*Blue Section*" in the second wave were hit by flak over the north of Zealand on the return flight.[397] The third wave consisting of the six 487 Squadron FB.VIs, led by Wing Commander F. H. Denton DFC* a New Zealander and his Australian navigator Flying Officer A. J. Coe in PZ402 had navigation problems. They approached Copenhagen from the northeast; a completely different direction to the planned flight path. This wave had been observed in front of the returning aircraft from the first wave as they left the target area. Delayed by some minutes they were caught up by DZ383 *Q-Query*, flown by Flying Officer R. E. 'Bob' Kirkpatrick with Sergeant R. Hearne that had departed the Lake Tissø area two minutes behind the other six Mosquitoes. By mistake, four crews in the third wave bombed the area around the school. Denton and Coe, who located *Shellhaus*, saw so much damage already that the pilot aborted his attack and jettisoned their bombs in the sea. Flak tore away the starboard flap and knocked out the hydraulic system but Denton managed to nurse his flak-damaged FB.VI back and belly-landed in England.[398] *Q-Query* also limped home after taking a flak hit over the target. Kirkpatrick recalls:

> "As we approached the city I could see a huge pall of black smoke dead ahead, and, at the same time, some Mossies in a tight left turn. Our courses were converging. As they straightened out towards the smoke I had only a second to decide to join them close enough to avoid the 11 second delay bombs, rather than risk a right turn with the cruddy windshield [which had become coated with salt spray low over the North Sea]. The Mossies leveled off on track and I tucked in close, just as their bomb doors opened. I opened mine and saw their bombs drop just before we entered the smoke. I dropped my bomb load, then we got a pretty good wallop in the smoke and after breaking out I lost contact with the other Mosquitoes. On the outskirts of the city, I saw two Mossies at about 3 o'clock on a northerly heading. I joined up with them only to see that one was smoking badly from the starboard engine.[399] The escorting Mosquito waved me off, as without guns, I would be just a burden and their course was not towards England. I turned back west just in time to see a sandbagged gun pit with two guns firing at the three of us. We had inadvertently got close to a large barracks, a fenced area with several low buildings. The best and quickest evasion was to go straight towards the gun pit and dive. I opened the bomb doors to get their attention and spoil their aim. As the doors opened the gunners abandoned their guns and ducked down. We were gone in a flash, right over them."[400]
>
> Kirkpatrick concludes:
>
> "On the return trip we sweated fuel for over an hour. When we spotted the English coast, and, not too far inland, an air base. I went straight in. I got the wheels down, but nothing for flaps or brakes, so I coasted to a stop on the grass by the runway. We had found a B-24 base [Rackheath] near Norwich. Hearne and I were escorted by MPs to the control tower to explain our presence."[401]

140 Wing had one more low-level pinpoint raid to fly. On 17 April six FB.VIs of 140 Wing, led by Group Captain Bob Bateson DSO DFC** AFC and Ted Sismore, taxied out for a daylight strike on a school building on the outskirts of Odense, which was being used by the *Gestapo* as a HQ. Air Vice Marshal Basil Embry went along, as usual. The six Mosquitoes destroyed the *Gestapo* HQ and 18 days later Denmark was free. During April the retreat by the *Wehrmacht* had left medium bombers far to the rear of the battlefront, so at the end of the month 138 Wing advanced to Achmer.

On the night of 24/25 March 604, 605 and 410 "Cougar" Squadron RCAF crews shot down four more enemy aircraft. On the night of 25/26 March crews in 409 and 264 despatched two Bf 110s and a Ju 88 plus one "probable." There was a great deal of activity on 26/27 March with raids concentrated on the Rhine bridgehead at Emmerich and as a result, the Luftwaffe was forced up into the night sky, but with disastrous results.[402] Flight Lieutenant Al Gabitas of 488 Squadron RNZAF recalls:

> "At this stage of the war the Germans were feeling the effects of the Allied bombing on their synthetic petrol plants and were obviously trying to conserve fuel. This meant that their night flying activity tended to be concentrated on to particular nights, with long intervals of inactivity. The night of 26/27 March was to be a busy one with raids against the Rhine bridgehead at Emmerich. Flight Lieutenant Johnny Hall DFC, an Englishman on the Squadron, and his navigator Pilot Officer Taylor, contacted a Junkers 88 and brought it down 20 miles north of Emmerich after several bursts of cannon fire. But the Mosquito itself was damaged by flying debris and burst into flames as it landed on its belly at Gilze Rijn in Holland. Fortunately the top hatch slid back easily and the crew escaped unhurt."

Chunky Stewart and Bill Brumby were also on patrol over the bridgehead, in NF.XXX NT263. About 8 miles NW of Bocholt they intercepted a Bf 110, which, after a short burst, hit the ground with a brilliant explosion. Their radar set then became partially useless but even so, Brumby managed to pick up a contact, which turned out to be a He 111. Stewart gave the Heinkel a quick couple of bursts and it went into a steep dive. At the same time Stewart realized that he was being chased by a German night-fighter and he had to break off the engagement.

Flight Lieutenant Al Gabitas adds:

> "Following these successes there were many hours of patient patrolling and sky-searching and it was well into April [the night of 7/8] before Chunky and Bill were directed to a 'Bogey' over the Rhur. In the long chase that followed the rear gunner on the Me 110 opened fire on the Mosquito several times but Chunky was not able to get his sights on to the enemy or fire his guns. Presently a small fire started in the tail of the Messerschmitt and then grew larger until it dived into the ground and exploded. Although their guns were not fired, Chunky and Bill were credited with one enemy aircraft destroyed. The enemy had shot off his own tail. Thus Chunky, in a comparatively short time had brought his score up to five enemy aircraft destroyed and one damaged. Recognition of this achievement was to come with the award of DFC's to both Chunky and Bill. Unfortunately the paper work for the awards was rather slow and they were not announced until after the Squadron had been disbanded and left the Continent. I did not see Chunky again until 1949, by which time he was a full partner in his legal firm in Dunedin and making a name for himself in the profession. Sadly, he lived for only a few short years after the war and died suddenly in his hometown from a massive coronary. All those who knew him were profoundly shocked at the death in times of peace of one so apparently fit and comparatively young."

Meanwhile, 264 Squadron had moved back to France, to 148 Wing at Lille/Vendeville. Their move had coindiced with a snowstorm and the squadron had had to endure the weather with very little heating or comfort until the snow cleared early in February. Both January and February were complete operational blanks as the Luftwaffe was not keen to show himself at night at all, but near the end of February four pilots left for Gilse/Rijen to carry out operation "*Blackmail*." This was intensely secret at the time but it entailed carrying Dutchmen, Air Force and Army, and one woman over occupied Holland by day and night to maintain wireless communications with agents of their underground movement. This task was performed well and was particularly useful and had been refused by 2 Group who considered it to be too dangerous. March saw plenty of patrols being flown both from Lille and Gilse, but it was not until the 25th that any success was achieved, a Ju 88 destroyed and another damaged; the first combat since 10 August 10. March in fact saw a heavy toll of German aircraft by 2nd TAF Mosquito night-fighters. On 5/6 March Flight Lieutenant Don MacFadyen DFC RCAF in 406 ("Lynx") Squadron RCAF, flying NF.XXX NT325, destroyed a Ju 88G at Gerolzhofen.

When on 21 April "Ginger" Walsh and "Pat" Patterson in 487 Squadron in France flew an op to Emden, everything that could go wrong went wrong. Walsh remembers the event:

> "We took off and landed at Melsbroek first before come to the Rhine. We had a funnel only about two miles wide. A Mossie that had aborted flew back past us at a closing speed of more than 600mph and narrowly missed us! Crossing the Rhine we almost hit a barrage balloon that our boys were flying from a barge. We ended up at 1000-1500 feet in the middle of a German airfield. I compressed myself into a small space but nothing happened. We turned west and came back towards Hamburg. Finally, we dropped our bombs on a German town. 'Pat' threw the aircraft around but nothing happened. Back at Amiens our NZ Squadron Leader who was acting CO berated 'Pat' for bringing his ammo back.
>
> "'Pat' must have taken it to heart because four days later, on 25 April, when we were coming back from Emden, he lowered the nose and began firing. I told him three times that we were nearing our lines! His target could have been a haystack or it could have been Hitler. "Pat" continued firing off our ammo. We got light flak; the tracer was utterly fascinating and missed us but I had to do something. I reached up and fired off the red and yellow colors of the day from the Verey Pistol mounted in the roof of the cockpit. It did the trick! The cockpit filled with cordite and there was a big flash.
>
> "'Pat' I said, 'What the …. was that?'
>
> "I giggled and told him that I'd fired the Verey Pistol. You never gave away the colors of the day but it was of no consequence to me! The firing stopped. I had visions of a German down below looking at his flimsy [his 'colors of the day', which could be easily destroyed when no longer needed].
>
> "It was on this operation that Flight Lieutenant Johnny Evans and his navigator, Flying Officer Ifor Jenkins, were lost. Johnny had lost two pilot brothers killed in the war. I'd spent time in Montreal with Ifor. They put out a Mayday call:
>
> "'I'm on fire and losing height!' They'd got him.
>
> "Another voice said, 'You'll be all right'. Evans replied caustically, 'It's all right for you.' That was it - they were dead."

AN AIRFIELD REMEMBERED

We were hungry, tired and dirty,
From our shoulders rifles hung
Our clothes were torn our faces bronzed
By long hours in the sun,
Here was to be our Station,
For the war was not yet won,
When we came to Little Snoring,
That fateful June had just begun.

Living here among you we would
Join you at your play
And in the quiet of your Church
We knelt with you to pray,
We filled your Lane and Byways
With laughter and with song,
We shared each other's sorrows
As through life we journeyed on.

Where both men and maidens tended
To the harsh and warlike needs,
Of men who through the dark hours
Flew their man made steeds
The sky at night their hunting ground
In which they sought their prey,
Returning only when the night
Gave way to breaking day!

At times when hope was fading.
They would patient vigil keep,
Rejoicing if their Crew returned
But often they would weep
They wept for those who ere the sun
Had warmed the fresh turned clod,
Had fought their last battle
And were at peace with God

I returned to Snoring Airfield
The way was hard to find.
For over paths and taxiways
Nature had thrown a blind
Of grass and twisted bramble
Willow herb and clinging vine,
No longer there the Nissen Huts
In which men slept and dined.

Forsaken then the Hangars stood
Empty broken gaunt and grey
Only wheeling birds were there
To welcome me that day
And when some silent mystic hand
Rolled back the fleeting years
I saw this dead place fill with life
And my eyes were wet with tears.

For one vibrant fleeting moment
This vast Airfield was reborn,
Through misty eyes I saw it rise
From amid the standing corn
Men and buildings filled the skyline
At Dispersals stood the Planes,
Then like a wraith all sank to rest
Beneath the quilt of grain.

I trod again the winding path
Unlatched the old Oak door,
And found there in the House of God
That men had kept the score
Of all the kills the squadron made,
The honours men had won,
A humbled man I closed the door
My visit almost done.

I tried to find the work of him
Who when released from duties
Took paint and brush, from his hand
There grew a thing of beauty,
His Gallery was the Airmen's mess
His canvas bare brick wall,
All we who served on Snoring
His pictures can recall!

To ploughshares men shall beat their swords
To pruning hooks their spears
For us the Artist there portrayed
Our hopes for future years
I knew him well the Artist,
Who did those colors blend,
I knew what had inspired him
For you see he was my friend.

From my full well of memories
I drew long and deep that day,
Recalled the bitterness of war
And the price we had to pay,
That we might live in freedom
To worship without fear
Is that not what we fought for
And why we were stationed here?

Pilot Officer S. F. Ruffle,
23 & 515 Squadrons

Although this photo was specially staged and lit for the cameraman (Mosquito nightfighter crews never used tracer in their ammunition because if they did not hit their target immediately they would not want to advertise their presence and alarm their target), it nonetheless shows the formidable firepower of four Browning Mk.II .303 inch machine guns and four 20mm cannon available to Mosquito crews. (via Tom Cushing)

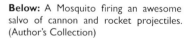

Far Left: Mosquito pilot and navigator beside their FB.VI in the summer of 1944.

Near Left: Flight Lieutenant J. H. 'Jack' Phillips DFC RCAF and Flying Officer Bernard M. Job DFC RAFVR of 418 (City of Edmonton) Squadron RCAF, 2 Group, 2nd TAF on the wing of FB.VI NT137/TH-T *Lady Luck* at Hartford Bridge, February 1945. Following the squadron's disbandment in March 1945 this aircraft was passed to 13 OTU with whom it suffered a landing accident on 28 May 1948 at Middleton St. George and it was relegated to an instructional airframe. (Bernard M. Job)

Below: A Mosquito firing an awesome salvo of cannon and rocket projectiles. (Author's Collection)

Above: Group Captain Pickard at the controls of a liaison aircraft. 'Pick' Pickard had joined the RAF in 1936 and in 1940, as a flight lieutenant, he had achieved an unwanted fame through his clipped, natural playing of the pilot of Wellington *F for Freddie* in the film *Target for Tonight.* After completing a bombing tour he commanded 161 Squadron at Tempsford assisting directly in the dangerous work of subversion and sabotage in France. On 27/28 February 1942 as a wing commander he led the force of a dozen 51 Squadron Whitley aircraft carrying British paratroops in the raid on Bruneval, which resulted in the capture of vital German radar secrets.

Top Left: Flight Lieutenant J.A.'Peter' Broadley DSO DFC DFM does up the harness straps for Group Captain Percy C. Pickard DSO DFC. (via Jerry Scutts)

Squadron Leader Ian McRitchie DFC RAAF and Flight Lieutenant R.W."Sammy" Sampson' of 464 Squadron RAAF by their FB.VI MM404/SB-T, which was downed by flak on Operation *Jericho,* the first of 140 Wing's notable pinpoint raids, on 18 February 1944. The Australian second flight leader was wounded in twenty-six places and he crash-landed at over 200 mph near Poix. McRitchie survived and was taken prisoner but Sampson did not survive the crash. (via John Rayner)

Pilot Officer Maxwell N. Sparks (left) and his navigator. Pilot Officer Arthur C. Dunlap of 487 Squadron RNZAF who crewed HX982/EC-T on the Amiens raid. (Arthur Dunlap via John Rayner)

Right: Group Captain Percy C. Pickard DSO DFC, CO 140 Wing, who died leading the famous Amiens Prison raid, 19 February 1944. (Author's Coll)

The model used for the daring raid on Amiens Prison in Operation *Jericho* on 18 February 1944. In January information had been received in London that 196 loyal Frenchmen were being held in captivity in Amiens prison, many under sentence of death. The most important Frenchman in the jail, which held 700 French men and women, of whom about 250 were political prisoners, was Monsieur Raymond Vivant, a key Resistance leader and *sous-préfet* at Abbeville. Monsieur Dominique Ponchardier, the dark haired, dark skinned leader of the whole of Occupied France of a group called the 'Sosies' had requested an urgent air strike to break open the 22 feet high and 3 feet thick walls surrounding the three-storey building, which rose to 66 feet and was built in the shape of a cross. There would be casualties, but better to die from RAF bombs than be shot by a German firing squad. Eleven members of the local *Frances Tireurs et Partisans Français* (FTPF) had been shot in the jail in December 1943. More prisoners, perhaps twenty, fifty or even a hundred, were due to be executed on 19 February. (IWM)

Amiens prison on fire after the raid. (via John Rayner).

487 Squadron RNZAF crews, some of whom took part in the Amiens raid, are interviewed by the BBC. Top, L-R: Pilot Officer D. R. 'Bob' Fowler, pilot of HX974/EG-J; Pilot Officer M. Barriball; Pilot Officer M. L. S. Darrall, pilot of HX909/EG-C. Bottom, L-R: Robin Miller NZ war correspondent; Pilot Officer Maxwell N. Sparks, pilot of HX982/EG-T; David Bernard (BBC) and Pilot Officer F. Stevenson, Pilot Officer Darrall's navigator an the operation. (via John Rayner)

The breached wall of the Amiens Prison. The first bombs were dropped on the outer walls on the east and north sides of the prison by the four 487 Squadron FB.VIs led by Wing Commander 'Black' Smith. Their bombs shot straight through or over the eastern wall and careered across the courtyard before crashing into the western wall on the far side. One of the bombs struck the main prison building. The two Mosquitoes attacking the northern wall from the north aimed for the right hand end and hit the junction of the northern and western wall. The five FB.VIs of 464 Squadron and Pickard's Mosquito closely followed them. Their target was the main building and the guards' quarters at the east and west ends of the prison. Wing Commander 'Bob' Iredale pinpointed the guards' quarters, let go his bombs so that they would skid right into the annex, with the sloping roof of the prison inches from the belly of his Mosquito, as he climbed over it. (via John Rayner)

Still taken from Wing Commander Bob Iredale's SB-F MM412 during the precision attack on Amiens Prison on 18 February 1944, one of the most famous operations of the war, when twelve FB.VIs of 464 Squadron RAAF and 487 Squadron RNZAF breached the prison walls at Amiens Prison, which was holding 700 French prisoners.The aircraft following is SB-A MM402 flown by Squadron Leader W. R. C. Sugden and his navigator, Flying Officer A. H. Bridger. (via Jerry Scutts)

Result of the precision attack on Amiens Prison 18 February 1944. Both the northern and southern perimeter walls were breached. The attack came in from the north so it must be assumed that the southern beach, left of the main gate, was caused by a bomb that skidded through the prison after being dropped from east or north. Pilot Officer D. R. Fowler of487 Squadron RNZAF, who flew EG-J/HX974, and Squadron Leader Ian McRitchie, of 464 Squadron RAAF, who flew MM404/SB-T, claim the same hole! (via GMS)

Photo reconnaissance picture of the prison after the raid. About 400 prisoners had escaped. After Arras was liberated in October 1944, 260 bodies were found buried outside the town. Among them were most of the Amiens prisoners who had deliberately stayed behind to take part in the work of mercy. They had been shot in April 1944. (IWM)

In 1946 a French film celebrating the Amiens raid opened in Paris, L-R: Mrs. I. S. Smith, Wing Commander I. S. 'Black' Smith. CO 487 Squadron RNZAF, who led the New Zealanders in FB.VI LR333/EG-R; Monsieur Dominique Ponchardier, who sent a message of thanks to the Air Ministry in London in March 1944; Mrs and Squadron Leader Ian McRitchie. (via John Rayner)

Flight Lieutenant Adam Szajdzicki, navigator, in 305 (Polish) Squadron. (Adam Szajdzicki)

NF.XIII HK382/T of 29 Squadron at Hunsdon, 1944. 29 Squadron had begun conversion from the Beaufighter to the Mosquito NF.XII in the summer of 1943 for the continuance of night intruder operations over occupied Europe and by the end of 1943 had destroyed about 600 enemy aircraft. *Intruder* operations continued in 1944, apart from October/November, when the Mosquitoes were used briefly for night interception of V1 flying bombs. Intruding then continued unabated until VE Day 1945. (Frank Pringle)

FBVI HX917 EG-E joined 487 Squadron RNZAF in July 1943 and was lost on 5 July 1944. (RAF Swanton Morley)

FB.VI MM417/EG-T of 487 Squadron RNZAF. On 26 March 1944 this aircraft, which was being flown by the CO, Wing Commander Irving S.'Black' Smith RNZAF was shot up (accidentally) by a following Mosquito flown by Claude Pocock, who was on his first *Noball* operation. MM417 landed at Hunsdon whereupon it broke up into three pieces. That evening, still thinking he had been hit by enemy fire, Smith and his navigator, Ronnie Marsh went to examine the wreck. Marsh dug some 20mm ammunition out of the wing and examination of NS828's camera gun film proved that Pocock had shot down his CO! (IWM)

464 Squadron RAAF and 487 Squadron RNZAF Squadrons remained at Thorney Island until December 1944 while 21 Squadron did not join them at Rosières-en-Santerre, France until February 1945. Pictured with ground crew are 21 Squadron pilot and navigator, Sid Moulds (2nd from left) and pilot Ted Bellis. (via Les Bulmer)

FB.VI LR366 of 613 'City of Manchester' Squadron in 138 Wing, 2 Group refuelling at RAF Swanton Morley, Norfolk early in 1944 during night interdictor training at the 2 GSU (Group support Unit) base. 613 Squadron flew their first Mosquito operation on 31 December 1943, an attack on a VI site in northern France. In 1944-45, as part of 2nd TAF, the squadron flew mainly night tactical operations against targets in France, as well as daylight precision maids on high security Nazi targets, the most notable of these being the attack on the Gestapo HQ at The Hague, April 1944 and the *SS* barracks at Egletons in August. 613 moved to Hartford Bridge in October and in November they moved again, to Cambrai-Epinoy, France, to harass German units. LR366 joined 107 Squadron and failed to return from the Arnhem operation on 17 September 1944 when the Mosquitoes of 138 Wing, 2nd TAF bombed German barracks as part of Operation *Market Garden*. (via Philip Birtles)

A FB.VI taxies out for a night operation.

NF.XXX NT585 of 125 (Newfoundland) Squadron at RAF Coltishall over Norfolk late in 1944. This particular nightfighter had previously served with 307 (Polish) Squadron. Its final frontline service was with 151 Squadron until 1946 and then sold for scrap in July 1948. (Richard Doleman)

One of the 150 NF.IIs delivered to the RAF between April and October 1942 by de Havilland Hatfield, DD744 seen here with four guns fitted like the all-black NF.II behind, is in a high-visibility silver finish during its time with either No.1 or 301 Fighter Training Unit (FTU). Later converted to PR.II the fighter was flown to North Africa by the Overseas Aircraft Delivery Unit (OADU) and used by 60 Squadron SAAF on the unit's first sortie from Castel Benito, near Tripoli on 15 February 1943. (DH via Philip Birtles)

Falaise Gap in a speeding Mosquito 'on D-Day plus about twenty feet! (Vic Hester)

Top: NF.XIII HK425/KP-D *Lonesome Polecat* of 409 'Nighthawk' Squadron RCAF on the unit's grass dispersal at Twente in Holland was built at Leavesden in the second half of 1943 and delivered to 95 Squadron when the unit converted from Beaufighter VIFs to Mosquito NF.XIIIs in October-November that year. HK425 was passed to 409 Squadron when it too converted from Beaufighter VIFs to NF.XIIIs, in March 1944. On 6/7 October 1944 Flying Officer Al Webster (left) and Flying Officer Ross H. Finlayson **[Above]** destroyed a Bf 110 in this aircraft, followed on 25/26 November 1944 with a claim for a Ju 88 by Flying Officer A. I. E. Britten RCAF and Flight Lieutenant L. E. Fownes over Rheindahlen. By the end of the war Britten and Fownes had destroyed five aircraft. *Lonesome Polecat*'s final victory was on 18/19 December when Finlayson and Webster destroyed a Ju 88 in this aircraft. The nose art was inspired by a drunken Indian character from a very popular comic strip of the day, Finlayson having added the name to the aircraft and then asked his parents to send him a copy of the comic from Canada for copying. However, before the publication arrived, one of his ground crew painted the skunk on the nose ahead of the titling, and it was considered to be so well done that Finlayson left it on. HK425 was SOC on 21 November 1945. (Ross Finlayson)

Bottom Right: NF.XIII MM560/F of 409 'Nighthawk' Squadron RCAF at Le Culot in Belgium on the morning of 7 October 1944 following Finlayson and Webster's shooting down of Koch's Bf 110. MM560 was normally flown by Squadron Leader Hatch, CO 'A' Flight but as the two Canadians had no aircraft of their own, they would take any Mosquito that was serviceable. All told, MM560/F is known to have featured in the destruction of four enemy aircraft. On 13/14 June 1944 Wing Commander J. W. Reid and Flight Lieutenant J. W. Peacock destroyed a He 177 10m East of Le Havre. On 18/19 August 1944 Squadron Leader Hatch and Flying Officer Eames destroyed a Ju 88/Ju 188 and on 30/31 December 1944 Squadron Leader Hatton and Flying Officer Rivers destroyed a Ju 88G. MM560 remained with the Canadians until written off in a belly landing at Lille/Vendeville on 13 March 1945 after the Mosquito's undercarriage had jammed during an air test. The NF.XXX parked in the distance behind MM560 is the 410 Squadron aircraft in which Flight Lieutenants Ben Erwin Plumer DFC and Hargrove had been vectored onto a second Bf 110 and lost an engine to return fire. Plumer weaved to dodge the German's bullets and the Bf 110 pilot lost control and crashed. (Ross Finlayson)

Squadron Leader Russ Bannock DFC and his navigator Flying Officer Bobbie Bruce DFC of 418 (City of Edmonton) Squadron RCAF, 2 Group, 2nd TAF, in front of their FB.VI HR147 *Hairless Joe* at Middle Wallop in August 1944. Bannock ended the war with nine confirmed victories, four damaged, two destroyed on the ground and eighteen and one shared V1s. *Hairless Joe's* art work was applied twice in fact for HR147 suffered damage to its nose in an operational mishap which saw the caricature and its background disc repainted. At this time one of the two rows of eight swastikas was replaced with 19 V1 symbols. *Hairless Joe* was sold for scrap in October 1954. (Bernard M. Job)

On 4 September 1944 Flight Lieutenant Ken W. Watson RAAF (**Right**) and Flying Officer Ken Pickup RAFVR of 540 Squadron were flying PR.IX LR429 when they were attacked over Nurnberg at 29,000 feet by Me 262s. For 15 minutes they evaded them before escaping at 1500 feet but not before hitting the tip of a Bavarian pine tree, which shattered the nose perspex and filled the cockpit with pine needles, making it very cold, uncomfortable and draughty. The crew flew on through the Brenner Pass to San Severo, Italy, where they safely recovered. After repairs LR429 was written off the next day in a crash-landing after the crew tried to return to Benson. Both men were unhurt and they completed their tours. On 3 June 1954 following a test flight to Cuxhaven Watson was killed landing a RAF Canberra when a Night Photo Flash bomb exploded in the bomb bay. (Pickup Coll)

Mosquito NFXXX MM767 of 410 'Cougar' Squadron RCAF rests on PSP (Pierced Steel Planking) in a muddy dispersal at either B48/Glisy or B51 Lille-Vendeville in the winter of 1944/45. On 29/30 October 1944 Lieutenant Archie A. Harrington USAAF and Pilot Officer D. G. Tongue shot down a Fw 190 flying this aircraft in the Venlo area. On 25/26 November this crew, again in MM767, destroyed three Ju 88Gs at Muntz, Jackerath and North of Hunxe thus raising their final score to seven. (Stephen M. Fochuk)

B.Mk.IV DZ383/? 'the query' (because it did not belong to any one of the three squadrons in 138 Wing, 2nd TAF at Lasham, Hants, 1943-44). A Polish airman's first attempt to paint a question mark went awry as he got it the wrong way round on one side! On 17 September 1944 DZ383 was flown by Flight Lieutenant Vic A. Hester of 613 Squadron, with cameraman Flying Officer Ted Moore to film an attack on a barracks at Arnhem ahead of the '*Market-Garden*' operation, then photograph the airborne drop at Arnhem. On the Shellhaus raid, 21 March 1945, Flying Officer R. E. 'Bob' Kirkpatrick, an American pilot in 21 Squadron flew D2383, with cameraman Sergeant R. Hearne from 4 FPU. Although damaged by flak over Copenhagen, Kirkpatrick nursed 'the query' back to Norfolk, where he force landed at the USAAF B-24 base at Rackheath, near Norwich.

B.VIs of 613 Squadron at Cambrai-Epinoy in 1945. (Philip Beck)

Crews in 305 Polish Squadron in front of NS844 *N-Nan,* which Pilot Officer Harry Randall-Cutler and Herbert Cohen flew on the daylight Operation *Clarion* on 22 February 1945 and which almost ended in disaster for them as Randall-Cutler recalls. 'We flew thirty-five operations - all at night - so it was marvelous to see this train in all its glory in daylight. When we arrived the engine quickly left the train in the station and steamed off around to a bend in the track where it stopped and the driver jumped out. We and another Mosquito crew strafed the train with cannon and machine gun fire, destroying eight wagons and then went after the engine, taking two or three runs on it from all directions and hitting it until all of our ammunition was gone. We cruised back at 250 feet, coming out just west of Nijmegen, where the Germans had flooded the area. I saw this haystack north of the river (our troops were on the other side). As we approached, I was astonished to see the sides of the haystack fall apart to reveal a 20mm gun emplacement! The gun crew held their fire as we flew right over the top of them and then they began firing at us. I gave a chunk of rudder to skid the aircraft and pulled the hail. The whole engine was soon black with oil. I throttled back and told Hugh to get ready to bale out. He replied, You must be joking!' I nursed *N-Nan* in a cruise quite comfortably back to base but we landed with a burst tyre and ground looped onto the grass. The aircraft was full of holes and so badly damaged I was told to get a new aircraft.' (Randall-Cutler)

B.XVI RV295 of 109 Squadron in 1944, which in addition to its flare marking duties for the heavies, its Mosquitoes carried bombs. On 21 April 1945 109 Squadron dropped the last bombs to fall on Berlin in WW2. During the last few days of the war the Squadron used marking techniques to select points for aircraft dropping supplies to the Dutch in various parts of Holland. (David M. Russell)

NF.XIII HK415/KP-R of 409 Squadron RCAF at Lille airfield in November 1944. Note that the hangars in the background behind the Spitfire have been camouflaged as farm buildings. On 18/19 December 1944 Flying Officers Al Webster and Ross H. Finlayson destroyed a Ju 88 in this aircraft, which Squadron Leader A. Parker-Rees and Flight Lieutenant Bennett of 96 Squadron were flying when they claimed a He 177 probable over Sussex on 24/25 February 1944 and a Me 410 at sea on 13/14 April 1944. HK415 was lost in a take-off accident at Lille airfield on 18 January 1945. (Ross Finlayson)

Canadian built B.XXV KB471. (via GMS)

A NF.XIX crew of 68 Squadron prepare for a night sortie in late 1944. The bulbous nose contains the AI.Mk.X radar equipment. This squadron was successful in shooting down four V1 carrying He 111H-22 aircraft over the North Sea during November-December 1944, the first on the night of 5/6 November 1944 by Flight Sergeant L. W. Neal and Flight Sergeant E. Eastwood in NF.XIX TA389. 68 Squadron destroyed another V1 carrying aircraft in January 1945. On the night of 19/20 October 25 flying bombs were air launched from over the North Sea. Four Mosquito crews succeeded in destroying five of them. Warrant Officer D. Lauchlan and Flight Lieutenant F. Bailey of 68 Squadron destroyed two of the *Divers* and Flight Sergeant A. Bullus and Flying Officer L.W. Edwards and Flying Officer G.T. Gibson and Sergeant B. M. Lack got another two V1s. Only one of the 25 air-launched V1s evaded the British ground and air defenses that night. On the night of 25/26 October when twelve V1s were launched. Squadron Leader M. J. Mansfeld and Flight Lieutenant S. A. Janacek took 68 Squadron's monthly V1 total to twelve and an unidentified crew destroyed another air-launched V1. DH)

Sergeant Colin 'Ginger' Walsh (left) and Flying Officer John Patterson of 487 Squadron RNZAF, 140 Wing, at Rosières-en-Santerre, who flew their first operation on 23 January 1945 from Thorney Island. (Colin Walsh)

Bombs rain down on the barracks at Caserne des Dunes, Poitiers on 1 August 1944. (via Paul McCue)

The attack on the Château de Fou by Mosquitoes of 107 Squadron on 2 August 1944. (IWM)

The bombed out barracks at Caserne des Dunes, Poitiers after the raid by twenty-four FB.VIs of 487 Squadron RNZAF and 21 Squadrons on 1 August 1944. (via Paul McCue)

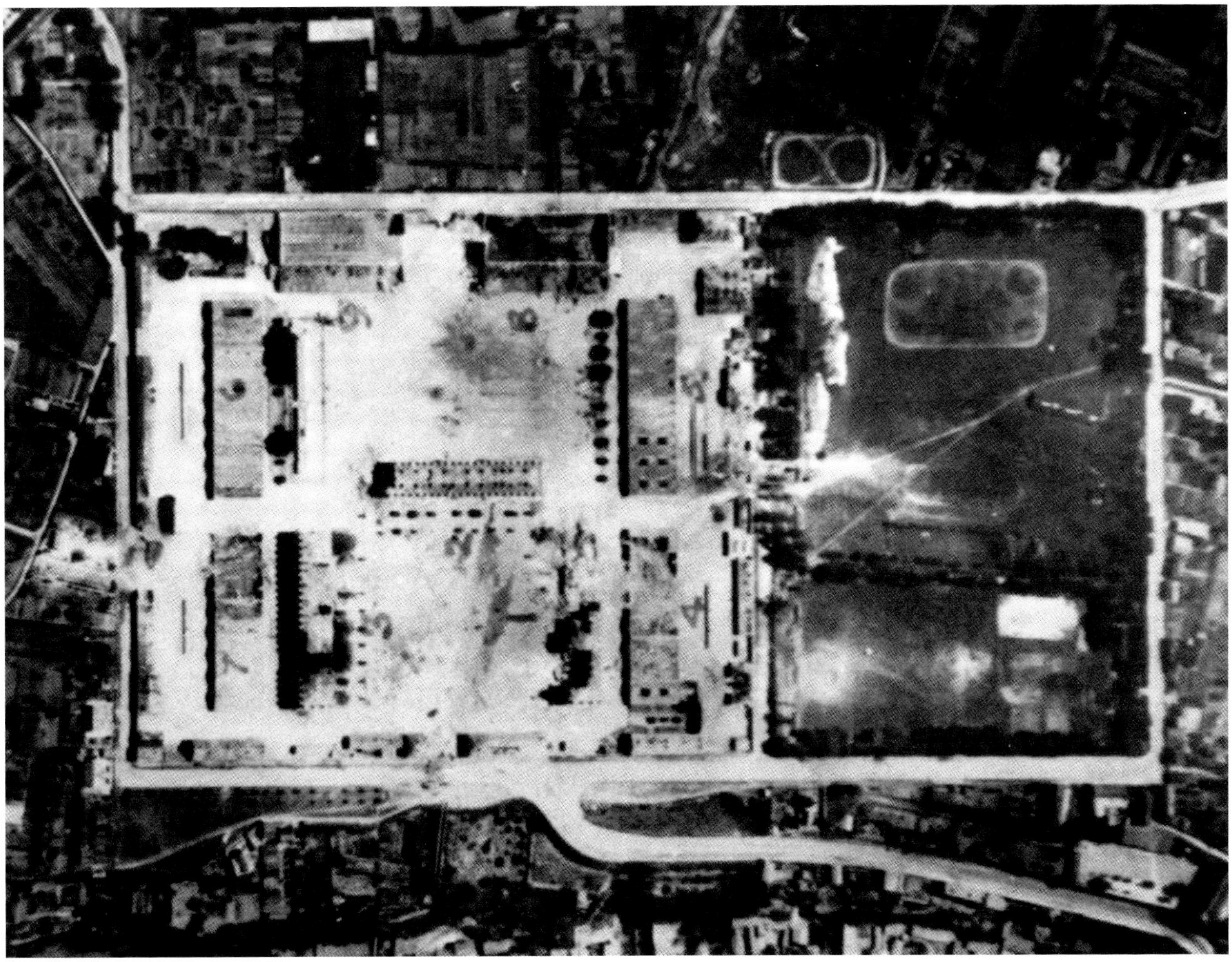

PR photo of the Caserne des Dunes barracks at Poitiers where the majority of the 2000-3000 Germans of the notorious 158th Security Regiment massing for an anti-*Maquis*/SAS sweep were billeted and which was bombed on 1 August 1944 by twenty-four FB.VIs of 487 Squadron RNZAF and 21 Squadrons escorted by Mustangs. (Group Captain I. S. Smith via Paul McCue)

The Glenn Miller AAF band prepare to play at RAF Twinwoods near Bedford, where a Mosquito can be seen to the right of the improvised bandstand. Twinwoods was a satellite of 51 OTU Cranfield and many aircrew who were trained here were posted to front-line Mosquito squadrons. (via Connie Richards)

464 Squadron FB.VIs at Thorney island in mid-1944. (Andy Thomas via Stuart Howe)

Above: 464 Squadron RAAF CO Squadron Leader Gordon 'Peter' Panitz DFC of Queensland, Australia and Flying Officer Richard Williams of NSW. Panitz and Williams were one of eighteen crews from 21, 464 and 487 Squadron RNZAF Squadrons who successfully attacked Bonneuil Matours, a collection of six buildings inside a rectangle just 170 x 100 feet, close to the village which had to be avoided, on 14 July, Bastille Day 1944. Wing Commander Panitz was KIA on 31 August 1944 attacking targets in France. (via Paul McCue)

Left: Mosquito II crews of 264 Squadron discuss last minute details of the night's operation before climbing aboard their aircraft at Predannack in late 1943. (DH)

FB.VIs 'B' and 'H' of 613 'City of Manchester' Squadron at A75/Cambrai-Epinoy France in late 1944. The squadron had moved here, together with 107 and 305 Squadrons of 138 Wing in November 1944 to be closer to the frontline for harassing operations against German units retreating further eastwards. (Philip Beck)

Flying Officer R. G. 'Bob' Stainton, a navigator in 29 Squadron at Ford in 1943. (Frank Pringle)

Flight Lieutenant Johnny Evans and Flying Officer Ifor Jenkins of 487 Squadron RNZAF who were lost on 25 April during an operation to Emden. Evans had lost two pilot brothers killed in the war. (Ginger Walsh)

Mosquito LR384 of 157 Squadron showing flak damage sustained on 22 July 1944 when it was flown home on one engine by Flying Officer Kneath, pilot and Flying Officer George Kelsey, navigator-radar operator. (George Kelsey)

HK425 of 409 ('Nighthawk') Squadron RCAF. (Ross Finlayson)

Pilot Officer Harry Randall-Cutler (right) and Pilot Officer Hubert Cohen of 305 (Polish) Squadron beside FB.VI LR303 *A-Apple* at Hartford Bridge in October 1944. 305 Squadron carried out night intruding over the continent from Hartford Bridge and Lasham that October before moving to Epinoy near Cambrai in November 1944. (Harry Randall-Cutler)

29 Squadron crews at Ford, Sussex in 1943 in front of Mosquito 'A', *"Dopey"* & *"Duke"*. (Frank Pringle)

Left: A Mosquito of 409 ('Nighthawk') Squadron RCAF coming into land with a crashed Mosquito in the foreground. (Ross Finlayson) **Right:** Swinging the tail of a 409 ('Nighthawk') Squadron RCAF (Ross Finlayson) **Below:** Pranged Mosquito of 409 ('Nighthawk') Squadron RCAF (Ross Finlayson)

Air crews in 409 ('Nighthawk') Squadron RCAF in the winter of 1944. (Ross Finlayson)

Left: Squadron Leader Paul V. Davoud DSO DFC (pointing) and his navigator, Flight Lieutenant Douglas Alcorn DFC (above) of 418 (City of Edmonton) Squadron RCAF with Squadron Leader C. C. Moran DFC during a debriefing session after a successful Intruder operation. On 27/28 June 1943 Squadron Leader Moran had claimed a Ju 88 and an He 111 destroyed at Avord, the pilot also blasting a train and a radio mast during the same sortie. By the end of the summer he had earned a deserved reputation as a 'train-buster', his technique usually consisting of a strafing run to stop the locomotive, before finishing it oft with bombs. Having attained wing commander rank, Paul Davoud led the squadron from June 1943 to January 1944. (Stephen M. Fochuk) **Middle:** Chief Engineer with Frank Pringle's navigator Flying Officer Wain Eaton of 29 Squadron in front of HK924 *"Goofy"*, 147/148 Wings of 2nd TAF at Drem. Scotland just prior to D-Day in 1944. In the run up to *D-Day*, 29 Squadron of the ADGB had been the first Mosquito unit equipped with the superior AI.Mk.VIII radar to be released for intruding over the Continent. Whilst still equipped with Beaufighter VIFs, the unit had had its first taste of offensive night operations in spring 1943 when it began *Night Rangers* over airfields in German-occupied France. After converting to the Mosquito in the summer 29 Squadron reverted to defensive operations in the ADGB, finally mounting its first *Intruders* over France on the night of 14 May 1944. (Frank Pringle) **Right:** Flying Officer 'Dickie' Locke of 29 Squadron at Ford in 1943 in front of *"Dopey" & "Duke"*. (Frank Pringle)

FB.VI *Moonbeam McSwine* of 418 (City of Edmonton) Squadron RCAF was flown by Lieutenant Lou Luma (smoking his pipe) and navigator Flying Officer Finlayson (right). Wing Commander Howard Douglas 'Howie' Cleveland (far left) and his navigator Flight Sergeant Earl Boal (middle) are the remaining aircrew in this photo taken at Ford in April 1944. (Stephen M. Fochuk)

Flying Officer Sid Seid DFC of 418 (City of Edmonton) Squadron RCAF leaning out of the cockpit of FB.VI TH-J with his dog 'Mostitch' and Flight Lieutenant Tommy Mathew alongside him on the wing. Seid, an American-Jew from California who enlisted in the RCAF was hell bent on destroying the Nazis, and would apparently stop at nothing to get at them. Sid's usual navigator was Flying Officer Dave Mcintosh DFC who postwar wrote a book entitled *Terror in the Starboard Seat* about his experiences flying with Sid Seid. The emblem seen painted on the cockpit access door was an unofficial 418 Squadron crest (Stephen M. Fochuk)

FB.VI NS850 TH-M *"Black Rufe"* of 418 (City of Edmonton) Squadron RCAF crewed by Squadron Leader Robert Allan Kipp and Flight Lieutenant Peter Huletsky at Holmsley South in June 1941. As this impressive scoreboard shows Kipp and Huletsky claimed ten aircraft shot down and one shared destroyed, one shared probable, one damaged, seven destroyed on the ground and eight damaged on the ground, the bulk of these being scored during December 1943-June 1944 in this aircraft. NS850 was written off in a landing accident at Hunsdon on 1 November 1944 when the fighter overshot the runway following an air test, its pilot having been forced to re-land with an engine feathered (Stephen M. Fochuk)

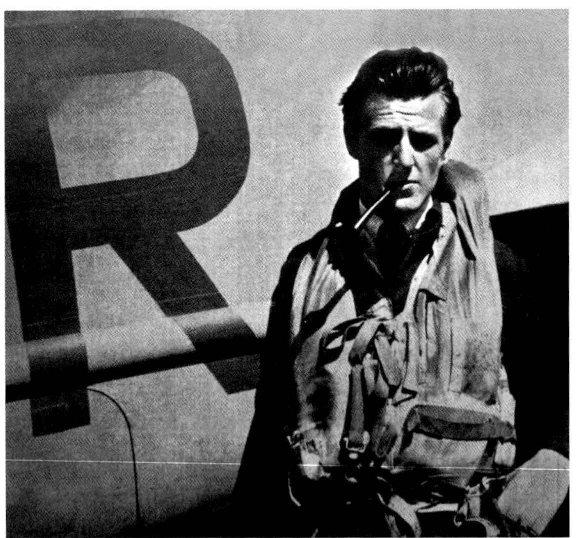

Flight Lieutenant George Esmond "Jamie" Jameson DFC RNZAF of 488 Squadron RNZAF, pilot of NF.XIII MM446 *R for Robert*, who with his navigator Flying Officer A. Norman Crookes on 24/25 June 1944 shot down a Me 410. On 28/29 June, Jameson and Crookes destroyed a Ju 88 ten miles NE of Caen as it was about to bomb British Forces landing at Arromanches. At the end of July the New Zealand squadron moved to Colerne near Bath, where Jameson was devastated to learn that his both his brothers had been killed. His elder brother was serving with the New Zealand Army in Tunisia and his younger brother died in a Beaufighter during training at East Fortune. Tragically a cable from New Zealand informed Jamie that his father had died on hearing the news of the death of two of his sons. Before Jameson departed for home he was determined to avenge the untimely deaths of his brothers and on the night of 29/30 July he and Crookes claimed three Junkers 88s and a Dornier Do 217 destroyed. "Jamie" Jameson's tenth victory on 488 Squadron RNZAF came on the night of 3/4 August when he shot down a Ju 88 which was about to dive-bomb British Army troops near St. Lô. Next day came news of his sailing date for New Zealand. On 6 August Jameson and Norman Crookes claimed a Ju 88 damaged 5 miles west of the Vire before notching his 11th victory, a Ju 88 15 miles east of Avranche. Jameson returned to New Zealand and the award of a DSO followed. Crookes, who after the war became a teacher in Kent, received a bar to his DFC. Jamie's score made him the highest scoring New Zealand fighter pilot of the war. "Jamie" Jameson died aged 76 in a bulldozer accident in 1998.

Refueling an FB.VI of 157 Squadron. (via Jerry Scutts)

AC1 Phillip Beck and LAC K. Kerslake, the 'boys with the 'gen', filling FB.VI 'W' of 613 Squadron with oxygen for a raid on Berlin. (Flight via Phillip Beck)

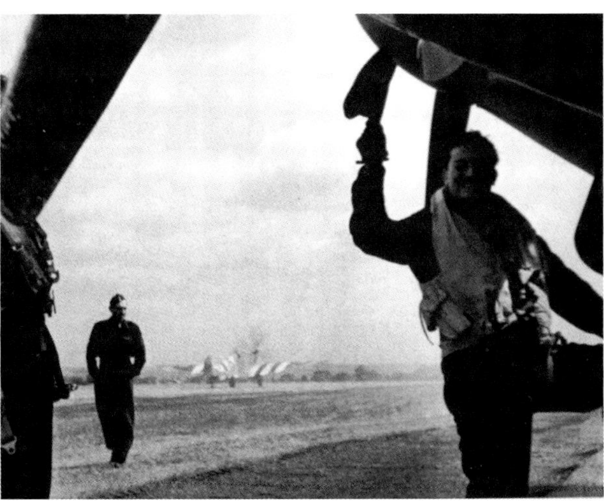

Squadron Leader Charles Patterson DSO DFC smiling for the camera before going aboard O-Orange on an airstrip in France in 1944. (Patterson)

Squadron Leader C. C. 'Charlie' Scherf DSO DFC, a RAAF *Intruder* pilot, flying Mosquitoes, who in the sixteen weeks following 27 January 1944 destroyed fifteen enemy aircraft in the air and nine on the ground. He was awarded the DFC in April 1944 when he had destroyed four enemy aircraft, a Bar to the DFC next month, when he had added five more "kills" to his score and the DSO a few weeks later, by when he had scored six more "kills" in the air - one of the most rapid runs of successes recorded in the European theater of war. (RAAF)

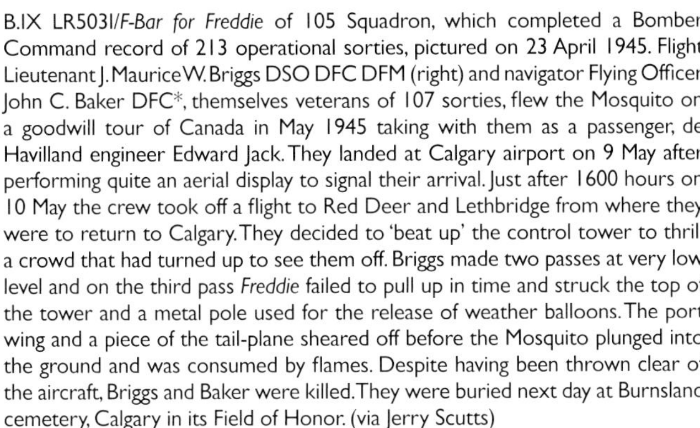

B.IX LR503I/*F-Bar for Freddie* of 105 Squadron, which completed a Bomber Command record of 213 operational sorties, pictured on 23 April 1945. Flight Lieutenant J. Maurice W. Briggs DSO DFC DFM (right) and navigator Flying Officer John C. Baker DFC*, themselves veterans of 107 sorties, flew the Mosquito on a goodwill tour of Canada in May 1945 taking with them as a passenger, de Havilland engineer Edward Jack. They landed at Calgary airport on 9 May after performing quite an aerial display to signal their arrival. Just after 1600 hours on 10 May the crew took off a flight to Red Deer and Lethbridge from where they were to return to Calgary. They decided to 'beat up' the control tower to thrill a crowd that had turned up to see them off. Briggs made two passes at very low level and on the third pass *Freddie* failed to pull up in time and struck the top of the tower and a metal pole used for the release of weather balloons. The port wing and a piece of the tail-plane sheared off before the Mosquito plunged into the ground and was consumed by flames. Despite having been thrown clear of the aircraft, Briggs and Baker were killed. They were buried next day at Burnsland cemetery, Calgary in its Field of Honor. (via Jerry Scutts)

Pilot Officer Harry Randall-Cutler in the pilot's seat of his 305 Squadron Mosquito. (Randall-Cutler)

Below: 21 Squadron FB.VI ground crew who served from 1941 to the end of the war at Melsbroek, Belgium in 1944-45. (via F. R. Lucas)

1st Lieutenant James Forrest 'Lou' Luma of 418 (City of Edmonton) Squadron RCAF. Luma was born in Helena, Montana, on 27 August 1922. After joining the RCAF he was posted to England in January 1943, where after a sorting-out process, through some sort of error or mix-up, Luma received an exceptionally high grade in a night-vision test. As a result, he was assigned to night intruders, though at the time he had no idea what a night intruder was. At 60 OTU he learned to fly the Mosquito and practised air-to-air gunnery and air-to-ground gunnery. After several weeks at OTU intruder trainees were instructed to informally pair off into crews. Colin Finlayson, a Canadian from British Columbia and Luma agreed to crew up together. While at OTU Luma decided to transfer to the US Army Air Forces. The official policy at the time, agreed to by the Americans and British, was that a crew would not be broken up, so after he was sworn in as a 1st Lieutenant he was permitted to return to the RCAF to finish his tour of operations before returning to the USAAF. Luma was a USAAF pilot on detached duty with the RCAF. After finishing OTU Luma and Fin were assigned to 418 Squadron RCAF. When Luma finished his tour in April 1944 he had scored five victories in the air and two destroyed and four damaged aircraft on the ground and he was awarded both a British and US DFC.

NF.II DZ716 UP-L of 605 Squadron in the spring of 1943. In February that year the Bradwell Bay-based squadron had begun replacing its Bostons and Havocs with NF.IIs. The squadron flew its first successful operation on the night of 4/5 May when six Mosquito *Night Intruders* patrolled over Dutch airfields awaiting the arrival of Luftwaffe bombers returning from a raid on Norwich. Flying Officer Brian Williams and Pilot Officer Dougie Moore duly shot down Do 217E-4 (Wk-Nr 4353) U5+CK of III./KG 2, piloted by Leutnant Ernst Andres, which was returning to Eindhoven. Two more Do 217M-Is were destroyed by NF.IIs of 605 Squadron on 13/14 and 25/26 July 1943. DZ716 was destroyed in a crash-landing at Castle Camps on 7 July (via Ron Mackay)

FB.VI HJ821 of 418 (City of Edmonton) Squadron RCAF on final approach to land.

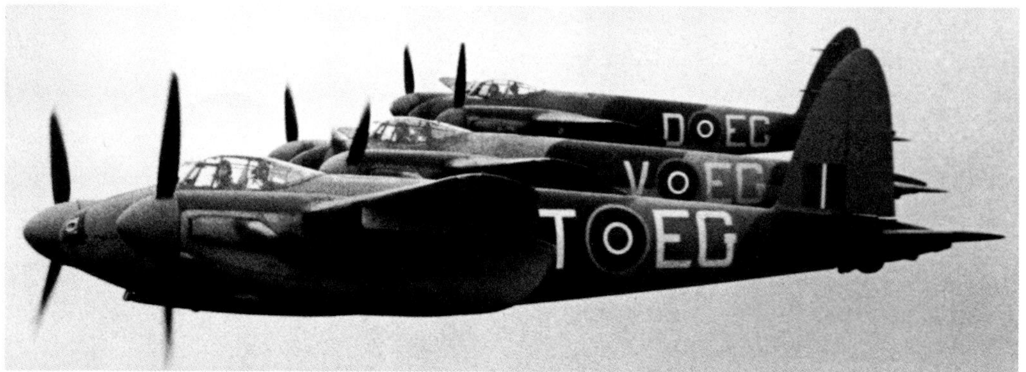

FB.VIs MM417/EG-T, EG-V and EG-D of 487 Squadron RNZAF on 29 February 1944 each carrying two 500lb bombs beneath their wings. (via GMS)

The rail yards at Lyon, France under attack by two Mosquitoes of 107 Squadron in July 1944. (Vic Hester)

Pilots of 1655 Mosquito Training Unit (PFF) at Warboys April-June 1944. Back Row L-R: Cassel (KIA in May-June course); Pinkerton; Locatelli (to 109 Squadron); Maloney (to 105 Squadron); Flying Officer Leonard Priestley Whipp (to 105 Squadron. On 19 October 1944 he jettisoned a 4000lb bomb after taking off from Bourn on a night sortie with fatal results killing him and his navigator Pilot Officer Clifford Bertenshaw); Gibbs; Hooper; Flying Officer George Simpson Henderson (to 635 Squadron – Lancaster pilot, KIA 12/13 August 1944 near Liege); Front Row L-R: u/k (KIA); Flight Lieutenant George Kenneth Whiffen (to 105 Squadron MIA 5/6 July 1944 on op to Scholven-Buer when he and Flying Officer Douglas Knight Williams DFC attacked and marked an oil target in ML913/E but they were never seen again); Flight Lieutenant P. Sleight (to 105 Squadron); David M. Russell (to 109 Squadron); Gump (to 109 Squadron); Halborrow (lost while on May-June 1944 course); Coke-Kerr. (David M. Russell Coll via Theo Boiten)

FB.VI with port propeller feathered. 'Flying on one engine was almost like flying on two but with a bit less power' recalls 'Dutch' Holland. 'Once, when I had many more hours under my belt, I flew formation with one feathered, on another aircraft flying on two…In all the Mosquito flying which I was privileged to enjoy, I never once had an engine failure. Another feature, which we appreciated, was the flat bulletproof windscreen, which not only gave a sense of security but provided a fine field of view and a good surface for the windscreen wiper.

Pilots of 107 Squadron in 1944. Left to right: Wing Commander Mike Pollard, CO; Flying Officer De Rosier (USA): Flying Officer J. Ballachey (Canada); Flying Officer Sanderson (Canada); Flying Officer Karl Aiken (Jamaica); Flying Officer Taylor (Canada) and Flight Lieutenant McClure (Canada). (J. Ballachey via Paul McCue)

On 2 August 1944 the survivors of the 158th Security Regiment billeted in the Château de Fou, an *SS* police HQ south of Châtellerault were killed when the barracks was bombed by twenty-three FB.VIs of 107 and 305 Squadrons. It is estimated that 80% of the regiment were killed in the three raids. (Vic Hester)

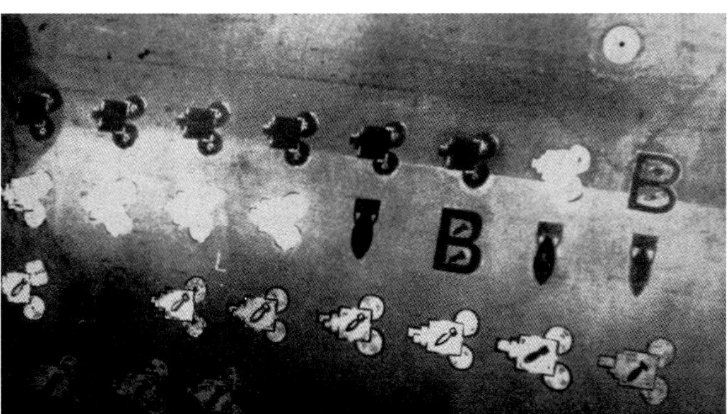

Flight Lieutenant Tony Wickham DFC (left) and Flight Lieutenant B.T. 'Banger' Good, Armaments Officer, 21 (City Of Norwich) Squadron, pose for the *'Illustrated London News'* at Thorney Island, 19 December 1944 in front of FB.VI *'Kay'*. Wickham had flown the 30 January 1943 daylight raid on Berlin and went on to serve in 618 Squadron on the *Highball* project before being posted to 21 Squadron with his navigator, Pilot Officer W. E. D. Makin on 8 September 1944. On 18 February 1944, Wickham flew the FPU B.IV, DZ414, on the Amiens raid, making three passes over the burning prison, so that his cameraman, Pilot Officer Leigh Howard, could film the flight of some 255 of the 700 prisoners held captive. (via Les Bulmer) **[Left]** Camera and bomb symbols on the nose of DZ414 *O-Orange*. This Mosquito was used for standard ops as well as ciné ops, hence the night bombs, the first 'B' for the first night raid on Berlin by Mosquitoes in full moon – Hitler's birthday present. DZ414 was hit by flak during the bombing run. (Vic Hester)

FB.VI TH-Y of 418 Squadron RCAF taxies out for an *Intruder* sortie. The Canadians converted fully from NF.IIs to FB.VIs during the spring and summer of 1943. (via Tom Cushing)

Mosquito FB.VIs of 464 Squadron RAAF shuddering and shaking with vibration caused by high speed a low level zooming across the Channel to attack targets in France. (Vic Hester)

NF.XXX MV529 is prepared for test flying at Leavesden in September 1944. Following its delivery to the RAF, the Mosquito saw service with 25 Squadron at Castle Camps until it was destroyed in a mid-air collision with fellow squadron aircraft MT494 on 23/24 January 1945. MV259 was crewed by Squadron Leader J. Arnsley DFC and Flight Lieutenant O. M Reid DFC at the time of the collision, which occurred over Camps Hall, Cambridgeshire during an AI practice interception. The second crew involved were Flight Lieutenants O. L. Ward DFC and E. D. Eyles. (BAe via Philip Birtles)

FB.VI NS837 YH-C crewed by Flight Lieutenant Mike Benn DFC and Flying Officer W.A. Roe, which overshot the runway at Thorney Island on the night of 22/23 June 1944. The aircraft was led in to the approach by another Mosquito but it touched down too far along the runway and went through the sea wall. Benn died of his injuries. Roe, who was slightly injured, later crewed up with Flight Lieutenant Lloyd and they were shot down and taken prisoner on 7 August 1944. (Les Bulmer via F. R. Lucas)

Leavesden-built NF.XXX MM748 equipped with AI.Mk.X radar in a thimble nose radome. The NF.XXX first entered service with 219 Squadron in June 1944. Six more squadrons were so equipped by the end of the year, including three, which served in 100 Group on *Intruder* operations. (BAe)

Flight Lieutenant 'Les' Bulmer (back row, third from left) and his pilot, Flight Lieutenant Ed McQuarrie RCAF (front row, third from left), pictured at No.3 Mosquito Course, 36 OTU, Greenwood, Nova Scotia, in 1943. Together with Flying Officer Harry Batt RCAF (back row far left), Flight Lieutenant George Murray DFC (front row far left) they joined 21 Squadron, 140 Wing, at Hunsdon on 15 February 1944. Pilot Officer Humblestone (back row 2nd from left) and Flight Lieutenant Evans RCAF (front row 2nd from left) survived one tour and Evans returned to Canada but Humblestone went missing on his first op of his 2nd tour with another pilot. Flying Officer Wakeman an American who joined the RCAF before the USA came into the war (front row 3rd from right) and Pilot Officer Holmes (behind him) joined 464 Squadron RAAF and were killed when they crashed into the Thames on take-off from Gravesend. Flying Officer Hole (front row 2nd from right) and Sergeant West (behind him) were killed on a *Gee-H* course at Swanton Morley when the aircraft exploded in mid-air. Flying Officer Reeves (front row right) and Pilot Officer Prout (behind him) were posted to the Far East and were KIA. (Les Bulmer)

NF.IIs of 605 Squadron. The aircraft second from left is DZ717. Leading is DZ718. (RAF)

Ground crew paint black and white invasion stripes on B.Mk.IV (Modified) DZ633AZ-D, which was delivered to 627 Squadron at Woodhall Spa on 12 August 1944. 627 Squadron took part in marking and bombing attacks over Germany, being transferred to 5 Group in April 1944 to provide target marking for independent maids on strategic targets. 627 also carried out PR duties for 5 Group and participated in day bombing maids, remaining at Woodhall Spa until 1 October 1945. DZ633 led a charmed life. On 31 August 1944 it was hit by flak over Rollencourt and damaged in both wings but managed to reach Woodhall Spa and on 17 September 1944 it was hit again by flak, this time over the Boulogne area during a photo recce. One engine was hit and had to be feathered and the aircraft landed back at base on one engine. On 31 December 1944 DZ633 was hit during the raid on the *Gestapo* HQ at Oslo. Flight Lieutenant Wallace "Johnno" S. Gaunt DFC* was hit in the thigh from a cannon shell and the pilot, Flight Lieutenant Peter F. Mallender DFC gave him first aid pending a ground loop landing at Peterhead. The aircraft was repaired and returned to operations on 12 February 1945. (via Andy Thomas)

Pilot Officer Harry Randall-Cutler and Pilot Officer Hubert Cohen of 305 Polish Squadron beside LR303 *A-Apple* at Hartford Bridge in October 1944. 305 Squadron carried out Night Intruding over the continent from Hartford Bridge and Lasham that October before moving to Epinoy near Cambrai in November 1944. (Harry Randall-Cutler)

Above: Flight Lieutenant Eric Atkins DFC* KW* (middle) of 305 (Ziemia Wielkopolska) (Polish) Squadron in 1945. (Eric Atkins)

Left: FB.VI HJ821/TH-W of 418 (City of Edmonton) Squadron RCAF approaching Ford at the end of a sortie in early 1944. The Canadians flew their first FB.VI operation on 7 May 1943 and by the end of the year they were flying Intruder and *Day Ranger* operations over France and the Low Countries. (via Tom Cushing)

418 (City of Edmonton) Squadron RCAF crews face the camera in front of a well-worn FB.VI. American Lieutenant James F. Luma is seventh from left in his distinctive USAAF uniform. On 21 March 1944 Luma and Flying Officer Colin Finlayson shot down a W34 liaison aircraft and a Ju 52/3m transport and damaged two Gotha Go 242 glider transports and two Bf 109s on the ground at Luxeuil airfield. (via Tom Cushing)

On the night of 24 April 1946 Pilot Officers L. E. Fitchett and A. C. Hardy of 409 'Nighthawk' Squadron RCAF destroyed a Ju 52 but upon their return to B.108 Rheine just as dawn was breaking they were struck by fire from another aircraft and their port engine set alight. Their attacker overshot and Hardy quickly recognized it as another Mosquito from an Intruder squadron in the UK before Fitchett carried out an emergency crash-landing. That afternoon the CO of the Intruder squadron in question flew over to Rheine to apologize. Fitchett later lost his life flying Beaufighters with the embryonic Israeli air force during the Jewish State's first war with Egypt in 1948. Hardy became a professor of architecture at Manchester University (Ross Finlayson)

Applying black and white invasion stripes to a Mosquito of 2nd TAF just prior to D-Day. (British Newspaper Pool)

Flight Lieutenant Bert Willers (left) and Flight Lieutenant Les Bulmer of 21 Squadron supposedly going over the route while their FB.VI is warmed up behind in this staged photo taken by James Jarche for *Illustrated* magazine. Les Bulmer recalled that he did not seem to appreciate that crews did not get into a Mosquito with the engines running and he also had to borrow a pair of flying boots because apparently, he did not look the part of an intrepid aviator without them! 21 Squadron operated as part of 140 Wing, 2nd TAF, which gained a distinctive reputation for pinpoint bombing raids. On 6 February 1945, the squadron moved to Rosieres and remained on the continent until the end of the war. (via Les Bulmer)

Mosquitoes of 409 ('Nighthawk') Squadron RCAF at Lille, France in 1944. The nearest aircraft is NF.XIII HK425 KP-R. (Ross Finlayson)

FB.VI in flight. With the formation of the 2nd Tactical Air Force in June 1943, greater emphasis was placed on the offensive capabilities of the FB.VI night fighter squadrons. Indeed, by early 1944 their main contribution towards the eventual Allied victory in Europe was being performed on *Day Ranger* operations over France. (BAe)

A Wellington XIII of 69 Squadron, Spitfire PR.XI of 16 Squadron and a PR.XVI Mosquito of 140 Squadron at Melsbroek in Belgium in March 1945. All three squadrons formed 34 (PR) Wing in 2nd TAF. (Flight)

On Tuesday 11 April 1944 six Mosquito FB VIs of 613 Squadron led by the CO, Wing Commander R. N. 'Bob' Bateson DFC attacked the Dutch Central Population Registry in The Hague. The *Gestapo* building was completely destroyed in what an Air Ministry bulletin later described as "probably the most brilliant feat of low-level precision bombing of the war". (BAe Hatfield)

On 19 August 1944 613 Squadron Mosquito crews, led by Squadron Leader Charles Newman carried out a daring low level attack on a school building at Egletons, fifty miles SE of Limoges, believed to be in use as an *SS* troops barracks. Fourteen of the Mosquitoes located and bombed the target, scoring at least twenty direct hits and the target was almost completely destroyed. One Mosquito, crewed by Flight Lieutenant House and Flying Officer Savill, was hit in the starboard engine over the target area and failed to return but the crew survived and returned to the squadron just five days later. (Vic Hester)

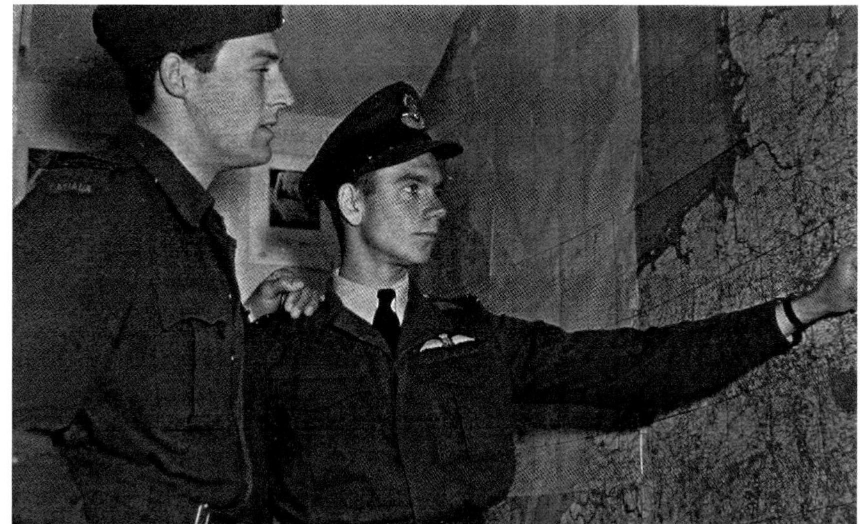

Flight Lieutenant 'Ted' Johnson DFC RCAF (right) with his navigator Flight Lieutenant N. J. 'Jimmy' Gibbons DFC of 418 (City of Edmonton) Squadron RCAF (Ted Johnson)

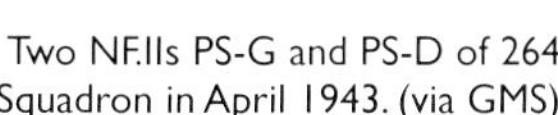

Two NF.IIs PS-G and PS-D of 264 Squadron in April 1943. (via GMS)

V1 flying low over England before it was destroyed by the chasing Mosquito.

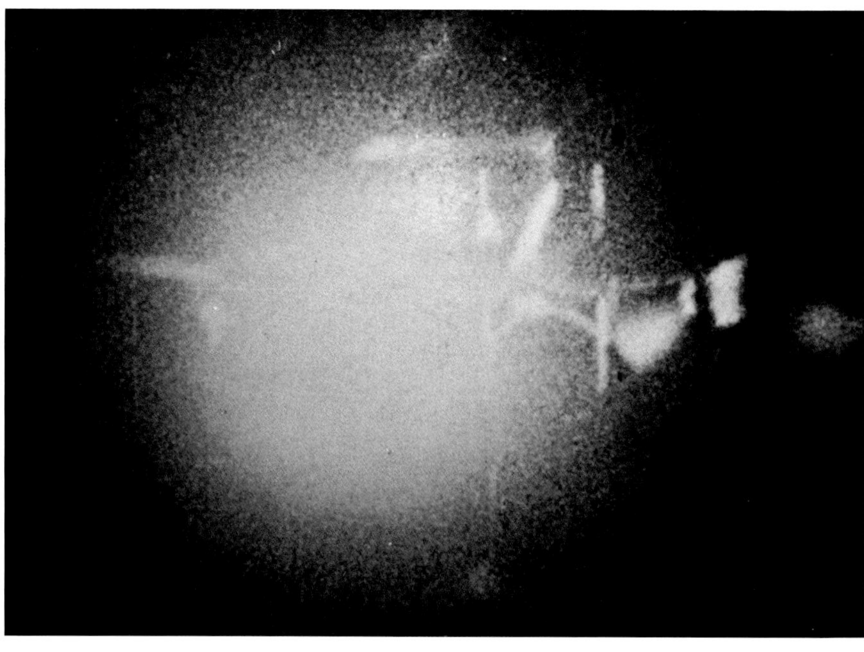

Feldwebel Robert Koch's Bf 110 (Wrk. Nr. 440130) G9+MN of 5./NJG1 explodes near Peer, Belgium at about 2320 hours on 7 October 1944, as a result of an attack by Flying Officer Ross Finlayson and Flying Officer Al Webster of 409 'Nighthawk' Squadron RCAF in NF.XIII MM560. In the minutes prior to this interception Koch had made a 180° turn to port and set course for his base at Düsseldorf, totally unaware that the Canadian nightfighter had been alerted to his presence by Allied GCI. The NF.XIII crew approached unobserved from astern, the GCI controller bringing them in to visual range because the Mosquito's radar had gone 'wonky'. Once close enough to see the contact, it was discovered that the enemy aircraft boasted external wing tanks, leading Finlayson to believe that his target was a four-engined aircraft. He therefore misjudged the closing speed and distance between himself and the Bf 110, scoring hits in the port wing and fuselage with his first burst but ending up right below the Messerschmitt with his wheels and flaps extended. However, before Koch had time to take evasive action, a second burst was fired, which rendered the Bf 110's controls useless and set the port wing alight, whereupon the pilot, who was flying his 70th operation, the first 26 of which were made with ZG2 in Russia during the summer of 1942, gave the order to bale out. Koch was slightly injured whilst taking to his parachute but his *Bordfunker*, Unteroffizier Heinz Ferster and gunner Unteroffizier Ernst Darg were both KIA. Koch, who had seven four-engined RAF bombers to his credit (February-August 1944) had previously been shot down near St. Trond during a daylight mission on 14 October 1943 by a USAAF P-47 shortly after joining 6./NJG1. He baled out wounded and did not fly again until February 1944 and in August joined 5./NJG1. A highly experienced Bf 110 pilot, Koch had also flown with 7./NJG1. (Ross Finlayson)

Giles cartoon in the *Sunday Express* 5 March 1944. "Come out of the road—you'll get run over."

NF.XXX MM695/G of the Central Fighter Establishment at Tangmere in the early summer of 1945. Previously it had served with 219 Squadron at Hunsdon and ended its days as an instructional airframe with No.1 radio School. The 'G' after its serial number indicated special equipment fitted, which had to be guarded at all times while on the ground. Next are FB.VI RF876 and NF.36 RL256.

Lieutenant James Luma DFC and his regular navigator Flying Officer Colin Finlayson of 418 (City of Edmonton) Squadron RCAF examining the hole in their Mosquito following a successful sortie over the continent in 1944. (Stephen M. Fochuk)

Squadron Leader David John 'Blackie' Williams DFC (left) and his navigator, Flying Officer Clarence Joseph Kirkpatrick DFC of 406 ('Lynx') Squadron RCAF in front of *"Blackie" & "Kirk"*. Williams, a native of Vancouver, joined the RCAF in 1940 and began his tour flying Hampdens with 408 Squadron. On the night of 27/28 August 1942 during a night raid on Kassel he shot down a Ju 88 with the fixed pilot's gun and then repulsed an attack by a Bf 109 on the return flight home. Flight Lieutenant Williams was awarded a DFC soon after this sortie and he went on to complete his tour the following October. Following a spell with 410 Squadron as a flight commander and conversion onto fighters at 54 OTU 'Blackie' was promoted to squadron leader in August 1943 and posted to 406 ('Lynx') Squadron RCAF as a flight commander. He subsequently attained wing commander rank in July 1944 and was given command of the unit. By this time he had shot down a He 177 while flying a Beaufighter, two Do 217s on 29/30 April flying a Mosquito NF.XII and 1_ Do 217s in NF.XXX MM731 during a Day Ranger on 21 July. The half was for a Do 217 that he had hit in one engine and set alight before he had broken off as the crew were baling out, only for another Mosquito to cut in, fire, and claim the credit for shooting it down. Williams was awarded a DSO in September 1944 and he finished the war with five and one shared destroyed (Stephen M. Fochuk)

Thirty-one-year-old Wing Commander Robert Carl 'Moose' Fumerton DFC from Fort Coulonge, Quebec, destroyed 14 enemy aircraft (12 of them defending Malta flying Beaufighters with 89 Squadron in 1942. Fumerton had claimed the first RCAF night victory of the war (a Ju 88) flying Beaufighter IF R2336 with 406 ('Lynx') Squadron RCAF on 1/2 September 1942. In August 1943 he was given command of 406 'Lynx' Squadron and he scored his 14th victory on the night of 14/15 May 1944 in a Mosquito NF.XII southeast of Portland, in Dorset. 'Moose' was to lead 406 ('Lynx') Squadron RCAF until July 1944 and he finished the war as the top-scoring Canadian nightfighter ace with 14 destroyed and one damaged. (Stephen M. Fochuk)

Flight Lieutenants Landrey and 'Steve' Stephens of 157 Squadron at Hunsdon in 1943. (Brian Whitlock Blundell Coll)

Flight Lieutenant Rayne 'Joe' Dennis Schultz DFC* from Bashow, Alberta and Flying Officer Vernon A. Williams DFC at Coleby Grange who scored their first victory in FB.VI HP849 on 15/16 August 1943 and on the night of 10/11 December shot down three Do 217s over the Sea between Clacton and Dunkirk in NF.II DZ292. Schultz and Flying Officer Christie scored four more victories flying NF.XIIIs and XXXs before the end of the war. (Stephen M. Fochuk)

Top: 409 ('Nighthawk') Squadron RCAF of Fighter Command, 148 Wing, 85 (Base) Group, 2nd TAF, at B51 Lille-Vendeville, France on 31 January 1945. (RCAF via Philip Birtles) **[right]** Squadron Leader 'Ted' Sismore DSO DFC* AFC was 'Bob' Bateson's navigator in FB.VI RS570 EG-X on the Shellhaus raid. (Derek Carter Coll)

Wing Commander Howard Douglas Cleveland, a native of Vancouver, joined the RCAF in October 1940. 'Howie' assumed command of 418 (City of Edmonton) Squadron RCAF at the outset of 1944 and with Flight Sergeant Frank Day DFM, scored four and one shared destroyed in the air and five and one shared destroyed and one damaged on the ground. His final scores came during an intruder mission over the Baltic on 16 May 1944 in FB.VI MM421 *Lil' Abner* when Cleveland destroyed a Do 217 on the ground and then forced a He 111 to crash into Kiel Bay without firing a shot. MM421 was hit in the engine by return fire however and the wing commander was injured and Day killed in the resulting crash-landing in Sweden. 'Howie' Cleveland was repatriated to Britain in June, where he received his DFC. In August he returned to Canada, reporting in January 1945 to the Ninth Air Force on attachment, before taking command of 418 Squadron once again in May 1945. He returned to Canada in September 1945. (Stephen M. Fochuk)

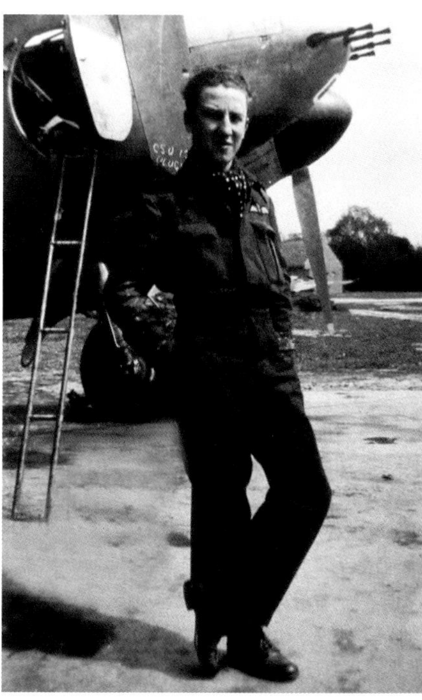

Eric Smith of 107 Squadron in front of his FB.VI at Epinoy, France late in 1944. (Stephen M. Fochuk)

A native of Montreal. Donald Aikins MacFadyen joined the RCAF in May 1940. His first score came while flying FB.VIs with 418 (City of Edmonton) Squadron RCAF when he was awarded a 'probable' on 22/23 December 1943 against a UEA. MacFadyen followed this up in early 1944 with the destruction of an Me 410, a Ju 52/3m and five V1s., MacFadyen also exploited the FB.V1s (in this case MM426) excellent ground strafing capabilities, which included a haul on 21 March 1944 of eight Go 242s damaged and a ninth destroyed, along with a Do 217, during a long range *Day Ranger* to Hagenau airfield, in France. Flight Lieutenant MacFadyen, accompanied by Flight Lieutenant 'Pinky' Wright, had also shot down a By 131 attempting to land at Luxeuil airfield prior to attacking Hagenau. Promoted to squadron leader, MacFadyen joined 406 ('Lynx') Squadron RCAF in November 1944, where he flew the NF.XXX on night Intruders. He was awarded a DFC and bar, an American DFC and the DSO during his two tours, and he finished the war with a tally of seven aircraft and five Via destroyed in the air, and five aircraft destroyed, one probable and seventeen damaged on the ground (Stephen M. Fochuk)

(Left) The Honorable Michael J. Wedgewood-Benn DFC, at 22, was the eldest of three sons of (right) William Wedgwood Benn DSO DFC Ld H (*Legion d'Honeur*) and CdG (*Croix de Guerre*), a WWI veteran pilot and prominent politician who was created Viscount Stansgate on 22 December 1940. (Tony Benn)

Wing Commander Howard Douglas 'Howie' Cleveland CO of 418 (City of Edmonton) Squadron RCAF. (Stephen M. Fochuk)

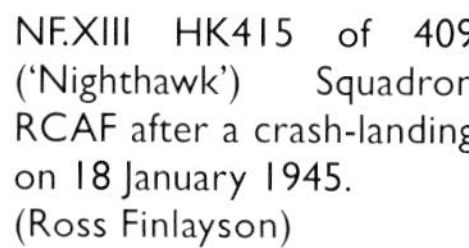

NF.XIII HK415 of 409 ('Nighthawk') Squadron RCAF after a crash-landing on 18 January 1945. (Ross Finlayson)

Prior to D-Day 2nd TAF Mosquito and Boston and B-25 Mitchell crews spent two-week stints under canvas at Swanton Morley in Norfolk to experience the kind of field conditions that were anticipated in France after the breakout from the bridgehead and rudimentary airstrips laid. (John Bateman)

FB.VI, one of 1066 Mosquitoes built by Standard Motors at Coventry during the war. (ARP)

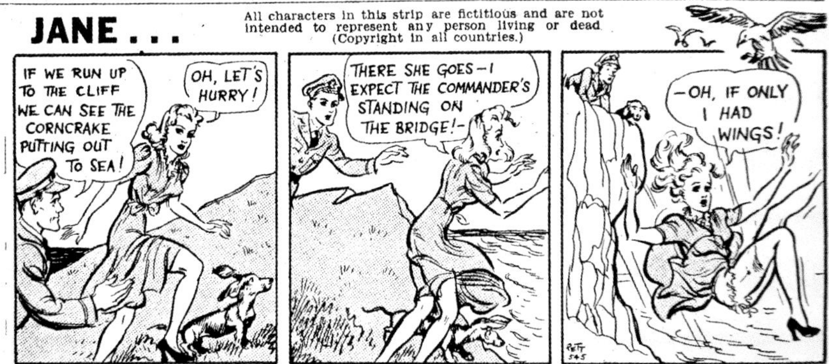

THE DAILY MIRROR
Friday, August 30, 1940
JANE . . .
All characters in this strip are fictitious and are not intended to represent any person living or dead (Copyright in all countries.)
IF WE RUN UP TO THE CLIFF WE CAN SEE THE CORNCRAKE PUTTING OUT TO SEA!
OH, LET'S HURRY!
THERE SHE GOES—I EXPECT THE COMMANDER'S STANDING ON THE BRIDGE!—
—OH, IF ONLY I HAD WINGS!

In the summer of 1945 Mosquitoes delivered British newspapers to UK forces in NW Europe on the day of issue. Codenamed *'Jane'*, a reference to the *Daily Mirror* cartoon character, who tended to drop all her clothes at frequent intervals, the service was required to operate with regularity regardless of weather conditions. Former LNSF pilots with at least one full tour of night bombing operations under their belt, or else 1200 hours of instrumental flying with 200 hours documented instrument flying, piloted the Mosquitoes. Eventually, they were air-dropping newspapers instead of landing to off-load them.

On 21 March 1945 Mosquito fighter-bombers of 464 Squadron RAAF took part in daylight low-level precision attacks on *Gestapo* Headquarters at Copenhagen. The attack was so accurate that none of the buildings next door and behind were seriously damaged. Nearly 200 *Gestapo* men and Danish collaborators were killed and all the documents kept in the building were burnt. The first picture was taken by a member of the Danish Resistance shortly after the bombing and the second picture was taken by an Australian officer on 22 May 1945 after the liberation of Copenhagen, showing the wreckage of the headquarters building. Australians and other 2nd TAF men visited the ruins after victory and were met by Minister Morgens Fog, leader of the Danish Freedom Council, who was a prisoner in the building when it was hit, but escaped death. He congratulated the Mosquito men.

Top and near right: On the Shellhaus raid three FB.VIs hit by flak had to ditch and all three crews perished. Flight Lieutenant Pattison and Flight Sergeant Pygram's FB.VI in 487 Squadron RNZAF was hit by fore from the cruiser *Nurnberg* at anchor in Copenhagen harbor. Flying Officer Palmer and Squadron Leader Becker of 487 Squadron and Flying Officer R. G. 'Shorty' Dawson RAAF and Flying Officer Fergus Murray of 464 Squadron RAAF were the other two Mosquito crews lost. Dawson (left) and Murray (right) are seen here in Malta in 1943 when they were serving with 23 Squadron. (Tom Cushing Coll) **[Far right]** Wing Commander R. W. 'Bob' Iredale DFC* RAAF, a former CO, 36 Wing of 464 Squadron RAAF, who took part in the wrecking of the Shellhaus building, talks amid the ruins with a member of the Danish Freedom organization. (RAAF)

On 31 October 1944 a precision attack was carried out on Aarhus University, the HQ for the *Gestapo* in the whole of Jutland, Denmark, by twenty-five FB.VIs of 21, 464 Squadron RAAF and 487 RNZAF Squadrons, each carrying eleven-second delayed action bombs, and led by Group Captain Peter Wykeham-Barnes. The operation was carried out at such a low altitude that Squadron Leader F. H. Denton of 487 Squadron hit the roof of the building, losing his tail wheel and the port half of the tail plane. Denton nursed the Mosquito across the North Sea and managed to land safely. The university and its incriminating records were destroyed.

Above and right: On 31 October 1944 25 FB.VIs of 21, 464 RAAF and 487 RNZAF Squadrons led by Group Captain Peter Wykeham-Barnes destroyed the *Gestapo* HQ at Aarhus University in Denmark with 11-second delayed action 500lb bombs. The buildings in the foreground are intact. (IWM)

MOSQUITO MUTTERINGS

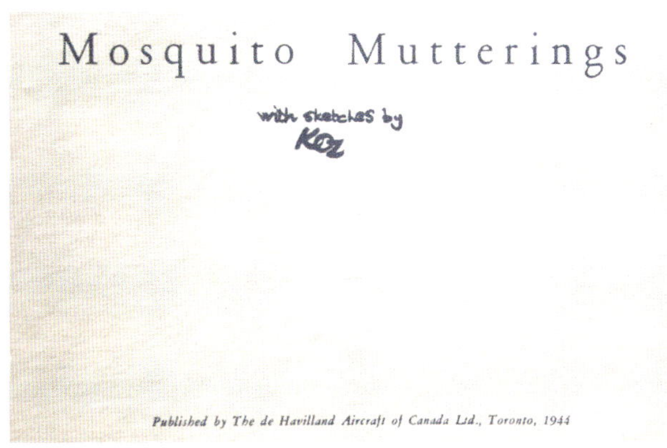

Mosquito Mutterings
with sketches by
KOZ
Published by The de Havilland Aircraft of Canada Ltd., Toronto, 1944

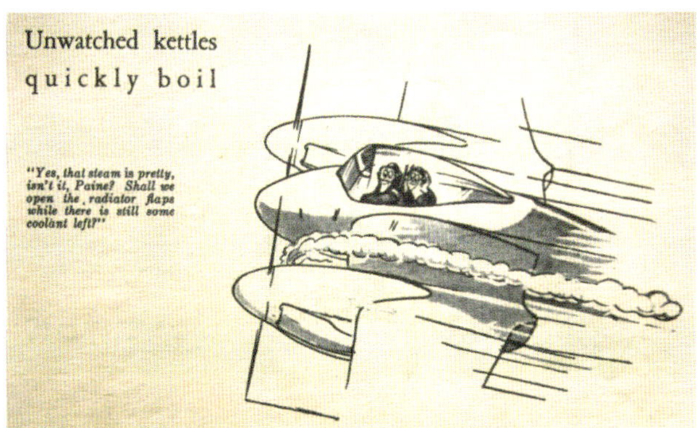

Unwatched kettles
quickly boil
"Yes, that steam is pretty, isn't it, Paine? Shall we open the radiator flaps while there is still some coolant left?"

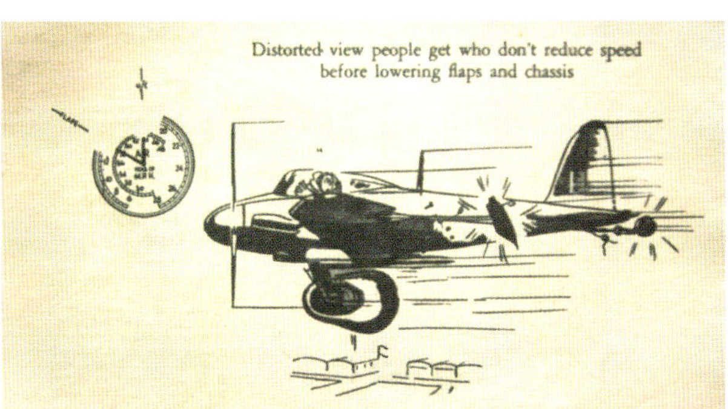

Distorted view people get who don't reduce speed
before lowering flaps and chassis

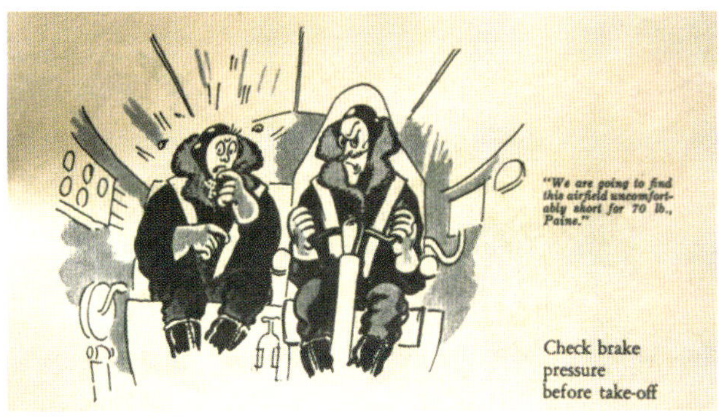

"We are going to find this airfield uncomfortably short for 70 lb., Paine."
Check brake
pressure
before take-off

If you ask for it you'll get the lot,
(Don't top up coolant when the engine's hot).

Eyes on the job, this job
OIL
Use the dip-stick next to the filler neck to ensure leaving the correct air space in the oil tank.

"I wonder why they say you shouldn't tow by the tailwheel when the tailplane's off. To me she seems as light as a feather."

"Just look at the mud and exhaust all over our nice flaps! Reely, Paine, you did ought to have raised them after we slowed down."

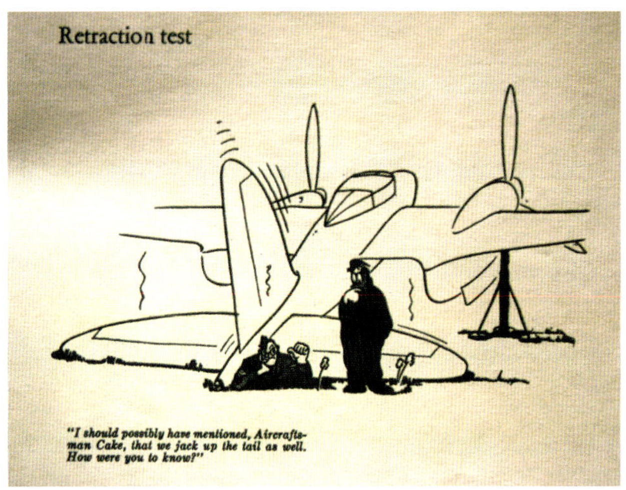
Retraction test
"I should possibly have mentioned, Aircraftsman Cake, that we jack up the tail as well. How were you to know?"

Pennants are the pilot's pigeon
"Yes, you took off with your undercart locked, so only the tail wheel retracted when you selected 'up.' So the light stayed green, so you didn't put the lever down again, so the tail wheel stayed up—sir."

"The last man who used a 400 lb. bottle on a 40 lb. tyre actually disintegrated."

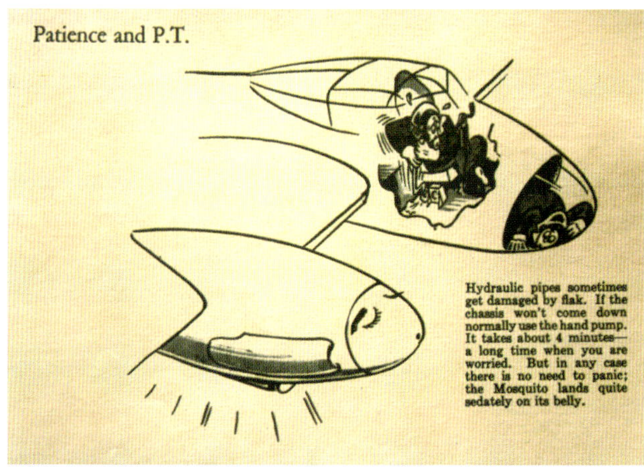
Patience and P.T.
Hydraulic pipes sometimes get damaged by flak. If the chassis won't come down normally use the hand pump. It takes about 4 minutes—a long time when you are worried. But in any case there is no need to panic; the Mosquito lands quite sedately on its belly.

"She floats all rightly, but—
—all the same it was nice of them to make sure the dinghy box and emergency-hatch fixings worked. Where are the cards, Paine?"

Single-engine safety
Don't waffle along with your nose in the air
Or you'll boil your good engine and sink in despair
But keep up your airspeed,* give plenty of power
And you'll cruise on one engine for hour after hour
*At least 170 I.A.S.

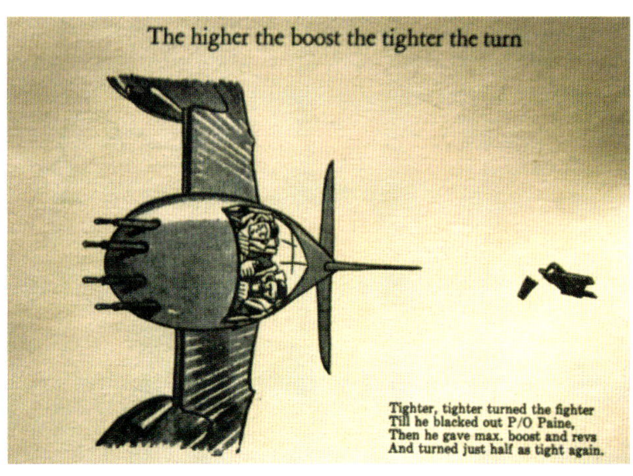
The higher the boost the tighter the turn
Tighter, tighter turned the fighter
Till he blacked out P/O Paine,
Then he gave max. boost and revs
And turned just half as tight again.

Never feather
both together

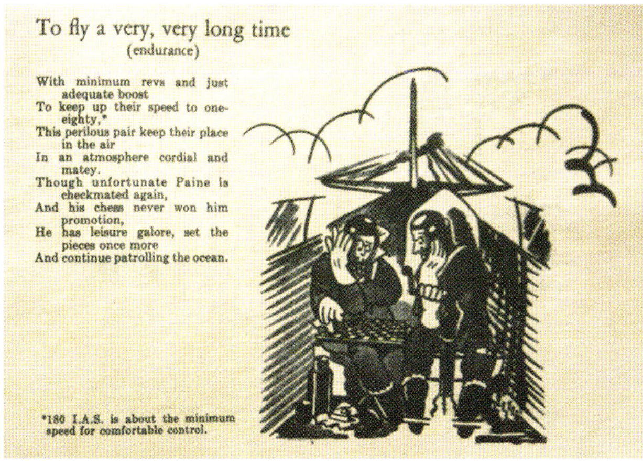
To fly a very, very long time
(endurance)
With minimum revs and just adequate boost
To keep up their speed to one-eighty,*
This perilous pair keep their place in the air
In an atmosphere cordial and matey.
Though unfortunate Paine is checkmated again,
And his chess never won him promotion,
He has leisure galore, set the pieces once more
And continue patrolling the ocean.
*180 I.A.S. is about the minimum speed for comfortable control.

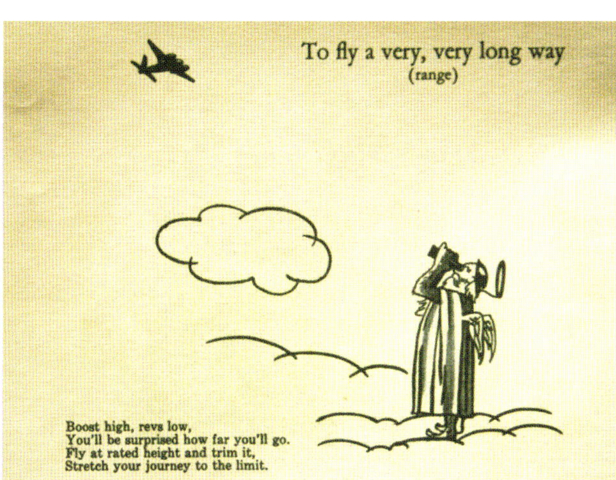
To fly a very, very long way
(range)
Boost high, revs low,
You'll be surprised how far you'll go.
Fly at rated height and trim it,
Stretch your journey to the limit.

Controls
(fighter version)
"Perhaps, sir, if I were to attend to the undercart you would have more time for your Grieg Concerto stuff."

Do they have bears at Scapa Flow, skip?
Always re-swing after change of compass

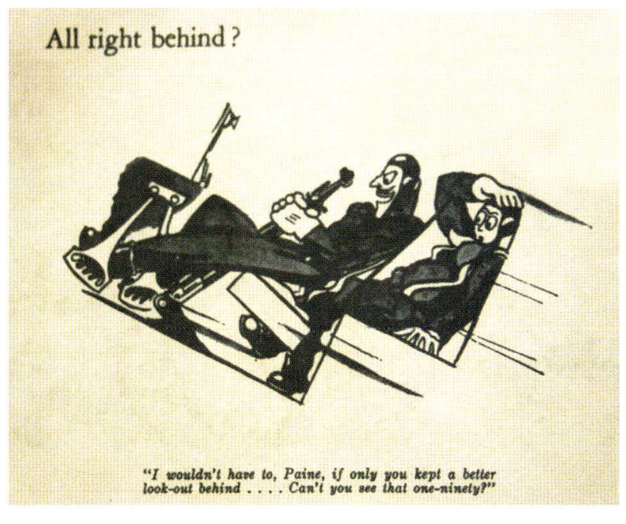
All right behind?
"I wouldn't have to, Paine, if only you kept a better look-out behind . . . . Can't you see that one-ninety?"

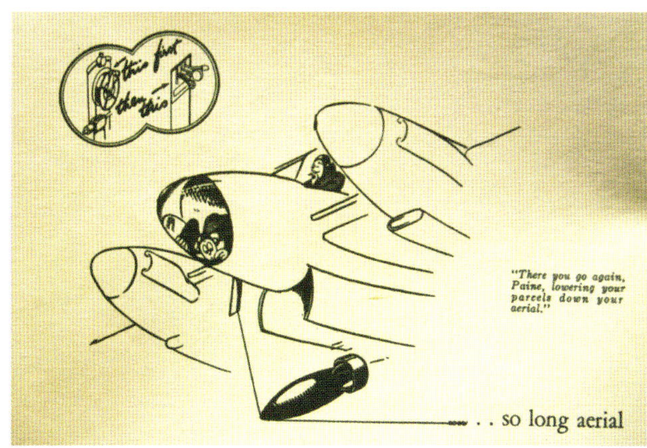
this first
then this
"There you go again, Paine, lowering your parcels down your aerial."
. . so long aerial

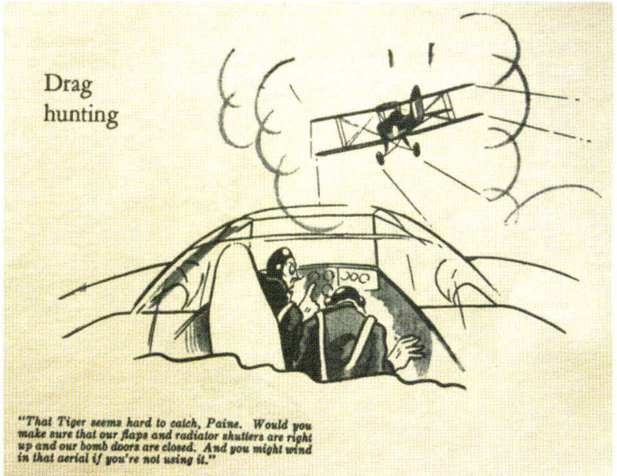
Drag hunting
"That Tiger seems hard to catch, Paine. Would you make sure that our flaps and radiator shutters are right up and our bomb doors are closed. And you might wind in that aerial if you're not using it."

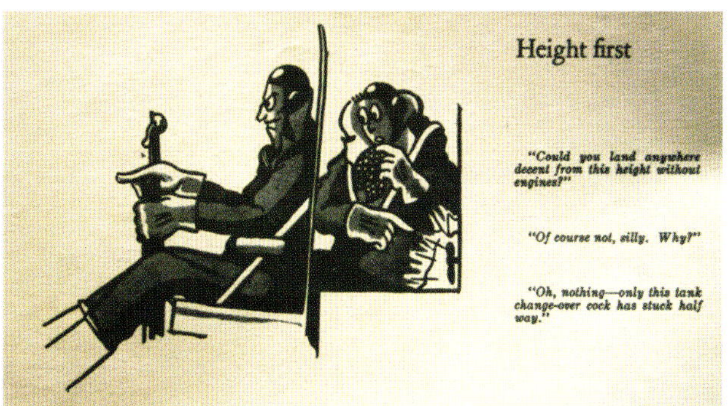
Height first
"Could you land anywhere decent from this height without engines?"
"Of course not, silly. Why?"
"Oh, nothing—only this tank change-over cock has stuck half way."

Pennants
are the
pilot's pigeon
"Yes, you took off with your undercart locked, so only the tail wheel retracted when you selected 'up.' So the light stayed green, so you didn't put the lever down again, so the tail wheel stayed up—sir."

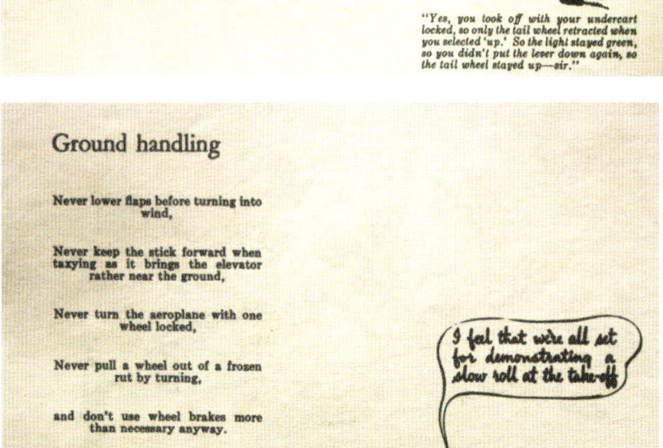
Ground handling
Never lower flaps before turning into wind,
Never keep the stick forward when taxying as it brings the elevator rather near the ground,
Never turn the aeroplane with one wheel locked,
Never pull a wheel out of a frozen rut by turning,
and don't use wheel brakes more than necessary anyway.
I feel that we're all set for demonstrating a slow roll at the take-off
What's wrong with this picture?

Take your
pump handle
"No, maybe we won't need it but it makes a nice mascot."

Going aboard
"That's the way, Pilot Officer Paine, and if the gun-sight bracket busts off just pull yourself up by the cannon trigger."

"WHAT A LOVELY SUMMER'S DAY - NOT A BREATH OF WIND."
Please throttle back before disconnecting stârter mechanic.

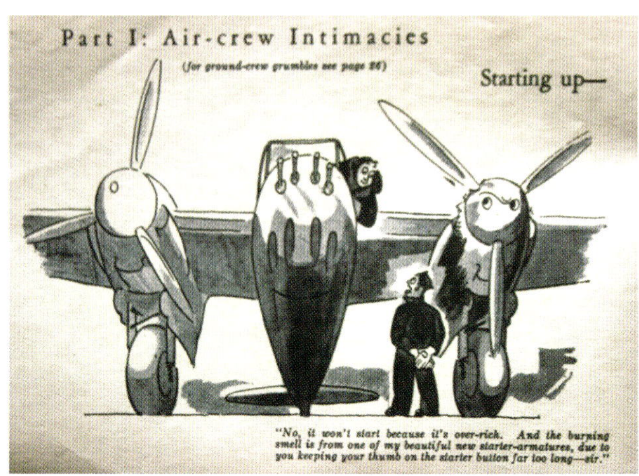
Part I: Air-crew Intimacies
(for ground-crew grumbles see page 86)
Starting up—
"No, it won't start because it's over-rich. And the burning smell is from one of my beautiful new starter-armatures, due to you keeping your thumb on the starter button far too long—sir."

—and down
"And by the way, sir, the chassis, flap and bomb door knobs should really be in neutral first."

No minor key
Remember the key for the filler caps,
You may have to land among strangers, p'r'aps.

Color Gallery

B.XVI ML963 *K-King*, which flew 571 Squadron's first sortie on 12/13 April 1944 to Osnabrück. Major repair work on the aircraft had recently been carried out following severe flak damage sustained on the operation to Scholven, 6 July 1944, when it was flown by Warrant Officer Russell Longworth and Pilot Officer Ken Davidson. (ML963 had also been damaged on 12 May, on a raid on Brunsbuttelkoog, repaired on 25 May and returned to the Squadron on 26 June). ML963 returned to the squadron on 18 October 1944. On 1 January 1945 it was used by Flight Lieutenant Norman J. Griffiths and Flying Officer W. R. 'Bill' Ball in the precision raids on railway tunnels in the Eiffel region during the Battle of the Bulge. Their 4000lb delayed-action bomb totally destroyed a tunnel at Bitburg. ML963 FTR from Berlin on 10/11 April 1945 following an engine fire. The 'Cookie' was jettisoned and Flying Officer Richard Oliver and Flight Sergeant L. Max Young, who baled out near the Elbe, returned safely. (Charles E. Brown)

Bomb aimer in a Mosquito B.IV.

On 9 May 1943 Ju 88C-6 D5+EV of 10./NJG3 was flown from Kristiansund/Kjevik in Norway to Dyce, near Aberdeen after its crew defected during an aborted interception of a Courier Service Mosquito off Denmark. The fiancée of the pilot, *Flugzeugführer* Oberleutnant Herbert Schmid, was Jewish and had been arrested and transported to a concentration camp, while his *Bordfunker*, Oberfeldwebel Paul Rosenberger, was of Jewish descent. *Bordschütze/Bordmechaniker* Oberfeldwebel Erich Kantwill went along with the defection. This aircraft was equipped with the FuG 202 *Liechtenstein* BC AI. Examination by TRE (Telecommunications Research Establishment) at Malvern, Worcestershire scientists enabled them to confirm that the *Serrate* homing device operated on the correct frequencies to home in on the FuG 202 *Liechtenstein BC* and FuG 212 *Liechtenstein* radars. *Serrate* could only home in on *Liechtenstein* AI radar and then only if it was turned on. The Ju 88C-6 is now on display at the RAF Museum, Hendon. (Author)

B.IV DZ476 XD-S *for Scottie* (note the dog and the black spinners) of 139 Squadron normally flown by Flying Officer G. S. W. Rennie RCAF and Pilot Officer W. Embry RCAF. The Canadian pairing flew DZ476 as one of the 'shallow diver' crews on raids to the railway engine sheds at Aulnoye on 4 March 1943 (a flak burst during this trip hit the fuselage and severed the rudder control cables), to the John Cockerill Steel and Armament Works at Liège on 12 March and to the engine sheds at Paderborn four days later. In April 1943 Rennie and Embry were one of eleven crews posted from Marham to Skitten to form 'A' Flight within the newly created 618 Squadron. They finished their tour and returned to Canada on 8 August 1944. DZ476 remained with 139 Squadron until on 1 April 1944 this Mosquito swung in a crosswind and suffered undercarriage collapse at Upwood.

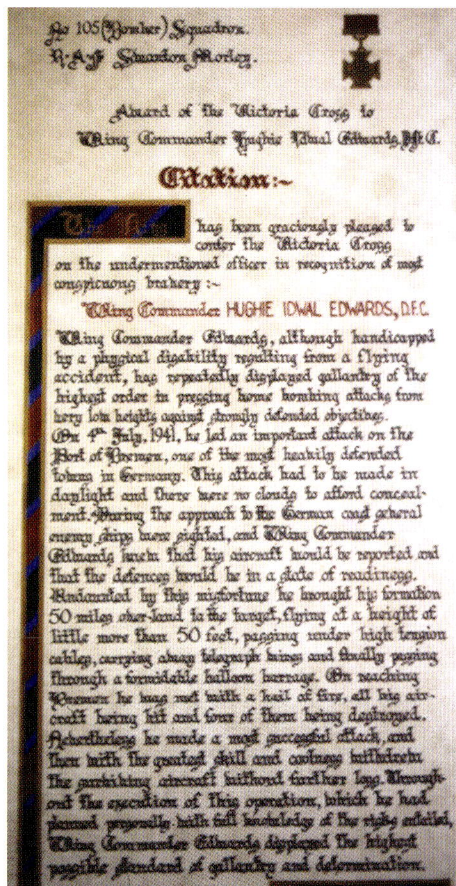

No 105 (Bomber) Squadron.
R.A.F. Swanton Morley.

Award of the Victoria Cross to
Wing Commander Hughie Idwal Edwards, D.F.C.

Citation:–

[illegible] has been graciously pleased to confer the Victoria Cross on the undermentioned officer in recognition of most conspicuous bravery :–

Wing Commander HUGHIE IDWAL EDWARDS, D.F.C.

Wing Commander Edwards, although handicapped by a physical disability resulting from a flying accident, has repeatedly displayed gallantry of the highest order in pressing home bombing attacks from very low heights against strongly defended objectives.
On 4th July, 1941, he led an important attack on the Port of Bremen, one of the most heavily defended towns in Germany. This attack had to be made in daylight and there were no clouds to afford concealment. During the approach to the German coast several enemy ships were sighted, and Wing Commander Edwards knew that his aircraft would be reported and that the defences would be in a state of readiness. Undaunted by this misfortune he brought his formation 50 miles over-land to the target, flying at a height of little more than 50 feet, passing under high tension cables, carrying away telegraph wires and finally passing through a formidable balloon barrage. On reaching Bremen he was met with a hail of fire, all his aircraft being hit and four of them being destroyed. Nevertheless he made a most successful attack, and then with the greatest skill and coolness withdrew the surviving aircraft without further loss. Throughout the execution of this operation, which he had planned personally with full knowledge of the risks entailed, Wing Commander Edwards displayed the highest possible standard of gallantry and determination.

Citation for Wing Commander Hughie Edwards VC DFC.

139 Squadron at Marham. Wing Commander Peter Shand DSO DFC in white jacket stands before XD-G DZ421, which flew with the squadron from 31 December 1942 until it passed to 627 Squadron on 21 April 1944. It crashed at Wistow in Yorkshire on 25 July 1944 when it was being operated by 1655 MTU. Shand and his navigator Pilot Officer Christopher Handley DFM were shot down and killed over the Ijsselmeer on the night of 20/21 April 1943 by Oberleutnant Lothar Linke, *Staffelkapitän* 12./NJG1. DZ373 XD-B, next in the line, was hit by flak and caught fire before it crashed on the runway of Woensdrecht airfield and Sergeant Robert Pace and Pilot Officer George Cook were killed. Next in line are XD-T DZ423 and XD-K DZ428.

Wing Commander Hughie Edwards VC DFC at RAF Marham.

Five B.IVs of 139 Squadron in echelon rear formation. Nearest aircraft is XD-G DZ421 flown by the CO, Wing Commander Peter Shand DSO DFC. Next is DZ407/R, which joined 139 Squadron from 105 Squadron on 22 December 1942 and which failed to return from the raid on Burmeister & Wain on 27 January 1943 when Sergeant Richard Clare and Flying Officer Edward Doyle hit a balloon cable and tree at East Dereham after the starboard engine failed.

Wing Commander Guy Gibson VC DSO* DFC* On the night of 19/20 September 1944 the designated Master Bomber was unavailable and Gibson and 23-year old navigator Squadron Leader James Brown Warwick DFC, an Irishman and veteran of two tours, took off from Woodhall Spa in B.XX KB267/E., a 627 Squadron Mosquito, to act as Controller for the raid on Rheydt. While returning over Walcheren both engines of Gibson's Mosquito cut (according to Anton de Bruyn, a night watchman at the local sugar factory in Steenbergen, who witnessed the incident) and the aircraft crashed near the sea wall killing both crew. Gibson and his navigator are buried at Bergen-op-Zoom. The most likely theory for the incident is that the fuel transfer cocks were not operated in the correct sequence and the engines ran out of fuel. (IWM)

'Hun' scoreboard at Swannington showing aerial kills for 85 and 157 Squadrons in 1944. The board is now on permanent display in the Stafford Sinclair (100 Group) Memorial Room at the City of Norwich Aviation Museum at Norwich Airport. (Author)

B.IV Series ii DK338 on a test flight before delivery to of 105 Squadron. It was damaged beyond repair on 1 May 1943. (Charles E. Brown)

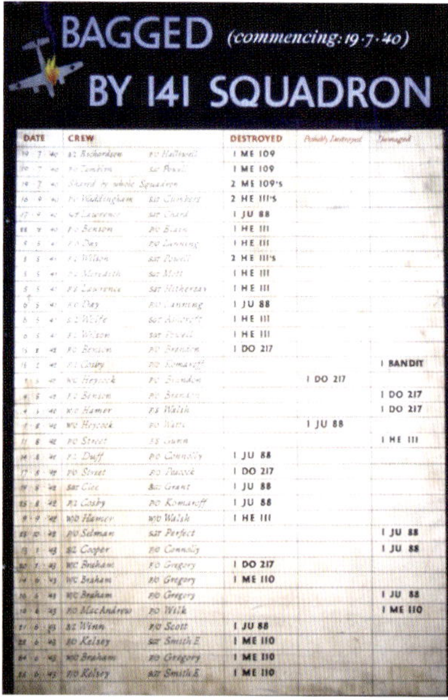

Left: 239 Squadron Record of Victories at the former RAF West Raynham. (Author) **Middle:** Bagged by 141 Squadron board commencing (19.7.40) at the former RAF West Raynham. (Author) **Right:** 141 Squadron *Ranger Effort* 20 March 1943-30 September 1944. (Author)

Napalm

DATE | CREWS | TARGET

Juterbog
Munich-Neubiberg
Flensburg

Napalm

DATE | CREWS | TARGET

Neuruppen
Schleissheim
Munich-Neubiberg
Flensburg
Schlesmig
Sylt
Lubeck
Munich-Neubiberg
Munich-Reim
Kohn

141 Squadron *Ranger Effort* 20 March 1943-30 September 1944. (Author)

Painting of Group Captain Percy C. Pickard DSO DFC CO 140 Wing and his navigator Flight Lieutenant J. A. 'Peter' Broadley DSO DFC DFM.

Artist Henry Peter's painting of NF.II DZ240 flown by 'Butch' Welham and 'Gus' Hollis of 141 Squadron shooting down a Ju 88 south of Tilburg on 27/28 June 1944, possibly Ju 88G-1 Werke Nr 710455 of 4./NJG3, which crashed at Arendonck, Belgium. Unteroffizier Eugen Wilfert and crew were KIA. Welham and Hollis also destroyed a Me 410 on 14/15 June flying the same aircraft. (via Welham)

Heinkel He 111H-16 5K+HS of 8./KG3 air launching a V1 flying bomb against Southampton just after sunset in July 1944. (Woodcock)

PR.XVI MM345/Z in the 653rd Bomb Squadron, 25th Bomb Group. The group's Mosquitoes were used in a number of roles, including agent dropping (code-named Restocking, in the hope that the German *Abwehr* would think they were connected with *Bluestocking* weather missions). j399

PR.XVI NS777 of 140 Squadron, 2nd TAF possibly at Melsbroek, early in 1945. This Mosquito was one of several acquired by the French Air Force on 15 June 1946. (Charles E. Brown)

Swannington airfield in the 1990s. (Author)

The final 100 Group operation of the war took place on 2/3 May 1945 when a record 106 aircraft took part in napalm attacks on Flensburg and Höhn airfields in Schleswig-Holstein, Westerland and Jägel. Leslie Holland, who flew this operation, has captured the scene in his very impressive painting of the raid. (Leslie Holland)

Derelict Bylaugh Hall near Swanton Morley, Norfolk in 1994. The now restored Hall reflects its former glory when it served as Headquarters. 2 Group and from 18 January 1944 onwards Headquarters 100 Group. (Author)

A painting of the bombing of the Shellhaus by J. Stafford-Baker.

Derelict Bylaugh Hall in 1994 viewed through the broken windows of a Nissen hut in its grounds. (Author)

The Stained-glass window in Ely Cathedral, which is a memorial to the crews of the RAF Groups who flew from East Anglia in WW2. The roll of honor lists 525 men killed in action. (Author)

A weather-beaten hangar and a cobweb ridden and rusty piece of agricultural machinery which both continue to survive the ravages of harsh Norfolk winters, pictured at Great Massingham in November 2005. Now a private airfield, it is easily accesible as part of the perimeter track is a public footpath but apart form the runways only a single T2 hangar remains. On the western side of the village there is a water tower and a well-preserved RAF gymnasium. The Fox and Pheasant and Royal Oak, popular wartime pubs in Great Massingham, are now private residences. Weasenham Hall nearby, was requisitoned by the RAF to billet the aircrews at the end of 1940 following a heavy German bombing raid on 27 October after which it was decided that aircrew accommodation should be dispersed. (Author)

Little Snoring airfield is still in use. In St. Andrew's church near the airfield the 23 and 515 Squadron victory boards can be found. (Author)

Little Snoring Control Tower, which remains in a relatively intact condition. (Author)

Little Snoring Marker Stone. (Author)

Rare villa style control tower at Swanton Morley, now preserved for posterity. The base is now a Army camp.(Author)

The main camp at Swanton Morley (top left of the grass airfield) now Robertson Barracks and bottom right on the Worthing side of the airfield is the former RAF 100 Group Mosquito servicing (T2) hangar. The first ever raid by American airmen on a German target was flown from this Norfolk base on 4 July 1942. The BSDU arrived at Swanton Morley from Foulsham having been formed at West Raynham on 10 April 1944 under the command of Wing Commander Rupert F. H. Clerke DFC, initially with four Mosquitoes later increased to nine. The BSDU had moved to Foulsham in June, to develop, test and produce a wide variety of radar and radio equipment for 100 Group. In addition to the technical development and production side, a Mosquito Flight of nine aircraft was established to carry out operational and non-operational trials appertaining to fighter equipment. Among the inventions BSDU developed and introduced into service, a range of tail warning devices, homers such as *Serrate* IV, IVA; IVB; V; *Hookah* and interrogators like *Perfectos* I, IA, IB and II. During the period June 1944 to April 1945 BSDU carried out 114 operational sorties in Mosquitoes over the continent to test the various fighter devices. The crews who flew these operations were experienced 100 Group pilots and navigators. (Author)

'The haunted former cinema at Swanton Morley. (Author)

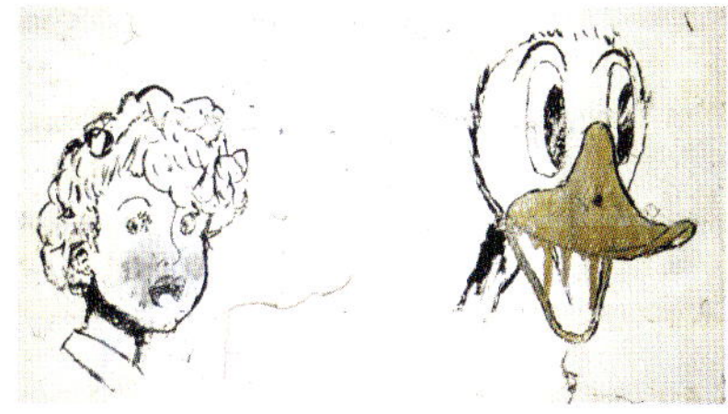

'*Jane*' the famous *Daily Mirror* strip cartoon character still survives in the haunted former cinema at Swanton Morley. (Author)

In the haunted former services' cinema at Swanton Morley are cartoons of men fencing, a 'Desperate Dan' character, a duck, a Highland Fling and a young girl. (Author)

Eerie light shines on the two lighthouses, which marked the projector apertures in the far wall in the haunted cinema at Swanton Morley. (Author)

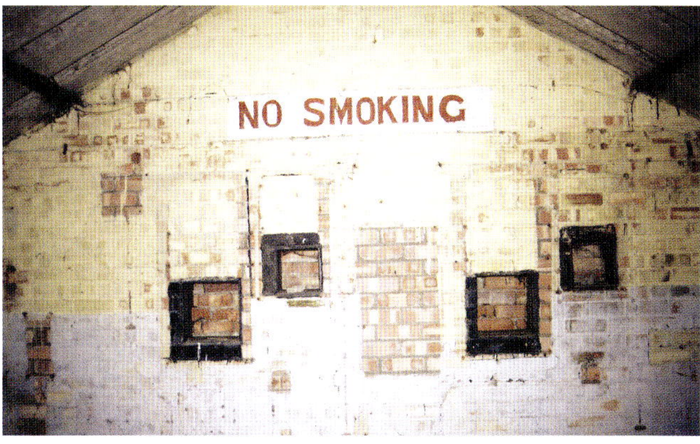

The projection apertures now bricked up in the haunted cinema at Swanton Morley. (Author)

Foulsham airfield in the 1970s. (Author)

The grave of Flying Officer Jeffery N. Edwards, 22-year-old navigator in 157 Squadron. He is buried in the churchyard of St Peter's Church, Haveringland part of the former airfield at Swannington. Edwards was killed on 22 December 1944 when a Mosquito NF.XIX piloted by Flight Lieutenant William Taylor crashed while attempting to land after informing Flying Control over the R/T that they had no aileron control (Author)

Three hangars remain intact at Foulsham and in between them are several buildings, either disused or in use by local industry. (Author)

Overgrown Nissen hut in the grounds of Bylaugh Hall. (Author)

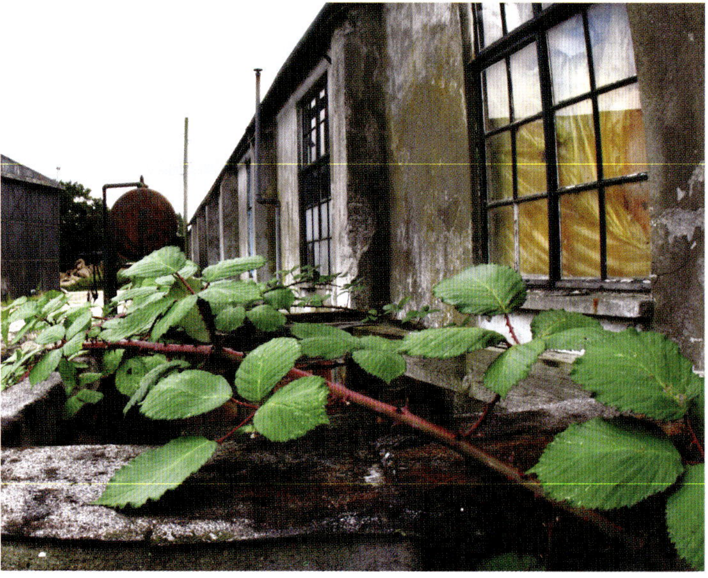

Overgrown buildings at Foulsham. (Author)

Aerial view of Foulsham in 2007. (Author)

Nissen Huts in the snow. (Author)

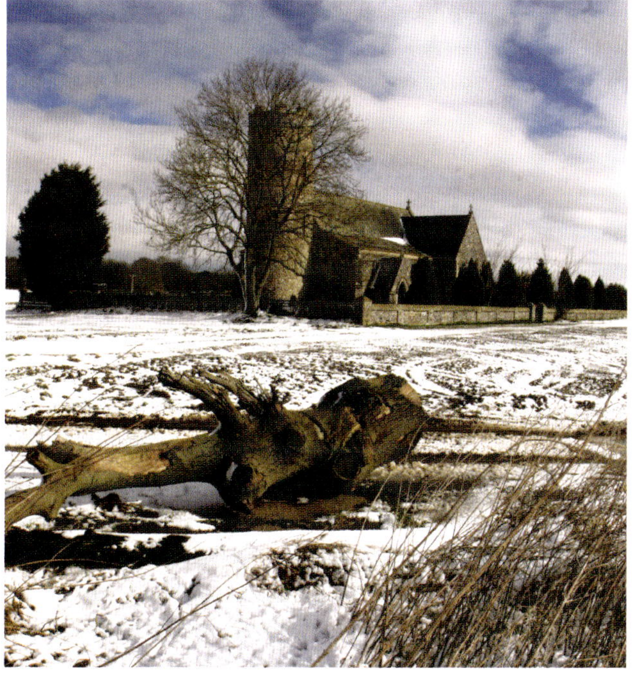

St. Peter's church, Haveringland on whose land part of RAF Swannington airfield was sited. (Author).

The former RAF Officers Mess at Horsham St. Faith just before demolition. (Author)

The old control tower at the former RAF Swannington. (Author)

Norwich Airport is today a thriving regional airport with a valuable link to Schiphol in Holland and its international routes. The runway and perimeter track layout is a valuable legacy of the halcyon days when the airfield was RAF Horsham St. Faith. (Author)

Another view of the old control tower at the former RAF Swannington. (Author)

Hut still standing – just – at Swannington in 2007. (Author)

Former wartime hut at Swannington. (Author)

A hut open to the skies at Swannington airfield. (Author)

Wartime huts at Swannington in 2006. (Author)

Reflections in time. An old and decayed hut at Swannington in 2008. (Author)

Appendix 1

Mosquito Variants

F.II Day and night long-range fighter and intruder built with long nacelles. Powered by two 1460hp Merlin 21, 22 or 23s. W4052 prototype first flew 15 May 1941. Fitted with AI.Mk.IV. Armed with four 20mm Hispano cannon and four .303 inch Browning machine guns in the nose. In turn, W4052 was fitted experimentally with a four-gun Bristol B.XI dorsal turret and a bellows-operated segmented airbrake around the mid-fuselage and later a Mosquito II was fitted experimentally with a *Turbinlight* in the nose. 25 (Special) Intruder models were built for 23 Squadron with AI radar equipment deleted. As late as 1943-44 many surviving aircraft were refurbished, re-engined, had AI.Mk.IV and V radar sets installed, and were given to 100 Group. A few aircraft were converted for photo-reconnaissance duties. 494 built; 97 converted to NF.XII and 100 converted to NF.XVII; six converted to T.III.

T.III Unarmed dual control trainer. First flew January 1942. 358 built, including six from F.II. Powered by Merlin 21, 23 or 25s.

FB.VI Day and night fighter-bomber, intruder, and long range fighter powered by two 1460hp Merlin 21 or 23, or two 1635hp Merlin 25s. First flew 1 June 1942. Prototype HJ662/G was converted from B.IV DZ434. Production aircraft first flew in February 1943. Altogether, 2289 (almost one-third of total Mosquito production) were built, including 1065 by Standard Motors Ltd and 56 by Airspeed Ltd; 19 of these were completed as FB.XVIIIs, two converted to Sea Mosquito TR.33 prototypes. Armed with four 20mm cannon and four .303in machine guns and able to carry two 250lb bombs in enclosed bomb bay plus two more (later, two 500lbs), or eight 60lb rocket projectiles under the wings. Alternatively, one mine or depth charge beneath each wing.

NF.X Night-fighter powered by two-stage Merlin 61 engines. Although ordered in quantity, the NF.X never went into production.

FB.XI Fighter-bomber version similar to the B.VI but with two-stage 1565hp Merlin 61s. Not ordered into production.

NF.XII Prototype (DD715) and the 97 NF.XII night-fighters built were all conversions of the NF.II. Powered by two 1460hp Merlin 21 or 23 engines. Main distinguishing feature was a thimble-nose containing a powerful transmitter with a parabolic reflector for the 10cm wavelength AI.Mk VIII radar, which removed the need for any external aerials. First flew in August 1942. Armed with four 20mm cannon only.

NF.XIII Night-fighter powered by Merlin 21,23 or 25s with universal wing similar to that of the Mk.VI. AI.Mk.VIII in thimble' or Universal (bull) Nose. First flew in August 1943. 260 built.

NF.XIV Night-fighter based on the NF.XIII and intended to be powered by two-stage Merlin 67 or 72 engines, but was never put into production, being superseded by the NF.XIX and NF.XXX.

NF.XV High-altitude fighter, capable of reaching 45,000 feet, built in response to the Threat posed by the Ju 86 high altitude bomber. Prototype (MP469) was the first Mosquito with a pressurized cabin, and first flew on 8 August 1942, later being fitted with AI.Mk.VIII radar, as were the four NF.XVs built - all modified B.IVs with two-stage 1680hp Merlin 72/73 or 170hp 76/77 engines driving three- or four-bladed airscrews. The NF.XVs were armed with four .303 inch machine guns in underbelly pack. MP469 was delivered to the newly formed High Altitude Flight at Northolt on 16 September 1942, but this, and the Fighter Interception Unit at Ford, which received DZ366, DZ385, DZ409 and DZ417, March-August 1943, never had need to use them as the Ju 86s ceased operations over Britain. All five were used by 'C' Flight of 85 Squadron at Hunsdon and later some went to Farnborough for pressure cabin research.

NF.XVII 100 night-fighter variants converted from NF.II and powered by 1460hp Merlin 21 or 23 engines. Fitted with SCR720/729 or AI.Mk.X radar. First flown, March 1943.

FB.XVIII Ground attack and anti-shipping fighter-bomber with four cannon deleted and replaced by a Molins 57mm 6 pounder cannon weighing 1580lb, while retaining the four .303 inch Browning machine guns. Twenty-four 57mm rounds for the cannon, which had a muzzle velocity of 2950ft/second were carried. The eighteen *Tsetses* built started as FB.VIs, whose two 1635hp Merlin 25s, were retained. Prototype (HJ732/G) was converted from FB.VI and was first flown on 8 June 1943.

NF.XIX Night-fighter powered by two Merlin 25s and fined with AI.VIII or X/SCR720 and 729 in 'thimble' or Universal Nose similar to the NF.XIII. First flown, April 1944. 280 built.

FB.21 Canadian version of the FB.VI superseded by the FB.26. Three built.

T.22 Canadian version of the T.III developed from the FB.21. Six built. Powered by two 1460hp Packard-built single-stage Merlin 33 engines.

FB.24 Canadian high-altitude fighter-bomber version based on the FB.21, with two 1620hp Packard-built single-stage Merlin 301s but not ordered into production.

FB.26 Uprated Canadian version of the FB.VI fighter-bomber, improved from the FB.21, powered by two 1620hp Packard-built single-stage Merlin 225s. 300 built, plus a further 37 were converted to T.29 standard.

T.27 Dual control trainer version developed from the T.22 with more powerful (two 1620hp) Packard-built single-stage Merlin 225 engines. 49 built.

T.29 Thirty-seven dual control trainers converted from the FB.26, powered by two Packard-built single-stage Merlin 225s.

NF.XXX Night-fighter development of the NF.XIX, which appeared in March 1944. Powered by two-stage 1680hp Merlin 72s, 1710hp Merlin 76 or 1690hp Merlin 113s. Fitted with AI Mk X. 529 built.

NF.31 NF 30 with two 1750hp Packard-built single-stage Merlin 69s but it never went into production.

TR.33 Torpedo-reconnaissance fighter-bomber for Royal Navy carrier-borne operations. Two prototypes (LH359 and LR387) were converted from Mk.VIs to meet Specification 15/44, with arrestor hook and reinforced fuselage for deck landing and 1635hp Merlin 25s driving bur-bladed airscrews, but the wings were non-folding. Two more (TS444 and TS449), fitted with upward folding wings and arrestor hook (and extra bulkhead over the arrestor hook attachment point), were built for handling trials. The first production TR.33, TW227, flew for the first time on 10 November 1945. From the 14th TR.33 onwards, manual folding wings were introduced and the rubber blocks in compression undercarriage were replaced by Lockheed oleo-pneumatic shock absorbers to reduce the rebound in deck landings. Slightly smaller wheels were also fitted. The TR.33 could carry an 18-inch Mk.XV or XVII torpedo, or a mine, or a 2000lb bomb under the fuselage, plus two 500lb bombs in the bomb bay and either two 50-gallon fuel-tanks beneath the wings, or two 30-gallon tanks and four RPs. A thimble nose housed ASH radar, while the four 20mm cannon were retained. Two detachable RATO (Rocket Assisted Take Off) bottles either side of the fuselage, which fell away after firing, could also be fitted. 50 TR.33s were built but an order for 47 more was cancelled.

NF.36 Night-fighter development of the NF.XXX, with improved AI radar and four 20mm cannon. Powered by two 1690hp Merlin 113 (starboard)/114 (port) or 1710hp 113A (starboard)/114A (port). 163 built, a few being converted to Met.35s. The first NF.36 (HK955) flew in May 1945. NF.36s were retired from service n 1953.

TR.37 Torpedo-fighter/bomber, of which only fourteen were built. The prototype, TW240, a modified TH.33, first flew in 1946. The TH.37 differed from the TR.33 only in having a British ASV (Air to Surface Vessel) Mk XIII in thimble nose radome slightly larger than the TR.33. 14 built at Chester. Powered by two 1635hp Merlin 25s.

NF.38 Night-fighter with Merlin 1710hp 114As. One prototype (RL248) converted from NF.36. Some models were fitted with AI.Mk.IX radar. Yugoslavia acquired most of the 101 built.

TT.39 High-speed shore-based Naval target tug. Two prototypes (ML995 and PF569), plus twenty-four more were converted from existing B.XVI aircraft by General Aircraft Ltd, under their designation GAL.59 to Royal Navy Specification 0.19/45 to replace the Miles M.33 Monitor TT.11. The B.XVI's two 1680hp Merlin 72/73 engines were retained but the extended (and glazed) nose (which housed the camera operator) resulted n the airscrew blades having to be cropped. The third crewmember, a rear-facing observer/drogue operator, sat in a dorsal cupola aft of the wings. Drogue targets were streamed from a hydraulically operated winch the bomb bay, powered by a retractable wind driven generator in the forward bomb bay. A radar altimeter was fitted for radar-calibration exercises. The TT.39 first entered service with Fleet Requirements Units from 1948.

FB.40 212 Australian-built versions of the FB were the product of de Havilland Australia Ltd. Six were converted to PR.40; 28 to PR.41s; one to FB.42, and twenty-two to T.43s. Powered by 1460hp Packard-built single-stage Merlin 31,33s.

FB.42 Single Australian fighter-bomber converted from FB.40 (A52-90) to become A52-300 PR.41 prototype). Powered by two 1750hp Packard-built single-stage Merlin 69s.

T.43 22 Australian trainer versions similar to T.III converted from FB.40s (A52-1050 to A-52 1071). Powered by two 1460hp Packard-built single-stage Merlin 33s.

Appendix 2

Mosquito Air-To-Air Victories

1942-April 1945

DATE	TYPE	SERIAL	SQN	ENEMY	A/C DETAILS	PILOT-NAVIGATOR/RADAR OP
29/30.5.42	II	W4099	157 Sqn	Do 217E-4	S of Dover.	S/L C. Ashfield (Do 217E-4 of KG2)
29/30.5.42	II	DD608	151 Sqn	Do 217E-4	(Prob) North Sea	P/O J. A. Wain-F/Sgt T. S. G. Grieve (Do 217E-4 of KG2)
28/29.6.42	II		264 Sqn	Do 217E-2	over Creil	F/O Hodgkinson (Uffz Rudolf Blankenburg, KG2).
24/25.6.42	II	W4097	151 Sqn	2 x Do 217E-4	The Wash	W/C I. S. Smith DFC-F/L Kemon-Sheppard (Do 217E-4 5454 of II/KG40 and Do 217E-4 of I/KG2)
25/26.6.42	II	DD61 6	151 Sqn	He 111 H-6	North Sea.	P/O J. A. Wain-F/Sgt T. S. G. Grieve
26/27.6.42	II	DD609	151 Sqn	Do 217E-4	North Sea.	F/L Moody-P/O Marsh (Do 217E-4 U5+ML of 3./KG2 flown by Fw Hans Schrödel)
6/7.7.42	II	DD670/S	23 Sqn	Do 217 16m E	Chartres.	W/C B. R. O' B. Hoare DFC*-P/O S J Cornes
8/9.7.42	II	DD670/S	23 Sqn	Do 217/ He 111	Etampes/ Evreux	S/L K. H. Salisbury-Hughes
21/22.7.42	II	W4090	151 Sqn	Do 217E-4 off	Spurn Head	P/O Fisher (Ofw Heinrich Wolpers and crew, Do 217E-4 U5+IH 3./KG2)
27/28.7.42	IIs			DD629 & DD608		
			151 Sqn	2xDo 217E-4	North Sea	S/L Pennington & P/O Fielding. (Fw Richard Stumpf of I/KG2 and Lt Hans-Joachim Mohring of 3./KG2)
27/28.7.42	II	W4099	157 Sqn	He 111	North Sea	S/L G. Ashfield
29/30.7.42	II	DD669	151 Sqn	Do 217E-4	North Sea	F/O A. I. McRitchie-F/Sgt E. S. James (Do 217E-4 U5+GV, flown by Ofw Artur Hartwig of II/KG2,)
30/31.7.42	II	DD670/S	23 Sqn	UEA	Orleans	W/C B. R. O'B. Hoare DFC*-W/O J. F. Potter
30/31.7.42	II	DD639	264 Sqn	Ju 88A-4	Nr Malvern Hills	S/L C. A. Cooke-P/O R. E. MacPherson.Ju 88A-4 of KüFlGr 106.
22/23.8.42	II	DD612	157 Sqn	Do 217E-4	Worlingworth	W/C Gordon Slade-P/O P. V. Truscott Slade (Do 217E-4 U5+LP of 6./KG2, flown by 29-year-old ex-Lufthansa pilot Oblt Hans Walter Wolff, Deputy Staffelkapitan)
8/9.9.42	II	DD669	151 Sqn	Do 217E-4	Orwell, Cambs	F/O A. I. McRitchie-F/Sgt E. S. James (Do 217E-4 F8+AP, on loan to 3./KG2 and piloted by Fw Alfred Witting)
10/11.9.42.	II		'B' 23 Sqn	UEA 12m S	Enschede	W/C B. R. O'B. Hoare DFC*-W/O J. F. Potter
17/18.9.42	II	DD610	151 Sqn	Do 217E-4 Cr.	Docking	F/L H. E. Bodien DFC-Sgt G. B. Brooker. U5+UR of 7./KG2 piloted by Fw Franz Elias crashed at Fring. All four crew taken prisoner.
30.9.42	II	DD607	157 Sqn	Ju 88A-4 30m	off Dutch coast	S/L R. F. H. Clerke
26.10.42	II	DD716	157 Sqn	Ju 88D-1	off Beachy Head	F/O E. H. Cave
7/8.1.43	II		23 Sqn	Comiso Ju 88 of II/KG30		W/C N. J. Starr DFC
15/16.1.43	II	DD609	151 Sqn	Do 217E-4 Cr.	Boothby Graffoe	Sgt E. A. Knight RCAF-Sgt W. I. L. Roberts (Do 217E-4 U5+KR of 7./KG2. Lt Günter Wolf, pilot, Uffz Helmut Knorr, Uffz Kurt Semitschka, dorsal gunner, & Ogfr Karl-Heinz Krusewitz) all KIA
17/18.1.43	II	VY-V 85	Sqn	Ju 88A-14 SE	England	W/C G. L. Raphael DFC*-W/O W. N. Addison DFM (Ju 88A-14 of IV.KG3 or III/KG6)
22.1.43	II	HJ929 410	Sqn	Do 2 17E-1 (Prob) Ju 88 of II/LG1		W/C P. G. Wykeham-Barnes DSO DFC*-F/O G. E. Palmer DFC
7/8.3.43	II		23 Sqn	Ju 88	Catania	W/C P. G. Wykeham-Barnes DSO DFC*-F/O G. E. Palmer DFC Ju 88 of II/LG1
18/19.3	II	W4099	157 Sqn	Ju 88A-14	off Harwich	F/O G. Deakin-P/O de Costa
18/19.3.43	II	HK936	410 Sqn	Do 217E8-4	King's Lynn	F/O D. Williams-P/O P. Dalton (Do 217 U5+AH Werke No 5523) I/KG2 flown by Uffz Horst Toifel, Uffz Heinrich Peter, gunner, Ludwig Petzold radio operator, Ogfr Georg Riedel, observer.
28/29.3.43	II	W4079 1	57 Sqn	Do 217E-4	off Southwold	F/O J. R. Beckett-F/Sgt Phillips (Do 217E-4 U5+NM (Werk No 4375) of 4./KG2, flown by Fw Paul Huth. Huth, Uffz Werner Hans Burschel, dorsal gunner, Oblt Gottfried Thorley, observer, and Uffz Konrad Schuller, radio operator, all KIA. Victory shared with a 68 Squadron Beaufighter piloted by F/O Vopalecky with F/Sgt Husar; both Czech)
30.3.43	II		264 Sqn	He 111 8m N	Redon	S/L M. H. Constable-Maxwell
9/10.4.43	II		23 Sqn	Ju 88 of III/KG76	Catania	W/C P. G. Wykeham•Barnes DSO DFC*-F/O G. E. Palmer DFC. Ju 88 of III/KG76
13/14.4.43	II	DZ243	157 Sqn	Do 217E-4		
14/15.4.43	XII	VY-F	85 Sqn	Do 217E-4	Clacton-on-Sea	S/L W. P. Green-F/Sgt A. R. Grimstone DFM (Do 217E-4 F8+AM of 4./KG40)
14/15.4 .43	XII	VY-G	85 Sqn	Do 217E-4	Clacton-on-Sea	F/L G. L. Howitt-F/O G. Irving (Do 217E-4 U5+DP of 6./KG2 flown by Uffz Franz Tannenberger)
14/15.4.43	II	DD730	157 Sqn	Do 217E-4	SW Colchester	F/L J. G. Benson DFC-F/L L. Brandon DFC (Dornier 217E-4 U5+KP flown by Uffz Walter Schmurr of 6./KG2. Uffz Franz Witte, radio operator-gunner KIA. Schmurr, Lt Karl-Heinrich Hertam, observer and Uffz Martin Sehwarz, gunner, baled out. Witte's body was found in the wreckage).
24/25.4.43	XII		85 Sqn	Ju 88 nr		Bromley, Kent F/O J. P. M. Lintott-Sgt G. G. Gilling-Lax (Ju 88A-14 3E+HS of 8./KG6 disintegrated in the air and the wreckage fell in Bromley, Kent)
4/5.5.43	II		605 Sqn	Do 217K1 x 2	Eindhoven	F/O B. Williams-P/O D. Moore (Do 217K-l U5+AA (Werk Nr 4415) of 6./KG2. Lt Ernst Andres, pilot, seriously injured, Maj Walter Bradel, Kommodore of KG2 KIA in the crash at Landsmere, near Amsterdam. Flg Wernerker also killed, although he may have died in the Mosquito attack, and rest of the crew injured. All recovered, Andres being promoted to Oblt and receiving the Ritterkreuz on 20 April 1944. He was killed with 5./NJG4 on 11 February 1945

DATE	TYPE	SERIAL	SQN	ENEMY	A/C DETAILS	PILOT-NAVIGATOR/RADAR OP
13/14.5.43	II		157 Sqn	Do 217E4 10m		NE Colchester P/O R. L. Watts-Sgt J. Whewell (157 Squadron shot down two Do 217E-4s of KG2 piloted by Lt Stefan Szamek and Lt Gerd Strufe). A Do 217E-4 of II/KG2 was intercepted by a Mosquito NF.II of 157 Squadron from Hunsdon, flown by Sgt R. L. Watts with Sgt J. Whewell, and shot down after an exchange of fire. A fire started in the Dornier's starboard engine and it crashed about 10 miles NE of Colchester at 0207 hrs. Near Norwich, a Do 217K-1 of 4./KG2 flown by Uffz Erhard Corty was claimed at about 0250 hrs)
16/17.5.43	XII	'A'	85 Sqn	Fw 190A-4/U-8	nr Dover	S/L W. P. Green-F/Sgt A. R. Grimstone DFM
16/17.5.43	XII	'G'	85 Sqn	Fw 190A-4/U-8	15m S. Hastings	F/L G. L. Howitt-F/O G. Irving
16/17.5.43	XII	'L'	85 Sqn	Fw 190A-4/U-8 Fw 190A-4/U-8 (Prob)	Dover Straits "	F/O B. J. Thwaites-P/O W. P. Clemo DFM*
16/17.5.43	XII	'D'	85 Sqn	Fw 190A-4/U-8	off Gravesend	F/O J. D. Shaw-P/O A. C. Lowton
18/19.5.43	XII	'Z'	85 Sqn	Fw190A-5	Kent	F/O J. P. M. Lintott-Sgt G. G. Gilling-Lax
21/22.5.43	XIII	'V'	85 Sqn	Fw 190A 25m	NW Hardelot	S/L E. D. Crew DFC*-F/O F. French
29/30.5.43	XII	'S'	85 Sqn	Ju 88S-1	Isfield nr Lewes	F/O J. P. M. Lintott-Sgt G. G. Gilling-Lax (3Z+SZ of I/KG66)
5.6.43	XII		29 Sqn	Ju 88A-14	off Ostend	
11.6.43	XII		256 Sqn	Do 217	South of Ford	F/O Burnett
11.6.43	II		85 Sqn	25 Ju 88	Bay of Biscay	F/L J. Singleton-F/O W. G. Haslam
12/13.6.43	XIX	MM630/E	157 Sqn	Ju 188	Foret de Compeigne	F/L J.G. Benson DFC-F/L Brandon DSO DFC
13/14.6.43	XII	DZ302/R	85 Sqn	Fw 190A-5	Wrotham	W/C J. Cunningham DSO* DFC*-F/L C. F. Rawnsley DFC DFM* (W/C Cunningham, CO 85 Squadron, who had shot down 16 enemy aircraft while flying Beaufighters, pursued Fw 190A-5 CO+LT of 3./SKG10 over his own airfield and shot it down. The Fw 190, flown by Lt Ullrich, crashed at Nettlefold Farm, Borough Green near Wrotham, but incredibly, the pilot had been catapulted through the canopy in the death dive of the aircraft and was taken prisoner)
14/15.6.43	XVII	HK315	219 Sqn	Ju 88	Harwich area	F/L M. J. Gloster DFC-F/L J. F. Oswold DFC
17/18.6.43	XII		85 Sqn	Fw 190 (Prob)		Capt J. Räd RNWAF-Capt L. Lövestad RNWAF DFM*
19.6.43	II		151 Sqn	Ju 88	Bay of Biscay	F/L H. E. Bodien DFC
21/22.6.43	XII	'E'	85 Sqn	Fw 190	River Medway	F/L W. H. Maguire-F/O W. D. Jones (Fw 190 GP+LA of 2./SKG 10)
2/3.7.43	XII	HK166 FIU		Ju 88D-1	45m S Bognor	W/C R. A. Chisholm DFC-F/O N. L. Bamford DFC
3/4.7.43	II	DD739	157 Sqn	Do 217	St Trond	F/L J.G. Benson DFC-F/L L. Brandon DFC
9.7.43	XII	'Z'	85 Sqn	Do 217K-1 nr	Detling	F/O J. P. M. Lintott-Sgt G. G. GillIng-Lax (Lintott's 4th victory - Do 217K-1 U5+FP, piloted by Oblt Hermann Zink of 6./KG2. Zink and his crew were all KIA. The GCI controller who had put Lintott onto the raider saw two blips on his CRT merge and stay together for 7 minutes: then they had faded. 2 mls from where the Dornier fell the Mosquito crew were also found dead in the wreckage of their aircraft)
11/12.7.43	II	HJ944	410 Sqn	Do 217 10m	E Humber	S/L A. G. Lawrence DFC RCAF-F/Sgt H. J. Wilmer DFM
13/14.7.43	XII	'T' 8	5 Sqn	Me 410A-1	off Felixstowe	F/L E. N. Bunting-F/O F. French (Me 410A-1 U5+KG flown by Fw Franz Zwißler (pilot) and Ofw Leo Raida (bordfunker) of 16./KG2. Bunting closed to within 200 yd, but the Mosquito got caught in the Germans' slipstream and he could not aim his guns. He dived below and closed in again before firing two short bursts. The Me 410 burst into flames at once and fell into the sea 5 miles off Felixstowe. It was the first Me 410 to be shot down over Britain)
13/14.7.43	II	HJ944	410 Sqn	RCAF Do 217	off Humber Estuary	(Do 217M-l, U5+EL of 3./KG2, flown by Uffz Willy Spielmanns)
13/14.7.43	II		605 Sqn	Do 217M-1nr	Eindhoven	F/O R. R Smart-F/O J. K. Sutcliffe (On Intruder over Holland, shot down Do 217M-1 U5+CK of 2./KG2 Uffz Hauck and his crew crashed in the vicinity of Eindhoven)
15/16.7.43	XII	'G'	85 Sqn	Me 410 A-1	off Dunkirk	F/L B. J. Thwaites-P/O W. P. Clemo DFM* (Me 410 U5+CJ of V/KG2, flown by Hptm Friederich-Wilhelm Methner and Uffz Hubert Grube)
18.7.43	XII		256 Sqn	Fw 190	Channel	
25/26.7.43	II		605 Sqn	Do 217M-1	Soesterberg	F/L C. Knowles-F/O A. Eagling (Do 217M-1 U5+KL, flown by Lt Manfred Lieddert of 3./KG2)
26/27.7.43	XII	VY-A	85 Sqn	Ju 88 25m	E Ramsgate	S/L W. P. Green DFC-F/Sgt A. R. Grimstone DFM
29/30.7.43	XII		256 Sqn	Me 410A-1 20m	S Beachy Head	W/C G. R. Park (Oblt Helmut Biermann and Uffz Willi Kroger in Me 410A-1 U5+BJ. They fell into the sea 20 miles south of Beachy Head
July 43	XII		29 Sqn	Ju 88	NE of Foreness	
15/16.8.43	XII		256 Sqn	2 x Do 217M-1 30m	SE Selsey	W/C G. R. Park (Uffz Karl Morgenstern and Uffz Franz Bundgens' Do 217M-ls in the sea off Worthing. Park's third 'kill' of the night occurred when he shot down Uffz Walter Kayser's Do 217M-l)
15/16.8.43	XII		256 Sqn	2 x Do 217M-1	France	F/Sgt Brearley (Fw Theodor Esslinger fell near Evreux and Lt Franz Bosbach crashed near St André)
15/16.8.43	VI	HP849	410 Sqn	Do 217M 17m	off Beachy Hd	P/O R. D. Schultz-F/O V. A. Williams (Do 217M-1 U5+GT of 9./KG2 flown by Uffz Josef Schultes and crew (all KIA)
17/i8.8.43	VI	'O'	605 Sqn	Bf 109 E	Schleswig	F/L D. H. Blomely DFC-F/O R. "Jock" Birrel
22/23.8.43	XII	'V'	85 Sqn	Me 410-A-1	Chelmondiston	S/L G. E. Howitt DFC-P/O J. C. O. Medworth (Me 410A-1, U5+AF of 15./KG2 crewed by Fw Walter Hartmann and Obgefr Michael Meurer. Meurer baled out and came down at Stratton Hall, while Hartman's body was later found in a field, his parachute unopened)
22/23.8.43	XII	DZ302/R	85 Sqn	Fw 190	nr Dunkirk	
22/23.8.43	XII	HK197	29 Sqn	Me 410-A-1	E of Manston	F/L C. Kirkland-P/O R. C. Raspin
22/23.8.43	XII	HK175	29 Sqn	Me 410 A-1nr	Dunkirk	
22/23.8.43	XII	HK164	29 Sqn	Me 410A-1	North of Knocke	
23/24.8.43	XII	DZ302/R	85 Sqn	Fw 190	off Dunkirk	W/C J. Cunningham DSO* DFC*-F/L C. F. Rawnsley DFC DFM*
24/25.8.43	XII	'G'	85 Sqn	Me 410A-1		Capt J. Räd RNWAF-Capt L. Lövestad RNWAF DFM* (U5+EG, a Me 410A-1 of 16./KG2, flown by Fw Werner Benner with Uffz Hermann Reimers). Victory was officially shared with W/C R. E. X. Mack DFC in a XII of 29 Sqn.
6/7.9.43	XII	'K'	85 Sqn	Fw 190A-5	France	
6/7.9.43	II	'V'	85 Sqn	Fw 190A-5 3m	E Clacton	S/L G. E. Howitt DFC-F/L C. Irving DFC
8/9.9.43	XV	DZ302/R	85 Sqn	Fw 190A-5	off Aldborough	W/C J. Cunningham DSO* DFC*-F/L C. F. Rawnsley DFC DFM*
8/9.9.43	XII	'L'	85 Sqn	2 x Fw 190A-5 of I/SKG10	off N Foreland	F/L B. J. Thwaites-P/O W. P. Clemo DFM*
11/12.9.43	XIX	MM630/E	157 Sqn	2 x Ju 188	Zeeland	F/L J. G. Benson DFC-F/L. Brandon DSO DFC
15/16.9.43	XII	'T'?	85 Sqn	Ju 88A-14	Tenterden	F/O E. R. Hedgecoe-P/O J. R. Witham. Ju 88A-14 3E+FP of 6./KG6. Mosquito was crippled by return fire, and the crew baled out, their aircraft crashing at Tenterden, Kent.

DATE	TYPE	SERIAL	SQN	ENEMY	A/C DETAILS	PILOT-NAVIGATOR/RADAR OP
15/16.9.43	XII	'T'?	85 Sqn	Ju 88A-14	off Boulogne	F/L E. N. Bunting-F/O F. French (Ju 88A-14 of II/KG6)
15/16.9.43	XII	HK204	488 Sqn	Do 217M	E of Foreness	F/L Watts (9./KG2 Do 217M-1, flown by Ofw Erich Mosler shot down into the sea SE of Ramsgate.
15/16.9.43	XII	HK203	488 Sqn	He 111	North of Bradwell	
15/16.9.43	XII	HK189	29 Sqn	Me 410	off Beachy Head	F/O Jarris. Ofw Horst Muller and Uffz Wolfgang Dose in Me 410A-1 U5+AF of 15./KG2 off Beachy Head during a raid on Cambridge)
21.9.43	VI	'C'	605 Sqn	2 x Ju 88	W Skaggerak	S/L D. H. Blomely DFC-F/O J. Birrel
22.9.43	XI		85 Sqn	Me 410	off Orfordness	
26.9.43	II	DZ757	410 Sqn	Do 217	Dutch coast	F/L M. A. Cybulski DFC-F/O H. H. Ladbrook DFC
27/28.9.43	VI	'R'	605 Sqn	Do 217	Dedelsdorf	W/C B. R. O'B Hoare DSO DFC*-W/C J. F. Potter
2/3.10.43	XII		85 Sqn	2 x Do 217K	off Humber Est.	P/O T. Weisteen RNWAF-F/O F. French
6.10.43	XII		488 Sqn	Do 217M-1	Canterbury	
7/8.10.43	II	DZ260	157 Sqn	Me 410A-1	(Dam?) off Shoeburyness	F/Sgt Robertson
7/8.10.43	XII	'E'	85 Sqn	Me 410A-1 15m	off Hastings	F/L W. H. Maguire-Capt L. Lövestad RNWAF. Me 410A flown by Fw Georg Slodczyk and Uffz Fritz Westrich of 16./KG2 Westrich's body was picked up off Dungeness on 13 October and buried at sea.
7/8.10.43	XII		85 Sqn	Me 410A-1		F/L B. J. Thwaites-P/O W. P. Clemo DFM*. Me 410A flown by Fw Wilhelm Sohn and Uffz Günther Keiser of 14./KG2, which crashed at Ghent.
8/9.10.43	XII		85 Sqn	Ju 88S-1	off Foulness	F/O S. V. Holloway-W/O Stanton (Ju 88S-1 3E+US of 8./KG6)
8/9.10.43	XII		85 Sqn	Ju 88S-1 10m	S Dover	F/L E. N. Bunting-F/O F. French (Ju 88S-1 3E+NR of 7./KG6 into the sea 10 miles S of Dover at 2020 hrs; Fw W. Kaltwasser, Obgefr J. Jakobsen and Uffz J. Bartmuss were killed)
12.10.43	XII		151 Sqn	Me 410	Zrch/Little Warley	F/L E. N. Bunting-F/O F. French (Bunting and F/L C. P. Reed Me 410 U5+LF of 15./KG2) flown by FF (pilot) Ofw Lothar Bleich (k) and Uffz Ernst Greiecker (inj)
20.10.43	XII		29 Sqn	Fw 190A-1	South of Beachy Head	
20.10.43	XII		29 Sqn	Me 410A-1	over Channel	
20/21.10.43	XII	HK163	29 Sqn	Me 210 (prob)		F/L R. C. Pargeter-F/L R. L. Fell. Dungeness-Ashford
22.10.43	XII		29 Sqn	Fw 190A	East of Beachy Head	
30/31.10.43	XII	'G'	85 Sqn	Ju 88S-1 20m	SE of Rye	F/L R. L. T. Robb-F/O R. C. J. Bray. Ju 88S of III./KG6 either WNr 1404853E+KS, or WNr 140585 3E+AS.
30/31.10.43	XII	'J'	85 Sqn	Ju 88S-I 20m	S of Shoreham	F/O H. B. Thomas-W/O C. B. Hamilton
1.11.43	XII		29 Sqn	Ju 88S-1? Nr	Andover	
2/3.11.43	XII	'K'	85 Sqn	Fw 190	S of Canvey Island	F/O E. R. Hedgecoe-P/O J. R. Witham
5/6.11.43	II	HJ917	410 Sqn	Me 41010m	S of Dungeness	F/O C. F. Green-P/O E.G. White
6/7.11 .43	XII	'W'	85 Sqn	Fw 190A 2/3m	S of Hastings	
8/9.11.43	XII	HK163	29 Sqn	Me 410A-1	nr Beachy Head	F/O Russell-Steward-F/O G. K. Main
8/9.11.43	XII	'E'	85 Sqn	Me 410A-1	nr Eastbourne	S/L W. H. Maguire DFC-F/O W. D. Jones. WNr 10244 U5+BF of 15./KG2; Maj Wilhelm Schmitter Knight's Cross with Oak leaves, and his bordfunker, Uffz Felix Hainzinger, both killed when the a/c crashed into Shinewater Marsh).
8/9.11.43	XIII	HK367	488 Sqn	Me 410A-1	off Clacton	F/O Reed-P/O Bricker
9.11.43	VI	'O'	605 Sqn	Bf 110 20m	W Aalborg	S/L D. H. Blomely DFC-F/O J. Birrel
18/19.11.43II		HJ705		FIU Bf 110	Mannheim	W/C R. A. Chisholm DFC-F/L P. C. Clarke
20.11.43	II		157 Sqn	Ju 290 8 mls	N Estaca Point-	W/C J. A. Mackie-F/O L. Scholefield
20.11.43	II		157 Sqn	Ju 88 (prob)	15-40 mls N Cape Ortegal-	F/L Dyke-W/O C. R. Aindow
20/21.11.43	XIII	HK403	29 Sqn	Fw 190	Broadbridge Heath	F/L R. C. Pargeter-F/L R. L. Fell
20/21.11.43	XII	HK177	151 Sqn	Me 410	off Esparto Point	
22.11.43	II	HJ651	307 Sqn	Fw 200 120m	NE Shetlands	F/Sgt Jaworski
25/26.11.43	XII	HK228	488 Sqn	Me 410	off Calais	F/L P. F. L. Hall-F/O R. D. Marriott
9.12.43	II	EW-R	307 Sqn	Ju 88D-1		
10/11.12.43	II	DZ29	410 Sqn	3 x Do.217M-1 C	lacton-Dunkirk	F/O R. D. Schultz-F/O V. A. Williams (Do 217Ms of KG2)
10/11.12.43	II	HJ944	410 Sqn	Do 217	nr Chelmsford	
19/20.12.43	XIII	HK457	488 Sqn	Me 410A-1	nr Rye	P/O D.N. Robinson RNZAF
20/21.12.43	VI		418 Sqn	UEA	Delune a/f nr Metz	P/O J. T. Caine RCAF-P/O E. W. Boal RCAF
22/23.12.43	VI	HX812/T	418 Sqn	UEA (Prob)	Orleans a/f	F/L D. A. MacFadyen RCAF-F/L Wright
23/24.12.43	VI	'H'	605 Sqn	UEA	Fassberg airfield	F/L A. D. Wagner DFC-P/O E. T. Orring
2.1.44	XIII	HK461	488 Sqn	Me 410	Straits of Dover	
2/3.1.44	XIII	HK374	85 Sqn	Me 410	Sandwich	W/C J. Cunningham DSO* DFC*-F/L C. F. Rawnsley DFC DFM*
2/3.l.44	II		96 Sqn	Fw 190	Rye	F/L N. S. Head-F/O A. C. Andrews
4/5.1.44	XII		85 Sqn	Ju 88	off Dieppe	F/O E. R. Hedgecoe-P/O J. R. Witham DFM*
4/5.1.44	XIII		96 Sqn	Ju 888-1 3m	S of Hastings	W/C E. D. Crew DFC-W/O W. R. Croysdill
10/11.1	VI	'E'	605 Sqn	Ju 188 4m	E Chieves	W/C B. R. O'B Hoare DSO DFC*-W/O J. F. Potter
15/16.1.44	XIII		96 Sqn	Fw 190	Dungeness	S/L A. Parker-Rees-F/L Bennett
21/22.1.44	XII	HK197	29 Sqn	Fw 190	S of Beachy Head	
21/22.1.44	XII	HK168	29 Sqn	Ju 88	S of Beachy Head	
21/22.1.44	XII	'N'	85 Sqn	Ju 88	off Rye	
21/22.1.44	XIII	HK414	96 Sqn	Ju 88	Paddock Wood Stn	Sub-Lt J. A. Lawley-Wakelin-Sub-Lt H. Williams
21/22.1.44	XIII	HK425	96 Sqn	Ju 88	Tonbridge	
21/22.1.44	XIII	HK372	96 Sqn	2xJu 88 (Prob)	S of Bexhill	F/L N. S. Head-F/O A. C. Andrews
21/22.1.44	XII	HK193	151 Sqn	He 177A-3	nr Hindhead	W/O H. K. Kemp-F/Sgt J. R. Maidment. The first He 177 to be shot down over the British Isles, He 177A-5 Werk Nr 15747 of I/KG40, crashing at Whitmore Vale near Hindhead, Surrey. Only the tail assembly about 3ft forward of the fin survived relatively undamaged.
21/22.1.44	XI		85 Sqn	He 177A-3 6m	SE of Hastings	F/O C. K. Nowell-F/Sgt F. Randall (He 177 of 2./KG40)
21/22.1.44	XIII	HK380/Y	488 Sqn	Do 217M-1		F/L J. A. S. Hall-F/O J. P. W. Cairns 13m off Dungeness +Ju 88A-14 Sellindge, Kent
21/22.1.44	VI	'D'	418 Sqn	Bf 110 20m	SW Wunsdorf	1st Lt J. F. Luma US-F/O A. Eckert
27.1.44	VI		418 Sqn	Ju 88	Clermont-Farrand a/f	F/L J. R.F. Johnson RCAF
				Ju W34 x 2 10m	SE Bourges	" "

DATE	TYPE	SERIAL	SQN	ENEMY	A/C DETAILS	PILOT-NAVIGATOR/RADAR OP
27.1.44	VI		418 Sqn	Ju 88	Clermont-Farrand a/f	P/O J. T. Caine RCAF-P/O E. W. Boal RCAF
				Ju W34 x 2 10m	SE Bourges	" "
27.1.44	VI	'R'	418 Sqn	Fw 200	SE Avord a/f	F/L C. C. Scherf RAAF
28/29.1.44	XIII	HK432	410 Sqn	Ju 88		
28/29.1.44	XIII	HK397	96 Sqn	Ju 88	nr Biddenden	F/O S. A. Hibbert-F/O G. D. Moody
28/29.1.44	II			HJ941/X 141 Bf 109	nr Berlin	F/O H. E. White DFC-F/O M. S. Allen DFC
28/29.1.44	II	HJ644	239 Sqn	Bf 110	near Berlin	F/O N. Munro-F/O A. R. Hurley
30/31.1.44	II	HJ712/R	141 Sqn	Bf 110	near Berlin	F/L G. J. Rice-F/O J. G. Rogerson
30/31.1.44	II	HJ711/P	169 Sqn	Bf 110	Brandenburg area	S/L J. A. H. Cooper-F/L R. D. Connolly. Bf 110G-4 Wrk Nr 740081 D5+LB of Stab III/NJG3, which crashed at Werneuchen, 20km E of Berlin. Oblt Karl Loeffelmaan, pilot KIA. Fw Karl Bareiss, radar op and Ofw Oscar Bickert, both WIA, baled out.
3/4.2.44	XIII	'P'	85 Sqn	Do 217 20m	E The Naze	F/O H. B. Thomas-W/O C. B. Hamilton
3/4.2.44	XIII	HK463	410 Sqn	Do 217M-1	off Orfordness	F/O E. S. P. Fox RCAF-F/O C. D. Sibett RCAF
3/4.2.44	XIII	HK367	488 Sqn	Do 217	off Foulness Pt	F/Sgt C. J. Vlotman-Sgt J. L. Wood
4/5.2.44	VI		605 Sqn	UEA	(Prob) Chievres	W/C B. R. O'B Hoare DSO DFC*-W/C J. F. Potter
5/6.2.44	II	HJ707/B	169 Sqn	Bf 110	North Sea off England	P/O W. H. Miller-P/O F. C. Bone
8.2.44	II		157 Sqn	Bv.222	Lake Biscarosse	S/L H. E. Tappin DFC-F/O I. H. Thomas
12.2.44	II	DZ687/A	157 Sqn	Fw 200	Instep Criegal	F/O R. D. Doleman-F/L McAllister
12/13.2.44			29 Sqn	Me 410	off Fecamp	
13.2.44	VI	'X'	418 Sqn	He 177 3m	S Bordeaux	1st Lt J. F. Luma US-F/O C. Finlayson
13/14.2.44	XIII	HK426	96 Sqn	Ju 188	nr Whitstable	W/C E. D. Crew-W/O W. R. Croysdill
13/14.2.44	XIII	HK466		Ju 88S-1	nr Romford	S/L J. D. Somerville-F/O G. D. Robinson. Ju 88S-1 Z6+HH of I/KG66.
13/14.2.44	XIII	HK429	410 Sqn	Ju 188 10-20m	off E. Anglia	F/O R. D. Schultz DFC-F/O V. A. Williams DFC
15/16.2.44	II	DZ726/Z	141 Sqn	He 177	Berlin	F/O H. E. White DFC-F/O M. S. Allen DFC
18/19.2.44	VI	'S'	605 Sqn	Ju 188	Brussels-Melsbroek	F/O I. Williams-F/O F. Hogg
18/19.2.44	VI		418 Sqn	2 x Me 410	Juvincourt a/f	S/L R. A. Kipp DFC RCAF-F/L P. Huletsky RCAF
19.2.44	II		157 Sqn	1 Ju 290	on Instep patrol	F/L R. J. Coombs-F/O G. H. Scobie/F/L R. D. Doleman-F/L L. Scholefield
19/20.2.44	XIII	HK396	96 Sqn	Me 410	S of Dungeness	
20/21.2.44	II	DZ270	239 Sqn	Bf 110	near Stuttgart	F/O T. Knight-F/O D. P. Doyle
20/21.2.44	XVII	HK285	25 Sqn	Ju 188	E Essex.	P/O J. R. Brockbank-P/O D. McCausland. Ju 188E-1 U5+LN flown by Lt Ewald Bohe of 5/KG2. The Ju 188E, blazing furiously, commenced a deep death dive through the clouds to crash at Park Farm, Wickham St. Paul, Essex. The time of the 'kill', 2203 hrs, was logged; the first 'kill' attributed to a Mosquito NF.XVII. Bohe, Ofw Karl Bittgen (BO), Uffz Günther Güldner (BF) Uffz Wilhelm Pyttel (BM) and Gftr Hugo Schweitzer (BS) KIA.
20/21.2.44	XVII	HK255	25 Sqn	Do 217K-10 50m	E Lowestoft	F/L. J. Singleton DFC-F/O W. G. Haslam. Victim either Do 217K-1 U5+AR of 7./KG2, which was shot down at 2236 hrs Oblt Wolfgang Brendel, Fw Bruno Preker, Ofw Bruno Schneider and Uffz Heinz Grudßus all posted as 'Missing'. Or, Do 217M1 of 9.KG2. Uffz Walter Schmidt, (pilot): Uffz Fritz Frese; Ogefr Siegrfried Briesning and Ogefr Heinz Bodzien (all KIA).
20/21.2.44	XVII		85 Sqn	Ju 188	(Prob) Lydd	S/L B. J. Thwaites DFC-F/O W. P. Clemo DFM*
22/23.2.44	XVII	HK285	25 Sqn	He 177A-3	nr Yoxford.	F/L A. S. H. Baillie-F/O J. M. Simpson. He 177A-3 of 3./KG100. Ofw Wolfgang Ruppe (fflugzeugfuhrer (pilot), Uffz Ernst Werner bordschutze (gunner), Uffz Freidrich Beck, bordfunker (radio operator) Uffz Georg Lobenz, kampf beobachter (observer), Bordschutzen Obgefr Georg Markgraf, & Obgefr Bordwart (ground crew) KIA. Emil Imm, heck schutz (tail gunner) survived. (Baillie-Simpson KIA 12/13 June 44 on Night intruder to Deelen in XVII HK288, crashed at Eupen)
22/23.2.44	XVII	'Y'	85 Sqn	Me 410	off Dungeness	F/L B. Burbridge-F/L F. S. Skelton
22/23.2.44	XVII		85 Sqn	Me 410	35m S Dungeness	F/O E. R. Hedgecoe-P/O J. R. Witham
22/23.2.44	XIII	HK370	96 Sqn	Me 410	W Uckfield	S/L G. L. Caldwell- F/O Rawling
22/23.2.44	XIII	HK521	410 Sqn	Ju 88A-4	N Sea	S/L C. A. S. Anderson-F/Sgt C. F. A. Bodard
				Ju 188E-1	nr Rochford	" "
22/23.2.44	VI		605 Sqn		E/a Melsbroek	Flt Off B. F. Miller USAAF-F/O J. C. Winlaw RCAF
23/24.2.44	XVII		25 Sqn	Do 217	off E. Anglia	
23/24.2.44	XVII	HK293	25 Sqn	Ju 188	off Yarmouth	
23/24.2.44	XVII	'O'	85 Sqn	Ju 88	(Prob) Beachy Head	W/C J. Cunningham DSO* DFC*-F/O C. F. Rawnsley DFC DFM*
23 /24.2.44	VI		605 Sqn	Ju 88	Chievres airfield	F/O L. Williams-F/O F Hogg
24/25.2.44	VI	NS830/G	418 Sqn	Me 410	Würzburg a/F	F/L D. A. MacFadyen RCAF-F/L Wright
24/25.2.44	VI	'R'	418 Sqn	2 x Ju 88	Ansbach a/f	F/L C. C. Scherf RAAF
24/25.2.44	XIII	HK413	29 Sqn	Do 217M	Dorking Hills, Surrey	S/L C. Kirkland-F/O R. Raspin
24/25.2.44	XIII	HK515	29 Sqn	Ju 188E	Framfield, Sussex	F/O W. W. Provan-W/O Nichol
24/25.2.44	XIII	HK422	29 Sqn	Ju 88A-4+Ju 188		F/L R. C. Pargeter-F/L R. L. Fell. Ju 88A-4 of 8./KG6 was downed at Withyham, Sussex. Ju 188 fell at Thame?
24/25.2.44	XII	HK168	29 Sqn	Do 217M	Willesborough, Kent	F/O J. E. Barry-F/O G. Hopkins
				Me 410 (Prob)		" "
24/25.2.44	XII		29 Sqn	He 177 30-35 mls	S of Ford-Beachy Head area	F/L E. Cox-W/O Kershaw
24/25.2.44	XIII	HK370	96 Sqn	Me 410	off Beachy Head	F/L D. L. Ward-F/L E. D. Eyles Me 410 of 2/KG54 B3+CK; crew PoW
24/25.2.44	XIII	HK415	96 Sqn	He 177	(probable) Sussex	S/L A. Parker-Rees-F/L Bennett
24/25.2.44	XII	HK228	488 Sqn	He 177A-3	Lamberhurst.	F/L P. F. L. Hall-F/O R. D. Marriott. He 177A-3 of 3./KG).
24/25.2.44				FIU He 177	at Sea (Prob)	
25/26.2.44	II	DZ254/P	169 Sqn	Bf 110	SW Mannheim	F/L R. G. Woodman-F/O P. Kemmis
25/26.2.44	XVII	HK293	25 Sqn	Ju 188 off	Yarmouth	
26.2.44	VI		418 Sqn	Bo 242	St Yan	S/L H. D. Cleveland RCAF-F/Sgt F. Day DFM
26.2.44	VI	'F'	418 Sqn	Go 242/He 111Z	Dole/Tavaux a/f	F/L C. C. Scherf RAAF
29.2/1.3.44	XVII	'S'	85 Sqn	He 177	English Channel	
29.2/1.3.44	XIII	HK469	96 Sqn	Fw 190	off Dieppe	

DATE	TYPE	SERIAL	SQN	ENEMY	A/C DETAILS	PILOT-NAVIGATOR/RADAR OP
1/2.3.44	XIII	HK499	96 Sqn	Me 410 50m	SE Beachy Head	F/L J. W. Gough-F/L Matson
1/2.3.44	XIII	HK377 1	51 Sqn	He 177A-3	Cr. Hammer Wood	W/C G. H. Goodman-F/O W.F.E. Thomas
1/2.3.44	XIII	MM448	151 Sqn	Ju 188	at Sea	S/L Harrison
1/2.3.44	XIII	HK232	151 Sqn	Ju 88	at Sea	F/L Stevens
5.3.44	VI	LR364/E	613	He 177	Châteaudun	W/C J. R. D. Braham DSO DFC**-F/L W. J. Gregory DFC
5.3.44	VI	515 He 177			Bretigny? Melun	W/C E. F. F. Lambert DFC-F/L E. W. M. Morgan DFM. He 177A-3 Wrk.Nr. 332214 5J+RL of 3./KG100 crashed near Châteaudun/France. Lt Wilhelm Werner (pilot); Uffz Kolemann Schoegl (WOp); Uffz Gustav Birkebmaier (Flt. Eng); Uffz Alfred Zwieselsberger (AG); Uffz Josef Kerres (AG) all KIA.
5/6.3.44	VI	'J'	605 Sqn	Fw 190+2 Me 410	Gardelegen a/f	F/L A. D. Wagner DFC-F/O E. T. Orringe
6.3.44	VI	'Y'	418 Sqn	Fw 190	Pau	1st Lt J. F. Luma US-F/O C. Finlayson
14/15.3.44	XIII	HK406	96 Sqn	Ju 88A-4	Hildenborough	F/L N. S. Head-F/O A. C. Andrews
				Ju 188	Channel	F/L N S Head-F/O A C Andrews
14/15.3.44	XIII	HK466	410 Sqn	Ju 88	off East Coast	
14/15.3.44	XIII	HK521	410 Sqn	Ju 88A-4	Hildenborough	1st Lt A. A. Harrington US-Sgt D. G. Tongue (Ju 88A-14 B3+CK of 2./KG54
14/15.3.44	XIII	HK432	410 Sqn	Ju 88	off East Coast	
14/15.3.44	XIII	MM476/V	410 Sqn	Ju 188E-1		S/L E. N. Bunting DFC-F/L C. P. Reed DFC (Ju 188E-l U5+BM, flown by Lt Horst Becker of 4./KG6 broke up in the air and crashed in flames at White House Farm, Great Leighs, nr Chelmsford. Becker, Uffz G. Bartolain, Uffz A. Lange, Uffz G. Göcking and Ofw H. Litschke, killed)
14/15.3.44	XIII		488 Sqn	Ju 188E-1		
14/15.3.44	XIII	NK523	410 Sqn	Ju 88		S/L W. P. Green DFC-F/Sgt A. R. Grimstone DFM
14/15.3.44	XVII	HK255	25 Sqn	Ju 88	E Southwold	F/L J. Singleton DFC-W/O W. G. Haslam (Ju 88 of KG30)
18/19.3.44	II	HJ710/T	141 Sqn	2 x Ju 88	near Frankfurt	F/O H. E. White DFC-F/O M. S. Allen DFC
18/19.3.44	II	DZ761/C	141 Sqn	Ju 88	near Frankfurt	F/O J. C. N. Forshaw-P/O F. S. Folley
				Ju 88C-6		Wrk.Nr. 750014 R4+CS of 8./NJG2, shot down by Mosquito of 141 Squadron, crashed at Arheilgen near Darmstadt, 25km S of Frankfurt. Ofw Otto Müller (pilot); Ogefr Erhard Schimsal (radar op); Gefr Gunter Hanke (AG) all KIA.
19/20.3.44	XVII	HK255	25 Sqn	3 x Ju 88 50m	NNE Cromer	F/O J. Singleton DFC-F/O W. G. Haslam
19/20.3.44	XVII	HK278	25 Sqn	Do 217	NNW Cromer	F/L D. H. Greaves DFC-F/O T. M. Robbins DFC
		He 177A-3			off Skegness	" "
19/20.3.44	XII	HK119/ J 307 He 177			nr Humber Estuary	P/O J. Bruchoci-F/L Ziolkowski
19/20.3.44	XII		264 Sqn	Do 217M-1	Cr. Alford, S. Lincs	F/O R. L. J. Barbour-F/O G. Paine
19/20.3.44	VI	'U'	418 Sqn	Ju W34+Ju 52/3m	Luxeuil a/f	1st Lt J. F. Luma USA -F/O C. Finlayson
21/22.3.44	XVII	HK322	25 Sqn	Ju 188 35m	SE Lowestoft	F/L R.L. Davies-F/O B. Bent
			Ju 88 25m	SE Lowestoft	"	"
21/22.3.44	XIII	HK456	410 Sqn	Ju 88A-4	Latchington, Essex	F/O S. B. Huppert-P/O J. S. Christie (Ju 88A-4 of 4./KG30)
21/22.3.44	XIII	HK365	488 Sqn	Ju 188	at Sea	F/Sgt C. J. Vlotman-Sgt J. E. Wood
				Ju 88	nr Herne Bay	" "
21/22.3.44	XIII	HK380/Y	488 Sqn	Ju 88A-14		F/L J. A. S. Hall-F/O J. P. W. Cairns. Ju 88A-14 3E+GS of 8./KG6 from Melsbroek fell on Earls Colne airfield where the aircraft and one of its 500-kg HE bombs exploded, damaging three B-26 Marauders of the 323rd BG, US 9th AF.
21/22.3.44	XIII	MM476	488 Sqn	Ju 88A-4+Ju 188E1		S/L E. Bunting DFC-F/L C. P. Reed DFC. Ju 88A-4 4D+AT flown by Ofw Nikolaus Mayer of 9./KG30 from Varêlbusch. cr at Blacklands Hall, Cavendish, Suffolk where the bomber's fuel tanks exploded. Fw K. Maser and Fw Karl-Heinz Elmhorst had baled out and were taken prisoner. Mayer and Ofw W. Szyska died in the crash. Ju 188E-1 3E+BK of 2./KG6, flown by Lt G. Lahl hit the ground and exploded near Butlers Farm at Shopland, Essex shortly after 0110 hrs. Lahl, Uffz J. Fromm, Uffz R. Budrat and Obgefr Schiml were killed. Uffz E. Kosch baled out, injured, and was taken prisoner.
21/22.3.44	XVII	HK359	456 Sqn	Fw 190	off S Coast	
21/22.3.44	XVII	HK297/V	456 Sqn	Ju 88	Rye	F/L K. A. Roediger RAAF-F/L R. J. H. F. Dobson
21/22.3.44	XIII		604 Sqn	Ju 88A-4	Chelmsford	F/L J. C. Surman-F/Sgt C. E. Weston
22/23.3.44	II		239 Sqn	Bf 110	Frankfurt	S/L E. W. Kinchin-F/L D. Sellers
22/23.3.44	XIII	MM451	96 Sqn	Fw 190	SE of Pevensey	F/L N. S. Head-F/O A. C. Andrews
22/23.3.44	XVII	HK286/A	456 Sqn	Ju 88A-4	nr Arundel	W/C K. M. Hampshire DSO RAAF-F/L T. Condon
23/24.3.44	XII	VY-R	85 Sqn	Fw 190	off Hastings	S/L B. J. Thwaites DFC-F/O W. P. Clemo DFM*
24.3.44	VI	LR374/W	613 Sqn	Ju 52/3m 15m	S Aalborg	W/C J.R.D. Braham DSO DFC**-S/L Robertson
			Ju 64 6m	S Aalborg	"	" "
24/25.3.44	XVII	HK293	25 Sqn	Ju 188E-1		F/L V. P. Luinthune DFC-F/O A. B. Cumbers DFC (Ju 188E-1, U5+AN, flown by Uffz Martin Hanf of 5./KG2. Hanf and his four crew died in a watery grave 45 miles SE of Lowestoft
24/25.3.44	XII	'O'	85 Sqn	Ju 188	off Hastings	F/O E. R. Hedgecoe-F/O N. L. Bamford
24/25.3.44	XVII	'M'	85 Sqn	Do 217+Ju 88	Straits	F/L B. Burbridge-F/L F. S. Skelton
24/25.3.44	XVII	HK286/A	456 Sqn	Ju 88	Walberton, Sussex	W/C K. M. Hampshire DSO RAAF-F/L T. Condon
24/25.3.44	VI	'R'	605 Sqn	Bf 109	Stendal-Burg	W/C B. R. O'B Hoare DSO DFC*-F/O R. C. Muir
24/25.3.44	II	DD717/M	141 Sqn	Fw 190	Berlin	F/L H. C. Kelsey DFC*-F/O E. M. Smith DFC DFM
27/28.3.44	XIII	HK	425 Sqn/ 96 Sqn	Fw 190	at Sea	
27/28.3.44	XVII	HK260	219 Sqn	Ju 88	Hestar Combe	S/L Ellis-F/L Craig
27/28.3.44	XVII	HK286/A	456 Sqn	Ju 88A-4	nr Beer	W/C K. M. Hampshire DSO RAAF-F/L T. Condon
				Ju 88A-14	nr Ilminster	" " "
27/28.3.44	XVI	HK323		Ju 88	nr Beer	S/L B. Howard-F/O J. R. Ross
30/31.3.44	II	DZ661	239 Sqn	Ju 88	Nuremberg	F/Sgt J. Campbell DFM-F/Sgt R. Phillips. Ju 88C-6 Wrk.Nr. 360272 D5+ of 4./NJG3 crashed 10km SW of Bayreuth. Oblt Ruprecht Panzer (pilot) WIA; radar op & AG baled out safely.
4.4.44	VI	LR355/H	613 Sqn	Bucker 131	St Jean-d'Angely	W/C J. R. D. Braham DSO* DFC**-F/L W. J. Gregory DFC
5.4.44	VI	'F'	418 Sqn	Bf 110/Fw 58	Lyon	F/L C. C. Scherf RAAF

DATE	TYPE	SERIAL	SQN	ENEMY	A/C DETAILS	PILOT-NAVIGATOR/RADAR OP
6.4.44	XIII	MM448	151 Sqn	Ju 88	off St Nazaire	W/C G.H. Goodman-F/O W.F. Thomas DFM
11/12.4.44	II	DZ263	239 Sqn	Do 217	Aachen	S/L N. E. Reeves DFC*-W/O A. A. O'Leary DFC** DFM
12.4.44	VI		418 Sqn	Fw 190 12m	SE Verdun	F/L C. M. Jasper-F/L O. A. J. Martin DFC RCAF
13.4.44	VI	LR313/B	613 Sqn	He 111/Fw 58	Esbjerg/Aalborg	W/C J. R. D Braham DSO* DFC** F/L W. J. Gregory DFC
13/14.4.44	XIII	MM497	96 Sqn	Ju 88	nr Le Touquet	P/O Allen? DFM
13/14.4.44	XIII	HK497	96 Sqn	Ju 88	off Dungeness	S/L A. Parker-Rees-F/L Bennett
13/14.4.44	XIII	HK415	96 Sqn	Me 410	at Sea	S/L A. Parker-Rees-F/L Bennett
13/14.4.44	XIII			Me 410	off Dungeness	F/L D. L. Ward-F/L E. D. Eyles
14.4.44	VI		418 Sqn	2 x Ju 52/3m	Kattegat	P/O J. T. Caine RCAF-P/O E. W. Boal RCAF
14.4.44	VI		418 Sqn	2 x Ju 52/3m	Kattegat	S/L R. A. Kipp DFC RCAF-F/L P. Huletsky RCAF
16.4.44	VI		418 Sq		Caudron Goeland (+2 on ground). Luxeuil a/f	F/L C. M. Jasper-F/L O. A. J. Martin DFC RCAF
18/19.4.44	XVII	'B'	85 Sqn	Ju 88	Sandgate	F/L B. Burbridge-F/L F. S. Skelton
18/19.4.44	XVII	HK349/R	85 Sqn	Ju 188E-1	nr Dymchurch	W/C C. M. Miller DFC**-Capt L. Lövestad RNWAF (5./KG2 Ju 188E-1 U5+KN, piloted by Fw Helmuth Richter)
18/19.4.44	XIII	MM499	96 Sqn	Me 410-1	Brighton	W/C E. D. Crew DFC*-W/O W. R. Croysdill. Me 410A-1 of 1./KG51. Oblt Richard Pohl (k) Fw Wilhelm Schubert (k) KG2)?
18/19.4.44	XIII	MM495	96 Sqn	Ju 884-4	nr Margate	S/L W. P. Green DFC-F/Sgt A. R. Grimstone DFM
18/19.4.44	XIII		96 Sqn	Ju 88A-4	Cr. nr Cranbrook	P/O Allen-F/Sgt Patterson
18/19.4.44	XIII	MM551/X	488 Sqn	Ju 88 60m	E Bradwell	F/L J. A. S. Hall-F/O J. P. W. Cairns
18/19.4.44	XIII	MM813	488 Sqn	Ju 88	at Sea	W/O R. F. D. Bourke
18/19.4.44	XVII	HK237	25 Sqn	Me 410	off Southwold	F/L R. M. Carr-F/L Saunderson (Ju 188E-1 U5+DM of 4./KG2 flown by Hptm Helmuth Eichbaum.
18/19.4.44	XIII	MM456/D	410 Sqn	He 177		F/O S. B. Huppert-P/O J. S. Christie (He 177 of 3./KG100 flown by Fw Heinz Reis, which fell near Saffron Walden.
18/19.4.44	XIII		410 Sqn	Ju 88		F/O Snowdon-F/Sgt McLeod
18/19.4.44	XVII		456 Sqn	Me 410-1	nr Horsham	F/L C. L. Brooks-W/O R. J. Forbes
18/19.4.44	II	DD799	169 Sqn	Bf 110	Compiègne	F/O R. G. Woodman-F/O P. Kemmis
20.4.44	XVII	HK354	25 Sqn	Ju 188	at Sea	
20.4.44	XIII	HK480 2	64 Sqn	He 17740m	ENE Spurn Hd	F/O F/L H. J. Corré-P/O C. A. Bines
20.4.44	XIII	MM446/Q	151 Sqn	Ju W34	N Biscarosse	W/C G.H. Goodman-F/O W.F. Thomas
20/21.4.44	II	DD732/S	141 Sqn	Do 21	7 N of Paris	F/L H. E. White DFC*-F/L M. S. Allen DFC*. Either Do 217N-1 Wrk Nr 51517 of 5/NJG4, which crashed near Meulan N of Paris. Ofw Karl Kaiser, pilot WIA, and Uffz Johannes Nagel, radar op WIA, baled out; Gefr Sigmund Zinser (AG) KIA or Do 217E-5 Wrk.Nr. 5558 6N+EP of 6./KG100, crash place u/k. Fw Heinz Fernau (pilot), Hptm Willi Scholl (observer), Uffz Josef Bach (WOp), Ofw Fritz Wagner (flt eng), all MIA.
20/21.4.44	II		169 Sqn	Bf 110	Ruhr	F/L G. D. Cremer-F/O B. C. Farrell
22/23.4.44	II	W4085	169 Sqn	Bf 110	Bonn area	F/L R. G. Woodman-F/O P. Kemmis
22/23.4.44	II	W4076	169 Sqn	Bf 110	Köln	P/O W. H. Miller-P/O F.C. Bone
23/24.4.44	II	HJ712/R	141 Sqn	Fw 190	Flensburg	F/L G. J. Rice-P/O R. S. Mallett
23/24.4.44	XVII	HK355	125 Sqn	Ju 88A-14 4m	S Melksham	W/C E. G. Barwell DFC-F/L D. A. Haigh
23/24.4.44	XVII	HK299	125 Sqn		off SW Coast	
23/24.4.44	XVII	HK301	125 Sqn		off SW Coast	
23/24.4.44	XVII	HK286/A 456		Ju 88	in sea, nr Swanage	W/C K. M. Hampshire DSO RAAF-F/L T. Condon
25/26.4.44	XVII	'B'	85 Sqn	Me 410	S Selsey Bill	F/L B. Burbridge-F/L F. S. Skelton
25/26.4.44	XVII	HK299	125 Sqn	Do 217	at Sea	
25/26.4.44	XVII	HK353	456 Sqn	Ju 88	S Selsey	F/L K. A. Roediger RAAF-F/L R. J. H. F. Dobson
26.4.44	VI		515 Sqn	UEA	Gilze a/f	S/L H. B. Martin DSO DFC-F/O J. W. Smith
26.4.44	VI		515 Sqn	UEA	Le Culot a/f	W/O T. S. Ecclestone-F/Sgt J. H. Shimmon
26.4.44	VI		515 Sqn	UEA	Brussels Evere	" "
26/27.4.44	II	W4078	239 Sqn	Bf 110	Essen	F/O W. R. Breithaupt-F/O J. A. Kennedy DFM
26/27.4.44	XVII	HK286/A	456 Sqn	Ju 88	at Sea	
26/27.4.44	XVII	HK297/V	456 Sqn	Ju 88	at Sea	
26/27.4.44	XVII	HK264	456 Sqn	Ju 88	at Sea	
26/27.4.44	XVII	HK346/D	125 Sqn	Ju 188	S St Catherines Pt	W/C J. G. Topham DFC*-F/L H. W. Berridge DFC
27/28.4.44	II	W4076	169 Sqn	Bf 110	SE of Strasbourg	P/O P. L. Johnson-P/O M. Hopkins
27/28.4.44	II		239 Sqn	Bf 110/Ju 88	Montzon-Aulnoye	F/O R. Depper-F/O G. C. Follis
27/28.4.44	II	DD622	239 Sqn	Bf 110	Montzon-Aulnoye	S/L N. E. Reeves DFC*-W/O A. A. O'Leary DFC** DFM
27/28.4.44	VI		605 Sqn	UEA	(Prob) Couron	F/O R. E. Lelong RNZAF-P/O J. A. McLaren
27/28.4.44	VI		418 Sqn	UEA	Toul /Croix de Metz	S/L H D. Cleveland RCAF-F/Sgt F. Day DFM
28/29.4.44	XVII	HK346/D	125 Sqn	Ju 88	off Cherbourg	W/C J. G. Topham DFC*-F/L H. W. Berridge DFC
28/29.4.44	XVII	HK286/A	456 Sqn	Do 217(Prob)		W/C K. M. Hampshire DSO RAAF-F/L T. Condon (86m off Curmington)
29.4.44	VI	22 'H'		613 Fw	190 NW Poitiers	W/C J. R. D. Braham DSO* DFC**-F/L W.J. Gregory DFC
29/30.4.44	XII	'O'	406 Sqn	2 x Do 217	off Plymouth	W/C D. J. Williams DFC RCAF-F/O Kirkpatrick DFM
2.5.44	VI	'X'	418 Sqn	Ju 86P (+4 on ground) Griefswald		F/O C. C. Scherf RAAF
2/3.5.44	VI 418		Sqn 4x	Fw 190	SW Saarbourg	S/L R. A. Kipp DFC RCAF-F/L P. Huletsky RCAF
4.5.44	XIII	MM446/Q	151 Sqn	4 x He 111	Dijon area	W/C G. H. Goodman-F/O W.F. Thomas
6/7.5.44	VI		605 Sqn	Me 210	St Dizier airfield	W/C N. J. Starr DFC
7.5.44	VI	'G'	21 Sqn	Ju 188	Roskilde, 30m N Copenhagen	W/C J. R. D. Braham DSO* DFC**-F/L D. Walsh DFC
8/9.5.44	II	DD709	169 Sqn	Bf 110	Braine-le-Comte	S/L R. G. Woodman DFC-F/O P. Kemmis. Bf 110 of I./NJG4 crewed by Lt. Wolfgang Martstaller and his radar operator/air gunner who had taken off from Florennes at 0300 hrs shot down Lancaster ND587 of 405 Squadron before their combat with Woodman. The Bf 110 belly-landed in a field. Martstaller was KIA in a crash at St. Trond aerodrome in August 1944.
8/9.5.44	VI	605	Sqn	Ju 88	Creilsham	F/O R. E. Lelong RNZAF-P/O J. A. McLaren

DATE	TYPE	SERIAL	SQN	ENEMY	A/C DETAILS	PILOT-NAVIGATOR/RADAR OP
10/11.5.44	II	W4078	239 Sqn	Bf 110	Near Courtrai	F/O V. Bridges DFC-F/Sgt D. G. Webb DFM. Bf 110 3C+F1 Wrk Nr 740179 of I./NJG4, which crashed at Ellezelles, Belgium. Oblt Heinrich Schulenberg, pilot and Ofw Hermann Meyer, radar operator, baled out near Flobeq. Meyer was wounded and badly concussed and spent 3 weeks in hospital and 4 more weeks at home.
11/12.5.44	II	DZ726/Z	141 Sqn	Ju 88	N of Amiens	F/L H. E. White DFC*-F/L M. S. Allen DFC*
11/12.5.44	II	DZ240/H	141 Sqn	Ju 88	SW of Brussels	F/L L. J. G. Le Boutte-F/O R. S. Mallett. Ju 88 of 6./NJG2. Wilhelm Simonsohn, pilot, Uffz Franz Holzer, flight engineer and Uffz Günther Gottwick, wireless operator-air gunner all baled out. A/c crashed near Mechlen, north east of Brussels.
12.5.44	VI	NS885/B	21 Sqn	Fw 190	Herning, 10m WSW Aalborg	W/C J. R. D. Braham DSO* DFC**-F/L W. J. Gregory DFC
12/13.5.44	II	W4078	239 Sqn	Bf 110	Hasselt-Louvain	F/O W. R. Breithaupt-F/O J. A. Kennedy DFM
12/13.5.44	II	W4092	239 Sqn	Ju 88	Belgium	F/O V. Bridges DFC-F/Sgt D. G. Webb DFM. Ju 88C-6 Wrk Nr 750922 D5+ of 5./NJG3 crashed at Hoogcruts near Maastricht. Uffz Josef Polzer, Ogefr Hans Klünder, radar op, KIA. Gefr Hans Becker (AG) WIA.
14.5.44	VI		418 Sqn	He 111	Nancy-Croix Metz	F/L C. M. Jasper-F/L O. .A. J. Martin
14/15.5.44	XVII	HK325	125 Sqn	Ju 88	off Cherbourg	
14/15.5.44	XVII	HK318	125 Sqn	Me 410	N of Portland Bill	
14/15.5.44	III	'D'	406 Sqn	Ju 88	20m SE Portland	W/C R. C. Fumerton DFC*-
14/15.5.44	XVII	HK246	456 Sqn	Ju188A2	Cr. Larkhill, Wilts	F/O A. S. McEvoy-F/O M. N. Austin
14/15.5.44	XIII	MM551/X	488 Sqn	Ju 188A2		F/L J. A. S. Hall-F/O J. P W. Cairns (Henstridge, Somerset)
14/15.5.44	XIII	HK381	488 Sqn	Ju 88	at Sea	F/O R. W. Jeffs-F/O E. Spedding
				Do 217K1	Cr. nr Yeovilton	" "
14/15.5.44	XIII	HK527		604 Do 217	at Sea	F/L J. C. Surman-P/O C. E. Weston
14/15.5.44	XIII		264 Sqn	Ju 188	nr Alton	F/L C. M. Ramsey DFC-F/O J. A. Edgar DFM. Crew baled out and Edgar was killed.
14/15.5.44	VI		418 Sqn	He 177	Mont de Marson a/f	S/L R. A. Kipp DFC RCAF-F/L P. Huletsky RCAF
15/16.5.44	XIII		264 Sqn	Me 410	Over the Channel	S/L P. B. Elwell-F/O F. Ferguson
15/16.5.44	XIII	MM526 604		Ju 188	SW Isle of Wight	W/C M. H. Constable-Maxwell DFC
15/16.5.44	II	DZ748	169 Sqn	Bf 110/2 x Ju 88	Cuxhaven area	P/O W. H. Miller-P/O F.C. Bone
15/1 6.5.44	XVII	HK297	456 Sqn	Ju 884-4	Medstead	F/O D. W. Arnold-F/O J. B. Stickley
16.5.44	VI		418 Sqn	He 111	Kiel Bay area	S/L H. D. Cleveland RCAF-F/Sgt F. Day DFM (KIA)
16.5.44	VI	'T'	418 Sqn	He 111/Fw 190/ He 177/Hs 123/Ju 86P		S/L C. C. Scherf DFC* RAAF
19/20.5.44	VI		605 Sqn	He 219	Florennes	W/C N. J. Starr DFC-P/O J. Irvine
22/23.5.44	XVII	HK316	125 Sqn	Ju 188	S St Catherine's Pt	F/O K. T. A. O'Sullivan
22/23.5.44	XVII	HK252	125 Sqn	Ju 88	nr Southampton	
22/23.5.44	XVII	HK286/A	456 Sqn	Ju 88	S Isle of Wight	W/C K. M. Hampshire DSO DFC RAAF-F/L T. Condon
22/23.5.44	XVII	HK353/M	456 Sqn	Ju 88	nr Southampton	
22/23.5.44	II	DZ309	239 Sqn	Bf 110	Dortmund	F/L D. L. Hughes-F/O R. H. Perks
22/23.5.44	II		169 Sqn	Bf 110	Groningen area	W/C N. B. R. Bromley OBE-F/L P. V. Truscott. Bf 110G-4 Wrk Nr 720050 D5 of 3.NJG3 crashed at Hoogeveen S of Groningen. Fw Franz Müllebner (FF), Uffz Alfons Josten (radar op); Gefr Karl Rademacher (AG) all WIA & baled out.
24/25.5.44	II	DZ265	239 Sqn	Bf 110	Aachen	F/L D. J. Raby DFC-F/Sgt S. J. Flint DFM
24/25.5.44	II	DZ309	239 Sqn	Bf 110	Aachen	F/L D. L. Hughes-F/O R. H. Perks Bf 110G-4 Wrk Nr 730106 2Z+AR of 7./NJG6 poss. shot down by either of these two crews at 0230 hrs in forest between Zweifall & Mulartshuette SE of Aachen. Oblt Helmut Schulte (FF) baled out, Uffz Georg Sandvoss (radar op) KIA, Uffz Hans Fischer (AG) baled out. Bf 110G-4 Wrk.Nr. 720387 2Z+HR of 7./NJG6, poss. shot down by Raby/Flint or Hughes/Perks, crashed at 0235 hrs at the Wesertalsperre near Dipen, S of Aachen. Crew: Uffz Oskar Voelkel (pilot); Uffz Karl Hautzenberger (radar op); Uffz Günther Boehxne (AG) all baled out.
24/25.5.44	II	DZ297	239 Sqn	Ju 88	15m ESE of Bonn	F/O W. R. Breithaupt-F/O J. A. Kennedy DFM
24/25.5.44	II	DZ297	239 Sqn	Ju 88	15m ESE of Bonn	F/O W. R. Breithaupt-F/O J. A. Kennedy
24/25.5.44	XVII	HK345	219 Sqn	Ju 88 (Prob)		F/O D. T. Tull (55m E Orfordness)
27.5.44	XVII	HK346	456 Sqn	Me 410 nr	Cherbourg	
27/28.5.44	II	DD622	239 Sqn	Bf 110F	Aachen	S/L N. E. Reeves DFC*-P/O A. A. O'Leary DFC** DFM. Bf 110F Wrk.Nr. 140032 G9+CR of 7./NJG1 crashed at Spannum in Friesland Province/Neth. at 0115 hrs. Uffz Joachim Tank (pilot, 26), slightly wounded. Uffz Günther Schroeder (radar op, 19) & Uffz Heinz Elwers (AG, 24), KIA.
27/28.5.44	II	HJ941/X	141 Sqn	Bf 109	W of Aachen	F/L H. E. White DFC*-F/L M. S. Allen DFC*
28.5.44	XIII	HK462/E	410 Sqn	Ju 88	nr Lille	
28.5.44			605 Sqn	Ju 52	off Sylt	F/L Welch-F/L L. Page DFM
28/29.5.44	XVII	HK257	25 Sqn	Me 410	50m off Cromer	W/C C. M. Wight-Boycott DSO- F/L D. W. Reid (Me 410 Hornisse 9K+KP, of KG5I, flown by Fw Dietrich (KIA) and Uffz Schaknies (KIA)
29.5.44	XVII	HK286/A	456 Sqn	Me 410		
31.5/1.6.44	II	DZ297	239 Sqn	Bf 110	Near Trappes	F/O V. Bridges DFC-F/Sgt D. C. Webb DFM
31.5/1.6.44	II	DZ256/U	239 Sqn	Bf 110	West of Paris	F/L D. Welfare DFC*-F/O D. B. Bellis DFC*
1/2 6.44	II	DZ265	239 Sqn	Bf 110	Northern France	F/L T. L. Wright-P/O L. Ambery
1/2 6.44	XIX	'K'	85 Sqn	Ju 88	(Prob) Ipswich	F/L B. A. Burbridge DFC-F/L F. S. Skelton DFC
3/4 6.44	XVII	HK248	219 Sqn	He 219	Dutch Islands	F/O D. T. Tull
5/6.6.44	VI		605 Sqn	Me 410	7m SE Evreux a/f	F/O R. E. Lelong RNZAF-P/O J. A. McLaren
5/6.6.44	XIII		409 Sqn	Ju l88	{Prob} S Coast	F/O H. F. Pearce-F/O Moore
5/6.6.44	II	DD789	239 Sqn	Ju 88	off Friesians	F/O W. R. Breithaupt-F/O J. A. Kennedy DFM. Ju 88 G-1 Wrk.Nr. 710454 of 5./NJG3, crashed 20km N of Spiekeroog. Uffz Willi Hammerschmitt (pilot), Uffz Friedrich Becker (radar op) and Fw Johannes Kuhrt (AG) all KIA.
5/6.6.44	II	DZ256/U	239 Sqn	Bf 110	North of Aachen	F/L D. Welfare-F/O D. B. Bellis. Poss. Bf 110 Wrk.Nr. 440272 G9+NS of 8./NJG1 shot down at great height, crashed at 0054 hrs on Northern beach of Schiermonnikoog. Uffz Adolf Stuermer (22), pilot, KIA; Uffz Ludwig Serwein (21) Radar Op MIA; Gefr Otto Morath (23) AG, KIA.
6/7.6.44	VI		418 Sqn	3 x Ju 52 & 1 Ju 188	Orléans & Châteaudun airfields, France.	F/L S. H. R. Cotterill DFC RCAF-Sgt McKenna

DATE	TYPE	SERIAL	SQN	ENEMY	A/C DETAILS	PILOT-NAVIGATOR/RADAR OP
6/7.6.44			29 Sqn	Ju 52/3m & UEA	over Coulommiers	F/L G. E. Allison-F/O R. G. Stainton
6/7.6.44	XVII	HK286/A	456 Sqn	He 177	3m S Barfleur?	W/C K. M. Hampshire DSO DFC RAAF-F/L T. Condon
6/7.6.44	VI		605 Sqn	Ju 88	Orleans-Bricy a/f	F/L E. L. Williams DFC*-F/O S. Hatsell
6/7.6.44	VI	HR155/X	418 Sqn	Ju 52/	3m N Coulommiers a/f	F/L D. A. MacFadyen DFC RCAF-F/L Wright
7/8.6.44	XVII	HK319	219 Sqn	Me 410 10m	E Harwich	F/O D. T. Tull
7/8.6.44	XVII	HK248	219 Sqn	Ju l88	15m ESE Harwich	W/C P L. Burke AFC*
7/8.6.44	XVII	HK290/J	456 Sqn	2 x He 177	off Normandy coast	S/L B. Howard-F/O J. R. Ross
7/8.6.44	XVII	HK302	456 Sqn	He 177	off Normandy	P/O Hodgen
7/8.6.44			29 Sqn	Ju 188 Ju 88	S of Paris	F/L J. Barry-S/L Porter
7/8.6.44			29 Sqn	UEA	Dreux	F/O F. E. Pringle-P/O W. Eaton
7/8.6 3.44	XVII	HK354	25 Sqn	Me 410	nr Happisburgh	F/L D. H. Greaves DFC-F/O T. M. Robbins DFC
8/9.6.44	XIII	MM500	604 Sqn	Bf 110	NE of Laval	F/L J. C. I. Hooper DFC-F/O Hubbard DFM
8/9.6.44	II	DD741	169 Sqn	Do 217	Paris area	W/C N. B. R. Bromley OBE-F/L P. V. Truscott. Poss. Do 217K-3 Wrk.Nr. 4742 6N+OR of Stab III./ KG100 claimed in Paris area but crash-place u/k. Oblt Oskar Schmidtke (pilot); Uffz Karl Schneider (Observer); Uffz Helmuth Klinski (WOp); Uffz Werner Konzett (flt. eng), all MIA.
8/9.6.44	II	DD303/E	141 Sqn	UEA	Rennes	F/O A. C. Gallacher DFC-W/O G. McLean DFC
8/9.6.44			29 Sqn	Ju 88		F/O Wigglesworth-Sgt Blomfield
9/10.6.44	XII	MK403	29 Sqn	Ju 88	8m S Beachhead	F/L R. C. Pargeter-F/L R. L. Fell
9/10.6.44			29 Sqn	Ju l88		Lt Price
9/10.6.44	XVII	HK353/M	456 Sqn	He 177	off Cap Levy	S/L R. B. Cowper DFC RAAF-F/L W. Watson
			Do 217	off Cap de la Hague	"	"
9/10.6.44	XIII	MM460	409 Sqn	Ju 188	40m SE Le Havre	S/L R. S. Jephson-F/O C. D. Sibbett
9/10.6.44			410 Sqn	Ju l88		F/O Snowden-Lt Wilde
10/11.6.44	XIII		264 Sqn	Ju 88/Fw l90 (Prob)		F/O F/L H. J. Corré-P/O C. A. Bines
10/11.6.44	XIII	MM453	409 Sqn	Ju l88		F/O R. L. Fullerton-F/O Castellan
10/11.6.44			409 Sqn	2 x Ju 88		P/O C. J. Preece-F/O Beaumont
10/11.6.44	XVII	HK249/B	456 Sqn	He l77	(Prob) 40m S Brighton	S/L G. E. Howitt DFC-F/L G. Irving DFC
10/11.6.44	XIII	MM547	409 Sqn	Fw 190		F/Sgt S.H. J. Elliott-F/l R. A. Miller
10/11.6.44	VI		605 Sqn	Ju l88	SE Coulommiers	F/O R. E. Lelong RNZAF-P/O J. A. McLaren
10/11.6.44	VI		605 Sqn	Me 410	Châteaudun	W/C N. J. Starr DFC
11/12.6.44	II	DZ256/U	239 Sqn	Bf 110	North of Paris	F/L D. Welfare DFC-F/O D. B. Bellis DFC*
11/12.6.44	XIII	MM555	409 Sqn	Ju 188	Over France	F/O K. Livingstone
11/12.6.44	XIII	MM523	409 Sqn	Do 217E	Over France	F/O A.W. Sterrenberg
11/12.6.44	II	DZ256/U	239 Sqn	Bf 110	North of Paris	F/L D. Welfare DFC*-F/O D. B. Bellis DFC*
11/12.6.44	XIX	MM642/R	85 Sqn	Bf 110	10m NE Melum a/f	W/C C. M. Miller DFC**-F/O R. O. Symon DFC
12/13.6.44	XIII	HK512	264 Sqn	Ju 188	over beaches	F/L M. M. Davison DFC-F/O A. C. Willmott DFC
12/13.6.44	XIII	HK475	264 Sqn	Ju 188	over beaches	F/L Beverley-F/O Sturley
12/13.6.44	XVII	HK286/A	456 Sqn	Ju 88		W/C K. M. Hampshire DFC DSO RAAF-F/L T. Condon
12/13.6.44	XIX	MM630/E	157 Sqn	Ju 188	Fôret De Compiègne	F/L J. G. Benson DFC-F/L L. Brandon DFC
12/13.6.44	XIX		85 Sqn	Bf 110	near Paris	F/L M. Phillips-F/L D. Smith
12/13.6.44	XIII	MM526	604 Sqn	He 177	l5m NE Cherbourg	F/L R. A. Miller DFC-P/O P. Catchpole
12/13.5.44	XIII	MM500	604 Sqn	Ju 88		F/L J. C. I. Hooper DFC-F/O Hubbard DFM
12/13.6.44	VI		605 Sqn	Ju 88	(Prob) Chievres airfield	F/L E. L. Williams DFC-F/O S. Hatsell
12/13.6.44	XIII	HK366/O	410 Sqn	2 x Do 217	Over Beachhead	W/O W. F. Price
12/13.6.44	XIII	HK459/A	410 Sqn	He 177	Over Channel	P/O L. J. Kearney-F/O Bradford
12/13.6.44	XIII	HK466/J	410 Sqn	Ju 88	10m off Le Havre	F/O R. L. Snowden-F/O Wilde
12/13.6.44	XIII	MM476/V	488 Sqn	Ju 88	Caen-Bayeux	S/L E. N. Bunting DFC*-F/L C. P. Reed DFC*
13/14.6.44	XIII	HK502	264 Sqn	He 177	Over Channel	S/L I. H. Cosby-F/L E. R. Murphy
13/14.6.44	XIII	MM560/F	409 Sqn	He 177	10m E of Le Havre	W/C J. W. Reid-F/L J. W. Peacock
13/14.6.44	II	DZ254/P	169 Sqn	Ju 88	Near Paris	W/O L. W. Turner-F/Sgt F. Francis
14/15.6.44	XVII	HK282	456 Sqn	He 177	off Fecamp	
14/15.6.44	XIII		410 Sqn	Ju 88		S/L I. A. March-F/L Eyolfson
14/15.6.44			604 Sqn	Fw 190	(Prob) Carentan	F/O Wood-F/L Elliott
14/15.6.44			604 Sqn	He 177		F/L F. C. Ellis
14/15.6.44	VI		418 Sqn	He 111	S end Bagenkop Isle	S/L R. A. Kipp DFC RCAF-F/L P. Huletsky RCAF
14/15.6.44	XIII	HK476/O	410 Sqn	Mistel (Mistletoe) (Ju 88A-4/		F/L W. G. Dinsdale RCAF-P/O J. E. Dunn RCAF piggy-back Bf 109F-4 guided bomb 25 miles SE of Caen
14/15.6.44	XVII	HK356/D	456 Sqn	Ju 88	at Sea	S/L R. B. Cowper DFC RAAF-F/L W. Watson
14/15.6.44	XIII	HK502	264 Sqn	Mistel (Mistletoe) (Ju 88A-4/		F/L H. J. Corré-P/O C. A. Bines piggy-back Bf 109F-4 guided bomb off Normandy
14/15.6.44	XIII	MM513/D	488 Sqn	Ju 88	10m SW St Lô	F/O P. F. L. Hall-F/O R. D. Marriott
14/15.6.44	VI		418 Sqn	Bf 110	Avord airfield	S/L. R. Bannock RCAF-F/O R. R. Bruce
14/15.6.44	II	DZ240/H	141 Sqn	Me 410	North of Lille	W/O H. W. Welham-W/O E. J. Hollis
14/15.6.44	XIX	MM671/C	157 Sqn	Ju 88	Near Juvincourt	F/L J. Tweedale-F/O L. I. Cunningham
14/15.6.44	XIX	'Y'	85 Sqn	Ju 188	SW Nivelles	F/L B. A. Burbridge DFC-F/L F. S. Skelton DFC. Ju 188 flown by Maj Wilhelm Herget, Kommandeur I./ NJG4. By the end of the war 58 of the 73 victories Herget gained were at night.
14/15.6.44	XIX	'J'	85 Sqn	Ju 88	near Creil	F/L H. B. Thomas-P/O C. B. Hamilton
14/15.6.44	XVII	HK315	219 Sqn	Ju 88	Harwich area	F/L M. J. Gloster DFC-F/L J. P. Oswold DFC
15/16.6.44	XIX	'C'	85 Sqn	Bf 110	St Trond a/f	S/L F. S. Gonsalves-F/L B. Duckett. Bf 110 Wrk.Nr. 5664 G9+IZ of 12./NG1 crashed 9km W of Tongres (between St. Trond and Maastricht). Uffz Heinz Bärwolf (pilot, injured, baled out); Uffz Fischer (WOp/Radar op) baled out. Ogfr Edmund Kirsch (23, AG) KIA.
15/16.6.44	XIX	MM671/C	157 Sqn	Ju 88	Creil-Beauvais	F/L J O. Mathews-W/O A. Penrose

DATE	TYPE	SERIAL	SQN	ENEMY	A/C DETAILS	PILOT-NAVIGATOR/RADAR OP
15/16.6.44	VI		605 Sqn	Bf 1100/Fw 190	Le Culot	F/L E. L. Williams DFC-F/O S. Hatsell
16/17.6.44	XIII		410 Sqn	Ju 88	SE of Valongues	F/O I. S. Girvan-Lt Cardwell
16/17.6.44	XVII	HK344	219 Sqn	Me 410		F/O Faraday
16/17.6.44	XIII		29 Sqn	UEA & a Do 217		F/O Crone
16/17.6.44	XIII		264 Sqn	Ju 188	or La Haye de Pais	F/L M. M. Davison DFC- F/L A.C. Willmott DFC
16/17.6.44	II	W4076	169 Sqn	Ju 88	Pas de Calais	F/O W. H. Miller-F/O F. Bone. Poss. Ju 88 Wrk.Nr. 710590 of 1./NJG2 crashed in Pas de Cancale/France. Hptm Herbert Lorenz (pilot), Fw Rudolf Scheuermann (radar op.) and Flg Harry Huth (AG) all KIA.
16/17.6.44	XIII	MM476/V	488 Sqn	Fw 190	St Lô	S/L E. N. Bunting DFC*-F/O C. P. Reed DFC*
17/18.6.44	XIX		85 Sqn	Bf 110	Eindhoven	F/O P. S. Kendall DFC*-F/L C. R. Hill. Bf 110 of NJG1 shot down at 0230 hrs & cr. at Soesterberg airfield. Müller & 2(?) others KIA.
17/18.6.44	II	W4092	239 Sqn	Ju 88	Near Eindhoven	F/O G. F. Poulton-F/O A. J. Neville. Ju 88G-1 Werke Nr 710866 R4+NS of 8./NJG2 which crashed at Volkel airfield. Lt Harald Machleidt (pilot) (k). Uffz Kurt Marth (radar op) WIA, Gefr Max Rinnerthaler (AG) KIA.
17/18.6.44	XIII	HK466/J	410 Sqn	Ju 188	6m off Le Havre	F/L C. E. Edinger-F/O C. C. Vaessen
17/18.6.44	XIII	MM499/C	410 Sqn	Ju 188	nr Caen	S/L I. A. March-F/L Eyolfson
17/18.6.44	XIII	MM439	488 Sqn	Fw 190	Quinville area	F/O D. N. Robinson RNZAF-F/O K. C. Keeping
17/18.6.44	XIII	MM558/S	488 Sqn	Ju 88	30m S Radox Mather	F/L P. F. L. Hall-F/O R. D. Marriott
17/18.6.44	XVII	HK250	219 Sqn	Ju 88 (Prob)	18m N Ostend	F/L G. R. I. Parker DSM-W/O D. L. Godfrey
17/18.6.44	XIII		264 Sqn	Ju 88	Domtront-Argentan	F/L M. M. Davison DFC-F/L A. C. Willmott DFC
17/18.6.44	XIII	HK473	264 Sqn	Fw 190		F/L I. H. Cosby-F/L E. R. Murphy
17/18.6.44	XIII		264 Sqn	2 x Ju 188	Over Beachhead	F/O J. P. de L. Brooke-P/O J. Hutchinson
17/18.6.44	XIII		264 Sqn	Ju 188		F/O J. C. Duffy-F/Sgt Newhouse
17/18.6.44	XIII	HK428	29 Sqn	Ju 88		F/Sgt Johnson
18/19.6.44	XIII	HK470/X	410 Sqn	Ju 88	Over Beachhead	F/O G. E. Edwards-F/Sgt Georges
18/19.6.44	XIII	MM571/Y	410 Sqn	Ju 88	Vire area	1st Lt .A. A. Harrington USAAF-Sgt D.G. Tongue
18/19.6.44	XVII	HK346/D	125 Sqn	2 x Ju 88	Beachhead area	W/C J. G. Topham DFC*-F/O H. W. Berridge DFC
19/20.6.44			488 Sqn	Fw 190	S. Falaise	P/O C. J. Vlotman-F/Sgt Wood
19/20.6.44	XIII		264 Sqn	Ju 88	Over Channel	S/L F. J. A. Chase-F/O A. P. Watson
20/21.6.44	XIII	MM573/B	409 Sqn	Ju 88 (Prob)		F/L M. C. Taylor-W/O Mitchell
20/21.6.44	XIII		29 Sqn	Bf 110	Coulanniers	F/L Price-S/L Armitage
20/21.6.44	XIII		29 Sqn	Ju l88 (Prob)	Bourges	F/Sgt Benyon-F/Sgt Pearcy
21/22.6.44	II	DZ2950	239 Sqn	He 177	Ruhr	F/O R. Depper-F/O R. G. C. Follis
21/22.6.44	XIII	MM552	604 Sqn	Ju l88 (Prob)	SSE Ventnor IoW	F/L P. V. G. Sandeman-F/O W. H. R. A. Coates
21.6.44	VI	PZ203/X	515 Sqn	Bf 110G-4		S/L P. W. Rabone DFC-F/O F. C. H. Johns. Bf 110G Wrk Nr 440076G9+NS of 8./NJG1, which had just taken off from Eelde a/f, shot down at 1519 hrs. Uffz Herbert Beyer (21) pilot, Uffz Hans Petersmann (21) radar op, & Ogfr Franz Riedel (20) AG, all KIA.
22/23.6.44			488 Sqn	Ju l88	E.Bayeux	P/O O. J. McCabe-W/O Riley
22/23.6.44	XVII	HK23	125 Sqn	3 x Ju 88	at Sea	F/O W. J. Grey
22/23.6.44	XVII	HK262	125 Sqn	2 x Ju 88	at Sea	Sub Lt H. J. Petrie RNZVR-Lt F. A. Noyes RNZVR
22/23.6.44	XIII	MM527	604 Sqn	Ju 88	NW Le Havre	F/O J. S. Smith-F/O Roberts
22/23.6.44	XIII		264 Sqn	Ju 88	N Rouen	F/O J. C. Trigg-F/L Smith
23/24.6.44	XVII	HK257	25 Sqn	Ju 88	NW Orfordness	W/C C. M. Wight-Boycott DSO-F/O D.W. Reid
				Ju 188F1	Cr. Chillesford	" "
23/24.6.44	XIII	MM554?	409 Sqn	Ju 188		F/O W. H. Vincent-F/L Thorpe
23/24.6.44	XIX	'Y'	85 Sqn	Ju 88		F/L B. A. Burbridge DFC-F/L F.S. Skelton DFC
23/24.6.44	XIII	HK500/T	410 Sqn	Jul88	15m NW Beachhead	W/O R. Jones-W/O Gregory
23/24.6.44	XIII		264 Sqn	2 x Fw 19011 (Prob)		S/L P. B. Elwell-F/O F. Ferguson
24.6.44	XVII	HK262	125 Sqn	Ju 88	Isle de St Marcouf	
24.6.44	XVII	HK310	125 Sqn	Ju 88	W of Le Havre	
24/25.6.44	II	DD759/R	239 Sqn	Ju 88	Paris-Amiens	F/L D. Welfare-F/O D. B. Bellis
24/25.6.44	XIII	MM554?	409 Sqn	Ju 188		W/O W. G. Kirkwood-W/O Matheson
24/25.6.44	XIII	MM466	488 Sqn	Me 410	20m SW Bayeux	F/L G. E. Jameson DFC RNZAF-F/O A. N. Crookes
24/25.6.44	XVII	HK355	125 Sqn	Ju 88	W St Marcouf	W/C E. G. Barwell DFC-F/L D. A. Haigh
25/26.6.44	XVII	HK287	125 Sqn	Ju 88	E Le Havre area	F/L Simcock
25/26.6.44	XIII	MM518	409 Sqn	Ju 188/Do 217		F/L D. T. Steele-F/O Storrs
27.6.44	VI		418 Sqn	Ju 88	2m N Rostock	F/L C. M. Jasper-F/L O. A. J. Martin DFC RCAF
27/28.6.44	II	HJ911/A	141 Sqn	Ju 88	Cambrai	S/L G. J. Rice-F/O J. G. Rogerson
27/28.6.44		DZ240/H	141 Sqn	Ju 88	S of Tilburg	W/O H. Welham-W/O E. Hollis. Poss Ju 88G-1 Wrk.Nr 710455 of 4./NJG3, crashed at Arendonk/Belgium. Uffz Eügen Wilfert (pilot), KIA; Ogefr Karl Martin (radar op.), KIA; Gefr Rudolf Scherbaum (AG), KIA.
27/28.6.44	II	DD759/R	239 Sqn	Me 410	E of Paris	F/L D. Welfare-F/O D. B. Bellis
27/28.6.44	II		239 Sqn	Fw 190	Near Brussels	W/C P. M. J. Evans-F/O R. H. Perks DFC
27/28.6.44	II	DD749	239 Sqn	Ju 88	Near Brussels	F/L D. R. Howard-F/O F. A. W Clay
27/28.6.44	VI	PZ188/J	515 Sqn	Ju 88	Eindhoven	P/O C. W. Chown RCAF-F/Sgt D. G. N. Veitch. Ju 88 Wrk Nr. 300651 B3+LT of 9./NJG54 during landing approach at Welschap (after a mine-laying operation in the invasion area) at 0213 hrs. The Ju 88 crashed into a house, killing 3 children and Uffz Gotthard Seehaber, pilot, Gefr Kurt Voelker, Ogefr Walter Oldenbruch & Ogefr Hermann Patzel.
27/28.6.44	XIII		264 Sqn	Ju l88	Seine estuary	F/L Turner-F/O T. V. Arden
27/28.6.44	II	HJ911/A	141 Sqn	Ju 88	Cambrai	S/L G. J. Rice-F/O J. G. Rogerson
27/28.6.44		DZ240/H	141 Sqn	Ju 88	S of Tilburg	W/O H. Welham-W/O E. Hollis. Poss. Ju 88G-1 Wrk.Nr 710455 of 4./NJG3, crashed at Arendonk/Belgium. Uffz Eügen Wilfert (pilot), KIA; Ogefr Karl Martin (radar op.), KIA; Gefr Rudolf Scherbaum (AG), KIA.
28/29.6.44		VI NT150	169 Sqn	Bf 110	nr Mucke	P/O H. Reed-F/O S. Watts
28/29.6.44	XIII	MM589	409 Sqn	Ju 188		W/O W. G. Kirkwood-W/O Matheson
28/29.6.44	XIII	MM466	488 Sqn	Ju 88	10m NE Caen	F/L G. E. Jameson DFC RNZAF-F/O A. N. Crookes
29/30.6.44	XIII		264 Sqn	Ju 188	Seine Bay	F/O R. Barbour-F/O G. Paine

DATE	TYPE	SERIAL	SQN	ENEMY	A/C DETAILS	PILOT-NAVIGATOR/RADAR OP
30.6.44	VI	PZ203/X	515 Sqn	He 111	Jägel/Schleswig	S/L P. W. Rabone DFC-F/O F. C. H. Johns
30.6.44	VI	PZ188/J	515 Sqn	Ju 34		P/O C. W. Chown RCAF-F/Sgt D. G. N. Veitch
30.6/1.7.44	VI	DZ265	239 Sqn	Ju 88	Le Havre	F/L D. J. Raby DFC-F/Sgt S. J. Flint DFC Probably Ju 88 Wrk.Nr. 711114 of 5./NJG2 crashed SE of Dieppe/ France. Uffz Erich Pollmer WIA. Other crew details u/k.
2/3.7.44	XIII	MM526	604 Sqn	Ju 188	15m W of Le Havre	F/L R. A. Miller DFC-P/O P. Catchpole
2/3.7.44	XIII	MM465	604 Sqn	Ju 88	10m N Ouistreham?	W/C M. H. Constable-Maxwell DFC-F/L Quintin
2/3.7.44			488 Sqn	Ju l88		W/O T. G. C. Mackay
2/3 7.44	XIII	MM517	604 Sqn	Ju 88	15m N of Le Havre	S/L D. C. Furse-F/L J. H. Downes
3/4 7.44	XIII	MM447	410 Sqn	Ju 188	NE Raz de la Pierce	F/L C. E. Edinger RCAF-F/O C.C. Vaessen
3/4 7.44	XIII	MM570/B	410 Sqn	Ju 188/Me 410		F/L S. B. Huppert-F/O J. S. Christie
3/4 7.44	XIII	HK479	264 Sqn	Ju 188		S/L I. H. Cosby-F/L E. R. Murphy
4/5 7.44	XVII	HK325	125 Sqn	Do 217 (Poss Ju 188)	Le Havre	S/L L. W. G. Gill-F/O D. C. Hutchins
4/5.7.44	XVII	HK356/D	456 Sqn	He 177	30m S Selsey Bill	S/L R. B. Cowper DFC RAAF-F/L Watson
4/5.7.44	XVII	HK249/B	456 Sqn	He 177	N of Cherbourg	
4/5.7.44	XVII	HK282	456 Sqn	He 177	In Channel	
4/5.7.44	XVII	HK282	456 Sqn	Do 217	at Sea	
4/5.7.44	II		169 Sqn	Bf 110	Villeneuve	F/L J .S. Fifield-F/O F. Staziker
4/5.7.44	XIII		264 Sqn	Ju 88/Me 410	Normandy	F/L C. M. Ramsay DFC-F/L D. J. Donnet DFC
4/5.7.44	II	DZ298	239 Sqn	Bf 110	NW Paris	S/L N. E. Reeves DFC*-P/O A. A. O'Leary DFC** DFM
4/5.7.44	VI	PZ163/C	515 Sqn	Ju 88	Near Coulommiers	W/O R. E. Preston-F/Sgt F. Verity
4/5.7.44	II	DD725/G	141 Sqn	Me 410	Near Orleans	F/L J. D. Peterkin-F/O R. Murphy
5/6.7.44	II	DZ298	239 Sqn	Bf 110	near Paris	S/L N. E. Reeves DFC*-W/O A. A. O'Leary DFC** DFM
5/6.7.44	II	W4097	239 Sqn	2 x Bf 110	Paris	S/L J. S. Booth DFC*-F/O K. Dear DFC Bf 110G-4 110028 C9+HK of 2./NJG5, which crashed near Compiègne, is believed to be one of the two aircraft shot down by Booth and Dear. Lt Joachim Hanss, pilot and Fw Kurt Stein, bordschütz, were killed. Uffz Wolfgang Wehrhan, radar operator, wounded.
5.7.44	XVII	HK312/G	456 Sqn	He 177	In Channel	
5/6.7.44	XIII	MM552	604 Sqn	Me 410	15m SW of Caen	W/O J. E. Moore-W/O J. A. Hogg
5/6.7.44	VI	NT121	169 Sqn	Ju 88	South of Paris	F/O P. G. Bailey-F/O J. O. Murphy. Ju 88 Wrk.Nr. 751065 R4+ of 5./NJG2 crashed near Chartres/France. Ofw Fritz Farrherr (pilot) KIA; Gefr Josef Schmid (Radar op) WIA baled out; Ogefr Heinz Boehme (AG) KIA.
5/6.7.44	XIII		264 Sqn	Ju l88		F/O Trigg-F/L G. E. Smith
7/8.7.44	XIII	MM504	409 Sqn	Ju l88		F/O Pearce-P/O Smith
7/8.7 44	II	HJ911/A	141 Sqn	Bf 110	NW of Amiens	S/L G. J. Rice-F/O J. G. Rogerson. Poss. Bf 110G-4 Wrk.Nr. 730006 D5+ of 2./NJG3 crashed 5km W of Chièvres/ Belgium. Pilot u/k & Gefr Richard Reiff WIA, baled out. Ogefr Edmund Hejduck KIA.
7/8.7.44	II	DD789	239 Sqn	Fw 190	Pas de Calais	W/C P. M. J. Evans-F/L T. R. Carpenter
7/8.7.44	II	DZ29S8	239 Sqn	Bf 110	Near Charleroi	F/L V. Bridges DFC-F/Sgt D. G. Webb DFM
7/8.7.44	XIII		410 Sqn	Me 410	nr Paris	S/L I. A. March-F/L Eyolfson
7/8.7.44	XIII	MM570	410 Sqn	Ju 88		F/L S. B. Huppert-F/O J. S. Christie. a/c FTR – Starboard engine hit by debris from the Ju 188 during the shoot down. Huppert KIA. Christie baled out. Safe)
7/8.7.44	XIII		29 Sqn	UEA		F/O Bennett-W/O Gordon
8/9.7.44	XIII	MM465	604 Sqn	Ju 88	10m W Le Havre	W/C M. H. Constable-Maxwelll
				Do 217 (Prob)	S Bank Seine	
9/10.7.44	XIII		264 Sqn	Ju 88	25m NE Bayeux	S/L F. J. A. Chase-F/O A. F. Watson
10.7.44	VI	PZ188/J	515 Sqn	Ju 88	Zwishilnahner a/f	F/O R. A. Adams-P/O F. H. Ruffle) shared
10.7.44	VI	PZ420/O	515 Sqn			F/O D. W. O. Wood-F/O K. Bruton) shared
10/11.7.44	XIII		264 Sqn	Do 217 (Prob)		S/L P. B. Elwell-F/O F. Ferguson
11/12.7.44	XVII		219 Sqn	Ju 88	20m ENE Rouen	F/O D. T. Tull
11/12.7.44	XVII	HK248	219 Sqn	Ju l88		W/C P. L. Burke AFC
12/13.7.44	XIII	HK451	264 Sqn	Ju 88	Seine Estuary	F/O R. Barbour-F/O G. Paine
12/13.7.44	XIX	TA401/D	157 Sqn	Ju 88	SE Étampes	F/L J. O. Mathews-W/O A. Penrose
14.7.44	VI	RS993/T	515 Sqn	Ju 34	Stralsund, NE Ger.	F/L A. E. Callard-F/Sgt E. D. Townsley
14/15.7.44	XIX		157 Sqn	Bf 110	20m NE Juvincourt	Lt Sandiford RNVR-Lt Thompson RNVR (anti Diver)
14/15.7.44	VI	NT112/M	169 Sqn	Bf 109	Auderbelck	W/O L. W. Turner-F/Sgt F. Francis
14/15.7.44	XVII	HK248	219 Sqn	Ju l88	SW Caen	W/C P. L. Burke AFC
17/18.7.44	VI		605 Sqn	UEA	Schwabish Hall	W/C N. J. Starr DFC-P/O J. Irvine
17/18.7.44	VI		418 Sqn	UEA	Altenburg a/f	S/L R. Bannock RCAF-F/O R R. Bruce
17/18.7.44	XIII		604 Sqn	Ju 88		F/L G. A. Hayhurst-W/O Gosling
18/19.7.44	XIII	MM512	409 Sqn	Do 217		F/O McPhail-P/O Smith
18/19.7.44	XIII	MM589	409 Sqn	Ju 88		W/O Kirkwood-W/O Matheson
18/19.7.44	XIII		29 Sqn	UEA		W/O A. Cressweli
19.7.44	XXX		219 Sqn	Ju 188	Over Beachhead	
20/21.7.44	VI	NT113	169 Sqn	Bf 110G-4	near Courtrai	W/C N. B. R. Bromley OBE-F/L R Truscott DFC. Bf 110G-4 Wrk Nr 730218 G9+EZ of 12./NJG1 crashed near Moll, Belgium. Ofw Karl-Heinz Scherfling (25) pilot, a Ritterkreuztraeger since 8 April 1944 & who had 33 night victories, KIA. Fw Herbert Winkler, (31, AG), Fw Herbert Scholz (25, radar op), baled out seriously injured. Fw Herbert Winkler (31, AG) KIA.
20/21.7.44	VI	NT146	169 Sqn	Ju 88	Homburg area	P/O H. Reed-F/O S. Watts
20/21.7.44	VI	NTl21	169 Sqn	Bf 110	Courtrai	F/L J. S. Fifield-F/O F. Staziker
21.7.44	XXX	MM731	406 Sqn	2 x Do 217		W/C D. J. Williams DFC RCAF
23/24.7.44	II	HJ710/T	141 Sqn	Ju 88	SW of Beauvais	P/O I. D. Gregory-P/O D. H. Stephens. Poss. Bf 110G-4 Wrk.Nr. 730117 G9+GR of 7./NJG1, shot down by Mosquito NF at 0125 hrs, crashed 5km N of Deelen a/f. Lt Josef Hettlich (pilot); Fw Johann Treiber (WOp/Radar Op.) both slightly injured & baled out. AG also baled out. Or, Bf 110 Wrk.Nr. 441083 G9+OR of III./NJG1 or 7./NJG1, shot down by Mosquito NF at 0147 hrs during landing at Leeuwarden a/f, crashed at Rijperkerk N of Leeuwarden. Hptm Siegfried Jandrey (30, pilot) & Uffz Johann Stahl (25, Radar op) KIA. Uffz Anton Herger (24, AG) injured.

DATE	TYPE	SERIAL	SQN	ENEMY	A/C DETAILS	PILOT-NAVIGATOR/RADAR OP
23/24.7.44	VI	NS997/C	169 Sqn	Bf 110G-4	near Kiel	F/L R. J. Dix-F/O A. J. Salmon. Bf 110G-4 Wrk Nr 730036 G9+ER of 7./NJG1 was shot down at very low level around midnight. The 110 crashed near Balk in Friesland Province, Holland. Fw Heinrich-Karl Lahmann (25, pilot) & Uffz Günther Bouda (21 AG) both baled out. Uffz Willi Huxsohl (21, radar op) KIA.
23/24.7.44	II	DZ661	239 Sqn	Bf 110	Kiel	F/O N. Veale-F/O R. D. Comyn. At 0125 hrs Bf 110G-4 730117 G9+GR of 7./NJG1 was shot down N of Deelen airfield. Lt Josef Hettlich, pilot, Fw Johann Treiber (RO) and the air gunner all baled out safely.
23/24.7.44	XIII		29 Sqn	Bf 110	nr Leeuwarden a/f	F/L A. C. Musgrove-F/O G. Egerton-Hine. 441083 G9+OR of 7./NJG1, which was shot down at 0147 hours during landing at Leeuwarden airfield and which crashed at Rijperkerk, just to the N of the base. Hptm Siegfried Jandrey, 30, pilot, and Uffz Johann Stahl, 25, radar operator, were killed. Uffz Anton Herger, 24, air gunner, was injured.
24/25.7.44	XIII	MM504	409 Sqn	Ju 88		W/O MacDonald-F/Sgt King
25/26.7.44	XIII	MM587	409	Ju 88		W/C Reid-F/L Peacock
25/26.7.44	VI	RS961/H		515 Me 410	Knocke, Belgium	S/L H. B. Martin DSO DFC-F/O J. W. Smith
25/26.7.44	VI	PZ178	23 Sqn	UEA	Laon Pouvron	F/L D. J. Griffiths-F/Sgt S. F. Smith
25/26.7.44	XVII		219 Sqn	Ju 88 50	ENE La Havre	F/O D. T. Tull
26/27.7.44	XIII	MM510	409 Sqn	Ju 88	Over Caen	S/L R. S. Jephson-F/O J. M. Roberts (Mos hit by debris in the shoot down. Both crew KIA)
26/27.7.44	XIII		29 Sqn	Ju 188	Melun	F/O F. E. Pringle-F/O W. Eaton
26/27.7.44	XIII		604 Sqn	Ju 88	Granville	F/O J. C. Truscott-F/O Howarth
28/29.7.44	XIII	MM500	604 Sqn	Ju 88	Lisieux-Bernay	F/L J. P. Meadows-F/O McIlvenny
28/29.7.44	XIII	MM526	604 Sqn	Ju 88	3m E Bretal	F/L R. A. Miller DFC-P/O P. Catchpole
28/29.7.44	XIII	MM513/D	488 Sqn	2 x Ju 88	10m NW Vire	F/L R. F. L Hall-F/O R. D.Marriott
28/29.7.44	XIII	MM439	488 Sqn	Ju 188	10-15m N Mayenne	F/O D. N. Robinson RNZAF-F/L W. T. M.Clarke DFM
28/29.7.44	II	HJ712/R	141	2 x Ju 88	Metz/Neufchâteau	F/L H. E. White DFC*-F/L M. S. Allen DFC*
28/29.7.44	II	HJ741/Y	141 Sqn	Ju 88	Metz area	P/O I. D. Gregory-P/O D. H. Stephens. Ju 88G-1 Wrk.Nr. 713649 R4+KT of 9./NJG2, possibly shot down by Mosquito of 141 Sqn (White & Allen or Gregory/Stephens), crashed 20km SSW of Toul, France. Hptm August Speckmann (pilot), KIA; Ofw Arthur Boos (radar op) WIA. Ofw Wilhelm Berg (flt eng) & Uffz Otto Brueggenkamp (AG) both KIA.
28/29.7.44	XIII		410 Sqn	Ju 88	Beachhead	F/L W. A. Dexter-Lt Richardson
29/30.7.44	XIII	MM466	488 Sqn	3 x Ju 88	5-6m S Caen	F/L G. E. Jameson DFC RNZAF-F/O A. N. Crookes DFC
			Do 217	5-6m S Lisseaux	"	"
29/30.7.44	XIII		264 Sqn	Ju 188 (or 88)	15m SE St Lô	S/L F. J. A. Chase-F/O A. F. Watson
29/30.7.44	XIII	MM621	604 Sqn	Ju 88	30m S of Cherbourg	F/L Miller
30/31.7.44	XIII	MM589	409 Sqn	Ju 88		W/O Kirkwood
30/31.7.44	XIII	MM501	410 Sqn	Ju 88		P/O D. M.Mackenzie-P/O C. F. A. Bodard
30/31.7.44	XIII		29 Sqn	Ju 88	nr Paris	F/O F. E. Pringle-F/O W. Eaton
30/31.7.44	XIII		604 Sqn	Ju 88	SE of Caen	S/L. B. Maitland-Thompson-W/O Pash
31.7.44	XXX		219 Sqn	Ju 188		
31.7/1.8.44	XIII		410 Sqn	Ju 88		F/O J. Maday-F/O J. R. Walsh
1/2.8.44	XIII	MM498	488 Sqn	Ju 88	10m E of St Lô	F/L P. F. L. Hall-F/O R. D. Marriott
1/2.8.44	XIII	MM477/U	410 Sqn	RCAF Ju 188	NE Tessy	S/L J. D. Somerville-F/O G. D. Robinson
1/2.8.44	XIII		604 Sqn	Ju 188	SE Caen	F/L F. C. Ellis-F/O P.C. Williams
2/3.8.44	XIII	HK532	488 Sqn	Do 217-	4m S of Avranches	F/L A. S. Browne-W/O T. F. Taylor
2/3.8.44	XIII	MM439	488 Sqn	Ju 188-	8m S of Avranches	W/O T. G. C. Mackay-F/Sgt A. A. Thompson
2/3.8.44	XIII	MM477/U	410 Sqn	RCAF Do 217	6m NW Pontorson	S/L J. D. Somerville-F/O G. D. Robinson
2/3.8.44	XIII		264 Sqn	Ju 188 (or 88)	10m W Argentan	S/L F. J. A. Chase-F/O A. F. Watson
2/3.8.44	XIII		410 Sqn	Ju 188		F/L B. E. Plumer RCAF-F/O V. W. Evans
3/4.8.44	XXX		219 Sqn	2 x Ju 188	Seine Estuary	F/L P. G. K. Williamson DFC RAAF-F/O F. E. Forrest
3/4.8.44	XIII	MM466	488 Sqn	Ju 88	8m N St Lô	F/L G. E. Jameson DFC RNZAF-F/O A. N. Crookes DFC ((Claim 2nd Ju 88)
3/4.8.44	XIII	HK504	488 Sqn	Ju 88	ENE of Vire	
3/4.8.44	XIII	MM513	488 Sqn	Do 217	NW of Barnes	
3/4.8.44	XIII	MM502	488 Sqn	Do 217	W of Angers	
3/4.8.44	XIII	HK420	488 Sqn	Ju 88	W Avranches	W/O G. S. Patrick-F/Sgt J. J. Concannon
3/4.8.44	XIII	MM552	604 Sqn	Do 217	5m S of Granville	F/L R. J. Foster DFC-F/L M. F. Newton DFC
3/4.8.44	XIII	'S'	264 Sqn	Ju 88		S/L I. H. Cosby DFC-F/L E. R. Murphy
3/4.8.44	XIII		264	Ju 88		F/L Beverley-F/O P. C. Sturling (Mosquito FTR; crew baled out)
3/4.8.44	XIII		604 Sqn	Do 217	S Granville	F/L R. J. Foster DFC-F/O M. F. Newton
3/4.8.44	XIII	MM554?	409 Sqn	Ju 188		F/L. E. Spiller-F/O Donaghue
3/4.8.44	XIII	MM508?/K	409 Sqn	Ju 188		W/O MacDonald-W/O Colborne
3/4.8.44	XIII		410 Sqn	Bf 110	NE Avranches	F/L W. G. Dinsdale-P/O J. E. Dunn
4/5.8.44	XIII	MM512	409 Sqn	Ju 188		W/O Joss-W/O Lailey
4/5.8.44	XIII		409 Sqn	Ju 88 (Prob)		P/O F. S. Haley
4/5.8 44	XIII	MM514/B	604 Sqn	Ju 188 & Ju 88	nr Barnes	F/L J. A. M. Haddon-F/O R. J. McIlvenny
4/5.8.44	XIII	MM449	410 Sqn	HS 126		F/L W. G. Dinsdale-P/O J. E. Dunn
4/5.8.44	XIII	MK403	29 Sqn	Ju 188	Orly airfield	F/L R. C. Pargeter-F/L R. L. Fell
4/5.8.44	XIII	HK504/M	488 Sqn	Ju 88	ENE Vire	W/C R. C. Haine DFC-F/L A. P. Bowman
4/5.8.44	XIII		488 Sqn	Ju 188	NE St Lô	F/O A. L. Shaw-F/Sgt L. J. Wyman
5/6.8.44	XII	MM513/D	488 Sqn	Do 217K-2	20m from Beacon	F/L P. F. L. Hall-F/O R. D. Marriott
5/6.8.44	XIII		488 Sqn	Do 217K-2		F/Sgt T. A. Mackan
5/6.8.44	XIII	MM514	604 Sqn	Ju 188/Ju 88	Rennes area	F/L J. A. M. Haddon-F/O R. J. McIlvenny
6/7.8.44	XIII	MM466	488 Sqn	Ju 88	15m S Avranches	F/L G. E. Jameson DFC RNZAF-F/O A. N. Crookes DFC
6/7.8.44	XIII	HK420	488 Sqn	Ju 188	SW Avranches	F/L A. E. Browne-W/O T. F. Taylor ((+2 UEA flew into ground trying to evade) One of these poss. Hptm Helmut Bergmann of 8/NJG4 MIA Invasion area.
6/7.8.44	XIII	MM500	604 Sqn	Ju 188		F/O R. M. T. MacDonald-F/Sgt C.G. Baird
6/7.8.44	XIII	MM465	604 Sqn	Ju 88	S Avranches	W/C F. D. Hughes DFC**-F/L L. Dixon DFC*
6/7.8.44	XIII	MM449/B	604 Sqn	2 x Do 217 & Bf 110		F/L J. C. Surman-P/O C. E. Weston

DATE	TYPE	SERIAL	SQN	ENEMY	A/C DETAILS	PILOT-NAVIGATOR/RADAR OP
6/7.8.44	XXX		219 Sqn	Ju 188	Argentan area	F/L P. G. K. Williamson DFC RAAF-F/O F. E. Forrest
6/7.8.44	XIII	MM566/R	410 Sqn	RCAF Ju 88	St Hilaire	S/L J. D. Somerville-F/O G. D. Robinson
6/7.8.44	XIII		410 Sqn	Ju 88		F/L R. M. Currie-F/O A. N. Rose (Hptm Helmut Bergmann, St.Kapt 8./NJG4 (36 night victories, Knight's Cross 9.6.44, MIA 6/.8.44 in Bf 110G-4 Wrk Nr 140320 3C+CS from sortie to Invasion Front area Avranches-Mortain, poss shot down by Mosquito NF)
7.8.44	XIII	MM550	FIU	Ju 88	Melun-Bretigny	Lt P. Twiss RN-F/O R. J. Lake AFC
7/8.8.44	XIII	MM555	409 Sqn	Ju 188		W/O Henke-F/Sgt Emmerson
7/8.8.44	XIII	MM429	604 Sqn	2 x Do 217	nr Rennes	F/O J. S. Smith-F/O L. Roberts
7/8.8.44	XIII	HK525	604 Sqn	Ju 188	S of Nantes	F/O R. M. T. MacDonald-F/L S. H. J. Elliott
7/8.8.44	XIII	MM517	604 Sqn	Ju 188	E of Falaise	F/L J. R. Cross-W/O H. Smith
				Ju 88	nr Conde	" "
7/8.8.44	XIII	HK524	29 Sqn	Bf 110	Melun, W Orly	F/O W. W. Provan-W/O Nichol
7/8.8.44	XXX		219 Sqn	2 x Ju 188	W Vire	F/L M. J. Gloster DFC-F/L J. F. Oswold DFC
7/8.8.44	XIII		264 Sqn	Ju 88		F/L Davidson-F/O Willmott
8/9.8.44	II	DZ256/U	239 Sqn	Fw 190	St Quentin	F/L D. Welfare-F/O .B. Bellis
8/9.8.44	II		239 Sqn	Bf 109	N France	F/L D. J. Raby DFC-F/Sgt S. J. Flint DFM
8/9.8.44	VI	NT156/Y	169 Sqn	Fw 190	E Abbeville	F/L R. G. Woodman DFC-F/L P. Kemmis
8/9.8.44	XIII	MM528/H	604 Sqn	Do 217		F/O T. R. Wood-F/O R. Leafe
8/9.8.44	XXX		219 Sqn	2 x Ju 188		
9/10.8.44	XXX		219 Sqn	Fw 190	E Evereux	F/L M. J. Gloster DFC-F/L J. F. Oswold DFC
10/11.8.44	XIII		264 Sqn	Ju 188	Caen	S/L F. J. A. Chase-F/O A. F. Watson
10/11.8.44	XXX		219 Sqn	Ju 88	10m SW Le Havre	F/L G. R. I. Parker DSM-W/O D. L. Godfrey
			Fw 190	5m S Le Havre		" "
10/11.8.44	XIII	MM504	409 Sqn	Fw 190		S/L Hatch-F/O Eames
10/11.8.44	XIII	MM523	409 Sqn	Do 217		F/O Collins-F/O Lee
10/11.8.44	VI	NT176/H	169 Sqn	Bf 109	Over Dijon	F/O W. H. Miller DFC-F/O F. C. Bone DFC
10/11.8.44	XIII		264 Sqn	Ju l88		F/O Daker-F/Sgt J.A. Heathcote
10/11.8.44	XIII		410 Sqn	Ju 88		W/C G. A. Hiltz-F/O J. R. Walsh
11/12.8.44	XXX		219 Sqn	Ju 88		
11.8.44	XIII	HK429	604 Sqn	Do 217 (Prob)		F/L R. A. Miller DFC-P/O P. Catchpole (both inj in the combat)
11/12.8.44	XIII	MM619	409 Sqn	Fw 190		W/O Henke-F/Sgt Emmerson
12/13.8.44	VI	NT173	169 Sqn	He 219	nr Aachen	F/O W. H. Miller DFC-F/O F. C. Bone DFC
14/15.8.44	XIII	MM477/U	410 Sqn	Ju 88	15m W Le Havre	S/L J. D. Somerville-F/O G. D. Robinson
14/15.8.44	XIII	MM491	409 Sqn	Ju 88		F/O Collins-F/O Lee
14/15.8.44	XIII	MM466/B	488 Sqn	Ju 88	20-30m S of Caen	F/L J. A. S. Hall DFC-F/O J. P. W. Cairns
15/16.8.44	XXX		219 Sqn	Ju 88 1	5m W Le Havre	F/L G. R. I. Parker DSM-W/O D. L. Godfrey
15/16.8.44	XIII	HK377	488 Sqn	Ju 88	SE of Caen	P/O McCabe-W/O F. Newman
16/17.8.44	XIII	MM590/H	409 Sqn	Ju 188		W/O MacDonald-W/O Colborne
16/17.8.44	XXX		219 Sqn	Ju 188	nr Caen	F/L M. J. Gloster DFC-F/L J. F.Oswold DFC
16/17.8.44	VI	HB213/G	141 Sqn	Bf 110	Ringkobing Fjord	W/O E. A. Lampkin-F/Sgt B. J. Wallnutt
18/19.8.44	XIII	MM560/F	409 Sqn	Ju 88/Ju 188		S/L Hatch-F/O Eames
18/19.8.44	XIII	MM622	488 Sqn	Do 217		F/O M. G. Jeffs-F/O A. N. Crookes DFC
19/20.8.44	XIII	MM589	409 Sqn	Do 217		S/L. R. Hatton-F/L Rivers
19/20.8.44	XXX	MM744	410 Sqn	2 x Ju 88		F/O J. Fullerton-F/O B. E. Gallagher
20/21.8.44	XIII	MM439	488 Sqn	Ju 188	15m S of Caen	F/L D. N. Robinson RNZAF-W/O W. N. Addison DFC DFM
26/27.8.44	VI	NT146/T	169 Sqn	Ju 88	near Bremen	W/O L. W. Turner-F/Sgt F. Francis. Ju 88G-1 Wrk.Nr. 710542 D5+BR of 7./NJG. crashed near Mulsum 42km E of Bremen. Lt Achim Woeste (pilot), KIA. Uffz Heinz Thippe, WIA, baled out. Gefr Karl Walkenberger, WIA, baled out. Uffz Anton Albrecht KIA.
27.8.44.44	XIII	HK304	25 Sqn	Bf 109	Northern France	
28/29.8.44	VI		605 Sqn	UEA	Chievres airfield	F/O R. E. Lelong RNZAF-P/O J. A. McLaren
29/30.8.44	II	W4097	239 Sqn	Ju 88	near Stettin	F/L D. L. Hughes-F/L R. H. Perks
1/2.9.44	XIII		410 Sqn	Fw 190		F/L I. E. MacTavish-F/O A. M. Grant
1/2.9.44	XIII	MM566/A	488 Sqn	Ju 188	10-15m W La Havre	W/C R. C. Haine DFC-F/L A. P. Bowman
6/7.9.44	VI	PZ338/A	515 Sqn	Bf 109	Odder, Denmark	W/C F. F. Lambert DFC-F/O R. J. Lake AFC
11/12.9.44	XVII		FIU	Ju 88	10m S Bonn	F/O D. T. Tull-F/O P Gowgill
11/12.9.44	XIX	'Y'	85 Sqn	Ju 188	Baltic Sea	S/L B. A. Burbridge DFC-F/L F. S. Skelton DFC
11/12.9.44	VI	HR180/B	141 Sqn	Bf 110	SW of Mannheim	F/L P. A. Bates-P/O W. G. Cadman
11/12.9.44	XIX	MM630/E	157 Sqn	2 x Ju 188	Zeeland	S/L J. G. Benson DFC-F/L L. Brandon DFC
11/12.9.44	XIX	'A'	85 Sqn	Bf 109G	Limburg area	F/L P. S. Kendall DFC*-F/L C R. Hill DFC*
12/13.9.44	XIX	MM643/F	157 Sqn	Bf 110	Frankfurt	F/L R. D. Doleman-F/L D. C. Bunch DFC
12/13 9.44	II		239 Sqn	Bf 110	Ranschhack	F/O W. R. Breithaupt DFC-F/O J. A. Kennedy DFC DFM
12/13.9.44	XIII	HK469	29 Sqn	Bf 110	SE Frankfurt	F/O W. W. Provan-W/O Nichol
12/13.9.44	VI		418 Sqn	UEA	Kitzingen	S/L R. Bannock RCAF-F/O R. R. Bruce
12/13.9.44	XXX		219 Sqn	Ju 88	Dutch border	F/L L Stephenson DFC-F/L G. A. Hall DFC
13/14.9.44	XIX	'D'	85 Sqn	Bf 110	nr Koblenz	F/L W. House-F/Sgt R. D. McKinnon. Bf 110G-4 Wrk.Nr.440384 G9+EN of 5./NJG1 which took off from Düsseldorf A/F at 2234 hrs crashed at Birresborn in the Eiffel at 2335 hrs. Oblt Gottfried Hanneck, pilot, baled out WIA. Uffz Thdch Sacher (radar op) & Uffz Willi Wurschitz (radar op/AG) both KIA.
16/17.9.44	XXX	MM743	410 Sqn	UEA		F/L C. E. Edinger RCAF-F/O CC. Vaessen
16/17.9.44	XIII		FIU	UEA	Ardorf a/f	F/O E. R. Hedgecoe DFC-F/O N. L. Bamford
17/18.9.44	XIX	'J'	85 Sqn	2 x Bf 110		F/O A. J. Owen-F/O J. S. V. McAllister DFM. Bf 110 G-4 Wrk.Nr. 740358 G9+MY of 11./NJG1 crashed E of Arnhem/Holland. Uffz Walter Sjuts KIA; Uffz Herbert Schmidt KIA; Uffz Ernst Fischer KIA. Bf 110G-4 Wrk.Nr. 740757 G9+GZ of 12./NJG1 crashed E of Arnhem/Holland. Uffz Heinz Gesse, Uffz Josef Kaschub & Ogefr Josef Limberg all KIA.

DATE	TYPE	SERIAL	SQN	ENEMY	A/C DETAILS	PILOT-NAVIGATOR/RADAR OP
23/24.9.44	XVII		FIU	Bf 110	10m SE Münster	F/O D. T. Tull-F/O P. J. Cowgill DFC
23/24.9.44	XXX		219 Sqn	Bf 110	7-10m NE Cologne	S/L W. P Green DFC-F/L D. A. Oxby DFM**
24/25.9.44	XIII	MM462/T	604 Sqn	He 219	55m S Nijmegen	F/L R. J. Foster DFC-F/L M.F. Newton DFC He 219 (I/NJG1?)
25.9.44	XIII	MM589	409 Sqn	He 111H22	Over N Sea	W/O L. E. Fitchett-F/Sgt A. C. Hardy (crash-landed near Lille after damage from debris from He 111)
25/26.9.44	XVII		125 Sqn	He 111H22	Over N Sea	F/O W. A. Beadle-F/O R. A.Pargeter
26/27.9.44	VI	PZ301/N	515 Sqn	He 111	Zellhausen a/f	S/L H. F. Morley-F/Sgt R. A. Fidler
26/27.9.44	XXX	MM743	410 Sqn	Ju 87	12m N Aachen	1st Lt A. A. Harrington USAAF-P/O D. G. Tongue
26/27.9.44	XVII	HK257	25 Sqn	Ju 188	40m 5 Harwich	W/C C. M. Wight-Boycott DSO-F/L D. W. Reid
27/28.9.44	VI		418 Sqn	2 x Bf 108	Barrow airfield/sea	S/L R. Bannock RCAF-F/O R. R. Bruce
27/28.9.44	XIX	'J'	85 Sqn	Ju 188 (Prob)	SW Kaiserlautern	F/O A. J. Owen-F/O J. S. V. McAllister DFM
28/29.9.44	XXX		219 Sqn	Ju 87	over Low Countries	F/L G. R. I. Parker DSM-W/O D. L. Godfrey
28/29.9.44	XIX	'Y'	85 Sqn	Ju 188		F/L M. Phillips-F/L D. Smith
28/29.9.44	XVII	HK357	25 Sqn	2 x He 111H22	over N Sea	W/C L. J. C. Mitchell-F/L D. L. Cox
29/30.9.44	XIX		157 Sqn	Me 410 (Prob)	10m ESE Yarmouth	F/L Vincent-F/O Money
2/3.10.44.	VI		605 Sqn	Bv 138	Jasmunder Bay	F/O R. E. Lelong RNZAF-P/O J.A. McLaren
2/3.10.44	XXX		219	3 x Ju 87	E Nijmegen	S/L W. P Green DFC-F/L D. A. Oxby DFM**
5/6.10.44	XVII	HK239	25 Sqn	He 111H-22	over N Sea	F/L J. R. F. Jones-F/O R. Skinner
5/6.10.44	XIII		409 Bf 110			S/L S. J. Fulton-F/O A. R. Ayton
5/6.10.44	XXX	MM760	410 Sqn	Ju 88	16m NE Namur	F/L C. S. Edinger RCAF-F/O C. C. Vaessen
6/7.10.44	XIII	MM560	409 Sqn	Bf 110	over Peer, Belgium	F/O R. H. Finlayson-F/O J. A. Webster. Bf 110 G9+MN of 5./NJG1. Fw Robert Kock, who was on his 70th operation baled out and was slightly injured. Uffz Heinz Forster, bordfunker and Uffz Ernst Darg, gunner were KIA.
6/7.10.44	XIII	MM574	409 Sqn	Ju 88		P/O F. S. Haley-P/O S. J. Fairweather (baled out)
6/7.10.44	XVII	HK317/Y	456 Sqn	Ju 188	20m NW of Nijmegen	
15/16.10.44	XIX	'D'	85 Sqn	Bf 110		F/L C. K. Nowell-W/O Randall
6/7.10.44	XX		219 Sqn	Bf 110	N Arnhem	F/L G. R. I. Parker DSM-W/O D. L Godfrey
6/7.10.44	XXX		219 Sqn	Ju 87		F/L J. C. E. Atkins DFC-F/O D. R. Mayo
6/7.10.44	VI	NT234/W	141 Sqn	Ju 88	S of Leeuwarden	F/L A. C. Gallacher DFC-P/O D. McLean DFC. Ju 88G-1 Wrk.Nr. 710639 D5+EV of 10./NJG3 crashed near Groningen. Oblt Walter Briegleb (pilot) WIA; Fw Paul Kowalewski (radar op) KIA; Uffz Brandt (flt eng) WIA; Uffz Bräunlich (AG) WIA.
6/7.10.44	XVII	HK257	25 Sqn	He 111H-22	40m S Southwold	F/L A. E. Marshall DFC DFM-F/O C. A. Allen
6/7.10.44	XIII		410 Sqn	Bf 110		F/L B. E. Plumer RCAF-F/L Hargrove
7/8.10.44	XIII		410	Sqn Ju 188		F/O Fullerton-F/O Gallagher
7/8.10.44	XIX	MM671/C	157 Sqn	Bf 110	W of Neumünster	F/L J. O. Mathews DFC-W/O A. Penrose DFC
8.10.44	VI	PZ181/E	515 Sqn	Bf 109	Eggebeck, Denmark	F/L F. T. L'Amie-F/O J. W. Smith
11.10.44	II	DZ256/U	239 Sqn	Seaplane	Tristed	F/L D. Welfare DFC-F/O D. B. Bellis DFC (on the water)
14.10.44	XVII	HK245	125 Sqn	He 219	nr Duisburg	
14/15.10.44	XIX	'Y'	85 Sqn	2 x Ju 88G	Gütersloh a/f	S/L B. A. Burbridge DFC*-F/L F. S. Skelton DFC*
14/15.10.44	VI	PZ245	239 Sqn	Fw 190	Meland	F/L D. R. Howard-F/O F. A. W. Clay
14/15.10.44	XIX	FIU		Ju 88G	W. Kassel	F/O D. T. Tull-F/O P. J. Cowgill DFC
15/16.10.44	XIX	'D'	85 Sqn	Bf 110		F/L C. K. Nowell-W/O Randall
19/20.10.44	XXX	NT250/Y	141 Sqn	Ju 88	SE of Karlsruhe	F/L G. D. Bates-F/O D. W. Field. Poss. Ju 88G-1 Wrk.Nr. 712312 2Z+EB of I./NJG6, which crashed at Vaihirgen/ Marksdorf ENE of Pforzheim/Germany. Oblt Wilhelm Engel (pilot) WIA; radar op safe.
19/20.10.44	VI	PZ175/H	141 Sqn	Ju 88	NW of Nuremberg	F/O J. C. Barton-F/Sgt R. A. Kinnear
19/20.10.44	XIX	TA404/M	157 Sqn	Ju 88	nr Mannheim	S/L R. D. Doleman DFC-F/L D. C. Bunch DFC. Poss. Ju 88G-1 Wrk.Nr. 714510 2Z+CM of 4./NJG6, which crashed at Murrhardt, SE of Heilbronn/Germany. Uffz Georg Haberer (pilot) & Uffz Ernst Dressel (radar op) both KIA.
19/20.10.44	XIX	'Y	85 Sqn	Ju 188	Metz	S/L B. A. Burbridge DFC*-F/L F. S. Skelton DFC*
19/20.10.44	VI	PZ275	239 Sqn	Bf 110	Strasbourg	W/O P. C. Falconer-F/Sgt W. C. Armor
22/23.10.44	XXX	MM792	219 Sqn	Ju 88	Verviers area	S/L W. P. Green DFC-F/L D. A. Oxby DFM**
25.10.44			68 Sqn	He 111H-22	Over N Sea	S/L M. J. Mansfeld-F/L S. A. Janacek
25.10.44	XVII	HK310	125 Sqn	He 111H-22	over N Sea	F/O W. A. Beadle-F/O R. A. Pargeter. Heinkel 111 of 2 Staffel, KG53 Legion Kondor piloted by Obfw Othmar Hammerce.
28/29.10.44	II	PZ245	239 Sqn	He 111	Dummer Lake	F/L D. R. Howard-F/O F. A. W. Clay
29.10.44	VI	PZ344/E	515 Sqn	Fw 190+Ju W34		F/L P. T. L'Amie-F/O J. W. Smith
29 10.44	VI	PZ217/K	515 Sqn	Bf 110		P/O T. A. Groves-F/Sgt R.B. Dockeray
29/30.10.44	XXX	MM767	410 Sqn	Fw 190	nr St Antonis	1st Lt A. A. Harrington USAAF-F/O D. G. Tongue
30/31.10.44	XVII	HK240	125 Sqn	He 111H-22	Over N Sea	S/L L. W. G. Gill-F/L D. A. Haigh. He 111H22 of 4./KG53. Fw Theodore Warwas & crew KIA.
1/2.11.44	XIX	'R'	85 Sqn	Ju 88	20m S Mülhouse	F/O A. J. Owen-F/O J. S. V. McAllister
2/3.11.44	XIII	HK469	29 Sqn	Bf 110	Handorf a/f	F/O W. W. Provan-W/O Nichol
4/5.11.44	XIX	TA401/D	157 Sqn	Bf 110	Osnabrück	W/C K. H. P. Beauchamp-P/O Money
4/5.11.44	II		239 Sqn	Bf 110	Bochum	F/O J. N. W. Young-F/O R. H. Siddons
4/5.11.44	XIX	TA401/D	85 Sqn	Bf 110	Bochum	S/L R. G. Woodman DFC-F/O A. F. Witt
4/5.11.44	XIX	'B'	85 Sqn	Ju 88	S E Bielefeld	F/O A. J. Owen-F/O J. S. V. McAllister DFM
4/5.11.44.						Bf 110 of II./NFG1, shot down by Mosquito NF at 1900 hrs at 20,000 feet. Uffz Gustav Sario (pilot) injured & baled out; Uffz Heinrich Conrads (radar op) & Ogefr Roman Talarowski (AG) both KIA. Bf 110G-4 Wrk.Nr. 440648 G9+PS of 8./NJG1 possibly shot down by Mosquito NF, crashed at Bersenbrück, 30km N. of Osnabrück/Germany. Fw Willi Ruge (pilot) WIA, baled out; Uffz Helmut Kreibohm (radar op) & Ogefr Anton Weiss (AG) both KIA. Bf 110 Wrk.Nr. 730272 G9+E2 of IV./NJG1 shot down by Mosquito NF SW of Wezel/Germany. Lt Heinz Rolland (26, pilot, 15 night victories); Fw Heinz Krüger (25, WOp/Radar Op); Uffz Karl Berger (22, AG) all KIA.
4/5.11.44	XXX	MM802	151 Sqn	Ju 87		P/O Oddie-F/L Gibbs
4/5.11.44	XXX	MM820	488 Sqn	Bf 110		W/O J. W. Marshall-F/O P. P. Prestcott
4/5.11.44	XIX	'Y'	85 Sqn	Ju 88G	30m S. Bonn	S/L B. A. Burbridge DSO DFC*-F/O P. S. Skelton DSO DFC*
			Ju 88	5m SE Bonn		

DATE	TYPE	SERIAL	SQN	ENEMY	A/C DETAILS	PILOT-NAVIGATOR/RADAR OP
			Bf 110	N of Hangelar		Bf 110 of II./NJG1 which crashed into the River Rhine nr Hangelar airfield at 2150 hrs. Oblt Ernst Runze, pilot, KIA. Ogefr Karl-Heinz Bendfield, radar operator, and air gunner baled out.
			Ju 88	N of Hangelar		
5/6.11.44	XIX	TA389	68 Sqn	He 111H22	Over N Sea	F/Sgt L. W. Neal-F/Sgt E. Eastwood. A Heinjel of 6th Staffel KG53 piloted by Lt Heinz Redde and a 7th Staffel machine flown by Uffz Walter Schulz were lost, one the result of a successful interception, the other the result of an accident.
6/7.11.44	XIX	'N'	85 Sqn	Ju 188		S/L F. S. Gonsalves-F/L B. Duckett
6/7.11.44	XXX	'Y'	85 Sqn	Bf 110	S Bonn a/f	F/O B. R. Keele DFC-F/O H. Wright
6/7.11.44	XIX	'A'	85 Sqn	Ju 88 (prob)		Capt T. Weisteen RNWAF
6/7.11.44	XIX	TA391/N	157 Sqn	Ju 188 (prob)		Osnabrück/Minden F/O H. P. Kelway-Sgt Bell
6/7.11.44	XIX	TA404/M	157 Sqn	Bf 110	S of Koblenz	S/L R. D. Doleman DFC-F/L D. C. Bunch DFC
6/7.11.44	II	DD789	239 Sqn	Ju 188	Osnabrück	F/O G. E. Jameson-F/O L. Ambery
6/7.11.44	XXX	MM726	151 Sqn	Ju 188		F/O Turner-F/O Partridge (This night Ju 88G-6 Wrk.Nr. 620396 R4+KR of Stab/IV./NJG3, shot down by Mosquito and crashed at Marienburg/Germany. Hptm Ernst Schneider (pilot) KIA; Ofw Mittwoch (radar op) baled out; Uffz Kaase (AG) baled out. Ju 88G-6 Wrk.Nr. 620583 R4+TS of 11./NJG3, shot down by a Mosquito NF and crashed SW of Paderborn/Germany. Oblt Josef Förster (pilot), safe; Fw Werner Moraing (radar op) WIA; Fw Heinz Wickardt (AG) WIA.)
9/10.11.44	VI		605 Sqn	2 x Ju 87		F/O R. R. Smart-P/O P. O. Wood
9/10.11.44	VI	He 111				F/O Lomas-F/O Fleet
10/11.11.44	XVII 1		25 Sqn	He 111H22	over N Sea	F/O G. F. Simcock-F/O N. E. Heijne. He 111H-22 A1+AB Werke Nr 162080 of Gruppe Stab I/KG53.
10/11.11.44	XVII		68 Sqn	He 111H22	Over N Sea	F/Sgt A. R. Brooking-P/O R. B. Finn
10/11.11.44	XXX	MT492	25 Sqn	He 111H22	70m S Lowestoft	F/O D. H. Greaves DFC-F/O F. M. Robbins DFC
10/11.11.44	XIX	TA402/F	157 Sqn	Ju 88	Frankfurt-Koblenz	S/L J. G. Benson DFC*-F/L L. Brandon DFC*
10/11.11.44	XXX	PZ247	169 Sqn	Ju 188	NE Germany	S/L R. G. Woodman DFC-F/O A. F. Witt
11/12.11.44	XIX	MM671	157 Sqn	Ju 88	(Prob) Bonn	F/O J. O. Mathews DFC-W/O A. Penrose DFC. Ju 88 Wrk.Nr. 712268 of 1./NJG4, crashed near Giessen/ Germany. Pilot and radar op baled out. Gefr Alfred Graefer (AG) KIA.
11/12.11.44	XIX	'B'	85 Sqn	Fw 190	30m SE Hamburg	F/O A. J. Owen-F/O J. S. V. McAllister DFM
17/18.11.44	XVII		456 Sqn	He 111H22	75 miles E of Lowestoft	F/O D. W. Arnold-P/O J. B. Stickley. He 111H-16 A1+NN of 5th Staffel, KG53 flown by Fw Rudolf Ripper.
18/19.11.44	XXX	MM813	219 Sqn	Ju 87		F/L J. C. E. Atkins DFC-F/O D. R. Mayo
21/22.11.44	XIX	'N'	85 Sqn	Bf 110	Near Würzburg	S/L B. A. Burbridge DSO DFC*-F/L F. S. Skelton DSO DFC*
			& Ju 88	Over Bonn		
25/26.11.44	XXX	MM767	410 Sqn	3 x Ju 88G	Muntz	1st Lt A. A. Harrington USAAF-F/O D. G. Tongue (Jacberath & N of Hunxe)
25/26.11.44	XIII	HK425/D	409 Sqn	Ju 52	Rheindahlen	F/O R. I. E. Britten RCAF-F/L L. E. Fownes
25.11.44	XVII	HK29S0/J	456 Sqn	He 111H22	75m S Lowestoft	F/O F. S. Stevens-W/O W. A. H. Kellett
29/30.11.44	XIII	MM622	409 Sqn	2 x Ju 88	over Holland	W/O E. F. Cole-F/O W. S. Martin (a/c dam by debris c/l & SOC)
30.11.44	VI	HR242	169 Sqn	He 177	Liegnitz	W/C H. G. Kelsey DFC*-F/O E. M. Smith DFC DFM (on the ground)
30.11/1.12.44	XIX		85 Sqn	Ju 88		S/L F. S. Gonsalves DFC-F/L B. Duckett
30.11/1.12.44	XIX		157 Sqn	Ju 188 5030N 0920E		F/O R. J. V. Smythe-F/O Waters
30/11/1.12.44	XIII		410 Sqn	Ju 88		F/O D. M. Mackenzie-F/O C. F. A. Bodard
?.11.44		FIU He 111H22				S/L W. H. Maguire DFC-F/L W. D. Jones DFC
2/3.12.44	XIX	'A'	85 Sqn	Bf 110		Capt T. Weisteen RNWAF. Bf 110G-4 Wrk.Nr. 180382 of 12./NJG4 took off Bonninghardt at 2047 hrs, crashed at 2145 hrs near Lippborg (near Hamm/Germany). Lt Heinz-Joachim Schlage (pilot) safe. Fiebig & Uffz Kundmüller KIA.
2/3.12.44	XIX		157 Sqn	Ju 88	Osnabrück	F/L W. Taylor-F/O Edwards. Poss. Ju 88 Wrk.Nr. 714819 3C+WL of 3./NJG4, which crashed at Rheine. Ofhr Erhard Pfisterhammer (pilot) WIA; Uffz Wolfgang Sode (radar op) WIA; AG u/k probably safe.
4.12.44	XXX	MM790	219 Sqn	Bf 110	nr Krefeld	F/O L. Stephenson DFC-F/L G. A. Hall DFC
4/5.12.44	XXX	'B'	85 Sqn	Bf 110	50m ENE Heilbronn	Capt S. Heglund DFC*-F/O R.O. Symon DFC
4/5.12.44	XIX	MM671/C	157 Sqn	Ju 88	Dortmund a/f	F/L J. O. Mathews DFC-W/O A. Penrose DFC
4/5.12.44	XIX		157 Sqn	Bf 110	Limburg	F/L W. Taylor-F/O Edwards
4/5.12.44	XXX	'C'	85 Sqn	2 x Bf 110	Germesheim	F/L R. T Goucher-F/L C. H. Bulloch
4/5.12.44	XXX	'H'	85 Sqn	Ju 88	nr Krefeld	F/O A. J. Owen-F/O J. S. V. McAllister DFM. Prob. Ju 88G-1 Wrk.Nr. 714152 of 6./NJG4 (85 Squadron's 100th victory), which crashed near Krefeld/Germany. Uffz Wilhelm Schlutter (pilot) WIA; Uffz Friedrich Heerwagen (radar op) & Gefr Friedrich Herbeck (AG) both KIA.
6/7.12.44	XXX	'O'	85 Sqn	Bf 110	West of Münster	F/O E. R. Hedgecoe DFC-F/Sgt J. R. Whitham. Poss. Bf 110G-4 Wrk.Nr. 140078 G9+HZ of 12./NJG1, shot down by Mosquito & crashed 10km NW of Münster-Handorf/Germany. Hptm Hans-Heinz Augenstein Knight's Cross 9.6.44 (St.Kpt 12./NJG1, 46 night victories, of which 45 were four-engined RAF bombers) KIA. Fw Gunther Steins (radar op) KIA; Uffz Kurt Schmidt (AG) WIA, baled out.
6/7.12.44	XIX	MM671/C	157 Sqn	Bf 110	Near Limburg	F/L J. O. Mathews DFC-W/O A. Penrose DFC
				Ju 88	15m SW Giessen	
6/7.12.44	XIX	TA404/M	157 Sqn	Bf 110	Giessen	S/L R. D. Doleman DFC-F/L D. C. Bunch DFC
6/7.12.44	XIX	MM638/G	BSDU	Bf 110	W of Giessen	S/L N. E. Reeves DSO DFC*-F/O M. Phillips
12/13.12.44	XIX	'A'?	85 Sqn	Ju 88		Capt E. P. Fossum-F/O S. A. Hider
12/13.12.44	XXX	'O'	85 Sqn	2 x Bf 110	20m S Hagen/Essen	F/L E. R. Hedgecoe DFC-F/Sgt J. R. Whitham (with FIU)
12/13.12.44	XXX	'Z'	85 Sqn	Ju 88	Gütersloh a/f	S/L B. A. Burbridge DSO DFC**-F/L F. S. Skelton DSO DFC**. Ju 88G-1 Wrk Nr. 714530 of 6./NJG4, crashed at Gütersloh airfield. Uffz Heinrich Brune, pilot, Uffz Emil Hoftharth, radar op & Uffz Wolfgang Rautert (AG) all KIA.
				Bf 110	2m W of Essen	
17/18.12.44	XIX	MM627/H	157 Sqn	Bf 110	5112N 0635E	W/O D. A. Taylor-F/Sgt Radford
17/18.12.44	XIX	MM653/L	157 Sqn	Bf 110		F/Sgt J. Leigh
17/18.12.44	XXX	'J'	85 Sqn	Bf 110	40m from Ûlm	F/L R. T. Goucher-F/L C. H. Bullock
18/19.12.44	XIII	MM569	409 Sqn	Bf 110		P/O F. S. Haley-W/O McNaughton
18/19.12.44	XIII	HK415	409 Sqn	Ju 88		F/O R. S. Finlayson-F/O J. A. Webster
18/19.12.44	XIII	MM456/M	409 Sqn	Ju 88	Kaiserworth area	W/C J. O. Somerville DFC-F/O G. D. Robinson DFC

DATE	TYPE	SERIAL	SQN	ENEMY	A/C DETAILS	PILOT-NAVIGATOR/RADAR OP
18/19.12.44	XIX	MM640/I	157 Sqn	He 219	Osnabrück area	F/L W. Taylor-F/O J. N. Edwards. Poss. He 219A-0 Wrk Nr 190229 G9+GH of I./NJG1. Uffz Scheuerlein (pilot) baled out, Uffz Günther Heinze (radar op) KIA. Taylor and Edwards were killed on 22/23 December trying to land at Swannington.
18/19.12.44	XXX	MV527	410 Sqn	Ju 88	S Bonninghardt	F/O G. E. Edinger RGAF-F/O C. C. Vaessen
18/19.12.44	XXX	MV549	85 Sqn	Bf 110		F/O D. T. Tull DFC (KIA)-F/O P. J. Cowgill DFC (KIA) accidentally rammed Bf 110 G9+CC of Stab IV/NJG1 flown by Hptm Adolf Breves (Fw Telsnig (radar op) Uffz Ofers (AG) as the latter was landing at Düsseldorf a/f at 22.30hrs. Breves landed safely but Tull & Cowgill were killed in the crash of their Mosquito
21/22.12.44	XIX	TA401/D	157 Sqn	Ju 88	N of Frankfurt	W/C K. H. P. Beauchamp DSO DFC-F/L L. Scholefield
22/23.12.44	XXX	MM792	219 Sqn	Ju 88		W/C W. P. Green DSO DFC-F/O D. A. Oxby DFM**
22/23.12.44	XXX	'B'	85 Sqn	2xJu 88+Bf 110	Saarbrücken area	F/O A. J. Owen-F/O J. S. V. McAllister DFM. Ju 88 Wrk.Nr. 621441 2Z+HK of 2./NJG6 crashed at Larxistuhl/Germany. Ofw Max Hausser (pilot) KIA; Ofw Fritz Steube (radar op) KIA; Fw Ernst Beisswenger (AG) WIA. Ju 88G-6 Wrk.Nr. 621436 2Z+DC of II./NJG6 crashed at Lebach, N of Saarbrücken/Germany. Uffz Werner Karau, aircrew function unknown, KIA; 2 others safe?
22/23.12.44	XXX	'P'	85 Sqn	Bf 110	Koblenz-Gütersloh	S/L B. Burbridge DSO* DFC*-F/O F. S. Skelton DSO* DFC*
22/23.12.44	XIX	TA404/M	157 Sqn	Ju 88	5m W Limburg	S/L R. D. Doleman DFC-F/L D. C. Bunch DFC
23/24.12.44	XXX	MM702?	219 Sqn	Ju 88		F/O W. B. Allison-W/O Mills
23/24.12.44	XXX	NT297?	219 Sqn	Ju 88		F/O R. L. Young-F/O N. C. Fazan
23/24.12.44	XXX	MM706	219 Sqn	Ju 88	S Huy	S/L W. P. Green DSO DFC-F/L D. A. Oxby DFM**
23/24.12.44	XXX	NT263	488 Sqn	Ju 188		W/C R. G. Watts-F/O I. C. Skudder
23/24.12.44	XXX	MM822	488 Sqn	Ju 88/188	10m W Maeseyck	F/L K. W. Stewart-F/O H. E. Brumby
23/24.12.44	XXX	MT570/P	488 Sqn	Me 410	US Sector	F/L J. A. S. Hall DFC-F/O J.P.W. Cairns DFC
23/24.12.44	XVII	HK247	125 Sqn	He 111H22	Over N Sea	F/L R. W. Leggett-F/O E. J. Midlane. He 111H22 of 7./KG53 Legion Kondor flown by Uffz Robert Rosch crashed at Lent in Holland. Four crew KIA. 1 gunner survived.
23/24.12.44	XVII		68 Sqn	He 111H-22	Over N Sea	F/Sgt A. Bullus-F/O L. W. Edwards. The Heinkel was flown by Unteroffizier Herbert Neuber of 7/KG53.
23/24.12.44	XIII	MM461	409 Sqn	Ju 188		F/L McPhail-F/O Donaghue
23/24.12.44	XXX		157 Sqn	Ju 88	Near Koblenz	F/L R. J. V. Smythe-F/O Waters
23/24.12.44	XIX	'N'	85 Sqn	Bf 110	Mannheim-Mainz	F/L G. C. Chapman-F/L J. Stockley
23/24.12.44	XIII		410 Sqn	2 x Ju 88		F/O D. M. Mackenzie-F/O C. F. A.Bodard
24/25.12.44	XIII	MM462/T	604 Sqn	He 219		
24/25.12.44	XXX	MM698	219 Sqn	Ju 188	12m S Eindhoven	F/L G. R. I. Parker DSM DFC-W/O D. L Godfrey DFC DFM
				Ju 188	34m E Arnhem	
24/25.12.44	XXX	MM790	219 Sqn	Bf 110	near Hasselsweiler	F/L L. Stephenson DFC-F/L G. A. Hall DFC
24/25.12.44	XXX		410 Sqn	Ju 87		S/L MacTavish-F/O Grant
24/25.12.44	XXX	MV527	410 Sqn	Ju 87	Wassemberg area	F/L C. E. Edinger DFC RCAF-F/O .C. Vaessen DFC
24/25.12.44	XXX		410 Sqn	Ju 88		F/O J. A. Watt-F/L Collis
24/25.12.44	XIX	MM671/C	157 Sqn	Ju 88G	3m SW Köln	F/L J. O. Mathews DFC-W/O A. Penrose DFC
24/25.12.44	XIX	TA404/M	157 Sqn	2 x Bf 110	Köln/Duisburg	S/L R. D. Doleman DFC-F/L D. C. Bunch DFC. Bf 110G-4 G9+CT Wrk Nr 740162 of 9./NJG1 flown by Hptm Heinz Strüning, Ritterkreuz mit Eichenlab (Knight's Cross with Oak Leaves) and 56 night victories in NJG1 & NJG2 crashed at Bergisch Gladbach. Bordfunker and bordschütze baled out safely. Strüning hit the tail of his Bf 110 and was killed. 2nd Bf 110 was G9+GR of 7./NJG1 which crashed near Soppenrade at 1922 hrs. Pilot and bordfunker survived. Gfr Wilhelm Ruffleth inj.
24/25.12.44	XIX	MM676/W	157 Sqn	Bf 110	5038N 0752E	S/L J. G. Benson DFC*-F/L L. Brandon DFC*
24/25.12.44	XXX	'A'	85 Sqn	Bf 110	20m N Frankfurt	Capt S. Heglund DFC*-F/O R. O. Symon DFC
24/25.12.44	XXX	MM693	406 Sqn	Ju 88	nr Paderborn	W/C R. Bannock DFC* RCAF-F/L R. R. Bruce DFC
25/26.12.44	XXX	MM706	219 Sqn	Bf 110		F/L E. A. Campbell-W/O G. Lawrence
26/27.12.44	XXX	MM792	219 Sqn	Ju 87	S Huy	S/L W. P. Green DSO DFC-F/L D. A. Oxby DFM**
26/27.12.44	XXX		488 Sqn	Ju 188 (Prob)		F/L H. D. C. Webbe-F/O I. Watson DFC
27/28.12.44	XXX		410 Sqn	Ju 88G	Helchteren area	F/L W. G. Dinsdale-F/O J. E. Dunn
27/28.12.44	XIII	MM466/G	409 Sqn	2 x Ju 88G	Kaltenkirchen	F/O R. I. E. Britten RCAF-F/L L. E. Fownes
30/31.12.44	XIII	MM560/F	409 Sqn	Ju 88G		S/L Hatton-F/O Rivers
31.12.44	XIX	TA389	68 Sqn	He 111	Over N Sea	
31.12/1.1.44	XIII	MM569/J	604 Sqn	2 x Ju 87		
31.12/1.1.45	VI	RS518/L	515 Sqn	Ju 88	Lovns Bredning	S/L C. V. Bennett DFC-F/L R. A. Smith. Ju 88 of 4./NJG2. Oblt August Gyory (k). Enemy spun in and dropped into Lim Fijord.
31.12/1.1.45	XIX	MT491/E	169 Sqn	He 219	Köln area	F/L A. P. Mellows-F/L S. L. Drew (att 85 Sqn) He 219A-2 Wrk.Nr. 290194 G9+KL of 3./NJG1, crashed at Schleiden, 50km SW of Köln. Oblt Heinz Oloff (pilot) & Fw Helmut Fischer (radar op) both WIA & baled out.
31.12/1.1.45	VI	RS507/C	239 Sqn	Ju 88	Alhorn area	S/L J. Tweedale-F/O L. I. Cunningham
31.12/1.1.45	XIX	'R'	169 Sqn	He 219		F/L L. F. Endersby (att 85 Sqn)
31.12/1.1.45	XXX		410 Sqn	Ju 188	nr Antwerp	S/L Currie-F/L Rose
31.12/1.1.45	XXX		410 Sqn	Ju 88G		F/L Dexter-F/O D. G. Tongue
31.12/1.1.45	XXX		219 Sqn	2 x Ju 188		S/L J. P. Meadows-F/L H. M. Friend
1/2.1.45	XXX	MM790	219 Sqn	Bf 110		F/L F. T. Reynolds-F/O F. A. van den Heuvel
1/2.1.45	XIII	HK529	604 Sqn	He 219	Mönchengladbach	S/L D. C. Furse-F/L J. H. Downes
1/2.1.45	XIII	HK526/U	604 Sqn	3 x Ju 88		F/L R. J. Foster DFC-F/L M. F. Newton DFC
1/2.1.45	XXX	'R'	85 Sqn	Ju 188	10m N of Münster	F/L R. T. Goucher-F/L C. H. Bullock. 2nd enemy was Ju 88G-6
				Ju 88G	10m E of Dortmund	Wrk Nr 621364 2Z+CP of 5./NJG6 which crashed at Dortmund killing Oblt Hans Steffen, pilot, Uffz Josef Knon, Uffz Helmut Uttler and Uffz Frierich Krebber.
1/2.1.45	XXX		85 Sqn	Ju 88		F/O L. J. York
2/3.1.45	XXX	'N'	169 Sqn	Ju 188	near Frankfurt	F/L R. G. Woodman DFC-F/L B. J. P. Simpkins DFC (85 Sqn)
2/3.1.45	XIX	TA393/C	157 Sqn	Ju 88	3m W Stuttgart	F/L J. O. Mathews DFC-W/O A. Penrose DFC
2/3.1.45	XXX	'X'	85 Sqn	Ju 88	15m SW Ludwigshafen	S/L B. A. Burbridge DSO DFC* F/L F. S. Skelton DSO DFC*
4.1.45	XIII	MM563	604 Sqn	Ju 88	W Hostmar	F/O P. W. Nicholas-F/O W. M. G. Irvine

DATE	TYPE	SERIAL	SQN	ENEMY	A/C DETAILS	PILOT-NAVIGATOR/RADAR OP
5/6.1.45	XXX	NT283/Y	406 Sqn	He 111H-22	Josum a/f	W/C R. Bannock DFC* RCAF-F/L R. R. Bruce DFC. Hptm Siegfried Jessen, Staffelkapitän, 9/KG53.
5/6.1.45	XXX	'B'	85 Sqn	Bf 110	25m N Münster	Capt S. Heglund DFC*-F/O R. O. Symon DFC
5/6.1.45	XIX	TA394/A	157 Sqn	He 219	S Hanover	S/L J. G. Benson DFC*-F/L L. Brandon DFC*. He 219A-0 Wrk.Nr. 190188 G9-CK of 2./NJG1 cr. 5km S of Wesendorf/Germany. Ofw Josef Stroelein (pilot) KIA. Uffz Kenne (radar op) baled out safely.
5/6.1.45	VI	RS881/C	515 Sqn	Ju 88	Jägel a/f	F/L A. S. Briggs-F/O Rodwell. Poss. Ju 88 Wrk.Nr. 620513 R4+CD of III./NJG2, which crashed in Denmark (at Jägel airfield?) Oblt Bruno Heilig (pilot), Uffz Günther Kulas (radar op), Gefr Johann Goliasch (flt eng) & Ogefr Horst Jauernig (AG) all KIA.
6.1.45	XVII	HK296	68 Sqn	He 111H22	Over N Sea	W/O A. Brooking-P/O R. B. Finn (FTR)
6.1.45	XXX		488 Sqn	Bf 110	Holland	F/L F. A. Campbell-W/O G. H. Lawrence
7.1.45	XXX	MM792	219 Sqn	2 x Ju 87		
13/14.1.45	XIII	MM459	604 Sqn	Ju 188	Rotterdam area	W/C P. O. Hughes DFC*-F/O Dixon
14/15.1.45	XXX	'Y'	85 Sqn	Ju 188	Frankfurt	F/L K. D. Vaughan-F/L R. D. MacKinnon
14/15.1.45	VI	HR294/T	141 Sqn	UEA	Jüterborg	F/L R. Brearley-F/O J. Sheldon
16/17.1.45	VI	RS507/C	239 Sqn	Bf	109 Fassberg	F/L T. Smith-F/O A. Cockayne
16/17.1.45	XXX	'Y'	85 Sqn	He 219	Ruhr	F/L K. D. Vaughan-F/Sgt R. D. MacKinnon. Poss. Ju 88G-1 Wrk.Nr. 710818 D5+EP of Stab/NJG3 which crashed 3km SE of Friedberg (N of Frankfurt). Ofw Johann Fels (pilot), Uffz Richard Zimmer (radar op) & Gefr Werner Hecht (AG) all KIA.
16/17.1.45	VI	HR200/E	141 Sqn	Bf 110	Magdeburg	F/L D. H. Young-F/O J. J. Sanderson
16/17.1.45	VI	HR213/G	141 Sqn	Bf 110	SW Magdeburg	F/O R. C. Brady-F/L M. K. Webster
16/17.1.45	XIX	TA446/Q	157 Sqn	Ju 188	Fritzler	F/L A. Mackinnon-F/O G. Waddell
17/18.1.45	XXX	MM696	219 Sqn	Ju 88	l0m E Aachen	F/L P. G. K. Williamson DFC RAAF-F/O F. E. Forrest
22/23.1.45	XXX	MM703	219 Sqn	2 x Ju 87		F/L G. R. I. Parker DFC DSM-W/O D. L. Godfrey DFC DFM
23/24.1.45	XIII	MM466/G	409 Sqn	Ju 88	Over Scheldt	P/O M. G. Kent-P/O Simpson
23/24.1.45	XIII	MM456/M	409 Sqn	Ju 188E-1 3m	W Dienst	W/C J. D. Somerville DFC-P/O A.C. Hardy (Ju 188E-1 A3+QD Wrk.Nr. 260452 of Kommando Olga crewed by FF (pilot) Ogfr Heinz Hauck, Observer Gfr Kurt Wuttge, Uffz Max Grossman (BF) & Fw Heinrich Hoppe (dispatcher) shot down after dropping 2 Leute (trusted people) in Holland. All crew PoW)
26.1.45	VI	FIU Bf 109				F/L E. L. Williams
26.1.45	VI	FIU Bf 109				F/L P. S. Crompton
1/2.2.45	XIX		157 Sqn	Bf 110	(Prob) Oberolm	S/L Ryall-P/O Mulroy
1/2.2.45	XXX	NT252	169 Sqn	Bf 110	Stuttgart	F/L A. P. Mellows DFC-F/L S. L. Drew DFC. Prob. Bf 110 Wrk.Nr. 730370 2Z+EL of 3./NJG6, which crashed 25km S of Stuttgart. Oblt Willy Rathmann (pilot), Fw Erich Berndt (radar op) and Uffz Alfred Obry (AG) all KIA.
2/3.2.45	XXX	MV548/Z	85 Sqn	Ju 88		W/C W. K. Davison
1/2.2.45	XXX	NT309/C	239 Sqn	Bf 110	Mannheim	W/C W. F. Gibb DFC-F/O R. C. Kendall DFC. Bf 110G-4 Wrk.Nr.730262 G9+CN of 5./NJG1, probably shot down by Mosquito of 157 or 239 Sqn, belly-landed 2km W of Kettershausen. Oblt Gottfried Hanneck (pilot) WIA. Fw Pean (radio/radar op) and Uffz Gloeckner (AG) baled out safely.
1/2.2.45	XXX	MM792	219 Sqn	Ju 88	2m SW Rheydt	W/C W. P Green DSO DFC- F/L D. A. Oxby DFC DFM**
2/3.2.45	VI	RS575/V	515 Sqn	Ju 88	Vechta	W/C H. C. Kelsey DFC*-F/L E. M. Smith DFC DFM
3/4.2.45	XXX		219 Sqn	Ju 88		P/O M. G. Kent-P/O Simpson
3/4.2.45	XXX		410 Sqn	He 219		F/L B. E. Plumer DFC-F/L Hargrove
7/8.2.45	XXX	NT330/P	239 Sqn	Bf 110	Ruhr	F/L A. J. Holderness-F/L W. Rowley DFC.
7/8.2.45	XXX	NT361/N	239 Sqn	Bf 110	Ruhr	F/L D. A. D. Cather DFM-F/Sgt L. J. S. Spicer DFM. Bf 110G-4 Wrk.Nr. 730322 G9+HR of 7./NJG1 crashed W of Soest (Ruhr). Fw Heinz Amsberg (pilot) & Uffz Matthias Dengs (radar op) both KIA. Gefr Karl Kopperberg (AG) WIA, baled out.
13/14.2.45	XIX	MM684/H	BSDU	2 x Bf 110	Frankfurt area	F/L D. R. Howard DFC-F/L F. A. W. Clay DFC. Bf 110 Wrk.Nr. 480164 C9+ of 5./NJG5 crashed near Bodenbach (Frankfurt area). Fw Heinrich Schmidt (pilot), Uffz Erich Wohlan (radar op) and Uffz Adam Zunker (AG) all KIA.
14/15.2.45	XXX	MV532/S	85 Sqn	Ju 88	Schwabish Hall a/f	F/L F. D. Win RNZAF-F/O T. P. Ryan RNZAF
20/21.2.45	XXX	NT361/N	239 Sqn	Fw 190	Worms	W/C W. F. Gibb DFC-F/O R. C. Kendall DFC DFM
21/22.2.45	XXX	NT263	488 Sqn	Ju 88	Groenlo	F/L K. W. Stewart-F/O H. E. Brumby
21/22.2.45	XXX	NT325/N	406 Sqn	Bf 110	E Stormede a/f	F/L D. A. MacFadyen DFC RCAF
24/25.2.45	XXX	MM792	219 Sqn	Ju 87		W/C W. P. Green DSO DFC-F/O D. A. Oxby DFC DFM**
24/25.2.45	VI	605 Sqn	2 x Fw	190	Ludwigslost a/f	F/O R. E. Lelong DFC RNZAF-P/O J. A. McLaren DFC
28.2.45	XXX	NT325/N	406 Sqn	UEA (Prob)	Hailfingen	S/L D. A. MacFadyen DFC RCAF
3/4.3.45	XXX	NT368	68 Sqn	Ju 188	at Sea	F/L D. B. Wills
3/4.3.45 J	XXX	NT381		Ju 188	at sea	F/L R. B. Miles
3/4.3.45	XXX	NT415	125 Sqn	Ju 188	at Sea	W/C Griffiths
5/6.3.45	XXX	NT361/N	239 Sqn	2xJu 88	Chemnitz/Nuremberg	W/C W. F. Gibb DFC-F/O R. C. Kendall DFC DFM. Ju 88G-6 Wrk.Nr. 622319 C9+GA of Stab/NJG5 flown by Obstlt Walter Borchers KIA (Kommodore NJG5, (59 victories - 16 by day, 43 by night) Knight's Cross 29.10.44 KIA. Lt Friedrich Reul (radar op) KIA (crashed near Altenburg 25km NW of Chemnitz in Thuringia). Ju 88G-6 Wrk.Nr. 622318 C9+NL of 3./NJG5 crashed near Chemnitz. Uffz H. Dorminger (FF), Uffz Max Bartsch (BF), Ogfr Franz Wohlschlögel (BMF); Uffz Friedrich Rullmann (BS) all MIA.
5/6.3.45	XXX	NT325/N	406 Sqn	Ju 88	G Gerolzhofen	F/L D. A. MacFadyen DFC RCAF
7/8.3.45	VI	'S'	23 Sqn	Fw 190	Stendahl	F/O E. L. Heath-F/Sgt J. Thompson
8/9.3.45	XXX	MV555	85 Sqn	Ju 188		F/L I. A. Dobie-W/O A. R. Grimstone DFM
12/13.3.45	XXX		410 Sqn	Ju 88 (Prob)	Dunkirk area	F/L J. W. Welford-F/O R. H. Phillips
14/15.3.45	VI	HR213/G	141 Sqn	UEA	Lachen, Germany	F/O (2nd Lt) R. D. S Gregor-F/Sgt P. S. Baker
14/15.3.45	XIX	TA397/R	157 Sqn	Ju 88G	Lützkendorf	S/L R. D. Doleman DSO DFC-F/L D. C. Bunch DFC
15/16.3.45	XXX	NT309	85 Sqn	Ju 88	Hanover area	Capt E. P. Fossum-F/O S. A. Hider
15/16.3.45	XIX	TA393/C	157 Sqn	Ju 88	20m S Würzburg	F/L J. O. Mathews DFC*-W/O A. Penrose DFC*
16/17.3.45	XXX	NT330	239 Sqn	Ju 188	Nuremberg	S/L D. L Hughes DFC-F/L R. H. Perks DFC. Pilot Maj Werner Hoffmann?
18/19.3.45	XXX	NT364/K	157 Sqn	Ju 88	Hanau	W/O D. Taylor-F/Sgt Radtord

DATE	TYPE	SERIAL	SQN	ENEMY	A/C DETAILS	PILOT-NAVIGATOR/RADAR OP
18/19.3.45	XXX	NT271/M	239 Sqn	He 219	Witten	W/C W. F. Gibb DFC-F/O R. C. Kendall DFC DFM. Prob. He 219 of NJG1 Hptm Baake (pilot & Kommandeur I./NJG1) and Uffz Bettaque (radar op) both safe.
18/19.3.45	XXX	MV548/Z	85 Sqn	Bf 110		F/L F. D. Win RNZAF-F/O T. P. Ryan RNZAF
20/21.3.45	XXX	NT450	125 Sqn	Ju 188	at Sea	F/L Kennedy
20/21.3.45	XXX	NT324/T	85 Sqn	Bf 110+He 219V14		F/L G. C. Chapman-F/Sgt J. Stockley. Poss. He 219V-14 Wrk.Nr. 190014 of 3./NJG1. Oblt Heinz Oloff (pilot & St.Kpt. 3./NJG1); radar op u/k.
21/22.3.45	XIII	MM466/G	604 Sqn	Bf 110	Dhunn area	
21/22.3.45	XIII		409 Sqn	Bf 110		F/O R. I. E. Britten DFC RCAF-F/O L. E. Fownes DFC
21/22.3.45	XXX		488 Sqn	Bf 110		F/O K. Fleming-F/O K. L. Nagle
23/24.3.45	XXX		219 Sqn	Fw 190		F/L J. C. E. Atkins DFC-F/O D. R. Mayo
24/25.3.45	VI		605 Sqn	Ju 88	Erfurt	F/L A. D. Wagner DFC-F/L E. T. Orringe
24/25.3.45	XIII		604 Sqn	Bf 109	Haltern	F/L L. J. Leppard-F/L Houghton
24/25.3.45	XXX		410 Sqn	Bf 110		F/L G. R. Leask-F/L J. W. Rolf
24/25.3.45	XXX		410 Sqn	Ju 88G		S/L MacTavish-F/O Grant
25/26.3.45	XIII	MM513/J 409		Ju 88	Dortmund area	F/O R. I. E. Britten DFC RCAF-F/O L. E. Fownes DFC
25/26.3.45	XIII		264 Sqn	Ju 88	25m NNE Wesel	F/L C. M. Ramsay DFC-F/L D. J. Donnet DFC
25/26.3.45	XIII		264 Sqn	Ju 88 (Prob)		F/O A. Recina-F/Sgt R. A. W. Smith
25/26.3.45	XXX		219 Sqn	2 x Bf 110		F/L Ruffley-F/O Fagan
26/27.3.45	XIII	MM497	604 Sqn	Ju 88		F/O T. R. Wood-F/O R. Leafe
26/27.3.45	XXX	NT263	488 Sqn	Bf 110	8m NW Bocholt	F/L K. W. Stewart-F/O H. E. Brumby
26/27.3.45	XXX	NT314/P	488 Sqn	Ju 88	20m N Emmerich	F/L J. A. S. Hall DFC-P/O Taylor (Mosquito crash landed)
26/27.3.45	XXX		219 Sqn	Ju 188		F/O Reed-F/O Bricker
26/27.3.45	XXX		410 Sqn	Bf 110		F/L B. E. Plumer DFC-F/L Bradford
27/28.3.45	XXX		219 Sqn	He 177		F/O Reed-P/O Bricker
30/31.3.45	XIII		264 Sqn	Fw 190	SE Münster	W/C E. S. Smith AFC-F/L P. C. O'Neil-Dunne
3.4.45	XXX		239 Sqn	Ju 188		S/L D. L. Hughes DFC-F/L R. H. Perks DFC
4/5.4.45	XXX	NT540/C BSDU		Bf 109	W Magdeburg	S/L R. G. Woodman DFC-F/L A. J. Neville DFC
4/5.4.45	XXX	'C'	85 Sqn	Ju 188	Near Magdeburg	F/L C. W. Turner-F/Sgt G. Honeyman
7/8.4.45	XXX	'Q'	85 Sqn	Fw 190	NW Mobiis	W/C W. K. Davison DFC-F/L D. C. Bunch DFC (85/157 Sqns)
7/8.4.45	XXX	NT263	488 Sqn	UEA	20m SE Osnabrück	F/L K. W. Stewart-F/O H. E. Brumby
8/9.4.45	XXX	NT494/N	85 Sqn	Ju 88	20m W Lützkendorf	F/L H. B. Thomas DFC-F/O C. B. Hamilton
9/10.4.45	VI	RS575/V	515 Sqn	Ju 188	SE Hamburg	W/C H. C. Kelsey DFC*-F/L E. M. Smith DFC DFM
10/11.4.45	XXX		239 Sqn	He 111		W/C P. O. Falconer-F/Sgt W. G. Armor
13/14.4.45	XXX	NT334/S	85 Sqn	He 219	Kiel	F/L K. D. Vaughan-F/Sgt R. D. MacKinnon
14/15.4.45	XXX		239 Sqn	Ju 88	Potsdam	S/L D. J. Raby DFC-F/O S. J. Flint DFM
15/16.4.45	VI	PZ398/C	515 Sqn	Ju 52/3M	Nr Schleissheim	P/O L. G. Holland-F/Sgt R. Young
17/18.4.45	XXX	MV557 55		Ju 88	Munich area	W/C W. K. Davison DFC-F/L D. C. Bunch DFC (85/157 Sqns)
19/20.4.45	XXX	NT276/B	BSDU	Ju 88	S Denmark	F/L D. R. Howard DFC-F/L F. A. W. Clay DFC
9/10.4.45	XXX		219 Sqn	He 177	Ruhr	F/O Lang-F/O Fagan
10/11.4.45	XXX		239 Sqn	He 111		W/C P. O. Falconer-F/Sgt W. G. Armor
10/11.4.45	XXX	MM744	410 Sqn	Ju 188	Damme area	F/L R. D. Schultz DFC*-F/O J. S. Christie DFC
11/12.4.45	XXX		FIDS	Ju 88	20m NNW Berlin	F/L F. R. L. Mellersh DFC*
13/14.4.45	XXX	N1334/S	85 Sqn	He 219	Kiel	F/L K. D. Vaughan-F/Sgt R. D. MacKinnon
14/15.4.45	XXX		239 Sqn	Ju 88	Potsdam	S/L D. J. Raby DFC-F/O S. J. Flint DFM
15/1 6.4.45	VI	PZ398	515 Sqn	Ju 52/3M	Nr Schleissheim	P/O L. G. Holland-F/Sgt R. Young
17/1 8.4.45	XXX	MV557 55		Ju 88	Munich area	W/C K. Davison DFC
19/20.4.45	XIX	NT276/B	BSDU	Ju 88 S	Denmark	F/L D. R. Howard DFC-F/L F. A. W. Clay DFC
20/21.4.45	XIII	MM521	264 Sqn	Ju 88	20m W Berlin	F/O P. N. Lee-F/O R. Thomas
21/22.4.45	XIII		264 Sqn	2 x Ju 290	20m W Berlin	F/O J. Daber-W/O J. A. Heathcote
21/22.4.45	XIII		264 Sqn	Ju 188		W/O A. S. Davies-F/Sgt C. T. Fisher
21/22.4.45	XXX		488 Sqn	Ju 52		P/O G. S. Patrick-W/O J. J. Concannon
21/22.4.45	XXX	MV527	410 Sqn	2 x Ju 188	Ferrbellen area	F/L R. D. Schultz DFC*-F/O J. S. Christie DFC
21/22.4.45	XIII		264 Sqn	Ju 88 (Prob)	35m NW Berlin	F/O C. M. Ramsay DFC-F/L D. J. Donnet DFC
21/22.4.45	XIII		264 Sqn	He 111		F/O W. A. Craig-F/O A. L. Tauwhare
21.4.45	VI		23 Sqn	Ju 188		W/O East-F/Sgt Eames
22/23.4.45	XIII		264 Sqn	Ju 88G	20M W Berlin	F/L C. M. Ramsay DFC-F/L D. J. Donnet DFC
23/24.4.45	XIII		264 Sqn	He 111	Between Elbe-Berlin	F/O W. H. Foster-F/O F. H. Dagger
23/24.4.45	XXX	NT512	488 Sqn	Ju 52		
23/24.4.45	XXX	NT327	488 Sqn	Ju 88		
23/24.4.45	XIII	HK506/H	409 Sqn	2 x Ju 52		F/O J. H. Skelly-P/O P. J. Linn
23/24.4.45	XIII	HK429/D	409 Sqn	2 x Ju 87/Fw 190		F/O E. E. Hermansen-F/L D. J. T. Hamm
23/24.4.45	XIII	MM588/T	409 Sqn	Ju 52		P/O J. Leslie-P/O C. M. Turgood
23/24.4.45	XXX	NV548/Z	406 Sqn	Ju 88	Witstock	W/C R. Bannock DFC* RCAF-F/L R. R. Bruce DFC
24/25.4.45	XIII	MM517/S	409 Sqn	Ju 29		W/C R. F. Hatton-F/L R. N. Rivers
24/25.4.45	XIII		409 Sqn	Ju 52		P/O L. E. Fitchett-P/O A. C. Hardy (Mosquiro crash land/base)
24/25.4.45	VI		605 Sqn	Ju 88	Neuburg a/f	F/L A. D. Wagner DFC*-F/O E. T. "Pip" Orringe DFC
24/25.4.45	XXX		488 Sqn	Ju 52		S/L F. W. Davison DFC-F/L E. Hickmore
24.4.45	XXX		29 Sqn	Me 262a		W/O Dallinson
24/25.4.45	VI	RS575/V	515 Sqn	Do 217	6m N Libeznice	W/C H. C. Kelsey DFC*-F/L E. M. Smith DFC DFM
				Do 217	Prague, Czech	" " "
25/26.4.45	XIII	HK466	264 Sqn	Fw 190	W Berlin	P/O J. Hutton-P/O H. E. Burraston
25/26.4.45	XXX	NT527	488 Sqn	Fw 189		F/O J. W. Marshall-P/O P. F. Prestcott
2/3.5.45	VI	'K'	605 Sqn	Fw 190	Lecke, Denmark	F/O B. Williams DFC-W/O S. Hardy

Appendix 3

Top Scoring V1 Flying Bomb Destroyers (Mosquito crews)

V1s	Pilot	Squadron		Aircraft
152	S/L R. N. CHUDLEIGH	96		NF.XIII
61	F/Sgt J. BRYAN	96		NF.XIII
57	F/L D. A. MACFADYEN	418	RCAF	Mosquito II
53	F/O P. de l BROOKE	264		NF.XIII
51	F/L. J. W. GOUGH	96		NF.XIII
21	W/C E. D. CREW	96		NF.XIII
39	F/L F. R. L. MELLERSH	96		XII
18½	W/C R. BANNOCK	418	RCAF	Mosquito II
13	W/C W. P. GREEN	96		NF.XIII
12	F/L I. A. DOBIE	96		NF.XIII
12	F/L J. C. MUSGRAVE	605		VI
12	F/L D. L. WARD	96		XIII
9	F/L K. A. ROEDIGER	456	RAAF	XVII
9	S/L A. PARKER-REES	96/501		NF.XIII/Tempest V
8	F/O B. C. BENSTED	605		FB.VI
8	F/L.G. J. WRIGHT	605		FB.VI
8	F/L E. L. WILLIAMS	FIU/	501/605	Tempest V/ 605 Mosquito FB.VI
8	S/L N. S. HEAD	96		NF. XIII
7.51	F/L. C. J. EVANS	418	RCAF	Mosquito II
7	P/O W. A. MCLARDY	96		XII
6	F/L R. C. WALTON	605		VI
6	S/L P. L. CALDWELL	96		NF.XIII
6	W/C J. G. BENSON	157		NF.XIX
6	F/L G. R. I. PARKER	219		XXX
5	F/O P. S. LEGGAT	418	RCAF	Mosquito II
5	F/L.N. S. MAY	418	RCAF	Mosquito II
5	F/O J. D. WRIGHT	418	RCAF	Mosquito II
5	S/L B. HOWARD	456	RAAF	NF.XVII
5	F/L J. C. WORTHINGTON	605		FB.VI
5	S/L H. M. CHISHOLM	157		NF.XIX
5	F/L.J. O. MATHEWS	157		NF.XIX

Appendix 4

Mosquito Squadrons

1 Photo Reconnaissance Unit (8 7 40-26 6 43)

Command Assignments: 16 Group Coastal Command; Bomber Command, 26 6 43-
Aircraft: PR I; PR II; PR IV; PR IX; PR XVI, PR 32.

History: No 1 PRU was renamed as such from the PDU (Photographic Development Unit), 8 July 1942. First Mosquito (PR 1) operation, 17 9 42. Disbanded 19 10 42 and PRU reformed as five PR squadrons, Nos 540 & 544 being equipped with Mosquitoes. Re-numbered No 106 (PR) Wing 26 6 43. Re-numbered again, 15 5 44, as No 106 (PR) Group (15 5 44-7 5 45).

4 Squadron (NC: UP)

Motto: *In futurum videre* ('To see into the future')
Command Assignments: No 35 (R) Wing, No 84 Group, 2nd TAF (PR), WW2. BAFO Germany, 31.8.45
Aircraft: ('B' Flight) PR.XVI, 8.43-11.5.44. FB.VI, 9.45-7.50.

Stations:		Squadron Commanding Officers:	
Volkel, Holland	31 Aug 1945	S/L C D Harris St John DFC	May 1945
Gilze Rijen, Holland	Sept 1945-	W/C M P C Corkery	Sep 1945
Gütersloh, Germany	8 Nov 1945-	W/C R L Jones	May 1946
Wahn, Germany	13 Nov 1945-	S/L B Everton-Jones	Nov 1947
Wünsdorf, Germany	10.7.50-7.50	S/L C P N Newman DFC	Sep 1949

History: Up until August 1943 flew Lysanders and Tomahawks on general army co-operation and PR work. Began receiving Spitfire XIs and XIIIs and Mosquito XVIs for purely high-level PR duties. Early 1944 gave up its Mustangs which, it used on Rhubarbs across the Channel, and went over to PR duties in 2nd TAF using just Spitfires and Mosquito PR XVIs ('B' Flight). First Mosquito PR sortie flown, 20 March. Among the tasks allotted was the need to map all V-l sites in northern France. Last Mosquito sortie flown, 20 May 1944, further conversion to Spitfires having already begun, 11 May. Some Typhoons were received for low-level PR duties, October 1944. Disbandment occurred 31 August 1945. That same day 605 Squadron, equipped with FB.VIs at Celle, was re-numbered 4 Squadron. FB.VIs were operated in the strike role in BAFO for five years before replacement by the DH Vampire fighter-bombers in 1950.

8 Squadron (HV)

Motto: *Uspiam et passim* ('Everywhere unbounded')
Command Assignments: Middle East
Aircraft: FB.VI, 9.46-5.47.

Stations:		Squadron Commanding Officers:	
Khormaksar, Aden	1/9/46-5/4 7	W/C P E St E. O'Brien DFC	9/46-2/47
		S/L F W M Jensen DFC AFC	Feb 1947

History: Formed from B-24 Liberator (SD) flight which disbanded 15/11/45. 1 September 1946 114 Squadron at Khormaksar re-numbered 8 Squadron, equipped with FB.VIs. Used to police the Aden Protectorate and the border with Yemen and other neighbouring states. March 1947, Mosquitoes replaced with Tempests.

11 Squadron (OM)

Motto: *Ociores acrioresque aquilis* ('Swifter and keener than eagles)
Command Assignments: BAFO, Germany
Aircraft: FB.VI, 10.48-8.50.

Stations:		Squadron Commanding Officers:	
Wahn, Germany	4.10.48-1948	F/L J Welsh	Jun 48
Celle, Germany	9.49-9.50	S/L I W Hutchison	Oct 48
Wünsdorf, Germany	August 1950	S/L J M Rumsey	Mar 49
		S/L D H Seaton	Aug 50

History: Equipped with Spitfires in Japan 5/46-2/48. 4/10/48 107 Squadron in BAFO at Wahn, Germany, re-numbered 11 Squadron, FB.VIs being used until 11 August 1950 when re-equipped with Vampire FB.5s.

13 Squadron

Motto: *Adjuvamus tuendo* (We assist by watching)
Command Assignments: PR, Middle East

Aircraft: PR. IX/PR.XVI/PR.34, 8.46-2.52.

Stations:

Ein Shemer	1/9/46-
Kabrit	11.12.46
Fayid	5.2.47
Kabrit	21.2.51-52

Squadron Commanding Officers:

W/C A H W Ball DSO DFC	Sep 1946
W/C A M Brown DFC*	Nov 1946
S/L RN Hampson	Mar 1947
S/L J C T Hewell DFC DSO	Dec 1948
S/L L V Bachellier AFC	Dec 1949

History: Disbanded as a Boston squadron, Greece, 19/4/46. 1 September 1946 680 Squadron at Ein Shemer, Palestine, re-numbered 13 Squadron with PR.34s. Provided PR for the Egyptian and Canal Zone area and throughout the Middle East. Early 1952, PR.34s were replaced by Meteor PR.l0s.

14 Squadron (CX)

Motto: "I spread my wings and keep my promise"
Command Assignments: Coastal Command, 6.45-31.3.46. BAFO, Germany, 4.46-51
Aircraft: FB.VI, 6.45-3.46. XVI/B.35, 4.46-l0.47.B.35 12.47-2.51.

Station:

Banff (143 renumbered)	1.6.45
Wahn (128 renumbered)	1/4/46
Disbanded	1/4/4 6
Celle	9/49
Fassberg	11.50-2/51

History: WW2 Coastal Command Wellington Squadron. Disbanded, 1 June 1945 and 143 Squadron at Banff was renumbered 14 Squadron the same day. For nine months 14 Squadron operated B.IV aircraft before disbanding, 31 March 1946. Next day at Wahn, 14 Squadron reformed in BAFO by renumbering 128 Squadron, which operated the B.XVI, later equipping with the B.35. February 1951 re-equipped with the DH Vampire FB.5.

18 Squadron

Command Assignments: Suez Canal Zone
Aircraft: FB.VI, 3.47-11.47

Stations:

Kabrit, Egypt	March 1947
Mingaladon	March 1947
Changi	Sept 1947

Squadron Commanding Officers:

S/L D R Lumley-George	March 1947

History: Disbanded, Ein Shemer, Palestine, 15 September 1946, having flown Lancaster GR.3s. Reformed, Kabrit, 15 March 1947 as light bomber unit equipped with FB.VIs. Moved to Changi, Singapore, September 1947 where it remained until being renumbered 1300 (Met) Flight, 15 November 1947.

21 (City Of Norwich) Squadron (YH)

Motto: *"Virribus vincimus'* ("By strength we conquer")
Command Assignments: 140 Wing, 2 Group, 2nd Tactical Air Force/BAFO, Germany
Aircraft: FB.VI, 9.43-10.47.

Stations:

Sculthorpe	10/43-
Hunsdon	31/12/43
Gravesend	23/4/44
Thorney Island	23/6/44
Rosieres	6/2/45
Melsbroek	18/4/45
Gütersloh	3/11/45
Münster/Handorf	27/6/46
Gütersloh	9/8/46-7/11/47

Squadron Commanding Officers:

W/C R M North DFC AFC	June 1943
W/C I G Dale DFC	May 1944
W/C D E Dennis DSO DFC DFM	July 1944
W/C I G Dale DFC	Oct 1944
W/C V R Oates	Feb 1945
W/C P A Kleboe DSO DFC AFC	Mar 1945
W/C A G Wilson DFC	Apr 1945
W/C L J Joel DFC	May 1946

History: Throughout the early part of the war sustained high losses flying Blenheims, then Venturas, before conversion to the FB.VI September 1943. Operated as part of 140 Wing, 2nd TAF, gaining a distinctive reputation for pinpoint bombing raids. Moved to the continent, December 1944, remaining there until the end of the war, then becoming a part of BAFO. Flew a courier service between Nürnberg and Blackbushe for the Nürnberg war trials before disbanding, 7 November 1947.

22 Squadron

Motto: *"Preux et audacieux"* ('Valiant and brave')
Command Assignments: Ear East
Aircraft: FB.VI, 5.46-8.46

Stations:

Seletar, Malta	1/5/46-15/8/46

Commanding Officers:

W/C A Pleasance CBE DFC	May 1946

History: 89 Squadron at Seletar, Singapore renumbered 22 Squadron 1 May 1946, but it existed as such for only three months, equipped with FB.VIs, before disbanding, 15 August that year. (Reformed, 1955 equipped with the Pioneer).

23 Squadron (YP)

Motto: *"Semper agressus"* ("Always on the attack")
Command Assignments: Fighter Command/100 Group (Special Duties later Bomber Support)
Aircraft: NF.II, 7.42-8.43, B.VI, 6.43-9.45, NF.30, 8.45-2.47, NF.36, 10.46-12.51.

Stations:

Ford	July 1942
Manston	6 August 1942
Bradwell Bay	13 September 1942
in transit to Malta	7 December 1942
Luqa, Malta (with dets at Pomigliano & Alghero)	28 December 1942
At sea	8 May 1944-1 June 1944
Little Snoring	19 June 1944
Disbanded	25 September 1945
Reformed Wittering	10 October 1946
Coltishall	23 November 1947
Det Church Fenton	19 November 1949
Coltishall	22 September 1950
Horsham St Faith	15 January 1952
Coltishall	4 July 1952

Squadron Commanding Officers:

W/C B R O'B Hoare DSO DFC*	March 1942
W/C P G Wykeham-Barnes DSO DFC*	Sept 42
W/C J B Selby DSO DFC	April 1943
W/C P R Burton-Giles DSO DFC	Sept 1943
W/C A M Murphy DSO DFC C de G	Dec 43
W/C S P Russell DFC	Dec 1944
W/C P G K Williamson DFC	Sept 1946
W/C D L Norris-Smith	July 1947
W/C V S H Duclos DFC	Oct 1949
W/C A J Jacomb-Hood DFC	Dec 1951

History: Operated Blenheims and Havoc's in the night fighter/night intruder role until July 1942 before beginning conversion to NF.IIs, stripped of their Al Mk. IV radar, and with increased fuel capacity, for Intruder operations. First Mosquito sortie flown 6/7 July 1942 by the CO, W/C Sammy Hoare in S-Sugar. On 7/8 July he shot down a Do217 16m E of Chartres with three short bursts of cannon fire. On 8/9 July S/L K. H. Salisbury-Hughes in S-Sugar destroyed a Do217 over Etampes and a He 111 at Evreux. 8/9 September, three Mosquitoes were lost on Intruder sorties. 30 December 1942-September 1943, 23 Squadron flew hundreds of intruder sorties against the Axis in Italy, North Africa and Sicily. January-March 1943 lost 5 aircraft and crews, while 17 aircraft were claimed "destroyed", the first, a Ju 88, falling to S/L Philip Russell/P/O E G Pullen, 8 January during an Intruder to Tunis airfield. During the moon period two sorties each night were flown against road convoys of Rommel's retreating army along the North African coast. 19 January, 14 FB.VIs attacked Rommel's convoys on the heavily congested roads between Tripoli and Gabes and left one road jammed with burning vehicles and fires that could be seen for 40 miles. December 1942-September 1943 flew 38 co-operation sorties with torpedo carrying Wellingtons and Beauforts. After the fall of Sicily, operated over Italy in FB.VIs from Gerbini. Little night enemy air activity meant most operations were bombing and cannon attacks on targets of opportunity. Moved to Pomigliano, near Naples, October 1943; final sorties being flown, April 1944. At the end of June 1944 joined 100 Group, reverting to Fighter Command post-war, for a time as night-fighter unit, until disbandment, 25 September 1945. Re-formed, 1946, remaining the leading squadron in the night fighter force, 12 Group, operating NF.36s, until conversion to the Vampire NF10, 1951.

25 Squadron (ZK)

Motto: *"Eeriens tego"* ("Striking I defend")
Command Assignments: Fighter Command
Aircraft: NF.II, 11.42-3.44, FB.VI, 8.43-9.43, NF.XVII, 12.43-11.44, NF.30, 9.44-9.46 FB.VI, 1/2.45, NF.36, 9.46-9.51.

Stations:

Church Fenton	17/5/42
Acklington	19/12/43
Coltishall	5/2/44
Castle Camps	27 October 1944
Boxted	11 January 1946
West Malling	5 September 1946-9/51

Squadron Commanding Officers:

S/L E G Watkins AFC	Sept 1942
S/L J L Shaw	March1943
W/C S N L Maude DFC	April 1943
W/C C M Wight-Boycott DSO	Oct 1943
W/C L J C Mitchell	Sept 1944
W/C W Hoy DFC	April 1945
S/L R Goucher DFC	Dec 1945

History: FB.VI replaced Beaufighters, 1942, for night Rangers over France and the Low Countries. Ground targets such as trains were also attacked. Detachment in Cornwall flew long-range patrols in the Bay of Biscay, mid-1943. Towards end of 1943 new radar equipment was fitted for operations at night to intercept German night fighters threatening the bomber streams. Continued this role throughout 1944 using NF.XVIII. Intruder patrols then became a feature. May 1944, enemy intruders over Britain, in particular He 111-22 V1 launchers, were dealt with effectively, before reverting to home defense and intruder patrols once again. 1946-1951 spent as one of the squadrons in the all-weather defense of the UK. NF.36s were flown until 1951 when replaced by the Vampire NF.10.

27 Squadron

Motto: *"Quam celerrime ad astra"* ("With all speed to the stars") Command Assignments: India
Aircraft: NF.II, 4.43-6.43, FB.VI, 12.43-4.44.

Stations:

Agartala	Feb 1943
Parasharam	Feb 1944

Squadron Commanding Officers:

W/C H C Daish DFC	Dec 1942
W/C E J B Nicolson VC	Aug 1943

History: Equipped with the Beaufighter, 1943, but two NF.IIs were acquired for evaluation purposes in Burmese conditions. By year end one flight had converted to the Mosquito but after several operations, December 1943-January 1944, were withdrawn, squadron reverting to an all-Beaufighter squadron once more.

29 Squadron (RO)

Motto: *"Impiger et acer"* ("Energetic and keen")
Command Assignments: Fighter Command (ADGB) to 148 Wing, 85 (Base) Group, 2nd TAF, 1.5.44. To 147 Wing, June 1944. Back to ADGB 26.8.44
Aircraft: NF.XII, 5.43-4.44, NF.XIII, 10.43-2.45, NF.XXX, 2.45-1946, NF.36, 8.46-6.50. NE.XXX, 6.50-10.51.

Stations:		**Squadron Commanding Officers:**	
West Malling	October 1942	W/C R E X Mack DFC	June 1943
Bradwell Bay	13 May 1943	W/C P W Arbon DFC	Feb 1944
Ford	4 September 1943	W/C G E Powell-Sheddon DFC	April 1944
Drem	1 March 1944	W/C J W Allan DSO DFC	Dec 1944
West Malling	1 May 1944	S/L T C Wood DFC	Dec 1945
Hunsdon	19 June 1944	S/L D Hawkins DFC	Feb 1947
Colerne	22/26 Feb 1945-	S/L M J B Young DFC	Mar 1949
Manston	11 April 1945	S/L M Shaw DSO	July 1949
West Malling	1 January 1946		
Tangmere	November 1946-Janaury 1951		

History: Began converting from the Beaufighter to the Mosquito XII, summer 1943, for the continuance of night intruder operations over occupied Europe. By end of 1943 had destroyed about 600 enemy aircraft. Intruder operations continued in 1944, apart from October/November, when the Mosquitoes were used briefly for night interception of V1 flying bombs. Intruding then continued unabated until VE Day 1945. Me 262 jet fighter was shot down before the end of the war in Europe. Post war, remained in Fighter Command, being selected in 1950 as the first in the RAF to convert to the Meteor NF.11.

36 Squadron (248 Squadron re-numbered)

Motto: *"Rajawali raja langit"*
Command Assignments: Coastal Command 1946-1947
Aircraft: FB.VI, 10.46-10.47.

Stations:		**Squadron Commanding Officers:**	
Thorney Island	1 October 1946-	W/C J V Hoggarth	Oct 1946
	14 October 1947	W/C F H Stubbs DFC	Apr 1947
		W/C G E Home	Aug 1947

History: 248 Squadron, Coastal Command at Thorney Island, 1 October 1946, re-numbered 36 Squadron, being used in coastal strike equipped with FB.VI until 15 October 1947, when the squadron disbanded.

39 Squadron

Motto: *"Die Noctuque"* ("By day and night")
Command Assignments: Canal Zone, Egypt, 1950
Aircraft: FB.VI, 10.45-9.46, NF.36, 3.46-3.53.

Stations:		**Squadron Commanding Officers:**	
Fayid	September 1949	S/L R D Doleman DSO DFC	Apr 1949
Kabrit	21 February 1951-March 1953	S/L J C Cogill DSO DFC	Oct 1951
		S/L J J O'Meara DSO DFC	Feb 1954

History: Began a slow re-equipment October 1945, with the FB.VI, alongside Martin Marauders. Disbanded, Khartoum, 8 September 1946. Re-formed at Eastleigh Airport, Nairobi, Kenya 1 April 1948 with Hawker Tempests. Disbanded again, 28 February 1949. Next day, reformed, Fayid, Canal Zone, with 8 NF.36s, a T.III and ten crews. For four years acted as night fighter defense of the Suez Canal and surrounding area, its NF.36s being replaced by Meteor NF.13s, March 1953.

45 Squadron (OB)

Motto: *"Per ardua surgo"* ("Through difficulties I arise")
Command Assignments: India
Aircraft: FB.VI 2.44-5.46.

Stations:		**Squadron Commanding Officers:**	
Yelahanka, India	12 February 1944	W/C H C Stumm DFC	Jan 1944
Dalbhumgarth	29 May 1944	W/C R J Walker	May 1944
Ranchi	August 1944	S/L V S H Duclos DFC	Mar 1945
Kumbhirgram	September 1944	W/C Etherton DFC	July 1945
Joan	26 April 1945	S/L C O L Dyke	Mar 1946
Cholavaram	May 1945	W/C E W Snell DFC	April 1946
Madras, St Thomas' Mt	October 1945-May 1946	S/L D P Marvin DFC	June 1946
Negombo, Ceylon	May 1946	W/C C C O Key	Nov 1946

History: Operated first Blenheims and then Vengeance aircraft in Burma 1942 until end of 1943, when withdrawn from the front line for re-equipment with the FB.VI. Structural problems with the aircraft prevented operations until September 1944. Bombing attacks on the Japanese in Burma continued until May 1945 before the return to India. Moved to Ceylon, 1946, re-equipping with Beaufighters and Brigands.

46 Squadron

Motto: "We rise to conquer"
Command Assignments: Mediterranean
Aircraft: NF.XII, 8.44-11.44

Stations:		**Squadron Commanding Officers:**	
Idku, Egypt	May 1942-Dec 1944	S/L C E Robertson	Aug-Nov 1944
		W/C R W Denison	Nov-Dec 1944

History: All surviving Gladiators and most of the crews lost aboard Glorious, 7 June 1940, which was sunk on return from the campaign in Norway. Re-equipped with Hurricanes and fighting in the Battle of Britain, night patrols were flown in 1941 before going overseas again. Pilots were absorbed by hard pressed Hurricane squadrons in Malta, May 1941 while ground crew went on to Egypt less aircraft and aircrew to be put to work servicing other unit's aircraft there. May 1942, a flight of 89 Squadron at Idku was expanded into a new 46 Squadron using Beaufighters for intruder operations as far afield as Sicily and Palestine. Began receiving NF.XII aircraft for the task, August 1944, and in September 11 enemy aircraft were accounted for in five days. Operations practically ceased in November. Converted to Short Stirling Vs for transport duties, England, January 1945.

47 Squadron (KU)

Motto: *"Nih nomen roboris omen"* ("The name of the Nile is an omen of our strength")
Command Assignments: India-Burma/Malaya
Aircraft: FB.VI, 10.44-11.44, 2.45-2.46.

Stations:

Yelahanka, India	12 February 1944
Ranchi, India	November 1944
Kumbhirgam, India	January 1945
Kinmagon, Burma	April 1945
Hmawbi, Burma	August 1945
Kemajoran, Java	November 1945
Butterworth, Malaya	January 1946

Squadron Commanding Officers:

W/C W D L Eilson-Young	Nov 1943
S/L J H Etherington DFC	May 1945
W/C V S H Bucles	June 1945
W/C C H Melville-Jackson DFC	Oct 1945

History: Began conversion from Beaufighters to FB.VIs, October 1944. Structural problems however, meant no Mosquito operations were flown and by the end of the year conversion back to Beaufighters had taken place. Mosquitoes were re-introduced, February 1945. Problems with the wooden aircraft in the hot climate were experienced again and the squadron was rendered non-operational from May-August. Sent to Java on ground-attack duties to deal with Indonesian separatists at the end of the Pacific War, disbandment took place, 21 March 1946, Butterworth, Malaya.

55 Squadron

Motto: *"Nil nos tremefacit"* ("Nothing makes us afraid")
Command Assignments: Greece
Aircraft: FB.XXVI, 7.46-1.11.46.

Stations:

Hassani, Greece	July 1946-1 November 1946
Disbanded	

History: Operated in WW2 as a bomber squadron, before converting from Bostons to FB.XXVIs, July 1946. Squadron disbanded however, 1 November before commencing operations.

58 Squadron (OT)

Motto: *"Alis nocturnis"* ("On the wings of the night")
Command Assignments: PRU, Gt Britain, Oct 1946 - mid-1953
Aircraft: PR.34, 10.46-8.52, PR.34A, 10.51-1.54. PR.35, 11.51-4.54

Stations:

Benson	August 1947
Wyton	March 1953-1954

Squadron Commanding Officers:

W/C A D Panton	Oct 1946
W/C A Gadd DFC	Sep 1947
S/L J M Rumsey	Nov 1947
S/L M M Mair	Feb 1949
S/L A D MacLaren DFC	May 1951
S/L J C Bishop DFC	June 1951
S/L R A Hoskin DFC AFC	April 1952

History: Re-formed, Benson, 1 October 1946 in the PR role, the first task to photo-survey Gt Britain for the Ordnance Survey using Anson C19s and Mosquito PR.34s. Mid-1953, both were replaced by the English Electric Canberra.

60 Squadron SAAF

Motto: *"Per ardua ad aethera tendo"* ("I strive through difficulties to the sky")
Command Assignments: North African Tactical Air Force (No 285 Wing/No 336 Wing). Mediterranean Allied PR Wing, Italy.
Aircraft: Mk IV, 2 43-11 43; PR IX, VI, PR XVI, 8.43-45.

Stations:

Caste) Benito	Jan 1943
Senen	March 1943
Sorman	May 1943
San Severo	Dec 1943

Squadron Commanding Officers:

Maj O C Davies DFC	Feb 1943
Maj E U Brierley	June 1943
Lt Col O C Davies DFC	April 1944
Maj D W Allam	April 1944
Maj P P Daphne DFC	Jan 1945

History: Equipped with Baltimores and Marylands, 1942, for PR operations in support of the British 8th Army in the Western Desert. Two PR IV Mosquitoes arrived, February 1943, reputedly on the insistence of Gen Montgomery, to photograph the Mareth Line between Tunisia and Libya. Fitted with American K.17 cameras, ideal for mapping photographs, these were first used operationally on 15 February. Col Owen Glynn Davies was instrumental in getting his squadron equipped with Mosquitoes. In July 1943 a detachment operated from Lentini, south of Catania, Sicily. By November ten PR IXs, and a Mk VI for training, were on the strength of 'B' Flight. (LR480 is displayed at the South African National Museum of Military History at Saxonwold). In February 1944, the first of 14 PR XVIs (and two F IIs) arrived. PR flights were made, 1944-45, as far afield as Austria, the Balkans, and southern Germany, Me 262 jets accounting for some of the squadron's aircraft. Towards the end of the war carried out mapping survey work over Austria, the Alps, Italy and France. Post-war further survey work was carried out in Greece until 15 July 1945, ten surviving Mosquitoes were flown to Zwarkop, SA.

68 Squadron (WM)

Motto: *"Vzdy Pripaven"* ("Always Ready")
Command Assignments: Fighter Command
Aircraft: NF.XVII, 6.44-4.45, NF.XIX, 7.44-2.45, NF.XXX, 6.44-20.4.45.

Stations:

Castle Camps	June 1944
Coltishall	Oct 1944
Wittering	Feb 1945
Coltishall	Feb 1945
Church Fenton	Mar 1945

Squadron Commanding Officers:

W/C D Hayley-Bell DFC	Oct 1943
W/C C Howden DFC	Aug 1944
W/C L W G Gill	Feb 1945

History: 1941-1943 operated Blenheim night fighters and in turn, Bristol Beaufighters, until, after D-day, re-equipped with NF.XVIII Mosquitoes. These were used immediately against V1 offensive over southern England at night. Disbanded, Church Fenton, 20 April 1945 (re-forming 1952 with Meteor NF.lls).

69 Squadron (WI)

Motto: "With vigilance we serve"
Command Assignments: BAFO, Germany
Aircraft: FB.VI, 8.45-3.46, B.XVI, 4.46-11.47.

Stations:

Cambrai/Epinoy, France	Aug 1945-March 1946
Wahn	April 1946-Nov 1947

History: Disbanded, Eindhoven, 7 August 1945. Next day 613 Squadron at Epinoy, France was renumbered 69 Squadron. Operated FB.VIs for seven months on light bomber duties in France before disbandment, 28 March 1946. Re-formed four days later by re-numbering 180 Squadron at Wahn, Germany using B.XVIs. With these, became the first Mosquito squadron to be stationed at Gatow on police duties, but main task was to provide a courier service between Nuremberg and Hartford Bridge (Blackbushe) during the War Trials. Disbanded, Wahn, 6 November 1947.

81 Squadron

Motto: *"Non solum nobis"* ("Not only by us")
Command Assignments: Malaya, September 1946-15 December 1955
Aircraft: PR.XVI, 9.46-9.47, PR.34, 9.46-5.53, PR34A, 9.52-1.56.

Stations:

Seletar	Sept 1946
Changi	Oct 1947
Tengah	Feb 1948
Seletar	March 1950

Squadron Commanding Officers:

W/C J R H Merrifield DFC	Sept 1946
S/L B A Fairhurst DFC	June 1947
S/L P D Thompson DFC DFM	Jan 1949
S/L J Morgan DSO	Sept 1951
S/L W P Swaby	Feb 1953
S/L S McCreith AFC	Aug 1955

History: 1 September 1946 684 Photo-Reconnaissance Squadron in Malaya, which operated the PR.34, renumbered 81 Squadron at Seletar. Now made responsible for long-range photo-reconnaissance and survey over the East Indian area. 1 August 1947, Spitfires from 34 Squadron were added to the strength and 81 Squadron became the most important and only PR unit, in the Ear East Air Force. PR duties were never more important than during the Firedog anti-terrorist operation, which began July 1949. During the campaign, became the last squadron in the RAF to fly the Spitfire operationally (1 April 1954) and the Mosquito (15 December 1955). The Mosquito was replaced in PR service when 81 Squadron converted to Meteor PR.10 and Hunting Pembroke.

82 (United Provinces) Squadron (UX)

Motto: "Super omnia ubique" ("Over all things everywhere")
Command Assignments: India
Aircraft: EB VI, 7.44-3.46.

Stations:

Kolar, India	July 1944
Ranchi, India	Oct 1944
Chharra, India	Dec 1944
Kumbhirgram, India	Dec 1944
Cholavaram, India	May 1945
St Thomas' Mount, Madras	Oct 1945

Squadron Commanding Officers:

W/C L V Hudson	July 1944
W/C E W Snell DFC	Dec 1944

History: Converted from the Vultee Vengeance to the FB.VI, July 1944 after using the dive-bomber very effectively since June 1943 against Japanese positions in Burma. Mosquito operations began December 1944 and were used until May 1945 before a return to India was made to prepare for the intended invasion of Malaya. Remained in India until disbanded at St. Thomas' Mount, Madras 15 March 1946.

84 Squadron (PY)

Motto: *"Scorpiones pungunt"* ("Scorpion Sting")
Command Assignments: India-Malaya
Aircraft: FB.VI, 2.45-12.46.

Stations:

Quetta, India	July 1944
Yelahanka	Oct 1944

Squadron Commanding Officers:

W/C R E Jay	Nov 1944
S/L M H Constable-Maxwell DSO DFC	June 1945

Chharra	April 1945
St Thomas Mount	June 1945
Cuindy, India	Sept 1945
Seletar, Singapore	Sept 1945
Kemajoran, Java	Jan 1946
Kuala Lumpur, Malaya	May 1946
Seletar	Sept 1946

History: Equipped in India-Burma February 1944 with Vengeance dive-bombers, which after just five months on operations, were withdrawn pending replacement by the FB.VI. Before becoming operational, failures of the Mosquito in the hot climate delayed introduction into service and the war finished before participation in the war against the Japanese. Operated post-war against Indonesian separatists in Java before return to Malaya began 1946 for Firedog operations against CTs using Beaufighters.

85 Squadron (VY)

Motto: "*Noctu diuque venamur*" ("We hunt by day and night")
Command Assignments: Fighter Command/100 Group (Special Duties later Bomber Support)
Aircraft: NF.II, 8.42-5.43, NF.XII, 2.43-2.44, FB.VI, 8.43-9.43, NF.XV, 3.43-8.43, NF.XVII, 11.43-10.44, NF.XIX, 5.44-12.44, NF.30, 9.44-1.46, NF.36, 1.46-11.51.

Stations:

Hunsdon	May 1941
West Malling	May 1943
Swannington	May 1944
West Malling	July 1944
Swannington	August 1944
Castle Camps	June 1945
Tangmere	Oct 1945
West Malling	April 1947

Squadron Commanding Officers

W/C C L Raphael DFC	May 1942
W/C J Cunningham DSO* DFC*	Jan 1943
W/C C M Miller DFC	Mar 1944
W/C E S Gonsalves DFC	Oct 1944
W/C W K Davison DFC	Jan 1945

History: One of the most famous fighter squadrons in both world wars beginning WW2 with Hurricanes, then Defiants and later Havocs. August 1942 began equipping with NF.IIs and was very successful in combatting enemy intruder operations over southern England. 28 February 1943, the first NF.XII was delivered to Hunsdon and the type flown operationally for the first time, 24 March. May 1944, transfer to 100 Group Bomber Support at Swannington, Norfolk took place, but in July a quick return south to West Malling ensued again, for a month on anti-Diver patrols against V1s. From August 1944 intruder operations in 100 Group were recommenced and continued until the end of the war before reverting to Fighter Command again in 1945. Operated Mosquitoes from West Malling until 1951 when Meteor NF.IIs replaced them.

86 Squadron RAAF

Command Assignments: RAAF
Aircraft: Mk 40 (modfied); PR XVI

Stations: Coomalie Creek; Broome, Western Austrailia.

History: Reformed from No 1 PRU RAAF on 10 September 1945, equipped with modified FB 40s. No 1 PRU had originally been based in the Northern Territtory of Australia to cover the Dutch East Indies, including East Java, Borneo East, the Celebes, the Halmaheras, Timor, Kai Islands, and later the Philippines, especially Davao Gulf and Leyte Gulf. FB 40s were modified to carry cameras and the first PR 40 sortie flown from Coomalie Creek, 54 miles south of Darwin, 1 June 1944. By 1945, Broome, 1500 miles from Coomalie Creek, was being used enabling the Mk 40s and seven British-built PR XVIs (from a batch of 23: A52-600/622), to reach targets in East Java, 2,300 miles distant, on flights lasting up to 9hrs duration.

87 Squadron RAAF

Command Assignments: No 87 Wing, RAAF
Aircraft: PR 40/FB Mk.40 (modfied); PR XVI

Stations: Coomalie Creek; Parks, NSW.

History: Operated 6 PR 40s (delivered May-October 1944) and 20 FB 40s (delivered 1944-45), on PR in the NW area of the Pacific to photograph Japanese-held territories, including Borneo. The first 12 of 16 PR XVIs received from Britain, March 1945, when No 87 flew a number of sorties to find and successfully photograph the Japanese heavy cruiser Isuzu and her three escorts en route to Koepang, Timor Island. PR XVIs used almost exclusively for the rest of the war although Mk 40s were still used on sorties to Java and East Borneo. Two PR XVIs and one Mk 40 under the command of Squadron Leader K J 'Red' Gray DFC detached to RAF Station Brown, Cocus Island, from June 1945, to photograph Singapore, but bad weather restricted the unit to just one flight, to Christmas Island. Post war, used PR 41 (28 built A52-300/A52-327, delivered 29 5 47-22 7 48), on a large-scale air survey of Australia. (A52-319 is displayed at the Australian War Memorial, Canberra). Disbanded 1946.

89 Squadron

Motto: "*Dei auxilio telis meis*" ("By the help of God, with my own weapons")
Command Assignments: India
Aircraft: FB.VI, 2.45-4.46, NF.XIX, 5.45-4.46

Stations:

Baigachi	August 1944
Hmawbi	Sept 1945
Seletar	Sept 1945

Squadron Commanding Officers:

W/C E Collingridge	Nov 1944
S/L A E Browne	July 1945
S/L A G A Good	Sept 1945

History: Withdrawn from front-line service February 1945 to convert from Beaufighters to the NF.XIX. However, the war in the Far East was over before Mosquito operations could begin. Operating from Singapore flew leaflet-dropping sorties over the Dutch East Indies until it gave up its aircraft, January-February 1946. 1 May 1946 re-numbered 22 Squadron.

96 Squadron (ZJ)

Motto: *"Nocturni obambulamus"* ("We stalk by night") Command Assignments: Fighter Command
Aircraft: NF.XII, 6-11.43, NF.XIII, 10.43-3.45.

Stations:

Honiley	October 1942
Church Fenton	August 1943
Drem	Sept 1943
West Malling	Nov 1943
Ford	June 1944
Odiham	Sept 1944

Squadron Commanding Officers:

W/C E D Crew DFC	June 1943

History: After flying Hurricanes in 1940, and then Defiants in 1941, converted to the Beaufighter in 1942. June 1943, changed over to the NF.XII and in November that year, moved south to West Malling to provide fighter defense for Kent. Following the D-Day invasion, June 1944 provided fighter defense for the Normandy bridgehead. During the summer, destroyed 49 V1s on anti-Diver patrols in southern England. Disbanded, 12 December 1944, 18 days later reforming as a transport squadron equipped with the Halifax III.

98 Squadron (VO)

Motto: "Never failing"
Command Assignments: Sept 1945 - 30 April 1947, 2 Group; 1 May 1947 - 84 Group
Aircraft: B.XVI, 9.45-1.7.48, B.35, 8.48-2.51

Stations:

Melsbroek	Sept 1945
Wahn	March 1946
Celle	Sept 1949
Fassberg	Nov 1950

Squadron Commanding Officers:

W/C V E Marshal	Feb 1945
W/C E W Thornewill	Feb 1946
W/C D B Cericke	Feb 1947
S/L P W Cook	Nov 1947
S/L D R M Frostick	July 1949
S/L J M Rumsey	Aug 1950

History: Operated from 1943 onwards in 2nd TAF using first Bostons, and later Mitchell aircraft. Moved to Belgium October 1944 for the final drive into Germany and continued to support the Allied advance until the end of the war in Europe, May 1945. From then on became a part of BAFO. When the Mitchells were returned to the USA under the terms of Lend-Lease, the squadron quickly re-equipped with B.XVI aircraft. Remained a bomber squadron in Germany until February 1951 when conversion began to a light ground-attack role operating with Vampires, later Venom's.

105 Squadron (GB)

Motto: *"Eortis in praeliis"* ("Valiant in battles")
Command Assignments: 2 Group, 1940-summer 1943; 8 (PFF) Group - 1945
Aircraft: B.IV, 11.41-3.44, B.IX, 6.43-8.45, B.XVI, 4.44-1.46

Stations:

Swanton Morley Oct 1940
Horsham St Faith Dec 1941
Marham Sept 1942
Bourn March 1944
Upwood June 1945

Squadron Commanding Officers:

W/C P H A Simmons DFC	Oct 1941
W/C H I Edwards VC DFC	Aug 1942
W/C C P Longfield	Feb 1943
W/C J de L Wooldridge DFC DFM	Mar 1943
G/C H J Cundali DFC AFC	July 1943
G/C K J Somerville DSO DFC AFC	Sept 1944
W/C T W Horton DSO DFC	June 1945
W/C C N Collard DSO DFC	Oct 1945
W/C C O Lister	Nov 1945
W/C D G Stokes	Dec 1945

History: One of the Blenheim squadrons in 2 Group, which bore the brunt of the German onslaught in France, 1940. Losses continued to mount during the next phase of operations, 1940-41, during which the squadron went over to almost suicidal anti-shipping strikes in the North Sea. After a disastrous sojourn on Malta, 1941, remnants returned to the UK and in October-November awaited the arrival of the first Mosquito bombers in the RAF. Early months of 1942 worked up on the revolutionary new aircraft and the first Mosquito bombing operation was not flown until 31 May 1942, when a single B.IV bombed Cologne immediately after the 1000 bomber raid on the city. Low level raids then became the order of the day. 25 September, Gestapo HQ in Oslo audaciously attacked with such precision that the building was completely destroyed and many of its inhabitants killed. Crews and aircraft drawn from 105 used to help equip sister squadron, 139, at Marham. First daylight raid on Berlin was flown 30 January 1943 succeeding in preventing a broadcast by Reichsmarschall Göring for over an hour. Transferred to 8 (PFF) Group June 1943, and B.IXs equipped with Oboe. Carried out precision marking for the 'heavies' for the rest of the war. By June 1944 B.XVIs had arrived and were used until disbandment, Upwood, 1 February 1946.

107 Squadron (OM)

Motto: *"Nous y serons"* ("We shall be there")
Command Assignments: 138 Wing, 2 Group 2nd Tactical Air Force/BAFO, Germany
Aircraft: FB.VI 2.44-11.48.

Stations:

Lasham	Feb 1944
Hartford Bridge	Oct 1944
Epinoy	Nov 1944
Melsbroek	July 1945
Gütersloh	Nov 1945
Wahn	Dec 1947-Oct 1948

Squadron Commanding Officers:

W/C M E Pollard	Nov1943
W/C W J Scott AFC	July 1944
W/C W C Maher DFC AFM	1945
W/C D P Hanafin	Aug 1946
W/C B Kemp	Dec 1946
W/C Banning-Lover	June 1947

History: 1939-1941, equipped with Blenheims in 2 Croup. Converted to the Boston, January 1942. Early in 1944, now part of 2nd TAF in the south of England, Bostons began to be replaced with FB.VIs for use on daylight intruder operations. A move to France, November 1944, resulted in continued action against the retreating German forces until the end of the war. Operated as a light bomber unit in BAFO May 1945-4 October 1948, when disbandment by re-numbering as 11 Squadron took place.

108 Squadron

Motto: *"Viribus contractis"* ("With gathered strength")
Command Assignments: Malta
Aircraft: NF.XII, 2.44-7.44, NF.XIII, 4.44-3.7.44.

Stations:		**Squadron Commanding Officers:**	
Luqa, Malta	Feb 1944	W/C A J Banham	Dec 1943

History: New 108 Squadron formed at Sandur, 10 March 1943 with Blenheims for night fighter defense of the Nile delta. Blenheims replaced by NF.XIIs at the start of 1944. That summer began night intruder patrols from advanced base at Alghero before withdrawal to Egypt for Nile delta defense duties again and conversion to Beaufighters. Disbanded, Italy, 28 March 1945.

109 Squadron (HS)

Motto: *"Primi hastati"* ("The first of the legion")
Command Assignments: 2 Group/B (PFF) Croup, Bomber Command
Aircraft: B.IV, 12.42-7.44, B.IX, 4.43-12.45, B.XVI, 10.45-12.48, B.35 48-7.52

Stations:		**Squadron Commanding Officers:**	
Wyton	Dec 1942	W/C H E Bufton DFC AFC	July 1942
Marham	July 1943	W/C R M Cox AFC	Mar 1944
Little Staughton	April 1944	W/C T E Grant DSO DFC	May 1944
Woodhall Spa	Oct 1945	W/C R C E Law DFC	Dec 1944
Wickenby	Oct 1945	W/C C W Scott DFC	Sept 1945
Hemswell	Nov 1945		
Coningsby	Nov 1946		
Hemswell	March 1950		

History: Remained largely an experimental unit throughout 1941, encompassing the Wireless Intelligence Development Unit to investigate and identify German radio beams and to find ways of jamming them. Development Flight moved to Tempsford, 1942 while Reconnaissance Flight went to Upper Heyford, where it became the embryo of the later Radar Reconnaissance units, and the Investigation Flight went to Boscombe Down. What remained of 109 Squadron was established at Stradishall, April 1942, to bring Oboe into full operational service as a navigation aid for Bomber Command. Moved to Wyton, August, where at the end of the year, received the first Oboe equipped B.IVs. On a raid on Düsseldorf, 31 December 1942/1 January 1943, sky-marking using Oboe was trialled for the first time by two sky-markers for eight Lancasters of the PFF acting as bombers. Became the premier marking squadron in the RAF, carrying out the most raids and flying the most sorties in 8 Group, which it joined on 1 June 1943. On 10 December the first B.XVI for the RAF was received at Marham, although 692 Squadron were the first to use it operationally, 5 March 1944. In addition to its flare marking duties for the heavies, its Mosquitoes carried bombs. 23 December 1944 S/L R. A. M. Palmer DFC lost his life in an Oboe-equipped Lancaster borrowed from 582 Squadron when he led a formation-attack on the Cologne railway marshalling yards. His Lancaster was hit by flak and set on fire but Palmer got his bombs away before his aircraft went down out of control. He was awarded a posthumous Victoria Cross. 21 April 1945 dropped the last bombs to fall on Berlin in WW2. During the last few days of the war used marking techniques to select points for aircraft dropping supplies to the Dutch in various parts of Holland. Disbanded, 30 September 1945, Little Staughton. Next day, 627 Squadron at Woodhall Spa, re-numbered 109 Squadron and together with 139 Squadron, formed the last remaining Mosquito wing in Bomber Command. B.35s replaced the XVIs, 1948, which were replaced with EE Canberra's, 1952.

110 (Hyderabad) Squadron (VE)

Motto: *"Nec timeo nec sperno"* ("I neither fear nor despise")
Command Assignments: India-Burma
Aircraft: FB.VI, 11.44, 1.45-4.46

Stations:		**Squadron Commanding Officers:**	
Yelahanka, India	October 1944	W/C A E Saunders	Sept 1944
Joari, India	March 1945	S/L P C Joel	May 1945
Kinmagan, Burma	May 1945	W/C A E Binks DFC	Nov 1945
Hmawbi, Burma	Aug 1945	Seletar, Singapore	October 1945
Labaun, Borneo	December 1945		

History: Ironically, a 110 Squadron detachment using Vengeance IVs, briefly co-operated with the chemical warfare establishment at Porton Down, 1944, testing certain chemicals against mosquitoes in West Africa. Meanwhile, at the squadron 's main base at Yelahanka, India, its motley collection of Airspeed Oxfords was about to be replaced with FB.VIs. In November the squadron was finally at full complement but glue problems with the Mosquitoes resulted in all the aircraft being grounded. It was not until January the following year that suitable replacements enabled the squadron to enter first line service again, in time for the final assault on Rangoon. W/C Saunders, the CO, actually took the final surrender of the capital, 14 August 1945. Having dropped the first bombs of the war, 110 dropped the last bombs in WW2, 20 August 1945. From September based at Labaun, Borneo, and from here carried out low level strafing attacks on a new enemy, across the border, in Indonesia. Disbanded, Labaun, 15 April 1946.

114 (Hong Kong) Squadron (RT)

Motto: "With speed I strike"
Command Assignments: Aden
Aircraft: FB.VI, 9.45-9.46.

Stations:	
Khormaksar, Aden	Sept 1945

History: Operated first Blenheims and later Bostons, in raids from the UK, and from 1943 onwards, from North Africa and Italy. September 1945 moved to Aden to re-equip with FB VIs for policing duties in the protectorate. Carried out operations from Khormaksar for a year before being disbanded there, 1 September 1946, re-numbering as 8 Squadron.

125 (Newfoundland) Squadron (VA)

Motto: *"Nun quam domandi"* ('Wever to be tamed")
Command Assignments: Fighter Command
Aircraft: NF. XVII, 2. 44-3. 45, NF.30, 3. 45-6. 46.

Stations:

Valley, Wales	November 1943
Hum	March 1944
Middle Wallop	July 1944
Coltishall	Oct 1944
Church Fenton	April 1945

Squadron Commanding Officers:

W/C J C Topham DSO DFC*	Oct 1943
W/C C L Howitt DFC	Dec 1944
W/C V R Snell	Oct 1945

History: Early 1944 began converting from the Beaufighter VIE to the NF.XVII. By June 1944 on station to provide fighter defense over the Normandy Beachhead and also to escort the transport and glider forces on D-Day. Shortly thereafter, operated at night in the war against the V1. Moved to Coltishall, Norfolk, October 1944 for anti-intruder duties often engaging German night fighter bombers and He 111H22-V-l launch aircraft. Final victory, 20 March 1945, brought grand total to 44 aircraft shot down, five probably destroyed and four damaged. Moved to Church Fenton, April 1945, disbanding there 20 November 1945 by re-numbering as 264 Squadron.

128 (Hydedrabad) Squadron (M5)

Motto: *"Eulminis instar"* "Like a thunderbolt")
Command Assignments: B (PFF) Group, 15 Sept 1944-19 Sept 1945/2 Group-1 April 1946
Aircraft: B.XX, 9.44-12.44. B.XXV/XVI, 10/11.44-3.45.

Stations:

Wyton	September 1944
Warboys	June 1945
Melsbroek	October 1945
Wahn	March 1946

Squadron Commanding Officers:

W/C K J Burrough DFC	Sept 1944

History: Disbanded, Hastings, Sierra Leone 8 March 1943. Re-formed, 15 September 1944, Wyton, as a Pathfinder unit in B (PFF) Group. Equipped with B.XXs before standardizing on the B.XVI. From then until the end of the war operated as part of the LWSE, sometimes flying specialist raids such as the attack on 1 January 1945 when four Mosquitoes, all of which carried a 4000lb delayed-action bomb, took part in the skip-bombing of railway tunnels in the Eifel region between the Rhine and the Ardennes. A fifth aircraft despatched crashed on take off, killing the crew. After VE Day remained in Bomber Command, until September 1945, transferring then to BAFO, being based at Melsbroek, Brussels. Retained B.XVIs as part of 2 Group. Also operated an air mail service between Nuremberg and Blackbushe during the War Trials, 1946. Disbanded, Wahn, 1 April 1946, by re-numbering as 14 Squadron.

139 (Jamaica) Squadron (XD)

Motto: *"Si placet necamus"* ("We destroy at will") Command Assignments: 2 Group/B (PFF) Group
Aircraft: B.IV, 10.42-7.44, B.IX, 9.43-9.44. B.XX, 11.43-9.45, B.XVI, 11.44-10.48, B.35, 7.48-12.52

Stations:

Horsham St Faith	June 1942
Oulton	June 1942
Horsham St Faith	June 1942
Marham	Sept 1942
Wyton	July 1943
Upwood	Feb 1944
Hemswell	Feb 1946
Coningsby	Nov 1946
Hemswell	3.50-1.56

Squadron Commanding Officers:

W/C P Shand DFC	July 1942
S/L V.R.G. Harcourt DFC RCAF	Apr 1942 (KIA 21.5.43)
WIC R W Reynolds DSO DFC	May 1943
W/C G H Womersley DSO DFC	Apr 1944
WIC J R G Ralston DSO AFC DFM	Mar 1945

History: Disbanded, 30 April 1942, Chittagong, Burma by its absorption into 62 Squadron. Reformed 8 June, Horsham St Faith, Norwich as the second B.IV squadron in the RAF, mainly from personnel and aircraft from its sister squadron, 105, also based there. A few Blenheim Vs were also used for working up purposes. Began to receive additional IVs in September after the two squadrons relocated to Marham. Soon became operational alongside 105 Squadron on low level bombing operations in France and the Low Countries. Followed in the footsteps of 105 Squadron, 30 January 1943, over Berlin, successfully disrupting a Nazi radio broadcast. June 1943 was transferred to 8 (PFF) Group to fly night bombing operations for the rest of the war (sustaining the most losses (23) of all the Mosquito squadrons). Early 1944 received H_2S-equipped B.XIVs and used this radar to perfect accuracy at target finding and marking. Post-war was retained for low-level target marking, using Mosquitoes in this role until November 1953, when they were superseded by the EE Canberra.

140 Squadron

Motto: 'Foresight'
Command Assignments: No 34 (PR) Wing, HQ, 2nd TAF, .11 43-5 45
Aircraft: PR IX, 11.43-7.44, PR XVI, 12.43-8.45.

Stations:

Hartford Bridge	March 1943
Northolt	April 1944
Balleroy (A12)	Sept 1944
Amiens-Glisy (B48)	Sept 1944
Melsbroek	Sept 1944

Squadron Commanding Officers:

W/C R I Mallafont-Bowen	Nov 1943
W/C C F M Chapman	Sept 1944
W/C F O S Dobell	Oct 1944
W/C D R M Frostick	April 1945

Eindhoven (B 78)	Feb 1945
Acklington	July 1945
Fersfield	Sept-Nov 1945

History: 17 September 1941, 1416 Flight at Benson became 140 Squadron, equipped with Blenheim IVs and Spitfire Is fitted with cameras for night and day PR duty respectively over France. Late in 1942 based a detachment at St. Eval for PR coverage of the French ports using Blenheims, for a time, and later the Lockheed Ventura was also used in a limited capacity. June 1943 became part of 34 Wing, 2nd TAF and duties switched to detailed photography of coastal installations and targets, as well as general mapping. November 1943, a number of PR.IXs introduced for long-range PR, followed, by PR.XVIs equipped with Gee and Rebecca. Using this equipment was able to carry out blind night photography. History: June 1943, became part of No 34 Wing, 2nd TAF, detailed photography of coastal installations and targets, as well as general mapping. November 1943, a number of PR IXs introduced for long-range PR, followed, by PR XVIs equipped with Gee and Rebecca. Using this equipment was able to carry out blind night photography. First night sortie flown, 4 May 1944. After the invasion moved to the continent, first to Amiens, France, and in September, to Belgium. Early in 1945 experimented with night photography controlled by a mobile radar post, but the experiment needed further development to realize its full potential. In April 1945 the squadron switched to visual reconnaissance over the German and Danish coasts as these areas were being liberated. Returned to England, July 1945. Disbanded, Fersfield, 10 November 1945.

141 Squadron (TW)

Motto: *'Caedimus Noctu'* ("We Slay By Night")
Command Assignments: 11 Group, Fighter Command; 100 Group (Special Duties later Bomber Support), December 1943-1945; Fighter Command, 17 June 1946-
Aircraft: NF.II, 11.43-8.44, FB.VI, 8.44-4.45, NF.XXX, 3.45-9.45, 6.46-8.47. NF.36, 8.47-1.52.

Stations:

Wittering	April 1943
West Raynham	December 1943
Little Snoring	July 1945
Coltishall	June 1946
Church Fenton	November 1949
Coltishall	September 1950

Squadron Commanding Officers:

W/C K C Roberts AFC	Oct 1943
W/C F F Davies DFC	Feb 1944
W/C C V Winn DSO DFC	June 1944

History: Converted to the Beaufighter, August 1941 for defensive night fighting over the British Isles. 1942 moved over to the offensive with Instep patrols in the Bay of Biscay and intruder patrols over France. Such was fighting spirit and leadership, it was the first fighter squadron chosen, November 1943, to join 100 Group (Special Duties, later Bomber Support). That month the first NF.IIs arrived and in August began to replace these with the FB.VI for intruder operations over occupied Europe. With the war in Europe over, moved to Little Snoring, Norfolk to return to the Fighter Command fold. 1946, moved the short distance to Coltishall before transferring to Church Fenton, 1949. NF.36s were replaced by Meteor NF.lls, 1951.

142 Squadron (4H)

Motto: "Determination"
Command Assignments: 8 (PFF) Group Light Night Striking Force
Aircraft: B.XXV, 10.44-9.45.

Stations:

Gransden Lodge	25 October 1944

Squadron Commanding Officers:

W/C B C D Nathan	Oct 1944

History: Disbanded, Regina, Italy, 5 October 1944, giving up its Wellington X bombers. 25 October a new 142 Squadron was formed, at Gransden Lodge, as part of 8 Group (PFF), equipped with B.XXVs. Served in the Light Night Striking Force, target-marking and bombing at night, until the end of the war. Disbanded 28 September 1945.

143 Squadron (NE)

Motto: *"Vincene est vievere"* ("To conquer is to live")
Command Assignments: Banff Strike Wing
Aircraft: II., 10.44-11.44, FB.VI, 10.44-6.45.

Stations:

Banff	October 1944

Squadron Commanding Officers:

W/C E H McHardy DSO DFC	Nov 1943
W/C J M Maurice DSO DFC	Dec 1944*
W/C C N Foxley-Norris DSO	Feb 1945

*Pseudonym for Frenchman W/C M. Guedj DSO DFC

History: September 1942-mid-1944 equipped with Beaufighters, which were employed very successfully in the anti-shipping role in enemy waters. October 1944, operations off the Dutch coast ceased with a moved north to join the Banff Strike Wing and conversion to the FB.VI. First Mosquito operation took place 7 November, when two aircraft carried out a search for enemy aircraft between Obrestad and Lindesnes. 21 April 1945, nine torpedo-carrying Ju 88s in a formation of 18 were shot down. Also shared in the sinking of five U-boats, April-May 1945. After the war flew ASR searches. Disbanded, 25 May 1945 by renumbering as 14 Squadron.

151 Squadron (DZ)

Motto: *"Eoy pour devoir"* ("Fidelity into duty")
Command Assignments: Fighter Command
Aircraft: NF.II, 4.42-7.43, XII, 5.43-4.44, FB.VI, 8.43-9.43, NF.XIII, 11.43-9.44, NF.30, 8.44-10.46.

Stations:

Wittering	December 1940
Colerne	April 1943
Middle Wallop	August 1943

Squadron Commanding Officers:

W/C I S Smith DFC	Feb 1942
W/C D V Ivins	Mar 1943
W/C S P Richards AFC	May 1943

Colerne	November 1943	W/C G H Goodman DSO DFC	Oct 1943
Predannack	March 1944	W/C W R L Beaumont DFC	Dec 1944
Castle Camps	October 1944		
Hunsdon	November 1944		
Bradwell Bay	March 1945		
Predannack	May 1945		
Exeter	June 1946		
Colerne	September 1946		
Weston Zoyland	October 1946		

History: After operating first Defiants then Turbinlight Havocs, began converting to the NF.II, April 1942, becoming operational at the end of May. Patrols were flown from Wittering to over the North Sea where enemy bombers attacking England were intercepted. Went over to the offensive, 1943, intruding over enemy occupied Europe. By the summer these had increased to Day and Night Ranger operations into northwest France and the Western Approaches. Late in 1944 moved to Castle Camps and then Bradwell Bay to provide night defense for the invasion forces. Fighter support for night bombing operations were commenced, 1945. Post war, reverted to 10 Group. Disbanded, Weston Zoyland, 10 October 1946.

157 Squadron (RS)

Motto: "Our cannon speak our thoughts"
Command Assignments: Fighter Command, 1942-1944; 100 Group (Special Duties later Bomber Support) May 1944-16 August 1945
Aircraft: NF.II, 1.42-6.44, FB.VI, 7.43-4.44, NF.XIX, 5.44-4.45, NF.3O, 2.45-8.45.

Stations:		Squadron Commanding Officers:	
Debden	December 1941	W/C R G Slade	Dec 1941
Castle Camps	December 1941	W/C V J Wheeler MC DFC	Jan 1943
Bradwell Bay	March 1943	W/C J A Mackie	Aug 1943
Hunsdon	May 1943	W/C H D U Denison	Mar 1944
Predannack	November 1943	W/C W K Davison DFC	June 1944
Valley	March 1944	W/C K H P Beauchamp DSO DFC	Sept 1944
West Malling	July 1944		
Swannington	August 1944		

History: Fought with distinction as a fighter squadron in WI at the end of which it was disbanded. Reformed, Debden, 13 December 1941, moving to the satellite at Castle Camps four days later, where, in January 1942, became the first night fighter squadron to receive NF.IIs. First operation took place on 27 April and night patrols began in earnest, the first victory occurring in May. March 1943 began training for intruder operations, some FB.VIs added for this role in July. A detachment was sent to Predannack for long-range patrols in the Bay of Biscay and bombers support operations were also flown. The first victory on this work was achieved in November. That month the entire squadron moved to Predannack for interception patrols in the Bay of Biscay and the Western Approaches. Moved to Anglesey, spring 1944 for two months before equipping with NF.XIXs for service with 100 Group. There was a brief interlude combating V1s on anti-Diver patrols, July 1944, before flying bomber support operations in August that year. The last bomber support operation was flown on the night of 2/3 May 1945. Disbanded, Swannington, 16 August 1945.

162 Squadron (CR)

Motto: "One time, one purpose"
Command Assignments: 8 Group (PFF)
Aircraft: B.XXV, 12.44-7.46, B.XX, 1945.

Stations:		Squadron Commanding Officers:	
Kabrit, Egypt	January 1944	W/C J D Bolton DFC	Dec 1944
		W/C M K Sewell DFC	April 1945

History: A detachment of 109 Squadron in the Canal Zone equipped with Wellingtons to check on enemy radar stations and jam them, became 162 Squadron on 4 January 1942. Blenheims were received for calibration of British radio and radar while the Wellingtons jammed the enemy's tank radios. Disbanded at Idku on 25 September 1944, and on 18 December, reformed at Bourn as part of the Light Night Striking Force in 8 (PFF) Group with B.XXs and B.XXVs. In 1945 the squadron re-equipped with H_2S-equipped Mosquitoes, and flew PFF and bombing operations right up until the end of the war. In July 1945 moved to Hartford Bridge transferring to Transport Command, and flew an air delivery letter service - Operation Jane to many bases on the continent. Disbanded, Hartford Bridge, 14 July 1946.

163 Squadron

Command Assignments: 8 (PFF) Group, Light Night Striking Force
Aircraft: B.XXV/B.XVI, 1.45-8.45.

Stations:		Squadron Commanding Officers:	
Wyton	25 January 1945	W/C I G Broom DFC	Jan 1945

History: Original 163 Squadron disbanded at Asmara, Eritrea on 16 June 1943. Re-formed at Wyton on 25 January 1945 on B.XXVs, under the command of W/C (later AM) Ivor Broom DFC, flying first LNSF operation on the night of 28/29 January when four B.XXVs dropped Window at Mainz ahead of the PFF force. Disbanded, Wyton, 10 August 1945.

169 Squadron (VI)

Motto: "Hunt and destroy"
Command Assignments: Fighter Command; 1 October-November 1943; 100 Group (Special Duties later Bomber Support), December 1943-10 August 1945
Aircraft: NF.II, 1.44 - 7.44, FB.VI, 6.44 - 4.45, NF.XIX, 1.45 - 8.45.

Stations:		Squadron Commanding Officers:	
Ayr	October 1943	W/C E J Gracie DFC	Oct 1943
Little Snoring	December 1943	W/C R C Slade	Feb 1944

Great Massingham	June 1944	W/C N B R Bromley OBE	April 1944
		W/C T A Heath DFC AFC	Sept 1944
		W/C N E Reeves DSO DFC	Jan 1945

History: A new 169 Squadron was reformed at Ayr, 1 October 1943 as a night fighter squadron using Beaufighters and Mosquito IIs. December that year joined 100 Group, at Little Snoring, Norfolk. Intruder operations using AI radar and Serrate homing equipment were flown. May 1944, some intruder operations were begun and eventually this became the primary role until the winter of 1944-45, when bomber stream sorties were again flown. Operations continued until the end of the war. Disbanded, Great Massingham, 10 August 1945.

176 Squadron

Motto: *"Nocte custodimus"* ("We guard by night")
Command Assignments: India
Aircraft: FB.VI, 6.45-8.45, NF.XIX, 7.45-5.46.

Stations:
Baigachi, India July 1945-1 June 1946

Squadron Commanding Officers:

W/C C M Merrifield AFC	Jan 1945
S/L L W H Welch DFC*	Sept 1945

History: In WW2 flew Beaufighters and Hurricanes from India and Ceylon against the Japanese before being withdrawn as non-operational in August 1944. A few night defense duties were flown from India-Burma, until July 1945, when again was withdrawn from operations for working up on NF.XIXs at Baigachi. By the time it was operational the war ended, and so, in January 1946, flying stopped. Disbanded, 1 June 1946.

180 Squadron (EV)

Motto: *"Sauviter in modo fontier in re"* ("Agreeably in manner, forcibly in act")
Command Assignments: BAFO, Germany
Aircraft: B.XVI, 9.45-4.46.

Stations:

Wahn, Germany.	Sept 45-31.3.46

History: From September 1942 to VE Day, operated North American Mitchells in 2 Group and 2nd TAF, and when these aircraft had to be returned under the terms of Lease-Lend, began re-equipment, September 1945, with B.XVIs. March 1946, was based at Wahn as part of BAFO, but immediately disbanded, 31 March by being re-numbered 69 Squadron.

192 Squadron (C Flight) (DT)

Motto: "Dare to discover"
Command Assignments: ELINT; 100 Group (Special Duties later Bomber Support)
Aircraft: B.IV, 11.42—8.45, B.XVI (six in C Flt only), 3.45-8.45.

Stations:		Squadron Commanding Officers:	
Gransden Lodge	Jan 1943	W/C C D V Willis DFC	Jan 1943
Feltwell	April 1943	W/C E P M Fernbank DFC	May 1944
Foulsham	Nov 1943-August 45	E W Donaldson DSO DFC	June 1944

History: 1474 Flight at Gransden Lodge became 192 Squadron 4 January 1943, using Wellingtons and about six Mosquitoes ('C' Flight) to identify the types and numbers of German radars and wavelengths used against Allied bombers. Detachments were sent to the Mediterranean for similar duties and in April operations in support of Coastal Command were flown in the Bay of Biscay from Davidstowe Moor. At the end of 1943 was absorbed into 100 Group and RCM flights became the norm. October 1944 concentrated on locating signals for German missiles investigating Egon during bombing raids, and Knickebein and Benito radio guidance systems. Provided RCM for 100 Group until 22 August 1945, disbanding at Foulsham. Reformed, 15 July 1951 as part of the Central Signals Establishment at Watton for operational signals research.

199 Squadron

Motto: "Let tyrants tremble"
Command Assignments: 90 Signals Group (Radio Counter Measures)
Aircraft: NF.36, 12.51-3.53.

Stations:

Watton	15 July 1951
Hemswell	April 1952

History: Operated in WW2 as a ECM and RCM unit in 100 Group using Short Stirlings and Halifaxes, before being disbanded, 29 July 1945 at its wartime base at North Creake, Norfolk. Reformed at Watton as part of 90 Signals Group for RCM duties again, equipped with a mix of Avro Lincoln's and NF.36s. Mosquitoes replaced by Canberra's, March 1954.

211 Squadron

Motto: *"Touj ours a prop os"*
Command Assignments: India-Burma-Thailand
Aircraft: FB.VI, 5.45-1.46.

Stations:

Yelahanka, India	May 1945
St. Thomas Mount	July 1945
Don Muang, Thailand	September 1945

History: Fought in Greece, Syria and Java before disbanding, 19 February 1942, Kalidjati. Reformed, Phaphamau, India, 14 August 1943, and operated Beaufighters in Burma from beginning 1944-early 1945 when in June, re-equipped with FB.VIs at Yelahanka. Moved to Don Maung, September 1945, disbanding there, 28 February 1946.

219 (Mysore) Squadron (FK)

Motto: "From dusk till dawn"
Command Assignments: 12 Group, Fighter Command, 1944; 147 Wing, 85 (Base) Group, 2nd TAF, 28.8.44-7.5.45 1945; 12 Group, Fighter Command, 1945-1.9.46. Egypt, 1951-3.53.
Aircraft: NF.II/, NF.XVII, 2.44-11.44, NF.XXX, 6.44-9.46. NF.36, 4.51-3.53.

Stations:

Woodvale	February 1944
Honiley	February 1944
Bradwell Bay	May 1944
Hunsdon	August 1944
Amiens-Glisy	October 1944
Gilze-Rijen	March 1945
Enschede	June 1945
Twente	July 1945
Wittering	August 1945
Acklington	November 1945
Church Fenton	1 September 1946

Squadron Commanding Officers

W/C A D McN Boyd DFC	Mar 1943
W/C W P Green DSO DFC	Aug 1944*
W/C B Maitland-Thompson	Apr 1945
W/C A Carlisle	Aug 1945
W/C Pain DFC AFC	Oct 1945
S/L P C K Williamson DFC	Feb 1946

*Killed testing a Mosquito 1.3. 45

History: A light bomber squadron at the outset of war with Blenheims, later operating Beaufighters in England and North Africa until 1944, before returning to the UK in January to re-equip with NF.XVIIs in 2nd TAF. In October 1944 moved to France and thence to Gilze-Rijen in February 1945. Returned to England. Disbanded Church Fenton, 1 September 1946. Re-formed Kabrit, Egypt, April 1951, with NF.36s before conversion to Meteor NF.13s, March 1953. Disbanded when Canal Zone evacuated early in 1955.

235 Squadron (LA)

Motto: *"Jaculamur humi"*
Command Assignments: Banff Strike Wing
Aircraft: FB.VI, 6.44-7.45.

Stations

Portreath	June 1944
Banff	8.9.44-10.7.45

Squadron Commanding Officers:

W/C R H McConnell DSO DFC	July 1943
W/C J V Yonge	May 1944
W/C R A Atkinson DSO DFC	Oct 1944
W/C A H Simmonds DFC	Dec 1944

History: After using Beaufighters on anti-shipping operations, in June 1944 began converting to the FB.VI and early in September joined the Banff Strike Wing in Scotland. Anti-shipping strikes were carried out, 16 June-3 May 1945. Disbanded, Banff, 10 July 1945.

239 Squadron (HB)

Motto: *"Exploramus"* ("We explore")
Command Assignments: Fighter Command, September 1943-November 1943; 100 Group (Special Duties later Bomber Support), December 1943-1 July 1945
Aircraft: NF.II, 12.43-9.44; FB.VI, 12.43-2.45; NF.XXX, 1.45-5.45. NF.30, 1.45-7.45.

Stations:

West Raynham	11.12.43

Squadron Commanding Officers:

W/C P M J Evans DFC	Sept 1943
W/C W E Gibb	Sept 1944

History: Reformed, 18 September 1940 and for two years operated a wide range of aircraft, including Lysanders (Army Co-operation), Fairey Battles, Hurricanes, Curtiss Tomahawks and Mustang I tactical reconnaissance aircraft. September 1943 moved north to re-equip with NF.IIs, before joining 100 Group at West Raynham, Norfolk November 1943. FB.VIs followed and also NF.XXXs, all of which were used for intruding over enemy territory right up until the end of the war. Disbanded, West Raynham, 1 July 1945.

248 Squadron (DM:WR)

Motto: *"Il faut en finer"*
Command Assignments: Banff Strike Wing
Aircraft: FB.VI, 12.43-12.45, FB.XVIII, 10.43-1.45.

Stations:

Predannack	Jan 1943
Portreath	Feb 1944
Banff	Sept 1944
Chivenor	July 1945
Thorney Island May 1946	

Squadron Commanding Officers

W/C F E Burton DFC	July 1943
W/C O J M Barron DFC	Feb 1944 (KIA 11.4.44)
W/C A D Phillips DSO DFC	April 1944
W/C D G Sise DSO DFC	July 1944
W/C R K Orrock DFC	March 1945
W/C JI N Jackson-Smith DFC	March 1945
W/C J V Hoggarth	Oct 1945

History: Operating in Coastal Command first using Blenheims, later Beaufighters, on anti-shipping strikes in the Bay of Biscay and off Norway until December 1943. Began re-equipping with FB.VIs, late 1943, joining the Banff Strike Wing, flying anti-shipping strikes from there until the end of the war in Europe. Post war, moved south to Chivenor and then Thorney Island. Disbanded there, 30 September 1946.

249 (Gold Coast) Squadron (GN)

Motto: *"Pugnis et calcibus"* ("With fists and heels")
Command Assignments: Mediterranean/Middle East

Aircraft: FB.26, 4.46-12.46.

Stations:

Eastleigh, Kenya	Feb 1946
Habbaniya, Iraq	June 1946

History: Operated in WW2 with Hurricanes, in the Battle of Britain, and later, the Mediterranean and the Balkans before re-equipping with the Mustang III and IV. Disbanded, Brindisi, 18 August 1945, re-forming as a bomber squadron by renumbering 500 Squadron at Eastleigh (Nairobi), 23 October 1945. First received Martin Baltimore's, then in February 1946 re-equipped with FB.VIs for general survey work, before moving to Iraq in June, where Hawker Tempest fighter-bombers were taken on charge. February 1950, Vampires replaced these.

254 Squadron (QM)

Motto: *"Eljuga vakkta ok ljosta"*
Command Assignments: North Coates Wing
Aircraft: Five FB.XVIII 'Tsetse' on detachment from 618 Squadron, 3.45-11.5.45

Stations:

North Coates	early 1945
Thorney Island	3.46-1.10.46

Squadron Commanding Officers:

W/C D L Cartridge DSO DFC	Sept 1944
W/C C J S Dinsdale DFC	Mar 1946

History: Primarily, served in WW2 as a fighter squadron, being equipped in turn with Blenheim Ifs and Beaufighters for coastal strike operations in Coastal Command. In October 1942 became part of the North Coates Strike Wing and in 1944 was operating Wellingtons and Beaufighters. Early in 1945 also received five FB.XVIIIs armed with the 57mm Molins gun, and used these on anti-U-boat patrols, March-May 1945. Disbanded, Thorney Island, 1 October 1946.

255 Squadron (YD)

Motto: "Ad auroram" ("To the break of dawn")
Command Assignments: Italy
Aircraft: NF.19, 1.45-4.46, NF.30, 4.45-4.46.

Stations:

Foggia Main, Italy	Jan 1944
Rosignano, Italy	Feb 1945
Hal Ear, Malta	Sept 1945
Gianaclis, Egypt	Jan 1946

Squadron Commanding Officers:

W/C J W R Kempe	Nov 1944
W/C J R H Lewis DFC	July 1945

History: Operated as a fighter squadron in the UK, equipped, in turn, with Defiants and then Beaufighter IIs. August 1942, posted to North Africa where with Beaufighter VIfs provided fighter cover for Torch and subsequent campaigns in North Africa. 1943-1944 operated from Italy on intruder operations. 1945 re-equipped with NF.l9s. After a short sojourn in Malta and then Egypt, disbanded, Gianaclis, 30 April 1946.

256 Squadron (JT)

Motto: *"Addimus vim vinibis"* ("Strength to strength")
Command Assignments: Italy/Mediterranean
Aircraft: NF.XII, 4.43-8.43, NF.XIII, 11.43-8.45; XII, 2.45-5.45, FB.VI 4.45-8.45,NE.XIX, 9.45-9.46

Stations:

Ford	Apr 1943
Woodvale	Aug 1943
Luqa	Oct 1943
La Sehia	Apr 1944
Foggia	Sep 1944
Forli	Feb 1945
El Ballah	Sep 1945
Deversoir	Dec 1945
Nicosia	July 1946

Squadron Commanding Officers:

W/C T N Hayes Oct 1942	
W/C G R Park DFC	June 1943
W/C P M Dobree-Bell	Feb 1944
W/C H W Elliot DSO DFC	Oct 1944
W/C H E Tappin DFC	Mar 1945
W/C D Giles DFC	Dec 1945
W/C A P Dottridge DFC	Jan 1946

History: After using Defiants and then Hurricanes, in the summer of 1942 converted to Beaufighters. May 1943, re-equipped again, this time with NF.XIIs and a detachment was posted to Malta in July. This proved so successful that in October the rest of the squadron joined them on Malta. Provided the Malta night defense, with a forward detachment at Alghero for intruding over Italy and southern France. September 1944 moved to Foggia and continued intruding over Italy until the surrender. September 1945 moved to Egypt, and in July 1946, to Cyprus. Disbanded, Nicosia, 12 September 1946.

264 (Madras Presidency) Squadron (PS)

Motto: "We defy"
Command Assignments: Fighter Command (ADGB) To 141 Wing, 85 (Base) Group 2nd TAF, 19 Dec 43 (Administered as such from 10.3.44). Left 141 Wing 19.6.44. To 148 Wing, 26.6.44. To UK on rest, 23.9.44. 148 Wing, 8.1.45-7.5.45. 12 Group Fighter Command, 20.11.45-51
Aircraft: NF.II, 5.42-3.43, FB.VI, 8.43-12.43, NF.XIII, 12.43-8.45; NF.XXX, 5.45-3.46, NE.36, 3.46-1.52

Stations:

Colerne	May 1941
Predannack	Apr 1943
Fairwood Common	July 1943
Coleby Grange	Nov 1943
Church Fenton	Dec 1943
Hartford Bridge	May 1944
Hunsdon	July 1944
A8 (France)	Aug 1944
B17 (Caen-Carpiquet)	Sept 1944
Predannack	Sept1944

Squadron Commanding Officers

W/C H M Kern DFC	May 1942
W/C W J Alington	Mar 1943
W/C E S Smith AFC	Apr 1944
W/C E C Barwell DFC*	June-Aug 1945

Colerne	Dec 1944
Odiham	Dec 1944
B5l (Lille)	Jan 1945
B77 (Gilze-Rijen)	Apr 1945
Rheine	May 1945
Twente	June 1945
Church Fenton	Nov 1945
Acklington	Feb 1950
Church Fenton	Sep 1950
Linton-on-Ouse	Aug 1951

History: Operated Defiants during the Dunkirk operation and during the height of the Battle of Britain but losses to the rear turreted fighters proved catastrophic and the squadron was switched to night defense. May 1941 went over to intruder operations on a small scale but in May 1942 began to gain real teeth with the introduction of NF.IIs. Nightly patrolled in the West Country and by day in the Bay of Biscay and Western Approaches. 1943 went over fully to intruding over the continent and in October flew bomber support sorties for the Main Force. 1944, NF.XIIIs arrived and for a time defensive patrols were flown. June, went over to the offensive again with night patrols over the beachhead. A stint on anti-Diver patrols and beachhead work until September, followed, then a move to Predannack to coven the Western Approaches once more. January 1945 returned to 2nd TAF, moving to Lille/Vendeville and patrolling the Schelde Estuary at night before moving to patrol the Rhine. At the end of the war was based at Twente. Disbanded there, 25 August 1945. 20 November 1945 reformed by taking 125 Squadron's number plate and was equipped with NF.XXXs in 12 Group, Fighter Command, 1951, re-equipped with Meteor NF.lls.

268 Squadron (EG)

Motto: "Adjidaumo" ("Tail-in-the-air")
Command Assignments: 2nd Tactical Air Force/BAFO, Germany, Sept 1945-March 1946
Aircraft: FB.VI, 9.45-3.46.

Stations:

Cambrai/Epinoy, Fr.	Sept 1945
disbanded 31.3.46	

History: Used for Army Co-Operation, being equipped in turn, with Lysanders, Curtiss Tomahawks, Mustang Is and Typhoons, and Spitfire XIVs. 19 September 1945, disbanded at Celle by renumbering as 16 Squadron but re-formed at Cambrai/Epinoy, 16 October 1945 by re-numbering 487 Squadron, which was equipped with FB.VIs. Disbanded there 31 March 1946.

305 (Ziemia Wielkopolska) (Polish) (SM)

Command Assignments: 138 Wing, 2 Group, 2nd Tactical Air Force; BAFO, Germany
Aircraft: FB.VI, 12.43-11.46.

Stations:

Lasham, Hants	Nov 1943
Hartford Bridge, Hants	Oct 1944
Lasham, Hants	Oct 1944
Hartford Bridge, Hants	Oct 1944
A75 (Carnbrai/Epinoy)	Nov 1944
Volkel, Holland	July 1945
Gilze-Rijen, Holland	Sept 1945
Melsbroek (Brussels)	Nov 1945
Wahn, Gr	March 1946
Faldingworth, Lincs	Oct 1946

Squadron Commanding Officers:

W/C K Konopasek	July 1943
W/C B Orlinski	Aug 1944
W/C S Grodzicki	Feb 1945

History: The fourth Polish bomber squadron to be formed in England in WW2. After using Fairey Battles and then Wellington night bombers 1943, transferred to day bombing, moving to 2 Group and re-equipping at Swanton Morley with Mitchell IIs. These were only used for a short time. In November conversion to FB.VIs at Lasham followed. These were used on daring daylight low-level strikes on the continent in support of the ground forces. Moved to Cambrai-Epinoy November 1944 and continued to operate up to the defeat of German forces, May 1945. At Wahn, became part of BAFO, until returning to England, at Faldingworth in October 1946. Disbanded there, 6 January 1947.

307 (Lwow) Squadron (EW)

Command Assignments: Fighter Command
Aircraft: NF.II, 1.43—3.44; FB.VI, 9.43-1.44, NF.XII, 1.44-4.44, NF.XXX, 10.44-1.47.

Stations:

Exeter	4.41-4.43
Fairwood Common	4.43-8.43
Predannack	Aug 1943
Drem	Nov 1943
Coleby Grange	March 1944
Church Fenton	May 1944
Castle Camps	Jan 1945
Coltishall	May 1945
Horsham St Faith	8.45-2.1.46

Squadron Commanding Officers:

W/C J Michalowski VM KW DFC	8.42-3.43
W/C J Orzechowski	April 1943
W/C M Lewandowski	Jan 1944
W/C G K Ranoszek	5.44-3.45
W/C S Andrzejewski	3.45-2.46
W/C J Damsz	3.46-2.1.47

History: The only Polish night fighter squadron formed in the UK in WW2. After using Defiants and Beaufighters, in late 1942 re-equipped with the NF.II at Fairwood Common. Moved to Drem, Scotland, November 1943 and then south again, to 12 Group, to serve until the end of the wan. Post war remained in Fighter Command, at Horsham St. Faith, with NF.XXXs. Disbanded, 2 January 1947.

333 (Norwegian) Squadron ('B' Flight only) (KK)

Motto: *"Eon konge fedreland og flaggets heder"* Command Assignments: Banff Strike Wing
Aircraft: NF.II, 5.43-10.43, FB.VI, 9.43-11.45

Stations:		**Squadron Commanding Officers**	
Banff	Sept 1944-May 1945	Cdn E Lambnechts	May 1943

History: Formed, Leuchars, Scotland, 10 May 1943 from 1477 (Norwegian) Flight. One flight then operated NF.IIs as a coastal fighter squadron, the other operating Catalinas from Woodhaven. FB.VIs followed and these were used for fighter sweeps over Norway and for making attacks on U-boats. Mosquito flight joined the Banff Strike Wing September 1944 and took pant in large-scale attacks on enemy shipping off Norway. They also dropped mines in Norwegian waters. Moved to Stavanger May 1945. Disbanded into the Royal Norwegian Air Force, 21 November 1945.

334 (Norwegian) Squadron (VB)

Command Assignments: Banff Strike Wing
Aircraft: FB.VI, 5.45-10.45

Stations:	
Gardermoen (Oslo)	May 1945
Stavanger/Sola	Oct 1949

History: Formed from the Mosquito Flight of 333 Squadron, 30 May 1945. Within a fortnight moved to Stavanger to become part of the Royal Norwegian Air Force, 21 November 1945.

400 Squadron

Motto: *"Percussi vigiles"*
Command Assignments: No 39 (R) Wing, No 83 Group, 2nd TAF
Aircraft: ('A' Flight) PR XVI, 12 43-12 5 44

Stations:		**Squadron Commanding Officers:**	
Redhill	Oct 1943	W/C R A Ellis DFC	Sept 1943
Kenley	Dec 1943	S/L M C Brown DFC	Nov 1944
Odiham	Feb 1944	S/L J A Morton DFC	July 1945
Sommervieu	July 1944		
B21/Ste Honorine-de-Ducy	Aug 1944		
B34/Avrilly	Sept 1944		
B66/Blakenburg	Sept 1944		
B78/Eindhoven	Oct 1944		
B90/Petit-Brogel	March 1945		
B108/Rheine	April 1945		
B116/Wunsdorf	April 1945		
B154/Soltau	April 1945		
B156/Luneberg	May 1945		
B160/Copenhagen	July 1945		
B156/Luneberg	Aug 1945		

History: Arrived in the UK, February 1940 and located at Old Sarum equipped with Westland Lysanders, was known as 110 City of Toronto Auxiliary Squadron. At Odiham 1 March 1941, renumbered 400 Squadron, which was successively equipped with Curtiss Tomahawks and Mustang Is. 'A' flight began conversion onto Spitfire XIs, and 'B' Flight began re-equipment with Mosquito PR.XIs purely for reconnaissance duties, 4 January 1944. 'B' Flight's first Mosquito sortie flown, 26 March 1944, the last (43rd), 2 May 1944 'B' Flight's Mosquitoes replaced with Spitfires, mid-May 1944. Moved to France, July 1944, and established a base at Sommenvieu. Flew PRU sorties until the German surrender, May 1945. After VE Day remained in Germany with BAFO. Disbanded, Luneberg, 7 August 1945.

404 ('Buffalo') Squadron RCAF (EO)

Motto: Ready to Fight"
Command Assignments: Banff Strike Wing
Aircraft: FB VI, 4.45-5.45

Stations:		**Squadron Commanding Officers:**	
Banff	3.4.45	W/C E W Pierce	Aug 1944

History: Formed, Thorney Island 15 April 1941. Successively equipped with Blenheim IVf and Bristol Beaufighters for fighter duties with Coastal Command. Re-equipped with FB.VIs March 1945 but used these for only a short time before the end of the wan. Disbanded, Banff, 25 May 1945, becoming pant of the post war RCAF in Canada, operating Lancaster MP.10s.

406 ('Lynx') Squadron RCAF (HU)

Motto: "We kill by night"
Command Assignments: Fighter Command/2nd TAF?
Aircraft: NF.XII, 7. 43-12. 44; NF.30, 7. 44-8. 45

Stations:		**Squadron Commanding Officers:**	
Winkleigh, Devon	April 1944	W/C R C Fumerton DFC*	Aug 1943
Colerne	Sept 1944	W/C D J Williams DSO DFC	July 1944
Manston	Nov 1944	W/C R Bannock DFC*	Nov 1944
Predannack	June 1945	W/C R C Cray DFC*	May 1945

History: Formed, Acklington, 10 May 1941 and operated, in turn, Blenheims and Beaufighters. Added night intruding duties, spring 1943, before reverting to fighter patrols again for the invasion of France. Re-equipped with NF.XIIs, April 1944, continuing to operate in an offensive capacity over German night fighter bases to the end of the wan in Europe. After the wan, based at Predannack. Disbanded there, 1 September 1945.

409 ('Nighthawk') Squadron RCAF(KP)

Motto: *"Media nox menides nosten"* ("Midnight is our noon")
Command Assignments: Fighter Command. 148 Wing, 85 (Base) Group, 2nd TAF, 30.3. 44-1. 7. 45
Aircraft: NF.XIII, 3.44-6.45,

Stations:

Acklington	March 1944
West Malling	May 1944
Hunsdon	June 1944
B17/Canpiquet	Aug 1944
B24/St. Andre	Sept 1944
B48/Clisy	Sept 1944
B68/Le Culot	Oct 1944
B51/Vendeville	Oct 1944
B108/Rheine	April 1945
B77/Cilze-Rijen	May 1945
B106/Twente	June 1945

Squadron Commanding Officers:

W/C J W Reid	Feb 1943
W/C M W Beveridge DFC	Aug 1944
W/C J D Somerville DSO DFC	Oct 1944
W/C R E Hatton	Man 1945

History: Formed at Digby on 7 June 1941 and was equipped, in turn, with Defiants and Beaufighter IIfs and VIfs. In 1943 flew Ranger missions over the continent and in March 1944 converted to NF.XIIIs, moving, in May to West Malling as part of 2nd TAF. Some anti-Diver patrols were flown in the summer of 1944 but intruder operations from the UK and later France formed the mainstay of operations until the end of hostilities in Europe. Disbanded, Twente, 1 July 1945.

410 ('Cougar') Squadron RCAF (RA)

Motto: *"Noctivaga"* ("Wandering by night")
Command Assignments: Fighter Command. 141 Wing, 85 Group, 2nd TAF, 12.5.44. 147 Wing, 85 Group, 18.6.44-7 May 1945
Aircraft: NF.II, 10.42-12.43, FB.VI, 7.43-9.43; NF.XIII, 12.43-8.44, NF.XXX, 8.44-6. 45.

Stations:

Acklington	Oct 1942
Coleby Grange	Feb 1943
West Malling	Oct 1943
Hunsdon	Nov 1943
Castle Camps	Dec 1943
Hunsdon	Apr 1944
Zeals	June 1944
Colerne	July 1944
Hunsdon	Sep 1944
B48/Glisy	Sep 1944
B51/Vendeville	Nov 1944
Glisy	Jan 1945
B77/Gilze-Rijen	Apr 1945

Squadron Commanding Officers:

W/C E W Hillock	Aug 1942
W/C C H Elms	May 1943
W/C C A Hiltz	Feb 1944
W/C E P Heybroek	Apr 1945

History: The second Canadian night-fighter squadron, after 409, to form in the UK. Came together at Ayr, 30 June 1941 and operated Defiants, before converting to Beaufighters, April 1942. These were replaced by NF.IIs, October 1942, and in February 1943 moved to Coleby Grange for intruder operations from forward bases. Moved to Hunsdon, October 1943, then Castle Camps where regular patrols were flown in defense of southern England. At the end of 1943 re-equipped on the NF.XIII and then moved to Zeals, Somerset, for operations over the Normandy beachhead at night. Joined 2nd TAF in France, September 1944. For the rest of the war flew offensive night patrols, being based at Gilze-Rijen. Disbanded there, 9 June 1945.

418 (City of Edmonton) Squadron RCAF (TH)

Motto: *"Piyautailili"* ("Defend even unto death")
Command Assignments: Fighter Command. To 136 Wing, 2nd TAF, 21.11.44-7.5.45
Aircraft: FB.VI, 5.43-9.45.

Stations:

Ford	Mar 1943
Holmsley South	Apr 1944
Hum	July1944
Middle Wallop	July1944
Hunsdon	Aug 1944
Hartford Bridge	Nov 1944
B71/Coxde, Belgium	Mar 1945
B8O/Volkel, Holland	Apr 1945

Squadron Commanding Officers:

W/C J H Little DFC	1942
W/C P Y Davoud DFC	June1943
W/C D C S MacDonald DFC	Jan 1944
W/C R J Bennell	Feb 1944
W/C A Barker	Mar 1944
W/C R Bannock DFC	Oct 1944
W/C J C Wickett	Nov 1944
W/C D B Annan	Feb 1945
W/C H D Cleveland DFC	May 1945

History: Formed, Debden as an Intruder squadron, 15 November 1941 equipped with Boston III aircraft. Operated Bostons on intruder missions over the continent March 1942-March 1943, moving to Ford for re-equipping on the FB.VI, the first unit to receive the type, 18 February. First FB.VI operation took place, 7 May 1943. By the end of 1943 was flying intruder and Day Ranger operations over France and the Low Countries. In April-May 1944 shot down 30 enemy aircraft in the air and destroyed a further 38 aircraft on the ground. July-21 August, destroyed 123 V-ls, and finished the war with the distinction of destroying more enemy aircraft both in the air and on the ground, than any other Canadian squadron, in both night and daylight operations. Moved to 2 Group, 2nd TAF November 1944 for daylight operations against the retreating German armies. Disbanded, Volkel, Holland, 7 September 1945.

456 Squadron RAAF (RX)

Command Assignments: 10 Group/11 Group, Fighter Command.
Aircraft: NF.II, 12.42-2.44, FB.VI, 7.43-2.44, NF.XVII, 1.44-12.44, NF.30, 12 44-6. 45.

Stations:		**Squadron Commanding Officers:**	
Valley	June1941	W/C E C Wolfe DFC	Mar 1942
Middle Wallop	Mar 1943	W/C M H Dwyer	Dec 1942
Colerne	Aug 1943	W/C G Howden DFC	June 1943
Fairwood Common	Nov 1943	W/C K M Hampshire DSO	Dec 1943
Ford	Feb 1944	W/C B Howard DFC	Nov 1944
Church Fenton	Dec 1944	S/L R B Cowper	May-June 1945
Bradwell Bay	3.45-15.6.45		

History: Formed, Valley, 30 June 1941 as a Defiant night-fighter unit but it quickly converted to Beaufighters. Began converting to the NF.II, spring 1943, moving to Middle Wallop, March 1943, for day and night intruder operations over France. That summer also operated out of Predannack for patrols in the Bay of Biscay. Moved to Fairwood Common, November, re-equipping with NF.XVIIs. Moved again, February 1944, to Ford, to be nicely placed for anti-Diver patrols once the V1s started arriving over southern England that summer. Moved to Church Fenton, December 1944, for re-equipping on the NF.XXX for anti-intruder patrols over the UK. March 1945, transferred to Bradwell Bay for bomber-support duty but the war ended before the Australians could get into their stride. Disbanded, 15 June 1945.

464 Squadron RAAF (SB)

Motto: *"Aequo animo"* ("Equanimity")
Command Assignments: 140 Wing, 2 Group, 2nd Tactical Air Force
Aircraft: FB.VI, 8.43-9.45.

Stations:		**Squadron Commanding Officers:**
Sculthorpe	July 1943	W/C J Meakin DFC Apr 1943
Hunsdon	Dec 1943	W/C R W Iredale DFC Dec 1943
Gravesend	Apr 1944	W/C G Panitz DFC June 1944
Thorney Island	June 1944	W/C A W Langton DFC Aug 1944
B87/ Rosières-en-Santerre	Feb 1945	W/C N Vincent DFC Jan 1945
B58/Melsbroek	Apr 1945	

History: Formed, Feltwell in 2 Group, 1 September 1942, equipped with Lockheed Ventura I light bombers These proved disastrous on daylight operations over Europe and in August 1943, long overdue replacements, FB.VIs, began to arrive. Operated in 2nd TAF, first from Sculthorpe, and later southern England, in daylight low-level operations in 140 Wing, whose specialty was pin-point raids on Nazi high-security buildings, the most famous being the raid on Amiens prison, 18 February 1944. Moved with the wing, February 1945, to Rosières-en-Santerre, France for operations against the retreating German armies. Disbanded, Melsbroek, Brussels, 25 September 1945.

487 Squadron RNZAF (EG)

Motto: *"Kite mutunga"* ("Through to the end")
Command Assignments: 140 Wing, 2 Group, 2nd Tactical Air Force
Aircraft: FB.VI, 8.43-9.45.

Stations:		**Squadron Commanding Officers:**	
Sculthorpe	July 1943	W/C A C Wilson	May 1943
Hunsdon	Dec 1943	W/C I S Smith DFC	Feb 1944
Gravesend	April 1944	W/C R C Porteus	Aug 1944
Thorney Island	June 1944	W/C R W Baker	Jan 1945
B87/Rosières-en-Santerre	Feb 1945	W/C E H Denton DFC	Feb 1945
B58/Melsbroek	April 1945	W/C W P Kemp	Aug 1945
Epinoy/Cambrai	July 1945		

History: Formed, Feltwell, 15 August 1942, equipped with the Lockheed Ventura. This lamentable aircraft was finally withdrawn from 2 Group after suffering heavy losses in daylight operations on the continent and in the early summer of 1943 replacement with the FB.VI began in earnest. Became part of the famous 140 Wing which carried out a number of pin-point raids on Nazi high-security targets, 1944-45, including the raid on Amiens prison, 18 February, culminating in low level strikes on Nazi buildings in Denmark. Was part of the wing at Rosières-en-Santerre February 1945, before moving, to Belgium for the final assault on Germany by 2nd TAF. Returned to France, July 1945. Disbanded, Cambrai-Epinoy, October 1945 by being re-numbered (in error) as 16 Squadron, RAF, then 268 Squadron, retrospectively, from 19.11.45

488 Squadron (ME)

Motto: *"Ka ngarue ratau"* ("We shake them")
Command Assignments: Fighter Command. 147 Wing, 85 (Base) Group 2nd TAF 12.5.44-26 April 1945. Disbanded 26.4.45
Aircraft: NF.XII 8.43-5.44, NF.XIII, 10.43-10.44, NF.30, 10.44-4.45.

Stations:		**Squadron Commanding Officers:**	
Ayr	Sep 1942	W/C J Nesbitt-Dufort DSO	Mar 1943
Drem	Aug 1943	W/C A R Bunton-Gyles DFC	July 1943
Bradwell Bay	Sep 1943	W/C P H Hamley	Sep 1943
Zeals	May 1944	W/C R C Haine DFC	Jan 1944
Colerne	July1944	W/C R C Watts	Oct 1944
Hunsdon	Oct 1944		
B48/Glisy	Nov 1944		
B77/Gilze Rijen, Holland.	Apr 1945		

History: First formed, Rongotai, September 1941 with CAC Wirraways before moving to Singapore in October that year. Then used Brewster Buffaloes and Hurricanes before being evacuated to Batavia following the debacle in Malaya and Singapore. By end of February the shattered remnants had been withdrawn to New Zealand, and there absorbed into 14 Squadron RNZAF. 488 re-formed at RAF Church Fenton, 25 June 1942, as a night-fighter squadron, equipped with Beaufighter IIIfs before moving to Ayr for the night defense of the Clyde. By August 1943 re-equipment on the NF.XII had begun for the continuance of intruder operations over France and Belgium but not before victories had been recorded against German intruders over Scotland. Then operated from Bradwell Bay, before being transferred, April 1944, to 2nd TAF. Moved to Zeals to provide coven for the Normandy operation, and was also used to help combat V1s being fired at London and southern England. Moved to Amiens/Glisy November 1944 to take part in the final assault on Germany. Moved up to Gilze-Rijen, Holland April 1945, disbanding there, 26 April 1945.

489 Squadron RNZAF (P6)

Motto: *"Whakatangata kia kaha"*
Command Assignments: Banff Strike Wing
Aircraft: FB.VI, 6.45.

Stations:		Squadron Commanding Officers:	
Banff	6.1945-1.8.45	W/C D H Hammond	Feb 1945

History: Operated Blenheims and later Beaufighters on anti-shipping strikes in WW2 converting to the FB.VI, June 1945 when the war was over. Disbanded, Banff, 1 August 1945.

500 (County of Kent) Squadron (RAA)

Motto: "Quo fata vocent" ("Whither the fates may call")
Command Assignments: Auxiliary Air Force
Aircraft: NF.XIX, 3.47-7.48, NF.30, 2.47-11.49.

Stations:		Squadron Commanding Officers	
West Malling	10.5.46-Aug 48	S/L P Green OBE AFC	Aug 1946
		S/L M C Kennard DFC	Feb 1949

History: Disbanded, Kenya, 23 October 1945. Re-formed as a NF.XXX fighter squadron in the Auxiliary role at West Malling 10 May 1946. In 1948 became the first auxiliary squadron to fly jets when it began trading in its NF.30s for Gloster Meteor E.3s.

502 (County of Ulster) Squadron (RAC)

Motto: *"Nihil timeo"* ("I fear nothing")
Command Assignments: Auxiliary Air Force
Aircraft: B.XXV, 7.46-early 1947, NF.3O, 8.47-6.49

Stations:		Squadron Commanding Officers:	
Aldergrove, N.I.	17.7.46	S/L W H McGiffin	July 1946

History: Disbanded, Stornaway, 25 May 1945. Re-formed, Aldergrove, 17 July 1946 as a light bomber squadron equipped with B.XXVs. December 1947, became a fighter squadron when it was decided that all auxiliary squadrons should become fighter squadrons, and the NF.XXX night-fighter became standard equipment. June 1948 reclassified again, this time as a day fighter squadron and the Mösquitoes were traded in for Spitfire F.22s.

504 (County of Nottingham) Squadron (RAD)

Motto: *"Vindicat in ventis"* ("It avenges in the wind")
Command Assignments: Auxiliary Air Force

Stations:		Squadron Commanding Officers
Syerston	10.5.46	S/L A H Rook DFC AFC May 1946
Hucknall	11.46	

History: Disbanded, Colerne 10 August 1945 to form 245 Squadron. Re-formed Syerston, 10 May 1946, as a Mosquito light bomber squadron in the Auxiliary Air Force. After training on the T.III, was reclassified as a fighter unit and given NF.XXXs. 1948, plans changed again, being re-classified as a fighter unit, now with Spitfire F.22s, in keeping with the AAF strategy.

515 Squadron (3P)

Motto: *"Ceieniter fenite ut hostes necetis"*
Command Assignments: 100 Group (Special Duties later Bomber Support), January 1944-10-June 1945
Aircraft: NF.II, 2.44-5.44, FB.VI, 3.44-6.45

Stations:		Squadron Commanding Officers:	
Little Snoring, Norfolk	15.12.-l0.6.45	W/C F F Lambert DSO DFC	Jan 1944
		W/C H C Kelsey DFC	Dec 1944

History: 1 October 1942 the Defiant Flight at the A&ARE, Boscombe Down was used to form 515 Squadron, which moved to Heston. Led the development of experimental jamming operations and in June 1943 Bristol Beaufighters were added. Was transferred, January 1944, to 100 Group, where, at Little Snoring, re-equipment with FB.I/Is for intruder operations over the Reich began. Operated very successfully in this role for the remainder of the war until disbanded, 10 June 1945.

521 Squadron

Command Assignments: Meteorology
Aircraft: Mk.IV, 8.42-3.43

Stations:	
Bircham Newton, Norfolk	1.8.42-31.3.43

History: Formed from 1401 Flight, Bircham Newton, 1 August 1942. Throughout WW2 operated as a meteorological squadron flying a diverse range of aircraft including the Gladiator, Hudson, Spitfire, and two Mk.IVs (for Pampa reconnaissance operations over Europe). Disbanded, Bircham Newton, 31 March 1943 into 1401 and 1409 Flights. Re-formed, Docking, 1 September 1943, being equipped with Gladiators, Hudson's, Hampdens, and in turn, Venturas.

527 Squadron (WN)

Motto: "Silently We Serve"
Command Assignments: CSE
Aircraft: B.35, 9.52-1.56

Stations:		**Squadron Commanding Officers**	
Watton, Norfolk	1.5.52-21.8.1958		

History: Formed, Castle Camps, 15 June 1943 for calibration duties using various aircraft including the Wellington, Blenheim, Hurricane and even the DH Hornet Moth. Disbanded, Watton, 15 April 1946. Re-formed there, 1 August 1952 from the 'N' and 'R' Squadrons of the Central Signals Establishment. Among the aircraft employed were a few B.35s. Disbanded, 21 August 1958 by renumbering as 245 Squadron.

540 Squadron (DH)

Motto: *"Sine qua non"*
Command Assignments: No 1 PRU, 19 10 42- ; No 106(PR) Wing, 26 6 43-15 5 44; No 106(PR) Group, 15 5 44-7 5 45
Aircraft: PR.IV, 10.42-5.43; PR.XI, 6.43-5.44; PR.XVI, 6.44-9.46; PR.34, 12.47-12.52

Stations:		**Squadron Commanding Officers:**	
Leuchars	Oct 1942	W/C M J B Young DFC	Oct 1942
Benson	Feb 1944	W/C Lord Douglas-Hamilton OBE	May1943
Coulommiers	March 1945	W/C J R H Merrifield DSO DFC	Mar1944
Benson	Nov 1945	W/C A H W Ball DSO DFC	Sep 1944
Benson	Dec 1947		

History: 19 October 1942 two flights of the PRU, H and L Flights, at Leuchars, were merged to form 540 Squadron. Principally tasked to cover the passage of German capital shipping, operating far and wide throughout Northern and Western Europe and the Mediterranean on this task. 1943, battle-damage assessment and target reconnaissance at such places as Peenemünde were added tasks. Beginning in 1944 went over totally to reconnaissance of the German rail transportation system in preparation for D-Day. By the end of the year detachments had been established at Gibraltar, Agadir, Lossiemouth, Yagodnik, Russia, Dyce and Leuchars for reconnaissance of enemy shipping. Moved to Coulommiers, France, March 1945, for a complete photo-reconnaissance of the country. Finished this assignment, November 1945, returning to Benson, disbanding there, 30 September 1946. Reformed, Benson, 1 December 1947 with PR.34s, which were used on PR and survey duties until December 1952 when Canberra PR.3s took over.

544 Squadron

Motto: *"Quaero"*
Command Assignments: No 1 PRU, 19 10 42- ; No 106(PR) Wing, 26 6 43-15 5 44; No 106(PR) Group, 15 5 44-7 5.45
Aircraft: PR.IV, 4.43-9.43; PR.IX, 10.43-10.45

Stations:		**Squadron Commanding Officers:**	
Benson	April 1943-Oct 13 1945	S/L W R Acott	Oct 1942
		S/L J R H Merrifield DFC	July 1943
		W/C D C B Walker	Oct 1943
		W/C D W Steventon DSO DFC	Nov 1943
		S/L E L Dodd DSO DFC AFC	Sep 1945

History: Formed, Benson, 19 October 1942 equipped with Ansons, Wellington IV and Spitfire PR.IV aircraft for PR and night photography roles. In April 1943 PR.IVs replaced the Wellingtons and before the year was out, PR.IXs completed re-equipment. All were used on day and night photographic missions over Germany, Western Europe, southern France, and Austria using an advance base at San Severo in Italy. Early in 1944 Mosquitoes ranged over Norway, and July 1944, were flying regularly to Moscow for sorties over eastern Germany and Poland. In addition, the Black Sea ports and the Balkans were also covered. 1945, some of the Mosquitoes had their cameras removed and were used to fly diplomatic mail sorties over liberated Europe. After VE Day, allocated to Tiger Force for the invasion of Japan but after VJ-Day was switched to aerial survey work over Holland and Belgium. Disbanded, Benson, 13 October 1945.

571 Squadron (8K)

Command Assignments: 8 (PFF) Group/Light Night Striking Force
Aircraft: B.XVI, 4.44-9.45, B.IX, 6.44—7.44

Stations:		**Squadron Commanding Officers**	
Downham Market	7.4.44	W/C J M Birkin DSO DFC AFC	April 1944
Graveley	4.44	W/C R J Gosnell DSO DFC	Nov 1944
Oakington	24.4.44	W/C R W Bray DFC	March 1945
Warboys	20.7.45-20.9.45		

History: Formed, Downham Market 7 April 1944 with B.XVIs as a squadron in No 8 Group (PFF). B.XVI was capable of carrying the 4000lb bomb in the bomb bay, many being delivered to German cities 1944-45. September 1944 introduced the LORAN AP/AN navigational aid in Mosquito aircraft in 8 Group. New Year's Day 1945, five Mosquitoes, each carrying a 4000lb delayed-action bomb, took part in the skip-bombing from 100-200ft, of 14 railway tunnels in the Eifel region between the Rhine and the Ardennes. One bomb totally destroyed a tunnel. In July 1945 moved to Warboys, disbanding there, 20 September 1945.

600 (City of London) Squadron (BQ)

Motto: *"Praeter sescentos"* ("More than six hundred")
Command Assignments: Italy
Aircraft: XIX, 12.44-8.45

Stations:		**Squadron Commanding Officers:**	
Cesenatico, Italy	12.44	W/C L H Styles DFC	March 1944
Foggia		W/C A H Drummond	Dec 1944
Campoformido	5. 45-		
disbanded	21. 8. 45		

History: Converted to the NF.XIX from Beaufighters shortly before the end of the war with Italy, at the end of 1944. Only three more victories were scored before the Italian surrender. Disbanded, Campoformido, 21 August 1945.

604 (County of Middlesex) Squadron (NC)

Motto: *"Si vis pacem, para bellum"* (If you want peace, prepare for war")

Command Assignments: Fighter Command. 141 Wing, 2nd TAF, 26.4.44-2.5.44. To 147 Wing, 85 (Base) Group, 2nd TAF until 23.9.44. To UK for rest. To 148 Wing, 85 Group, 2nd TAF 31.12.44. Non-operational from 15.4.45 (disbanded 18.4.45).

Aircraft: XII/XIII, 2.44-4.45

Stations:

Church Fenton	April 1944
Hum	May 1944
Colerne	July1944
Zeals	July1944
A8/Picauville	Aug 1944
B17/Carpiquet	Sep 1944
Predannack	Sep 1944
Odiham	Dec 1944
B51/Vendeville	Dec 1944

Squadron Commanding Officers:

W/C M Constable-Maxwell DFC	Apr 1944
W/C F D Hughes DFC	July1944

History: Operated Bristol Blenheims and became one of the four original Beaufighter squadrons before converting to the NF.XIII at Scorton, April 1943. Moved to Church Fenton, April 1944 and in May took Mosquitoes to Hurn to help provide night defense over Normandy for the Allied armies. Within a few weeks had shot down 15 enemy aircraft. Moved to Picautville 6 August to provide further fighter cover and in September returned to England, moving to Predannack in Cornwall. Returned to France, December 1944, this time being based at Lille-Vendeville. In the first four months of 1945 destroyed 32 aircraft. Disbanded, Lille, 18 April 1945.

605 (County of Warwick) Squadron (UP: RAL)

Motto: *"Nun quam dormio"* ("I never sleep")

Command Assignments: Fighter Command. To 136 Wing, Tactical Air Force, 21 November 1944-31.8.45. Royal Auxiliary Air Force, 10 May 1946-1948

Aircraft: NF.II, 2.43-7.43, FB.VI, 7.43-8.45; NF.XIX, 4.47-11.48, NF.XXX, 4.47-1.49

Stations:

Ford	Jne 1942
Castle Camps	Mar 1943
Bradwell Bay	Oct 1943
Manston	Apr 1944
Hartford Bridge	Nov 1944
B⁷1/Coxyde	Mar 1945
B80/Volkel	Apr 1945
Honiley	May 1946

Squadron Commanding Officers

W/C G Denholm DFC	Aug 1942
W/C C D Tomalin DFC AFC	May 1943
W/C B R O'B Hoare DSO DFC	Sep 1943
W/C N J Starr DFC	Apr 1944
W/C R A Mitchell DFC	Sep 1944
W/C A W Home DFC AFC	Mar 1945
S/L R J Walker	June 1946

History: First organisation had an inauspicious beginning, being captured at Tasik Majala, Java March 1942. New formation flew a few defensive sorties from Malta, January-February 1942, before also disappearing at the end of February. Third organisation formed, Ford, 7 June 1942, as an intruder unit equipped with Bostons and Havocs proved more successful. Began to re-equip with NF.IIs for home defense duties) February 1943, at Bradwell Bay. Intruder operations were flown from April 1944 onwards from Manston, until in November, transferred to 2nd TAF for operations on the continent. Moved to Coxyde, Belgium, March 1945, and later Volkel, disbanding there, 31 August 1945 by renumbering as 4 Squadron. Re-formed as Birmingham's auxiliary squadron once more, 10 May 1946, at Honiley. Finally flying began again, 11 months later, now equipped with NF.XXXs. Re-classified as a fighter squadron, 1948 and Vampires eventually replaced the Mosquitoes.

608 (North Riding) Squadron (6T:RAO)

Motto: *"Omnibus ungulis"* ("With all talons")

Command Assignments: 8 (PFF) Group, Light Night Striking Force/Auxiliary Air Force, July 1946-1948.

Aircraft: B.XX, 8.44-8.45, B.XVI, 3.45-8.45; T.III, 7.46-47, NF.XXX, 7.47-10.48

Stations:

Downham Market	8.44-8.45
Thornaby-on-Tees, Yorks	31.7.46-

Squadron Commanding Officers

W/C W W C Scott	Aug 1944
W/C R C Alabaster DSO DFC	Nov 1944
W/C K Gray	Apr 1945
S/L W A Brown DFC	July1946

History: Original 608 Squadron disbanded Montercorvino, Italy 31 July 1944. Re-formed 1 August 1944, Downham Market, Norfolk, equipped with B.XXs in 8 (PFF) Group. Bombing operations began on 6 August. In March 1945 re-equipped with B.XVIs, which could canny a 4000lb bomb. Disbanded, Downham Market, 24 August 1945. Reformed, 10 May 1946 as a night-fighter unit in the Auxiliary Air Force, equipped with NF.30s. Changed to a day fighter squadron, 1948, the Mosquitoes being replaced with Spitfire F.22s.

609 (West Riding) Squadron (RAP)

Motto: "Tally ho"

Command Assignments: Auxiliary Air Force

Aircraft: NF.XXX, 7.46-4.48

Stations:

Church Fenton, Yorks	10.5.46
Yeadon, Yorks	1946-1948

Squadron Commanding Officers:

S/L P A Womersley DFC	May 1946

History: Disbanded, Wunsdorf, Germany, 15 September 1945. Re-formed as an Auxiliary unit, Yeadon, 10 May 1946. From June 1947 equipped with NF.XXXs. Changed for Spitfire LF.l6Es, April 1948, upon re-designation to a fighter squadron.

613 (City of Manchester) Squadron (SY)

Motto: *"Semper parati"* ("Always ready")

Command Assignments: 138 Wing, 2 Group, 2nd Tactical Air Force

Aircraft: FB.VI 10.43-8.45

Stations:		**Squadron Commanding Officers**	
Lasham	Oct 1943	W/C K H Blair DFC	Oct 1943
Hartford Bridge	Oct 1944	W/C R N Bateson DFC	Feb 1944
A75/Epinoy	Nov 1944	W/C C W M Newman DFC	June 1944
		W/C P B Lucas DSO DFC	Dec 1944

History: Formed, Ringway, Manchester, 1 March 1938 for Army Co-Operation duties using Hawker Hinds. After using Lysanders and Curtiss Tomahawks and then Mustangs, in October 1943 moved to Lasham and equipped with FB.VIs for a new role. First Mosquito operation flown, 31 December 1943, an attack on a V1 site in northern France. In 1944-45, as part of 2nd TAF, flew mainly night tactical operations against targets in France, as well as daylight precision maids on high security Nazi targets, the most notable of these being the attack on the Gestapo HQ at The Hague, April 1944 and the SS barracks at Egletons in August. Moved to Hartford Bridge in October. November, moved again, to Cambrai-Epinoy, France, to harass German units. Disbanded, Epinoy, 8 August 1945 by being renumbered as 69 Squadron. Re-formed, Ringway, as the City of Manchester Squadron in the Auxiliary Air Force, 10 May 1946.

616 (South Yorkshire) Squadron (RAW)

Motto: *"Nulla rosa sine spina"* ("No rose without a thorn")
Command Assignments:
Aircraft: NF.30, 11.46-12.48

Stations:		**Squadron Commanding Officers**	
Finningley	10.5.46-12.48	S/L K Holden DFC	June 1946

History: Had the distinction, July 1944, of being the RAF's first jet squadron when it equipped with Gloster Meteors. Disbanded, Lübeck, 29 August 1945. Reformed as an auxiliary unit at Finningley, 31 July 1946 with NF.XXXs. Appropriately, considering its wartime history, in 1948 these were replaced with Gloster Meteors again.

617 (Dam Busters) Squadron

Motto: *"Aprs moi, le deluge"* ("After me, the flood")
Command Assignments: 5 Group Bomber Command
Aircraft: FB.VI/B.XVI, 8.43-1945

Stations:	**Squadron Commanding Officers**
Coningsby	W/C C L Cheshire VC DSO DFC
Woodhall Spa	

History: April 1944, this famous 5 Group Lancaster squadron used Mosquitoes for low level marking duties after Lancasters had been tried. 617 first operated a Mosquito in the low level marking method, 5/6 April 1944, when W/C Leonard Cheshire with F/O Pat Kelly successfully marked an aircraft factory at Toulouse from 800-1000 feet with two red spot flares on his third run. Cheshire used the same aircraft, ML976 N, 10/11 April when he marked the St. Cyr German signals depot during a dive from 5000 to 1000 feet. These successes led to 617 Squadron receiving four FB.VI and B.XVIs, which were first used for marking the Paris-Juvisy marshalling yards, 18/19 April, with 3 Oboe Mosquitoes of 8 Group. La Chapelle was marked 20/21 April, by three out of the four 617 Squadron Mosquitoes despatched. Brunswick, 22/23 April became the first German city to be marked by the low-level marking method. Sir Arthur Harris, who had sanctioned the release of the four Mosquitoes, said they could be retained if Munich was hit heavily on the night of 24/25 April. Operating from Manston because of the long range involved, the four Mosquitoes were successful. Cheshire, in NS993, dived from 12,000 feet to 3000 feet and then flew repeatedly over the city at little more than 700 feet, coming under fire for 12 minutes as he left the target area. S/L Dave Shannon in ML976/L dived from 15,000 to 4000 feet but his markers hung up. NS992 got four spot flares away. Cheshire's contribution to the success of the Munich operation was mentioned in his Victoria Cross citation, 8 September 1944. Altogether, 617 Squadron 's Mosquitoes flew 75 sorties without loss.

618 Squadron

Command Assignments: "Highball" development
Aircraft: B.IV, 4.43-11.45, B.VI, 7.44-9.44, PR.XVI, 7.44-3.45

Stations:		**Squadron Commanding Officers**	
Skitten 1	April 1943	W/C C H B Hutchinson DFC	1 April 1943
Benson	Sept 1943		
Wick	June 1944		
Fisherman's Bend, Australia	Dec 1944		
Narromine, Australia	Feb 1945		

History: Formed, 1 April 1943, one month before 617 Squadron's attack on the German dams, 16/17 May, for the sole purpose of using 950lb, 35" diameter, Highball weapons against the Tirpitz and other 'major naval units and other shipping at sea." Each Mosquito would carry two Highballs, which were 9" smaller in diameter than the 'Upkeep' bombs dropped by the Lancasters. Much of 1943 spent perfecting Dr Barnes Wallis' weapon and flying assimilation sorties but development was protracted, by September 1943 reduced to a cadre at Benson, later being re-tasked for mine-laying in the Pacific. June 1944 brought up to full strength. Fairey Barracudas from Crail were used for practice deck landings on HMS Implacable followed by Mosquito landings at sea. With 27 Mosquitoes, set sail for Australia, 31 October 1944, in the carriers Fencer and Striker, arriving in Melbourne, 23 December, and setting up base at Fisherman's Bend, January 1945. Moved to Narromine, February, to begin operations and in May 12 FB.VIs arrived, but a shortage of suitable shipping targets saw the squadron remain in Australia until 14 July 1945 when it disbanded at Narromine.

627 Squadron (AZ)

Motto: "At first sight"
Command Assignments: Bomber Command: 8 (PFF) Group, Nov 1943-March 1944/5 Group, April 1944—Sept 1945
Aircraft: B.IV, 11.43-12.44, B.XVI, 6.44-12.44, B.XX, 8.44-8.45, B.IX, 1.45-8.45

Stations:		**Squadron Commanding Officers**	
Oakington, Cambs	12.11.43	W/C R P Elliott DSO DFC	Nov 1942
Woodhall Spa, Lincs	4.44 - 9.45	W/C C W Curry DFC	Jne 1944
		W/C B R W Hallows DFC	Jan 1945
		W/C R Kingsford-Smith DSO DFC	Apr1945

History: Formed, 12 November 1943 from a nucleus of 139 Squadron equipped with B.IVs. Participated in marking and bombing attacks over Germany, being transferred to 5 Group, April 1944 to provide target marking for independent maids on strategic targets. Also carried out PR duties for 5 Group and participated in day bombing maids. Remained at Woodhall Spa until 1 October 1945, disbanding there by renumbering as 109 Squadron.

680 Squadron

Command Assignments: Photo-reconnaissance, Middle-East/Mediterranean
Aircraft: PR.IX, 2.44-, PR.XVI, 2.44-9.46.

Stations:

Matariya	Dec1943
San Severo	August 1944
Deversoir	Feb 1945
Aqir	Feb 1946
Em Shemer	Aug 1946

Squadron Commanding Officers:

W/C J R Whelan DFC	Feb 1943
W/C J C Paish	Oct 1944

History: 1 February 1943, 2 PRU re-numbered 680 Squadron, part of the new Mediterranean Air Command, formed 23 February. Received PR IX LR444, 16 February 1944 (MIA 28 2 45 over Crete: Plt Off Ted Ousley killed when parachute candled, Wt Off Cyril Butterworth survived), followed next day by the first of nine PR XVIs by April. Beginning 7 May 1944, carried out PR in the eastern Mediterranean and Greece ('B' Flt, Tocra) and Balkans ('A' Flt, San Severo) using PR IXs, PR XVIs. To San Severo, August 1944. Mosquitoes ranged over the Balkans and Hungary, finishing the war mapping Italy. Moved to Egypt February 1945 to work solely as a survey squadron, moving to Palestine to survey that country, finally disbanding, Em Shemer, 13 September 1946 by renumbering as 13 Squadron.

681 Squadron

Command Assignments: Photo-reconnaissance, India-Burma
Aircraft: Mk.II, 8.43-10.43, VI, 8.43-12.43, PR.IX, 8.43-12.43.

Stations:

Dum Dum (Calcutta)	2.1.43

History: Formed at Dum Dum (Calcutta), 2 January 1943. Went on to use Hurricanes Spitfire IVs, and B-25 Mitchells before adding a few Mosquitoes as a temporary measure in August 1943. Operated just Spitfire IVs and XIs in 1944. Disbanded, India, 1 August 1946 by renumbering as 34 Squadron.

682 Squadron

Command Assignments: Photo-reconnaissance North Africa
Aircraft: II, VI, 4 43-8 43.

History: Formed at Maison Blanche, 1 February 1943, by renumbering No 4 PRU. Equipped with Spitfires, in April some PR Mosquitoes for longer-range operations were acquired, the first Mosquito operation, over the French Alps, being flown, 20 May. Almost all PR sorties in July were over Italian airfields. By August all Mosquitoes withdrawn.

683 Squadron

Motto: *"Nihil nos latet"* (Nothing Escapes us)
Command Assignments: Photo Reconnaissance, Middle East
Aircraft: II/VI, 5.43-7.43.

Stations:

Luqa, Malta	1.2.43

Squadron Commanding Officers:

History: Formed, Luqa, 8 February 1943 from B Flight of 69 Squadron. Initially equipped with Spitfire IVs and later XIs, before adding F.IIs and FB.VIs, May 1943 for a month of operations over Italy and Sicily starting on the 13th. Disbanded, San Severo, 22 September 1945. Reformed 1950 as a Lancaster unit.

684 Squadron

Motto: *"Invisus videns"*
Command Assignments: Photo-reconnaissance, India-Burma
Aircraft: II, 11.43-12.43, Mk.VI, 11.43-8.44, PR.IX, 10.43-7.44, PR.XVI, 2.44-2.46, PR.34, 7.45-9.46.

Stations:

Dum Dum (Calcutta)	Sep 1943
Comilla	Oct 1943
Dum Dum (Calcutta)	Jan 1944
Alipore	May 1944
Saigon	Oct 1945
Don Muang (Bangkok)	Jan 1946

Squadron Commanding Officers:

S/L B S Jones	Sep 1943
W/C W B Murray DFC	1943
W/C W E M Lowry DFC	Nov 1944
W/C K J Newman DFC	Nov 1945
W/C J R H Merrifield DSO DFC	Apr 1946

History: Formed, Dum Dum, 29 September 1943, from the twin-engined Flights of 681 Squadron and equipped from the outset with F.IIs, FB.VIs and PR.IXs as well as Mitchell III aircraft. Flew long-range PR sorties during the Burma campaign, regularly going to the Andaman Islands, Rangoon and the Burma-Thailand railway. Survey flying using IXs and XVIs from Calcutta took place before a move to Alipore for the remainder of the war. Detachments sent to the Cocos Islands, Ceylon and Burma until VJ Day. Then continued to operate PR.34s, providing a high-speed courier service to the far flung units in the Far East before moving to Bangkok, January 1946, to take up survey duties. Disbanded 1 September 1946 by renumbering as 81 Squadron.

692 (Fellowship of the Bellows) Squadron (P3)

Motto: *"Polus dum sidera pascet"* ("So long as the sky shall feed the stars")
Command Assignments: 8 (PFF) Group Bomber Command, Light Night Striking Force
Aircraft: B.IV, 1.44-6.44, B.XVI, 5.3.44-9.45

Stations:

Graveley, Hunts	1.1.44

Squadron Commanding Officers:

W/C W C Lockhart DSO DFC	Jan1944

Gransden Lodge, Beds	6.45-20.9.45	W/C S D Watts DFC	Mar1944
		W/C J Northrop DFC AFC	July 1944

History: Formed, Graveley, 1 January 1944, equipped with B.IVs. Operated as part of the LNSF, flying first operation 1/2 February, when three B.IVs set off for Berlin, one of which bombed the city. Had the distinction of being the first Mosquito squadron to drop a 4000lb bomb over Germany when DZ647, a modified B.IV, released one during a raid on Düsseldorf on 23/24 February. The first B.XVI with bulged bomb bay for a 4000lb bomb, was used operationally, 5/6 March, on a raid on Duisburg. 4000lb bombs were dropped on Berlin for the first time, 13/14 April. Crews mined the Kiel Canal 12/13 May, for the first time. Most operations were flown at low level (the squadron also dropped mines), including, on New Year's Day 1945, when six Mosquitoes, each carrying a 4000lb delayed-action bomb, skip bombed railway tunnels in the Eifel region between the Rhine and the Ardennes from 100-200ft. Disbanded, Gransden Lodge, 20 September 1945.

25th Bomb Group USAAF (653rd and 654th Squadrons)

Command Assignments: 8th Air Force
Aircraft: T. III/PR.XVI

Stations:		**Commanding Officers:**	
Watton, Norfolk	22.4.44-23.7.45	Lt Col Joseph A. Stenglein	23 Sept 44
		Col Leon W. Gray	23.9.44-14.4.45
		Lt Col John R. Hoover	14.4.45-19.6.45
		Maj Ernest H. Patterson	19.6.45-Aug 45

History: Specialist weather/photo reconnaissance and strategic unit, first activated at Cheddington as the 802nd Reconnaissance group (Provisional), moving immediately to Station 376, Watton. Had begun to function, 28 March 1944, however, prior to activation, as the 8th Heavy Weather Recon Squadron (Provisional), equipped with B-17 aircraft (later to become 652nd Weather Recon Squadron (heavy). Soon became apparent that the varied nature of the group's missions would prove too cumbersome for a photo-reconnaissance organization, and the group was re-activated, 9 August 1944, as the 25th Bombardment Group (Recon, Special). Apart from weather missions (Blue-stocking) over the Atlantic and the Continent, the group flew missions over enemy territory by day (Dilly) and night (Joker) on still and motion picture photographic missions, and carried out target scouting, Chaff dispensing (Gray-Pea), OSS Red-stocking agent contact (Joan-Eleanor) sorties, Command pilot (Red Tail) flights, as well as PR of drone bombing. Group left England for the USA, August 1945. Inactivated, Drew Field, Florida, 8 September.

MISCELLANEOUS UNITS

- 1 PRU
- 1 PRU RAAF
- 8 PR OTU
- 87 and 94 Squadrons RAAF
- 5 OTU RAAF
- 13 Squadron RCAF
- 6,8 (PR),13,16,51,54,60 and 132 OTUs (Operational Training Units)
- 226,228,229,231 and 237 OCUs (Operational Conversion Units)
- 1655 Mosquito Training Unit (MTU)
- 1660 Conversion Unit (CU)
- 1672 Mosquito Conversion Unit (MCU)
- 703 RU Squadron
- 728 Fleet Requirements Unit
- 762 RU Squadron
- 771 RU Training Squadron
- 772 RU Training Squadron
- 790 RU Squadron
- 811 RU Training Squadron
- 1,3,3/4,5,226,229,233,236,and 238 Civil Anti-Aircraft Co-Operation Units (CAACU)
- APS Sylt
- 1300 Flight; 1317 Flight; 1401 Flight;1409 Flight; 1474 Flight
- 1692 Bomber Support Training Flight
- 204 Advanced Flying School
- Air Torpedo Development Unit (ATDU)
- Armament Practice School (APS)
- BSDU (Bomber Support Development Unit)
- Bomber Development Unit
- Bombing Trials Unit
- Central Bomber Establishment
- Central Gunnery School
- Central Fighter Establishment
- Central Signals Establishment
- Empire Air Armament School (EAAS)
- Empire Test Pilots School
- Fighter Interception Unit (FIU)
- Signals Flying Unit
- Special Installation Unit
- Night-fighter Development Wing
- Photographic Development Unit
- Pathfinder Navigation Training Unit (PFFNTU)
- Special Installation Unit
- Special Flying Unit

Appendix 5

Mosquito Fighter/Fighter-Bomber/Bomber/PR Squadrons England and the Continent 1944-45

Squadron		Location	Aircraft Type	Command
4		England	XVI/Spitfire XI	2nd TAF
21		England/Continent	FB.VI	ADGB/2nd TAF
23		England	FB.VI	To 100 Group May 44
25		England	FB.VI/NF.XVII	ADGB
29		England/Continent	NF.XIII	ADGB/2nd TAF/ADGB
85		England	NF.II/XII/FB.VI/NF.XV/XVII/XIX	Ftr Cmd. To 100 Group May 44
96		England	NF.XIII	ADGB
105		England	B.IX/XVI	8 (PFF)
109		England	B.IV/IX/XVI	8 (PFF)
107		England/Continent	FB.VI	138 Wing, 2 Group, 2nd TAF
125	'Newfoundland'	England	NF.XVII	ADGB
139		England	B.IV/IX/XVI/XX	8 (PFF)
141		England	NF.II	Ftr Cmd. To 100 Group 11.43
151		England	NF.XIII	ADGB
157		England	NF.II/FB.VI/NF.XIX/NF.XXX	Ftr Cmd. To 100 Group May 1 44
169		England	NF.II/FB.VI/NF.XIX	Ftr Cmd. To 100 Group 7 Dec 43
192		England	B.IV/B/XVI/Wellington X	100 Group
219		England/Continent	NF.XVII	ADGB/2nd TAF
239		England	NF.II	Ftr Cmd.To 100 Group Dec 43
264	'Madras Presidency'	England/Continent	NF.XIII	ADGB/2nd TAF
305	*Ziemia Wielkopolska*	England/Continent	FB.VI	138 Wing, 2 Group, 2nd TAF
307	City of Lvov' (Polish)	England	NF.II/XII	ADGB
400	'City of Toronto'	England/Continent	B.XVI	39 (R) Wing, 83 Group, 2nd TAF
406	'Lynx' RCAF	England	NF.XII/NF.XXX	ADGB
409	'Nighthawk' RCAF	England/Continent	NF.XIII	Ftr Cmd/148 Wing, 2nd TAF
410	'Cougar' RCAF	England/Continent	NF.XIII/NF.XXX	141 & 147 Wings, 2nd TAF
418	'City of Edmonton'RCAF	England/Continent	FB.VI	136 Wing 2nd TAF
456	RAAF	England	NF.II/FB.VI/NF.XVII/NF.XXX	10 & 11 Groups Ftr Cmd
464	RAAF	England/Continent	FB.VI	140 Wing 2 Group 2nd TAF
487	RNZAF	England/Continent	FB.VI	140 Wing 2 Group 2nd TAF
488	RNZAF	England/Continent	NF.XII/XIII/NF.XXX	Ftr Cmd/ADGB/147 Wing2ndTAF
515		England	FB.VI	To 100 Group 15 Dec 43
540		England	B.IX/XVI	106 PR Group
544		England	B.IX/XVI	106 PR Group
571		England	B.XVI	8 (PFF)
605	'County Of Warwick'	England/Continent	FB.VI	ADGB/136 Wing, 2nd TAF
613	'City of Manchester'	England/Continent	FB.VI	138 Wing, 2 Group, 2nd TAF
604	'County Of Middlesex'	England/Continent	NF.XII/XIII	ADGB/141 Wing 2nd TAF
617	Dam Busters	England	FB.VI	5 Group
627		England	B.IV	5 Group
692		England	B.IV/XVI	8 (PFF)
8	OTU	Scotland	PR.I/NF.II/IV/VI/PR.VIII	106 PR Group
1692	Flight	England	NF.II	100 Group

Appendix 6

100 Group RAF

(Special Duties later Bomber Support)

Order of Battle

(HQ Bylaugh Hall Norfolk)

Squadron	Base	Aircraft	1st Op in 100 Group
141	West Raynham	Beaufighter VI NF.II/FB.VI/NF.XXX	December 1943
192	Foulsham Wellington B.III, Halifax III/V	NF.II/B.IV/B.XVI/	December 1943
239	West Raynham	NF.II/FB.VI/NF.XXX	20 January 1944
515	Little Tnoring/Great Massingham	NF.II/FB.VI	3 March 1944
169	Little Snoring	NF.II/FB.VI/NF.XIX	20 January 1944
214	Sculthorpe/Oulton	Fortress II/III	20/21 April 1944
199	North Creake	Stirling III/Halifax III	1 May 1944
157	Swannington	NF.XIX/NF.XXX	May1944
85	Swannington	NF.XII/NF.XVII	5/6 June 1944
23	Little Snoring	FB.VI	5/6 July 1944
223	Oulton	Liberator VI/Fortress II/III	cSept 1944
171	North Creake	Stirling II/Halifax III	15 Sept 1944
462 RAAF	Foulsham	Halifax III	13 March 1945

Appendix 7

German Ranks and their Abbreviations

German Ranks	US equivalent	RAF Equivalent
Reichsmarschall	no equivalent	no equivalent
Generalfeldmarschall	General (5-Star)	
Generaloberst	General (4-Star)	
General der Flieger	Lieutenant General	
Generalleutnant	Major General	
Generalmajor	Brigadier General	
Oberst	Colonel	Group Captain (G/C)
Oberstleutnant (Obstlt)	Lieutenant Colonel	Wing Commander (W/C)
Major	Major	Squadron Leader (S/L)
Hauptmann (Hptm)	Captain	Flight Lieutenant (F/L)
Oberleutnant (Oblt)	1st Lieutenant	Flying Officer (F/O)
Leutnant (Lt)	2nd Lieutenant	Pilot Officer (P/O)
Stabsfeldwebel (StFw)	Flight Officer	Warrant Officer (W/O)
Oberfähnrich (Ofhr)	no equivalent	no equivalent
Oberfeldwebel (Ofw)	Master Sergeant	Flight Sergeant
Fähnrich (Fhr)	Officer candidate	no equivalent
Feldwebel (Fw)	Sergeant	Sergeant
Unteroffizier (Uffz)	Staff Sergeant	Corporal
Obergefreiter (Ogfr)	Corporal	Leading Aircraftsman (LAC)
Gefreiter (Gefr)	Private First Class	Aircraftsman 1 (AC1)
Flieger (Flg)	Private Second Class	Aircraftsman 2 (AC')

APPENDIX 8

RAF SLANG TERMS IN COMMON EVERYDAY USE

A 48 A 48-hour leave of absence.

ADJ Adjutant

BANG-ON Something very good or very accurate.

BATTLE BLOOMERS WAAF Issue Knickers - name originally given to them by the WAAFs themselves

BEST BLUE Best uniform

BIG CITY, THE Berlin

BINDING Moaning, Complaining

BIRD SANCTUARY WAAF quarters - usually well away from the rough airmen!

BLOOD WAGON Ambulance

BODS People, Bodies

BOUGHT IT. Killed, failed to return

CHEESE CUTTER Peaked Cap

CHEESED OR CHEESED OFF Fed up, bored

CHIEFY Head of Aircraft Ground Crew - generally well respected

CLAPPED OUT Worn out, well past its best

CRATE Aircraft

COOKIE 4000lb Bomb

DICEY Dangerous. A dicey do. An op when there was heavy opposition

DICING (DICING WITH DEATH) Mainly operational flying but sometimes, just flying. Are we dicing tonight? Are we on the Battle Order?

DITCH To land in the Drink.

DRINK The sea

DUFF GEN Bad information.

ERKS Aircraftsmen - usually reserved for the lowest

FANS Propeller on aircraft. No fans - no engines.

FLIGHT A Flight Sergeant

FLIGHTS Where aircrew collected particularly on operational squadrons while waiting for the 'gen'. Cards and other games of chance were played here. More generally, any place around hangers where matters connected with flying took place.

FLIGHT OFFICES usually occupied by the CO, Flight Commanders and their slaves

FLYING ORIFICE Observers Brevet - the polite versions

FRUIT SALAD Lots of medal ribbons particularly on Americans.

GETTING FINGER OUT extracting the digit. Originally RAF slang term now in common use. In RAF it implied sitting on ones hands – politely

GET WEAVING Get a move on - from aircraft taking avoiding action from fighters.

GONE FOR A BURTON These terms were always used when anyone failed to return. Killed. Failed to return. It was never said that 'old so and so was killed last night'.

GONG Medal.

GOOD SHOW did well

GOING LIKE THE CLAPPERS moving very fast indeed.

GOT THE CHOP killed

GOT THE GEN have got the true information

GREMLIN A mythical mischievous creature invented by the RAF, to whom is attributed the blame for anything that goes wrong in the air or on the ground. There are different sorts of gremlins skilled in different sorts and grades of evil. The origin of the term is obscure, but has been stated variously to go hack as far as the Royal Naval Air Service; to have some connection with the RAF in Russia and the Kremlin; and to have come from India, where, it is alleged, in the early 1920s an officer was opening a bottle of Fremlin's Ale when the overheated gas blew out the cork, taking him by surprise. Meaning to say, 'A goblin has jumped out of my Fremlin's', he spoonerised and said: 'A gremlin has jumped out of my Foblin's'. In his book *It's a Piece of Cake!: RAF Slang Made Easy* (Sylvan Press, c1942).

HAD IT something coming to its end. For a person - 'He's had it' - he's died or is likely to

HAIRY dangerous or very exiting

HAPPY VALLEY the Ruhr

KITE Aircraft

Meat Wagon: Ambulance

Milk Run Regular run (USAAF equivalent - 'easy mission')

On a Fizzer On a charge in front of senior

Passion Bafflers WAAF Issue Knickers - name originally given to them by the WAAFs themselves

Penguin Non aircrew - often used for someone not popular.

A Piece of Cake Very Easy

Poor Show Bad behaviour. Not done well

Prang a crash, usually of aircraft. To prang - to crash or to prang a target - to hit it well. A wizard prang - a good raid.

Queen Bee WAAF Commanding Officer

Scrambled Egg Gold on caps of Senior Officers.

Second Dickey Second Pilot

Shaky do Near miss or lucky escape.

Shoot a line to brag, enlarge, blow ones own trumpet.

Sky Pilot padre

Snappers Enemy Fighters

Spot On Something very good or very accurate.

Sprog(s) New recruit(s).

Sprog crew A new crew.

A Stooge A boring flight.

Stooge Around Loiter. Hang around, fly around waiting for happening.

Stores Basher Someone who worked in Stores.

Suffering from the Twitch (particularly pilots), - To be avoided at all costs.

10/10ths complete cloud cover

Twitch Nervy. Bags of twitch' - suffered when in danger particularly from fighters.

Waafery WAAF quarters - usually well away from the rough airmen!

Winco Wing Commander usually Squadron Commanding Officer

Wingless Wonder Usually very unpopular non-aircrew

Glossary

* (Medal) and Bar (second award of the medal specified)
'Dicke Autos' 'Fat Cars' (Four engined heavy bombers)
'Heavies' RAF/USAAF four-engined bombers
A/c abbreviation for aircraft
AA Anti-Aircraft
AAA Anti-Aircraft Artillery
Abschuss Claim for a victory in air combat
Abschüsse: Claims for victories in air combat
Abschussbeteiligung Contribution to a claim for a victory in air-combat
AF Air Force
AFC Air Force Cross
AI Airborne Interception (radar)
Alarmstart 'Scramble'
AM Air Marshal
Anerkannter Abschuss Officially confirmed air-combat victory claim
AOC Air Officer Commanding
ASH AI Mk.XV narrow-beam radar used for low-level operations
ASR Air-Sea Rescue
ATS Air Training Squadron
AVM Air Vice-Marshal

BBC British Broadcasting Corporation
BEM British Empire Medal
BG Bomb Group (USAAF)
Blip Radar echo or response
BM *Bordmechaniker* (flight engineer) (German)
Bogey Unidentified aircraft
Bordfunker or Funker German Radar/radio operator
BS Bomb Squadron (USAAF)
BSDU Bomber Support Development Unit (RAF)

Capt Captain
CCU Combat Crew Unit
Chaff American *Window*
CO Commanding Officer
CoG Center of Gravity
Col Colonel
cr. abbreviation for crashed
CRT Cathode Ray Tube
C-scope CRT showing frontal elevation of target

Day Ranger Operation to engage air and ground targets within a wide but specified area, by day
DCM Distinguished Conduct Medal
Deutsches Kreuz (DK) German Cross
DFC Distinguished Flying Cross
DFM Distinguished Flying Medal
Diver V1 flying bomb operation
Drem lighting
System of outer markers and runway approach lights
DSC Distinguished Service Cross
DSO Distinguished Service Order
Düppel German codename for *Window* after a town near the Danish border where RAF metal foil strips were first found.

e/a Enemy Aircraft
Eichenlaub (El) (Knight's Cross with) Oak Leaves
Einsatz Operational flight
Eisernes Kreuz I, II (EK I, EK II) Iron Cross (1st and 2nd Class)
Emil Emil German codename for AI
Ergänzungsgruppe (EGr) Replacement or complement wing
ETA Estimated Time of Arrival
Experte(n) Expert. An ace/aces (five or more confirmed victories)
Express-Express German R/T code for 'hurry up'

FF *Flugzeugführer* (pilot)
F/L Flight Lieutenant
F/O Flying Officer
F/Sgt Flight Sergeant
Fähnrich (Fhr) Flight Sergeant
Feindberührung Contact with an enemy aircraft
Feldwebel (Fw) Sergeant
FIDO Fog Investigation and Dispersal Operation
Firebash 100 Group Mosquito sorties using incendiaries/napalm against German airfields
Flak *(Flieger Abwehr Kanone(n)* Anti-Aircraft Artillery
Flensburg German device to enable their night fighters to homeon to *Monica*
FNSF Fast Night Striking Force
Freelance Patrol with the object of picking up a chance contact or visual of the enemy
FTR abbreviation for failed to return
Führer Leader

G/C Group Captain
GCI Ground Control Interception (radar)
Gee British medium-range navigational aid using ground transmitters and an airborne receiver
Gen General
General der Flieger Air Marshal
Generalfeldmarschall Marshal of the Air Force
Generalleutnant Air Vice-Marshal
Generalmajor Air Commodore
Generaloberst Air Chief Marshal
Geschwader Roughly equivalent to three RAF wings. Comprises three or four *Gruppen* Gruppe containing three or four *Staffeln*, eg: *IV./NJG1* (the fourth *Gruppe* in *Nachtjagd Geschwader* 1), *12./NJG1* (the *12th Staffel* (in the fourth *Gruppe*) of *Nachtjagd Geschwader* 1)
GP General Purpose bomb
Gruppenkommandeur Commander or Captain, a Gruppe command position rather than a rank

H_2S British 10-cm experimental airborne radar navigational and target location aid
Hauptmann (Hptm)
Flight Lieutenant
HE High Explosive (bomb)
HEI High Explosive Incendiary
Helle Nachtjagd illuminated night fighting
Herausschuss Claim for a bomber shot out of formation
HMS His Majesty's Ship
Horrido! German for 'Tallyho'
HRH His Royal Highness

IAS Indicated Air Speed
IFF Identification Friend or Foe

Intruder Offensive night operation to fixed point or specified target
IO Intelligence Officer

Jagdbomber (Jabo) Fighter-bomber
Jagdgeschwader **(JO)** Fighter wing, includes three or four *Gruppen*
Jagdwaffe Fighter Arm or Fighter Force
Jager Fighter
Jägerleitoffizier JLO, or GCI-controller

Kampfgeschwader (KG) Bomber Group
Kommandeur Commanding officer of a *Gruppe*
Kommodore Commodore or Captain, a *Geschwader* command position rather than a rank
KüFlGr *Küstenfliegergruppe*: Coastal Flying Wing (German)
Kurier R/T code for 'Allied heavy bomber'

LAC Leading Aircraftsman
Leutnant (Lt) Pilot Officer
Liechtenstein Early form of German AI radar
LMF Lack of Moral Fibre
LNSF Light Night Striking Force
LORAN Long-Range Navigation
Lt Cmdr Lieutenant Commander
Lt Col Lieutenant Colonel
Lt Lieutenant
Luftflotte Air Fleet (German)
Luftwaffe (LW) Air Force

M/T Motor Transport
Mahmoud (British) High-level bomber support sortie
Maj Gen Major General
Maj Major
Major (German) Squadron Leader
Mandrel American airborne radar jamming device
Maschinen Gewehr (MG) Machine gun
Maschinen Kanone (MK) Machine cannon
MC Medium Capacity bomb
MCU Mosquito Conversion Unit
Met. Meteorological
MiD Mention In Dispatches
Monica British active tail warning radar device
MTU Mosquito Training Unit

Nachtjagdgeschwader (*NJG*) Night fighter Group
Nachtjäger Night-fighter
NCO Non-Commissioned Officer
NFS Night Fighter Squadron
Night Ranger Operation to engage air and ground targets within a wide but specified area, by night
Noball Flying bomb (V1) or rocket (V2) site
nr. Abbreviation for number

OBE Order of the British Empire
Oberfähnrich (Ofhr) Warrant Officer
Oberfeldwebel (Ofw) Flight Sergeant
Oberleutnant (Oblt) Flying Officer
Oberst (Obst) Group Captain
Oberstleutnant (Obstlt) Wing Commander
Objektnachtjagd Target Area Night Fighting
Oboe Ground-controlled radar system of blind bombing in which one station indicated track to be followed and another the bomb release point
Op Operation (mission)
OSS Office of Strategic Services. The US intelligence service activated during the Second World War and disbanded on 1 October 1945
OT Operational Training
OTU Operational Training Unit

P/O Pilot Officer
Pauke! Pauke!'Kettledrum! Kettledrum!' (R/T code for 'Going into attack!')
PFF Path Finder Force
PoW Prisoner of War
PR Photographic Reconnaissance
PRU Photographic Reconnaissance Unit

R/T Radio Telephony
RAAF Royal Australian Air Force
RAE Royal Aircraft Establishment
RAFVR Royal Air Force Volunteer Reserve
RCAF Royal Canadian Air Force
RCM Radio CounterMeasures
Reflex Visier (Revi) Gunsight
Reichsluftfahrtministerium (RLM) German Air Ministry
Reichs(luft)verteidigung Air Defense of Germany
Ritterkreuz (träger) (RK/RKT) Knight's Cross (holder)
RN Royal Navy
RNorAF Royal Norwegian Air Force
RNVR Royal Naval Volunteer Reserve
Rotte Tactical element of two aircraft
Rottenflieger Wingman, the second man in the *Rotte*
RP Rocket Projectile

S/L Squadron Leader
SAAF South African Air Force
SAS Special Air Service
SASO Senior Air Staff Officer
Schlachtgeschwader (SG) Ground attack Group
Schräge Musik 'Slanting Music'; night fighters' guns firing upwards
Schwarm Flight of four aircraft
Schwarmführer Flight leader
Schwerten (S) (Knight's Cross with Oak Leaves and) Swords
SD Special Duties
Serrate British equipment designed to home in on Liechtenstein AI radar.
SKG Schnelles Kampfgeschwader: Fast Bomber Group (German)
SOE Special Operations Executive
Stab Staff flight
Staffel Roughly equivalent to a squadron, designated sequentially within the *Geschwader* by Arabic figures, eg: *4./NJG1*
Staffelkapitän (St.Kpt) Captain, a *Staffel* command position rather than a rank
Sub/Lt Sub-Lieutenant

TIs Target Indicators
TNT TriNitroToluene
Transportgeschwader (TO) Transport Group

UEA Unidentified Enemy Aircraft
U/S Unserviceable
UHF Ultra-High Frequency
Uhu *'Owl'* Heinkel He 219 night fighter aircraft
Unteroffizier (Uffz) Corporal
USAAF United Sates Army Air Force

VC Victoria Cross
VHF Very High Frequency
Viermot (4-mot) Four-engined bomber abbreviation of *viermotorig*–four engined.
Viktor R/T code for 'have received and understood message'

W/C Wing Commander
W/O Warrant Officer
WAAF Women's Auxiliary Air Force
Wilde Sau *'Wild Boar'*: Free-lance night fighting, originally by single-engined aircraft, mainly over the RAF's target, relying on freelance interceptions from a running commentary aided by the lights from fires and from searchlights
Window Metal foil strips dropped by bombers to confuse German radar

Y-Service *Ypsilon*, *Y-Verfahren*, *Ypsilonverfahren*: *Luftwaffe* ground-controlled navigation by means of VHF

Zahme Sau *'Tame Boar'*: Tactic of feeding German twin-engined fighters into the bomber stream as soon as its track was properly established on the way to or from the target, and by means of broadcast running commentary on situation in the air
Zerstörer 'Destroyer', heavy twin-engined fighter-bomber aircraft (Bf 110/210/410)
Zerstörergeschwader (ZG) Bf 110 unit roughly equivalent to four RAF squadrons (*Geschwader* consisted of 100-120 a/c; each *Geschwader* had a *Geschwader Stab* and three or four *Gruppen*, with 25 to 35 a/c each; each *Gruppe* had three *Staffeln* of ten a/c each).
Zweimot Twin-engined aircraft

Endnotes

Chapter 1: Low Levellers and the Shallow Raiders

1 MAA *The Mossie* No.36 September 2004

2 W4064/C FTR on 31 May 1942 when it was hit by flak on the operation to Cologne and was ditched 10 km SW of Antwerp, at Bazel on the bank of the Schelde. Pilot Officer William Deryck Kennard and Pilot Officer Eric Raymond Johnson were killed.

3 Simmons was later killed flying a Turkish Air Force Mosquito.

4 A further 60 Mosquito bombers were on order, but they would not start to arrive until the following February. For now, 105 Squadron had to make do with W4066, the first Mosquito bomber to enter RAF service. This aircraft arrived at Swanton Morley on 17 November watched by the AOC 2 Group, Air Vice Marshal d'Albiac and his staff. Three other B.IVs - W4064, W4068 and W4071 - were delivered at intervals to Swanton Morley by Geoffrey de Havilland Jr. and Pat Fillingham.

5 George Parry and Jack Houlston had been sent to Boscombe Down to test-fly the prototype Mosquito and evaluate the aircraft for squadron service. Parry recalls. 'There were no handling notes; only a few roneoed pages. On 25 November I flew W4057 for the first time, with Houlston in the right-hand seat. After the Blenheim the Mosquito was unbelievable. The maximum recommended speed was 420 mph indicated air speed, but at 20,000 feet this was equivalent to 520 mph. However, the short nacelles caused a bit of buffeting on the tailplane and it also felt tail-heavy. I had to use nose-down to get the aircraft on the deck. We found out why in the Mess. Geoffrey de Havilland was there having lunch. We went up to him and he asked us what we thought. We mentioned the problems with buffeting and he replied that the short nacelles caused it. They were going to lengthen them, he said. He looked nonplussed when I mentioned about it being tail-heavy. Then he exclaimed: 'We put 1000lb of ballast in for the CoG, and I forgot to tell you!' On 27 December Flight Lieutenant Parry flew W4066 to an altitude of 30,000ft. On 5 January he carried out fuel consumption tests in W4068 at a more sedate 10,000-feet. Mosquito spares at this time were non-existent, although the squadron was expected to become fully operational with 16-18 crews and a dozen aircraft within a six-month period. At least the enterprising crews solved the question of spares, as 'George' Parry recalls. 'Roy Maisey, Chief Engineer at de Havilland, lived with us. We piled all the old bits of aircraft into an Anson on 9 January 1942 and I flew it down to Hatfield with Houlston and two others, where we swapped them, with de Havilland's permission, for brand-new parts. On another occasion I flew back with the aircraft filled with timber! Finally, the Air Ministry wrote and said, 'The degree of serviceability of 105 Squadron is amazing', and thereafter, spares schedules were issued and we had to abide by the rules!

6 In London they were interrogated by MI9 at the transit camp at the Grand Central Hotel in Marylebone and eventually issued with a certificate to take to RAF Uxbridge. Then they were free to send a telegram home and were taken to Air Ministry. They were given a written note stating their identity, had a couple of interviews, and asked where they wanted to be posted. Tommy Broom was told 105 Squadron had now moved to RAF Marham and 1655 Mosquito Training Unit was being formed and he agreed to be posted there. Costello-Bowen was killed in August 1943 while CFI at 1655 MTU when he was a passenger in a Ventura flown by Flying Officer Abbot, pilot of an Oxford. After a rest as Chief Ground Instructor 1655 MTU, Tommy Broom resumed operations with Flight Lieutenant Ivor Broom (no relation) with 571 Squadron, 128 Squadron, and then 163 Squadron; Ivor as Wing Commander and Tommy as Squadron Leader. They did another 58 operations (21 to Berlin). This was in 8 Group Pathfinder Force. Ivor later became Air Marshal Sir Ivor Broom KCB CBE DSO DFC** AFC.

7 KIA 13 November 1942.

8 Piffer, an Austrian was killed on 17 June 1944 when USAAF P-47 Thunderbolts shot his Fw 190A-8 'White 3' near Argentan. He was posthumously awarded the *Ritterkreuz* (Knight's Cross) on 20 October 1944 for his 26 victories in the West. *Defending The Reich: The History of JG1*, Eric Mombeek (JAC Publications 1992).

9 Rowland, a post war captain for BEA, learned this at a stopover in Hamburg in 1963. Klein had later lost a leg in a crash-landing after he was shot down by a P-51 Mustang. In July 1993 Parry met Fenten face-to-face also, when the German flew his light aircraft to Horsham St Faith (Norwich Airport) and they flew a memorable flight around the city!

10 Oberfeldwebel Timm was KIA on 28 May 1944 flying Bf 109G-6 'Yellow 3'.

11 By the end of November 1942 105 Squadron had flown 282 operational sorties and lost 24 aircraft.

12 107 houses and 96 shops were completely destroyed and 107 Dutch workers and civilians living around the factory were killed and 161 wounded.

13 See *The Mosquito Log* by Alexander McKee. Souvenir Press. 1988.

14 *The Mossie, Mosquito Aircrew Association*, Vol.18 January 1998.

15 Flying Officer C. Vernon Pereira, a Trinidadian, flew 80 ops on Mosquitoes on 139 and 105 Squadrons and he was awarded the DFC and Bar.

16 Flight Sergeant Frederick Alfred Budden and Sergeant Frank Morris in DZ420/F, which crashed northwest of Tours at Vengeons.

17 By the end of the year he had taken up an appointment in Air Command Far East Asia and held the rank of SASO (Senior Air Staff Officer) until the end of 1945. He remained in the post-war RAF and was awarded the OBE in 1947. In 1958 he was promoted to Air Commodore and finally retired from the service in 1963. He returned to Australia, was knighted and in 1974 became Governor of West Australia.

18 Four Fw 190s intercepted the Mosquitoes on the homeward journey and Flying Officer A. N. Bulpitt and his navigator, Sergeant K. A. Amond were last seen being pursued by two Fw 190s and crashed into the sea. The Mosquito flown by Flying Officer J. H. Brown and Flying Officer Pounder slowed down to signal to another Mosquito that his bomb doors were open. Brown made off for the coast down a winding valley pursued by two Fw 190s in line astern that caught the Mosquito crossing the coast and the leader scored hits in the fuselage just forward of the tail plane. The Fw 190s continued to follow the Mosquito out to seas for about 20 miles while Brown took violent evasive action. When they ran out of ammunition the Fw 190s were immediately replaced by two more and the combat finally ended 50 miles out to sea. Pounder then set course for Leuchars and they made landfall about 3 miles south. Brown made four attempts at a landing without hydraulics to operate the undercarriage and with no air speed indicator, rudder controls or elevator trim. He finally made a successful crash-landing. Six days later Brown and Pounder had a similar experience after being hit by flak over the Renault works at Le Mans and they returned with tail trim, rudder controls, hydraulics and wireless all out of action. They returned to Marham at 2015 hours and circled before finally crash-landing on the second attempt 'with no trouble' as Brown put it.

19 II./JG1 at Woensdrecht was equipped with 35 Fw 190A-4s of which twenty were serviceable.

20 9.8 tons of bombs were dropped on the John Cockerill works. Pace and Cook crashed into the Ooster Schelde off Woensdrecht.

21 Flight Sergeant Peter J. D. McGeehan DFM and Flying Officer Reginald C. Morris DFC were killed.

22 Mosquito DZ477 flown by Sergeant Massey DFM and Sergeant 'Lofty' Fletcher DFM was hit by flak in the port wing close to the fuselage. Petrol began to pour out and they feathered the port engine on case of fire. After leaving the target the port engine would not unfeather and they had to carry on, on one engine. As they approached the enemy coast a cone of searchlights tried to pick them up but they were too low to be caught in the beams though they must have been silhouetted as there was a considerable amount of light flak and they were hit again in the fuselage. The controls became very sloppy and 30 miles from the coast the remaining engine began to run rough. They then switched in to emergency and obtained assistance to land at Docking in Norfolk. They were unable to land on the flarepath due to a violent swing, which materialised as the starboard engine was throttled back but they landed alongside it and finally crashed into a windsock. They were uninjured buy the aircraft was written off.

23 Fog Investigation and Dispersal Operation. Wooldridge spent three months in command of 105 and on 25 June he was posted to 3 Group at RAF Stradishall. On 1 September 1943 he was posted back to the PWD. His replacement at Marham was 109 Squadron's Wing Commander Henry John 'Butch' Cundall AFC (later Group Captain Cundall CBE DSO DFC AFC. Wooldridge wrote *Low Attack* and after the war he composed music, worked as a conductor, with the Philharmonia Orchestra especially, and wrote many plays, orchestral suites, incidental film music and film scores. His most famous was *Appointment in London* (1952), for which he wrote the music and also the squadron song. Wooldridge died in a car accident on 27 October 1958.

24 On 3 April Flying Officer J. H. Brown and Flying Officer Pounder were killed on the raid on the locomotive repair shops at Malines in Belgium when their Mosquito was hit by coastal flak and finished off three minutes later by two Fw 190s.

25 *Bommen Vielen op Hengelo* by Henk F. Van Baaren, translated in *The Mossie* - MAA, Vol. 16, April 1997.

26 They were buried at Maubeuge Center cemetery on 5 April. On 30 July 1943 Mackenstedt crash-landed his Fw 190A-5 after being hit by return fire from a 8th Air Force B-17 and he died of his injuries in hospital. (See *The JG26 War Diary*, Vol.2 1943-45, Donald Caldwell (Grub Street 1998).

27 Mosquitoes of 140 Wing, 2nd TAF flew the 11th and final RAF raid on Hengelo on 18 March 1944 when they bombed the Hazemeyer works.

28 On 28/29 June 1942 Oberleutnant Reinhold Knacke, Staffelkapitän, 1./NJG1 had been the first *Nachtjagd* pilot to claim a Mosquito kill, when he shot down DD677 of 23 Squadron at Haps, Southern Holland).

29 Shand remains missing while the body of his navigator was washed ashore at Makkum. Linke, with 24 night and 3 day victories was killed on the night of 13/14 May 1943. After shooting down two Lancasters (W4981 of 83 Squadron and ED589 of 9 Squadron) and Halifax DT732 of 10 Squadron over Friesland, he suffered an engine fire. He baled out near the village of Lemmer in Friesland but he struck the tail unit of his Bf 110 and was killed. Linke's *Bordfunker* Oberfeldwebel Walter Czybulka baled out safely.

30 Flight Lieutenant Harold Sutton DFC and Flying Officer John Morris and Flying Officer Fred Openshaw and Sergeant Alfred Stonestreet, of 139 Squadron.

31 Unable to find the target by DR Patterson identified and attacked Weimar railway station from 300ft. Patterson completed two tours of daylight operations on Mosquitoes and he was awarded the DSO early in 1944. Squadron Leader Blessing DSO DFC RAAF was KIA on 7 July 1944 on a PFF marking sortie over Caen.

32 *The Mossie,* Mosquito Aircrew Association, Vol.21, January 1999.

33 Flying Officer F. M. 'Bud' Fisher DFC and his navigator Flight Sergeant Les Hogan DFM were prevented from attacking the target by the balloon barrage bombed the town from 200ft. (Fisher and Hogan were KIA on the night of 29/30 September 1943 when their Mosquito crashed near West Raynham returning from the raid on Bochum). Flying Officer Don C. Dixon, an Australian from Brisbane and his navigator Flying Officer W. A. Christensen, a fellow Australian from New South Wales, attempted three runs on the target. They were also prevented from bombing by the balloons and intense flak and they dropped their bombs on a goods train at Lastrup. Pilot Officer Ronald Massie and Sergeant George Lister who were last seen as the formation entered cloud prior to reaching the target, crashed near Diepholz and were killed.

34 By March 1945 Roy Ralston was CO of 139 Squadron and still managed to fly on operations. He had been awarded the DSO for 'outstanding leadership and determination' and he was awarded a bar to his DSO after his 83rd op, promoted to wing commander and given command of 1655 Mosquito Training Unit at Marham. At the end of the war Ralston was listed for a permanent commission but a medical examination revealed that he had TB and he was invalided out of the RAF in 1946. Wing Commander Ralston DSO* DFC DFM AFC died on 8 October 1996.

35 Flight Lieutenant William S. D. 'Jock' Sutherland and Flying Officer George Dean of 139 Squadron in Mosquito DZ605/D were seen to bomb their target. On their return they flew into high voltage overhead electric cables when attempting to land at RAF Coltishall and they crashed at Wroxham railway station. Both crew were killed. Flying Officers Alan Rae DFM and Kenneth Bush of 105 Squadron in DZ483/R died when their Mosquito crashed as they tried to land at Marham on one engine.

Chapter 2: Defensive and Offensive Night Fighting

36 On 27 May 1940 Embry had been shot down over France in a Blenheim and three times had been captured, but never made a PoW. On the second occasion, unarmed, he fought his way out; then, with a 'borrowed' German rifle had killed three Germans, and escaped to England.

37 He later became CO of 487 Squadron, which carried out the Amiens Prison raid. After the war he stayed in the RAF, retiring as a Group Captain in 1966.

38 On the night of 10 August Wain and Grieve took off in DD623 to make an interception. The aircraft crashed into the sea and the crew were lost. No report was made and the cause of the loss was not known.

39 In February 1943 418 (City of Edmonton) Squadron RCAF converted to the Mosquito.

40 Nightly 264 patrolled in the West Country and by day they operated in the Bay of Biscay and the Western Approaches. On 21 March 1943 during a Bay of Biscay patrol, two Ju 88s were destroyed, the second of which being the Squadron's 100th German aircraft destroyed. On 29 March a He 111 was probably destroyed during an *Intruder* patrol. April added nothing to the score by many locomotives and ground targets were damaged and destroyed. May saw the squadron at Predannack for Bay of Biscay patrols and *Day Rangers* (concentrating on Laon and Juvincourt), with fair success. June was excellent over the Bay. On the 13th a Fw 190 was damaged after an encounter with three of the single-engined fighters. On the 20th a Ju 88 was probably destroyed, and on the night of the 20th/21st 'a real picnic was enjoyed' as the squadron diarist wrote it, by Wing Commander Allington when three Blohm und Voss seaplanes were sighted. A BV 138 was destroyed in the air and two six-engined BV 222s were destroyed in the sea with another BV 138 destroyed on the water. Another BV 222 was damaged and a minesweeper and hangars left in flames. Wing Commander Allington was awarded a bar to his DFC for leading the sortie. On 27/28 June a Do 217 was claimed as 'damaged' and on the 28/29th, Flying Officer A.J. Hodgkinson forced down Unteroffizier Rudolf Blankenburg of KG2 over Creil as he made for home in a Do 217E-2 after a raid on Weston-Super-Mare.

41 On 21/22 July Pilot Officer Fisher shot down a Do 217E-4 flown by Oberfeldwebel Heinrich Wolpers and his crew of I/KG2 off Spurn Head. On 27/28 July Squadron Leader Pennington and Pilot Officer Field each claimed a bomber destroyed. Feldwebel Richard Stumpf of I/KG2 and Leutnant Hans-Joachim Mohring of 3./KG2 were their victims. On 29/30 July, when the Luftwaffe bombed Birmingham, Australian pilot Flying Officer A. I. McRitchie and Flight Sergeant E. S. James attacked a Do 217E-4 flown by Oberfeldwebel Artur Hartwig of II/KG2 and it crashed into the sea.

42 Sammy Hoare's first successful intruder in a Havoc, was on the night of 3/4 May when he got a He 111 for sure and a Ju 88 as a probable.

43 Sammy Hoare's first NF.II sortie on 5/6 July proved somewhat uneventful in that no sightings were made, but the night following, 6/7 July he and Pilot Officer Cornes despatched a Dornier Do 217 16 miles east of Chartres with three short bursts of cannon fire. On 8/9 July Squadron Leader K. H. Salisbury-Hughes flying *S-Sugar,* destroyed a Do 217 over Etampes and a He 111 at Evreux. On 30/31 July Sammy Hoare in *S-Sugar* destroyed an unidentified enemy aircraft at Orleans. On 8/9 September three Mosquitoes were lost on *Intruder* sorties over the Continent. Then, on 10/11 September, Sammy Hoare and J. F. Potter, flying *B-Bertie*, destroyed another UEA 12 miles south of Enschede. In December 1942 23 Squadron were posted to Malta for *Intruder* operations against the Axis. Sammy Hoare left 23 Squadron prior to its departure overseas to set up a specialized Intruder training "school" at No 51 OTU at Cranfield, Bedfordshire.

44 Tim'Woodman was born in Trowbridge, Wiltshire, on 3 June 1914, becoming an engineering apprentice at Hadens in Trowbridge until 1936, when he joined the Air Ministry's Mechanical and Electrical Design staff. He transferred to pilot training in 1940, being sent to Canada for much of this and being commissioned in February 1941. In June he returned to the UK and attended 52 OTU on Hurricanes, then being posted to 410 Squadron RCAF on Defiants and then Beaufighter IIs. As a Flight Lieutenant he was seconded to Bristol Aircraft in June 1942 as a production test pilot on Beaufighters until August, when he rejoined 410. In December he was posted to 96 Squadron, where he remained until November 1943, when he went to 169 Squadron to undertake 100 Group bomber-support operations or Mosquitoes.

45 This was Bodien's fourth victory. He had destroyed three aircraft flying Defiant Is on 151 Squadron in 1941 and had damaged a Do 217 near Clacton on the night of 8/9 September 1942. Squadron Leader Bodien's fifth and final victory of the war came on a daylight sortie in a Mosquito II on 19 June 1943 when he shot down a Ju 88 in the Bay of Biscay.

46 Rupert Francis Henry Clerke, the stepson of Air Chief Marshal Sir Edgar Ludlow-Hewitt, was born on 13 April 1916 and educated at Eton College. He received a Permanent Commission in the RAF in July 1937 and a year later joined 32 Squadron. By 1940 he had become a flight commander in 79 Squadron flying Hurricane I fighters. He was awarded a one third share in downing a He 111 off Sunderland on 9 August and a one fifth share for a Bf 110 and a Do 17 'probable' over the North Sea on 15 August. On 28 August he scored his first outright victory when he destroyed a He 59 and he was also awarded a Bf 109E 'probable'. In July 1941 he was posted to 1 PRU at RAF Benson where, on their first sortie, on 16 September, the old Etonian and his navigator, 32-year old Sergeant Sowerbutts, a pre-war Margate barber, were forced to abandon the operation when they were pursued by three Bf 109s but the PR.I easily outpaced them at 23,000ft and returned safely. Clerke and Sowerbutts made the first successful Mosquito PR.I sortie the next day when they set out at 1130 hours for a daylight photo reconnaissance of Brest, La Pallice and Bordeaux, before arriving back at Benson at 1745 hours. On 15 October Clerke undertook a record-breaking flight from Wick to Benson and on 4 November he made the first major overseas flight in the Mosquito, photographing targets in Italy en route and landing in Malta where he remained for several days. Clerke returned to fighters early in 1942 and became a flight commander in 157 Squadron flying the Mosquito II. His second outright victory followed on 30 September when he destroyed a Ju 88A-4 of I/KG6 off the Dutch coast. Two more victories followed in February and June 1943 when he was CO of 125 Squadron flying Beaufighter VIs. He was awarded the DFC in July. *Aces High: A Tribute to the Most Notable Fighter Pilots of the British and Commonwealth Forces in WWII.* Christopher Shores and Clive Williams (Grub Street London 1994)

47 U5+KR of 7./KG2.

48 A teetotal non-smoker, Gordon Learmouth Raphael was born in Brantford, Ontario on 25 August 1915, being educated in Quebec and then in Chelsea, London, where he attended the College of Aeronautical Engineers. He joined the RAFVR in September 1935, being commissioned in January 1936. Called up on the outbreak of war, he joined 77 Squadron in Bomber Command, flying Whitleys. Involved in the early leaflet raids over Germany, he became the first Canadian to be Mentioned in Despatches in February 1940. During May he was promoted Flight Lieutenant and awarded the DFC. His aircraft was attacked whilst making for an oil refinery target at Hanover on the night of 18/19 May, one engine being set on fire and Raphael was wounded in the foot. The rear gunner managed to claim the attacking Bf 110 shot down, but the Whitley had to be ditched in the sea. The destroyer HMS Javelin rescued the crew

and Raphael was hospitalized. On recovery in July he was posted to 10 Squadron, again on Whitleys. During the night of 16/17 August his bomber was again attacked by a Bf 110 during an attack on Jever, but once again this was claimed shot down by the rear gunner. In December 1940 he was posted as a flight commander to 96 Squadron as it was forming to become a night fighter unit, but early in May he was moved to 85 Squadron, which had just re-equipped with Douglas Havoc's. He was immediately successful, claiming four victories and a probable before the end of the year. He was awarded a Bar to his DFC in July after his third confirmed success, whilst in May 1942 he was promoted to command the squadron. He remained in command until January 1943, receiving a DSO the following month. He then commanded RAF Castle Camps, and subsequently RAF Manston from where during June 1944 he shot down two V1 flying bombs. He was killed on 10 April 1945 when the Spitfire he was flying collided with a Dakota. *Aces High: A Tribute to the Most Notable Fighter Pilots of the British and Commonwealth Forces in WWII.* Christopher Shores and Clive Williams (Grub Street London 1994)

49 John Cunningham was born in South Croydon, Surrey, on 27 July 1917 where he lived with his widowed mother. Following education at the Whitgift School, he attended the De Havilland Technical School in 1935, which was staffed mainly by the School's students. In November that same year he joined 604 Squadron, Auxiliary Air Force. Due to go onto the production side at De Havillands, instead, because of his Auxiliary training, he took over test flying from Geoffrey De Havilland, and became No.4 pilot in the test team during 1938. 604 were mobilized that year for two weeks at the time of the Munich Crisis, and in August 1939 were mobilized again, this time on a war-permanent basis. During May 1940 he was detached to Northolt to test the air-dropping of bombs on bomber formations, thereby missing the unit's day operations over Holland. The Squadron then began night fighter operations, and when the first Beaufighters began to arrive late in the year, he gained the first victory in one of these aircraft during the night of 19/20 November, with AC JR Phillipson as his radar operator. Thereafter he began to claim frequently during the winter months and spring of 1941. After his first three successes Phillipson, now a Sergeant (and later a Warrant Officer), was replaced by Sergeant C. F. Rawnsley, who had been Cunningham's gunner when the unit had been equipped with Hawker Demons, but who had now trained as a radar operator. Thereafter successes mounted rapidly, including three He 111s in one night, 15/16 April 1941. On the night of 7/8 May Cunningham claimed a He 111 near Weston Zoyland while HM King George VI was in the operations room, listening to the engagement. By early June 1941 his total had reached 13. In August he became CO of the squadron, but only three more successes would be recorded by the end of May 1942, when he and Rawnsley, the latter now commissioned, were rested. Cunningham now became Wing Commander Training at 81 Group, the Fighter Command Training Group at Aston Down. *Aces High: A Tribute to the Most Notable Fighter Pilots of the British and Commonwealth Forces in WWII.* Christopher Shores and Clive Williams (Grub Street London 1994)

50 *Night Fighter* by C. F. Rawnsley & Robert Wright. Elmfield Press.

51 Rawnsley was awarded the DSO in late 1944.

52 *Night Fighter* by C. F. Rawnsley & Robert Wright. Elmfield Press.

53 *Night Fighter* by C. F. Rawnsley & Robert Wright. Elmfield Press.

54 Geoffrey Leonard Howitt was born in Wallington, Surrey on 29 January 1914, obtaining a private pilot's 'A' licence in 1933. He attended the College of Aeronautical Engineering in Chelsea and became a Class 'F' Reservist in September 1936, transferring to the RAFVR in October 1937 and training at Gatwick, Rochester and Hatfield. Called up in September 1939, he was posted to 245 Squadron as a Sergeant in November and was commissioned in April 1940. In October he was posted to 615 Squadron but had found air-firing by day difficult to master and volunteered for night flying, being posted to 85 Squadron in November. Now flying Havoc Is, he was able to claim two victories during summer 1941, only the failure of his guns preventing a third success to be achieved. In August he was posted to 51 OTU, Cranfield, as an instructor and promoted Flight Lieutenant, receiving a DFC the following month. He returned to 85 Squadron in April 1942 on Havocs and subsequently on Mosquitoes, but few hostile aircraft were to be found. In December 1942 he was sent on the CGS course at Sutton Bridge. *Aces High: A Tribute to the Most Notable Fighter Pilots of the British and Commonwealth Forces in WWII.* Christopher Shores and Clive Williams (Grub Street London 1994)

55 Peter Green had joined 85 Squadron as a flight commander on 18 August 1942 from 277 Air-Sea Rescue Squadron.

56 Skelton was born at Pirbright, Surrey on 26 August 1920. His father, a garden designer, died when Bill was 15 and relations financed the remainder of his time at Blundells. These included the Duke of Somerset, who carried the Scepter at the Coronation of King George VI in 1937 and employed young Bill as a page to carry his coronet. By this time Skelton had left school and had started training as an accountant; he later claimed to have been one of only a handful of people who used public transport to attend the Coronation rehearsals. Skelton enlisted in the RAF in 1940 and he was commissioned the following year.

57 In February 1943 605 Squadron at Bradwell Bay began replacing its Bostons and Havocs with the NF.II. On 16 February 151 Squadron, which had equipped with the NF.II at Wittering in April 1942, began *Night intruder* operations over France flying Mosquitoes fitted with *Monica*, a tail warning device. 151 continued to fly *Night Ranger* operations over the continent from May 1943-April 1944 using NFXIIs attacking all targets. Starting in March 1943, 'C' Flight in 85 Squadron at Hunsdon were presented with five NF.XV high-altitude fighters, which had been pressed into service in response to the threat posed by the Ju 86 high altitude bomber. The prototype (MP469) was the first Mosquito with a pressurized cabin, and first flew on 8 August 1942, later being fitted with AI.Mk.VIII radar, as were the four NF.XVs built - all modified B.IVs with two-stage 1680hp Merlin 72/73 or 1710hp 76/77 engines driving three or four-bladed air screws. The NF.XV, which was capable of reaching heights of 43,000ft+, was armed with four .303-in machine guns in underbelly pack. In August the NFXVs were re-allocated to Farnborough for use in pressure cabin research. That same month 85 Squadron finally began *Intruder* patrols with the NF.II. However, they would have to wait until October that year before getting their first scent of a kill, a Ju 88 damaged and a Do 217 probably destroyed.

58 Edward Dixon Crew was born in Higham Ferrers, Northamptonshire, on 24 December 1917. He was educated at Felstead School, Essex and Downing College, Cambridge, where he joined the University Air Squadron. Commissioned in the RAFVR in October 1939, he joined 604 Squadron in July 1940 on completion of training, to become a night fighter pilot. Initially, he teamed up with Sergeant Norman Guthrie as radar operator and they claimed five victories together during the spring and summer of 1941. Crew was awarded a DFC on 29 July 1941, but at that point Guthrie was posted away. Flying now with Basil Duckett, he gained three further successes during spring 1942, becoming 'A' Flight commander during May. A Bar to his DFC was received in June. In October 1942 he was posted to command the Radio Development Flight, but returned to operations in March 1943 as a flight commander in 85 Squadron.

59 It was Do 217E-4 U5+NM 4375 of IV/KG2 flown by Feldwebel Paul Huth.

60 The Do 217 crashed a few minutes later in the sea off Horsey, at 22:05 hours. Huth, Burschel, Oberleutnant Gottfried Thorley, the observer and Unteroffizier Konrad Schuller, the radio operator, were all killed. The victory was shared with a 68 Squadron Beaufighter piloted by Flying Officer Vopalecky and Flight Sergeant Husar; both Czech.

61 Hillock completed his tour on 20 May and was succeeded by Wing Commander G. H. Elms.

62 On 22 December 1940 Benson had claimed the first confirmed night victory for the Defiant and next three victories were on Beaufighter Ifs and Mosquito IIs with Brandon and his radar operator. Benson had been one of the replacements posted to 141 Squadron in July 1940 after the debacle of 19 June when six Defiants were destroyed and one damaged by Bf 109s. He suffered a suspected fractured skull following a crash in his Defiant during a night landing in January 1941 but fully recovered and had crewed up with Brandy Brandon to form another highly successful Mosquito night-fighter team.

63 Unteroffizier Franz Witte, the radio operator-gunner, was dead. The Dornier crashed at Layer Breton Heath, five miles southwest of Colchester. Schmurr, Leutnant Karl-Heinrich Hertam, the observer, and Unteroffizier Martin Sehwarz, the gunner, baled out. Witte's body was found in the wreckage.

64 Predannack was also used by a detachment of 25 Squadron NF.IIs detached to 264 Squadron. 25 Squadron had received NF.IIs in October 1942 and had started freelance *Ranger* sweeps over the continent. In June Mosquitoes of 456 and 605 Squadrons began successful, albeit small scale, Bomber Support *Flower* attacks on German night fighter airfields during raids by main force bombers. *Flowers* supported bombers by disrupting enemy Flying Control Organisations. Long Range *Intruder* aircraft fitted with limited radar equipment are used, and these proceed to the target at high altitude, diving down whenever they see airfields illuminated. This type of operation if correctly timed, prevented the enemy Night Fighters who were already short of petrol from landing at their bases.

65 Werk No 4415).

66 Popular with his crews, Bradel was a former cavalry officer who had flown in the Spanish Civil War, first as a Staffelkapitan, later as a Grupperkommandeur and, finally, as a *Geschwaderkommodore* in the Condor Legion. He held the Spanish War Medal and the Spanish Gold Cross with Swords. In Norway Bradel was employed as leader of a transport staffel, bringing up supplies and equipment to the mountain troops near Narvik. He then took part as a bomber pilot in operations against England, and later in the Balkan campaign (he was said to have been the first to land and take possession of Athens airfield) and the operations against Crete. In the course of the latter he claimed to have sunk a British destroyer with bombs. On the Eastern front his chief exploit seems to have been a low-level attack on 500 Soviet tanks in the battle for Grodno. On 17 September 1941 he was awarded the *Ritterkreuz* (Knight's Cross).

67 Late in 1942 Williams was sent to an Aircrew Refresher Course at Brighton, a euphemism for a 'bad boys school'. He was perplexed, and took his parachute and 'Mae West' with him. Instead, early morning PT on the beach, drill all day and frequent haircuts awaited him. One of his fellow defaulters, a Pole, had been caught with a girl in his bed after he had left his shoes - and those of his lady friend - outside his door for his batman! After three weeks the 'bad boys' were returned to their units - if they had behaved. Williams stayed for 10 weeks! Then he was posted, to 605 Squadron at Castle Camps, where he flew his first Mosquito op on 10 March. They patrolled over the Dutch airfields to await the raiders' return. 605 squadron and 418 (City of Edmonton) Squadron RCAF were the first Mosquito night *Intruder* squadrons sent to attack Luftwaffe airfields on the continent. The former had taken over 23 Squadron's Bostons and Havocs and had begun *Intruder* operations over French airfields in July 1942. In February 1943 605 began equipping with the Mosquito, and by May 1943, when 418 received its first Mosquito, the County of Warwick squadron was making its presence felt.

68 Bradel probably died of injuries he sustained because he had not been strapped in. Flieger Wernerker was also killed, although he may have died in the Mosquito attack, and the rest of the crew was injured. All recovered, Andres being promoted to Oberleutnant and receiving the *Ritterkreuz* on 20 April 1944. He was killed with 5./NJG4 on 11 February 1945.

69 Night fighter Mosquitoes of 157 Squadron shot down two Do 217E-4s of KG2 piloted by Leutnant Stefan Szamek and Leutnant Gerd Strufe, on 13/14 May. A Do 217E-4 of II/KG2 was intercepted by a NF.II of 157 Squadron from Hunsdon, flown by Sergeant R. L. Watts and Sergeant J. Whewell, and shot down after an exchange of fire. A fire started in the Dornier's starboard engine and it crashed about 10 miles northeast of Colchester at 0207 hours. Near Norwich, a Do 217K-1 of 4./KG2 flown by Unteroffizier Erhard Corty was claimed at about 0250 hours.

70 *Night Fighter* by C. F. Rawnsley & Robert Wright (Elmfield Press).

71 Grimstone, who was awarded the DFM and Green, the DFC, scored their third victory on 26/27 July when they destroyed a Ju 88 25 miles east of Ramsgate. It was Peter Green's last victory with 85 Squadron as he left in August to command the AI Beaufighter Flight at Drem.

72 Adolph Gysbert 'Sailor' Malan, who was born in Wellington, South Africa on 3 October 1910, was one of 23 South African pilots in the Battle of Britain. His nickname came about as a result of service as a Third Officer with the Union Castle Steamship Line. He commenced pilot training in England in 1936 and was posted to 74 Squadron in December that year. His DFC was awarded on 11 June 1940 for five victories, two confirmed and three unconfirmed. During the night of 19/20 June 1940 when the first major night raid by the Luftwaffe on England took place, in conditions of bright moonlight, he was able to claim two of the intruders shot down, for which a Bar to his DFC followed in August. In action through July and August, he was promoted to command the squadron on 8 August. The unit was then withdrawn to Kirton-in-Lindsey to rest and here he wrote his so *Ru/es of Air Fighting,* which was produced and distributed throughout Fighter Command. In October the squadron returned to the south and received some of the first Spitfire IIs, seeing considerable action throughout the autumn. On Christmas Eve 1940 he received the award of a DSO, the citation crediting him with 18 confirmed and 6 possible victories. On to March 1941 he was appointed as one of the first Wing Leaders for the offensive operations planned for that year, leading the Biggin Hill Wing throughout the sweeps of May-July. A Bar to his DSO followed on 22 July, at that time recording his total as 28, plus 20 damaged or probables. In mid-August he was appointed CFI at 58 OTU, Grangemouth, by this time being listed as Fighter Command top scorer, with a total variously reported as 32 or 35 victories. In October he departed for the USA on a lecture tour, and to liaise with the USAAC, together with five other leading RAF fighter pilots. Whilst there he took part in the annual maneuvers, flying P-38s and P-39s. Returning to the UK in December, he became commanding officer of the Central Gunnery School at Sutton Bridge, where he remained for a year, being promoted Group Captain in October 1942. in January 1943 he returned to Biggin Hill as commanding officer, remaining until October, when he took command of 19 Fighter Wing in the new 2nd TAF. *Aces High: A Tribute to the Most Notable Fighter Pilots of the British and Commonwealth Forces in WWII.* Christopher Shores and Clive Williams (Grub Street London 1994)

73 Only 50 of these very fast bombers were built. Most examples, which first entered service with *I/KG66* at Chartres, were rebuilt versions of the A-4 with power-boosted BMW 801G-2 engines fitted with the GM-1 nitrous oxide injection system. Stripped of its ventral gondola and most of its armor, and reduced to just one MG131 machine gun, the Ju 88S-1 was difficult to catch. Lintott had to climb to 29,000 feet in stages before he finally saw 3Z+SZ of I/KG66, his victim. A single hit in one of the three high-pressure nitrous oxide storage tanks in the rear bomb bay was enough to blow the aircraft to smithereens.

74 *Night Fighter* by C. F. Rawnsley & Robert Wright (Elmfield Press).

75 Also on 13/14 July, a 410 Squadron RCAF Mosquito shot down Unteroffizier Willy Spielmanns' Do 217M-l of 3./KG2 into the sea off the Humber Estuary. Flying Officer Smart of 605 Squadron flying an *Intruder* over Holland shot down a Do 217M-1 of 2./KG2, which that night had bombed Hull. Unteroffizier Hauck and his crew crashed in the vicinity of Eindhoven. Altogether, KG2 lost four Dorniers that night.

76 Offensive patrols in July 1943 saw no combats. The first patrols of August 1943 included a successful attack on armed trawlers, one being destroyed. On the 7th 264 Squadron left for Fairwood Common, where they carried out *Night Rangers* and ASR cover patrolled and on the 18th 264 dropped its first bombs on Laon airfield. Bomber support patrols were carried out from Castle Camps. During September detachments were sent there and to Bradwell Bay and for raids on enemy airfields Coltishall, and Ford were sometimes used. In November 264 operations largely meant liaison with the Navy at Swansea and a move to Exeter for *Day Rangers* several trains were successfully attacked. On 17 November 264 squadron moved again, this time to Coleby Grange in Lincolnshire and Coltishall was used as a forward base for bomber patrols. In mid-December 1943 264 moved to Church Fenton to re-equip with MkX AI equipment, which it retained until after the end of the war.

77 Wing Commander Geoffrey Park, CO of 256 Squadron shot down Unteroffizier Karl Morgenstern and Unteroffizier Franz Bundgens' Do 217M-ls into the sea off Worthing. The wing commander then destroyed Unteroffizier Walter Kayser's Do 217M-l and damaged a third Dornier. Flight Sergeant Brearley, also of 256 Squadron, shot down two Do 217Ms over France; Feldwebel Theodor Esslinger fell near Evreux and Leutnant Franz Bosbach crashed near St André. Pilot Officer Rayne Dennis Schultz of 410 Squadron RCAF blasted a Do 217M-1 of 9./KG2 and sent his namesake, Unteroffizier Josef Schultes and his crew to their doom.

78 Howitt finished his second tour in October 1943, receiving a Bar to his DFC and a posting to 63 OTU, Honiley. In April 1944 he commenced a third tour as 'A' Flight commander in 456 Squadron, RAAF, until December 1944, when he was promoted to command 125 Squadron on NF.XXXs. He was released in October 1945 and joined the Air Registration Board.

79 Two Me 410s were lost this night, one of which was a Me 410A-1 of 16./KG2, flown by Feldwebel Werner Benner and Unteroffizier Hermann Reimers. Wing Commander R. E. X. Mack DFC and Flight Lieutenant B. C. Townsin were KIA during a patrol over the Channel in NF.XIX HK371 on 22/23 February 1944.

80 *Night Fighter* by C. F. Rawnsley & Robert Wright (Elmfield Press).

81 *Night Fighter* by C. F. Rawnsley & Robert Wright (Elmfield Press).

82 Murray and Littlewood were killed at Honiley, Warks, on 30 July on a navigation flight in an Oxford

83 In NF.II HJ705.

84 On 8/9 November Maguire and Jones shot down a Me 410A of 15./KG2 near Eastbourne. Major Wilhelm Schmitter *Ritterkreuz und Eichenlaub* (Knight's Cross with Oak leaves) and his *bordfunker* Unteroffizier Felix Hainzinger were killed when the aircraft crashed into Shinewater Marsh. Both Maguire and Jones were awarded DFCs at the end of 1943 and in July 1944 they were posted to the FIU. Maguire was to command this unit later in the year and in late November intercepted and shot down a V1 carrying He 111. On 17 February 1945 he and his navigator, Dennis Lake were carrying out rolling manoeuvres in a Mosquito to test a new altitude indicator when on the second roll, the aircraft rapidly lost height, hit a house and disintegrated.

85 Wight-Boycott had shot down a Heinkel 111 on 20/21 September 1941 flying a 219 Squadron Beaufighter If. On 17/18 January 1943 Wing Commander Wight-Boycott, flying a 29 Squadron Beaufighter, shot down two Ju 88s and a Do 217 and damaged another. On one remarkable night, 17/18 January 1943, he destroyed two Do 217s and a Ju 88 and damaged three other Dorniers. The following night the Wing Commander shot down two more Dornier 217s and a Ju 88.

86 *Mahmoud* was the code-name for a special kind of operation which was devised after it was realized that the Luftwaffe were operating radar equipped night-fighters against the 'heavies' of Bomber Command. In August 1943, this had led to a decision to release some Beaufighters with AI Mk IV radar over enemy territory as bait for enemy night-fighters in their known assembly areas. The British fighters flew individually over the continent to try and induce German night fighters to intercept them. Mosquito night fighters also flew *Mahmoud* operations, but were less successful at pretending to be bombers, as the Germans soon recognized the speed difference. AI Mk IV had an all round scan, so it was possible for the radar observer to detect on his CRT (Cathode Ray Tube) an enemy night-fighter trying to intercept them from astern. The British pilot would then carry out a 360-degree turn to try and get on the tail of the enemy and shoot him down. With the more powerful centimetric AI being used in Mosquitoes it was necessary to add *Monica* tail warning devices, as these later Mks of AI did not scan to the rear. Later in the war when the RAF received details of the Luftwaffe night-fighter assembly point beacons from the Resistance, *Mahmoud* sorties by single aircraft were also made against them.

Chapter 3: "Musical Mosquitoes"

87 *Oboe* was the codename for a high-level blind bombing aid, which took its name from a radar-type pulse which sounded rather like the musical instrument. (All non-*Oboe*-equipped squadrons in 8 Group were termed 'non-musical'!) Mainly because of this device, Bennett's force was able to conduct *eine kleine nacht musik* almost every night over Germany. Pulses were transmitted by Type 9000 ground stations at Hawkshill Down (Walmer), Kent, Trimingham near Cromer and Winterton both in Norfolk, Sennen and Treenin Cornwall, Worthy Matravers and Tilly Whim (Swanage), Beachy Head and Cleadon (Newcastle). They could be received by a high-flying *Oboe*-equipped aircraft up to 280 miles distant. The 'cat' station sent the pilot and navigator a steady sequence of signals describing an arc passing through the target, with dots to port and dashes to starboard. If inside the correct line, dots were heard; if outside the line, dashes. A steady note indicated that the aircraft was on track. The 'mouse' station indicated distance from target, and was monitored by the navigator only. Flying the beam made considerable demands on the *Oboe* pilot, who for 15-20 minutes had to maintain constant airspeed, altitude and tate of change of heading. The navigator monitored the aircraft's position along the arc, and only he received the release signal, from the 'mouse' station, when the aircraft reached the computed bomb-release point. Ten minutes away he received in Morse, four 'A's; four 'B's at 8 minutes; four 'C's at 6 minutes and four 'D's at approximately 4 minutes. The bomb doors were then opened. Next was heard the release signal, which consisted of five dots and a 2½-second dash, at the end of which the navigator released the markers or bombs. The jettison bars were operated and the bomb doors closed. As the pilot could not hear the 'mouse' signals, the navigator indicated to him the stage reached by tracing with his finger on the windscreen in front of him, the 'As, 'B's and 'C's etc. When the release signal came through, the navigator held his hand in front of the pilot's face. Permitted limits were strict - up to 200 yards off aiming point and crews were expected to be at the target within a 4-minute time span, from 2 minutes early to 2 minutes late. Sixty seconds off time on release point were acceptable. Failure to meet these criteria and the crew were off the squadron! *Oboe* was to become the most accurate form of blind bombing used in WWII and in practice, an average error of only 30 seconds was achieved.

88 'Sky markers' were parachute flares to mark a spot in the sky if it was cloudy. The PFF markers' job was to 'illuminate' and 'mark' targets with colored TI's (target indicators) for the Main Force and other 8 Group Mosquitoes. Three types of marking, using names selected by D. C. T. 'Don' Bennett from the hometowns of three of his staff were later employed. *Parramatta* in New Zealand gave its name to the blind ground marking technique, which used only H_2S in bad visibility or broken cloud. *Newhaven* was ground marking by visual methods when crews simply aimed at the TIs on the ground and *Wanganui* in Australia lent its name to pure 'sky marking'. The TIs themselves were made in various plain colors and used vivid star-bursts of the same or a different color to prevent the enemy from copying them at their many decoy sites near major cities.

89 Born in Toowoomba, Queensland, Australia on 14 September 1910, Donald Clifford Tyndall Bennett was the youngest of four outstanding brothers, all of whom were were raised on the family cattle station at Condomine in Queensland. As a small boy, Don saw the Wright Brothers demonstrating their flying machine on the racecourse at Toowoomba and he never forgot the experience. In 1930 at the age of 20 he joined the RAAF as a cadet and in the following year came to England, obtained a commission in the RAF and in 1932 he became an instructor at the RAF flying-boat base at Calshot. He transferred to the Reserve in 1935 and in the same year, while returning to Australia from Britain wrote *The Complete Air Navigator*, which became a standard work. He joined Imperial Airways and at age 26 was made captain of the largest aircraft of the day. He pioneered many of their overseas routes, including the Kangaroo Route to Australia. In 1938 as an airline captain, he flew the *Mercury,* the upper component of the *Mayo* composite aircraft, from Foynes, County Limerick to the St. Lawrence River at Boucherville, Montreal and on to New York, achieving a record east to west crossing of the North Atlantic. For this feat he won the Johnston memorial Trophy, awarded by the Guild of Air Pilots and Air Navigators for the best feat of air navigation during the year. Later, he flew *Mercury* from Dundee in Scotland to South Africa, establishing a long-distance record for seaplanes, which still stands today. On the eve of war found him in command of the *Cabot,* the big flying boat, which was to carry the mail from Southampton to New York. Soon after the Germans invaded Norway the *Cabot* and her sister flying boat *Caribou* were destroyed by the enemy in the Norwegian fjords. Bennett was among the founders of the North Atlantic Ferry Service, at first known as Atfero, which was responsible for flying American and Canadian warplanes to Britain, and he personally led the first flight of seven Hudson aircraft in mid winter to make the ocean crossing, something never attempted before. In May 1940 Bennett, still a civilian pilot, flew the Polish leader, General Sikorski, from Bordeaux in an armed civil flying-boat to England, two days after the capitulation. He was re-commissioned in the RAFVR in 1941 and was called on for service on the active list. As captain of a Halifax bomber on 27/28 April 1942, Bennett, then a wing commander, won the DSO for courage, initiative and devotion to duty when, after being shot down attacking the *Tirpitz* in Trondheim Fjord, Norway, he and his second pilot, Sergeant N. Walmsley, escaped to Sweden. Five weeks later he made his way back to Britain in the nose of a Lockheed Hudson. In July Bennett was appointed to command the newly formed Pathfinder Force. At first there were only four squadrons but in 1943 this was expanded and the Pathfinder Force was given full Group status and became 8 Group. He was promoted to Air Vice Marshal and at 32 was the youngest Group commander in the RAF. He turned PFF, whose only identification symbol, worn only when not flying, was a gilt eagle worn below the flap of the left breast pocket, into an elite force. After the war, feeling he could better serve Britain in the civil aviation world, he declined the offer of Governor Generalship of Australia, as a Viscount, a decision which no doubt lost him all chance of being honored by the crown as he was the only British Commander in the field, be it Navy, Army or Air Force, who was not Knighted after the war. AVM Donald Bennett CB CBE DSO FRAes died in Slough, Buckinghamshire on 15 September 1986.

90 There were eventually several types of TI from 250lb to the 'Pink Pansy' model weighing 2,300lb, which made use of a 4000lb bomb casing. It got its name from the red pyrotechnic added to the basic marker mixture of benzol, rubber and phosphorus. There ware also TIs of good ballistic form arranged to eject colored roman candles either in the air or on impact with or without explosives. A 250lb TI lit up a radius of 100 yards.

91 A complete account of the raid on Wuppertal on 29/30 May 1943 can be found in *Battle Over the Reich* by Alfred Price (Ian Allan Ltd 1973). Wuppertal was the target for 630 aircraft on 24/25 June when Elberfeld, the other half of the town, unharmed on 29/30 May, was bombed. The Pathfinder marking was accurate and the Main Force bombing began well but the creepback became more pronounced than usual; 30 aircraft bombed targets in more western parts of the Ruhr. About 3000 houses were destroyed and another 2500 dwellings severely damaged. about 1800 people were killed and 2400 injured. *The Bomber Command War Diaries* by Martin Middlebrook and Chris Everitt (Midland 1985).

92 See *The Bomber Command War Diaries* by Martin Middlebrook and Chris Everitt (Midland 1985).

93 British 10-cm experimental airborne radar navigational and target location aid.

94 Wolstenholme (who became famous after the war as a BBC sports commentator) flew Blenheims on 107 Squadron earlier in the war. On 21 May 1941 he made it back to Massingham with his observer, Sergeant J. C. 'Polly' Wilson RNZAF dead in his seat after their Blenheim was hit by flak on the operation to Heligoland. Wilson was laid to rest in the lovely country churchyard at Little Massingham close by the airfield.

95 Later Group Captain Cundall CBE DSO DFC AFC.

96 *Mosquito at War* by Chaz Bowyer. (Ian Allan 1984) and *Mosquito Thunder* by Stuart R. Scott. (Sutton Publishing 1999)

97 British Empire Medal.

98 Pilot Officer R. A. Hosking in a PR Mosquito had photographed a V1 site at Bois Carré, ten miles northeast of Abbeville, on 28 October 1942. This was the first V1 flying bomb launching site in France to be analysed on photographs, and the buildings shown were meant for storage of flying-bomb components. The *Vergelrungswaffe* I (Revenge Weapon No 1) was a small, pilotless aircraft with a 1870lb HE warhead that detonated on impact. On 5 December 1943 the bombing of the V1, or *Noball* sites, became part of the Operation *Crossbow* offensive. By 12 June 1944, 60 weapons sites had been identified. Hitler's 'rocker blitz' began on 13 June when ten V1s, or 'Doodlebugs', as they became known, were launched against London from sites in northeastern France.

99 Squadron Leader Blessing DSO DFC RAAF was KIA on 7 July 1944 on a PFF marking sortie over Caen.

100 Stead had joined 58 Squadron in July 1941 and he flew six sorties in 1941 as co-pilot to Leonard Cheshire VC before returning to 58 Squadron. He was posted to 196 Squadron, completed his first tour in June and began his second in October 1943. Hauptmann Dietrich Schmidt, scored 40 night victories in NJG1. He was awarded the *Ritterkreuz* and survived the war.

101 B-17G 42-97480 and Lieutenant Otto H. Brandau's crew failed to return from a raid on Germany on 13 April 1944. Four crew were KIA and six were taken prisoner.

102 The Mk.IV Mosquito with a 'Cookie' on board was 'just' capable of a take-off on a main runway with favourable wind and once in the air the aircraft handled sluggishly until 'bomb gone' when the altimeter unwound itself at an alarming rate. At take off time many a fitter and rigger could be seen sheltering as soon as the aircraft taxied out for take-off. Aircrews learned that the safety height to fly when 4000lb bombs were exploding was a minimum of 4000ft.

103 Eaton's immediate award of the DFC for this operation was announced on 17 April 1944. He went on to complete ninety operations by 18 March 1945. On 7/8 March also Flight Lieutenant Angus Caesar-Gordon DFM dropped 105 Squadron's first 4000lb 'Cookie', in the Duisburg area after the primary target at Hamborn could not be identified. (On 11/12 March a 105 Squadron Mosquito flown by Squadron Leader J. S. W. Bignall and Flying Officer G. F. Caldwell took off from Graveley in company with two Mosquitoes of 109 Squadron and dropped a 'Cookie' on the Verstahlwerke steel works at Hamborn). On 10 July 1944 Grenville Eaton and Jack Fox took off on their first daylight operation when the port engine blew up as they reached the end of the runway, an event that was usually fatal. Eaton somehow flew a circuit and landed safely on one engine but when Fox dropped prematurely through the escape hatch the propeller killed him.

104 Flight Lieutenant Norman Clayes DFC and his observer, Flying Officer Frederick Ernest Deighton were killed returning from an operation to Châteaudun on 12/13 May 1944 when a Verey pistol was discharged in the Mosquito as they came into land.

Chapter 4: Find Mark and Strike

105 The other eight squadrons were equipped with Lancasters.

106 Later Group Captain DFC* AFC AE.

107 Squadron Leader E. I. J. Bell DFC and Flying Officer J. G. R. Battle, who were shot down on 8 January 1944.

108 Fast, manoeuvreable and with devastating firepower of six cannon the *,Owl'* was fitted with *SN-2* radar and the world's first operational nosewheel undercarriage and ejection seats for the 2 crew. I./NJG1 had been equipped with the anti-Mosquito version of the He 219 *Uhu,* a modified version of the He 219A-2 which was lightened by the reduction in armament from 6 to 4 20-mm MG 151/20 cannon and had its performance improved by the installation of a nitrous oxide fuel injection system to its engines. It had FuG 2205-N26 airborne radar system, a service ceiling of 37,000 feet and was one of the few Luftwaffe night fighters fast enough to catch the Mosquito. During the first 10 days of operations in June 1943 with I./NJG1, which operated from Venlo and Münster, it proved the only Luftwaffe piston-engined night-fighter capable of taking on the Mosquito on equal terms, the unit claiming 6 Mosquitoes destroyed (+ claims for 25 4-engined bombers). But like the Me 262 jet fighter in the day-fighter arm was never available in sufficient numbers to have a significant effect on the course of the air war. In late May 1944 the *Uhu* was abandoned in favour of the Ju 88G series, an aircraft that had sufficient performance to take on 4-engined bombers but incapable of combatting the ,Wooden Wonder'. Only 268 *Uhus* were built, 195 of which were delivered to operational units. The majority went to I./NJG1 and to NJGr10, a specialist anti-*Moskito Gruppe* at Werneuchen near Berlin.

109 DZ354/D crashed near Herwijnen in Holland on the North bank of the Waal River. Both crew were later buried in the Herwijnen General cemetery.

110 On 21/22 January 1944 *Eichenlaubträger* Hauptmann Manfred Meurer, Kommandeur I/NJG1 and his *Funker, Ritterkreuzträger* Oberfeldwebel Gerhard Scheibe were killed when their He 219A-0 'Owl' was hit by debris from their 2nd victim and they crashed to their deaths 20 km E of Magdeburg. In less than two years Meurer had claimed 65 night victories, including 40 heavy bombers and two Mosquitoes in 130 sorties.

111 In October 1944 Group Captain Hugh S. L. 'Cocky' Dundas reached the rank at age 24.

112 *The Dam Busters* by Paul Brickhill (Evans Bros London 1951).

113 Born on 24 February 1895, the third son of Baron Cochrane of Cults in Fifeshire, Cochrane was educated at the Royal Naval Colleges at Osborne and Dartmouth before entering the Royal navy in 1912, transferring to the RAF in 1918. He became the first Chief of the Air Staff of the Royal New Zealand Air Force in 1936. In 1942 Cochrane became AOC 3 Group Bomber Command and with the sacking by Air Chief Marshal Harris of AVM Alec Coryton in February 1943, he assumed command of 5 Group. Cochrane had been a flight commander on 45 Squadron commanded by Harris in Mesopotamia in 1922-24 when the unit flew Vickers Vernons and Victorias on troop carrying duties. (Cochrane retired from the RAF as Vice-Chief of the Air Staff in 1952 and died in 1977 aged 82).

114 *At First Sight; A Factual and anecdotal account of No.627 Squadron RAF.* Researched and compiled by Alan B. Webb. 1991.

115 Three *Oboe* Mosquitoes of 8 Group also took part in the operation.

116 The target at La Chapelle was marked by three 617 Squadron Mosquitoes. Six Lancasters failed to return from this raid. Main Force targets included Cologne and four rail targets in France and Belgium. 247 Lancasters of 5 Group and 22 Mosquitoes were despatched to the rail target at La Chapelle. Another 175 aircraft attacked Lens, while 196 aircraft attacked rail yards at Ottignies in Belgium. Four Lancasters were lost on the Cologne raid. None of the aircraft attacking Ottignies were lost.

117 The raid was not successful. The initial marking by 617 Squadron Mosquitoes was accurate but many of the main force of Lancasters did not bomb these, partly because of a thin layer of cloud, which hampered visibility, and partly because of faulty communications between the various bomber controllers. Many bombs were dropped in the center of the city but the remainder of the force bombed reserve H_2S-aimed TIs, which were well to the south. Damage caused was not extensive.

118 When 637 aircraft bombed Karlsruhe and 234 Lancasters and 16 Mosquitoes raided Munich.

119 Sir Arthur Harris had sanctioned the release of the Mosquitoes to 617 Squadron and insisted they could be retained only if Munich was hit heavily. While no award of the Victoria Cross was ever made for a Mosquito sortie, Cheshire's contribution to the success of the Munich operation on 24/25 April, when he led four Mosquitoes of the Marking Force in 5 Group, was mentioned in his VC citation on 8 September 1944. The crews who took part were: Cheshire and Pat Kelly; Squadron Leader Dave Shannon DSO and Len Sumpter; Flight Lieutenant Terry Kearns and Flight Lieutenant Hone Barclay, and Flight Lieutenant Gerry Fawke and Flight Lieutenant Tom Bennett. The four aircraft flew to Manston on the Kent coast to begin the operation. Once over the target they proved highly successful, Cheshire diving from 12,000 to 3000 feet and then flying repeatedly over the city at little more than 700 feet, coming under fire for 12 minutes before leaving the area. Shannon dived from 15,000 to 4000 feet but his markers hung up, while the fourth Mosquito got four spot flares away.

120 During the week in which these early low-level marking efforts against German targets were taking place, Bill Hickox and Benny Goodman were suddenly called to the CO's office. They were trying desperately to fathom what they could have done wrong when they were ushered in to Roy Elliott's presence. He got up from his chair, grinned broadly and announced that they had each been awarded the DFC. This was a proud moment for them, particularly since these were the first DFCs awarded to members of 627 Squadron.

121 No.5 Group was the first wave of 163 Lancasters and was to attack the Southeast part of the camp while 153 bombers of 1 Group made up the second wave. Their target was the northwest section of the camp. Thirty aircraft were to concentrate on an area near the workshops. Five Special Duties Lancasters of 192 Squadron at Binbrook and six Mosquitoes and three ECM Halifaxes of 100 Group also took part.

122 Mailly actually accommodated a *Panzer* regiment HQ, 3 *Panzer* battalions belonging to regiments on the Eastern Front and elements of two more as well as the permanent training school staff.

123 Later Group Captain DFC* AFC AE.

124 Marking began at 2358 hours. Zero hour was 0005. The first two Mosquitoes arrived early at the rendezvous and flew on for 30 miles before returning to the site. Flares had already been dropped by 87 and 93 PFF Squadrons and these lit up the area so that Cheshire, dropping to 1500 feet from 3000 feet, had no problem in locating his two red spot flares on target. Cheshire was not happy with their position and called up Squadron Leader Dave Shannon in the accompanying Mosquito to mark the site that needed to be bombed more accurately, dropping his red spot fires accurately at 0006 hours. Cheshire told the Master Bomber to hold the main attack off until he was satisfied. After Shannon had dived down to 600 feet to lay the markers, Cheshire gave the master bomber the go ahead. The green TI dropped by the *Oboe* controlled Mosquito was timed at 2359 hours and fell 800 meters north of the center of the target. Shannon's marking was completed seven minutes later. The target was marked on time.

125 Flight Lieutenant Terry Kearns flew the fourth 617 Squadron Mosquito.

126 Squadron Leader Tom Bennett DFM writing in *Not Just Another Milk Run; The Mailly-le-Camp Bomber Raid* by Molly Burkett & Geoff Gilbert (Barny Books 2004). No.5 Group, which supplied nearly all the marker aircraft and the entire first wave, lost 14 of its 173 Lancasters. No.1 Group, which dispatched 173 Lancasters also, in the second wave of the attack and which were subjected to the greatest delay at Mailly, lost 28 bombers. One Mosquito *Intruder* and one RCM Halifax were also shot down. Approximately 1500 tons of bombs were dropped on Mailly and 114 barrack buildings, 47 transport sheds and workshops and some ammunition stores were hit. 218 Germans were killed or missing and 156 were wounded. 102 vehicles were destroyed, including 37 tanks. Damage to the buildings was German assessed as '80% destroyed, 20% worth repairing'. The only French civilian casualties in the village of Mailly nearby occurred when a Lancaster crashed into the house.

127 Bill Hickox has written that when the shattering news that their beloved leader, Roy Elliott, was being replaced, it was not by one of their own Flight Commanders, but by a stranger from HQ 5 Group, Wing Commander George W. Curry DFC (Wing Commander Curry DSO* DFC* met his death during a Battle of Britain display some time after the war). Hickox's loyalty was still with Don Bennett and 8 Group, so he was unhappy with this final take-over by 5 Group. Consequently, he took the opportunity of completing his second tour with a grand total of 81 operations and returned to 8 Group with a posting to the Mosquito Training Unit at Warboys. See *At First Sight; A Factual and anecdotal account of No.627 Squadron RAF.* Researched and compiled by Alan B. Webb. 1991.

128 The target was found by Flight Lieutenant Ronald L. Bartley who after dropping his red spot fire 50-60 yards 245 degrees from the Marking Point was followed by Benny Goodman, who laid two further reds which fell 200 yards 360 degrees and could not easily be seen as they landed on the edge of a wood near the gun battery. Flight Lieutenant D. W. Peck DFC then backed up the original marker with two red spots, which were assessed as being 100 yards 240 degrees. Finally, Flight Lieutenant J. F. Thomson DFC RNZAF laid a green TI on the reds and this was assessed as being 300 yards 240 degrees from the Marking Point. See *At First Sight; A Factual and anecdotal account of No.627 Squadron RAF.* Researched and compiled by Alan B. Webb. 1991.

129 B.XX KB267/E.

130 See *At First Sight; A Factual and anecdotal account of No.627 Squadron RAF.* Researched and compiled by Alan B. Webb. 1991.

131 *Barnes Wallis' Bombs: Tallboy, Dambuster & Grand Slam* by Stephen Flower (Tempus 2004).

132 PFF Mosquitoes made 124 sorties to 'mark' the dropping zones.

Chapter 5: LNSF

133 On 18/19 November 1943 'Bomber' Harris began his nightly offensive against Berlin. This series of raids, which were to last until the end of January 1944, brought added demands for bomb damage assessment (BDA). Flights over Germany were being made ever more difficult by enemy action, bad weather and other factors such as smoke from still burning factories and houses - it took no less than 31 PR Spitfire and six PR Mosquito sorties before the results of the bombing of Berlin on 18/19 November were obtained. BDA became such an issue with both the RAF and USAAF bomber commands that PR aircraft were required to cover targets within hours of a raid being carried out - sometimes even before the returning bombers had landed.

134 On 7 April 1944 571 Squadron was formed at Downham Market. A shortage of Mosquitoes meant that 571 had to operate at half-strength for a time. On the night of 13/14 April two crews from 571 and six Mosquitoes from 692 attacked Berlin for the first time carrying two 50-gallon drop tanks and a 4000-lb bomb. On 1 August 1944 608 Squadron at Downham Market joined LNSF. On 25 October 142 Squadron re-formed at Gransden Lodge and that same night they flew their first operation when their only two B.XXVs were despatched to Cologne. On 18 December 162 Squadron re-formed at Bourn with B.XXVs and soon accompanied the veteran 139 Squadron on target-marking duties. 163 Squadron, the 11th and final Mosquito unit in 8 Group, reformed at Wyton on 25 January 1945 on B.XXVs. Commanded by Wing Commander (later Air Marshal) Ivor Broom DFC the squadron flew its first LNSF operation just four days later when four Mosquitoes dropped 'Window' at Mainz ahead of the PFF force.

135 Back soloed in the Mosquito after only 55 minutes' dual in August. 'Bing' Bingham was killed on a night cross-country exercise from Wyton on 22 August when his Mosquito hit a hill.

136 Weather over Belgium and eastern France was 0/10ths to 4/10ths thin cloud while Holland and the Ruhr were cloudless.

137 Mosquito spoof attacks on Cologne, Frankfurt and Kassel were identified for what they were because to the German defenses they were apparently flying without H_2S. As the bomber stream was clearly recognized from the start, 246 twin- and single- engined night fighters were sent up to engage the heavies.

British jamming of the first interception of the bomber stream in the area south of Bonn was successful but from there on in the bomber stream was hit repeatedly and the majority of the losses occurred in the Giessen-Fulda-Bamberg area. A staggering 82 bombers were lost en route to and near the target.

138 At Nürnburg there was 10/10ths cloud at 1600 to 12,000 feet but the cloud veiled at 16,000 feet with generally good altitude visibility.

139 See *At First Sight; A Factual and anecdotal account of No.627 Squadron RAF.* Researched and compiled by Alan B. Webb. 1991. Sixty-four Lancasters and 31 Halifaxes (11.9 per cent of the force dispatched) were lost (and ten bombers crash-landed in England); the worst Bomber Command loss of the war.

140 B.IV DZ608 of 692 Squadron flown by Flying Officer I. S. H. MacDonald RAAF and Flying Officer E. B. Chatfield DFC.

141 MM125.

142 MM125 was shot down at about 0055 hours (continental time) as it approached the Dutch Coast at 27,000-feet. Wellington was taken prisoner. It was the crew's first operation on 571 Squadron. Downey, who was approaching his 26th birthday, had enlisted in the RAFVR in November 1938 and when war broke out he was called up in December 1939. Qualifying as a bomber pilot at 16 OTU he was posted to 83 Squadron, which was flying Hampdens at Finningley, Yorkshire. During December 1940-July 1941 he completed 32 ops before he was posted to instruct at 16 OTU (where he volunteered for 2 ops whilst with the unit). In 1941 he was awarded the DFM for saving his crew and his aircraft when his Hampden suffered an engine failure on take off. Joe married LACW Margaret Mary Monk in 1941 and in 1943 they had a son, Patrick. In 1942 Joe volunteered for another tour and was posted to 218 Squadron, which was flying Stirlings and during November 1942-April 1943 he completed a further 23 ops.

143 Nabrich, *Staffelkapitän* of *3./NJG1*, was killed in his vehicle during a strafing attack by RAF fighter-bombers on *Eichstrasse 54* from Handorf to Telgte on 27 November 1944. Feldwebel Fritz Habicht was WIA on 3/4 February 1945 when he and his pilot, Hauptmann Alexander Graf Rességuier de Miremont baled out of He 219A-2 290070 G9+CH. Over the Ruhr they were pursuing a Lancaster (possibly Lancaster I PD221 BQ-R of 550 Squadron) coned by 4 searchlights but as they went to attack 2 of the searchlights suddenly moved and illuminated the *Uhu*. The Lancaster gunners set the He 219A-2 on fire while the night-fighter crew's fire caused the Lancaster to go down nr. Roermond. (PD221 cr. nr. Westerbeek, Noord Brabant, 9 km SW of Boxmeer. Flying Officer R. G. Nye and crew were KIA). Habicht jettisoned his canopy and his pilot ejected. Habicht's ejection seat handle had been shot off in the attack but he nevertheless managed to get free of the a/c and immediately pull the ripcord of his parachute. He had been hit in the shoulder and chest in the attack and he suffered worse injuries when he hit some tall trees but Habicht survived although his operational flying was over. He had been involved in 17 victories.

144 13 *Tame Boar* crews were credited with 21 *Viermot* kills.

145 in ML960.

146 After a week or so in the station hospital Russell was given leave and returned to Little Staughton. Having suffered quite severe burns to his wrists on leaving the aircraft, Barker was grounded until on 4/5 October, when on only their second trip together after the 28/29 June incident, Russell and Barker's Mosquito was hit by flak N of Luxembourg returning from an attack on a precision tool shop at Heilbronn. MM153 was beyond control, pitching and going down in a spin. Both men baled out over liberated Belgium near Verviers and they returned to 109 Squadron. Russell was then attached to the Mosquito Service Unit at Upwood, which brought his operational flying to an end.

147 In an attempt to rack up more losses in the bomber streams, Oberleutnant Hans-Joachim 'Hajo' Herrmann, a bomber pilot, began forming a *Kommando* on 27 June 1943 using Fw 190A fighters fitted with 300-litre (66-gallon) drop tanks for *Wilde Sau* attacks on heavy bombers over the *Reich*. Hermann had reasoned that the light of the massed searchlights, Pathfinder flares and the flames of the burning target below could easily identify enemy bombers over a German city. By putting a mass concentration of mainly single-seat night-fighters over the target, his pilots could, without need of ground control, visually identify the bombers and shoot them down. Three *Geschwader*, *JG300, JG301* and *JG302*, which formed *30 Jagddivision*, were raised to carry out *Wilde Sau* tactics. These units were equipped with the Focke Wulf 190F-5/U2 and the Bf 109G-6/U4N. Additional *FuG 25a* and *FuG l6zy* radio equipment and the *FuG 350 Naxos Z* radar-receiving set were installed. The *30 Jagddivision* operated until March 1944, picking up *H2S* radar emissions from up to thirty miles away.

148 Müller took his score to 23 kills with four victories while in command of I./NJGr10.

149 B.XVI MM147 of 692 Squadron, which crashed West of Granzow, 9 km NNW of Kyritz at 0155 hours. Flight Lieutenant Burley DFC (KIA). Flight Lieutenant E. V. Saunders DFC baled out (PoW).

150 *The Mosquito Log* by Alexander McKee. Souvenir Press. 1988. Krause, later *Kommandeur* of III./NJG11, claimed a Lancaster shot down on 4/5 November 1944 during a Bomber Command raid on Bochum and survived the war despite 3 parachute jumps.

151 Major Hans Karlowski of 2./NJG1 shot down PF380 flown by Wing Commander S. D. Watts DSO DFC MiD and Pilot Officer A. A. Matheson DFM RNZAF off Terschelling and the crew were lost without trace.

152 Squadron Leader Terry Dodwell's death remains something of a mystery. MM136 had been intercepted and shot down by Hauptmann Heinz Strüning of 3/NJG1, flying in a modified He 219 *Uhu* (Owl) night fighter. (Unteroffizier Wittmann of 1./NJG10 claimed a Mosquito at Gardelegen-Berlin at about the same time as Strüning. It could be that both claims were for the same Mosquito, as only one FTR from the Berlin raid and no others were lost this night). MM136 crashed near Laudin, 35 miles west of Berlin. Squadron Leader Terence Edgar Dodwell RAFVR, DFC* was 29 years old. He had completed part of a Mosquito tour with 1409 Met Flight before joining 571 Squadron. Before this he had completed a tour with Squadron Leader Peter Ashley on 110 Hydedrabad Squadron, flying Mk IV Blenheims. He left a widow, Olive, who lived in Thorpe Bay, Essex. The Germans buried him in the small cemetery at Laudin and later removed and reburied him in the cemetery at Heerstrasse in Berlin. Two nights later, on 20/21 July, during a LNSF raid on Hamburg by 26 Mosquitoes, Strüning shot down another 571 Squadron B.XVI (ML984, crewed by Flight Lieutenants Thompson and Jack Calder RCAF). Thompson baled out but Calder was killed.

153 Squadron Leader C. R. Barrett DFC and Flying Officer E. S. Fogden of 608 Squadron (KIA) and Pilot Officer G. R. Thomas and Flying Officer J. H. Rosbottom of 692 Squadron (KIA) both crashed near. Nauen.

154 Flight Lieutenant B. H. Smith RCAF and Sergeant L. F. Pegg KIA.

155 One of Welter's victims was a 515 Squadron FB.VI in 100 Group flown by Squadron Leader C. Best DFC and Flight Sergeant H. Dickinson (KIA). Squadron Leader J. H. McK Chisholm and Flight Lieutenant E. L. Wilde of 157 Squadron disappeared w/o trace. Reichenbach's victim was a FB.VI of 239 Squadron, 2nd TAF flown by Flying Officer E. W. Osborne and Pilot Officer G. V. Acheson (KIA). Welter claimed another Mosquito N of Wittenberg on 18/19 September (B.XV DZ635 of 627 Squadron, which crashed at Schiffdorf in the E outskirts of Bremerhaven. Flight Lieutenant N. B. Rutherford AFC and Pilot Officer F. H. Stanbury KIA) when 1 Mosquito FTR from a heavy raid on Bremerhaven.

156 Duisburg received a pounding by RAF bombers on 14 October in Operation *Hurricane* when nearly 9000 tons of bombs fell on the city in less than 48 hours. On the night of 14/15 October, which was fine and cloudless, 1,005 RAF heavies attacked Duisburg for the second time in 24 hours in two waves and dropped 4,040 tons of high explosive and 500 tons of incendiaries and losing seven heavies. Bomber Support and forces on minor operations played their part with 141 training aircraft flying a diversionary feint towards Hamburg and turning back before reaching Heligoland and 46 Mosquitoes raiding Hamburg, Berlin, Mannheim and Düsseldorf while 132 aircraft of 100 Group flew RCM, *Serrate* and *Intruder* sorties. Unteroffizier Hans Durscheidt of I./NJG10 in a Fw 190 claimed a Mosquito, which failed to return from the raid on Berlin and crashed north of Duisburg. XVI MM184 of 692 Squadron. Flying Officer F. H. Dell (Evd) and Flying Officer R. A. Naiff (KIA).

157 On the night of 23/24 October Bomber Command despatched 1,055 aircraft to Essen to bomb the Krupps works. This was the heaviest raid on the already devastated German city so far in the war and the number of aircraft - 561 Lancasters, 463 Halifaxes and 31 Mosquitoes - was also the greatest to any target since the war began. Altogether the force dropped 4,538 tons of bombs including 509 4000 pounders on Essen. More than 90% cent of the tonnage carried was high explosive because intelligence estimated that most of Essen's housing and buildings had been destroyed in fire raids in 1943. Five Lancasters and three Halifaxes FTR from the raid.

158 His parents had emigrated to Theodore, Saskatchewan, Canada in late 1918 and Herbert Edward Boulter was born there on 15 April 1923. On 14 February 1937 his father died and in 1938 Bertie and his mother sailed for England and they took residence in Norwich, where his mother originated. On 15 April 1941 on his 18th birthday, Bertie enlisted in the RAF.

159 Altogether, they would fly 20 trips to the "Big City" and all would follow roughly the same pattern.

160 Medium Capacity.

161 On the night of 24/25 October there was no Main Force activity. Sixty-seven Mosquito bombers visited Hanover and other cities while 25 Lancasters and nine Halifaxes again sowed mines in the Kattegat and off Oslo.

162 'I have a certain pride in what I did, but I don't expect others to share it. I hope my 18 visits to Berlin had accomplished something. On our return trip we faced the terrors of murderous flak concentrations and the new formidable adversary in the form of the first jet fighters rising into the skies over Germany. As I think of all the fine men who lost their lives, I almost feel guilty at being alive. Most airmen who made it through a tour of 30 operations were grounded and glad of it I managed to survive 77 operations, flouting the law of probabilities - among 40,000 Canadians killed in WWII, fully 10,000 were in bombers. Andy and I were to attend an Investiture at Buckingham Palace on 12 December 1944 to receive the DFC from His Majesty. However, we were both very anxious to return to Canada and our families. We therefore forfeited this honor and boarded the *Queen Elizabeth* in Liverpool for New York. About the time the investiture was being held, I was meeting Phyl in Montreal for the continuation of' our honeymoon.'

163 Pilot Officer Norman Mackie began his first tour with 83 Squadron at Scampton in May 1941, flying a total of 23 operations on Hampdens before converting to the Manchester and finally completing is tour of 200 hours in March 1942. The award of the DFC was gazetted in May 1942 whilst he was 'on rest' instructing at 29 OTU. Mackie rejoined 83 Squadron for a second tour in November 1942. In the meantime his squadron had been incorporated into the Path Finder Force, flying Lancasters from Wyton. Acting Squadron Leader Mackie was shot down on his 20th Lancaster sortie on 11/12 March 1943 by Feldwebel Gerhard Rase of 6./NJG4 at Signy-en-l'Angle (Marne) as the first of his four night *Abschüsse* (victories) and his radar operator Unteroffizier Rolf Langhoff in a Bf 110 night-fighter from St. Dizier. Norman Mackie was captured by a *Wehrmacht* patrol on the second night after baling out and was imprisoned in a room in their command port with his flying boots removed. He managed to force a boarded up window and to escape without raising the alarm. With the help of French Resistance groups he reached Switzerland in early April. At first he as imprisoned in the Prison de St. Antoine, Geneva but he was later released and classed as an internee. During the second half of 1943 he worked for the British Air Attache before making a clandestine departure from Switzerland on 6 December 1943. He and his fellow escaper made it to Spain on 20 December. A short spell of imprisonment followed in Figueras but eventually Mackie was released and he reached England via Gibraltar on 17 January 1944. On return to the UK he briefly served as a Lancaster Flying Instructor at PFF NTU before he was appointed as Squadron Leader Flight Commander to form 571 Squadron in 8 Group on 23 April 1944. He went on to complete another 40 ops, being awarded the DSO before he was finally rested in December 1944. *Night Airwar: Personal Recollections of the conflict over Europe, 1939-45* by Theo Boiten (Crowood 1999).

164 235 Lancasters and 7 Mosquitoes of 5 Group would be bombing the Mittelland Canal and 128 Lancasters of 3 group would be bombing Koblenz.

165 During the afternoon of 6 November a large heavy daylight attack was made on the Nordstern synthetic oil plant at Gelsenkirchen. 707 heavies were despatched, supported by 31 Mosquitoes and a fighter escort. 514 bombers caused widespread damage to the plant and a second raid was planned for the evening with 48 Mosquitoes, one of which was *L-London* and the Henley-Clark crew. The first aircraft, flown by Wing Commander Jerry Gosnell and Flight Sergeant Stan Emmett, would take off at 1738 hours.

Chapter 6: The Fast Night Strikers

166 See *Mosquito To Berlin: The Story of Ed 'Bertie' Boulter DFC, One of Bennett's Pathfinders* by Peter Bodle FRAeS and Bertie Boulter DFC. Pen & Sword 2007.

167 Ed Boulter adds. 'After Nuremberg if anything was going to happen it felt like it was going to happen to me. On 16 December ops were cancelled after we took off and we had to jettison the 4000lb bomb in the North Sea. On 18 December I hit some H/T cables after take off because I didn't climb enough and chopped off part of the Plexiglas nose. Again we jettisoned the 4000lb bomb in the North Sea before landing at Woodbridge. After a hairy take off on 5 March 1945 Jim Churcher decided he'd had enough. He was entitled to call it a day and did so. That night when we went out to the aircraft there was snow on the ground and the fitters were working on the starboard engine with a canvas windshield and torches. I contacted the squadron CO and asked what I should do, because it looked like the aircraft would be another half an hour. He said, "Don't worry you are to go to Berlin." On take off the starboard engine was misfiring and the aircraft was trying to roll to the right. Luckily, it kept running. We climbed away and dropped our cookie in the North Sea. I accepted Jim quitting. He felt that "someone was trying to tell us something" and after 21 trips, decided enough was enough. I sympathized with him. Being the pilot I had the benefit of not flying with an idiot flyer like me! I couldn't quit.'

168 XVI MM190 of 128 Squadron. Flight Lieutenant R. C. Onley and Flying Officer G. B. Collins RAAF KIA.

169 The only Mosquito lost was a 306 Squadron NF.XXX that was hit by a V2 in mid air during an *Intruder* patrol!

170 48 Mosquitoes of 8 Group were to bomb the coking plant and 32 to the Meidrich benzol plant, 571 Squadron dispatching six Mosquitoes to each of the targets. Sergeant John Clark and his pilot, Warrant Officer Bill Henley, were one of the crews attacking the benzol plant.

171 Next day an analysis of the photo recce photographs showed that at least 70 per cent of crews had hit the target and that considerable damage had been done to the distillation plant. No aircraft were lost.

172 On 18 December the LNSF, or Fast Night Striking Force (FNSF), as it had become known at Bennett's insistence, was increased when 162 Squadron reformed at Bourn with B.25s. Soon it was accompanying 139 Squadron on target-marking duties. Charles Parker recalls. 'Bennett thought we should be called the Fast Night Strike Force because we carried a 4000lb bomb load to the target - fast, unlike the American B-17s and B-24s. I don't think Bennett had a very high opinion of the Americans. On at least one occasion he ordered Mosquitoes to take off and form up over Cambridge at 500ft, to show the good folk of that city that there were RAF squadrons in the area besides Americans! Also, if he ever heard squadrons using the American phonetic alphabet (which ultimately replaced the RAF alphabet), a wigging would go to the squadron CO.'

173 136 aircraft – 67 Lancasters, 54 Halifaxes and 15 Mosquitoes – of 4, 6, and 8 Groups were despatched and no aircraft were lost.

174 In April 1945 the award of a posthumous Victoria Cross was made to Squadron Leader Robert Anthony Maurice Palmer His body is buried in the Rheinberg War Cemetery with the other men who died aboard the Lancaster. Only the tail gunner escaped death, by taking to his parachute. On 21 April 1945 109 Squadron dropped the last bombs to fall on Berlin in WW2.

175 Wing Commander Curry dive bombed from 1,300ft and hit the Northeast corner of the buildings. Two of the other Mosquitoes dive bombed and released their 2 x 1000 MC bombs and the two others dived from 1,300 to 1000ft and dropped their loads of 4 x 500 pounders, some of which fell on the southern building.

176 See *At First Sight; A Factual and anecdotal account of No.627 Squadron RAF.* Researched and compiled by Alan B. Webb. 1991.

177 There was too much smoke and Mallender jettisoned his bombs. Three others returned with their bomb loads while one Mosquito bombed the North building, which was completely wrecked. The sixth and final Mosquito in the second wave attacked the North West building at 1,300ft but it was already damaged so the pilot undershot on target.

178 Peter Mallender was awarded the DFC on 1 January 1945 and promoted squadron Leader to command A Flight on 8 February 1945. It was 45 years before he learned that dear old *'D-Dog"* was repaired and lived to a 'ripe old age'. Flying Officer Bob Boyden concludes. 'The trip back to Peterhead was uneventful. Those Mosquitoes were really smooth and reliable and much credit must go to the manufacturers and, of course, our aircraft mechanics who worked hard to keep them flying. All aircraft returned to Peterhead and all had some flak damage. Mine also had a cracked landing light cover, which they said had been caused by the concussion of the bombs. The next morning we did a fly-past in front of the control tower as we headed back to base. A few officers of high rank met us and shook hands and said a few words. I received the DFC for this trip and years later, when I read the citations, I felt proud to have taken part in this once in a lifetime adventure.' Bob Boyden was awarded the DFC on 2 March 1945 and a bar followed on 17 July 1945. See *At First Sight; A Factual and anecdotal account of No.627 Squadron RAF.* Researched and compiled by Alan B. Webb. 1991.

179 HM409

180 *K for King* came to an untimely end on 2 February 1945 when, returning from a Berlin sortie it was diverted in bad weather to Rougham, an airfield operated by the USAAF and home of the 94th Bomb Group flying B 17s. The aircraft overshot the runway and collided with a civilian car; no one was hurt. The crew were Flying Officer Phillip Back and Flying Officer Derek Smith.

181 A 128 Squadron Mosquito crashed on take-off, killing the crew. A record of the bombing was to be made using cameras mounted in the front and rear of the Mosquitoes to record explosions at the entrance and exit of each tunnel.

182 Twelve tunnels were blocked in the Eifel and Ardennes area, holding up German lines of communication. Six out of seven Mosquitoes of 692 Squadron bombed tunnels near Mayen, losing Flight Lieutenant George Nairn and his navigator Sergeant Danny Lunn to light flak.

183 Five Mosquitoes from the Berlin raid crashed in England and three crashed in Belgium.

184 Later Air Marshal Sir Ivor, KSB CBE DSO DFC AFC.

185 'The story then died for 50 years until we were invited to attend the launch of Martin Bowman's book *'The Men Who Flew the Mosquito'* at Swanton Morley on 2 February 1995. Philip still had his licence so we flew in together from his home at Sisland, east of Norwich in his part-owned Cessna 172. Of course, this created considerable interest, especially as it was exactly 50 years on from our Rougham experience. After the launch, we were interviewed by Anglia Television and the *Eastern Daily Press* with the interview appearing on 'Anglia Tonight' that evening. This item was seen by Dick and Sybil Rayner, two occupants of the car, living at Holland-on-Sea, who got in touch with Anglia, who wanted to get us all together. I had returned home to Oxfordshire that night but Philip met them on 3 February at the 'Flying Fortress' pub at Rougham where Martin Bowman had first discovered details of the event during his researches. This get-together was again featured on 'Anglia Tonight' and the Rayners were able to give us copies of press cuttings and pictures which had been taken by the Americans.' (On 12 March 1945 Derek Smith completed his tour of 50 ops as a navigator on Mosquitoes and he was awarded a bar to his DFC. On 14 March Philip Back and Alex 'Sandy' Galbraith RNZAF, Joe Northrop's navigator, were posted to 139 Squadron. Philip Back flew his 51st op on 25 March and flew nine more before the war's end).

186 See *At First Sight; A Factual and anecdotal account of No.627 Squadron RAF.* Researched and compiled by Alan B. Webb. 1991.

187 Dresden had been targeted as part of a series of particualy heavy raids on German cities in Operation *Thunderclap* with a view to causing as much destruction, confusion and mayhem as possible The other cities were Berlin, Chemnitz and Leipzig, which like Dresden, were vital communications and supply centers for the Eastern Front. *Thunderclap* had been under consideration for several months and was to be implemented only when the military situation in Germany was critical. The campaign was to have started with an American raid on Dresden on 13 February but bad weather over Europe prevented any US involvement until the 14th.

188 In addition the US 8th Air Force despatched 450 B-17s of which 316 attacked Dresden shortly after 12 noon on 14 February.

189 In the case of the 5 Group attack the outward route consisted of no less than eight legs with feints towards the Ruhr, Kassel, Magdeburg and Berlin using Window at the same time. To assist the night operations of Bomber Command various 'spoof' attacks were made by Mosquitoes on Dortmund, Magdeburg and Hanover and 344 Halifaxes attacked an oil plant at Böhlen near Leipzig at the same time as the first attack. In addition to the above the routing and. feints carried out by the Main Forces involved caused night fighter reaction to be minimal. An indication of the effectiveness of these operations was that out of over 1000 aircraft taking part against Dresden only six were lost. Two more Lancasters crashed in France and one in England.

190 Winston Churchill later tried to distance himself from Dresden and declared that, 'The destruction of Dresden remains a serious query against the conduct of Allied bombing.' This was the same Winston S. Churchill who on 22 June 1941 had said, 'We shall bomb Germany by day as well as night in ever-increasing measure, casting upon them month by month a heavier discharge of bombs and making the German people taste and gulp each month a sharper dose of the miseries they have showered upon mankind.'

191 XXV KB409 powered by Packard Merlins. More than a few crews preferred the Mosquito IV aircraft with Rolls Royce engines. They had a smoother purr than the Packards and did not cut out as the Packards did when going into a dive due to the design of the Stromberg carburettor.

192 William Topper was awarded the DFC on 9 March 1945. Flight Lieutenant Garth Davies was awarded the DFC on 21 September 1945.

193 Twenty-eight of the thirty-two Lancasters dispatched carried *Tallboy* bombs and one from 617 Squadron dropped the first 22,000lb *Grand Slam* bomb.

194 An unusually high loss percentage, as the average losses usually only amounted to 0.99 % of the fast Berlin raiders.

195 Hudson, born in Kaponga, New Zealand on 16 November 1915, suffered from polio in early childhood, which affected both his legs but he overcame this and in High School played 1st Class cricket and rugby and participated in cross-country runs to build up his stamina. (*571 Mosquito Squadron History* by Barry Blunt).

196 Becker's victim was FB.VI MM131 XD-J of 139 Squadron, which had taken off from Upwood at 1912 hours for Berlin. Squadron Leader H. A. Forbes DFC, the navigator/bomb aimer escaped and was taken prisoner but no trace has ever been found of his pilot, Flight Lieutenant André A. J. van Amsterdam, a Dutch escapee decorated with the DFC and the Dutch AFC.

197 Bill Henley died tragically a few months after the war flying as a passenger in a Dakota returning from Malta. They flew through a layer of stratus cloud over Marseilles, unaware that there was a cumulo-nimbus embedded in it and the aircraft was torn to pieces.

198 See *The Men Who Flew The Mosquito* by Martin W. Bowman (Pen & Sword 2003).

Chapter 7: The "Baby Blitz"

199 The *Greif* crashed at Whitmore Vale, near Hindhead, Surrey. Only the tail assembly about three feet forward of the fin survived relatively undamaged. Flying Officer C. K. Nowell and Flight Sergeant F. Randall of 85 Squadron claimed a He 177 of 2./KG40.

200 By 20/21 February 1944 Mosquito night fighters had, since the start of 1943, claimed to have shot down just over 100 Luftwaffe raiders.

201 One was a Ju 88A-4 of 8./KG6 shot down by Flight Lieutenant Reginald Clive Pargeter and Flight Lieutenant R. L. Fell of 29 Squadron (which claimed six this night) at Withyham, Sussex. A 3./KG100 *Greif* was shot down by Flight Lieutenant Peter F. L. Hall and Flying Officer R. D. Marriott of 488 Squadron and it fell at Lamberhurst, Kent.

202 B3+CK; crew all PoW.

203 On 30 March Peter Green was posted to 96 Squadron, claiming one victory and 13 V1s shot down whilst with this unit. On 11 august 1944 he was given command of 219 Squadron in 2nd TAF's 85 Group and here he teamed with Flight Lieutenant Douglas 'Douggie' Oxby, as his radar operator. Oxby has been described by Jimmy Rawnsley as 'a young, slightly built, with a twinkling almost roughish eye, and a keen wit that seemed always just about to bubble over. I could well imagine that in the air his commentary would come rippling over in an exuberant but unflurried stream.' Oxby had already seen service with 89 Squadron in the Mediterranean and had assisted in many successful operations. Operating over Europe the Green-Oxby team achieved considerable success. During the night of 2/3 October 1944 they claimed three Ju 87s shot down over Nijmegen, the award of a DSO for Green following in December. By the end of February 1945 he had added a further five victories but on 1 March, while testing a Mosquito, he crashed near Amiens and was killed. At the end of the war Oxby was awarded a DSO to add to his DFC and DFM, as the RAF's top-scoring radar operator, having taken part in 21 successful interceptions. *Aces High: A Tribute to the Most Notable Fighter Pilots of the British and Commonwealth Forces in WWII*. Christopher Shores and Clive Williams (Grub Street London 1994).

204 Becker, Unteroffiziers G. Bartolain, A. Lange and G. Goecking and Oberfeldwebel H. Litschke were killed.

205 One of two Do 217s of 2./KG2 destroyed was shot down by a Mosquito of 264 Squadron and crashed at Legbourne, Lincolnshire, at 2204 hours. An He 177A-3 of 2./KG100 was destroyed by a Mosquito of 25 Squadron and crashed into the sea off Skegness at 2146 hours. Two other Ju 88s, one from II/KG54, and a Ju 188 of 2./KG66, crashed into the sea near the Humber Lightship.

206 The AI.Mk.IX, a British development, was abandoned when the superior American SCR 720 became available. *Confound and Destroy* by Martin Streetly (MacDonald & Janes 1978).

207 Two Ju 88s of II/KG54 and a Ju 88 of 7./KG6 were lost this night.

208 At around the same time Flight Lieutenant J. A. S. Hall and Flying Officer J. P. W. 'Jock' Cairns of 488 Squadron RNZAF shot down a Ju 88A-14 of 8./KG6 from Melsbroek and it fell on Earls Colne airfield where the aircraft and one of its 500-kg high explosive bombs exploded, damaging three B-26 Marauders of the 323rd Bomb Group, US 9th Air Force.

209 Lahl, Unteroffiziers J. Fromm and R. Budrat and Obergefreiter Schiml were killed. Unteroffizier E. Kosch baled out injured and was taken prisoner. Bunting added a Bar to his DFC and he had nine enemy aircraft confirmed destroyed. Included in this total was a Ju 88 on 12/13 June and a Fw 190 on 16/17 June. Edward Bunting was shot down and killed when NF.XIII MM467 was hit by British flak guns at Beachy Head on 29/30 July 1944 while chasing a radar contact. His radar operator Flying Officer E. Spedding was also killed.

210 A 4./KG2 Ju 188E-1 flown by Hauptmann Helmuth Eichbaum was shot down off Southwold by Flight Lieutenant R. M. Carr and Flight Lieutenant Saunderson of 25 Squadron at Coltishall; while a 5./KG2 Ju l88E-1 piloted by Feldwebel Helmuth Richter was shot down by Wing Commander C. M. Miller DFC, CO 85 Squadron at West Malling. Flying Officer S. B Huppert of 410 Squadron RCAF at Hunsdon shot down an He 177 of 3./KG100 flown by Feldwebel Heinz Reis, which fell near Saffron Walden. Two Ju 88s were destroyed by Pilot Officer Allen and Squadron Leader Green DFC of 96 Squadron and its new CO, Wing Commander Edward D. Crew DFC* shot down a Me 410A-1 of 1./KG51 over Brighton. Flight Lieutenant. J. A. Hall and Warrant Officer R. F. D. Bourke of 488 Squadron RNZAF each claimed a Ju 88.

Chapter 8: Star and Bar

211 After Colonel Leon Gray, who assumed command of the 25th Bomb Group on 23 September 1944 and Colonel (later General) Budd Peaslee.

212 Ralph Fisher was reported MIA one week later, 21 January 1945, on another "*Bluestocking*" meteorological mission.

213 Pecquet had been born in France in 1912, and in 1940 was one member of a French AA battery credited with 17 aircraft shot down. He served with the US 11th Armoured Division and had trained as an OSS paratrooper at Ringway.

Chapter 9: "Divers" and "Doodlebugs," Widows and Orphans

214 Over the coming weeks Tempests, Spitfires and Mosquitoes chased the 300-420 mph pilotless bombs in the sky. Tempests of the Newchurch Wing destroyed 580 'Doodlebugs', as they were dubbed by the press or *Divers,* as they were code-named, while Spitfire XIVs brought down a further 185. NF.XIIIs of 96 Squadron based at Ford shot down 174, and Mosquitoes of 418 (City of Edmonton) Squadron RCAF, stationed at Holmsley South, Hurn and Middle Wallop, destroyed a further 90. Ground batteries in the '*Diver* Box' accounted for the rest.

215 In the spring and summer of 1940 Barwell had been a Defiant I pilot on 264 Squadron and he and Pilot Officer J.E.M. Williams and Sergeant Martin his gunners, had scored six victories. Barwell added one more victory plus a probable in 1941 before flying Beaufighter IIs and then Mosquito XVIIs with 125 Squadron. Barwell and Flight Lieutenant D. A. Haigh as radar operator destroyed two Ju 88s at night and a V1 over the sea in 1942 while flying the Mosquito. *Aces High: A Tribute to the Most Notable Fighter Pilots of the British and Commonwealth Forces in WWII.* Christopher Shores and Clive Williams (Grub Street London 1994).

216 It was during April 1943 when Photo Reconnaissance Mosquitoes returned with photos of Peenemünde, that the attention of RAF intelligence was aroused. On their 22nd sortie with 540 Squadron, flown on 22 April 1943 in DZ473, 22-year old Canadian pilot Flight Lieutenant Bill White and his navigator, 23-year old Flight Lieutenant Ron Prescott completed one of the most memorable flights of their extensive operational careers. They were sent to photograph the railyards at Stettin, Germany's biggest Baltic port and which had been bombed two days before on the night of the full moon by 339 'heavies', as well as the Politz oil refinery and Swinemunde on the Baltic coast. Twenty-four fires were still burning at Stettin when the PR Mosquito aircraft flew over the target a day-and-a-half later, approximately 100 acres in the center of the town having been devastated. White recalls. 'On leaving Stettin, we left our cameras running all down the north coast of Germany, and when the film was developed, it was found to contain pictures of Peenemünde.' The interpreters of the CIU (Central Intelligence Unit) at Medmenham studied the photos brought back by the crew. From the type of buildings seen and the elliptical earthworks originally photographed in May 1942 that were also present they concluded that Peenemünde must be an experimental center , probably connected with explosives and propellants. One of the prints from the 22 April 1943 sortie showed an object 25-feet long projecting from what was thought to be a service building, although it had mysteriously disappeared on the next frame! A sortie flown on 14 May 1943 by Squadron Leader Gordon Hughes and Flight Sergeant John R Chubb brought back more photos. Further investigation of the photos from the 22 April sortie revealed that road vehicles and railway wagons near one of the earthworks were carrying cylindrical objects measuring about 38ft long. On 17 May it was concluded that German rocket development had not only probably been underway for some time but was also 'far advanced'. A sixth sortie to Peenemünde on 2 June 1943 in DZ419 unearthed scant new information. But ten days later a sortie flown by Flight Lieutenant Reggie A Lenron in DZ473 resulted in the first definite evidence that the previously unidentified objects were in fact V2 rockets. One was photographed near to a building adjacent to one of the elliptical earthworks lying horizontally on a trailer. On 23 June Flight Sergeant E. P. H. Peek brought back photos so clear that two rockets could be seen lying on road vehicles inside the elliptical earthwork. The news was relayed immediately to Prime Minister Winston Churchill. PRU Mosquitoes photographed Peenemünde again on 27 June and 22 and 26 July. It was now almost certain that Hitler was preparing a rocket offensive against southern England, and it had to be forestalled with all speed. On 17/18 August 1943 596 Lancasters, Halifaxes and Stirlings set our to destroy the experimental rocket site. Although the ground controllers were fooled into thinking the bombers were headed for Stettin and a further 'spoof' by Mosquitoes aiming for Berlin drew more fighters away from the Peenemünde force, forty Lancasters, Halifaxes and Stirlings (6.7% of the force) were shot down but 560 bombers reduced the target to rubble by dropping almost 1800 tons of bombs. Next morning Flying Officer R. A. Hosking of 540 Squadron (in LR413) reconnoitered the target area, and returned again the following day. The raid had put the production of V2 rockets back by at least two months. Although the attack forced the Germans to relocate development and production of V2s to an underground facility in Austria, raids continued against secret weapons' sites in France, including the V2 preparation and launch sire at Watten, which was bombed by the USAAF on 27 August. A PRU sortie three days later revealed that the target was not completely destroyed, so a follow-up raid was flown on 7 September, which devastated the complex and forced the Germans to concentrate development at Wizernes. This site was in turn attacked and destroyed by Lancasters of 617 Squadron on 17 July 1944. While PR never did reveal how the V2s were launched, during October 1944-March 1945 544 Squadron Mosquitoes and other PR aircraft, identified several launching sites in Holland and ground intelligence showed that they were to be launched vertically.

217 On 4/5 July 1944 Bill Gill and his navigator Flying Officer D. C. Hutchins destroyed a Dornier Do 217 20 miles Southwest of Le Havre.

218 A1+AB Werke.Nr 162080. See *Air-launched Doodlebugs: The Forgotten Campaign* by Peter J. C. Smith (Pen & Sword 2006).

219 A1+NM Werke.Nr 161924 of 4 *Staffel.*

220 Douglas Haig Greaves was born in Leeds, West Yorkshire on 4 April 1917, working in his father's printing company before the war. He also did some private flying at the Yorkshire Aero Club, Yeadon. He married in 1939 and joined the RAF in November of that year, completing his training on Hurricanes. He was then posted to Church Fenton to train as a night fighter and in March 1941 joined 68 Squadron, with Sergeant F. Milton Robbins as his radar operator. In September 1941 the pair were posted to 255 Squadron and late in 1942 flew to North Africa with this unit. Here they enjoyed immediate success over Bone. During the night of 16/17 December they closed on one He 111, dropping flaps and undercarriage to allow them to get very close. When fired on, the bomber exploded in a mass of flame, which they flew through, the fire burning away the fabric on ailerons and rudder and covering the windscreen with soot. They got back but had to crash-land on Bone airfield. They were both awarded DFCs early in 1943, Robbins now a Warrant Officer. Their tour ended late in April and they returned to the UK, being posted to TFU, Defford. In January 1944, Greaves now a Flight Lieutenant and Robbins a Flying Officer, they were posted to 25 Squadron. Both were awarded Bars to their DFC in February 1945 and were promoted again, Greaves to Squadron Leader and Robbins to Flight Lieutenant.

221 A1+BM WerkeNr 700862.

222 See *Final Flights: Dramatic wartime incidents revealed by aviation archaeology* by Ian McLachlan (PSL 1989). A second USN crew, Lieutenant Sam Peebles and Ensign Dick Grinnals, were also KIA on 22 November 1944. This left only one USN crew with 68 Squadron of those sent to Coltishall to gain night-fighting experience, Lieutenant John W. Kelly and Lieutenant Tom Martin; both were recalled to the USA two days after the loss of Peebles and Grinnals.

Chapter 10: The Serrate Squadrons Strike

223 Addison's HQ would not move to the county until 3 December when it was established at RAF West Raynham, eight miles from Fakenham. A permanent HQ, at Bylaugh Hall near Swanton Morley would not be ready for occupation on 18 January 1944, when 2 Group HQ moved to Mongewell Park near Wallingford in Berkshire, becoming part of 2nd Tactical Air Force.

224 Its Blind Approach Training Development Unit had started to fly on the German *Ruffian* and *Knickebein* beams. 192 had been formed at Gransden Lodge on 4 January 1943 from 1474 Flight for the ELINT role with three Mosquito Mk IVs, two Halifax Mk IIs and eleven Wellington Mk Xs to monitor German radio and radar. The squadron had always been part of the Y-Service and, as such, its primary object had been a complete and detailed analysis from the air of the enemy signals organization. Throughout 1944 and early 1945 192 Squadron crews listened in on enemy radio frequencies and jammed enemy VHF transmissions. They even afforded the RAF control of German fighters.

225 The TRE (Telecommunications Research Establishment) at Malvern, Worcestershire had developed the homer using a receiver known as *Serrate,* which actually homed in on the radar impulses emitted by the *Lichtenstein (Emil-Emil)* interception radar. *Serrate* got its name from the picture on the CRT (cathode ray tube). When within range of a German night-fighter, the CRT displayed a herringbone pattern either side of the time trace, which had a serrated edge. *Serrate* came to be the codename for the high-level Bomber Support operations. On 9 May 1943 a Ju 88R-1 of IV/NJG3 was flown from Kristiansund/Kjevik in Norway to Dyce, near Aberdeen, after its crew defected during an aborted interception of a Courier Service Mosquito off Denmark. The fiancée of the pilot, Flugzeugführer Oberleutnant Herbert Schmidt, was Jewish and had been arrested and transported to a concentration camp, while his *Bordfunker*, Oberfeldwebel Paul Rosenberger, was of Jewish descent. *Bordschutze* Oberfeldwebel Erich Kantvill, a Nazi, went along with the defection. This aircraft was equipped with the *FuG 202 Lichtenstein* BC AI. Examination by TRE scientists enabled them to confirm that the *Serrate* device operated on the correct frequencies to home in on the *FuG 202 Lichtenstein BC* and *Lichtenstein FuG 212* radars. *Serrate* could only home in on *Lichtenstein* AI radar and then only if it was turned on. The Beaufighters would also be equipped with Mk IV AI radar, which would be used in the closing stages of a *Serrate* interception because *Serrate* could not positively indicate range. The Mk IV was also needed to obtain contacts on enemy night-fighters that were not using their radar.

226 239 had been reformed at Ayr in September 1943. Its previous function had been Army Co-operation, so that all aircrew for its new role of the offensive night fighting had to be posted in. With Wing Commander P. M. J. Evans DFC as Squadron Commander. Squadron Leaders Black and E. W. Kinchin as flight commanders and Flight Lieutenants Carpenter and 'Jacko' Jacobs DFC* as N/R Leader and navigation officer respectively the eighteen crews began their training. On 9 December 239 Squadron moved to West Raynham and on 11 December two operational Mosquito IIs equipped with Mk IV AI forward-looking and backward-looking *Serrate* equipment and the *Gee* navigational aid, arrived. The squadron trained at every available opportunity when the weather allowed.

227 The squadron had been reformed at Ayr on 15 September under the command of Wing Commander Edward John "Jumbo" Gracie DFC. Gracie was described as 'a little fire-eater' who, as a Flight commander flying Hurricanes in 56 Squadron in the Battle of Britain, was credited with the destruction of five enemy aircraft destroyed, two probables and two damaged before he was shot down and sustained a broken neck. He recovered and added to his score in 1941. The idea of using the Hurricane as a night intruder aircraft probably originated with Gracie. As a Flight Commander with 23 Squadron in April 1941, Gracie made a few sorties in a Hurricane I from Manston to the Lille and Merville areas. He then did not have any actual successes but he saw enemy aircraft on at least one occasion and showed the possibilities of single engined intrusion. The experiment was copied by other squadrons. Later, in 1942, the Mediterranean, Gracie flew Spitfires from the carriers *Eagle* and *Wasp* to reinforce units on Malta. He finally commanded a Wing at Takali before returning to England to command 169 Squadron. The groundcrew were all retained from the old Mustang squadron and aircrew were posted in, mostly made up of volunteers from night-fighter squadrons. A Mosquito II and a Beaufighter were delivered towards the end of October, followed by further Beaufighters. All aircrew underwent a course with 1692 Flight at Drem and all pilots went on to the Rolls Royce Engine Handling Course.

228 515 had, since 1942, tested the *Mandrel* jamming device on RAF night and US 8th Air Force daylight bombing raids. Despite problems with the Mosquitoes, many of which were war-weary and their engines often proving unreliable, 515 Squadron's Beaufighters and Blenheims had been replaced by Mosquito B.IIs, beginning on 29 February, for training on the type. Some of 605 Squadron's Mosquitoes were operated by 515 on detachment at Bradwell Bay and it was in one of these aircraft that the CO, Wing Commander Freddie Lambert and Flight Lieutenant E. Morgan, shot down an He 177 in the first squadron sortie.

229 On 17/18 August 1943 when Bomber Command attacked the secret experimental research establishment at Peenemünde on the Baltic, which was developing the V1 pilotless flying bomb and the V2 rocket the German night-fighter force operated in large numbers employing large-scale *Zahme Sau* (Tame Boar) tactics for the first time. *Zahme Sau* had been developed by Oberst Victor von Lossberg of the Luftwaffe's Staff College in Berlin. The *Himmelbett* ground network provided a running commentary for its night-fighters, directing them to where the Window concentration was at its most dense. Although the ground controllers were fooled into thinking the bombers were headed for Stettin and a further *Spoof* by Mosquitoes aiming for Berlin drew more fighters away from the Peenemünde force, some forty Lancasters, Halifaxes and Stirlings, or 6.7 per cent of the force, were shot down.

230 One returned early with equipment failures and 22-year-old Flight Lieutenant Basil Johnny' Brachi and his navigator 37 year old Flying Officer Angus P MacLeod of 239 Squadron, failed to return. During a patrol to Berlin their Mosquito lost its starboard engine over enemy territory and then the port engine started cutting out and finally quit over the North Sea. Crews in 239 and 141 Squadrons conducted an extensive sea search but the two crewmen were never found. MacLeod's body was later washed ashore in Holland where he is buried.

231 As a 17-year-old, Harry White had enlisted in the RAF in 1940 having lied about his age. On 4 August 1941, Sergeant White, as he then was, crewed up with 18-year old AC2 Michael Seamer Allen at 54 OTU Church Fenton. In September 1941, they were posted from the OTU to 29 Squadron at West Malling where they started defensive night patrols in Beaufighters. Harry White was then only 18 and a half. After only six weeks, they were posted to 1455 Flight (later renumbered 534 Squadron) at Tangmere, a Havoc and Boston Turbinlite squadron. In practice, the Turbinlite was none too successful but Mike Allen regarded the 15 months that he and White spent on Havocs as invaluable training in the art of night fighting. Michael Allen was born on 15 March 1923 at Croydon, Surrey, and educated at Hurstpierpoint College, Sussex. He then studied mechanical engineering at night school before being apprenticed to Fairey Aviation. Aeronautical engineering apprentices often had difficulty being accepted for aircrew training in wartime as their employers had first claim on their specialist skills. Allen's father, however, was also in the aviation business and was able to persuade Fairey to release his son. (He and Allen's mother were subsequently killed when a V2 rocket destroyed their house in July 1944). Harry White was commissioned as a Pilot Officer on 26 March 1942. He and Allen operated on Turbinlites on home defense until 19 January 1943 with no success at all but before he was 21, Harry White's bravery had earned him a DFC and bar. When the Turbinlite units were disbanded, Harry and his navigator were posted back to a Beaufighter squadron, 141 at Ford. Much to their disappointment, they were attached to a Ferry Unit at Lyneham and spent four frustrating months ferrying new Beaufighters from Britain to Egypt, eventually rejoining 141 at Wittering on 15 June 1943.
White and Allen's first victory was a Bf 110 flown by Major Herbert Rauth of II./NJG4, a 31 victory *Ritterkreuzträger*, on 15/16 July 1943 flying a Beaufighter. On 17/18 August 1943 they destroyed a Bf 110 (WNr 6228 of III/NJGI flown by Hauptmann Wilhelm Dormann, a pre-war *Lufthansa* pilot and former *Wilde Sau* pilot with 14 victories) and a Bf 110 of 1V/NJGI flown by Leutnant Gerhard Dittmann and Unteroffizier Theophil Bundschuh. They were both killed. White and Allen scored their fourth kill when they destroyed a Ju 88 on 6/7 September.

232 Cooper and Connolly's victim was Bf 110G-4 Wrk Nr 740081 D5+LB of *Stab III/NJG3,* which crashed at Werneuchen, 20km East of Berlin. Oberleutnant Karl Loeffelmaan, pilot, was killed and Feldwebel Karl Bareiss, radar operator and Oberfeldwebel Oscar Bickert, *bordschutze,* who were both WIA, baled out. Five Mosquitoes of 141 Squadron were on patrol and one of the crews destroyed a Bf 110. In the early 1930s Lance Corporal Joe Cooper had been a cavalryman in the 4th Hussars. When it mechanized in 1936, Cooper decided he did not wish to drive tanks - he wanted to fly aeroplanes -so he borrowed £25 from a friend and bought his discharge from the Army He applied for, and surprisingly got, a short service commission in the RAF. 'I'd left school at fourteen without the School Certificate but to their credit, the RAF took me in', he recalls. Apart from being a keen horseman, Cooper was an accomplished boxer and he became Lightweight Boxing Champion of the RAF in 1938/39. Cooper soloed on the Tiger Moth and went on to fly Audaxes and Harts, Blenheim night-fighters and then Beaufighters in 141 Squadron where he was B Flight Commander. Flying a Beaufighter Cooper and Connolly damaged a Ju 88 on the night of 18 January 1943.

233 Forty-three bombers were lost on 15/16 February and Wing Commander Jumbo Gracie and his navigator Flight Lieutenant Wilton W. Todd were shot down in the Hanover area. Six weeks later news was received that Gracie had been killed. Todd was a PoW in *Stalag Luft III.* (He later designed the memorial to the fifty airmen murdered by the *Gestapo.*

234 Truscott, who was from Canterbury, had been Slade's observer on 22/23 August 1942 when they notched the first blood to 157 Squadron by shooting down a Do 217 of KG2 over Suffolk. London-born Slade had joined the RAF in 1933 and had learned the deadly art of night fighting in 604 Squadron at West Malling under Wing Commander John Cunningham. Slade's tenure of 169 would be short - just under three months - but Truscott remained with the squadron, until he was killed flying with Wing Commander Neil Bromley, Slade's successor. (Group Captain Slade OBE, FRAS left the RAF in July 1946 and took the post of Chief Test Pilot for Fairey Aviation, retiring as Chairman of Fairey Hydraulics in 1977.)

235 A seventh, He l77A-3 Wrk.Nr. 332214 5J+RL of 3./KG100, was destroyed by Wing Commander Freddie Lambert and Flight Lieutenant E. W. M. Morgan DFM of 515 Squadron, on 5 March. It crashed near Châteaudun, France killing Leutnant Wilhelm Werner, pilot and Unteroffiziers Kolemann Schoegl, *bordfunker,* Gustav Birkebmaier, flight engineer, Alfred Zwieselsberger and Josef Kerres *bordschütze*.

236 One of these was Ju 88C-6 Wrk.Nr. 750014 R4+CS of 8./NJG2, which crashed at Arheilgen near Darmstadt, 25 kilometers South of Frankfurt. Oberfeldwebel Otto Müller, pilot, Obergefreiter Erhard Schimsal, *bordfunker* and Gefreiter Gunter Hanke, *bordschütz*, were killed.

237 On 20/21 April Kinchin and Sellars were shot down and killed by Oberleutnant Fritz Krause of 1./NJGr10 flying a *Neptun*-equipped Fw 190A-5 over Berlin.

238 Vandenplassche evaded capture and made a remarkable home run via the Pyrenees. Spain and Gibraltar He arrived back in Britain on 2 May. Mamoutoff is buried at Choloy War Cemetery. (Vandenplassche was killed in May 1953 flying a Belgian jet)

239 Flight Sergeants J. Campbell DFM and R. Phillips of 239 Squadron shot down Ju 88C-6 Wrk Nr 360272 D5+? Of *4./NJG3*, which crashed ten kilometers SW of Bayreuth. Oberleutnant Ruprecht Panzer, pilot, WIA, *bordfunker* and *bordschütz*, all baled out safely.

240 A staggering total of 95 bombers (11.9 per cent) were lost from a force of 795 dispatched to Nürnburg, Bomber Command's worst night of the war. Woodman and Kemmis destroyed a Bf 110 at Compeigne on 18/19 April 1944.l

241 White and Allen's victim was either Do 217N-1 Wrk Nr 51517 of *5/NJG4*, which crashed near Meulan, north of Paris. Oberfeldwebel Karl Kaiser, pilot and Unteroffizier Johannes Nagel, *bordfunker* both WIA, baled out. Gefreiter Sigmund Zinser, *bordschütz*, MIA. Or it was Do217E-5 Wrk. Nr. 5558 6N+EP of 6./KG100, with the loss of Feldwebel Heinz Fernau (pilot), Hauptmann Willi Scholl (observer), Unteroffizier Josef Bach, *bordfunker,* and Oberfeldwebel Fritz Wagner (flight engineer).

242 Thirty-seven bombers were lost this night.

243 Both men are buried in Rheinberg War Cemetery, only about 45 kilometers from Essen. The following night, 27/28 April, 239 Squadron Mosquitoes landed back at West Raynham and submitted claims for three enemy aircraft destroyed. John Forshaw's chosen replacement Squadron Leader Victor Lovell DFC and his navigator, Warrant Officer Robert Lilley DFC failed to return from a patrol to Stuttgart/Friedrichshafen.

244 Five French targets were bombed in 452 sorties and 12 aircraft were lost - seven Halifaxes and four Lancasters.

245 Lancaster ND587/D crashed at 0345 hours at Gallaix (Hainaut) 12 km E Tournai.

246 In a letter to his parents on 12 May, Martstaller wrote. 'The sky was fully lit, so we could easily see the Tommy. We saw at least ten bombers. However, we could only concentrate on one aircraft. When I was near him and fired (and my burst of fire bloody well blinded me!) the Schwinehund fired off a flare with a signal pistol, so that an enemy night fighter could post us).'

247 Martstaller was killed in a crash on St Trond aerodrome in August 1944.

248 Bf 110 3G+E1 Wrk Nr. 740179 crashed at Ellezelles, Belgium. Oberleutnant Heinrich Schulenberg, pilot and Oberfeldwebel. Hermann Meyer, *bordfunker* baled out near Flobeq.

249 Le Boutte had joined the *l'Aviation Militaire* (Belgian Armed Forces) in April 1919. In 1924 he joined the *Militaire Vliegwezen* (Air Component of the Belgian Amy). Le Boutte had a successful career, rising to *Capitaine Aviateur* (Captain-Flyer) and commander of the IIIrd Group of the 2nd Regiment by 1930. As CO of this Unit, he became the first leader of a Belgian aerobatic team. In June 1935, he became Major and CO of a Group of the *1st Luchtvaartregiment* based at Evere. This unit was equipped with Fairey Foxes and later, Fairey Battles. In January 1940 Le Boutte was sent to the Belgian Congo on an assignment to form three squadrons at Leopoldville, Stanleyville and Elizabethville. Having successfully completed his mission in Congo, he left this Belgian colony on 16 May 1940 but the war and the rapid advance of the German Armed Forces in the West interrupted his voyage home and he became stranded in Algiers. On 1 June his diplomatic passport enabled him to embark on a ship heading for Marseilles, where he visited the Belgian government in exile then residing in Poitiers. Belgian officials there ordered him to return to Belgium, together with a group of Belgian pilots. Very reluctantly, Le Boutte obeyed the order. Le Boutte went into hiding in Belgium but the Germans tracked him down. However Le Boutte told them that he was an Official State Photographer and they believed him! This incident convinced Le Boutte that he should try and escape to England. On 3 January 1941 he began a long journey via France and Spain to Gibraltar, but Franco's soldiers captured him and he was thrown into jail. Living conditions were very harsh and Le Boutte lost a lot of weight. Almost every day fellow prisoners were executed. After 10 weeks he was transferred to the notorious prison at Miranda. He survived the ordeal in this jail too and after four months he was released. Five days later he reached Liverpool. Having finally arrived in England, Le Boutte was soon greeted with bad news - aged forty-three and wearing glasses, the RAF medical board declared him unfit for all flying duties. Disillusioned, Le Boutte sought advice from his Belgian friends who had successfully joined the British Armed Forces. While visiting one of his friends, Le Boutte stole his identity card and set off for the recruiting center for night fighter aircrew at Uxbridge. The interviewing board was impressed by his flying career, hardly glancing at 'his' identity card, and the medical board declared him 'perfectly fit'. Le Boutte immediately joined the RAF as pilot officer. He did not care for his rank of Major, as he only wanted fly! His training on Oxfords and Blenheims was soon successfully completed and at OTU he crewed up with young Sergeant Harry Parrot, who wanted to improve his French. Despite his age and the fact that he wore glasses, Le Boutte was finally commissioned into the RAF as a Pilot Officer in January 1942 and that summer Le Boutte and Parrot were posted to 141 Squadron.

250 This was Le Boutte's first and only kill during his time on 141 Squadron. In June Lucien Le Boutte, who on 24 May had been awarded the DFC (as was his navigator, Mallett) was officially 'tour expired' Mallet himself was on his third tour. Le Boutte, who had flown over fifty *Instep, Ranger,* night-fighter and *Serrate* patrols and damaged three trains in strafing attacks, was given a staff position in London, reaching the rank of Wing Commander DFC CdeG. After the war Group Captain Le Boutte served in Brussels at SHAEF and he was one of the founder members of the Belgian Air Force. He served with distinction until retirement in 1956.

251 They destroyed Ju 88G-6 Wrk Nr 750922 of 5./NJG3, which crashed at Hoogcruts near Maastricht. Unteroffizier Josef Polzer, pilot and Obergefreiter Hans Klünder, radar operator were killed and Gefreiter Hans Becker, *bordschütz* was wounded.

252 They had got a Bf 110 on 5/6 February and another on 22/23 April.

253 Flight Lieutenant D. L. Hughes and Flying Officer R. H. 'Dickie' Perks of 239 Squadron destroyed a Bf 110. Bf 110G-4 720050 05+2 of 3./NJG3, was shot down by Wing Commander N. B. R. Bromley OBE and Flight Lieutenant Philip V. Truscott of 169 Squadron. Feldwebel Franz Müllebner, pilot, Unteroffizier Alfons Josten, radar operator and Gefreiter Karl Rademacher, air gunner, were all wounded in action and baled out successfully. The Bf 110 crashed at Hoogeveen, south of Groningen.

254 Bf 110G-4 of 7./NJG6. Wrk Nr 730106 2Z+AR crashed at 0230 hours in forest between Zweifall and Mulartshuette, SE of Aachen and Oberleutnant Helmut Schulte, pilot, and Unteroffizier Hans Fischer, air gunner, both baled out. Unteroffizier Georg Sandvoss, radar operator, was killed. The other Bf 110G-4, Wrk.Nr. 720387 2Z+HR, flown by Unteroffizier Oskar Völkel, crashed five minutes later at the Wesertalsperre near Eupen, south of Aachen. Völkel and Unteroffiziers Karl Hautzenberger, radar operator and Günther Boehxne, air gunner, baled out safely

255 The A Flight Commander, Squadron Leader Neil Reeves DSO DFC and Pilot Officer A. A. O'Leary DFC** DFM destroyed Bf 110F WrkNr 140032 G9+CR of 7./NJGI. It crashed at Spannum in Friesland province in Holland at 0115 hours. Unteroffizier Joachim Tank, the 26-year-old pilot, was slightly wounded. Unteroffiziers Günther Schröder, the 19 year old radar operator, and Heinz Elwers, the 24 year old air gunner, were killed.

256 Although the second Messerschmitt Bf 109 had escaped, the eleventh victory of Harry White and Mike Allen was duly recorded in 141 Squadron's record book. On 14 June Harry White and Mike Allen (and Howard Kelsey and Smitty Smith) were posted to the Bomber Support Development Unit (BSDU) at Foulsham. White and Allen flew 21 and 20 operations respectively while with BSDU, testing new radar equipment for 100 Group. On 28/29 July 1944 Harry White and Mike Allen returned briefly to West Raynham to fly *Serrate* patrols with nine other Mosquitoes of 141 Squadron. During the sortie they shot down two Ju 88s to take their final tally to thirteen, the highest score in the Squadron's history. Harry White was promoted Squadron Leader and became A Flight Commander. He remained with 141 until it disbanded at Little Snoring in September 1945.

257 Bailey was taken in by the Dutch Underground but his immediate concern was for his wife Jean who was eight months pregnant on 29 May and how she would react to the news that he was "missing". Bailey spent three months with the Dutch Underground - even taking part in a raid on a post office to augment supplies of ratio cards and money - before being sent down the escape lines to Belgium in August 1944. Unfortunately the line had been infiltrated. Bailey, an American Fortress pilot by the name of Bill Lalley from Lowell, Michigan and Viv Connell a RAAF Lancaster navigator from Broken Hill, NSW, were taken prisoner by the Germans. 2nd Lieutenant William J. Lalley was co-pilot of B-17 42-3513 of the 326th Bomb Squadron, 92nd Bomb Group flown by 2nd Lieutenant Russell M. Munson, which was shot down on 29 April on the mission to Berlin and which crashed at Millingen in Holland. Munson and the other eight members of the crew survived to become prisoners of war. Flight Sergeant Viv Connell was navigator of ND752, one of seven 75 Squadron RNZAF Lancasters that were shot down on 20/21 July 1944 on the raid on Homberg. Connell and one other man survived from Flying Officer H. J. Burtt's crew. They had taken off from Mepal in Cambridgeshire at 2330 hours and the Lancaster crashed at 0140 hours near Tilburg. W. R. Chorley, *Royal Air Force Bomber Command Losses of the Second World War* (six vol, Midland Counties Leicester 1992-1998)

258 Their victim possibly, was Wrk.Nr. 440272 G9+NS of 8./NJG1 which crashed at 0054 hours on the Northern beach of Schiermonnikoog. Unteroffiziers Adolf Stuermer the 22-year old pilot, Unteroffizier Ludwig Serwein, the 21-year old radar operator and Gefreiter Otto Morath, the 23-year old air gunner, were killed. Flying Officers Bill Breithaupt DFC and J. A. Kennedy DFC of 239 Squadron claimed a Ju 88G-1 off the Friesians. Their victim was Wrk.Nr. 710454 of 5./NJG3, which crashed 20 kilometers North of Spiekeroog. Unteroffiziers Willi Hammerschmitt, pilot and Friedrich Becker, *bordfunker,* and Feldwebel Johannes Kuhrt, *bordschütze* were killed.

259 The campaign to acquire the British designed, American-made AI Mk X culminated in the arrival in 100 Group of 85 and 157 Squadrons at Swannington. At the beginning of May, 85 Squadron equipped with AI Mk X and already well trained in its use had been engaged in defensive night fighting, while 157 equipped with AI Mk XV had supported Coastal Command's daylight anti-*U-Boat* patrols in the Bay of Biscay. AI Mk X, unlike Mk IV had no backward coverage at all. From the point of view of the Mosquito's own safety, some kind of backward warning equipment had to be fitted before it could be used on high-level operations. To provide a quick interim answer BSDU began a modification of *Monica I.* Until the tail warner was fitted, 85 and 157 Squadrons would be trained for low-level airfield intrusions. This would mean that the AI Mk X squadrons would eventually be in a position to play a dual role - either high-level or low-level work, which would help considerably in the planning of bomber operations.

260 Possibly Do 217K-3 Wrk Nr 4742 6N+OR of *Stab* III./KG100. Oberleutnant Oskar Schmidtke, pilot and Unteroffiziers Karl Schneider, observer; Helmuth Klinski, *bordfunker* and Werner Konzett, flight engineer were killed.

261 It took Benson's personal tally to five. Flight Lieutenants Micky Phillips and Derek Smith of 85 Squadron destroyed a Bf 110 near Paris.

262 On 25 June some Mosquitoes from 85 and 157 Squadrons were detached to West Malling for *anti-Diver* patrols. On 20 August they resumed bomber support duties from Swannington.

263 *Night Fighter* by C. F. Rawnsley & Robert Wright. Elmfield Press.

264 Gonsalves and Duckett's victim was Bf 110 5664 G9+IZ of 12./NJG1. It crashed nine kilometers west of Tongres, between St. Trond and Maastricht. Unteroffizier Heinz Bärwolf, pilot, who was injured, and Unteroffizier Fischer, radar operator, baled out. Obergefreiter Edmund Kirsch, the 23-year old *bordschütz*, was killed. Flight Lieutenant Jimmy Mathews and Warrant Officer Penrose of 157 destroyed a Ju 188 the same night. On 15/16 June also Flight Lieutenant Jimmy Mathews and Warrant Officer Penrose of 157 destroyed a Ju 188.

265 Ju 88 710590 Hauptmann Herbert Lorenz (pilot), Feldwebel Rudolf Scheuermann, *bordfunker* and Flieger Harry Huth, *bordschütze* were killed.

266 Kendall and Hill's victim was a Bf 110 of NJG1. Muller, the pilot, and two others were killed.

267 The first was Ju 88 G-1 710866 R4+NS of 8./NJG2. It crashed at Volkel airfield. Leutnant Harald Machleidt, pilot, and Gefreiter Max Rinnerthaler, *bordschütze,* were killed and Unteroffizier Kurt Marth, *bordfunker,* was wounded.

268 Wrk Nr 440076 G9+NS.

269 Beyer, Unteroffizier Hans Petersmann, the 21-year-old radar operator and Obergefreiter Franz Riedel, the 20-year old *bordschütz*, were killed. It was Rabone's seventh victory of the war. Born in England and raised in New Zealand, Rabone had been a pilot in 88 Squadron on Fairey Battles and in May 1940 his aircraft was hit by flak during an attack on a bridge at Maastricht. He baled out behind enemy lines before escaping in civilian clothes with a refugee column. Returning to England he was shot down again on 12 June by a Bf 109 during a raid on a Seine bridge and he baled out once more. In August 1940 Rabone transferred to RAF Fighter Command and flying Hurricane Is in 145 Squadron, shot down a Bf 109E off Dungeness. Rabone added two more victories in late 1940. In October he had joined 422 Flight, which became 96 Squadron in December as a night fighter unit, flying Hurricanes and Defiants. On 13 April 1941 Rabone and his gunner had to bale out over the Derbyshire Peak District after an engine failure. After a spell on Havocs in 85 Squadron By the summer of 1943 Rabone was flying Mosquito IIs in 23 Squadron in the Mediterranean and on 15 August, while flying a Spitfire Vc carrying spare parts to Palermo, Sicily, he shot down a Ju 88. Flying a Mosquito II on 8 September he destroyed another Ju 88 and a Heinkel 111 and damaged another Heinkel. On 30 June/1 July Rabone destroyed a He 111 and a Ju W34 at Jägel and Schleswig to take his score to nine confirmed victories. In mid-July Rabone rejoined 23 Squadron and his run of luck finally ran out when he and Johns failed to return from a *Day Ranger* on 24 July. Rabone's body was washed ashore on Heligoland Island three months later.

270 In December 1942, Wing Commander John Randall Daniel 'Bob' Braham DSO DFC* not yet 23, assumed command of 141 Squadron, then flying Beaufighters. An outspoken individualist, unsurpassed in his sheer aggressive fighting spirit and relentless determination, Bob Braham was already a living legend, having shot down twelve enemy aircraft, eleven of them at night. The son of a WWI RFC pilot, Braham shot down his first aircraft during the Battle of Britain and at 23 had become the youngest wing commander in the RAF. 'The Night Destroyer', as he was dubbed in the press, had an overdeveloped sense of modesty and could see no reason for the press having an interest in him. It is perhaps because he shunned publicity wherever possible, that he is not as well known as some other aces of WW2. Posted with Braham to 141 Squadron from 29 Squadron was Flying Officer William J. 'Sticks' Gregory DFC DFM his navigator and radio/radar operator, who had partnered Braham in seven kills. Gregory earned his nickname as a result of having been a drummer in Debroy Somer's band. Flight Lieutenant Jacko Jacobs partnered Braham in four of his victories. In April 1943 Air Marshal Sir Trafford F. Leigh-Mallory AOC Fighter Command had been impressed with the aggressive spirit Braham had instilled in his squadron in so short a time and had informed him that 141 Squadron had been selected as the first *Serrate* squadron for Bomber Support operations over enemy territory.

271 They added to their score on 8/9 August when they destroyed a Fw 190 near St Quentin (their seventh victory) and damaged two Bf 109s. On 11 October they were credited with the destruction of a seaplane on the water at Tristed.

272 Welham and Hollis' victim was possibly Ju 88G-1 Wrk.Nr 710455 of 4./NJG3, which crashed at Arendonk, Belgium. Unteroffizier Eügen Wilfert (pilot), Obergefreiter Karl Martin, radar operator and Gefreiter Rudolf Scherbaum, *bordschütz,* were KIA. Three aircraft were destroyed by 239 Squadron without loss or early return to bring its total to twenty-nine. Flight Lieutenant Denis Welfare DFC* and Flying Officer Taffy Bellis DFC* shot down a Me 410 east of Paris and a Fw 190 was destroyed by their CO, Wing Commander Paul M. J. Evans and navigator Flying Officer R. H. 'Dickie' Perks DFC.

273 Paddy Engelbach ended up a prisoner of war and came upon old acquaintances from 141 Squadron behind the wire. One of them was Wing Commander Bob Braham for whom he had searched on 26 June after Braham had been shot down during a *Day Ranger* to Denmark. Engelbach returned to 141

Squadron at the end of the war and in his flying logbook when recording his search for Braham, he inserted, *'Found him in Dulag Luft!'* Paddy Engelbach was killed taking off in a DH Venom from West Raynham in February 1955. At that time he was Commanding Officer of 23 Squadron.

274 Seehaber, Gefreiter Kurt Völker, Obergefreiters Walter Oldenbruch and Hermann Patzel were killed.

275 Unteroffizier Erich Pollmer was WIA. (Other crew details unknown).

Chapter 11: *MOSKITOPANIK!*

276 Ju 88 751065 R4+? of 5./NJG2 was shot down by Flying Offcers P. G. Bailey and J. O. Murphy of 169 Squadron and it crashed near Chartres. Oberfeldwebel Fritz Farrherr, pilot and Obergefreiter Heinz Boehme, *bordschütz*, were killed. Gefreiter Josef Schmid, radar operator, was WIA and baled out. Bf 110G-4 110028 C9+HK of 2./NJG5 crashed near Compeigne. It is believed that this was one of the two aircraft shot down this night by Squadron Leader J. S. Booth DFC* and Flying Officer K. Dear DFC of 239 Squadron. Leutnant Joachim Hanss, pilot, and Feldwebel Kurt Stein, *bordschütz*, were killed. Unteroffizier Wolfgang Wehrhan, radar operator, was wounded

277 Sticky was born on 26 September 1917 at Cockermouth in Cumberland. After spending his early life in South Africa, his father's health forced the Murphy's to return to England where Alan went to Seafield Preparatory School at Lytham on the northwest coast until about 1931. Whilst there he played cricket and soccer. Murphy was an outstanding athlete. He jumped high and long, as well as being a top hurdler and 440-yard man. He represented the RAF at athletics, and in a triangular match between Cranwell, Woolwich and Sandhurst, he created a long-standing record for the long jump of 23 feet 1¼ inches in 1938. Commissioned as a pilot Officer in July 1938, Sticky continued his training on 185 Squadron with the Fairey Battle, then trained others in the north of Scotland at an OTU as Station Navigation Officer. In March 1941, Sticky joined 1419 Special Duty Flight at Stradishall, with the primary duty then of dropping secret agents throughout Occupied Europe for intelligence and Resistance activities. Sticky Murphy became one of the pioneer pilots in 138 Squadron, one of the 'Moon Squadrons', which flew the short take-off and landing Lysander to infiltrate and exfiltrate 'Joes' in Europe. On 1 June 1942, he was rested and attached to the Air Ministry but flew various types of aircraft and enjoyed his married life *in* the London area. On 20 June 1943 after almost a year, he arrived at High Ercall for conversion to Mosquitoes, and for a rapid course on intruding. Passing this course, he was given an 'Exceptional' grading by Wing Commander 'Mouse' Fielden, who had been Sticky's Commanding Officer on 161 Squadron. In late September 1943, Sticky landed in Malta to join the veteran 23 Squadron which had been the scourge of the Axis Powers in the area throughout that year, harassing the retreating enemy armies and air forces in North Africa, and in Sicily and Italy throughout 1943. Sticky Murphy quickly became the commander of B Flight. He followed the squadron motto *Semper Aggressus* (Always have a Go) which he was more inclined to translate in terms of the ANZACs at Gallipoli, with their war cry 'Right lads. After the bastards!'

278 He had commanded 23 Squadron during March-September 1942 and on 6 July had flown the Squadron's first Mosquito *Intruder* sortie. In September 1943 he had assumed command of 605 Squadron, destroying a Do 217 on his first operation, and in January 1944 had notched the Squadron's 100th victory when he downed a Ju 188.

279 Their victim was most likely Bf 110G-4 730006 D5+? of 2./NJG3, which crashed 5km west of Chievres, Belgium. The German pilot and Gefreiter Richard Reiff, who was wounded, both baled out safely. Obergefreiter Edmund Hejduck was killed.

280 Harold Brownlow Morgan Martin, born at Edgecliff, New South Wales on 27 February 1918, was probably the RAF's greatest exponent of low-level bombing. In Australia he had been pronounced unfit to fly because of asthma but he worked his passage to England, where he joined the RAF in 1940. Martin was commissioned in 1941 and he then served with 455 Squadron RAAF. He was transferred to 50 Squadron, with whom he flew a further 23 operations before being taken off operational flying and awarded the DFC. Chosen by Wing Commander Guy Gibson to join the newly formed 617 Squadron, Martin flew on the Dams raid on 16/17 May 1943 for which he was awarded the DSO. At the Möhne Dam Guy Gibson went in and sent his mine successfully bouncing up to the concrete wall, where it sank and exploded. The next two Lancasters missed. *M-Mother*, flown by Flight Lieutenant John V. 'Hoppy' Hopgood DFC* was shot out of the sky and his mine exploded on the powerhouse on the other side of the dam. Flight Lieutenant Mick Martin DFC RAAF in *P-Popsie* got his mine away but the dam held. The fourth and fifth hits by Squadron Leader Melvyn 'Dinghy' Young DFC* and Flight Lieutenant David J. H. Maltby finally breached the dam at 0056 hours. In January 1944 Martin was awarded a bar to his DSO. On 12/13 February 1944 in an attack by ten Lancasters of 617 Squadron with 12,000lb blockbusters on the Anthéor Viaduct, near Cannes on the coastal railway line leading to Italy. When running in to attack at under 200 feet through heavy fire, Martin's Lancaster was hit repeatedly. 'Bob' Hay his bomb aimer was killed and the engineer wounded. The bomb release was destroyed and the controls badly damaged. Martin's Lancaster got clear of the defenses and he succeeded in flying the crippled bomber back through severe electrical storms to Elmas Field at Cagliari in Sardinia, where he made an excellent landing in difficult circumstances. The sides of the valley were very steep and the viaduct was defended by guns which damaged both Martin's and Leonard Cheshire's low level aircraft. Martin was awarded a second bar to his DFC in November 1944. By the end of the war he was the only Australian airman to have won five British awards in the conflict. He was granted a permanent commission in 1945 and commanded 2nd TAF and RAF Germany from 1967 to 1970, retiring from the RAF in 1974 as Air Marshal Sir Harold Martin KCB DSO* AFC. He died on 3 November 1988.

281 Bf 110G-4 730036 G9+ER of 7./NJG1, was shot down by Flight Lieutenant R. J. Dix and Flying Officer A. J. Salmon of 169 Squadron at very low level around midnight. The 110 crashed near Balk in Friesland Province in Holland. Feldwebel Heinrich Karl Lahmann, the 25 year-old pilot, and Unteroffizier Günther Bouda, the 21-year old *bordschütz*, both baled out. Unteroffizier Willi Huxsohl, the 21-year-old radar operator, was killed. This same night two other NJG1 night fighters were lost. At 0125 hours Bf 110G-4 730117 G9+GR of 7./NJG1 was shot down north of Deelen airfield. Leutnant Josef Hettlich, pilot, Feldwebel Johann Treiber, radar operator and the *bordschütz* all baled out safely. (Flying Officers N. Veale and R. O. Comyn of 239 Squadron claimed a Bf 110 this night). The third Bf 110 lost was 441083 G9+GR of III./NJG1 or 7./NJG1, which was shot down at 0147 hours during landing at Leeuwarden airfield and which crashed at Rijperkerk north of the base. Hauptmann Siegfried Jandrey the 30-year-old pilot and Unteroffizier Johann Stahl, 25, radar operator, were killed. Unteroffizier Anton Herger (24) *bordschütz* was injured.

282 Ju 88G-1 713649 R4+KT of 9./NJG2, flown by Hauptmann August Speckmann, pilot (KIA), with Oberfeldwebel Wilhelm Berg, flight engineer (KIA), and Unteroffizier Otto Brüggenkamp, *bordschütz* (KIA) and Oberfeldwebel Arthur Boos, radar operator (WIA), was shot down over France. It was probably one of the Ju 88s destroyed by Gregory and Stephens and Harry White DFC* and Mike Allen DFC* of 141 Squadron.

283 On the night of 4/5 July when FB.VIs of 23 Squadron flew their first *intruder* operation with sorties against enemy airfields, 100 Group Mosquitoes shot down four enemy aircraft. Ju 88 751065 R4+2 of 5./NJG2 was shot down by Flying Officer P. G. Bailey and Flying Officer J. O. Murphy of 169 Squadron and it crashed near Chartres. Oberfeldwebel Fritz Earrherr, pilot and Ogefr Heinz Boehme, air gunner, were killed. Gefr Josef Schmid, radar operator, was WIA and baled out. Bf 110G-4 110028 C9+HK of 2./NJG5 crashed near Compeigne. It is believed that this was one of the two aircraft shot down this night by Squadron Leader J. S. Booth DFC* and Flying Officer K. Dear DFC of 239 Squadron. Leutnant Joachim Hanss, pilot and Feldwebel Kurt Stein, air gunner, were killed. Unteroffizier Wolfgang Wehrhan, radar operator, was wounded. Squadron Leader Graham J. Rice and Flying Officer Jimmy G. Rogerson of 141

Squadron meanwhile, had taken off from West Raynham at 2317 hours on a *Serrate* patrol in support of Bomber Command attacks on St Lou D'Esserent and Vaires. They returned with a claim for a Bf 110 destroyed approximately 8 miles northwest of Amiens at 0050 hours at 10,000 feet. On 20/21 July Bf 110G-4 730218 G9+EZ of 12./NJG1 was another victim of Wing Commander Neil Bromley and Philip Truscott of 169 Squadron. The aircraft crashed near Moll in Belgium. Oberfeldwebel Karl-Heinz Scherfling, the 25-year-old pilot, who was a *Ritterkreuztraeger* since 8 April 1922 and who had 33 night victories, was killed. So too was Feldwebel Herbert Winkler, the 31-year old air gunner. Feldwebel Herbert Scholz, the 25-year-old radar operator, baled out seriously injured. On the night of 23/24 July Bf 110G-4 730036 G9+ER of 7./NJG1, was shot down by Flight Lieutenant R. J. Dix and Flying Officer A. .J. Salmon of 169 Squadron at very low level around midnight. The 110 crashed near Balk in Friesland Province in Holland. Feldwebel Heinrich Karl Lahmann, the 25 year old pilot, and Unteroffizier Günther Bouda, the 21 year old air gunner, both baled out. Unteroffizier Willi Huxsohl, the 21-year-old radar operator, was killed. This same night two other NJG1 night fighters were lost. At 0125 hours Bf 110G-4 730117 G9+GR of 7./NJG1 was shot down north of Deelen airfield. Leutnant Josef Hettlich, pilot, Feldwebel Johann Treiber, radar operator and the air gunner all baled out safely. (Flying Officer N. Veale and Flying Officer R. O. Comyn of 239 Squadron claimed a Bf 110 this night). The third Bf 110 lost was 441083 G9+OR of III./NJG1 or 7./NJG1, which was shot down at 0147 hours during landing at Leeuwarden airfield and which crashed at Rijperkerk, just to the north of the base. Hauptmann Seigfried Jandrey (30) pilot and Unteroffizier Johann Stahl (25) radar operator, were killed. Unteroffizier Anton Herger, 24, air gunner, was injured. A Mosquito of 2nd TAF possibly shot down this aircraft. Pilot Officer Doug Gregory and Pilot Officer D. H. Stephens of 141 Squadron returned to West Raynham with a claim for one Ju 88 destroyed 'Gregory fired just 48 rounds to down the Ju 88. Doug Gregory and Stephens were airborne from West Raynham again on the night of 28/29 July for another stint at 'bashing the beacons' when the bombers' target was Stuttgart. They destroyed a Ju 88 16 miles NW of Metz. (Ju 88G-1 713649 R4+KT of 9./NJG2, flown by Hauptmann August Speckmann, pilot (KIA), with Oberfeldwebel Wilhelm Berg, flight engineer (KIA), and Unteroffizier Otto Brüggenkamp, air gunner (KIA) and Oberfeldwebel Arthur Boos, radar operator (WIA), was shot down over France. It was probably one of the two Ju 88s destroyed by Gregory and Stephens and Harry White DFC* and Mike Allen DFC* of 141 Squadron.

284 Turner and Francis' victim, which was brought down by 480 rounds of cannon fire, was Ju 88G-1 710542 D5+BR of 7./NJG3 flown by Leutnant Achim Woeste. He and Unteroffizier Anton Albrecht were KIA. Unteroffizier Heinz Thippe and Gefreiter Karl Walkenberger, who were both wounded in the action, baled out. The aircraft crashed near Mulsum, 42 kilometers east of Bremen. Turner adds, 'The large number of cannon rounds used was, in the main, due I fear to a feeling of extreme anger at the time. Just before take off I had read the Press reports of the discovery of the extermination ovens at Lubeck and I was so incensed that I was determined that any *Nazi* within range was not going to aid that war effort.'

285 Their victims – both of which crashed east of Arnhem, Holland - were Bf 110G-4 Wrk.Nr. 740358 G9+MY of 11./NJG1 (Unteroffiziers Walter Sjuts; Herbert Schmidt and Ernst Fischer were KIA) and Bf 110G-4 Wrk.Nr. 740757 G9+GZ of 12./NJG1. Unteroffiziers Heinz Gesse and Josef Kaschub and Obergefreiter Josef Limberg were KIA.

286 *Night Fighter* by C. F. Rawnsley & Robert Wright. Elmfield Press. Phillips and Smith failed to return on 6/7 November. They were investigating a radar contact and at the moment they got a visual on it and realized that it was a British bomber it opened fire and set one of the Mosquito's engines on fire. The next moment a He 219 came up behind them and shot them down. Phillips and Smith baled out. Captured, they spent the last six months of the war in *Stalag Luft I.* After they were released and had returned home Derek Smith died following an operation.

287 440384 G9+EN.

288 The 110 crashed at Birresborn in the Eifel at 2335 hours.

289 11./NJG1 lost Bf 110 G-4 740358 G9+MY when it was shot down east of Arnhem by Ginger Owen and Flying Officer McAllister DFM of 85 Squadron. Walter Sjuts and Unteroffiziers Herbert Schmidt and Ernst Fischer were killed. The same RAF crew also shot down Bf 110G-4 740757 G9+GZ of 12./NJG1 in the same area. Unteroffiziers Heinz Gesse and Josef Kaschub and Obergefreiter Josef Limberg were killed.

290 Their victim was Bf 110G-4 440384 G9+EN of 5./NJG1 piloted by Oberleutnant Gottfried Hanneck. The 110 crashed at Birresborn in the Eifel at 23.35 hours. Unteroffizier Erich Sacher, radar/radio op and Unteroffizier Willi Wurschitz, who on this sortie served as air gunner but normally was a radar operator, were killed in the crash. Hanneck was a very experienced pilot who served with various Luftwaffe units flying 40 different aircraft types for five years before he joined 5./NJGl at Deelen in April 1944. On his 4th operational sortie, on the night of 11 May 1944 he shot down his first RAF night bomber and had gone on to claim another five '4-Mots'.

291 On 17/18 September 11./NJG1 lost Bf 110 G-4 740358 G9+MY when it was shot down east of Arnhem by Flying Officer Alan G. 'Ginger' Owen DFM and Flying Officer J. S. V. McAllister DFM of 85 Squadron. Walter Sjuts, Unteroffizier Herbert Schmidt and Unteroffizier Ernst Fischer, were all killed. The same RAF crew also shot down Bf 110G-4 740757 G9+GZ of 12./NJG1 in the same area. Unteroffizier Heinz Gesse, Josef Kaschub and Obergefreiter Josef Limberg were all killed. Ginger Owen and Victor McAllister had joined 85 Squadron in July 1944 after a rest period after seeing action on Beaufighter IIIs on 600 'City of London' Squadron and after Ginger's brother Don had been killed while flying as a navigator with 85 Squadron from West Malling.

292 On 6/7 October Ju 88G-1 710639 D5+EV of 10./NJG3 was shot down by Flight Lieutenant Gallacher and Pilot Officer McLean of 141 Squadron. It crashed near Groningen. Oberleutnant Walter Briegleb, pilot, Unteroffizier Brandt, flight engineer, and Unteroffizier Braeunlich, air gunner, were WIA. Feldwebel Paul Kowalewski, radar operator, was killed. On 7/8 October, Flight Lieutenant Jimmy Mathews and Warrant Officer Alan "Penny" Penrose of 157 Squadron picked up a contact at six miles range west of Neumünster while on a high level support sortie. Mathews narrowed the range and as they got a visual at 1000 yards the target straightened out. It was recognized as a Me 410 with long range tanks. Mathews opened fire with a short burst from 100 yards dead behind. Strikes were seen and a small explosion occurred in the starboard engine. Another burst and the starboard engine caught fire. It dived burning to the ground and exploded. On the night of 19/20 October Squadron Leader 'Dolly' Doleman and Flight Lieutenant 'Bunny' Bunch DFC of 157 Squadron returned to Swannington from a High Level Support Patrol to Nuremberg with a claim for a Ju 88. Their possible victim was Ju 88G-1 714510 27+CM of 4./NJG6, which crashed at Murrhard SE of Heilbron, Germany. Unteroffizier Georg Haberer (pilot) KIA; Unteroffizier Ernst Dressel (radar op) KIA.

293 Their victim was Ju 88G-1 710639 D5+EV of 10./NJG3, which crashed near Groningen. Oberleutnant Walter Briegleb, pilot, Unteroffiziers Brandt, flight engineer and Bräunlich, air gunner were WIA. Feldwebel Paul Kowalewski the radar operator was killed.

294 Their victim was possibly Ju 88G-1 Wrk.Nr. 712312 2Z+EB of I./NJG6, which crashed at Vaihirgen/Marksdorf ENE of Pforzheim, Germany. Oberleutnant Wilhelm Engel (pilot) was WIA; radar operator safe.

295 Doleman and Bunch's possible victim was Ju 88G-1 714510 2Z+CM of 4./NJG6, which crashed at Murrhard SE of Heilbronn, Germany. Unteroffiziers Georg Haberer (pilot) and Ernst Dressel (radar op) were killed. The other 100 Group Mosquito victory in October was on the 15/16th when Flight Lieutenant C. K. Nowell and Warrant Officer Randall of 85 Squadron bagged a Bf 110.

296 L'Amie and Flying Officer Smith were killed on 21 November 1944.

297 The reason for the lack of success was a result of the *Nachtjagd* bringing *FuG 220 Lichtenstein SN-2* AI radar into service. It was not affected by Window and the *Serrate* homer fitted to the Mosquitoes was calibrated to the frequencies of the old *Lichtenstein* AI sets. For some time, *Serrate* crews had noticed on operations that the enemy night-fighters quickly took evasive action when picked up on AI radar. By May 1944, the majority of German night-fighters had been fitted with *SN-2* sets and backward-looking warning devices were introduced. When the frequency band of the SN-2 was discovered in June, work was at once started to develop a homer, later called *Serrate* Mk IV. (*Serrate* Mk IV would not be used operationally until January 1945.) The development of another homing device, *Perfectos,* was started in June 1944 and the first *Perfectos* operations were carried out in November. On 4/5 November two Bf 110s that were shot down probably fell to 100 Group Mosquito crews. Bf 110 of II./NJG1 was shot down at 1900 hours at a height of 20,000 feet. Unteroffizier Gustav Sario, pilot, was injured and baled out. Unteroffizier Hienrich Conrads, the radar operator and Ogefr Roman Talarowski, air gunner, were both killed. Another Bf 110 of II./NJG1 was shot down by Squadron Leader Branse Burbridge DSO* DFC* and Flight Lieutenant F. S. Skelton DSO* DFC* of 85 Squadron into the River Rhine near Hangelar airfield at 2150 hours. Oberleutnant Ernst Runze, pilot was killed and Ogefr Karl Heinz Bendfield, radar operator, baled out safely. Two other Bf 110s were also shot down this night. Bf 110G-4 440648 G9+RS of 8./NJG1 was possibly shot down by a Mosquito night fighter. It crashed at Bersenbrück, 30km north of Osnabrück, Germany. Feldwebel Willi Ruge, pilot was wounded and baled out. Unteroffizier Helmut Kreibohm, radar operator, and Ogefr Anton Weiss, air gunner, were both killed. Also shot down this night by a Mosquito was Leutnant Heinz Rolland, the 26-year-old pilot of IV./NJG1, who had 15 victories at night. Rolland, Feldwebel Heinz Krueger, 25 year old radar operator, and Unteroffizier Karl Berger, 22 year old air gunner, were all killed when their Bf 110 crashed SW of Wezel, Germany. On 6/7 November, two Ju 88G-6 aircraft were lost. 620396 R4+KR of Stab/IV./NJG3 was shot down by a Mosquito and crashed at Marienburghsn, Germany. Hauptmann Ernst Schneider, pilot, was killed. Oberfeldwebel Mittwoch, radar operator and Unteroffizier Kaase both baled out safely. 620583 R4+TS of 11./NJG3 was shot down in air combat and crashed SW of Paderborn. Oberleutnant Josef Foerster, pilot survived. Feldwebel Werner Moraing, radar operator, and Feldwebel Heinz Wickardt were both wounded. This same night Squadron Leader Dolly Doleman and Flight Lieutenant 'Bunny' Bunch DFC of 157 Squadron returned to Swannington in their NFXIX with a claim for a Bf 110 destroyed'

298 Stewart completed 50 trips on ops with 23 Squadron at Little Snoring and returned to Canada as an instructor, all before reaching the age of 21. The Stewart-Beaudet crew went to 45 enemy aerodromes, 36 of them in Germany.

Chapter 12: *"Ritterkreuz Height"* or Die!

299 Bf 110 of *II./NJG1* was shot down at 1900 hours at a height of 20,000 feet. Unteroffizier Gustav Sario, pilot, was injured and baled out. Unteroffizier Heinrich Conrads, the radar operator and Obergefreiter Roman Talarowski, air gunner, were both killed. Bf 110G-4 440648 G9+RS of 8./NJG1 crashed at Bersenbrück, 30 kilometers north of Osnabrück, Germany. Feldwebel Willi Ruge, pilot was wounded and baled out. Unteroffizier Helmut Kreibohm, radar operator and Obergefreiter Anton Weiss, air gunner were both killed. Also shot down this night by a Mosquito was Leutnant Heinz Rolland, the 26-year old pilot of IV./NJG1, who had fifteen victories at night. Rolland, Feldwebel Heinz Krueger, 25-year old radar operator, and Unteroffizier Karl Berger, 22-year old air gunner, were killed when their Bf 110 crashed SW of Wezel, Germany.

300 Although 100 Group Mosquitoes claimed six enemy aircraft this night it had been a sorry 24 hours for Bomber Command. Despite the actions of the Mosquito crews (239 Squadron and 157 Squadrons also destroyed an enemy aircraft apiece) and a Window *Spoof* by 100 Group, out of a combined 1081 sorties during the day (to Solingen) and night, thirty-one bombers were lost, the highest for some time.
Altogether, Squadron Leader Branse Burbridge DSO* DFC* and Bill Skelton DSO* DFC* destroyed 22 enemy aircraft before they finished their second tours early in 1945 and finished the war as the top-scoring night-fighter crew in the RAF. (Bob Braham and Wing Commander John Cunningham both destroyed nineteen enemy aircraft at night). Post-war, Branse Burbridge and Skelton left the RAF to study Theology at Oxford and Cambridge respectively. Burbridge became a lay preacher. Skelton read History and Theology at Trinity Hall and came under the influence of Launcelot Fleming, the Dean, a distinguished Royal Navy chaplain during the war and later Bishop of Norwich. Skelton, a moderate evangelical, completed his training for the ministry at Ridley Hall, Cambridge. From 1950 to 1952 he was a curate at Ormskirk, Lancashire, then returned to Cambridge as chaplain of Clare College.

301 Arthur Witt was KIA on a night training exercise with his pilot Flight Lieutenant T. W. Redfearn on 26/27 January 1945 near Oulton, Norfolk in a NF.XXX.

302 Two Ju 88G-6 aircraft were lost. 620396 R4+KR of Stab/IV./NJG3 was shot down by a Mosquito and crashed at Marienburghsn, Germany. Hauptmann Ernst Schneider, pilot, was killed. Oberfeldwebel Mittwoch, radar operator, and Unteroffizier Kaase both baled out safely. 620583 R4+TS of 11./NJG3 was shot down in air combat and crashed SW of Paderborn. Oberleutnant Josef Foerster, pilot survived. Feldwebels Werner Moraing, radar operator and Heinz Wickardt were both wounded.

303 On 11/12 November Flying Officers Ginger Owen and Victor McAllister DFM of 85 Squadron shot down a Fw 190 thirty miles SE of Hamburg and Flying Officer Jimmy Mathews DFC and Warrant Officer Penny Penrose of 157 Squadron claimed a Ju 88 'probable' a Bonn. Ju 88 Wrk.Nr. 712268 of 1./NJG4 crashed near Giessen. The pilot and radar operator baled out safely but Gefreiter Alfred Gräefer, *bordschütze,* was KIA.

304 On 2/3 December Captain Weisteen of 85 Squadron shot down Bf 110G-4 180382 of 12./NJG4, which had taken off from Bonninhardt at 2047 hours. It crashed at 2145 near Lippborg near Hamm. Leutnant Heinz-Joachim Sclage, pilot survived, but the other two were killed. Flight Lieutenant W. Taylor and Flying Officer J. N. Edwards of 157 Squadron shot down a German night fighter, possibly Ju 88 714819 3C+WL of 3./NJG4, which crashed at Rheine. Ofhr Erhard Pfisterhammer, pilot, Unteroffizier Wolfgang Sode, radar operator and the air gunner, were all WIA. On the night of 4/5 December there was a *spoof* on Dortmund while the Main Force attacked Heilbronn and Karlsruhe. German night fighters were sent to the *spoof* and they waited in the area for about 15 minutes for the attack to start. However, they found nothing but high intruders and their losses were high. On this night 100 Group Mosquitoes shot down five and probably destroyed another. Flight Lieutenant R. T. 'Dickie' Goucher and Flight Lieutenant C. H. 'Tiny' Bulloch of 85 Squadron destroyed two of them, while Flying Officer 'Ginger' Owen DFM and Flying Officer J. S. V. McAllister DFM, also of 85 Squadron, scored the squadron's 100th victory when they shot down Ju 88G-1 714152 of 6./NJG4, which crashed near Krefeld. Unteroffizier Wilhelm Schlutter, pilot, was wounded and Unteroffizier Friedrich Heerwagen, radar operator and Gefr Friedrich Herbeck, air gunner, were both killed. Captain Svein Heglund DFC* and Flying Officer Robert O. Symon of 85 Squadron returned to from Swannington this night from a High Level Support Patrol in the Karlsruhe area with a claim for a Bf 110 *near Rothenburg.* On 6/7 December Flight Lieutenant J. O. Mathews DFC and Warrant Officer A. Penrose DFC of 157 Squadron destroyed a Bf 110 and a Ju 88 (712268 of I./NJG4, which crashed near Giessen killing the air gunner, Gefreiter Alfred Graefer). Squadron Leader Dolly Doleman and Flight Lieutenant 'Bunny' Bunch DFC of 157 Squadron returned to Swannington with a Claim for one Bf 110 destroyed. Flight Lieutenant Edward R. Hedgecoe DFC and Flight Sergeant J. R. Whitham, who were attached to the Fighter Interception Unit, destroyed a 110 west of Munster, possibly Bf 110G-4 740078 G9+HZ of 12./NJG1, which crashed 10 kms NW of Handorf. This aircraft was flown by Hauptmann Hans-Heinz Augenstein, *St.Kapitan*, 12./NJG1, who was killed, along with Feldwebel Günther Stems, his radar operator. Augenstein had 46 night victories, including 45 RAF night bombers and had been awarded the Knight's Cross on 9 June 1944. Unteroffizier Kurt Schmidt, *bordschütze*, who was WIA, baled out successfully. Hedgecoe and Whitham destroyed two more Bf 110s on

the night of 12/13 December, when 100 Group shot down five more German night fighters, Squadron Leader Branse Burbridge DSO* DFC* and Flight Lieutenant F. S. Skelton DSO* DFC* of 85 Squadron added a Ju 88 and a Bf 110 to their rising score. The Ju 88 G-1 714530 of *6./NJG4*, crashed at Gütersloh airfield. Unteroffizier Heinrich Brune, pilot, Unteroffizier Emil Hoffharth, radar operator, and Unteroffizier Wolfgang Rautert, air gunner, were all killed. Wing Commander Beauchamp, DSO DFC, CO 157 Squadron flying with Flight Lieutenant Scholefield, returned to Swannington from a patrol in support of Bomber Command attacks on Essen with a claim for a Bf 110 damaged at Aschaffenburg.
Three Bf 110s were destroyed on the night of 17/18 December. On 18/19 December, Flight Lieutenant William Taylor and Flying Officer J.N. Edwards destroyed He 219A-O 190229 G9+GH of 1./NJG1. The *Uhu* (Owl) crashed at Suedlohn killing Unteroffizier Günther Heinze, radar operator. Unteroffizier Scheürlein, pilot, baled out safely. (Edwards was killed on 22 December during landing back at Swannington with Taylor). On the night of 22/23 December Swannington celebrated in huge style when 85 Squadron's Burbridge and Skelton shot down a Bf 110 and 'Ginger' Owen DFM and Flying Officer J.S.V. McAllister DFM scored a hat trick of victories, with two Ju 88s and a Bf 110. Ju 88 621441 27+HK of II./NJG6 crashed at Landstuhl killing Oberfeldwebel Max Hausser, pilot, Oberfeldwebel Fritz Steube, radar operator and Feldwebel Ernst Beisswenger, air gunner. Ju 88G-6 621436 2Z+DC also of II./NJG6, crashed at Lebach, north of Saarbrücken. Unteroffizier Werner Karau survived while the other two crew were killed. Squadron Leader Dolly Doleman and his navigator Flight Lieutenant 'Bunny' Bunch also returned to the Norfolk station with a claim for a Ju 88 destroyed.

305 The German night fighter was possibly Ju 88 714819 3C+WL of 3./NJG4, which crashed at Rheine. Oberfähnrich Erhard Pfisterhammer, pilot, Unteroffizier Wolfgang Sode, radar operator and the air gunner, were WIA.

306 Weisteen's victim was Bf 110G-4 180382 of 12./NJG4, which had taken off from Bonninhardt at 2047 hours. It crashed at 2145 near Lippborg near Hamm. Leutnant Heinz-Joachim Schlage, pilot survived, but Fiebig and Unteroffizier Kundmüller were killed.

307 Altogether 112 aircraft of 100 Group were aloft, including a Liberator of 223 Squadron, captained by Flight Lieutenant Haslie on the Squadron's first target patrol at Karlsruhe.

308 The Ju 88 G-1, Wrk Nr 714530 of *6.NJG4*, crashed at Gütersloh airfield. Unteroffizier Heinrich Brune (pilot); Unteroffizier Emil Hoffharth, *bordfunker*, and Unteroffizier Wolfgang Rautert, *bordschütze* were killed.

309 He 219A-O Wrk Nr 190229 G9+GH of 1/NJG1.

310 Doleman fired 52 SAPI and 48 HEI rounds to dispatch the enemy night fighter.

311 Ju 88 621441 27+HK of II./NJG6 crashed at Landstuhl killing Oberfeldwebel Max Hausser, pilot, Oberfeldwebel Fritz Steube, radar operator and Feldwebel Ernst Beisswenger, air gunner. Ju 88G-6 621436 2Z+DC also of II./NJG6, crashed at Lebach, north of Saarbrücken. Unteroffizier Werner Karau survived while the two other crew were killed

312 2nd TAF was also active this night with 139 Mosquitoes being dispatched on bombing attacks on targets in North and South-west Germany. One Mosquito was lost. Also, 37 Mosquitoes of the 2nd TAF patrolled the areas of Aachen, Arnhem and the Dutch Friesian Islands, and flew 'close support' sorties over the front lines. None of these Mosquitoes was lost and they shot down 2 Ju 87s, 2 Ju 188s, 1 Ju 88 and 1 Me 110. In addition they 'bagged' 50 trucks and 6 trains.

313 Flight Lieutenant Jimmy Mathews and Warrant Officer Alan Penrose of 157 Squadron blasted a Ju 88 of 5/NJG2 with a 1½ second burst, which resulted in the starboard engine bursting into flames. As it turned to port, three parachutes came out in quick succession and three bodies sailed to earth. The aircraft then spun down and crashed at Roermond three miles southwest of Köln.

314 Doleman fired 484 rounds of SAPI and HEI. One of their victims was Bf 110G-4 740162 G9+OT, flown by Hauptmann Heinz Strüning, *Ritterkreuz mit Eichenlaub* (Knight's Cross with Oak leaves), *Staffelkapitan* of *9./NJG1,* which was shot down at 2200 hours and crashed at Bergisch Gladbach/ Rheinland. The *bordfunker* and *bordschütze* baled out safely but the thirty-two year old ace, who had fifty-six night victories, was killed when he hit the tail of his 110. Strüning's body was found two months later. Luftwaffe losses included Bf 110 of *7/NJG1,* which crashed near Roermond killing the crew; one Ju 88 of 5/NJG2 which crashed near Roermond, one of the crew was killed, three became PoW's. This may have been the aircraft claimed by Mathews & Penrose of 157 Squadron. One Ju 88 of *5/NG1* crashed south of Afferden, one KIA, two MIA, one PoW.

315 Their victim was He 219A-2 290194 G9+KL of 3./NJG1 crashed at Schleiden, fifty kilometers SW of Cologne. Oberleutnant Heinz Oloff, pilot, and Feldwebel Helmut Fischer, radar operator who were WIA, both baled out and survived. Oloff was shot down and killed by Flight Lieutenant G. C. Chapman and Flight Sergeant J. Stockley of 85 Squadron on the night of 20/21March 1945.

316 621364 27+CP of 5./NJG6. Oberleutnant Hans Steffen, pilot and Unteroffiziers Josef Knon, Helmut Uttler and Friedrich Krebber, were killed.

317 Harry White was promoted Squadron Leader and became A Flight Commander. He remained with 141 until it disbanded at Little Snoring in September 1945.

318 It was Heglund's 15th and final victory of the war. He finished the war as the top scoring Norwegian pilot with 15 and one shared victories.

319 It crashed at five kilometers south of Wesendorf. Oberfeldwebel Josef Stroelein, pilot, was killed. Unteroffizier Kenne, radar operator, baled out safely. Ju 88 620513 R4+CD of III./NJG2 is possibly the aircraft shot down by Flight Lieutenant A. S. Briggs and Flying Officer Rodwell of 515 Squadron. It crashed at Jägel airfield. Oberleutnant Bruno Heilig, pilot, Unteroffizier Günther Kulas, radar operator, Gefreiter Johan Goliasch, flight engineer, and Obegefreiter Horst Jauernig, air gunner, were killed.

320 169 Squadron flew its first NF.XIX operation on 21 January This same night 239 Squadron operated NF.XXX Mosquitoes for the first time.

321 Their victim was possibly Ju 88G-1 710818 D5+EP of *Stab/NJG3*, which crashed 3 kilometers SE of Friedberg, north of Frankfurt. Oberfeldwebel Johann Fels, pilot, Unteroffizier Richard Zimmer, radar operator and Gefreiter Werner Hecht, *bordschütze*, were killed.

322 Vaughan expended sixty-two SAPI and 56 HEI to destroy the Owl, which was 85 Squadron's fourth and final victory during the month.

323 Tommy Smith was treated at Fassberg sick quarters. The Germans confirmed his destruction of the two 109s he had shot at and also credited him with another 109 which spun in due to the presence of the intruding Mosquito. It crashed and burnt out, killing the pilot. Tommy stayed at Fassberg for a month before being transferred to *Dulag Luft* at Frankfurt for another month. He was bombed out by the RAF then transferred to Homemark, a convent hospital being used for RAF PoWs. On 28 March 1945, he and the other inmates were released by the US 3rd Army and flown home from Paris. At the PoW reception center at RAF Cosford, his assorted burns were treated in hospital. After discharge he was given a posting to Fighter Command HQ at Bentley Priory where the 'Prang Basher' once again took up crash investigation duties. When it came to demob he was invalided out of the RAF and sent to East Grinstead for further plastic surgery. It was there that he met a nursing sister who was to become his wife. Her name was Joy. After the war, a Feldwebel, who had befriended Tommy when he was blind, sent him photos of Cockayne's grave. It showed Tommy's grave, on the left, waiting for him! Tommy adds, 'The Huns were a tidy-minded lot and would have put the two of us alongside each other. Luckily I was "late for my own funeral".'

324 The first ground units of 100 Group were established on the continent at Wenduine, Belgium during January.

325 In Bf 110G-4 730262 G9+CN.

326 It is believed that Hanneck's adversary was either a 157 or 239 Squadron Mosquito. Squadron Leader Ryall and Pilot Officer Mulroy of 157 Squadron claimed a Bf 110 "probable" at Oberolm, while Wing Commander Walter Gibb DSO DFC and Flying Officer R.C. Kendall DFC of 239 Squadron destroyed a Bf 110 at Mannheim.

327 Mellows fired 72 rounds of SAPI and 68 rounds of HEI to down the Bf 110, probably Bf 110 730370 2Z+EL of 3./NJG6, which crashed 25 kms south of Stuttgart. Oberleutnant Willy Rathmann, pilot, Feldwebel Erich Berndt, radar operator and Ogefr Alfred Obry, air gunner were killed. Howard had fired 80 rounds of HEI and 80 round SAPI on the sortie. One of the downed aircraft, Bf 110 480164 C9+ of 5./NJG5, crashed near Bodenbach in the Frankfurt area. Feldwebel Heinrich Schmidt, pilot, Unteroffizier Erich Wohlan, radar operator and Unteroffizier Adam Zunker, air gunner were killed. 239 Squadron crews were prominent on the night of 7/8 February when the Main Force targets was Cleve.and Hussum. Flight Lieutenant O. A. O. Cather DFM and Flight Sergeant L. J. S. Spicer BEM shot down Bf 110G-4 730322 G9+HR of 7./NJG1, which crashed west of Soest in the Ruhr. Feldwebel Heinz Amsberg, pilot and Unteroffizier Matthias Oengs, radar operator were killed, while Gefreiter Karl Kopperberg, air gunner, who was WIA, baled out. Flight Lieutenant A. J. Holderness and Flight Lieutenant Walter Rowley DFC meanwhile, returned to West Raynham after a patrol in the Dressel area with a claim for a Bf 110. On the night of 13/14 February when the bombers' targets were Dresden and Leipzig, Flight Lieutenant Donald R. 'Podge' Howard DFC and Flying Officer 'Sticky' Clay DFC who were attached to the BSDU at Swanton Morley to evaluate AI.Mk.X and *Serrate IV* returned after a very eventful patrol of beacons *Kolibri, Ida, Elster, Nachtigall* and *Otto.* They put in claims for two Bf 110s shot down near Beacon *Kolibri.*

328 Bates was twenty-three years old and Cadman, the son of Major William H. Cadman MBE of nearby Redenhall, Norfolk was just twenty-two. Both men are buried at Hanover War Cemetery Apart from the air-to-air victory they had destroyed one locomotive, damaged three more, and damaged a ship and a train.

329 Flight Lieutenant D. A. D. Cather DFM and Flight Sergeant L. J. S. Spicer BEM shot down Bf 110G-4 730322 G9+HR of 7./NJG1, which crashed west of Soest in the Ruhr. Feldwebel Heinz Amsberg, pilot, and Unteroffizier Matthias Dengs, radar operator were killed, while Gefreiter Karl Kopperberg, air gunner, who was WIA, baled out.

330 Podge Howard fired 80 rounds of HEI and 80 rounds of SAPI on the sortie. One of the downed aircraft, Bf 110 480164 C9+ of 5./NJG5, crashed near Bodenbach in the Frankfurt area. Feldwebel Heinrich Schmidt, pilot, Unteroffiziers Erich Wohlan, radar operator and Adam Zunker, air gunner were killed.

331 13 Halifaxes, 9 Lancasters, a B-17 and Mosquito XIX MM6l0/H of 169 Squadron flown by Squadron Leader V. J. Fenwick and Flying Officer J. W. Pierce who were returning from a bomber support sortie to Kamen were shot down. Five of these aircraft crashed in Norfolk. The Mosquito crashed at The Avenue, Buxton, Norfolk. Both crew were killed.

332 Altogether, 33 Ju 88G night intruders were lost during *Gisela.* Five Luftwaffe aircraft crashed on British soil and eight other crews were reported missing. Three more crews perished in crashes on German territory, six crews baled out due to lack of fuel and eleven crashed on landing.

333 The first two, both Ju 88s, occurred on the night of 5/6 March and both were credited to Wing Commander Walter Frame Gibb DSO DFC the CO and Flying Officer R. C. 'Killer' Kendall DFC. They made quite sure of their claim to the fiftieth by destroying two Ju 88s. The first, Ju 88G-6 622319 C9+GA of Stab/NJG5 flown by Oberstleutnant Walter Borchers, which crashed near Altenburg, 25 kilometers NW of Chemnitz. Borchers, *Ritterkreuzträger* (29 October 1944), *Kommodore*, NJG5, a 59 victory ace of which 16 had been scored by day and 43 by night, and his radar operator, Leutnant Friedrich Reul were killed. The second Ju 88 to fall to Gibb's guns was Ju 88G-6 622318 C9+NL of 3./NJG5, which also crashed near Chemnitz. Unteroffizier Hans Dorminger, pilot, Max Bartsch and Friedrich Rullman and Obergefreiter Franz Wohlschloegel were killed.

334 Heath fired 200 rounds of 20-mm cannon (fifty rounds per cannon).

335 Hauptmann Baake, pilot and *Kommandeur* of I./NJG1 and his radar operator, Unteroffizier Bettaque baled out safely.

336 Chapman and Stockley landed back at Swannington at 0652 hours to claim a Bf 110 and He 219 destroyed. The He 219V14 190014, of 3./NJG1 was flown by Oberleutnant Heinz Oloff, *Staffel Kapitan,* 3./NJG1. It will be remembered that Mellows and Drew shot down Oloff on the night of 31 December/1 January 1945.

337 Napalmgel came in three different consistencies - thick, medium and thin. Winnie Winn carried out two further trials over West Raynham's grass expanses, on 12 and 13 April, in front of large audiences. As a result of the trials, it was discovered that the thick gel failed to ignite.

338 The American 8th Air Force also used Napalm for the first time on 15 April. Nearly 850 Flying Fortresses and B-24 Liberators dropped more than 460,000 gallons of it in 75-85 gallon liquid-fire tanks along with more than 6000 100lb conventional incendiaries on 22 German gun batteries along the east bank of the Gironde estuary at Point de Grave in the Royan area, which was denying the Allies the use of the port of Bordeaux. Each napalm tank was about 8 feet long and one and a half feet in diameter and when it exploded it covered an area of 60 square yards, taking the oxygen out of the air and destroying everything.

339 Seven 141 Squadron Mosquitoes each carrying two 100-gallon drop tanks filled with napalm, eight Mosquitoes of 169 Squadron from Great Massingham, four Mosquito IVs of 23 Squadron and four of 515 Squadron from Little Snoring and one 141 Squadron aircraft for high-level AI.Mk.X patrol over the target. The eight Mosquitoes from 23 and 515 Squadrons and the eight Mosquitoes of 169 Squadron were to drop flares and HE on München/Neubiberg with 141 adding to the destruction.

340 Miller and Squadron Leader Wright both returned to Great Massingham with a tank hung up but landed safely. On 28 June Miller lost an engine near Bircham Newton. He extinguished the fire and put down at Great Massingham where he overshot and crashed. He and his navigator were unhurt. Immediately afterwards. Miller jumped into his car, and headed for London where he proceeded to score 56 not out at Lords!

341 On the afternoon of 6 May Flight Sergeants Williams and Rhoden crashed on a cross-country training flight at Devil's Dyke (Spitalgate) near Brighton. Both men were killed. They were 169 Squadron's final casualties of the war. With Hitler dead and the European war over, celebrations got into full swing before crews began training for the Japanese war or got demobbed or transferred to other duties in the service.

Chapter 13: 2nd TAF and the German Winter of Discontent

342 Luma was born in Helena, Montana, on 27 August 1922. After joining the RCAF he was posted to England in January 1943, where after a sorting-out process, through some sort of error or mix-up, Luma received an exceptionally high grade in a night-vision test. As a result, he was assigned to night intruders, though at the time he had no idea what a night intruder was. At 60 OTU he learned to fly the Mosquito and practised air-to-air gunnery and air-to-ground gunnery. After several weeks at OTU intruder trainees were instructed to informally pair off into crews. Colin Finlayson, a Canadian from British Columbia and Luma agreed to crew up together. While at OTU Luma decided to transfer to the US Army Air Forces. The official policy at the time, agreed to by the Americans and British, was that a crew would not be broken up, so after he was sworn in as a 1st Lieutenant he was permitted to return to the RCAF to finish his tour of operations before returning to the USAAF. Luma was a USAAF pilot on detached duty with the RCAF. After finishing OTU Luma and Fin were assigned to 418 (City of Edmonton) Squadron RCAF.

343 9 other Mosquito victories went to 29 Squadron crews in NF.XII HK197 and NF.XII HK168 who got a Fw 190 and a Ju 88 respectively S of Beachy Head. NFXII 'N' of 85 Squadron destroyed a Ju 88 off Rye. Warrant Officer H. K. Kemp-Flight Sergeant J. R. Maidment of 151 Squadron in NF.XII HK193 got He 177A-5 Wk Nr 15747 of I/KG40 which crashed at Whitmore Vale, nr Hindhead, Surrey, the first He 177 to be shot down over the British Isles. Sub-Lieutenant J. A. Lawley-Wakelin-Sub-Lieutenant H. Williams of 96 Squadron in NF.XIII HK414 destroyed a Ju 88 at Paddock Wood Stn. Flight Lieutenant N. S. Head-Flying Officer A. C. Andrews of 96 Squadron in NF.XIII HK372 claimed 2 Ju 88 'probables' S of Bexhill and another 96 Squadron crew in NF.XIII HK425 got a Ju 88 at Tonbridge. Flying Officer C. K. Nowell-Flight Sergeant F. Randall of 85 Squadron in a NFXI destroyed He 177A-3 of 2./KG40 6m SE of Hastings. Flight Lieutenant J. A. S. Hall-Flying Officer J. P. W. Cairns of 488 Squadron in NF.XIII HK380/Y destroyed a Do 217M-1 13 miles off Dungeness and a Ju 88A-14 at Sellindge, Kent.

344 KIA 4.1.45.

345 A cousin of Wing Commander Bell-Irving.

346 The Honorable Michael J. Wedgewood-Benn DFC at 22, was the eldest of three sons of William Wedgwood Benn DSO DFC Ld-H (*Legion d'Honeur*) and CdG (*Croix de Guerre*), a WWI veteran pilot and prominent politician who was created Viscount Stansgate on 22.12.40.

347 One of the great RAF navigators in WWII, after fighting in the French 61st Regiment of Artillery in WWI and at the beginning of WWII Livry-Level DSO DFC* CdG* DFC (USA) did at least four tours of operational flying in Coastal Command, on special duties and in 2 Group Mosquitoes. He could not be persuaded to have a break from operational flying. On 31 August 1944 'Buck' Taylor and his navigator, Flight Lieutenant Johnson were shot down on a *Night Intruder* to Strasbourg-Sarreborg when they attacked a train. Flak set fire to their port engine and the wing collapsed. They baled out and evaded capture, returning to England on 29 September 1944. Taylor rejoined 21 Squadron on 28 October after a spell in the RAF Hospital, Swindon. By January 1945 Squadron Leader Taylor DFC* Ld-H CdG* MiD had flown a total of 48 low level day and night bombing sorties.

348 *Bommen Vielen Op Hengelo* by Henk F. van Baaren, translated into English in *The Mossie* Vol. 16 April 1997.

349 A native of Montreal, Donald Aikins MacFadyen joined the RCAF in May 1940. His first score came whilst flying FB.VIs with 418 (City of Edmonton) Squadron RCAF when he was awarded a 'probable' on 22/23 December 1943 against a UEA. MacFadyen followed this up in early 1944 with the destruction of a Me 410, a Ju 52/3m and five V1s. Promoted to squadron leader. MacFadyen joined 406 'Lynx' Squadron in November 1944, where he flew the NF.XXX on *Night Intruders*. He was awarded a DFC and bar, an American DFC and the DSO during his two tours, and he finished the war with a tally of seven aircraft and five V1s destroyed in the air and five aircraft destroyed, one probable and seventeen damaged on the ground.

350 Kipp was awarded the DFC in May 1944 and a DSO in July while Huletsky was awarded the DFC and bar. By 14 June they had scored ten aircraft and one shared destroyed, one shared probable and one damaged plus 7 destroyed on the ground and 8 damaged on the ground. At the end of June 1944 they were posted to ADGB HQ and were later posted to the Fighter Experimental Flight at Ford, where they remained until July 1945, seeing more action during March-July that year and scoring several ground victories. Kipp returned to Canada and was released in October 1945. He rejoined the RCAF a year later but was killed in a flying accident in a DH Vampire at St Hubert on 25 |July 1949. *Aces High: A Tribute to the Most Notable Fighter Pilots of the British and Commonwealth Forces in WWII*. Christopher Shores and Clive Williams (Grub Street London 1994)

351 During April-May 1944 418 (City of Edmonton) Squadron RCAF shot down 30 enemy aircraft in the air and destroyed a further 38 aircraft on the ground. 418 scored their 100th victory in May and in June flew anti-*Diver* patrols at night.

352 Scherf left the service in April 1945 to return to the family ranch but found it difficult to settle back to civilian life, starting to drink heavily. He was killed in a car accident on 13 July 1949. *Aces High: A Tribute to the Most Notable Fighter Pilots of the British and Commonwealth Forces in WWII*. Christopher Shores and Clive Williams (Grub Street London 1994)

353 Starr had taken command of the squadron on 11 April after a successful career with 23 Squadron in the Mediterranean where he had destroyed two Ju 88s and damaged two other aircraft. On 6/7 May he scored his first victory for the 'County of Warwick' Squadron by destroying a Bf 110 at St. Dizier airfield for this third kill overall.

354 Starr destroyed a Me 410 and a UEA in 1944 to take his final score to 6 destroyed, 1 probable, 2 damaged, 2 destroyed on the ground + 1 V1 destroyed. Starr was killed early in January 1945 when he was flying as a passenger aboard an Avro Anson, which crashed nr Dunkirk killing everyone on board. He was en route to get married at the time.

355 Flying Officer Pearce and Flying Officer Moore in a 409 Squadron NF.XIII claimed a 'probable'. The only Mosquito kill was by Flying Officer R. E. Lelong RNZAF and Pilot Officer J. A. McLaren, of 605 Squadron in a FB.VI who destroyed a Me 410 7 miles SE of Evreux airfield.

356 On 6/7 June Flight Lieutenant E. L. Williams DFC of 605 Squadron in a FB.VI shot down a Ju 88 at Orleans-Bricy airfield. Flight Lieutenant Don MacFadyen DFC RCAF and Flight Lieutenant 'Pinky' Wright, of 418 (City of Edmonton) Squadron RCAF, flying HR155, destroyed a Ju 52/3m north of Coulommiers airfield. Wing Commander Keith M. Hampshire DSO, CO, 456 Squadron RAAF and Flight Lieutenant T. Condon, in NF.XVII HK286, destroyed a He 177 three miles east of Barfleur. Flight Lieutenant Allison and Flying Officer Stanton of 29 Squadron destroyed a Ju 52/3m and an UEA over Coulommiers. 604 Squadron alone destroyed ten aircraft on 7 and 8 June (on 6 August 604 became the first fighter squadron to move to France.) On 7/8 June when Mosquito night fighters shot down eight enemy aircraft over France 456 Squadron destroyed four He 177s and three more on the 8th. On 8/9 June Flight Lieutenant J. C. I. Hooper DFC and Flying Officer Hubbard DFM of 604 Squadron, in NF.XIII MM500, destroyed a Bf 110 NE of Laval and Flying Officer Wigglesworth and Sergeant Blomfield of 29 Squadron downed a Ju 88. On the night of the 9/10th, 29 Squadron destroyed two more enemy aircraft and 409 and 410 Squadrons destroyed two Ju 188s. 456 Squadron shot down a He 177 and a Do 217. (On 5 July the Australians claimed three enemy aircraft to bring its score to 30 victories since 1 March). By the end of June the night-fighters and fighter-bombers of 85 Base Group had destroyed 76 enemy aircraft and claimed five probables. In June 264 Squadron claimed 16 A/C destroyed, one probable and three damaged all in the vicinity of the beaches. On 19/20 June Squadron Leader F. J. A. Chase and Flying Officer A. P. Watson destroyed a Ju 88 over the Channel. July opened well and 264 Squadron claimed six more destroyed by the 14th with a probable and a couple damaged. On the night of the 14th 264 changed over from the Beachhead patrols to defensive patrols against flying bombs. A very busy fortnight followed, during which they destroyed 19 - no mean feat with the lack of speed superiority by the Mosquito. Flying Officer P. del Brooke distinguished himself by getting six. His final score was 53 V1s destroyed. On 26 July 264 Squadron moved to Hunsdon, while 142 Wing, who had recently taken over from 141, went on ahead to France.

357 The FB.VIs of 21, 464 and 487 Squadrons in 140 Wing, 2nd TAF were to remain at Thorney Island until December 1944 when the Australian and New Zealand squadrons both sent advance detachments to Rosières-en-Santerre, France. At Lasham meanwhile, 2nd TAF's other Mosquito fighter-bomber wing – 138 - comprised 107, 305 (Polish) and 613 Squadrons, which late the previous year had re-equipped with FB.VIs after flying Bostons, Mitchell IIs and Mustangs respectively. It was planned to transfer 138 Wing to airfields in France when the outbreak from the Normandy beachhead came. 2nd TAF was further strengthened early in 1944 85 (Base) Group was formed for the purpose of providing fighter cover over the continent leading up to and after, *D-Day*. 85 Group was created by the transfer from Fighter Command of 29, 264, 409 'Nighthawk' Squadron RCAF, 410 'Cougar' Squadron RCAF, 488 Squadron RNZAF and 604 Squadrons. The first Mosquito fighter squadron to transfer to 85 Group was 264 Squadron, in January 1944, which went to 141 Wing. (The last, 219 Squadron - would transfer from Fighter Command to 147 Wing on 28 August). As part of the newfound offensive, the main work for the NF.XIIs and NF.XIIIs of 85 Group and the FB.VIs of 138 and 140 Wings was *Day* and *Night Ranger* operations and *intruder* sorties from England.

358 Two 604 Squadron Mosquito crews claimed a probable Fw 190 near Carentan and a He 177. 25 miles SE of Caen Flight Lieutenant Walter G. 'Dinny' Dinsdale RCAF and Pilot Officer Jack E. Dunn RCAF of 410 Squadron RCAF in NF.XIII HK476/O were the first crew to shoot down a *Mistel* (Mistletoe) (piggy-back Bf 109 and a bomb-laden Ju 88) (*Vater und Sohn*) of KG101. Off Normandy Flight Lieutenant J. H. Corre and Pilot Officer C. A. Bines of 264 Squadron in NF.XIII HK502 also shot down one of the guided bombs. Squadron Leader I. A. March and Flight Lieutenant Eyolfson of 410 Squadron in a NF.XIII, a Ju 88. Squadron Leader Robert A. Kipp DFC RCAF and Flight Lieutenant P. Huletsky RCAF of 418 (City of Edmonton) Squadron RCAF in a FB.VI, a He 111 S end Bagenkop Isle. Flying Officer Peter F. L. Hall and Flying Officer R. D. Marriott of 488 Squadron in NF.XIII MM513/D destroyed a Ju 88 10m SW St Lô.

359 Bannock was a pre-war civilian pilot and had been an instructor and ferry pilot until finally getting a posting to England in February 1944. After completing a Mosquito OTU course at High Ercall and Greenwood, Nova Scotia he joined 418 (City of Edmonton) Squadron RCAF at Holmsley South in May. 418 Squadron had been engaged in *Night Intruding* against enemy airfields as well as conducting low level *Day Rangers* against airfields when operating in pairs. While at Greenwood he teamed up with navigator, Robert Bruce, who recalls. 'In 1939 I was a graduate of Edinburgh University with a first in Music, a brilliant outlook and no money. Deeply influenced by the poetry of Wilfred Owen, who was KIA in November 1918, I joined the Friends Ambulance Unit (as gallant a bunch as any military). But after 2½ years I knew the war was ruinous and I must be part of the ruin. I was accepted for aircrew training. I was almost 28. Russ on the other hand was young in years - 23 - and old in flying experience and leadership. I arrived at Holmsley South about the 10th of June, Russ a few days earlier.' Bannock and Bruce went on to destroy 8 more e/a and 18 and 1 shared V1s.

360 Topham had been awarded a Ju 88 probable on 15/16 August 1940 flying the Blenheim If on 219 Squadron. He and Berridge destroyed nine enemy aircraft flying Beaufighters on the squadron during 1941-42. Topham scored his 10th victory of the war with 125 Squadron on 26/27 April 1944 (a Ju 88) and he damaged a Me 410 on 27/28 May. He was awarded the DSO in September 1944.

361 *Terror in the Starboard Seat* by Dave McIntosh.

362 On 28 June Wing Commander 'Daddy' Dale and other squadron personnel attended Mike Benn's funeral. As soon as he heard he news William Wedgwood Benn, who was also in the RAF at that time with the Allied Control Commission in Italy, returned home. Mike's younger brother Anthony who was training as a pilot in Rhodesia at the time received a telegram reporting his brother's death. Tony Benn became a Sub-lieutenant in the RNVR but the war ended before he could see action. De-mobbed in 1946, he became Viscount Stansgate upon the death of his father but later renounced the title to become the well-known Labour politician.

363 MM466.

364 Jamie had flown Beaufighter IIs and VIs in 125 Squadron and had his first combat during night raids on Cardiff and Swansea in the summer of 1942. After a Heinkel 111 had bombed his own airfield, Jamie pursued the enemy aircraft and shot it down into the Bristol Channel. He landed to find that the bombs had killed the WAAF fiancée of his squadron friend. In August Jamie destroyed another He 111 and while on detachment in the Shetlands he claimed a Ju 88 as "damaged" although later information indicated that the bomber had crashed on landing at Stavanger. He was credited with the destruction of a Do 217 on 11/12 February 1943 and he then went on "rest", becoming a gunnery instructor. In January 1944 he joined 488 Squadron, which lost nine crews in flying accidents for just two enemy aircraft destroyed. Morale was very low and although Jameson and Crookes patrolled night after night along the East coast, very little activity had come their way.

365 In July the six Mosquito fighter squadrons in 2nd TAF shor down 55 enemy aircraft and claimed two probables. In July 1944 NF.XVIIs of 219 Squadron in Fighter Command based at Bradwell Bay shot down six Ju 88/188s in and around the beachhead. Flying Officer D. T. Tull got two of them. In August 77 enemy aircraft were destroyed in the air by the seven night-fighter and fighter-bomber squadrons. On 1/2 August Canadians Squadron Leader James D. Somerville and Flying Officer G. D. Robinson of 410 Squadron RCAF in NF.XIII MM477/'U' equipped with AI VIII shot down of a Ju 88 NE of Tessy at 0100 hours. The night following, 2/3 August 1944, Squadron Leader F. J. A. Chase and Flying Officer A. F. Watson of 264 Squadron got their 5th enemy aircraft since *D-Day* when they destroyed a Ju 188 (or 88) 10m west of Argentan. Somerville and Robinson in MM477/U scored their third victory when they shot down a Do 217 6 miles NW of Pontorson at 2255 hours. On the night of 6/7 August Somerville and Robinson in NF.XIII MM566/'R' equipped with AI VIII shot down a Ju 88 at St Hilaire to take their personal victory score to four. On the night of 14/15 August Squadron Leader Somerville DFC and Flying Officer G. D. Robinson DFC of 410 Squadron RCAF in NF.XIII MM477/'U' equipped with AI VIII got their fifth victory, a Ju 88 15 miles due West of Le Havre. Somerville was promoted to wing commander and given command of 409 Squadron RCAF.

366 Flying Officer William Wright Provan, another 29 Squadron pilot.

367 In 1938 Bob Stainton had been a brilliant captain of the Sussex cricket team.

368 George Allison was killed on 22 July on the squadron's first *Day Ranger*. His navigator Sub Lieutenant (A) C. W. Porter FAA also died.

369 In fact, the soldiers clubbed to death were a reconnaissance party of the SAS, code-named '*Bulbasket*', who were dropped south-west of Châteauroux on 5 June to harass the *2nd SS Panzer Division* on its move from Toulouse to Normandy. The main party was dropped on 11/12 June and joined up with the Maquis. On 3 July their main camp in the Foret de Verrieres was attacked by German troops. Nine SAS members got away but 31 SAS and Lieutenant Tom Stevens, a USAAF evader who had joined them, were taken prisoner. One officer was wounded before capture and was tied to a tree and publicly beaten to death in Verrieres. Three SAS prisoners were also wounded and taken to hospital in Poitiers, where they were given lethal injections. The remainder, including the American and two other SAS captured previous to this engagement, were shot in the Foret de Saint Sauvant near the village of Rom. The German unit responsible for this atrocity was believed to be the 158th Security Regiment from Poitiers. The SAS survivors signalled the UK with the information of their disaster and that the unit responsible was billeted at Bonneuil Matours.

370 Wing Commander R. H. Reynolds DSO DFC led the four FB.VIs of 487 Squadron.

371 Wing Commander Reid and Flight Lieutenant Peacock of 409 Squadron in NF.XIII MM587 got a Ju 88 while Flying Officer D. T. Tull of 219 Squadron in a NF.XVII got a Ju 88 50 miles ENE La Havre for his 4th victory. Tull's first victory was a He 219 on 3/4. June 1944 (He 219) followed by a Me 410 (7/8. June 1944) Ju 88 (11/12 July 1944). Posted to the FIU he scored 4 more kills, 3 on Mosquitoes (Ju 88 11/12 September 1944, Bf 110 23/24 September 1944, Ju 88G 14/15 October 1944) He 111 flying a Beaufighter VI on 25/26 October 1944. He and navigator Flying Officer P. J. Cowgill DFC were KIA on 18/19 December 1944.

372 2nd TAF decided that rather than have all its fighter units flying tactical reconnaissance, its three recce Wings should each contain a PR unit. B Flight of 4 Squadron in 35 Wing (84 Group) and A Flight of 400 Squadron RCAF in 39 Wing (83 Group) therefore received PR XVIs for the role. At the end of May 1944 both flights reverted back to Spitfire IXs but 140 Squadron, operating in 34 PR Wing (HQ), retained all its PR XVIs, which they had equipped with *Gee* and *Rebecca* so as to fly long-range blind night photography operations, first from Northolt, and later, the continent.

373 140 Squadron provided photo coverage throughout the winter of 1944-45, moving to France in September to keep in touch with the action. In January 1945 Flight Lieutenant Kirk got a new navigator, Flight Lieutenant Anthony Guy Humphryes, who was the unit's navigation leader. Kirk recalls. 'We did 17 operations together. Our best joint effort was on the night of 24 February, when were sent to photograph the railway sidings at Monchengladbaeh. We approached the target three times. Each time, just as we were set to release the flashes, the "natives" were decidedly hostile. Lots of little red balls kept coming up at us, starring off apparently quite slowly, then, as they got nearer, whizzing very rapidly by. I didn't think we'd get very good pictures while all this was going on. We had a moment's consultation as to how best to cope with the situation. 'I decided to do the run in reverse. I asked Tony to navigate us to the far end of the run and give me a reciprocal course to steer. He put his skills to work, and at the correct moment we turned onto the target, straightened up, and raced over the marshalling yard. Down went the flashes one after another, going off like bolts of summer lightning. We didn't mind the gunners shooting at our tail as we left. Perhaps the million candlepower flashes put them off a bit! Next morning, the photos delighted the interpreters, as well as Tony and I. This night, added to our other efforts, earned us a DFC each.'

374 "Jamie" Jameson died aged 76 in a bulldozer accident in 1998.

375 Bergmann's Bf 110G-4 Wrk Nr 140320 3C+CS probably shot down by Flight Lieutenant John C. Surman and Pilot Officer C. E. Weston of 604 Squadron in Mosquito NF.XIII MM449/B who also claimed 2 Do 217s. (Only in 1956, Bergmann's badly burnt remains, which had been recovered from a crash site nr. St. James in mid-August 1944, were formally identified. Since then, the *Nachtjagd Experte* rests in the large German military cemetery of Marigny, Manche). Flight Lieutenant A. E. Browne-Warrant Officer T. F. Taylor of 488 Squadron in NF.XIII HK420 destroyed a Ju 188 SW of Avranches and also claimed two UEA, which flew into ground trying to evade. Other 604 Squadron victories went to: Flying Officer R. M. T. MacDonald-Flight Sergeant C. G. Baird in NF.XIII MM500, a Ju 188 and Wing Commander F. D. Hughes DFC**-Flight Lieutenant L. Dixon DFC* in NF.XIII MM465 a Ju 88 S Avranches and Flight Lieutenant P. G. K. Williamson DFC RAAF-Flying Officer F. E. Forrest of 219 Squadron in a NF.XXX a Ju 188 in the Argentan area and Flight Lieutenant R. M. Currie-Flying Officer A. N. Rose of 410 Squadron in a NF.XIII a Ju 88. On a night when the Main Force was grounded, Mosquito XX KB118 of 139 Squadron flown by Flying Officer B. E. Hooke (PoW) and Flying Officer J. Stevenson (KIA) FTR from a raid by 40 Mosquitoes on Castrop-Rauxel. Mosquito NF.XIII MM621 of 604 Squadron, 2nd TAF was lost in an engagement with a Me 410 over France and was also hit by flak. Flight Lieutenant J. C. Cooper DFC and Flying Officer S. C. Hubbard DFM KIA. Oberfeldwebel Willi Glitz of Stab./NJG2 claimed a Mosquito at 'BJ-BI' at 2340 hours.

376 Three NF.XIII crews in 604 Squadron claimed 5 victories. Near Rennes Flying Officer J. S. Smith-Flying Officer L. Roberts in MM429 destroyed 2 x Do 217s. Flying Officer R. M. T. MacDonald-Flight Lieutenant S. H. J. Elliott in HK525 got a Ju 188 S of Nantes. Flight Lieutenant J. R. Cross-Warrant Officer H. Smith in MM517 destroyed a Ju 188 E of Falaise and a Ju 88 near Conde. Warrant Officer Henke-Flight Sergeant Emmerson of 409 Squadron in NF.XIII MM555 claimed a Ju 188. Flying Officer W. W. Provan-Warrant Officer Nichol of 29 Squadron in NF.XIII HK524 got a Bf 110 at Melun, W Orly. Flight Lieutenant Davidson-Flying Officer Willmott of 264 Squadron in a NF.XIII got a Ju 88. Flight Lieutenant Michael John Gloster DFC and Flight Lieutenant James F. Oswold DFC of 219 Squadron in a NF.XXX got 2 x Ju 188 W Vire. (On 9/10 August Gloster and Oswold got a Fw 190 E Évreux and on 16/17 August 1944 a Ju 188 near Caen. Gloster scored 10 e/a destroyed including 3 He 111s flying a Beaufighter VIf in N. Africa 5/6 December 1942. Gloster and Oswold were awarded bars to their DFCs in November 1944.

377 Flying Officer T. R. Wood and Flying Officer R. Leafe of 604 Squadron in NF.XIII MM528/H got a Do 217 and a 219 Squadron NF.XXX crew got 2 Ju 188s.

378 Jasper ended the war with four enemy aircraft destroyed, 3 V1s destroyed, 3 aircraft destroyed on the ground and one damaged on the ground.

379 On the night of 29/30 August, Russ Bannock and Bob Bruce, paired with Flying Officer Sid Seid, a Californian, and Dave McIntosh, blew up a Ju 88 on the ground at Copenhagen-Kastrup and a Bf 110 at Vaerose airfield. Seid, who scored hits on a line of three aircraft, observed a mechanic working around the tail section of the Bf 110 as they approached. "After one look at us," Seid recalled, "the 'Erk' broke all speed records during a sprint in an easterly direction. During my attack, another 'Erk' was observed descending a high ladder near the roof of a hangar. Upon seeing us the speed of his descent was suddenly and forcibly increased by a backward fall from near the top of the ladder. I claim this 'Erk' as "probably destroyed."

380 Wellings was returning to ops on Mosquitoes with 107 Squadron and did not have a navigator so he asked Hemmings if he would fly with him? Hemmings readily agreed and his transfer to 138 Wing at Lasham was arranged. On 13 August 1940 Wellings had gained an eleventh hour reprieve when, taxiing out for the suicidal trip to Aalborg airfield in Denmark, he and his crew were recalled because their posting had just come through. Wellings, who had a son named James and was married to Stella who lived about twenty miles from Lasham, often rode home on his motorbike on stand down nights to 'spend a night between the sheets', as he called it, as at Lasham they were living under canvas tents with blankets only with a view to moving into France wherever airfields could be cleared.

381 'Ted was very reserved, to a point of being thought unfriendly. Pre-war he was a cameraman with leading British film companies. He joined up and went to Canada for pilot training in 1942. He was pulled out just after qualifying to become part of a most extraordinary unit called the "Pinewood Military Film Unit". The men and ladies of this unit were all pre-war professionals at their trade/art, and who were now all in military service. The cameramen probably did more operations than most of us and spent more time over the target to get their pictures. Post war Ted became a Director of Photography who made at least four James Bond films, *Genevieve* and *A Man For All Seasons* - for which he got an Oscar.'

382 *Market-Garden* was aimed at cutting the German-occupied Netherlands almost in half and to prepare the way for the invasion of Germany that would bypass the northern flank of Germany's Westwall fortifications (The Siegfried line). The Allied plan was to capture bridges on the Rhine in Holland at Veghel, Grave, Nijmegen and Arnhem, using Britain's 1st and America's 82nd and 101st Airborne Divisions. They were to cut off the Germany Army in the Belgian sector and save the bridges and the port of Antwerp for the American army units and British XXX Corps advancing north from the Dutch border.

383 Of over 10,200 British airborne troops landed in the Arnhem area, 1,440 were killed or died of their wounds. 3000 were wounded and taken prisoner and 400 medical personnel and chaplains remained behind with the wounded and about 2500 uninjured troops also became PoWs. There were also 225 prisoners from the 4th Battalion, the Dorsetshire Regiment. About 450 Dutch civilians were killed. The operation also cost 160 RAF and Dominions aircrew, twenty-seven USAAF aircrew and 79 Royal Army Service Corps dispatchers were killed and 127 taken prisoner. A total of 55 Albemarle, Stirling, Halifax and Dakota aircraft of 38 and 46 Groups failed to return and a further 320 damaged by flak and seven by fighters while 105 Allied fighter aircraft were lost.

384 Five days later, on 7 October, two Mosquitoes of 605 Squadron destroyed ten enemy aircraft near Vienna and damaged six more. Roy Lelong finished the war with seven confirmed victories, 1 probable, 3 damaged and three V1s destroyed. After the war he joined the RAF and in 1952 he went on exchange to the US 5th Air Force in Korea. He then flew Hunters with 43 Squadron and in 1955 took command of 257 Squadron.

385 On 29 October 47 Lancasters – 18 from 9 Squadron and 18 from 617 Squadron, attacked the *Tirpitz* which was moored near the Norwegian port of Tromsö. 32 Lancasters dropped *Tallboy* bombs on estimated position of the capital ship (30 seconds before the attack a bank of cloud came in to cover the ship) but no direct hits were scored. One of 617 Squadron's Lancasters, which was damaged by flak, crash-landed in Sweden and its crew were later returned to Britain. On 12 November 30 Lancasters of 9 and 617 Squadrons attacked the *Tirpitz* again and at least two *Tallboys* hit the ship, which capsized to remain bottom upwards. Approximately 1000 of the 1900 men on board were killed or injured. One Lancaster, of 9 Squadron, was severely damaged by flak and landed safely in Sweden with its crew unhurt.

386 'Peter and I did have one interesting Interlude in Stockholm, where we chanced to meet the farmer and-his wife who had-received-us-so warmly upon our unceremonious arrival at Harplinge and we tried to return the compliment. After this we did not fly together again, going our separate ways. Mine led to Transport Command and the Far East. After the war all who participated in these raids received commemorative cufflinks from the Danish government.'

387 On the night of 22/23 December Wing Commander Peter Green DSO DFC and Flight Lieutenant Oxby DFM** of 219 Squadron, in NF.XXX MM792, shot down a Ju 88, and bagged another, south of Huy, on the night of 23/24 December. Two other crews in 219 Squadron destroyed two more Ju 88s. Altogether, 2nd TAF NF.XXX and NF.XIII crews knocked down ten enemy aircraft on 23/24 December. Flight Lieutenant McPhail and Flying Officer Donaghue of 409 Squadron destroyed a Ju 188, Flying Officer Mackenzie and Flying Officer Bodard of 410 Squadron brought down two Ju 88s. Four others and one damaged fell victim to 488 Squadron RNZAF at B48/Amiens-Glisy. Wing Commander R. G. Watts, the CO and Flying Officer I. C. Skudder got a Ju 188, Flight Lieutenant Johnny Hall DFC and Flying Officer J. P. W. Cairns DFC shot down a Me 410 in the US Sector. The two other victories this night (both Ju 88s) went to Flight Lieutenant Kenneth William "Chunky" Stewart, a solicitor from Dunedin and his navigator Flying Officer H. E. 'Bill' Brumby in NF.XXX MM822. On Christmas Eve 1944 18 German aircraft were shot down, five of them by four Mosquito crews of 100 Group. The rest were shot down by Mosquitoes of 2nd TAF, which dispatched 139 Mosquitoes on that night to targets in southwest Germany. 613 Squadron dispatched some 30 Mosquitoes; LR374, crewed by Warrant Officer Baird, pilot, and Sergeant Whateley-Knight, navigator, failed to return from a sortie to harass German movement behind the enemy thrust in the Ardennes. Also, 37 Mosquitoes of 2nd TAF patrolled the areas of Aachen, Arnhem and the Dutch Friesian Islands, and flew close support sorties over the front lines. None of these Mosquitoes were lost, and they destroyed 50 vehicles and six trains. 410 Squadron RCAF at Lille/Vendeville (B.51) dispatched nine Mosquitoes on front-line patrols between 1750 hours on Christmas Eve and 0530 hours on Christmas Day. Three of the Canadian crews claimed two Ju 87s of *Nachtschlachtgruppe* 1 (used for harassment of troops and transport) and a Ju 88 destroyed. In the Wassemberg area Flight Lieutenant Charles Emanuel 'Pop' Edinger DFC and Flying Officer C. C. Vaessen DFC in NF.XXX MV527 destroyed one of the Stukas and Squadron Leader I. E. MacTavish and Flying Officer A. M. Grant, flying NF.XXX MT485, got the other. A Ju 88 victory went to Flying Officer J. A. Watt and Flight Lieutenant E. H. Collis. Watt fired a total of 410 rounds to down their victim, a Ju 88 of 2./NJG2, which crashed near Roermond killing pilot Tetzlaff. Three crew survived and were made PoW. Two crews in 219 Squadron claimed three victories. Flight Lieutenant G. R. I. 'Sailor' Parker DFC DSM and Warrant Officer D. L. Godfrey DFC DFM in NF.XXX MM698 fitted with AI Mk.X. claimed 2 Ju 188s destroyed. Flight Lieutenant L. Stephenson DFC and Flight Lieutenant G. A. Hall DFC of 219 Squadron claimed a Bf 110 destroyed. The other victories on Christmas Eve went to Wing Commander Russ Bannock DFC*, now CO, 406 Squadron, in NF.XXX MM693, shot down 10 Kms west of Paderborn, Ju 88G-1 714132 3C+CT of 9./NJG4, crewed by Oberfeldwebel Manfred Ludwig and Feldwebel Hans Fischl (both KIA). Flight Lieutenant R. J. Foster DFC and Flight Lieutenant M. F. Newton DFC of 604 Squadron in NF.XIII MM462 from Odiham claimed a He 219 as probably destroyed, approximately 5 miles east of Nijmegen.

388 *LG1* lost three Ju 88s this night, including one flown by the *Gruppe Kommandeur*, Hauptmann Hecking (301348 L1+GK) and one flown by Oblt Huber, *Stafelführer 6./LG1*, in 331294 L1+NP. On 3/4 February Kent and Simpson added to their score by downing a Ju 88. Flight Lieutenant B. E. Plumer DFC and Flight Lieutenant Hargrove of 410 Squadron, in a NF.XXX, despatched a He 219 *Uhu*.

389 In NF.XIII MM456.

390 260542 A3+QD.

391 Hauck, his observer, Gefreiter Kurt Wuttge, *bordfunker*, Unteroffizier Max Grossman, and Feldwebel Heinrich Hoppe, the despatcher, baled out and were taken prisoner.

392 On the night of 21/22 February and east of Stormede airfield Flight Lieutenant Don A. MacFadyen DFC RCAF of 406 Squadron, in NF.XXX NT325, destroyed a Bf 110. Flight Lieutenant K. W. 'Chunky' Stewart and Flying Officer Bill Brumby of 488 Squadron RNZAF were patrolling over Holland when they were warned by ground control that they were being followed by a strange aircraft. Flight Lieutenant Al Gabitas, a fellow NZ pilot on the squadron, recalls. "A sort of dog fight ensued in complete darkness between the two night-fighters guided entirely by their own radar. With a great deal of weaving about Chunky managed to get behind the other aircraft. After brief visual contact it was identified as a Junkers 88G night-fighter. Following a quick burst of cannon fire on a fairly wide deflection it blew up in mid-air. This was a dual to the death between evenly-matched opponents in which the outcome was determined by superior flying and gunnery skills and more than a slight edge on the technology.' The enemy machine exploded near Groenlo. Three more victories were recorded on the night of the 21/22nd and they went to 2nd TAF Mosquito crews. A 604 Squadron NF.XIII crew despacthed a Bf 110 in the Dhunn area, and Flying Officer R. I. E. Britten DFC RCAF and Flight Lieutenant L. E. Fownes DFC of 409 Squadron in a NF.XIII, shot down a Bf 110. The third victory of the night, a Bf 110, went to Flying Officer K. Fleming and Flying Officer K. L. Nagle of 488 Squadron. On 24/25 February, Wing Commander Peter Green DSO DFC and Flight Lieutenant D. Oxby DFC DFM** of 219 Squadron, flying NF.XXX MM792, shot down a *Stuka*, and on the 28th, Squadron Leader Don MacFadyen DFC in NF.XXX NT325, claimed a UEA 'probably destroyed' at Hailfingen.

393 2 Group put up every available aircraft, flying 215 sorties, 176 from the Continent and the remainder by 136 Wing in England. It was to be the last time that the Mosquitoes operated in daylight in such numbers. 138 and 140 Wings lost nine Mosquitoes and many more were damaged. 2 Group lost a total of 21 Mosquitoes on *Clarion,* with 40 damaged.

394 On 29 January 1945 21 Squadron had flown from Thorney Island to Fersfield. Norfolk for a secret briefing on an attack on the *Gestapo* HQ in Copenhagen but the weather deteriorated and was unsuitable for low flying over the sea, so the operation was postponed for 24 hours. On 31 January the raid was again postponed for a further 24 hours, and next morning, 1 February, Air Vice Marshal Embry announced that he could not afford to have his aircraft hanging around doing nothing for any longer. The operation would have take place at a later date.

395 In LR388, the 5th Mosquito.

396 As the Mustangs crossed the target area, the second loss of the day occurred. Flak tracer shells bracketed Flight Lieutenant David Drew DFC's Mustang, the aircraft had sustained a hit - evident by a thin black line of smoke appearing from the underside of the aircraft. Drew banked his Mustang and turned north. It disappeared over the rooftops and crashed in Fælled Park. Drew was killed, he was later buried at Bispebjerg Churchyard together with Kleboe and Hall.

397 SZ999 crewed by Flying Officer Ronald G. 'Shorty' Dawson RAAF and Flying Officer Fergus T. Murray, ditched near Lisleje Strand. RS609 crewed by Flying Officer John H. "Spike" Palmer RAAF and Sub Lieutenant Hans H. Becker, a Norwegian, ditched in Samsø Belt. There were no survivors from either aircraft. Becker's body was discovered in an unmarked grave on the Danish Island of Samsø. Becker was Jewish and all his family were eradicated by the holocaust.

398 Coe was killed in a flying accident on 6 April 1945. Squadron Leader W. P. Kemp RNZAF and Flight Lieutenant R. Peel in PZ339 and New Zealanders' Flying Officers G. L. Peet and L. A. Graham in SZ985 returned safely. Flight Lieutenant R. J. Dempsey and Flight Sergeant E. J. Paige RAAF in PZ462 had one engine damaged by a single bullet in the coolant system over the west coast of Jutland and flew 400 miles home with the engine feathered.

399 NT123, Flight Lieutenant David V. Pattison and Flight Sergeant Frank Pygram's Mosquito had been hit by flak from the cruiser *Nürnburg* moored in the harbor.

400 Pattison broke R/T silence with the message "*Z-Zebra- Christmas*" the code for a forced landing in Sweden. The aircraft had been hit on the port engine, which began to burn fiercely. Flying towards the Oresound, with hopes of making it across the water to neutral Sweden, the aircraft lost height rapidly and control was difficult. The Mosquito was last seen as it ditched in Oresound 1 km ESE of the Swedish Hveen Island. The crew was spotted standing on the wing, but the weather conditions made it impossible to launch a rescue boat. Both men were posted as missing believed killed in action - no bodies were ever recovered. The wreck of the Mosquito has since been precisely located at a depth of 115 feet.

401 Pilot Officer R. C. Hamilton RAAF's Mustang in 64 Squadron sustained damage over the target area and he lost oil pressure before being forced to ditch in Ringkøbing Fiord near Tarm, Jutland. Hamilton survived to be taken prisoner and he was later sent to *Stalag Luft I* at Barth in Germany. In all, four Mosquitoes and two Mustangs FTR for the loss of nine air crew. Of the 26 prisoners on the sixth floor, 18 escaped. The remaining prisoners died in the building. Some of those that had survived the attack were injured or killed by jumping from the fifth floor into the street below. If the entire Mosquitoes' bombs had been dropped on *Shellhaus* it is doubtful that anyone would have survived. Tragically at *the Jeanne D'Arc School* 86 children were killed and 67 wounded, 16 adults also lost their lives with 35 more injured. Several other people were killed elsewhere as a direct result of the attack. Had the air-raid warning been sounded on time, civilian casualties may have been much less. The *Gestapo* lost their precious archive material and their Headquarters. The total number of dead was 72, with 26 members of the *Gestapo* and some 30 being Danish collaborators. The remainder were innocent Danes. An official number has never been revealed. The escape of so many Danish patriots provided the Resistance with the much-needed breathing space. The tragedy at the *Jeanne d'Arc School* marred this success, as one can never balance the lives of innocent children against those of resistance fighters, nevertheless there has never been any retribution shown towards the RAF for this costly operation. After the war, a fitting memorial was raised to the children and adults killed at the *Jeanne d'Arc School*. Likewise, at the new *Shellhaus* building there is a memorial to the Resistance members that lost their lives. Today at *Shellhaus*, there is a memorial to the nine air crew members that laid down their lives in the fight for Denmark's freedom.

402 Flying Officer T.R. Wood and Flying Officer R. Leafe of 604 Squadron in NF.XIII MM497 shot down a Ju 88. Flying Officer Reed and Flying Officer Bricker of 219 Squadron, flying a NF.XXX downed a Ju 188. Flight Lieutenant B. E. Plumer DFC and Flight Lieutenant Bradford of 410 Squadron, flying a NF.XXX destroyed a Bf 110.